55 *Victorian Prose Writers Before 1867,* edited by William B. Thesing (1987)

56 *German Fiction Writers, 1914-1945,* edited by James Hardin (1987)

57 *Victorian Prose Writers After 1867,* edited by William B. Thesing (1987)

58 *Jacobean and Caroline Dramatists,* edited by Fredson Bowers (1987)

59 *American Literary Critics and Scholars, 1800-1850,* edited by John W. Rathbun and Monica M. Grecu (1987)

60 *Canadian Writers Since 1960, Second Series,* edited by W. H. New (1987)

61 *American Writers for Children Since 1960: Poets, Illustrators, and Nonfiction Authors,* edited by Glenn E. Estes (1987)

62 *Elizabethan Dramatists,* edited by Fredson Bowers (1987)

63 *Modern American Critics, 1920-1955,* edited by Gregory S. Jay (1988)

64 *American Literary Critics and Scholars, 1850-1880,* edited by John W. Rathbun and Monica M. Grecu (1988)

65 *French Novelists, 1900-1930,* edited by Catharine Savage Brosman (1988)

66 *German Fiction Writers, 1885-1913,* 2 parts, edited by James Hardin (1988)

67 *Modern American Critics Since 1955,* edited by Gregory S. Jay (1988)

68 *Canadian Writers, 1920-1959, First Series,* edited by W. H. New (1988)

69 *Contemporary German Fiction Writers, First Series,* edited by Wolfgang D. Elfe and James Hardin (1988)

70 *British Mystery Writers, 1860-1919,* edited by Bernard Benstock and Thomas F. Staley (1988)

71 *American Literary Critics and Scholars, 1880-1900,* edited by John W. Rathbun and Monica M. Grecu (1988)

72 *French Novelists, 1930-1960,* edited by Catharine Savage Brosman (1988)

73 *American Magazine Journalists, 1741-1850,* edited by Sam G. Riley (1988)

74 *American Short-Story Writers Before 1880,* edited by Bobby Ellen Kimbel, with the assistance of William E. Grant (1988)

75 *Contemporary German Fiction Writers, Second Series,* edited by Wolfgang D. Elfe and James Hardin (1988)

76 *Afro-American Writers, 1940-1955,* edited by Trudier Harris (1988)

77 *British Mystery Writers, 1920-* edited by Bernard Benstock Thomas F. Staley (1988)

78 *American Short-Story Writers, 1910,* edited by Bobby Kimbel, with the assistance of liam E. Grant (1988)

79 *American Magazine Journalists, 1850-1900,* edited by Sam G. Riley (1988)

80 *Restoration and Eighteenth-Century Dramatists, First Series,* edited by Paula R. Backscheider (1989)

81 *Austrian Fiction Writers, 1875-1913,* edited by James Hardin and Donald G. Daviau (1989)

82 *Chicano Writers, First Series,* edited by Francisco A. Lomelí and Carl R. Shirley (1989)

83 *French Novelists Since 1960,* edited by Catharine Savage Brosman (1989)

84 *Restoration and Eighteenth-Century Dramatists, Second Series,* edited by Paula R. Backscheider (1989)

85 *Austrian Fiction Writers After 1914,* edited by James Hardin and Donald G. Daviau (1989)

86 *American Short-Story Writers, 1910-1945, First Series,* edited by Bobby Ellen Kimbel (1989)

87 *British Mystery and Thriller Writers Since 1940, First Series,* edited by Bernard Benstock and Thomas F. Staley (1989)

88 *Canadian Writers, 1920-1959, Second Series,* edited by W. H. New (1989)

89 *Restoration and Eighteenth-Century Dramatists, Third Series,* edited by Paula R. Backscheider (1989)

90 *German Writers in the Age of Goethe, 1789-1832,* edited by James Hardin and Christoph E. Schweitzer (1989)

91 *American Magazine Journalists, 1900-1960, First Series,* edited by Sam G. Riley (1990)

92 *Canadian Writers, 1890-1920,* edited by W. H. New (1990)

93 *British Romantic Poets, 1789-1832, First Series,* edited by John R. Greenfield (1990)

94 *German Writers in the Age of Goethe: Sturm und Drang to Classicism,* edited by James Hardin and Christoph E. Schweitzer (1990)

95 *Eighteenth-Century British Poets, First Series,* edited by John Sitter (1990)

96 *British Romantic Poets, 1789-1832, Second Series,* edited by John R. Greenfield (1990)

[97] *...nlightenment ...0-1764,* edited ...Christoph ...

[98] *...First Series,* edited by Robert Beum (1990)

99 *Canadian Writers Before 1890,* edited by W. H. New (1990)

100 *Modern British Essayists, Second Series,* edited by Robert Beum (1990)

101 *British Prose Writers, 1660-1800, First Series,* edited by Donald T. Siebert (1991)

102 *American Short-Story Writers, 1910-1945, Second Series,* edited by Bobby Ellen Kimbel (1991)

103 *American Literary Biographers, First Series,* edited by Steven Serafin (1991)

104 *British Prose Writers, 1660-1800, Second Series,* edited by Donald T. Siebert (1991)

105 *American Poets Since World War II, Second Series,* edited by R. S. Gwynn (1991)

106 *British Literary Publishing Houses, 1820-1880,* edited by Patricia J. Anderson and Jonathan Rose (1991)

107 *British Romantic Prose Writers, 1789-1832, First Series,* edited by John R. Greenfield (1991)

108 *Twentieth-Century Spanish Poets, First Series,* edited by Michael L. Perna (1991)

109 *Eighteenth-Century British Poets, Second Series,* edited by John Sitter (1991)

110 *British Romantic Prose Writers, 1789-1832, Second Series,* edited by John R. Greenfield (1991)

111 *American Literary Biographers, Second Series,* edited by Steven Serafin (1991)

112 *British Literary Publishing Houses, 1881-1965,* edited by Jonathan Rose and Patricia J. Anderson (1991)

113 *Modern Latin-American Fiction Writers, First Series,* edited by William Luis (1992)

114 *Twentieth-Century Italian Poets, First Series,* edited by Giovanna Wedel De Stasio, Glauco Cambon, and Antonio Illiano (1992)

115 *Medieval Philosophers,* edited by Jeremiah Hackett (1992)

116 *British Romantic Novelists, 1789-1832,* edited by Bradford K. Mudge (1992)

(Continued on back endsheets)

British Children's W
1800–1880

British Children's Writers, 1800–1880

Edited by
Meena Khorana
Morgan State University

A Bruccoli Clark Layman Book
Gale Research Inc.
Detroit, Washington, D.C., London

The paper used in this publication meets the minimum requirements
of American National Standard for Information Sciences–Permanence
Paper for Printed Library Materials, ANSI Z39.48-1984. ™
∞

Library of Congress Cataloging-in-Publication Data

British children's writers, 1800–1880 / edited by Meena Khorana.
   p. cm. – (Dictionary of literary biography; v. 163)
"A Bruccoli Clark Layman book."
Includes bibliographical references and index.
ISBN 0-8103-9358-1 (alk. paper)
1. Children's literature, English – Dictionaries. 2. English literature – 19th century –
Bio-bibliography – Dictionaries. 3. Children's literature, English – Bio-bibliography –
Dictionaries. 4. Authors, English – 19th century – Biography – Dictionaries. 5. English
literature – 19th century – Dictionaries. I. Khorana, Meena. II. Series.
PR990.B747 1996
820.9'9282'0934 – dc20   96–10276
                                   CIP
[B]

10 9 8 7 6 5 4 3 2 1

To my husband, Shami

Contents

Plan of the Series ix
Introduction xi

Lucy Aikin (1781–1864) 3
    Linda J. Turzynski

R. M. Ballantyne (1825–1894) 8
    Joel D. Chaston

William Blake (1757–1827) 21
    Alan Richardson

Robert Browning (1812–1889) 30
    A. Waller Hastings

Randolph Caldecott (1846–1886) 37
    Michael Scott Joseph

Lucy Lyttelton Cameron (1781–1858) 48
    Naomi J. Wood

Lewis Carroll (1832–1898) 56
    Karen Patricia Smith

Dinah Maria Craik (1826–1887) 70
    Diana A. Chlebek

Walter Crane (1845–1915) 76
    George R. Bodmer

Maria Edgeworth (1768–1849) 83
    Adele M. Fasick

Juliana Horatia Ewing (1841–1885) 91
    Patricia Demers

Frederic William Farrar (1831–1903) 100
    Brendan A. Rapple

William Godwin (1756–1836) and
  Mary Jane Godwin (1766–1841) 110
    Ann R. Montanaro

Thomas Hughes (1822–1896) 119
    Douglas Ivison

Jean Ingelow (1820–1897) 127
    Carolyn Sigler

Annie Keary (1825–1879) 132
    Kay E. Vandergrift

Charles Kingsley (1819–1875) 136
    Brendan A. Rapple

William Henry Giles Kingston (1814–1880) 148
    Nicola D. Thompson

Charles Lamb (1775–1834) and
  Mary Lamb (1764–1847) 159
    Judy Anne White

Edward Lear (1812–1888) 167
    Celia Catlett Anderson

Mark Lemon (1809–1870) 177
    Karen Patricia Smith

George MacDonald (1824–1905) 183
    Roderick McGillis

Frederick Marryat (1792–1848) 194
    Nigel Spence

Emma Marshall (1828–1899) 202
    A. Waller Hastings

Harriet Martineau (1802–1876) 210
    Lois Rauch Gibson

Favell Lee Mortimer (1802–1878) 217
    Frederick Rankin MacFadden Jr.

Francis Edward Paget (1806–1882) 222
    Jan Susina

Mayne Reid (1818–1883) 228
    Peter D. Sieruta

William Roscoe (1753–1831) 234
    Michael Scott Joseph

Christina Georgina Rossetti (1830–1894) 239
    Jan Susina

John Ruskin (1819–1900) 247
    Marilynn Strasser Olson

Anna Sewell (1820–1878)........................259
Lopa Prusty

Mary Martha Sherwood (1775–1851) 267
Janis Dawson

Catherine Sinclair (1800–1864)............................282
Judith Gero John

Hesba Stretton (Sarah Smith)
(1832–1911) 287
Leslie Howsam

Ann Taylor (1782–1866) and
Jane Taylor (1783–1824) 292
Judith A. Overmier

William Makepeace Thackeray (1811–1863)......297
Craig Howes

Charlotte Elizabeth Tonna ("Charlotte Elizabeth")
(1790–1846) 307
Lois Rauch Gibson and Madelyn Holmes

Charlotte Maria Tucker ("A.L.O.E.")
(1821–1893) 316
Judith Overmier

Charlotte Mary Yonge (1823–1901)....................323
Claudia Nelson

Appendix: Children's Illustrators, 1800–1880 ...339
Gwyneth Evans

Books for Further Reading....................355
Contributors..359
Cumulative Index 363

Plan of the Series

. . . Almost the most prodigious asset of a country, and perhaps its most precious possession, is its native literary product — when that product is fine and noble and enduring.

Mark Twain*

The advisory board, the editors, and the publisher of the *Dictionary of Literary Biography* are joined in endorsing Mark Twain's declaration. The literature of a nation provides an inexhaustible resource of permanent worth. We intend to make literature and its creators better understood and more accessible to students and the reading public, while satisfying the standards of teachers and scholars.

To meet these requirements, *literary biography* has been construed in terms of the author's achievement. The most important thing about a writer is his writing. Accordingly, the entries in *DLB* are career biographies, tracing the development of the author's canon and the evolution of his reputation.

The purpose of *DLB* is not only to provide reliable information in a convenient format but also to place the figures in the larger perspective of literary history and to offer appraisals of their accomplishments by qualified scholars.

The publication plan for *DLB* resulted from two years of preparation. The project was proposed to Bruccoli Clark by Frederick C. Ruffner, president of the Gale Research Company, in November 1975. After specimen entries were prepared and typeset, an advisory board was formed to refine the entry format and develop the series rationale. In meetings held during 1976, the publisher, series editors, and advisory board approved the scheme for a comprehensive biographical dictionary of persons who contributed to North American literature. Editorial work on the first volume began in January 1977, and it was published in 1978. In order to make *DLB* more than a reference tool and to compile volumes that individually have claim to status as literary history, it was decided to organize volumes by topic, period, or genre. Each of these free-standing volumes provides a biographical-bibliographical guide and overview for a particular area of literature. We are convinced that this organization — as opposed to a single alphabet method — constitutes a valuable innovation in the presentation of reference material. The volume plan necessarily requires many decisions for the placement and treatment of authors who might properly be included in two or three volumes. In some instances a major figure will be included in separate volumes, but with different entries emphasizing the aspect of his career appropriate to each volume. Ernest Hemingway, for example, is represented in *American Writers in Paris, 1920–1939* by an entry focusing on his expatriate apprenticeship; he is also in *American Novelists, 1910–1945* with an entry surveying his entire career. Each volume includes a cumulative index of the subject authors and articles. Comprehensive indexes to the entire series are planned.

With volume ten in 1982 it was decided to enlarge the scope of *DLB*. By the end of 1986 twenty-one volumes treating British literature had been published, and volumes for Commonwealth and Modern European literature were in progress. The series has been further augmented by the *DLB Yearbooks* (since 1981) which update published entries and add new entries to keep the *DLB* current with contemporary activity. There have also been *DLB Documentary Series* volumes which provide biographical and critical source materials for figures whose work is judged to have particular interest for students. One of these companion volumes is entirely devoted to Tennessee Williams.

We define literature as the *intellectual commerce of a nation:* not merely as belles lettres but as that ample and complex process by which ideas are generated, shaped, and transmitted. *DLB* entries are not limited to "creative writers" but extend to other figures who in their time and in their way influenced the mind of a people. Thus the series encompasses historians, journalists, publishers, and screenwriters. By this means readers of *DLB* may be aided to perceive literature not as cult scripture in the keeping of intellectual high priests but firmly positioned at the center of a nation's life.

*From an unpublished section of Mark Twain's autobiography, copyright by the Mark Twain Company

DLB includes the major writers appropriate to each volume and those standing in the ranks immediately behind them. Scholarly and critical counsel has been sought in deciding which minor figures to include and how full their entries should be. Wherever possible, useful references are made to figures who do not warrant separate entries.

Each *DLB* volume has a volume editor responsible for planning the volume, selecting the figures for inclusion, and assigning the entries. Volume editors are also responsible for preparing, where appropriate, appendices surveying the major periodicals and literary and intellectual movements for their volumes, as well as lists of further readings. Work on the series as a whole is coordinated at the Bruccoli Clark Layman editorial center in Columbia, South Carolina, where the editorial staff is responsible for accuracy of the published volumes.

One feature that distinguishes *DLB* is the illustration policy – its concern with the iconography of literature. Just as an author is influenced by his surroundings, so is the reader's understanding of the author enhanced by a knowledge of his environment. Therefore *DLB* volumes include not only drawings, paintings, and photographs of authors, often depicting them at various stages in their careers, but also illustrations of their families and places where they lived. Title pages are regularly reproduced in facsimile along with dust jackets for modern authors. The dust jackets are a special feature of *DLB* because they often document better than anything else the way in which an author's work was perceived in its own time. Specimens of the writers' manuscripts are included when feasible.

Samuel Johnson rightly decreed that "The chief glory of every people arises from its authors." The purpose of the *Dictionary of Literary Biography* is to compile literary history in the surest way available to us – by accurate and comprehensive treatment of the lives and work of those who contributed to it.

The *DLB* Advisory Board

Introduction

The nineteenth century, especially the Victorian period, was the great age of experimentation in children's literature. At no other time in the history of children's literature was there such a flowering of genres and styles or such an importance placed on theories on child raising and education or on books written especially for children. However, when the children's literature of this period is examined in its larger historical context, forces and tendencies that had been long in the making are revealed.

The nineteenth century, which had inherited insular conventions from the previous era, was a transitional period of doubts and contradictions in governmental power, religious beliefs, the economic base of society, and social values. While at home England was becoming more democratic, she was fiercely imperialistic toward her expanding colonies; while democracy gave importance to the rights of the individual, wealth was concentrated in the hands of the few; while industrialization increased the economic prosperity of the nation, it also led to exploitation, grinding poverty, and unsanitary conditions for the workers; and while the growing importance of science made technological advancements and a more progressive outlook possible, it also resulted in bitter controversy between science and religion. The resulting confusion produced a tenacious adherence to accepted norms of social and moral behavior, hence the derogatory epithet *Victorianism* — connoting old fashionedness, hypocrisy, prudishness, complacency, bigotry, and middle-class respectability — came to be applied especially to the second half of the nineteenth century.

All these divergent trends find expression in the works of children's writers published between 1800 and 1880. Of the forty-one entries in this volume, seven are detailed essays on the major figures of the period: Lewis Carroll, George MacDonald, R. M. Ballantyne, Mary Martha Sherwood, Charlotte Mary Yonge, Juliana Horatia Ewing, and Randolph Caldecott. There are extended essays on Thomas Hughes, John Ruskin, Anna Sewell, William Henry Giles Kingston, Edward Lear, Maria Edgeworth, William Makepeace Thackeray, and Charles Kingsley; and there is an appendix on children's illustrators. The remaining twenty-five entries cover significant writers and illustrators such as Harriet Martineau, Francis Edward Paget,

Frederic William Farrar, Frederick Marryat, Lucy Lyttelton Cameron, Charlotte Elizabeth Tonna, and Walter Crane. Collectively, the works of these authors reflect the impact of social, political, historical, religious, and pedagogical conditions on books for children. While the Georgian period (until 1837) was a direct outcome of the late eighteenth century, the first half of Queen Victoria's reign reflects significant changes in the general outlook toward children and their literature.

The most powerful societal influence on children's literature, as David Grylls points out in *Guardians and Angels* (1978), a study of parent/child relationships in the nineteenth century, was a heightened awareness of the uniqueness of children and the emphasis on psychological and social factors contributing to the growth of a child. That children's upbringing was important to society is evident from the fact that writers, educators, philosophers, clergy, and suffragettes all expressed their views on the subject. This focus on children resulted in the development of a publishing industry with books written, illustrated, and produced especially for children. In his survey of British children's literature, *Children's Books in England: Five Centuries of Social Life* (1982, revised edition), F. J. Harvey Darton asserts that relative to the population there were many children's writers and books in nineteenth-century England. Juvenile writers were especially prolific: Sherwood is credited with writing more than 400 titles; Kingston wrote 150 adventure stories; Emma Marshall produced 200 works; Yonge wrote nearly 200 tracts; and Charlotte Maria Tucker created more than 100 works of popular fiction.

The void created by the increasing demand for suitable reading material for children was filled by the entry of many women into the field of children's literature. Though domestic servants provided increased leisure for educated middle-class women, they had few outlets for intellectual pursuits apart from writing or teaching. Since telling stories, teaching manners, disciplining, and providing moral guidance to children were associated with motherhood, women naturally assumed the role of writing for children, bringing a fresh understanding of, and interest in, childhood to their stories. However, the stigma that it was somehow "unwomanly" to show intelligence or that it was not socially respectable for middle-class women to earn money prompted them to write under male pseudonyms, initials, or anonymously. Magazines, which were a popular mode of literary publication, swelled in number and provided a convenient outlet for the growing numbers of women writers.

Educators and thinkers of the late eighteenth century had begun to give serious consideration to education as a tool for influencing the minds and behavior of children. In France, Jean-Jacques Rousseau in *Emile* (1762) outlined his theory that children should be raised in an environment that will allow them to develop according to their nature and simple impulses. This was a revolutionary idea, because children were typically raised with stern morality and fear of punishment. In England there were conflicting attitudes toward child raising, ranging from a belief in original sin to rationalism to authoritarianism. Thomas Day and Richard Lovell Edgeworth embraced Rousseau's philosophy; however, they believed children had to be influenced by adult reasoning and direction. Day's *The History of Sanford and Merton* (1783–1789) intended to curb the natural exuberance of children with a rigid moral code, hard work, and self-denial. In contrast, Maria Edgeworth, who embodied her father's theories, glorified reason and practicality. The Edgeworths did not believe that constraints should be externally imposed, but rather that children should be allowed to develop virtues and expel vices because of the consequences associated with their actions. Edgeworth's short stories in *The Parent's Assistant* (1795) and *Early Lessons* (1801), especially "The Purple Jar," give fictional life to her theory that discipline should come from the inner person. Happily, Edgeworth's observations of her eighteen siblings and experience with creating stories for them provided her with the skill to combine believable human characters with situations that instruct as well as amuse.

The Sunday School Movement, initiated in 1780 by Robert Raikes to provide rudimentary education for poor and laboring children, and organizations such as the National Society for Promoting the Education of the Children of the Poor in the Principles of the Established Church also had a great impact on children's literature of the Georgian era. Sunday schools and day schools were established with the dual agenda of the educational and moral upliftment of poor children and their parents. According to Kirsten Drotner, by the 1850s 75 percent of working-class children between the ages of five and fifteen attended Sunday schools. Prominent educators such as Sarah Trimmer (*Reflections Upon the Education of Children in Charity Schools*, 1792); Hannah More, who started Cheap Repository Tracts; John Aikin, a schoolmaster and Unitarian doctor of divinity; and Anna Laetitia Barbauld (*Lessons for Children from Two to Three Years Old*, 1778; *Hymns in Prose for Children*, 1781) wrote religious tracts because they believed that moral instruction should be an essential ingredient of formal learning. Magazines and tracts, intended not to amuse and entertain but to instruct and enlighten, were published by religious societies such as the Religious Tract Society (founded 1799), the Christian Tract Society, the Society for Distributing Evangelical Tracts Gratis (founded 1799), the British and Foreign Bible Society (founded 1804), and the Society for Promoting Christian Knowledge (founded 1805). These tracts, directed mainly at lower-class children, were bought by churches and missionary societies for distribution in workhouses, prisons, Sunday schools, and day schools or as prize books. According to Samuel Pickering, these societies collectively published "several hundred thousands [tracts] annually for the moral benefit of Britons."

This pioneering work was carried on by a host of women writers such as Margaret Gatty, Charlotte Elizabeth Tonna, Mary Pilkington, Mary Elliott, Elizabeth Sandham, Alicia Catherine Mant, Mary Robson Hughes, Priscilla Wakefield, Barbara Hofland, and Agnes Strickland, to whom Percy Muir refers as that "monstrous regiment of women" in *English Children's Books, 1600–1900* (1954). These writers, who were active in community projects such as teaching poor children and workers, establishing schools or taking in pupils, adopting orphans, and engaging in charitable works, naturally embraced the moral tale as an extension of their roles as mothers and teachers of the young. Rejecting the natural impulses of a child, they emphasized that children should be raised with strict discipline in order to avoid corrupting influences. They wanted to inculcate in children the puritanical virtues of discipline, selflessness, industry, temperance, and austerity. Hence their didactic stories feature moral vices or virtues, stereotypical characters, and thin plots engineered to drive home the moral lessons. Edward Augustus Kendall should be mentioned along with these women writers as a writer of moral tales and animal stories, such as *Lessons of Virtue* (1801), *Keeper's Travels in Search of His Master* (1798), and *Canary Bird: A Moral Fiction* (1799), intended to impart moral, humanitarian, and otherwise useful instruction for the young. This doctrinaire approach led to a suspicion of fairy tales and imaginative writing as the sources of evil and mischief in children. Sherwood (*The History of the Fairchild Family,* 1818–1847), a prominent writer of moral tales, embodied the prevalent theory that parents are the representatives of God and that children owe them complete obedience and reverence.

Catherine Sinclair, a notable exception to such writers, attacks moral stuffiness in *Holiday House* (1839) by depicting high-spirited and playful children whom she considered "now almost extinct." Some freshness was also introduced through the poems of Ann and Jane Taylor, whose collections — such as *Original Poems for Infant Minds* (1804), *Rhymes for the Nursery* (1806), and *Hymns for Infant Minds* (1808) — reveal the familiar situations and experiences of childhood with insight and gentle humor. While the Taylor sisters introduced the moral fable in verse, they also gave importance to entertainment and viewing the world from the child's perspective. Their example was followed by Charles and Mary Lamb (*Poetry for Children,* 1809), Elizabeth Turner (*The Daisy; or, Cautionary Stories in Verse,* 1807; *The Cowslip,* 1811), and Sara Coleridge (*Pretty Lessons in Verse, for Good Children,* 1834).

The moralistic tone of the Georgian period led to the insertion of religious propaganda in children's books. The purpose of these tracts was to propagate orthodox doctrines and precepts of the faith, to prevent children from succumbing to evil influences, and to emphasize the possibilities of heavenly reward and salvation. Because religious controversy among the three dissenting factions of the Anglican Church — High, Low, and Broad — was rampant during the nineteenth century, no author could avoid asserting his or her religious views in books for impressionable young readers. Margaret Maison's *The Victorian Vision* (1961), her study of the religious novel, aptly states that "Fiction became the pulpit, the confessional and the battlefield for countless Victorians . . . to portray the religious movements of their time, to be a vehicle for all manner of theological and ecclesiastical propaganda to conduct debates and controversies, and to tell the world of their doubts and conflicts, their spiritual travels and phases of faith." Although blatantly dogmatic and intolerant, religious writings found eager publishers and ready markets because they served a distinct social and ecclesiastical purpose. Stories that illustrate deathbed conversions, suffering for the sake of faith, illustration of biblical stories and catechism, warnings to sinners of the wrath of God, confessions and penance, and spiritual awakenings all come under the category of the religious novel.

The High Church group, especially after the Oxford Movement led by John Keble, John Henry Newman, and Edward Bouverie Pusey, aimed at reviving the ceremonies and doctrines of the early church. Some of the prominent High Church writers for children were Emma Marshall, Ewing, Elizabeth Sewell (*Margaret Percival,* 1847), and Yonge (*The Castle Builders,* 1854), who wrote of sacrifice and complete submission to the authority of the church and warned against the attractions of Catholicism. Sewell's novels, in particular, document the impact of religious controversy on the lives of ordinary people. Francis Edward Paget, in contrast, focused on the need to restore churches, encourage church attendance and baptisms, and discontinue the pew system because it emphasized distinctions among classes.

Low Church, or evangelical writers, de-emphasized ritual and ceremony in church services and attacked High Church clergy for being sympathetic to Rome. Evangelicals, who were active in establishing Sunday schools, teaching, and writing tracts, appear oppressively moralistic when judged by twentieth-century standards. They subscribed to the doctrine of original sin, which stated that the child was inherently evil and needed to be saved. Sherwood (*The Indian Pilgrim,* 1818; *The Infant's Progress,* 1821; *Stories Explanatory of the Church Catechism,* 1817), Lucy Lyttelton Cameron (*The Two Lambs,* 1816), Favell Lee Mortimer (*Line Upon Line,* 1848; *Here a Little and There a Little,* 1861), Tucker (*The Mine; or, Darkness and Light,* 1858; *Claudia,* 1869), and Tonna (*Conformity,* 1841; *Falsehood and Truth,* 1841) employ realistic or allegorical themes to denounce worldly pleasures, encourage submission to God and Christ, and suggest conversion to Low Church beliefs. Mortimer's descriptions of God's wrath and the horrors awaiting the erring child are so graphic that her books are considered sadistic by modern standards. Like the other evangelicals, she inspires fear of punishment, guilt, religious fervor, and repentance in young readers. In *The Peep of Day* (1833) she instructs children on their bodies thus: "You have a little body. God has covered your bones with flesh. Your flesh is soft and warm. Will your bones break? Yes, they would, if you were to fall down from a high place, or if a cart were to go over them."

A favorite motif in the religious novel is the melodramatic death of a virtuous child. Through deathbed scenes the dying child is exploited to teach religious lessons to relatives, friends, and sinners. Often the innately good child who is raised in an un-Christian environment dies as a result of the neglect, abuse, or wickedness of adults. For instance, the "glorious" deaths of innocent and pious children in Stretton's *Jessica's First Prayer* (1867) and *Pilgrim Street, a Story of Manchester Life* (1867) and in Sherwood's *Margaret Whyte* (1800s) and *Little Henry and His Bearer* (1814) lead to the confession, conversion, and salvation of onlookers. Drotner in *English Children and Their Magazines, 1751–1945* (1982) concludes that the high infant mortality rate in nineteenth-century England – a fourth of all deaths were of children under the age of one – made it easy for tract writers to instill the fear of death as the ultimate punishment. Farrar's *Eric* (1858) is a painful recounting of the moral deterioration of a young schoolboy who finally repents on his deathbed.

Broad Church writers, who represented the nonconformist element of the Anglican Church, introduced freshness, imagination, and respect for natural human passions in books for children. Martineau wrote about her theistic beliefs in *Devotional Exercises for the Use of Young Persons* (1823) and *Deerbrook* (1837). Kingsley, an ordained priest, introduced religious tolerance and reconciliation of orthodox theology and science, especially Charles Darwin's *Origin of the Species* (1856). He believed that the fear of punishment and eternal damnation that had preoccupied moralists and evangelicals inhibited the personality and natural potential of children; instead, in *The Water Babies* (1863) he demonstrates that moral conduct is influenced by environment. He uses symbolic baptisms, bodily cleanliness, and cathartic experiences as metaphors for spiritual purity and moral righteousness. Likewise, MacDonald's antidogmatic beliefs were expressed in his denunciation of the material concerns of the organized church, his belief in an all-loving God, and his search for mystical harmony with creation. In *At the Back of the North Wind* (1871) he creates a mysterious and all-pervading female figure who is both a benevolent and a wrathful agent of the creator.

Children's writers were also engaged in social reform and political propaganda. Once again, the presence of women writers was strongly felt. Martineau, a Unitarian philanthropist, stated: "I want to be doing something with the pen since no other means of action in politics are in a woman's power." In analyzing the social novel by nineteenth-century British women, Joseph Kestner in *Protest and Reform* (1985) argues that literature provided women with the only socially acceptable avenue for political and social activism. Since women could not vote, they used fiction to influence public opinion and governmental policy. The industrial revolution, which led to a shift in the economic base of society from rural to urban and from cottage industries to mass production by machines, gave rise to social abuses. Men and women used the novel as a platform for humanitarian causes: Dickens and Hesba Stretton exposed the wretched lot of the poor (*A Christmas Carol,* 1843; *Little Meg's Children,* 1868), Charlotte Elizabeth Tonna and Stretton the deplorable living and working conditions in mines and factories (*Helen Fleetwood,* 1841; *The Children of Cloverley,* 1865), Ballantyne the horrors of the slave trade (*Black Ivory,* 1873), Maria Edgeworth and Stretton the abuse of Irish tenants and agricultural reforms (*Castle Rackrent,* 1800; *Fern's Hollow,* 1864), Charles Kingsley and Hannah More child abuse and child labor (*The Water Babies,* 1863; *The Lancashire Collier Girl,* 1795), and Anna Sewell and MacDonald the ill treatment of horses and coachmen (*Black Beauty,* 1877; *At the Back of the North Wind*).

The solutions offered in these novels reflect the political ideologies of the individual authors. While Martineau subscribed to Jeremy Bentham's principle of laissez-faire, which sanctioned unrestricted enterprise or nonintervention by government, others such as Tonna, who researched case histories in the "Blue Books," and Ruskin demanded that the state ameliorate the plight of the working class. Dinah Maria Craik developed the doctrine of self-help and wrote novels of upward mobility (*John Halifax, Gentleman,* 1856) in which the protagonist bridges the social gap through financial success and hard work. Because of their interest in scientific research and involvement in the Christian Socialist Movement, Kingsley, Ruskin, and Hughes were interested in civic projects as expressions of their Christian faith, called the cult of "Muscular Christianity."

Another genre that evolved in the first half of the nineteenth century because of the entry of women into the field of writing was the domestic novel. It replaced the "courtesy book" or "manual of conduct" on the training and socialization of girls, making novels gender-specific for the first time in the history of British children's literature. Domestic stories, often termed "trivial" by detractors, provided a leisurely depiction of everyday family life, child-raising practices, and relationships among different segments of the community. Although these books targeted female readers, men such as Ruskin, Kingsley, Alfred Tennyson, and Rudyard Kipling acknowledged enjoying the books of Yonge and Ewing.

By owning property, establishing schools to equip girls with marketable skills, demanding just payment for their writing, performing social services, expressing subversive views on marriage, and claiming equality with men, writers such as Tonna (*The Wrongs of Woman*, 1843), Marshall, Ewing, Sewell, Martineau, Craik (*A Woman's Thoughts About Women*, 1858), and Stretton championed the causes of better education, greater career opportunities, economic independence, and equal political rights for women. Ironically, while they wrote either to support themselves or to supplement the family income, their domestic stories depict the limited experience and dependent roles of women and children in the family and community. The heroines of Yonge (*The Daisy Chain*, 1862; *Abbey Church*, 1844), Sewell (*Ursula*, 1858), Marshall (*The Happy Days at Fernbank*, 1861), Martineau (*Deerbrook*, 1837), and Ewing (*Six to Sixteen*, 1875) center their lives around domestic chores, parish work, and responsibility toward siblings. They are embodiments of the Victorian ideal of womanhood: loyal, submissive, self-sacrificing, patient, well-mannered, disciplined, and restrained.

This ideal was no doubt influenced by Rousseau's and Day's theories that girls' education should train them to please and serve men. Women such as Mrs. William Ellis concurred with this position. In *The Women of England* (1843) she claims: "The first thing of importance is to be content to be inferior to men – inferior in mental power in the same proportion that you are inferior in bodily strength." A woman's training had to do with attracting a husband, and marriage was her ultimate goal. Privileged girls attended finishing schools, which taught the drawing room accomplishments of playing a musical instrument, singing, dancing, acting, speaking foreign languages, and reciting poetry – all essential for attracting suitors. Dr. Gregory's advice in *A Father's Legacy to his Daughters* was: "But if you happen to have any learning, keep it a profound secret, especially from the men, who generally look with a jealous and malignant eye on a woman of . . . cultivated understanding."

If stories aimed at girls were restricted to the narrow confines of the home and parish community, boys' fiction moved outdoors, away from the domestic milieu. Exciting, fast-paced adventures take their bold and courageous heroes to far-off places. Interest and sense of immediacy are heightened through detailed descriptions of the arctic region (Kingston's *Peter the Whaler*, 1851; Ballantyne's *The World of Ice*, 1859, and *Ungava*, 1857), stormy seas (Frederick Marryat's *Mr. Midshipman Easy*, 1836, and *Masterman Ready*, 1841–1842; Kingston's *The Three Midshipmen*, 1873), the American frontier

(Mayne Reid's *The Rifle Rangers*, 1850; *The Desert Home*, 1852), or exotic locales (Kingston's *The Two Supercargoes*, 1878, and *Hendricks the Hunter*, 1879; Ballantyne's *The Coral Island*, 1858). Historical stories also re-create the thrill of explorations, military exploits, and the adventure and drama of living in the past. Martineau transports readers to the French Revolution, Norway, and Haiti (*The Playfellow: A Series of Tales*, 1841); Yonge to tenth-century France and fifteenth-century Germany (*The Little Duke*, 1854; *The Dove in the Eagle's Nest*, 1866); and Kingsley to the defeat of the Spanish Armada and William the Conqueror's invasion of England (*Westward Ho!*, 1855; *Hereward the Wake*, 1866). Just as domestic stories defined femininity, adventure stories embodied the ideals of masculinity: heroism, daring, strength, valor, endurance, and moral uprightness.

Another genre for boys was made up of stories about life at public schools. With a growing middle class, prosperity as a result of the industrial revolution, and the need to train colonial officials for the overseas empire, public boarding schools gained in popularity because they produced the ideal Victorian gentleman. They were prestigious institutions where upper- and middle-class children were groomed for the leadership of English society. The microcosmic setting of the all-male boarding school, regimentation and strict obedience of authority, and class consciousness were believed to inculcate the values of manliness, control over emotions, and discipline in boys. Sports were an important aspect of this mystique of manhood, of playing by the rules, physical fitness, and team spirit. School stories, beginning with Martineau's *The Crofton Boys* (1841), describe loyalty to school, "ragging" of new pupils, and "fagging" for seniors as rites of passage that build character and integrity.

The school story also became the forum for the debate on educational reforms that social critics such as Dickens and Thackeray were demanding. Hughes's *Tom Brown's School Days* (1857) and Farrar's *Eric; or, Little by Little* (1858) support the educational ideology of Thomas Arnold, who became headmaster of Rugby in 1828. Arnold emphasized the importance of teaching Christian morality, instituted the monitorial, or prefect, system (established on the principles of peer discipline and self-government first outlined by Andrew Bell in 1789) to reduce the authoritarian rule of schoolmasters, and revised the outdated curriculum. In *St. Winifred's* (1862) Farrar criticizes the classical curriculum as neglecting to give students training in the liberal disciplines of physical sciences, history, and modern languages. Critics of the Arnoldian system, however, point out that the strict discipline and brutality that were formerly attributed to schoolmasters were now exercised by the prefects.

Public-school stories were read not only in England but also by the children of British officials in the colonies. In India schools such as Bishop Cotton, Auckland House, La Martiniere, Sherwoods, Mount Carmel, and Woodstock were established for colonial children who could not return "home" to study. Ironically, while critics, such as John Reed in *Old School Ties* (1964), held the nineteenth-century public schools responsible for the decline of the British Empire because they mass-produced snobbish students lacking in individuality, imagination, and original thought, British-style schools in the former colonies still cater to the Westernized, English-speaking elite. Likewise, public-school stories and the antics of cult heroes such as Billy Bunter had so strong a hold on youthful imagination that the genre is still being imitated in postcolonial times. For instance, in Nigeria, Anezi Okoro's *One Week, One Trouble* (1972) and Cyprian Ekwensi's *Trouble in Form Six* (1966) glorify the mischievous pranks of pupils and the hierarchical structure of public schools.

As the boundaries of the British Empire extended during the Victorian period and as Britons traveled to foreign lands on military or civil service assignments, another popular genre in children's fiction emerged – the colonial novel. Directed at British children, these novels inculcated patriotic fervor by promoting the message of empire and colonization. They fulfilled readers' curiosity about "wild" and "inhospitable" lands and "exotic" cultures. In an attempt to rationalize British rule, colonial stories presented biased and often inaccurate descriptions of setting and people. They denigrated native cultures as being primitive, warmongering, and lawless, while British officials were portrayed as self-sacrificing, responsible, and just. Colonial novels also justified the British ideology of control of industrial raw materials and markets for manufactured products, political domination, and superiority of British values and civilization. In Ballantyne's *Black Ivory* (1873), for instance, the British navy fulfills its altruistic mission of saving East Africans from Arab slave traders and states that colonial rule will bring peace and prosperity to the savage land. There is no mention of the European slave trade on the west coast. These books established colonial stereotypes that are still prevalent in children's literature.

Expansionism and religious fervor naturally gave rise to missionary stories, which combine an evangelical message with that of empire building. Authors such as Tonna, Tucker, Mortimer, Sherwood, Kingston, and Cameron sincerely believed that through imperialism and Christianity the British were fulfilling their religious duty of saving heathen souls from meaningless, barbaric rituals. Religious novels and tracts were translated into the languages of Africa, Asia, Australia, Europe, and North America for the purpose of conversion and missionary work. Sherwood's *Little Henry and His Bearer* (1814), set at the time of the East India Company, is about imparting religious instruction to British memsahibs, children, and soldiers in military barracks in India, as well as converting Indians. Its sequel, *The Last Days of Boosy* (1842), serves as an excuse for denouncing Hinduism and the "evil" nature of its followers. Religious zeal also led Tucker in *Harold's Bride* (1889) and Mortimer in the short stories "The History of Ta-ma-ha-ha" and "King Radama," in *Far-Off* (1852), to describe in graphic detail "heathen" customs and persecution of Christian converts.

In the 1850s, changing social, political, economic, and religious conditions led to a distinct paradigm shift in the attitude of Victorians toward children. The evangelical belief in the inherent sinfulness of children was discarded for the more romantic and idealized view held by William Wordsworth, William Blake, and Samuel Taylor Coleridge that childhood was a time of innocence and purity. Far from considering parents perfect role models, attention was focused on the influence of parental behavior on a child's character and well-being. It is the impoverished environment, exploitation, and bad examples, stated Dickens, Kingsley, MacDonald, Ruskin, Jean Ingelow, Craik, and others, that make children deviate from the blissful state in which they were born.

Due to the efforts of enlightened thinkers, humanitarians such as Lord Shaftesbury, and social reform novelists, children were provided with legal rights. An 1842 act curtailed female labor and labor by children under ten in mines; the factory legislation of 1850 and 1867 ensured limited work hours, healthy environment, and compulsory education for children in factories; the Chimney Sweeper's Act of 1864 brought needed redress for the horrible conditions suffered by children in the profession; the Infant Life Protection Act of 1872 expressed concern over the rising rate of infanticide; and rural children were protected under the Gangs Act of 1867 and the 1873 Agricultural Children's Act, both aimed at restricting the employment of children under eight and providing compulsory education. The London Society for the Prevention of Cruelty to Children, founded largely due to the efforts of Stretton, paid attention to child abuse. Although these policies were not strictly enforced, by the end of the nineteenth century more lower-class children were going to school instead of working in factories, mines, and fields. The Education Act of 1870 included girls in the compulsory elementary education scheme, and by 1880 all children between the ages of five and thirteen had to attend school. The literacy rate accordingly rose to 94 percent for men and 90 percent for women by 1891.

The debate on educational methodology once again became heated, and imagination and enjoyment were considered important to the full development of a child. Literature became respectful of the innate worth of its young readers. Fairy tales, which had been rejected by moralists and educators such as Trimmer, Rousseau, Day, Edgeworth, and Barbauld as having a corrupting influence on children, started to make an appearance in English nurseries in the 1830s and 1840s. Earlier collections such as the English translation of Charles Perrault's *Stories from Times Past, with Morals — Tales of My Mother Goose* (1726?), Benjamin Tabart's multivolume *Collection of Popular Stories for the Nursery* (1804) and *Popular Fairy Tales* (1809), and William Godwin's *Fables, Ancient and Modern* (1805) had represented an undercurrent or subversive element in children's literature. With the English translations of the Grimm brothers' *German Popular Stories* (1823) and Danish folklorist Hans Christian Andersen's tales in 1846, fairy tales helped to oust the highly moralistic tone of juvenile literature. Soon collections of Scottish, French, Danish, Norse, Scandinavian, African, Russian, Italian, and Arabic stories were translated into English. Among the notable books for children were Kingsley's *The Heroes* (1855), an engaging retelling of three Greek legends, and Annie Keary's recounting of Norse myths in *The Heroes of Asgard* (1857). The lighthearted tone of traditional stories aimed to entertain children rather than to instruct and inculcate fear of punishment.

Just as realism was the special purview of women, male writers defended the imaginative aspects of the fairy tale and made great contributions to the development of modern fantasy. As philosophers, humanitarians, professors, and ordained priests, they used the literary fairy tale as an avenue for expressing their views on art, religion, social evils, and child raising. The growing popularity of fairy tales led some writers, such as George Cruikshank, to use this genre to promote abstinence, prohibition of liquor, free trade, and popular education. In "Fraud on the Fairies" (1853) Dickens states that fairy tales should not be exploited for "utilitarian" or didactic purposes. In the preface to his 1869 edition of the Grimms' *German Popular Stories* Ruskin also wrote strongly in favor of the innocence and simplicity of the original fairy tales instead of the "moral" fairy tale. In "The Fantastic Imagination" MacDonald says that if a fairy tale has "proportion and harmony it has vitality, and vitality is truth. The beauty may be plainer in it than truth, but without the truth the beauty could not be, and the fairytale would give no delight." He believes fantasy releases the reader's feelings and thoughts, each according to his own ability and inclination, to give significance to the fairy tale.

Nina Auerbach and U. C. Knoepflmacher in *Forbidden Journeys* (1992), a study of traditional and literary fairy tales by Victorian women writers, state that women writers moved subversively to fantasy writing because the stereotyping of gender roles confined them to writing didactic books of social realism, while male authors openly appropriated the fairy tale. They further state that Victorian women writers, "Unwilling to be stereotyped as fantasists, eager to be valued for their social realism . . . found themselves prevented from overtly acknowledging the importance of their own creative efforts of the fantasy lore bequeathed to them by their anonymous foremothers." There were a few scattered fantasy works by women in the early decades of the nineteenth century, such as Sherwood's *The Rose* (1818) and *The Lady in the Arbour* (1827), but they were generally moralistic in tone. Craik, who championed the cause of fairy tales, states in "The Age of Gold" that fairy tales are essential in fostering imagination and providing pleasure, while moralistic books destroy the creative impulse.

It was with Paget's *Hope of the Katzekopfs* (1844), Ruskin's *King of the Golden River* (written 1841, published 1851), and Dickens's five Christmas books (*A Christmas Carol*, 1843; *The Chimes*, 1844; *The Cricket on the Hearth*, 1845; *The Battle of Life*, 1846; *The Haunted Man*, 1848) that the severe moral tone of books for children was countered with fairy-tale conventions. While still heavily didactic, these early fantasies offered children moral choices but in an entertaining and refreshing manner. They were the first to introduce supernatural beings, allegorical themes, magic and enchantment, and manipulation of chronological time in children's literature. By focusing on the Christmas season, Dickens in *A Christmas Carol* effects the spiritual regeneration of the misanthropic Scrooge by making him relive and reflect on the key events of his life, the impact of neglect at home and school, and the corrupting influences of money and power.

The commercial success of Dickens's Christmas books, which rivaled the popularity of gift books and annuals, led to a host of imitators, such as Thackeray (*Christmas Books,* 1857), Catherine Gore (*The Snow Storm,* 1845; *The Inundation, or Pardon and Peace,* 1848), and George P. R. James (*The Last of the Fairies,* 1848). While Dickens's stories are about love, humanity, selflessness, and social responsibility to the poor, Thackeray's text and illustrations in *Mrs. Perkins' Ball* (1847) cast an ironic gaze upon human frailty. However, it was with his "fireside pantomimes" (*The Ring and the Rose,* 1855; *Rebecca and Rowena,* 1850), influenced by Paget's *Hope of the Katzekopfs,* that Thackeray employed fairy-tale motifs. Paget's fantasy also influenced Dickens's *Holiday Romance* (1868) and Craik's *Alice Learmont* (1851), *The Adventures of a Brownie* (1872), and *The Little Lame Prince* (1875).

The next milestone in mid-Victorian children's literature was the publication of Lewis Carroll's *Alice's Adventures in Wonderland* (1865) and its sequel *Through the Looking-Glass, and What Alice Found There* (1871). Carroll infused greater imagination and freedom in children's books and was the first to create a fantasy world with its own whimsical logic, vocabulary, and narrative structures. Juliet Dusinberre in *Alice to the Lighthouse: Children's Books and Radical Experiments in Art* (1987) points out that Carroll was also the first writer who refused to determine the ultimate meaning of the text. Both the Alice books are popular with modern-day educators because they anticipate the current pedagogical theory of Matthew Lipman, founder of the Institute for the Advancement of Philosophy for Children, in Montclair, New Jersey, that children need to be taught thinking skills. In her adventures through the two wonderlands Alice is confronted with some challenging situations that involve critical thinking, philosophic reasoning, and problem-solving strategies: What will happen to Alice when the Red King stops dreaming about her? Do words mean only what you want them to mean? Can all sentences be reversed and still mean the same thing? Carroll's play with time in the Bruno and Sylvie stories also anticipates modern science-fiction movies such as *Back to the Future* (1985). The Alice books had an immediate impact on writers such as Jean Ingelow (*Mopsa the Fairy,* 1869) and Christina Rossetti ("The Goblin Market," 1862; *Speaking Likenesses,* 1874).

Lear challenged the accepted poetic style for children with his *Book of Nonsense* (1846) and subsequent volumes of nonsense verse, stories, botany, and alphabets (1871, 1872, 1877). Lear takes everyday topics such as courtship, domestic life, cookery, and science and turns them into sheer fun by using pompous Latinized names or by stressing bodily imperfections and human frailty. Like Carroll, Lear delights readers with apparently meaningless words, puns, inverted logic, and incongruent placement of ideas and situations. Through the mediums of humor and grotesquerie he comments on how tender his reader's hold is on reality and how a whimsical perspective can make the commonplace world appear topsy-turvy or ridiculous.

Perhaps the most visionary writer of this period was MacDonald, whose evocative fantasies present a Romantic view of life — respect for humble folk, simplicity, a democratic outlook, beauty in nature. In *At the Back of the North Wind, The Princess and the Goblin* (1871), and *The Princess and Curdie* (1872) he describes fanciful journeys leading to inner growth and self-knowledge. MacDonald also explores the themes of universal love, male and female archetypes (*The Day Boy and the Night Girl,* 1879), psychological insight, and spiritual and mystical unity. With Carroll and MacDonald children's books became androgynous: heroism, bravery, and going on quests are not necessarily male attributes.

As the attitude toward children's education and books changed during the second half of Queen Victoria's reign, the emphasis of magazines also shifted from didacticism to entertainment. Instead of being distributed to poor children and cottagers by charitable institutions, magazines were now sold for profit. As children became viable consumers, and as literacy among lower-class children increased, magazines became gender-specific and began to cater to the needs and reading tastes of children. Popular writers such as Mayne Reid, Kingston, Marryat, Kingsley, Ballantyne, G. A. Henty, and J. B. Reed published their adventure/school stories in magazines directed at adolescent girls and boys. While at the beginning of the century there were approximately eleven juvenile periodicals, such as *The Lilliputian Magazine,* started in 1751 by John Newbery, after the 1860s, children's magazines, many of them weeklies, started to inundate the market. Some of the most prominent magazines to be established at this time were *Merry and Wise: A Magazine for Young People* (started in 1865), *Every Boy's Magazine* (1862), *Aunt Judy's Magazine* (1866), *The Boys of England* (1866), *Little Folks* (1871), *Good Words for the Young* (1868), and the *Boy's Own Paper* and *Girl's Own Paper,* started by the Religious Tract Society in 1879 and 1880 respectively.

At the beginning of the nineteenth century book illustration had already become a commercial business, and there were several engraving firms and printing shops run by popular artists such as the Dalziel brothers, Alfred Crowquill, Samuel Williams, Thomas Bewick, Edmund Evans, Joseph Swain, and William James Linton, who specialized in engraving their own designs as well as the works of other artists. Due to technical improvements the woodcuts and wood and copperplate engravings of the eighteenth and early nineteenth centuries were replaced by lithography, chromolithography, color printing, steel-plate engraving, and photomechanical or process engraving. As techniques became increasingly sophisticated, the importance of illustrations as a visual medium that delights as well as stimulates the imagination of the young was recognized.

Evans, a leading publisher of color books for children, engaged Randolph Caldecott, Walter Crane, and Kate Greenaway — called the "famous triumvirate" — for his many fine toy books and picture books. Aesthetically, the artwork became more graceful and the lines more lively. Children's books displayed a variety of styles, ranging from the comic art of John Leech, John Tenniel, Richard Doyle, and Hablot Knight Browne; to the naturalism of Charles Bennett and Greenaway; to the symbolic images of William Blake; to the ethereal paintings of the artist Arthur Hughes; to the grotesque exaggerations and caricatures of Lear; to the realism and gentle humor of Caldecott; and to the highly ornate and decorative style of Crane. The relationship between text and illustrations also shifted from ornamentation to accurate representation to interpretation and extension of text. Caldecott in particular could enter the text imaginatively and amplify it with elegant pictures of country landscapes, animals, rural life, and the moods and personalities of characters. Caldecott's contribution to children's book illustration and to the development of the picture book as a genre has been recognized in the annual Caldecott Medal (established in 1938), given to the most distinguished picture book in the United States.

The nineteenth century undoubtedly made great contributions to the development of children's literature, moving children's books from the severe and instructional tone of the late eighteenth century to the child-centered outlook that characterizes modern times. Twentieth-century children's literature is a direct outcome of the experimentation and innovations of the previous century. Between 1800 and 1880 all the major genres for children except drama had evolved, and, in Drotner's words, it was the "golden era in which new genres were being adopted for different age groups." There were concept books, toy books, picture storybooks, moral tales, realistic stories, historical fiction, adventure stories, school stories, nonsense verse, modern fantasy, informational books, annuals and gift books, and series books. Whether a book was intended for moral instruction, entertainment, or aesthetic pleasure, both text and illustrations paid attention to childhood as an important phase of life. The authors discussed in this volume also influenced the next generation of late-Victorian and Edwardian children's writers and established literary trends not only in England but in Europe, America, Australia, Africa, and Asia as well. For instance, the influence of Marryat and Ballantyne can be detected in the adventure stories of Henty, Robert Louis Stevenson, and William Haggard; Carroll in the fantasies of Kenneth Grahame, Beatrix Potter, and Kipling; Ballantyne and Kingston in the colonial novels of Henty, Kipling, William Haggard, and Edgar Rice Burroughs; and Hughes in the public-school stories of Talbot Baines Reed and James Hilton.

It was in the nineteenth century that children's publishing became a viable economic enterprise: Mortimer's *The Peep of Day* (1833) sold more than a million copies in the original version and was translated into thirty-eight languages; at the height of his career Marryat received more than a thousand pounds for each book; Dickens's Christmas books were a huge commercial success; Kingston's *The Three Midshipmen* was republished at least one hundred times before the 1940s; and Hughes's *Tom Brown's School Days* (1857) went into five editions within the first eight months and a total of fifty editions during the author's lifetime. While most nineteenth-century children's authors are now forgotten or read only by children's literature scholars or social historians, the works of some have remained in print and form the canon of children's literature: Dickens's *A Christmas Carol,* Carroll's Alice books, Anna Sewell's *Black Beauty,* MacDonald's *At the Back of the North Wind,* Lear's nonsense poetry, Caldecott's picture books, Browning's "Pied Piper of Hamelin," Jane Taylor's "The Star" ("Twinkle, Twinkle Little Star"), the Lambs' *Tales from Shakespear,* Ballantyne's *The Coral Island,* and Hughes's *Tom Brown's School Days.* These works continue to delight children with their universal themes, breadth of vision, and ability to touch the imagination.

— *Meena Khorana*

Acknowledgments

This book was produced by Bruccoli Clark Layman, Inc. Karen L. Rood is senior editor for the *Dictionary of Literary Biography* series. Sam Bruce was the in-house editor.

Production coordinator is James W. Hipp. Photography editors are Julie E. Frick and Margaret Meriwether. Photographic copy work was performed by Joseph M. Bruccoli. Layout and graphics supervisor is Emily Ruth Sharpe. Copyediting supervisor is Laurel M. Gladden. Typesetting supervisor is Kathleen M. Flanagan. Systems manager is George F. Dodge. Laura Pleicones and L. Kay Webster are editorial associates. The production staff includes Phyllis A. Avant, Ann M. Cheschi, Melody W. Clegg, Patricia Coate, Joyce Fowler, Stephanie C. Hatchell, Kathy Lawler Merlette, Jeff Miller, Pamela D. Norton, Delores Plastow, William L. Thomas Jr., and Allison Trussell.

Walter W. Ross and Steven Gross did library research. They were assisted by the following librarians at the Thomas Cooper Library of the University of South Carolina: Linda Holderfield and the interlibrary-loan staff; reference-department head Virginia Weathers; reference librarians Marilee Birchfield, Stefanie Buck, Stefanie DuBose, Rebecca Feind, Karen Joseph, Donna Lehman, Charlene Loope, Anthony McKissick, Jean Rhyne, Kwamine Simpson, and Virginia Weathers; circulation-department head Caroline Taylor; and acquisitions-searching supervisor David Haggard.

The publishers acknowledge the generous assistance of William R. Cagle, director of the Lilly Library, Indiana University, and his staff, who provided many of the illustrations in this volume. Their work represents the highest standards of librarianship and research.

The editor is indebted to Caroline C. Hunt (editorial adviser for the DLB volumes on British children's writers) for her generous assistance and guidance throughout the preparation of this volume; to Laura M. Zaidman for her valuable advice; and to all the contributors for their excellent scholarship and cooperation. The editor especially appreciates the help of colleagues and administrators at Morgan State University, particularly Burney Hollis, Dean of the College of Arts and Sciences, and Eugenia Collier, Chair, Department of English and Language Arts, for their continued support and encouragement. Thanks are also due to Betsy Van Auker and the interlibrary staff at Howard County Public Library for their efficient service in locating books.

British Children's Writers, 1800–1880

Dictionary of Literary Biography

Lucy Aikin
(6 November 1781 – 29 January 1864)

Linda J. Turzynski
Rutgers University

See also the Aikin entry in *DLB 144: Nineteenth-Century British Literary Biographers.*

BOOKS: *Epistles on Women, Exemplifying Their Character and Condition in Various Ages and Nations: With Miscellaneous Poems* (London: Printed for J. Johnson, 1810; Boston: Wells & Wait, 1810);

Juvenile Correspondence, or Letters, Designed as Examples of the Epistolary Style, for Children of Both Sexes (London: J. Johnson, 1811; Boston: Cummings & Hilliard, 1822);

Lorimer: A Tale (London: Printed for Henry Colburn, Sold by G. Goldie, Edinburgh, and J. Cumming, Dublin, 1814; Philadelphia: Carey / Boston: Wells & Lilly, 1816);

Memoirs of the Court of Queen Elizabeth, 2 volumes (London: Printed for Longman, Hurst, Rees, Orme & Brown, 1818; Boston: Wells & Lilly, 1821);

Memoirs of the Court of King James the First, 2 volumes (London: Longman, Hurst, Rees, Orme & Brown, 1822; Boston: Wells & Lilly, 1822);

Memoir of John Aikin, M.D.: With a Selection of His Miscellaneous Pieces, Biographical, Moral, and Critical, 2 volumes (London: Baldwin, Cradock & Joy, 1823; Philadelphia: A. Small, 1824);

An English Lesson Book, for the Junior Classes (London: Printed for Longman, Rees, Orme, Brown & Green, 1828); republished as *Holiday Stories for Young Readers* (London: Groombridge, 1858);

Memoirs of the Court of King Charles the First, 2 volumes (London: Longman, Rees, Orme, Brown, Green & Longman, 1828; Philadelphia: Carey, Lea & Blanchard, 1833);

Lucy Aikin; silhouette by J. Kendrick

The Life of Joseph Addison (London: Longman, Brown, Green & Longmans, 1843; Philadelphia: Carey & Hart, 1846);

Holiday Stories for Young Readers (London: Groombridge, 1858);

Memoirs, Miscellanies, and Letters of the Late Lucy Aikin, Including Those Addressed to the Rev. Dr. Channing from 1826 to 1842, edited by Philip Hemery Le Breton (London: Longman, Green, Longman, Roberts & Green, 1864);

The One Syllable Sunday Book, as Mary Godolphin (London, 1870).

OTHER: *Poetry for Children: Consisting of Short Pieces To Be Committed To Memory,* edited by Aikin (London: Printed for Richard Phillips, 1801);

Louis François Jauffret, *The Travels of Rolando: Containing, in a Supposed Tour round the World, Authentic Descriptions of the Geography, Natural History, Manners and Antiquities of Various Countries,* 4 volumes, translated by Aikin (London: Printed for Richard Phillips, 1804);

Jean Gaspar Hess, *The Life of Ulrich Zwingli,* translated by Aikin (London: J. Johnson, 1813);

Anna Laetitia Barbauld, *The Works of Anna Laetitia Barbauld,* edited, with a memoir, by Aikin (2 volumes, London: Longman, Hurst, Rees, Orme, Brown & Green, 1825; 3 volumes, Boston: Reed, 1826);

Barbauld, *A Legacy for Young Ladies: Consisting of Miscellaneous Pieces, in Prose and Verse,* edited by Aikin (London: Printed for Longman, Hurst, Rees, Orme & Green, 1826; Boston: Reed, 1826);

Elizabeth Ogilvy Benger, *Memoirs of the Life of Anne Boleyn, Queen of Henry VIII,* includes "Memoir of Miss Benger" by Aikin (London: Printed for Longman, Hurst, Orme & Brown, 1827);

The Juvenile Tale Book: A Collection of Interesting Tales and Novels for Youth, includes contributions by Aikin (London, 1837);

John Aikin, *Selected Works of the British Poets with Biographical and Critical Prefaces,* edited by Lucy Aikin (London: Longman, Brown, Green & Longmans, 1845);

John Aikin, *The Arts of Life,* edited by Lucy Aikin (London: Longman, Brown, Green, Longmans & Roberts, 1858);

Daniel Defoe, *Robinson Crusoe in Words of One Syllable,* edited by Aikin as Mary Godolphin (London & New York: Routledge, 1868 [i.e., 1867]);

Thomas Day, *Sandford and Merton: In Words of One Syllable,* edited by Aikin as Mary Godolphin (London & New York: Cassell, Petter & Galpin, 1868?);

Aesop's Fables: In Words of One Syllable, edited by Aikin as Mary Godolphin (New York: Miller, 1869; London: Cassell, Petter & Galpin, 1873);

John Bunyan, *The Pilgrim's Progress in Words of One Syllable,* edited by Aikin as Mary Godolphin (London: Routledge, 1869; New York: McLoughlin, 1884);

Johann David Wyss, *The Swiss Family Robinson, in Words of One Syllable,* edited by Aikin as Mary Godolphin (London: Routledge, 1869; Philadelphia: Altemus, 1899).

Like her celebrated aunt, Anna Laetitia Barbauld, Lucy Aikin felt a strong interest in providing accessible and suitable books for children. Her interest in providing proper literary models for young people to follow is evident in *Poetry for Children: Consisting of Short Pieces To Be Committed to Memory* (1801) and her engaging *Juvenile Correspondence* (1811), which espoused a more intimate, relaxed style for young writers than the typical models of the day. The versatility of Aikin's writing is reflected in the different genres she attempted: historical biography, fiction, poetry, letters, and the curious adaptations of classic literature published posthumously under the name Mary Godolphin.

Born in Warrington, England, on 6 November 1781, Lucy Aikin enjoyed all the opportunities and advantages of growing up in a literary family. She was the daughter of Dr. John Aikin, author and physician, and Martha Jennings Aikin, a cousin to John. Family influences were always to be important for Lucy Aikin; the strongly nurturing background of her early years provided her with a model of family living reflected in all her writings for young people.

Although Aikin was called a "little Dunce" by her grandmother for not learning to read as quickly as her precocious aunt and older brothers — a reproach that she remembered until the end of her life — she rapidly came into her own as both a writer and a scholar. Her lively intelligence was encouraged at home, where her father was her principal tutor, since experience had shown that the local school could profit her but little. The education she received was not normally vouchsafed to girls in the eighteenth century: she had a thorough grounding in the English classics and was fluent in Latin, French, and Italian. She shared her father's taste for history and biography, and she would later repay his instruction by becoming his biographer. Her studies in history served her well in the writing of her popular court memoirs, which described life during the reigns of Elizabeth I, Charles I, and James I.

In 1792, after being identified as the author of two fiery pamphlets attacking the repeal of the Corporation and Trust Acts, John Aikin moved his family and practice from Yarmouth to London. Lucy Aikin's Unitarian principles, which she inherited from her father, remained with her all of her life and are forcibly and eloquently expressed in her long correspondence with Dr. William Ellery Channing, a Unitarian minister who lived in Boston. On account of failing health, John Aikin moved again in 1797, this time to Stoke Newington, where Lucy Aikin remained until his death.

Aikin began writing early, contributing articles and reviews to magazines when she was seventeen. When she was twenty, her anthology *Poetry for Children* appeared. It included original work – poems by Aikin and by her aunt, Barbauld – but principally presented selections from English Augustan writers, including Alexander Pope, John Dryden, Joseph Addison, and John Gay. William Shakespeare is also represented, as is John Milton; in later editions poems by William Wordsworth appear.

Aikin favors both the moral and the pathetic in her own poetry and in the poems she selects from others. One of the two Shakespearean selections is the following quatrain: "What stronger breast-plate than a heart untainted? / Thrice is he arm'd that hath his quarrel just; / And he but naked, though lock'd up in steel, / Whose conscience with injustice is corrupted." Even a casual reader of Shakespeare will recognize that this is not the Bard at his most stirring, melodic, or memorable – even the sentiments expressed are said more movingly elsewhere. Soundness of message, briefly and clearly expressed, is what matters in this collection – comparatively feeble virtues, given the poetic richness of the Shakespearean canon. Aikin's taste for the pathetic is revealed in her choice of William Cowper's "The Goldfinch Starved in His Cage" (1782), John Bicknell and Thomas Day's "The Dying Negro" (1773), and John Thelwall's "The Orphan Boy" (1800).

In her own poetry Aikin explores similar territories. In "The Beggar Man," the opening piece of the anthology, an old man dressed in rags appears at a farmer's cozy homestead, begging for shelter. The farmer and his family welcome their guest freely, while the children "chafed his frozen hands in theirs." He weeps his thanks, and the poem concludes:

> The children too began to sigh,
> And all their merry chat was o'er;
> And yet they felt, they knew not why,
> More glad than they had done before.

The children's awakening consciousness of the joyful power of virtue is an image typical of Aikin's work, as is the rosy picture of a sympathetic and affectionate family. In another original poem, "Prince Leboo," a young black Pacific islander sails to "gay busy London" with some English sailors whom he has helped rescue. He is delighted with the metropolis and plans to bring back the fine English merchandise to his native Pelew. This, alas, is not to be, for "death has arrested him far from Pelew, / And strangers have wept o'er the gentle Leboo!"

What is striking about these poems today is that, apparently, little concession is paid to the youth of their intended audience. Neither the diction nor the subjects reflect what would now be judged appropriate for children – death, in particular, is treated more openly than in modern children's literature. Yet, whatever the modern reader may think of Aikin's selections, one cannot with justice accuse her of being insensitive to the special concerns of young readers. In the preface to *Poetry for Children* she muses, "But when we consider how many of the subjects of verse are unintelligible to children, or improper for them – how few poems have been written, or how few poets could be trusted to write, to them – we shall not be surprised to find it a frequent complaint with judicious instructors, that so few pieces proper for children to commit to memory are to be found either in the entire works of poets, or in selections made from them, purposely for the use of young people." Further criteria for her selection include brevity – meaning that the poem could be learned in one or two lessons – and intrinsic worth; additionally, the style of the poem "should have nothing in it that a well-educated child might not, their matter nothing that he should not, understand."

Even in this early work Aikin is fully aware of the advantages of education and the role the home and parents should play in the proper rearing of their young. The careful and attentive tutoring the author had received as a girl is the model she advocates with great energy, and the sensitive and responsive children portrayed in *Po-*

etry for Children are clearly versions of the young Lucy.

This same well-educated, well-intentioned child of good moral purpose is the pattern for the childish writers in *Juvenile Correspondence*. The letters, designed as models for children to emulate, offer a frank, chatty, and open style, one that reveals the trust and affection between the correspondents. In letter 5 Edward Monkton describes for his mother a fight in which he participated. He recounts that the other boy, Thompson, had been hitting a girl younger than himself. Upon being called "an impertinent little prig for meddling," Edward went into "a great passion" and hit Thompson in the nose. Thompson lied about the cause of the fight, but little Eliza set the matter straight for the adult inquisitors. Edward concludes that while he did not think that his uncle was too angry over the matter – its nature having been established satisfactorily – he nevertheless told Edward that he had been "rather too hot," and he hoped Edward would be "more calm another time, and take care not to give the first blow."

All of Aikin's moral strategies are at work here. First, there is the manly candor about an undeniably unfortunate incident, the fight itself. Its natural evil, however, is partly redeemed by its championship of weakness and innocence, while the uncle's corrective provides a better course should similar situations occur in the future. Finally, there is the laudable act of confessing to his "dear mama," with every confidence of her forgiveness. The letter provides not only an epistolary model but a behavioral one.

After her father's death in 1822, Lucy Aikin and her mother settled in Hampstead, where they lived until her mother died in 1830. She continued alone in Hampstead until 1844, when she moved to London to join her nephew C. A. Aikin and his family. After two years she joined the Wimbledon household of her niece, Mrs. Philip Hemery Le Breton, where she lived until 1852. In that year the whole family returned to Hampstead, where Aikin spent the rest of her life. She died of influenza on 29 January 1864. Aikin never married but always remained closely attached to her family, whose presence reverberates in her literary contributions.

Aikin's one-syllable redactions of literary classics, written under the pseudonym Mary Godolphin and published after her death, deserve special attention, for they combine most vividly the impulses that inspired the author. The books she chose to rewrite were adventurous enough to interest young readers, while at the same time providing sound moral instruction. They were designed not only to make literature available to beginning readers – and thereby inspire them with a delight in reading – but to adults with limited literacy as well. In the preface to her 1867 adaptation of Daniel Defoe's *Robinson Crusoe* (1719), Aikin explains her intentions: "But although, as far as the subject matter is concerned, the book can lay no claims to originality, it is believed that the idea and scope of its construction are entirely novel, for the One Syllable literature of the present day furnishes little more than a few short, unconnected sentences, and those chiefly in spelling books."

Any abridgment inevitably sacrifices something, and Aikin's are no exception. Occasional distortions occur, but they were probably considered a small price to pay for making the story more widely available. Aikin's careful work with these classics is evident in an example from her version of *Robinson Crusoe* and the original. In Defoe's account of Friday's death, the passage reads,

> Whether they understood him or not, that I knew not. . . . but immediately Friday cried out they were going to shoot, and, unhappily for him, poor fellow, they let fly about three hundred of their arrows, and, to my inexpressible grief, killed poor Friday, no other man being in their sight. The poor fellow was shot with no less than three arrows, and about three more fell very near him; such unlucky marksmen they were!

Aikin's rendition gives this as

> It may be that they did not know what he said, but as soon as he spoke to them I heard him cry out that they would shoot. This was too true, for they let fly a thick cloud of darts, and to my great grief poor Friday fell dead, for there was no one else in their sight. He was shot with three darts, and three more fell quite near him, so good was their aim.

Aikin has been successful in keeping the sense of the passage intact, as well as keeping true to her avowed purpose in making the reading more simple. What is lost is the sophistication and irony of Defoe's language, as he styles the deadly archers "unlucky marksmen" – unlucky, of course, for the dead Friday; Aikin's "so good was their aim" merely emphasizes the accuracy of the marksmen.

The same hierarchy of guiding principles that governed the selections in *Poetry for Children* operates in these books: the moral concern – in this case the democratization of literature – outweighs the purely literary one. While the one-syllable books might now be considered a wrongheaded experiment both pedagogically and aesthetically, the passion for literacy that inspired them is admirable. Aikin's attention to her originals and her obvious respect for them keep this pioneering effort well within the bounds of honest abridgments.

While Aikin's purposes are explicit in her children's writings, her success in achieving them is questionable. In his influential *Fantasy and Reason: Children's Literature in the Eighteenth Century* (1985) Geoffrey Summerfield complains that "it was almost invariably [Charles] Lamb's feebler self that was engaged in the writing of books for children," and he points to *Poetry for Children* as one of the "wretched precedents" of Lamb's compositions. His testiness notwithstanding, Lucy Aikin's perception of children as a special audience and her determination to provide a special literature for them deserve sympathetic recognition. Her ultimate success should not, perhaps, be measured so much by her own compositions as by the precedents she provided her literary inheritors.

Letters:

Memoirs, Miscellanies and Letters of the Late Lucy Aikin: Including Those Addressed to the Rev. Dr. Channing from 1826 to 1842, edited by Philip Hemery Le Breton (London: Longman, Green, Longman, Roberts & Green, 1864);

Correspondence of William Ellery Channing, D.D., and Lucy Aikin, from 1826 to 1842, edited by Anna Laetitia Le Breton (Boston: Roberts, 1874).

Reference:

Geoffrey Summerfield, *Fantasy and Reason: Children's Literature in the Eighteenth Century* (Athens: University of Georgia Press, 1985).

R. M. Ballantyne

(24 April 1825 – 8 February 1894)

Joel D. Chaston
Southwest Missouri State University

BOOKS: *Hudson's Bay; or, Everyday Life in the Wilds of North America* (Edinburgh: Blackwood, 1847; New York: Nelson, 1857);

Snowflakes and Sunbeams; or, The Young Fur Traders, illustrated by Ballantyne (London, Edinburgh & New York: Thomas Nelson, 1856), republished as *The Young Fur Traders* (London: Blackie, 1950);

Three Little Kittens: A Nursery Tale, illustrated by Ballantyne, as Comus (London, Edinburgh & New York: Thomas Nelson, 1856);

The Butterfly's Ball and the Grasshopper's Feast, by William Roscoe, expanded and illustrated by Ballantyne, as Comus (London, Edinburgh & New York: Thomas Nelson, 1857);

The Life of a Ship from the Launch to the Wreck, illustrated by Ballantyne (London, Edinburgh & New York: Thomas Nelson, 1857);

Mister Fox, illustrated by Ballantyne, as Comus (London, Edinburgh & New York: Thomas Nelson, 1857);

My Mother, illustrated by Ballantyne, as Comus (London, Edinburgh & New York: Thomas Nelson, 1857);

Ungava: A Tale of Esquimaux Land, illustrated by Ballantyne (London, Edinburgh & New York: Thomas Nelson, 1857);

The Coral Island: A Tale of the Pacific Ocean, illustrated by Ballantyne (London, Edinburgh & New York: Thomas Nelson, 1858);

Handbook to the New Gold Fields: A Full Account of the Richness and Extent of the Fraser and Thompson River Gold Mines (London: Hamilton, Adams, 1858; Edinburgh: Thomas Nelson, 1858);

Martin Rattler; or, A Boy's Adventure in the Forests of Brazil (London, Edinburgh & New York: Thomas Nelson, 1858);

The Robber Kitten, illustrated by Ballantyne (London, Edinburgh & New York: Thomas Nelson, 1858);

Environs and Vicinity of Edinburgh (London, Edinburgh & New York: Thomas Nelson, 1859);

R. M. Ballantyne; painting by John Ballantyne (National Portrait Gallery, London)

How Not to Do It, A Manual for the Awkward Squad (Edinburgh & London: Constable, 1859);

Mee-a-ow!; or, Good Advice to Cats and Kittens (London, Edinburgh & New York: Thomas Nelson, 1859);

Ships: The Great Eastern and Lesser Squad (Edinburgh & London: Constable, 1859);

The Lakes of Killarney (London, Edinburgh & New York: Thomas Nelson, 1859);

The World of Ice; or, The Whaling Cruiser of "The Dolphin" and the Adventures of Her Crew in the Polar Region (London, Edinburgh & New York: Thomas Nelson, 1859);

Discovery and Adventure in the Polar Seas and Regions, by Sir John Leslie and Hugh Murray, expanded by Ballantyne (London, Edinburgh & New York: Thomas Nelson, 1860);

Ensign Sopht's Volunteer Almanac for 1861 (Edinburgh: Constable, 1860);

The Golden Dream; or, Adventures in the Far West (London: J. Nisbet, 1860);

The Volunteer Levee; or, The Remarkable Experiences of Ensign Sopht, illustrated by Ballantyne (Edinburgh: Constable, 1860);

The Dog Crusoe and His Master (London, Edinburgh & New York: Thomas Nelson, 1861);

The Gorilla Hunters: A Tale of the Wilds of Africa (London, Edinburgh & New York: Thomas Nelson, 1861);

The Red Eric; or, the Whaler's Last Cruise (London: Routledge, 1861);

Away in the Wilderness; or, Life Among the Red Indians and Fur Traders of North America (London: J. Nisbet, 1863);

The Wild Man of the West: A Tale of the Rocky Mountains, illustrated by John Baptist Zwecker (London: Routledge, 1863);

Fast in the Ice; or, Adventures in the Polar Regions (London: J. Nisbet, 1863);

Fighting the Whales; or, Doings and Dangers on a Fishing Cruise (London: J. Nisbet, 1863);

Gascoyne – The Sandal-Wood Trader, A Tale of the Pacific (London: J. Nisbet, 1864);

Chasing the Sun, or, Rambles in Norway (London: J. Nisbet, 1864);

The Lifeboat: A Tale of our Coast Heroes (London: J. Nisbet, 1864);

Freaks on the Fells; or, Three Months' Rustication, And Why I Did Not Become a Sailor (London: Routledge, 1865);

The Lighthouse: Being the Story of a Great Fight between Man and Sea (London: J. Nisbet, 1865);

Shifting Winds; A Tough Yarn (London: J. Nisbet, 1866; Philadelphia: Porter & Coates, 1866);

Silver Lake; or, Lost in the Snow (London: Jackson, Walford, & Hodder, 1867; Philadelphia: Lippincott, 1868);

Deep Down: A Tale of the Cornish Mines (London: J. Nisbet, 1868; New York: Burt, 1868);

Fighting the Flames: A Tale of the London Fire Brigade (London: J. Nisbet, 1868; Philadelphia: Lippincott, 1868);

Photographs of Edinburgh with Descriptive Letterpress (Glasgow: Andrew Duthie, 1868);

The Battle and the Breeze, or, The Fights and Fancies of a British Tar (London: J. Nisbet, 1869);

The Cannibal Islands; or, Captain Cook's Adventures in the South Seas (London: J. Nisbet, 1869);

Digging for Gold; or, Adventures in California (London: J. Nisbet, 1869);

Erling the Bold: A Tale of the Norse Sea-Kings, illustrated by Ballantyne (London: J. Nisbet, 1869);

Hunting the Lions (London: J. Nisbet, 1869);

Lost in the Forest; or, Wandering Will's Adventures in South America (London: J. Nisbet, 1869);

Over the Rocky Mountains; or, Wandering Will in the Land of the Red Skin (London: J. Nisbet, 1869);

Saved by the Lifeboat; or, A Tale of Wreck and Rescue on the Coast (London: J. Nisbet, 1869);

Sunk at Sea; or, The Adventures of Wandering Will in the Pacific (London: J. Nisbet, 1869);

The Floating Light of the Goodwin Sands: A Tale (London: J. Nisbet, 1870);

Up in the Clouds; or, Balloon Voyages (London: J. Nisbet, 1870);

The Iron Horse; or, Life on the Line. A Tale of the Grand National Trunk Railway (London: J. Nisbet, 1871);

The Pioneers: A Tale of the Western Wilderness Illustrative of the Adventures and Discoveries of Sir Alexander MacKenzie (London: J. Nisbet, 1872);

The Norsemen in the West; or, America Before Columbus (London: J. Nisbet, 1872; New York: Thomas Nelson, 1872);

Black Ivory: A Tale of Adventure among the Slavers of East Africa (London, Edinburgh & New York: Thomas Nelson, 1873);

Life in the Red Brigade. A Story for Boys (London: Routledge, 1873);

Chit-Chat by a Penitent Cat (London, Edinburgh & New York: Thomas Nelson, 1874);

The Ocean and Its Wonders (London: Thomas Nelson, 1874);

The Pirate City: An Algerine Adventure (London: J. Nisbet, 1874; New York: Thomas Nelson, 1874);

Rivers of Ice: A Tale Illustrative of Alpine Adventure and Glacier Action (London: J. Nisbet, 1875);

The Story of the Rock; or, Building on the Eddystone (London: J. Nisbet, 1875);

Under the Waves; Diving in Deep Waters (London: J. Nisbet, 1876);

The Settler and the Savage: A Tale of Peace and War in South Africa (London: J. Nisbet, 1877; New York: Thomas Nelson, 1877);

In the Track of the Troops: A Tale of Modern War (London: J. Nisbet, 1878);

Jarwin and Cuffy: A Tale (London: Warne, 1878; New York: James Pott, 1882);

Six Months at the Cape; or, Letters to Periwinkle from South Africa (London: J. Nisbet, 1878);

Philosopher Jack: A Tale of the Southern Seas (London: J. Nisbet, 1879);

The Lonely Island; or, The Refuge of the Mutineers (London: J. Nisbet, 1880; New York: Thomas Nelson, 1880);

Post Haste: A Tale of Her Majesty's Mails (London: J. Nisbet, 1880; New York: Thomas Nelson, 1880);

The Red Man's Revenge: A Tale of the Red River Flood (London: J. Nisbet, 1880);

The Collected Works of Ensign Sopht — Late of the Volunteers (Edinburgh: Constable, 1881);

The Giant of the North; or, Pokings Round the Pole (London: J. Nisbet, 1881; New York: Thomas Nelson, 1881);

My Doggie and I (London: J. Nisbet, 1881);

The Kitten Pilgrims; or, Great Battles and Grand Victories, illustrated by Ballantyne (London: J. Nisbet, 1882);

The Battery and the Boiler; or, Adventures in the Laying of Submarine Electric Cables (London: J. Nisbet, 1883; New York: Thomas Nelson, 1883);

Battles with the Sea, or, Heroes of the Lifeboat and Rocket (London: J. Nisbet, 1883);

Dusty Diamonds Cut and Polished. A Tale of City-Arab Life and Adventure (London: J. Nisbet, 1883; New York: Thomas Nelson, 1883);

The Madman and the Pirate (London: J. Nisbet, 1883);

The Young Trawler: A Story of Life and Death and Rescue on the North Sea (London: J. Nisbet, 1884);

The Island Queen; or, Dethroned by Fire and Water. A Tale of the Southern Hemisphere (London: J. Nisbet, 1885);

The Rover of the Andes: A Tale of Adventure in South America (London: J. Nisbet, 1885; New York: Thomas Nelson, 1885);

Twice Bought: A Tale of Oregon Gold Fields (London: J. Nisbet, 1885);

Red Rooney; or, The Last of the Crew (London: J. Nisbet, 1886);

The Prairie Chief (London: J. Nisbet, 1886);

The Big Otter: A Tale of the Great Nor'West (London: J. Nisbet, 1887);

The Fugitives; or, The Tyrant Queen of Madagascar (London: J. Nisbet, 1887; New York: Thomas Nelson, 1887);

Blue Lights; or, Hot Work in the Sudan (London: J. Nisbet, 1888; New York: Thomas Nelson, 1888);

The Middy and the Moors: An Algerine Story (London: J. Nisbet, 1888); republished as *Slave of the Moors* (London: Latimer, 1950);

Blown to Bits, or The Lonely Man of Rakata (London: J. Nisbet, 1889);

The Crew of the "Water Wagtail": A Story of Newfoundland (London: J. Nisbet, 1889);

Charlie to the Rescue: A Tale of the Seas and the Rockies, illustrated by Ballantyne (London: J. Nisbet, 1890);

The Garret and the Garden; or, Low Life High Up. And Jeff Benson; or, The Young Coastguardsman (London: J. Nisbet, 1890);

The Buffalo Runners. A Tale of the Red River Plains, illustrated by Ballantyne (London: J. Nisbet, 1891);

The Coxwain's Bride; or, The Rising Tide. A Tale of the Sea and Other Tales, illustrated by Ballantyne (London: J. Nisbet, 1891);

The Lively Poll; A Tale of the North Sea (London: J. Nisbet, 1891);

The Hot Swamp: A Romance of Old Albion (London: J. Nisbet, 1892; New York: Thomas Nelson, 1892);

Hunted and Harried: A Tale of the Scottish Covenanters (London: J. Nisbet, 1892; Boston: Bradley, 1893);

The Walrus Hunters: A Romance of the Realms of Ice (London: J. Nisbet, 1893; New York: Thomas Nelson, 1893);

Personal Reminiscences in Book-Making (London: J. Nisbet, 1893).

OTHER: Patrick Fraser Tyler, *The Northern Coasts of America, and the Hudson's Bay Territories, With Continuation by R. M. Ballantyne — A Narrative of Discovery,* edited by Ballantyne (Edinburgh: Thomas Nelson, 1853).

One of the most popular, prolific, and influential writers of nineteenth-century boys' adventure stories and historical fiction, R. M. Ballantyne wrote around one hundred books, many set in exotic locations such as the South Seas, Africa, the Arctic, the Rocky Mountains, and South America. While most of his novels are episodic and are occasionally melodramatic, Ballantyne helped to establish firmly the realistic adventure story for young people, introducing readers to a variety of cultures and geographic locations. A few of his novels, most notably *The Coral Island: A Tale of the Pacific Ocean* (1858), *The Dog Crusoe and His Master* (1861), *Martin Rattler; or, A Boy's Adventure in the Forests of Brazil* (1858), *Snowflakes and Sunbeams; or, The Young Fur Traders* (1856), and *Ungava: A Tale of the Esquimaux Land* (1857), have greatly influenced subsequent writers, especially Robert Louis Stevenson, J. M. Barrie, and William Golding.

Robert Michael Ballantyne was born in Edinburgh, Scotland, on 24 April 1825, the ninth child of Alexander "Sandy" Thomson Ballantyne and Anne Randall Scott Grant. During his childhood Ballantyne's family was involved in publishing. His uncle James was the main publisher for novelist Sir Walter Scott, while, among other ventures, his father managed *The Kelso Mail*. Both his father and uncle were financially ruined by Scott's bankruptcy in 1826. Ballantyne was educated for two years at the Edinburgh Academy, but because of his family's financial difficulties he was taught at home by his mother and sisters beginning in 1838.

At his father's suggestion, sixteen-year-old Ballantyne became an apprentice clerk to the Honourable Hudson Bay Company in 1841. He spent the next six years in the United States and Canada trading with Indians. Ballantyne arrived in York Factory, the company's main headquarters, in August 1841 and left ten days later for Fort Garry in Red River Settlement. The following June he was transferred to Norway House, a post on Lake Winnipeg, then back to York Factory in 1843 where he first tried his hand at writing by producing a poem about Hudsons Bay. Although most of his duties with Hudsons Bay Company involved office work, Ballantyne frequently went hunting, fishing, trapping, and canoeing, developing an interest in wilderness survival that inspired many of his books.

On his return to Edinburgh, Ballantyne learned that his father had died, and he assumed the responsibility of putting his family's affairs in order. While Ballantyne was working as a clerk for the North British Railway Company, Mary Grieg, a family friend, offered to subsidize the publication of letters he had written to his mother from Canada. He revised the letters, forming a narrative that was published in late 1847 as *Hudson's Bay; or, Everyday Life in the Wilds of North America*. Ballantyne also drew several of the book's original illustrations.

Hudson's Bay follows Ballantyne's career from his initial appointment and journey to York Factory to his discharge; Ballantyne comes across as a young romantic, much like the heroes of his later novels. He describes various outposts and the company's operations, as well as details about the lives of the Cree Indians. He often focuses on his various journeys into the wilderness, including canoe trips up various rivers, as well as hunting, camping, and sleighing. Ballantyne shows the dis-

comforts and joys of exploring new lands but ultimately suggests that an adventurous life is preferable to one spent doing mundane tasks.

Most of the book's original readers were family members and friends; when all debts were paid, Ballantyne netted about twenty pounds. The book was read by James Blackwood, the editor of *Blackwood's Magazine*, who agreed to print a second edition of one thousand copies. This edition did not sell well, partly because it was marketed for adults.

In the fall of 1848 Ballantyne's sister, Madalina, died. According to biographer Eric Quayle, this prompted a new interest in religion, as well as his subsequent election as an elder in the Free Church of Scotland in 1849. In the summer of 1849 Ballantyne took a job with paper manufacturer Alexander Cowan and Company, then bought a junior partnership with Thomas Constable and Company, the publishing firm once run by his uncle. While at Thomas Constable, he edited Patrick Fraser Tyler's *The Northern Coasts of America, and the Hudson's Bay Territories, With Continuation by R. M. Ballantyne — A Narrative of Discovery* (1853), adding three chapters to the end. Although Ballantyne was not originally credited for this work, his name was added to the title page in 1854. William Nelson, who published this book, then suggested that Ballantyne write a novel for boys based on his own experiences, but the project was delayed after the death of Ballantyne's mother. Eventually, Ballantyne left his job with Thomas Constable, and after a three-month holiday in Norway he finished *Snowflakes and Sunbeams; or, The Young Fur Traders*, later retitled *The Young Fur Traders*.

The book's basic plot is one that Ballantyne employed in other novels: a young, well-intentioned but impetuous young man longs for excitement instead of a boring life in a mundane occupation. Against the better judgment of his guardian, he travels to an exotic locale, faces great dangers and difficulties, and finally returns home. In *The Young Fur Traders* Charley Kennedy does not want to spend his life working as a clerk for Hudson's Bay Company. He and his sister, Kate, have been raised near Lake Winnipeg in a colony called Red River Settlement. Reluctantly, Charley's father agrees to let him become involved in the hunting and trading part of the company after he demonstrates his courage by taming a new horse. Charley and Harry Somerville, a clerk, soon find themselves on their way to York Fort to receive their assignments. Before their arrival, however, they befriend an Indian named Redfeather.

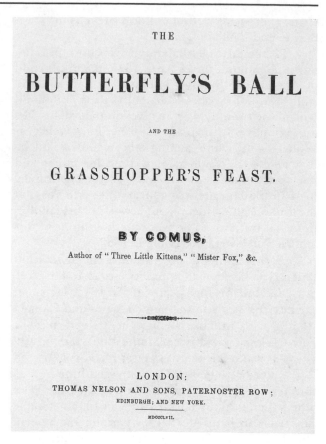

Frontispiece and title page for Ballantyne's expanded, illustrated edition of William Roscoe's popular poem (courtesy of the Lilly Library, Indiana University)

Charley is soon sent on a mission to establish good relations between the traders and an Indian camp. Meanwhile, Harry Somerville, who has remained at York Fort, hunts arctic foxes in his spare time. Charley and Harry keep in contact through letters. After many adventures they return to Red River Settlement, where Harry has been reassigned. Harry then marries Kate, and the novel ends with the assurance that he and Charley will always be friends, although they may be separated.

Like most of Ballantyne's novels, *The Young Fur Traders* is episodic, focusing on adventure and excitement while dispensing advice to readers on how to live. The one safeguard against all evil, the reader is told, is the love of God. The book also describes in detail life in the Canadian wilderness. For example, Ballantyne tells readers how to make "robbiboo," a combination of flour, water, and dried buffalo flesh. The novel also treats one of Ballantyne's favorite themes, strong friendships that weather separations over great distances and long periods of time. Ballantyne suggests that such

friendships can overcome racial barriers, as is the case with Harry and Charley and Redfeather.

Based on the success of *The Young Fur Traders*, Ballantyne's publisher expressed interest in other manuscripts. As a result Ballantyne submitted a series of short stories he had invented for his nieces, including *The Three Little Kittens: A Nursery Tale* (1856), *Mister Fox* (1857), *My Mother* (1857), and *The Butterfly's Ball and the Grasshopper's Feast* (1857). Ballantyne requested, however, that the publisher not use his real name, so these stories originally appeared under the pseudonym "Comus." These books were popular throughout Ballantyne's life, especially *The Three Little Kittens,* which he immediately followed with two other "kitten" books, *The Robber Kitten* (1858) and *Mee-a-ow!; or, Good Advice to Cats and Kittens* (1859). Years later Ballantyne added two more titles to the series, *Chit-Chat by a Penitent Cat* (1874) and *The Kitten Pilgrims; or, Great Battles and Grand Victories* (1882), a simplified version of John Bunyan's *Pilgrim's Progress* (1678), replacing the main character, Christian, with two kittens.

Ballantyne soon returned to writing adventure fiction. His next novels, *Ungava* and *The Coral Island,* are two of his most popular and influential works. Like *Hudson's Bay* and *The Young Fur Traders, Ungava* focuses on the Hudson's Bay Fur Company. George Stanley is asked to travel far north and establish a new post in Ungava, a desolate arctic location. Most of the men at Moose Flat are reluctant to make the move, but eventually George puts together a group of fifteen people, including the novel's protagonist, his ten-year-old-daughter, Edith, known as "Eda," and a young trader, Frank Morton. The book chronicles the group's canoe trip to Ungava, during which Frank Morton rescues the blacksmith, Bryan, from a polar bear. At Ungava the group builds Fort Chimo, named after Eda's dog, who, among other things, protects Eda and two Inuit girls from a wolf. During the last half of the book Eda's role grows. She helps rescue Frank after he is attacked by a wolf, and she then becomes lost. She is rescued by a group of Inuit who care for her until she is found by her friends. In the last chapter Edith, now seventeen, meets Frank Morton again and the two are married.

The book features descriptions of the Arctic and a discourse on the ways snow affects emotions, and it celebrates the courage of explorers. The novel also has an important subplot involving the Inuit and their quarrel with the Allat, resulting in the kidnapping of an Inuit woman. While the trappers express prejudices against both of these groups of people, Ballantyne questions some stereotypes through Edith's generally positive interactions with the Inuit. Edith Stanley's depiction as a courageous, strong-willed young girl is a departure from the author's usual all-male cast of characters.

Ballantyne's most famous novel, *The Coral Island,* is unusual in its use of a first-person narrator. It is related by Ralph Rover, who at the age of fifteen determines to set sail for the South Seas. With his parents' blessing he becomes a crew member of the "Arrow," along with two other youths, eighteen-year-old Jack Martin and a mischievous fourteen-year-old boy named Peterkin Gay. When the ship is wrecked while rounding Cape Horn, the three boys are marooned on "The Coral Island," a tropical paradise. Based more on Ballantyne's imagination than on firsthand knowledge, the first half of the story is a schoolboy's dream. The three boys survive with the help of a penknife, a single ax, and trees filled with coconuts. Jack becomes their leader, helping them to catch fish, establish headquarters in a cave, and explore a nearby island of penguins. The boys are threatened by

Title page for Ballantyne's best-known novel, the story of a fifteen-year-old boy who sails to the South Seas (courtesy of the Lilly Library, Indiana University)

sharks and dine on crabs, wild pigs, and exotic fruits.

The second half of the novel is both more serious and more didactic. Two warring groups of "savages" show up and the boys become involved in the battle. Ralph is kidnapped, but he and a crew member, Billy, escape. In the process, Billy is wounded and dies, but not without getting some religion from Ralph. Ralph is reunited with his friends and helps save a Tongan named Avatea from cannibals. The boys eventually see the natives converted to Christianity by a missionary, and they ultimately set sail for home.

The popularity of this novel is at least in part because of its three young protagonists, whose likable banter and unfailing humor make them more believable than some of Ballantyne's other characters. In addition, for much of the novel the three boys have to use their own wits to save themselves.

Roger Lancelyn Green has argued that *The Coral Island* is "the best 'wrecked island' story of all." It was certainly one of the most influential. The novel's South Seas island is the prototype for those described in three better-known books: Stevenson's *Treasure Island* (1883), Barrie's *Peter Pan* (1904), and Golding's *The Lord of the Flies* (1955). Golding, who subverts the popular genre of the robinsonnade, chose Ballantyne's novel as his most obvious target. His characters make direct reference to *The Coral Island,* and the two most important characters are named Ralph and Jack. One result of the publication of *The Coral Island* was the author's determination to write only about locales he had visited. In *Personal Reminiscences in Book-Making* (1893), Ballantyne credits this resolve to a glaring mistake in *The Coral Island*: at one point, his characters bore a hole in a coconut with a penknife and extract a liquid that tastes like lemonade.

In 1858 Ballantyne and his older brother John joined the Edinburgh Volunteers, the equivalent of the Territorial Army. At the end of the year Ballantyne further secured his popularity as a writer with the publication of *Martin Rattler; or, A Boy's Adventure in the Forests of Brazil*. The strength of this book lies in its lush details, which help make many of the more-preposterous episodes believable. One of Ballantyne's most popular works, it provides readers with a likable hero and lets them vicariously experience an exotic land. J. B. Foreman argues that the novel's language is "surprisingly modern" and that the book effectively brings geography to life.

The protagonist, Martin Rattler, is described by his aunt as a "bad boy." Martin, however, has many positive qualities. Early on he stands up to Bob Croaker, a bully, in order to save his pet kitten. The fight is observed by a sailor, Barney O'Flannagan, who becomes Martin's friend. Four years later, at the age of fourteen, the boy is accidentally carried out to sea on Barney's ship, the *Firefly*. Martin becomes a cabin boy, but the ship is attacked by pirates and he and Barney are marooned on the coast of Brazil.

After several adventures on their way into the Brazilian interior, Martin and Barney are captured by Indians and are separated when they make their escapes. When the two are reunited, Barney has assumed the name "Baron Fagoni" and is running a diamond mine. In the end Martin returns home to his aunt, who has mourned his disappearance, and he is just in time to save her life. As a result of his trip, Martin has found the value of the Bible and prospers, spending evenings reminiscing with Barney about their adventures in Brazil.

Because of Ballantyne's success both Thomas Nelson and Thomas Constable provided the author with the opportunity to earn extra money by turning out several rather pedestrian nonfiction books, including *Handbook to the New Gold Fields: A Full Account of the Richness and Extent of the Fraser and Thompson River Gold Mines* (1858), *Ships: The Great Eastern and Lesser Squad* (1859), *Environs and Vicinity of Edinburgh* (1859), and *The Lakes of Killarney* (1859). Around this time Ballantyne also produced a humorous booklet for his fellow officers in the Edinburgh Rifle Volunteer Corps titled *How Not to Do It, A Manual for the Awkward Squad* (1859), which he followed with *The Volunteer Levee or, The Remarkable Experiences of Ensign Sopht* (1860), *Ensign Sopht's Volunteer Almanac for 1861* (1860), and *The Collected Works of Ensign Sopht – Late of the Volunteers* (1881).

At this point in his career Ballantyne wrote every day and published several books each year. Two books on the Arctic appeared in 1859–1860: *The World of Ice; or, The Whaling Cruiser of "The Dolphin" and the Adventures of Her Crew in the Polar Region* and an expansion of *Discovery and Adventure in the Polar Seas and Regions* by Sir John Leslie and Hugh Murray. *The World of Ice* treats young Fred Ellice's search for his father, who sailed away on a shipping vessel and never returned. Fred, along with his young surgeon friend Tom Singleton and an old sailor named Buzzby, joins the *Dolphin,* bound for the Arctic. Much of the book details the crew's life in the Arctic and the animals they observe, such as seals, walruses, deer, rabbits, and polar bears. The crew also builds igloos and experiences the disappearance of the sun during winter.

While Ballantyne had by this time established a formula plot that he would follow repeatedly, *The World of Ice* is distinct in that it concentrates on the attempt by the crew to create civilization in the wilderness. Captain Guy leads church services; the doctor gives readings from Shakespeare twice a week; and Fred edits a weekly illustrated newspaper, produces a play called "Blunderbore; or, the Arctic Giant," and becomes writing master in the school the crew starts. They are also beset by dangers such as wild animals, the weather, and icebergs. In the end they find Fred's father, return to England (where Fred's long-lost mother has been found), and Tom marries Fred's sister, Isobel.

In *The Golden Dream; or, Adventures in the Far West* (1860) Ballantyne takes his readers to the California gold rush. The novel opens with a dream, in which eighteen-year-old Ned Sinton finds himself in a cave filled with men and women who have turned to gold. Just before he awakens, he, too, is transformed. His dream does not stop him, however, from leaving England for California, trying to make it rich from the gold rush. Ned soon discovers the transitory nature of his wealth: every time he and his friends get money they invariably lose it. Moreover, because of the gold rush they find themselves paying small fortunes for such ordinary items as eggs.

The novel criticizes America's support of slavery and, as usual, suggests the value of reading the Bible and keeping the Sabbath holy. It also draws on Ballantyne's interest in art (Ned becomes richer from painting portraits than from panning for gold). In the end Ned and his friend, Tom Collins, leave the other miners to see the wonders of California, including enormous waterfalls, grizzly bears, and giant trees. Ned and most of his companions eventually make their way back to England where Ned marries, finding pleasure in the golden grain he raises and in living by the golden rule.

The Dog Crusoe and His Master focuses on a Newfoundland puppy in the Mustang Valley near the Missouri River. Crusoe's owner offers to give a silver rifle, the puppy, and its mother to the winner of a shooting contest. The winner, Dick Varley, trains Crusoe until the dog can rescue objects from a lake and "speak" with his head, tail, and eyes. Dick accompanies two men, Joe Blunt and Henri, on a trip to the Rocky Mountains to establish good relations with the Indians they encounter.

The rest of the book narrates Dick's travels, during which he experiences buffalo hunts, a narrow escape from the Pawnee, and the discovery of a wild mustang, which, with the help of Crusoe, he tames. Along the way, Crusoe demonstrates his worth by saving a Pawnee child from going over a waterfall. Dick is reunited with his friends, and they all temporarily join a group of trappers before returning to Mustang Valley. While Ballantyne seems mostly interested in describing wild animals and the Rocky Mountains, he does throw in a little religion by having Dick read the small Bible his mother has given him. The character of Crusoe prefigures other valiant dogs in books for children and young adults, such as Albert Payson Terhune's *Lad: A Dog* (1926), Eric Knight's *Lassie Go Home* (1940), Jim Kjelgaard's *Big Red* (1948), Fred Gipson's *Old Yeller* (1956), Wilson Rawls's *Where the Red Fern Grows* (1961), and Phyllis Reynolds Naylor's *Shiloh* (1991).

Ballantyne's publisher urged him to write a story about gorillas because of the popularity of Paul du Chaillu's *Explorations in Equatorial Africa* (1861) and Charles Darwin's *On the Origin of Species* (1859). Ballantyne used the occasion to write a se-

quel to his ever-popular book, *The Coral Island*. In *The Gorilla Hunters: A Tale of the Wilds of Africa* (1861), Ralph Rover is twenty-two years old and working as a naturalist, having inherited a small fortune. At the beginning of the novel he is reunited with Jack Martin and Peterkin Gay, who has become a famous hunter.

The three men embark on an African safari to hunt gorillas, and they encounter several native villages and befriend Makarooroo, an African who has learned English from Christian missionaries, and help him rescue Okandaga, his intended mate, after she is charged with witchcraft. Meanwhile, Ralph and his friends observe lions and giraffes; Jack is wounded by a rhinoceros; and their oxen are bitten by tsetse flies and left to die.

Finally, in chapter ten, they find a gorilla track, which causes Ralph to recall the emotions Robinson Crusoe felt when he discovered a footprint on his deserted island in Daniel Defoe's novel. By the time they leave gorilla country, they have shot almost forty gorillas, each carefully measured and studied by Ralph. He does feel some pity for the gorillas and saves several young ones, an act that prompts Jack to remark that Ralph is too tenderhearted for an African hunter.

Throughout the book Ralph gives readers a good dose of his own philosophy of life. He warns them against becoming "muffs" (boys who are too mild, gentle, and timid) and argues that they should take risks in order to prepare for the world. Ralph decides that most Christians do not understand the condition of the natives in Africa and vows to contribute to missionary funds when he returns. In addition he suggests that there should be tolerance between all religions and races. During the course of the novel Ralph gains respect for Makarooroo, who becomes their guide and whom they nickname "Mak." While Jack suggests that Mak and his people are stupid, Ralph realizes that Mak has knowledge of the wilds that the others lack. Even so, Mak is subservient to the white men, calling them "Massa."

Glynn Proctor of *The Red Eric; or, the Whaler's Last Cruise* (1861) is similar to Ned Sinton. While he can be reckless, he ultimately proves courageous and generous. Glynn accompanies Captain Dunning, an American whaler, on his last voyage. The captain has insisted on taking his young daughter, Ailie, along, against the wishes of his two unmarried sisters who are raising her. They warn him of the fate of Robinson Crusoe, who was shipwrecked "in consequence of his resolutely, and obstinately, and willfully and wickedly going to sea!" The crew of

Ballantyne, his wife, Jeanie, and their six children in 1883

Captain Dunning's ship, the *Red Eric,* have various adventures, including a sojourn on the African coast, during which a whale they have killed is stolen by another ship. The *Red Eric* is subsequently wrecked on a sandbar; along the way, Glynn shows his courage, saving Ailie from drowning when she is knocked overboard. Several episodes focus on Ailie, who is slowly educated about life and death in the wilds.

Like *The Golden Dream,* *The Red Eric* ends didactically. Captain Dunning and his crew sue the men who stole their whale and are largely successful because they are scrupulously honest and do not lie and exaggerate as do their opponents. They are awarded £2,000, which Captain Dunning turns over to Glynn, the first to strike the whale. Glynn buys a farm, which he and the captain run. A few years later he marries Ailie. In typical Ballantyne fashion, the hero becomes content with a pastoral, rural life.

The Wild Man of the West: A Tale of the Rocky Mountains (1863) is full of coincidence and melodrama and is reminiscent of *The Dog Crusoe and His Master.* Its hero, sixteen-year-old March Marston, is deemed "mad" by many of the settlers at Pine Point on the banks of the Yellowstone River. March is

reckless and daring, particularly when it comes to jumping horses. Early in the novel, like Dick Varley, he bids his mother farewell and goes off with trappers who are traveling to the Rocky Mountains. By the book's end March has returned to his true home, and several secret identities have been revealed. Once again, Ballantyne laces his work with religious sermons. A weaker book than some of the others Ballantyne wrote at the time, it shows how the author sometimes overworked the same material.

Around 1863 Ballantyne met James Watson, proprietor of James Nisbet and Company, at a literary dinner, which led to his submitting a book to this publisher: *Gascoyne — The Sandal-Wood Trader, A Tale of the Pacific* (1864). James Nisbet and Company was to become Ballantyne's primary publisher for the rest of his career. Watson agreed that Ballantyne could submit several short books as part of a series called Ballantyne's Miscellany, and the author quickly produced the first four volumes: *Fighting the Whales* (1863), *Away in the Wilderness* (1863), *Fast in the Ice* (1863), and *Chasing the Sun* (1864). He claimed they were intended for adults and for the poor. Six years later he began adding new titles to the series, which was then targeted for a middle-class market. Later titles include *Sunk at Sea; or, The Adventures of Wandering Will in the Pacific* (1869), *Digging for Gold; or, Adventures in California* (1869), *Hunting the Lions* (1869), *Up in the Clouds; or, Balloon Voyages* (1869), *The Pioneers: A Tale of the Western Wilderness Illustrative of the Adventures and Discoveries of Sir Alexander MacKenzie* (1872), *Over the Rocky Mountains; or, Wandering Will in the Land of the Red Skin* (1869), and *Lost in the Forest; or, Wandering Will's Adventures in South America* (1869). All of these stories mix religion and adventure. The series became popular, and new editions were published well into the twentieth century.

After the drowning of several relatives, Ballantyne became concerned with the unsafe ships of his day and addressed the issue in *The Lifeboat: A Tale of our Coast Heroes* (1864). More than usually didactic, this book includes a chapter detailing the history of lifeboats and an object lesson in which a miser is nearly destroyed by his own disregard for human life. Once again, Ballantyne's main theme is bravery, as his hero, Guy Foster, saves lives and thwarts smugglers. Because of the excitement of its plot and likable characters, the novel is more than just an appeal to support the Royal National Lifeboat Institution. It was extremely popular and quickly went through several editions. After its publication Ballantyne presented a series of lectures in Edinburgh and Leith, contributing the profits to a fund to provide for more lifeboats.

The success of *The Lifeboat* prompted Ballantyne to search for a related topic. As a result he spent time in the Bell Rock Lighthouse to gather material for *The Lighthouse: Being the Story of a Great Fight between Man and Sea* (1865), which also sold well, though it was not as successful as *The Lifeboat*. Once again, Ballantyne provides factual information enlivened by a subplot about smugglers. The novel is filled with details about the construction of the lighthouse, and its ultimate value in various storms and fog-ridden evenings is demonstrated.

Ballantyne had always wanted to take a walking tour from London to Edinburgh and realized his dream in 1864, when he made the 426-mile journey beginning on 28 April 1864 and ending on 25 May. After completing this trip Ballantyne tried to publish the journal he had kept but was unsuccessful because a similar book had been published by an American, Elihu Burritt. In 1865 Ballantyne published *Freaks on the Fells,* a slightly fictionalized account of his adventures while fishing in the Scottish Highlands.

In early 1866 Ballantyne met twenty-one-year-old Jane "Jeanie" Dickson Grant in Edinburgh, and on 31 July they were married. The Ballantynes spent their honeymoon traveling through North Wales. It was during this period, according to Eric Quayle, that Ballantyne met the young Robert Louis Stevenson, who would grow up to pay the elder writer tribute in the poem that prefaces *Treasure Island.*

Shifting Winds; A Tough Yarn, which deals with the Shipwrecked Mariners Society, appeared in 1866, shortly after Ballantyne's marriage. He then went on a lecture tour covering much of Scotland, during which he wrote *Silver Lake; or, Lost in the Snow* (1867), originally serialized in a magazine for young readers. In August 1867 Ballantyne visited London, where he was able to study firsthand the fire brigade in preparation for writing *Fighting the Flames: A Tale of the London Fire Brigade* (1868). Shortly after his visit to London, Ballantyne was part of rescue efforts during a fire in Edinburgh for which he received a medal. The same year Ballantyne wrote the text for *Photographs of Edinburgh with Descriptive Letterpress* (1868), a collection of architectural photographs.

Ballantyne and his wife took a holiday in Cornwall, where he visited the Bottallack copper and tin mine, spending part of each day underground. The result was *Deep Down: A Tale of the Cornish Mines* (1868). On one level *Deep Down* can be read as a documentary history of the Bottallack mine. Ballantyne provides a history of the mine and details about its operation, the dress of the miners, their pay, and their private lives. The novel describes several accidents (including one in which five men are killed), tin smelting, and Cornish landscape and customs. Woven into these sections are three main plots. In one the protagonist, Oliver Trembath, comes to Cornwall as an assistant surgeon. Oliver becomes interested in the mine, makes friends with Charlie Tregarthen who tells him about Cornwall, and marries Rose Ellis, his adopted cousin. In another plot Tom Donnithorne, Oliver's uncle, has financial difficulties and is nearly ruined by George Augustus Clearmout, who has started a fake mining operation called the Great Wheal Dooem Mining Company. At the same time, most of the major characters become involved with Jim Cuttance, a smuggler who saves Oliver's life and eventually helps Charlie defeat Clearmout.

As Ballantyne suggests in the novel's preface, his primary concern is to present "some of the most interesting and picturesque scenes, incidents, and facts, connected with mining life in the west of the country." Ballantyne shows great respect for the work that the miners do, although Oliver does tell the mine's manager that working underground away from the sun is not healthy. Like earlier books, this one benefits from Ballantyne's personal experience and research and, as a result, *Deep Down* is valuable as a document of life in the Cornish tin mines.

On 25 June 1869 the Ballantynes' first child, Frank Grant Ballantyne, was born. That summer Ballantyne wrote *Erling the Bold: A Tale of the Norse Sea-Kings,* which he had researched while on a trip to Norway. In his preface Ballantyne suggests that "much of the religious, civil, and political liberty" of England, including representative legislation and trial by jury may be "traced to the Norsemen of old." The novel focuses on two Norse warriors, Erling and Glumm, who lead their people against Danish attacks and those of their own king, Harald Haarfager. Living among them is a hermit named Christian, who slowly begins to convert them to Christianity. After several battles, Erling and Glumm save the women they love, Hilda and Ada, from the king. Finally, they leave Denmark to escape their despot king, eventually settling in Iceland at the beginning of the tenth century. Ballantyne's view of the Vikings is sympathetic; indeed, he argues that if Erling had been born in another time he would have been a gentle, peaceful man.

In 1870 Ballantyne spent time on a lightship, *The Gull,* and a tugship, *Aid,* while writing *The Floating Light of the Goodwin Sands* (1870). In May 1871 Ballantyne's second child, Edgar "Ted" William McKenzie Ballantyne, was born. At this time Ballantyne was doing research with the Edinburgh Central Railway Station in preparation for writing *The Iron Horse; or, Life on the Line,* published in November. It is less exotic than some of Ballantyne's novels, focusing on the daily life of individuals associated with the Grand National Trunk Railway. As a whole the book is somewhat lighter and more intentionally humorous than many of Ballantyne's adventure stories.

Ballantyne followed *The Iron Horse* with *The Pioneers* (1872), which follows the trail of Sir Alexander Mackenzie, and *The Norsemen in the West; or, America Before Columbus* (1872), about the pre-Columbian West Indies. More successful was Ballantyne's attack on slave trading, *Black Ivory: A Tale of Adventure among the Slavers of East Africa* (1873). The first edition of three thousand copies sold out almost immediately, and an order for another three thousand was quickly made. The book has been reprinted as recently as 1969, and Jean-Louis Brindamour praises its "fascinating information about the many tribes of Africa; their mores and their ways," suggesting that "once read it is not easily forgotten."

Ballantyne's purpose in writing *Black Ivory* was to give his readers a "true picture in outline of the Slave-Trade as it exists at the present time on the east coast of Africa" and to encourage "the total abolition of the African slave trade." The novel begins with the shipwreck of an English vessel, the *Aurora,* on the coast of East Africa, focusing on the subsequent adventures of young Harold Seadrift, the ship's owner, and one of the crew, Disco Lillihammer. Like the heroes of *The Gorilla Hunters,* they soon encounter Arab slave traders, who capture them to ensure their silence. When the pair escape they are involved in helping to free and reunite with their families some slaves, including the beautiful Azinanté.

Throughout the novel Ballantyne tries to educate his readers about Africa, stressing that there are great differences between various tribes. Harold also has the opportunity to educate Africans about England, as when he retells *Robinson Crusoe,* "Cinderella," and "Jack the Giant Killer" to Chief Yambo. By the end of the novel Azinanté has found her husband and child and is employed by the Maraquita, daughter of the governor of an area in East Africa; Harold has fallen in love and decided to relocate to the Cape of Good Hope, taking

Jumbo, a former slave, as his valet; and Captain Romer is still roaming the eastern seas trying to free slaves. The novel ends with a heartfelt plea to readers to help abolish slavery. Ballantyne explains there is an "urgent need for action. There is death where life should be; ashes instead of beauty; desolation in place of fertility, and even while we write, terrible activity in the horrible traffic in — 'Black Ivory.' "

Jean "Jane" Randall Howard Ballantyne, Ballantyne's first daughter, was born on 23 April 1873. The whole family soon moved to Switzerland. Soon after, Ballantyne left his family in Montreux while he traveled to Algiers, where he researched and wrote *The Pirate City* (1874). Ballantyne claims that the book's purpose is to "present a true picture of life and events in the Pirate city of Algiers, as exhibited about the first quarter of the present century." This he accomplishes by focusing on a family of Sicilians: fifty-year-old Francisco Rimini; his twenty-three-year-old son, Lucien, who is slated to become a priest; and his nineteen-year-old son, Mariano, who is active and mischievous. On a voyage to Malta, the three Riminis are taken hostage when their ship is attacked by pirates. At the urging of the Jewish trader, Bacri, their lives are spared, but they and two young women, Paulina and Angela from another ship, are taken to Algiers, where they are imprisoned and made slaves. The book chronicles their escape and recapture by the pirates, as well as the rise and fall of three "Deys," or pirate kings. In 1816 Algiers was attacked by Britain and forced to free 1,642 slaves. This, according to Ballantyne, is a blow from which the Pirate City will never recover and results in the freedom of the Riminis and their friends, as well as the marriage of Mariano and Angela.

As usual the novel is filled with social commentary and Ballantyne's personal and religious views. Lucien argues for religious tolerance, particularly on the part of the Christians toward Jews, and a British woman, Mrs. Langley, attacks slavery. Ballantyne is less sympathetic toward the Mohammedans, many of whom are pirates. At one point the narrator relates that "Mohammedan Women, far more than English, have need of a 'Women's Rights Society.' " The book describes in detail the houses and markets of Algiers, along with a variety of customs of the day, undoubtedly gleaned from the author's visit to the former Pirate City.

In 1875 Ballantyne's fourth child, Robert James Grant "Hans" Ballantyne, was born. That year the author published *Rivers of Ice* and traveled to England in preparation for a trip to South Africa. While in England he had the opportunity to go diving, providing material for *Under the Waves; Diving in Deep Waters* (1876). He continued to South Africa, which helped him in writing *The Settler and the Savage* (1877) and the autobiographical *Six Months at the Cape* (1878).

The Settler and the Savage is an interesting fictionalized history of the Kaffir Wars in South Africa from the point of view of a group of British, Scottish, and Dutch settlers. The novel opens in 1820. Charlie Considine, a typical Ballantyne hero, immigrates to South Africa from England and soon finds himself lost on the frontier, where he is helped by a young Dutch African colonist, Hans Marais.

Much of the novel concerns daily life in the South African "bush," including meals of ostrich eggs and meat, encounters with cobras and baboons, a flood, a plague of locusts, leopard attacks, an afternoon sketching elephants, and kidnappings by "Hottentots." The novel then skips ahead to 1834 to the Kaffir uprisings. The story concludes with the wedding of Charlie Considine and Bertha Marais. Unlike some of Ballantyne's other books, the work does not show much respect for the native people encountered by the protagonists. Ballantyne is somewhat sympathetic to the Hottentot Ruyter, but then he suggests that Ruyter's people are among the lowest of the human race.

Ballantyne returned to his family in Switzerland in 1876. In 1877 his daughter Alice Christina Hogarth Ballantyne was born. That year Ballantyne visited a battleship to write a book about the navy, *In the Track of the Troops: A Tale of Modern War* (1878). The following year he did firsthand research with postal workers in London in order to write *Post Haste: A Tale of Her Majesty's Mails* (1880). In 1879 the Ballantynes moved back to London, where they eventually built a new home, "Duneanes." Another daughter, Isobel McKenzie Ballantyne, was born in 1882.

During the 1880s Ballantyne continued his stream of novels. In general these books are not memorable, merely reworking plots and themes explored in Ballantyne's earlier novels. Typical of these later books is *Red Rooney; or, The Last of the Crew* (1886), in which Ballantyne once again treats the Arctic and its people. The preface states a fairly didactic purpose: to break down stereotypes about Eskimos, showing that they also have joys, sorrows, fears, and aspirations. In general the author does a good job, although he is not especially subtle: at one point Ballantyne actually asks readers to imagine that they are Eskimos in order to understand their

Cover for Ballantyne's last novel, one of the many works about the Arctic and its people (courtesy of the Lilly Library, Indiana University)

feelings. He clearly feels that the Eskimos would benefit from becoming Christians and that the rum some of them drink can be their downfall. Nevertheless, he allows the Eskimos to criticize the "Kablunets" (foreigners), who they feel live in an odd land where there are no whales or polar bears and where they eat grass (wheat).

In 1890 Ballantyne showed the first symptoms of Ménière's disease, which would eventually kill him. He continued to write and publish, even while seeking relief from his illness in places such as Bath. During this time he wrote *Charlie to the Rescue: A Tale of the Seas and the Rockies* (1890), *The Garret and the Garden; or, Low Life High Up* (1890), and *The Coxwain's Bride; or, The Rising Tide* (1891). *The Hot Swamp: A Romance of Old Albion,* set in ancient Bath, was published in 1892. Shortly after, Ballantyne began work on another arctic novel, *The Walrus Hunters: A Romance of the Realms of Ice* (1893).

During this period Ballantyne's daughter Jane gathered some of her father's autobiographical fragments and short stories and had them published as *Personal Reminiscences in Book-Making.* The book, which includes a variety of material, was not well received. The first six chapters are anecdotes related to the writing of Ballantyne's early books, and in the first chapter he readily admits that this book is "a rambling account of some of the curious incidents which have occurred in connection with his writing" and that he does not intend to inflict on his readers a full autobiography. In this chapter he discusses briefly his career with Hudson's Bay Company, the circumstances that led him to write *The Young Fur-Traders* and *The Coral Island,* as well as his mistake about coconut milk and his turn to religion. The following five chapters describe his real-life adventures researching *The Lifeboat, Fighting the Flames, Deep Down, The Lighthouse,* and *Erling the Bold.* These highly anecdotal chapters are followed by six fictional short stories. In addition, there are two short essays, one on making the best of one's life and another praising a doctor who runs a home for boys.

In October 1893 Ballantyne traveled to Italy, where in Jane's care he stayed at a clinic. They soon decided to go home, however, and traveled to Rome, where they were supposed to stay for a few days. There, on 8 February 1894, Ballantyne died. Shortly after his death, the boys of Harrow School began to raise money to erect a statue to Ballantyne. Robert Louis Stevenson, still a fan, encouraged them to give most of the money to Ballantyne's family, providing instead a tombstone from the fund.

The power of Ballantyne's work, especially *The Coral Island,* can be seen in its influence on other writers. In the verse at the beginning of *Treasure Island,* Stevenson pays tribute to "Ballantyne the Brave." J. M. Barrie, author of *Peter Pan,* writes that "Ballantyne was for long my man, and I used to study a column in *The Spectator* about 'forthcoming books,' waiting for his next as for the pit door to open. He wrote many (I think I looked upon him as the author of 'The Hundred Best Books' and wondered why that list ever needed to be a subject of controversy) but all lagged behind *The Coral Island.*"

Ballantyne's books are also important because, while sometimes far-fetched, they provide generally accurate scientific and geographic information, attempting to educate readers realistically about other countries, cultures, and times. While his work sometimes reflects the prejudices of his time, Ballantyne also asks his readers to try to see life from the perspective of non-British peoples. His early books, particularly *Hudson's Bay, The Coral Island,* and *Martin Rattler,* create effective and believable young protagonists and can still be read with enjoyment. Clearly, Ballantyne's books represent a movement toward the many realistic adventure stories and historical novels written for children in the twentieth century.

Biographies:

L. C. Rodd, *The Young Fur Trader: The Story of R. M. Ballantyne* (Melbourne: F. W. Cheshire, 1966);

Eric Quayle, *Ballantyne the Brave: A Victorian Writer and His Family* (London: Rupert Hart-Davis, 1967).

References:

Jean-Louis Brindamour, "Foreword," in Ballantyne's *Black Ivory* (Chicago: Afro-Am Books, 1969), p. ii;

Sheila Egoff, *The Republic of Childhood: A Critical Guide to Canadian Children's Literature in English* (Toronto: Oxford University Press, 1967);

J. B. Foreman, "Introduction," in Ballantyne's *Martin Rattler* (London: Collins, 1960), pp. 11–14;

Roger Lancelyn Green, *Tellers of Tales: British Authors of Children's Books from 1800 to 1964* (New York: Watts, 1965);

Susan Naramore Maher, "Recasting Crusoe: Frederick Marryat, R. M. Ballantyne and the Nineteenth-Century Robinsonade," *Children's Literature Association Quarterly,* 13 (Winter 1988): 169–175;

Paulette Michel Michot, "The Myth of Innocence: *Robinson Crusoe, The Coral Island,* and *The Lord of the Flies;* A Belgian Tribute on His Eightieth Birthday," in *William Golding: The Sound of Silence,* edited by Jeanne Delbaere (Liège: University of Liège, 1991), pp. 35–44.

William Blake

(28 November 1757 – 12 August 1827)

Alan Richardson
Boston College

See also the Blake entries in *DLB 93: British Romantic Poets, 1789–1832, First Series* and *DLB 154: The British Literary Book Trade, 1700–1820.*

BOOKS: *Poetical Sketches* (London: Privately printed, 1783; facsimile, London: William Griggs, 1890);

There is No Natural Religion, series a and b (London: Printed by William Blake, 1788?; facsimile, 2 volumes, London: William Blake Trust, 1971);

All Religions Are One (London: Printed by William Blake, 1788?; facsimile, London: William Blake Trust, 1970);

Songs of Innocence (London: Printed by William Blake, 1789); revised and enlarged as *Songs of Innocence and of Experience* (London: Printed by William Blake, 1794; facsimile, London: William Blake Trust, 1955);

The Book of Thel (London: Printed by William Blake, 1789; facsimile, London: William Blake Trust, 1965);

The Marriage of Heaven and Hell (London: Printed by William Blake, 1793?; facsimile, London: William Blake Trust, 1960);

Visions of the Daughters of Albion (London: Printed by William Blake, 1793; facsimile, London: William Blake Trust, 1959);

For Children: The Gates of Paradise (London: Printed by William Blake, 1793); revised and enlarged as *For the Sexes: The Gates of Paradise* (London: Printed by William Blake, 1818?; facsimile, London: William Blake Trust, 1968);

America. A Prophecy (Lambeth: Printed by William Blake, 1793; facsimile, London: William Blake Trust, 1963);

Europe (Lambeth: Printed by William Blake, 1794; facsimile, London: William Blake Trust, 1969);

The First Book of Urizen (Lambeth: Printed by William Blake, 1794; facsimile, London: William Blake Trust, 1975);

William Blake; engraving after a portrait by Thomas Phillips

The Song of Los (Lambeth: Printed by William Blake, 1795; facsimile, London: William Blake Trust, 1975);

The Book of Los (Lambeth: Printed by William Blake, 1795; facsimile, London: William Blake Trust, 1975);

The Book of Ahania (Lambeth: Printed by William Blake, 1795; facsimile, London: William Blake Trust, 1973);

Milton (London: Printed by William Blake, 1804 [i.e., 1808?]; facsimile, London: William Blake Trust, 1967);

Jerusalem (London: Printed by William Blake, 1804 [i.e., 1820?]; facsimile, London: William Blake Trust, 1951);

A Descriptive Catalogue of Pictures, Poetical and Historical Inventions, Painted by William Blake in Water Colours, being the Ancient Method of Fresco Painting Restored: and Drawings (London: Printed by D. N. Shury, 1809);

Illustrations of the Book of Job, in Twenty-One Plates, Invented and Engraved by William Blake (London: Printed by William Blake, 1826); facsimiles: *The Illustrations of the Book of Job,* edited by Lawrance Binyon and Geoffrey Keynes (New York: Pierpont Morgan Library, 1935) and in *Blake's Job: William Blake's Illustrations to the Book of Job,* by S. Foster Damon (Providence: Brown University Press, 1966);

Blake's Illustrations of Dante. Seven Plates, designed and engraved by W. Blake (London, 1838);

Vala, or The Four Zoas (London: Oxford University Press, 1963);

Tiriel (London: Oxford University Press, 1967);

Pickering Manuscript (New York: Pierpont Morgan Library, 1972);

The Notebooks of William Blake, edited by David Erdman and Donald Moore (London: Oxford University Press, 1973);

An Island in the Moon (Cambridge: Cambridge University Press, 1987).

Collections: *The Writings of William Blake,* 3 volumes, edited by Geoffrey Keynes (London: Oxford University Press, 1925); revised as *The Complete Writings of William Blake* (London: Oxford University Press, 1957; revised, 1966);

The Complete Poetry and Prose of William Blake, edited by David Erdman (Berkeley: University of California Press, 1965; revised, 1982);

The Illuminated Blake, Annotated by David Erdman (Garden City, N.Y.: Anchor/Doubleday, 1974);

William Blake's Writings, 2 volumes, edited by G. E. Bentley Jr. (Oxford: Clarendon Press, 1978).

SELECTED BOOKS ILLUSTRATED:William Enfield, *The Speaker: Or, Miscellaneous Pieces, Selected from the Best English Writers, and Disposed Under the Proper Heads, with a View to Facilitate the Improvement of Youth in Reading AND Speaking* (London: J. Johnson, 1781) – includes one plate by Blake;

C. G. Salzmann, *Elements of Morality, for the Use of Children,* translated by Mary Wollstonecraft (London, J. Johnson, 1791) – includes 17 plates engraved by Blake;

Wollstonecraft, *Original Stories from Real Life; with Conversations, Calculated to Regulate the Affections, and Form the Mind to Truth and Goodness* (London: J. Johnson, 1791) – includes 6 plates designed and engraved by Blake;

Charles Allen, *A New and Improved History of England, from the Invasion of Julius Caesar to the End of the Thirty-Seventh Year of the Reign of King George the Third* (London: J. Johnson, 1797) – includes 4 plates engraved by Blake;

Leonard Euler, *Elements of Algebra,* 2 volumes (London: J. Johnson, 1797) – frontispiece to volume 1 engraved by Blake;

Allen, *A New and Improved Roman History from the Foundation of the City of Rome, to Its Final Dissolution as the Seat of The Empire* (London: J. Johnson, 1798) – includes 4 plates engraved by Blake;

Salzmann, *Gymnastics for Youth: or a Practical Guide to Healthful and Amusing Exercises for the Use of Schools* (London: J. Johnson, 1800) – includes 10 plates attributed to Blake;

Robert John Thornton, *The Pastorals of Virgil, with a course of English Reading, Adapted for Schools: in which All the Proper Facilities Are Given, Enabling Youth to Acquire the Latin Language,* third edition (London: Rivington, 1821) – includes 6 engravings and 17 woodcuts by Blake, and 1 additional engraving from Blake's design.

William Blake, poet, painter, illustrator, and printer, is one of the most compelling and idiosyncratic figures in the history of British culture. His works, little known until their rediscovery some forty years after his death, have eluded one interpretive category after another, including genre, period, and even conventional distinctions between literature and the graphic arts. In considering Blake's relation to the British tradition of writing for children, the difficulties in classifying his work become even more pronounced, as it remains unclear whether Blake wrote for children at all. Are the *Songs of Innocence* (1789) and *For Children: The Gates of Paradise* (1793) books intended for children, parodies of children's books, or sophisticated versions of children's genres aimed primarily at adults? Despite lasting uncertainty regarding the intended audience of these works, Blake has become a crucial presence in modern interpretations of early children's literature as a brilliant adapter and implicit critic of the writing for children available in his time, and as an exemplar of what children's poetry and picture books could become.

William Blake was born on 28 November 1757 in London, and he would live most of his life in or near the city. His father, James Blake, was a hosier (selling stockings, gloves, and haberdashery) who maintained a precarious competency somewhere above working-class poverty and below middle-class prosperity. His mother, Catherine Harmitage Blake, was thirty, a year older than her husband, when they married in 1752; she gave birth to seven children during the next fifteen years, two dying in infancy. The youngest, Robert (born in 1767) became William's favorite sibling.

Although city bred, Blake lived within walking distance of the fields, hills, and rustic villages then bordering on London, and as a child he wandered urban streets and rural lanes alike. According to his first biographer, Alexander Gilchrist, Blake's visionary tendencies were already manifest when, at around age nine, he looked up in the course of a country ramble to see a tree filled with angels. Still younger, at age four, Blake had allegedly screamed when he saw God "put his head to the window." Blake's parents, probably Baptists (at least by the mid 1760s), did not encourage these visions: William's insistence once nearly led to a beating (for lying) by his father, who generally found corporal punishment useless with a boy of his son's high temper. Neither did he force William to attend school, for which Blake later expressed gratitude.

If fundamentally self-taught, however, Blake did receive instruction in drawing, painting, and engraving, a marketable skill that his father encouraged. At age ten Blake began drawing lessons at Henry Pars's academy; at fourteen he was apprenticed to James Basire, a master engraver who held to an unfashionable preference for clean outline. One of Blake's assignments as apprentice was to sketch the tombs at Westminster Abbey, exposing him to a variety of Gothic styles from which he would draw inspiration throughout his career. After completing his apprenticeship at twenty-one, Blake briefly enrolled (1779–1780) in the Royal Academy, though the theory and practice of its president, Sir Joshua Reynolds, were antithetical to Blake's emerging aesthetic ideals.

More congenial (at least for a time) was the circle of young artists Blake met through the painter and collector George Cumberland, which included Thomas Stothard and John Flaxman. Blake began receiving his first independent engraving jobs, including a design for William Enfield's *The Speaker,* an anthology of recitation pieces for students, commissioned by the radical publisher Joseph Johnson in 1780. Johnson would eventually become Blake's major link to the relatively new world of publishing and writing for children.

On 18 August 1782 Blake married Catherine Boucher, who signed the marriage register with an *X*. Under her husband's tutelage she became an able assistant and something of a disciple. The marriage seems to have been stable and successful, but for some reason the Blakes had no children. Catherine once remarked, "I have very little of Mr. Blake's company; he is always in Paradise"; she came to have visions like those of her husband, who described her (in *Milton,* 1804) as his "Shadow of Delight." Through Flaxman, Blake found early supporters in the Reverend Anthony Stephen Mathew and Harriet Mathew, a fashionable couple who hosted gatherings of artists, musicians, and writers in their Soho parlor. There Blake would sing lyrics from *Poetical Sketches* (1783) and perhaps from *Songs of Innocence* to tunes of his own devising that, sadly, went unrecorded.

The printing of *Poetical Sketches,* Blake's first published volume, was underwritten by the Mathews and Flaxman in 1783; the condescending "Advertisement" by the Reverend Mathew describes it as the work of "untutored youth," replete with "irregularities and defects," but redeemed by "poetic originality." Modern readers have found in *Poetical Sketches* a remarkable series of experiments in various styles and modes, including imitations of traditional ballads, the works of Edmund Spenser, and Elizabethan lyrics; verses in the manner of "Ossian" (the Celtic bard fabricated by James Alan McPherson); and poems in the "sensibility" register of William Collins, Christopher Smart, and Thomas Gray. The Mathews also helped Blake open a small print-selling shop in 1784 with James Parker, a fellow apprentice of Basire's, at 27 Broad Street (next to Blake's family home), but the partnership was soon dissolved.

Given Blake's fierce sense of artistic independence and his often fiery temperament, it is hardly surprising that he eventually broke with the patronizing Mathews and went on to satirize them in *An Island in the Moon* (composed in 1784). This work, unpublished in Blake's lifetime, is a sometimes trenchant, sometimes airy satire in prose and verse; its targets are not only avant-garde conversation parties of the type held by the Mathews but also the scientific, philosophical, and educational ideas, innovations, and jargons likely to be encountered there.

The one-sided dialogues between wise adults and docile children characteristic of late-eighteenth-century children's authors such as Eleanor Fenn are

Title page for Blake's first successful attempt to combine his poetry and illustrations as "illuminated writing" (copy N, Doheny Collection, auctioned by Christie, Manson, and Woods International, 21–22 February 1989)

parodied in the exchanges between the pedant Obtuse Angle and Aradobo, a hopeful youth ever in quest of information. Blake also includes parodies of versified alphabets in the style of the Newbery books and the simplistic style of writing for small children recently introduced by Anna Laetitia Barbauld and Sarah Trimmer. The last chapter of the unfinished manuscript includes versions of three songs that became better known as "Holy Thursday," "Nurse's Song," and "The Little Boy Lost" in the *Songs of Innocence*. Blake's satire on modern children's literature and education seems to have led him toward a different and more telling mode of imitating and implicitly commenting on his era's innovative writing for and about children.

Following Blake's withdrawal from print-selling in 1785, he and Catherine moved to Poland Street, where he struggled to succeed as an independent engraver and continued training his brother Robert (who had made himself part of the family at 27 Broad Street) in drawing, painting, and engraving. Robert fell ill during the winter of 1787 and died, most likely of consumption, after being lovingly tended by William, who went the last fortnight without sleep keeping vigil at his brother's bedside. As Robert died, William saw his spirit rise up and ascend through the ceiling, "clapping its hands for joy." Exhausted and (presumably) depressed, William slept through three days and nights. He felt that Robert's spirit continued to visit him and later claimed that in a dream Robert taught him the secret of stereotype printing (etching text and illustration in relief on a single copper plate), which Blake developed for use in *Songs of Innocence* and other "illuminated" works. In contrast to the specialization that increasingly marked the engraving and illustrating professions, relief etching allowed Blake personally to control nearly every aspect of book production and marketing, and he remained uniquely independent of the established book trade.

Blake's first trials of stereotype, or "illuminated printing," as he referred to it — the companion pieces *All Religions Are One* (1788?) and *There is No Natural Religion* (1788?) — are brief aphoristic works that readers have found helpful in first approaching Blake's difficult "prophetic" books, a series in which the author's religious, political, and social thought, his dazzling poetic mythmaking, and his ongoing self-representation all become intertwined.

Songs of Innocence, a work of a different kind, represents Blake's first major success with illuminated writing. It originally included twenty-three lyrics, four of which were eventually transferred to its companion text, *Songs of Experience,* published as the second part of an enlarged edition, *Songs of Innocence and of Experience* (1794). Blake continued to print separate copies of the 1789 volume, however.

The title page of *Songs of Innocence* features a mother or nurse holding an open book, which two children, a boy and a girl, are eagerly reading. The group is sheltered by an apple tree (the branches of which frame the word *Innocence* in the title) with a vine growing around its trunk, suggesting the children's dependence on the adult and perhaps also the folds of a serpent and the inevitable loss of innocence. The image clearly refers to the children's-book tradition, but whether it is meant to announce *Songs of Innocence* as a work for children, as a work that reflects and comments upon children's books, or (like Lewis Carroll's Alice books) as both remains an open question.

The first lyric, "Introduction," raises similar questions. The speaker, a pastoral poet, is "Piping songs of pleasant glee" when he sees perched on a cloud a laughing child muse, who commands him first to "Pipe a song about a Lamb" – pastoral and Christian traditions had often been combined in English poetry, including in poems for children – then to sing the songs, and finally to write them "In a book that all may read." Does the child muse mean a book that the simplest reader can comprehend or one that readers at all levels, children and adults, can appreciate in various ways? A specialized children's literature market had arisen in England only a half-century previously, and many popular chapbooks intended for a mixed audience of children and adults were still in circulation. Although Blake exploits the thematic, stylistic, and formal conventions of children's books throughout *Songs of Innocence,* he may also be attempting to recapture a not so distant time before children and adults had been segregated into distinct readerships.

Songs of Innocence refers to the developing tradition of children's literature in various ways. As verses wedded to graphic images, some of them overtly symbolic, specific songs such as "The Blossom" and "The Little Boy Lost" evoke the tradition of emblem books aimed at children, best known from the republication of John Bunyan's *A Book for Boys and Girls* (1686) as *Divine Emblems* (1724). As songs for children with religious content and associations, lyrics such as "The Lamb," "A Cradle Song," and "The Divine Image" recall such children's poems as Isaac Watts's *Divine Songs, Attempted in Easie Language for the Use of Children* (1715), the hymns for children included among Charles Wesley's works, and Barbauld's *Hymns in Prose for Children* (1781), and critics have detected echoes from all of these writers scattered throughout the *Songs of Innocence.* With their simple vocabulary, short phrases and easy syntax, familiar imagery, and use of repetition and refrain, "The Ecchoing [*sic*] Green," "Spring," and "Infant Joy" reflect the simplified, accommodating style of children's writing that Barbauld, Trimmer, and Fenn were pioneering in the 1780s. And in their concern with questions of slavery, poor and working children, and compassion for others, "The Little Black Boy," "The Chimney Sweeper," "Holy Thursday," and "On Another's Sorrow" take up issues that socially conscious writers such as Barbauld, Thomas Day,

"The Lamb," one of Blake's best-known poems, in the 1789 version of Songs of Innocence *(copy N, Doheny Collection, auctioned by Christie, Manson, and Woods International, 21–22 February 1989)*

and Mary Wollstonecraft were bringing into writing for children.

Wollstonecraft's *Original Stories from Real Life,* published by Joseph Johnson in 1788, was in fact illustrated by Blake when republished in 1791. Blake also engraved plates (from designs by Daniel Chodowiecki) for Wollstonecraft's translation of C. G. Salzmann's *Elements of Morality,* another children's book published by Johnson in 1791. Similar commissions from Johnson included engravings for Leonard Euler's *Elements of Algebra* (1797), Charles Allen's histories for children of England and Rome published in 1797–1798, and Salzmann's *Gymnastics for Youth* (1800).

Blake had begun frequenting Johnson's shop, a meeting place for authors, designers, and radicals, in the late 1780s under the wing of Henry Fuseli, a Swiss artist and at the time Blake's close friend and supporter. There Blake met Wollstonecraft, William Godwin, and other radical and liberal writers, perhaps including Barbauld (another of Johnson's authors). Through Johnson's circle Blake would have had greater and more direct access to the world of progressive thought on education and children's reading than he had encountered at the Mathews' parties.

Although none of the poems in *Songs of Innocence* is overtly satiric (unlike some of their counterparts in *Songs of Experience*), it is clear that Blake's relation to both traditional Christian writers for children and the progressive children's authors cultivated by Johnson was often a critical one. Some readers have insisted on taking *Songs of Innocence* in a straightforward fashion, particularly those who consider it primarily a children's book, but others have found signs of parody or critique even in the most seemingly naive and simple of the lyrics. "The Divine Image," for example, can be read as a children's lyric in the tradition of Bunyan and Watts, enjoining the Christian child to pray to "God our father dear," who exemplifies the qualities of "Mercy Pity Peace and Love." But one could also read this poem as an instance of Blake's radical humanism, his insistence that God exists in and through human beings, and that no human being (Christian or not) stands beyond the pale of God's mercy: "And all must love the human form / In heathen, turk or jew."

The critical edge of this song emerges through implicit contrast with earlier Christian poetry for children: Bunyan, for example, depicts the unredeemed child in *Divine Emblems* as a "swarthy Ethiopian" or "Black-a-more," and Watts gives "Praise for Birth and Education in a Christian Land" (as opposed to heathen "Ignorance and Darkness") in the *Divine Songs*. Blake's "Holy Thursday" could be read as an uncomplicated celebration of the Charity School movement, which gave rudimentary educations, clean uniforms, and a sense of order and decency to poor children. But details such as the children's regimented marching, the disciplinary "wands" of the beadles who shepherd them, and their placement above the "aged men" who have appointed themselves "wise guardians of the poor" suggest an implicit indictment of the condescending, self-interested, and frequently harsh treatment that poor and working children of the time frequently met at the hands of their would-be benefactors.

Much more has been made of the relation, however critical, of Blake's lyrics to "official" children's literature than of his evident interest in and relish for what can be called, in contrast, the

"underground" world of oral forms – nursery rhymes, riddles, folk songs, fairy lore, folktales – and of the popular chapbooks that drew significantly upon the same traditions. These forms were still, in Blake's time, largely uncensored, often aimed at a mixed audience of children and adults, and represented a traditional lower-class culture under assault from the "guardians of the poor," religious and progressive alike. The rhythms of Blake's songs owe as much to Mother Goose as to Watts or Wesley, and at a time when many educators and children's writers were working to lure children away from the streets and village greens, Blake took up the burden of popular rhymes. In the popular traditions Blake found ample precedent for including verbal ambiguity, covert satire, and sexual imagery in children's forms, whereas "official" children's literature had been increasingly marked by a program of formal simplicity and sanitized content.

In August 1790 the Blakes moved across the Thames to Lambeth, a suburban area with open meadows and swamps. There Blake wrote and etched the *Songs of Experience,* dating the combined *Songs of Innocence and of Experience* volume 1794, with the subtitle "Shewing the Two Contrary States of the Human Soul." In thus framing the two works, Blake forestalled attempts to read them in terms of a progression from a simplistic to a more sophisticated viewpoint, or a biographical shift from a youthful and naive attitude to an experienced and cynical one. Instead Blake – who wrote in *The Marriage of Heaven and Hell* (1793?) that "Without Contraries is no progression" – has been understood as insisting that neither an innocent nor an experienced perspective is in itself adequate to the complexities of human life. Each underscores and corrects the partialities and deficiencies of the other: a comprehensive vision allows on the one hand for the unguarded openness to life, the sense of a benign, quasi-parental providence, and the simple joys associated with innocence, and on the other for the acknowledgment of human perversity and cruelty, the questioning of natural and providential design, and the impatience with social repression associated with experience. Moreover, these contraries can be found inhering within individual lyrics in either group of songs. Some of the *Songs of Innocence* were given explicit counterparts in the Experience volume: there are "contrary" versions of "Holy Thursday," "The Chimney Sweeper," "Nurse's Song," and "The Lamb." But it would be oversimplifying to try to read the two volumes in terms of a series of one-to-one correspondences, and Blake rearranged

Two of the matched poems in Songs of Innocence and Experience *(copy* Z, *Rosenwald Collection, Library of Congress)*

the plates in every copy he produced, each arrangement suggesting new interpretive possibilities.

Around this time Blake produced an emblem book, *For Children: The Gates of Paradise,* which has sometimes been considered a children's book owing to its title, its relation to earlier emblem books for children, and the fact that Fuseli is thought to have given a copy to a five-year-old girl; on the title page Blake printed the name and business address of Joseph Johnson, by then well-known as a publisher for children. Yet in his prospectus "To the Public," dated 10 October 1793, Blake listed this work simply as "The Gates of Paradise, a small book of engravings. price 3*s*," distinguishing neither it nor *Songs of Innocence* (priced still higher at 5 shillings) as a children's book. In any case the relation of *The Gates of Paradise* to the tradition exemplified by Bunyan's *Divine Emblems* is evidently a critical one. Whereas Bunyan's and later emblem books for children painstakingly spell out the meaning of each emblem and its moral application, Blake's captions

are brief and suggestive, giving far more interpretive latitude to and demanding far more work of the reader. Blake reworked this volume some twenty-five years later as *For the Sexes: The Gates of Paradise,* expanding the captions and adding two plates of "Keys" and an epilogue.

Blake's extraordinary poetic and artistic career, as well as his criticizing and reversing of conventional pieties and wisdom, helped to develop his image as revolutionary poet and latter-day prophet. As a graphic artist Blake is best known for his illustrations inspired by the works of earlier poets; these illustrations (which include drawings and watercolors as well as engravings) are not mere ornaments to the poems they illustrate but constitute critical appreciations of them.

Blake's life was marked by conflict and the lack of widespread artistic recognition or lasting commercial success. He quarreled with one friend and patron after another. Blake's precarious commercial fortunes as an artist and engraver were not mended by the exhibition he mounted in his brother James's house on Broad Street in 1809–1810 and for which he wrote his *Descriptive Catalogue of Pictures* (1809), and he spent the next seventeen years working to stave off utter poverty.

Blake died on 12 August 1827 in a two-room flat in a house owned by relatives of his wife; Catherine survived him by four years. In his final years Blake had found a small group of disciples in young artists such as Samuel Palmer and George Richmond, who wrote Palmer of Blake's death: "Just before he died his countenance became fair. His eyes Brighten'd and He burst out Singing of the things he saw in Heaven."

Blake was known in his time primarily as an artist and engraver, but he had no great reputation and was highly regarded only by a few. As a poet he was virtually unknown – his insistence on printing his own works effectively excluded him from the established world of publishing and reviewing – but a few contemporaries encountered and left brief comments on his works. Samuel Taylor Coleridge, who had been lent a copy of *Songs of Innocence and of Experience,* considered the author a "man of Genius," and Wordsworth made his own copies of several songs. Charles Lamb sent a copy of "The Chimney Sweeper" from *Songs of Innocence* to James Montgomery for his *Chimney-Sweeper's Friend, and Climbing Boys' Album* (1824), and Robert Southey (who, like Wordsworth, considered Blake insane) attended Blake's exhibition and included the "Mad Song" from *Poetical Sketches* in his miscellany, *The Doctor* (1834–1837).

The publication of Alexander Gilchrist's *Life of William Blake: Pictor Ignotus* (1863) brought new interest to Blake's poetry, which was taken up by important literary figures such as A. C. Swinburne, Dante Gabriel Rossetti, and William Butler Yeats, who edited Blake's poetry in 1893. Selections from *Songs of Innocence and of Experience* were included by Francis Turner Palgrave in *The Children's Treasury of Lyrical Poetry* (1875) and by Samuel Eliot in *Poetry for Children* (1880) and have been featured in anthologies of children's verse ever since. A children's edition of *Songs of Innocence,* cloyingly reillustrated by Harold Jones, was published in 1961. Nancy Willard's *A Visit to William Blake's Inn: Poems for Innocent and Experienced Travellers* (1981) is a recent children's book inspired by Blake's *Songs* and has also been adapted for a video format (1986).

Blake's contribution to the children's literature of his own time must be considered negligible at best, given how few readers (children or adults) encountered his books. However, Blake's work has taken on major significance for the history and criticism of writing for children in at least two ways: as a brilliant adapter, parodist, and implicit critic of early children's literature, Blake helped set the terms for any retrospective understanding of both its achievements and its limitations; and as a creator of poems in children's forms virtually unrivaled for their high aesthetic standards, compelling rhythms and imagery, and subtle complexities, Blake provided an important example and challenge to late-nineteenth- and twentieth-century children's writers. There is little doubt that Blake will continue to inspire the children's writers – and the children – of future ages.

Letters:

Letters from William Blake to Thomas Butts 1800–1802, facsimile, edited by Geoffrey Keynes (London: Oxford University Press, 1926);

The Letters of William Blake, third edition, revised and amplified, edited by Keynes (Oxford: Clarendon Press, 1980).

Bibliographies:

Geoffrey Keynes, *A Bibliography of William Blake* (New York: Grolier Club, 1921);

Keynes and Edwin Wolf, *William Blake's Illuminated Books: A Census* (New York: Grolier Club, 1953);

Keynes, *Engravings by William Blake: The Separate Plates* (Dublin: E. Walker, 1956);

G. E. Bentley Jr. and Martin Nurmi, *A Blake Bibliography: Annotated Lists of Works, Studies, and Blakeana* (Minneapolis: University of Minnesota Press, 1964);

Bentley, *Blake Books* (Oxford: Clarendon Press, 1977).

Biographies:

Alexander Gilchrist, *Life of William Blake: Pictor Ignotus,* 2 volumes (London: Macmillan, 1863; enlarged, 1880);

Mona Wilson, *The Life of William Blake* (London: Nonesuch Press, 1927); third edition, edited by Geoffrey Keynes (London: Oxford University Press, 1965);

Michael Davis, *William Blake: A New Kind of Man* (Berkeley: University of California Press, 1977);

James King, *William Blake: His Life* (New York: St. Martin's Press, 1991).

References:

Hazard Adams, *William Blake: A Reading of the Shorter Poems* (Seattle: University of Washington Press, 1963);

John Adlard, *The Sports of Cruelty: Fairies, Folk-Songs, Charms and Other Country Matters in the Work of William Blake* (London: Woolf, 1972);

G. E. Bentley, ed., *William Blake: The Critical Heritage* (Boston: Routledge & Kegan Paul, 1975);

Margaret Bottrall, ed., *William Blake, Songs of Innocence and Experience: A Casebook* (London: Macmillan, 1970);

Vivian de Sola Pinto, "William Blake, Isaac Watts, and Mrs. Barbauld," in *The Divine Vision: Studies in the Poetry and Art of William Blake,* edited by de Sola Pinto (London: Gollancz, 1957);

Martha Winburn England, "Wesley's Hymns for Children and Blake's *Songs,*" in *Hymns Unbidden: Donne, Herbert, Blake, Emily Dickinson and the Hymnographers,* by England and John Sparrow (New York: New York Public Library, 1966), pp. 44–62;

David V. Erdman, *Blake: Prophet Against Empire,* third edition (Princeton: Princeton University Press, 1977);

Stanley Gardner, *Blake's Innocence and Experience Retraced* (London: Athlone Press, 1986);

D. G. Gillham, *Blake's Contrary States: The "Songs of Innocence and of Experience" as Dramatic Poems* (Cambridge: Cambridge University Press, 1966);

Robert F. Gleckner, *The Piper and the Bard: A Study of William Blake* (Detroit: Wayne State University Press, 1959);

Heather Glen, *Vision and Disenchantment: Blake's Songs and Wordsworth's Lyrical Ballads* (Cambridge: Cambridge University Press, 1983);

E. D. Hirsch Jr., *Innocence and Experience: An Introduction to Blake* (New Haven: Yale University Press, 1964);

John Holloway, *Blake: The Lyric Poetry* (London: Edward Arnold, 1968);

Edward Larrissy, *William Blake* (Oxford: Blackwell, 1985);

Zachary Leader, *Reading Blake's Songs* (Boston: Routledge & Kegan Paul, 1981);

Harold Pagliaro, *Selfhood and Redemption in Blake's Songs* (University Park: Pennsylvania State University Press, 1987);

Morton D. Paley, ed., *Twentieth Century Interpretations of Songs of Innocence and of Experience* (Englewood Cliffs, N.J.: Prentice-Hall, 1969);

Alan Richardson, *Literature, Education, and Romanticism: Reading as Social Practice, 1780–1832* (Cambridge: Cambridge University Press, 1994);

Geoffrey Summerfield, *Fantasy and Reason: Children's Literature in the Eighteenth Century* (Athens: University of Georgia Press, 1984);

Joseph Wicksteed, *Blake's Innocence and Experience* (New York: Dutton, 1928).

Papers:

The British Library houses a significant collection of Blake's illuminated works, including Blake's notebook and the manuscripts for *Tiriel* and *Vala, or The Four Zoas.* A second important collection of illuminated works that also includes the manuscript of *An Island in the Moon* resides in the Fitzwilliam Museum (Cambridge, England). The Tate Gallery (London) boasts a major collection of Blake's graphic works. Prominent collections of Blake's works in the United States can be found at the Huntington Library in California, Harvard University, the Library of Congress, and the Pierpont Morgan Library in New York.

Robert Browning

(7 May 1812 – 12 December 1889)

A. Waller Hastings
Northern State University

See also the Browning entry in *DLB 32: Victorian Poets Before 1850.*

BOOKS: *Pauline: A Fragment of a Confession,* anonymous (London: Saunders & Otley, 1833);

Paracelsus (London: Wilson, 1835); edited by C. P. Denison (New York: Baker & Taylor, 1911);

Strafford: An Historical Tragedy (London: Longman, Rees, Orme, Brown, Green & Longmans, 1837);

Sordello (London: Moxon, 1840);

Bells and Pomegranates. No. I. – Pippa Passes (London: Moxon, 1841);

Bells and Pomegranates. No. II. – King Victor and King Charles (London: Moxon, 1842);

Bells and Pomegranates. No. III. – Dramatic Lyrics (London: Moxon, 1842); edited by J. O. Beatty and J. W. Bowyer (New York: Houghton, 1895);

Bells and Pomegranates. No. IV. – The Return of the Druses: A Tragedy in Five Acts (London: Moxon, 1843);

Bells and Pomegranates. No. V. – A Blot in the 'Scutcheon: A Tragedy in Five Acts (London: Moxon, 1843); edited by W. Rolfe and H. Hersey (New York: Harper, 1887);

Bells and Pomegranates. No. VI. – Colombe's Birthday: A Play in Five Acts (London: Moxon, 1844);

Bells and Pomegranates. No. VII. – Dramatic Romances & Lyrics (London: Moxon, 1845);

Bells and Pomegranates. No. VIII. – and Last. Luria; and A Soul's Tragedy (London: Moxon, 1846);

Poems: A New Edition, 2 volumes (London: Chapman & Hall, 1849; Boston: Ticknor, Reed & Fields, 1850);

Christmas-Eve and Easter-Day (London: Chapman & Hall, 1850; Boston: Lothrop, 1887);

Two Poems by Robert Browning and Elizabeth Barrett Browning (London: Chapman & Hall, 1854);

Men and Women (2 volumes, London: Chapman & Hall, 1855; 1 volume, Boston: Ticknor & Fields, 1856);

Robert Browning (National Portrait Gallery, London)

Dramatis Personae (London: Chapman & Hall, 1864; Boston: Ticknor & Fields, 1864);

The Poetical Works of Robert Browning, 6 volumes (London: Smith, Elder, 1868);

The Ring and the Book (4 volumes, London: Smith, Elder, 1868–1869; 2 volumes, Boston: Fields, Osgood, 1869);

Balaustion's Adventure, Including a Transcript from Euripides (London: Smith, Elder, 1871; Boston: Osgood, 1871);

Prince Hohenstiel – Schwangau, Saviour of Society (London: Smith, Elder, 1871);

Fifine at the Fair (London: Smith, Elder, 1872; Boston: Osgood, 1872);

Red Cotton Night-Cap Country; or, Turf and Towers
(London: Smith, Elder, 1873; Boston: Osgood, 1873);

Aristophanes' Apology, Including a Transcript from Euripides: Being the Last Adventures of Balaustion (London: Smith, Elder, 1875; Boston: Osgood, 1875);

The Inn Album (London: Smith, Elder, 1875; Boston: Osgood, 1876);

Pacchiarotto and How He Worked in Distemper, with Other Poems (London: Smith, Elder, 1876; Boston: Osgood, 1877);

La Saisiaz, and the Two Poets of Croisic (London: Smith, Elder, 1878);

Dramatic Idyls (London: Smith, Elder, 1879);

Dramatic Idyls: Second Series (London: Smith, Elder, 1880);

Jocoseria (London: Smith, Elder, 1883; Boston & New York: Houghton, Mifflin, 1883);

Ferishtah's Fancies (London: Smith, Elder, 1884; Boston: Houghton, Mifflin, 1885);

Parleyings with Certain People of Importance in Their Day (London: Smith, Elder, 1887; Boston & New York: Houghton, Mifflin, 1887);

Asolando: Fancies and Facts (London: Smith, Elder, 1889; Boston & New York: Houghton, Mifflin, 1890);

Complete Poetic and Dramatic Works of Robert Browning, Cambridge Edition, edited by G. W. Cooke and H. E. Scudder (Boston & New York: Houghton, Mifflin, 1895);

The Complete Works of Robert Browning, Florentine Edition, edited by Charlotte Porter and Helen A. Clarke, 12 volumes (New York & Boston: Crowell, 1898);

The Works of Robert Browning, Centenary Edition, 10 volumes, edited by Frederic G. Kenyon (London: Smith, Elder / Boston: Hinkley, 1912);

New Poems by Robert Browning and Elizabeth Barrett Browning, edited by Kenyon (London: Smith, Elder, 1914; New York: Macmillan, 1915);

Robert Browning: The Ring and the Book, edited by Richard D. Altick (London: Penguin / New Haven: Yale University Press, 1971);

Robert Browning: The Poems, 2 volumes, edited by John Pettigrew, supplemented and completed by Thomas J. Collins (London: Penguin / New Haven: Yale University Press, 1981).

OTHER: John Forster, *Lives of Eminent British Statesmen,* volume 2, undetermined contribution to biography of Thomas Wentworth, Earl of Strafford, by Browning (London: Longman, Orme, Brown, Green & Longmans, 1836);

Letters of Percy Bysshe Shelley, introduction by Browning (London: Moxon, 1852), pp. 1–44;

The Agamemnon of Aeschylus, translated by Browning (London: Smith, Elder, 1877);

Thomas Jones, *The Divine Order: Sermons,* introduction by Browning (London: Isbister, 1884);

"Sonnet: Why I Am a Liberal," in *Why I Am a Liberal,* edited by A. Reid (London: Cassell, 1885).

Although the early part of Robert Browning's creative life was spent in comparative obscurity, he has come to be regarded as one of the most important poets of the Victorian period. His dramatic monologues and the psychohistorical epic *The Ring and the Book* (1868–1869), a novel in verse, have established him as a major figure in the history of English poetry. His claim to attention as a children's writer is more modest, resting as it does almost entirely on one poem, "The Pied Piper of Hamelin," included almost as an afterthought in *Bells and Pomegranites. No. III. – Dramatic Lyrics* (1842) and evidently never highly regarded by its creator. Nevertheless, "The Pied Piper" moved quickly into the canon of children's literature, where it has remained ever since, receiving the dubious honor (shared by the fairy tales of Hans Christian Andersen and J. M. Barrie's *Peter Pan,* 1911) of appearing almost as frequently in "adapted" versions as in the author's original.

Browning was born on 7 May 1812 in Camberwell, a middle-class suburb of London; he was the only son of Robert Browning, a clerk in the Bank of England, and a devoutly religious German-Scotch mother, Sarah Anna Wiedemann Browning. He had a sister, Sarianna, who like her parents was devoted to her poet brother. While Mrs. Browning's piety and love of music are frequently cited as important influences on the poet's development, his father's scholarly interests and unusual educational practices may have been equally significant, particularly in regard to Browning's great children's poem. The son of a wealthy banker, Robert Browning the elder had been sent in his youth to make his fortune in the West Indies, but he found the slave economy there so distasteful that he returned, hoping for a career in art and scholarship. A quarrel with his father and the financial necessity it entailed led the elder Browning to relinquish his dreams so as to support himself and his family through his bank clerkship.

Browning's father amassed a personal library of some six thousand volumes, many of them collections of arcane lore and historical anecdotes that the

Drawing of the Pied Piper by William Macready Jr., for whom Browning wrote "The Pied Piper of Hamelin" in 1842 (Armstrong Browning Library, Baylor University)

poet plundered for poetic material, including the source of "The Pied Piper." The younger Browning recalled his father's unorthodox methods of education in his late poem "Development," published in *Asolando: Fancies and Facts* (1889). Browning remembers at the age of five asking what his father was reading. To explain the siege of Troy, the elder Browning created a game for the child in which the family pets were assigned roles and furniture was recruited to serve for the besieged city. Later, when the child had incorporated the game into his play with his friends, his father introduced him to Alexander Pope's translation of the *Iliad*. Browning's appetite for the story having been whetted, he was induced to learn Greek so as to read the original.

Much of Browning's education was conducted at home by his father, which accounts for the wide range of unusual information the mature poet brought to his work. His family background was also important for financial reasons; the father whose own artistic and scholarly dreams had been destroyed by financial necessity was more than willing to support his beloved son's efforts. Browning decided as a child that he wanted to be a poet, and he never seriously attempted any other profession. Both his day-to-day needs and the financial cost of publishing his early poetic efforts were willingly supplied by his parents.

Browning's early career has been characterized by Ian Jack as a search for an appropriate poetic form, and his first published effort, *Pauline: A Fragment of a Confession* (1833), proved in retrospect to be a false start. Browning's next poetic production, *Paracelsus* (1835), achieved more critical regard and began to move toward the greater objectivity of the dramatic monologue form that Browning perfected over the next several years. Browning also wrote several plays intended for the stage, along with closet dramas; however, he was not suited to be a playwright. His chief theatrical patron, William Macready, was already becoming disillusioned by the plays' lack of success and the poet's persistent difficulties in creating theatrical plots.

Before that estrangement, however, the alliance between Browning and Macready had one salutary effect: it provided the occasion for Browning's composition of "The Pied Piper." In May 1842 Macready's son Willie was sick in bed; Willie liked to draw and asked Browning to give him "some little thing to illustrate" while in confinement. The poet responded first with a short poem, "The Cardinal and the Dog," and then, after being impressed with Willie's drawings for it, with "The Pied Piper of Hamelin."

The story of the Pied Piper was evidently well known in Browning's home. The poet's father began his own poem on the subject in 1842 for another young family friend, discontinuing his effort when he learned of his son's poem. The primary source of the story was a seventeenth-century collection, Nathaniel Wanley's *Wonders of the Little World* (1678). Browning claimed many years later that this was the sole source, but William Clyde DeVane notes that some significant details in Browning's account, including an erroneous date for the event described, occur in an earlier work, Richard Verstegen's *Restitution of Decayed Intelligence in Antiquities* (1605), but not in Wanley.

Whatever its sources, "The Pied Piper" reflects the hand of a master storyteller. The poem tells a story of civic venality and retribution. Desperate to rid the city of rats, the corrupt and repulsively corpulent mayor engages the mysterious piper to charm the vermin away; the piper plays a tune that draws the rats from their holes and leads them to the river Weser, where they drown. Only one especially hardy rat escapes death — by swimming across the river — to tell a cautionary tale to other rats; the rat's story enables Browning to provide an explanation for the piper's magic, as the rat tells how the sound of the pipe evoked all kinds of wonderful rattish treats:

> I heard a sound as of scraping tripe,
> And putting apples, wondrous ripe,
> In a cider-press's gripe;
> And a moving away of pickle-tub boards,
> And a leaving ajar of conserve-cupboards,
> And a drawing the corks of train-oil flasks,
> And a breaking the hoops of butter-casks.

With the rats destroyed and their nests blocked up, the mayor and corporation of Hamelin feel secure in reneging on their agreement with the piper and refuse to pay him the thousand guilders he demands. Where they had offered fifty times the piper's requested fee before the rats were eliminated, they now offer only fifty guilders, thinking of all the fine wines they might purchase with the money saved. After all, the mayor claims, the piper cannot restore the rats to life.

The angry piper then blows a new tune and lures the children of Hamelin to follow him — not, this time, to the river but to the Koppelberg, a mountain west of the city, which opens up to swallow all but one, a lame boy who cannot walk fast enough to pass through the opening before it closes. The child, saved by his physical limitations, neatly parallels the rat who survives destruction by its superior fitness and serves a similar function of revealing the secret of the piper's song, which had promised an idyllic world of play for all who followed.

The Hamelin city officials offer rewards and send searchers in all directions to find the missing children, but to no avail. Browning explains how the story passes into local tradition, illustrated in stained glass and commemorated in all legal memorandums from that day onward. His account also notes, as does the Verstegen source text, the existence of a pocket of Saxons in Slavic Transylvania that may be descended from the lost children of Hamelin and it ends with the moral that people should keep their promises.

"The Pied Piper" has a great deal of charm, and both its theme and its moral reflect the mainstream of Victorian thought. Browning, however, seems to have held the poem in little esteem and reportedly only included it in *Dramatic Lyrics* because of the need for additional verse to fill out the sixteen-page pamphlet. Indeed, this narrative poem does not seem to fit comfortably with the dramatic monologue form of the other poems in the book, which include such widely anthologized pieces as "My Last Duchess" and "Porphyria's Lover." While "The Pied Piper" found its own audience and John Forster's review of *Dramatic Lyrics* in *The Examiner* quoted favorably nearly half the poem, critical attention has usually focused on the other poems in the volume, the shorter dramatic monologues in which Browning finally found the form that would establish him as a major poet of his time and a significant influence on modern poetry.

While "The Pied Piper" differs from most of Browning's adult poetry, much of its charm and delight derive from the same poetic tools that Browning deployed in his more serious work. However, techniques that are praised in "The Pied Piper" are frequently perceived as defects in the adult poems.

Kate Greenaway's frontispiece for the 1888 edition of
Browning's "The Pied Piper of Hamelin"

Victorian critics disliked his predilection for outrageous (and sometimes unpronounceable) rhymes and the excessive use of single rhymes, as in the vivid account of the rat infestation that opens "The Pied Piper":

> Rats!
> They fought the dogs and killed the cats,
>   And bit the babies in the cradles,
> And ate the cheese out of the vats,
>   And licked the soup from the cooks' own ladles,
> Split open the kegs of salted sprats,
>   Made nests inside men's Sunday hats,
> And even spoiled the women's chats.

Earlier critics tended to see Browning's rhyme patterns as appropriate for light verse such as children's poems, where the emphasis is on entertainment, but as a defect in adult poetry, with its philosophical or religious concerns. The source of "The Pied Piper" in arcane reference works from past centuries also suggests one of the problems Browning had in achieving an audience for his adult poetry: he was frequently attacked for obscurity in his verse, and much of that obscurity derives from his unreferenced allusions to the vast body of arcana that he had read.

Another narrative poem, " 'How They Brought the Good News from Ghent to Aix,' " appeared in Browning's collection of dramatic monologues *Bells and Pomegranates. No. VII. – Dramatic Romances & Lyrics* (1845). While not expressly written for children, this poem was printed separately in a child's edition after Browning's death and for many years was commonly included in children's school texts; it remains popular for its galloping anapestic rhythm and exciting description of a cross-country equestrian race. The poem presents an entirely imaginary seventeenth-century mission to relieve the city of Aix-la-Chapelle in Germany. Three riders are dispatched from Ghent, in Belgium, to carry an important message; two of the riders' horses fail, and the third, that of the speaker, accomplishes the mission to universal acclaim. What the message is, other than to secure the freedom of the German city, is never stated.

Besides introducing the world to "The Pied Piper" and establishing the poet's modus operandi for his future verse, *Dramatic Lyrics* also had a lasting effect on Browning's personal life. Elizabeth Barrett admired the book, and in her 1844 poem "Lady Geraldine's Courtship" she expressed the esteem in which she held Browning by linking him to William Wordsworth and Alfred Tennyson as one of the great poets of the age. She met Browning and the two poets fell deeply in love; unfortunately, Elizabeth's father, Edward Moulton Barrett, would not countenance any of his children marrying and leaving the home. On 12 September 1846 they were secretly married, and one week later they eloped to the Continent.

Browning wrote relatively little during the marriage, in part because the family frequently moved and, because of Elizabeth's frail health, he was usually busy making all the arrangements for housing and transportation. The Brownings had one child, Robert Wiedemann Barrett Browning, called "Pen," born in 1849 (the same year Browning's mother died). Both parents doted on the boy, and Robert Browning took particular responsibility for his son's education — yet another diversion from poetic production. The poet who some years earlier had produced a major children's poem to amuse the son of a friend made no similar creations for his own son, however, but continued to work on longer philosophical poems for an adult audience.

Browning became in his later years that curious phenomenon, the Victorian sage — widely regarded for his knowledge and his explorations of philosophical questions of great resonance in Victorian life. He witnessed the creation (by F. J. Furnivall in 1881) of the Browning Society, dedicated to the study of the poet's work and thought. Just before his death in 1889, Browning finally published the other poem written for young Willie Macready, "The Cardinal and the Dog." This fifteen-line poem, like "The Pied Piper," originated in one of the legends recounted in Wanley's *Wonders of the Little World*. It tells how Cardinal Crescenzio, a representative of the pope at the Council of Trent, was frightened by the apparition of a large black dog that only he could see, after which he became seriously ill; on his deathbed he again saw the dog. The poem has elicited little critical response and has seldom been anthologized; its interest today lies primarily in its role as a warm-up to "The Pied Piper."

Anyone as widely adulated as Browning was during the later years of his life is bound to suffer a decline in critical valuation. Along with other Victorians, Browning was dismissed by influential figures among the modernists, including T. S. Eliot (although Ezra Pound paid tribute to Browning as one of his literary fathers). Following World War II, however, Browning's reputation has been salvaged by a more objective generation of critics who note his poetic failings but also trace his influence on the poetic forms and concerns of his twentieth-century successors. Through all the vicissitudes of critical reputation, however, Browning's major contribution to the canon of children's literature, "The Pied Piper of Hamelin," has retained its popular audience.

Letters:

Letters of Robert Browning Collected by Thomas J. Wise, edited by Thurman L. Hood (New Haven: Yale University Press, 1933);

Robert Browning and Julia Wedgwood: A Broken Friendship as Revealed in Their Letters, edited by Richard Curle (London: Murray & Cape, 1937);

New Letters of Robert Browning, edited by William Clyde DeVane and Kenneth Leslie Knickerbocker (New Haven: Yale University Press, 1950);

Dearest Isa: Browning's Letters to Isa Blagden, edited by Edward C. McAleer (Austin: University of Texas Press, 1951);

Browning to His American Friends: Letters between the Brownings, the Storys, and James Russell Lowell, 1841–1890, edited by Gertrude Reese Hudson (London: Bowes & Bowes, 1965);

Learned Lady: Letters from Robert Browning to Mrs. Thomas FitzGerald 1876–1889, edited by McAleer (Cambridge, Mass.: Harvard University Press, 1966);

The Letters of Robert Browning and Elizabeth Barrett, 1845–1846, 2 volumes, edited by Evan Kintner (Cambridge, Mass.: Harvard University Press, 1969);

The Brownings to the Tennysons, edited by Thomas J. Collins (Waco: Armstrong Browning Library, Baylor University, 1971);

The Brownings' Correspondence, 10 volumes to date, edited by Philip Kelley and Ronald Hudson (Winfield, Kans.: Wedgestone, 1984–   ).

Bibliographies:

L. N. Broughton, C. S. Northrup, and R. B. Pearsall, *Robert Browning: A Bibliography, 1830–1950*

(Ithaca, N.Y.: Cornell University Press, 1953);

Warner Barnes, *Catalogue of the Browning Collection at the University of Texas* (Austin: University of Texas Press, 1966);

Pearsall, "Robert Browning," *New Cambridge Bibliography of English Literature,* volume 3 (Cambridge: Cambridge University Press, 1969);

William S. Peterson, *Robert and Elizabeth Browning: An Annotated Bibliography, 1951–1970* (New York: Browning Institute, 1974);

Philip Kelley and Ronald Hudson, eds., *The Brownings' Correspondence: A Checklist* (New York: Browning Institute / Winfield, Kans.: Wedgestone, 1978).

Biographies:

Edward Gosse, *Robert Browning: Personalia* (London, 1890);

Edward Dowden, *The Life of Robert Browning* (London: Dent, 1904);

Mrs. Sutherland Orr, *Life and Letters of Robert Browning,* revised by F. G. Kenyon (London: Smith, Elder, 1908);

W. Hall Griffin and Harry Christopher Minchin, *The Life of Robert Browning* (London: Methuen, 1910);

Betty Miller, *Robert Browning: A Portrait* (London: John Murray, 1952);

Maisie Ward, *Robert Browning and His World,* 2 volumes (London: Cassell, 1967–1969);

William Irvine and Park Honan, *The Book, the Ring, and the Poet* (New York: McGraw-Hill, 1974);

John Maynard, *Browning's Youth* (Cambridge, Mass.: Harvard University Press, 1977).

References:

Harold Bloom, ed., *Robert Browning* (New York: Chelsea Press, 1985);

Forrest D. Burt, "Browning's 'Pied Piper of Hamelin: A Child's Story' and 'The Cardinal and His Dog': Considering the Poet's Early Interest in Drama and Art," *Studies in Browning and His Circle,* 16 (1988): 30–41;

William Clyde DeVane, *A Browning Handbook,* second edition (New York: Appleton-Century-Crofts, 1955);

Arthur Dickson, "Browning's Source for *The Pied Piper of Hamelin,*" *Studies in Philology,* 23 (July 1926): 327–332;

Ian Jack, *Browning's Major Poetry* (Oxford: Oxford University Press, 1973);

Barbara Melchiori, *Browning's Poetry of Reticence* (Edinburgh: Oliver & Boyd, 1968);

Bernard Queenan, "The Evolution of the Pied Piper," *Children's Literature,* 7 (1978): 104–114;

Clarence Tracy, ed., *Browning's Mind and Art* (New York: Barnes & Noble, 1970).

Papers:

There is no central depository for Robert Browning's papers. A listing of all manuscripts and their locations can be found in Philip Kelley and Betty A. Coley, *The Browning Collections* (Winfield, Kans.: Wedgestone, 1984).

Randolph Caldecott

(22 March 1846 – 12 February 1886)

Michael Scott Joseph
Rutgers University Libraries

BOOKS: *R. Caldecott's Picture Books* (London: Routledge, 1878–1885);

The Babes in the Wood (London: Routledge, 1879);

R. Caldecott's Picture Book, Containing The Diverting History of John Gilpin, The House that Jack Built, The Babes in the Wood, and An Elegy on the Death of a Mad Dog (London & New York: Routledge, 1879);

Sing a Song for Sixpence (London: Routledge, 1880);

The Three Jovial Huntsmen (London: Routledge, 1880);

The Farmer's Boy (London: Routledge, 1881);

The Queen of Hearts (London: Routledge, 1881);

R. Caldecott's Picture Book (No. 2) Containing The Three Jovial Huntsmen, Sing a Song for Sixpence, The Queen of Hearts, The Farmer's Boy (London & New York: Routledge, 1881);

R. Caldecott's Collection of Pictures & Songs Containing: The Diverting History of John Gilpin, The House that Jack Built, An Elegy on the Death of a Mad Dog, The Babes in the Wood, The Three Jovial Huntsmen, Sing a Song for Sixpence, The Queen of Hearts, The Farmer's Boy (London & New York: Routledge, 1881);

Routledge's Christmas Number (London & New York: Routledge, 1881);

Hey Diddle Diddle, and Baby Bunting (London: Routledge, 1882);

The Milkmaid. An Old Song Exhibited & Explained in Many Designs (London: Routledge, 1882);

Scenes humoristiques (Paris: Hachette, 1882);

The Fox Jumps Over the Parson's Gate (London: Routledge, 1883);

A Frog He Would A-Wooing Go (Folk-song) (London: Routledge, 1883);

The Hey Diddle Diddle Picture Book, by Randolph Caldecott. Containing – Where Are You Going My Pretty Maid, Hey Diddle Diddle and Baby Bunting, A Frog He Would A-Wooing Go, The Fox Jumps Over the Parson's Gate (London: Routledge, 1883);

Randolph Caldecott (engraving by Edmund Evans)

A Sketch-Book of R. Caldecott's (London & New York: Routledge, 1883);

Randolph Caldecott's "Graphic" Pictures (London & New York: Routledge, 1883);

Come Lasses and Lads (London: Routledge, 1884);

Ride a Cock-Horse to Banbury; and A Farmer Went Trotting Upon His Grey Mare (London: Routledge, 1884);

The Panjandrum Picture Book, Containing Come Lasses and Lads, Ride a Cock-Horse to Banbury Cross and A Farmer Went Trotting Upon His Grey Mare, Mrs. Mary Blaize, The Great Panjandrum Himself (London & New York: Routledge, 1885);

R. Caldecott's Second Collection of Pictures and Songs. Containing The Milkmaid, Hey Diddle Diddle, and Baby Bunting, The Fox Jumps Over the Parson's

Gate, A Frog He Would A-Wooing Go, Come Lasses and Lads, Ride a Cock-Horse to Banbury Cross, and A Farmer Went Trotting Upon His Grey Mare, Mrs. Mary Blaize, The Great Panjandrum Himself. All exhibited in beautiful engravings (London & New York: Routledge, 1885);

Fox-Hunting; by a Man in a Round Hat (London, 1886);

A Few Sketches by the Late Randolph Caldecott with Compliments (London, 1886);

The Christmas Card Sketch Book (London: Marion, 1886);

The Complete Collection of Pictures & Songs (London & New York: Routledge, 1887);

Facsimiles of Original Sketches (Manchester: Galloway, 1887);

More "Graphic" Pictures, by Randolph Caldecott (London & New York: Routledge, 1887);

Nouvelles scenes humoristiques (Paris: Hachette, 1887);

Randolph Caldecott's "Graphic" Pictures. Complete Edition (London & New York: Routledge, 1887–1891);

Randolph Caldecott's Last "Graphic" Pictures (London & New York: Routledge, 1888);

The Complete Collection of Randolph Caldecott's Contributions to the "Graphic" (London & New York: Routledge, 1888);

Catalogue of a Loan Collection of the Works of Randolph Caldecott at the Brasenose Club (Manchester: John Heywood, 1888);

Gleanings from "Graphic" (London & New York: Routledge, 1889);

The Complete Collection of Randolph Caldecott's Contributions to the "Graphic" (London & New York: Routledge, 1889);

Randolph Caldecott's Sketches (London: S. Low, Marston, Searle & Rivington, 1890);

Sporting Society, or, Sporting Chat and Sporting Memories (London: Bellairs, 1897);

Lightning Sketches for "The House that Jack Built" (Westminster, 1899; New York: Warne, n.d.);

Randolph Caldecott's Painting Book (London & New York: Frederick, 1902).

BOOKS ILLUSTRATED: Henry Blackburn, *The Harz Mountains; A Tour in the Toy Country* (London: S. Low, Marston, Searle & Rivington, 1873);

Frederick Marryat, *Frank Mildmay or the Naval Officer* (London & New York: Routledge, 1873);

Louisa Morgan, *Baron Bruno; or, The Unbelieving Philosopher, and Other Fairy Stories* (London: Macmillan, 1875);

Washington Irving, *Old Christmas from Washington Irving's Sketch-book* (London: Macmillan, 1875);

Irving, *Bracebridge Hall* (London: Macmillan, 1877);

William Cowper, *The Diverting History of John Gilpin, Showing How He Went Farther Than He Intended, and Came Safe Home Again* (London: Routledge, 1878);

Alice Vansittart Strettel Carr, *North Italian Folk; Sketches from Town and Country Life* (London: Chatto & Windus, 1878; New York: Scribner & Welford, 1878);

Oliver Goldsmith, *An Elegy on the Death of a Mad Dog. Written by Dr. Goldsmith, Pictured by R. Caldecott, Sung by Master Bill Primrose* (London: Routledge, 1879);

Henry Blackburn, *Breton Folk: An Artistic Tour in Brittany* (London: S. Low, Marston, Searle & Rivington, 1880; Boston: Osgood, 1881);

Hannah Jane Locker-Lampson, *What the Blackbird Said; a Story, in Four Chirps* (London & New York: Routledge, 1881);

Frederick Locker-Lampson, *London Lyrics* (London: Chiswick Press, 1881; New York: White, Stokes & Allen, 1886);

Juliana Horatia Gatty Ewing, *Jackanapes* (London: Society for Promoting Christian Knowledge, 1883; New York: E. & J. B. Young, 1883?);

Edwin Waugh, *Poems and Songs* (Manchester: John Heywood, 1883);

Waugh, *Rambles in the Lake Country and Other Travel Sketches* (Manchester: John Heywood, 1883);

Aesop, *Some of Aesop's Fables with Modern Instances . . . from New Translations by Alfred Caldecott* (London & New York: Macmillan, 1883);

F. C. Burnand, H. Savile Clark, R. E. Fracillon, and others, *Society Novelettes* (London: Vizetelly, 1883);

Ewing, *Daddy Darwin's Dovecot: A Country Tale* (London & Brighton: Society for Promoting Christian Knowledge, 1884; New York: E. & J. B. Young, 1884);

Oliver Goldsmith, *An Elegy on Mrs. Mary Blaize, the Glory of Her Sex* (London: Routledge, 1885);

Jean de la Fontaine, *Fables de la Fontaine* (London: Macmillan, 1885);

Samuel Foote, *The Great Panjandrum Himself* (London: Routledge, 1885);

Ewing, *Lob Lie-by-the-Fire; or, The Luck of Lingborough* (London: Society for Promoting Christian Knowledge, 1885; New York: E. & J. B. Young, 1885);

A. Y. D., *The Owls of Lynn Belfry. A Tale for Children* (London: Field & Tuer/Leadenhall, 1886);

Hallam Tennyson, Baron, *Jack and the Bean-Stalk; English Hexameters* (London & New York: Macmillan, 1886);

Irving, *Old Christmas and Bracebridge Hall* (London & New York: Macmillan, 1886);

Blackburn, *Artistic Travel* (London: Sampson Low, Marston, 1892);

Blackburn, *The Art of Illustration* (London: W. H. Allen, 1894).

The Caldecott Medal, bestowed annually since 1938 upon the "most distinguished American picture book for children in the United States," has helped make Randolph Caldecott's name synonymous with children's book illustrations of excellence. Frederick G. Melcher and the American Library Association chose to commemorate Caldecott through this singular honor for his remarkable books of illustrated nursery rhymes, folktales, and comic poems. Published from 1876 to 1885, these works indelibly mark the genesis of the modern picture book.

Caldecott's sixteen picture books reflect a delight in English village life, rural traditions, nature, and unpredictability. They also reveal a severe economy of style, as well as an understanding of color as a means to express character and as a purely decorative element in the high Victorian mode. Caldecott's genius for storytelling was preeminent among nineteenth-century illustrators. Combining a gift of insight with a gift for invention — by which he would take the most dramatic features of a text and harmonize them with incidents and subplots from his own imagination — he took children's book illustration far beyond textual ornamentation. In Caldecott's work the illustrator becomes an equal partner to the author, and through his illustrations readers experience not merely the surface activities of the text but the breadth and nature of the world from which the text arose.

Randolph Caldecott was born 22 March 1846 in the city of Chester. His father, John Caldecott, worked as a hatter, tailor, and woolen-draper in the Rows on Bridge Street, and living, as the family did, above the shop afforded the young artist an opportunity to drink in the color and excitement of the market. Like his brother, Alfred, Randolph Caldecott attended the King Henry VIII school, where he achieved the status of head-boy. However, Randolph preferred modeling wildlife in bits of wood and pieces of clay to the labors of school. He had become, by age six, an avid sketcher. His master, Mr. James Harris, used to show off a Caldecott sketch of Aeneas filially bearing off his father, An-

chises, from the burning ruins of Troy, so impressed was he by the child's precocious draftsmanship. But Caldecott's choice of subject matter tended away from classical themes and more toward animals and nature. Throughout boyhood, as indeed throughout his tragically shortened life, he favored rustic scenery and lonely haunts over the bustling life of the city.

Like most prudent middle-class tradesmen, Caldecott's father did not encourage his son's art but instead secured for him, when he was fifteen, a position in the Whitchurch Office of the Whitchurch and Ellesmere Bank. As tedious as bank work must have been, life in rural Shropshire nicely matched Caldecott's temperament. For much of the six years (1861–1867) he dwelled there, he found ample occasion for cultivating such rural pastimes as fishing, shooting, and attending the markets and the cattle fairs, all the while sketching and collecting a store of visual memories of the towns and villages of North Shropshire and South Cheshire.

As serene as his life may have been in Whitchurch, Caldecott's artistic ambitions could not be entirely satisfied by a rural life, and he obtained a position in the city of Manchester at the Manchester and Salford Bank. Caldecott became an evening student at the Manchester School of Art. He further mingled with fellow artists and writers, such as Frederick Shields, Alfred Waterhouse, and Edwin Waugh, as a member of the exclusive Bracenose Club, designed "to promote the association of gentlemen of literary, scientific or artistic professions, pursuits or tastes," according to its motto.

Leaving the steamy rooms of the club, Caldecott often wandered through town gaining impressions of the bustling, murky metropolis and then returned home to fill notebooks with sketches, until the arrival of a new workday sent him back to the bank. Colleagues at the bank recalled finding drawings of horses, dogs, and other such subjects on the back of receipt slips, old envelopes, and the blotter on Caldecott's desk. The drawings he published in the local papers *Will o' the Wisp* and *The Sphinx* showed the influence of the English caricaturist tradition going back to William Hogarth in the artist's preference for the line, for narration, and for satire.

In 1870, at age twenty-four, Caldecott traveled to London. Encouraged by the warm reception accorded his drawings, he made his home there in 1872. The summer of Caldecott's first year in London, he accompanied Henry Blackburn and his family to the German Harz Mountains. His many cartoonlike sketches of the landscape and amusing en-

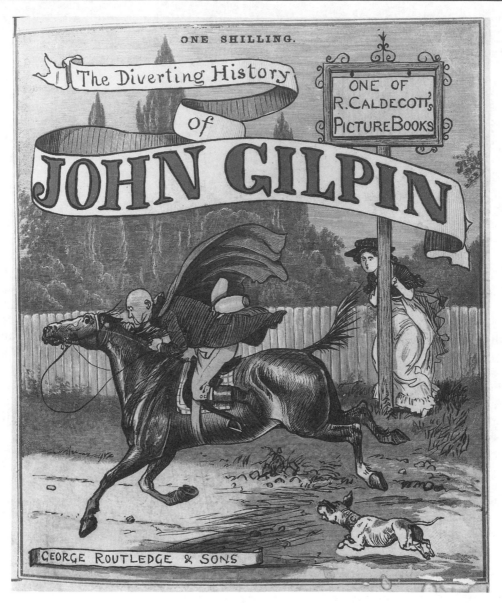

Cover for Caldecott's second picture book, which was an immediate popular and critical success
(courtesy of the Lilly Library, Indiana University)

counters with the local population were gathered together the following year and published in Blackburn's *The Harz Mountains; A Tour in the Toy Country* (1873). The book reveals both Caldecott's awareness of the congenial style of Richard Doyle and a spirit of spontaneity that anticipates his picture-book drawings. One also notes the artist's tendency to seize upon the grotesque, later to distinguish some of his most admired inventions, such as the concluding sketch for "Hey Diddle Diddle" in *Hey Diddle Diddle, and Baby Bunting* (1882) and the attack of the cats in *A Frog He Would A-Wooing Go* (1883).

The Harz Mountains opened several important doors for Caldecott. Through his publication in *Harper's Monthly Magazine* in 1873, he obtained access to an American audience; success as a book illustrator also provided him with an alternative to the wearying business of journal illustration, the rigorous demands of which suited neither Caldecott's personality nor the frail health he had suffered since a boyhood bout with rheumatic fever.

On 23 January 1874 James D. Cooper sought out Caldecott in his rooms on Great Russell Street, opposite the British Museum. A highly regarded wood engraver and printer who styled himself "the old woodpecker," Cooper proposed a Christmas volume of Washington Irving's stories to be culled from *The Sketchbook of Geoffrey Crayon* (1819). Caldecott, who felt at heart a kinship with the time of Irving and a predilection to render the types of that age, agreed. *Old Christmas from Washington Irving's Sketch-book* (1875), published by Macmillan, includes 120 original drawings that demonstrate a fondness for the Regency period — which Caldecott had nourished by studying color-plate books — and an eye for local architecture. They also demonstrate the artist's lively fancy, his passing appreciation of John Leech, and his gift for sustained interpretation.

Old Christmas introduced Caldecott to a wider, sympathetic audience. Blackburn encouraged sales of his young friend's book by reviewing it favorably, and the *Graphic* published Caldecott's first color illustrations, based upon his *Old Christmas* drawings, in their Christmas issue. Cooper produced another book of Irving's with illustrations by Caldecott, *Bracebridge Hall* (1877). While perhaps not as popular as its predecessor, it confirmed Caldecott's stature as a major illustrator with a large popular appeal. The book marked another turning point in Caldecott's career, as he began his association with Edmund Evans, the virtuoso color printer. Although Caldecott's previous children's book, Louisa Morgan's *Baron Bruno; or, The Unbelieving Philosopher, and Other Fairy Stories* (1875), had been somewhat unpromising, through Evans's brilliant technique Caldecott's picture books would become the high-water mark of late-nineteenth-century children's illustration.

Edmund Evans had been printing highly successful sixpenny children's books illustrated by Walter Crane for a dozen years, using woodblocks for both design and tint. Although slightly out-of-date, the technology best suited the nature of the illustrations he printed. Crane's book illustrations, inspired by the principles of Aestheticism, owed much of their beauty and success to the effects of Evans's printing and engraving prowess. In 1877, when Crane refused to go on with the work, Evans, convinced that the young illustrator of the Irving books possessed the talent required to maintain the high standard of his picture books, invited Caldecott to continue in Crane's place. Caldecott agreed to produce two picture books per year, although he had the price raised to a shilling.

In 1879 Routledge and Sons published *The House that Jack Built* and *The Diverting History of John Gilpin* in editions of approximately ten thousand copies. *The House that Jack Built,* the first of Caldecott's picture books, featured eight full-page color illustrations and many line drawings, printed in sepia. (This formula would remain essentially unchanged throughout the series.) Based on the traditional nursery rhyme and well traveled as it was, having been part of the chapbook repertoire for more than a century, the book nevertheless surprised readers with its unusual forcefulness and freehanded embellishment of the text. Caldecott's drawings introduced subplots, embedding a mock tragedy and inflating the significance of the dog's death, into the simple narrative, prompting the reader to rediscover its deeper meanings and rich nuances. Through his embellishments Caldecott nearly succeeds in transforming the rhyme into a fable. He had in fact been illustrating Aesop for James D. Cooper, although the work was not published until 1883, but his *House that Jack Built* possesses a stronger sense of dramatic form as well as a consistently detached and ironic tone. It is precisely Caldecott's gift for harmonizing opposites — the profound and the casual, the comic and tragic, the fabulous with the realistic, superficial monotonousness with registers of deeper feeling, a spareness of line and a rich overflow of imaginative embellishment — that resonates throughout his oeuvre.

The Diverting History of John Gilpin, the second of the picture books, displayed Caldecott's strong grounding in both the English village life he knew as a boy and in the English caricaturist tradition, echoing George Cruikshank's engaging approach to the same poem a half century earlier. Unlike the first picture book, *John Gilpin* utilizes a text of certain origin and considerable length, and William Cowper's poem of sixty-three busy quatrains did not lend itself to the extraordinary literary manipulations of Caldecott's work on the nursery rhyme. One of Caldecott's strategies in illustrating *John Gilpin* was to create scenery out of the English countryside and to delineate architecture, domestic furnishings, and fulsome costumes down to the smallest detail, in order to invest the poem with a sense of place and dramatic verisimilitude. He introduces details that re-create the homey and boisterous life of the English village, demonstrating Caldecott's genius for stagecraft and for visualizing the physics to which the nature of the poem is responsive.

Caldecott's work won immediate and unanimous praise, although it was natural enough for reviewers to compare him with his immediate predecessor, Walter Crane. The London *Times* concluded an enthusiastic commentary by declaring, "In a few strokes, dashed off apparently at random, [Cal-

Cover for one of the picture books Caldecott produced in 1879, a
story of two orphans who are taken into the woods to
be slain (courtesy of the Lilly Library,
Indiana University)

decott] can portray a scene or incident to the full as correctly and completely, and far more lucidly than Mr. Crane in his later and far more elaborate style." The *Nation* wrote, "Mr. R. Caldecott's latest caricatures should not be overlooked by purveyors for the nursery. His *John Gilpin* and *The House that Jack Built* (Routledge) are *sui generis,* and irresistibly funny as well as clever. One hardly knows which to admire most — the full page color prints, or the outline sketches in the brown ink of the text. Happy the generation that is brought up on such masters as Mr. Caldecott and Mr. Walter Crane."

Reviewers may have perceived Evans's two young protégés as rivals, but after Thomas Armstrong introduced them in 1877 Randolph Caldecott and Walter Crane became friends. (In fact, they were the same age and both descended from old Chester families, and they found much in common.) In his book *An Artist's Reminiscences* (1907), Crane's memories of his friend tenderly relate how Caldecott would delay riding on horseback until the early evening so that he could play with Crane's children before their bedtime. Caldecott was also befriended by the other great illustrator of his generation, Kate Greenaway, to whom he was introduced in 1878. One sees in such works as *Sing a Song for Sixpence* (1880) and

Hey Diddle Diddle, and Baby Bunting the influence of Greenaway upon Caldecott's depiction of children, despite Caldecott's evident amusement at the sugary excesses of the Greenaway style.

In 1879, the same year that he exchanged his digs on Great Russell Street for Wybournes, a house at Kemsing, a tiny village near Sevenoaks, Kent, Caldecott produced a second pair of picture books: *The Babes in the Wood,* a melodramatic ballad, and *An Elegy on the Death of a Mad Dog,* an ironic poem by Oliver Goldsmith. Much of the work was undertaken while the artist was in Italy, a trip that would also inspire a collection of comic illustrations published the following year in the *Graphic* as "A Visit to Venice."

The Babes in the Wood presented Caldecott with a difficult assignment. The story is heavy with pathos, portraying two luckless toddlers who are first orphaned and then fetched away to be slain. When one of the hired murderers refuses to fulfill his hateful task, the orphans look on in horror as the two villains fight to the death. Although the less hardhearted combatant prevails, the orphans gain nothing but the dubious consolation of being allowed to expire naturally, alone and hungry, in the dark wood.

Caldecott observes the gravity of the text by restricting his palette to dark and somber hues and including thick black lines in his designs to convey the harshness, as well as the antiquity, of the tale, but his Norfolk doctors are a study in satiric absurdity. Never completely recovering his own health from an early bout with rheumatic fever — and sick at the time he was at work — Caldecott perhaps allowed his feelings of helplessness to be expressed in the owlish countenances of the feeble avatars of the medical profession. He further personalized the text by depicting the father, "sore sick and like to die," with his own features and depicting one of the "ruffians strong" with the features of Edmund Evans. Although Caldecott hardly varied from the conventionally pathetic treatment, the *Nation* complained that "the artist has shown a grievous want of taste in treating humorously the tragedy of the Babes."

Dogs constitute the picture books' most favored category of domestic animal, after which, in diminishing prominence, come horses, geese, and pigs. In *An Elegy on the Death of a Mad Dog* Caldecott took the opportunity to reveal himself as a true dog lover — in the final color illustration he delineates sixteen different breeds. The book also demonstrates the artist's pleasure in creating self-contained cartoons, a skill that had served him well in his newspaper work. In one scene he shows an excited seeing-eye dog barreling headlong down the street as its poor master, who has been posing as a blind man in order to beg, races along behind, glaring murderously at his innocent companion.

In 1880 Caldecott married Marian Brind, a neighbor of his at Wybournes. They were not to have children. *Sing a Song for Sixpence* and *The Three Jovial Huntsmen,* adapted from Edwin Waugh's "Old Cronies," were the picture-book offerings for that year. Perhaps owing to his newfound domestic felicity, they are among Caldecott's most dynamic and inspired creations. The subject of the latter, one of the best known of Caldecott's picture books, had been featured in an oil painting the artist had exhibited at the Royal Academy in 1878 and which had earned him his first serious attention as a painter. The subject of the poem – three inebriated old huntsmen bumbling along through meadow and town and picaresquely jumbling everything they see – brought out the full flavor of Caldecott's comic genius. Never quite balanced in the saddle or quite able to manage their hunting horns, Caldecott's huntsmen convey the rowdy, sour whimsicality of a country tradition pleasantly gone to seed.

Sing a Song for Sixpence represented another opportunity for Caldecott to train his interpretative skills upon a traditional rhyme. With the first full-color illustration of a grandmother holding a coin and recounting a story to her grandchildren, the artist invents a frame story. Readers are to understand that they are overhearing the story, either as it is recounted or more probably as one of the children in the circle comprehends it. Thus, the nonsensical details of the rhyme and its drifting focus are natural reflections of a child's perceptions: the king and queen are imagined as children, and the counting-house is decorated with framed illustrations of Robinson Crusoe and Jack the Giant-Killer, reflecting the parlor where the story is being told, which is decorated with illustrations of Little Bo Peep, Red Riding Hood, and the Babes in the Woods.

Caldecott also invented a woodsman and his family to explain how the blackbird pie came to be. By depicting children of modest circumstances who divert themselves by setting traps and baking pies, Caldecott brilliantly sets off the luxurious and self-indulgent pastimes of the child-king, "counting out his money," and child-queen, "eating bread and honey." The repeated depiction of children, including the audience of the frame story, imparts a sense of a loosely knit community, so that the text of *Sing a Song for Sixpence* assumes the significance of a children's myth. Such a trope spoke to the popular idea disseminated by Jacques Rousseau and warmly

embraced by the Victorians that childhood constituted its own inherently coherent world. This is, of course, at the heart of Greenaway's generation of innocent mignonettes who go about peacefully through green meadows in unsupervised, harmonious perfection. Caldecott's community is formed upon the basis of a shared story.

The following year Evans raised Caldecott's royalty payment to a penny farthing, beginning with the picture books *The Farmer's Boy* (1881) and *The Queen of Hearts* (1881). The former marks one of Caldecott's purest odes to country life, for which he used sketches he made at Wybournes, including the puppies of his own dachshund, Lalla Rook. Inspiration for *The Queen of Hearts* derived, in contrast, from the 1840 publication of *Chatto's History of Playing Cards. The Farmer's Boy* turns upon one of Caldecott's most sublime ironies. By delineating the farmer boy's manners and costume effeminately at the beginning and abruptly presenting a handsome and virile young man in his final illustration, Caldecott shows that the character's effeminacy has matured into manly delicacy.

The Queen of Hearts, in sharp relief to the naturalism of *The Farmer's Boy,* gains strength from its painterly concern for decoration, its dazzlingly vibrant colors, the physical beauty of its characters, and its creation of subplots to embellish the story synthetically. Just as *John Gilpin* resonates with the noise and excitement of a bucolic English village, *The Queen of Hearts* mirrors the elegant, idealized habits of the court. With characteristic boldness, Caldecott portrays the queen draped in revealingly cut voluptuous garments and envisions a knave more susceptible to emotion, who is variously caricatured in transports of guilt, sorrow, and remorse. The main narrative is further deepened by Caldecott's decision to supply offspring to each pair of playing card parents. It is they, most fittingly, for whom the tarts were intended. Therefore, it is fatherly protectiveness and not royal pique that triggers the King of Hearts's vengeful wrath.

One of the pair of picture books published the following November, *Hey Diddle Diddle, and Baby Bunting* recalls in its decorative schemes and use of color the work of the French illustrator Grandville. One can also recognize in the illustrations for "Baby Bunting" the tower of Saint Oswald's parish church and the town of Malpas. "Hey Diddle Diddle" is a masterpiece of embellishment. Like *Sing a Song for Sixpence,* it introduces a frame story: a musical cat, perhaps an analog for the author, obtains a fiddle so he may entertain a roomful of children. They join hands and dance about under the attentive gaze of a

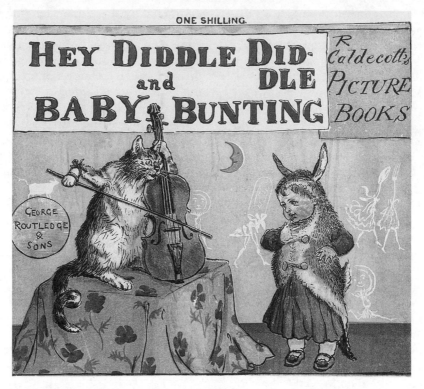

*Cover for one of Caldecott's 1882 picture books, a clever retelling of two well-known
nursery rhymes (courtesy of the Lilly Library, Indiana University)*

serving maid standing behind a table filled with luscious desserts. Caldecott then turns to the central
narrative, enriching it with a subplot involving a
milkmaid.

In the final full-color illustration, the dish and
spoon run off together while the plates, a decanter
of wine, and a vase are shown gyrating wildly to the
music of the fiddling cat. The final page presents a
shock – the dish lies shattered in pieces, mourned
by his sister dishes, while the spoon is being hustled
off by a mother-fork and an angry father-knife.
With this final embellishment Caldecott succeeds in
subverting the poetical text, puncturing the stuffiness of the insulated Victorian idyll. By transforming the cat into a type of enchanted fiddler, an emblem well-known in folklore for its mischievous and
unpredictable powers, Caldecott manages with as-
tonishing effectiveness to bring out the essential
mystery and musicality of "Hey Diddle Diddle."
When his sketch of the dish and spoon was shown
to Kate Greenaway, she praised it by lamenting that
she had not such cleverness.

In *The Milkmaid. An Old Song Exhibited & Explained in Many Designs* (1882) Caldecott again
turned his attention to rural courtship, as he had in
The Farmer's Boy. Emphasizing the proud milkmaid's

rejection of the young squire's bungled suit, he at-
taches seven drawings, including two that are full-
page and in color, for the concluding line: " 'Nobody asked you, Sir!' she said." Where the original
rhyme makes only a mild swipe at aristocratic
haughtiness, in which the milkmaid asserts her dignity in the face of insensitive aristocratic rejection,
Caldecott's romantic illustrations glorify the milkmaid's unsophisticated existence. Her life – associated with simplicity, the out-of-doors, natural
beauty, dance, female camaraderie, and quick justice – forms the ideal, and the squire, a perfect foil
for the smiling innocent in *The Farmer's Boy,* merits
the reader's scorn for falling short of it.

In September 1882 Caldecott and Marian
Brind left Wybournes for Broomfield, at Frensham,
Surrey. While he continued to work upon picture
books, from 1882 to 1885 the artist also entered
into a fruitful collaboration with the author Juliana
Horatia Gaddy Ewing, producing *Jackanapes* (1883),
Daddy Darwin's Dovecot: A Country Tale (1884), and
Lob Lie-by-the-Fire; or, The Luck of Lingborough (1885).
Ewing proved an exacting and occasionally temper-
amental associate, although a perceptive and stead-
fast admirer of Caldecott's art. The relationship
began in 1879 when Caldecott was asked to provide

an illustration around which Ewing could construct a story. Picture and story appeared together in *Aunt Jody's Magazine* in October 1879. With hopes of enlarging the story into a book, Ewing solicited further drawings from Caldecott, who did not seriously begin work until 1883. Their association ended with the author's sudden death in May 1885, while *Lob Lie-by-the-Fire* was still incomplete. (When it was published in November, the *Nation* declared Caldecott's drawings to be below his best work.)

While working on *Jackanapes* and completing sketches for *The Graphic, The English Illustrated Magazine,* and *Punch,* Caldecott continued in the development of his extraordinary picture books, two more of which were published in 1883: *A Frog He Would A-Wooing Go,* based on a traditional folk song, and *The Fox Jumps Over the Parson's Gate.* With these titles Caldecott raised the price of his picture books' royalty to three halfpence.

A Frog He Would A-Wooing Go is a loving satire in which, once again, rustic courtship supplies the predominant theme. Following the treacherous code of "Hey Diddle Diddle," published the previous year, *A Frog He Would A-Wooing Go* ends in disaster as bloodthirsty pussycats come crashing in upon Miss Mouse's quaint domicile, sending the courtier fleeing. Caldecott introduces a human family into the story – another feature the book shares with "Hey Diddle Diddle" – to add a layer of subtle irony. Their pretty Sunday outfits and wholesome family manner notwithstanding, the family appears stiff and wooden and far less human than the gallant frog, who for all his natty sangfroid and romantic optimism still ends up a duck's dinner.

The Fox Jumps Over the Parson's Gate celebrates the fox hunt as a symbol of mundane routine transcended in the pursuit of excitement and fun. Occupational as well as social conventions are flouted as villagers break away from their daily grind, whether it be a church service or a simple gardening task. The text is a scattering of stanzas lacking a discursive context. Caldecott's illustrations provide the main narrative, the disruption of a wedding service and its eventual happy completion. But even as he celebrates the beauties of spring and the amusing pastimes of country life, Caldecott's art harbors a darker sentiment as well. In a tableau of the wedding party leaving the church – for which the artist sketched the stone porch and entrance of the church of Saint Martin-of-Tours, where he and Marian Brind were wed – there is a child in green with a white ruff collar and a black hat, gesturing open-handedly from his seat upon a tombstone bearing the name "Caldecott." The unexpected waif

intrusively arrests the progress of the wedding procession, just as a fox hunt had done earlier. By withholding from the reader the easy satisfaction of a placidly happy moment, Caldecott suspends the reader's attention and thus immeasurably enhances the power of the work.

In yoking together images of transient pleasure with those that soberly assert the verities of life, Caldecott drew from an early-nineteenth-century aesthetic sensibility predating Victorian sentimentality. A singular understanding of the union of the forces of life and death may be said to define the structure of many memorable nursery rhymes, and the picture books of 1883–1885 suggest that one of Caldecott's intentions was to suit the weft of his illustrations to this ineluctable design. Indeed, while critics have praised Caldecott's cheer and lightheartedness, they have also marveled at the psychological complexity and honesty of his vision. In this sense Caldecott's work perpetuates a strain of hardheaded realism prevalent in English children's book illustration since the time of Thomas Bewick. Mirroring authentic nursery rhymes in their method of operation, this realism is the quality in Randolph Caldecott that recoiled from the oversimplified, the superficial, the censored, and the merely escapist.

Springtime and rural courtship again served as contexts in *Come Lasses and Lads* (1884), in which Caldecott reprises the image of fiddler as a central emblem. Unlike the animated cat in "Hey Diddle Diddle," the human fiddler in this book suffers loneliness, fatigue, imperfection, and dejection. Caldecott's musician epitomizes the ambiguousness of a work that strikes a balance between age and cruel melancholy on the one hand, and gaiety, music, tender affection, grace, and comedy on the other. Its dependence upon traditional rites notwithstanding, *Come Lasses and Lads* embodies a modern sensibility and a complex texture. Caldecott's inclusion of a transvestite Maid Marian is an unusual addition given the context of nineteenth-century children's illustration.

In his other 1884 offering Caldecott again demonstrated his strong preference for combining elements of high contrast by selecting two nursery rhymes radically dissimilar in tone and sense: *Ride a Cock-Horse to Banbury; and A Farmer Went Trotting Upon His Grey Mare.* For the former rhyme Caldecott offers a paean to female beauty, conceiving of his "fine lady" in the exquisite, worshipful manner of the Pre-Raphaelite Brotherhood. In contrast, Caldecott's bare illustrations for "A Farmer Went Trotting" frame a concern for human frailty. His farmer, drawn in the likeness of the farmer from *The House that Jack Built,* is a figure of helplessness. A raven becomes the symbol of the farmer's dolorous fate: to be destroyed by a supernatural agency of irresistible force.

Caldecott's final picture books, Goldsmith's *An Elegy on Mrs. Mary Blaize, the Glory of Her Sex* (1885) and Samuel Foote's *The Great Panjandrum Himself* (1885), are also his strangest. His illustrations for the former, the less unusual of the two, shift the balance of the rhyme by giving the title character a profession. Caldecott makes her a pawnbroker, allowing for the ironic treatment of her charity, most notably in the stanza

> The needy seldom pass'd her door,
> And always found her kind;
> She freely lent to all the poor –
> Who left a pledge behind.

Caldecott mingles pedestrian, middle-class shrewdness with mawkish emotion, however. As the pawnbroker does business with a fading gallant who is hoping to interest her in a heart-shaped charm, Mary's mysteriously adoring smile betrays an inner life in which she imagines herself the object of somewhat more romantic attentions. She emerges as a lonely matron, an undiscovered treasure, whose imagination transforms the objects of her trade into the stage props of a more personally fulfilling interior drama.

Caldecott develops the metaphor of Mary Blaize's sentimental alchemy by transmuting the pawnbroker's symbol into three-stem cherries, which appear in a color illustration of the character handing out the fruit to an eager and delighted group of children. The theme of *tempora mutantur* (times are changing) more deeply etches the pathos of *Mary Blaize.* In three illustrations Caldecott's treatment of the character's death attains added resonance by making allusions to earlier picture books. The first illustration, in which three doctors diagnose, with comic gravity, Mary's terminal disorder, mirrors the artist's scorn for the Norfolk doctors of *The Babes in the Wood.* The second illustration, in color, depicts Mary's body resting in a chair, her face a death mask. The illustration typifies Caldecott's mature artistic boldness. His fascination with both mortality and art are reflected simultaneously: beside the still form of Mary Blaize a cat steals nourishment from his mistress's bowl, conjuring up an image of the cat from "Hey Diddle Diddle," whose feral energies broke over the dam of convention and cozy decorum. Mary Blaize's cat, no longer checked by the aged mistress,

is an analog of continuity and the aggressive instinct to survive – one of the major themes sounded in Caldecott's first picture book, *The House that Jack Built.* The nature of survival and of what survives may be inferred from the final illustration. The pallbearers convey Mary Blaize's casket, emblazoned with three-stem cherries, to the graveyard, where a parson waits, book in hand, at the gate. This incongruous touch lends both formal dignity and liberating novelty to the occasion and is an affirmation of Mary Blaize's social identity.

The collection of non sequiturs and subversions culled from Foote and published under the title *The Great Panjandrum Himself* begins in medias res, as a young maid goes to the garden to cut a cabbage leaf for the "surprise filling" of an apple pie. Having proven a failure as a cook, the maid has "very imprudently married the barber." Her flawed, if not perverse, judgment seems to be at the heart of the story, and, running contrary to the disapproving narrative tone, it proves to sustain her and to supply the book with a joyful and untroubled wedding. Despite its lowly nature, the marriage is sanctioned by no less a personage than the Great Panjandrum himself, the epitome of learning, reason, and judgment. The Great Panjandrum cuts an absurdly grandiose figure. His imposing size, the details of his exaggerated features, and the universal wonderment his figure elicits combine to make an impression of supreme inappropriateness.

Caldecott's comic and complex epithalamium picks up themes of the country wedding and the awkward or inappropriate courtship treated in his earlier books. By affirming the delectability of the imprudent union, *The Great Panjandrum Himself* offers a successful alternative to the squire's clumsy surrender to prudence in *The Milkmaid,* while the graceful progress of its wedding procession seems to flow from the bucolic diversions of *Come Lasses and Lads* and the halting progress of *The Fox Jumps Over the Parson's Gate.*

In fact, the latter book is tellingly evoked in an illustration accompanying the pivotal line "and she very imprudently married the Barber": Caldecott revisits the memorable scene of bride and groom moving past a small figure astride a gravestone. The married couple coming out of the church in *The Fox* are caught off guard and distressed to find the gamin saluting them from atop Mr. Caldecott's tombstone, but the barber and the maid in *The Great Panjandrum Himself* have passed the small figure. Indeed, it is the roadsider who reacts to *them* – he is gladdened by the procession. Caldecott apparently includes this allusive image for the purpose of validating the congeniality of the couple's future. Moreover, this figurative child-man would seem to anticipate the Great Panjandrum, whose sophisticated grandeur may cast him in the role of outsider but does not impede his rolling around on the floor in play with the children, thus becoming a child-man himself. In the work of an artist who wrestled with melancholy and the shadow of mutability, this image, made bold by its repetition, seems sincerely life-affirming.

In early November 1885, before Routledge had published *Mary Blaize* and *The Great Panjandrum Himself*, the Caldecotts left England for America. Although Randolph left with a commission from the *Graphic* to execute sketches of scenes there, the trip was made for the artist's health as well. The itinerary was rigorous. The Caldecotts were to dock in New York, proceed south to Philadelphia, Baltimore, Washington, Richmond, Savannah, and Florida, then turn west for New Orleans and California; after a stop in Colorado they were to return to New York, then visit Boston and return home by May. On 12 February 1886, however, during a seizure of acute gastritis, Caldecott collapsed and died in Saint Augustine, Florida. He was shy of his fortieth birthday by less than a month.

Had Caldecott lived he may not have chosen to produce more picture books; his letters do not clearly indicate his intention. The arduousness of selecting two titles every spring and early summer, then planning and producing the original drawings, persuaded the artist that he ought to attempt a book of a more profitable character. He wrote to Evans in 1885, "I have an idea of another single book at 2s. 6d. or so which might be successful." Caldecott left no sketches or notes, however, as clues to what he had in mind, but the vigor and beauty of his last picture books reveal a mature talent capable of growth.

In order to consider Randolph Caldecott's life fairly, one must note the extraordinary influence he had on others. In his illustrations for *Old Christmas* and *Bracebridge Hall*, he pioneered the style of book illustration called the "Cranford style," which Hugh Thompson admired and popularized in his illustrations for the novels of Mrs. Gaskell. The work of Beatrix Potter shows a spirited preference for Caldecott's joining of wit to energy. Her exposure to Caldecott occurred at a tender age and left a lasting impression, and her father purchased Caldecott's spontaneous ink-and-brush drawings for *A Frog He Would A-Wooing Go* and the original sketches to *The Three Jovial Huntsmen*. By artfully cultivating

the expressive capacities of the line rather than relying upon heavy chromatic effects, and in their painstaking efforts at making the perfect marriage between text and picture, L. Leslie Brooke, Edward Ardizzone, and William Nicolson all disclose a strong affinity with Caldecott, as does the work of Edwin Abbey and the young Howard Pyle. Perhaps no artist has come nearer to matching Caldecott's surprising habit of blending the fanciful with the observable than Maurice Sendak, who has written of himself: "When I came to picture books, it was Randolph Caldecott who really put me where I wanted to be."

Letters:

Yours Pictorially: Illustrated Letters of Randolph Caldecott, edited by Michael Hutchins (London: Warne, 1976).

Biography:

Henry Blackburn, *Randolph Caldecott: A Personal Memoir of His Early Art Career* (London: S. Low, Marston, Searle & Rivington, 1886).

References:

Brian Alderson, *Sing a Song for Sixpence* (Cambridge: Cambridge University Press, 1986);

Rodney K. Engen, *Randolph Caldecott, Lord of the Nursery* (New York: Jupiter, 1981);

Nancy Finlay, *Randolph Caldecott, 1846–1886* (Cambridge, Mass.: Houghton Library, 1986);

Maurice Sendak, "Randolph Caldecott: An Appreciation," in *The Randolph Caldecott Treasury*, selected and edited by Elizabeth T. Billington (London & New York: Warne, 1978), pp. 11–14.

Papers:

Major collections of Randolph Caldecott's sketchbooks and correspondence are housed at the Houghton Library of Harvard University. Page proofs and woodblocks are in the de Grummond Collection at the University of Southern Mississippi. The original drawings for *Old Christmas* are housed at Columbia University. Other important repositories of Caldecott material are the UCLA Research Library; the Huntington Library; the Fitzwilliam Museum, Cambridge; the Victoria and Albert Museum; the University of Indiana; the City Library, Sheffield; and the Shropshire Country Library.

Lucy Lyttelton Cameron

(29 April 1781 – 6 September 1858)

Naomi J. Wood
Kansas State University

BOOKS: *The Work-House; or, A Religious Life the Only Happy One, Being an Interesting History of Susan and Esther Hall* (Bath: S. Hazard, 1802);

The Two Lambs, an Allegorical History (Burlington, N.J.: Allinson, 1816; fourteenth edition, Wellington, Salop: Houlston, 1821);

The Raven and the Dove (Wellington, Salop: Houlston, 1817; Boston: Samuel T. Armstrong and Crocker & Brewster, 1823);

History of Fidelity and Profession, an Allegory (Wellington, Salop: Houlston, 1818; New York: Samuel Wood & Sons, 1820);

The Caskets; or, The Palace and the Church (Wellington, Salop: Houlston, 1818; Boston: Samuel T. Armstrong and Crocker & Brewster, 1823);

The Holiday Queen (Wellington, Salop: Houlston, 1818);

The Mother's Grave, second edition (Wellington, Salop: Houlston, 1819);

The Nosegay of Honeysuckles (Portland: William Hyde, 1820; ninth edition, Wellington, Salop: Houlston, 1822);

Vain Wishes (London: Whittemore and Wightman & Cramp, 1820?);

The Polite Little Children (Andover, Mass.: Mark Newman, 1820; fourth edition, Wellington, Salop: Houlston, 1821);

Memoirs of Emma and Her Nurse; or, The History of Lady Harewood (Wellington, Salop: Houlston, 1820; revised edition, Philadelphia: American Sunday School Union, 1827);

The Pink Tippet, 4 parts (London: Whittemore and Wightman & Cramp, 1820?);

The History of Marten and his Two Little Scholars at a Sunday-School, second edition (Wellington, Salop: Houlston, 1821; revised edition, Philadelphia: American Sunday School Union, 1825);

The Lost Child (Wellington, Salop: Houlston, 1821; Philadelphia: American Sunday School Union, 1828);

The Sunday-School Teachers, Houlston's Series of Tracts, no. 6 (London: Houlston, circa 1821–1849);

Proper Spirit, Houlston's Series of Tracts, no. 9 (London: Houlston, circa 1821–1849);

An Honest Penny Is Worth a Silver Shilling, Houlston's Series of Tracts, no. 10 (London: Houlston, circa 1821–1849);

The Seeds of Greediness, Houlston's Series of Tracts, no. 22 (London: Houlston, circa 1821–1849;

New York: Protestant Episcopal Sunday School Union, n.d.);

Crooked Paths; or, The Gains of Dishonesty, Houlston's Series of Tracts, no. 25 (London: Houlston, circa 1821–1849; New York: Protestant Episcopal Sunday School Union, n.d.);

The Two Wives, Houlston's Series of Tracts, nos. 33, 34, 2 parts (London: Houlston, circa 1821–1849);

The Novice, Houlston's Series of Tracts, nos. 43, 44 (London: Houlston, circa 1821–1849);

My Bible and My Calling, Houlston's Series of Tracts, nos. 53, 54 (London: Houlston, circa 1821–1849; New York: General Protestant Episcopal Sunday School Union, 1830s);

What Is Liberty? or, The Easy Yoke and the Heavy One, Houlston's Series of Tracts, nos. 63, 64 (London: Houlston, circa 1821–1849; New York: General Protestant Episcopal Sunday School Union, n.d.);

Mistrust, Houlston's Series of Tracts, no. 74 (Wellington, Salop: Houlston, circa 1821–1849);

The Self-Seeker, Houlston's Series of Tracts, no. 83 (London: Houlston, circa 1821–1849);

The History of Samuel Thomson, Houlston's Series of Tracts, no. 84 (London: Houlston, circa 1821–1849);

The Railroad, Houlston's Series of Tracts, no. 97 (Wellington, Salop: Houlston, circa 1821–1849);

The Story of the Kind Little Boy, fifth edition (Wellington, Salop: Houlston, 1822; Philadelphia: American Sunday School Union, 1825);

The Strawberry-Gatherers, fourth edition (Wellington, Salop: Houlston, 1822);

Cleanliness Is Next to Godliness (London: Whittemore and Wightman & Cramp, 1823);

The Singing Gallery (London: Whittemore and Wightman & Cramp, 1823);

The Two Death-Beds (London: Whittemore and Wightman & Cramp, 1823);

The Young Mother (London: Whittemore and Wightman & Cramp, 1823);

The Warning Clock; or, the Voice of the New Year (Wellington, Salop: Houlston, 1823);

The Faithful Little Girl (Wellington, Salop: Houlston, 1823);

The Caution; or, Infant Watchfulness, second edition (Wellington, Salop: Houlston, 1824);

The Sister's Friend, or, Christmas Holidays Spent at Home (Boston: Samuel T. Armstrong and Crocker & Brewster / New York: John P. Haven, 1824; London: L. B. Seeleys, 1831);

The Two Mothers; or, Memoirs of the Last Century (Wellington, Salop: Houlston, 1824);

The Willoughby Family (Wellington, Salop: Houlston, 1824);

The Cradle (London: Whittemore and Wightman & Cramp, 1824);

The Evening Visit (London: Whittemore and Wightman & Cramp, 1824);

The Village Nurse (London: Whittemore and Wightman & Cramp, 1824);

Memory (Philadelphia: American Sunday School Union, 1825; second edition, Wellington, Salop: Houlston, 1826);

The Baby and the Doll; or, Religion and Its Image (Wellington, Salop: Houlston, 1826);

The History of Margaret Whyte, or, the Life and Death of a Good Child (Wellington, Salop: Houlston, 1827);

The Mountain of Health; or, The Hour Improved, third edition (Wellington, Salop: Houlston, 1827; New York: Mahlon Day, 1838);

The Berkshire Shepherd, second edition (Wellington, Salop: Houlston, 1827);

Dialogues for the Entertainment and Instruction of Youth, Part the First, eighth edition (Wellington, Salop: Houlston, 1827);

Amelia (Wellington, Salop: Houlston, 1827);

The Fruits of Education; or, The Two Guardians (Wellington, Salop: Houlston, 1827);

The History of Little Frank and His Sister (Wellington, Salop: Houlston, 1827);

The Mother's Nosegay (Wellington, Salop: Houlston, 1827);

The Little Dog Flora, with Her Silver Bell (Wellington, Salop: Houlston, before 1828);

The Three Flower-Pots, seventh edition (Wellington, Salop: Houlston, 1828);

The Bunch of Violets (Wellington, Salop: Houlston, 1828);

Addresses to Children, On the Beatitudes (Wellington, Salop: Houlston, 1828);

The Two Virginian Nightingales (Wellington, Salop: Houlston, 1828);

Forms of Pride; or, The Midsummer Visit (London & Wellington: Houlston, 1829);

Content and Discontent (London: Houlston, 1830);

The Oaken-Gates Wake, 4 parts (London: Houlston, 1830?);

Lectures for Little Children, second edition (London: Houlston, 1836);

The Use of Talents (London & Wellington, Salop: Houlston, 1837);

Dialogues for the Entertainment and Instruction of Youth, Part the Second, seventh edition (London & Wellington, Salop: Houlston, 1837);

Our Neighborhood (London: Houlston, 1839);

Entertainment and Instruction for Youth (London: Houlston, circa 1840);

Englishwomen in Past and Present Times (London: R. B. Seeley & W. Burnside, 1841);

The Young Backslider; or, the Blighted Flower (London: Hamilton, Adams, 1842);

The Farmer's Daughter (London: Houlston & Stoneman, 1843; New York: Appleton, 1843);

The Pastor's Stories (Boston: Waite, Peirce, 1845);

The Broken Doll; or, the Trial with Two Faces (London: Houlston & Stoneman, circa 1848);

Lucy and Her Robin (London: Houlston & Stoneman, 1848);

Things in Common (London: Wertheim & Macintosh, circa 1848);

Christmas Recollections; or, the History of Catherine Humphries (London: J. Nisbet, 1850);

The Bee-Hive Cottage (New York: General Protestant Episcopal Sunday School Union, 1857);

Fanny and Marten (London: Houlston & Wright, 1860);

Sophia; or, The Source and Benefit of Affliction, eighth edition (London: Houlston & Wright, circa 1860);

A Visit to an Infants' School, new edition (London: Houlston & Wright, circa 1860);

I Can Do Without It (New York: Protestant Episcopal Sunday School Union, n.d.).

OTHER: *The Nursery and Infants' School Magazine,* edited by Cameron (circa January 1831–1852).

The works of Lucy Lyttelton Cameron, writer of tracts and books for children and the poor, were widely circulated in the early part of the nineteenth century. She chiefly wrote allegorical and realistic stories for children that her contemporaries recommended as suitable for the intended audience. Her best-known work, an allegorical tract titled *The Two Lambs* (1816), ran into multiple editions in both England and the United States and was translated into several languages, including French, Italian, Bulgarian, and Hindi. Cameron was committed to disseminating Evangelical principles through her writing. According to a contemporary of hers, educator Thomas Arnold, she achieved her aim: "The knowledge and the love of Christ nowhere be more readily gained by young children, than from . . . some of the short stories of Mrs. Cameron, such as 'Amelia,' the 'Two Lambs,' the 'Flower Pot.'"

Today Cameron is most often mentioned alongside her better-known elder sister, Mary Martha Butt Sherwood, as the prime expression of the spirit of Evangelical writing for children during the nineteenth century. Cameron's goal as a writer, a mother, and an educator was to bring her audience to a saving knowledge of God, Christ, and the Anglican Church.

Lucy Lyttelton Butt, the third and youngest child of the Reverend Dr. George and Martha Sherwood Butt, was born on 29 April 1781. Her godmother was Lucy, Lady Valentia, who gave her the name Lucy Lyttelton after her own family. Cameron's father was a handsome, genial, and gregarious clergyman whose humane religious views mirrored those of his century and his class. A native of Lichfield, he knew and socialized with Samuel Johnson, Richard Lovell Edgeworth, Erasmus Darwin, Anna Seward, and other prominent members of the intellectual culture of the time. He ministered to George III as chaplain and entertained his working-class dissenting parishioners with equal ease and grace. Cameron's mother was different: a homely, shy, exacting woman who early accorded herself the prerogatives of age, and who loathed familiarity among near relatives, Mrs. Butt was in many ways the opposite of her husband. Their daughters, Mary and Lucy, blended their father's intellectual curiosity and energy with intense religious commitment and a somber Evangelical expression that seems to have been derived in spirit, if not in doctrine, from their mother.

Cameron remembered her childhood as a happy one, especially their situation at Stanford, a lovely country place. The lambs she recalled "skipping in the park" outside her mother's bedroom window may have provided the initial image for *The Two Lambs,* which contrasts lovely, Edenic pasture with a scrabbling existence elsewhere. When Lucy Butt was seven years old her father was given a more profitable living in the industrial town of Kidderminster. Although Dr. Butt and the children relished the change, their mother was less enthusiastic. The contrast in surroundings and society — Stanford's lovely landscapes and aristocratic milieu exchanged for Kidderminster's noisy streets and merchant-class community — was profoundly distasteful to her, and she increasingly withdrew from all society except that of her family.

The Butt daughters were educated at home by their mother. Lucy began learning Latin at age seven, as well as French, the Bible, geography, and history. Because of her delicate health, Lucy was spared the iron collar and backboard that her sister was forced to wear to improve her posture; however, her mother did not stint her lessons in other ways. In the Butts' spartan nursery no fire was allowed, even in the winter, and the children could neither speak in company nor sit in the presence of their mother. The children made up for these strictures by their active imaginative lives; from an early age Mary told Lucy stories, and Lucy soon began to follow suit. When Mary was ten and Lucy only four, they pretended they were sister-queens and would have long conversations about their situations, homes, and children. In adolescence this creativity turned to writing, and both sisters began writing novels at about the same time.

A strong undercurrent of their lives was religion. From her first sight of a funeral at age three, Cameron remembered fearing God's wrath and the idea of death, ideas that occupied her both positively and negatively throughout her long life. She was a devout child who read the Bible and other religious books avidly, and she was prepared to defend her faith in more than words. Mary Martha Sherwood recorded in her memoirs that, when a younger boy told Lucy that he did not believe that Jesus Christ had existed, Lucy promptly "struck him with all her little might, rolled him down on the carpet, and beat him with all her strength." In later years she was less physical but no less vehement in the cause of Christianity and the Church of England.

The most far-reaching event of Cameron's youth was the death of her father when she was fourteen years old. At that time she had been to school in Reading (the same school that educated Jane and Cassandra Austen) and – in her later evaluation – was growing increasingly worldly. She had been enjoying her expanded society, the new faces, the house parties, the balls, and a life much like that described in Jane Austen's novels. At her father's death the family moved out of their beautiful home at Stanford and into a wretched house in the town of Bridgnorth, taken sight unseen because it was inexpensive. Mrs. Butt retreated from society and began living frugally, carrying what had already been marked parsimony to its extreme.

From living the lives of gay young gentry, Lucy and Mary were suddenly isolated from all their society and limited in their means. Their days at Bridgnorth were long and featureless, except for their studies: "We used to sit at hard study from ten till one, when we went a-walking: we dined at three, and from five till eight, or later, with the short interruption of tea, we generally read aloud to my mother." The girls were starved not only for com-

pany but even for food: during one year their mother decided to economize by giving them an allowance of bread that had to last the week. These measures later turned out to have been unnecessary, as Mrs. Butt managed to save £1,200 during her widowhood.

Both sisters responded to the strictures of this new life by increased religious seriousness. Mary wrote years later, "Lucy and I had begun to suspect that a life of worldly pleasure was not agreeable to God"; and indeed, there was not much opportunity for worldly pleasure during this period. The sisters concentrated on resigning themselves to the will of God, developing the spirit of self-sacrifice apparently required of them. Cameron was particularly zealous; her sister recounts that in order to discipline her desire for any satisfaction, however small, "she studied to render what food she ate disagreeable to the palate" by pouring cold beer on already distasteful suet pudding. Cameron started a journal in the spirit of John Wesley, who urged those who sought after righteousness to record their daily spiritual state. In the journal she began her lifelong practice of annually tabulating her spiritual failures and achievements and of drawing up lists of new disciplines she intended to follow.

Cameron was later to believe that Providence had arranged this period for her benefit. She wrote,

How sweet to me are the remembrances of that period I spent at Bridgnorth! There I was hidden from the world . . . at a period when I might have learned to love its service. Had I been differently situated, – had we gone, at my father's death, as was once thought of, to live at Bath, I might have been fostered in vanity, love of admiration, etc., to which I had strong inclinations. But, against my own will, my God had mercy upon me, whilst I repined too often at those domestic crosses, which were to prove my choicest blessings.

These spiritual lessons of submission, of bowing to a higher will, and of suppressing personal preference were to become the major themes of Cameron's writing.

Cameron's sixteenth year was the year most crucial to her later development, according to the author's own account. Suffering extreme disappointment from a mysterious affair, Cameron repeatedly resolved not to indulge in "castles in the air" and "wandering thoughts." She concluded after the experience (which she never fully describes in her writings) that her only option was to place her life entirely in God's hands. In the midst of this sorrow and deprivation, however, Cameron found one of her life's great vocations: teaching children and the poor. The local Low Church curate asked Lucy and Mary Butt to teach in his Sunday school. Sunday schools were a new and rather controversial project: while conservatives inveighed against any education of the poor as tantamount to Jacobinism, Evangelicals saw such education as the way to control the poor by guiding their development in the "proper" directions of submitting to the will of God and of the state. The new project did wonders for Lucy; she "entered fully into the active delights of teaching," the only delights she would never renounce.

Inspired by a family friend, Mrs. King, who not only advocated Sunday school but also the other teachings of Hannah More, the sisters began to write tracts. Drawing on their own experiences and their observations of the students in their Sunday schools, they wrote for their students in "a style of composition which was almost peculiarly our own – narratives of people in low life, free from vulgarisms." Mary wrote her third novel, *The History of Susan Gray* (1802), and Lucy began *The History of Margaret Whyte, or, the Life and Death of a Good Child* (written 1798–1799; earliest extant edition, 1827). For the next twenty years most of her publications (published under the initial "L.," in the discreet manner of the time) would identify her authorship by this book. Although no copies of the first edition exist, it was obviously published before 1802, since her next book, *The Work-House; or, A Religious Life the Only Happy One, Being an Interesting History of Susan and Esther Hall* (1802), recommends it as being by the author of "Margaret Whyte."

Margaret Whyte is the story of a pious village girl falsely accused of the theft of some corn. In fact, she had been trying to persuade another child, a mischievous orphan boy named Richard, not to steal the corn; failing that, she took some of her own corn that she had legally gleaned and was replacing the stolen goods when a passerby saw and reported her. For months afterward, Margaret is in deep disgrace with all the authority figures in the community, but she is able to use this fact to influence Richard for the good. When she tells him what she is suffering for his sake, he is so moved that he begins to try to become a better boy. Margaret later falls into a decline, in part because of the strain brought on by being falsely accused, and as she is dying, Richard is moved to confess. At rest because her name has been cleared, Margaret dies peacefully, offering good counsel to the mourners. Her funeral is well attended, and her influence lives on in the children she had worked so hard to convert.

Although the book is obviously geared to a Sunday school audience, its themes obliquely mirror the issues in Cameron's life. Margaret's inflexible adherence to a rigid code of behavior and her outspoken tendency to rebuke those around her for their sins were certainly part of the author's behavior. Furthermore, the rewards for being good in the story are great: Margaret is a central figure in the village, loved for her good behavior and mourned heartily when she is dead; her influence cannot be overestimated. Surely one of the satisfactions of writing the book was Cameron's exploration of the fantasy of being wholly loved and recognized for all the sacrifices she had made.

Cameron's diary reveals the dissatisfaction she was trying to exorcise through her writing. She berates herself for too much intercourse with the world and too much complaining. She speaks repeatedly of the desires that the world awakens and of her efforts to suppress them. Her repeated prayers for peace and calmness and against passion and desire show how difficult it was for her to live up to the model she had taken. In 1803 she became seriously ill, but her illness was a comfort to her because it enhanced the spiritual state she was trying to achieve: "I can hardly tell how unimportant youth, beauty, flattery, riches, seemed to me. Oh, that we could always see the world in the same point of view, as we do on a sick bed!"

In 1803 Mary Butt wed her cousin Henry Sherwood, and Cameron was alone with her mother. By this time even Mrs. Butt had decided that the accommodations at Bridgnorth were unacceptable, and they had moved to a more pleasant house in Stockton. There Cameron continued working with Sunday schools, although the minister of this parish was not supportive and indeed was rather negligent. Cameron recounts that the time for church was so sporadic that on Sundays they had to wait tensely with their bonnets on for the bells to ring and rush out of the house immediately if they were to catch the hurried service. Cameron's energy was appreciated by the community, however, and her Sunday school thrived. While in Stockton she wrote the tract that gained her the most fame, *The Two Lambs, an Allegorical History* (earliest extant British edition, 1821). While it is uncertain when the book was first published, it was overwhelmingly popular with tract societies and was disseminated all over the world.

Only thirty-two pages long, the story is a simple allegory about two lambs named "Peace" and "Inexperience." After a close brush with death at the jaws of a ravening lion, they are rescued by the Shepherd, who cleans them with his blood, flowing from wounds he has sustained in the rescue. He

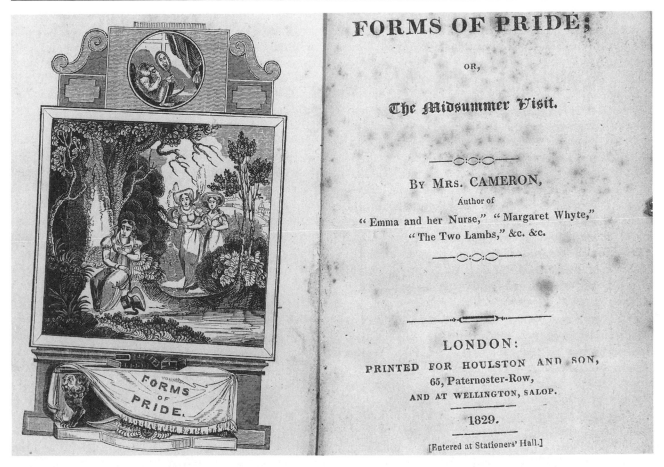

FORMS OF PRIDE;

OR,

The Midsummer Visit.

By Mrs. CAMERON,

Author of

" Emma and her Nurse," " Margaret Whyte,"

" The Two Lambs," &c. &c.

LONDON:

PRINTED FOR HOULSTON AND SON,

65, Paternoster-Row,

AND AT WELLINGTON, SALOP.

1829.

[Entered at Stationers' Hall.]

Frontispiece and title page for one of Cameron's moral tales (courtesy of the Lilly Library, Indiana University)

then brings them to a beautiful pasture, where they may live in security and plenty as long as they do not stray into the mountains on either side. All is well for a time, but then Inexperience begins to look longingly at the far mountains and to speak with the goats and sheep who roam there and who tempt him to come with them, calling his present situation "intolerable restraint." Inexperience believes the goats and follows.

He soon discovers that the delights he was promised are all disappointing, and after another close encounter with the lion, he is convinced that he has more liberty with the Shepherd. He runs all night toward the fold and collapses at the "narrow gate." He watches longingly as the Shepherd tenderly carries Peace in his bosom to a pleasant pasture guarded by a golden gate. The lion roars behind him, but the Shepherd also appears, saying, "Fear not, little lamb, I am able to save unto the uttermost all that come unto me." The lamb throws

himself at the Shepherd's feet. The narrator concludes by relating that "this happy lamb was always afterwards convinced, that in *His* fold only there is rest, and that in keeping of His commandments there is quietness and assurance forever!"

The tract is suspenseful and the conclusion moving; it is not surprising that it was so popular. Its message offering peace and security in Christ against the treacherous offerings of the world was one that evidently struck a chord with many readers. Cameron was later told by several different people that the work first persuaded them to think seriously about their salvation. After one such encounter, a grateful Cameron wrote, "Ought I not to thank God for this and similar testimonies to the usefulness of my poor writings?" It is not difficult to see how the author used the hard lessons and material of her own life to offer a similar message to her readers: what looks like liberty is deceptive, because people who offer happiness apart from the limitations of God only evoke greater desire; peace is only to be found in submitting to Christ and allowing him to dictate desire.

In 1804 she became engaged to the Reverend C. R. Cameron, one of her brother's best friends, and they were married on 12 June 1806. The couple moved to Snedshill, Shropshire, a mining town, where their congregation was primarily made up of colliers and miners. They began trying to reform their district with all the energy Evangelicals brought to the task in the early nineteenth century, pressuring the community to stop pagan customs – "Oaken Gates' Wake; bull-baiting and cock-fighting," among them – and to become good Christians. Cameron incorporated many of these interactions, characters, and issues into her stories, faithfully recording anecdotes of good and bad deaths, evidences of providence, and other material in her diary.

In marked contrast with her old life, Cameron was incessantly busy. The year after she was married she gave birth to her first child, Charles, the first of twelve children. Her diaries for the next fifty years record the many ways in which she tried to use her time to its fullest advantage for the work of God. Cameron was deeply committed to her vocation as a mother and sometimes records being criticized by her peers for spending too much time with her children. Her care seems to have reaped the benefits she desired: four sons became ministers and three daughters missionaries.

In her diary Cameron describes the trouble she had finding time for all her tasks – furnishing education and social services to the community, dealing with her frequent pregnancies, raising her children, and trying to do right by her servants. It is surprising that she found time in 1816 to begin composing "penny books for the poor." Cameron had been acting as a go-between for her sister and F. Houlston, a local bookseller who published religious material. She received stories in letters from her sister, edited them, and then passed them on. Mary Sherwood's *The Story of Henry and His Bearer* (1815) was already phenomenally popular.

By seizing every opportunity she had to write and by writing down all the true stories that came her way, Cameron was able to produce a tremendous amount of prose. In her diary she wrote, "A plan has occurred to me, for enabling me to write half-an-hour a-day; – 300 half-hours make 150 hours. In that time I may write 1800 pages, equal at least to about 40 tracts." Using this method, in 1816 she wrote *The Raven and the Dove* (1817) – a thirty-six-page tract – in only four hours.

Memoirs of Emma and Her Nurse; or, The History of Lady Harewood (1820) is another of Cameron's best-known tales. Like *Margaret Whyte,* it features a poor and pious village girl doing her duty, but it also offers glimpses of the everyday life of the nobility. Lady Harewood is the pious but neglected wife of a careless lord. She handpicks Jane, a village girl from the Sunday school, to be the nurse of her daughter. Soon afterward Lady Harewood gives birth to a son and dies; her last request is that Jane be allowed to nurse little Emma. Jane becomes the focus of the tale as she resists the temptations of the godless household and suffers various disappointments in her work. Her devotion to Emma is rewarded when the child, after a respiratory illness, is able to die virtuously, having brought her father, Sir Arthur, to an understanding of the wrongs he did her mother. Jane's struggles to be good are more realistically delineated and psychologically acute than those in *Margaret Whyte.* Clearly Cameron has developed as a writer and psychologist. The basic message, however, remains the same: whatever happens is the will of God, and it is the duty of the Christian to submit cheerfully and without complaint.

Like Cameron's previous works, *Memoirs of Emma and Her Nurse* was published and frequently reprinted by tract societies in both England and the United States. In 1873 an "advertisement" of Cameron's works from the publisher related just how popular *Memoirs of Emma and Her Nurse* and similar tales were: "The sale of successive editions, amounting to upwards of 60,000 copies of these favourite Tales, and the continued demand for them has induced the Publishers to issue this new illustrated edition."

By 1831 Cameron was editing *The Nursery and Infants' School Magazine,* a monthly magazine for which she was responsible at least until 1852, when she noted as part of her "Plans Temporal" for the year: "To finish my magazine; to get all my papers, etc., in such order as that all may be found, easy and comfortable, to others, at my departure hence to my blessed home." One of her last novels, *Fanny and Marten* (earliest extant edition, 1860) grew out of her work for *The Nursery and Infants' School Magazine.*

Cameron never became rich from her labors; in fact, she never received any money for *The Two Lambs,* an injustice of which she was fully aware. She noted that "had I received what I ought to have done in common honesty, I should have been rich: but it is sweeter far to depend on God for everything." Nevertheless, at the end of her life she was satisfied knowing that her work had borne the fruit she desired. In 1854, four years before her death, she visited Manchester, where "An agent of the Tract Society . . . told me that a few years ago, the number of wicked books circulated for the poor, far exceeded the good ones, but he believed now it was not the case, and a publisher of some bad work had said that he was obliged, in order to sell it, to put something good in it." Late in life she received a visit from the American bishop of Maryland, who "pleased me by saying, he was well acquainted with my little books. Oh, eternity! oh, heaven! why are my thoughts so little there?" She died in Swaby, Lincolnshire, on 6 September 1858.

Historians of children's literature mention Lucy Lyttelton Cameron only in tandem with her sister, usually as a lesser talent. However, her contemporaries recognized in her work the precise spiritual qualities they desired for their children. Cameron's writing for children grew directly out of her larger Christian vocation; her early disappointments and struggles provided the impetus for a spiritual quest requiring submission and acquiescence to a higher authority at all costs. These themes are obsessively repeated in her voluminous writings, and if they seem harsh to a twentieth-century reader, there is no doubt that she held herself to the same standard she proffered to her young readers.

Biography:

Life of Mrs. Cameron: Partly an Autobiography, and from Her Private Journals, edited by Charles Cameron (London: Darton, 1862; revised edition, London: Houlston, 1873).

References:

M. Nancy Cutt, *Mrs. Sherwood and her Books for Children* (London: Oxford University Press, 1974);

F. J. Harvey Darton, ed., *The Life and Times of Mrs. Sherwood (1775–1851). From the Diaries of Captain and Mrs. Sherwood* (London: Wells Gardner, Darton, 1910);

Sophia Kelly, *The Life of Mrs. Sherwood, Chiefly Autobiographical, with Extracts from Mr. Sherwood's Journal During His Imprisonment in France and Residence in India* (London: Darton, 1857).

Papers:

The Osborne Collection at the Toronto Public Library has *The Cameron Commonplace Book,* once owned by Lucy Lyttelton Cameron's son Charles.

Lewis Carroll
(Charles Lutwidge Dodgson)
(27 January 1832 – 14 January 1898)

Karen Patricia Smith
Queens College, City University of New York

See also the Carroll entry in *DLB 18: Victorian Novelists After 1885.*

BOOKS: *The Fifth Book of Euclid, Treated Algebraically, So Far as It Relates to Commensurable Magnitude, With Notes,* as Charles L. Dodgson (Oxford & London: J. Parker, 1858);

Rules for Court Circular (a New Game of Cards for Two Or More Players, anonymous (London, 1860);

A Syllabus of Plane Algebraical Geometry, Systematically Arranged, with Formal Definitions, Postulates, and Axioms, anonymous (Oxford: J. Wright, 1860);

The Formulae of Plane Trigonometry, Printed with Symbols (Instead of Words) to Express the "Goniometrical Ratios," as Dodgson (Oxford: James Wright, 1861);

An Index to "In Memoriam," anonymous (London: Edward Moxon, 1862);

The Enunciations of the Propositions and Corollaries Together with Questions on the Definitions, Postulates, Axioms, &c. in Euclid, Books I and II, as Dodgson (Oxford: T. Combe, 1863);

A Guide to the Mathematical Student in Reading, Reviewing, and Working Examples, as Dodgson (Oxford: John Henry & James Parker, 1864);

The Dynamics of a Particle, with an Excursus on the New Method of Evaluation, as Applied to π, anonymous (Oxford: J. Vincent, 1865);

Alice's Adventures in Wonderland (London: Macmillan, 1865; New York: Appleton, 1866);

An Elementary Treatise on Determinants, with Their Application to Simultaneous Linear Equations and Algebraical Geometry, as Dodgson (London: Macmillan, 1867);

Phantasmagoria and Other Poems (London: Macmillan, 1869);

The New Belfry of Christ Church, Oxford, as D.C.L. (Oxford: James Parker, 1872);

Through the Looking-Glass, And What Alice Found There (London: Macmillan, 1872; Boston: Lee, Sheppard & Dillingham, 1872);

Lewis Carroll

The Vision of the Three T's. A Threnody by the Author of "The New Belfry," anonymous (Oxford: James Parker, 1873);

The Blank Cheque, a Fable, By the Author of "The New Belfry" and "The Vision of the Three T's," anonymous (Oxford: James Parker, 1874);

Facts, Figures and Fancies, Relating to the Elections to the Hebdomadal Council, the Offer of the Clarendon Trustees, and the Proposal to Convert the Parks into Cricket-Grounds, anonymous (Oxford: James Parker, 1874);

Suggestions as to the Best Method of Taking Votes, Where More Than Two Issues Are To Be Voted On, as C.L.D. (Oxford: Hall & Stacy, 1874); revised as *A Method of Taking Votes on More than Two Issues,* anonymous (Oxford, 1876);

An Easter Greeting to Every Child Who Loves "Alice," anonymous (N.p., 1876);

The Hunting of the Snark, An Agony in Eight Fits (London: Macmillan, 1876; Boston: James R. Osgood, 1876);

Rhyme and Reason? (Boston: James R. Osgood, 1876; London: Macmillan, 1883);

Word-links; a Game for Two Players, or a Round Game, as Dodgson (N.p., 1878);

Doublets; a Word Puzzle (London: Macmillan, 1879);

Euclid and His Modern Rivals, as Dodgson (London: Macmillan, 1879);

Lawn Tennis Tournaments; the True Method of Assigning Prizes with a Proof of the Fallacy of the Present Method, as Dodgson (London: Macmillan, 1883);

Christmas Greetings from a Fairy to a Child (London: Macmillan, 1884);

The Principles of Parliamentary Representation, as Dodgson (London: Harrison, 1884);

Twelve Months in a Curatorship, by One Who Has Tried It, anonymous (Oxford: E. Baxter, 1884);

A Tangled Tale (London: Macmillan, 1885);

Alice's Adventures Under Ground, Being a Facsimile of the Original MS. Book Afterwards Developed into "Alice's Adventures in Wonderland" (London & New York: Macmillan, 1886);

The Game of Logic (London & New York: Macmillan, 1886);

Three Years in a Curatorship. By One Whom It Has Tried, anonymous (Oxford: E. Baxter, 1886);

Not All X are Y, anonymous (London: Richard Clay, 1887);

Curiosa Mathematica, Part I: A New Theory of Parallels, as Dodgson (London: Macmillan, 1888);

The Nursery Alice (London: Macmillan, 1889; New York: Macmillan, 1890);

Sylvie and Bruno (London & New York: Macmillan, 1889);

Eight or Nine Wise Words About Letter-Writing (Oxford: Emberlin, 1890);

The Wonderland Postage-Stamp Case (Oxford: Emberlin, 1890);

Curiosissima Curatoria, as Rude Donatus (Oxford: G. Sheppard, 1892);

Curiosa Mathematica, Part II: Pillow-Problems Thought Out During Sleepless Nights, anonymous (London: Macmillan, 1893);

Sylvie and Bruno Concluded (London & New York: Macmillan, 1893);

Syzygies and Lanrick, a Word-puzzle and a Game for Two Players (London & Bungay: Richard Clay, 1893);

A Fascinating Mental Recreation for the Young. Symbolic Logic (London: Macmillan, 1895);

Resident Women-students, anonymous (Oxford: G. Sheppard, 1896);

Symbolic Logic. Pt. I: Elementary (London & New York: Macmillan, 1896);

Three Sunsets and Other Poems (London: Macmillan, 1898);

The Lewis Carroll Picture Book: A Selection from the Unpublished Writings and Drawings of Lewis Carroll Together with Reprints from Scarce and Unacknowledged Work, edited by Stuart Dodgson Collingwood (London: Unwin, 1899); published in facsimile as *Diversions and Digressions of Lewis Carroll* (New York: Dover, 1961);

Feeding the Mind (London: Chatto & Windus, 1907).

Editions: *Novelty and Romancement; A Story by Lewis Carroll* (Boston: B. J. Brimmer, 1925);

Further Nonsense Verse and Prose, edited by Langford Reed (London: T. Fisher Unwin, 1926);

The Collected Verse of Lewis Carroll (The Rev. Charles Lutwidge Dodgson) (New York: Dutton, 1929; London: Macmillan, 1932);

For the Train, Five Poems and a Tale, by Lewis Carroll [pseud] Being Contributions to "The Train," 1856–1857, with the original illustrations by C. H. Bennett and W. MacConnell; Together with some Carrollean Episodes concerning Trains. Arranged, with a preface, by Hugh J. Schonfeld (London: Denis Archer, 1932);

The Rectory Umbrella and Mischmasch (London: Cassell, 1932; New York: Dover, 1971);

The Russian Journal, and Other Selections from the Works of Lewis Carroll, edited by John Francis McDermott (New York: Dutton, 1935);

Hiawatha's Photographing (Berkeley, Cal.: Archetype Press, 1939);

How the Boots Got Left Behind; A Letter to Mary From C.L. Dodgson "Lewis Carroll" (San Francisco: White Knights Press, 1943);

The Diaries of Lewis Carroll, edited by Roger Lancelyn Green (London: Cassell, 1953; New York: Oxford University Press, 1954);

84

it without lobsters, you know. Which shall sing?"

"Oh! you sing!" said the Gryphon, "I've forgotten the words."

So they began solemnly dancing round and round Alice, every now and then treading on her toes when they came too close, and waving their fore-paws to mark the time, while the Mock Turtle sang, slowly and sadly, these words:

"Beneath the waters of the sea
Are lobsters thick as thick can be —
They love to dance with you and me,
    My own, my gentle Salmon!"

The Gryphon joined in singing the chorus, which was:

"Salmon come up! Salmon go down!
Salmon come twist your tail around!
Of all the fishes of the sea
    There's none so good as Salmon!"

Page from "Alice's Adventures Under Ground," a manuscript book that Carroll wrote, illustrated, and presented to Alice Liddell on 26 November 1864; the text formed the basis for Alice's Adventures in Wonderland, published the following year (from Alice's Adventures Under Ground: Being a Facsimile of the Original Ms. Book Afterwards Developed into "Alice's Adventures in Wonderland," 1886).

Useful and Instructive Poetry (London: Geoffrey Bles, 1954; New York: Macmillan, 1954);

The Book of Nonsense, edited by Roger Lancelyn Green (London: Dent, 1956; New York: Dutton, 1956);

The Wasp in a Wig. A "Suppressed" Episode of Through the Looking-Glass and What Alice Found There (New York: Lewis Carroll Society of North America, 1977);

The Complete Diaries of Lewis Carroll, edited by Edward Wakeling (Oxford: Lewis Carroll Birthplace Trust, 1993).

Self-effacing, yet having an expressive critical ability; reveling in the possibilities of fancy, though thoroughly at home with the sophisticated nuances of logic and mathematics, Lewis Carroll (Charles Lutwidge Dodgson) was an individual who, through his rare and diversified literary gifts and power of communication, would leave an indelible mark upon the imaginations of children and accessible adults both during his generation and in generations to come. His best-known works, *Alice's Adventures in Wonderland* (1865) and *Through the Looking-Glass, And What Alice Found There* (1872) are still enjoyed by readers throughout the world and have been adapted for radio, television, and motion pictures.

Born in the small parish of Daresbury on 27 January 1832, Charles Lutwidge Dodgson (better known by his pseudonym, Lewis Carroll) was the son of Charles Dodgson, archdeacon, and Frances Jane Lutwidge. The third of eleven children, Dodgson's secluded, quiet, and protected early childhood stands in ironic contrast to the impact he was to have on the world of Victorian children's literature. In *The Life and Letters of Lewis Carroll* (1898), Carroll's nephew Stuart Dodgson Collingwood wrote that his uncle "invented the strangest diversions for himself . . . made pets of the most odd and unlikely animals, and numbered certain snails and toads among his intimate friends."

Nurtured by a loving mother and father whose virtues he never failed to appreciate, Dodgson was able to practice the art of writing at an early age. It proved to be a satisfying outlet, which could be honed in solitary moments or within the forum of the family magazine. While at the Richmond School in 1845, Dodgson composed *Useful and Instructive Poetry,* his first family magazine (published in 1954), for the edification of his seven-year-old brother, Wilfred Longley Dodgson, and his five-year-old sister, Louisa Fletcher Dodgson. Of his writing in general, Mr. Tate, his instructor, was later to comment that the younger Dodgson was given toward some "creativity in replacing the inflexions of nouns and verbs, as detailed in our grammars," a fault which Dr. Tate reassured the elder Dodgson his son would most likely outgrow.

The poem "My Fairy" in *Useful and Instructive Poetry* seems to reflect some of the frustrations Dodgson may have experienced over one issue or another. The fairy persona takes on the aspect of a censoring adult who attempts to interfere with Charles no matter which way he turns. Finally, in dismay, the voice of youth cries out against the restrictive adult persona in the last verse:

> "What may I do?" at length I cried,
> Tired of the painful task.
> The fairy quietly replied,
> And said, "You must not ask."

"Rules and Regulations," in addition to commenting upon correctness in writing, also contains remonstrations. It refers to the problem of stammering, which plagued Dodgson throughout his life, emphasizing his shyness and becoming a major factor when he considered acceptance of any public-speaking engagements:

> Learn well your grammar,
> And never stammar,
> Write well and neatly,
> And sing most sweetly,
> Be enterprising,
> Love early rising,
> Go walk six miles,
> Have ready smiles,
> With lightsome laughter,
> Soft flowing after.

Indeed, the passage might well be taken as Victorian commentary on the expectations of childhood.

According to Carroll's preface to his family magazine *Mischmasch* (published together with *The Rectory Umbrella,* 1932), "The Rectory Magazine," which made its first appearance possibly around 1847, caused so much excitement in his household that most of his family members were sufficiently motivated to contribute to it. Of the dating of the magazine, biographer Anne Clark suggests that "the real clue to the year of initiation may lie in Charles' use of pseudonymous initials VX for his serial 'Sidney Hamilton.' Reversal of initials was a frequent device of his, and if the magazine dated from 1847, his age expressed in Latin would have been XV. The state of maturity of the contents is consistent with this dating." *Useful and Instructive Poetry* and

Alice, Lorina, Harry, and Edith Liddell, circa 1859

"The Rectory Magazine" were followed by other youthful magazines such as "The Comet" in 1848 and later "The Rosebud," "The Star," and "The Will-o' The Wisp." Carroll indicates in his preface to *Mischmasch* that the quality of these endeavors was poor and apparently generated little interest.

In 1846, at the age of fourteen, Dodgson was sent to Rugby. When he left the school in December 1849, it could well be said that he had satisfied the academic hopes his family had for him. In May 1850 he matriculated at Christ Church, Oxford, and thus embarked upon an association that was to remain constant until his death. Clark tells of the regimented environment in force at Oxford that strictly controlled thought and dress. Despite such strictures Dodgson seemed able to conform to the degree required for that margin of "academic safety," though, as Clark points out, "The many absurdities in the *Oxford University Statutes* were not lost on a humorist of Charles Dodgson's calibre." Indeed, such references were to find their way into his epic *The Hunting of the Snark* (1876) later on.

From 1849 to 1853 Dodgson produced *The Rectory Umbrella*, eight manuscript magazines, of which four are extant. The manuscripts display an amazing degree of versatility and attest to his ease and familiarity with nursery rhymes, classical poets, and William Shakespeare. Dodgson displayed a talent for writing engaging prose as well as verse. Detail, remarkable for its inclusion in an informal family magazine, is evident in such practices as the use of footnotes both as commentary on the action and as a scholarly apparatus.

That Dodgson had a sensitivity for animals is seen in such pieces as "Moans from the Miserable, or The Wretch's Wail," written from the point of view of rabbits who publicize their dismay and anger at being carried around by their ears. Later, his concerns would take a much more serious turn, as indicated in his essays on vivisection, "Vivisection as a Sign of the Times" and "Some Popular Fallacies About Vivisection," first printed in the *Pall Mall Gazette* (12 February 1875) and *Fortnightly Review* (1 June 1875), and later published in Collingwood's biography *The Life and Letters of Lewis Carroll* and Alexander Woollcott's *The Complete Works of Lewis Carroll* (1936).

Fancy was a strong element of the pieces appearing in *The Rectory Umbrella*. The brief essay titled "Pixies," under the general heading "Zoological Papers," was written as though such beings actually existed and foreshadows the preface of *Sylvie and Bruno Concluded* (1893), in which Carroll speaks convincingly of the existence of fairies. While illustrating was to remain an unsuccessful pursuit for the author, *The Rectory Umbrella* includes some amusing drawings, such as those done for "The Walking Stick of Destiny," some of which are reminiscent of the style of Edward Lear.

As his diaries and letters indicate, Dodgson was a meticulous young man. In his diary entries for 1855, when he was twenty-three, Dodgson reveals his frustration for failing to do his mathematics, having been enticed into the more attractive activities of reading and sketching. Dodgson's disciplined, and at times exacting, nature was only one side of a complex personality. He was also known for his unfailing good humor and was the sort of person who, despite his innate reticence, could be entertaining at dinner gatherings.

The beginning of the year 1851 brought Dodgson's long-awaited residence at Oxford, but this event was sadly followed by the death of his beloved mother at the age of forty-seven — a woman whom everyone agreed had been a superb mother and wife. In July 1851 Dodgson had an opportunity to visit the Great Exhibition, which had opened on 1 May. Its effect upon him was profound and moved him to write in a mood of great excitement to his sister, Elizabeth, on 5 July. He described the place as "a sort of fairyland," and near the conclusion of his lengthy letter stated, "I have to go to the Royal Academy so must stop: as the subject is quite inexhaustible, there is no hope of ever coming to a regular finish." Dodgson reveled in anything that excited the powers of imagination, and the Great Exhibition, with its spectacular exhibits, located in the Crystal Palace in South London, certainly did that; in fact, nothing like it had ever been seen either in England or abroad before.

At the end of that year at Oxford Dodgson's scholarly efforts earned him a Boulter Scholarship, which brought with it the small annual sum of £20. In December 1852 he was to earn a studentship, worth £25 a year. In 1856 he received a master of arts, and in 1857 he was appointed as a tutor, with an income of £300 per year.

A significant event occurred on 22 December 1861, when Dodgson was ordained as a member of the clergy. However, he would not proceed to the priesthood since he deemed himself unsuited. In a relatively short time then, Dodgson had distinguished himself as a student and clergyman, and had won for himself a stable and permanent living. He settled in nicely with the duties of lecturing, studying, and training private students.

His new duties notwithstanding, Dodgson was able to manage his time sufficiently to pursue his literary interests. In 1856 and 1857 he composed a set of literary pieces specifically for the journal *The Train*. These included "Solitude," "Novelty and Romancement," "The Three Voices," "The Sailor's Wife," "Hiawatha's Photographing," "Upon the Lonely Moor," and "Ye Carpette Knyghte." Their tones range from serious to humorous; Dodgson's disposition toward parody was expressed through "Hiawatha's Photographing," which retained the meter of its famous counterpart, and "Upon the Lonely Moor," which parodied William Wordsworth's poem "Resolution and Independence" (1802). "Upon the Lonely Moor" was later to serve as a model for the White Knight's ballad in *Alice's Adventures in Wonderland* (1865).

From 1858 until the publication of *Alice's Adventures in Wonderland,* Dodgson's output included mathematical and literary topics, including *The Fifth Book of Euclid* (1858), *A Syllabus of Plane Algebraical Geometry* (1860), *The Formulae of Plane Trigonometry* (1861), *The Enunciations of . . . Euclid, Books I and II* (1863), and *A Guide to the Mathematical Student* (1864). The number of such publications would grow as his career advanced, striking a peculiar and interesting juxtaposition between the abstract but acceptable world of numbers and the intangible and less credible one of fancy.

As was the case with many of his literary contemporaries, Dodgson also contributed widely to newspapers and magazines. Beginning in 1854 with two anonymous contributions to the *Oxonian Advertiser,* he published a wide variety of fiction, nonfiction, and poetry in newspapers and magazines, including the *Whitby Gazette,* the *Comic Times,* the *Oxford Critic,* the *Illustrated London News, College Rhymes, Strand Magazine, All the Year Round, Aunt Judy's Magazine, Oxford University Herald, Pall Mall Gazette,* and the *Monthly Packet.* With characteristic reticence about the value of the work he had produced, Dodgson at first refused to sign his name to his work, choosing instead to use the initials *BB.* Later, after having been prodded by Edmund Yates, editor of *The Train,* to select a pseudonym, Dodgson offered him several possibilities, among them "Lewis Carroll," a version of his first and middle names. A serious poem titled "The Path of Roses," which appeared in the May 1856 issue of *The Train,* was the first contribution to bear officially the Carroll pseudonym, by which the author is popularly known today.

In his diary entry for 2 June 1855 Carroll noted with regret that Thomas Gaisford, dean of Christ Church since 1831, had died on that day. Five days later he also noted rather matter-of-factly that "*The Times* announces that Liddell of Westminster is to be the new Dean; the selection does not seem to have given much satisfaction in the college." The appointment ultimately became a most fortunate one for Carroll, for Dean Liddell's three-year-old daughter, Alice, would profoundly influence the course of Carroll's literary career. According to Roger Lancelyn Green, Carroll had an odd relationship with the Liddell family. He apparently was not well liked by Mrs. Liddell, who seemed rather suspicious of his motives for associating with her children.

That the Victorians considered such relationships suspect is obvious from the reminiscences of Enid Shawyer, whose company Carroll unsuccessfully sought when she was a child of twelve. Her mother was suspicious of Carroll, perhaps in light of some of Carroll's whimsical notes to her daughter. In a letter dated 7 April 1891 Carroll wrote:

> So you think you've got the courage to come a walk by yourself with me? Indeed! Well, I shall come for you on April 31st at 13 o' clock, and first I will take you to the Oxford Zoological Gardens, and put you into a cage of LIONS, and when they've had a good feed, I'll bring you to my rooms, and give a regular beating, with a thick stick, to my new little friend. Then I'll put you into the coal-hole, and feed you for a week on nothing but bread and water. Then I'll send you home in a milk-cart, in one of the empty milk-cans. And after that, if ever I come for you again, you'll scream louder than a COCKATOO!

The letter should not be read in the light of late-twentieth-century concerns regarding child abuse, but rather with the author's sometimes extreme

Alice, the March Hare, the Dormouse, and the Mad Hatter; one of John Tenniell's illustrations for Alice's Adventures in Wonderland

sense of humor in mind. Even so, such writing was probably enough to raise the eyebrows of some Victorian parents.

Further, on 16 April 1891 Carroll wrote to Mrs. Stevens in what appears to be a state of mild alarm. Apparently Winnie, Enid's sister, had seen some photographs of nude children taken by Carroll while Carroll and Winnie were visiting a friend. Anticipating the mother's reaction, he carefully attempted to explain the photographs to Mrs. Stevens and assured her that any photographs he might take of her daughter Enid would be in full dress. Subsequently, Enid was permitted to accompany Carroll to tea for a few hours. In her study titled *Swift and Carroll: A Psychoanalytic Study of Two Lives* (1955), Phyllis Greenacre asserts that Carroll's desire to photograph little girls in the nude beyond infancy was out of the ordinary during the Victorian period, and suggests that his abrupt abandoning of photography in 1880 may have been related to speculations regarding his hobby.

There is no doubt that Carroll felt more at home with little girls than with little boys or with adults: in his letter dated 31 March 1890 to Edith Blakemore, he confesses that with little boys, "I'm out of my element altogether." In the same correspondence he refers to having at least one hundred child friends. He always maintained that his friendships, while their intensity was unusual, were to take place with the strictest propriety, although his letters to children occasionally adopted an uncomfortable familiarity.

Langford Reed, in his biography *The Life of Lewis Carroll* (1932), maintains that the author's dealings with children were innocent. Commenting on the complexities of Carroll's personality, Reed observes that the children who knew Carroll felt that he shared a commonality with them that was almost on the level of a sacred kinship. In most cases it appears that either Carroll or their own children were able to convince parents of the author's innocent intentions.

Thus, despite any reservations the elder Liddells may have had about Carroll's attraction to their daughters, he was allowed to take them on outings that they, apparently, enjoyed. The sunny, placid afternoon of 4 July 1862 is firmly fixed as a literary event in the minds of all those interested in Carrolleana, as the date when Carroll, at that point an ordained deacon, told the story that became *Alice's Adventures in Wonderland* to Alice Liddell during a boat ride. Carroll apparently began writing the text almost immediately. Canon Duckworth, a close friend of the author, present in the boat as oarsman on that eventful day (and who later appeared as the duck in the story), wrote that Carroll reported to him that the written text was actually begun on the night following the boat ride. Duckworth reports that the manuscript was seen by Henry Kingsley, brother of Charles Kingsley, who was visiting Dean Liddell. Kingsley was so impressed with the manuscript that he urged Mrs. Liddell to inform Carroll that he should have it published.

The seed having been planted, Carroll contacted Duckworth and asked him to read over the manuscript to determine its worth. Duckworth enthusiastically recommended that Carroll proceed and suggested that he send the manuscript to the illustrator John Tenniel. At this point Carroll still had not finalized the title. In a 10 June 1864 letter to Tom Taylor, a dramatist acquaintance of Carroll's, Carroll indicates several titles he was considering. Having considered such combinations as "Alice Among the Elves," "Alice Among the Goblins," and "Alice's Doings in Elf-land," Carroll states at the close of the letter that he prefers the title "Alice's Adventures in Wonderland," showing that he was looking more for affirmation than for new ideas.

Alice's Adventures in Wonderland was an audacious and thoroughly imaginative fairy tale without fairies. It makes bold references to the practices and politics of the day, and mentions specific friends and acquaintances of the author — not always in a complimentary fashion. Roger Lancelyn Green in "The Making of *Alice*: 1860-3" discusses some of the individuals and incidents responsible for the eventual shaping of the story. Lorina and Edith, sisters of Alice Liddell, serve as inspirations for the Lory and the Eagle respectively, while their two younger sisters, Rhoda and Violet, appear as the Rose and the Violet. Theophilus Carter, who had been affiliated with Christ Church but who ran a furniture shop in Oxford at the time the story was written, appears as the Mad Hatter. Carroll apparently had had a falling out with him, and used his literary talents to gain revenge.

Alice's Adventures in Wonderland was a story told to, and later written down for, privileged little girls at a time when only the middle and upper classes had primary access to leisurely pursuits and to the powerful medium of the book. While his strong Christian ethic informed an overall democratic approach, Carroll was generally uninformed about the less advantaged child, an attitude that occasionally manifests itself in a lack of sensitivity, though the author probably would have been appalled to have been considered insensitive.

The character Alice is a reflection of the children with whom Carroll had close contact. She is also, to some extent, a composite of the child audience toward whom most fantasy writers of the period were directing their work, even though some contemporary literary characters, such as Tom the chimney sweep in Charles Kingsley's *The Water Babies: A Fairy Tale for a Land-Baby* (1863), are clearly on the low end of the socio-economic scale. Alice, who makes reference to her nurse in both *Alice's Adventures in Wonderland* and its sequel, *Through the Looking-Glass, And What Alice Found There* (1872), demonstrates her sense of etiquette through her monologue about curtsying to the inhabitants she will meet at the bottom of the rabbit hole. While in Wonderland, she never once makes a complaint about being hungry or without adequate clothing in her waking life. She was a child with whose circumstances the Liddell children and the scholarly Canon Duckworth could easily identify. Lillian Smith has pointed out in *The Unreluctant Years: A Critical Approach to Children's Literature* (1991) that modern readers should be aware of the double-layered, literal/symbolic implications of the tale, since there were present in the original audience two levels of listeners. The gifted Carroll may thus have fashioned the story subconsciously to accommodate both types of listeners, which perhaps, along with the humorous activities that Alice and her fantastic escorts engage in, explains the universal appeal of this story.

The basic plot involves Alice's desire to enter a wonderful garden that she sees after having wandered into a magic hall. Alice eventually attains her goal and enters the garden. During the course of her travels through Wonderland she meets a strange combination of people and anthropomorphic animals.

The book is infused with Carroll's unique sense of humor and reflects his love of punning and sophisticated plays on language. The illustrations that accompanied the text were immediately popular, for Tenniel managed to capture Carroll's spirit of whimsy, as in the Cheshire cat episode in the chapter "Pig and Pepper," and outrageous exaggeration, as in Alice's sudden changes in size in the chapters "Down the Rabbit Hole" and "The Rabbit

Sends in a Little Bill." That Carroll and Tenniel both shared a passion for artistic accuracy is demonstrated in a 19 July 1865 letter, in which Tenniel expresses his dissatisfaction with the printing of his illustrations. Shortly thereafter, Carroll requested that Macmillan reprint the book, and he began recalling the inscribed copies he had sent to friends. The book was reprinted later that year to the satisfaction of both the author and the artist.

The hidden nuances and the more obvious aspects of invention in *Alice's Adventures in Wonderland* have been examined, and the text and presumed subtext guessed at, affirmed, and alternately uplifted and debased from a literary as well as a psychological point of view. *Alice's Adventures in Wonderland* remains not only Carroll's personal tour de force, but also the most influential classic in Victorian children's literature, despite the fact that many critics claim that the sequel, *Through the Looking-Glass, And What Alice Found There,* is a more inventive and imaginative work. Nevertheless, at the time when the first Alice book arrived, nothing like it had ever been seen before.

Carroll carefully collected the notices about *Alice's Adventures in Wonderland* in the newspapers. He was also concerned about how well the book would sell. In his 19 November 1865 letter to Alexander Macmillan, he asked the publisher not only to keep him abreast of any notices that appeared about the Alice books, but also of Macmillan's perception of how well the sales were progressing. There was little cause for concern, because Green reports that during Carroll's lifetime 180,000 copies were sold.

Gratified by the reception of the first story, Carroll wrote to Macmillan in August of the following year that he had an idea for a sequel, eventually titled *Through the Looking-Glass, And What Alice Found There.* It was published in 1871 (dated 1872), again illustrated by Tenniel, and was perhaps even more inventive than the first book. Through a mirror Alice enters a "Looking-glass world" on the other side. This world is laid out in chessboard fashion, and Alice's adventures are so many moves upon this giant chessboard. While some readers might interpret the story as an argument that all humans are pawns in the gigantic game of life (a stance that violates Carroll's Christian ethic), Alice has an opportunity to live out the experience literally, in a relatively short period of time, as she makes her way toward the eighth square, where she hopes to be crowned queen.

Once again, as in the previous book, Alice comes into contact with unusual people and anthropomorphic flora and fauna. In particular, the "Wool and Water" episode is memorable for its imagina-tive portrayal of a dark little shop in which objects float from one shelf onto another and, ultimately, through the ceiling. In this three-part scene — with Alice first in the shop; then outside, rowing down a little stream; and then back in the shop again — the reader is led ever deeper into a world of nonreality. Carroll permits his heroine to test her senses of sight, sound, smell, and touch, but does not allow her to experience taste. Therefore, Alice, and ultimately the reader, is stopped from totally experiencing this episode as reality. Alice buys a little egg in the shop, but is not allowed to eat it. Instead, the sheep places it at a distance from her and informs Alice that in this shop people must get things for themselves. The egg turns into Humpty Dumpty before she can get it, and Alice is thrown headlong into another adventure.

Both of the Alice tales give voice to the Victorian desire to overcome restrictive environments, demonstrated to some degree through Carroll's use of parody to open traditionally closed literary formats. Beverly Lyon Clark asserts that Carroll's use of both open and closed fields, as well as his unique integration of text and poetry, constitutes a new approach in Victorian writing for children. Physically, the movement in the two stories is from indoor settings to outdoor environments. In *Alice's Adventures in Wonderland* Alice passes through the restrictive environment of a rabbit hole and yearns to be free in the wonderful garden. Her most vibrant adventures take place primarily in the outdoors; her indoor experiences are generally more frustrating and uncomfortable, although the outdoor adventures have their own share of difficulties. The same is the case in *Through the Looking-Glass.* Alice passes through the closed-in setting of the looking-glass house and heads immediately for the outdoors. Since that entire country is laid out in chessboard fashion, Alice cannot see the limits of her existence as she proceeds along her journey. Therefore, the environment has no discernible boundaries.

The quest for freedom is one of the primary themes of the two works. Whether one considers the journey as being in concert with Alice's rather precocious mind-set (which might have led her into trouble in a Victorian environment), or, delving further, the concept of the dream story as representing a liberating ideal, there is a distinct air of unbridled joy about these works. They seem to invite readers of all ages and from all times to revel with Carroll in places and with people and creatures who are not bound by the usual rules and regulations.

Carroll's complex personality has made it appear to many critics that he was living a double life:

the pragmatic world of the Oxford don and the secret shadowy world of fantasy. While he often stated that he wished to avoid the limelight and preferred not to be recognized as Lewis Carroll, the author of the Alice tales, Carroll recognized (and probably enjoyed) the convenience of being able to accomplish certain goals because he was who he was. In his diary entry for 25 June 1870 he notes that he gained an introduction to Lord and Lady Salisbury; he admits the introduction was probably because of his authorship of *Through the Looking-Glass*. In other instances Carroll turned down dinner invitations because he did not wish to be deluged with people asking him about Alice.

As the Alice stories left their imprint on the life of Carroll, so they have left their indelible mark upon readers in places far away in time and space from Victorian Great Britain. In his survey of the translations of *Alice in Wonderland* titled *Alice in Many Tongues: The Translations of Alice in Wonderland* (1964), Warren Weaver identifies forty-seven languages into which the book had been translated either in whole or in part by 1963. Charles C. Lovett, editor of *Knight Letter*, the newsletter of the Lewis Carroll Society of North America, recently identified sixty-two languages into which either the entire *Alice's Adventures in Wonderland* or *Through the Looking-Glass, And What Alice Found There* had been translated. The accessibility of the Alice books, both in terms of language availability and the fact that they have never been out of print, has helped ensure a lasting place for these books in the libraries of children in both western and nonwestern cultures.

Critics also continue to be fascinated with the works and explore ways in which to illuminate the intricacies of their texts and backgrounds for adults as well as for children. In *The Other Alice: The Story of Alice Liddell and Alice in Wonderland* (1993) Christina Bjork and Inga-Karin Eriksson present the story of Carroll's friendship with Alice Liddell and the creation of the ensuing fantasy in a well-researched format accessible to young people.

Between the writing of the two Alice books, Carroll was also busy writing mathematical works, including *The Dynamics of a Particle* (1865), *The New Method of Evaluation* (1865), and *An Elementary Treatise on Determinants* (1867). During this time he also took a memorable tour of the Continent, including parts of Russia. His impressions were later recorded in "Journal of a Tour of Russia 1867," published as *The Russian Journal, and Other Selections from the Works of Lewis Carroll* (1935).

Aside from the Alice books, however, Carroll's most memorable work during this period was a collection of comic and serious poetry under the title *Phantasmagoria and Other Poems* (1869), which featured the long and amusing poem of the same title. In this seven-canto poem, in which a ghost calls upon a middle-aged gentleman, Carroll exercises some of his finest abilities as a humorous poet. The ghost is in Carroll's study primarily to haunt, but ends up presenting a rationale for ghostly house selection and the manner in which these things are done in the spirit world.

Despite the sophisticated treatment of the subject matter, Carroll apparently intended the poem to be read by children, though Langford Reed surmises that most of the verses were above the heads of a child audience. In his letter of 5 April 1881 to A. B. Frost, his eventual illustrator, Carroll commented that Frost's drawing of the ghost pleading for mercy from an enraged host was too frightening for young readers as the man had " 'murder' written in his face." Frost's drawings for the poem continued to be amazingly realistic, superimposed with a kind of comic impossibility that well suited the fantastic subject. Though Carroll had previously approached several other illustrators, including Sir John Tenniel, Linley Sambourne, George Du Maurier, E. and A. Fairfield, F. W. Lawson, and Walter Crane, none of whom was able and/or willing to take on the assignment, he greatly admired the illustrations ultimately provided by Frost. He wrote in his 5 April letter, "It is difficult to find words which will express, as strongly as I wish, how *thoroughly* I admire your pictures to the ghost-poem. They really are *wonderful.*"

At the close of 1872, the year *Through the Looking-Glass* was published, Carroll published a letter of gratitude to his child readers of *Alice's Adventures in Wonderland*. In it he reconciles his role as Lewis Carroll, author of a famous fairy tale, and Charles Dodgson, deacon and lecturer at Christ Church. He thanks his child readers for their support of his fairy tale, and also wishes them a wonderful Christmas season that is "bright with the presence of that unseen Friend, who once on earth blessed little children," gently reminding them of the true meaning of the holiday season. Carroll, throughout his lifetime, would always remember the child, and he wrote hundreds of letters to young admirers.

In April 1876 *The Hunting of the Snark* was published. Henry Holiday provided the illustrations. This elaborate nonsense poem actually had its origins in somewhat mystical circumstances. Two years earlier, while at Guildford assisting in the care of a sick relative, Carroll was out walking when a line seemed to occur to him out of nowhere. That

A preliminary sketch (1887) made by Carroll for his 1894 work Sylvie and Bruno Concluded *(courtesy of the Lilly Library, Indiana University)*

line, "For the Snark *was* a Boojum, you see," would eventually form the ending of *The Hunting of the Snark*. In his essay "Alice on the Stage" (1887) Carroll explains that he did not at the time, nor did he years later upon going back to the poem, understand its meaning. "I have received courteous letters from strangers, begging to know whether 'The Hunting of the Snark' is an allegory, or contains some hidden moral, or is a political satire: and for all such questions I have but one answer, 'I *don't know*!'" Despite this apparent affirmation of its "nonsense only" intention, many readers have drawn parallels between the poem's content and individuals Carroll encountered and situations that occurred during his lifetime. For instance, Anne Clark points out strong connections between some of the characters in the poem and people mentioned in *Notes by an Oxford Chiel,* published two years earlier in 1874.

The reception of *The Hunting of the Snark* was disappointing. Carroll may have come to believe that the work had missed its mark with his youthful audience. In April 1876 he wrote to one of his child friends, Florence Balfour, and asked her to let him know whether she liked and understood the poem, since "some children are puzzled with it." Further, in August 1879 Carroll heard from nineteen-year-old Mary Brown, who requested that he explain the Snark

to her, but Carroll answered that he could not. Perhaps the best response he was to give on the subject was to the inquiry by the Lowrie children: he stated, "words mean more than we mean to express when we use them: so a whole book ought to mean a great deal more than the writer meant."

The Hunting of the Snark is in eight parts, or "fits," as Carroll called them. The story involves the quest of a ship's crew of nine, captained by an obsessed Bellman, who are in search of the creature called "the Snark." Hunting the creature seems to be akin to hunting the fabled unicorn, as Snark sighting seems to be an extremely rare event. But the creature they seek is dangerous as well as marvelous, since it is reported that some Snarks are Boojums, who have the ability to cause unlucky victims to vanish. Despite this knowledge, they decide to press on, until the Baker, who has wandered off on his own, at last sights a Snark. Too late, he shouts his warning and then vanishes, leaving the reader to ponder over the solemn news that "the Snark *was* a Boojum, you see."

Many readers are compelled to ignore Carroll's admonition that the poem means nothing. Such a well-defined narrative with a quest and a conclusion seems to cry out for interpretation. Broadly speaking, one may guess the search for the unattainable, which even when known to be ridiculous and dangerous, is a goal still felt to be worth the seeking.

In 1879 the author published what many deem to be his most accessible mathematical work entitled *Euclid and His Modern Rivals*. Utilizing a dramatic format, Carroll presents a case for preserving Euclid's manual in its entirety without modifications, by having Euclid appear as a ghost to convince the mathematics examiner of the efficacy of this approach. Collingwood makes the point in his biography that this fanciful presentation was by far more effective in getting across Carroll's point than a scholarly essay on the same topic would have been. Carroll had the potential of being most successful when he could combine humor and fancy in his writing, regardless of subject.

In December 1882 Carroll was drafted into a post that would occupy the next nine years of his life: Curator of the Common Room at Christ Church. According to Anne Clark, Carroll was responsible for purchase, storage, and inventory of wine, food, supplies, and furniture, as well as the salaries and supervision of servants. Carroll was a fastidious individual who had a passion for record keeping and accountability. Hence, a great deal of his time for the next nine years was spent in attempting to refine the system. Additionally, Carroll discovered (and had no doubt anticipated) that the inherent rigors of an administrative position do not necessarily ensure the gratitude of one's colleagues. He found himself engaged in many conflicts over issues, in many instances petty ones. After nine years, on 4 March 1892, Carroll gladly resigned from the position when a colleague, Thomas Banks Strong, agreed to take his place. The 26 April entry in Carroll's diary reveals his sense of relief: "after nine years' interval, I have my time wholly at my own disposal." During this time he produced the pamphlet *Twelve Months in a Curatorship, by One Who Has Tried It* (1884), followed by *Three Years in a Curatorship. By One Whom It Has Tried* (1886), which were not, as the titles imply, without a substantial dose of Carroll's characteristic sense of humor. Despite the distractions inherent in such a position, Carroll was able to maintain a schedule of writing projects.

Besides the two Alice books Carroll's most substantial works for the child audience were *Sylvie and Bruno* (1889) and its sequel, *Sylvie and Bruno Concluded* (1893). Both books are long and complex in format and offer a difficult mix of fact and fancy within the context of a fairy tale. They serve as curious contrasts to *The Nursery Alice* (1889), intended to make *Alice in Wonderland* more accessible to the young. Carroll willingly sacrificed concern for accessibility with the Sylvie and Bruno books — though it is interesting to note that when parts of the books were told orally to the earl of Salisbury's children, the youthful audience was delighted. The written versions were later published in *Aunt Judy's Magazine*. As full-length fantasy novels, however, the stories became part of an intricate interweaving of fancy with philosophical and theological musings.

Carroll states in his preface to *Sylvie and Bruno* that in writing this book he had embarked upon a new type of venture — one that he hoped would be well received. Carroll hoped to entertain, but, above all, the stories were meant to introduce children to "some of the graver thoughts of human life." It is precisely this factor that causes the two works to be a bit didactic and labored. The story includes several plots. First is that of the Warden of Outland, who is in danger of being usurped by his evil brother, the Sub-Warden. Because of his bookish and rather absent-minded tendencies, the Warden is in danger of losing his post and possibly his life. He has two enchanting children, Sylvie and Bruno, whose fairy adventures form a major part of the novel. The Warden is invited to be ruler of Elfland and leaves the affairs of Outland in the hands of his

Carroll's grave, Guildford Cemetery, Surrey

brother who, taking advantage of the Warden's timely disappearance, spreads rumors of his death.

Simultaneously, the author intervenes with a first-person "story" of his own. Carroll's intervention complicates the tale, introducing a parallel story in which the narrator (who suffers from a heart condition and is guest of Arthur Forester, a doctor friend), fades in and out of Sylvie and Bruno's adventures in fairyland. Arthur Forester is in love with Lady Muriel Orme, one to whom the narrator appears also to be attracted. Further complications involve a cousin, Eric Lindon, to whom Lady Muriel becomes engaged but (as the reader discovers in *Sylvie and Bruno Concluded*) does not marry. The narrator becomes involved in the ordinary and fairy concerns of Sylvie and Bruno when he is in a dreamlike state, but exists simultaneously within his adult world filled with heavily philosophical and theological concerns and conversations.

Carroll sought to work out many of his preoccupations in these books: including questions about fatalism, free will, and ritual in religious practice. Additionally, adult characters engage in political and moral discussions that have little relevance or application to childhood. The best parts of the book are the adventures of Sylvie and Bruno, which are clearly within the realm of fancy. In the chapter titled "An Outlandish Watch," the narrator's experiences with a magical watch are a solid fantasy, situated within a realistic environment. While witnessing an accident, the narrator tries to manipulate time by moving the hands of the watch backward. The effect, however, is disastrous, since this merely causes the accident to take place again at the appointed hour, and the narrator witnesses the mishap over and over again each time he moves the hands of his watch backward. Through this experience, the narrator comes to realize how powerless he is against the inevitability of time. The idea is both fascinating and wrenching and allows Carroll to explore both his preoccupation with time and his belief in the inevitability of God's will. Ultimately, *Sylvie and Bruno* is a children's story subsumed within an adult framework; Carroll himself was to refer to the story as "a huge unwieldy mass of litterature [*sic*]."

The story of *Sylvie and Bruno* is continued in *Sylvie and Bruno Concluded*. The narrator meets the title characters in Kensington Gardens, and his fantastic encounters with them and the other cohorts of their fantastic world continue. Arthur Forester marries Lady Orme, only to be separated from her when he volunteers to travel to a village plagued by a dread disease. It is erroneously reported that Arthur is dead, and Lady Muriel mourns his passing. In the parallel story, the Warden returns to Outland, but not to regain his place, which was usurped in the last book. Rather, he allows his sheepish brother to rule and announces his intention to return to Elfland with his children. This scene fades to reveal Lady Muriel knocking at the narrator's door to inform him excitedly that her husband, Arthur, whom she had thought dead, has been found alive by her former suitor, Eric Lindon. Carroll neatly wraps up all the details and creates a firm conclusion.

The plot of the second book is less reliant on fantastic events, and Carroll seems more determined to pursue adult concerns. One wonders what children of the time made of conversations such as the one on how much money was raised at a Charity-Bazaar. This discussion quickly moves from morals and ethics to the economics of the situation, as Arthur and the narrator debate the "two distinct species" of Charity-Bazaars, where market value and fancy prices are involved. In such episodes Carroll appears to have placed his youthful audience to one side. *Sylvie and Bruno Concluded* is therefore less satisfying than its predecessor.

The preface to the work, however, is intriguing, as Carroll defines what he sees as the three states of fairy and discusses the ability of humans to see fairies and vice versa. He presents a tabulation in which he outlines the "abnormal states," and this tabulation acts as a foundation for the blending of fact and fantasy that the reader experiences while reading the books. Each volume also includes an index, an unusual apparatus in a fictional work. Both books are unique presentations, of interest for Carroll's rather daring experiment with form.

The Sylvie and Bruno books are Carroll's last full-length works for children. Following *Sylvie and Bruno Concluded,* he was to produce shorter works, including several publications on logic. *A Fascinating Mental Recreation for the Young* (1895) was an eight-page circular advertising the author's *Symbolic Logic, Part I,* which was to appear in 1896. The following year, Carroll delivered "An Address for Children" at St. Mary Magdalen Church during a children's service. It presented four accounts of acts of kindness and love designed to serve as examples to be emulated by boys and girls.

Early in January 1898 Carroll received word of the death of his brother-in-law Charles Stuart Collingwood. It was his intention to attend the funeral, but within the week Carroll developed a case of influenza, causing his plans to be halted abruptly. He died on 14 January 1898. Two weeks following his death, Dean Paget was to state aptly of Carroll during the course of a sermon: "The brilliant, venturesome imagination, defying forecast with ever fresh surprise; the sense of humour in its finest and most naive form; the power to touch with lightest hand the undercurrent of pathos in the midst of fun; the audacity of creative fancy, and the delicacy of insight – these are rare gifts; and surely they were his." It is for these gifts and their resulting contributions that Lewis Carroll occupies a seminal place in the history of children's literature.

Letters:

Two Letters to Marion from Lewis Carroll (Bristol: Fanfare Press, 1932);

A Selection of the Letters from Lewis Carroll (the Rev. Charles Lutwidge Dodgson) to His Child-friends; Together with "Eight or Nine Words about Letter-Writing," edited by Evelyn M. Hatch (London: Macmillan, 1933);

Morton Cohen, ed., *The Letters of Lewis Carroll,* 2 volumes (New York: Oxford University Press, 1979).

Bibliographies:

Sidney Herbert Williams and Falconer Madan, *The Lewis Carroll Handbook* (Folkestone, Kent: Dawson, 1979);

Rachel Fordyce, *Lewis Carroll: A Reference Guide* (Boston: G. K. Hall, 1988).

Biographies:

Stuart Dodgson Collingwood, *The Life and Letters of Lewis Carroll* (New York: Century, 1898);

Langford Reed, *The Life of Lewis Carroll* (London: W. & G. Foyle, 1932);

Isa Bowman, *Lewis Carroll As I Knew Him* (New York: Dover, 1972);

Anne Clark, *Lewis Carroll: A Biography* (New York: Schocken, 1979);

Morton N. Cohen, *Lewis Carroll: A Biography* (London: Macmillan, 1995).

References:

Nina Auerbach, "Alice and Wonderland, A Curious Child," *Victorian Studies,* 17 (1973): 31–47;

Christina Bjork and Inga-Karin Eriksson, *The Other Alice: The Story of Alice Liddell and Alice in Wonderland* (Stockholm: R & S Books, 1993);

Kathleen Blake, *Play, Games, and Sport: The Literary Works of Lewis Carroll* (Ithaca & London: Cornell University Press, 1974);

Beverly Lyon Clark, "Carroll's Well-Versed Narrative: *Through the Looking-Glass,*" in *Soaring with the Dodo: Essays on Lewis Carroll's Life and Art,* edited by Edward Guiliano and James R. Kincaid (N.p.: Lewis Carroll Society of North America, 1982), pp. 65–76;

William Empson, "Alice in Wonderland: The Child as Swain," in *Aspects of Alice: Lewis Carroll's Dreamchild as Seen Through the Critics' Looking-Glasses,* edited by Robert Phillips (New York: Vintage, 1977), pp. 344–373;

Jean Gattégno, *Lewis Carroll: Fragments of a Looking-Glass,* translated by Rosemary Sheed (New York: Crowell, 1976);

Donald J. Gray, "The Uses of Victorian Laughter," *Victorian Studies,* 10 (1966): 145–176;

Phyllis Greenacre, *Swift and Carroll: A Psychoanalytic Study of Two Lives* (New York: International Universities Press, 1955);

Edward Guiliano, ed., *Lewis Carroll: A Celebration* (New York: Potter, 1982);

Guiliano, ed., *Lewis Carroll Observed: A Collection of Unpublished Photographs, Drawings, Poetry, and New Essays* (New York: Potter, 1976);

Guiliano and James R. Kincaid, eds., *Soaring with the Dodo: Essays on Lewis Carroll's Life and Art* (Charlottesville: Lewis Carroll Society of North America/University Press of Virginia, 1982);

Alice Hargreaves and Caryl Hargreaves, "Alice's Recollections of Carrollian Days," *Cornhill Magazine,* 73 (1932): 1–12;

Richard Kelly, *Lewis Carroll,* revised edition (Boston: Twayne, 1990);

Charles C. Lovett, ed., "Special Supplement: Translations of Alice," *Knight Letter,* The Lewis Carroll Society of North America, no. 46 (Winter 1994): 4–5;

Graham Ovenden, ed., *The Illustrators of Alice* (London: Academy / New York: St. Martin's Press, 1972);

Robert Phillips, ed., *Aspects of Alice: Lewis Carroll's Dreamchild As Seen Through the Critic's Looking-Glasses 1865–1971* (New York: Vanguard / London: Gollancz, 1971);

George Pitcher, "Wittgenstein, Nonsense, and Lewis Carroll," *Massachusetts Review,* 6 (1965): 591–611;

Robert M. Polhemus, "Carroll's *Through the Looking-Glass:* The Comedy of Regression," in *Comic Faith: The Great Tradition from Austen to Joyce* (Chicago & London: University of Chicago Press, 1980);

Elizabeth Sewell, *The Field of Nonsense* (London: Chatto & Windus, 1952);

Lillian Smith, *The Unreluctant Years: A Critical Approach to Children's Literature* (Chicago: American Library Association, 1991), pp. 143–147;

Robert D. Sutherland, *Language and Lewis Carroll* (The Hague: Mouton, 1970);

Warren Weaver, *Alice in Many Tongues: The Translations of Alice in Wonderland* (Madison: University of Wisconsin Press, 1964).

Papers:

Lewis Carroll materials are in collections around the world. The largest collection of materials is the M. L. Parrish collection at Princeton University, New Jersey. Other important collections are at the University of Texas at Austin; the New York Public Library (Berg); the New York University Library; the Elmer Holmes Bobst Library (Berol); the Bodleian Library; the British Library; Christ Church College, Oxford; the Columbia University Library; the Harcourt Amory Collection at Harvard University; and the Huntington Library.

Dinah Maria Craik

(20 April 1826 – 12 October 1887)

Diana A. Chlebek
University of Akron

See also the Craik entry in *DLB 35: Victorian Poets After 1850.*

BOOKS: *Michael the Miner* (London: Religious Tract Society, 1846);

How to Win Love: or Rhoda's Lesson (London: Arthur Hall, 1848);

The Ogilvies: A Novel (3 volumes, London: Chapman & Hall, 1849; 1 volume, New York: Harper, 1850);

Cola Monti: or The Story of a Genius (London: Hall, 1849);

Olive, 3 volumes (London: Chapman & Hall, 1850);

The Half-Caste: An Old Governess's Tale (London & Edinburgh: W. & R. Chambers, 1851);

The Head of the Family (1 volume, New York: Harper, 1851; 3 volumes, London: Chapman & Hall, 1852);

Alice Learmont: A Fairy Tale (London: Chapman & Hall, 1852; Boston: Mayhew & Baker, 1859);

Bread Upon the Waters: A Governess's Life (London: Governesses' Benevolent Institution, 1852);

Avillion and Other Tales (3 volumes, London: Smith & Elder, 1853; 1 volume, New York: Harper, 1854);

Agatha's Husband: A Novel (3 volumes, London: Chapman & Hall, 1853; 1 volume, New York: Harper, 1853);

A Hero: Philip's Book (London: Addey, 1853);

The Little Lychetts (London: Sampson Low, 1855);

John Halifax, Gentleman (3 volumes, London: Hurst & Blackett, 1856; 1 volume, New York: Harper, 1856);

Nothing New: Tales (London: Hurst & Blackett, 1857; New York: Harper, 1857);

A Woman's Thoughts About Women (London: Hurst & Blackett, 1858; New York: Rudd & Carleton, 1858);

A Life for a Life (3 volumes, London: Hurst & Blackett, 1859; 1 volume, New York: Harper, 1859);

Dinah Maria Craik (courtesy of Special Collections, Thomas Cooper Library, University of South Carolina)

Poems (London: Hurst & Blackett, 1859; Boston: Ticknor & Fields, 1860);

Romantic Tales (London: Smith, Elder, 1859);

Domestic Stories (London: Smith, Elder, 1859);

Our Year: A Child's Book in Prose and Verse (Cambridge: Macmillan, 1860; New York: Harper, 1860);

Studies From Life (London: Hurst & Blackett, 1861; New York: Harper, 1861);

Mistress and Maid (2 volumes, London: Hurst & Blackett, 1863; 1 volume, New York: Harper, 1863);

The Fairy Book (London: Macmillan, 1863; New York: Harper, 1870);

Christian's Mistake (London: Hurst & Blackett, 1865; New York: Harper, 1865);

A New Year's Gift for Sick Children (Edinburgh: Edinburgh & Douglas, 1865);

A Noble Life (2 volumes, London: Hurst & Blackett, 1866; 1 volume, New York: Harper, 1866);

Two Marriages (2 volumes, London: Hurst & Blackett, 1867; 1 volume, New York: Harper, 1867);

The Woman's Kingdom (1 volume, New York: Harper, 1868; 3 volumes, London: Hurst & Blackett, 1869);

A Brave Lady (3 volumes, London: Hurst & Blackett, 1870; 1 volume, New York: Harper, 1870);

The Unkind Word and Other Stories (2 volumes, London: Hurst & Blackett, 1870; 1 volume, New York: Harper, 1870);

Fair France: Impressions of a Traveller (London: Hurst & Blackett, 1871; New York: Harper, 1871);

Little Sunshine's Holiday (London: Sampson Low, 1871; New York: Harper, 1871);

Hannah (London: Hurst & Blackett, 1872; New York: Harper, 1872);

The Adventures of a Brownie as Told to My Child (London: Low, Marston, Low & Searle, 1872; New York: Harper, 1872);

My Mother and I (London: Isbister, 1874; New York: Harper, 1874);

Songs of Our Youth (London: Daldy, Isbister, 1875; New York: Harper, 1875);

Sermons Out of Church (London: Daldy, Isbister, 1875; New York: Harper, 1875);

The Little Lame Prince and His Travelling Cloak (London: Macmillan, 1875);

The Laurel Bush: An Old-Fashioned Love Story (New York: Harper, 1876; London: Daldy, Isbister, 1877);

Will Denbigh, Nobleman (Boston: Roberts Brothers, 1877);

A Legacy: Being the Life and Remains of John Martin, Schoolmaster and Poet (2 volumes, London: Hurst & Blackett, 1878; 1 volume, New York: Blackett, 1878);

Young Mrs. Jardine (3 volumes, London: Hurst & Blackett, 1879; 1 volume, New York: Harper, 1880);

Thirty Years: Being Poems New and Old (London: Macmillan, 1880; Boston: Houghton Mifflin, 1881); republished as *Poems* (London: Macmillan, 1888);

Children's Poetry (London: Macmillan, 1881);

His Little Mother and Other Tales (London: Hurst & Blackett, 1881; New York: Harper, 1881);

Plain Speaking (London: Hurst & Blackett, 1882; New York: Harper, 1882);

An Unsentimental Journey Through Cornwall (London: Macmillan, 1884);

Miss Tommy: A Medieval Romance (London: Macmillan, 1884; New York: Munro, 1884);

About Money and Other Things (London: Macmillan, 1886; New York: Harper, 1887);

King Arthur — Not a Love Story (London: Macmillan, 1886; New York: Harper, 1886);

Work for Idle Hands (London: Spottiswoode, 1886);

Fifty Golden Years: Incidents in the Queen's Reign (London & New York: R. Tuck, 1887);

An Unknown Country (London: Macmillan, 1887; New York: Harper, 1887);

Concerning Men and Other Papers (London: Macmillan, 1888).

OTHER: Francois Guizot, *M. de Barante, A Memoir,* translated by Craik (London: Macmillan, 1867);

Twenty Years Ago: From the Journal of a Girl in Her Teens, edited by Craik (London: Sampson Low, 1871);

Is It True? Tales Curious and Wonderful, edited by Craik (London: Sampson Low, 1872).

The literary opus of Dinah Maria Craik has come to be regarded as a significant reflection of Victorian expectations and values. Her children's books are important explorations of the sentiments of the innocent and the dispossessed. *The Little Lame Prince and His Travelling Cloak* (1875) and *The Adventures of a Brownie as Told to My Child* (1872) especially represent a strain of juvenile fantasy that reacted against a flood of moralistic books that attempted to stifle the natural ebullience of children. In the context of both the history of children's literature and the sociology of childhood, Craik's work underscores a turning point in the attitude toward the young, particularly regarding the role children play in sensitizing adults to the moral and creative possibilities of an imaginative sensibility.

Craik was born Dinah Maria Mulock on 20 April 1826 at Stoke on Trent in Staffordshire. Early in life, as the eldest child of a frail mother, Dinah Mulock, and an unstable and irresponsible clergyman father, Thomas Mulock, the girl took responsibility for the care of her two younger brothers, Thomas and Benjamin. Her insecure childhood was a mixture of conventional religious and genteel education and unrestricted independence in leisure ac-

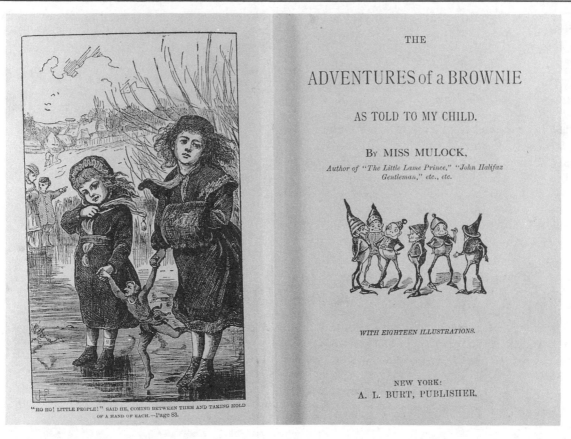

THE

ADVENTURES of a BROWNIE

AS TOLD TO MY CHILD.

By MISS MULOCK,

Author of "The Little Lame Prince," "John Halifax Gentleman," etc., etc.

WITH EIGHTEEN ILLUSTRATIONS.

NEW YORK:
A. L. BURT, PUBLISHER.

"HO HO! LITTLE PEOPLE!" SAID HE, COMING BETWEEN THEM AND TAKING HOLD OF A HAND OF EACH.—Page 83.

Frontispiece and title page for an early American reprint of Craik's 1872 book inspired by the author's adopted daughter, Dorothy (courtesy of Special Collections, Thomas Cooper Library, University of South Carolina)

tivities. In later recollections of her youth, such as the essay "Going Out to Play" (1858), she recalls the free access she and her brothers were given to roam the countryside and indulge in tomboyish romps. This type of unsupervised childhood, in which boys and girls alike were allowed to play in rough clothes at country children's games, was unusual for a Victorian middle-class family. The independence Mulock learned during these years later played an important role in forming both her assertive, resilient personality and her advanced ideas about the status of women in society.

In early adolescence, during a period when sickness forced her family indoors, Mulock discovered the treasures of the English novel and devoured the works of Jane Austen, Sir Walter Scott, Charles Dickens, Amelia Opie, and Sir Edward Bulwer-Lytton. From this valuable literature, as she later described in her essay on reading for children, "Want Something To Read" (1858), her "imaginative and romantic tendencies sprung up full-grown, as it were, in a day." Thus inspired, by age twelve she was writing her own stories and poems. In 1839, when her father relinquished financial respon-

sibility for his family, her mother opened a school in Newcastle. Mulock became her assistant and thus, at the age of thirteen, received her first lessons in financial independence for women, a credo that she would promote frequently in her novels and essays.

After her mother died in 1845 and her father refused to support the children, Mulock embarked upon a writing career in London to support herself and her two brothers. Her first literary efforts appeared in *Chamber's Edinburgh Journal.* Thus, along with her peers Margaret Gatty and Margaret Oliphant, she became part of a productive society of Victorian female authors who wrote out of financial necessity rather than for amusement. In 1846 the Religious Tract Society published Mulock's first book, *Michael the Miner,* one of five didactic children's novels that she wrote during the next decade. The story, modeled after the tracts of Hannah More, details the daily struggle of a poor and industrious boy to help support his destitute family.

Two more sentimental moral tales were published in quick succession. *How to Win Love: or Rhoda's Lesson* (1848) describes the transformation of a sullen adolescent into a selfless, loving step-daughter. Through a near-fatal bout with illness, Rhoda learns the lessons of love and generosity from her angelic second mother. The motto "God Helps Those Who Help Themselves" embellished the title page of Mulock's third children's novel, *Cola Monti: or The Story of a Genius* (1849). It underscored the moral of self-help embodied in the poor hero's struggle to avoid the easy, corruptive life of a hanger-on in the margins of artistic society. Instead, Cola Monti works hard to become a successful commercial artist and eventually wins acclaim in an exhibition at the Royal Academy. In a similar vein, the novels *A Hero: Philip's Book* (1853) and *The Little Lychetts* (1855) teach children the values of self-reliance, perseverance, and charity through various object lessons that focus on loss of privilege or material well-being.

The reception accorded the children's tales was comparable to that of Mulock's first domestic novels for adults published during this period: *The Ogilvies: A Novel* (1849) and *Olive* (1850). Her fiction was extremely popular with the masses but received mixed critical reviews. Generally, the characters of her books were praised as uplifting and often as original, but her narrative plots were described as contrived and repetitious. A contemporary critique of the strengths and weaknesses of her books in the *British Quarterly Review* praises the "purity of moral tone" in her writing but laments its lack of "artistic power" and "poetic richness."

In a departure from the didactic strain of children's stories, Mulock wrote her first fairy tale, *Alice Learmont* (1852), in 1851. Her essay on children's literature, "The Age of Gold" (1860), espoused the necessity of cultivating youthful imagination through reading fanciful tales in childhood. Mulock's fantasy is an especially skillful and eerie combination of literary invention and Scottish traditional tale that embellishes the motif of the changeling, the human child stolen by evil fairies to pay their seven years' tribute to the devil. The author presents the legend as an allegory of the child's maturation into adulthood through the sacrifice of the parents. In Mulock's story Alice's mother struggles to guide her daughter through the torturous transformation from a bewitched, indifferent fairy's child into a caring, loving human adult.

Mulock's popularity with the public, success as an independent professional in the literary world, and generous encouragement of her peers won her friends and supporters among famous artists and authors of her time. Elizabeth Gaskell,

Margaret Oliphant, and Jane Carlyle admired her self-assurance and spirit, particularly when it came to financial acumen in dealing with publishers to obtain fair payment for her work. In addition, she asserted an unusual degree of independence when she established her own household as a single woman, complete with a social circle of distinctive female and male friends and peers. Her father's irresponsible attitude toward the family and the necessity of earning her own way early in life had taught Mulock to look to herself for both economic and emotional support. While she admitted the attractions of romantic fulfillment, she stolidly recognized the falsity of Victorian myths of wedded bliss.

Mulock's literary skills matured and attained fulfillment with the publication of *John Halifax, Gentleman* (1856). The novel was an immediate success with the public, making the author's name a household word in Britain and abroad. As well as functioning as a historical allegory of the rise of the English middle class, this study of a poor apprentice's climb to the ranks of the gentry through hard work and fair play crystallizes the author's philosophy of self-reliance. Henry James's review of the book reflects much of the critical opinion it received; he concedes that despite the book's sentimentality, Mulock's John Halifax towers above all criticism through his status as the predominant symbolic figure of his era – the self-made man. The novel's theme of genteel self-help, epitomized in Mulock's own life of early hardship and struggle for professional status, struck a chord with her popular audience and became the underlying concept that unified her fiction for adults and her stories for children.

With her next publication, a series of essays titled *A Woman's Thoughts About Women* (1858), Mulock expanded her ideas on self-reliance to the sphere of the "woman question" that so fascinated British society during this period. She pressed a practical rather than philosophic approach to the issue of women's social status. With her emphasis on the need for greater career opportunities and better education for women as opposed to the conventional insistence on marriage as the sole female occupation, Mulock struck a blow both for herself and for all literary and artistic career women. Finally, in 1864, the literary success of *John Halifax, Gentleman* and her authority as a writer of respected position were symbolically recognized with the endowment of a Civil List Pension from Queen Victoria. She donated the full proceeds from this endowment to a fund that supported struggling young writers. Mulock was also generous in her efforts to advance the careers of fellow authors through the influence of her professional renown and contacts with the publishing world. In 1863 she persuaded her publishers Hurst and Blackett to take on George Macdonald's novel *David Elginbroad* after his own publishers had refused it; the book became a best-seller and established Macdonald as a writer.

Throughout the 1860s Mulock contributed stories and poems for children to journals such as *Chamber's Edinburgh Journal* and *Once a Week*. In 1869 George Macdonald invited her to write for the new children's magazine he was editing, *Good Words for the Young*. Most of her verse for children, like her poetry for adults, is sentimental and deals with commonplace themes and ideas. *Our Year: A Child's Book in Prose and Verse* (1860), an almanac of nature poetry and stories, is a typical embroidery of familiar events, characters, and scenery written in the simple, repetitive forms that appealed to the popular taste.

Mulock's marriage in 1865 to George Lillie Craik, a man eleven years her junior, opened up a new phase of her life. Although she continued to write, even above her husband's objection, she began to cultivate more fully the domestic side of her personality. The Craiks purchased a house in Kent with the author's literary earnings and in 1869 adopted a foundling. Out of concern and love for the destitute, Craik had always used her influence with the public to advocate shelters and nurseries for poor children in urban areas. The adoption of Dorothy, "the gift of God," was a highly unconventional transaction, but Craik could thus make both a social statement on behalf of the underprivileged young and satisfy her maternal instincts. The little girl became the focus of her mother's emotional fulfillment and a literary inspiration. *The Adventures of a Brownie as Told to My Child,* an episodic fantasy about the pranks of a household elf attached to a particular family, recoups the interest in old legends that was aroused with the publication of the author's previous fairy tale, *Alice Learmont*. In describing the brownie's conspiracies with the family's children, Craik's simple retelling and cozy narrative tone encourage imaginative play in the therapeutic vein that she proposed in her essay "Going Out to Play" — that is, amusement for the sheer pleasure of the moment.

The culmination of Craik's writing for children came with the publication in 1875 of another book inspired by Dorothy, *The Little Lame Prince and his Travelling Cloak*. The story, in parable form, recounts the magical journey to spiritual and material fulfillment of Prince Dolor, who is crippled at birth through the carelessness and indifference of adults. He is disinherited and imprisoned by his evil uncle but eventually escapes exile and reclaims his kingdom through the intercession of a fairy godmother, who endows him with exceptional powers of movement and observation.

Craik's advice to the reader regarding the hidden moral of *The Little Lame Prince* is almost misleading in its diffidence: "If any reader, big or little, should wonder whether there is a meaning in this story, deeper than that of an ordinary fairy tale, I will own that there is." But she further tantalizes her audience by warning, "I have hidden it so carefully that the smaller folk, and many larger folk will never find it out, and meantime the book may be read straight on, like Cinderella." In truth, the story goes far beyond a sentimental fantasy about a child dispossessed of his right to physical and social advantages through the actions of selfish adults. The conventional fairy-tale beginning and end of Craik's romance frames a journey of self-development taken by the child protagonist. Dolor's adventures on the flying cloak are virtual lessons in natural philosophy acquired through the enhancement of his physical faculties — feet, eyes, and ears. For when his intelligent curiosity is piqued by observations of the natural world as he flies above the earth, he also seeks to gain deeper knowledge of mankind and of himself.

The prince's first move toward freedom and wisdom begins, literally, with a leap of moral courage when he springs onto the cloak for a first magic journey that will break his ties to a comfortable, albeit deadening, incarceration in the tower. His fantastic flights over the world are also exercises in imagination that teach the values of an active life, as opposed to a passive dependence on adults who exploit his infirmity. As he travels further abroad, his perceptions of the world whet his appetite for more knowledge. His greatest satisfaction on the journeys comes through empathy with the flora and fauna he encounters. Craik stresses that it is through an affective innocence that the child discovers his world. Thus, Dolor's capacity for feeling, like that of the Dickensian child-hero, becomes a validating measure of human worth. Craik stresses that the prince's infirmity and dispossession are as much a result of his father's and nurse's indifference as of his uncle's greed and cruelty. All are manifestations of adult tyranny over children.

It is through innocence, a capacity to feel deeply, and fresh observations of the world that the prince achieves his rightful place in society, for example, the restoration of his kingdom. Moreover, the elements of his voyage to self-fulfillment are protected from adult interference. The magic cloak cannot be touched by grown-ups, and the fairy godmother, his benefactress, has the ability to vanish from the grasp of malicious adults. In the final analysis, the lame prince's story remains deeply embedded in the Victorian ethos of self-reliance; his magical journeys to transcendence and good deeds spring from a desire to make the fullest possible use of his abilities. At the end of the novel Craik underscores the dual nature of her hero's existence. As an adult monarch with his lameness and innocence masked, Dolor remains solidly in the realm of duty and responsibility and tends to matters of state with good sense. However, the child within him can stay in touch with the world of romance and of the spirit by retreating to his private abode at the top of the castle.

Early reviewers faulted the novel with excessive sentimentality and an overly bleak atmosphere. However, modern critics such as Elaine Showalter have reassessed the story as an allegory representing both imagination and the act of creativity. The prince is thus perceived as a stand-in for Craik, who as a Victorian female author found her independence through professional self-fulfillment – that is, through the ability to concretize in writing her observations of and empathy with her fellow beings. A great success in its own time, the novel has never waned in popularity with the young and has been printed in many editions.

Appropriately, Craik's last years were focused on giving assistance to the poor in her district and to needy authors. In addition, before her death of heart failure on 12 October 1887, she published *King Arthur – Not a Love Story* (1886), a novel advocating more liberal adoption laws. To the end she continued to use her public status and private means to help those less fortunate than she. Scholars now recognize that her works present explorations rather than statements on the human condition, particularly in the light of her own struggle for professional fulfillment. During her lifetime Craik's literary renown was established primarily through her adult novels; most of these works, with their stylistic and intellectual limitations, have now faded in obscurity. However, her juvenile books, *The Little Lame Prince* and *The Adventures of a Brownie,* have achieved the status of classics. They endure because they continue to invite readers to keep in touch with the most precious moments and feelings of childhood.

Biographies:

Henrietta Keddie, *Three Generations: The Story of a Middle-Class Scottish Family* (London: John Murray, 1911);

Aleyn Lyell Reade, *The Mellards and Their Descendants* (London: Privately printed at the Arden Press, 1915).

References:

Charles H. Frey, "Dinah Maria Mulock Craik, *The Little Lame Prince,*" in his *The Literary Heritage of Childhood* (Westport, Conn.: Greenwood Press, 1987), pp. 93–98;

Sally Mitchell, *Dinah Mulock Craik* (Boston: Twayne, 1983);

Louisa Parr, *Women Novelists of Queen Victoria's Reign* (London: Hurst & Blackett, 1897);

Elaine Showalter, "Dinah Mulock Craik and the Tactics of Sentiment: A Case Study in Victorian Female Authorship," *Feminist Studies,* 2 (Spring 1975): 5–23.

Papers:

Manuscripts and letters by Dinah Maria Craik are in the Morris L. Parrish Collection at Princeton University Library; the Berg Collection at the New York Public Library contains some of Craik's correspondence.

Walter Crane
(15 August 1845 – 14 March 1915)

George R. Bodmer
Indiana University Northwest

BOOKS: *Farmyard Alphabet* (London: Warne, circa 1865–1866);

Cock Robin (London: Warne, circa 1865–1866);

The Railroad Alphabet (London: Warne, circa 1865–1866);

The House that Jack Built (London: Warne, circa 1865–1866);

Dame Trot and Her Comical Cat (London: Warne, circa 1865–1866);

The Waddling Frog (London: Warne, circa 1865–1866);

Sing a Song of Sixpence (London: Warne, 1866);

Chattering Jack (London: Routledge, 1867);

How Jessie Was Lost (London: Routledge, 1867);

1, 2, Buckle My Shoe (London: Routledge, 1867);

The Old Courtier (London: Routledge, 1867);

Multiplication Tables in Verse (London: Routledge, 1867);

Grammar in Rhyme (London: Routledge, 1868);

Annie and Jack in London (London: Routledge, 1868);

The Alphabet of Old Friends (London: Routledge, circa 1870–1874);

Baby's Own Alphabet (London: Routledge, circa 1870–1874);

The Frog Prince (London: Routledge, circa 1870–1874);

The Hind in the Wood (London: Routledge, circa 1870–1874);

The Sleeping Beauty (London: Routledge, circa 1870–1874);

King Luckieboy's Party (London: Routledge, 1871);

This Little Pig Went to Market (London: Routledge, 1871);

The Fairy Ship (London: Routledge, 1871);

Old Mother Hubbard (London: Routledge, 1873);

My Mother (London: Routledge, 1874);

The Forty Thieves (London: Routledge, 1874);

The Absurd ABC (London: Routledge, 1874);

Jack and the Beanstalk (London: Routledge, 1874);

Cinderella (London: Routledge, 1874);

Valentine and Orson (London: Routledge, 1874);

Little Red Riding Hood (London: Routledge, 1874);

Photograph by Fred Hollyer

Puss in Boots (London: Routledge, 1874);

Goody Two Shoes (London: Routledge, 1874);

Beauty and the Beast (London: Routledge, 1874);

Walter Crane's New Toybook (London: Routledge, 1874);

Walter Crane's Picturebook (London: Routledge, 1874);

The Yellow Dwarf (London: Routledge, 1874);

Bluebeard (London: Routledge, 1875);

Princess Belle Etoile (London: Routledge, 1875);

Mrs. Mundi at Home (London: Marcus Ward, 1875);

The Terrestrial Ball (London: Marcus Ward, 1875);

Aladdin (London: Routledge, 1876);

The Quiver of Love: A Collection of Valentines Ancient and Modern, by Crane and Kate Greenaway (London: Marcus Ward, 1876);

The Baby's Opera, A Book of Old Rhymes with New Dresses (London: Routledge, 1877);

The Baby's Bouquet, A Fresh Bunch of Old Rhymes and Tunes (London: Marcus Ward, 1878);

Slateandpencilvania: Being the Adventures of Dick on a Desert Island (London: Marcus Ward, 1885);

Little Queen Anne and Her Majesty's Letters (London: Marcus Ward, 1885);

Pothooks and Perseverance, or the ABC Serpent (London: Marcus Ward, 1885);

Baby's Own Aesop, Being the Fables Condensed in Rhyme, with text by William Linton (London: Routledge, 1886);

The Sirens Three (London: Macmillan, 1886);

Legends for Lionel in Pen and Pencil (London: Cassell, 1887);

Flora's Feast: A Masque of Flowers (London: Cassell, 1889);

Walter Crane's Painting Book (London: Routledge, 1889);

Renascence: A Book of Verse (London: Elkin Mathews, 1891);

Queen Summer or the Tournament of the Rose (London: Cassell, 1891);

The Claims of Decorative Art (London: Lawrence & Bullen, 1892);

Of the Decorative Illustration of Books Old and New (London: George Bell, 1896);

The Bases of Design (London: George Bell, 1898);

A Floral Fantasy in an Old English Garden (London: Harper, 1899);

Line and Form (London: George Bell, 1900);

Moot Points, by Crane and Lewis F. Day (London: B. T. Batsford, 1903);

A Flower Wedding Described by Two Wallflowers (London: Cassell, 1905);

An Artist's Reminiscences (London: Methuen, 1907; Detroit: Singing Tree, 1968).

BOOKS ILLUSTRATED: John R. Wise, *The New Forest* (London: Smith & Elder, 1863);

Agnes de Havilland, *Stories from Memel for the Young* (London, 1864);

Mayhew Brothers, *The Magic of Kindness or the Wondrous Story of the Good Huan* (London: Cassell, 1869);

Mary Molesworth, *Tell Me a Story* (London: Macmillan, 1875);

Ennis Graham, *The Cuckoo Clock* (London: Macmillan, 1877);

Molesworth, *Grandmother Dear: A Book for Boys and Girls* (London: Macmillan, 1878);

Molesworth, *The Tapestry Room* (London: Macmillan, 1879);

Mary A. de Morgan, *The Necklace of Princess Fiormunde and Other Stories* (London: Macmillan, 1880);

Wise, *The First of May, A Fairy Masque* (London: Southeran, 1881);

Molesworth, *The Adventure of Heir Baby* (London: Macmillan, 1881);

Hans Grimm and Jacob Grimm, *Household Stories from the Collection of the Brothers Grimm,* translated by Lucy Crane (London: Macmillan, 1882);

Molesworth, *Rosy* (London: Macmillan, 1882);

Theodore Marzials, *Pan Pipes. A Book of Old Songs* (London: Routledge, 1883);

Molesworth, *Us. An Old Fashioned Story* (London: Macmillan, 1883);

Molesworth, *Christmas Tree Land* (London: Macmillan, 1884);

J. M. D. Meiklejohn, *The Golden Primer* (London: Blackwood, 1884);

Mrs. Burton Harrison, *Folk and Fairy Tales* (London: Ward & Downey, 1885);

Molesworth, *Four Winds Farm* (London: Macmillan, 1887);

Molesworth, *Little Miss Peggy. Only a Nursery Story* (London: Macmillan, 1887);

Oscar Wilde, *The Happy Prince and Other Tales* (London: Nutt, 1888);

Molesworth, *A Christmas Child: A Sketch of a Boy's Life* (London: Macmillan, 1888);

Molesworth, *A Christmas Posy* (London: Macmillan, 1888);

Molesworth, *The Rectory Children* (London: Macmillan, 1889);

Molesworth, *The Children of the Castle* (London: Macmillan, 1890);

Nathaniel Hawthorne, *A Wonderbook for Boys and Girls* (London: Osgood & McIlvaine, 1892);

Margaret Deland, *The Old Garden and Other Verses* (London: Osgood & McIlvaine, 1893);

William Shakespeare, *Two Gentlemen of Verona* (London: Dent, 1894);

William Morris, *The Story of the Glittering Plain or the Land of Living Men or the Acre of the Undying* (London: Kelmscott, 1894);

F. S. Ellis, *The History of Reynard the Fox: With Some Account of His Family* (London: Nutt, 1894);

Edmund Spenser, *The Faerie Queen* (London: Allen, 1894);

Elizabeth Harrison, *The Vision of Dante: A Story for Little Children and a Talk to Their Mothers* (Chicago: Chicago Kindergarten College, 1894);

Shakespeare, *The Merry Wives of Windsor* (London: Dent, 1896);

Spenser, *The Shepherd's Calendar* (London: George Bell, 1898);

Nellie Dale, *The Walter Crane Reader: First and Second Primers* (London: Dent, 1899);

Judge Parry, *Don Quixote of La Mancha* (London: Blackie, 1900);

Charles Lamb, *A Masque of Days* (London: Cassell, 1901);

E. J. Gould, *The Children's Plutarch* (London: Watts, 1906);

Dale, *The Dale Reader's Book II* (London: George Philip, 1907);

Arthur Kelly, *The Rosebud and Other Tales* (London: Unwin, 1909);

Henry Gilbert, *King Arthur's Knights: The Tales Retold for Boys and Girls* (Edinburgh: T. C. & E. C. Jack, 1911);

Morris, *William Morris to Whistler: Papers and Addresses on Art and Crafts and the Commercial* (London: George Bell, 1911);

Gilbert, *Robin Hood and the Men of the Greenwood* (Edinburgh: T. C. & E. C. Jack, 1912);

Mary MacGregor, *The Story of Greece as Told to Boys and Girls* (Edinburgh: T. C. & E. C. Jack, 1913);

Gilbert, *The Knights of the Round Table* (Edinburgh: T. C. & E. C. Jack, 1915);

Gilbert, *Robin Hood and His Merry Men* (Edinburgh: T. C. & E. C. Jack, 1915).

Walter Crane was a Victorian illustrator, designer, poet, teacher, Socialist, and painter whose advocacy of affordable colored picture books helped influence the look of nineteenth-century British children's literature. He was born on 15 August 1845 in Liverpool, the third of five children to Marie and Thomas Crane. His father was a painter and portraitist who had also operated a lithographic press with his two brothers. Because of Thomas Crane's ill health and futile attempts to make a success of his art, the family moved often. Nevertheless, Crane remembered his childhood fondly and the times he spent catching butterflies, blowing up things in the garden with gunpowder, lying on the floor of his father's studio drawing, completing the study sketches his father made, and copying pictures from his father's books. Crane became known at a young age as an accomplished artist, and he received the position of apprentice as a result of some illustrations he had made that came to the attention of critic John Ruskin and William James Linton, a student of Thomas Bewick and one of the best wood engravers of his time.

In January 1859, when he was still thirteen, Crane entered his three-year apprenticeship to wood engraver Linton at the height of that craft's popularity. What he found was a busy shop where workers cut the drawings into the end grain of boxwood blocks for illustrations in popular magazines and books. Many of these engravers were deaf and dumb, and to speed the process the block was often cut in sections, with one craftsman doing the background while a more experienced or skillful man might do the faces. Crane was hired to draw directly upon the ends of scraps of the boxwood, using a clean sharp line that could be cut accurately. In his memoirs Crane mentions his various tasks in Linton's employ: drawing animals at the zoo, doing medical drawings, fixing the pictures on the wood for others, and making sketches of notorious cases in court for the popular press. He notes, "The least enjoyable work I can remember was certainly the drawing of an incredible number of iron bedsteads for a certain catalogue." There is every reason to believe that Linton liked young Crane, treated him well, and tried to encourage his artistic development. They later worked together on book projects, and after Linton moved to the United States, Crane attempted unsuccessfully to obtain a pension for him from the British government. Crane in turn learned the mechanics of how images could be printed and, subsequently, worked closely with the printers of his work.

After the three years of his apprenticeship were completed (he would have been sixteen), Crane tried to survive on freelance work. His father had died in the summer of 1859, which obviously straitened the family's finances and made this work crucial. At the same time, Crane attended art classes at Heatherley's Art School at night, which put him in contact with other artists who grouped together to sell their pictures. His work at this time consisted largely of vignettes, landscapes, and groups of people in society dress for the covers or chapter headings of books, and his drawings show a thin, feathery line characteristic of engravings of the 1860s.

What Crane needed to learn at this stage was to produce a firm line and simplify the details in his images; these qualities would eventually characterize his picture books and would show off the color that made them unique. Later the artist wrote that the gift of some Japanese color woodcuts helped to develop his style. He recognized the vivid and dramatic effect of the definite black outline and flat, brilliant, yet delicate colors of Japanese art; and he "endeavored to apply these methods to the modern fanciful and humorous subjects of children's toy-books and to the methods of wood-engraving and machine-printing."

In 1863 Crane met the printer Edmund Evans, with whom he was to do much of his most creative work. Beginning by drawing the covers of cheap, sensational novels for Evans, in 1865 he began a series of colorful inexpensive picture books, the six-penny "toy books." Evans was a printer who was always looking for projects and worked with various artists (most notably the Victorian triumvirate: Crane, Kate Greenaway, and Randolph Caldecott); he printed the paper pages, which were then published by such houses as George Routledge, his sons, and Routledge's brother-in-law Frederick Warne. Evans worked closely with his artists, educating them in the mechanics of producing pictures and in turn trying to follow their desires for particular colors and effects. The first series of toy books with Crane, which eventually reached around fifty titles in the next thirty years, was published in 1865–1866 and included *Sing a Song of Sixpence; Farmyard Alphabet; Cock Robin; The Railroad Alphabet; The House that Jack Built; Dame Trot and Her Comical Cat;* and *The Waddling Frog.*

Crane's illustrations for these and the later toy books were usually outlined figures in a darker color, perhaps black but often green, brown, or blue. He would initially make the illustrations on the woodblocks for engraving; next he would make decisions about the strong, bright colors to be added in subsequent printings. He pictured people in elaborate costumes, with his animals usually more animated and frolicsome. The pictures were commonly framed by a line, and the words were often written into the picture in script or outlined in a box. Allegorical designs often worked their way into Crane's images, especially on the title page: a brooding black cat, a lost shoe, or a threatening spindle that emblematizes the story might appear. As a mature artist Crane characteristically filled his pictures with elaborate furniture and objects and made birds and vines snake along borders and margins. There is much to look at on the pages, both de-

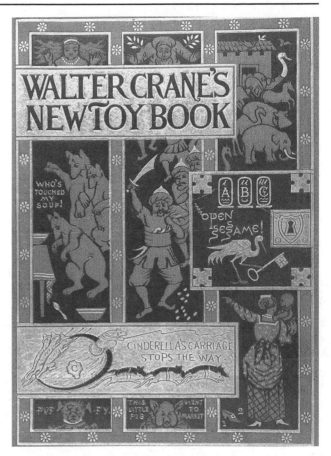

Illustrated cover for one of the two 1874 collections of Crane's toy books (courtesy of the Lilly Library, Indiana University)

tail and motion, but all is easy to see, clearly outlined and colored. These elements not only made Crane's books best-sellers but increased the public's desire for affordable colored picture books.

Wood engravings, which traditionally avoided large areas of pure black (uncut wood) or pure white, were filled with shadows, cross-hatching, and stippling. As Crane moved toward a simpler, more open line in his picture-book illustrations, he filled the backgrounds and foregrounds of his pictures with textured wallpapers, carpets, vases, and decorations: for instance, *1, 2, Buckle My Shoe* (1867) shows a decorative Japanese screen in the background. Of this development in his style he writes, "I was in the habit of putting in all sorts of subsidiary detail that interested me, and often made them the vehicle for my ideas in furniture and decoration. This element, indeed, in the books soon began to be discovered by architects and others interested in or directly connected with house decoration, and this brought me some occasional commissions for actual work in that way in the form of friezes or frieze panels."

Preliminary sketch (courtesy of the Lilly Library, Indiana University) and final illustration for "King Cole" in
The Baby's Opera *(1877)*

Consequently, Crane designed such decorative objects as tiles, jugs for the Wedgwood firm, vases, embroidery patterns, murals and mosaics, and textiles and tapestries. He created his first wallpaper pattern in 1875, partly in defense against those who had already copied designs from his picture books. His first wallpaper patterns featured Mother Goose rhymes for the nursery, but he also produced flowing geometric figures with swans and leaves, similar to those of William Morris, and produced more than fifty different wallpaper designs. With Morris he helped found the Arts and Crafts Society in 1888 and served as its first president. Likewise with Morris, he campaigned for Socialism, making speeches and drawing political cartoons. He joined the Fabian Society in 1885.

Crane married Mary Frances Andrews in 1871, and they lived in Italy until 1873, where he met other artists and studied European paintings. The couple had two sons, Lionel and Lancelot, a daughter, Beatrice, and a boy and girl who died in infancy. While Crane was in Italy, the technology of printing from photographically produced plates was developed, making it possible for him to continue his work with Evans on the toy books. Of this process he writes in his autobiography, "The drawings were made on card in black and white and sent to London through the post to Mr. Evans, who had them photographed on to the wood and engraved, returning me the proofs to colour. This method of

working [is] now beginning to supersede the old practice of drawing direct on the block for the engraver."

Crane returned from Italy to find himself a household name in England, for in his absence his publishers had issued a series of his toy books in a popular single volume called *Walter Crane's Picturebook* (1874). Since it was the custom to sell the pictures to the publishers outright, Crane realized no profit from this new edition. Consequently, it was over a disagreement about royalties with Routledge that Crane started in a new direction, producing *The Baby's Opera, A Book of Old Rhymes with New Dresses* in 1877. This book, engraved and printed by Evans and published by Routledge, sold for five shillings, substantially more than the toy books. With colorful full-page pictures as well as marginal drawings, it is a compilation of thirty-six nursery rhymes and songs such as "Oranges and Lemons," "Little Jack Horner," and "King Cole." Despite its price it was an instant best-seller, showing that the market could bear more-ambitious works, and led to such books by Crane as *The Baby's Bouquet, A Fresh Bunch of Old Rhymes and Tunes* (1878) and *Baby's Own Aesop, Being the Fables Condensed in Rhyme* (1886), the latter with words by Crane's former master, William Linton. Another important collaboration began with Mary Molesworth's *Tell Me a Story,* published by Macmillan in 1875. During the next fifteen years Crane illustrated more than a

MANY HAPPY RETURNS OF THE DAY

AND BEATRICE FINDS SHE HAS
ARRIVED IN BIRTHDAY-LAND
TO HER GREAT JOY.

THE END.

Final page of "Beatrice's Voyage of Discovery," a manuscript book Crane wrote and illustrated for his daughter in 1879–1880
(courtesy of the Lilly Library, Indiana University)

dozen books by the prolific and popular Molesworth.

Crane's rambling five-hundred-page autobiography, *An Artist's Reminiscences* (1907), seems to note the buyer of every painting he sold and each eminent Victorian he met. Nevertheless, it is a valuable source of information about the author's life, his journeys, and nineteenth-century British society. It also records his friendships with Edward Burne-Jones, William Morris, Bernard Shaw, Oscar Wilde, and Ford Madox Brown, among others. As an artist Crane is particularly observant of the clothes and whiskers people wore, and as a Socialist he notes the poor treatment of factory workers, ship stokers, and black servants in Boston, as well as dis-

playing a keen feeling for the American labor movement and the Haymarket Riot. Living through a period of great change, he also describes the newness of encountering typewriters, telephones, motorcars, and tourists with portable lightweight cameras. The autobiography is amply illustrated with sonnets Crane wrote in honor of his friends and cartoons of his children and domestic life.

From the mid 1860s onward, the artist signed his pictures with a monogram or a rebus: a drawing of a small crane inside a *C*, with the initial *W* divided into two *V*s on either side. Crane noted the use of such an emblem by the fifteenth-century artist William Crane, yet his use of it probably owes more to the custom of using such signature designs by the Japanese and popularly used by fellow artists such as James Whistler, Aubrey Beardsley, and even the American illustrator W. W. Denslow.

In 1882 Crane illustrated *Household Stories from the Collection of the Brothers Grimm,* translated by his sister Lucy Crane. Published by Macmillan, the work is clearly an illustrator's project, since it contains a list of illustrations but no table of contents for the fifty-two fairy tales. The tales are illustrated in black and white, with headpieces and tailpieces and a decorated first letter; many have a full-page illustration with a blank page behind. Crane uses antique clothing for his characters, which, along with Lucy's quaint language and the old-fashioned black-and-white wood engravings, lends a sense of timelessness to the stories. The headpiece of "Rapunzel," for instance, shows a frieze in which the mature Rapunzel plays with her twin children while her blind husband wanders in the background, giving away the end of the story at the beginning. The tailpiece shows the witch's rampion, which gives the heroine her name, and the initial letter shows the father scooting backward into the garden to steal it. The casual reader is unlikely to remember or be aware of these elements, and they suggest a kind of reading requiring backtracking and study of details.

The full-page picture is the expected image of the prince climbing up Rapunzel's long, flowing hair, which here enwraps and holds him. The picture is largely filled in with doves and undulating trees, and a tapestry from the Arts and Crafts movement hangs out of the tower window. At the corners are emblems of the mutilating scissors and the female moon. The heroine awaits, her head bent in Pre-Raphaelite pose. The picture is marked with the Crane rebus as well as the name of the engraver, Swain. In his work Crane was ruled by a sense of the decorative (a word he often used), which he held in higher regard than might a modern artist. He wrote in *Line and Form,* (1900), "Beauty and character. – In these lies the gist of all design."

Crane's fame was growing, and Lewis Carroll proposed a collaboration, but Crane was unable to work on the project, Carroll's *Sylvie and Bruno* (1889), which was ultimately illustrated by Harry Furniss. Considering his efforts at organizing and leading artists and craftspeople, it is natural that Crane would turn his interests toward education. At the end of the century he revamped the curriculum as director of design at the Manchester School of Art and served as principal of the Royal College

of Art in South Kensington. Isobel Spencer notes that his books *The Bases of Design* (1898) and *Line and Form* were widely used as textbooks in British art classes until the middle of the twentieth century. Many of his books were aimed at educating younger readers, including *Multiplication Tables in Verse* (1867), *The Walter Crane Reader: First and Second Primers* (1899), and *The Golden Primer* (1884), which he produced with a professor of education and language from Saint Andrews University.

At the end of his life the artist received honors from Italy, France, and Germany, as well as his own country. Throughout his adult life Crane produced oil paintings and watercolors, submitting annually to the Royal Academy. His paintings, often on allegorical and mythological subjects, were criticized for their stiff figures and poor composition, and they did not enjoy the official recognition that his books and illustrations received.

Crane's wife died in January 1915, and the artist only lived another two months, dying in London on 14 March 1915 at the age of sixty-nine. Though he had received little formal training as an artist, Crane worked hard to gain acceptance for all aspects of his artistic endeavor, something which had evaded his father's grasp. Consequently, he felt his reputation suffered from his being categorized. In his autobiography he wrote, "and though a painter before I was a designer, I had been labelled 'Children's Books' or 'Arts and Crafts,' and it is preposterous for a man to expect to be recognized without his usual label – besides, it disturbs the commercial order of things."

References:
Rodney K. Engen, *Walter Crane as a Book Illustrator* (London: Academy Editions, 1975; New York: St. Martin's Press, 1975);

Greg Smith and Sarah Hyde, eds., *Walter Crane 1845–1915: Artist, Designer, and Socialist* (London: Humphries, 1989);

Isobel Spencer, *Walter Crane* (London: Studio Vista, 1975).

Papers:

Important collections of Walter Crane's letters and designs are located in the Caroline Miller Parker Collection in the Houghton Library, Harvard University; and the Catherine Tinker Patterson Collection in the Beinecke Rare Book and Manuscript Library, Yale University.

Maria Edgeworth

(1 January 1768 – 22 May 1849)

Adele M. Fasick
University of Toronto

See also the Edgeworth entries in *DLB 116: British Romantic Novelists, 1789–1832* and *DLB 159: British Short-Fiction Writers, 1800–1880.*

BOOKS: *Letters for Literary Ladies, to Which Is Added an Essay on the Noble Science of Self-Justification* (London: Printed for J. Johnson, 1795; corrected and enlarged, 1799; George Town: Published by Joseph Milligan, W. Cooper, printer, 1810);

The Parent's Assistant; or, Stories for Children (3 volumes, London: Printed for J. Johnson, 1796; expanded edition, 6 volumes, London: Printed for J. Johnson by G. Woodfall, 1800; 3 volumes, George Town: Published by Joseph Milligan, Dinsmore & Cooper, printers, 1809);

Practical Education, by Maria Edgeworth and Richard Lovell Edgeworth (2 volumes, London: Printed for J. Johnson, 1798; New York: Printed for G. F. Hopkins and Brown & Stansbury, 1801; revised edition, 3 volumes, London: Printed for J. Johnson, 1801); republished as *Essays on Practical Education,* 2 volumes (London: Printed for J. Johnson, 1811);

Castle Rackrent: An Hibernian Tale; Taken from the Facts, and from the Manners of the Irish Squires, before the Year 1782 (London: Printed for J. Johnson, 1800; revised, 1801; Boston: Printed & published by T. B. Wait & Sons, 1814);

Moral Tales for Young People, 5 volumes (London: Printed for J. Johnson, 1801; New York: Printed for W. B. Gilley, 1810);

Belinda, 3 volumes (London: Printed for J. Johnson, 1801); revised edition, 2 volumes, edited by Anna Laetitia Barbauld (London: Printed for F. C. & J. Rivington, 1810; Boston: Printed for Wells & Lilly, 1814; corrected and improved edition, London: Printed for R. Hunter, 1821);

Early Lessons, 10 parts in 5 volumes (London: Printed for J. Johnson, 1801–1802) – comprises *Harry and Lucy,* parts 1–2; *Rosamond,*

Maria Edgeworth (engraving after a drawing by Joseph Slater)

parts 3–5; *Frank,* parts 6–9; "The Little Dog Trusty," "The Orange Man," and "The Cherry Orchard," part 10; 4 volumes (Philadelphia: Printed for J. Maxwell, 1821);

Essays on Irish Bulls, by Maria Edgeworth and Richard Lovell Edgeworth (London: Printed for J. Johnson, 1802; New York: Printed by J. Sevaine, 1803);

Popular Tales (3 volumes, London: Printed for J. Johnson by C. Mercer, 1804; 2 volumes, Philadelphia: Printed & sold by James Humphreys, 1804);

The Modern Griselda: A Tale (London: Printed for J. Johnson, 1805; corrected edition, London: Printed for J. Johnson, 1805; George Town:

Published by Joseph Milligan, W. Cooper, printer, 1810; corrected edition, London: Printed for J. Johnson, 1813; corrected edition, London: Printed for R. Hunter, 1819);

Leonora, 2 volumes (London: Printed for J. Johnson, 1806; New York: I. Riley, 1806);

Essays on Professional Education, by Maria Edgeworth and Richard Lovell Edgeworth (London: Printed for J. Johnson, 1809);

Tales of Fashionable Life, 6 volumes; volumes 1–3: "Ennui," "Almeria," "Madame de Fleury," "The Dun," and "Manoeuvring" (London: Printed for J. Johnson, 1809); 2 volumes (George Town: Printed for Joseph Milligan, 1809); volumes 4–6: "Vivian," "Emilie de Coulanges," and "The Absentee" (London: Printed for J. Johnson, 1812);

Patronage (4 volumes, London: Printed for J. Johnson, 1814 [i.e., 1813]; 3 volumes, Philadelphia: Published by Moses Thomas, J. Maxwell, printer, 1814); revised as volumes 11 and 12 of *Tales and Miscellaneous Pieces,* 14 volumes (London: Printed for R. Hunter and Baldwin, Cradock & Joy, 1825);

Continuation of Early Lessons, 2 volumes (London: Printed for J. Johnson, 1814; Boston: Printed for Bradford & Read, 1815);

Comic Dramas in Three Acts (London: Printed for R. Hunter, 1817; Philadelphia: Thomas Dobson & Son, 1817) – comprises *Love and Law; The Two Guardians; The Rose, The Thistle, and the Shamrock;*

Harrington: A Tale and *Ormond: A Tale* (3 volumes, London: Printed for R. Hunter and Baldwin, Cradock & Joy, 1817; 2 volumes, New York: Printed for Kirk & Mercein, 1817; Philadelphia: Published by Moses Thomas and Van Winkle & Wiley, New York, 1817; corrected edition, London: Printed for R. Hunter and Baldwin, Cradock & Joy, 1817);

Rosamond: A Sequel to Early Lessons, 2 volumes (London: Printed for R. Hunter, 1821; Philadelphia: Printed for J. Maxwell, 1821);

Frank: A Sequel to Frank in Early Lessons (3 volumes, London: Printed for R. Hunter, 1822; 2 volumes, New York: Printed for William B. Gilley, 1822);

Harry and Lucy Concluded: Being the Last Part of Early Lessons (4 volumes, London: Printed for R. Hunter and Baldwin, Cradock & Joy, 1825; 3 volumes, Boston: Printed for Munroe & Francis, 1825; corrected edition, 4 volumes, London: Printed for R. Hunter and Baldwin, Cradock & Joy, 1827; revised and corrected

edition, London: Printed for R. Hunter and Baldwin, Cradock & Joy, 1837);

Little Plays for Children, volume 7 of *The Parent's Assistant* (London: Printed for R. Hunter, 1827); republished as *Little Plays . . . Being an Additional Volume of The Parent's Assistant* (Philadelphia: Thomas T. Ash, 1827) – comprises *The Grinding Organ, Dumb Andy, The Dame School Holiday;*

Garry Owen; or, The Snow-Woman (Salem, Mass.: John M. and W. & S. B. Ives, 1829); republished with *Poor Bob the Chimney-Sweeper* (London: Printed for John Murray, 1832);

Helen: A Tale (3 volumes, London: Printed for R. Bentley, 1834; 2 volumes, Philadelphia: Carey, Lea & Blanchard / Boston: Allen & Ticknor, 1834);

Orlandino, in Chambers' Library for Young People (Edinburgh: Printed for W. & R. Chambers, 1848; Boston: Gould, Kendall & Lincoln, 1848);

The Most Unfortunate Day of My Life: Being a Hitherto Unpublished Story, Together with the Purple Jar and Other Stories (London: Cobden-Sanderson, 1931).

Editions: *Tales and Miscellaneous Pieces,* 14 volumes (London: Printed for R. Hunter and Baldwin, Cradock & Joy, 1825);

Tales and Novels (18 volumes, London: Printed for Baldwin & Cradock, 1832–1833; 9 volumes, New York: Harper, 1832–1834);

Tales and Novels (9 volumes, London: Printed for Whitaker, Simpkin, Marshall, 1848; 10 volumes, New York: Harper, 1852);

Tales and Novels, 10 volumes (London: Routledge, 1893).

OTHER: "An Essay on the Noble Science of Self-Justification," in *Letters for Literary Ladies,* anonymous (London: J. Johnson, 1795);

"The Mental Thermometer," in *The Juvenile Library,* volume 2 (London: Printed for T. Hurst, 1801), pp. 378–384;

"Little Dominick," in *Wild Roses; or, Cottage Tales* (London: Printed for T. Marden, 1807), pp. 53–60;

Mary Leadbeater, *Cottage Dialogues Among the Irish Peasantry, with Notes and a Preface by Maria Edgeworth* (London: Printed for J. Johnson, 1811);

Charles Sneyd Edgeworth, *Memoirs of the Abbé Edgeworth; Continuing His Narrative of the Last Hours of Louis XVI,* revised by Maria Edgeworth (London: Printed for R. Hunter, 1815);

Richard Lovell Edgeworth, *Readings on Poetry,* preface and last chapter by Maria Edgeworth (London: Printed for R. Hunter, 1816; corrected edition, London: Printed for R. Hunter, 1816; Boston: Published by Wells & Lilly and sold by Van Winkle & Wiley, New York, and by M. Carey, Philadelphia, 1816);

Memoirs of Richard Lovell Edgeworth, Esq.; Begun by Himself and Concluded by His Daughter, Maria Edgeworth, 2 volumes, volume 2 by Maria Edgeworth (London: Printed for R. Hunter, 1820; corrected edition, London: Printed for R. Hunter, 1821; Boston: Wells & Lilly, 1821);

"On French Oaths," in *The Amulet: A Christian and Literary Remembrancer,* volume 2, edited by S. C. Hall (London: W. Baynes, 1827), pp. 297–303;

"Garry-Owen; or, The Snow-Woman," in *The Christmas Box,* edited by T. Crofton Croker (London: Ebers / Edinburgh: Blackwood, 1829).

SELECTED PERIODICAL PUBLICATIONS –
UNCOLLECTED: "The Stranger in Ireland, or, a Tour in the Southern and Western Parts of that Country in the Year 1805, by John Carr, Esq.," anonymous review by Maria Edgeworth and Richard Lovell Edgeworth, *Edinburgh Review,* 10 (April 1807): 40–60;

"The Freed Negro: A Poem in Four Stanzas," *La Belle Assemblée: Being Bell's Court and Fashionable Magazine,* 25 (April 1822): 128;

"Thoughts on Bores," anonymous, in *Janus, or, The Edinburgh Almanack* (Edinburgh: Oliver & Boyd, 1826);

"Two Unpublished Manuscripts by Maria Edgeworth," edited by Christina Colvin, *Review of English Literature,* 8 (October 1967): 53–61.

Maria Edgeworth was one of the most popular writers of the early nineteenth century. Although her fame during her lifetime was based on her adult novels, especially those set in Ireland, Edgeworth also published many influential stories for children, and these stories outlasted her adult fiction. In writing for children, Edgeworth tried to demonstrate how children could be educated for a useful and moral life. Unlike some of the other didactic writers of children's stories, Edgeworth was able to make her child characters realistic and natural. Her stories were appealing enough to be kept in print through the nineteenth century and into the first half of the twentieth century.

Maria Edgeworth was born on 1 January 1768 (the date is sometimes given as 1767, but Marilyn Butler and Christina Colvin establish 1768 as the correct date) in Oxfordshire at the home of her maternal grandfather, Paul Elers. Her father, Richard Lovell Edgeworth, the son of an Anglo-Irish family, had married Anna Maria Elers while he was still a student at Oxford. The young couple were not happy together, and Maria's early years were spent mostly with her grandparents and her mother's aunts. When Maria was six years old her mother died, leaving her father free to marry Honora Sneyd. The family then returned to Ireland and lived at Edgeworthstown in the county of Longford, where the Edgeworth family had been settled for more than two hundred years.

At the age of eight Maria was sent to school in England, but both her father and her stepmother continued to play a large part in her education through regular correspondence. Honora died in 1780 when Maria was twelve. She had been ill for some time and had advised her husband to marry her sister. He moved quickly to carry out his wife's wishes, and Elizabeth Sneyd became Maria's next stepmother. The choice was a happy one. Maria and her brothers and sisters soon loved their new stepmother.

Maria continued at school in England until 1782, when she moved permanently to Ireland. At fifteen she was able to assist her father in running the family estate. Richard Edgeworth believed in letting his family know all about the business of the estate, so meetings with tenants and workmen were often held in the common sitting room. This experience no doubt helped Maria gain a strong sense of everyday life in Ireland and to understand the attitudes and feelings of working-class people.

Both Mr. and Mrs. Edgeworth believed in educating children by letting them share in the life and work of the household. As the family grew (Elizabeth had nine children), Maria played a growing role in educating the children. She would amuse the younger children by telling stories and then writing them out on a slate. The children's questions and comments helped her to shape the tales, some of which were later incorporated into her published works. Her father took great interest in these stories, and Maria would submit sketches for his approval before she wrote full versions.

In the 1790s Edgeworth published her first works: *Letters for Literary Ladies* (1795); *The Parent's Assistant* (1796); and *Practical Education* (1798), which was written with her father. Her stepmother died in 1797, and six months later her father married Eliza-

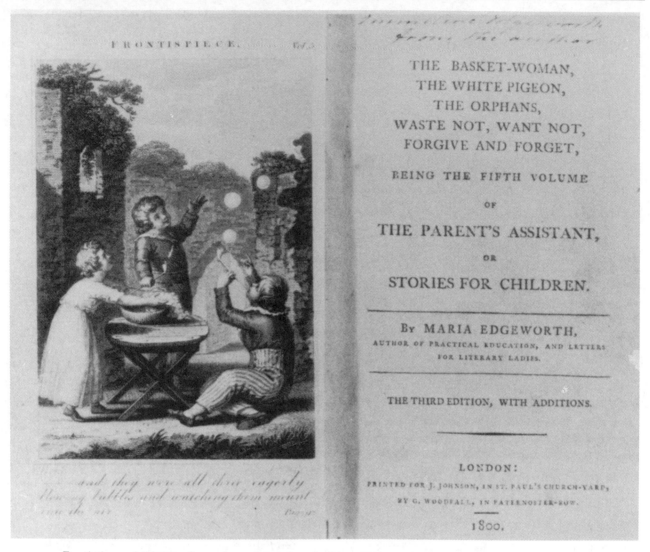

Frontispiece and title page for a volume of the enlarged edition of Edgeworth's first collection of children's stories

beth Beaufort, who was a year younger than Maria. This youthful stepmother might well have caused Maria some pangs of jealousy, but within a short time the two were close friends. Maria retained her central position in the family, helping to educate the children, writing with her father, and assisting in the management of the estate. Her association with her father in his work and writing was the major intellectual focus of her life. Her children's stories grew directly out of her life and experience and reflected the family values of Edgeworthstown: a belief in rationality, a faith in the beneficial influence of sensible and concerned parents, and an appreciation of the intrinsic fascination of the real world.

Edgeworth's earliest stories from *The Parent's Assistant* were clearly aimed at moral development. The tales are populated with heroes and heroines whose virtuous deeds are rewarded and with villains who are punished at the end. In "Lazy Lawrence" the hardworking widow's son, Jem, achieves fortunes, while Lawrence, who always seeks to avoid work, becomes involved with criminals and is sentenced to a month in Bridewell prison. "Simple Susan" (1798), one of Edgeworth's best-known stories, presents an almost perfect heroine, beloved by everyone except for Lawyer Case and his ill-bred children. Susan is sorely tried, but in the end her virtues are rewarded. The kindness she has shown to others is returned, and all her problems are resolved.

Edgeworth's more characteristic stories, however, especially in the volumes that followed *The Parent's Assistant,* allow wrongdoers to repent rather than suffer punishment. The result of this repentance is acceptance into the society of the family community. Cooperation is stressed far more than competition. "The Bracelets" (written, 1788; published, 1796) is a subtle and complex story of two friends, Cecilia and Leonora, who are the foremost candidates for the prize of a bracelet awarded to the best worker at their school. Cecilia wins the cherished prize, but her day of triumph is marred when she thoughtlessly breaks another child's toy; she eventually suggests that at the end of the month another prize be given, this one for the most amiable girl.

Edgeworth characterizes the two girls as virtuous in different ways: "Leonora was the most anxious to avoid what was wrong, Cecilia the most ambitious to do what was right." Each girl strives to win the bracelet; Leonora is unfailingly kind and therefore wins "passive love" from the girls, but Cecilia being more active and energetic inspires "active love" by her generosity. Edgeworth compares Cecilia's virtue, which is more suited to a man than a woman, to Leonora's more appropriately female attributes. Both types of virtue are valued, and the vote for the most amiable is a tie. In the end the two girls are reconciled, but the schoolmistress has the final say on what constitutes female virtue: "Remember, that many of our sex are capable of great efforts, of making what they call great sacrifices to virtue or to friendship; but few treat their friends with habitual gentleness, or uniformly conduct themselves with prudence and good sense."

Maria Edgeworth wrote the first of her adult novels, *Castle Rackrent* (1800), without the help of her father, although she continued to collaborate with him on stories for children. Occasionally these stories are linked in a series, as in the Rosamond, Frank, and Harry and Lucy sections of *Early Lessons* (1801–1802). These tales were meant for young children just learning to read and to reason. For older children she wrote longer stories, many of which appeared in the five volumes of her *Moral Tales for Young People* (1801).

The character of Rosamond, said to be based on the author, is Edgeworth's most memorable achievement. Rosamond makes her first appearance in the oft-reprinted "The Purple Jar" (from *Early Lessons*), in which the little girl asks her mother to buy her the beautiful purple jar she sees in a shop window rather than replace her worn-out shoes. The mother agrees but warns Rosamond that she will have to wear her old shoes for another month. When Rosamond returns home and tries to put her flowers in the purple jar, she discovers that the jar is only a plain glass one filled with colored water. For the rest of the month Rosamond must bear with her

worn-out shoes and even misses going on a visit to the glasshouse with her father and brother because of them. By the story's end Rosamond regrets her choice and proclaims, "I am sure, no, not quite sure, but I hope I shall be wiser another time."

As the series progresses Rosamond grows in wisdom and prudence. In "Rosamond's Day of Misfortunes" she hates getting up on a chilly morning and is convinced that it will be a day of misfortune. Her ever-reasonable mother helps Rosamond see that her misfortunes are of her own making. She is encouraged to go outside and run around to make herself warm. There she finds a robin, which she brings into the house to feed. She would like to keep it in a cage but is persuaded by her sister, Laura, that the bird would be better off outdoors. Reluctantly Rosamond lets the bird go and is rewarded when it returns to the window day after day to be fed. The lesson Rosamond learns is that by doing something unpleasant she may gain much greater pleasure in the end.

In story after story Rosamond gradually learns the virtues that her parents hope to instill in all their children. She learns to plan ahead, planting seeds and bulbs at the appropriate times so that she will have flowers in the spring. She learns to be kind to all creatures, even the rabbit who eats the flowers in her garden. After taking an irrational dislike to an elderly woman visitor who has a deformed finger, Rosamond discovers that the woman was injured while saving her granddaughter in a fire. Rosamond acknowledges that she should not make quick judgments about people.

As the stories progress Rosamond grows older and is able to participate in family outings, such as a visit to a cotton factory in "The Silver Cup." Rosamond is considered too young to understand all of the processes involved, but she is encouraged to go around the plant in a logical order, rather than flitting from one place to another, so that she can learn as much as possible. In another story, "The India Cabinet," Rosamond is shown a cabinet containing shells and other curiosities. Although tempted to examine the wonders of the cabinet by herself, Rosamond is persuaded by her mother that she will enjoy them more if she waits for the owner, Mrs. Egerton, to explain them. Once again her restraint leads to greater pleasure.

Although Edgeworth stresses the unfashionable virtues of prudence, reason, and restraint in these stories, her tone is neither oppressive nor dull. Rosamond and her two brothers are lively, believable children, and her sister, although a paragon of virtue, is kind, understanding, and never self-righteous. Their parents spend a great deal of time with the children and seem to enjoy talking with them and participating in activities, but they set limits. The stories seem to be an idealized portrait of the Edgeworth household – without the overwhelming number of children, maiden aunts, and other distractions that must have been part of life at Edgeworthstown. It is easy to understand how the Rosamond stories with their gentle adventures and everyday activities could appeal to generations of children in England and North America.

In "The Cherry Orchard" (1801) disagreeable Owen is ostracized because he kicks sand on the other children and then in a fit of anger tramples the cherries they have bought. When the children have a chance to earn money by plaiting straw for hats, all of the children except Owen work together. Owen must work alone and thus does not complete his work in time to go to the cherry orchard. After his promise to become better tempered, the children test his resolve and then decide to help him. His reward is admission to the cherry orchard and to the social group. Owen, like all of the children in Edgeworth's tales, is shown in the midst of family and friends. The happiness of the group is essential to the happiness of individual members. Competition is scarcely mentioned, while cooperation is highly praised. Children who are good-natured are well liked by other children; those who are ill-tempered or dishonest are disliked until they reform.

Edgeworth's stories for older readers are longer and more complex than the Rosamond and Frank stories. While still emphasizing the importance of family life and the primacy of relationships within the family, these tales introduce a broader social context. "The Prussian Vase" in *Moral Tales for Young People,* for example, is designed to demonstrate the virtues of the British judicial system. The story tells how Frederick II of Prussia moved several manufacturers from Dresden to Berlin in order to set up porcelain works there. Sophia Mansfeld, who has been forced to leave her elderly parents and her lover, languishes and is unable to work. She wins a contest by making the finest Prussian vase and is free to leave until Frederick discovers that the inscription on the bottom of the vase includes the words "the tyrant." He orders Laniska (who had written the inscription for the illiterate Sophia) arrested but is finally prevailed upon to permit a trial by jury. Upon closely examining the circumstances under which the vase was moved from the workshop to the kiln, it is revealed that Laniska is not guilty. The story exemplifies the value of ra-

tional thinking as a way of solving problems. Except for some objectionable anti-Semitism, it might hold its own today.

Edgeworth's female characters also move into the more complex world of adult life. In the second part of "Mademoiselle Panache" (in *Early Lessons*) two eighteen-year-old girls are preparing for their first season as marriageable young women. Helen Temple has been carefully educated by her mother, while Lady Augusta still has her French governess, Mademoiselle Panache, because her mother has been too indolent to dismiss her. Lady Augusta's family is visited by twenty-one-year-old Lord George and his tutor Mr. Dashwood, while Mr. Mountague visits the Temples and is quite attached to the kind Helen Temple. Lady Augusta flirts with Lord George and wins his affections, but in the long run her affectations and flirtations disgust him, and he withdraws his attentions. Augusta becomes entangled with the vulgar and ambitious Dashwood and eventually elopes with him. Only then is her mother awakened to the disaster she has caused by her reliance on Mademoiselle Panache. In contrast, the years of careful, patient teaching of Helen Temple have resulted in what Edgeworth sees as the ideal relationship between a parent and her adult daughter.

In Maria Edgeworth's well-ordered world, parents, like children, are invariably rewarded for doing right and punished for doing wrong. It is a comforting world, and there is little wonder that thousands of people enjoyed reading about it, but Edgeworth did not take a sentimental view of life. The trials her characters endure are difficult. Their problems are not solved by a miraculous fairy godmother. Children have to work long and hard to achieve success, as with Simple Susan, who spends hours baking bread and carrying it around the community to sell. Girls such as Helen Temple spend years learning how to behave, curbing their tempers and learning to be kind and patient with the poor, old, and sick. Even young children have to pay for their mistakes, as when Rosamond limps around in broken shoes for a month. Edgeworth's world is one of justice, not of easy triumphs.

After her father's death in 1817, Edgeworth wrote less. She completed her father's memoirs, but it was not until 1822 that she wrote more children's stories, producing sequels about Rosamond, Frank, and Harry and Lucy. Edgeworth's productivity was great, but it becomes remarkable when the circumstances of her writing are noted. She worked in the common sitting room surrounded by the interruptions of family life. The desk at which she worked for many years was inscribed by her father two years before his death with the following words: "On this humble desk were written all the numerous works of my daughter, Maria Edgeworth, in the common sitting-room of my family . . . while endeavoring to inform and instruct others, she improved and amused her own mind and gratified her heart, which I do believe is better than her head." In addition to her published works, Edgeworth wrote many letters, some of which were collected and published after her death. They give a vivid picture of life in Ireland and her tours of Europe. She remained active in running the family estate, and her management was instrumental in saving the estate from the debts incurred by her brother Lovell, who inherited it from their father. During the last years of her life, Edgeworth spent much time and effort trying to mitigate the effects of the Irish famine. She was active and busy until a few days before her death on 22 May 1849.

Edgeworth's writings were very influential. Critics have suggested that Jane Austen modeled some of her characters after those of Edgeworth's heroines. Walter Scott acknowledged his debt when he declared that *Castle Rackrent* inspired him to write his novels of Scotland. Maria Edgeworth moved the didactic tale for children out of the realm of sermon and into the world of literature. She started with an attempt to demonstrate her father's educational theories, but her stories were far more than educational treatises. She created a world that children could recognize, populated by characters who felt and thought as real children did. Her legacy lives on in the best of children's literature today.

Edgeworth in 1841

Letters:

The Life and Letters of Maria Edgeworth, 2 volumes, edited by Augustus J. C. Hare (London: E. Arnold, 1894);

Maria Edgeworth, Chosen Letters, edited by F. V. Barry (London: Cape, 1931);

Romilly-Edgeworth Letters, 1813–1818, edited by Samuel Henry Romilly (London: John Murray, 1936);

Letters of Maria Edgeworth and Anna Letitia Barbauld: Selected from the Lushington Papers, edited by Walter Sidney Scott (London: Golden Cockerel Press, 1953);

The Education of the Heart: The Correspondence of Rachel Mordecai Lazarus and Maria Edgeworth, edited by Edgar E. MacDonald (Chapel Hill: University of North Carolina Press, 1977);

Maria Edgeworth in France and Switzerland: Selections from the Edgeworth Family Letters, edited by

Christina Colvin (New York & Oxford: Oxford University Press/Clarendon Press, 1979).

Bibliography:

Bertha Coolidge Slade, *Maria Edgeworth, 1767–1849: A Bibliographical Tribute* (London: Constable, 1937).

Biographies:

Grace Atkinson Oliver, *A Study of Maria Edgeworth: With Notices of her Father and Friends* (Boston: A. Williams, 1882);

Helen Zimmern, *Maria Edgeworth* (London: W. H. Allen, 1883);

Emily Lawless, *Maria Edgeworth* (London: Macmillan, 1904);

Isabel Constance Clarke, *Maria Edgeworth: Her Family and Friends* (London: Hutchinson, 1950);

Elisabeth Inglis-Jones, *The Great Maria: A Portrait of Maria Edgeworth* (London: Faber & Faber, 1959);

Desmond Clarke, *The Ingenious Mr. Edgeworth* (London: Oldbourne, 1965);

Marilyn Butler, *Maria Edgeworth: A Literary Biography* (Oxford: Clarendon Press, 1972).

References:

Joanne Altieri, "Style and Purpose of Maria Edgeworth's Fiction," *Nineteenth Century Fiction,* 23 (December 1968): 265–278;

Marilyn Butler and Christina Colvin, "A Revised Date of Birth for Maria Edgeworth," *Notes and Queries,* 18 (September 1971): 339–340;

Donald Davie, *The Heyday of Sir Walter Scott* (London: Routledge & Kegan Paul, 1961), pp. 65–77;

Tom Dunne, *Maria Edgeworth and the Colonial Mind* (Cork: University College, 1984);

Thomas Flanagan, *The Irish Novelists, 1800–1850* (New York: Columbia University Press, 1958);

Kathleen L. Fowler, "Apricots, Raspberries, and Susan Price! Susan Price!: Mansfield Park and Maria Edgeworth," *Persuasion: Journal of the Jane Austen Society of North America,* 13 (December 1991): 28–32;

O. Elizabeth McWhorter Harden, *Maria Edgeworth* (Boston: Twayne, 1984);

Harden, *Maria Edgeworth's Art of Prose Fiction* (The Hague: Mouton, 1971);

Michael Hurst, *Maria Edgeworth and the Public Scene* (Coral Gables: University of Miami Press, 1969);

Elizabeth Kowaleski-Wallace, *Their Fathers' Daughters: Hannah More, Maria Edgeworth, and Patriarchal Complicity* (New York: Oxford University Press, 1991);

Emily Lawless, *Maria Edgeworth* (London: Macmillan, 1904);

Patrick Murray, *Maria Edgeworth: A Study of the Novelist* (Cork: Mercier Press, 1971);

Mitzi Myers, "The Dilemmas of Gender as Double-Voiced Narrative, or, Maria Edgeworth Mothers the Bildungsroman," in *The Idea of the Novel in the Eighteenth Century,* edited by Robert W. Uphaus (East Lansing, Mich.: Colleagues, 1988), pp. 67–96;

Myers, "Romancing the Moral Tale: Maria Edgeworth and the Problematics of Pedagogy," in *Romanticism and Children's Literature in Nineteenth Century England,* edited by James Holt McGavran Jr. (Athens: University of Georgia Press, 1991), pp. 96–128;

Myers, "Socializing Rosamond: Educational Ideology and Fictional Form," *Children's Literature Association Quarterly,* 14 (Summer 1989): 52–58;

Percy Howard Newby, *Maria Edgeworth* (Denver: Allan Swallow, 1950);

James Newcomer, *Maria Edgeworth* (Lewisburg: Bucknell University Press, 1973);

Newcomer, *Maria Edgeworth the Novelist* (Fort Worth: Texas Christian University Press, 1967);

Alice Paterson, *The Edgeworths: A Study of Later Eighteenth Century Education* (London: University Tutorial Press, 1914).

Papers:

The National Library of Ireland, Dublin, is the major repository of correspondence from Maria Edgeworth and members of her family as well as family manuscripts. Correspondence with her Swiss correspondents is in the Bibliothèque Publique et Universitaire, Geneva.

Juliana Horatia Ewing

(3 August 1841 – 13 May 1885)

Patricia Demers
University of Alberta

See also the Ewing entry in *DLB 21: Victorian Novelists Before 1885.*

BOOKS: *Melchior's Dream and Other Tales* (London: Bell & Daldy, 1862);

Mrs. Overtheway's Remembrances (London: Bell & Daldy, 1869);

The Brownies and Other Tales (London: Bell & Daldy, 1870);

A Flat Iron for a Farthing (London: Bell, 1872);

Lob Lie-by-the-fire, or The Luck of Lingborough, and Other Tales (London: Bell, 1874);

Six to Sixteen (London: Bell, 1875);

Jan of the Windmill; A Story of the Plains (London: Bell, 1876);

A Great Emergency and Other Tales (London: Bell, 1877);

We and the World (London: Bell, 1880);

Old-Fashioned Fairy Tales (London: Bell, 1882);

Brothers of Pity and Other Tales of Beasts and Men (London: Society for Promoting Christian Knowledge, 1882);

Blue and Red, or The Discontented Lobster (London: Society for Promoting Christian Knowledge, 1883);

The Dolls' Wash; Rhymes (London: Society for Promoting Christian Knowledge, 1883);

A Week Spent in the Glass Pond by the Great Water Beetle (London: Wells, Darton, 1883);

Master Fritz; Rhymes (London: Society for Promoting Christian Knowledge, 1883);

Jackanapes (London: Society for Promoting Christian Knowledge, 1883);

Our Garden; Rhymes (London: Society for Promoting Christian Knowledge, 1883);

A Soldier's Children; Rhymes (London: Society for Promoting Christian Knowledge, 1883);

A Sweet Little Dear; Rhymes (London: Society for Promoting Christian Knowledge, 1883);

Three Little Nest-Birds; Rhymes (London: Society for Promoting Christian Knowledge, 1883);

The Blue Bells on the Lea (London: Society for Promoting Christian Knowledge, 1884);

Daddy Darwin's Dovecote (London: Society for Promoting Christian Knowledge, 1884);

Dolls' Housekeeping; Rhymes (London: Society for Promoting Christian Knowledge, 1884);

Little Boys and Wooden Horses; Rhymes (London: Society for Promoting Christian Knowledge, 1884);

Papa Poodle and Other Pets; Rhymes (London: Society for Promoting Christian Knowledge, 1884);

Tongues in Trees; Rhymes (London: Society for Promoting Christian Knowledge, 1884);

"Touch Him If You Dare": A Tale of the Hedge; Rhymes (London: Society for Promoting Christian Knowledge, 1884);

Poems of Child Life and Country Life (London: Society for Promoting Christian Knowledge, 1885);

The Story of a Short Life (London: Society for Promoting Christian Knowledge, 1885);

Mary's Meadow and Other Tales (London: Society for Promoting Christian Knowledge, 1886);

Dandelion Clocks and Other Tales (London: Society for Promoting Christian Knowledge, 1887);

The Peace Egg and A Christmas Mumming Play (London: Society for Promoting Christian Knowledge, 1887);

Snap-Dragons, and Old Father Christmas (London: Society for Promoting Christian Knowledge, 1888);

Verses for Children, 3 volumes (London: Society for Promoting Christian Knowledge, 1888);

Works, 18 volumes (London: Society for Promoting Christian Knowledge, 1894–1896).

Juliana Horatia Ewing was a storyteller par excellence. Writing only for children and concentrating on the experiences of youngsters in either the nursery or the schoolroom, Ewing showed a natural sympathy and grace reminiscent of Hans Christian Andersen, an exquisite and careful attention to the details of family life, and a deep identification with her characters. No aspect of a child's experience was too small or insignificant for Ewing; she tended to favor pensive, aesthetically inclined, tractable, but high-spirited central characters who enjoy gardening, animals, and adventure. Ewing's upbringing in a staunch Church of England circle and her unquestioned fidelity to Anglicanism never translated into wearying didacticism in her tales, verse, and full-length novels. As a clergyman's daughter who became a soldier's wife, Ewing also wrote with firsthand knowledge and real affection about the military; life in a camp bungalow, the frequency of moves from one station to another, and the continuing efforts to beautify new surroundings and create a garden were elements of her experience reflected in her writing.

There is a delicacy about Ewing's tales, as there was about the author, who because of a childhood susceptibility to quinsy (inflammed tonsils) was dubbed by her mother the "Countess of Homeopathy." She believed firmly in the law of reticence; aware of "the blunder of throwing away powder and shot," she insisted that "a real artist needs strong warrants of Conscience when he dips into . . . the highest hopes, the deepest sufferings of humanity." However, although Ewing did not shy away from these heights and depths in criticizing authoritarian or negligent adults and inadequate educational systems in her family stories, she was no joyless crusader. Sparkling wit, geniality, and an unshakable belief in human goodness mark all her work.

She won a loyal following among contemporary writers and artists for the young and those of the next generation influenced by her; John Ruskin was a regular subscriber to *Aunt Judy's Magazine,* the periodical started by Ewing's mother, in which most of Ewing's tales first appeared; Charlotte Mary Yonge was an admirer and an early supporter of her work; and Randolph Caldecott, who agreed to illustrate some of her work, observed that Ewing possessed "a larger bump of imagination than falls to the skulls of most critics." In the wake of Ewing's success, Louisa Molesworth considered her books to be "universally loved," and Rudyard Kipling admitted having almost memorized whole stories by Ewing, while Arnold Bennett was convinced that Kipling's portraits of military life owed a great deal to his having read Ewing as a child.

Born on 3 August 1841, the second of the eight surviving children of Dr. Alfred Gatty, vicar of Ecclesfield, and Margaret (Scott) Gatty, the daughter of Nelson's chaplain, Juliana Horatia Gatty was a true child of the manse. The life of the Ecclesfield vicarage, with its High Church principles, family loyalties, and middle-class prejudices, was the first and one of the most prevailing influences on her work. Juliana and her sisters were educated at home by their mother; the boys were sent to public schools (Eton, Winchester, Marlborough, and Charterhouse). "Julie," as her siblings called her, was a natural leader. Her sister Horatia Katherine Frances Eden pictured Julie as "at once the projector and manager of all our nursery doings."

As reflections of what she knew best, the responsibilities of family life loom large in Ewing's first stories. Throughout her writing career she stressed the importance of family and friendly mentors and the transformational potential of special or instructive experiences. She was also fond of the device of nesting a story within a story, a technique at which she became expert. Thanks to her mother's reputation, Ewing gained an entrée to Yonge's magazine, *Monthly Packet,* where her first stories, "A Bit of Green," "The Blackbird's Nest," and "Melchior's Dream," were published (in July, August, and December 1861).

From the beginning, amid the solemn moral trappings of these tales, Ewing was distinguished as a fine storyteller who developed fully the emotional life of her characters. The doctor's son in "A Bit of Green," whose plans for a vacation in the country have been thwarted by his father's busy schedule, learns a valuable lesson by visiting one of his father's patients in the slums. Bill, a consumptive cripple who has never been outside the city, lives in a stark and ugly room; "but through the glass panes that were left, in full glory streamed the sun, and in the midst of the blaze stood a pot of musk in full bloom." The flowers and fragrance of this bit of green leave the once ill-humored narrator "lost in admiration." Ewing likely assimilated the paradigm of the privileged child learning from the experience of helping the less fortunate from the sentimental Evangelical novels of Mary Louisa Charlesworth, especially *Ministering Children* (1854). Although Ewing presents the moral about "the grace of Thankfulness," especially after Bill "was transplanted into a heavenly garden," without much subtlety, she succeeds in creating a believable child narrator.

The girl narrator of "The Blackbird's Nest" is similarly credible: she finds three birds and imagines that she will "walk about with them on [her] shoulders like Goody Twoshoes, and be admired by everybody." The curate tries to dissuade her, and when she discovers her pets "cold and dead," he helps to console her by relating an incident of his own youthful presumptuousness. Ewing succeeds in meshing fancy with noninsistent mentoring.

An adult friend and a story within a story both figure in "Melchior's Dream," but this narrative — the most refined of the early trio — is expansive and nuanced, allowing a young boy fed up with his siblings to journey into the future and preview their various torments. The lad quickly feels the point of the story about his alter ego, admitting, "it hit me rather hard" and confessing, "I want to say that though I didn't mean all I said about being an only son, (when a fellow gets put out he doesn't know what he means), yet I know I was quite wrong, and the story is quite right." Christian moralizing, unobtrusive yet scripturally sound and therefore appealing to both High Church and chapel tastes, concludes "Melchior's Dream," which alludes to "a bet-

ter Home than any earthly one, and a Family that shall never be divided."

Yonge's *Monthly Packet* published two more stories by Ewing: "The Yew Lane Ghosts" (1865) and "The Brownies" (1865). The former displays a terrific capacity for creating suspense, a feature Ewing chose not to develop in her later work. Although she offered no explanation for not continuing in this vein, speculations include her possible discomfort with stage-managing the supernatural and with almost unregenerate malevolence. When the friends of a lad who is being terrorized by a village bully rally round to help him, they manage, with the help of chemicals, to produce their own "scenic effects." They succeed in frightening Bully Tom into penitence by creating a grotesque, headless apparition.

Confining its effects to the domestic sphere, "The Brownies," dedicated to "my very dear and honoured Mother," is not nearly as horrific. A poor tailor's idle sons become true helpers and are mistaken for Brownies, "a race of tiny beings who . . . take up their abode with some worthy couple . . . and take little troubles out of hands full of great anxieties."

Two major sources of power and agency in Ewing's literary life were her mother and her husband. As a bookish young woman, Margaret Gatty had made presents to friends of her own illuminated and translated versions of Dante. Even as the mother of a large family, she pursued her scientific interest in varieties of seaweed. Her parables, allegories, and tales do not hesitate to instruct and moralize. Quickly realizing the superior literary ability of her daughter, she encouraged Julie from the outset. *Aunt Judy's Magazine,* so called after the family nickname for Juliana, was the main outlet for most of Julie's stories. It was also a needed source of income for the Gatty ménage, which could not exist on the vicar's scanty salary. Ewing eventually shared her mother's pecuniary anxieties too, since both women ended up paying the debts incurred by their husbands.

Besides being influenced by her mother's tastes and talents for writing and translating and understanding the need of these activities to pay for her brothers' school fees, Julie followed another family tradition in facing and surmounting opposition to her marriage plans. Just as the suitors of Mrs. Scott and Mrs. Gatty had been rejected initially, so too Maj. Alexander "Rex" Ewing, a soldier in the commissariat and ten years her senior, was not immediately welcomed by the Gattys. Julie, by contrast, was rhapsodic about her fiancé, confiding to a correspondent in December 1866: "A beautiful

The south screen of Ecclesfield Church, where Ewing's father served as vicar

musician – good linguist – well read, etc. – a dab at meteorology, photography, awfully fond of dogs, good rider, finally a high free mason (a knight Templar) and . . . a *mesmerist!* . . . He suits me to a shade." They were married on 1 June 1867 and sailed for Canada, Rex's new assignment, on 8 June.

Marriage was a form of liberation for Ewing, who was freed from duties around the vicarage and from the need to contribute to the family purse; she was also freed to start a life of adventure as a military wife. As Christabel Maxwell relates, Ewing wrote to her family that she had "found a double of [her]self and that it feels like the addition of a few new faculties – a large accession of *strength* – and a sort of mental companion, footman, courier, lady's maid, lover, and attendant geni rolled into one."

Ironies surround this liberation, however. Ewing ended up facing greater financial anxieties than those she had left behind; the separation from her family and especially from her mother led to serious bouts of homesickness. Yet her clear enjoyment of the life of a military camp, the friendships with other military families, and the spirited theatrical entertainments to which she often contributed

also meant that Ewing was a much more productive writer, publishing eleven short stories before her marriage and more than twice that amount plus three novels in her first six years as an army wife.

The Ewings arrived in Fredericton during the celebrations for Confederation, "a very gay week" according to the young bride's letter home; they left two years later as the last British troops withdrew from New Brunswick. Margaret and Thomas Blom have edited a portion of Ewing's letters and sketches from Canada, and these documents reveal a largely idyllic period, during which the newlyweds discovered snowshoeing and canoeing, benefited from the warm and protective hospitality of the Anglican community who were familiar with both Mrs. Ewing's and Mrs. Gatty's works, and learned of basic domestic needs, such as the thawing of meat for twenty-four hours before cooking and the necessity of wool blankets. Rex studied Hebrew with the bishop of Fredericton, and Julie was so enchanted by the autumn foliage that she sent a box of scarlet maple leaves to her sisters in Yorkshire as decorations for the harvest home festivities at the Ecclesfield church. They called their first home in Fredericton, rented from the president of the University of New Brunswick, Reka Dom, Russian for "River House" and the title of a story that Ewing wrote while in Canada.

Mrs. Gatty's editorship of *Aunt Judy's Magazine* – which she launched in 1866 and continued until her death in 1873, after which her daughters took over the enterprise and continued publication until 1885 – supplied a stable venue for her daughter's stories. The five interrelated stories comprising *Mrs. Overtheway's Remembrances* (1869) – "Ida," "Mrs. Moss," "The Snoring Ghost," "Reka Dom," and "Kerguelen's Land" – first appeared serially in *Aunt Judy's Magazine* from 1866 to 1868.

A solitary child and her comforting neighbor unite these stories. Ewing reveals the loneliness of Ida, whose mother died when the child was an infant and whose father's ship sank before he could return home to her six years later. Despite the chiding of her insensitive Nurse, Ida continues to watch the punctual comings and goings of the little lady across the street, whom she decides to call Mrs. Overtheway. The woman's flowers and kindly appearance fascinate the withdrawn girl, and when Mrs. Overtheway becomes a visitor, she tells the girl stories about her own life as a girl, a young woman, and a bride. Mrs. Overtheway takes Ida back to her own childhood in "Mrs. Moss," the story of a famous beauty who had lost her physical attractiveness through adversity but who enters into a joyous spiritual friendship with her young visitor.

"The Snoring Ghost" is not macabre; on the contrary, it is in every sense a family story of the experiences of the young Mrs. Overtheway and her sister during their stay at a friend's home. Although the girls are dismissed and patronized by the flighty, shallow Lucy Thompson, they realize the value of the upbringing they have received, while at the same time they are relieved to discover that the ghostly noise, attributed to a murderous early owner of the estate, really emanates from barn-door owls nesting in the drain pipe.

"Reka Dom" shows Ewing's ability to compact a whole saga into a story, in this case about a house where the young Mrs. Overtheway and her family lived. The six gardens attached to it, which become plots to be explored "like a tour in fairy land" for Mary's (Mrs. Overtheway's) brothers and sisters, originally belonged to an English-Russian family, and it is a son of this family, Ivan Smith, who eventually becomes Mrs. Overtheway's (Mrs. Smith's) husband.

"Kerguelen's Land" uses exchanges between Father Albatross and Mother Albatross about their discovery of the survivors of a shipwreck to advance the narrative line. Ewing manages an unexpectedly happy conclusion to the tale in the safe return of Ida's father and the wistful memories of Mrs. Overtheway about "the pale, eager, loving little face that turned to her in its loneliness."

In England the most settled posting for Major Ewing was Aldershot, where the couple stayed until 1877. In Julie Ewing's stories details of military and family life mingled more noticeably. One of her finest early portraits of this blending is "The Peace Egg" (1871), the account of a Christmas change of heart brought about not by Dickensian ghosts but by ebullient children. A crusty old widower has disinherited his daughter because she went against his wishes and married a soldier. After years of foreign postings the Captain and his wife and family are at last back in England and living close to the cantankerous gentleman who is, unknown to the children, their own grandfather. Ewing conveys this information in the opening pages and then lets the emotional pilgrimage begin. Her loyalties as a narrator clearly lie with the young couple and their military life. In contrast to the misanthropy of the old man's existence, their marriage is a secure partnership, built on uncomplaining thoughtfulness and handiness on both sides. The children, whose performance of the nursery mumming play melts the obduracy of their neighbor and effects the reconcilia-

tion of their parents and newly discovered grandfather, are precocious and self-possessed. Class differences also work to favor and promote the mummers. When the old man's "timid-looking" maid opens the door to the Christmas troupe and tries to shoo them away, the poor woman's employer thunders in support of the mummers. The transformation of this authoritarian employer into a fond grandpapa and the hatching of "happy peacemaking" and "general rejoicing" from "The Peace Egg" may, in fact, be a little hard to believe, but Ewing's attraction to harmony determines the sort of resolution for which she always strives.

An increasingly remarkable feature of Ewing's work is her skill in observing the patterns of family life, an aptitude that came into prominence in stories without the normal complement of natural parents: *Lob Lie-by-the-Fire, or The Luck of Lingborough* (1874), *Six to Sixteen* (1875), and *Jan of the Windmill; A Story of the Plains* (1876; originally published as "The Miller's Thumb" in *Aunt Judy's Magazine* from November 1872 to October 1873). The kind ministrations of generous women propel the narrative in these stories. When two spinster sisters from Lingborough Hall find a male baby beneath a broom bush, the reactions of Miss Betty and Miss Kitty point to the practical common sense of their Christian philanthropy. The first major decision the ladies must make concerns the name of the lad. Countering Miss Kitty's wish for a "pretty" and "romantic" name, Miss Betty opts for simple functionality; as she reasons, "The boy is to be brought up in that station in life for which one syllable is ample. . . . I propose to call him Broom. He was found under a bush of broom, and it goes very well with John, and sounds plain and respectable."

Concepts of plainness and respectability trigger most of the episodes of this extended tale, which relates how young John runs away from the abusive bailiff to whom he is apprenticed and how he finally finds his way back to Lingborough thanks to the intervention of a dying Highland soldier. It is a long homeward journey for John Broom, one that brings good luck to Lingborough. Although Broom settles as a respected citizen and raises a family in the area, "it is doubtful if John Broom was ever looked upon by the rustics as quite 'like other folk.' The favourite version of his history is that he was Lob under the guise of a child."

The realism is not magical but decidedly down-to-earth in *Six to Sixteen*, the diarylike entries of the orphaned Margaret Vandaleur, who comes to live with the Arkwrights and finds a sisterly companion in Eleanor Arkwright. One winter these teenaged girls decide to follow the "fad" of writing autobiographies, "merely to be lives of our own selves, for nobody but us two to read when we are both old maids." Although Margaret, coming upon her story a year later, regards it as but "a dusty relic of an old fad," Ewing's "sketch of domestic life" chronicles the eventful life of a Victorian orphan — from her childhood spent at a military camp in India to her private schooling at the home of her guardian, a Yorkshire vicar. With accurate strokes Ewing pictures the self-appointed director of all army wives, Mrs. Minchin, a notorious gossip; Margaret's Aunt Theresa, whose foolish gadding as Minchin's protégée leads to the neglect of her own daughter; the housekeeper Keziah, whose refreshing common sense sets the tone for the welcoming Arkwright home; and the knowledgeable mistress of this home, who unconventionally performs her maternal duties while also pursuing her interests as an amateur zoologist. Clearly this digressive account of the journey from girlhood to adolescence draws on many of Ewing's experiences and memories as an older sister who was likely part Eleanor and part Keziah.

Jan of the Windmill, one of Ewing's most successful novels, outlines the rewards, both monetary and aesthetic, that the foster child Jan brings to the family of an industrious miller, Abel Lake. Ewing concentrates not only on the minutiae of family life but also on the generally acknowledged superiority of the young boy with an artistic temperament over his adoptive and working-class parents. It is really a novel of cloaked identities, a juvenile Samuel Richardson or Henry Fielding novel, with Jan's aristocratic lineage being revealed at the end and an appropriate daughter of a squire being chosen as his wife. Ewing's deference to the gentry in matters of taste and morals, sometimes problematic for late-twentieth-century readers, is not veiled in any way, and the racist slurs that went unquestioned in her mid-Victorian Anglican milieu crop up too. When describing the appearance of the mysterious infant as the nurse delivers him to the Abel home, Ewing writes, "The contrast between the natural red of the baby's complexion and its snowy finery was ludicrously suggestive of an over-dressed nigger to begin with."

The death of her mother on 4 October 1873 was a severe blow to Ewing, who was deprived of her earliest and most intuitive mentor. As she admitted in a letter to her husband shortly after, "I have a feeling as if she were an ever-present *conscience* to me . . . which I hope by God's grace may never leave me." Her elegy, "In Memoriam, Marga-

ret Gatty" (1873), clarifies how her mother had fostered many of Ewing's interests. Gatty's pencil drawings of trees and her determination to "attack bits of waste or neglected ground from which everybody else shrank" promoted her daughter's love of gardens and beautification. Gatty loved animals; "the household pets were about her to the end." Despite the lingering effects of the stroke that gradually robbed her of the use of limbs and voice, Gatty maintained "a strong sense of humour" and "a child's pure delight in little things."

Ewing's ideas on literary models were certain and deliberate. Walter Scott had her vote over George Eliot because of his control of tone, his "artlessness and roughness." She liked the narrative sweep, the sense of historical saga, and the layered social scene in Scott as opposed to the intense character studies of Eliot. In a letter of 16 March 1880 she disclosed what she considered the "two qualifications for a writer of fiction" that Scott possessed in abundance: "Dramatism and individuality amongst his characters." Although she deemed Eliot's writing "glorious," she concluded pointedly: "Imagination limited — Dramatism — nil!" Her assessment of Eliot seems uncharacteristically extreme and limited; perhaps Ewing, as a writer for the young, learned the most from Scott's control of narrative incident.

John Ruskin was an admired contemporary who treated "Aunt Judy" with great respect and attentiveness on his visits to Herne Hill. Ewing confided in a letter to her family (11 October 1879) that she found Ruskin "*far* more *personally* lovable than . . . expected." "We are so utterly at one on some points," she declared. "I mean it is uncommonly pleasant to hear things one has long thought very vehemently, put to one by a Master! . . . And then to my delight I found him soldier-mad!!"

One of Ewing's best-known soldier stories, *Jackanapes* (1883; first published in *Aunt Judy's Magazine,* October 1879), combines dramatism and individuality to touching effect. It was prompted by the news of the death of the Prince Imperial during the Zulu War in June 1879 and the need Ewing felt to offer some explanation of military honor to skeptical civilians. Her control of a narrative stretching from infancy to adulthood reflects the lessons learned about panoramic design from Scott. Jackanapes (whose real but unused name is Theodore), the orphan son of a soldier killed at the battle of Waterloo, is raised by his great-aunt, Miss Jessamine.

The novel's emphasis is on the wholeness and balance of experience. While it is true that the hero has a lion's share of virtue, he has been brought up to appreciate both manly and womanly traits. Ewing indulges in observations about Jackanapes's education that sound like a philosophical aside from Eliot herself:

> In good sooth, a young maid is all the better for learning some robuster virtues than maidenliness and not to move the antimacassars. And the robuster virtues require some fresh air and freedom. As, on the other hand, Jackanapes (who had a boy's full share of the little beast and the young monkey in his natural composition) was none the worse, at his tender years, for learning some maidenliness — so far as maidenliness means decency, pity, unselfishness, and pretty behaviour.

In adult life Jackanapes dies on the battlefield while saving his childhood friend Tony Johnson. Selfless to the end, he expires defending and explaining his friend to the Major. It is thanks to Tony and his filial ministrations to the frail Miss Jessamine that the blow of her nephew's loss is cushioned. The praise that Jackanapes receives from all quarters echoes in Ewing's closing remarks about eternal verities, "things such as Love, and Honour, and the Soul of Man, which cannot be bought with a price, and which do not die with death." This credal statement constitutes Ewing's formulation of true military honor.

The ways in which the incorporation of a child within a community reflects on the group's specific values, openness, aspirations, and restrictions are the underlying concerns of all Ewing's final books. The "country tale" of *Daddy Darwin's Dovecote* (1884; first published in *Aunt Judy's Magazine,* November 1881) deserves to be compared with Eliot's *Silas Marner* (1861). As Eppie brightened the miserly Silas's life, so too Daddy Darwin's adoption of the workhouse lad Jack March brings prosperity to the dovecote and happiness to many in the region. Ewing shows an acute awareness of the social rounds of both working and middle classes in this Yorkshire country setting. The precise details of the schedule of the parson's well-meaning daughter show how much Ewing was drawing on her own memories of the Ecclesfield vicarage and the accounts of her younger sisters who continued to run it and look after their father. Within the overwhelmingly Christian norms of this country community, it is fitting that Jack's faithful, honest commitment to Daddy Darwin extends and continues the church-centered rhythms of their simple lives.

In *The Story of a Short Life* (1885; first published in *Aunt Judy's Magazine,* May–October 1882) involvement in the life of the nearby barracks trans-

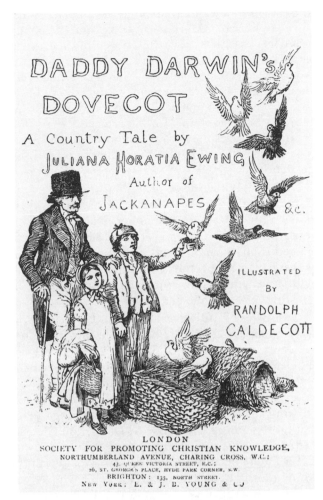

Title page for Ewing's 1884 book, about a kindly man's adoption of a workhouse lad

forms the spoiled and peevish Leonard into a saintly sufferer. Ewing's love of military life, despite the exhaustion entailed in its constant uprootings, shines through; she enjoyed the camaraderie of the barracks, the display of parades, the good fellowship of army theatricals, and the overall discipline of a camp. Ironically, Ewing proved to be a stronger advocate of the military life than her husband, who often pined to return to musical studies.

The frequent moves, however, did take their toll on Ewing. After Aldershot, shorter assignments at Bowdon, York, and Fulford followed. Poor health prevented her from joining Rex in Malta in 1879. She also stayed behind while he took up his next position in Ceylon in 1881. Rex was likely not aware of the depth of his wife's loneliness and sense of isolation; in her own way Julie soldiered on, although she had confided to her mother from Fredericton in 1869 that "the natural terrors of an untravelled and not herculean woman about the ups and downs of a wandering, homeless sort of life like ours are not so comprehensible by him, he having travelled so much, never felt a qualm of sea-sickness, and less than the average of home-sickness, from circumstances." In May 1883 the Ewings were finally together when they moved outside Taunton in a home they named Villa Ponente, named, as Horatia Eden explains, for "its aspect towards the setting sun." Despite her precarious health, Ewing – as always – threw herself into the digging of the garden.

Along with a love of animals, another common trait of the children in Ewing's stories is their passion for flowers. In one of her final works, "Letters from a Little Garden" (1884–1885), Ewing admitted that "harmony and gradation of colour always give me more pleasure than contrast." Hers was an earth-bound botanism that delighted in growing, picking, and arranging flowers.

Flowers fulfill several roles in Ewing's work. More than a mere scenic backdrop, they are often reflectors of personality and initiators of action. The childhood custom of blowing dandelion clocks ("you blow till the seed is all blown away, and you count each of the puffs – an hour to a puff") to tell the time accounts for the difference between Peter Paul, the young Dutch boy in "Dandelion Clocks" (1876), and his two sisters. Ewing relates, "it was Peter Paul's peculiarity that he always did want to know more about everything; a habit whose first and foremost inconvenience is that one can so seldom get people to answer one's questions." Even when he returns years later, after a life of wandering and adventure, Peter Paul realizes how far his own restlessness keeps him from his sisters' matronly contentment. "But he did not now ask why dandelion clocks go differently with different people."

An earlier story, "The Blind Hermit and the Trinity Flower" (1871), often compared to "Dandelion Clocks," makes the three-petaled flower an emblem of the dying man's faith and perseverance. Ewing noted in a letter dated 25 October 1871 that "this is one of my greatest favourites amongst my efforts." Charlotte Yonge, she added, "prefers it to anything I have ever done." The "mystic Three" controls the growth of the *Trillium erythrocarpum*. As the Hermit explains to his young apprentice, "Every part was threefold. The leaves were three, the petals three, the sepals three. The flower was snow-white, but on each of the three parts it was stained with crimson stripes, like white garments dyed in blood." In this moving legend the trillium's form forecasts the hermit's prayer of resignation: "If THOU wilt. When THOU wilt. As THOU wilt!"

"Mary's Meadow" (1883–1884) is another poignant flower story. Its late appearance makes it an almost final credal statement from Ewing. The child who plants flowers to beautify wayside places brings about reconciliation between her father and the squire and also inherits a once-contested plot of land. Taking a cue from her chosen epigraph from George Herbert's "The Garden" (1633), with its acknowledgment that "we are but flowers that glide," Ewing imbues the aesthetic vision of the young heroine with a truly creative potential: Mary not only makes flowers grow, but she also unites feuding parties. Taking their cue from this character, readers of *Aunt Judy's Magazine* formed a "Parkinson Society," with the aim of cultivating older species of flowers and disseminating information on gardens "to try and prevent the extermination of rare wild flowers as well as of garden treasures." Ewing was the first president of this society.

Finally, as her strength deteriorated, even the salubrious air of Bath did not help Ewing. After two unsuccessful and mysterious operations (either blood poisoning or cancer is a plausible speculation), she died there on 13 May 1885. She was buried with a military funeral in her parish churchyard of Trull, near Taunton, "in a grave," Eden relates, "literally lined with moss and flowers."

Juliana Horatia Ewing was, in many respects, the product of an era and of a specific community. Her friendships with Yonge and Ruskin and associations with the illustrators Randolph Caldecott (who illustrated *Lob Lie-by-the-Fire, Jackanapes,* and *Daddy Darwin's Dovecote*) and Gordon Browne all had a distinctive establishment cast. Kipling loved her work and learned from her warm characterizations of family life, as did E. Nesbit and Louisa Molesworth.

In her monograph on Ewing, Gillian Avery distinguishes between mother and daughter by suggesting that, unlike Mrs. Gatty, Ewing, "blessed with far more leisure and fewer responsibilities, wrote because she loved it." Ewing was a gifted and enchanting storyteller, even in childhood. Her writing seems to have supplied emotional and intellectual companionship throughout her life, particularly during periods of homesickness, loneliness, and depression. Writing not only permitted Ewing to participate in a rich imaginative universe, but also kept her close and sympathetically attuned to the feelings and perceptions of a generally happy childhood.

Some critics complain about the thinness of her plots and how they depend on stock devises. Ewing's stories are usually bulging with action — within the conventions of the Victorian maternal voice, blending entertainment and instruction to promote the goal of family unity and concord. But she definitely wanted to captivate young readers with more than the conventional. Whether animating toys or insects, whether detailing the routines of the barracks (which, thanks to Rex's tuition, she represented with great accuracy), or whether vivifying the yearnings of children as different as Ida, Jackanapes, Leonard, Jack March, and John Broom, Ewing makes an investment in characters and places. She is determined to tell a story, but she is prepared to linger, comment, and digress en route.

As a major contributor to the expansion of Victorian children's literature, which was releasing itself from an explicitly religious mission, Ewing helped to create a wider horizon for Society for Promoting Christian Knowledge publications. Writing for and appealing to both boys and girls, she made the detailed realism of her setting and the compassionate examination of the child character's emotional life the salient devices of her narrative art. Although F. J. Harvey Darton notes that with Ewing "literary qualities outweighed didactic excrescences," he concludes that her appeal to later generations is "limited." In Lance Salway's estimate her work now seems "excessively sentimental." Today Ewing may only be known to students of Victorian culture and historical children's literature, but the delicate nuance of her finest stories will always be enjoyed by a select readership.

Letters:

Elizabeth S. Tucker, *Leaves from Juliana Horatia Ewing's "Canada Home"* (Boston: Roberts Brothers, 1896);

Margaret Howard Blom and Thomas E. Blom, eds., *Canada Home: Juliana Ewing's Fredericton Letters 1867–1869* (Vancouver: University of British Columbia Press, 1983).

Biographies:

Horatia Katherine Frances Eden, *Juliana Horatia Ewing and Her Books* (London: Society for Promoting Christian Knowledge, 1896);

Christabel Maxwell, *Mrs. Gatty and Mrs. Ewing* (London: Constable, 1949);

Marghanita Laski, *Mrs. Ewing, Mrs. Molesworth and Mrs. Hodgson Burnett* (London: Arthur Barker, 1958).

References:

Gillian Avery, *Mrs. Ewing* (London: Bodley Head, 1961);

Jacqueline Bratton, *The Impact of Victorian Children's Fiction* (London: Croom Helm, 1981);

F. J. Harvey Darton, *Children's Books in England; Five Centuries of Social Life,* third edition, revised by Brian Alderson (Cambridge: Cambridge University Press, 1982), pp. 276–292;

Donna McDonald, *Illustrated News; Juliana Horatia Ewing's Canadian Pictures 1867-1869* (Toronto & London: Dundurn Press, 1985);

Louisa Molesworth, "Juliana Horatia Ewing," *Contemporary Review,* 49 (May 1886): 675–686;

Judith A. Plotz, "A Victorian Comfort Book: Juliana Ewing's *The Story of a Short Life,*" in *Romanticism and Children's Literature in Nineteenth-Century England,* edited by J. H. McGavran Jr. (Athens: University of Georgia Press, 1991), pp. 168–189;

Lance Salway, *A Peculiar Gift: Nineteenth Century Writings on Books for Children* (Harmondsworth, Middlesex: Kestrel Books, 1976);

Robert Lee Wolff, *Nineteenth-Century Fiction: A Bibliographical Catalogue* (New York: Garland, 1982).

Frederic William Farrar

(7 August 1831 – 22 March 1903)

Brendan A. Rapple
Boston College

BOOKS: *The Influence of the Revival of Classical Studies on English Literature During the Reigns of Elizabeth and James I. An Essay Which Obtained the Le Bas Prize for the Year 1856* (Cambridge: Macmillan, 1856);

The People of England. A Lecture Delivered before the Harrow Literary Institution, October 13th, 1857 (London: Longman, Brown, Green, Longmans & Roberts, 1857);

"The Christian Doctrine of the Atonement Not Inconsistent with the Justice and Goodness of God." An Essay, Which Obtained the Norrisian Prize for 1857 (Cambridge: Cambridge University Press, 1858);

Eric, or, Little by Little: A Tale of Roslyn School (Edinburgh: Black, 1858; New York: Rudd & Carleton, 1859);

Julian Home: A Tale of College Life (Edinburgh: Black, 1859; Philadelphia: Lippincott, 1860);

Lyrics of Life (London: Macmillan, 1859);

An Essay on the Origin of Language, Based on Modern Researches and Especially on the Works of Renan (London: Murray, 1860);

St. Winifred's; or, The World of School (London: Black, 1862; New York: Follett, Foster, 1863);

Chapters on Language (London: Longmans, Green, 1865);

A Brief Greek Syntax and Hints on Greek Accidence: With Some Reference to Comparative Philology, and with Illustrations from Various Modern Languages (London: Longmans, Green, 1867);

On Some Defects in Public School Education, A Lecture Delivered at the Royal Institution, on Friday, February 8th, 1867 (London: Macmillan, 1867);

Seekers After God (London: Macmillan, 1868; New York: Lovell, 1882);

The Fall of Man, and Other Sermons, Preached before the University of Cambridge, and on Various Public Occasions (London: Macmillan, 1868; New York: Macmillan, 1871);

Families of Speech: Four Lectures Delivered Before the Royal Institution of Great Britain in March, 1869 (London: Longmans, Green, 1870);

Frederic W. Farrar

The Witness of History to Christ. Five Sermons Preached Before the University of Cambridge, being the Hulsean Lectures for the Year 1870 (London & New York: Macmillan, 1871);

The Three Homes: A Tale for Fathers and Sons, as F. T. L. Hope (London: Cassell, 1873; New York: Dutton, 1896);

The Life of Christ (London & New York: Cassell, Petter & Galpin, 1874);

The Silence and the Voices of God, with Other Sermons (London: Macmillan, 1874; New York: Dutton, 1875);

"In the Days of Thy Youth." Sermons on Practical Subjects Preached at Marlborough College from 1871 to

1876 (London: Macmillan, 1876; New York: Macmillan, 1876);

Between the Living and the Dead. A Sermon Preached in Westminster Abbey (London: Tweedie, 1878);

Eternal Hope; Five Sermons Preached in Westminster Abbey, November and December, 1877 (London: Macmillan, 1878; New York: Macmillan, 1878);

Language and Languages. Being "Chapters on Language" and "Families of Speech" (London: Longmans, 1878; New York: Dutton, 1878);

Saintly Workers; Five Lenten Lectures Delivered in St. Andrew's, Holborn, March and April, 1878 (London: Macmillan, 1878; New York: Dutton, 1878);

The Life and Work of St. Paul, 2 volumes (London: Cassell, 1879; New York: Dutton, 1879);

Ephphatha; or, The Amelioration of the World. Sermons Preached at Westminster Abbey, with Two Sermons Preached in St. Margaret's Church at the Opening of Parliament (London: Macmillan, 1880; New York: Macmillan, 1880);

Mercy and Judgment: A Few Last Words on Christian Eschatology, with Reference to Dr. Pusey's "What Is of Faith?" (London: Macmillan, 1881; New York: Dutton, 1881);

Words of Truth and Wisdom (London: Bogue, 1881; New York: Dutton, 1883);

The Early Days of Christianity, 2 volumes (London & New York: Cassell, Petter, Galpin, 1882);

General Aims of the Teacher, and Form Management. Two Lectures Delivered in the University of Cambridge in the Lent Term, 1883, by Farrar and R. B. Poole (Cambridge: Cambridge University Press, 1883);

With the Poets. A Selection of English Poetry (London: Suttaby, 1883; New York: Funk & Wagnalls, 1883);

The Messages of the Books, Being Discourses and Notes on the Books of the New Testament (London: Macmillan, 1884; New York: Dutton, 1885);

Eulogy on General Grant Delivered at Westminster Abbey, London, August 4th, 1885 (New York: Dutton, 1885?);

Success in Life. Prefaced by a Brief Biography (Boston: Cupples, Upham, 1885);

Sermons and Addresses Delivered in America (London: Macmillan, 1886; New York: Dutton, 1886);

Dante (New York: Alden, 1886);

History of Interpretation; Eight Lectures Preached before the University of Oxford in the Year MDCCCLXXXV on the Foundation of the Late Rev. John Bampton (London: Macmillan, 1886; New York: Dutton, 1886);

Lectures and Addresses (New York: Alden, 1886);

Africa and the Drink Trade, by Farrar and W. T. Hornaby (New York: National Temperance Society, 1887);

Everyday Christian Life; or, Sermons by the Way (London: Isbister, 1887; New York: Whittaker, 1887);

Solomon: His Life and Times (London: Nisbet, 1887; New York: Randolph, 1888);

Lives of the Fathers: Sketches of Church History in Biography, 2 volumes (Edinburgh: Black, 1889; New York: Macmillan, 1889);

Sermons (London: Sonnenschein, 1889; New York: Whittaker, 1889);

The Passion Play at Oberammergau (London: Heinemann, 1890; New York: Lovell, 1890);

The Minor Prophets (London: Nisbet, 1890; New York: Randolph, 1890);

Truths to Live By. A Companion to "Everyday Christian Life" (London: Isbister, 1890; New York: Whittaker, 1890);

Darkness and Dawn; or, Scenes in the Days of Nero. An Historic Tale (London: Longmans, Green, 1891; New York: Longmans, Green, 1891);

Social and Present Day Questions (London: Hodder & Stoughton, 1891; Boston: Bradley & Woodruff, 1891);

The Voice from Sinai: The Eternal Bases of the Moral Law (London: Isbister, 1892; New York: Whittaker, 1892);

The First Book of Kings (London: Hodder & Stoughton, 1893; New York: Armstrong, 1893);

The Lord's Prayer: Sermons Preached in Westminster Abbey (London: Isbister, 1893; New York: Whittaker, 1893);

Our English Minsters, by Farrar and others (London: Isbister, 1893);

The Life of Christ as Represented in Art (London: Black, 1894; New York: Macmillan, 1894);

The Second Book of Kings (London: Hodder & Stoughton, 1894; New York: Armstrong, 1894);

The Book of Daniel (London: Hodder & Stoughton, 1895; New York: Armstrong, 1895);

Gathering Clouds, a Tale of the Days of St. Chrysostom, 2 volumes (London & New York: Longmans, Green, 1895);

My Brother and I: Selected Papers on Social Topics, by Farrar and others (New York: Hunt & Eaton, 1895);

Women's Work in the Home as Daughter, as Wife, and as Mother (London: Nisbet, 1895; Philadelphia: Altemus, 1895);

The Bible and the Child, by Farrar and others (London & New York: Macmillan, 1896);

The Young Man Master of Himself (London: Nisbet, 1896);

The Paths of Duty: Counsels to Young Men (Boston: Crowell, 1896);

The Bible, Its Meaning and Supremacy (London & New York: Longmans, Green, 1897);

Men I Have Known (New York & Boston: Crowell, 1897);

Progress in the Reign of Queen Victoria: A Brief Record of Sixty Years (London: Bliss, Sands, 1897);

Prophets of the Christian Faith, by Farrar and others (London: Clarke, 1897);

Sin and Its Conquerors; or, The Conquest of Sin (New York: Revell, 1897);

Allegories (London & New York: Longmans, Green, 1898);

Great Books: Bunyan, Shakespeare, Dante, Milton, The Imitation &c. (London: Isbister, 1898; New York: Crowell, 1898);

The Herods (London: Service & Paton, 1898; New York: Herrick, 1898);

Temperance Reform as Required by National Righteousness and Patriotism (London: Nisbet, 1899);

Texts Explained; or, Helps to Understand the New Testament (London: Longmans, 1899; New York: Dodd, Mead, 1899);

True Religion: Sermons (London: Freemantle, 1899);

The Life of Lives; Further Studies in the Life of Christ (London: Cassell, 1900; New York: Dodd, Mead, 1900);

Ruskin as a Religious Teacher (Bournville: Saint George, 1904).

Editions: *Treasure Thoughts, from the Writings of F. W. Farrar,* edited, with an introduction, by Rose Porter (Boston: Lothrop, 1886);

Farrar Year Book. Selections From the Writings of the Rev. Frederic W. Farrar, compiled by W. M. L. Jay (New York: Dutton, 1895).

OTHER: *Essays on a Liberal Education,* edited by Farrar (London: Macmillan, 1867);

Phillips Brooks: The Man, the Preacher, and the Author. Based on the "Estimate," by Newell Dunbar. With an Introduction by Joseph Cook, and a Supplementary Chapter from the Ven. Frederic W. Farrar. To Which are Added Selections from the Writings of the Late Great Divine (London: Marshall, 1893; Boston: Hastings, 1893).

Frederic William Farrar, the quintessence of stereotypical Victorianism, attained high prominence in diverse fields of endeavor. A schoolteacher for many years, a headmaster of a distinguished school, and a prolific writer on educational topics, he played a dominant role in introducing such subjects as science and modern literature into the classical curriculum of England's public schools, thereby helping to foster the modern humanist ideal. He was one of the age's most respected and beloved pulpit preachers, and his published sermons were read throughout the nation. As dean of Canterbury, England's premier deanery, he wrote widely influential theological works, in particular a best-selling life of Christ. Amid these manifold activities, Farrar also found time to write a series of best-selling novels of school and college life for juveniles, which were influential in rendering this literary genre one of the most popular in the latter part of the nineteenth century.

Frederic William Farrar was born on 7 August 1831 in Bombay, where his father was a chaplain of the Church Missionary Society. At the age of three Farrar was sent to England with his older brother, Henry, to live with two aunts in Aylesbury. From age six to seven he attended Aylesbury Latin school. Having moved in 1838 to the Isle of Man with his parents, who were on furlough from India, he was enrolled in King William's College. Farrar drew heavily from his experiences at this institution in writing *Eric, or, Little by Little: A Tale of Roslyn School* (1858). Though the school was not of the first rank academically, Farrar, mainly through his own aptitude and diligence, did well at his studies; he was also appointed head boy.

In 1847 Farrar's father obtained the curacy of St. James, Clerkenwell, and the family moved to London. Farrar enrolled in King's College, where he continued his academic success, taking first place in the matriculation and honor examinations. He graduated with a B.A. from London University. In October 1850 he went to Trinity College, Cambridge, with a sizarship and a King's College scholarship; he was awarded a Trinity scholarship in 1852. Farrar was proud that he supported his Cambridge days entirely by scholarships and exhibitions and that his education never cost his family a penny. He attained high intellectual prominence at university, winning the chancellor's gold medal in 1852 for English verse for his poem "The Arctic Regions and the Hopes of Discovering the Lost Adventurers." He was elected to the Apostles, a prestigious and intellectually elite society. In 1854 he graduated with a B.A. with a first class in the classical tripos and as a *junior optime* in the mathematical tripos. The following year he won the Le Bas Prize for his essay "The Influence of the Revival of Classical Studies on English Literature during the Reigns of Elizabeth and James I." A year later he

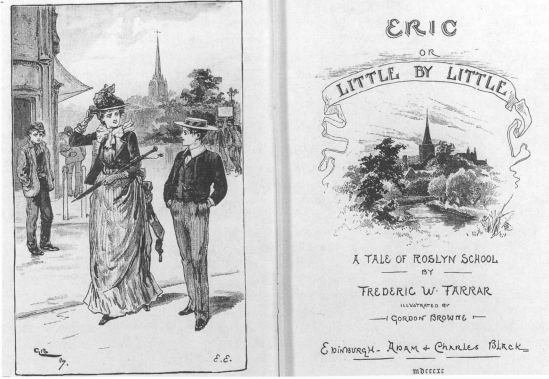

Cover, frontispiece, and title page for an 1890 edition of the novel that brought Farrar to public attention (courtesy of the Lilly Library, Indiana University)

was awarded the Norrisian Prize for an essay on the Atonement and was also elected a Fellow of Trinity College. In 1857 he proceeded to the M.A. degree.

Farrar's great promise had been recognized outside Cambridge even before the results of his undergraduate degree were announced. In 1854 G. E. L. Cotton, the Arnoldian headmaster of Marlborough College and later bishop of Calcutta, invited Farrar to take a teaching position at Wiltshire College. Cotton, who wanted masters of high scholarly ability, strong religious and moral principles, and palpable leadership qualities, saw in Farrar a likely candidate. Farrar was a successful teacher: the boys appreciated his consistent stressing of the need to inculcate both intellectual and moral virtue, and, despite his manifest disinterest in sports, he proved popular. As Canon Henry Bell, a pupil at Marlborough at the time, later remarked: "Farrar came, and brought the boys who were in his Form a new idea of life, and the conviction that we were made for something better and higher than to be caned and cuffed."

Farrar left Marlborough in late 1855 to take up an assistant mastership at Harrow School, where he remained for fifteen years. With the publication of his novel *Eric, or, Little by Little* he first came to public attention. The book, published only a year after Thomas Hughes's *Tom Brown's Schooldays* (1857), quickly caused controversy. *The Saturday Review* indignantly observed, "We can scarcely imagine a less healthy book to put into a boy's hand," and *The Quarterly Review* in 1860 complained that the story and personages were unlikely and that "if the contact of evil had effects as deadly, as certain, and as durable as [*Eric*] represent[s], the world would be one mass of contamination." *Blackwood's* was the most severe in an 1861 review: "A more utter failure . . . can hardly be conceived. Seldom has a book been written with such an excellent intention, by a scholar and a gentleman, which is so painful to read." Charlotte Yonge in her 1869 survey of children's literature dismissed *Eric* as "that morbid dismal tale." Although not all reviews of *Eric* were unfavorable, its critical reception was distinctly less successful than that accorded to the more genial, less evangelical, and less sentimental *Tom Brown's Schooldays*. Nevertheless, Farrar's novel was a best-seller, going through thirty-six editions in the author's lifetime.

The book's central theme is the gradual moral deterioration of the "truthful, ingenuous, quick," though "far from blameless" Eric Williams, who is enrolled at Roslyn School. Eric at first behaves well, though he sometimes fails to do the right thing for fear of losing popularity, but he gradually yields to wrongdoing. He reforms, but within a year he resumes his bad habits. Above all, he fails to care adequately for his younger brother, Vernon, who is gradually being corrupted by a bad set. After arriving drunk at school prayers, Eric narrowly escapes expulsion by promising to reform. Still, calamities continue. Vernon is killed in a fall from a cliff. Soon after, Eric is falsely suspected of stealing money. Unable to face the suspicion, he runs away to sea as a cabin boy. After suffering terrible hardships he makes his way back to his aunt's house. He learns that his good name is secure at school, but he also discovers that his mother in India, distraught at Vernon's death and Eric's disappearance, has died. Feeling responsible, Eric expires, repenting his wicked ways.

Eric is a late product of a long tradition of evangelical children's literature, dominant themes of which include the gloomy stressing of children's natural inclination to wrongdoing, the depiction of scene after scene of death, and the constant urging of repentance. In the preface to the twenty-fourth edition (1889), Farrar states that he wrote the book "with but one single object – the vivid inculcation of inward purity and moral purpose, by the history of a boy who, in spite of the inherent nobleness of his disposition, falls into all folly and wickedness, until he has learnt to seek help from above." There are many authorial asides and reflections – reminiscent of passages in *"In the Days of Thy Youth"* (1876), a collection of Farrar's school sermons – in which the author criticizes Eric for his failure to disapprove of dirty talk and preaches about an unnamed evil, which, he claims, has brought many an English boy to perdition. Jonathan Gathorne-Hardy is surely correct in his contention that this "evil" is masturbation.

As is evident in *Eric,* Farrar was well aware of the problems pervading public schools. The Clarendon Commission, which reported on these schools in 1864, saw their principal faults to be an outmoded curriculum, an inadequate administration, and a poor use of endowments. Farrar, while sympathizing with these conclusions, viewed the chief problem to be one of morality. He was adamant that the prime duty of teachers was not merely to impart the principles of scholarly disciplines but also to teach virtue and to help save their charges' souls. Farrar was greatly influenced by Thomas Arnold and the reforms he had helped foster in England's public schools. One of Roslyn's major shortcomings, according to Farrar, was the absence of the monitorial system, which Thomas Arnold had believed was a prime necessity for the good moral climate of a public school. At the very least, monitors at Roslyn would have curtailed some of the bullying and may have helped Eric to tread a more noble path.

Though Farrar's literary style is in many respects superior to that of Hughes, characterization in *Eric* is not as well developed nor as realistic as that of *Tom Brown's Schooldays*. P. G. Scott has argued eloquently that the characters and events of Farrar's novels accurately mirror the life of certain schools of the time, and Reginald Farrar, the author's son, in 1904 chastised critics who contended that the boys were far from realistically portrayed: "Their virtues, and even their vices, are idealised, but the heroes are such boys as Farrar was himself, and . . . of an epoch where alike the virtues and the vices of boys were more primitive and less sophisticated." Although Farrar may have succeeded in capturing the general temper of public school life of the 1830s, it may also be argued that he failed to flesh out his characters' personalities, to present them as other than personifications of virtue and vice.

Part of the reason for the success of Farrar's novel was its popularity among Victorian parents. Its depiction of the constant moral struggle faced by adolescents and its stress on the necessity to foster godliness and good learning undoubtedly recommended it to adults as a suitable present for their children. It is not so clear that it was invariably liked by boys. *Blackwood's Magazine* in 1861 stated categorically that it was "certainly not popular" with schoolboys. Many readers were probably deterred by its insistent didacticism and preaching, and as the century advanced and the maintenance of sangfroid and a stiff upper lip became essential qualities for Victorian males, others must have looked askance at Farrar's sentimentality. As *The Saturday Review* contemptuously complained: "everything is served up with tear sauce." Clearly, the Roslyn boys bear little relationship to those better-known public-school boys, whether in fiction or real life, who invariably maintain a strict code of independence and self-restraint. However, in a letter to his friend E. S. Beesly, Farrar himself acknowledged that the emotionalism of *Eric* was excessive: "The lacrimosity is, I know, too much, and arises from the state of mind in which I wrote it"; Farrar is here referring to his depressed state after the death of his mother. Moreover, Farrar, who had scant interest in sport, gives little attention to games in *Eric*. To the countless boys brought up during the second half of the nineteenth century, when sports mania pervaded public schools and descriptions of games became an essential ingredient of most school novels and stories, their absence in Farrar's work must have been a real deterrent.

Still, Farrar was a deft storyteller. Many young readers enjoyed the adventures, chases, fights, schoolboy talk, the attempts of pupils to outwit their teachers, and the tricks they played within and without the classroom. Nor should the modern reader suppose that no child appreciated or benefited from the book's evangelical, exhortatory tone. In his biography of his father, Reginald Farrar prints letters from young men testifying that the strong moral message of *Eric* had helped ameliorate their lives. Though Farrar probably intended the work primarily for middle-class boys, its high sales for many years imply that it was read by other classes. It is understandable that working-class children who would never be able to attend public school would avidly read *Eric*, to see how the "other half" lived.

In 1860 Farrar married Lucy Mary Cardew, third daughter of Frederic Cardew of the East India Company. It was a happy marriage that produced five sons and five daughters. The previous year Farrar had published *Julian Home: A Tale of College Life*, a novel set at university rather than public school. It is the story of the fortunes of a group of pupils at St. Werner's College, Camford. Just as St. Werner's is clearly based on Trinity College, Cambridge, which Farrar had attended, so Julian Home, the novel's central character, is probably modeled on the author as an undergraduate. A scholarly, high-principled, religious young man of poor family, Julian is juxtaposed with the initially popular, though weak-willed, Vyvyan Bruce. While the industrious Julian goes on, as did Farrar, to excel academically, Vyvyan, despite his intelligence and many talents, sinks ever deeper into a trough of baseness and is eventually expelled. However, in accordance with Farrar's theological principles, Vyvyan is not damned, but after becoming repentant and "a wiser, sadder, and better man," he immigrates to New Zealand to begin a new life. Again Farrar wishes to stress that salvation inevitably follows repentance.

Julian Home, like Farrar's earlier novel, may have been attractive to the young, but it was more so to their parents, through its emphases on the vanquishing of evil by virtue, the inevitable success accompanying hard work and study, and the importance of moral and spiritual rectitude. However, some readers must have been irked by the priggish, self-justificatory personalities of some characters, especially the invariably right Julian. Though there are some dramatic scenes, Farrar rarely misses an opportunity to sermonize. While it is difficult to imagine youth enjoying this novel today, it was popular in the nineteenth century and went through multiple editions. *Julian Home* was also unusual among school stories for including romantic love interests. In fact, *Blackwood's Magazine* in 1861 termed the novel feminine, as opposed to the masculine *Tom Brown's Schooldays,* and argued that the abundance of lovemaking rendered it particularly interesting to a female audience.

In 1862 Farrar published his second novel of public school life, *St. Winifred's; or, The World of School.* As Farrar's son observed, while much of *Eric* was based on the author's schoolboy experiences in the Isle of Man, *St. Winifred's* was more influenced by his career as a teacher at Marlborough and Harrow. The novel's central character is Walter Evson, who, though full of promise, becomes involved in all sorts of mischief. The situation culminates in his burning the only copy of a master's commentary on a Hebrew text, the fruit of his life's labors. After the master forgives him in true Christian manner, Walter vows to reform and reveals his genuine mettle and nobility of character in a daring rescue of schoolfriends trapped atop a mountain. In short, Walter becomes what Farrar considered to be the model schoolboy type.

St. Winifred's, like *Eric* and *Julian Home,* is a moral tale displaying a patent didacticism and portraying characters as mere exemplars of virtue or vice. However, compared to *Eric* at any rate, it is restrained, with only one deathbed scene. While *St. Winifred's* is in some respects a more realistic novel and has been subject to less criticism than *Eric,* it is, as Isabel Quigley has written, "in both senses less amusing; less memorable, quotable, absurd and gripping. *Eric's* intensity is missing, as well as its quaintness." Nevertheless, *St. Winifred's* was successful, going through twenty-six editions by the time of Farrar's death and being translated into French and Romanian.

During his fifteen years at Harrow, Farrar wrote widely on education, particularly on curricular concerns. In 1867 he published the successful *A Brief Greek Syntax and Hints on Greek Accidence* and edited an influential series of papers by distinguished authors, entitled *Essays on a Liberal Education.* His paper "Of Greek and Latin Verse-Composition as a General Branch of Education" was another incisive attack on some of the absurdities perpetrated on schoolboys in the name of classical education. He argued that the time devoted to teaching grammar and composition or in translating passages of En-

glish into Greek or Latin would be far better used on such subjects as comparative philology, history, modern languages, English language and literature, Hebrew, and, above all, science.

Farrar strongly believed that an understanding of the laws and phenomena of nature is an essential attribute of any true education. Though he did not teach science, he founded a natural history society at Harrow to stimulate interest in such subjects as botany among pupils who were not attracted to the usual classical fare. His main scientific endeavors focused on linguistic research, however. He published widely on the topic, his principal works being *An Essay on the Origin of Language, Based on Modern Researches and Especially on the Works of Renan* (1860), *Chapters on Language* (1865), and *Families of Speech: Four Lectures* (1870). The last two were reprinted in a single volume, *Language and Languages* (1878). *The Origin of Language* so impressed Charles Darwin that he proposed Farrar for a Fellowship of the Royal Society; he was elected in 1866. Farrar, in turn, thought so highly of Darwin that he arranged for his burial in Westminster Abbey over the objections of many ecclesiastics. He also preached Darwin's funeral sermon.

When Farrar was only an assistant master at Harrow he received in 1869 the distinction of being made an honorary chaplain to the queen. In 1873 he was promoted to chaplain-in-ordinary. Two years earlier he had been appointed to take over the headmastership of Marlborough College from A. G. Bradley. During his five and a half years in this position Farrar revealed that he was not as gifted an administrator as his brilliant predecessor. He was a skillful teacher, however, though by temperament he was more proficient and at ease instructing the older and better prepared boys of the sixth form rather than younger students.

While Marlborough's headmaster, Farrar published *The Life of Christ* (1874), based on extensive research, including modern German scholarship, and owing much to a trip by the author to Palestine during the Easter of 1870. This was probably his most widely read work. It went through many editions, twelve in the first year alone, and was translated into several languages, including Japanese and Russian. The first of a trilogy, this work was followed by *The Life and Works of St. Paul* (1879) and *The Early Days of Christianity* (1882). *The Life of Christ* was not Farrar's first religious work; he had previously published the popular *Seekers after God* (1868), an account of religious thought in the non-Christian thinkers Seneca, Epictetus, and Marcus Aurelius, as well as two collections of sermons, *The*

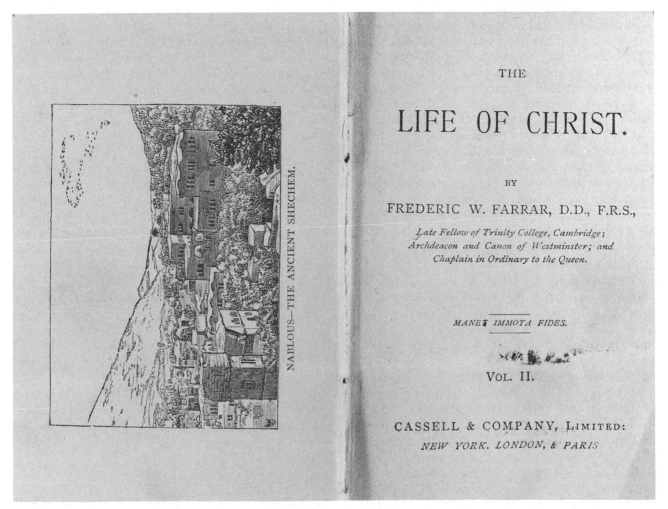

NABLOUS—THE ANCIENT SHECHEM.

THE

LIFE OF CHRIST.

BY

FREDERIC W. FARRAR, D.D., F.R.S.,

Late Fellow of Trinity College, Cambridge;
Archdeacon and Canon of Westminster; and
Chaplain in Ordinary to the Queen.

MANET IMMOTA FIDES.

VOL. II.

CASSELL & COMPANY, Limited:
NEW YORK. LONDON, & PARIS

Frontispiece and title page for Farrar's most widely read work, based on his extensive research in biblical history

Fall of Man, and Other Sermons (1868) and *The Silence and the Voices of God, with Other Sermons* (1874). In 1870 he delivered the Hulsean Lectures, *The Witness of History to Christ* (1871), at Cambridge.

In 1873 Farrar published *The Three Homes: A Tale for Fathers and Sons* under the pseudonym F. T. L. Hope (from "faintly trust the larger hope," a line from Alfred Tennyson's *In Memoriam,* 1850). It was 1896 before he publicly acknowledged authorship. The book is another story of school life, though it differs from *Eric* and *St. Winifred's* in that the action takes place during vacation time. It displays some of the same shortcomings pervading Farrar's other juvenile novels: sentimentality, excessive moralizing, a propensity for melodrama, and stereotypical characters who are too often vehicles for moral attributes. Still, the story is more genial than *Eric* and contains sufficient action to have whetted the interest of nineteenth-century boys. Part of its appeal to that great majority of readers who had not the means or the background to attend elite independent schools was in supposedly revealing how the scions of the rich and ruling classes lived. In addition, some readers probably empathized with the flagrant lack of understanding displayed by Ralph Douglas's father in dealing with his son; as is clear from the novel's subtitle, "A Tale for Fathers and Sons," Farrar intended that this intergenerational misunderstanding should be a particular message of the novel. The book sold well and by Farrar's death had gone through eighteen editions and had sold more than thirty thousand copies.

In 1876 Farrar accepted Prime Minister Benjamin Disraeli's offer of the post of canon of Westminster and rector of St. Margaret's, London. Farrar subsequently became one of the most popular preachers in the nation. Five sermons he delivered at Westminster Abbey in 1877, which repudiated the commonly held belief that God would condemn multitudes of souls to everlasting torment in hell, were extremely influential. Farrar published these sermons the following year in the widely read *Eternal Hope* and expanded upon the theme in *Mercy and Judgment* (1881). During this period, also, Farrar became a forceful advocate of the temperance movement. In 1883 he was appointed archdeacon of Westminster. Two years later he made a long and successful lecture tour of Canada and the United States. He was elected chaplain of the House of Commons in 1890, an appropriate honor for the rector of St. Margaret's, which was generally held to be the Commons's church.

Farrar wrote two historical novels in 1891 and 1895 about the early church, a fictional extension of his trilogy about early Christianity. Though these novels were not intended specifically for children, they were probably read by young people. The first, the lengthy *Darkness and Dawn; or, Scenes in the Days of Nero* (1891), went through eight editions by 1898. The "Darkness" of the title refers to the decadence of the once-brilliant Roman Empire, the "Dawn" to the birth and gradual spread of Christianity. He juxtaposes the simplicity, the virtue, and the hope of Christianity with the excesses, the evil, and the despair of Roman paganism. However, the discerning reader recognizes Farrar's biased viewpoint and that, while Nero and his ilk are justly treated, the general condemnation of nearly all non-Christian Romans is unfair.

Whereas *Darkness and Dawn* describes the triumphal overcoming of paganism by Christianity, Farrar's second historical novel, *Gathering Clouds, a Tale of the Days of St. Chrysostom* (1895) is the sadder story of how the pagan world in the fourth century A.D. reinvaded and prevailed over the Christian church. While the earlier novel is a well-constructed work, with its many subplots expertly interwoven, the same cannot be maintained for *Gathering Clouds*. The book does not possess the charm of its predecessor: its events are not so gripping, nor are its characters as convincingly delineated.

In 1895 Farrar was appointed dean of Canterbury. It was a well-deserved honor, though he might have expected a bishopric. Most likely, his occasional diversions from conservative theology rendered him an uncertain choice in the eyes of some in the establishment. He attended to his duties as dean with his accustomed diligence and enthusiasm. One of his major accomplishments during these years was the highly successful restoration of the cathedral. Toward the end of the century Farrar developed muscular atrophy. He died on 22 March 1903 after a long life of tireless and devoted service to the church, to education, and to literature.

Even before the close of the Victorian Era there was a distinct falling off in interest among the young for Farrar's particular brand of literary style, content, and message. Today Farrar's juvenile novels are virtually unknown among the age group for which they were intended. They have failed entirely to generate the interest still afforded such contemporary children's works as Lewis Carroll's *Alice's Adventures in Wonderland* (1861), Charles Kingsley's *The Water-Babies* (1863), or Hughes's *Tom Brown's Schooldays*. Even if the title *Eric, or, Little by Little* is nowadays recognized among adults, it is a recognition likely to be accompanied by a sneer. Percy Muir is representative of most modern critics in his declaration that any immortality attained by *Eric* is "only of derision." Literary tastes inevitably change, and it is now the fate of Farrar's juvenile works that their appeal is limited to the scholar and academic.

Biography:

Reginald Farrar, *The Life of Frederic William Farrar* (London: Nisbet, 1904).

References:

Geoffrey Bocca, "*Eric, or Little by Little* (1858): Frederic William Farrar," in his *Best Seller: A Nostalgic Celebration of the Less-Than-Great Books You Have Always Been Afraid to Admit You Loved* (New York: Wyndham, 1981), pp. 42–58;

Jonathan Gathorne-Hardy, *The Public School Phenomenon 597–1977* (London: Hodder & Stoughton, 1977);

Bruce Haley, *The Healthy Body and Victorian Culture* (Cambridge, Mass.: Harvard University Press, 1978);

Mary Hobbs, "Fair Play for Eric!," *Times Literary Supplement,* 30 November 1967, p. 1150;

A. Jamieson, "F. W. Farrar and Novels of the Public Schools," *British Journal of Educational Studies,* 16 (October 1968): 271–278;

Hugh Kingsmill, *After Puritanism 1850–1900* (London: Duckworth, 1929);

P. W. Musgrave, "*Tom Brown* and *Eric*," in his *From Brown to Bunter: The Life and Death of the School Story* (London & Boston: Routledge & Kegan Paul, 1985), pp. 47–82;

David Newsome, *Godliness and Good Learning: Four Studies on a Victorian Ideal* (London: Cassell, 1961);

Eugene Parsons, "Frederic William Farrar," *Methodist Quarterly Review,* third series, 29 (October 1903): 714–724;

Isabel Quigly, "The School Story as Moral Tale: Hughes and Farrar," in her *The Heirs of Tom Brown: The English School Story* (London: Chatto & Windus, 1982), pp. 42–76;

Jeffrey Richards, "Paradise Lost: *Eric, or, Little by Little,*" in his *Happiest Days: The Public Schools in English Fiction* (Manchester: Manchester University Press, 1988), pp. 70–102;

J. D. Rogers, "Dean Farrar as Headmaster," *Cornhill Magazine,* new series 14 (May 1903): 597–608;

"School and College Life: Its Romance and Reality," *Blackwood's Magazine,* 89 (February 1861): 131–148;

P. G. Scott, "The School Novels of Dean Farrar," *British Journal of Educational Studies,* 19 (June 1971): 163–182;

Charlotte M. Yonge, "Children's Literature, Part III. Class Literature of the Last Thirty Years," *Macmillan's Magazine,* 20 (September 1869): 448–456.

William Godwin
(3 March 1756 – 7 April 1836)
and
Mary Jane Clairmont Godwin
(1766 – 1841)

Ann R. Montanaro
Rutgers University

See also the William Godwin entries in *DLB 39: British Novelists, 1660–1800; DLB 104: British Prose Writers, 1660–1900, Second Series; DLB 142: Eighteenth-Century British Literary Biographers;* and *DLB 158: British Reform Writers, 1789–1832.*

BOOKS – by William Godwin: *The History of the Life of William Pitt, Earl of Chatham,* anonymous (London: G. Kearsley, 1783);

A Defence of the Rockingham Party, in their Late Coalition with the Right Honorable Frederic Lord North, anonymous (London: J. Stockdale, 1783); facsimile in *Four Early Pamphlets, 1783–1784,* edited by Burton R. Pollin (Gainesville, Fla.: Scholars' Facsimiles and Reprints, 1966);

An Account of the Seminary that will be opened on Monday the Fourth Day of August at Epsom in Surrey, for the Instruction of Twelve Pupils in the Greek, Latin, French, and English Languages, anonymous (London: T. Cadell, 1783); facsimile in *Four Early Pamphlets 1783–1784;*

Sketches of History, in Six Sermons, some copies anonymous (London: T. Cadell, 1784); as Godwin (Alexandria, Va., 1801);

The Herald of Literature; or, A Review of the Most Considerable Publications that will be made in the Course of the Ensuing Winter: With Extracts, anonymous (London: John Murray, 1784); facsimile in *Four Early Pamphlets 1783–1784;*

Instructions to a Statesman. Humbly inscribed to the Right Honourable George Earl Temple, anonymous (London: John Murray, J. Debrett & J. Sewell, 1784); facsimile in *Four Early Pamphlets 1783–1784;*

Damon and Delia: A Tale, anonymous (London: T. Hookham, 1784);

William Godwin; painting by Henry W. Pickersgill (National Portrait Gallery, London)

Italian Letters; or, The History of the Count de St. Julian, 2 volumes, anonymous (London: G. Robinson, 1784);

Imogen: A Pastoral Romance. From the Ancient British, 2 volumes, anonymous (London: W. Lane, 1784);

The History of the Internal Affairs of the United Provinces, from the Year 1780, to the Commencement of Hostilities in June 1787, anonymous (London: G. Robinson, 1787);

The English Peerage; or, A View of the Ancient and Present State of the English Nobility, 3 volumes, anonymous (London: G. G. & J. Robinson, 1790);

An Enquiry concerning Political Justice, and its Influence on General Virtue and Happiness, 2 volumes (London: G. G. & J. Robinson, 1793); revised as *Enquiry concerning Political Justice, and its Influence on Morals and Happiness,* 2 volumes (London: G. G. & J. Robinson, 1796; Philadelphia: Bioren & Madan, 1796); revised again, 2 volumes (London: G. G. & J. Robinson, 1798);

Things As They Are; or, The Adventures of Caleb Williams (3 volumes, London: B. Crosby, 1794; 2 volumes, Baltimore: H. & P. Rice, 1795; revised edition, 3 volumes, London: G. G. & J. Robinson, 1796; revised again, 3 volumes, London: G. G. & J. Robinson, 1797); revised as *Caleb Williams* (1 volume, London: H. Colburn & R. Bentley, 1831; 2 volumes, New York: Harper, 1831);

Cursory Strictures on the Charge delivered by Lord Chief Justice Eyre to the Grand Jury, October 2, 1794, anonymous (London: D. I. Eaton, 1794); facsimile in *Uncollected Writings (1785–1832),* edited by Jack W. Marken and Pollin (Gainesville, Fla.: Scholars' Facsimiles and Reprints, 1968);

A Reply to an Answer to Cursory Strictures, supposed to be wrote by Judge Buller. By the Author of Cursory Strictures, anonymous (London: D. I. Eaton, 1794);

Considerations on Lord Grenville's and Mr. Pitt's Bills, concerning Treasonable and Seditious Practices, and Unlawful Assemblies. By a Lover of Order, anonymous (London: J. Johnson, 1795); facsimile in *Uncollected Writings (1785–1832);*

The Enquirer. Reflections on Education, Manners, and Literature. In a Series of Essays (London: G. G. & J. Robinson, 1797; Philadelphia: Robert Campbell, 1797; revised edition, Edinburgh: John Anderson / London: W. Simkin & R. Marshal, 1823);

Memoirs of the Author of A Vindication of the Rights of Woman (London: J. Johnson/G. G. & J. Robinson, 1798; revised edition, London: J. Johnson, 1798); republished as *Memoirs of Mary Wollstonecraft Godwin, Author of "A Vindication of the Rights of Woman"* (Philadelphia: James Carey, 1799);

St. Leon: A Tale of the Sixteenth Century (4 volumes, London: G. G. & J. Robinson, 1799; 2 volumes, Alexandria, Va.: J. & J. D. Westcott,

Portrait of a woman believed to be Mary Jane Clairmont Godwin (location of original unknown)

1801; revised edition, 1 volume, London: H. Colburn & R. Bentley, 1831);

Antonio: A Tragedy in Five Acts (London: G. G. & J. Robinson, 1800; New York: D. Longworth, 1806);

Thoughts. Occasioned by the Perusal of Dr. Parr's Spital Sermon, preached at Christ Church, April 15, 1800: Being a Reply to the Attacks of Dr. Parr, Mr. Mackintosh, the Author of an Essay on Population, and Others (London: G. G. & J. Robinson, 1801); facsimile in *Uncollected Writings (1785–1832);*

Bible Stories. Memorable Acts of the Ancient Patriarchs, Judges, and Kings: Extracted from their Original Historians. For the Use of Children, 2 volumes, as William Scholfield (London: R. Phillips, 1802; Albany, N.Y.: Charles R. & George Webster, 1803); republished as *Sacred Histories; or, Insulated Bible Stories,* 2 volumes (London: R. Phillips, 1806);

Life of Geoffrey Chaucer, the Early English Poet, including Memoirs of his Near Friend and Kinsman, John of Gaunt, Duke of Lancaster: With Sketches of the Manners, Opinions, Arts and Literature of England in the Fourteenth Century, 2 volumes (London: R. Phillips, 1803);

Fleetwood; or, The New Man of Feeling (3 volumes, London: R. Phillips, 1805; 2 volumes, New York: I. Rilcy, 1805; Alexandria, Va.: Cotton & Stewart, 1805; revised edition, 1 volume, London: R. Bentley, 1832);

Fables, Ancient and Modern. Adapted for the Use of Children, 2 volumes, as Edward Baldwin (London: T. Hodgkins, 1805; New York: Increase Cooke, 1807);

The Looking Glass: A True History of the Early Years of an Artist. Calculated to Awaken the Emulation of Young Persons of Both Sexes, in the Pursuit of Every laudable Attainment: particularly in the Cultivation of the Fine Arts, as Theophilus Marcliffe (London: T. Hodgkins, 1805);

Life of Lady Jane Grey, and of Lord Guildford Dudley, her Husband, as Theophilus Marcliffe (London: T. Hodgkins, 1806);

The History of England. For the Use of Schools and Young Persons, as Edward Baldwin (London: T. Hodgkins, 1806);

The Pantheon; or Ancient History of the Gods of Greece and Rome. Intended to facilitate the Understanding of the Classical Authors, and of the Poets in General, as Edward Baldwin (London: T. Hodgkins, 1806);

Faulkener, A Tragedy (London: R. Phillips, 1807);

Essay on Sepulchres; or, A Proposal for erecting some Memorial of the Illustrious Dead in All Ages on the Spot where their Remains have been interred (London: W. Miller, 1809; New York: M. & W. Ward, 1809);

The History of Rome: From the Building of the City to the Ruin of the Republic, as Edward Baldwin (London: M. J. Godwin, 1809);

Outlines of English History. For the Use of Children from Four to Eight Years of Age, as Edward Baldwin (London: M. J. Godwin, 1814);

Lives of Edward and John Philips. Nephews and Pupils of Milton. Including Various Particulars of the Literary and Political History of their Times (London: Longman, Hurst, Rees, Orme & Brown, 1815);

Letters of Verax, to the Editor of the Morning Chronicle, on the Question of a War to be commenced for the Purpose of putting an End to the Possession of Supreme Power in France by Napoleon Bonaparte (London: R. & A. Taylor, 1815); facsimile in *Uncollected Writings (1785–1832);*

Mandeville. A Tale of the Seventeenth Century in England (3 volumes, Edinburgh: A. Constable / London: Longman, Hurst, Rees, Orme & Brown, 1817; 2 volumes, New York: W. B. Gilley, 1818; Philadelphia: M. Thomas, 1818);

Letter of Advice to a Young American: On the Course of Studies it might be Most Advantageous for him to Pursue (London: M. J. Godwin, 1818); facsimile in *Uncollected Writings (1785–1832);*

Of Population. An Enquiry concerning the Power of Increase in the Numbers of Mankind, being an Answer to Mr. Malthus's Essay on that Subject (London: Longman, Hurst, Rees, Orme & Brown, 1820; New York: Augustus M. Kelley, 1964);

History of Greece: From the Earliest Records of that Country to the Time in which it was reduced into a Roman Province, as Edward Baldwin (London: M. J. Godwin, 1821);

History of the Commonwealth of England. From its Commencement, to the Restoration of Charles the Second, 4 volumes (London: H. Colburn, 1824–1828);

Cloudesley: A Tale (3 volumes, London: H. Colburn & R. Bentley, 1830; 2 volumes, New York: Harper, 1830; Albany, N.Y.: O. Steele/Little & Cummings, 1830);

Thoughts on Man, his Nature, Productions and Discoveries. Interspersed with some Particulars respecting the Author (London: Effingham Wilson, 1831; New York: Augustus M. Kelley, 1969);

Deloraine (3 volumes, London: R. Bentley, 1833; 2 volumes, Philadelphia: Carey, Lea & Blanchard, 1833);

Lives of the Necromancers; or, An Account of the Most Eminent Persons in Successive Ages, who have claimed for themselves, or to whom has been imputed by Others, the Exercise of Magical Powers (London: F. J. Mason, 1834; New York: Harper, 1835);

Essays, Never Before Published, by the late William Godwin, edited by C. Kegan Paul (London: H. S. King, 1873).

Editions: *The Elopement of Percy Bysshe Shelley and Mary Wollstonecraft Godwin, as Narrated by William Godwin,* edited by H. Buxton Forman (London: Bibliophile Society, 1911; Boston, Mass.: Privately printed, 1912);

Memoirs of Mary Wollstonecraft, edited by W. Clark Durant (London: Constable / New York: Greenberg, 1927);

Memoirs of Mary Wollstonecraft, with a preface by John Middleton Murry (London: Constable / New York: R. R. Smith, 1928);

Imogen: A Pastoral Romance. From the Ancient British, edited by Jack W. Marken (New York: New York Public Library, 1963);

Italian Letters: or, The History of the Count de St. Julian, edited by Burton R. Pollin (Lincoln: University of Nebraska Press, 1965);

Four Early Pamphlets (1783–1784), edited by Pollin (Gainesville, Fla.: Scholars' Facsimiles & Reprints, 1966);

Uncollected Writings (1785–1832), edited by Marken and Pollin (Gainesville, Fla.: Scholars' Facsimiles and Reprints, 1968);

Caleb Williams, edited by David McCracken (Oxford: Oxford University Press, 1970; revised, 1982);

The Collected Novels and Memoirs of William Godwin, 8 volumes, edited by Mark Philp, Pamela Clemit, and Maurice Hindle (London: Pickering & Chatto, 1992);

The Political and Philosophical Writings of William Godwin, 7 volumes, edited by Philp, Clemit, and Martin Fitzpatrick (London: Pickering & Chatto, 1993);

St. Leon: A Tale of the Sixteenth Century, edited by Clemit (Oxford: Oxford University Press, 1994).

OTHER: *Memoirs of the Life of Simon Lord Lovat, Written by Himself, in the French Language and now first translated, from the Original Manuscript,* translated by Godwin (London: G. Nichol, 1797);

Posthumous Works of the Author of A Vindication of the Rights of Woman, 4 volumes, edited by Godwin (London: J. Johnson, 1798);

Mylius's School Dictionary of the English Language. To which is prefixed A New Guide to the English Tongue by Edward Baldwin, as Edward Baldwin (London: M. J. Godwin, 1809);

Outlines of English Grammar, partly abridged from Hazlitt's New and Improved Grammar of the English Tongue, edited by Godwin as Edward Baldwin (London: M. J. Godwin, 1810);

Valperga; or, The Life and Adventures of Castruccio, Prince of Lucca; A Novel by Mary Shelley, revised by Godwin (London: G. & B. W. Whittaker, 1823);

Preface to *Transfusion; or, The Orphans of Unwalden, by the late William Godwin Jun.,* 3 volumes (London: J. Macrone, 1835; New York: Wallis & Newell, 1835).

BOOK – by Mary Jane Clairmont Godwin: *Dramas for Children, or, Gentle Reproofs for Their Faults* (London: M. J. Godwin, 1808).

OTHER: *The Adventures of Andolocia with the Purse and Cap of His Father Fortunatus: A Tale for the Nursery,* edited by Mary Jane Clairmont Godwin (London: Tabart, 1804);

The Adventures of Valentine and Orson: A Tale for the Nursery, edited by Godwin (London: Tabart, 1804);

Beauty and the Beast: A Tale for the Nursery, edited by Godwin (London: Tabart, 1804);

Blue Beard, of Female Curiosity; and Little Red Riding-Hood, edited by Godwin (London: Tabart, 1804);

The Children in the Wood: A Tale for the Nursery, edited by Godwin (London: Tabart, 1804);

Cinderella, or, The Little Glass Slipper: A Tale for the Nursery, edited by Godwin (London: Tabart, 1804);

The History of Fortunatus, edited by Godwin (London: Tabart, 1804);

The History of Fortunio and His Famous Companions, edited by Godwin (London: Tabart, 1804);

The History of Goody Two-Shoes and The Adventures of Tommy Two-Shoes, edited by Godwin (London: Tabart, 1804);

The History of Jack the Giant-Killer, edited by Godwin (London: Tabart, 1804);

The History of Prince Fatal and Prince Fortune and The Story of the Three Wishes, edited by Godwin (London: Tabart, 1804);

The History of Robin Hood, edited by Godwin (London: Tabart, 1804);

The History of the White Cat, edited by Godwin (London: Tabart, 1804);

The History of Tom Thumb: A Tale for the Nursery, edited by Godwin (London: Tabart, 1804);

The History of Whittington and His Cat, edited by Godwin (London: Tabart, 1804);

Hop o' My Thumb: A Tale for the Nursery, edited by Godwin (London: Tabart, 1804);

Nourjahad, or, The Folly of Unreasonable Wishes: An Eastern Tale, edited by Godwin (London: Tabart, 1804);

Riquet with the Tuft: A Tale for the Nursery, edited by Godwin (London: Tabart, 1804);

The Sleeping Beauty in the Wood, edited by Godwin (London: Tabart, 1804);

The Story of Griselda, edited by Godwin (London: Tabart, 1804);

Aladdin, or, The Wonderful Lamp: A Tale for the Nursery, edited by Godwin (London: Tabart, 1805);

Ali Baba, or The Forty Thieves: A Tale for the Nursery, edited by Godwin (London: Tabart, 1805);

Richard Coeur de Lion: An Historical Tale, edited by Godwin (London: Tabart, 1805);

The Voyages of Sinbad the Sailor: A Tale for the Nursery, edited by Godwin (London: Tabart, 1805);

Belisarius, the Roman General, edited by Godwin (London: Tabart, 1807);

The History of Jack and the Bean-Stalk, edited by Godwin (London: Tabart, 1807);

Tabart's Moral Tales: in Prose and Verse; Selected and Revised from the Best Authors, 4 volumes, edited by Godwin (London: Tabart, 1809);

Johann David Wyss, *The Family Robinson, or, Journal of a Father Shipwrecked, with his Wife and Children, on an Uninhabited Island,* translated by Mary Jane Godwin (London: M. J. Godwin, 1814).

William Godwin and his second wife, Mary Jane Clairmont Godwin, made a lasting contribution to children's literature both as writers and publishers. William Godwin achieved fame as a novelist, biographer, and philosopher. He had a progressive approach to education and his works for children reflect his commitment to treat children with respect and affection and to encourage them to read widely, particularly in literature and history. Mary Jane translated and edited fiction for children. As publishers they were responsible for the notable works of Charles and Mary Lamb and the lasting tale *The Family Robinson* (1814).

William Godwin was the seventh of thirteen children of dissenting minister John Godwin and his wife, Ann. He was educated at London's Haxton Academy and at the age of twenty-two entered the ministry. Despite his orthodox training he was an independent minister who did not follow customary procedures, was not particularly popular, and changed congregations often.

After only a few years Godwin's religious beliefs were in turmoil and he left the ministry, turning to writing. He was prolific; within three years he produced a biography, a volume of sermons, a translation of memoirs, a pamphlet on education, a three-volume novel against the tyranny of the rich, a book of literary parody, two radical political pamphlets, digests of two years of British and foreign history, and reviews. Godwin was also a compulsive diarist, completing a total of thirty-two small notebooks between 1788 and 1836.

In 1791 Godwin married feminist Mary Wollstonecraft, the author of *A Vindication of the Rights of Woman* (1792). She died following the birth of their child, and Godwin was left with two children to raise: the infant Mary and Wollstonecraft's three-year-old daughter, Fanny Imlay. In the years following Wollstonecraft's death Godwin courted and proposed marriage to

several women. He sought a companion who would assist with his daughters' upbringing and leave him free to write.

In Godwin's diary of 5 May 1801 he records meeting Mary Jane Clairmont. Godwin was eager to wed, yet at the time of their marriage in 1802 he scarcely knew Mary Jane. He soon found that she lacked Wollstonecraft's talent and charm and had unpredictable moods and a bad temper. Godwin's friends, who had known his first wife, were bitterly disappointed with Mary Jane. Yet, despite her disagreeable characteristics, she and Godwin had a satisfactory relationship in the early years of their marriage. Few verifiable facts exist to detail Mary Jane Godwin's early life. When she married Godwin she was introduced as a widow with two children, Charles Gaulis Clairmont and Clara Mary Jane Clairmont. On Charles's birth certificate Mary Jane described herself as a daughter of Andrew Peter Devereux, and it is known she had lived in France as a child.

After Godwin and Mary Jane married, Godwin had to relinquish the career of writing moral philosophy that he had planned and instead find work that would provide for his family. Following the birth of William Godwin Jr. the year after their marriage, the merged household had five children under the age of eight. Mary Jane Godwin had been employed by Benjamin Tabart as an editor and writer of children's books, but her name did not appear on any title page. At the time of her marriage to Godwin she gave up her position but continued working at home to contribute to the family finances. She translated and edited about thirty stories from France, Germany, and England for Tabart's multivolume Popular Stories series (1804–1809). Some were written in simple prose, and others were turned into verse for younger children. William Godwin's diary records that he read and revised his wife's work.

Bible Stories. Memorable Acts of the Ancient Patriarchs, Judges, and Kings . . . For the Use of Children (1802) was published by Richard Phillips. Although published as by "William Scholfield," biographer William St. Clair produces substantial evidence to attribute the title to William Godwin. While the writer's public life and writing had made his name synonymous with atheism, sedition, and sexual immorality, he related the biblical stories as historical documents, avoiding any endorsement or condemnation of Christianity. The two-volume work must have been a commercial success, as it was still being advertised in 1831 and was pirated at least twice in the United States.

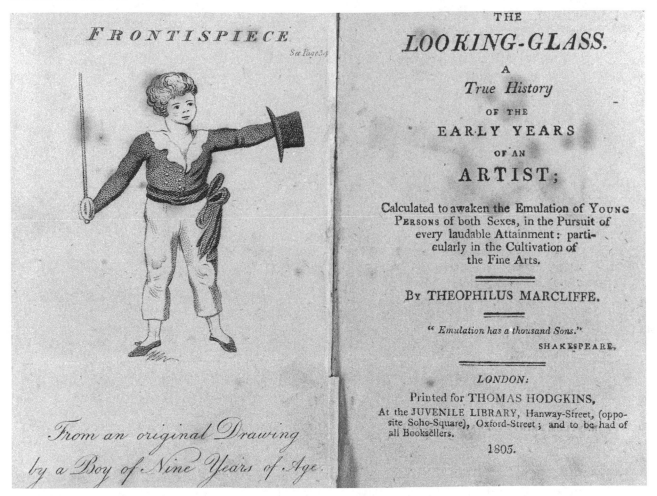

FRONTISPIECE

See Page 34

From an original Drawing by a Boy of Nine Years of Age.

THE
LOOKING-GLASS.
A
True History
OF THE
EARLY YEARS
OF AN
ARTIST;

Calculated to awaken the Emulation of YOUNG
PERSONS of both Sexes, in the Pursuit of
every laudable Attainment: particularly in the Cultivation of
the Fine Arts.

BY THEOPHILUS MARCLIFFE.

" Emulation has a thousand Sons."
SHAKESPEARE.

LONDON:
Printed for THOMAS HODGKINS,
At the JUVENILE LIBRARY, Hanway-Street, (opposite Soho-Square), Oxford-Street; and to be had of
all Booksellers.
1805.

Frontispiece and title page for one of Godwin's didactic biographies for young readers, published under his Marcliffe pseudonym (courtesy of Special Collections, Thomas Cooper Library, University of South Carolina)

Godwin had personal experience educating children and found contemporary children's books wanting. He wrote in the preface to *Bible Stories:* "These modern improvers have left out of their system that most essential branch of human nature – the imagination. Our youth, according to the most approved recent systems of education, will be excellent geographers, natural historians, and mechanics; . . . in a word, they are exactly informed about all those things, which if a man or a woman were to live or die without knowing, neither man nor woman would be an atom the worse."

Neither Godwin's writing nor his wife's editing and translating produced the income needed to support their large family. Several of Godwin's rich friends who admired his writing were invited to become subscribers to help the Godwins start a business, and in 1805 they opened the Juvenile Library, a shop specializing in books for children. Since

Godwin's notorious political views would not inspire confidence in him as a publisher of children's books, the shop was opened in the name of Thomas Hodgkins, an experienced manager who was also employed to run it. The store carried schoolbooks, copybooks, quills, pens, inkstands, slates, maps, and stationery in addition to juvenile books. Many books sold in the shop were written by Godwin – using the pseudonyms Theophilus Marcliffe and Edward Baldwin – and his friends.

Fables, Ancient and Modern (1805) was the first title to appear under the pseudonym Edward Baldwin. Published by Thomas Hodgkins, the two volumes include seventy-three copper-plate illustrations. The work was successful and went through many printings, including a one-volume edition and a French translation by Mary Jane Godwin. In the introductions, aimed at adults, William Godwin wrote, "In the present volumes I have uniformly represented myself to my own thoughts as relating the several stories to a child. I have fancied myself taking the child upon my knee, and have expressed them in such language as I should have been likely to employ, when I wished to amuse the child, and make what I was talking to take hold upon his attention."

Fables, Ancient and Modern was based on those of Aesop, but Godwin updated some stories and added others. Not satisfied to let the tales end abruptly or to leave the interpretation to the reader, he clearly spelled out the moral of each. In "The Fox and the Raven," for example, a cunning fox tricks a crow out of a piece of cheese. Godwin concludes: "foxes are never taught what is good and what is naughty. But, if I were a little boy or a little girl, I would rather go without cheese all the days of my life, than gain it by such cheating and wicked speeches as this fox is said to have made." Godwin also wrote in the preface to *Fables, Ancient and Modern* that he "endeavored to make almost all my narratives end in a happy and forgiving tone, in that tone of mind which I would wish to cultivate in my child."

Godwin only wrote two books using the pseudonym Theophilus Marcliffe; both teach the virtues of education, hard work, and self-help. *The Looking Glass: A True History of the Early Years of an Artist* (1805) describes artist William Mulready's success in overcoming his humble origins. The book's cover claimed that the work would act as a mirror, "in which every Good Little Boy and Girl may see what He or She is; and those who are not yet Quite Good may find what They ought to be." *Life of Lady Jane Grey, and of Lord Guildford Dudley, her Husband* (1806) tells the story of a young lady who "at twelve years of age understood eight languages, was for nine days Queen of England, and was beheaded in the Tower in the seventeenth year of her age, being at that time the most amiable and accomplished woman in Europe." A later edition of *Life of Lady Jane Grey* lists Edward Baldwin as the author, even though the advertisements still attributed the work to Theophilus Marcliffe.

The books Godwin wrote as Edward Baldwin — scholarly books on history, mythology, and grammar — were more popular than those he wrote as Marcliffe. In *The History of England, For the Use of Schools and Young Persons* (1806) the author determines that his pages should not be too detailed or "crowded with a variety of articles"; instead, they should present an overview of the great landmarks of British history in a refreshing manner. The historical narrative begins with the early Britons and ends with the death of William Pitt in 1806. The book was extremely popular and went through eight editions by 1836. Godwin also published an abridged version entitled *Outlines of English History* (1814), which went through three editions in the author's lifetime.

Baldwin's *The Pantheon: or Ancient History of the Gods of Greece and Rome* first appeared in 1806. It was an attempt to displace Andrew Tooke's translation of Françoise Antoine Pomey's *Pantheon* (1694), then the standard schoolbook of Greek mythology. Godwin's respect for ancient religion, myth, and poetry was reflected in this lively survey of the principal Greek and Roman gods. But Godwin was a businessman, and in 1810, in order to fill a school order, he agreed to have four illustrations reengraved because they were thought to be too explicit. In the subsequent editions the nudity of Venus, Apollo, Mercury, and Mars was covered. Baldwin's *Pantheon* was widely used as a school text and went through nine editions by 1836.

Despite continuous financial difficulties, Godwin moved his family and the Juvenile Library to larger London quarters at 41 Skinner Street in 1807. Over the main door was a statue of Aesop relating his fables to children. An illustration of the carving was used in some of Godwin's books as a trademark. By 1870 the reputation of the Juvenile Library was sufficiently established for it to be registered in Mary Jane's name as M. J. Godwin and Company. The company had a strong list of titles including education, fables, romance, and moral tales offered at a range of prices.

From the beginning of their publishing career the Godwins' product line had included titles written by William Godwin's well-known friends. Charles and Mary Lamb were among the most productive contributors. Mary Lamb wrote *Mrs. Leicester's School* and edited *Poetry for Children* (1807). Their *Tales from Shakespear* appeared in two volumes in 1807, with illustrations by Mulready. It sold out immediately and was republished separately in twenty parts. However, despite their successful publishing partnership, neither of the Lambs liked Mary Jane Godwin. Charles Lamb complained that she drove her husband's friends from the house, and he portrayed her, in an essay under thin disguise, as a "spiteful, gossipy, and jealous woman."

Other examples of the Godwin firm's productions for young readers are Charles Lamb's *The King and Queen of Hearts* (1805) and *Rays from the Rainbow* (1808); Eliza Fenwick's *Lessons for Children; or, Rudiments of Good Manners, Morals, and Humanity*

View of Skinner Street from Fleet Market, 1805. Godwin moved the Juvenile Library into the building on the left in 1807.

(1808), *Stories of Old Daniel: or Tales of Wonder and Delight* (1808), and *Continuation of the Stories of Old Daniel* (1820); and Lady Mountcashel's *Stories for Little Boys and Girls in Words of One Syllable* (circa 1820) and *Six Stories for the Nursery in Words of One or Two Syllables* (1824). Many of these books included engravings by William Mulready and on occasion by William Blake. Daniel Defoe's *Robinson Crusoe,* first published in 1719, was very popular and was so widely copied that an entire genre of "robinsonnades" imitated it – among the imitations was Johann David Wyss's *Swiss Family Robinson* (1812–1813), introduced to English readers by M. J. Godwin and Company as *The Family Robinson, or, Journal of a Father Shipwrecked, with his Wife and Children, on an Uninhabited Island* (1814). It was published in two volumes, translated by Mary Jane. The second edition, published under the now-familiar title, was a commercial success.

William Godwin's *History of Greece* was begun in 1809 but was not completed until 1821. He greatly admired the achievements of the Greeks because whatever "bold and admirable conception"

occurred in their minds, they attempted to realize. The work must have sold well, as new editions were published in 1828, 1829, 1836, and 1862.

Mary Jane Godwin's place in the annals of children's literature is deserved for the part she played in preparing books for publication and in stimulating others to write. She also contributed a title of her own, *Dramas for Children, or, Gentle Reproofs for Their Faults* (1808); the author is identified on the title page as the "editor of Tabart's *Popular Stories.*" The dramas, a series of morality plays, were intended as much for reading as for presentation. They all embody lessons about conduct or warnings against wrongdoing, as some of the titles convey: "The Dangers of Gossiping," "The Fib Found Out," and "The Spoiled Child." The reward for good children, as told in *Dramas for Children,* was to be taken to 41 Skinner Street and allowed to choose a book by the famous Mr. Baldwin. The second edition was published in 1817, with four plates by George Cruikshank.

The Juvenile Library was one of the foremost publishers and distributors of books for children. Its list contained more than twenty volumes that were clearly and entertainingly written and handsomely bound and illustrated. Unfortunately, by 1822 Godwin had exhausted the patience and credit of his friends and was bankrupt. For many years Percy Bysshe Shelley had been his main benefactor, but Shelley cut off his financial support after eloping with Godwin's daughter, Mary. Although the business had done well, in the early years it had been heavily financed by loans, and often new loans had to be secured to pay off earlier ones. Godwin's constant need to borrow money destroyed most of his self-respect. His children were grown: Jane was estranged from the family, Fanny had committed suicide, and the two sons were on their own. Mary, the author of *Frankenstein* (1818), returned with her children to live with her father and stepmother after Shelley's death. The Godwins gave up the Skinner Street establishment. Mary Jane made sporadic efforts to publish children's books from an address in the Strand in the 1820s, but Godwin himself appears to have had little to do with the business. William Godwin died on 7 April 1836 and was buried in the same grave as Mary Wollstonecraft. Mary Jane Godwin died in 1841 and was buried alongside her husband.

William Godwin is widely recognized for his contributions to political philosophy, but his writing for children receives little attention from biographers. As publishers, however, both he and Mary Jane made an important contribution to children's literature. M. J. Godwin and Company's publications such as *Fables, Ancient and Modern*, *Tales from Shakespear*; and *The Family Robinson* added significantly to the body of literature written for children. Of all their publications, however, only the *Fables* and the retitled *Swiss Family Robinson* remain in print.

Biographies:

C. Kegan Paul, *William Godwin: His Friends and Contemporaries,* 2 volumes (London: King, 1876);

Ford K. Brown, *The Life of William Godwin* (London: Dent, 1926);

Peter H. Marshall, *William Godwin* (New Haven: Yale University Press, 1984);

William St. Clair, *The Godwins and the Shelleys: The Biography of a Family* (New York: Norton, 1989);

George Woodcock, *William Godwin: A Biographical Study* (Montreal: Black Rose Books, 1989).

References:

Burton R. Pollin, *Godwin Criticism: A Synoptic Bibliography* (Toronto: University of Toronto Press, 1967);

William St. Clair, "William Godwin as Children's Bookseller," in *Children and Their Books: A Celebration of the Work of Iona and Peter Opie,* edited by Gillian Avery and Julia Briggs (Oxford: Clarendon Press, 1989), pp. 165–179;

Sue Taylor, "M. J. Godwin & Co.," *Horn Book,* 20 (March–April 1944): 79–87.

Thomas Hughes

(20 October 1822 – 22 March 1896)

Douglas Ivison
Université de Montréal

See also the Hughes entry in *DLB 18: Victorian Novelists After 1885.*

BOOKS: *History of the Working Tailors' Association* (London: George Bell, 1850);

A Lecture on the Slop-System, Especially As It Bears Upon the Females Engaged in It (Exeter: Pollard, 1852);

King's College and Mr. Maurice (London: Nutt, 1854);

Tom Brown's School Days, anonymous (Cambridge: Macmillan, 1857); republished as *Schooldays at Rugby* (Boston: Ticknor & Fields, 1857);

The Scouring of the White Horse; or, The Long Vacation Ramble of a London Clerk (Cambridge: Macmillan, 1858; Boston: Ticknor & Fields, 1859);

Tom Brown at Oxford (17 monthly parts, Boston: Ticknor & Fields, 1859–1861; 3 volumes, London: Macmillan, 1861);

Account of the Lock-out of Engineers, 1851-2 (Cambridge: Macmillan, 1860);

Tracts for Priests and People, No. 1: Religio Laici (Cambridge: Macmillan, 1861); republished as *A Layman's Faith* (London: Macmillan, 1868);

The Cause of Freedom: Which Is Its Champion in America, The North or the South? (London: Emancipation Society, 1863);

Alfred the Great, 3 parts (London: Macmillan, 1869; Boston: Osgood, 1871);

Memoir of a Brother (London: Macmillan, 1873; Boston: Osgood, 1873);

Lecture on the History and Objects of Co-operation (Manchester: Central Co-Operative Board, 1878);

The Old Church: What Shall We Do with It? (London: Macmillan, 1878);

The Manliness of Christ (London: Macmillan, 1879; Boston: Osgood, 1880; enlarged edition, London: Macmillan, 1894);

True Manliness, edited by E. E. Brown (Boston: D. Lothrop, 1880);

Rugby, Tennessee: Being Some Account of the Settlement Founded on the Cumberland Plateau by the Board of

Thomas Hughes

Aid to Land Ownership (London & New York: Macmillan, 1881);

Memoir of Daniel Macmillan (London: Macmillan, 1882);

Address on the Occasion of the Presentation of a Testimonial in Recognition of his Services to the Cause of Co-operation, 6 December 1884 (Manchester: Co-Operative Printing Society, 1885);

Life and Times of Peter Cooper (London: Macmillan, 1886);

Church Reform and Defence (London: Richard Clay, 1886);

James Fraser, Second Bishop of Manchester: A Memoir, 1818–85 (London: Macmillan, 1887);

Co-Operative Production (Manchester: Central Co-Operative Board, 1887);

David Livingstone (London: Macmillan, 1889);

Co-Operative Faith and Practice, by Hughes and E. Vansittart Neale (Manchester: Co-Operative Union, 1890);

Fifty Years Ago: A Layman's Address to Rugby School (London: Macmillan, 1891);

Vacation Rambles (London: Macmillan, 1895);

Early Memories for the Children (London: Thomas Burleigh, 1899).

OTHER: James Russell Lowell, *The Biglow Papers,* edited, with a preface, by Hughes (London: Trubner, 1859);

Comte de Paris, *The Trades' Unions of England,* edited, with a preface, by Hughes (London: Smith, Elder, 1869);

Frederick Denison Maurice, *The Friendship of Books and Other Lectures,* edited, with a preface, by Hughes (London: Macmillan, 1874);

A Manual for Co-Operators, edited, with a preface, by Hughes and E. Vansittart Neale (London: Macmillan, 1881);

G. T. T. Gone to Texas: Letters from Our Boys, edited, with a preface, by Hughes (London: Macmillan, 1884).

SELECTED PERIODICAL PUBLICATION – UNCOLLECTED: "The Ashen Faggot, A Tale for Christmas," *Macmillan's Magazine,* 5 (January 1862): 234–252.

With *Tom Brown's School Days* (1857), one of the first novels expressly written for boys, Thomas Hughes created both the genre of the public-school novel and the schoolboy-hero. He established the conventions followed by all subsequent public-school novels, and his protagonist, Tom Brown, became a model for the heroes of subsequent school and sports stories, both in Britain and the United States, and even for the heroes of popular adult novels of the time. At the same time, Hughes's portrayal of life at Rugby under the leadership of its headmaster, Dr. Thomas Arnold, defined the public-school experience for the novel's readers. In fact, as Isabel Quigley has written in *The Heirs of Tom Brown: The English School Story* (1982), *Tom Brown's School Days* "came to be regarded as fact" and became "a blue-print for the public schools." Not only did this story for boys influence the development of the British educational system, but, with its emphasis on manliness and athleticism, it also had a profound impact on British society as the United Kingdom moved into an era of increasing militarism and imperialism. After the massive success of his first novel Hughes quickly published two less successful novels, *The Scouring of the White Horse; or, The Long Vacation Ramble of a London Clerk* (1858) and *Tom Brown at Oxford* (1859–1861), and then turned to other activities. Yet for the rest of his life he would be known as "the author of *Tom Brown's School Days,*" a status that provided him with the opportunity to pursue his goals as a writer, politician, and activist.

Hughes was born on 20 October 1822 in the quiet village of Uffington, sixty miles west of London in the Berkshire Downs. This part of England is redolent with history, its best-known landmark being the White Horse carved into the chalk side of a hill near Uffington. The question of its origin remains a matter of debate, but during Hughes's childhood many people believed that the White Horse was a monument created in celebration of King Alfred's defeat of the Danes at the Battle of Ashdown in 871. This reminder of the area's rich and colorful history was clearly visible from Hughes's childhood home and was to be a significant landmark in much of his writing, forming the subject matter of his second novel.

Hughes felt himself to be grounded in the area's history through his family, as four generations of his ancestors had served as vicars of Uffington. His father, John Hughes, had attended Westminster school and Oriel College, Oxford, then returned to Uffington, where he married Margaret Wilkinson. John Hughes published prose and verse in magazines such as *Blackwood's* and *Ainsworth's,* and he edited the *Boscobel Tracts* (1830), which recounted the experiences of Charles I after the defeat of his forces at the Battle of Worcester; his work was praised by such well-known literary figures as Mary Russell Mitford and Sir Walter Scott. Hughes later drew an idealized picture of his father as Squire Brown and admired his "true popular sympathies." Another important influence on the young Hughes was his paternal grandmother, Mary Ann Hughes, through whom he met literary celebrities such as Scott.

Thomas Hughes was the second of eight children, and his older brother, George, was to have a great and long-lasting impact on his life. After George's death, Hughes published *Memoir of a Brother* (1873) as a tribute. In 1830 the eight-year-old Thomas and his brother George were sent to Twyford School, a private preparatory school near Winchester. Twyford was progressive in placing an emphasis on gymnastics and also on the reading and memorization of poetry, providing Hughes

Tom and Harry East give Flashman his comeuppance; illustration by Arthur Hughes for the 1869 edition of Tom Brown's
School Days

with the opportunity to learn many of the longer poems of his favorite writer, Sir Walter Scott.

In February 1834 the Hughes brothers enrolled at Rugby School, selected by John Hughes because Dr. Thomas Arnold, whom he had known at Oxford, had recently become headmaster. Although the conservative John Hughes disagreed with Arnold's politics, he had great faith in both the ability and character of the influential educational reformer. His decision was to have a great impact on young Thomas's life. Since becoming headmaster Arnold had rescued Rugby from a period of decline, instituting several reforms to reduce the bullying and unruly behavior of the students and assigning more authority to the school's instructors and senior pupils. His goal was to create an environment in which the boys who entered the school would leave as men ready to lead the nation, sharing his commitment to Christian ideals of virtue and moral behavior.

Although Hughes was not a member of the inner circle closest to Arnold, the headmaster did have a great influence on him. As Hughes would later document in *Tom Brown's School Days,* he was instantly gripped by the doctor's weekly Sunday evening sermons: Arnold "was a man whom we felt to be, with all his heart and soul and strength, striving against whatever was mean and unmanly and unrighteous in our little world" and "was fighting for us and by our sides, and calling on us to help him and ourselves and one another." Arnold inspired in Hughes the desire to participate, however he could, in the fight against evil, thereby deeply influencing the rest of his life.

Hughes liked Rugby so much that he did not want to leave when he was nineteen, the maximum age allowed at the school. Nevertheless, in 1842 he entered Oriel College, Oxford, which his father had attended and where Arnold had held a fellowship. There Hughes rejoined his brother George. In November Hughes's first known publication, a poem titled "Milton and the Swedish Lord," appeared in *Ainsworth's Magazine.* Oxford was a disappointment after Rugby, as the author would illustrate in *Tom Brown at Oxford.* He was later to admit that his first year had been wasted, and in keeping with the emphasis on athletics at Oriel College, Hughes's greatest accomplishments during that first year occurred

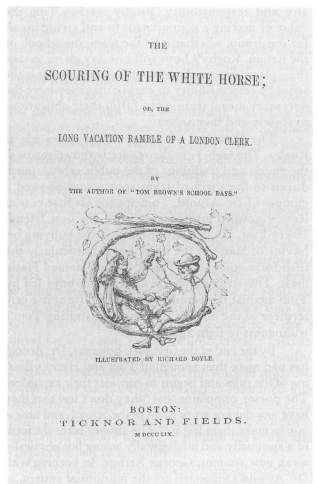

Frontispiece and title page for the American edition of Hughes's second novel

ual in promoting cooperation, as he makes clear in his preface: "We are sure that reverence for all great Englishmen, and a loving remembrance of the great deeds done by them in old times, will help to bring to life in us the feeling that we are a family, bound together to work out God's purposes in this little island, and in the uttermost parts of the earth." As in his Tom Brown stories, Hughes also makes a point of defending the value of sports and fighting as means of instilling manliness in men.

The initial critical response to the work was mostly positive, if somewhat less enthusiastic than that over *Tom Brown's School Days*. It sold six thousand copies in its first two weeks, but public interest quickly waned, and a third edition did not appear until 1889. Today it is largely forgotten. Although Hughes's evocation of an ideal England that never was does "exude an undeniable charm," as George J. Worth has written in *Thomas Hughes* (1984), it must be noted that as a novel *The Scouring*

of the White Horse is a failure: there is little sustaining narrative; the characterization is thin; and the writing is often didactic and ponderous. The most vivid scenes, as in Hughes's other fiction, are those describing sports and fighting.

Hughes's third and final novel was the much anticipated continuation of Tom Brown's adventures, *Tom Brown at Oxford,* which began to appear as a serial in the first issue of *Macmillan's Magazine* (November 1859) and was published in book form in 1861. A much longer work than either of Hughes's previous novels, it is poorly structured and rambling. Its first part chronicles Tom Brown's first year as an Oxford undergraduate. Like Hughes, Tom spends little of his time involved in intellectual endeavors, preferring to concentrate on trouble-making and rowing. A sport once again dominates Hughes's narrative, as the most fully realized scenes are those describing rowing, and the academic side of life at Oxford is mostly absent from the novel.

Hughes does not celebrate Oxford as he did Rugby, however. Tom greatly misses the presence of a figure like Arnold to provide guidance and ensure order, and without such a presence he experiences disillusionment and disappointment. As the novel progresses, he begins to realize that all is not well in Oxford or in England. Through his friend, the poor servitor Hardy, Tom is made aware of the prejudices that exist in his own college and begins to grapple with some of the issues facing society.

The second half of the novel is less concerned with life at Oxford, spending only one chapter each on Tom's second and third years as an undergraduate, as Hughes introduces a melodramatic love story and intrigue concerning the unjust treatment of a childhood friend, Harry Winburn. Hughes uses Winburn to introduce broader social questions into the narrative, and Tom sees his friend's problems as being symptomatic of the "condition of England."

At Oxford Tom is confronted with many solutions to this problem – Tractarianism, Utilitarianism, and Chartism, among others – and he explores and discards some of them. He must overcome his own naive idealism; after all, by carelessly interfering he becomes partially responsible for Harry Winburn's unjust treatment. In *Tom Brown at Oxford,* a less optimistic novel than Hughes's previous works, neither team sports nor rural life provides a suitable solution. The countryside has been tainted by squires and farmers who have forgotten the importance of community and cooperation in their pursuit of financial reward. Team sports, while remaining an important means of promoting cooperation among classes – as illustrated by Hardy's success in rowing – cannot solve all of England's problems. For Hughes, athleticism must be tempered with Christian belief, producing a "muscular Christian" who "does not hold that mere strength or activity are in themselves worthy of any respect or worship, or that one man is a bit better than another because he can knock him down."

Tom Brown at Oxford was not the massive success that its predecessor had been, yet it was among the ten best-selling books in the United States in 1861, and many editions were published in both Britain and the United States during the next few decades. It has remained out of print for much of the current century. Although the *Spectator* declared the book to be better than *Tom Brown's School Days,* many critics condemned it as a failure. The *Saturday Review* found it "more dull, purposeless and depressing as it proceeds." However, despite its flaws, much of the novel is of interest, especially its first

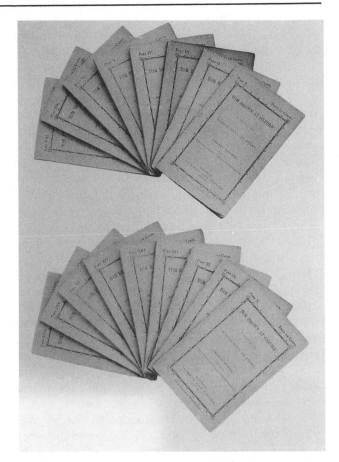

First publication, in parts, of the second Tom Brown novel

part, presenting as it does a detailed portrait of the sporting and social life at Oxford. In *The Sinews of the Spirit: The Ideal of Christian Manliness in Victorian Literature and Religious Thought* (1985) Norman Vance labels *Tom Brown at Oxford* "interesting and unjustly neglected." After publishing the short story "The Ashen Faggot, A Tale for Christmas" in the January 1862 issue of *Macmillan's Magazine,* Hughes was to publish no more fiction, although he did begin writing a novel during the 1880s.

Hughes's newfound celebrity provided him with a platform from which he could participate in public debate. He was gravely concerned with the challenges that faced his cherished Church of England, both from within and without, and gave speeches and lectures on the subject. He also published books on issues facing the church. As a result of his Christian convictions, and partly inspired by the American poet James Russell Lowell, Hughes was also a lifelong opponent of slavery and an advocate of the cause of American abolitionists. After the outbreak of the Civil War he quickly supported the cause of the North – a position contrary to the opinion of many in Britain. He frequently lectured on behalf of the Northern cause, introduced representatives of the Union to his friends, and in 1862 helped to establish the London Emancipation Society. From 1865 to 1874 he was a Liberal member of the House of Commons, often representing the interests of the cooperative societies and trade unions.

In *Alfred the Great* (1869), the first of six biographies he was to write, Hughes raises many of the issues addressed in his novels. For Hughes, Alfred was a Carlylean hero, creating order out of chaos and forming a nation in the spirit of Christ. As *The Scouring of the White Horse* had already made clear, Hughes saw Alfred as a symbol of commitment to a higher ideal, and it was this commitment, along with the cooperation that it would inspire, that Hughes consistently proposed as the solution to his society's difficulties. In all six biographies Hughes attempts to illuminate the exemplary in his subject's life, whether the subject be his brother George or David Livingstone. This focus, often combined with a lack of attention to detail, resulted in a lack of accuracy. Thus, despite their relative initial success, Hughes's biographies are neither informative nor of particular interest to today's reader.

During the 1870s Hughes became concerned about the lack of opportunity for the young men graduating from his beloved public schools. In response, he invested a great deal of money in the establishment of a Christian cooperative settlement in northeastern Tennessee on land purchased by the Board of Aid to Land Ownership, which he helped to found. Rugby, Tennessee, as Hughes named it, was officially opened on 5 October 1880 to high hopes; Hughes was so optimistic that he quickly settled his mother there. Because of a combination of incompetence, poor management, bad luck, and unrealistic expectations, however, the settlement was a complete failure, and its collapse was a financial disaster for Hughes, who was forced to vacate his London home and accept an appointment as a Chester County court judge in July 1882. He spent the rest of his life in Chester, remaining active as a social activist, lecturer, and writer. Suffering from a series of colds, Hughes was on his way to Italy to recuperate when he died on 22 March 1896 in Brighton.

Throughout his career as a writer, social activist, and public figure Hughes held true to his ideals of cooperation and community, which he felt could only be achieved through commitment to something greater than the individual: the team, the school, the nation, or Christianity. This commitment unites Hughes's often diverse writings, the causes he supported, and the organizations in which he participated. Hughes was not always successful in translating his ideas into action, and toward the end of his life he was cast aside by many of those whom he had tried to help, yet he remained optimistic, unwavering in his faith.

Despite his many accomplishments, Hughes is best remembered for *Tom Brown's School Days,* a classic of children's literature largely responsible for the advent of both the school story and the sports story. One of the most popular and widely read books of its day, it had an impact beyond the bookshelves, as its emphasis on athleticism and moral virtue would later be felt in the launching of the modern Olympics and the creation of the Boy Scouts at the turn of the century. Despite its flaws, *Tom Brown's School Days* remains an often vivid and exciting portrayal of a world that no longer exists.

Bibliography:

M. L. Parrish and Barbara Kelsey Maun, *Charles Kingsley and Thomas Hughes: First Editions (With a Few Exceptions) in the Library at Dormy House, Pine Valley, New Jersey* (London: Constable, 1936).

Biography:

Edward C. Mack and W. H. G. Armytage, *Thomas Hughes: The Life of the Author of Tom Brown's Schooldays* (London: Benn, 1952).

References:

Bruce Haley, *The Healthy Body and Victorian Culture* (Cambridge, Mass.: Harvard University Press, 1978), pp. 141–155;

Christian K. Messenger, *Sport and the Spirit of Play in American Fiction* (New York: Columbia University Press, 1981), pp. 159–164;

P. W. Musgrave, *From Brown to Bunter: The Life and Death of the School Story* (London: Routledge & Kegan Paul, 1985), pp. 47–65;

Isabel Quigley, *The Heirs of Tom Brown: The English School Story* (London: Chatto & Windus, 1982), pp. 42–68;

Jeffrey Richards, *Happiest Days: The Public Schools in English Fiction* (Manchester: Manchester University Press, 1988), pp. 23–69;

Norman Vance, *The Sinews of the Spirit: The Ideal of Christian Manliness in Victorian Literature and Religious Thought* (Cambridge: Cambridge University Press, 1985), pp. 134–165;

George J. Worth, *Thomas Hughes* (Boston: Twayne, 1984).

Jean Ingelow

(17 March 1820 – 20 July 1897)

Carolyn Sigler
Kansas State University

See also the Ingelow entry in *DLB 35: Victorian Poets After 1850.*

BOOKS: *A Rhyming Chronicle of Incidents and Feelings,* anonymous, edited by Edward Harston (London: Longman, Brown, Green & Longmans, 1850);

Allerton and Dreux; Or, The War of Opinion, anonymous, 2 volumes (London: Wertheim, 1851);

Tales of Orris (Bath: Binns & Goodwin / London: Marlborough, 1860); expanded version republished as *Stories Told to a Child* (London: Strahan, 1865; Boston: Roberts Brothers, 1866);

Poems (London: Longman, Green, Longman, Roberts & Green, 1863; Boston: Roberts Brothers, 1863);

Studies for Stories from Girls' Lives, anonymous (2 volumes, London: Strahan, 1864; 1 volume, Boston: Roberts Brothers, 1865);

Home Thoughts and Home Scenes, by Ingelow and others (London: Routledge, 1865; Boston: Tilton, 1865);

Songs of Seven (Boston: Roberts Brothers, 1866);

A Story of Doom, and Other Poems (London: Longmans, Green, 1867; Boston: Roberts Brothers, 1867);

A Sister's Bye-Hours, anonymous (London: Strahan, 1868; Boston: Roberts Brothers, 1868);

Mopsa the Fairy (London: Longmans, Green, 1869; Boston: Roberts Brothers, 1869);

The Monitions of the Unseen, and Poems of Love and Childhood (Boston: Roberts Brothers, 1871);

The Little Wonder-Horn: A New Series of "Stories Told to a Child" (London: King, 1872);

Off the Skelligs (4 volumes, London: King, 1872; 1 volume, Boston: Roberts Brothers, 1872);

Poems, first and second series, 2 volumes (London: Longmans, 1874, 1877);

Fated to be Free (3 volumes, London: Tinsley Brothers, 1875; 1 volume, Boston: Roberts Brothers, 1875);

The Shepherd Lady, and Other Poems (Boston: Roberts Brothers, 1876);

One Hundred Holy Songs, Carols, and Sacred Ballads (London: Longmans, Green, 1878);

Sarah de Berenger (1 volume, London: Low, Marston, 1879; Boston: Roberts Brothers, 1879; 3

volumes, London: Sampson, Low, Marston, Searle & Rivington, 1880);

Don John (3 volumes, London: Low, Marston, Searle & Rivington, 1881; 1 volume, Boston: Roberts Brothers, 1881);

Poems, third series (London: Longmans, Green, 1885); republished as *Poems of the Old Days and the New* (Boston: Roberts Brothers, 1885);

John Jerome, His Thoughts and Ways: A Book without Beginning (London: Low, Marston, Searle & Rivington, 1886; Boston: Roberts Brothers, 1886);

Very Young and Quite Another Story (London: Longmans, Green, 1890);

A Motto Changed (New York: Harper, 1894).

Jean Ingelow's London home is as lovingly cared for today as it was in the 1880s and 1890s by Ingelow herself. Yet, in a history-conscious city profusely dotted with bright blue markers indicating the homes of thousands of famous, infamous, and obscure literary figures, 6 Holland Villas Road, the home of one of the late nineteenth century's most popular and admired poets, remains markerless. This omission is particularly surprising given the degree of both popular and critical acclaim Ingelow achieved in her lifetime. Her books for both adults and children sold widely in Britain and were even more popular in America. Writers such as Alfred Tennyson, John Ruskin, Robert Browning, Henry Wadsworth Longfellow, and Christina Rossetti admired and befriended her and, along with many other literary figures, were frequent visitors to her Kensington home. In 1892, after Tennyson's death, many people suggested Ingelow as a candidate for poet laureate. Although she is generally dismissed today as a minor author of poetry and novels for adults, Ingelow's extraordinary work as a writer of early fantasy for children and her influence on and indebtedness to such contemporary writers as Lewis Carroll and Christina Rossetti deserve serious consideration and investigation.

Jean Ingelow, the eldest of eleven children, was born in the coastal town of Boston in Lincolnshire on 17 March 1820. Her father, William Ingelow, was a moderately prosperous banker and wine merchant, although he later suffered bankruptcy and near financial ruin. Her mother, Jean Kilgour, was of Scottish descent and strict Evangelical convictions. As a child Jean spent much of her time playing near the river by her parents' and grandfather's houses, learning the names of ships and listening to sailors singing and chanting as they loaded and unloaded the ships. She recaptured these early impressions in her poetry and prose, as in this early passage from her autobiographical novel *Off the Skelligs* (1842):

> One of my earliest pleasures was to watch the gangs of men who at high tide towed vessels up and down the river, where, being moored before these granaries, cargoes of corn were shot down from the upper stories into their holds. . . . I spent many a happy hour with my brother, sometimes listening to the soft, hissing sound made by the wheat in its descent; sometimes admiring the figure-heads of the vessels, or laboriously spelling out the letters of their names.

In 1834 William Ingelow, pursuing a business opportunity, moved his family to Ipswich in Suffolk. They lived in a large home above banking offices on the ground floor, and Jean Ingelow was given the rare luxury of having a room of her own. She and her siblings were educated at home by their mother and aunt, Rebecca Ingelow, a fiercely independent woman who had rejected marriage as an unbearable loss of liberty. Ingelow, who was close to her aunt, was probably influenced by her in her own decision as an adult not to marry.

At Ipswich the Ingelow children produced their own weekly magazine, *The St. Stephen's Herald,* on a toy printing press; it cost its subscribers a penny. Jean Ingelow was editor and also contributed poetry under the pen name "Orris." *The Herald* also afforded Ingelow, whose mother increasingly depended on her to help with the demands of their growing family, a much-needed excuse to write. Mrs. Ingelow could not disapprove of writing poetry to amuse the younger children, but her strict Evangelical principles and harried life caused her to frown on her daughter's writing strictly for her own pleasure. She even locked up the writing paper against such frivolous wastes, forcing Ingelow to write and conceal her verses on the backs of the white shutters in her room. Fortunately, Mrs. Ingelow's pragmatism also led her to recognize the extent of her daughter's talent when she discovered the shutter poems, and Ingelow was finally allowed to write unimpeded.

In the 1840s Ingelow was further encouraged in her writing by family friends, including the curate Edward Harston and his family, as well as by the Taylors, a literary family whom Jean loved to visit. Isaac Taylor was the author of *The Natural History of Enthusiasm* (1829), and his two daughters, Jane and Ann, had published *Original Poems for Infant Minds* (1804) and *Rhymes for the Nursery* (1806) – the latter included the immortal "Twinkle, Twinkle Little Star." Ingelow found another impetus to write in her desire to ease her parents' continuing financial difficulties, and in 1850, when the family moved to London, she was preparing her first slender collection of poems for publication.

A Rhyming Chronicle of Incidents and Feelings (1850) received little critical attention, although Tennyson (who had just succeeded Wordsworth as poet laureate) commented favorably on the collection in a letter to Ingelow's cousin Barbara Holloway. In 1851 *Allerton and Dreux; Or, The War of Opinion,* the first of her seven novels for adults, was published, and the following year Ingelow began contributing children's stories, under her childhood pen name Orris, to *Youth's Magazine,* edited by her old friend Isaac Taylor (Ingelow also briefly served as the publication's editor in 1855). In 1860 Ingelow published at her own expense *Tales of Orris,* a compilation of the stories written for *Youth's Magazine.* A collection of narratives for older girls called *Studies for Stories from Girls' Lives* (1864) was well received – in 1893 Helen Black in her *Notable Women Authors of the Day* described it as "full of wit and humour, of gentle satire and fidelity to nature. They are prose poems, written in faultless style and are truthful word-paintings of real everyday life."

Ingelow's voice as a storyteller strikes the reader forcefully: rich, complex, and with a clear sense of the author's imaginative, humorous, and sometimes frustrated personality as a writer. Ingelow's writings for children are particularly concerned with the tension between the worlds of imagination and domesticity and the need to achieve, often with great difficulty and loss, a balance between the two. Her tales often take the gently subversive point of view of the child, rather than the more conventional privileging of the adult viewpoint, and she frequently portrays adults as cranky, illogical, and unreasonable. In Ingelow's tales it is often adults who learn a "valuable lesson" – although the lessons themselves are conventional ones about independence, trust, love, and family. She constantly reminds her readers that children are deserving of respect as individuals with hopes and fears that are as valid – sometimes more valid – than those of adults.

In 1865, the year she met and became good friends with Christina Rossetti, Ingelow expanded her *Tales of Orris* as *Stories Told to a Child.* This work might seem easy to dismiss as a collection of conventional Victorian morality tales, yet they include subtle, gently subversive humor, and the narrator's

wry but sympathetic voice is a characteristic and significant device in the tales. Ingelow invariably demonstrates a perceptive compassion for the child's point of view while at the same time refusing to idealize childhood or child characters. In "The Grandmother's Shoe" Ingelow subverts conventional morality tales of naughty children who are taught lessons by watchful adults when the narrator describes the effect of the disapproving and suspicious gaze of her friend's grandmother:

> However good we might be, still we were ONLY children. We actually felt ashamed of ourselves in her presence to think that we were children! We knew we could not help it ... but she did not seem to think so; she sometimes had the appearance of thinking that we could help it if we liked, and were children on purpose!

Later, however, when the narrator and her friend Lucy try to "reform" to please Lucy's grandmother, their efforts ironically go all but unnoticed:

> How little, for all the sympathy of love, a child is known to his elders! How little during the ensuing week our childish troubles, our wavering endeavors to do right, our surprise at our own failures, were suspected in that orderly household.

In "Can and Could" Ingelow dramatizes the power of humble actions over inflated rhetoric. Could, a well-to-do gentleman, walks the streets shaking his head and exclaiming "What a shame!" and "What a disgrace!" over such problems as poverty and disease, while Can, a woman who is "not a grand personage," helps a poor child whose mother is ill. Ingelow claimed not to be in favor of women's rights (a claim that in 1892 shocked an interviewer from the London *Woman's Herald*), yet her awareness of women's power to affect their society in private but vital ways is consistently presented in her stories. For example, she satirically contrasts Can's and Could's achievements at the end of the day:

> Could having reached his comfortable home sat down before the fire and made a great many reflections; ... on the progress of civilisation, on the necessity for some better mode of education for the masses; ... he reflected on poverty, and made castles in the air as to how he might mitigate its severity, and then having in imagination made many people happy, he felt that a benevolent disposition was a great blessing, and fell asleep over the fire.
> Can made only two things. When she had helped to carry the child's basket, she kindly made her sick mother's bed, and then she went home and made a pudding.

The landing of the queen, an illustration for Ingelow's best-known children's book, Mopsa the Fairy *(1869)*

The Athenaeum described *Stories Told to a Child* as tales "which no child could hear without delight," and these mostly realistic stories often seem to have their bases in autobiography: many are set in Lincolnshire or Scotland, and all feature a first-person narrator who addresses the reader as if recalling an incident from memory. One story, "The Golden Opportunity," even features a little girl named Orris who humorously narrates a "great event . . . [the] birthday I first possessed a piece of gold," recalling the Ingelows' financial difficulties.

The author's most highly acclaimed collection of poetry for adults, *Poems* (1863), was well received upon its publication, and in 1867 Ingelow published a new collection, *A Story of Doom, and Other Poems.* In 1869 Ingelow published her best-known children's book, *Mopsa the Fairy,* one of the earliest in a flood of imitations and parodies of Lewis Carroll's *Alice's Adventures in Wonderland* (1865). A young boy named Jack, while his nurse reads and his baby sister

dozes, climbs a hollow hawthorn tree and falls inside, where he discovers a nest of fairies, including Mopsa, who becomes Jack's playmate, friend, and teacher. A large albatross named Jenny carries Jack and Mopsa off to Fairyland. She assures Jack, when he worries about his parents, that "when boys go to Fairyland, their parents are never uneasy about them."

The picaresque story that follows, in which Jack travels through a series of magical lands and helps to release the fairies from a diabolical spell and to restore Mopsa to her throne, is a vivid and haunting fantasy of female power. Jack's reluctant acceptance of his need to return home to the domestic power of his mother is paralleled by Mopsa's acceptance of her own authority as queen of the fairies. In the book's poignant final chapter, Mopsa achieves separation from Jack, her rescuer, by literally giving back his kiss in a subversive reversal of fairy-tale convention.

The book also experiments with linear time in ways that anticipate later fantasies. Jack discovers, in a chapter titled "Winding-Up Time," creatures that begin old and grow younger, that the "same thing never happens twice in Fairyland," and that Fairyland is not a place but rather a time long ago. Mopsa explains to him, "when the albatross brought you she did not fly with you a long way off, but a long way back – hundreds and hundreds of years. This is your world, as you can see; but none of your people are here, because they are not made yet." Although the novel ends with an emphatic "That's all," a clear indication that Jack will never return to Mopsa's world, the novel's epigraph offers a sense of transcendent hope through the power of imagination:

'Tis thy world, 'tis my world
City, mead, and shore,
For he that hath his own world
Hath many worlds more.

Ingelow's last collection for children, *The Little Wonder-Horn: A New Series of "Stories Told to a Child,"* was published in 1872. Like *Mopsa the Fairy,* it invokes the liberating fantasy of the fairy-tale genre, though at the same time fairy tales such as "The Ouphe of the Wood," "The Fairy Who Judged Her Neighbors," and "The Prince's Dream" often seem more didactic in their intent than the realistic tales in *Stories Told to a Child.* "The Prince's Dream" is similar in theme to "A Golden Opportunity," yet, though haunting and moving, it lacks the humor and optimism of the earlier tale. At the end of "The Prince's Dream" the protagonist remains trapped in his tower, as bleakly baffled about the power gold has over humankind as he was before the old man's lesson, while his mysterious teacher has abruptly vanished. In this tale — as in many of her stories for children — Ingelow attempts to reconcile the practical need for money with consequences of coveting wealth for its own sake. Like Charles Dickens, Ingelow was profoundly aware of the power of money from her own family's bouts with bankruptcy.

In 1872 Ingelow published her autobiographical adult novel, *Off the Skelligs,* which, unlike her more satiric children's works that favor the child's perspective, reveals an increasingly sentimental and nostalgic view of childhood:

> Some people appear to feel that they are much wiser, much nearer to the truth and to realities than they were when they were children. They think of childhood as immeasurably beneath and behind them. I have never been able to join in such a notion. It often seems to me that we lose quite as much as we gain by our lengthened sojourn here.

The last twenty-five years of Ingelow's life were marked with success and friendship. She continued to publish volumes of poetry and novels for adults until a few years before her death. She received respect and fellowship in high literary circles; welcomed visitors from England and abroad, particularly America, where she was extremely popular; and finally enjoyed financial security. Although characterizing herself in letters as a shy person, she seemed to have a gift for making others feel comfortable and for several years gave what she called "copyright dinners" at which she would entertain twelve needy people just released from a hospital.

Ingelow died on 20 July 1897. Her obituary in the London *Times* characterized her as a writer "whose works gave sincere pleasure to many and offence or pain to none." Yet, although *Mopsa the Fairy* has remained in print sporadically over the last century, most of Ingelow's other works for both adults and children have fallen into obscurity. New interest in the work of Ingelow and other Victorian women writers, exemplified in such collections as Nina Auerbach and U. C. Knoepflmacher's *Forbidden Journeys* (1992), may bring highly deserved critical attention to one of the nineteenth century's most gifted women writers.

References:

Nina Auerbach and U. C. Knoepflmacher, *Forbidden Journeys: Fairy Tales and Fantasies by Victorian Women Writers* (Chicago: University of Chicago Press, 1992);

Naomi Lewis, "A Lost Pre-Raphaelite," *Times Literary Supplement,* 8 December 1972, pp. 1487–1488;

Maureen Peters, *Jean Ingelow: Victorian Poetess* (Ipswich: Boydell Press, 1972);

Some Recollections of Jean Ingelow and Her Early Friends (London: Wells Gardner, 1901).

Annie Keary

(3 March 1825 – 3 March 1879)

Kay E. Vandergrift
Rutgers University

BOOKS: *Mia and Charlie: Or, A Week's Holiday at Rydale Rectory* (London: David Bogue, 1856); republished, illustrated by Birket Foster (New York, 1866);

Sidney Grey, A Tale of School Life (London, 1857; New York: General Protestant Episcopal Sunday School, n.d.); republished as *Sidney Grey; Or, A Year From Home* (London: Warne, 1883);

Heroes of Asgard and the Giants of Jotunheim, or, The Christmas Week and Its Story, by Keary and Eliza Keary (London: David Bogue, 1857); republished as *The Heroes of Asgard: Tales from Scandinavian Mythology* (London & New York: Macmillan, 1893); republished as *The Heroes of Asgard: Tales from Scandinavian Mythology,* illustrated by Huard (New York: Macmillan, 1900);

The Rival Kings, or, Overbearing (London: W. Kent, 1858);

Through the Shadows (London: Hurst & Blackett, 1859);

Blind Man's Holiday: Or, Short Tales for the Nursery, illustrated by John Absolon (London: Griffith & Farron, 1860; New York: Robert Carter, 1866);

Early Egyptian History for the Young; with Descriptions of the Tombs and Monuments, by Keary and Eliza Keary (Cambridge: Macmillan, 1861);

Janet's Home, 2 volumes (London: Macmillan, 1863);

Little Wanderlin, and Other Fairy Tales (London: Macmillan, 1865);

Clemency Franklyn, 2 volumes (London: Macmillan, 1866);

Oldbury, 3 volumes (London: Macmillan, 1869; Philadelphia: Porter & Coates, n.d.);

The Nations Around (London: Macmillan, 1870); republished as *The Nations Round Israel* (London: Macmillan, 1893);

Castle Daly: the Story of an Irish Home Thirty Years Ago, 3 volumes (London: Macmillan, 1875);

Annie Keary

A York and a Lancaster Rose (London: Macmillan, 1877);

A Doubting Heart, 3 volumes (London: Macmillan, 1879; New York: Harper, 1879);

Father Phim (London: Faith Press, 1879).

OTHER: "Phonic Writing," in *The Dawn of History: An Introduction to Pre-Historic Study,* edited by Charles Francis Keary (London: Mozley & Smith, 1878; New York: J. Fitzgerald, 1883), chapter 13;

"Picture Writing," in *The Dawn of History: An Introduction to Pre-Historic Study,* edited by Charles Francis Keary (London: Mozley & Smith, 1878; New York: J. Fitzgerald, 1883), chapter 12;

"Religion," in *The Dawn of History: An Introduction to Pre-History Study,* edited by Charles Francis

Keary (London: Mozley & Smith, 1878; New York: J. Fitzgerald, 1883), chapter 8;

"To Emily At Her Own Home, From the Cat," in *Enchanted Tulips and Other Verses for Children,* by Keary, Eliza Keary, and Maud Keary (London: Macmillan, 1914), pp. 52–55;

"Left Alone," in *Enchanted Tulips and Other Verses for Children,* by Keary, Eliza Keary, and Maud Keary (London: Macmillan, 1914), pp. 90–91;

"Winter," in *Enchanted Tulips and Other Verses for Children,* by Keary, Eliza Keary, and Maud Keary (London: Macmillan, 1914), pp. 70–72.

From a very early age Annie Keary turned the everyday events of a sheltered Victorian childhood into highly imaginative stories. She published twelve books for children and several domestic and historical novels for adults. Her children's writings include original fairy tales, nature stories, poetry, school stories, myths, history, and tales of everyday life in Victorian England.

Annie Keary was born on 3 March 1825 in Bilton, Yorkshire; she was the daughter of William Keary, an Irish soldier-turned-clergyman, and Lucy Plumer Keary, an English gentlewoman, both of whom encouraged their daughter to exercise her imagination. She was the youngest of six children, with four older brothers and one sister. Eliza Keary's 1882 memoir of her sister relates how some of Annie's fantasy characters became regular companions of their nursery play and later appeared as characters in her children's stories.

Keary spent her childhood in the town of Hull and was educated mostly at home, but she also attended a dame's school with one of her brothers and, briefly, a boarding school. Keary was partially deaf, and thus she could not hear the sermons that students were required to discuss in their compositions. She often horrified her teachers with her "creative" interpretations of those sermons. Because she was partially deaf, Keary paid attention to details and became a keen observer of people and things. This attention to detail was reflected in her stories.

Eliza Keary's memoir paints a picture of a young woman who dedicated much of her life to the care of others. Annie Keary sacrificed the one romantic love of her life to care for her brother's motherless children and later nursed both her parents through their final illnesses. Her own health was not strong, and she died of an unnamed disease, probably cancer, on her fifty-fourth birthday.

Many of Keary's works reflect the Victorian moralism that attempted to frighten young sinners onto the paths of righteousness by depicting horrific punishments, akin to the fates that befell the mythic monsters in the Norse tales she adapted. Nevertheless, her prose, especially in the later books, is not as ponderous or as preachy as much of that by her contemporaries. Instead, her stories were gentle tales of everyday child experiences. Throughout her life Keary retained a childlike delight in the imagination and in simple domestic pleasures reflected in her stories. She was especially adept at character development, often depicting very realistic protagonists who, although confined to a particular locale, were not really constricted by it.

Mia and Charlie: Or, A Week's Holiday at Rydale Rectory (1856), Keary's first published children's book, is set in Nunnington and describes many of the scenes of this village, where the author spent a summer (probably 1840) while her father was recuperating from a serious illness. This book also presents Keary's version of a local tale about a stepmother and a sickly child in an old manor house.

Both *Sidney Grey, A Tale of School Life* and *Heroes of Asgard and the Giants of Jotunheim, or, The Christmas Week and Its Story* were published the following year. *Sidney Grey,* a boys' school story, was probably Keary's most popular children's book during her lifetime. *Heroes of Asgard,* however, written with her sister, Eliza, is her most lasting contribution to children's literature. It was the first successful interpretation of Norse myths for children, has been reprinted many times, and is the most readily available of all of Keary's works. Included in this collection are two especially well-told stories, "Iduna Giving the Magic Apples" and "The Punishment of Lothi."

The Rival Kings, or, Overbearing (1858) is a story of a family in which two jealous sons must learn to accept their father's three adopted children. It includes an example of the Victorian tendency to use death to convey a moral to children: in this case, it is not the evil child who dies but a younger sibling he had mistreated. In spite of its heavy-handed morality, this is a much more child-centered and compelling story than many of its time.

Many of the short stories in *Blind Man's Holiday: Or, Short Tales for the Nursery* (1860) are told from the point of view of Little Helen, who resembles the author as a child. One of the autobiographical aspects of this collection is the inclusion of the powerful Mrs. Calkill, an imaginary character who was the consistent nursery companion of Keary and her brother. Religious overtones are strong, as in the story of the little girl who loses her glove in a garden and immediately kneels to pray for help and

Charles Kingsley

(12 June 1819 – 23 January 1875)

Brendan A. Rapple
Boston College

See also the Kingsley entries in *DLB 21: Victorian Novelists Before 1885* and *DLB 32: Victorian Poets Before 1850.*

BOOKS: *The Saint's Tragedy: or, The True Story of Elizabeth of Hungary, Landgravine of Thuringia, Saint of the Romish Calendar* (London: Parker, 1848; New York: International Book, 1855);

Twenty-five Village Sermons (London: Parker, 1849; Philadelphia: Hooker, 1854);

Introductory Lectures, Delivered at Queen's College, London (London: Parker, 1849);

Alton Locke, Tailor and Poet. An Autobiography (London: Chapman & Hall, 1850; New York: Harper, 1850);

Cheap Clothes and Nasty, as Parson Lot (London: Macmillan, 1850);

Yeast; a Problem (London: Parker, 1851; New York: Harper, 1851);

The Application of Associative Principles and Methods to Agriculture. A Lecture, Delivered on Behalf of the Society for Promoting Working Men's Associations, on Wednesday, May 28, 1851 (London: Bezer, 1851);

The Message of the Church to Labouring Men. A Sermon Preached at St. John's Church, Charlotte Street, Fitzroy Square, On the Evening of Sunday, June the 22nd, 1851 (London: Parker, 1851);

Phaethon; or, Loose Thoughts for Loose Thinkers (Cambridge: Macmillan, 1852; Philadelphia: Hooker, 1854);

Sermons on National Subjects Preached in a Village Church (London: Griffin, 1852);

Who Are the Friends of Order? A Reply to Certain Observations in a Late Number of Fraser's Magazine *on the So-Called "Christian Socialists"* (London: Lumley, 1852);

Hypatia: or, New Foes with an Old Face (London: Parker, 1853; New York: Lowell, 1853);

Alexandria and Her Schools. Four Lectures Delivered at the Philosophical Institution, Edinburgh (Cambridge: Macmillan, 1854);

Charles Kingsley and his wife, Fanny

Sermons on National Subjects. Second Series (London & Glasgow: Griffin, 1854);

Who Causes Pestilence? Four Sermons, with Preface (London & Glasgow: Griffin, 1854);

Westward Ho! or, the Voyages and Adventures of Sir Amyas Leigh, Knight, of Burrough, in the County of Devon, in the Reign of Her Most Glorious Majesty Queen Elizabeth (Cambridge: Macmillan, 1855; Boston: Ticknor & Fields, 1855);

Glaucus; or, The Wonders of the Shore (Cambridge: Macmillan, 1855; Boston: Ticknor & Fields, 1855);

Sermons for the Times (London: Parker, 1855; New York: Dana, 1856);

The Heroes; or Greek Fairy Tales, for My Children, illustrated by Kingsley (Cambridge: Macmillan, 1855; Boston: Warner, 1855);

Poems (Boston: Ticknor & Fields, 1856);

Two Years Ago (Cambridge: Macmillan, 1857; Boston: Ticknor & Fields, 1857);

Andromeda, and Other Poems (London: Parker, 1858; Boston: Ticknor & Fields, 1858);

Miscellanies (London: Parker, 1859);

The Good News of God; Sermons (London: Parker, 1859; New York: Burt, Hutchinson & Abbey, 1859);

The Massacre of the Innocents (London: Jarrold, 1859);

The Limits of Exact Science as Applied to History. An Inaugural Lecture, Delivered before the University of Cambridge (Cambridge & London: Macmillan, 1860);

Why Should We Pray for Fair Weather? A Sermon (London: Parker, 1860);

New Miscellanies (Boston: Ticknor & Fields, 1860);

Town and Country Sermons (London: Parker, 1861);

Ode Performed in the Senate-House, Cambridge, on the Tenth of June, M.DCCC.LXII. Composed for the Installation of His Grace the Duke of Devonshire, Chancellor of the University. Set to Music by W. Sterndale Bennett (Cambridge & London: Macmillan, 1862);

Speech of Lord Dundreary in Section D on Friday Last. On the Great Hippocampus Question, anonymous (Cambridge & London: Macmillan, 1862);

A Sermon on the Death of His Royal Highness, the Prince Consort, Preached at Eversley Church, December 22nd, 1861 (London: Parker, 1862);

The Water-Babies; A Fairy Tale for a Land-Baby (London & Cambridge: Macmillan, 1863; Boston: Burnham, 1864);

The Gospel of the Pentateuch. A Set of Parish Sermons (London: Parker, 1863);

The Roman and the Teuton. A Series of Lectures Delivered before the University of Cambridge (Cambridge & London: Macmillan, 1864; New York: Macmillan, 1890);

"What, Then, Does Dr. Newman Mean?" A Reply to a Pamphlet Lately Published by Dr. Newman (London & Cambridge: Macmillan, 1864);

Hints to Stammerers, by a Minute Philosopher (London: Longman, 1864);

David. Four Sermons Preached before the University of Cambridge (London & Cambridge: Macmillan, 1865);

Hereward the Wake, "Last of the English" (London & Cambridge: Macmillan, 1866; Boston: Ticknor & Fields, 1866);

The Temple of Wisdom. A Sermon (London: Macmillan, 1866);

Three Lectures Delivered at the Royal Institution, on the Ancien Regime as It Existed on the Continent before the French Revolution (London: Macmillan, 1867);

The Water of Life and Other Sermons (London: Macmillan, 1867; Philadelphia: Lippincott, 1868);

The Hermits (London: Macmillan, 1868; Philadelphia: Lippincott, 1868);

Discipline, and Other Sermons (London: Macmillan, 1868; Philadelphia: Lippincott, 1868);

God's Feast. A Sermon (London & Cambridge: Macmillan, 1868);

The Two Breaths (London: Jarrold, 1868);

Women and Politics (London: London National Society for Women's Suffrage, 1869);

The Address on Education, Read before the National Association for the Promotion of Social Science, at Bristol, on the 1st of October, 1869 (London: National Education League, 1869);

Madam How and Lady Why; or First Lessons in Earth Lore for Children (London: Bell & Daldy, 1870; New York: Macmillan, 1885);

At Last; A Christmas in the West Indies (London & New York: Macmillan, 1871);

Letter to a Public School Boy on Betting and Gambling (London: Society for Promoting Christian Knowledge, 1871?);

Town Geology (London: Strahan, 1872; New York: Appleton, 1873);

Poems; Including The Saint's Tragedy, Andromeda, Songs, Ballads, &c., Collected Edition (London: Macmillan, 1872; New York: Hurst, 1880?);

Plays and Puritans, and Other Historical Essays (London: Macmillan, 1873);

Prose Idylls, New and Old (London: Macmillan, 1873);

Frederick Denison Maurice, A Sermon Preached in Aid of the Girls' Home, 22 Charlotte Street, Portland Place (London: Macmillan, 1873);

Selections from Some of the Writings of C. Kingsley (London: Strahan, 1873);

Health and Education (London: Isbister, 1874; New York: Appleton, 1874);

Westminster Sermons (London: Macmillan, 1874);

Lectures Delivered in America in 1874 (London: Longmans, Green, 1875; Philadelphia: Coates, 1875);

Letters to Young Men on Betting and Gambling (London: King, 1877);

All Saints' Day and Other Sermons, edited by Rev. W. Harrison (London: Kegan Paul, 1878; New York: Scribner, Armstrong, 1878);

True Words for Brave Men: a Book for Soldiers' and Sailors' Libraries (London: Kegan Paul, 1878; New York: Whittaker, 1886);

Out of the Deep: Words for the Sorrowful, from the Writings of Charles Kingsley, edited by Fanny E. Kingsley (London & New York: Macmillan, 1880);

Daily Thoughts, Selected from the Writings of Charles Kingsley by His Wife (London: Macmillan, 1884);

From Death to Life. Fragments of Teaching to a Village Congregation. With Letters on the Life after Death, Edited by His Wife (London: Macmillan, 1887);

Words of Advice to School-Boys, Collected from Hitherto Unpublished Notes and Letters of the Late Charles Kingsley, edited by E. F. Johns (London: Simpkin/ Winchester: Warren, 1912);

The Tutor's Story; an Unpublished Novel, by the Late Charles Kingsley, revised and completed by Lucas Malet (Mrs. Mary St. Leger Harrison) (London: Smith, Elder, 1916; New York: Dodd, Mead, 1916).

OTHER: Charles B. Mansfield, *Paraguay, Brazil, and the Plate,* with a biographical sketch by Kingsley (Cambridge: Macmillan, 1856);

The History and Life of the Reverend Doctor John Tauler of Strasbourg; with Twenty-Five of His Sermons, with a preface by Kingsley (London: Smith, Elder, 1857);

Henry Brooke, *The Fool of Quality: or, The History of Henry Earl of Moreland,* with a biographical preface by Kingsley (London: Smith, Elder, 1859);

John Bunyan, *Pilgrim's Progress,* with a preface by Kingsley (London: Longman, 1860);

Rose Georgina Kingsley, *South by West; or, Winter in the Rocky Mountains and Spring in Mexico,* with a preface by Kingsley (London: Isbister, 1874).

The Reverend Charles Kingsley, writer of poetry; novels; historical works; sermons; religious tracts; scientific treatises; and political, social, and literary criticism, was one of the Victorian age's most prolific authors. His was by no means the stereotypical writer's ivory-tower existence, however, as his extensive practical activities in the public arena reveal. A parish priest for much of his life, Kingsley was also a prominent social reformer, political activist, and practical scientist, as well as the Regius Professor of Modern History at Cambridge,

chaplain to Queen Victoria, the private tutor to the future Edward VII, and the canon of Westminster. Clearly, he led a varied and interesting life and was well known among his contemporaries. Today Kingsley's abundant writings and diverse causes are largely forgotten, and few commentators would consider him in the front ranks of eminent Victorians. Although his condition-of-England novels, *Alton Locke, Tailor and Poet* (1850) and *Yeast; a Problem* (1851), still find a small readership and a few historians associate him with Christian Socialism, "muscular Christianity," or the great controversy with Cardinal Newman, Kingsley is primarily recalled for a single aspect of his career, one which he undoubtedly considered of minor importance – his writings for children. It is as the author of *The Water-Babies; A Fairy Tale for a Land-Baby* (1863), and to a lesser extent *Westward Ho!* (1855) and *The Heroes* (1855), that Kingsley has gone down in history.

Charles Kingsley was born on 12 June 1819 at Holne Vicarage near Dartmoor, Devonshire. His father, Charles, though reared to be a country gentleman, had taken Holy Orders because of the financial mismanagement of his inheritance. Kingsley's mother, Mary, more worldly and practical than his father, was born in the West Indies and came from a line of Barbadian sugar-plantation owners. During a short stay at a small preparatory school in Clifton, Kingsley witnessed the bloody 1831 Reform Bill riots in Bristol, which influenced his later social and political thought. Though there was talk of his going to Eton, in 1832 he was sent to Helston Grammar School in Cornwall, where the Reverend Derwent Coleridge, Samuel Taylor Coleridge's son, was headmaster. Kingsley was not academically outstanding, though he displayed great interest in art and natural science, especially botany and geology, and wrote much poetry. After the family moved to London in 1836 upon the elder Kingsley's being appointed rector of Saint Luke's, Chelsea, Charles Kingsley entered King's College as a day student. He did well and in the autumn of 1838 went to Magdalene College, Cambridge.

In July 1839 Kingsley met his future wife, Fanny Grenfell, the daughter of a prosperous family and several years his senior. At that time she was under the influence of the Tractarian movement, which argued for a revival of doctrines, rituals, and traditions of the older church, and she was even considering entering an Anglican sisterhood in London. Kingsley was experiencing religious doubts at the time, revolting from the "bigotry, cruelty, and quibbling" of the Athanasian Creed. He found his prescribed academic course at Cambridge tedious and irrelevant, and during his second year he spent more time in sporting activities than in study. However, his relationship with Fanny gradually brought him back to a firm belief in God and the Anglican Church. Wishing to marry and having decided to enter the church, Kingsley began to study diligently in order to gain a good degree. His late academic exertions proved fruitful – he gained a first class in classics and a second in mathematics – though he suffered a mild breakdown, a presage of years to come.

After taking holy orders Kingsley in July 1842 became curate in Eversley, Hampshire. At about this time, influenced by F. D. Maurice's *Kingdom of Christ* (1838), he became convinced that true religion could not remain distinct from social and political issues or the temporal needs of mankind. Accordingly, in addition to performing religious services, Kingsley worked feverishly to improve the appalling physical, social, and educational conditions of his Eversley parishioners, which had been ignored by the lax previous rector. In January 1844 Kingsley married Fanny, the marriage proving a happy and physically satisfying one. This latter aspect, as Susan Chitty stresses in her biography, was of particular importance to Kingsley, a highly sexed man. In May his extensive work as curate at Eversley was rewarded by his appointment as rector. In November 1844 Kingsley's first child, Rose, was born. His eldest son, Maurice, was born in 1847, and his third child, Mary St. Leger, who later wrote novels under the name of Lucas Malet, was born in 1852.

The year 1848 was extremely busy for Kingsley. He published the blank verse drama *The Saint's Tragedy,* a life of Saint Elizabeth, a married medieval saint. F. D. Maurice secured for him the professorship of English literature and composition at the then-recently established Queen's College, London, a post he was obliged to resign one year later due to pressure of work. Influenced by the political events in Europe that year, Kingsley attended the Chartist demonstration in London, at which he displayed a political poster signed "a Working Parson." Though the message was by no means revolutionary, the fact that it was espoused by an Anglican priest was momentous. Soon, together with Maurice and the barristers John Malcolm Ludlow and Thomas Hughes, author of *Tom Brown's Schooldays* (1856), Kingsley was fully committed to the Christian Socialist movement. He was never particularly radical, however, and as he grew older he increasingly became an establishment figure. As Dean Howson of Chester Cathedral portrayed Kingsley

An illustration by Linley Sambourne for Kingsley's The Water-Babies *(1863)*

after his death: "I should have described him as a mixture of the Radical and the Tory, the aspect of character which is denoted by the latter word being, to my apprehension, quite as conspicuous as that which is denoted by the former." Certainly, in Kingsley's Christian Socialism the emphasis was always far more on the Christian than on the Socialism.

In 1848 Kingsley's long story *Yeast; a Problem,* concerned with the deplorable living conditions of England's agricultural laboring families, began appearing in *Fraser's Magazine.* It was published in book form in 1851. Kingsley also began to contribute to various Christian Socialist journals. His political activities became more widely known, and adverse reaction by the establishment was probably responsible for his rejection for a professorship at King's College. His hectic activity throughout 1848, combined with domestic financial worries, undoubtedly contributed to the severe breakdown in health that occurred in the autumn.

In 1849 a cholera epidemic started in Jacob's Island in Bermondsey, a district in London's East End that had already achieved notoriety in Charles Dickens's *Oliver Twist* (1837–1838). Kingsley and his friends, manifesting the practical stress of the Christian Socialist movement, worked incessantly in the district to arrest the outbreak. A desire to introduce greater awareness of sanitation and hygiene into his contemporaries' lives remained a lifelong preoccupation with Kingsley. Indeed, he became so well known for his work in sanitary reform and his eagerness to instill an appreciation of the rules of public health that he was asked in the spring of 1854 to speak before the House of Commons on the unhygienic conditions prevalent in urban areas and the low remuneration of parish medical officers. The following year he led a deputation on the issue of sanitary reform to the prime minister.

Kingsley's horror at the frequently atrocious sanitary conditions in Victorian cities accounts for some of the most striking episodes and passages in his novel *Alton Locke*. This work, purporting to be the autobiography of a working-class Chartist poet, had as a principal aim the exposure of the dreadful working conditions, especially the shocking lack of hygiene, of tailors in London's West End. Kingsley, under the pseudonym "Parson Lot," had earlier published a passionate account of the same subject in his pamphlet *Cheap Clothes and Nasty* (1850).

In 1853 Kingsley published his first historical novel, *Hypatia: or, New Foes with an Old Face,* in two volumes; it had earlier appeared serially in *Fraser's Magazine*. Set in fifth-century Alexandria, *Hypatia* is the story of various conflicts of Greeks, Jews, Romans, Egyptians, and Goths, particularly the rival claims of Christianity, Judaism, and Neoplatonic thought, against the background of the collapsing Roman Empire. It received varying reviews in England and was even condemned for immorality. However, it was much appreciated in Germany.

The Kingsley family spent the winter of 1853 and the following spring in the mild climate of Torquay to aid Fanny's poor health. On the seashore Kingsley gathered material for *Glaucus; or, The Wonders of the Shore* (1855), an introduction to natural history and one of the first books of its kind to be written specifically for children (it first appeared in November 1854 as a long article, "The Wonders of the Shore," in the *North British Review*). *Glaucus* reveals a keen appreciation of the marine world, and Kingsley amply displays his gift for conveying scientific knowledge in a simple, direct, and dramatic manner. As only a small minority of English children at this period received any scientific instruction in school, Kingsley's vivid descriptions of the appearance and activities of such creatures as the long sea worm, the red capsicum, and the holothurian undoubtedly provided a wonderful entry into a new

world for many readers. Moreover, his straightforward practical advice on how to stock and maintain an aquarium of marine creatures probably resulted in countless aquariums in Britain's parlors, playrooms, studies, and schoolrooms. Although Kingsley's theological asides, comments on current educational practices, and references to the likes of Heracleitus, Democritus, and Johann Wolfgang von Goethe probably held little interest for many children, his commentaries on such topics as the physical, moral, and intellectual qualities appropriate for a good naturalist or the essential role of physical science in an educational system are refreshingly clear and direct. *Glaucus* was praised by Prince Albert. It appeared in many editions and was later expanded and revised.

Manifest in *Glaucus* is the author's firm belief in evolution. Kingsley, uncommon among clerics battling with the religious and moral problems introduced by the onslaught of Darwinian theories, saw no conflict between the teachings of science and the teachings of religion. He believed that one could cast aside the traditional doctrine of creation while maintaining the theory of final causes. Indeed, he consistently emphasized that by studying science one was in effect studying the work of God and getting to know him better. As he wrote about *The Water-Babies:* "I have tried, in all sorts of queer ways, to make children and grown folks understand that there is a quite miraculous and divine element underlying all physical nature." Of course, Kingsley's knowledge of science was such that he became a fellow of both the Linnaean and Geological Societies and was even cited by Charles Darwin in *The Descent of Man* (1871). Like his fellow priest, novelist, and writer for children Frederic Farrar, he was also an active promoter of science – his works, even his sermons, being suffused with praise of biology, geology, botany, and all aspects of natural history. He was keen to express science's great boon to mankind, particularly in such spheres as health and sanitary reform. Convinced that the day was coming when an ignorance of basic science would be considered an inadequacy "only second to ignorance of the primary laws of religion and morality," Kingsley desired increased science content in school curricula. He also urged the establishment of science societies, naturalists' clubs, and science museums, such as the one he set up at Wellington College.

In the summer of 1854 the Kingsleys moved to Bideford on the north coast of Devon, where Kingsley wrote his historical romance *Westward Ho!,* more than a quarter of a million words long. Though not primarily intended for the young, this work was cer-

Kingsley in the garden at Eversley Rectory

tainly read and enjoyed by many young people. Set in the sixteenth century at the time of Queen Elizabeth I, it is a quintessential adventure story, full of the daring exploits of Elizabethan explorers in the New World, the glory of the English defeat of the Armada, the terrors of the Spanish Inquisition, and the pain of unrequited love. Kingsley began writing it just after England and France had entered the Crimean War on the side of Turkey. With the country in a patriotic fervor, the novel's propaganda was timely, and most readers would have had little difficulty in identifying Russians with the cruel Spaniards. Indeed, Kingsley intended *Westward Ho!* – "a most ruthless bloodthirsty book . . . (just what the times want, I think)" – to encourage recruiting for the war and to inspire his compatriots to recapture the courageous spirit of their Elizabethan forebears.

Westward Ho! was the type of book to appeal to young boys – "a sublimated school-boy's dream," in the words of Margaret Farrand Thorp. Many readers would identify with the hero, Amyas Leigh, who by his intrepid exploits helps achieve the great military victory of the English against the Spanish

Armada. Indeed, as Robert Bernard Martin suggests, the depiction of Amyas – physically powerful, more energetic and athletic than intellectual, brave, loyal, not too complex, lacking in imagination, gruff, and respectful in his dealings with females – was an Elizabethan version of the ideal Victorian public-school boy. Moreover, through Amyas, Kingsley lived vicariously the life he would have liked to lead.

Westward Ho! is successful in its realistic representation of characters, scenery, and historic events. In preparatory research Kingsley consulted many historical sources, especially Richard Hakluyt. Many real Elizabethan characters appear in the book – Edmund Spenser, Sir Philip Sidney, Sir Francis Drake, Sir Walter Ralegh, Sir Richard Grenville – and they are for the most part accurate representations. However, some of the most realistic portrayals in the novel are those characters whom Kingsley based on contemporary Devon characters. The settings, whether in England or the West Indies, are authentic. Though his knowledge was all based on secondary sources, as it was written fourteen years before he visited the region, Kingsley's descriptions of the landscape, flora, and fauna of the West Indies are realistic.

A problem with *Westward Ho!* lies in Kingsley's jingoistic and ethnic biases. He displays a distinct racism in his depiction of black West Indians and a hardly less prejudicial tone when writing of the Irish. He emphasizes cruelties perpetrated by the Spanish but glosses over English atrocities. Moreover, *Westward Ho!* is full of fervent Protestantism and virulent anti-Papist and anti-Jesuit biases. Kingsley particularly detests prayer to the Virgin Mary, and Catholic priests are portrayed as traitors. Queen Elizabeth, head of the English Protestant Church, is a noble and inspiring monarch, whereas the Catholic Mary Stuart, for whom Kingsley had a particular dislike, is painted as an abhorrent person. Kingsley's bigotry and lack of understanding of Roman Catholicism were later to prove irksome to John Henry Newman.

Though George Eliot condemned its moralizing, *Westward Ho!* was generally well received by critics. It has probably been the most widely read of all Kingsley's novels, with the notable exception of *The Water-Babies.* It was the first of the author's novels to be published by Macmillan and, becoming a best-seller, made a lot of money for both Kingsley and the publisher. It was instrumental in setting the newly established Macmillans on the road to financial success, and it placed Kingsley in the front ranks of popular writers and made him a worthy successor to Sir Walter Scott and William Makepeace Thackeray in the field of the historical novel. *Westward Ho!* also made Kingsley's work more socially acceptable; this time his propaganda suited the mood of the nation.

It is understandable that, as a classical scholar, Kingsley wished to tell the stories of the Greek myths. *The Heroes; or Greek Fairy Tales, for My Children,* a book of three Greek legends, was intended specifically for children; the first edition included eight handsome illustrations by the author. The first legend is the story of Perseus, the son of Zeus and Danaë who slew the Gorgon and rescued Andromeda. The second tells of the quest of Jason and the Argonauts for the Golden Fleece and Jason's relationship with Medea. The third is the story of how Theseus with the help of Ariadne killed the Minotaur in the labyrinth. Nathaniel Hawthorne had already published versions of Greek myths for children in his *A Wonder-Book for Boys and Girls* (1852) and *Tanglewood Tales* (1853), but Kingsley disliked these works, believing them to be excessively romanticized and lacking in the true Greek

spirit. His own versions are distinguished by a distinct nobility and are successful in capturing the grandeur of the original Greek myths. Kingsley's consummate storytelling is evident throughout, and passages of beautiful prose-poetry are abundant. The tales are told in a simple ballad tone, as Kingsley hoped that a metrical prose style would help children remember the myths with greater ease. It has often been said that *The Heroes* possesses an appeal for children similar to that of Charles and Mary Lamb's *Tales from Shakespeare* (1807). In the preface Kingsley asserts that "there are no fairy tales like these old Greek ones, for beauty, and wisdom, and truth, and for making children love noble deeds, and trust in God to help them through." Still, *The Heroes* was one of the first children's books that did not have as its primary motive the fostering of morality. Nor does it, unlike many of Kingsley's other works, exhibit much bowdlerization. The book went through many editions in Kingsley's own day and later. It has been translated into many languages, including modern Greek in 1888, Irish and Swahili in 1933, and Twi in 1937. For many children and adults it has served as an introduction to the ancient Greek world.

Another novel for adults, *Two Years Ago* (1857), greatly helped the economy of the Kingsley household. Set in the contemporary age, it exhibits Kingsley's views on such topics as the role of the artist in society, the great need for sanitation, the importance of science, and the abolition of slavery. It is also indicative of Kingsley's distancing himself from his prior keen espousal of the Christian Socialist cause, as his sympathy for working-class concerns is less evident.

Two Years Ago was also responsible for Kingsley's association in the public mind with the cult of "muscular Christianity," a phrase he detested. Weary of the controversies of the Oxford Movement and theological debates on what he considered to be mere niceties, Kingsley was indeed a muscular Christian, entering into social movements and helping the poor in a practical sense. He also consistently stressed the importance of strength, energy, and physical behavior in pleasing God – one's physical activity must complement one's spirituality, a muscular Christian duality that Kingsley himself perfectly manifested. Few people have placed greater trust in the maxim *Mens sana in corpore sano.* Believing that it was truly manly to use all God-given traits, Kingsley argued that human appetites and passions should be enjoyed, not suppressed. That is an important reason why he could never understand Roman Catholicism, believing that far too many of its male adherents were unmanning themselves by celibacy.

The year 1859 was important for Kingsley's career and ascendance on the social ladder. On Palm Sunday he was invited to preach before Queen Victoria and Prince Albert at Buckingham Palace. As Susan Chitty remarks, "On that day Parson Lot bowed himself off the stage, and Canon Kingsley, the darling of the Establishment, took his place. From then on there were no further outcries against the government and the landowners, and the canon's championship of the working class, already half-hearted, ceased almost completely." Soon afterward Kingsley was appointed chaplain to the queen. In the autumn of 1859 he had the further honor of preaching before the court at Windsor Castle. The following year royal favor was responsible for the offer of the Regius Chair of Modern History at Cambridge, a post Kingsley held until his resignation in 1869. In 1861 Kingsley was appointed as private tutor to the Prince of Wales, the future Edward VII. There is much evidence of the great popularity of his lectures among Cambridge students, though the acclaim probably owed more to style rather than high intellectual content. Kingsley was by no means a strong academic and suffered severe criticism for his historical methods and conclusions. A selection of his lectures, *The Roman and the Teuton* (1864), received especially acerbic censure.

From August 1862 to March 1863 Kingsley's best-known work for children, *The Water-Babies,* appeared serially in *Macmillan's Magazine,* coming out in book form in 1863. This novel, a marvelous compendium of diverse material, tells the story of little Tom, the poor child chimney sweep who, reborn as a water-baby, experiences wonderful adventures in the company of real and imaginary creatures. Though it is an uneven novel, it is clearly Kingsley's masterpiece. It would be a jaded child who failed to respond to Tom's early trials and tribulations or who did not delight in the wonderful depictions of the river and marine creatures encountered by Tom after his metamorphosis into a water-baby.

Much of the material of *The Water-Babies,* however, touches the story's principal theme only tangentially. Kingsley had at least two aims in writing this tale. It was begun as a simple story for his youngest child, Grenville Arthur, who was born in 1858. As his wife reports, Kingsley, upon being reminded one morning of a promise to compose a book for their boy, "made no answer, but got up at once and went into his study, locking the door. In half an hour he returned with the story of little Tom. This

was the first chapter of *The Water-Babies,* written off without a correction." That chapter is unaffected, direct, and delightful. The rest of the book is equally appealing, but it also displays the second of Kingsley's aims: to espouse his social, scientific, and educational views. Kingsley loaded the tale with his opinions on such subjects as the question of evolution; the greed of lawyers; architectural excesses; the tendency for scientists to obfuscate and argue incessantly over petty details; racial and national stereotypes; the appalling medical treatment often meted out by physicians; the unhealthiness of girls' fashions, with their tight stays and cramped boots and shoes; the frequent carelessness of nursemaids; the cruelty of many teachers and the corporal punishment all too prevalent in schools; the certification process of elementary-school teachers; pupils' and teachers' emphases on mechanical rote learning; the antieducational effects of the contemporary "payment by results" examination system; and the urgent need for legislation to protect chimneysweep and collier boys. Though such subject matter is beyond the interest of many children, Q. D. Leavis is apt in pointing out that *The Water-Babies,* in addition to constituting a fine story in itself, provides a good introduction for thoughtful children to diverse aspects of the Victorian Age, as well as treatments of important intellectual questions.

A pervasive theme of the book is the urgent need for young readers to develop proper sanitary habits, a particularly efficacious method of preventing disease. One of the good works undertaken by the mysterious Irishwoman, in reality the queen of all the water-babies, is "opening cottage casements, to let out the stifling air; coaxing little children away from gutters, and foul pools where fever breeds." The fact that the water-babies have had firsthand experience of man's filthy and unhygienic ways is the reason why the rock pools where they live are always so clean and spotless and the water so pure and healthy. Kingsley's abhorrence of sullied water is also seen to good effect in the song of the river, which tells of its journey from source to sea – from a state of being clear, cool, and undefiled, to one of filthy pollution by human and industrial waste, and back once more to being pure, taintless, and strong. A related theme reflects the belief of Kingsley, who reportedly had a fetish about personal cleanliness, in the virtuous properties of washing. Kingsley actually saw in water, preferably cold water, a moral agent that would help beget masculine vigor, doughty spirit, and yeoman mien, which he considered necessary to save England from her increasing effeminacy and soft ways. He was even convinced that if a boy took a cold bath every morning moral rectitude was bound to result — "a conviction," declares Chitty, "for which generations of English public schoolboys have had reason to curse him."

In addition to stressing the need for personal cleanliness and increased sanitation in society, Kingsley also intended the oft-repeated motif of this purifying by fresh water to allegorize Tom's Christian rebirth. Tom's drowning in the river not only washes his body of soot and grime but also cleanses his soul of the filth of original sin and ignorance. Tom, as was not uncommon in one of his class and education in early Victorian England, knows little if anything about religion. What is worse, he has clearly never been baptized. In fact, the black sooty dirt of his chimney sweep's body mirrors the filth of his unredeemed soul. The purity of body and soul are mutually dependent, a notion that necessarily exacerbates Kingsley's racist dislike, all too evident in the story, of the appearance of certain people, especially blacks and Irish.

Kingsley also wishes to point out a fundamental tenet of Christian theology. Though a soul becomes pure after the water of baptism, man's free will invariably plunges it again into a sinful state by wrongdoing. Still, a man can redeem himself by regaining and following the path of goodness and righteousness, especially by learning the efficacy of Christian charity. Thus, "poor little heathen Tom," hearkening in his fevered sleep to the words of the mysterious Irishwoman — "those that wish to be clean, clean they will be" — earnestly desires to wash himself thoroughly. Although Tom becomes spiritually and physically clean after tumbling into the stream, the pure state of his soul does not endure long. He soon begins to tease and torture the creatures of the river and sea. After he helps a lobster trapped in a pot to escape, however, he sees the other water-babies for the first time. His good deed of Christian charity redeems him, and he is rewarded. Though he repeatedly falls by the wayside, Tom always manages to return to the state of grace. His final redemption comes about through his successful completion of the long and arduous journey from river to sea to the Other-end-of-Nowhere to help the nasty Mr. Grimes, his former master, redeem himself. Tom learns from the Bunyanesque trials and tribulations of his journey the meaning of altruism and selflessness, so that he is finally regenerated as a mature man ready and willing to take his place in the Christian world.

Though it has perhaps not entered the same pantheon as another Victorian masterpiece of children's fantasy, Lewis Carroll's *Alice's Adventures in Wonderland* (1865), *The Water-Babies* has been the most enduring and loved of Kingsley's works. It is almost impossible to estimate how many thousands of children have read it or have had it read to them. It has been dramatized, filmed, and recorded as a book on tape. Though many have understandably criticized the book's sermonizing as uncongenial to children's tastes, Kingsley's social commentary had an important practical effect. The Chimney-Sweeper's Act of 1864 was largely the result of the outcry occasioned by the trials of little Tom at the hands of Mr. Grimes.

Kingsley's affection and respect for children are evident throughout *The Water-Babies* and indeed all his writings for the young. He was undoubtedly gifted in understanding children; the publisher Charles Kegan Paul observed that his "insight into school-boy life [is] most remarkable, and his sympathy with the young unflagging." According to Kingsley, children should always be happy: "there is no food, nor medicine either, like happiness." Fear was to play no part either at home or at school, as Kingsley believed that the body of a bullied or frightened child would never thrive. He held that if a child misbehaved or was weary at lessons it was often due to physical causes such as sickness, and not necessarily because of moral or spiritual inadequacies.

Kingsley had an unhappy childhood and did not wish the same for his offspring. Hence, he practiced what he preached and made his home a cheerful and secure place. Mrs. Kingsley remarked that her husband would become a happy boy when he was with his children and that he would ponder whether "there is so much laughing in any other home in England as in ours." Kingsley's eldest son also testified to his father's positive attitude to his children: " 'Perfect love casteth out all fear,' was the motto on which my father based his theory of bringing up his children; and this theory he put in practice from their babyhood till when he left them as men and women." No corporal punishment was allowed, since Kingsley considered that young people's lying frequently resulted from fear of punishment. He also held that, under such threats, children learned to fear not the sin but its punishment. Kingsley, unlike so many Evangelicals, was unwilling to assert the perfection of parents and the evil of children and made the sensible point that parents are often responsible for their children's faults by providing poor models. In *The Water-Babies* he quotes approvingly the old aphorism " 'Maxima debetur pueris reverentia' – The greatest reverence is due to children; that is, that grown people should never say or do anything wrong before children, lest they should set them a bad example."

In 1864 Kingsley, once again manifesting his anti-Catholic sentiments, made an unfortunate mistake by provoking an altercation in print with John Henry Newman, later cardinal. Kingsley was vanquished by a far more subtle and intellectual opponent, though posterity gained Newman's *Apologia Pro Vita Sua* (1864) as a result of the debate. The controversy undoubtedly contributed to one of Kingsley's periodic health crises, a breakdown that endured for about a year. He recovered sufficiently to write his last novel, *Hereward the Wake, "Last of the English"* (1866), which appeared serially in 1865 in *Good News*. Though not written specifically for the young, *Hereward the Wake* was appropriated by them, and in the latter part of the nineteenth century more copies were probably to be found in schoolchildren's satchels or lockers than in their parents' studies. Amid the multitudinous scenes of battle and mayhem, the novel's main story relates the career of the valiant Saxon Hereward, a muscular Christian par excellence, who, manifesting great daring and military expertise, leads English resistance to the invading armies of William the Conqueror and his Normans. As Amyas Leigh in *Westward Ho!* symbolizes the spirit of English manhood and vitality in restraining the Spanish enemy, so Hereward embodies English defiance of Norman aggression.

Hereward the Wake brought in less money to the financially strapped Kingsley household than had his earlier novels and is probably Kingsley's least successful novel artistically. The main problem is the narrow, bellicose focus of the work, in which battle follows battle in rapid succession. Allan John Hartley calls the work "a rude and savage portrait of a rude and savage age. The book is full of fighting and expresses cruelty and bloodthirstiness to the point of nausea." Few characters – apart from Hereward and his wife, Torfuda – are given rounded, credible personalities. For the most part individuals are depicted as mere fighting machines and caricatures of medieval warriors. If adult readers found the novel tedious, however, many children found it exciting, with its descriptions of battles, medieval weapons, bloodthirsty deeds, and audacious feats that crowd almost every page. In addition, it contains hardly any digressions on philosophical matters or current political and social affairs. Still, both young and mature readers probably became bored by this much-researched novel's many footnotes, which Kingsley, smarting from at-

Charles and Fanny Kingsley's grave at Eversley

tacks on his professorial ability, probably inserted to prove his historical acumen.

Madam How and Lady Why; or First Lessons in Earth Lore for Children (1870), Kingsley's last work specifically conceived for children, was first published as a series of easy science articles in *Good Words for the Young*. Geology and natural history are its main subjects, and Kingsley discusses at length such topics as earthquakes, volcanoes, corals, the Ice Age, the formation of rocks and mountains, the properties of chalk, the various transformations of a grain of soil, birds, and hay fields. He firmly intended not only that this work should inform children of geological facts, but also that it persuade them to go out into nature and gain practical experience of the scientific world. Kingsley, who has frequently been accused of antiintellectualism, was always chary of book knowledge. As he wrote in the preface: "mere reading of wise books will not make you wise men: you must use for yourselves the tools with which books are made wise; and that is – your eyes, and ears, and common sense." Although children with a scientific bent would have had no trouble understanding the subject matter, many might have been put off by the author's preachiness. One of his main motives in writing the book was religious: to teach the young that "God's Book, which is the Universe, and the reading of God's Book, which is Science, can do you nothing but good, and teach you nothing but truth and wisdom." Kingsley made a lot of money from this book, mainly due to the business sagacity of his wife, who arranged the deal under which he received £1,000 for all the rights.

Shortly after resigning from his Cambridge chair in 1869 Kingsley accepted the canonry of Chester, a preferment many – including himself and his wife – considered long overdue. In the same year he was made president of the Educational Section of the Social Science Congress at Bristol, and in his inaugural address he fervently opposed the pervasive voluntary action in education and advocated greater state control. Not surprising, he supported Forster's Elementary Education Act of the following year. Before assuming his new duties at Chester, Kingsley and his daughter Rose visited the West Indies, a trip that resulted in *At Last; A Christmas in the West Indies* (1871). At Chester, though increasingly a prey to ill health, Kingsley remained active in teaching, preaching, sanitary reform, and botanical and geological research. In 1870 he commenced a botany class, which grew into the Chester Natural Science Society. Further advancement came in 1873, when Kingsley was appointed the canon of Westminster Abbey. In the following year he undertook a long lecture tour throughout the United States for financial reasons. In ill health on his return, he contracted pneumonia and died at Eversley on 23 January 1875.

The American writer John Whittier, while praising Kingsley's literary work in an 1876 letter to Fanny Kingsley, wrote: "since I have seen *him,* the man seems greater than the author." This also seems to be the conclusion of many twentieth-century critics: much of the Kingsley research during the last few decades has focused on the man as opposed to his written works. This situation is perhaps understandable, for Kingsley was a striking and peculiar personality; moreover, he has had the misfortune, both in his own day and the present, to have his writings – be they novels, poems, sermons, or scientific treatises – have generally been relegated by critics to the second rank. That he was a good writer but not really of the first class seems to be the general verdict, a judgment that has resulted in few readers for most of Kingsley's works today.

Kingsley's writings for the young have followed similar readership trends. Tastes change, and it is not surprising that modern children eschew works intended for their Victorian ancestors. *The Heroes* has been supplanted by other retellings of the Greek tales; the science of *Glaucus* and *Madam How and Lady Why* no longer has appeal, and today's youth would reject the books' pervasive social commentary, sermonizing, and didacticism. Nor is *Westward Ho!* read much by present-day youngsters, though it is still available in a children's edition. The significant exception has been the consistently high readership, especially in the United Kingdom, for *The Water-Babies,* of which there are probably more editions, adaptations, and abridgments in print today than in Kingsley's own time. The work's simplicity, brilliant fantasy, and affection for the young, despite its frequent preaching, still capture the devotion of children. It is *The Water-Babies,* though its author would never have foretold it, that will ensure Kingsley a high rank in the history of children's literature.

Letters:

Charles Kingsley: His Letters and Memories of His Life, 2 volumes, edited by Fanny Kingsley (London: King, 1877);

Charles Kingsley's American Notes: Lectures from a Lecture Tour, 1874, edited by Robert Bernard Martin (Princeton: Princeton University Library, 1958);

Charles Kingsley and Wellington College: The Text of Fourteen Letters from Charles Kingsley and One from Maurice Kingsley to Edward White Benson, 1860–1872, compiled by Mark Baker (Eversley: Wellington College, 1975).

Bibliographies:

Margaret Farrand Thorp, "Bibliography of Charles Kingsley's Works," in her *Charles Kingsley 1819–1875* (Princeton: Princeton University Press, 1937; London: Oxford University Press, 1937), pp. 191–204;

Robert A. Campbell, "Charles Kingsley: A Bibliography of Secondary Studies," *Bulletin of Bibliography,* 33 (1976): 78–91, 104, 127–130;

Styron Harris, *Charles Kingsley: A Reference Guide* (Boston: G. K. Hall, 1981).

Biographies:

Stanley E. Baldwin, *Charles Kingsley* (Ithaca, N.Y.: Cornell University Press, 1934);

Margaret Farrand Thorp, *Charles Kingsley 1819–1875* (Princeton: Princeton University Press, 1937; London: Oxford University Press, 1937);

Una Pope-Hennessy, *Canon Charles Kingsley: A Biography* (London: Chatto & Windus, 1948);

Robert Bernard Martin, *The Dust of Combat: A Life of Charles Kingsley* (London: Faber & Faber, 1959);

Susan Chitty, *The Beast and the Monk: A Life of Charles Kingsley* (London: Hodder & Stoughton, 1975);

Brenda Colloms, *Charles Kingsley: The Lion of Eversley* (London: Constable, 1975).

References:

William J. Baker, "Charles Kingsley and the Crimean War: A Study in Chauvinism," *Southern Humanities Review,* 4 (Summer 1970): 247–256;

Michael Banton, "Kingsley's Racial Philosophy," *Theology,* 78 (January 1975): 22–30;

Owen Chadwick, "Charles Kingsley at Cambridge," *Historical Journal,* 18 (June 1975): 303–325;

Dorothy Coleman, "Rabelais and 'The Water Babies,' " *Modern Language Review,* 66 (July 1971): 511–521;

Valentine Cunningham, "Soiled Fairy: *The Water-Babies* in Its Time," *Essays in Criticism,* 35 (April 1985): 121–148;

Mary Wheat Hanawalt, "Charles Kingsley and Science," *Studies in Philology,* 34 (October 1937): 589–611;

Henry R. Harrington, "Charles Kingsley's Fallen Athlete," *Victorian Studies,* 21 (Autumn 1977): 73–86;

Allan John Hartley, *The Novels of Charles Kingsley: A Christian Social Interpretation* (Folkestone: Hour-Glass Press, 1977);

John C. Hawley, "*The Water-Babies* as Catechetical Paradigm," *Children's Literature Association Quarterly,* 14 (Spring 1989): 19–21;

Arthur Johnston, "*The Water Babies:* Kingsley's Debt to Darwin," *English,* 12 (Autumn 1959): 215–219;

Guy Kendall, *Charles Kingsley and his Ideas* (London & New York: Hutchinson, 1947);

Q. D. Leavis, "*The Water Babies,*" *Children's Literature in Education,* 23 (Winter 1976): 155–163;

C. N. Manlove, "Charles Kingsley (1819–75) and *The Water-Babies,*" in his *Modern Fantasy: Five Studies* (Cambridge & New York: Cambridge University Press, 1975), pp. 13–54, 262–271;

Charles H. Muller, "Spiritual Evolution and Muscular Theology: Lessons from Kingsley's Natural Theology," *University of Cape Town Studies in English,* 15 (March 1986): 24–34;

Stephen Paget, "The Water-Babies," in his *I Have Reason to Believe* (London: Macmillan, 1921), pp. 102–116;

Patrick G. Scott, "Kingsley as Novelist," *Theology,* 78 (January 1975): 8–15;

J. A. Sutherland, "*Westward Ho!:* 'A Popularly Successful Book,' " in his *Victorian Novelists and Publishers* (London: Athlone Press, 1976), pp. 117–132;

Malcolm Tozer, "Charles Kingsley and the 'Muscular Christian' Ideal of Manliness," *Physical Education Review,* 8 (1985): 35–40;

Larry K. Uffelman, *Charles Kingsley* (Boston: Twayne, 1979);

Uffelman and Scott, "Kingsley's Serial Novels, II: *The Water-Babies,*" *Victorian Periodicals Review,* 19 (Winter 1986): 122–131;

Norman Vance, *The Sinews of the Spirit: The Ideal of Christian Manliness in Victorian Literature and Religious Thought* (Cambridge: Cambridge University Press, 1985);

Colwyn E. Vulliamy, "Charles Kingsley and Christian Socialism," in *Writers and Rebels: From the Fabian Biographical Series,* edited by Michael Katanka (London: Knight, 1976; Totowa, N.J.: Rowman & Littlefield, 1976), pp. 159–191;

Michael Young, "History as Myth: Charles Kingsley's *Hereward the Wake,*" *Studies in the Novel,* 17 (Summer 1985): 174–188.

Papers:

The most important collections of papers of and material relating to Charles Kingsley are in the British Library, the Cambridge University Library, the Princeton University Library, and the New York Public Library.

William Henry Giles Kingston

(28 February 1814 – 5 August 1880)

Nicola D. Thompson
State University of New York, College at Cortland

BOOKS: *The Circassian Chief* (London: Bentley, 1843);

Lusitanian Sketches of the Pen and Pencil, 2 volumes (London: Parker, 1845);

The Prime Minister. An Historical Romance, 3 volumes (London: R. Bentley, 1845);

Pepe the Pirate; or, Perils of the Ocean (Boston: "Star Spangled Banner" Office, 1848);

Some Suggestions for the Formation of a System of General Emigration and for the Disposal of Convicts in the Colonies (London, 1848);

A Lecture of Colonization (London, 1849);

The Albatross; or, Voices from the Ocean (London: Hurst, 1849);

The Emigrant Voyager's Manual (London, 1850);

How to Emigrate; or, The British Colonists (London: Grant & Griffen, 1850);

Emigrant Manuals (London: Society for Promoting Christian Knowledge, 1851);

The Ocean Queen and the Spirit of the Storm (London: Bosworth, 1851);

Peter the Whaler: His Early Life and Adventure in the Arctic Regions (London: Grant & Griffith, 1851; New York: Francis, 1852);

The Pirate of the Mediterranean, 3 volumes (London: Newby, 1851);

Mark Seaworth; or, A Tale of the Indian Ocean (London: Grant & Griffith, 1852; New York: Francis, 1853);

Manco, the Peruvian Chief; or, An Englishman's Adventures in the Country of the Incas (London: Grant & Griffith, 1853; New York: Dutton, 187?);

Blue Jackets; or, Chips of the Old Block (London: Grant & Griffith, 1854);

The Emigrant's Home; or How to Settle (London: Groombridge, 1856);

Western Wanderings; or, A Pleasure Tour in the Canadas (London: Chapman & Hall, 1856);

Salt Water; or, The Sea Life and Adventures of Neil D'Arcy, the Midshipman (London: R. E. King, 1857; New York: C. S. Francis, 1858);

Fred Markham in Russia; or, The Boy Travellers in the Land of the Czar (London: Griffith & Farran, 1858; New York: Harper, 1858);

The Early Life of Old Jack (London: Nelson, 1859);

Old Jack: A Man-of-War's-Man and Sea Whaler (New York & London: Nelson, 1859);

Round the World: A Tale for Boys (London: Nelson, 1859; Boston: Crosby & Nichols, 1862);

Will Weatherhelm; or, The Yarn of an Old Sailor (London: Griffith & Farran, 1860; New York: Munro, 1886);

Digby Heathcote; or, The Early Days of a Country Gentleman's Son and Heir (New York & London: Routledge, 1860);

Ernest Bracebridge; or, School Days (London: Gall & Inglis, 1860; Boston: Ticknor & Fields, 1860);

The Cruise of the "Frolic"; or, Yachting Experiences of Barnaby Brine (London: Sampson Low, 1860; Boston: Tilton, 1866);

My First Voyage to Southern Seas (London: Nelson, 1860; New York: Nelson, 1874);

The Boy's Own Book of Boats (London, 1861; revised edition, London: Gall & Inglis, 1874?);

Jack Buntline; or, Life on the Ocean (London: Sampson Low & Marson, 1861);

My Travels in Many Lands Narrated for My Young Friends (London: Bosworth & Harrison, 1861);

True Blue; or, The Life and Adventures of a British Seaman of the Old School (London, 1862 [i.e., 1861]);

Marmaduke Merry the Midshipman; or My Early Days at Sea (London: Kent, 1862; Boston: Grosby & Nichols, 1864); republished as *The Midshipman Marmaduke Merry* (New York: Lovell, 1884);

The Fire-Ships, 3 volumes (London, 1862);

Hearty Words for British Sailors Afloat and Ashore (London, 1862); republished as *Ronald Morton* (New York: Routledge, 1872);

Twice Lost (London: Virtue Brothers, 1863; New York: Munro, 1878);

Our Sailors; or, Anecdotes of the Engagements and Gallant Deeds of the British Navy During the Reign of Her Majesty Queen Victoria (London: Guildford, 1863; New York: Dutton, n.d.);

Our Soldiers; or, Anecdotes of the Campaigns and Gallant Deeds of the British Army During the Reign of Her Majesty Queen Victoria (London: Guildford, 1863);

Adventures of Dick Onslow Among the Red Skins (London, 1863; Boston: Lee & Shepard, 1864);

Antony Waymouth; or, The Gentlemen Adventurers (Boston: Tilton, 1865; London: Warne, 1865);

The Gilpins and Their Fortunes: An Australian Tale (London: Society for Promoting Christian Knowledge, 1865; New York: Patt & Young, 1865);

Philip Mavor; or, Life Amongst Kaffirs (London: Society for Promoting Christian Knowledge, 1865);

Rob Nixon, The Old White Trapper (London: Society for Promoting Christian Knowledge, 1865; New York: Miller, 1866);

The Young Foresters and Other Tales (New York: Lovell, 1865);

Mountain Moggy; or, The Stoning of the Itch (London: Society for Promoting Christian Knowledge, 1866);

Washed Ashore: The Tower of Stormount Bay (London, 1866; New York: Warne, 1892);

Foxholme Hall: A Legend of Christmas and Other Amusing Tales (London: Strahan, 1867);

Infant Amusements; or, How to Make a Nursery Happy (London: Griffith & Farran, 1867);

Paul Gerrard, the Cabin Boy (London, 1867);

The Pirate's Treasure; A Legend of Panama; and Other Amusing Tales for Boys (London, 1867; New York: Virtue & Yorston, 1869);

Ralph Clavering; or, We Must Try Before We Can Do (London, 1867);

Count Ulrich von Lindburg (London, 1868; New York, 1902);

The Perils and Adventures of Harry Skupwith by Sea and by Land (London: Virtue, 1868);

Three Hundred Years Ago; or, The Martyr of Brentwood (Philadelphia: Lutheran Board of Publications, 1868; London: Partridge, 1868);

Adrift in a Boat (London: Hodder & Stoughton, 1869; New York: Worthington, n.d.);

John Deane: Historic Adventures by Land and Sea (New York: Dutton, 1869; London: Griffith & Farran, 1869);

The Last Look (London: Aylesbury, 1869);

Our Fresh and Salt Water Tutors (London: Sampson Low & Marston, 1869);

A Voyage Around the World (London: Nelson, 1869; New York: Nelson, 1870);

John Deane: Historic Adventures by Land and Sea (London: Griffith & Farran / New York: Dutton, 1869); republished as *John Deane of Nottingham: His Adventures and Exploits* (London: Griffith & Farran / New York: Dutton: 1878);

How Britannia Came to Rule the Waves (London: Gall & Inglis, circa 1870);

Adventures of Dick Onslow Among the Redskins. A Book For Boys (Boston: Tilton, 1870; London: Gall & Inglis, 1889);

At the South Pole; or, Adventures of Richard Pengelley (New York & London: Cassell, Petter & Galpin, 1870);

Little Ben Hadden; or, Do Right, Whatever Comes of It (London: Religious Tract Society, 1870);

Off to Sea; or, The Adventures of Jovial Jack Junker on His Road to Fame (New York & London: Cassell, Petter & Galpin, 1870);

The Royal Merchant; or, Events in the Days of Sir Thomas Gresham (London: Partridge, 1870); republished as *The Golden Grasshopper* (London: Religious Tract Society, 1880; Boston: Bradley, 1881);

Sunshine Bill (London: Society for Promoting Christian Knowledge, 1870);

Captain Cook: His Life, Voyages, and Discoveries (London: Religious Tract Society, 1871);

In the Eastern Seas; or, The Regions of the Bird of Paradise (London: Nelson, 1871; New York: Nelson, 1881);

In the Wilds of Africa: A Tale for Boys (London: Nelson, 1871; New York: Nelson, 1879);

The Fortunes of the "Ranger" and "Crusader" (London: Gall & Inglis, 1872);

On the Banks of the Amazon; or, A Boy's Journal of His Adventures in the Tropical Wilds of South America (London: Nelson, 1872; New York: Nelson, 1885);

Shipwrecks and Disasters at Sea (New York & London: Routledge, 1872);

A True Hero (London: Frome, 1872);

Ben Burton; or, Born and Bred at Sea (London, 1872);

The African Trader (London: Gall & Inglis, 1873);

Hurricane Hurry; or, The Adventures of a Naval Officer Afloat and on Shore (New York: Dutton, 1873; London: Griffith & Farran, 1873);

Janet M'Laren; or, The Faithful Nurse (London: Gall & Inglis, 1873);

Mary Liddiard; or, The Missionary's Daughter (London, 1873);

Michael Penguyne (New York: Pott & Young, 1873; London: Society for Promoting Christian Knowledge, 1873);

Millicent Courtney's Diary; or, The Experiences of a Young Lady at Home and Abroad (London: Gall & Inglis, 1873; Chicago: Revell, n.d.);

The History of Little Peter the Ship-Boy (London: Religious Tract History, 1873);

The Three Midshipmen (New York: Dutton, 1873; London: Griffith & Farran, 1873);

The Trapper's Son (London: Gall & Inglis, 1873);

Waihoura; or, The New Zealand Girl (London: Gall & Inglis, 1873; New York: Pott & Young, n.d.);

Alone on an Island (London: Routledge, 1874);

Charlie Laurel; a Story of Adventure by Sea and Land (London: Sunday School Union, 1874);

Eldol the Druid; or, The Dawn of Christianity in Britain (London, 1874);

Great African Travelers from Bruce and Mungo Park to Livingston and Stanley (New York & London: Routledge, 1874);

Roger Kyffin's Word (London: Guildford, 1874);

Stories of Animal Sagacity (London: Nelson, 1874);

The Brothers (London: Routledge, 1874);

The Fisher Boy; or, Michael Penguyne (Boston: Lothrop, 1874);

The Heroic Wife; or, The Wanderers of the Amazon (London: Griffith & Farran, 1874; New York: Routledge, 1880);

The Merchant of Harlem (London: Partridge, 1874);

The Two Shipmates (London: Society for Promoting Christian Knowledge, 1874);

The Western World (New York & London: Nelson, 1874);

The Settlers: A Tale of Virginia (London: Society for Promoting Christian Knowledge, 1875);

The South Sea Whaler (London: Nelson, 1875);

The Three Lieutenants; or, Naval Life in the Nineteenth Century (New York: Pott & Young, 1875; London, 1875);

The Child of the Wreck; or, The Loss of the Royal George (London, 1876);

Half-Hours with the Kings and Queens of England (London, 1876);

The Popular History of the British Navy from the Earliest Time to the Present (London: Gall & Inglis, 1876);

Saved from the Sea; or, The Loss of the "Viper" (London & New York: T. Nelson, 1876);

Snow-Shoes and Canoes; or, The Early Days of a Fur-Trader in the Hudson Bay Territory (London: Sampson Low, Marston, Searle & Rivington, 1876);

The Three Commanders; Active Service Afloat in Modern Days (London: Griffith & Farran, 1876; New York: Pott & Young, 1876);

Virginia: A Centennial Story (Boston: Lothrop, 1876);

The Wanderers; or, Adventures in the Wilds of Trinidad and Orinoco (London: Nelson, 1876; New York: Nelson, 1879);

The Young Rajah (New York & London: Nelson, 1876);

Clara Maynard; or, The True and the False (London, 1877);

Here, There, and Everywhere (New York: World, 1877);

Jovinian; or, The Early Days of Papal Rome (London: Hodder & Stoughton, 1877);

Owen Hartley; or, Ups and Downs (London: Society for Promoting Christian Knowledge, 1877);

Yachting Tools (London: Hunt, 1877);

The Voyage of the "Steadfast"; or, The Young Missionaries in the Pacific (London: Religious Tract Society, 1877);

The Young Llanero (London: Nelson, 1877; New York: Munro, 1878);

In the Rocky Mountains (New York & London: Nelson, 1878);

The Mate of the "Lily"; or, Notes from Harry Musgrave's Log Book (New York: Pott & Young, 1878; London: Society for Promoting Christian Knowledge, 1878);

Ned Garth; or, Made Prisoner in Africa (London: Society for Promoting Christian Knowledge, 1878; New York: Pott & Young, 1878);

The Rival Crusoes (London: Griffith, Farran & Brown, 1878);

The Two Supercargoes; or, Adventure in Savage Africa (London: Low, Marston, Searle & Rivington, 1878; Philadelphia: Lippincott, 1878);

With Age and Rifle; or, The Western Pioneers (London: Low, Marston, Searle & Rivington, 1878);

Kidnapping in the Pacific; or, The Adventures of Boas Ringdon (New York & London: Routledge, 1879);

Hendricks the Hunter; or, The Border Farm: A Tale of Zululand (London: Hodder & Stoughton, 1879; New York: Armstrong, 1884);

In New Granada; or, Heroes and Patriots (New York & London: Nelson, 1879);

Piccolo Paolo (London: Sunday School Union, 1879);

The Seven Champions of Christiandom (New York & London: Routledge, 1879);

The Frontier Fort; or, Stirring Times in the North-West Territory of British America (London: Society for Promoting Christian Knowledge, 1879; New York: Young, n.d.);

The Gentlemen Adventurers: The Story of Antony Waymouth (New York & London: Lock, 1879);

The Two Whalers; or, Adventures in the Pacific (New York: Pott & Young, 1879; London: Society for Promoting Christian Knowledge, 1879);

A Yacht Voyage Around England (London: Religious Tract Society, 1879; revised, 1890);

Adventures in the Far West (London: Routledge, 1880);

Among the Red Skins (London: Castle, 1880);

The Boy Who Sailed with Blake; and the Orphans (London: Sunday School Union, 1880);

The Cruise of the "Dainty" (London: Christian Knowledge Society, 1880; New York: Pott & Young, n.d.);

Dick Cheveley: His Adventures and Misadventures (London: Sampson Low, Marston, Searle &

Rivington, 1880; Philadelphia: Lippincott, 1887);

The Ferryman of Brill (New York & London: Cassell, 1880);

In the Forest (New York & London: Nelson, 1880);

In the Wilds of Florida: A Tale of Warfare and Hunting (New York & London: Nelson, 1880);

A Lily of Leyden (London: Christian Knowledge Society, 1880);

Norman Ballery; or How to Overcome Evil With Good (London: Gall & Inglis, 1880);

Notable Voyages from Columbus to Parry (London: Routledge, 1880); revised and enlarged as *Notable Voyages from Columbus to Nordenskiod* (London: Routledge, 1885); revised and enlarged again as *Notable Voyages from Columbus to Nansen* (London: Routledge, 1904);

Voyages and Travels of Count Funnibos and Baron Stilkin (London: Society for Promoting Christian Knowledge, 1880);

Wonders of the Mines (London: Gall & Inglis, 1880; New York: Revell, n.d.);

Wonders of the Oceans (New York & London: Gall & Inglis, 1880);

The Young Berringtons; or, The Boy Explorers (London: Cassell, 1880);

The Heir of Kilfinnan: A Tale for the Shore and Ocean (London: Sampson Low, 1881);

Peter Biddulph; or, The Rise and Progress of an Australian Settler (London: Sunday School Union, 1881);

Peter Trawl; or, The Adventures of a Whaler (London: Hodder & Stoughton, 1881; New York: Armstrong, 1882);

Roger Willoughby; or, The Times of Benbow (London: Nisbet, 1881; New York: Pott, 1890);

The Two Voyages; or, Midnight and Daylight (New York: Pott & Young, 1881; London: Society for Promoting Christian Knowledge, 1881);

Adventures in Africa (New York & London: Routledge, 1882);

Arctic Adventures (London: Routledge, 1882);

James Braithwaite the Supercargo (London, 1882; New York: Armstrong, 1883);

Adventures in India (London: Routledge, 1883);

Paddy Finn; or, The Adventures of a Midshipman Afloat and Ashore (London: Griffith & Farran, 1883; New York: Dutton, 1883);

Won from the Waves; or, The Story of Maiden May (London: Griffith & Farran, 1883; New York: Dutton, 1883);

The Log House by the Lake: A Tale of Canada (London: Society for Promotion of Christian Knowledge / New York: Young, 1884);

Adventures Among the Indians (Chicago: Bedford & Clark, 1884);

Adventures in Australia (London: Routledge, 1884); republished as *Australian Adventures* (London: Routledge, 1887);

Afar in the Forest (New York & London: Nelson, 1884);

From Powder Monkey to Admiral: A Story of Naval Adventure (New York: Armstrong, 1884; London: Humphrey Milford, 1918);

Travels of Dr. Livingstone (London: Routledge, 1886);

Travels of Mungo Park, Denham, and Clapperton (London: Routledge, 1886);

Villegagnon: A Tale of Huguenot Persecution (London: Sunday School Union, 1886);

Happy Jack, and Other Tales of the Sea (London: Gall & Inglis, 1889);

Uncle Boz and Other Tales of the Sea (London: Gall & Inglis, 1889);

The Voyages of the "Ranger" and "Crusader" and What Befell Their Passengers and Crews (London: Gall & Inglis, 1890);

Very Far West Indeed; or, The Adventures of Peter Burn (London: Cauldwell, 1891);

Exiled for the Faith: A Tale of the Huguenot Persecution (London: Sunday School Union, 1898);

The Cruise of the "Mary Rose"; or, Here and There in the Pacific (London: Religious Tract Society, 1901; Boston: Bradley, 1901);

The Young Whaler; or, The Adventures of Archibald Hughson (Boston: Lothrop, n.d.).

OTHER: Jules Verne, *The Mysterious Island,* translation attributed to Kingston (New York: Armstrong, 1876);

Verne, *Micheal Strogoff, the Courier of the Czar,* translation attributed to Kingston (New York: Scribner & Armstrong, 1877);

Johann David Wyss, *The Swiss Family Robinson,* translation attributed to Kingston (London: Routledge, 1879; Cleveland: World, 1947);

Verne, *Abandoned,* translation attributed to Kingston (New York: Dutton, 1924);

Richard Johnson, *Saint George and the Dragon,* adapted by Kingston (New York: Limited Editions Club, 1950).

William Henry Giles Kingston was arguably the most popular and respected English writer for boys in the second half of the nineteenth century. He was the foremost author of boys' books between 1850 and 1900, and he played a significant role in the popularity of the genre of boys' fiction in the Victorian period. Kingston wrote such classics of children's literature as *Peter the Whaler: His Early Life and Adventure in the Arctic Regions* (1851) and *The Three Midshipmen* (1873); he wrote *From Powder Monkey to Admiral* (1884), the first serial published in the *Boy's Own Paper* (1879); he founded (January 1880) and edited the boys' periodical *Union Jack*; and he edited the *Colonial Magazine* (1849–1852) and *Kingston's Magazine* (1859–1862). A *Union Jack* obituary (26 August 1880) described him as "the father of the school of writers of healthy stirring tales for boys." Kingston's more than 150 sea stories and other tales of adventure typically promote England's imperial expansion and an evangelical Christianity.

Kingston was born in London on 28 February 1814, the eldest son of Lucy Henry Kingston and Frances Sophia Rooke. He spent most of his youth in Oporto, Portugal, where his father was a merchant, but was educated in England. His father was a former sailor, and Kingston had several uncles and cousins in the Royal Navy. He married Agnes Kinloch in 1853; they had eight children.

During his long career as a writer, Kingston wrote three to four books a year on the average, and five to six a year in his last years. In addition to his work as an author and magazine editor, Kingston had an active philanthropic interest in emigration, the spiritual condition of seamen, and the volunteer movement. He received a Portuguese knighthood for negotiating a commercial treaty with Portugal and a British government pension in later life for his literary work.

Kingston left Oporto in 1824 at the age of ten to be educated in England. He attended Eagle House in Hammersmith, a school he described fondly in *The Three Midshipmen* as a "capital school though it was not a public one." He enjoyed his schooldays and his summer holidays, which he spent in Lymington, where he had many relatives. His favorite occupation in the summers was wandering around the ports, talking to sailors, and developing an enthusiasm for the sea and sailing that became a central part of his books.

After Kingston left school he had a private tutor until he ended his formal education in 1832 by going on a nine-month trip to France and Italy with a relative. His memoirs reveal that while in Paris he saw the opera and ballet; his ambivalent moralizing reaction to this experience gives some indication of the didactic and evangelical bent of his later stories for boys:

Front page for a popular boys' periodical featuring a serialized novel by Kingston

In the evening I saw for the first time, an opera and a ballet. Delightful as was the music, the impression the whole exhibition made on me was such that I should be very sorry to expose any young person over whom I could exercise any influence to a similar spectacle, and I cannot suppose that the glaring evil can in any way be counterbalanced by any benefit or pleasure to be derived by listening to the syren voices of the singers.

In 1833 Kingston returned to Portugal to work with his father in his business. From 1833 to 1842 he divided his time between Portugal and London. Kingston's literary articles, which formed only a small part of his writing activity in these years, were partly responsible for the signing of the treaty between Great Britain and Portugal on 3 July 1847. His first novel, *The Circassian Chief,* appeared in 1843, followed by two books on Portugal in 1845:

The Prime Minister and *Lusitanian Sketches of the Pen and Pencil,* a travel book.

In 1844 Kingston moved to England, where he continued his writing career. He became extremely active in emigration matters, in developing the Missions to Seamen, and in his involvement with the volunteer movement. Kingston's work on emigration took place mostly from the mid 1840s to the mid 1850s. In 1844 he edited *The Colonist, The Colonial Magazine,* and the *East Indian Review.* He was the honorary secretary of a colonization society, wrote *Some Suggestions for the Formation of a System of General Emigration and for the Disposal of Convicts in the Colonies* (1848), lectured on colonization in 1849, and wrote *How to Emigrate; or, The British Colonists* (1850). In more practical matters, Kingston inspected the arrangements for emigrants at seaports and examined many ships.

The evident love of the sea, patriotism, and intense religiosity that create the major themes in Kingston's books are clearly based on his personality and experiences. In 1856, for example, his evangelical tendencies led him to found the Society for Missions to Seamen. Kingston's own brand of patriotic devotion also led to his involvement in the volunteer movement. He took part in a civilian military unit that confronted the Chartists in their demonstration of 10 April 1848. He helped organize the Rifle Volunteers in 1859, and more than 160,000 men volunteered in a few weeks.

Kingston's biographer, Maurice Rooke Kingsford, asserts that there was "much of the lay-parson in Kingston." The *Boy's Own Paper,* to which he was a frequent contributor, was published by the Religious Tract Society, and Kingston wrote several small books for the Society for Promoting Christian Knowledge. His religious zeal is often evident in his enthusiastic attitude toward the maintenance and expansion of the British Empire and in his belief that the British had an innate racial superiority to any other people: Kingsford characterizes Kingston as "a maker and prophet of Empire" and writes that *Kingston's Magazine* "must be regarded as the magnum opus of his life. It was a gigantic effort in which he deliberately set himself the task to educate an Empire, and in actual fact he became a great imperial schoolmaster."

Kingston's literary strengths revolved around his ability to write fast-paced action stories informed by detailed knowledge of sailing and seamanship. If his strength is his focus on action, his weakness is his inability to create original or memorable characters. His male characters are almost indistinguishable, and his female characters, when they appear, are flat stereotypes.

Although his early books were received with some interest and appreciation, it was not until Kingston's first book for boys, *Peter the Whaler,* appeared in 1851 that his popularity really took off. In this novel Kingston was able to harness and unite his various enthusiasms, and the immediate acclaim with which the book was received made it clear that he had found his niche as a writer. From that point on Kingston devoted his career and energies to writing boys' travel, adventure, and historical stories, many of which were also sea tales. His fascination with the sea was part of a lifelong passion, cultivated by his many relatives in seafaring professions, his frequent journeys between England and Portugal as a child (Kingston reportedly crossed the Bay of Biscay four times before he was nine years old),

and his school holidays spent with relatives in Lymington.

The title character of *Peter the Whaler,* the son of an Irish clergyman, is sent to sea as a punishment for poaching. Before he leaves, Peter's father admonishes him not to forget his origins: "Wherever you wander, my son, remember you are a Briton, and cease not to love your native land." While on board the *Black Swan,* headed toward America, Peter has various adventures and learns to be a sailor; Kingston manages, in the process, to make many points about the terrible treatment of emigrants aboard such ships. He also preaches the virtues of following one's conscience in difficult circumstances: "Oh, let me urge my young friends, in their course through life, always to do what they know is right, fearless of consequences."

The remainder of the book deals with Peter's dramatic adventures on this and other ships. Some of the exciting episodes include being shipwrecked with friends on an iceberg, killing whales, shooting polar bears, and various adventures amid beautiful arctic scenery. When Peter and his friends find themselves in Eskimo territory and decide to stay there for the winter, Kingston displays his missionary zeal: "I should say that they [the Eskimos] are a most amiable, industrious, and peaceful people, whose minds are well prepared to receive the truths of Christianity, though at present they appear to have little or no notions whatever of any sort of religion, and none of a Supreme Being."

When spring arrives, Peter and his friends are rescued by a French ship; a near wreck allows the English sailors to demonstrate their superiority; Kingston notes, "In moments of sudden peril the French are apt to lose command over themselves." The ship is eventually wrecked on the west coast of Ireland, where most of the sailors drown, but Peter manages to return home. When Peter's father tells him that he has returned poor, Kingston ends the book with an unmistakable moral:

"No, father," [Peter] answered. "I have come back infinitely richer. I have learned to fear God, to worship Him in His Works, and to trust to His infinite mercy. I have also learned to know myself, and to take advice and counsel from my superiors in goodness." "Then," said my father, "I am indeed content; and I trust others may take a needful lesson from the adventures of PETER THE WHALER."

The book was greeted with instant delight by critics as well as young readers. *The Athenaeum* praised the book and assured "any one catering for boy-readers that they will find abundance of excitement in company of Peter the Whaler; but a word may be added to assure 'parents and guardians,' and also their fireside clients, that Mr. Kingston tells his story more than ordinarily well, – minutely and seriously, but without tediousness." Kingsford states that Kingston's secret was to "combine the grave and the gay, and it is clear that the dramatic and fast-moving nature of Peter's adventures made the book's moral agenda perfectly palatable to its original readers; parents, of course, were very pleased with the various moral subtexts. With the publication of this novel, Kingston became known as the foremost author of boys' sea stories of his day."

It was not until 1949 that any serious critical attacks were leveled at *Peter the Whaler*. Malcolm M. Willey's article in *The New Colophon,* "Peter The Whaler, Plagiarist," picked up several instances of close literary "borrowings" that had apparently gone unnoticed in the nineteenth century. Willey demonstrates that there are pages of parallels between *Peter the Whaler* and a book published thirty years before its first appearance, Capt. William Scoresby's *The First Arctic Regions and the Northern Whale-Fishery* (1820). By the time of Willey's attack, Kingston's reputation had receded into near obscurity, and the article caused little stir. In *The Collector's Book of Boys' Stories* (1973) Eric Quayle argues that the kind of "literary piracy" of which Kingston was guilty was extremely common in children's writers of the nineteenth century and that Kingston was probably not any more liable to "borrow" than his fellow writers.

By 1859 Kingston and his wife, Agnes, had four children, and in June they decided to move to Wimborne in Dorset, where the writer and his family enjoyed the countryside. Kingston developed his interest in naturalism and wrote articles on flowers and animals for *Kingston's Magazine*. During this period he continued his prolific writing career. *The Cruise of the "Frolic"* (1860) was, along with *The Three Midshipmen* and *The Two Supercargoes* (1878), one of Kingston's most popular and enduring novels. It is representative of Kingston in its themes, preoccupations, and literary style. Addressing its readers as "brother yachtsmen," the book begins with the depiction of a group of bachelors sailing at the Cowes Regatta and proceeds to recount their adventures at sea. Several stories within the story display an odd mixture of genres: a romantic, quasi-Gothic tale of the struggle between the heroic Edward Staunton and the villainous Daggerfeldt is told; there are travelogue sections set in Oporto, Lisbon, Cadiz, and Gibraltar; and at one point Kingston digresses

Frontispiece for Kingston's The Two Supercargoes; or, Adventure in Savage Africa *(1878)*

into an extended historical section on Portugal, which prompts him to remind himself that he is "writing the cruise of the 'Frolic,' and not a history of Portugal." As is customary with the author, there are many remarks about the superiority of Englishmen, the following conflation of masculinity, sailing, and violence being typical: "a finer set of broadshouldered, wide-chested fellows I never saw, as they stood around us with their necks bare and the sleeves of their blue shirts tucked up above the elbows, handling their weapons with the fond look which a child bestows on a newly-given toy." The book also contains conventional sentimentalities about women's roles as daughters, wives, and mothers, along with pious, evangelical statements: "I was led to look upward as the only source of happiness, and a pure and unfailing source it has ever since proved to me."

The Three Midshipmen, "the best of Kingston's creations" according to Kingsford, details the adventures of three old school friends as midshipmen: Alick Murray, Jack Rogers, and Terence Adair. The flavor of the book – and the nature of its appeal to

Victorian boys – is evident in the narrator's early foreshadowing of the boys' adventures:

> Who would have thought when we were together at dear old Eagle House, that they would, ere many years had gone over their heads, have actually crossed swords with real red-capped or turbaned Mahomedans, fought with true Greek romantic pirates, hunted down slaves and explored African rivers with voracious sharks watching their mouths, hungry crocodiles basking in their slimy shallows, and veritable negroes inhabiting their banks.

The book stresses Christian duty; attacks slavery, which it calls "a disgrace to every civilized country calling itself Christian;" and describes the idealized English hero, Jack, as the pinnacle of human creation: "as he stood cutlass in hand, with a profusion of light hair streaming back from his honest sun-burnt countenance, he was the picture of a true British sailor, and might have been likened to the noblest type of the king of the beasts." Like *Peter the Whaler*, *The Three Midshipmen* was a commercial, popular, and critical success; it was often reprinted from its first appearance until the 1940s.

Surprisingly, despite Kingston's industry and despite the popularity of his books, he was almost bankrupt in 1868. His financial grants from the Royal Literary Fund and the Queen's Civil List in that year suggest financial distress, as do the minutes of the Literary Fund. Kingsford attributes Kingston's "almost complete disappearance from public life" for the last ten years of his life to his financial problems. At least Kingston's marriage and family life were happy. His wife, Agnes, kept diaries of their domestic life; she apparently was responsible for the translations of Jules Verne's stories and of Johann David Wyss's *The Swiss Family Robinson* but wrote them under her husband's name, to whom they have traditionally been attributed.

In 1878 the family moved to Stormont Lodge in Willesden, and Kingston's amazing productivity continued unabated, despite financial problems and ill health. *The Two Supercargoes; or, Adventure in Savage Africa* was published that year. In his preface, Kingston asks his readers "to take an interest in the long-neglected and fearfully ill-treated inhabitants of that benighted land, and to assist those who are so heroically laboring for their amelioration with their contributions, if not by their personal efforts." The qualities valorized throughout the novel are "judgement, courage, and perseverance." *The Athenaeum,* in its review of 19 December 1877, proclaimed: "Boys will read Mr. Kingston's story with avidity, for it abounds in startling incidents, and is full of life and bustle." *The Athenaeum* complained, however, that the book would be more instructive if the author were more informed about Africa's geography and history: "A boy reading this book will imbibe notions about Africa, the slave trade, and gorillas, which are certainly not correct, and this is a pity."

Kingston was also actively involved in boys' magazines of the period. He was one of the authors of the *Boy's Own Magazine* (1855–1874), the forerunner to the *Boy's Own Paper* and a monthly magazine that, according to Kirsten Drotner, "marked the beginning of a change in juvenile papers from religious didacticism or secular rationalism toward moral entertainment where an extrovert imperial manliness mattered more than introspective piety or dry moralizing." Drotner's remarks are also applicable to Kingston's stories, where piety and moralizing are grafted onto "extrovert imperial manliness." Kingston subsequently became an active contributor to the Religious Tract's successful *Boy's Own Paper* (1879–1967), along with authors such as G. A. Henty, R. M. Ballantyne, Arthur Conan Doyle, and Jules Verne. Kingston's *From Powder Monkey to Admiral* became the paper's first serial in 1879. It was criticized for "encouraging warlike spirit," to which accusation Kingston mounted a spirited defense. In its first three months the *Boy's Own Paper* attained a circulation of nearly two hundred thousand; in five years its circulation rose to a quarter of a million. Kingston was also one of the early authors featured in the magazine *Little Folks,* founded in 1871.

Kingston maintained active editorial involvement in magazines. He edited the *Colonial Magazine* from 1849 to 1852, and in 1859 he started the illustrated monthly *Kingston's Magazine for Boys,* which ran until 1862. His editorial letter in the first issue gives a clear idea of his sense of mission, focus, and audience:

> My great aim is to give you a periodical . . . which you will value and look over years hence as an old familiar friend, when you may be battling with the realities of life under the suns of India, in the backwoods of Canada or the States, on the grassy downs of Australia. . . . The Magazine will contain interesting stories and descriptions of exciting adventure; and though I will not attempt to cram information and sage advice down your throats, I should very much neglect my duty as an Editor if I did not take every opportunity of offering you both one and the other.

In January 1880 Kingston founded the *Union Jack,* a weekly illustrated penny magazine for boys. One of his stories, "Paddy Finn," appeared in the first issue, along with a story by G. A. Henty titled

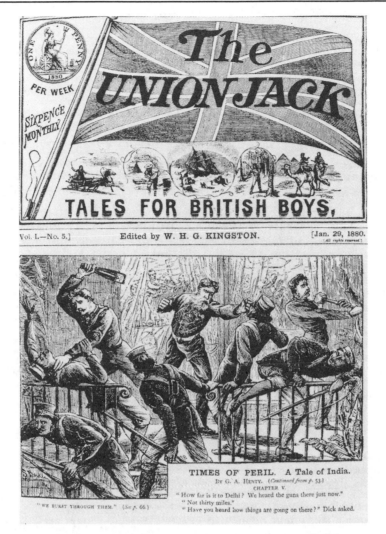

Front page for the boys' magazine founded and edited by Kingston

"Times of Peril: A Tale of India." Kingston became ill with cancer, however, and resigned the editorship in April 1880 to Henty.

On 2 August 1880 Kingston wrote a farewell letter to his *Boy's Own Paper* readers, in which he provided an overview of his life and work. Far from complaining about his serious illness and impending death, he expressed his faith:

> I want you to know that I am leaving this life in unspeakable happiness, because I rest my soul on my Saviour, trusting only and entirely to the merits of the Great Atonement, by which my sins have been put away forever.
>
> Dear boys, I ask you to give your hearts to Christ, and earnestly pray that all of you may meet me in Heaven.

More than five hundred thousand readers of the *Boy's Own Paper* read the letter, which aroused a public stir. Its effect was enhanced by the fact that it appeared in the *Boy's Own Paper* three days after the author's death on 5 August, imbuing the letter with a Lazarus-like profundity. Countless sermons cited the letter as a source of inspiration and moral encouragement and portrayed Kingston as an exemplar of evangelical Christianity.

Kingston's letter formed a dramatic end to an illustrious, prolific, and wide-ranging career. During the thirty years from 1850 to 1880 Kingston dominated the market as a writer of boys' fiction. Reviewers agreed that his books were exciting and enjoyable reading for boys and that they were morally sound. *The Athenaeum,* for example, in its 1860 review of *Digby Heathcote,* praised the book for the "admirable counsels scattered throughout the pages," concluding, "we could not desire a better or more entertaining book for boys."

Although by 1870 Kingston was beginning to receive occasional criticism for being too prolific and formulaic, most readers and critics throughout the latter half of the nineteenth century agreed on his merits. Kingsford relates that in 1884 a questionnaire about children's literature was circulated to 790 boys and 1,200 girls at English schools by Charles Walsh, and it determined that Kingston was the boys' second favorite author: he received 179 votes to Charles Dickens's 223. In 1888 critic Edward Salmon, discussing the "passion for romance," praised Kingston highly: "The best . . . as well as the most popular purveyor of literature to meet this special want, who has yet lived, was Kingston." In the prefatory poem to *Treasure Island* (1883) Robert Louis Stevenson cites Kingston as a predecessor in whose tradition he was following. In addition, Kingsford reports that *The Three Midshipmen* was reprinted at least one hundred times in England before the 1940s.

Obituaries were also generous in their assessment of Kingston's contribution to literature. The *Union Jack* stressed the salutary moral elements in and effects of Kingston's work and called him the "greatest boy's writer of his age." The *Athenaeum* described his novels as being "full of descriptions of other lands, and of hairbreadth escapes and perilous adventures by flood and field, written with vraisemblance," and stated with satisfaction that "there is not a page in any of his books which the most scrupulous parent would wish to take out, or a sentiment inculcated that is not thoroughly honest, upright, manly, and true."

Kingston's name emerges today mostly in the context of Victorian boys' literature and children's magazines, particularly in discussions about ideals of masculinity and attitudes to the British Empire in writings for boys. K. C. Laurie's 1947 review of Kingsford's biography summarizes Kingston's importance in terms of what he did "to mould impressionable youth and to determine the racial and spiritual tone of the British Empire." His work is little read today and is usually thought of as a literary curiosity. However, an anonymous 1976 article in *Extracts* favorably compares Kingston to Herman Melville: "If true fictional art lies . . . in the concentration of huge dollops of spine-tingling adventure in one exciting story, then Kingston in *Peter the Whaler* has it all over Melville. For he did in one novel what it took Melville six to do."

Contemporary critics occasionally agree with William H. P. Crewdson, who in a 1986 article called Kingston the greatest and "best-loved author of his day." In general, however, Kingston receives little serious critical consideration and is usually grouped with Ballantyne and other Victorian boys' writers by critics who may not have read his novels or considered his distinctive contribution to children's literature. Kingston's books played a crucial role in creating and promulgating the cult of idealized British masculinity that formed so central a part of mid- to late-nineteenth-century literature for boys. Clearly, Kingston's treatment of masculinity and the British Empire plays a significant role in the history of children's literature. Perhaps equally important is the fact that Kingston was one of the first authors for children to target one sex specifically, thus initiating a gender-based segregation of children's literature. While his books do not correspond closely with current tastes, Kingston deserves more sustained critical attention for his important contributions to the history of children's literature.

Biography:
Maurice Rooke Kingsford, *The Life, Work and Influence of William Henry Giles Kingston* (Toronto: Ryerson, 1947).

References:
Jack Cox, *Take a Cold Tub, Sir! The Story of the Boy's Own Paper* (Guildford: Lutterworth, 1983);

William H. P. Crewdson, "W. H. G. Kingston," *Antiquarian Book Monthly Review* (August 1986): 294–300;

Kirsten Drotner, *English Children and Their Magazines, 1751–1945* (New Haven & London: Yale University Press, 1982);

Patrick A. Dunae, "Boy's Literature and the Idea of Empire," *Victorian Studies,* 24 (Autumn 1980): 105–121;

K. C. Laurie, "The Life of W. H. G. Kingston," *Dalhousie Review,* 28 (1947): 409–410;

"W. H. G. Kingston and Melville: A Critical Comparison by an Englishman Spending the First of April in Pittsfield," *Extracts: An Occasional Newsletter,* no. 27 (September 1976): 8–10;

Malcolm M. Willey, "Peter The Whaler, Plagiarist," *New Colophon,* 2 (January 1949): 29–32.

Charles Lamb
(10 February 1775 – 27 December 1834)
and
Mary Lamb
(3 December 1764 – 20 May 1847)

Judy Anne White
Morgan State University

See also the Charles Lamb entries in *DLB 93: British Romantic Poets, 1789–1832, First Series* and *DLB 107: British Romantic Prose Writers, 1789–1832, First Series.*

BOOKS – by Charles Lamb: *Blank Verse,* by Lamb and Charles Lloyd (London: Printed by T. Bensley for J. & A. Arch, 1798);

A Tale of Rosamund Gray and Old Blind Margaret (Birmingham: Printed by Thomas Pearson, 1798; London: Printed for Lee & Hurst, 1798);

John Woodvil: A Tragedy (London: Printed by T. Plummer for G. & J. Robinson, 1802);

The King and Queen of Hearts (London: Printed for Thomas Hodgkins, 1805);

The Adventures of Ulysses (London: Printed by T. Davison for the Juvenile Library, 1808; New York: Harper, 1879);

Prince Dorus: Or, Flattery Put Out of Countenance (London: Printed for M. J. Godwin at the Juvenile Library, 1811);

Beauty and the Beast; or, A Rough Outside with Gentle Heart (London: Printed for M.J. Godwin at the Juvenile Library, 1811);

Mr. H., or Beware a Bad Name. A Farce in Two Acts [pirated edition] (Philadelphia: Published by M. Carey, printed by A. Fagan, 1813);

The Works of Charles Lamb, 2 volumes (London: Ollier, 1818);

Elia: Essays Which Have Appeared under that Signature in the London Magazine (London: Printed for Taylor & Hessey, 1823; [pirated edition] Philadelphia: Carey, Lea & Carey, printed by Mifflin & Parry, 1828);

Elia: Essays Which Have Appeared under that Signature in the London Magazine, Second Series [pirated edition] (Philadelphia: Carey, Lea & Carey, printed by J. R. A. Skerret, 1828);

Mary and Charles Lamb in 1834; portrait by F. S. Cary (National Portrait Gallery, London)

Album Verses, with a Few Others (London: Moxon, 1830);

Satan in Search of a Wife (London: Moxon, 1831);

The Last Essays of Elia (London: Moxon, 1833; Philadelphia: T. K. Greenbank, 1833).

BOOKS – by Charles and Mary Lamb: *Tales from Shakespear. Designed for the Use of Young Persons,* 2 volumes, attributed to Charles Lamb (London: Printed for Thos. Hodgkins at the Juvenile Library, 1807; Philadelphia: Bradford & Inskeep, printed by J. Maxwell, 1813);

Mrs. Leicester's School: Or, The History of Several Young Ladies Related by Themselves, anonymous (London: Printed for M. J. Godwin at the Juvenile Library, 1809; George Town: J. Milligan, 1811);

Poetry for Children, Entirely Original, 2 volumes (London: Printed for M. J. Godwin at the Juvenile Library, 1809; Boston: West & Richardson and E. Cotton, 1812).

Edition: *The Works of Charles and Mary Lamb,* 7 volumes, edited by E. V. Lucas (London: Methuen, 1903–1905; New York: Putnam, 1903–1905).

PLAY PRODUCTION: *Mr. H----,* by Charles Lamb, London, Theatre Royal, Drury Lane, 10 December 1806.

OTHER: *Specimens of English Dramatic Poets, Who Lived About the Time of Shakespeare: With Notes,* edited, with commentary, by Charles Lamb (London: Printed for Longman, Hurst, Rees & Orme, 1808; New York: Wiley & Putnam, 1845).

Although Charles Lamb was best known to his contemporaries for his essays published under the pseudonym "Elia," his place in the annals of children's literature rests on *Tales from Shakespear* (1807), which appeared under his name but which was mainly written by his sister, Mary. It has remained in print and has succeeded in drawing children into Shakespeare's world as well as into the individual universe of each play. However, the literary reputation of Charles and Mary Lamb has been influenced by the central facts of their lives: Mary's debilitating mental illness for much of her adult life and Charles's immeasurable affection for and enduring relationship with his sister, a relationship that led to successful collaboration on two collections of children's stories: *Tales from Shakespear* and *Mrs. Leicester's School* (1809).

Mary Lamb was born on 3 December 1764 in London. Her older brother, John, had been born a year earlier; Charles was born on 10 February 1775. Only these three of seven children born to John and Elizabeth Field Lamb survived infancy. John Lamb's employer and benefactor, Samuel Salt, installed the Lamb family in living quarters below his own at the London Temple, the vast complex where barristers lived and worked. The three chil-

dren enjoyed the benefits of fine schooling: Charles and Mary attended Mr. William Bird's school; John and Charles were accepted at the day school at Christ's Hospital.

The Lambs' parents and benefactors ensured that the children's education continued beyond the classroom. Salt allowed them to wander in his personal library; the three children thus developed a love of books unusual in the progeny of a servant. Mary and Charles were also allowed to attend theater performances at the age of five or six and became enthusiastic theatergoers. In addition, the matriarch of the Plumer family, their grandmother's employer, allowed the children to visit the rural Plumer estate, Blakesmere, where they profited not only from intellectual and aesthetic experiences in a mansion decorated with paintings, sculptures, and tapestries, but also from immersing themselves in a natural environment teeming with plant and animal life. All of these experiences would benefit the Lambs as writers.

Practical considerations prevented the two younger Lamb children from exploring further educational or other "idle" careers. In 1789 governors of the Christ's Hospital school decided that Charles should not go on to university, his stuttering being too great a handicap for a clergyman; instead, they secured for him an apprenticed clerkship at the office of a Mr. Paice. Charles found another job at the South Sea House a year later and after six months found employment at the East India House, where he would spend the rest of his working life.

After Salt's death in 1792 the Lambs were forced to leave the London Temple for a cramped dwelling in High Holborn. Both parents' health deteriorated rapidly afterward; Mrs. Lamb, presumably arthritic, became chair-bound, and Mr. Lamb began to show signs of senility. In addition, John, the eldest, moved out and left the rest of the family to fend for themselves.

At this time Charles shared some of his finest hours with his old schoolmate Samuel Taylor Coleridge, who returned to London in 1794. They spent evenings and weekends at the Salutation and Cat, where they drank ale and discussed philosophy and religion. Their relationship also led to the first publication of Charles's writings, as Coleridge generously added four of Lamb's sonnets to his own first volume of poetry.

Meanwhile, the family's burdens fell entirely upon Mary's shoulders. Young Charles was working on probation without pay, and so the sole surviving daughter took up her needle and entered the dressmaking business to support her family.

Charles's long hours at the East India House precluded his participation in the daily care of his parents and the elderly aunt who lived with them; Mary spent her remaining energies making her ailing elders comfortable. The family's survival came to depend on Mary's success as a businesswoman and a nurse. Thus was the stage set for a tragedy of major proportions: Mary's temporary insanity and murder of her mother in September 1796.

It was Charles who took command of his family's affairs from that day forward. He put his family's needs before his own. When Mary had been returned to his custody after treatment at a Hoxton asylum, he set up separate lodgings for her. He then moved his father and his aging Aunt Hetty to a house in Chapel Street, Pentonville. For months Charles, the devoted son and brother, worked long hours at the East India House and then returned home to care for his aged relatives. His Aunt Hetty died the following February; but the senile elder John Lamb survived another two years.

Charles's life at this time was not barren of intellectual inspiration, however, as he was acquainted with some of the leading writers of his day. In June 1797 he left London to visit Coleridge and his family at Nether Stowey. He also met William and Dorothy Wordsworth during his stay; the two had taken a house close to the Coleridge cottage. Years later Wordsworth would visit the Lambs frequently when he was in London, especially for one of Charles's noted evenings of feasting and discussion. In 1798 Charles also published a novelette, *A Tale of Rosamund Gray and Old Blind Margaret,* based on his unrequited love for a young woman named Ann Simons.

After his father's death in 1799, Charles felt that he would be able to devote his time away from the East India House to his sister and to his friends. His future, along with his sister's, seemed bright. The truth, however, was far from the utopian existence Charles had begun to envision. Although Mary was able to live with him, they were forced to move three times between 1799 and 1800 before settling again at the London Temple, as their reputation preceded them. In addition, Mary was never cured of her illness: her "retreats from reality" increased in number and duration as she got older and sometimes culminated in violence. Charles was consistently forced to make the heartbreaking decision to return Mary to the asylum. In his memoir Bryan Waller Procter wrote, "It was very affecting to meet them [on the way to the asylum], walking together, weeping together, carrying Mary's straight-jacket with them." Their relationship, however, never followed the contemporary standard of male dominance and female dependency. Each was inexorably bound to the other, though uncomfortably; Mary, in a 14 March 1806 letter to Sarah Stoddart, commented that "Our love for each other has been the torment of our lives hitherto." Many of their acquaintances noticed, in fact, that Charles seemed to be the more dependent of the two.

Charles found solace in his writing. In 1802 he wrote a five-act play in blank verse, which the manager of the Drury Lane rejected outright. Undaunted, Charles started another. In 1806 *Mr. H----* was produced at the Drury Lane, where it failed miserably. Luckily, the Godwins' entry into the business of publishing children's literature enabled a defeated Charles to concentrate on something besides his failures.

In 1805 William Godwin, the radical philosopher, and his second wife, Mary Jane Godwin, decided to launch a publishing company for children's literature. Shortly thereafter, the Godwins enlisted the Lambs, acquaintances and card partners, as contributors. Charles's first venture into juvenile literature resulted in an amusing adaptation of a rhyme, *The King and Queen of Hearts* (1805), illustrated by William Mulready. Charles's running commentary on the events of the rhyme transforms the children's rhyme into a full-blown farce. The Knave is a rogue caught in the act of stealing tarts by the Queen's servant, her spy, and when the King of Hearts "beats the Knave full sore," the tarts "for fear" pop out of the poor lad's pockets. Although Charles was a romantic in spirit, his retelling of this children's rhyme is more Victorian in its moral overtones. In *Charles Lamb and His Friends* (1944), Will Howe notes that Charles's first children's project was significant "in giving the author confidence of an ability to write for young readers."

Encouraged by the success of *The King and Queen of Hearts,* the Godwins engaged both Mary and Charles to write *Tales from Shakespear;* the adaptation of plays for children was then a novel idea. On 10 May 1806 Charles reported to his friend Thomas Manning that he and Mary were working on the project: "Six are already done by her . . . I have done 'Othello' and 'Macbeth' and mean to do all the tragedies. I think it will be popular among the little people." *Tales from Shakespear* consists of prose versions of twenty plays, fourteen by Mary and six by Charles. Mary and Charles proved themselves gifted in defining the essence of each tale for their young audience.

The strength of the collection lies in its concise, flowing prose and rich Elizabethan vocabulary. Characters essential to the plot and the tenor of the story are included as a rule, and the psychological undercurrents motivating the characters are recounted simply and effectively. Choices and motives are carefully explained, yet the Lambs succeed in avoiding the overly complex explanation in favor of letting their audience see what is about to happen. At the same time, however, the Lambs also remained steadfast in their intent to enlighten their young readers.

Mary's talent for infusing merriment and charm into her tales reveals itself in her treatment of the character Puck in *A Midsummer Night's Dream:* "the . . . old dame was gravely seating herself to tell her neighbours a sad and melancholy story, [when] Puck would slip her three-legged stool from under her, and down toppled the poor old woman, and then the old gossips would hold their sides and laugh at her, and swear they never wasted a merrier hour." The shared and involving nature of the passage plays upon the associative – that everyone knows such a prankster and that everyone wishes to know what the sprite might do next.

Charles's power as a storyteller resides in his ability to explain the psychological motives underlying an act. His representation of Lady Macbeth is succinct, yet provides a wealth of information: "She was a bad, ambitious woman, and so as her husband and herself could arrive at greatness, she cared not by what means. She spurred on the reluctant purpose of Macbeth . . . and did not cease to represent the murder of the king as a step absolutely necessary to the fulfillment of the flattering prophecy." The tone and sense of suspense, however, urge the reader on, despite the fact that Charles has revealed much about Lady Macbeth's nature.

The stories were originally published in discrete illustrated booklets; then a two-volume set was published under Charles Lamb's name, titled *Tales from Shakespear. Designed for the Use of Young Persons.* Godwin printed five editions during the first ten years of the series' existence in order to meet demand. The stories have been available to young readers since 1807.

Shortly after the publication of the tales, Mary began *Mrs. Leicester's School: Or, The History of Several Young Ladies Related by Themselves.* Structurally similar to Boccaccio's *Decameron* (1351), a favorite of the Lambs' friend William Hazlitt, this collection of stories centers on a meeting of new students. Each tells an autobiographical story, while Mrs. Leicester

acts as moderator and guide. Mary's personal experiences – her childhood visits to Blakesmere and her school days – provide the basis for the majority of the tales. Charles contributed the final three of the ten stories, although it is not known whether Mary encouraged him to complete the collection or whether she was unable to do so because of her illness.

Published anonymously in 1809, *Mrs. Leicester's School* was initially a success. Godwin released the book during the Christmas holidays, and the warmth and innocence of the schoolgirl stories reflected the zeitgeist of that December. Unlike *Tales from Shakespear,* however, the volume faded into obscurity after some twenty years and eight editions. Despite a prediction from Coleridge to the contrary, *Mrs. Leicester's School* was forgotten by the time of Charles's death.

Mary, enthusiastic now that she had a reading public – albeit a reading public who did not know her name, thanks to William Godwin's insistence that the tales be attributed to Charles alone – had scarcely attended to the publication of *Mrs. Leicester's School* before she turned to writing what would be her final book, *Poetry for Children, Entirely Original* (1809). The verses deal with commonplace childhood events, such as the loss of a beloved toy. Some of the poems speak directly to a child's literal sensibility: in "The Rainbow," for example, the narrator appeals to the child's sense of wonder to teach about the unity binding all nature and humanity. Others offer rigid moral lessons, reinforcing the familial values of love and mutual respect. At their best, the Lambs' poems – Charles and brother John also contributed to the collection – combine a fine moral sense with social consciousness: "The Force of Habit" bemoans the irony of a sensitive child's fear of the sounds of war – ceremonial guns fired in a park – and his growing up to become a military leader.

Poetry for Children thus recalls William Blake's *Songs of Innocence and of Experience,* the first volume of which had appeared in 1794. The imagery in *Poetry for Children* is not as concise or powerful as Blake's, however, nor is the sense of despair so strong. Informative and heartfelt in its sympathetic views of the powerless – children and the working class – the poetry is not so much visionary as descriptive. Nonetheless, the collection was popular when it was first published in 1809, although it did not long remain in demand.

Charles retreated to his own individual projects: for children he began an adaptation of *The Odyssey* titled *The Adventures of Ulysses* (1808); for adults

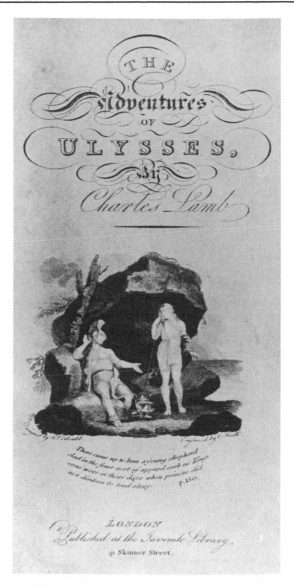

Title page for Charles Lamb's 1808 adaptation of
Homer's Odyssey

he completed *Specimens of English Dramatic Poets, Who Lived About the Time of Shakespeare: With Notes* (1808). About the former Charles wrote to Manning in February 1808 that his intent was to write "an introduction to the reading of Telemachus." He made little claim to absolute accuracy, allowing that he had used George Chapman's seventeenth-century translation of Homer as a basis for his adaptation. Charles's book is both lively and accessible. He narrates the story in chronological sequence, abandoning the flashback; he also includes an abundance of descriptive details and introduces a bit of psychology into the fast-paced plot. The book was destined to become a children's classic.

In 1811 Charles ventured yet again into the world of children's literature, publishing two lesser tales, *Prince Dorus: Or, Flattery Put Out of Countenance* and *Beauty and the Beast; or, A Rough Outside with Gentle Heart* (1811). *Prince Dorus*, like *Tales from Shakespear*, is grounded in the psychology of the self. The narrative has as its center the need for an individual to recognize and accept his own shortcomings. The prince is cursed at birth with an excessively large nose, and the curse is only broken when he accepts that his nose is immense. Psychology and morality merge here, as self-acceptance is encouraged. The tale is uneven in tone and technical quality. Lamb seems overwhelmed in his attempts to entertain and educate; his tone varies from whimsical to cautionary. In addition, the couplets of which *Prince Dorus* is composed are often stilted; it is unlikely that they would ring true for a young child. For all its faults, however, the tale has a certain charm. *Beauty and the Beast* benefits from a more dexterous poetic touch as well as the author's appreciation of the strengths and weaknesses of familial bonds.

There is little information on the Lambs' daily lives from 1809 to 1818, as few of their letters from that period have survived. They lived at Inner Temple Lane, in the shadow of their childhood lodgings, and evidently enjoyed one of the happiest and most successful periods of their lives, except for Mary's bouts with her chronic illness. In 1818 *The Works of Charles Lamb* was published in two volumes, with a dedication to Coleridge. That year the Lambs also moved to a home in Covent Garden, where they were to stay for five years.

During the next two years a pair of important young women entered the lives of the Lambs. In 1819 Charles fell in love with the actress Fanny Kelly, and after a brief courtship he proposed. Kelly rejected the proposal; she wrote to her sister that she could not put herself into "that atmosphere of sad mental uncertainty which surrounds his domestic life." Charles never again proposed marriage. The second of the two women brought greater happiness. In 1820 the Lambs spent their summer holiday at Cambridge, where they met Emma Isola, an eleven-year-old Italian English girl who captured their hearts. The pair gradually accepted full responsibility for young Emma's welfare, and when her father died in 1823 they apparently adopted her as their daughter. Until she married the publisher Edward Moxon, Emma provided companionship for Charles and an outlet for Mary's maternal indulgence.

The year 1820 also marked the beginning of Charles's association with the newly created *London Magazine*. For the next five years Charles wrote, under the pseudonym "Elia," an engaging series of informal essays that became the talk of the town. The original essays were collected in book form in 1823 and 1828, and again in 1833. In the essays Charles couples affectionate portraits of friends and relatives – especially his sister, loosely disguised as "Bridget Elia, my housekeeper" – with philosophical insight and folk wisdom. The pieces were hugely popular and influenced many subsequent essayists.

The years 1820–1821 were not without tribulation. In October 1821 John Lamb died. Although he had been estranged from Charles and Mary for

several years, they both loved him. Mary's health also continued to deteriorate. An 1821 trip to France, undertaken by the pair with enthusiasm, quickly turned to tragedy when Mary suffered a mental breakdown en route. This proved to be a precursor to the longer, more severe attacks that would plague her until the end of her life.

From 1826 until 1834 several changes occurred in the Lamb household. The family had left the city in 1823 and moved to Islington; in 1826 the Lambs and Emma Isola moved to Enfield, where they lived for six years; they then moved to Edmonton, where Charles and, later, Mary would find a final resting place. Charles finally retired from the East India House; he grew lonely for the city, however, and took rooms in London, preparing extracts from Elizabethan plays for William Hone's *Every-Day Book* (1826–1827). He also published *Album Verses, with a Few Others* in 1830 and a short play, *Satan in Search of a Wife,* in 1831.

The little triumphs did not quite erase the pain of Mary's ongoing tragedy. The length and severity of her attacks increased. Charles lamented to his friend Bernard Barton that " 'tis a tedious cut out of a life of sixty-four to lose twelve or thirteen weeks every year or two." By the time of his death in 1834, Charles had seen his sister reduced from a charming and literate companion to a confused old woman unable to meet the demands of daily living.

The year 1834 saw the lives of both Charles Lamb and his beloved friend Coleridge come to an end. Coleridge, who had been increasingly bedridden since 1830, died on 25 July 1834; his death was a great shock to Charles and Mary, who had not seen their friend for years. Five months later, on 27 December, Charles died of complications following a fall. He was fifty-nine years of age. He was buried in Edmonton Churchyard in a spot he and Mary had chosen on one of their walks. Mary lived on for another twelve years, first at Edmonton with a nurse and then, after a long illness in 1839, at St. John's Wood, where her nurse's sister had a home. She died on 20 May 1847, at the age of eighty-two, and was buried alongside her brother.

During the Lambs' lifetimes and after, critics scrutinized Charles – both his works and his life – and ignored Mary entirely, save the assumptions they made about her effect on her brother's disposition. As a whole, they expressed an unprecedented interest in examining "Saint Charles's " personality as carefully as his texts when preparing to render judgment upon his work. As Jane Aaron explains in *A Double Singleness* (1991), "The pet-Lamb cult served to distance Charles' behaviour from that required of the average male . . . his image could be cherished as one comfortably set apart, in its sweet domestic niche, from the self-assertive public world of the nineteenth-century middle-class male." As a result, the overwhelmingly male circles of critics in Georgian, and later Victorian and Edwardian, England responded vigorously to Charles Lamb the man as well as his essays.

Twentieth-century critics, however, also focusing mainly on his essays, find Charles Lamb's writing difficult to praise. The proliferation of celebratory anthologies in 1934, the centenary of Charles Lamb's death, drew the unsympathetic eyes of the modern British critics, who had promoted the study of English literature as a rigorous intellectual activity. Denys Thompson, in "Our Debt to Lamb" states that Charles Lamb's Elia essays represent "a falling away from the more rigorous eighteenth-century essay which attempted to improve the reader's 'spiritual manners' by disturbing his complacency." Much more damaging to Lamb's reputation were Thompson's claim, in his widely distributed scholastic guide to criticism, *Reading and Discrimination,* that Lamb had reduced the eighteenth-century essay to "a vehicle for charming whimsies" and his elimination of Lamb's essays in later editions of the guide. In America New Critics resented the overly subjective nature of Lamb's essays. Lamb's reputation has never fully recovered from such disparagement, and despite the continued vitality of the Charles Lamb Society, scholars and students today may complete Romantic or Victorian studies without having read a single Elia essay.

Mary Lamb, in contrast, was generally perceived by contemporary critics as a lifetime distraction to her brother's genius, his albatross. One might conclude that this was because Mary's works were published either under a pseudonym or under her brother's name; but consequent revelation of her authorship did nothing to improve her critical standing. Thomas McFarland, for example, as recently as 1987 in *Romantic Cruxes: The English Essayists and the Spirit of the Age,* disregarded Mary's literary accomplishments altogether. Perhaps future critics will learn to appreciate both Mary Lamb's contributions to children's literature and the importance of her collaboration with her brother Charles on children's projects.

Letters:

E. V. Lucas, ed., *The Letters of Charles Lamb, to Which are Added Those of His Sister Mary Lamb,* 3 volumes (London: Dent/Methuen, 1935);

The grave of Charles and Mary Lamb in the Edmonton churchyard

Edwin W. Marrs, ed., *The Letters of Charles and Mary Anne Lamb,* 3 volumes (Ithaca, N.Y.: Cornell University Press, 1975–1978).

Biographies:

E. V. Lucas, *The Life of Charles Lamb,* revised edition, 2 volumes (London: Methuen, 1921);

Will D. Howe, *Charles Lamb and His Friends* (Indianapolis: Bobbs-Merrill, 1944);

Katharine Anthony, *The Lambs: A Study of Pre-Victorian England* (London: Hammond, 1948);

Winifred F. Courtney, *Young Charles Lamb: 1775–1802* (London: Macmillan, 1982).

References:

Jane Aaron, "Charles and Mary Lamb: The Critical Heritage," *Charles Lamb Bulletin,* no. 59 (July 1987): 73–85;

Aaron, *A Double Singleness: Gender and the Writings of Charles and Mary Lamb* (Oxford: Clarendon Press, 1991);

Winifred F. Courtney, "Mrs. Leicester's School as Children's Literature," *Charles Lamb Bulletin,* no. 47–48 (July–October 1984): 164–169;

T. W. Craik, "Charles and Mary Lamb: Tales from Shakespear," *Charles Lamb Bulletin,* no. 49 (January 1985): 2–14;

David Foxon, "The Chapbook Editions of the Lambs' 'Tales from Shakespear,'" *Book Collector,* 6 (Spring 1957): 41–53;

Jean I. Marsden, "Shakespeare for Girls: Mary Lamb and Tales from Shakespeare," *Children's Literature: An International Journal, Annual of the Modern Language Association Division on Children's Literature,* 17 (1989): 47–63;

Thomas McFarland, *Romantic Cruxes: The English Essayists and the Spirit of the Age* (Oxford: Clarendon Press, 1987);

Joseph E. Riehl, "Charles Lamb's Mrs. Leicester's School Stories and Elia: The Fearful Imagination," *Charles Lamb Bulletin,* no. 39 (July 1982): 138–143;

Denys Thompson, "Our Debt to Lamb," in *Determinations: Critical Essays,* edited by F. R. Leavis (New York: Haskell, 1970), pp. 199–217;

Thompson, *Reading and Discrimination* (London: Chatto & Windus, 1934);

D. G. Wilson, "Lamb's Tales from Shakespear," *Charles Lamb Bulletin,* no. 49 (January 1985): 14–17.

Edward Lear

(12 May 1812 – 29 January 1888)

Celia Catlett Anderson
Eastern Connecticut State University

See also the Lear entry in *DLB 32: Victorian Poets Before 1850.*

BOOKS: *Illustrations of the Family of Psittacidae, or Parrots* (London: Privately printed, 1832);

Views in Rome and Its Environs: Drawn from Nature and on Stone (London: McLean, 1841);

Gleanings from the Menagerie and Aviary at Knowsley Hall (Knowsley: Privately printed, 1846);

Illustrated Excursions in Italy, 2 volumes (London: McLean, 1846);

A Book of Nonsense, as Derry Down Derry, 2 volumes (London: McLean, 1846); enlarged, as Lear, 1 volume (London: Routledge, Warne & Routledge, 1861; Philadelphia: Hazard, 1863);

Journals of a Landscape Painter in Albania, etc. (London: Bentley, 1851);

Journals of a Landscape Painter in Southern Calabria, etc. (London: Bentley, 1852);

Views in the Seven Ionian Islands (London: Privately printed, 1863);

Journal of a Landscape Painter in Corsica (London: Bush, 1870);

Nonsense Songs, Stories, Botany and Alphabets (London: Bush, 1870; Boston: Osgood, 1871);

More Nonsense, Pictures, Rhymes, Botany, Etc. (London: Bush, 1872);

Tortoises, Terrapins and Turtles Drawn from Life, by Lear and James de Carle Sowerby (London: Sotheran, Baer, 1872);

Laughable Lyrics: A Fourth Book of Nonsense Poems, Songs, Botany, Music, Etc. (London: Bush, 1877);

Queery Leary Nonsense: A Lear Nonsense Book, edited by Constance, Lady Strachey (London: Mills & Boon, 1911);

The Lear Coloured Bird Book for Children (London: Mills & Boon, 1912);

Lear in Sicily May–July 1847, edited by G. Proby (London: Duckworth, 1938);

Edward Lear

The Complete Nonsense of Edward Lear, edited by Holbrook Jackson (London: Faber & Faber, 1947; New York: Dover, 1951);

Edward Lear's Journals: A Selection, edited by Herbert Van Thal (London: Barker, 1952);

Indian Journal: Watercolours and Extracts from the Diary of Edward Lear (1873–1875), edited by Ray Murphy (London: Jarrolds, 1953; New York: Coward-McCann, 1955);

Teapots and Quails, and Other New Nonsenses, edited by Angus Davidson and Philip Hofer (London:

John Murray, 1953; Cambridge: Harvard University Press, 1953);

Edward Lear in the Levant: Travels in Albania, Greece and Turkey in Europe, 1848–1849, edited by Susan Hyman (London: John Murray, 1988).

Edward Lear's illustrated nonsense verse, narratives, alphabets, and botanies are early and central examples of a type of literature for children that endures because it conveys humorous, vigorous, and accessible images of a skewed reality. Known as the laureate of nonsense, for the last 150 years Lear's work has been equally enjoyed by adults. In the nineteenth century, no less a critic than John Ruskin called the limericks "refreshing, and perfect in rhythm" and asserted, "I really don't know any author to whom I am half so grateful, for my idle self, as for Edward Lear. I shall put him first of my hundred authors." In his 1927 essay on Lear, Aldous Huxley claims that the nonsense author is one of the "few writers whose works I care to read more than once," because "Lear had the true poet's feelings for words – words in themselves, precious and melodious, like phrases of music; personal as human beings."

Edward Lear was born on 12 May 1812 in the Holloway district of London, the twentieth child of the stockbroker Jeremiah Lear and his wife, Ann Skerrit Lear. In 1816 Jeremiah defaulted on the stock exchange, and although a friend paid the debts, the family was split by the financial fall. Edward Lear's sister Ann, twenty-two years his senior, became his virtual mother, and they remained close throughout her lifetime.

In addition to the turmoil of disrupted family life, Lear suffered from epilepsy, a condition he apparently kept secret from all but family members. He had virtually no formal education, a lacuna that Lear regarded as beneficial, because it fostered a more individualistic view of the world – in his case, a view in which humor encompassed both sorrows and joys. Biographer Vivien Noakes finds in the author's surviving juvenalia "a combination of humour with real sadness, and an interdependence of words and pictures."

In the 1820s on visits to his sister Sarah's house near Arundel, Lear met several rich patrons of the arts who influenced his ambition to be a painter. Because Lear was dependent on the small inherited income of his sister Ann, studying art in an academic setting was beyond his means, and at age fifteen he began to help support himself by selling sketches, drawing medical subjects, and teaching art. From 1828 to 1830 he drew birds for Prideaux Selby's and Sir William Jardine's *Il-lustrations of British Ornithology,* an experience that led to Lear's *Illustrations of the Family of Psittacidae, or Parrots* (1832), the only volume of a projected multivolume work. Such work led to an invitation in 1832 from Lord Stanley, later the thirteenth earl of Derby, to stay at Knowsley Hall, near Liverpool, to draw the estate's menagerie. At Knowsley Hall, Lear drew humorous pictures for the children of the household and then, after being introduced to the limerick form, combined verse with his nonsense pictures. These early illustrated limericks met with delight from the adults as well as the children and were among those published many years later in *A Book of Nonsense* (1846), under the pseudonym Derry Down Derry.

Lear worked at Knowsley Hall until 1837. During this period he also received some formal training in art but abandoned it to travel in Ireland and the Lake District, giving him not only his first experience in landscape painting but also a lingering case of bronchitis. His patron, Lord Stanley, sent him to Rome for a cure and a course in painting. Lear was successful in selling his work there and also published *Views in Rome and its Environs: Drawn from Nature and on Stone* (1841). Through this set of circumstances he established himself as a landscape painter and author-illustrator of travel journals and found the Mediterranean as the primary region for his artistic expeditions and eventual settlement. Lear's nonsense works reflect his early interest in drawing birds and animals and his travel experiences.

The pattern of Lear's personal life was also set during these early years. Although Lear seems to have been a homosexual in tendency if not in practice, he was never able to establish a lasting intimate relationship with either a man or a woman. He had many friends, among them Chicester Fortescue, later Baron Carlingford; Frank Lushington, later husband of Lady Waldegrave; Thomas Baring, later Lord Northbrook and governor general of India from 1873 to 1875; and the poet Alfred Tennyson and his wife, Emily. In addition, Lear became the "Adopty Nuncle" of many children, who found in him an adult who could match and surpass their sense of fun. His letters and journals reveal how natural it was for him to envision endless recombinations of the cosmos and its inhabitants as a method of counteracting the loneliness and insecurity he often felt in his personal life.

Lear is best known for his limericks, but he did not invent the form – in fact, he discovered it in 1831 when he read the anonymously published book of limericks, *Anecdotes and Adventures of Fifteen Gentlemen* (1823). The form is usually bawdy, but

Cover for the second part of Lear's 1846 collection of limericks

Lear's limericks, devoid of sexual innuendo, can be included with other types of nursery rhymes.

The limericks in *A Book of Nonsense* reveal both Lear's preoccupations and his temperament: birds, foreign places, and his view of himself as an outsider. One example of the many birds in his verse is the lead limerick about an Old Man who laments "Two Owls and a Hen, four Larks and a Wren, / Have all built their nests in my beard." Six more of the first set of limericks present birds. The illustration of the "Old Man, on whose nose, / Most birds of the air could repose" has the ill-omened number of thirteen animals perched there. If one compares the birds to a flock of children, it is possible to view Lear's verse as a haven for the vagaries of childhood.

Lear's predilection for foreign lands is seen more strongly in this early set of limericks than in his later nonsense. Among the 112 rhymes, almost fifty mention foreign locations, including Peru, Norway, Quebec, Prague, Calcutta, Corfu, Tartary, and Parma. The selection is eclectic and probably chosen partly for the rhyme, although

Lear often takes liberties in this area: most of the *-a* and *-ia* endings are rhymed with *-er* and *-ier*: *Smyrna* with *burn her*; *Ischia* with *friskier*; and *Columbia* with *some beer*. These and such rhymes as *Dorking* and *walking* may, however, simply indicate Lear's own pronunciation of the words.

A protagonist isolated from the community, one of the chief characteristics of Lear's nonsense writing, is amply demonstrated by the eccentrics in his early limericks. The old men, old women, and young girls stand in either fear or defiance of a ubiquitous "They." Lear, whose life as an expatriot bachelor placed him outside conventional Victorian society, seems frequently to identify with the protagonist. One could argue, as does Ina Rae Hark, that the outsider protagonist represents a rebellious child, but in some of Lear's limericks it is "They" who seem to be boisterous children, warning or twitting the foolish or cranky protagonist:

There was an old Man at a casement
Who held up his hands in amazement;

Manuscript for a limerick published in A Book of Nonsense *(from the folio album in the collection of Mr. and Mrs. Hans P. Kraus)*

When they said, 'Sir! you'll fall!' he replied 'Not at all!'
That incipient Old Man at a casement.

Lear, with his perpetual sense of fun but also with his shortcomings of health, his abhorrence of noise, and his dislike of large social gatherings, could easily identify with both the energetic young characters and the older disgruntled ones.

Susan Chitty describes "They" as a Kafka-esque "anonymous chorus." Huxley says "They" are "all Right-Thinking Men and Women . . . Public Opinion." Hark classifies the They-protagonist relationship, naming six categories of hostility and helpfulness. Commentators on Lear differ as to whether "They" or the eccentric protagonist wins. Discussing the violent acts in the limericks, Thomas Byrom concludes that "In extreme cases They succeed in killing him. But just as often, he retaliates." There are many examples of defeat or death. Twice a male protagonist is baked: the Old Man of Peru by his wife and an Old Man of Berlin by "They," who are pictured in the accompanying illustration as three women in aprons and bakers' caps. But, on occasion "They" actually help, as in the case of the Old Man of Nepaul, who splits in two — "They" mend him, using "some very strong glue."

The women fare better in these early limericks; only one, the Young Lady of Clare, dies. With few exceptions the females are more in control of the situation than the males — shown most dramatically in two contiguous limericks portraying an Old Man who is afraid of a cow and a Young Lady who distracts a bull. The illustrations make the balance of power even clearer: the "Cow" has large menacing horns and a fierce expression; the "Bull" has small stumpy horns and a meek expression. Lear's unsatisfactory relationship with his mother, his long dependency on his sister Ann, his homosexual inclinations, and his ambivalence about marriage — any or all of these factors could have contributed to the imbalance of gender power depicted in the early limericks.

A Book of Nonsense was popular, but Lear did not make much money on it, having signed away the rights for a small sum. He regarded his paintings and travel journals as more dependable means of livelihood. His reputation as a fashionable artist was undoubtedly aided by the fact that the publication of *Illustrated Excursions in Italy* (1846) led to Queen Victoria's request for Lear to give her a series of drawing lessons.

Queeriflora Babyöides

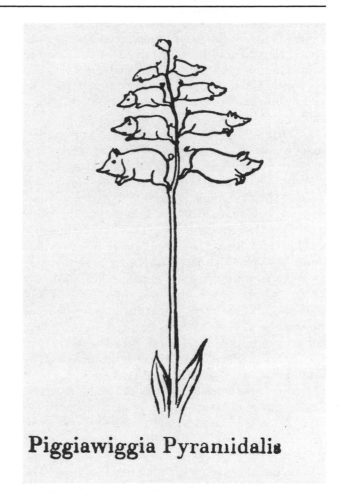

Piggiawiggia Pyramidalis

Two examples of "nonsense botany" from Lear's Nonsense Songs, Stories, Botany and Alphabets *(1870)*

Italy's political unrest touched Lear's life when he witnessed outbursts of revolution there, and in 1848 he extended the range of his travels to Greece, Albania, the Ionian Islands, Egypt, Malta, and Jerusalem. Except for the years 1849 to 1853 – when he lived in England and briefly enrolled in the Royal Academy Schools and studied under the Pre-Raphaelite painter William Holman Hunt – Lear continued to lead the itinerant life of a landscape painter and published more travel books: *Journals of a Landscape Painter in Albania, etc.* (1851), *Journals of a Landscape Painter in Southern Calabria, etc.* (1852), and *Views in the Seven Ionian Islands* (1863). Tennyson's poem "To E. L. on His Travels in Greece" praises Lear's work:

> Tomohrit, Athos, all things fair,
> With such a pencil such a pen,
> You shadow'd forth to distant men,
> I read and felt that I was there.

Lear, who could never resist a chance for humor, even at his own expense, parodied these lines:

> Tom-Moory Pathos; – all things bare –
> With such a turkey! Such a hen!
> And scrambling forms of distant men,
> O! – ain't you glad you were not there!

Lear did, however, hold Tennyson's poetry in high regard, setting twelve of his poems to music and illustrating others with appropriate landscape paintings. The poet's lines were later engraved on Lear's tombstone.

A Book of Nonsense went through several printings, and in 1861, the year Ann Lear died, an expanded edition was published. By this time Lear was quite willing to put his own name on the work. He paid for the printing expenses and subsequently sold his entire rights to it to his distributors, Routledge and Warne, for £125. The book went through nineteen editions in Lear's lifetime. Lear lived and traveled in various Mediterranean locations during the next nine years, publishing his last travel book, *Journal of a Landscape Painter in Corsica* (1870). In 1870 he also began construction on the

Villa Emily in San Remo, Italy, where, except for summers in nearby mountains, brief stays in England, and a trip to India, he lived for the next ten years. Some thought he had named the villa after Tennyson's wife, to whom Lear was a devoted friend, but he claimed it was named for his niece Emily.

Throughout his years as a wandering painter, Lear wrote and illustrated limericks and other forms of nonsense verse, usually for the children of friends or youthful acquaintances he met on his travels. His next book, *Nonsense Songs, Stories, Botany and Alphabets* (1870), collected these works. Included are "The Owl and the Pussycat" and eight other verses, which Lear designated "songs" (he provided a musical score for some). Although closer to traditional poetry for children than the limericks, the longer poems deal with more-mature topics and themes, such as courtship and the tensions between the need for domesticity and the need for unconventional rambling. Hark notes that the songs frequently take place in a fantasy land inhabited by fantasy creatures, while the limerick characters are people and the limerick settings can all be found on a map. She speculates that moving away from the everyday world in the songs seems to have been Lear's method of dealing with those aspects of his life that were painful.

With the exception of "Calico Pie," however, which can be called a lament about loneliness, the songs in the 1871 volume are among the happiest that Lear wrote. This lightheartedness does not so much reflect Lear's mental state at the time of publication as it does his happy relations with friends and acquaintances during the times when he wrote the pieces. The first three songs, "The Owl and the Pussycat," "The Duck and the Kangaroo," and "The Daddy Long-Legs and the Fly," each have improbable but satisfactory pairings, and any sorrowful tinge comes from the reader's knowledge that writing of such unions was merely wish fulfillment for Lear. In 1867 his hesitant courtship with Augusta "Gussie" Bethell, daughter of one of Lear's patrons, Richard Bethell, Lord Westbury, had ended with Lear's inability to propose to her, and, although he ostensibly wrote "The Owl and the Pussycat" for three-year-old Janet, the daughter of his friends Catherine and John Addington Symonds, biographer Chitty believes that Lear is the Owl and Gussie the Pussycat.

There are two successful escape poems, "The Nutcrackers and the Sugar-Tongs" and "The Jumblies," whose chancy voyage in a sieve ends triumphantly. Noakes says of Lear's attitude in "The Jumblies" and similar poems: "His realization of the rewards which can come from daring to take risks was something he sought to convey to children when he believed his traveling days were over and he began to write his nonsense songs." Hark describes "Mr. and Mrs. Spikky Sparrow," "The Broom, the Shovel, the Poker, and the Tongs," and "The Table and the Chair" as songs about those "who willingly live settled domestic lives and whose travels involve only afternoon excursions." Lear had an intermittent longing for a settled, domesticated lifestyle. In an 1871 letter to Chicester Fortescue and his wife, Lady Waldegrave, Lear laments approaching old age and writes, "I think of Marrying some domestic hen bird & then of building a nest in one of my olive trees, whence I should only descend at remote intervals during the rest of my life."

The most extreme nonsense language outside Lear's letters occurs in the prose pieces in the 1871 volume. There are recipes for "Nonsense Cookery," which instruct the reader how to make an "Amblongus Pie," "Crumbobblious Cutlets," and "Gosky Patties." In "The History of the Seven Families of the Lake Pipple-Popple," place-names are nonsense words: "Land of Gramblamble" and "City of Tosh." So are the names of some of the creatures who destroy the disobedient offspring of the Seven Families: "Plum-pudding Flea," "Blue Boss-Woss," and, nemesis of the cats, the "Clangle-Wangle," a speckled animal with a plumy tail, not to be confused with the Quangle Wangle, a spiky but warmhearted creature who travels with and aids "The Four Little Children Who Went Round the World." The children – Violet, Slingsby, Guy, and Lionel – were Gussie's niece and nephews, and Lear apparently wrote the story for them at about the time of his last failed attempt to propose.

This nonsense travel tale is an example of Lear's ability to parody the pompous language of second-rate authors of the era. The British middle and upper classes were great travelers in the nineteenth century, both for pleasure and on assignment to colonial outposts, and many of them felt compelled to publish their travel journals. The four children in Lear's poem respond to the fantastic landscapes and creatures they encounter with properly Victorian polysyllabic, hyperbolic, and frequently oxymoronic phrases. Among their landfalls is the country of the Blue-Bottle Flies, who live together "in the most copious and rural harmony" and in "perfect and abject happiness." Lear's descriptions are superb parodies of gushing travel books. Lear's prose nonsense, which often gets short shrift even

Drawing by Lear published on the cover of More Nonsense, Pictures, Rhymes, Botany, etc. *(1872) showing Lear identifying himself to a train passenger. The man had been telling other passengers that "Edward Lear" was merely a pseudonym used by Edward, Earl of Derby.*

in books devoted entirely to him, is rewarding to read and deserves more attention.

The 1871 volume contains the first published examples of Lear's alphabets. Although manuscript alphabets by Lear have surfaced, and there are undoubtedly more that have been lost, the nonsense books published in his lifetime contain only six ABCs. Abecedaria in the twentieth century are frequently high nonsense, but Lear's seem strangely sedate in comparison. Lear seems for once to accept the didactic element in children's literature, perhaps because the alphabet genre is the first stage of literacy for the child reader. The first of the three alphabets in *Nonsense Songs* has both the upper and the lower case of the featured letter and repetition of the sound, but only the gentlest of humor. The second alphabet does at least employ nonsense words, while the final alphabet contains only one genuinely funny example:

A was an ape,
Who stole some white tape

And tied up his toes
In four beautiful bows.

Nonsense Songs does, however, introduce the nonsense botany, a genre unto itself and apparently original to Lear. Consisting of a drawing of a nonsense plant, labeled with a pseudo-Latinate name, the botanies are fine examples of text and illustration that are simultaneously verbal and visual puns, as well as parodies of a scientific format. According to Noakes the earliest known example dates from 1860 in Lear's letter to Sir George Grove (the manuscript drawing since lost). In 1870 Lear wrote to a Mrs. Ker that he had found flowers in The Grasse Hills that "only grow about here & in the Jumbly Islands." Some drawings of nonsense specimens were submitted to Lord and Lady Fitzwilliam's children, for whom Lear wrote "The Seven Families of Lake Pipple-Popple." Some of the botanies may have been drawn for Hubert Congreve, a neighbor's son who lived briefly with Lear at the Villa Emily.

Lear's inspiration for the nonsense botanies is unknown. Noakes concludes that, "whatever the source of his drawings, in the classification of newly discovered species Lear was echoing methods with which he had been familiar during his ornithological days."

The botanies also reveal Lear's capabilities as an artist in a way that the deliberately crude but exuberant sketches for the nonsense prose and verse do not. For instance, "Piggiawiggia Pyramidalis," which seems at a superficial glance to be fragile gradated blossoms, is, on close inspection, revealed as nine prancing piglets, and "Tigerlillia Terribilis" (from the 1872 *More Nonsense, Pictures, Rhymes, Botany Etc.*) is a delicate drawing of five tigers clustered upright on a stem, which indeed looks like a partially opened tiger lily.

In Lear's third nonsense book (the second to include limericks), *More Nonsense, Pictures, Rhymes, Botany Etc.*, the limericks are as vigorous as ever, but there are some changes in the proportion of English and foreign place-names and in relations among the characters. Lear, exiled by his health from England and its damp climate, may express a longing for his native land in the increased use of English place-names. The balance of power between "They" and the protagonist, as well as between the sexes, has also changed. The various Old Men seem successfully to be avoiding the advice, taunts, and threats of "They," and the Young Ladies seem to be withdrawing from action. The Old Ladies, however, have become more aggressive. One, not pleased with her daughters, "dressed them in gray, and banged them all day." An old person of Jodd persists in perplexing the townspeople by squeaking to them on her whistle, and an "impulsive old person of Stroud" handles a pushing crowd quite effectively: "Some she slew with a kick, some she scrunched with a stick." Thomas Byrom speculates on the implications of the types of personalities and actions that are assigned by gender and age, wondering if the old ladies may "represent a malignant force." He wonders whether Lear "felt the more feminine part of him as the more potent, and a threat to his happiness and sanity." Byrom, however, sees no clear psychological portrait in Lear's verse.

The language of the limericks in both the 1846 and 1872 volumes is marked by deliberate incongruities, especially by nonsense adjectives and peculiar pairings of noun and adjective, usually in the last line. Examples from the 1846 edition are "intrinsic Old Man of Peru," "borascible person of Bangor," and "umbrageous old person of Spain." The 1872 collection includes an "eclectic old man

of Port Gregor" and an "abruptious old man of Thames Ditton." In her article "The Limericks and the Space of Metaphor" (1988), Ann Colley argues that these "metaphoric adjectives give the illusion of blending the various pieces" and that "Lear throws the weight of the limerick into that final adjective." Colley defends Lear's use of the limerick form, a use that purists consider flawed, because classic limericks build up to a punch line. Colley contends, however, that substituting a variation of the first line is Lear's method for turning the action back on itself and creating a microcosm where the eccentric protagonist can do a dance of advance or retreat. *More Nonsense, Pictures, Rhymes, Botany Etc.* also includes "Twenty-Six Nonsense Rhymes and Pictures," an alphabet with a nonsensical use of language and illustration. In it Lear emphasizes the letters only through alliteration: the "*B*ountiful *B*eetle," the "*C*omfortable *C*onfidential *C*ow," the "*D*olomphious *D*uck," the "*F*itzgiggious *F*ish," the "*M*elodious *M*eritorious *M*ouse," and so on.

The final phase of Lear's life began in the early 1870s. Giorgo Cocali, his servant since 1856, was becoming undependable. Foss, Lear's cat and the great comfort of his later years, entered the household in 1872. Lear had already published his last travel book and after 1872 he published only one more book of nonsense. He had intended to remain settled at the Villa Emily, but his friend Thomas Baring, Lord Northbrook, had been appointed governor general of India and invited Lear to visit him. After one failed attempt when various mishaps stopped him at Suez, Lear traveled in India from 1873 to 1875.

The last volume of Lear's work published during his lifetime, *Laughable Lyrics: A Fourth Book of Nonsense Poems, Songs, Botany, Music Etc.* (1877) reveals a wide array of moods. It includes what seems at first to be an ultra-Victorian alphabet, though it also displays hints of social criticism. The final entry in the 1877 volume is an unillustrated alphabet of the cumulative, House-that-Jack-Built type.

Among the nonsense tidbits Lear wrote for the children he met on his travels is an alphabet given in 1880 to Charles Pirouet, then a small boy. In a manner similar to that employed by Heinrich Hoffman in *Strewellpeter* (1847), a book of humorously didactic verses, Lear shakes his fingers jokingly at misbehaving children. However, most nineteenth-century Sunday-school tract writers and authors who wrote pious tales of warning were not joking.

Lear's joking has, however, a consistent touch of melancholy. Hark says that in several of the 1877 songs "two themes, wandering and loss, predominate." The lead poem, "The Dong with a Luminous Nose" (given only a title illustration by Lear, but effectively illustrated by Edward Gorey in 1969), is a lament for love lost, a parody of Thomas Moore's "The Lake of the Dismal Swamp" in particular and of the Romantic style in general. John Lehmann, in his study *Edward Lear and His World* (1977) asserts that the poem's "undertone of deep feeling that hints at the troubles of Lear's own emotional life" places it beyond simple parody. The Dong is also the prime example of Lear's obsession with noses and his various characters who sport a peculiar probiscus. As Joanna Richardson says in her biography of Lear, the nonsense laureate makes ample fun of his own perceived shortcomings: "He laughs at enormous beards, poor eyesight, excessively long legs, fatness, thinness. And, above all, because it is his own most obvious shortcoming, he makes fun of enormous noses."

Although there are no limericks in this collection, human characters return to the scene. Hark thinks that in his later years Lear had worked through enough of his personal problems with epilepsy, homosexual tendencies, and an isolated lifestyle to deal with such matters through the medium of human characters. He no longer needed the disguising technique of anthropomorphic animals. After the love lament of the Dong, "The Two Old Bachelors" provides an interlude of light comedy. The old men lose the food they caught (a muffin and a mouse) because they are so literally dim minded as to confuse *sage,* the herb, with *sage,* a wise man.

"The Courtship of the Yonghy-Bonghy-Bó," another narrative of failed courtship, is the most overtly autobiographical of all of Lear's verse. The Bó's proposal to the Lady Jingly Jones is rejected because, according to the Lady, "you've asked me far too late, / 'For in England I've a mate." Lear's biographers agree that the poem is in reference to his hesitant wooing of Gussie. Shortly after Lear let her sister persuade him that the match was unsuitable, Gussie married an elderly invalid, a far less suitable husband.

Of the 1877 songs "The New Vestments" (a poem in which a man clothed in food has his vestments ravaged away) most clearly contains the limericks' antagonistic violence. Two other poems, "The Cummerbund" and "The Akond of Swat," are, respectively, parodies of a nonsense ballad (the seeming nonsense words are terms used in India) and a humorous play on silly rhyming. In the sequel to "Discobbolos," Mr. Discobbolos ends the overabundant domesticity of living with twelve children by blowing up their walltop home. Hark holds that in poems such as the first "Discobbolos" and

"The Pobble Who Has No Toes" Lear developed "the theme of sage but limiting domesticity."

"The Quangle Wangle's Hat" is perhaps Lear's most optimistic poem to be published in his later years. In it the Learian menagerie gathers in a friendly community. Only one other poem (the posthumously published "The Scroobious Pip") has a comparable vision of unity. Left in an incomplete manuscript form, "The Scroobius Pip" was first published in *Teapots and Quails, and Other New Nonsenses* (1953) and later completed by Ogden Nash. If any one poem reflects Lear's mature philosophy of life, this one may. The Scroobious Pip is a pantheistic figure with fur, fins, wings, and antennae, and he refuses to answer queries from various animals about his identity. In the final verse the creatures praise his multiplicity by dancing around him, expressing an attitude similar to Lear's. His journals and letters make clear that he had little use for most organized religion. "The Scroobious Pip" seems to be Lear's "sermon" on the joyful acceptance of creation.

Looking back at Lear's work from the perspective of his last book of nonsense and the pieces published since his death, it is possible to see a connectedness in his attitudes and techniques. Throughout his life, humor was both his delight and his defense. Rather than bemoan disappointments, Lear preferred what he called the "spirit of Munchausenism," referring to Rudolph Raspe's eighteenth-century nonsense tales of Baron Münchausen. Although he believed that his landscapes were more important to his career than his nonsense pieces, Lear nevertheless took his verse more seriously than its seeming spontaneity suggests. He wrote that "bosh requires a good deal of care, for it is a sine quâ non in writing for children to keep what they have to read perfectly clear & bright, & incapable of any meaning but one of sheer nonsense."

Lear never realized the financial rewards from his immensely popular nonsense books. Robert Bush, his publisher (beginning with the 1871 volume), went bankrupt in 1880, owing Lear a backlog of royalties and having lost the printing plates. In 1880 Lear built a second home, Villa Tennyson, in San Remo after the construction of a new hotel blocked his sea view and studio light. He lived here until his death of chronic bronchitis and epilepsy on 29 January 1888.

Lear's impact on both children's literature and such adult genres as the theater of the absurd is great. His nonsense works have been continuously in print, whether with the original illustrations, in reillustrated collections, or in publications of selected or individual pieces. Besides the expected spate of scholarly articles and books in 1988, the centennial of Lear's death, literary critics continue to analyze his nonsense: Ann Colley's *Edward Lear and the Critics* (1993) is a recent collection of critical opinions. Lear's enduring fame as the laureate of nonsense has also caused art historians to reassess his landscape paintings and sketches. As Lehmann says, Lear has been "seen at last as a many-sided genius, one of the most original of the Victorian age."

Lear's chief impact on children's literature is that, along with Lewis Carroll, he broke the didactic mold into which books for juveniles were poured. But the absence of didacticism does not imply a lack of meaning. Lear's cleverness at mixing and matching diverse elements, whether of language or emotions, is endlessly intriguing. Everyone has witnessed a crying child jollied back into laughter by some silly sight or sound. This is precisely Lear's approach to discontent. In his diary he once noted, "I see life as basically tragic and futile and the only thing that matters is making little jokes." With his "little jokes" played in a completely fitted-out nonsense world, Lear has managed to jolly millions of young and old sorrowers into a smiling state.

Letters:
Letters of Edward Lear, edited by Lady Strachey (London: Unwin, 1907);
Later Letters of Edward Lear, edited by Lady Strachey (London: Unwin, 1911);
The Corfu Years: A Chronicle Presented Through Letters and Journals, edited by Philip Sherrard (Greece: Harvey, 1988);
Edward Lear: Selected Letters, edited by Vivien Noakes (Oxford: Clarendon Press, 1988).

Bibliography:
William B. Osgood Field, *Edward Lear on My Shelves* (Munich: Bremer Press, 1933).

Biographies:
Angus Davidson, *Edward Lear: Landscape Painter and Nonsense Poet* (London: John Murray, 1938);
Joanna Richardson, *Edward Lear* (London: Longmans, 1965);
Vivien Noakes, *Edward Lear: The Life of a Wanderer* (Boston: Houghton Mifflin, 1968);

Susan Chitty, *That Singular Person Called Lear: A Biography of Edward Lear, Artist, Traveller and Prince of Nonsense* (New York: Atheneum, 1989).

References:
George N. Belknap, "History of the Limerick," *Papers of the Bibliographical Society of America,* 75 (First quarter 1981): 1–32;
Anthony Burgess, "Nonsense," in *Explorations in the Field of Nonsense,* edited by Wim Tigges (Amsterdam: Rodopi, 1987), pp. 17–21;
Thomas Byrom, *Nonsense and Wonder: The Poems and Cartoons of Edward Lear* (New York: Dutton/ Brandywine, 1977);
Ann C. Colley, "Edward Lear's Limericks and the Reversals of Nonsense," *Victorian Poetry,* 26 (Autumn 1988): 285–299;
Colley, "The Limerick and the Space of Metaphor," *Genre,* 21 (Spring 1988): 65–91;
Colley, ed., *Edward Lear and the Critics* (Columbia, S.C.: Camden House, 1993);
Ina Rae Hark, *Edward Lear* (Boston: Twayne, 1982);
Philip Hofer, *Edward Lear as a Landscape Draughtman* (Cambridge, Mass.: Harvard University Press, 1967);
John Lehmann, *Edward Lear and His World* (London: Thames & Hudson, 1977);
Stephen Prickett, *Victorian Fantasy* (Bloomington: Indiana University Press, 1979);
Elizabeth Sewell, "Nonsense Verse and the Child," *Lion and the Unicorn,* 4 (Winter 1980–1981): 30–48;
Tigges, ed., *Explorations in the Field of Nonsense* (Amsterdam: Rodopi, 1987);
Mark West, "Edward Lear's *A Book of Nonsense:* A Scroobious Classic," in *Touchstones: Reflections on the Best in Children's Literature,* volume 2: *Fairy Tales, Fables, Myths, Legends, and Poetry,* edited by Perry Nodelman (West Lafayette, Ind.: Children's Literature Association, 1987), pp. 150–156.

Papers:
The largest collection of Edward Lear's manuscripts is at Harvard University.

Mark Lemon

(30 November 1809 – 23 May 1870)

Karen Patricia Smith
Queens College, City University of New York

BOOKS: *The Enchanted Doll* (London: Bradbury & Evans, 1849);

Prose and Verse (London: Bradbury & Evans, 1852);

The Heir of Applebite and Our Lodgers (London: Bradbury & Evans, 1856);

Betty Morrison's Pocket-Book (London: Bradbury & Evans, 1856);

A Christmas Hamper (London: Routledge, Warne & Routledge, 1860);

Tom Moody's Tales (London: Bradbury & Evans, 1863);

Wait for the End (London: Bradbury & Evans, 1863);

The Jest Book (London: Macmillan, 1864; London & New York: Macmillan, 1892);

The Legends of Number Nip (London: Macmillan, 1864);

Loved at Last (London: Bradbury & Evans, 1864);

Falkner Lyle (London: Hurst & Blackett, 1866);

Golden Fetters (London: Bradbury & Evans, 1867);

Up and Down the London Streets (London: Chapman & Hall, 1867; Philadelphia: Lippincott, 1867);

Leyton Hall, and Other Tales (London: Hurst & Blackett, 1867; Philadelphia: T.B. Peterson, n.d.);

Fairy Tales (London: Bradbury & Evans, 1868);

Tinykin's Transformations (London: Bradbury & Evans, 1869);

My Jest Book; The Choicest Anecdotes and Sayings (London, n.d.; New York: Dutton, 1907).

SELECTED PLAY PRODUCTIONS: *P.L.; or, 30,* London, Strand Theatre, 25 April 1836;

The Silver Thimble, London, Strand Theatre, 12 April 1841;

Punch (renamed *Star of the Street*), London, Strand Theatre, 17 September 1841;

Robinson Crusoe, London, Royal Olympic Theatre, 21 March 1842;

Open Sesame; or, A Night with the Forty Thieves, with à Beckett, London, Lyceum Theatre, 8 April 1844;

The Chimes; or, A Goblin Story of Some Bells that Rang an Old Year Out and a New Year In, with Gilbert

Mark Lemon

Abbott à Beckett, London, Royal Adelphi Theatre, 19 December 1844;

St. George and the Dragon, with à Beckett, London, Royal Adelphi Theatre, 24 March 1845;

Hearts Are Trumps, London, Strand Theatre, 30 July 1849;

Welcome Little Stranger, London, Royal Adelphi, 30 March 1857;

Petticoat Parliament; or, A Woman's Suffrage, London, Royal Olympic Theatre, 26 December 1867.

OTHER: Frederick Eltze, *New Table Book: Pictures for Young and Old Parties,* edited by Lemon (London: Bradbury, Evans, 1867).

SELECTED PERIODICAL PUBLICATIONS – UNCOLLECTED: "The Heir of Applebite" [serial], *Punch,* 1 (28 August 1841–13 November 1841);

"Spring-Time in the Court," *Household Words,* no. 9 (25 May 1850): 199;

"What Came of Killing a Rich Uncle One Christmas Time," *Punch,* 8 (December 1865): 2–11;

"The Small House Over the Water," *Punch,* 10 (December 1866): 5–16.

In the final pronouncement of his most successful fairy story for children, *Tinykin's Transformations* (1869), Mark Lemon confides to his young audience, "The fairies are said to have left us for good and aye; but there are some pretty creatures as beautiful as the fairies could possibly have been, often to be seen haunting the margin of Katrine Lake in Tilgate Forest, and playing under the green oaks of Brantridge Park." In so saying, this imaginative author, refusing to abandon the tenants of the fairy realm, fused the possibilities of fancy with the realistic British landscape, thus creating a vivid and fantastic excursion that had about it the ring of veracity. The communication of realism and imagination via the vehicles of drama, poetry, novel, fairy tale, lighthearted farce, and extravaganza were to characterize Lemon's prolific literary output.

Lemon was born on 30 November 1809 into the middle-class London home of Alice Collis and Martin Lemon. The elder Lemon was a successful hops merchant, a business at which Mark was later to try his hand, but at which he did not succeed. He attended the exclusive Cheam School in Surrey, an institution whose curriculum was centered upon the classics, related historical studies, and religious doctrine. All of these subjects were to serve as important influences in Lemon's later writings.

Lemon never lost the appreciation he had for his relatively comfortable upbringing. Through his poem "Spring-Time in the Court," published in *Household Words* in 1850, he contrasted his own upbringing with that of a poor London child:

> His toys are but an oyster-shell,
> Or pieces of broken delf;
> His playground is the gulley's side,
> With outcasts like himself!
> *I* used to play on sunny banks,
> Or else by pleasant streams;

> How oft – oh, God be thanked! how oft –
> I see them in my dreams.

Despite comfortable surroundings Lemon was not spared the pain of tragedy. His biographer, Arthur A. Adrian, relates that between the ages of eight and eleven Lemon experienced the passing of his father, grandfather, and grandmother. His environment, however, was stable enough to prevent him from becoming an embittered, sullen, or cynical adult. Contemporary accounts indicate that Mark Lemon was attractive in spirit and geniality. His charismatic personality served to make him a successful organizer. While not possessed of a profound literary imagination, he was sufficiently endowed with ability and keen wit to attract the attention and gain the appreciation of nineteenth-century audiences.

Lemon's public-school career apparently ended when he was fifteen, at which time he was apprenticed to his uncle Thomas Collis to learn the hops business. This decision was prompted more by practicality than by genuine interest and skill; clearly this type of work did not spark the young man's imagination. Later, a brief experience as a tavern keeper proved to Lemon, who had married Helen Romer in September 1839, that this should not be his permanent line of work. Despite the fact that his business was not doing well, such a decision could not have been easy for Lemon, particularly since his wife had just given birth on 20 October 1840 to his first child, Mark. By 1841 he had left the tavern-keeping business, and, with his wife's encouragement, he prepared to pursue writing as a primary career.

Lemon's first play, *P.L.; or, 30,* premiered at the Strand Theatre on 25 April 1836. Lemon started writing plays at a time when the lighthearted, farcical style that was to bring him modest success was appreciated by London audiences. Displaying a talent for creating character within a formulaic structure and a keen ear for comic dialogue, Lemon began to establish himself as a minor playwright. He was to have an impressive number of plays, melodramas, farces, and operas to his credit by 1867 – more than eighty of his productions were performed before the London public.

In 1841 Lemon entered a venture that was to change the course of his life and provide the stability he must have desired. A discussion with acquaintances Henry Mayhew, Joseph Last, and later Ebenezer Landells was to result in the creation of *Punch, or the London Charivari,* a Saturday weekly newspaper based on a French publication, *Charivari.* The endeavor excited Lemon, who had an interest

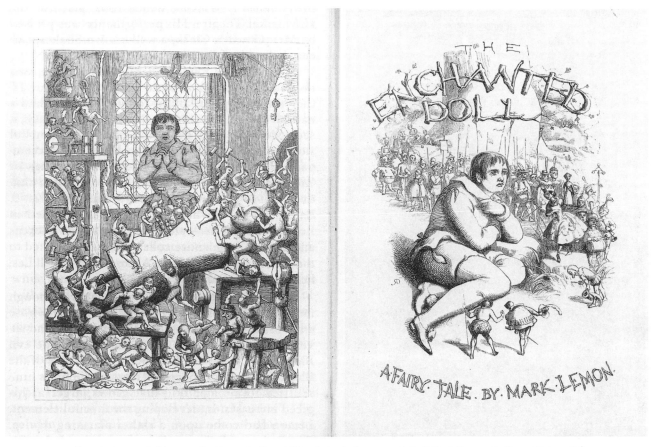

Frontispiece and title page for Lemon's first children's book (courtesy of the Lilly Library, Indiana University)

in journalism, and provided an important vehicle for his creative energies. Lemon's personal contributions took the form of serialized fiction, poetry, and essays on London politics and the social scene.

The introduction to the first issue, in 1841, promised coverage of a wide range of topics, including politics, fashions, fine arts, music, drama, and sports. In "The Moral of Punch," Lemon promised his readers that fun would be had in good taste since the magazine's pages would be "interspersed with trifles that have no other object than the moment's approbation – an end which will never be sought for at the expense of others, beyond the evanescent smile of a harmless satire." The Victorian sense of what constituted harmless satire, however, even in the light of the social context, is difficult to justify. Under this aegis appeared articles that ridiculed Jews, who were at the fringes of British society, and the American black populace. In "Nigger Peculiarities," an unsigned article appearing in the 30 October 1841 issue, Lemon ridicules the "spirit of imitation" of American blacks for the fashions and customs of white people.

Despite the questionable nature of some of his contributions to *Punch,* Lemon's personality, managerial skills, and ready wit were to build him a successful career as its editor for twenty-nine years. During that time he maintained a warm and collegial relationship with his publishers, Bradbury and Evans, who were later to publish his children's works. Some of the most revered and dynamic figures of the day were to leave their mark on the pages of *Punch,* including Charles Dickens (with whom Lemon had a close friendship until a publisher's dispute ended the relationship), John Tenniel, and William Makepeace Thackeray. It is as the editor of *Punch,* despite his voluminous production of plays, that Lemon is chiefly remembered.

The fanciful element of Lemon's work, which was to play a prominent role in the *Fairy Tales* (1868), surfaces in some of his plays and prose. On 19 December 1844 *The Chimes; or, A Goblin Story of Some Bells that Rang an Old Year Out and a New Year In,* written in collaboration with Gilbert Abbott à Beckett, was performed at the Adelphi Theatre. The production was a success, and indeed it appears to have

Lemon. While certainly not written with children in mind, the book was aimed at a young adult to adult audience. Its objective seems to have been one of pure fun; it contained blank pages, on which the reader was to indicate his or her likes and dislikes on a variety of topics, including favorite king or queen, statesman, author, artist, poet, opera, flower, or ambition. The idea was to allow the reader to be an active, rather than a passive, participant. The book includes twenty-four poems accompanied by black-and-white engravings.

In 1868 the firm of Bradbury and Evans published Lemon's *Fairy Tales*. The collection comprises "The Three Sisters," *Tinykin's Transformations* (published separately in 1869), and the previously published *Enchanted Doll*. Each of the stories, particularly *Tinykin's Transformations,* is in effect a short novel. In "The Three Sisters" Lemon pursues a theme common to his fairy tales, that of the overwhelming male figure who acts as an antagonist, precipitating the action of the story. This tale borrows motifs from the Charlemagne legends, displaying Lemon's Victorian proclivity for including references to the classics in literature for young people. After wandering several times into an enchanted forest and meeting three enchanted creatures (actually transformed princes), an old Baron offers them his daughters Wulfilda, Bertha, and Adelheid in return for his life and a chance to gain wealth. Rinaldo, a younger brother (also the name of a hero in the Charlemagne legends), searches for his sisters in the enchanted forest. After several trials he succeeds in disenchanting their three husbands and winning for himself a lovely bride.

"The Three Sisters" is a well-told story, but it lacks the power of *Tinykin's Transformations,* the third tale in the collection. Lemon's finest contribution to Victorian children's fantasy, *Tinykin's Transformations* is also his most child-centered story. Set in Tilgate Forest, an area near Lemon's Crawley residence, it tells the story of Tinykin, a six-year-old child who has the ability to perceive the presence of fairies. The story uses thematic material from Shakespeare, borrowing from *A Midsummer Night's Dream* (circa 1595–1596) and *The Tempest* (1611). Tinykin transforms into an ouzel, fish, deer, and mole, experiencing air, sea, earth, and below-earth adventures.

The story reflects Lemon's concern with social conditions. Tinykin is the son of Thomas the verderer, an arrogant and dissatisfied man who takes out his frustrations on his wife and child. There is a strong element of domestic violence in the story, as Thomas threatens or beats his wife and child on several occasions, but he is also portrayed as the victim of a fiery temper, drink, and an unreasonable employer – the king to whom he must report. Thomas is not totally despicable; the reader feels empathy for him when he softens and sheds tears at Tinykin's recoveries after his transformations, and these qualities cause Tinykin to come to his father's aid when he is unjustly imprisoned by the king. To win his release, Tinykin must locate the king's missing daughter and successfully perform three audacious trials. By the conclusion of this fanciful bildungsroman, Tinykin has changed from an innocent child into a mature young man who has successfully utilized all of his past experiences. This is Lemon's most well-developed children's story, offering moments of elegant prose and inventiveness and illustrating what the resourceful and reflective Lemon could render.

Lemon died on 23 May 1870 at Vine Cottage, Crawley, in Sussex. His contemporaries wrote of him as a dependable man of unfailing good humor. Lemon apparently did not expect greatness as a writer, but he hoped to make an acceptable contribution to the Victorian literary scene. While many argue that he will be primarily remembered as the editor of *Punch,* Lemon's prolific contributions to a variety of literary genres, signifying a fertile imagination and inventiveness, assure him a place in the history of children's literature.

Biography:

Arthur A. Adrian, *Mark Lemon: First Editor of Punch* (London: Oxford University Press, 1966).

References:

Walter Dexter, ed., *The Unpublished Letters of Charles Dickens to Mark Lemon* (London: Haltron & Smith, 1927);

M. H. Spielmann, "The Reader: Mark Lemon," *Bookman,* 37 (October 1909): 77–89.

George MacDonald

(10 December 1824 – 24 September 1905)

Roderick McGillis
University of Calgary

See also the MacDonald entry in *DLB 18: Victorian Novelists After 1885.*

BOOKS: *Within and Without: A Dramatic Poem* (London: Longman, Brown, Green & Longmans, 1855);

Poems (London: Longman, Brown, Green, Longmans & Roberts, 1857);

Phantastes: A Faerie Romance for Men and Women (London: Smith, Elder, 1858);

David Elginbrod (London: Hurst & Blackett, 1863);

Adela Cathcart (London: Hurst & Blackett, 1864);

The Portent: A Story of the Inner Vision of the Highlanders, Commonly Called the Second Sight (London: Smith, Elder, 1864);

Alec Forbes of Howglen (London: Hurst & Blackett, 1865);

Annals of a Quiet Neighborhood (London: Hurst & Blackett, 1867);

Dealings with the Fairies (London: Strahan, 1867);

The Disciple and Other Poems (London: Strahan, 1867);

Unspoken Sermons (London: Strahan, 1867);

England's Antiphon (London: Macmillan, 1868);

Guild Court (London: Hurst & Blackett, 1868);

Robert Falconer (London: Hurst & Blackett, 1868);

The Seaboard Parish (London: Tinsley Brothers, 1868);

The Miracles of Our Lord (London: Strahan, 1870);

At the Back of the North Wind (London: Strahan, 1871);

Ranald Bannerman's Boyhood (London: Strahan, 1871);

Works of Fancy and Imagination, 10 volumes (London: Strahan, 1871);

The Princess and the Goblin (London: Strahan, 1872);

The Vicar's Daughter: An Autobiographical Story (London: Tinsley, 1872);

Wilfrid Cumbermede (London: Hurst & Blackett, 1872);

Gutta Percha Willie: The Working Genius (London: Henry S. King, 1873);

George MacDonald

Malcolm (London: Henry S. King, 1875);

The Wise Woman: A Parable (London: Strahan, 1875); republished as *Princess Rosamund: A Double Story* (Boston: Lothrop, 1879); republished as *The Lost Princess: A Double Story,* illustrated by D. Watkins-Pitchford (London: Dent, 1965);

Dramatic and Miscellaneous Poems (New York: Scribners, 1876);

Exotics (London: Strahan, 1876);

St. George and St. Michael (London: Henry S. King, 1876);

Thomas Wingfold, Curate (London: Hurst & Blackett, 1876);

The Marquis of Lossie (London: Hurst & Blackett, 1877);

Paul Faber, Surgeon (London: Hurst & Blackett, 1879);

Sir Gibbie (London: Hurst & Blackett, 1879);

A Book of Strife in the Form of the Diary of an Old Soul (London: Unwin, 1880);

Mary Marston (London: Sampson Low, Marston, Searle & Rivington, 1881);

Castle Warlock: A Homely Romance (London: Sampson Low, Marston, Searle & Rivington, 1882);

The Gifts of the Child Christ, and Other Tales (London: Sampson Low, Marston, Searle & Rivington, 1882);

Orts (London: Sampson Low, Marston, Searle & Rivington, 1882); enlarged as *A Dish of Orts* (London: Sampson Low, Marston, 1893);

Weighed and Wanting (London: Sampson Low, Marston, Searle & Rivington, 1882);

Donal Grant (London: Kegan Paul, Trench, 1883);

Princess and Curdie (London: Chatto & Windus, 1883);

Unspoken Sermons: Second Series (London: Longmans, Green, 1886);

What's Mine's Mine (London: Kegan Paul, Trench, 1886);

Home Again (London: Kegan Paul, Trench, 1887);

The Elect Lady (London: Kegan Paul, Trench, 1888);

Unspoken Sermons: Third Series (London: Longmans, Green, 1889);

The Flight of the Shadow (London: Kegan Paul, Trench, Trubner, 1891);

A Rough Shaking (London: Blackie, 1891);

There and Back (London: Kegan Paul, Trench, Trubner, 1891);

The Hope of the Gospel (London: Ward, Lock, Bowden, 1892);

Heather and Snow (London: Chatto & Windus, 1893);

The Poetical Works of George MacDonald, 2 volumes (London: Chatto & Windus, 1893);

Scotch Songs & Ballads (Aberdeen: John Rae Smith, 1893);

Lilith: a Romance (London: Chatto & Windus, 1895);

The Hope of the Universe (London: Victoria Street Society for the Protection of Animals from Vivisection, 1896);

Rampolli: Growths for a Long Planted Root, Being Translations New and Old, Chiefly from the German: Along with a "Year's Diary of an Old Soul" (London: Longmans, Green, 1897);

Salted With Fire (London: Hurst & Blackett, 1897);

Far Above Rubies (New York: Dodd, Mead, 1899);

The Golden Key, illustrated by Maurice Sendak (New York: Farrar, Straus & Giroux, 1967);

The Light Princess, illustrated by Sendak (New York: Knopf, 1969);

The Day Boy and the Night Girl, illustrated by Nonny Hogrogian (New York: Knopf, 1988) — first book publication of "The History of Photogen and Nycteris: A Day and Night Marchen" (1879);

Little Daylight, adapted and illustrated by Erick Ingraham (New York: Morrow, 1988).

During the mid- to late-Victorian period, George MacDonald was a public personality and a well-known literary figure. Leading critical journals printed long articles on his work; in 1869 the *London Quarterly Review* called him "one of the most popular authors of the day." Both his fantastic and his realistic stories for children were popular and influential; undoubtedly, however, it is his fantasies that had and continue to have the greatest influence. These works represent the beginning of a continuing tradition of spiritually driven children's books that stand as one half of the Victorian legacy to twentieth-century children's books. The other half has its source in the nonsense of Lewis Carroll's Alice books. MacDonald's fantasies for children, especially *At the Back of the North Wind* (1871) and *The Princess and the Goblin* (1872), have influenced such major writers of children's books as E. Nesbit, C. S. Lewis, J. R. R. Tolkien, Maurice Sendak, and Madeleine L'Engle. As this short list indicates, MacDonald's presence is felt on both sides of the Atlantic. His books continue to appear in various forms and edited for modern readers, and at least two of his stories, *The Princess and the Goblin* and "The Light Princess," (1864) have appeared as films.

George MacDonald was born in Huntly, Aberdeenshire, on 10 December 1824. He was the second son of George and Helen MacDonald, and he was raised on a farm not far from the village. In *A Dish of Orts* (1895) MacDonald wrote that his "earliest definable memory" was the funeral of the duke of Gordon, and death was a constant presence in the author's life, as it was in the lives of most Victorians. His mother died of tuberculosis when he was eight years old, and only three years earlier a brother had been stillborn. MacDonald himself was diagnosed as tubercular in 1850, and several of his children died from the disease.

As a child, MacDonald wandered the hills about Huntly and investigated the great castle, with its black dungeon and marvelous spiral staircase rising from the ruins of a great tower. The countryside of MacDonald's youth provided material for much of his later work, and *Alec Forbes of Howglen* (1865) contains an explicit description of Huntly Castle's dungeon and stairs. This impressive ruin also appears in such works as *The Princess and the Goblin* (1872) and the poem "The Old Castle" (1893).

A serious child who, at thirteen, was president of the Huntly Juvenile Temperance Society, MacDonald early acquired the desire to preach, and he once berated the family maid for being a reprobate beyond redemption. He not only sat in judgment but he also dispensed punishment. On his return from school one day, the young MacDonald saw a boy smaller than himself mistreating a calf. He approached the boy, asked him to hold his coat, and then proceeded to thrash the offender with an umbrella. Years later, this same crusading spirit was still evident. Writing to his wife, Louisa, in 1888, MacDonald speaks of meeting a young lad who had just returned from Monte Carlo, "where he had been gambling": "I said I could not understand how a gentleman could consent to be the better for other people's losses, and that money got without value given I counted dirty."

In 1840 MacDonald entered King's College, Aberdeen, where he studied chemistry, natural philosophy, and modern literature and languages. At various times he contemplated going to Germany to further his scientific training or to study medicine, but he had to forgo such studies because of financial restrictions. The teaching standards in Aberdeen in MacDonald's time were not high, as the Reverend Robert Troup, a fellow student with MacDonald at Aberdeen and a member of the family through marriage, testifies in his book *The Missionary Kirk of Huntly* (1901).

Troup also recalls MacDonald "sitting by himself after the meal was over, silent and thoughtful, sometimes apparently musing, and sometimes reading while the others were talking." MacDonald's son Greville quotes a remark his father supposedly repeated often in his student days: "I wis we war a' dead." In his testimonial letter in aid of MacDonald's application for the chair of English literature at the University of Edinburgh in 1865, Sir William Geddes shifts perspective when he notes that MacDonald "did not much mix with students at college, and, indeed, hardly cared to descend into the ordinary arena of emulation." This loneliness and introspective attitude are indications of an inferiority complex evident in MacDonald throughout his life.

The years at King's College were crucial for the development of MacDonald's sense of mission in life, for it was then that he thought of becoming a poet. He projected a Byronic image, walking back

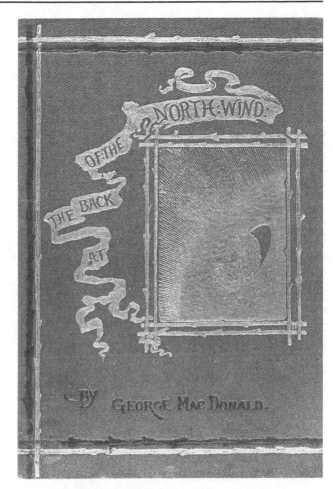

Cover for MacDonald's 1871 novel combining realism and fantasy

and forth along the shore of the North Sea "amid howling winds and the beating spray" and "addressing the sea and the waves and the storm." He also discovered the German and English Romantic writers. During the summer months of 1842 MacDonald catalogued a library in the north of Scotland. The location of the "certain castle," sometimes assumed to be Thurso Castle, is uncertain, but some have guessed that it housed the major works of German Romanticism. MacDonald may have discovered these writers at the King's College Library, however.

Several commentators have also speculated that MacDonald had an early and unhappy love affair, perhaps with his cousin Helen Mackay. Much of the poetry MacDonald wrote while at university was dedicated to her. The two formed a deep attachment, and Helen later claimed that she helped him "when he was puzzled and undecided as to what life he was fit for." With his cousin as his muse and his discovery of romantic literature – MacDon-

Diamond flying away with the North Wind; illustration by Arthur Hughes for MacDonald's At the Back of the North Wind

ald copied Samuel Taylor Coleridge's *The Rime of the Ancient Mariner* (1798) and portions of Percy Bysshe Shelley's *Wandering Jew* (1847) for her — he found the themes of spiritual unrest, search, and communion with nature that pervade his later work. The White Lady in *Phantastes: A Faerie Romance for Men and Women* (1858) might refer to Mackay, and perhaps MacDonald's first work for children, "The Light Princess," tries to put this relationship in perspective.

While at college, and indeed all his life, MacDonald was eccentric in his dress. He wore a radiant tartan coat that William Geddes, in a lecture titled "The 'Minstrel' and George MacDonald," describes as "the most dazzling affair in dress I ever saw a student wear." Although poor, MacDonald was always fastidious in his choice of clothes, and his appearance enhanced the poetic pose he maintained all his life. A gorgeous new smoking jacket, a new jewel, or a new cap were always his pride. MacDonald also took delight in fine rings. He possessed an intaglio antique of Psyche, which Ruskin gave him as an example of late Greek art; a blood-stone signet; a carbuncle; and a star sapphire. Through-

out his life he wore his hair longer than the contemporary styles dictated, and his well-known beard was initially grown at a time when beards were not approved by the majority; more than once he shaved it off to please his father or father-in-law. The beard, long hair, and splendid clothes styled MacDonald a poet, but not a poet such as James Hogg or Robert Burns. MacDonald's ambition was to leave the rural haunts of his childhood for the urban south of his jeweled island.

The way to London and literary fame, however, was not easy. After graduation in 1845 with the degree of M.A., MacDonald accepted a tutorship in Fulham, where he hoped to earn enough money to repay his Aberdeen debts. A fictional account of this period in his life is included in his novel *David Elginbrod* (1863). MacDonald, like his fictional counterpart Hugh Sutherland, not only disliked the children in his charge, but he also found the middle-class pretensions and condescensions of the parents insufferable. To make matters worse, he was beset with spiritual doubt, a record of which may be found in "Gennaro," an unpublished verse drama he wrote at this time. The work reflects the influence of the "Spasmodic School" of poetry fashionable in the 1840s and 1850s. It also introduces themes and motifs that would appear in MacDonald's published work: the Faust theme, pitting science against spiritual knowledge; the figure of the doppelgänger; and the presentation of the city as a place of alienation and despair. "Gennaro" proved therapeutic; the ending is bathetic, but it betokens the victory of its author over doubt and depression. Perhaps one factor in MacDonald's brighter emotional state was his introduction in early 1846 to the family of James Powell. Powell had six accomplished daughters, one of whom, Louise, married MacDonald five years later.

In 1848 MacDonald left his position as tutor to enter Highbury College to study for the ministry. With a pastorate MacDonald would be able to teach his message, of which he was increasingly confident. He explained to William Robertson-Nicoll of the *British Weekly* how the passion for his mission took hold of him: "Thoughts began to burn in me and words to come unbidden, till sometimes I had almost to restrain myself from rising in the pew where I was seated, ascending the pulpit stairs, and requesting the man who had nothing to say to walk down and allow me who had something to say to take his place." To complete his course at Highbury, MacDonald fought poverty, fatigue, headaches, and constant bronchitis. On completion of his studies he accepted a call to Arundel in 1850. There, according to Robertson-Nicoll, MacDonald "made his impression rather as a pastor than as a preacher. His charities were large and unsparing, and in times of sickness he was a constant and helpful visitor."

In MacDonald's view the ideal human was the simple and humble peasant, farmer, or tradesman in communion with the soul of life in every object of nature – best exemplified by Jesus – and he portrayed this ideal in the Petersons of *The Princess and the Goblin* and its sequel, the wise woman of such stories as "The Golden Key" and *The Lost Princess: A Double Story* (1965), and Diamond and his parents in *At the Back of the North Wind* (1871). Like Wordsworth, MacDonald felt he could perceive a poetic quality in the common man. How strange, then, to find him writing to his father to complain, "There are none I would call society for me [in Arundel] – but with my books now and the beautiful earth, and added to these soon, I hope, my wife – and above all that, God to care for me – in whom I and all things arc – I do not much fear the want of society." MacDonald neither felt completely comfortable in the intellectual milieu of university life nor in the rural society of Arundel. While there (1850–1853) his debts continued to mount. After his marriage on 8 March 1851, he accepted a fine house from his father-in-law, who not only furnished it but also paid the rent.

At Arundel an incident occurred that would provide a pattern for much of MacDonald's later fiction. In 1846 MacDonald had been introduced to Louisa Powell by his cousin Helen Mackay, then Mrs. Alexander Powell, and these two women served as models for MacDonald's fictional females. The relationship with his cousin remains mysterious – it is, perhaps, one of those "certain points" that several of Greville's consultants thought "too intimate for publication." That they had been intimate since MacDonald's college days is clear; it was Helen who comforted him in his loneliness and spiritual crises and who inspired him to write poetry. She was "a great beauty" and a favorite in the Powell home. After her marriage in 1844, Helen still kept a "delightful and proprietary right in her cousin George of whom she expected great things for the world's uplifting." Her own marriage was not happy.

Louisa Powell was the antithesis of her sister-in-law: quiet and plain. She could not match Helen's fascination. Before her marriage, she wrote to MacDonald about Helen: "I wish I were as *bewitching!*" The tensions Louisa felt were real.

Helen showed an "unwillingness to relinquish the influence she once had" with MacDonald. In 1850, not long before George and Louisa were married, an incident illustrating these strained relations occurred: MacDonald had given "Certain pocketbooks, full of boyhood's scribblings" to Helen, and he decided that Louisa should have them; perhaps thoughtlessly, he asked Louisa to retrieve them. Helen's reply was, "Very well, Louisa, I will make up a little packet for *him.*" Some of the poetry she burned, explaining that it "was for no eyes but her own." In later years, MacDonald would recall his cousin's "love of power."

Helen and Louisa lie behind the two women who appear time and again in MacDonald's novels: one vivacious, domineering, and strongly sexual; the other passive and maternal. The first type turns up as Agnes in the children's book *The Lost Princess,* and her most striking appearance is as Lilith in another book of the same name (1895). The second type appears as a grandmother in *Phantastes* and the Princess books, and as Eve in *Lilith.* She is the holy spirit manifested in the form of a dove; she is the "Ewig Weibliche," the creative or redemptive female principle.

In November 1850 MacDonald suffered a serious hemorrhaging from the lungs, and while convalescing at Newport, Isle of Wight, and later at Niton, he wrote his first important book, the dramatic poem *Within and Without.* Longmans published this work in May 1855. Greville notes that the "reception of the new writer was remarkable." The poem presents a concept central to MacDonald's thought. As the title suggests, the work deals with psychological and religious dualisms, focusing on the effect of external circumstances on the mental and spiritual states of the two main characters, Julian and Lilia. A tension exists for Julian between an ingoing will that seeks to find God by abandoning worldly things and an outgoing will that attempts to find God in the external world. Neither approach to God is satisfactory since each denies the other. MacDonald's is a practical mysticism that sees the supernatural in the natural, feels the will of God in the heart, and manifests itself in an acceptance of the burdens of others.

When MacDonald began *Within and Without,* he was a bachelor; when it appeared in print he had been married four years, and he had left the pastoral life in Arundel for the industrial north. During the two and a half years in Manchester, MacDonald met and became friends with A. J. Scott, then principal of Owens College, and he also came under the patronage of Lady Byron, Lord Byron's widow. She often gave him money, and she sent the family to Algiers for the winter of 1856–1857. When she died in 1860, the MacDonalds received a legacy of £300. MacDonald received money from his many friends all his life.

The most prominent among these friends were the Cowper-Temples, later Lord and Lady Mount-Temple. Mrs. Cowper-Temple was an ardent spiritualist, and, if MacDonald was not interested in spiritualism, he did take a keen interest in the supernatural. In a debate at Highbury College he introduced a discussion on ghosts, and when he lived in Hastings he attended the lectures of a Polish mesmerist, Zamoiski, the prototype for Von Funkelstein in *David Elginbrod*. MacDonald was also fascinated by the Highland belief in second sight, and he "reluctantly" admitted that he himself had no trace of this mystical power. MacDonald had a "longing after visions and revelations," and this explains his interest in fantasy and romance, his conception of life, and his literary theory. Not favored with the mystic experience, MacDonald used his imagination to project himself into visions, and he believed firmly in the existence of two corresponding and interpenetrating worlds, one natural and one supernatural. These two worlds are nowhere more evident in his work than in his children's book *At the Back of the North Wind*.

The first fruit of MacDonald's mystic imaginings is *Phantastes*, a symbolic adventure meant to suggest meaning rather than state it and by degrees to lead the reader to deep truths. Realism, however, was the fashion in mid-Victorian fiction. The *Athenaeum* reviled the author for having "lost all hold of reality"; and the *Spectator*, in a generally favorable review, is constrained to say that the work "places us in the wildest regions of fairy and fancy, and though some of the persons or incidents appear to be allegorical, yet we can rarely satisfactorily interpret them, and sometimes not at all." MacDonald's publisher, George Murray Smith, told him, "if you would but write novels, you would find all the publishers saving up to buy them of you! Nothing but fiction pays." MacDonald preferred poetry; his natural genius was for romance; but necessity forced him to write for money, and that meant novels.

Between 1858 and 1863 MacDonald did not publish a book, but he did publish stories, poems, and criticism in many of the leading journals. In 1860 he published in the first two volumes of the *Cornhill* (edited by William Makepeace Thackeray) a short story, "The Portent," which he later expanded and brought out as a short novel in 1864.

"My Uncle Peter" appeared in the *Queen* on 21 December 1861. His poems appeared in *Macmillan's Magazine, Good Words,* the *Illustrated London News,* and elsewhere. He wrote studies of William Shakespeare in 1863 and 1864, and he contributed an article on Shelley to the 1860 edition of the *Encyclopedia Britannica.* During these years MacDonald moved from Hastings to Tudor Lodge, Albert Street, Regent's Park, and he accepted a professorship at one of the first colleges for women, Bedford College, in 1859. He held the position until 1867, when he and others resigned in protest against outside examiners. In 1859 he met Charles Dodgson (Lewis Carroll) at the house of James Hunt, a philologist and speech therapist. In 1863 Dodgson asked MacDonald to read the manuscript of his story "Alice's Adventures Underground," and MacDonald encouraged him to publish it. His own stories – "Cross Purposes" (1867) and *Lilith* – draw upon this story (published as *Alice's Adventures in Wonderland,* 1865) for inspiration.

MacDonald's next book was his first novel, *David Elginbrod,* published on the recommendation of Margaret Oliphant by Hurst and Blackett in 1863. It was a success, being favorably compared by R. H. Hutton in the *Spectator* to Bulwer-Lytton's *Strange Story*. Both Hutton and the reviewer in the *Morning Post* criticized the book's deviation from realism, thus further ensuring that MacDonald would devote most of his creative energy to the writing of realistic novels. His genius for romance was driven underground to reemerge in his children's stories. Perhaps an impetus to his turning to children's stories was not only a growing family but also his collaboration with the Pre-Raphaelite painter Arthur Hughes, which began as early as 1861. An issue of the *Queen* includes two poems by MacDonald, "Born on Christmas-Eve" and "Died on Christmas Eve," which are accompanied by an Arthur Hughes illustration. Hughes remained a lifelong friend, and as late as 1905 he illustrated an edition of *Phantastes*.

The year 1863 was auspicious for MacDonald for reasons other than the appearance of his first novel. The family moved to 12 Earls Terrace, Kensington, a house later occupied by Walter Pater. MacDonald met John Ruskin, who was at this time at the height of his fame, and MacDonald had been acquainted with his work for many years. The two men became intimate friends. Ruskin helped MacDonald in many ways, criticizing his works and easing his financial burdens. Their friendship ended, however, with the death of Ruskin's beloved Rose La Touche in 1875.

During this period MacDonald experienced a burst of creative energy. In 1867, for example, he produced four books and scattered contributions to magazines. One of these books is *Dealings with the Fairies,* a collection of short fiction that MacDonald dedicated "To my children." It includes the best known of MacDonald's short fairy tales for young readers: "The Golden Key," "Cross Purposes," "The Light Princess," "The Shadows," and "The Giant's Heart."

The first two stories appear here for the first time, but the other three had been included in the 1864 version of the novel *Adela Cathcart,* and "The Giant's Heart" had originally appeared in the *Illustrated London News* in 1863. All of these stories remain in print today. MacDonald's inclusion of three of these tales in a novel ostensibly for adults confirms his statement in *A Dish of Orts* that he does "not write for children, but for the childlike, whether of five, or fifty, or seventy-five." From one perspective MacDonald is merely inscribing a double discourse in his work for children; his stories offer something for the child reader and something more for the adult reader.

This intentional appeal to a dual readership is familiar in such "classic" children's books as *Alice's Adventures in Wonderland;* it is what differentiates them from more-popular and ephemeral works. But MacDonald's stories do not contain an irony unavailable to the young reader. The delight of parody in a work such as "The Light Princess" is precisely the thrill of recognition a young reader will receive when reading it. And in most of these stories MacDonald has both a female and a male protagonist. Although he differentiates males and females on familiar Romantic lines, the stories nevertheless chronicle the journeys of both sexes, and girls take part in the adventures. At a time when publishing for the young was beginning to grow more gender-specific and when children's books generally were perceived as important to the cause of social stability, MacDonald went against the grain.

MacDonald's sophisticated breaking of barriers is most lightly evident in the pun-filled story of the light princess and most complexly evident in "The Golden Key." The former is a parody of the story of Sleeping Beauty, and it turns on a pun. Instead of cursing the princess with one hundred years of sleep, the wicked wise woman ensures that the princess will have no gravity, in both senses of the word: she will never be serious, nor will she have physical weight – she floats. MacDonald concentrates on the theme of sexual maturity, which comes only when the princess learns to feel sympathy for the young man willing to sacrifice himself for her. The story is both a searching criticism of "Sleeping Beauty" and other fairy tales that recount the growth of young girls and a satiric look at modern life, which privileges science and rationality over poetry and imagination.

"The Golden Key," in contrast, is a richly symbolic account of both the male and the female journey through life. The journey to the land from which the shadows come is mysterious and enchanting. Although Mossy and Tangle take different routes to the rainbow's end, they must finally proceed together to the land of origins. The key of the title echoes John Milton's golden key that opens the door of eternity in *Comus* (1637), and MacDonald envisages eternity as a reconciliation of antitheses: male/female, life/death, dream/reality, humanity/nature.

With the publication of *Dealings with the Fairies,* MacDonald became assured of high recognition as a writer for children. H. A. Page, writing in the *Contemporary Review* in 1869, claimed that MacDonald "more than any other in our country, has raised child-literature to the level of high art. He has a pure, graceful phantasy." Nearly twenty years later MacDonald's reputation remained strong; Edward Salmon writes in an article in *Nineteenth Century* (1887) that a "more capable pen than George MacDonald's has never created for children."

In 1869 MacDonald's alma mater, King's College, Aberdeen, conferred on him the honorary degree of LL.D. A year later he became editor of a magazine for children, *Good Words for the Young,* a post he relinquished in 1872, the year of his American tour. Ernest Rhys praises the magazine in *Wales England Wed: An Autobiography* (1934): "But what enchantment lay hidden in its pages! There were two long stories in it, one called *At the Back of the North Wind;* the other, *Ranald Bannerman's Boyhood,* had a Scottish countryside for its scene, and just that background of farm life and hill and stream that I relished."

Rhys's delight in the realistic *Ranald Bannerman's Boyhood* (1871) is apparently no longer shared by readers, but his interest in *At the Back of the North Wind* is. In print since it first appeared, the work combines a realistic depiction of childhood in both the mid-Victorian city and in its smaller towns, with the author's flare for the fantastic. Early in the book, young Diamond flies away, tucked in the hair of the North Wind, which is manifested in the shape of a grand lady. She takes Diamond to the land at her back, and this experience permeates the rest of

The goblins who threaten Princess Irene; illustration by Hughes for MacDonald's The Princess and the Goblin *(1871)*

the book, which remains firmly grounded in the realities of mid-Victorian life. Diamond is an ideal child (something akin to Charles Dickens's Little Dorrit), but despite his inveterate goodness he remains believable even in the most shocking circumstances.

The Princess and the Goblin was serialized in the magazine between November 1870 and June 1871. Its sequel, *Princess and Curdie* (1883), was serialized between January and June 1877 in another journal, titled *Good Things*. Both of these fairy tales have remained in print, and they might well lay claim to being MacDonald's most popular works, especially the former. *The Princess and the Goblin* is a fairy tale of the first order. It tells the story of Princess Irene; her adventures with a young miner boy named Curdie, who tries to defend her from goblins beneath the earth; and her relationship with her mysterious great-great-grandmother, who lives secretly in a tower of the princess's home.

The lighthearted humor of this book disappears in the sequel, however. The humor of *Princess and Curdie* is satiric and is vicious in its attack on social ills. MacDonald takes aim at politics, econom-

ics, spiritual stupidity and hypocrisy, and the greed of capitalist society. For this reason, and because of its violent content, the sequel has had fewer admirers than *The Princess and the Goblin*. It is, however, a visionary work, apocalyptic in its ending and uplifting in its powerful descriptions.

More stories for children appeared in the ten volumes of MacDonald's collected works published by Chatto and Windus in 1871, which include "The Carasoyn" and "Little Daylight." The first six sections of the first story had appeared in 1866 as "The Fairy Fleet" in the *Argosy,* and the second story forms chapter 28 of *At the Back of the North Wind.* Once again MacDonald brings together works for both young and older audiences, suggesting his resistance to categorizing his works as "for children" or "for adults."

MacDonald's work shows great sensitivity to children. The individual awakening of wonder that leads to knowledge appears in Hugh Sutherland's tutorship of Harry Arnold in *David Elginbrod,* and the childish pranks of Ranald and his friends in *Ranald Bannerman's Boyhood* are presented humanely and judiciously. The hardship many poor children experience is evident in *At the Back of the North Wind* and *Sir Gibbie* (1879). In both works MacDonald examines the dangerous world of the city streets and contrasts this with the healthful purity of the countryside and its people. MacDonald is also sensitive to a child's fears. This is perhaps best exemplified during the scene in which Irene, in *The Princess and the Goblin,* first loses herself in the upper regions of her house. The long corridors with their many closed doors and the pounding rain on the roof serve as objective correlatives for the young girl's fear. Despite this accurate portrayal of the anxiety and fear children experience, MacDonald insists on presenting the child as a romantic icon, a type of perfection. He writes about this at some length in his sermon "The Child in the Midst."

While many of MacDonald's children are idealized (Diamond; Gibbie; Irene; Curdie; Gutta Percha Willie; the prince in "The Light Princess"), it is also true that many of his characters are a mixture of good and bad (Richard and Alice in "Cross Purposes"; Tricksey Wee and Buffy Bob in "The Giant's Heart"). MacDonald also portrays children who suffer deprivation. Nanny in *At the Back of the North Wind* is a product of her hard background. Even more pronounced is MacDonald's depiction of the two girls in *The Lost Princess,* in which a wise woman takes into her strange home two naughty girls, one a princess and the other a shepherd's daughter. It is clear from this story that not all children are perfect diamonds in the rough. Agnes, the shepherd's daughter, proves impossible to teach. In this story MacDonald combines two traditions that strongly influenced children's literature in the nineteenth century: the evangelical tradition, which saw children as "brands of hell," tainted with original sin; and the Romantic tradition, which saw children as naturally pure and good, uncorrupted by social evils. When readers think of MacDonald, it is usually in terms of the latter tradition.

This idealization conflicts not only with MacDonald's fictional treatment of children, however, but also with what is known of MacDonald's treatment of his own children. In his autobiography Greville MacDonald remarks that "corporeal punishment, sometimes severe, was inevitable," and the result was that "it made an over sensitive child craving for love, so truly afraid of his father that more than once I lied to him." Greville was punished for failing to grasp intuitively the principles of Latin grammar and Euclid. Greville also remembers being "the shabbiest-drest boy in the school," while his father dressed in finery. What surfaces here is MacDonald's somewhat inconsistent pedagogical practice.

However inconsistent MacDonald may have been in his understanding and treatment of his own children, he did strike a responsive chord in his readers with his fantasies for children. All of these have remained in print, including his last one, now known as *The Day Boy and the Night Girl* (1988) but first published in the Christmas issue of the *Graphic* in 1879 as "The History of Photogen and Nycteris." In this story MacDonald's interest in the psychological (and spiritual) development of children is clearly evident. The plot concerns the witch Waltho, who abducts two children and raises the girl, Nycteris, in total darkness and the boy, Photogen, in daylight. MacDonald examines masculine and feminine principles as constructed through education rather than biology, and he shows how the two principles must be brought into harmony for a full and complete life. The story is a remarkable reflection of MacDonald's spiritual resiliency, coming as it does in the midst of a difficult two decades in his family.

After the successful American tour of 1872, MacDonald returned to Hammersmith, where the family remained until 1874. In the spring of 1875 they moved from the city to an old farmhouse near Guildford, and from there MacDonald wrote to Ruskin in May to say that "we are all but Psyches half awake, who see the universe in great measure only by reflection from the dull coffin-lid over us.

But I hope, I hope, I hope infinitely." This note of determined faith signals the beginning of a period of profound sadness for MacDonald. Earlier in the year his daughter Mary Josephine was afflicted with tuberculosis, the disease MacDonald later named "the family attendant." The family left London for Bournemouth, where they took a house they named Corage. This name and the name of the family's next and final home, Casa Coraggio, indicate the spiritual struggle and dogged faith of MacDonald's final years.

After "The History of Photogen and Nycteris," MacDonald wrote only one more children's book, the novel *A Rough Shaking* (1891). Its main character is one of MacDonald's idealized children, Clare Skymer, who finds himself in a distinctly evangelical version of the world, in which animals prove more worthy of affection than most humans. The book partakes of the spirit of the "street Arab" fictions for the young popularized by such writers as Hesba Stretton and Mrs. O. F. Walton. MacDonald had earlier written about such waifs in *At the Back of the North Wind* and *Sir Gibbie.*

In 1877 the MacDonald family moved to Italy and set up home at Palazzo Cattaneo in Nervi. There Mary Josephine died in April 1878. Her illness and death were a blow to MacDonald, and he wrote to the Cowper-Temples: "when I look forward and think how I shall look back on my own folly, I want to have some of the wisdom now." Later in the year the family moved again, this time to Porto Fino, and there MacDonald's son Maurice died in 1879. Once more the family was shaken by grief, but MacDonald tenaciously held to his faith. The next twelve years brought the deaths of MacDonald's daughter Grace (1884); his granddaughter Octavia (1891); his daughter-in-law (1890); and his most beloved child, Lilia (1891).

Despite the sorrow of these years, the family secured itself in its yearly activities, traveling through England in the summer to perform in their family productions of John Bunyan's *The Pilgrim's Progress* (1678) and other works, and settling in their grand new house in Bordighera, Italy, in the winter. Casa Coraggio was a gift from several friends, and there MacDonald spent the greater part of his final twenty-five years. The coming of the MacDonalds to Bordighera, according to Francis Brookfield, writing in the *Sunday Magazine* in 1905, "marked a real epoch" in the life of that town, and Casa Corragio became the center of social activity. In 1883 Lady Mount-Temple visited Casa Corragio, and she reported that the house was "the very heart

MacDonald and his favorite child, Lilia (photograph by Lewis Carroll)

of Bordighera, the rich core of it, always raying out to all around, and gathering them to itself."

On Sunday and Wednesday evenings the great house was open to any who wished to attend for hymn singing, a sermon, or talks on MacDonald's favorite literature. The family was also active in helping the poor. They gave a benefit concert to help with the completion of a Catholic church, and Christmas festivities for the local people were a yearly event. In Bordighera, MacDonald achieved his dream of having a home in which he could gather people together and "do his work without any reference to others" who opposed his teaching. He was, in Augustus Hare's words, "the king of the place" who "writes constantly and never leaves the house, except to see a neighbour in need of help or comfort."

MacDonald urged his son Greville to take up his medical practice in Bordighera, and he also convinced his daughter Lilia not to take up a career on the stage. Lilia was a gifted actress, but her parents would not consent to such a career. Nevertheless, she took a prominent part in family productions, playing such roles as Lady Macbeth (George played

Macbeth), Christiana (George was Greatheart), and Beauty in *The Beauty and the Beast.* Lilia broke her engagement rather than discontinue acting in public with her family. She remained faithful to them until, in 1891, while nursing a friend who had tuberculosis, she contracted the disease and died in her father's arms on 22 November.

The loss was tremendous, initiating a period of depression and spiritual unrest for MacDonald. In the year of Lilia's death MacDonald published *There and Back,* a book that indicates his mental and spiritual unrest. The young protagonist, Richard Lestrange, confronted by the suffering and cruelty of life, cannot bring himself to believe in God, and a large portion of the novel contains speculation on the nature of God and the reason for life's absurdity and apparent cruelty. To Richard, schism is everywhere, and he can find "no harmony, no right, no concord, no peace." Desperately he cries: "I have no one, no one, God, to speak to! and if thou wilt not hear, then there is nothing! Oh, be! be! God, I pray thee exist."

This, then, reflects MacDonald's state of mind while he worked on his last great book, the fantasy *Lilith.* He worked on it from 1890 until its publication in 1895, and the main character's loss of his loved one undoubtedly owes much to MacDonald's loss of his daughter. The prepublication versions of *Lilith* indicate that MacDonald connected this book with *Phantastes,* which likewise drew on his fascination with the fantastic, the mythic, and the symbolic. These two works, along with his handful of children's stories, are MacDonald's true legacy.

But MacDonald provided the last word on his literary biography when he published his final work, *Far Above Rubies* (1899), in the Christmas 1898 issue of the *Sketch.* Its relation to the author's early literary life is apparent. Through the fictional character Hector Macintosh, MacDonald assesses his youthful idealism and his tendency to ignore the practical realities of life in the ardor of his search for God. When the narrator writes that Hector "was intimate with none," although his mind "would dwell much upon love and friendship in the imaginary abstract," the reader is reminded of the lonely student at King's College. Later Hector falls in love, gets married, and writes a dramatic poem (*Within and Without*), and his second book is a volume of poems that suffers at the hands of reviewers. The story follows MacDonald's life to the early 1860s when a period of happiness, industry, and relative prosperity began.

The conclusion reveals MacDonald's desire to avoid polemic, presenting instead an uneasy tension between exhortation and symbolism. This is, perhaps, what gives his work, including his children's books, a unique voice. This originality has kept MacDonald's work alive for a small coterie of readers, while at the same time it has inhibited his work from entering the mainstream of literary studies. After *Far Above Rubies* MacDonald published nothing more. He slipped into silence for his remaining years, suffering, it appears, a stroke sometime in the late 1890s. He died on 24 September 1905, in Ashstead, Surrey; he was cremated at Woking and his ashes buried in Bordighera, Italy.

Letters:

An Expression of Character: The Letters of George MacDonald, edited by Glenn Edward Sadler (Grand Rapids, Mich.: Eerdmans, 1994).

Bibliographies:

J. M. Bulloch, "A Centennial Bibliography of George MacDonald," *Aberdeen University Library Bulletin,* 5 (February 1925): 679–747;

R. B. Shaberman, *George MacDonald's Books for Children: A Bibliography of First Editions* (London: Cityprint Business Centres, 1979).

Biographies:

Greville MacDonald, *George MacDonald and His Wife* (London: Allen & Unwin, 1924);

Kathy Triggs, *The Stars and the Stillness: A Portrait of George MacDonald* (Cambridge: Lutterworth, 1986);

Michael R. Phillips, *George MacDonald: Scotland's Beloved Storyteller* (Minneapolis: Bethany House, 1987);

William Raeper, *George MacDonald* (Tring, Hertfordshire: Lion, 1987);

Elizabeth Saintsbury, *George MacDonald: A Short Life* (Edinburgh: Canongate, 1987);

Rolland Hein, *George MacDonald: Victorian Mythmaker* (Nashville, Tenn.: Star Song, 1993).

References:

Humphrey Carpenter, "George MacDonald and the Tender Grandmother," in his *Secret Gardens: A Study of the Golden Age of Children's Literature* (London: Allen & Unwin, 1985), pp. 70–85;

Rolland Hein, *The Harmony Within* (Grand Rapids, Mich.: Eerdmans, 1982);

Greville MacDonald, *Reminiscences of a Specialist* (London: Allen & Unwin, 1932);

Ronald MacDonald, *From a Northern Window* (Edinburgh: James Nisbit, 1911);

Louis MacNeice, "The Victorians," in his *Varieties of Parable* (Cambridge: Cambridge University Press, 1965), pp. 76–101;

Colin Manlove, "Circularity in Fantasy: George MacDonald," in his *The Impulse of Fantasy Literature* (Kent, Ohio: Kent State University Press, 1983), pp. 70–92;

Manlove, "George MacDonald (1824–1905)," in his *Modern Fantasy* (Cambridge: Cambridge University Press, 1975), pp. 55–98;

Cynthia Marshall, "Allegory, Orthodoxy, Ambivalence: MacDonald's 'The Day Boy and the Night Girl,' " *Children's Literature,* 16 (1988): 57–75;

Roderick McGillis, "George MacDonald's 'Princess' Books: High Seriousness," in *Touchstones: Reflections on the Best in Children's Literature,* volume 1, edited by Perry Nodelman (West Lafayette, Ind.: Children's Literature Association, 1985), pp. 146–162;

McGillis, ed., *For the Childlike: George MacDonald's Fantasy for Children* (Metuchen, N.J.: Scarecrow Press, 1992);

Stephen Prickett, "Adults in Allegory Land: Kingsley and MacDonald," in his *Victorian Fantasy* (Bloomington: Indiana University Press, 1979), pp. 150–197;

William Raeper, *The Gold Thread: Essays on George MacDonald* (Edinburgh: Edinburgh University Press, 1990);

Richard Reis, *George MacDonald* (New York: Twayne, 1972);

David Robb, *George MacDonald* (Edinburgh: Scottish Academic Press, 1987);

Leslie Willis, "Born Again: The Metamorphosis of Irene in George MacDonald's *The Princess and the Goblin,*" *Scottish Literary Journal,* 12 (May 1985): 24–39;

Robert Lee Wolff, *The Golden Key: A Study of the Fiction of George MacDonald* (New Haven: Yale University Press, 1961);

Jack Zipes, "Inverting and Subverting the World with Hope: The Fairy Tales of George MacDonald, Oscar Wilde and L. Frank Baum," in his *Fairy Tales and the Art of Subversion* (New York: Wildman, 1983), pp. 97–111.

Frederick Marryat

(10 July 1792 – 9 August 1848)

Nigel Spence
University of New England

See also the Marryat entry in *DLB 21: Victorian Novelists Before 1885.*

BOOKS: *A Code of Signals for the Use of Vessels Employed in the Merchant Service* (London: J. M. Richardson, 1817);

Suggestion for the Abolition of the Present System of Impressment in the Naval Service (London: J. M. Richardson, 1822);

The Naval Officer; or, Scenes and Adventures in the Life of Frank Mildmay (3 volumes, London: Henry Colburn, 1829; 2 volumes, Philadelphia: E. L. Carey & A. Hart, 1833);

The King's Own (3 volumes, London: Henry Colburn & Richard Bentley, 1830; 2 volumes, Philadelphia: E. L. Carey & A. Hart, 1834);

Newton Forster; or, The Merchant Service (3 volumes, London: James Cochrane, 1832; 1 volume, New York: Wallis & Newell, 1836);

Peter Simple, 3 volumes (Philadelphia: E. L. Carey & A. Hart, 1833–1834; London: Saunders & Otley, 1834);

Jacob Faithful, 3 volumes (Philadelphia: E. L. Carey & A. Hart, 1834; London: Saunders & Otley, 1834);

The Pacha of Many Tales (2 volumes, Philadelphia: E. L. Carey & A. Hart, 1834; 3 volumes, London: Saunders & Otley, 1835);

Japhet in Search of a Father (4 volumes, New York: Wallis & Newell, 1835–1836; 3 volumes, London: Saunders & Otley, 1836);

The Pirate, and The Three Cutters (London: Longman, Rees, Orme, Brown, Green & Longmans, 1836); revised as *Stories of the Sea* (New York: Harper, 1836);

The Diary of a Blasé (Philadelphia: E. L. Carey & A. Hart, 1836);

Mr. Midshipman Easy (3 volumes, London: Saunders & Otley, 1836; 2 volumes, Boston: Marsh, 1836);

Frederick Marryat

Snarleyyow, or, the Dog Fiend (3 volumes, London: Henry Colburn, 1837; 1 volume, New York: Colyer, 1837);

The Phantom Ship (3 volumes, London: Henry Colburn, 1839; 1 volume, Boston: Weeks, Jordan, 1839);

A Diary in America, with Remarks on Its Institutions, 6 volumes (London: Longman, Orme, Brown, Green & Longmans, 1839; New York: Appleton, 1839);

Poor Jack (London: Longman, Orme, Brown, Green & Longmans, 1840; New York: Nafis, 1840);

Olla Podrida (3 volumes, London: Longman, Orme, Brown, Green & Longmans, 1840; 1 volume, New York: Routledge, 1874);

Joseph Rushbrook; or, The Poacher, 3 volumes (London: Longman, Orme, Brown & Green, 1841; Philadelphia: E. L. Carey & A. Hart, 1841);

Masterman Ready, or, The Wreck of the Pacific, Written for Young People (3 volumes, London: Longman, Orme, Brown, Green & Longmans, 1841–1842; 2 volumes, New York: Appleton, 1841–1842);

Percival Keene (3 volumes, London: Henry Colburn, 1842; 1 volume, New York: Wilson, 1842);

Narrative of the Travels and Adventures of Monsieur Violet, in California, Sonora, and Western Texas (3 volumes, London: Longman, Brown, Green & Longmans, 1843; 1 volume, New York: Harper, 1843);

The Settlers in Canada, Written for Young People, 2 volumes (London: Longman, Brown, Green & Longmans, 1844; New York: Appleton, 1845);

The Mission; or, Scenes in Africa, Written for Young People, 2 volumes (London: Longman, Brown, Green & Longmans, 1845; New York: Appleton, 1845);

The Privateer's-Man, One Hundred Years Ago (2 volumes, London: Longman, Brown, Green & Longmans, 1846; 1 volume, Boston: Roberts, 1866);

The Children of the New Forest (2 volumes, London: H. Hurst, 1847; 1 volume, New York: Harper, 1848);

The Little Savage (2 volumes, London: H. Hurst, 1848–1849; 1 volume, New York: Harper, 1849);

Valerie: An Autobiography (2 volumes, London: Henry Colburn, 1849; 1 volume, New York: Beadle & Adams, 1881).

Frederick Marryat was almost fifty and had long completed the work for which he must have imagined he would be remembered when he wrote his first book for children, *Masterman Ready* (1841–1842). Following a distinguished career of more than twenty years in the Royal Navy, Marryat had been editor and proprietor of a successful magazine and produced many well-received novels for adults. He called his children's books "my little income," regarding them as the product of his failing creative powers; they comprise half of his last ten novels. Nonetheless, the warmth of the immediate critical reception of *Masterman Ready* led Marryat to return to writing for children with *The Settlers in Canada* (1844) and *The Mission; or, Scenes in Africa* (1845) – both, like *Masterman Ready,* subtitled "Written for Young People." Marryat's other "young people's" books were *The Children of the New Forest* (1847) and *The Little Savage* (1848–1849), finished after the author's death, probably by his son Frank.

Marryat both derived from and contributed to the style of works associated with Tobias Smollett, Daniel Defoe, and Henry Fielding; in some matters of characterization he bears comparison with William Makepeace Thackeray and Charles Dickens; and certainly he anticipates Victorian writers of adventures for young people such as Robert Louis Stevenson, G. A. Henty, and R. M. Ballantyne. Marryat was a man of his age, however, and he seemed happiest "in the thick of the action," when rapid description and forceful writing were required. Marryat's story lines, whether serial adventures, picaresques, or robinsonnades – with the occasional industrial city or forest wilderness serving as an alternative to a desert island – rely on repetitive, stock characterizations and contrived, thinly constructed plots, while his sentimentality, predictability, and bursts of sententious didacticism do not always endear him to the modern reader. Marryat's flaws are often the result of haste, oversight, or lack of restraint, and his bluff, exciting, good-tempered narratives continue to justify Joseph Conrad's observation in *Notes on Life and Letters* (1921) that Marryat is "the enslaver of youth, not by the literary artifices of presentation, but by the natural glamour of his own temperament."

Marryat was born in London on 10 July 1792. His mother, Charlotte, was the daughter of a loyalist American, Frederick Geyer of Boston. His father, Joseph, was a merchant banker who served as chairman of the committee of Lloyd's, as colonial agent for Trinidad and Grenada, and as the member of Parliament for Horsham and later Sandwich. The couple had fifteen children, of whom ten survived to maturity.

Perhaps resentful of his elder brother, Joseph, and under the spell of Admiral Nelson and the pomp of his funeral after Trafalgar, Marryat is reported to have tried three times to run away to sea from Mr. Freeman's school at Ponder's End. Finally, in September 1806 his father found a place for the boisterous fourteen-year-old on the Royal Navy's thirty-eight-gun frigate *Impérieuse,* under Captain Lord Cochrane, later the tenth earl of Dundonald. On the *Impérieuse* for three years, Marryat was in more than fifty engagements and was wounded several times. The future novelist kept a journal, carefully recording life with Cochrane, his shipmates, and the routines, raids, and actions of the war against Napoleon. Marryat's youth passed on patrol and in action in the Mediterranean and off the North American coast. He attained the ranks of lieutenant in December 1812 and commander on 13 June 1815.

Marryat's first publication was *A Code of Signals for the Use of Vessels Employed in the Merchant Service* (1817), which, after its adoption by Lloyd's, came into general use and was not officially superseded until 1857. The French conferred the Legion of Honor on the author on 19 June 1833 for this work. Marryat was made a fellow of the Royal Society in 1817, apparently for his skills as a caricature artist, and in 1818 he was awarded a gold medal by the Royal Humane Society for saving lives at sea: on nearly a dozen occasions in his life Marryat entered the water – more than once from the deck of a ship at sea – to save a drowning person.

In January 1819 Marryat married Catherine Shairp, second daughter of Sir Stephen Shairp of Houston, Linlithgow, once chargé d'affaires in Saint Petersburg. The Marryats had four sons and seven daughters, but the marriage deteriorated by 1836 or 1837, and they separated in 1839; the novelist paid his wife £500 annually thereafter. Of their children, three of the sons died before their father; three of their daughters – Charlotte, Augusta, and Florence – would become novelists; Florence also wrote a biography of her father.

In June 1820 Marryat was ordered to Saint Helena, where the following year he sketched the face of the former emperor Napoleon before his postmortem. Marryat obtained some recognition as an artist in his own day, but his satiric cartoons ensured that it was not always complimentary. Marryat's *Suggestion for the Abolition of the Present System of Impressment in the Naval Service* (1822) also engendered well-placed opposition. Although the future William IV enjoyed Marryat's novels, there is evidence that he disagreed with the opinions in this work, which may have cost the captain a knighthood.

Marryat's next command would be the apogee of his naval career. In Burma his virtual invention of "gunboat diplomacy" by sending the steam warship *Diana* up coastal rivers, as well as the efficiency and élan that characterized his work, caused him to be nominated C.B. (Companion, Order of the Bath) on 26 December 1826.

Marryat was now a post-captain. Only seniority could advance him further. While on the *Ariadne* in the Atlantic during 1828, Marryat produced the manuscript of *The Naval Officer; or, Scenes and Adventures in the Life of Frank Mildmay* (1829), for which he received £400. This novel has many elements that are typical of the author's later works: it is a nautical picaresque, featuring a not-always-likable protagonist, a breezy narratorial tone, a surprising canine, and a great deal of action. Years after he had left the sea, Marryat retained the ability to evoke vividly the sights, scents, and sounds of a maritime environment. Most of his works, beginning with *The Naval Officer,* feature fond, powerful, and accurate re-creations of life at sea. Marryat was intimate with the "Great Age of Sail" in its final era, and he knew firsthand what his successors and imitators could only imagine. His service career not only left its mark on his fiction, but the veracity of his depiction of the mariner's world gave his works a life that has enabled them to endure.

Marryat's reputation was enhanced by his second published novel, *The King's Own* (1830), permitting him to explore the economic and social potential of a life ashore. For a time he found a patron in the duke of Sussex, and he acquired Sussex House in Hammersmith – which he later exchanged, over a bottle of champagne, for a seven-hundred-acre farm at Langham, on the Norfolk coast. In October 1830, at the age of thirty-eight, Marryat resigned from the navy.

The name Cochrane featured at the start of Marryat's second career, as it had his first, in the person of James Cochrane, publisher of Marryat's next novel, *Newton Forster; or, The Merchant Service* (1832). The novel is distinguished by a character called Hornblow, which may have inspired the name of C. S. Forester's Horatio Hornblower. James Cochrane also started the *Metropolitan* magazine in May 1831, with Marryat among the major investors. The captain succeeded the poet Thomas Campbell as its editor in 1832. Marryat cannily profited from a system that allowed him to publish his fiction in his own magazine and then lease it to publishers for volume publication; for four years almost every issue carried an installment of a Marryat novel. The captain pioneered the exploitation of the serial form, with novels punctuated by neatly judged points of anticipation, serendipitously climaxing at the end of an issue. His success is demonstrated by an incident during the serialization of Marryat's novel *Japhet in Search of a Father* (1835–1836): crossing in the mid Atlantic, an American ship signaled a British merchantman, not for aid but to ask: "Has Japhet found his father yet?"

As an advocate of the reform of Parliament as well as of the navy Marryat unsuccessfully spent

Frontispiece for The Pacha of Many Tales *(1834), one of*
Marryat's adventure novels

£7,000 in 1833 to stand for the seat of Tower Hamlets. This outlay, coupled with the expenses incurred in a lifestyle devoted to drinking, gaming, and the social round, marks the beginning of financial troubles that subsequently plagued the author.

The commencement of the publication of *Peter Simple* (1833–1834) brought Marryat increased recognition and a diverse readership. As biographer Oliver Warner noted in a 1953 article in the *Junior Bookshelf,* the book "has always been read by older children, and it used to be said to have been responsible for many entries into the navy." Marryat's next work was *Jacob Faithful* (1834), which features the same blend of melodrama and exaggeration of scene and character as *Peter Simple,* in the setting of the watermen who ply their trade on the Thames.

Marryat was committed to a literary life. He found considerable demand for the simple, action-filled yarns in which he specialized, and at his peak he could command in excess of £1,000 per novel. He sought inspiration traveling on the Continent, and at home he divided his residence between Brighton and London. He wrote prolifically, the stress of long hours causing blood vessels in his eyes to break. Marryat's handwriting was exceptionally small and became more so as years passed. At the end of his career there was reportedly only one compositor who could read his handwriting.

The glimpses posterity admits of Marryat show that, although to friends and family he was generous and good-natured, he had inherited some of the temperament of his grandfather – who had been nicknamed "Sal Volatile" – arguing, fighting in the street, and proposing to duel with other writers. His association with Madame D'Orsay's salon and his friendship with a Mrs. Stewart of Liverpool earned his wife's disapproval, and this conflict exacerbated the tension between Frederick and Catherine, two strong individuals of vastly different temperaments.

Establishing an avuncular style blending rollicking action, broad comedy, and continental and exotic locations, during the next two years Marryat wrote *The Pacha of Many Tales* (1834), *Japhet in Search of a Father, The Diary of a Blasé* (1836), and two tales published together, *The Pirate, and The Three Cutters* (1836), which in its American edition was entitled *Stories of the Sea* (1836). Also in 1836 appeared *Mr. Midshipman Easy,* for which Saunders and Otley paid Marryat £1,200. This novel is a well-paced comedy, which time has aptly placed with the books Marryat wrote for younger audiences. *Mr. Midshipman Easy* includes Marryat's most often recounted scene. In it a Dr. Middleton brings a wet nurse to take care of the newly born Jack. The woman has conceived out of wedlock, but the protestations of the punctilious

Ready and William; illustration by Fred Pegram for Marryat's
Masterman Ready *(1841–1842)*

Mrs. Easy are met by a cheeky curtsy and the excuse that the baby "was a very little one . . . and it died soon after it was born." Satisfied by the apparent sense of propriety demonstrated by the offending infant, all proceeds smoothly. Jack Easy finds adventure and romance, playing pranks from one end of the Mediterranean to the other. His eccentric parents, a "triangular duel," and fights and frolics on sea and land are among this novel's attractions.

Some of *Mr. Midshipman Easy* had been written while Marryat traveled in Europe. In 1835, with financial trouble imminent, he moved to Brussels. He continued to edit the *Metropolitan* from the Belgian capital, castigating his subeditor, a former naval officer and childhood friend, Edward Howard, with unrelenting vigor. The state of affairs not proving satisfactory, Marryat sold his interest in the maga-

zine to the publishers Saunders and Otley for £1,050 in 1836.

Marryat appears often to have been difficult. He frequently and volubly quarreled with those who purchased and presented his works. In 1836 he wrote to W. J. Otley in typical fashion: "I am Sinbad the Sailor and you are the Old Man of the Mountain clinging on my back, and you must not be surprised at my wishing to throw you off at the first convenient opportunity. . . . We all have our own ideas of Paradise, and, if other authors think like me, the more pleasurable portion of anticipated bliss is that there will be no publishers there." Marryat changed publishers for his next work, *Snarleyyow, or, the Dog Fiend* (1837), and although his succeeding novels were, in the main, either under the imprint of Henry Colburn or Longman and Company, it is tempting to wonder if Marryat's considerable commercial appeal was tempered for publishers by the problems of dealing with the querulous captain. The novel in question was written for adults, but its often-gruesome humor might yet find it a contemporary, younger audience.

In 1837 and 1838 Marryat was in America and Canada, where he toured and lectured. Although lionized at first by the American press, Marryat made several injudicious remarks, involved himself in Canadian and American politics, and caused an uproar that would have been even greater had the contents of Marryat's diary, which was published in 1839, been known. Edgar Allan Poe, in an essay in the *Southern Literary Messenger* in 1841, called the diary "the most extraordinary libel, which the press of England, fertile in such productions, has yet given the world." Marryat's unkind views of America were attacked on both sides of the Atlantic and defended by few. Today the work is all but forgotten.

Marryat lived mainly in London from 1839 until 1843, during which time he published several books: *The Phantom Ship* (1839), which he wrote in America; a collection of stories, including "Diary of a Blasé" (retitled "Diary on the Continent" in *Olla Podrida,* 1840); *Poor Jack* (1840); *Masterman Ready*; *Joseph Rushbrook* (1841); *Percival Keene* (1842); and *Narrative of the Travels and Adventures of Monsieur Violet* (1843). None of these works is among the author's best. The extravagant retired mariner is said to have gone through at least two "fortunes," and he had become dependent on the income generated by his pen to maintain his lifestyle.

In these literary outpourings Marryat's productivity often outstripped his inspiration. Those looking for the narrative and thematic art displayed by more-eminent Victorian novelists will be disappointed. Landscape and character alike are achieved with hurried strokes, and the narrative is fueled by familiar and formulaic conventions. Marryat's characters tame the world's trials with consistency, application, and a reliance on a benevolent fate that rarely fails them. Marryat's essentially "noble" if not always ethical hero might be an heir robbed of place by injustice or misfortune, or a youth determined to rise and be worthy of success. Rank and title, money and influence are attained through a combination of hard work, luck, sheer British pluck, and a cheerful smile. Marryat's novels are a mixture of historical drama, battles on land and sea, disguise, intrigue and violence, economics, patronage, and romance and marriage. If, as the author grew older, his choler and taste for the opinionated digression become more noticeable, he generally kept these excesses at bay in his children's books, ultimately contributing both to their persistent popularity and to the renown of their creator.

After *Olla Podrida* came the author's first real children's novel, *Masterman Ready*. Its prose is rough and sometimes hasty, but in this tale of castaways moments of peril and conflict pepper the narrative, and didacticism is sweetened by humor. Marryat adopts a brisk, genial tone to tell the tale of the Seagrave family, passengers on the *Pacific*, which runs aground after a storm on the way to Australia, depositing the survivors on a desert island. The aptly named Mr. Seagrave and his wife are the parents of William, twelve; Tommy, six; Caroline, seven; and Albert, who is not yet one. Providence allows the group the use of much material from the ship; the guidance of Ready, a pious but able old salt; the help of Juno, the children's black nurse, whose competence balances Mrs. Seagrave's frequent indispositions; and the companionship of faithful canines. Ready teaches the family to build shelter, make fire, fish, catch turtles, and blaze trails. Late in the book the stockade the group constructs is attacked by natives. Like every thoughtless scapegrace in Marryat's works, Tommy allows their water supply to run out; Ready is mortally wounded replenishing it and dies at prayer, imploring Mr. Seagrave to keep the consequences of the boy's foolishness from him. Captain Osborn of the *Pacific*, who presumed the family lost with his ship, arrives in time to recoup his abrogation of duty, and the castaways are rescued. *Masterman Ready* enjoyed a resurgence in popularity in the late-Victorian era with what A. A. Milne would remember as "combined desert island adventure with a high moral tone; jam and powder in the usual proportions."

In 1843 Marryat retired to Langham Manor. The land was unprofitable, and Marryat incorrectly imagined that he had the solution. The retired seafarer's failures were paralleled in his work; inspiration for adult themes seemed also to be waning. On the advice of the author William Harrison Ainsworth, Marryat was reduced to dredging up details from his own memories and reworking the logbooks of one Captain Elsdale to produce *The Privateer's-Man, One Hundred Years Ago* (1846), a poorly constructed piece, written without the author's habitual zest and amused tone. *Valerie: An Autobiography* (1849), Marryat's final book, experiments with a female narrator and was finished by another writer, probably Frank Marryat. In the meantime, Marryat had written four more children's books, in three of which Marryat's literary ebullience is at its height.

In *The Settlers in Canada* the vast Canadian forests are the setting for the adventures of a displaced English family. The Campbells have four sons: Henry, an Oxford man; Alfred, a young naval officer on leave; Percival, a thoughtful twelve-year-old; and John, ten, who resembles mischievous Tommy Seagrave of *Masterman Ready*. The Campbells have two female wards, Mary and Emma Percival; the latter is destined to marry Alfred. The drabness of the characterization of these individuals contrasts with Marryat's vivid portrayal of the wise and patient frontiersman Malachi Bone, a grizzled hunter who teaches the family all they need to survive. There are convincing descriptions of the Canadian wilds, of hunting and fishing, and of long winter nights in the family cabin. Specific incidents focus on an attack by a wolf, a forest fire, marauding bears, capture by Indians, battles with a villain named Angry Snake, and John's rescue from a freezing stream. Eventually the Campbells return to England, only to find themselves, like many castaways before them, yearning for the freedom of their exile.

Part of a remark by one of the Indian characters has become proverbial: "I think it much better as we all go along together, that every man paddle his own canoe." Marryat was quite a coiner of phrases, and his books popularized several: for instance, "There's no getting blood out of a turnip" from *Japhet in Search of a Father;* "As savage as a bear with a sore head" from *The King's Own;* and "I never knows the children. It's just six of one and half-a-dozen of the other" from *The Pirate.*

The Mission; or, Scenes in Africa is the one failure of Marryat's children's novels. The mission of the title is to find a woman lost in the shipwreck of the *Grosvenor* near Port Natal in 1782. The adventures of Alexander Wilmot and his friend, the naturalist

Emma Marshall

(29 September 1828 – 4 May 1899)

A. Waller Hastings
Northern State University

BOOKS: *The Happy Days at Fernbank, A Story for Little Girls* (London: Hogg, 1861);

Johnny Weston; or, Christmas Eve at the White House (London: Society for Promoting Christian Knowledge, 1862);

The Second Mother: Her Trials and Joys, by Marshall and Hannah Geldart (London: Seeley, Jackson & Halliday, 1862);

Rose Bryant: Passages in Her Maiden and Married Life (London: Jarrold, 1862);

Lessons of Love; or, Aunt Bertha's Visit to the Elms (London: Seeley, Jackson & Halliday, 1863);

Heart Service; or, The Organist's Children (London: Society for Promoting Christian Knowledge, 1863);

Mark Churchill; or, The Boy in Earnest (London: Society for Promoting Christian Knowledge, 1863);

Rainy Days and How to Meet Them (London: Partridge, 1863);

Consideration; or, How Can We Help One Another? (London: Jarrold, 1864);

Brothers and Sisters; or, True of Heart (London: Seeley, Jackson & Halliday, 1864);

Helen's Diary; or, Thirty Years Ago (London: Seeley, Jackson & Halliday, 1864);

Katie's Work (London: Jarrold, 1864);

The Mischief-maker and the Peace-maker (London: Jarrold, 1864);

Poppy's Easter Holidays, A Story for Children (London: Society for Promoting Christian Knowledge, 1864);

Brook Silverstone and The Lost Lilies (London: Seeley, Jackson & Halliday, 1865);

Ida, or Living for Others (London: Society for Promoting Christian Knowledge, 1865);

Roger's Apprenticeship; or, Five Years of a Boy's Life (London: Jarrold, 1865);

Millicent Legh: A Tale (London: Seeley, Jackson & Halliday, 1866);

The Crofton Cousins (London: Warne, 1866);

The Dawn of Life; or, Little Mildred's Story, Written by Herself (London: Jarrold, 1867);

Grannie's Wardrobe; or, The Lost Key (London: Society for Promoting Christian Knowledge, 1867);

The Old Gateway; or, The Story of Agatha (London: Seeley, Jackson & Halliday, 1867);

Theodora's Childhood; or, The Old House at Wynbourn (London: Warne, 1867);

Violet Douglas; or, The Problems of Life (London: Seeley, Jackson & Halliday, 1868);

Daisy Bright (London: Nisbet, 1868);

The Little Peat-Cutters; or, The Song of Love (London: Nisbet, 1868);

Grace Buxton; or, The Light of Home (London: Nisbet, 1869);

Little May's Legacy and The Story of a Basket (London: Seeley, Jackson & Halliday, 1869);

The Story of the Two Margarets (London: Jarrold, 1869);

Christabel Kingscote; or, The Patience of Hope (London: Seeley, Jackson & Halliday, 1870);

Edward's Wife: A Tale (London: Seeley, Jackson & Halliday, 1870);

Primrose; or, The Bells of Old Effingham (London: Nisbet, 1870);

Three Little Sisters (London: Nisbet, 1871);

Heights and Valleys: A Tale (London: Seeley, Jackson & Halliday, 1871);

Shellafont Abbey; or, "Nothing New" (London: Nisbet, 1871);

To-day and Yesterday; or, A Story of Summer and Winter Holidays (London: Nisbet, 1871);

Matthew Frost, Carrier; or, Little Snowdrop's Mission (London: Nisbet, 1872);

Between the Cliffs; or, Hal Forrester's Anchor (London: Nisbet, 1873);

Mrs. Mainwaring's Journal (London: Seeley, Jackson & Halliday, 1874);

A Lily Among Thorns (London: Seeley, Jackson & Halliday, 1874);

Now-a-days; or, King's Daughters (London: Seeley, Jackson & Halliday, 1874);

Three Little Brothers (London: Nisbet, 1875);

Life's Aftermath: A Story of Quiet People (London: Seeley, Jackson & Halliday, 1876);

Joanna's Inheritance: A Story of Young Lives (London: Seeley, Jackson & Halliday, 1877);

Mrs. Haycock's Chronicles: A Story of Life-Service (London: Hand & Heart, 1877);

Lady Alice; or, Two Sides of a Picture (London: Seeley, Jackson & Halliday, 1878);

Jon Singleton's Heir and Other Stories (London: Seeley, Jackson & Halliday, 1878);

Marjory; or, The Gift of Peace (London: Nisbet, 1878);

True and Strong; or, Mark Haywood's Work, with Other Home Tales (London: Hand & Heart, 1878);

A Knight of Our Own Day and Other Verses (Gloucester: Davies, 1879);

The Rochemonts: A Story of Three Homes (London: Seeley, Jackson & Halliday, 1879);

Stories of the Cathedral Cities of England (London: Nisbet, 1879); republished as *The Cathedral Cities of England* (London: Nisbet, n.d.);

A Chip of the Old Block, Being the Story of Lionel King, of Kingsholme Court (London: Nisbet, 1879);

Framilode Hall; or, Before Honour is Humility (London: Nisbet, 1879);

The Royal Law; or, The Words of the King: With Other Sunday Tales Illustrating Bible Truth (London: Hand & Heart, 1879);

Ruby and Pearl; or, The Children of Castle Aylmer: A Story for Little Girls (London: Nisbet, 1879);

Memories of Troublous Times, Being the History of Dame Alicia Chamberlayne of Ravensholme, Gloucestershire (London: Seeley, Jackson & Halliday, 1880);

The Birth of the Century; or, Eighty Years Ago (London: Nisbet, 1880);

Heather and Harebell: A Story for Children (London: Nisbet, 1880);

Light on the Lily; or, A Flower's Message (London: Nisbet, 1880);

A Rose without Thorns (London: Nisbet, 1880);

A Violet in the Shade (London: Nisbet, 1880);

Dorothy's Daughters (London: Seeley, Jackson & Halliday, 1881);

Dewdrops and Diamonds (London: Nisbet, 1881);

Benvenuta; or, Rainbow Colours (London: Seeley, Jackson & Halliday, 1882);

Rex and Regina; or, The Song of the River (London: Nisbet, 1882);

Dayspring: A Story of the Time of William Tyndale, Reformer, Scholar, and Martyr (London: Home Words Office, 1882);

Constantia Carew: An Autobiography (London: Seeley, Jackson & Halliday, 1883);

The Court and the Cottage: A Story for Girls (London: Griffith & Farran, 1883);

Poppies and Pansies: A Story for Children (London: Nisbet, 1883);

Little and Good; or, Manners Make the Man (London: Willoughby, 1883);

In Colston's Days: A Story of Old Bristol (London: Seeley, 1883);

Sir Valentine's Victory and Other Stories (London: Nisbet, 1883);

Mrs. Willoughby's Octave (London: Seeley, 1884);

Heathercliffe; or, It's No Concern of Mine (London: Nisbet, 1884);

Silver Chimes; or, Olive: A Story for Children (London: Nisbet, 1884);

My Grandmother's Pictures (London: Nisbet, 1884);

In the East Country with Sir Thomas Browne, Knight, Physician and Philosopher of the City of Norwich (London: Seeley, 1884);

Over the Down; or, a Chapter of Accidents (Walton-on-Thames: Nelson, 1884);

The Story of the Lost Emerald; or, Overcome Evil with Good (Walton-on-Thames: Nelson, 1885);

The Mistress of Tayne Court (London: Seeley, 1885);

Cassandra's Casket (London: Nisbet, 1885);

Michael's Treasures; or, Choice Silver (London: Nisbet, 1885);

No. XIII; or, The Story of the Lost Vestal (London: Cassell, 1885);

Salome; or, "Let Patience Have Her Perfect Work" (Walton-on-Thames: Nelson, 1885);

Under the Mendips: A Tale of the Times of More (London: Seeley, 1885);

The Tower on the Cliff: A Story Founded on a Gloucestershire Legend (London: Seeley, 1886);

Thoughts on Women's Suffrage (Bristol: Arrowsmith, 1886);

A Flight with the Swallows; or, Little Dorothy's Dream (London: Partridge, 1886);

Rhoda's Reward; or, "If Wishes Were Horses" (London: Cassell, 1886);

The Roses of Ringwood: A Story for Children (London: Nisbet, 1886);

The Life of Our Lord Jesus Christ; or, Little Sunny's Sweet Stories of Old, for Very Young Children (London: Nisbet, 1886);

In Four Reigns: The Recollections of Althea Allingham, 1785-1842 (London: Seeley, 1886);

The Two Swords: A Story of Old Bristol (London: Seeley, 1887);

Daphne's Decision; or, Which Shall It Be?: A Story for Children (London: Nisbet, 1887);

Eaglehurst Towers (London: Partridge, 1887);

Mistress Matchett's Mistake: A Very Old Story (London: Nisbet, 1887);

Dandy Jim (London: Partridge, 1887);

On the Banks of the Ouse; or, Life in Olney a Hundred Years Ago (London: Seeley, 1887);

"Only a Bunch of Cherries" (London: Partridge, 1887);

The Story of John Marbeck, a Windsor Organist of Three Hundred Years Ago: His Work and His Reward (London: Nisbet, 1887);

Alma; or, The Story of a Little Music Mistress (London: Sonnenschein, 1888);

Bristol Diamonds; or, The Hot Wells in the Year 1773 (London: Seeley, 1888);

Houses on Wheels: A Story for Children (London: Nisbet, 1888);

Dulcibel's Day Dreams; or, The Grand Sweet Song (London: Nisbet, 1888);

Oliver's Old Pictures; or, The Magic Circle (London: Nisbet, 1888);

Our Own Picture Book (London: Nisbet, 1888);

Bishop's Cranworth; or, Rosamond's Lamp (London: Shaw, 1888);

In the City of Flowers; or, Adelaide's Awakening (London: Seeley, 1888);

Chris and Tina; or, The Twins (London: Seeley, 1888);

Her Season in Bath. A Story of By-Gone Days (London: Seeley, 1889);

Laurel Crowns; or, Griselda's Aim: A Story for Brothers and Sisters (London: Nisbet, 1889);

The End Crowns All: A Life-Story (London: Shaw, 1889);

Golden Silence; or, Annals of the Birkett Family of Crawford-under-Wold (London: Nisbet, 1889);

Robert's Race; or, More Haste Less Speed (London: Shaw, 1889);

"The Line of Beauty"; or, The Pierpoints of Linwood (London: Home Words Office, 1889);

Under Salisbury Spire in the Days of George Herbert: The Recollections of Magdalene Wydville (London: Seeley, 1890);

Up and Down the Pantiles: A Story of Tunbridge Wells a Hundred Years Ago (London: Seeley, 1890);

Eventide Light; or, Passages in the Life of Dame Margaret Hoby, Only Child and Sole Heiress of Sir Arthur Dakyne, Kt, of Hackness, Near to Scarborough (London: Shaw, 1890);

Pictures Illustrative of the Lord's Prayer, with Appropriate Stories for Children (London: Nisbet, 1890);

Curley's Crystal; or, A Light Heart Lives Long (London: Shaw, 1890);

Eastward Ho!: A Story for Girls (London: Nisbet, 1890);

Fine Gold; or, Ravenswood Courtenay (London: Partridge, 1890);

The Mother's Chain; or, The Broken Link (London: Partridge, 1890);

Shakespeare and His Birthplace (London: Nister, 1890);

When I Was Young (London: Nisbet, 1890);

Winchester Meads in the Times of Thomas Ken, D.D., Sometime Bishop of Bath and Wells (London: Seeley, 1890);

A Romance of the Undercliff; or, The Isle of Wight in 1799 (London: Seeley, 1891);

In the Purple (London: Nisbet, 1891);

Those Three; or, Little Wings: A Story for Girls (London: Nisbet, 1891);

Hurly-Burly; or, After Storm Comes a Calm (London: Shaw, 1891);

Little Miss Joy (London: Shaw, 1891);

Little Queenie: A Story of Child-Life Sixty Years Ago (London: Shaw, 1891);

My Lady Bountiful (London: Nisbet, 1891);

Winifrede's Journal of Her Life at Exeter and Norwich in the Days of Bishop Hall (London: Seeley, 1891);

Bristol Bells: A Story of the Eighteenth Century (London: Seeley, 1892);

New Relations: A Story for Girls (London: Nisbet, 1892);

Pat's Inheritance (London: Nisbet, 1892);

Bluebell: A Story of Child Life Now-a-Days (London: Shaw, 1892);

In the Service of Rachel, Lady Russell: A Story (London: Seeley, 1892);

Christopher's New Home (London: Shaw, 1892);

The Eve of St. Michael and All Angels, and Other Verses (Bristol: Arrowsmith, 1893);

Boscombe Chine; or, Fifty Years After (London: Seeley, 1893);

The Bride's Home (London: Nisbet, 1893);

Nature's Gentleman; or, "Manners Makyth Man" (London: Nisbet, 1893);

The Close of St. Christopher's: A Story for Girls (London: Nisbet, 1893);

The Children of Dean's Court; or, Ladybird and Her Friends (London: Shaw, 1893);

Penshurst Castle in the Time of Sir Philip Sidney (London: Seeley, 1893);

Peter's Promise; or, Look Before You Leap (London: Shaw, 1893);

The First Light on the Eddystone: A Story of Two Hundred Years Ago (London: Seeley, 1894);

Lettice Lawson's Legacy, and Other Stories (London: Nisbet, 1894);

Lizette and Her Mission; or, Over the Moor (London: Nisbet, 1894);

Kensington Palace in the Days of Queen Mary II: A Story (London: Seeley, 1894);

Clement and Georgie; or, Manners Makyth Man (London: Shaw, 1894);

Mother and Son; or, "I Will" (London: Home Words Office, 1894);

The White King's Daughter: A Story of the Princess Elizabeth (London: Seeley, 1895);

The Lady's Manor; or, Between Brook and River (London: Nisbet, 1895);

The Master of the Musicians: A Story of Handel's Days (London: Seeley, 1895);

By the North Sea; or, The Protector's Grand-Daughter (London: Jarrold, 1895);

An Escape from the Tower: A Story of the Jacobite Rising of 1715 (London: Seeley, 1896);

Abigail Templeton; or, Brave Efforts: A Story of To-Day (Edinburgh: Chambers, 1896);

Only Susan: Her Own Story (London: Nisbet, 1896);

Sir Benjamin's Bounty (London: Nisbet, 1896);

A Little Curiosity (London: Shaw, 1896);

The Two Henriettas (London: Partridge, 1896);

A Haunt of Ancient Peace: Memories of Mr. Nicholas Ferrar's House at Little Gidding, and of his Friends Dr. Donne and Mr. George Herbert (London: Seeley, 1897);

Castle Meadow: A Story of Norwich a Hundred Years Ago (London: Seeley, 1897);

Lady Rosalind; or, Family Feuds (London: Nisbet, 1897);

In the Choir of Westminster Abbey: A Story of Henry Purcell's Days (London: Seeley, 1897);

The Lady of Holt Dene (London: Griffith, Farran, 1897);

Lady Maud's Help; or, The Story of Christian Moss (Walton-on-Thames: Nelson, 1898);

Better Late than Never (London: Griffith, Farran, 1898);

The Young Queen of Hearts: A Story of the Princess Elizabeth and Her Brother, Henry, Prince of Wales (London: Seeley, 1898);

Master Martin (London: Nisbet, 1898);

Under the Laburnums: A Story (London: Nisbet, 1898);

Rose Deane; or, Christmas Roses (Bristol: Arrowsmith, 1899);

Cross Purposes; or, The Deanes of Dean's Croft, completed by Beatrice Marshall and Evelyn E. Green (London: Griffith, Farran, 1899);

A Good-Hearted Girl; or, A Present-Day Heroine (Edinburgh: Chambers, 1899);

Time Tries (London: Nisbet, 1899);

The Parson's Daughter: Her Early Recollections and How Mr. Romney Painted Her, completed by Beatrice Marshall (London: Seeley, 1899);

A Pink of Perfection, completed by Emily Dibdin (London: Nisbet, 1900);

The Thin End of the Wedge: A Story (London: Jarrold, 1900);

How the Lost Purse Was Found (London: Religious Tract Society, 1902).

Emma Marshall was a popular and prolific children's writer in her day, producing nearly two hundred books and assorted short stories and poems during a long career. Although several of her works remained in print into the 1920s, all are now out of print, relegated to the rare-book shelves of the library, while Marshall's name is unknown to both the general reader and most experts on children's literature. The author's descent into obscurity may be because of her chosen genre of religious fiction, which tends to fall below the critical horizon in the twentieth century, or to the fact that she was compelled by financial necessity to overproduce, resulting in a corpus of inconsistent quality. At the height of her career, during the late 1880s and early 1890s, she published from seven to ten volumes each year.

Emma Martin was born on 29 September 1828 in Norwich, the seventh and last child of a middle-class family well situated within local society. Her father, Simon Martin, was a partner in a local bank; her mother, Hannah Ransome Martin, belonged to an old Quaker family with connections to the large and prominent Society of Friends' community in Norwich. Perhaps in part because her father was not a member of the Society of Friends, Marshall was not fully immersed in Quaker religion; however, her early exposure to the Friends' religious principles appears to have contributed to the tolerance and simplicity of faith evident in her later writing. Her novel *Life's Aftermath: A Story of Quiet People* (1876) depicts Quaker customs, but according to her daughter, Marshall relied on her older sisters' recollections for much of this material.

Since there was a significant gap in age between herself and her older siblings, Martin spent much of her childhood without regular playmates, relying instead on imaginary friends and occasional visitors for companionship. She also had a friend who came regularly to share in lessons from Martin's governess. Her comfortable home life ended when she was ten, when her father died and the family relocated to a smaller house outside town. From there she was sent to boarding school until the age of sixteen.

Like other young women of her age and time, Marshall read the works of Sir Walter Scott, Charles Dickens, and William Makepeace Thackeray, but she was particularly drawn to the poetry

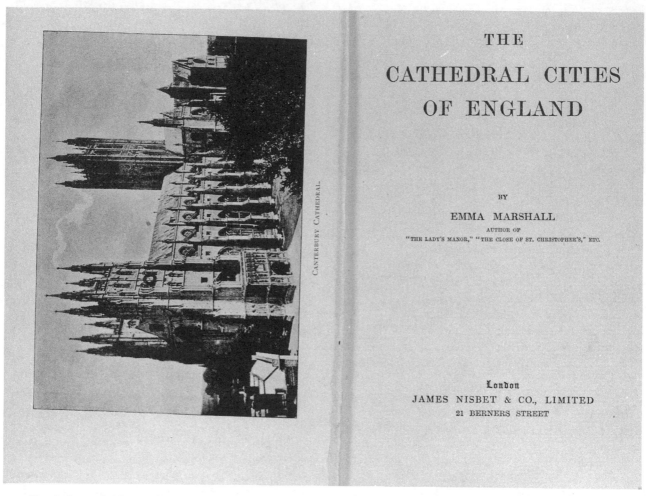

THE

CATHEDRAL CITIES

OF ENGLAND

BY

EMMA MARSHALL

AUTHOR OF

"THE LADY'S MANOR," "THE CLOSE OF ST. CHRISTOPHER'S," ETC.

London
JAMES NISBET & CO., LIMITED
21 BERNERS STREET

CANTERBURY CATHEDRAL

Frontispiece and title page for an early edition of Marshall's 1879 guide, which grew out of her fascination with church history

of Henry Wadsworth Longfellow, with whom she began a correspondence in 1851. The American poet encouraged her pursuit of a literary career, commenting favorably on several of her early works. Their friendship continued until his death in 1882, but various accidents of timing prevented the correspondents from meeting, despite Longfellow's visits to England and Marshall's to the United States. Other positive influences on Marshall's writing vocation included the writer John Addington Symonds, whom she met in 1849 when she and her mother moved to Clifton, near the home of Symonds's father. Symonds introduced her to the world of contemporary literature and the arts and later contributed to several lecture series promoted by Marshall, committed to higher education for women.

At Clifton, Emma Martin met and fell in love with Hugh Graham Marshall, the eldest son of an Anglican minister. Her mother opposed the romance on the grounds that Marshall's financial prospects were poor; nevertheless, the two were married by the groom's father in 1854. Emma Marshall, whose commitment to her mother's nominal Quakerism had always been tenuous, completed her religious migration by joining the Church of England during her engagement. Although her preference appears to have been for the High Church brand of Anglicanism, Marshall retained a broad sympathy and tolerance for other Protestant beliefs. These religious commitments are reflected in her writings, which are inclusively evangelical but clearly hostile to Catholicism.

In 1856 the Marshalls settled at Wells, where Hugh was appointed manager of the West of England Bank. Emma was drawn into the social life of a cathedral town, visiting regularly with clerical families and attending religious services several days a week. They had nine children: Lucy Agnes, born 1856; James Graham Wilberforce, born 1857; Legh Richmond, born 1859; Emma Beatrice, born 1861; Hugh Atherton, born 1863; Cyril Legh, born

1865; Douglas Hamilton, born 1867; Edith Mary, born 1869; and Christabel Gertrude, born 1871. Most of her married life was spent in various cathedral cities across the south of England, creating a fascination with the historical church that later manifested itself in several historical novels and in her 1879 guide, *Stories of the Cathedral Cities of England*.

Marshall's literary work began in earnest at Wells. Early in her marriage she wrote poetry, though she did not seek publication. In 1861, however, encouraged by two friends who had published short stories and challenged by her husband's skepticism about her writing vocation, she published her first novel, *The Happy Days at Fernbank, A Story for Little Girls*, written at night after her children (she had four by this time) were in bed.

The novel tells the story of two young girls of different economic circumstances – one is the daughter of an Anglican dean, the other the orphan of a clergyman who is being raised by her aunt – and it belongs to the genre Marshall was to concentrate on through her early career, the domestic or family story, in which children are presented with moral rules for life. Each of the protagonists must overcome a degree of self-centeredness, and they are helped by several interpolated stories as well as by their own experiences. The climax comes with the death of the orphaned girl, who has been so transformed by her experiences that she in turn effects the moral reforms of her aunt and the dean's daughter.

This first attempt at a children's novel was a moderate success, encouraging Marshall to produce a second book, *Johnny Weston; or, Christmas Eve at the White House* (1862); the popularity of this work may be judged by its having remained in print for twenty years. She also completed *The Second Mother: Her Trials and Joys* (1862), a book begun by her sister Hannah Geldart who had died before its completion. This book began her association with the evangelical publishing house of Seeley, Jackson, and Halliday, which became one of her two primary publishers.

Throughout her career Marshall wrote several books each year, almost all of them evangelical in inspiration but directed at different audiences. Vera R. Hughes divides Marshall's works into shorter children's tales, most of which eventually came to be published by Nisbet; more-sophisticated works for older children and adults of the upper middle classes, generally published by Seeley; and "Christian journalism," shorter works produced for parish magazines and as prize books for lower-class children.

Whatever the projected audience, much of this work consciously presents moral fables of weak human beings who must subdue selfish instincts to prevent suffering – their own and that of those who love them. An early example is *Violet Douglas; or, The Problems of Life* (1868), the story of a girl whose efforts to be good make her conscious of human frailty. Willie Douglas, Violet's weaker brother, fails to learn self-discipline in his youth and repents on his deathbed, causing his mother remorse for her failure to teach him.

Marshall's novels followed the model of *The Happy Days at Fernbank* in contrasting similar experiences among middle-class children and the "respectable poor" – which included both honest working-class folks and down-on-their-luck gentlefolk such as Mabel Hampden in *Violet Douglas*. Mabel's attempts to help her family by working as a seamstress are hampered by her ambiguous status: as a gentlewoman she cannot directly solicit work, but she is treated as the object of charity by better-off women who hire her services through a marketing association. Judith Rowbotham interprets this episode as an attempt to instruct more-fortunate readers (the book was published by Seeley, Marshall's "genteel" publishing house) in the proper respect to be shown to such workers.

Even this early in her career, despite her husband's modest success, Marshall's writing appears to have been influenced by economic necessity – in this case to save for her sons' education. *The Happy Days at Fernbank* was published shortly after the birth of her fourth child; she would eventually bear nine children. By the time the Marshalls left Wells in the summer of 1868, Emma Marshall had already produced some twenty books and seven children.

The departure from Wells resulted from Hugh Marshall's promotion to manage a larger branch of the bank at Exeter, another cathedral town. There, and later at Gloucester, Emma Marshall joined with other women to support and promote series of women's lectures – scholarly presentations for women born too early to benefit from the opening of women's colleges at Oxford and Cambridge. Many of these lecture series were on literature or art, but they reflected a wide range of intellectual interests, including some scientific topics.

Despite Hugh Marshall's promotion, the move to Exeter proved costly to the large and growing family, and much of what Emma Marshall had been able to save from her writing was lost through increased expenses and bad investments. However, more difficult financial times lay ahead. The family moved again in 1872 to a larger bank at Gloucester, but in 1878 the West of England Bank failed. As a

Frontispiece and title page for one of the novels in which Marshall used historical figures in domestic fiction (courtesy of the Lilly Library, Indiana University)

partner, Hugh Marshall not only lost his managerial salary but was also burdened with a share of the bank's debts.

The bank failure compelled the family to move to less expensive quarters and to sell much of its belongings; it also left the Marshalls' economic fate entirely on the shoulders of Emma Marshall's writing. Her literary output in the 1860s and early 1870s had already been fairly large, but she still had the leisure to develop plots and characterization at length. Following the bank failure, however, Marshall began to churn out book after book – six, eight, and even ten a year through the next fifteen years. Under such pressures, she understandably turned to conventional plots and poorly realized characters.

This prodigious output, evidence of both a high level of productivity and an obvious market for the works, has undoubtedly affected Marshall's literary reputation in this century. The sheer number of her publications is so intimidating that few critics have read more than one or two of her books – if in fact they have read any – and much of her opus is

admittedly hackwork, a "mechanical handling of old themes" as J. S. Bratton has described Marshall's *Eastward Ho!: A Story for Girls* (1890).

Eastward Ho! describes the social work of religious missionaries among the poor of the East End of London, a subject of considerable interest in late-Victorian England; its plot centers on a rebellious heiress who runs away to assist in this work. Hughes connects the upper-class, university-educated missionaries of the novel to several real-world models known to Marshall, suggesting that she consciously shaped her writing to appeal to readers' interests in contemporary events. The novel appears to have been popular: it remained in print until 1913 and was widely used as a prize book in lower-class Sunday schools.

Despite the writing problems associated with Marshall's accelerated literary production, it was during this later period that her best-known and most highly regarded works, her historic fiction for adolescents and adults, were written. They reflect Marshall's interest in the stories of the various provincial towns in which she lived, in the lives of religious and literary figures of the past, and in the tensions between various religious factions of her own time.

Winchester Meads in the Times of Thomas Ken, D.D., Sometime Bishop of Bath and Wells (1890) centers on the historical figure of the title, a nonjuring bishop during the Restoration and the uncle of Izaak Walton, and a fictional family, the Lilburns. The mother, Alice Lilburn, is a widow; her twin sons, Quentin and Hugh, are scholarship students at the school in Winchester and form the center of her existence. The mother's piety, the academic excellence of Hugh, and the physical energy of Quentin have caught the attention of Dr. Ken, a member of the cathedral chapter and an occasional instructor who has established a friendship with the family.

Alice Lilburn's brother, Ambrose, who had embraced the Puritan cause and emigrated from England to America, returns and asks her to supervise the education of his beautiful daughter, Judith, before going abroad again. Ambrose Lilburn's brand of religion is clearly rigid and restrictive, but his daughter, who clings to her principles despite the efforts of Alice and Dr. Ken to bring her into the Church of England, shows a softer, more idealistic side of Puritanism. Her obvious virtues and beauty attract both of her cousins and lead to Hugh's conversion to a more evangelical brand of Christianity, to the consternation of his mother and Dr. Ken.

The primary conflict is over which of the brothers Judith will marry. She clearly favors Hugh, but he, misreading her devotion and dedicating himself to religious good works, urges her to accept his brother, whose secular diplomatic career has nevertheless served the true cause of Protestantism against the Catholics. Meanwhile, Dr. Ken attempts to shape a path for true religious principles between the extremes of Puritan repression and a return to Rome. Thus, Marshall's broad sympathies for all sects of Protestantism and her distaste for Catholicism are explored in the context of the religious conflicts of the late seventeenth century. The family romance at the center of the novel and the philosophical stand of Dr. Ken against pressures from both sides are nicely balanced.

Other works of the period less successfully merge historic figures with domestic fiction. *Penshurst Castle in the Time of Sir Philip Sidney* (1893) has a potentially more compelling domestic conflict at its heart — the abduction of Mary Gifford's son by her husband, who had abandoned his wife and plans to raise his son as a Catholic. The distraught mother solicits the assistance of Sidney and others to find the missing child; but the potentially tragic situation is resolved abruptly when the father, on his deathbed, repents and returns the boy. The novel's attention then turns primarily to Sidney, dramatizing his short but spectacular career as courtier, soldier, and poet. The two strands are joined more artificially, and the characters are comparatively weak.

Despite a degree of literary success, Marshall's greatest efforts were not enough to keep the wolf from the door. While many of the books went into several printings and several were in print well into the 1920s, financial necessity led Marshall to trade long-term income for immediate payment. Many of the books' copyrights were sold to publishers outright; according to Hughes, only Seeley paid her continued royalties for subsequent editions. During the final decade of her life, with her children at university and medical school, Marshall was forced to make repeated applications to the Royal Literary Fund for financial relief, usually with success.

Extant applications demonstrate that Marshall was acutely aware of the strain of providing for her family's needs and her children's education through her writing. She asks the fund for support so that she might "take a few weeks rest next year, and prevent the *absolute* necessity of working so much in order to meet expenses." In her later years this strain told upon her health, and her appeals for assistance make frequent reference to illness; despite ill health, as her list of publications and her daughter's biography demonstrate, she remained active and was working on yet another book when she died of pneumonia on 4 May 1899. Several of the projects she had on hand were finished by her daughter Beatrice or friends.

Biography:

Beatrice Marshall, *Emma Marshall: A Biographical Sketch* (London: Seeley, 1900).

References:

J. S. Bratton, *The Impact of Victorian Children's Fiction* (London: Croom Helm, 1981);

Vera R. Hughes, "The Works of Mrs. Emma Marshall in Relationship to Her Life and the Educational Concepts of Her Times," dissertation, University of Liverpool, 1986;

Judith Rowbotham, *Good Girls Make Good Wives: Guidance for Girls in Victorian Fiction* (Oxford: Blackwell, 1989).

Harriet Martineau

(12 June 1802 – 27 June 1876)

Lois Rauch Gibson
Coker College

See also the Martineau entries in *DLB 21: Victorian Novelists Before 1885, DLB 55: Prose Writers Before 1867,* and *DLB 159: British Short Fiction Writers, 1800–1880.*

BOOKS: *Devotional Exercises for the Use of Young Persons* (London: Hunter, 1823; Boston: Bowles, 1833);

Addresses with Prayers and Original Hymns for the Use of Families and Schools (London: Hunter, 1826);

Principle and Practice; or, The Orphan Family (Wellington: Houlston, 1827; New York: W. B. Gilley, 1828);

The Rioters; or, A Tale of Bad Times (London: Houlston, 1827);

Mary Campbell; or, The Affectionate Granddaughter (Wellington: Houlston, 1828);

The Turn Out; or, Patience the Best Policy (London: Houlston, 1829);

The Essential Faith of the Universal Church: Deduced from the Sacred Records (London: Unitarian Association, 1831; Boston: Bowles, 1833);

Five Years of Youth; or, Sense and Sentiment (London: Harvey & Darton, 1831; Boston: Bowles & Greene, 1832);

Sequel to Principle and Practice (London: Houlston, 1831);

Illustrations of Political Economy (25 monthly parts, London: Fox, 1832–1834; 8 volumes, Boston: Bowles, 1832–1835);

The Faith as Unfolded by Many Prophets: An Essay Addressed to the Disciples of Mohammed (London: Unitarian Association, 1832; Boston: Bowles, 1833);

Providence as Manifested Through Israel (London: Unitarian Association, 1832; Boston: Bowles, 1833);

Poor Laws and Paupers (4 volumes, London: Fox, 1833–1834; Boston: Bowles: 1833);

Christmas-Day; or, The Friends (London: Houlston, 1834);

Harriet Martineau, circa 1835

Illustrations of Taxation, 5 volumes (London: Fox, 1834);

The Children Who Lived by the Jordan. A Story (Salem, Mass.: Landmark, 1835; London: Green, 1842);

The Hamlets (Boston: Munroe, 1836);

Miscellanies, 2 volumes (Boston: Hilliard, Gray, 1836);

Society in America, 3 volumes (London: Saunders & Otley, 1837);

The Guide to Service, 3 parts (London: Knight, 1838–1839);

How to Observe Morals and Manners (London: Knight, 1838; New York: Harper, 1838);

My Servant Rachel, a Tale (London: Houlston, 1838);

Retrospect of Western Travel (3 volumes, London: Saunders & Otley, 1838; 2 volumes, New York: Lohman, 1838);

Deerbrook: A Novel (3 volumes, London: Moxon, 1839; 2 volumes, New York: Harper, 1939);

The Martyr Age of the United States of America (Boston: Weeks, Jordan, 1839; Newcastle upon Tyne: Emancipation and Aborigines Protection Society, 1840);

The Hour and the Man. A Historical Romance, 3 volumes (London: Moxon, 1841); republished as *The Hour and the Man. An Historical Romance,* 2 volumes (New York: Harper, 1841);

The Playfellow: A Series of Tales (4 volumes, London: Knight, 1841; 1 volume, London & New York: Routledge, 1883);

Life in the Sick-Room: Essays by an Invalid (London: Moxon, 1844; Boston: Bowles & Crosby, 1844);

Dawn Island: A Tale (Manchester: Gadsby, 1845);

Letters on Mesmerism (London: Moxon, 1845); republished as *Miss Martineau's Letters on Mesmerism* (New York: Harper, 1845);

Forest and Game Law Tales, 3 volumes (London: Moxon, 1845–1846);

The Billow and the Rock (London: Knight, 1846);

The Land We Live In, by Martineau and Charles Knight, 4 volumes (London: Knight, 1847);

Eastern Life, Past and Present (3 volumes, London: Moxon, 1848; 1 volume, Philadelphia: Lea & Blanchard, 1848);

Household Education (London: Moxon, 1849; Philadelphia: Lea & Blanchard, 1849);

The History of England during the Thirty Years' Peace: 1816–1846, 2 volumes (London: Knight, 1849); republished as *The History of England from the Commencement of the XIXth Century to the Crimean War,* 4 volumes (Philadelphia: Porter & Coates, 1864);

Two Letters on Cow-Keeping (London: Charles Gilpin, 1850);

Introduction to the History of the Peace from 1800 to 1815 (London: Knight, 1851); republished as *History of England, A.D. 1800–1815; Being an Introduction to the History of the Peace* (London: Bell, 1878);

Letters on the Laws of Man's Nature and Development, by Martineau and Henry George Atkinson (London: Chapman, 1851; Boston: Mendum, 1851);

Letters from Ireland (London: Chapman, 1853);

Guide to Windermere, with Tours to the Neighbouring Lakes and Other Interesting Places (Windermere: Garnett / London: Whittaker, 1854);

A Complete Guide to the English Lakes (Windermere: Garnett / London: Whittaker, 1854);

The Factory Controversy: A Warning Against Meddling Legislation (Manchester: National Association of Factory Occupiers, 1855);

A History of the American Compromises (London: Chapman, 1856);

Sketches from Life (London: Whittaker / Windermere: Garnett, 1856);

British Rule in India: A Historical Sketch (London: Smith, Elder, 1857);

Corporate Tradition and National Rights: Local Dues on Shipping (London: Routledge / Manchester: Dinham, 1857);

Guide to Keswick and Its Environs (Windermere: Garnett / London: Whittaker, 1857);

The "Manifest Destiny" of the American Union (New York: American Anti-Slavery Society, 1857);

Suggestions towards the Future Government of India (London: Smith, Elder, 1858);

Endowed Schools of Ireland (London: Smith, Elder, 1859);

England and Her Soldiers (London: Smith, Elder, 1859);

Health, Husbandry and Handicraft (London: Bradbury & Evans, 1861); republished in part as *Our Farm of Two Acres* (New York: Bunce & Huntingdon, 1865);

Biographical Sketches (London: Macmillan, 1869; New York: Leopoldt & Holt, 1869);

Harriet Martineau's Autobiography, with Memorials by Maria Weston Chapman (3 volumes, London: Smith, Elder, 1877; 2 volumes, Boston: Osgood, 1877);

The Hampdens: An Historiette (London: Routledge, 1880).

OTHER: *Traditions of Palestine,* edited by Martineau (London: Longman, Rees, Orme, Brown & Green, 1830); revised and republished as *The Times of the Saviour* (Boston: Bowles, 1831);

The Positive Philosophy of Auguste Comte. Freely Translated and Condensed, 2 volumes, translated by Martineau (London: Chapman, 1853; New York: Appleton, 1854).

In her autobiography Harriet Martineau states emphatically that authorship was never "a matter of choice" for her. She wrote not "for amusement, or for money, or for fame, or for any reason but because I could not help it." Regardless of her subject –

religion, economics, history, social reform, education, family relations, biography, or philosophy — Martineau wrote because "things were pressing to be said" and she was "the person to say them." Many of her contemporaries agreed. Her work was praised by such literary luminaries as George Eliot, Elizabeth Barrett Browning, Thomas Carlyle, William Wordsworth, Charlotte Brontë, and Ralph Waldo Emerson, who were also her friends. Members of the government trying to gain public acceptance of proposed policies sought her journalistic and literary support.

Martineau's writings for children were as varied as those for adults, including devotional exercises and Sunday school stories, geographical and historical fiction, a boys' school story, and several moral tales (though these may have been for adults as well). Her best children's stories, "The Crofton Boys" and "Feats on the Fiord," originally published with two other tales as *The Playfellow: A Series of Tales* (1841), continued to appear in new editions until 1928 and 1941, respectively. Today, however, they are read primarily by adults for their historical significance.

Harriet Martineau was born on 12 June 1802, in Norwich, Norfolk, the sixth of eight children. Her father, Thomas Martineau, came from a long line of Huguenot surgeons, the first of whom had left Normandy soon after the 1685 revocation of the Edict of Nantes made France inhospitable to Protestants. Unlike his ancestors, Thomas Martineau manufactured cloth, chiefly bombazine. Harriet's mother, Elizabeth Rankin Martineau, was the daughter of a wholesale grocer and sugar refiner of Newcastle upon Tyne. The Martineaus, who were Unitarians, believed in educating both daughters and sons.

Harriet learned French and discovered the works of John Milton before beginning school; from ages seven to fourteen she derived such pleasure from *Paradise Lost* (1671) that she committed large portions of it to memory, reciting verses at bedtime to help her fall asleep. She describes this as her first experience of finding "moral relief through intellectual resource." She found similar happiness at Isaac Perry's school, which she began attending daily with her sister Rachel at age eleven. She especially enjoyed composition, arithmetic, and Latin; recitations of Latin verse began to replace Milton as her bedtime incantations.

She reports in her autobiography that she felt emotionally neglected at home, where her parents used the "taking down" method of child rearing and rarely praised or petted. This especially pained young Harriet, who longed for kind words or overt expressions of affection. Her distress was increased by an apparent milk allergy, an impaired sense of smell and taste, and increasing deafness, all of which were discounted by her parents. She was delighted at age sixteen to be sent to live for a year in Bristol with her "dear aunt Kentish," her mother's sister-in-law, and to be educated with her cousins there. Martineau believes that her "heart warmed and opened" in Bristol.

Nonetheless, Martineau admitted that she could be difficult: not only was she often nervous and given to jealousy, but her timidity vied with assertiveness, and steadfastness could become obstinacy. She reports a telling early example of sticking to principle. While still at Perry's school, Martineau objected when her teacher said "Shakspere" was an incorrect spelling of the great poet's name. She went home and found a volume in which it was spelled just that way and showed it to her teacher in front of the class; she also continued to spell the name "Shakspere" throughout her life. To her credit, she admitted in retrospect that she ought to have shown her teacher the book in private.

When she showed an interest in becoming a writer, her younger brother James, who later became a noted theologian, encouraged her to write for the Unitarian *Monthly Repository*. Her first publication, a letter to the editor of that periodical about "Female Writers of Practical Divinity," signed "V of Norwich," appeared in 1822. When her older brother read it aloud and praised it, Martineau acknowledged her authorship; he responded in admiration, "Now, dear, leave it to other women to make shirts and darn stockings; and do you devote yourself to this." It was some time, however, before she was able to do so; for many years, she spent her days sewing, as was considered appropriate for genteel ladies; Martineau notes that even Jane Austen was forced to keep a piece of muslin handy should guests arrive. Most of her own writing had to be done before breakfast or late at night. Still, the unaccustomed praise from her brother gave her the courage she needed: "That evening made me an authoress," she recalled.

She immediately began work on her first book, *Devotional Exercises for the Use of Young Persons* (1823). In her autobiography she recalls nothing of this book except her older brother reading the manuscript with anxious looks and gentle hints about "precision and arrangement of ideas." Her early biographer, F. Fenwick Miller, believed the book was more than a commonplace devotional because it reveals the theism that was to be Martineau's belief system for the following twenty years; but most readers find it unexceptional. More interesting is Martineau's comment in her preface that "being yet young," she is an appropriate author for the volume because different ideas and feelings move people at different ages of their lives. Seventeen years later, as she prepared to write a series of children's tales, she clearly felt a need for youthful input: she asked her friend Fanny Wedgewood's seven-year-old daughter, Snow, to make a list of the stories she and her six-year-old brother liked best and least; she asked the same of her many nephews and nieces.

The success of her first book led Martineau to complete another like it: *Addresses with Prayers and Original Hymns for the Use of Families and Schools* (1826) went to press as her father was dying. His "affectionate pleasure" in it and his high hopes for his daughter's continued success as an author were her only comfort in his last illness. He died in June 1826, two years after his oldest son, Thomas.

Following her father's death, Martineau became engaged to John Worthington, a friend of her brother James. Unsure of her ability to "undertake the charge of his happiness" and ambivalent about the engagement, Martineau described herself as "ill . . . deaf . . . in an entangled state of mind." When Worthington contracted "brain-fever" and died several months later, Martineau grieved, but years later she recalled her ambivalence and felt relieved that she had remained free of marriage and children. She added, "My work and I have been fitted to each other, as is proved by the success of my work and my own happiness in it."

During the following year Martineau wrote several short tales and tracts published anonymously by Houlston of Shropshire, titles which the publisher's sons apparently sold under the name of the more renowned Mrs. Sherwood. Martineau also wrote the longer *Principle and Practice; or, The Orphan Family* in 1827, sometimes described as her earliest children's story. Though neither Martineau nor Houlston advertised it as children's fiction, the book is similar in style and theme to three of her later Playfellow tales: it combines a survival tale with light didacticism and focuses on children who overcome difficult circumstances through courage, hard work, steadfastness, and faith. As in the later "Crofton Boys," a character suffers an amputation after an accident and must learn to go on. The book sold well enough to inspire a sequel four years later.

In *Reason Over Passion* (1986) Valerie Sanders calls both *Principle and Practice* and *Five Years of Youth* (1831) "short moral tales for young people," de-

Frontispiece for an 1895 edition of Martineau's The Crofton Boys, *originally published in* The Playfellow: A Series of Tales *(1841)*

scribing the latter tale of two daughters of an eccentric widower a kind of "junior *Sense and Sensibility*." In her autobiography, however, Martineau claims she wrote the book while awaiting the results of an essay competition, never looked at it again, and had "no inclination" to reread it.

In June 1829 the family business, which had been troubled since before Martineau's father's death, finally failed. Ironically, though this left Harriet with "precisely one shilling in [her] purse" and her mother and sisters equally destitute, they were suddenly freed of the strictures of gentility and thrown on their own resources; as a result, they worked, traveled, made friends, and, in Martineau's words, "lived instead of vegetated." Because her deafness precluded governessing and music, Martineau could pursue the career of her choice full-time. She quickly wrote to W. J. Fox, the editor of the *Monthly Repository*, who agreed to pay her fifteen pounds a year for reviews. She continued selling tracts to Houlston. She also entered an essay contest to present Unitarianism to Catholics, Jews, and Muslims and won all three prizes, gaining not only the prize money but also a renewed confidence in her future as an author.

These successes led to the series that firmly established her as a serious thinker and writer: *Illustrations of Political Economy* (1832–1834), twenty-five tales, each designed to reinforce a specific economic principle. Martineau was inspired by Jane Marcet's *Conversations on Political Economy* (1816) and the works of Adam Smith, Jeremy Bentham, and Thomas Malthus; her tales were based on thorough research and on actual events. Published between 1832 and 1834, they were so successful that publishers and literary "lionizers" courted her, but she chose instead to travel to the United States, committing herself to no books about her travels.

In America she wrote *The Children Who Lived by the Jordan* (1835) for a Sunday school festival and added an essay to an American edition of her early work; but she concentrated primarily on learning about American life and culture. Her antislavery sentiments led to some threats against her; still, her overall experience was positive, resulting in life-long friendships with the Emersons and the Chapmans (Maria Weston Chapman became her literary executor), and two books, *Society in America* (1837) and *Retrospect of Western Travel* (1838).

After completing these books, Martineau continued to publish short tales and didactic articles while preparing to write her first full-length novel, *Deerbrook* (1839), based on events and people she had known or heard about, a technique she used in all her writing; she believed all great writers did the same. She began the novel on her thirty-sixth birthday and was pleased when reviewers compared her completed work to that of Jane Austen. She accepted calmly Carlyle's condemnation of it as "trivial-didactic."

Following these very productive years, illness forced Martineau to cut short a European tour and move near her physician brother-in-law; she remained there for nearly six years. Treatment for her problems — an ovarian cyst and a uterine tumor — was limited mostly to opiates and rest, so the author "took to her bed," like so many other Victorians. But she did not rest idly. She carried on an impressive correspondence while writing several significant books: a historical novel about Haitian independence leader Toussaint-Louverture, *The Hour and the Man* (1841); the children's collection, *The Playfellow;* and *Life in the Sick Room* (1844), describing and reflecting upon her experience.

Before the Toussaint-Louverture book was published, Martineau recalls, she "planned the light and easy work . . . of a series of children's tales." She began the first, "Settlers at Home," while in high spirits about the reception of *The Hour and the Man,* but the tale is anything but cheerful. It is set in seventeenth-century Lincolnshire, in an area farmed by hard-working French and Dutch immigrants, who are hated by the xenophobic natives. Inspired by a true Thomas De Quincey story about surviving a snowstorm, Martineau decided that a flood would be a less hackneyed plot device. "Settlers at Home" is a well-constructed adventure, full of dramatic tension, which avoids both overt moralizing and sentimentality.

The Linacres are good, honest, industrious Dutch settlers with three children: Oliver, age eleven; Mildred, nine; and George, two. Despite occasional acts of vandalism and robbery by local "gypsies," their home and garden are comfortably attractive, and their family life is enviable until a sudden and terrible flood caused by jealous neighbors leaves the children, the young maid Ailwin, and the gypsy boy Roger in a Robinson Crusoe–like situation. Food becomes scarce as livestock die off and floating bodies pollute the river; even Roger's game begin to die and scavenging birds become omens of doom. Roger is alternately mean-spirited and helpful, won over finally by the love of baby George. This transformation recalls Martineau's descriptions of her own softening during the rare times she had felt such warmth as a child. Unfortunately, even Roger's attention cannot save the baby after the cow dies and there is no milk, but the others are rescued and restored to their parents, and Roger seems ready to reform and be adopted. The ending is bittersweet, for the Linacres' home is gone, George is dead, and there is no guarantee that the neighbors will repent; yet the faith and love of the Linacres remain unabated.

The second story of the set, "The Peasant and the Prince," is really two loosely connected tales about the French Revolution. The first part recounts the love story of the peasants Charles and Marie, juxtaposed with the passage through their district of fifteen-year-old Marie Antoinette, en route to her own marriage to the king. The Dauphine, shocked by the poverty and wretchedness around her, takes pity on the lovers and their families and relieves their suffering. But Jerome, a young soldier, has the last word: "It is all very well, and I am glad this one family is saved, but it is only one of a hundred thousand miserable families. What is to become of all the rest, who may not have the luck to see a royal bride pass their way?" His comments provide the bridge to the much longer second part, in which the peasants of the prologue never reappear; instead, the royal family's downfall is presented sympathetically. The king seems more ignorant than evil, and the Dauphin is an appealing little boy; the reader may easily forget the abject poverty and unjust conditions of the peasants.

Martineau notes in her autobiography that her mother remembered the French Revolution and sympathized with the royal family, while Martineau and most of her contemporaries found the "poor little Dauphin . . . an object of romantic interest." Martineau felt that "The Peasant and the Prince" was the least successful tale in *The Playfellow* because she wrote it on a friend's advice rather than on her own initiative. More likely it appealed less to children because the day-to-day life of imprisoned royalty is simply not very exciting to them. Poor people loved the book, however, calling it the "French revelation"; copies in lending libraries were well thumbed, according to Martineau.

The third tale, "Feats on the Fiord," so convincingly portrays Norway that at least one Norwegian assumed Martineau had lived there. An adventure tale filled with local color, it became the most popular success of the 1841 collection. An 1899 edition includes illustrations by Arthur Rackham, and a 1939 volume, *Tales for Children from Many Lands,* pairs it with *Robin Hood.* The story includes pirates, smuggling, a hidden cave, a pair of separated lovers, a heroic boy, a plot to kidnap a bishop, and a villain who has thrown two babies to the wolves to save his own life. Norwegian marriage customs, farm life, and folk beliefs about wood and water sprites add charm and verisimilitude, especially when Erica the housemaid insists on staying awake to "keep an eye on the cattle," lest the fairies reduce them to the size of mice and make them vanish through crevices in the ground. Christianity prevails over superstition, however, as the seemingly supernatural events turn out to have natural, even humorous, causes. Unlike the other Playfellow tales, this one has a happy ending unmarred by painful accident or premature death.

"The Crofton Boys," the last of the series, begins as an apparently happy tale of a little boy who longs to join his big brother at boarding school. He soon gets his wish but finds, as his mother had warned him, that school for the newest boy is more painful than fun. Worse yet, eight-year-old Hugh Proctor is just beginning to overcome his self-centeredness and immaturity and is gaining some acceptance, when an accident leads to the amputation of his foot. His stoicism and courage in learning to cope, his ability to forgive the boy responsible for the accident, and his steadfastness in working to become a better student and a better person demonstrate Hugh's increasing maturity. Throughout, Hugh is a fallible, believable child, and the description of life at school rings true: Martineau even received letters from schoolboys telling her so. It is worth noting that Martineau's tale precedes Thomas Hughes's *Tom Brown's School Days* (1857), with which it is often compared, by sixteen years.

When Martineau wrote "The Crofton Boys," she believed it would be her final publication. She enjoyed a kind of catharsis as she wrote it and claimed there were some things that she could not have written unless she believed herself near death. Perhaps she meant that she might have more carefully disguised events and relationships from her life. The amputation was based on the experience of her childhood friend Emily Cooper, to whom she wrote an apology; Emily's generous response eased Martineau's conscience. More significant, Hugh Proctor's mother is said to be a thinly disguised version of Martineau's mother, especially when Hugh worries in the midst of fun about what his mother's grave looks mean, or when he flinches inwardly at her severe looks upon his erring in his lessons. After his foot is amputated, however, his mother sits beside him, wipes away his tears, and comforts him as the young Harriet would like to have been comforted in her childhood agonies. Another echo of Martineau's life appears in the conversations between Hugh and his older sister, Agnes; like Martineau and her younger brother, the two are very close, but she dotes far more than he appreciates. In her autobiography Martineau bemoans the inequity of affection between brothers and sisters; she clearly identifies with Agnes Proctor.

Though Martineau expected to die soon after completing "The Crofton Boys," she was cured — either through some natural change in her medical condition, or by mesmerism, or both. She published a series of letters on mesmerism that led to a break with some friends and relatives, but she was adamant about its effects. She built a house in Ambleside, continued to write political tales, and began a new series of Playfellow tales with *The Billow and the Rock* (1846), which seems less like a children's book than nearly anything else she had written. Though it is historical fiction in a picturesque setting (1740s Scotland), few child characters appear, none of them central. Martineau retells the story of Lord and Lady Grange (she renames them Carse) whose political differences led Lord Grange to arrange for the kidnapping of his wife to prevent her revealing Jacobite secrets: she is loyal to King George. The psychologically complex narrative recounts Lady Carse's attempts to return from exile in the Hebrides to see her children and get revenge on their father; but she dies shortly after leaving the island, still at sea.

Martineau never completed the second Playfellow series, embarking instead on a journey to Egypt that led to the publication of *Eastern Life, Past and Present* (1848). Upon her return she declared her "age of fiction-writing" over, and turned to writing advice in *Household Education* (1849). Soon after, she attracted even greater controversy than her mesmerism letters had aroused when she co-authored *Letters on the Laws of Man's Nature and Development* (1851), presenting a position later called agnosticism. In 1853 Martineau translated and condensed Auguste Comte's *Positive Philosophy;* Comte was so pleased with it that he had her version translated into French.

Martineau spent the rest of her life in Ambleside, at first enjoying long walks among the lakes and later, when her health again failed, venturing rarely from home; but she never stopped writing — guidebooks, histories, articles for the *Daily News,* and countless letters. In 1855, again sure she was dying, Martineau wrote her autobiography, probably her most important work. Though she lived for twenty-one years longer, she never added to it, leaving the summary of her final years to Maria Weston Chapman. Fortunately, though Martineau asked friends to burn her letters, not all of them did, and the straightforward, outspoken writer of the autobiography is just as apparent in her correspondence.

Apart from her autobiography, Martineau's most significant works for the modern reader are surely her Playfellow tales, all forerunners of recognizable genres in children's literature: survival tales, in which children are forced to handle disaster without the assistance of adults; historical fiction; tales of other lands; and boys' school stories. Written between the early didactic era and the "golden age" of imaginative literature, Martineau's tales combine lively style, exciting plots, heroic characters, and light didacticism. Though rarely read by children today, these entertaining stories provide an important link in the history of children's literature.

Letters:
Elisabeth Sanders Arbuckle, ed., *Harriet Martineau's Letters to Fanny Wedgewood* (Stanford, Cal.: Stanford University Press, 1983);
Valerie Sanders, ed., *Harriet Martineau: Selected Letters* (Oxford: Clarendon Press, 1990).

Bibliography:
Joseph B. Rivlin, *Harriet Martineau: A Bibliography of Her Separately Printed Books* (New York: New York Public Library, 1947).

Biographies:
F. Fenwick Miller, *Harriet Martineau* (London: Allen, 1884);
Vera Wheatley, *The Life and Work of Harriet Martineau* (London: Secker & Warburg, 1957);
R. K. Webb, *Harriet Martineau: A Radical Victorian* (London: Heinemann, 1960);
Valerie Kossew Pichanick, *Harriet Martineau: The Woman and Her Work, 1802–1876* (Ann Arbor: University of Michigan Press, 1980).

References:
Susan Hoecker-Drysdale, *Harriet Martineau: First Woman Sociologist* (Oxford & New York: Berg, 1992);
Valerie Sanders, *Reason Over Passion: Harriet Martineau and the Victorian Novel* (Sussex: Harvester / New York: St. Martin's Press, 1986);
Gillian Thomas, *Harriet Martineau* (Boston: Twayne, 1985).

Favell Lee Mortimer

(14 July 1802 – 22 August 1878)

Frederick Rankin MacFadden Jr.
Coppin State College

BOOKS: *The Peep of Day; or, A Series of the Earliest Religious Instruction the Infant Mind Is Capable of Receiving,* anonymous (London: Hatchard, 1833; Boston: William Pierce, 1836); revised as *The New Peep of Day* (London & New York: Hodder & Stoughton, 1893);

Reading Disentangled (London: Roake & Varty, 1834);

Line Upon Line; or, A Second Series of the Earliest Religious Instruction the Infant Mind Is Capable of Receiving, anonymous (London: Hatchard, 1837; New York: American Tract Society, 1848);

The Night of Toil, anonymous (London: Hatchard, 1838; Philadelphia: Hooker, 1845);

More about Jesus, anonymous (London: Hatchard, 1839);

The History of Job, in Language Adapted to Children, anonymous (London: Hatchard, 1842);

Precept upon Precept; or, A Third Series of the Earliest Religious Instruction the Infant Mind Is Capable of Receiving, anonymous (London: Hatchard, n.d.; New York: J. S. Taylor, 1843);

Scripture Facts in Simple Language, anonymous, 2 volumes (N.p.: American Tract Society, 1848?);

The Countries of Europe Described, anonymous (London: Hatchard, 1849; Philadelphia: G. S. Appleton, 1850; New York: D. Appleton, 1850); republished as *Near Home; or, The Countries of Europe Described* (New York: R. Carter, 1857); revised as *Near Home; or, The Countries of Europe Described* (London: Hatchard, 1878);

Far Off: Asia and Australia Described, anonymous (London: Hatchard, 1852; New York: R. Carter, 1853); revised edition (London: Hatchard, 1864; revised again, 1875);

Far Off: Africa and America Described, anonymous (London: Hatchard, 1854; New York: R. Carter, 1854); revised (London: Hatchard, 1864; revised again, 1875);

Reading Without Tears; or, A Pleasant Mode of Learning to Read, anonymous, 2 volumes (London: Hatchard, 1857; New York: Harper, 1865);

George Richmond, R.A. del.   Chas H. Jeens. Sculp.

Favell Lee Mortimer

Here a Little and There a Little; or, Scripture Facts, anonymous (Philadelphia: Lippincott, 1861);

Lines Left Out; or, Some of the Histories Left Out in "Line upon Line," anonymous (London: Hatchard, 1862?);

Kings of Israel and Judah; Their History Explained to Children: Being a Continuation of "Lines Left Out," anonymous (London: Hatchard, 1872; New York: R. Carter, 1872); revised by J. E. Hodder Williams (London: Hatchard, 1923);

The Captivity of Judah, anonymous (London: Hatchard, 1876); revised (London: Longmans, 1894).

Favell Lee Mortimer was a tireless best-selling author of biblical, geographical, and reading texts for children. Her grandniece Rosalind Constable stated in a 1950 article that *The Peep of Day* (1833), Mortimer's most notable work, "sold over a million copies in the original edition, and was translated into thirty-eight languages." Near the turn of the twentieth century it was republished with its austere language tempered for modern young readers. Mortimer held to the moralistic trend in children's literature long after the fairy tale was supposed to have emerged triumphant. She inherited the mantle of moral education for children from the previous generation, led by Sarah Trimmer and Mary Sherwood, and it was the evangelistic branch represented by Sherwood to which Mortimer belonged, rather than the established branch of moral narrative found in Trimmer's works. Mortimer's purpose was to write accurately of morals and mores for readers up to age five, using firsthand, as well as documented, accounts from biblical and secular sources. Her vivid anecdotes and direct style won the widespread appreciation of parents and teachers.

Mortimer was born Favell Lee Bevan on 14 July 1802, the second of five daughters born to David and Favell Bourke Bevan. Mortimer's father was a banker with Barclay, Bevan, and Company, later known as Barclay's Bank, Limited. The family was Quaker, but Mortimer at twenty-five converted to Evangelicalism, the party of plain worship with a missionary imperative. This redirection of conscience led Bevan into a literary career perhaps by default. Her marital hopes were crushed when her spiritual protégé, Henry Manning, later cardinal, met a rector's daughter and married her. In 1841 Bevan married Thomas Mortimer, a popular preacher but apparently a cruel husband. After his death in 1850 the widow Mortimer spent the remainder of her life caring for the destitute and writing children's books to help fill the void of children she never had during her brief marriage. In 1827 she had begun reaching out to children through the parish schools she organized on her father's estates and through her books for young children.

Mortimer's writing peaked almost instantly with her most popular work, *The Peep of Day,* written to prepare young children's minds for the reading of the Scriptures. Its alternating design of exposition and interpretation formed the basic structural pattern of all her writing, including her reading, history, and geography texts. Her methodology was intended to provide the necessary sensory foundation upon which the pupil's knowledge of otherworldliness would later build.

Within the expository sections of her books Mortimer would frequently insert a catechistic format that gave an artificial classroom ring to certain passages. In *The Peep of Day,* for example, after the initial discussion of Creation and the child's body and soul as coming from mother and father, Mortimer poses a series of questions: "You have a little body. God has covered your bones with flesh. Your flesh is soft and warm. Will your bones break? Yes, they would, if you were to fall down from a high place, or if a cart were to go over them." In a later passage, she asks if they have seen the body of a sick child and then gives a graphic description: "The baby's flesh was almost gone, and its little bones were only covered with skin. . . . How good God has been to keep you strong and well." This painful moral was surprisingly kept in the 1893 expurgated edition of the book. Mortimer offers the trusting child a shield against the fiery scenes of God's wrath with the protective love of Jesus. This loving counterbalance to the threatening elements of her work always guaranteed a large favorable audience, as evidenced by the many editions of *The Peep of Day.*

Mortimer's central concern to instill a reverential fear of God in the young met some of her expurgator's desires, but it also went further than the taste of the 1890s would allow. On the one hand, the censors found descriptions of bones "only covered with skin" acceptable, but on the other hand, they were offended by a poem warning against such childish misdemeanors as scratching, biting, name-calling, lying, cursing, and swearing. The middle stanza reads:

Satan is glad
When I am bad,
And hopes that I
With him shall lie
In fire and chains
And dreadful pains.

The expurgators were not mollified by Mortimer's statement that her lyrics were meant "to render religious topics as attractive as possible." They winced not only at the picture of ill-behaved children but also at Mortimer's rendering of the Day of Judgment: "One day God will burn up this world we live in," she proclaims, after describing the lake

*Frontispiece for an 1860 revised edition of Mortimer's most
popular work,* The Peep of Day *(1833)*

of fire reserved for the devil and all wicked children.

To retain the marketability of *The New Peep of Day* (1893), the bishop of Durham provided a justification in his introduction: "Many people now advanced in middle life – I am one of them – associate *Peep of Day* with their earliest and tenderest memories. . . . To some, however, who love *The Peep of Day,* it has seemed advisable, on purpose that its usefulness may be the more abiding, to modify it in some detail." Constable relates how her mother recalled with horror the original excoriating edition of *The Peep of Day:* "Hers was not the only night nursery in England where the sleeping child's dreams were turned to nightmares by . . . description[s] of the hell that awaited the child 'who did what God forbid.' "

Mortimer's next work, *Reading Disentangled* (1834), a set of thirty-four enlarged phonics cards with illustrations, was so successful that it reached at least fifteen editions by 1873. In her biography of Mortimer, Louisa Meyer suggests that her aunt originated the use of phonics cards, much copied by other reading instructors. *Reading Without Tears* (1857), a well-known primer, was a reduction of the cards to two diminutive bound volumes, which sold eighty-one thousand copies by 1890. In her preface Mortimer makes some concessions to engaging the interest of the reader by suggesting that "colouring the letters would render them more attractive, and distinguish them better from the pictures. They might be coloured by degrees, as a reward to the little pupil for remembering their names." Constable's few recollections of the contents – "Pat a fat cat" and "I gave a lily to my sister" – suggest that the work was pleasant in tone, but it seemed sadistic to some readers. Like all of Mortimer's books, the sales figures give strong evidence that many generations of readers were affected by the author's tenderness rather than by her morbidity or sadism.

Her analysis of social and antisocial behavior, in combination with her spirit of caregiving, made her work universally translated and admired.

Mortimer's two-volume historical geography text, *Far Off* (1852, 1854), examines Asia, Australia, Africa, and America. Aimed at the early childhood market, the title sold gradually but steadily; in 1900 it reached a cumulative sale of fifty-five thousand copies. Mortimer's rhetorical program of exposition and interpretation was broadened to include history and geography in educating children. Discussion of factual topics for more than twenty peoples and lands includes general geographical features, animals indigenous to the regions, religions, brief histories of ruling families and governments, and slavery, current or past. There is no discoverable spiritualizing or allegorical treatment of animals.

Surprisingly, Mortimer's moral is often merely implied in the book's exposition. There is no preachiness, for example, in the story of the Australian gold digger who returned with a few gold nuggets only to find that his wife was but "a PALE CORPSE!" Mortimer's concluding reference to God as father to the fatherless is more in keeping with the trend of social work and humanitarianism than hard-line fundamentalism. However, throughout the book, without being either frequently or baldly intrusive, Mortimer pursues her main objective – spelled out so many years before in the subtitle of *The Peep of Day* – to offer "the earliest religious instruction the infant mind is capable of receiving."

For the moral anecdotes that illustrate the discursive segments of *Far Off*, Mortimer used accounts published in various missionary books and periodicals, and from these she gleaned several character types, examples of which appear in individual tales. In her culminating story, "The History of Ta-ma-ha-ha," set during the first half of the nineteenth century, a young New Zealand native prince named Rangi-Ka-tu-Kua ("The White Chief Bird of the Heavens"), or Katu for short, is disillusioned when the war gods seem powerless to eat his sacrificial food. Katu begins a quest for the true god. He refuses to participate in the next tribal war and brings a missionary to his village. Katu has become a baptized Christian and takes the name Thomson, or "Tamahaha" in Maori. He becomes the Christian king of his people, but only after his father is imprisoned by the colonists on suspicion of stirring up rebellion. The old king finally converts on his deathbed. Another story of conversion to Christianity is "The History of Little Jejana," in which a racist white South African woman, motivated by prejudice, impedes the religious instruction of Jejana, her

Hottentot servant. Mortimer defends the Boers in general and provides Jejana with a ministerial mentor and with a good Christian family as employers.

Far Off presents an interesting variety of behavioral choices, ranging through ethical, moral, and transformational actions. Besides the characters considered above, there is the eponymous protagonist of "Little Mickey," an Australian aborigine boy who learns the meaning of forgiveness when he realizes that he is forgiven after stealing food from his employer. In "The Young Savages" Wylie, also an Australian aborigine, proves loyal to an explorer rather than to two boys who have murdered and stolen. He fails the test of generosity, however, when he keeps his catches of game for himself. Wylie serves as an example not only of the Christian who is faithful to God but also, by implication, of the carnal Christian.

"The History of Zamba" is the best of the many vivid slave narratives in *Far Off*. Zamba, the noble, after marrying rather than enslaving the captive princess Zillah, is himself sold as a slave in Charleston, South Carolina, after being duped by the wily Captain Winton. Zamba is sold to a kindly tradesman, is freed, and then is reunited with Zillah. He becomes a storekeeper, embodying the middle-class Christian conscience that has been awakened in him in Charleston churches. He is ever aware of the much poorer plight of most of his enslaved black brethren. He is truly ready, Mortimer implies, for the social gospel of intercession, proving that "faith without works is dead."

Mortimer was not averse to providing graphic descriptions of bloody and violent scenes, as in *Here a Little and There a Little; or, Scripture Facts* (1861), a collection of Bible stories for children. "The First Murder" describes the death of Abel at the hands of his brother, Cain, while "Christ in the Garden" states that "the Son of God was in such great sorrow and trouble, that the blood came through his skin while he prayed, and it fell on the ground in great drops." The majority of the stories are more beatific, however, and "The Heavenly Babe and Its Mother," "Christ Shining on the Mountain," and "Christ Going up to Heaven" help alleviate any impression of sadism in the collection.

Strengthened by her benign stoicism, Mortimer continued to write and teach the orphans she had taken in, despite being afflicted in her late years with pulmonary and neurological disorders. In 1877 she laboriously composed her questions for an edition of the book of Kings, to the very end practicing her craft as the faithful servant of her pedagogy. Death came to her on 22 August 1878.

There can be no better testimony to the universal value of Mortimer's publications than the worldwide array of translations of her work, especially *The Peep of Day*. From 1863 to 1901, according to Meyer's biography, the Religious Tract Society published thirty-five translations of *The Peep of Day* in the diverse languages of Africa, Asia, Europe, and the Americas. Between 1887 and 1916 the translations of *Line upon Line* (1837) and *Precept upon Precept* appeared in Secwana, as did an Afrikaans translation of *Reading Without Tears*. Around the world, then, several generations of parents, teachers, and children were the beneficiaries of Mortimer's vivid, direct style and fetching narratives.

Mortimer's work still has relevance in at least one area, that of English as a second language. In 1867 Mortimer wrote, "*The Quarterly* has made me look foolish, but I always knew that the language of the nursery must appear ridiculous to the learned." She pointed out that the New Testament had been translated into pidgin, implying the value of a highly simplified vocabulary for introductory Bible teaching in the English language. Meyer cites the opinion of Rev. James Gilmour of Peking's Lower Mission that even for an oriental scholar far above his countrymen in knowledge, the ethnic allusions and involved epithets of the Bible should be prefaced by a reading of *The Peep of Day*. Mortimer was a precursor of the basic English movement, which after World War I produced such systems as C. K. Ogden's BASIC (British American Scientific International Commercial) English, Janet Aiken's system, and Dr. Michael West's fourteen-hundred-word system. Finally, while Mortimer's writings are too moralistic for today's tastes, she deserves a place in histories of children's literature. As Percy Muir writes of *The Peep of Day, Line Upon Line,* and *Reading Without Tears,* "Although these are strictly instructional in nature, their multitudinous reprintings demand their inclusion."

Biography:
Louisa C. Meyer, *The Author of 'The Peep of Day': Being the Life Story of Mrs. Mortimer, by her Niece Mrs. Meyer, with an Introduction by the Reverend F. B. Meyer, B.A.* (London: Religious Tract Society, 1901).

References:
Gillian Avery, *Nineteenth Century Children: Heroes and Heroines in English Children's Stories 1780–1900* (London: Hodder & Stoughton, 1965), p. 121;

Rosalind Constable, Letter to the Editor, *New Yorker* (4 March 1950): 79–83;

Percy Muir, *English Children's Books, 1600 to 1900* (New York: Praeger, 1954), pp. 123–124.

Francis Edward Paget

(24 May 1806 – 4 August 1882)

Jan Susina
Illinois State University

BOOKS: *Caleb Kniveton, the Incendiary* (Oxford: W. Baxter, 1833);

St. Antholin's; or Old Churches and New. A Tale for the Times (London: James Burns, 1841);

Tales of the Village, 3 volumes (London: James Burns, 1841; New York: Appleton, 1844);

Milford Malvoisin; or, Pews and Pewholders (Oxford: James Burns, 1842);

A Tract Upon Tomb-stones; or, Suggestions for the Consideration of Persons Intending to Set Up the Kind of Monument of the Memory of Deceased Friends (Rugeley: Joseph Masters, 1843);

The Warden of Berkingholt; or, Rich and Poor (Oxford: J. H. Parker, 1843);

The Pageant; or, Pleasure and Its Price, A Tale for the Upper Ranks of Society (London: James Burns, 1843);

Tales of the Village Children, First Series (London: Joseph Masters, 1844; New York: Appleton, 1844);

The Hope of the Katzekopfs. A Fairy Tale, as William Churne of Staffordshire (Rugeley: John Thomas Walter / London: James Burns, 1844); republished as *The Hope of the Katzekopfs; or, The Sorrows of Selfishness,* as Paget (London: Joseph Masters, 1845); revised as *The Self-Willed Prince; or The Hope of the Katzekopfs* (London: Wells, Gardner, Darton, 1916);

Sermons on Duties of Daily Life (Rugeley: John Thomas Walters, 1844; New York: J. A. Sparks, 1844);

The Christian Day (London: James Burns, 1845);

Tales of the Village Children, Second Series (London: Joseph Masters, 1845; New York: Appleton, 1845);

Room For All (London: Edwards & Hughes, 1845);

Luke Sharp; or, Knowledge Without Religion. A Tale of Modern Education (London: Joseph Masters, 1845; New York: General Protestant Episcopal Sunday School Union, 1846);

Sursum Corda: Aids to Private Devotion. Being A Body of Prayers Collected From the Writings of English Churchmen (London: Joseph Masters, 1847);

Sermons for the Saints' Days (London: Joseph Masters, 1848);

Prayers in Behalf of the Church and Her Children in Times of Trouble (London: Joseph Walters, 1850);

Daily Prayers for Labouring Lads (London: Joseph Masters, 1851);

Psalms, Hymns, Anthems, and Introits (Lichfield: Thomas George Lomax, 1853);

The Owlet of Owlstone Edge: His Travels, His Experience, and His Lucubrations (London: Joseph Masters, 1856);

Hobson's Choice: A Tale of a Journal (London: Parker, 1856);

Sermons for Special Occasions (London: Joseph Masters, 1858);

The Curate of Cumberworth and the Vicar of Roost (London: Joseph Masters, 1859);

Daily Prayers for Young Women, Who Have Been Taught in Church Schools (London: Joseph Masters, 1859);

Lucretia; or The Heroine of the Nineteenth Century. A Correspondence, Sensational and Sentimental (London: Joseph Masters, 1868);

Some Account of Elford Church: Its Decay, and Its Restorations, in Ancient and Recent Times (Lichfield: Thomas George Masters, 1870);

Some Records of the Ashtead Estate, and Its Howard Possessors with Notices of Elford, Castle Rising, Levens, and Charlton (Lichfield: A. C. Lomax, 1873);

Helps and Hindrances to the Christian Life. Plain Village Sermons for a Year, 2 volumes (London: Skeffington, 1874);

A Student Penitent of 1695 (London: Joseph Masters, 1875);

Faith and Patience, in Work and Warfare, Triumph and Reward; A Course of Daily Instruction on Hebrews XI and XII (London: Skeffington, 1875);

Tales for Young Men and Women, 2 volumes (Oxford: J. H. Parker, 1877);

Homeward Bound: The Voyage and the Voyagers, the Pilot and the Port (London: Joseph Masters, 1876).

OTHER: *The Juvenile Englishman's Library,* 21 volumes, edited by Paget and J. F. Russell (Cambridge: John Thomas Walters, 1844–1849).

Francis Edward Paget is best known as one of the writers of Tractarian fiction, those children's and adult texts produced by members of the Oxford Movement that were intended to illustrate the doctrines of the Anglican High Church. Paget and William Gresley wrote novels during the 1830s and 1840s that were little more than thinly coated religious tracts against the perceived dangers of the growing secularization of the Church of England. Paget did not view himself primarily as a novelist, but as a minister using fictional polemics as a way to promote his religious beliefs; he alternated novels with the publication of sermon and prayer collections. With the novels of Paget and Gresley the High Church tradition of theological fiction became differentiated from its Evangelical counterpart. While Paget's writing is vastly superior to that of Gresley, his early Tractarian texts for children are marred by similar faults of heavy didacticism and poor characterization; they remain, however, an influential bridge to the later work of the most prolific and most skillful of the Tractarian novelists, Charlotte Yonge.

While Paget's religious novels are rarely read today, they established the foundations for a genre that was to be developed more successfully by Yonge and Elizabeth Sewell. In a similar fashion, his best children's book, *The Hope of the Katzekopfs. A Fairy Tale* (1844), which Roger Lancelyn Green has called "the first real fairy story of its kind, written in English," is an important predecessor to the later English literary fairy tales, and it influenced the production of William Makepeace Thackeray's *The Rose and the Ring* (1854), Andrew Lang's *Prince Prigio* (1889), and Rudyard Kipling's *Rewards and Fairies* (1910). Paget's work as the editor of the twenty-one volumes of *The Juvenile Englishman's Library* (1844–1849) did much to improve the climate for the reception of literary fairy tales as appropriate reading material for Victorian children.

Paget was the eldest son of the soldier Sir Edward Paget. He was educated at Westminster School and Christ Church, Oxford, where he took a B.A. in 1828 and an M.A. in 1830 and held a studentship until 1835. He attended Oxford University during the critical period of the Oxford Movement and was an active participant in the reforms of the Church of England. Appointed rector of Elford in 1835, Paget remained there the rest of his life, marrying Fanny Chester, the daughter of a clergyman, in 1840.

His first novel, *Caleb Kniveton, the Incendiary* (1833), traces the actions of the protagonist, who sets fire to a rick yard in revenge. His wife and child die in the fire, however, and Caleb ends his days as the village idiot. Besides being a lurid warning against what Paget calls "the fearful depravity of a revengeful spirit," the novel functions as a powerful critique of the social upheaval and consequences of industrialization, suggesting that the lack of religious faith in the working classes leads directly to personal and community chaos, a theme to which he would in his children's novel *Luke Sharp; or, Knowledge Without Religion* (1845).

His second novel, *St. Antholin's; or, Old Churches and New* (1841), promotes the Tractarian concern for careful restoration of Anglican churches and the dangers of cheap modern church architecture. Paget supervised the restoration of his beloved church in Elford in 1848, and restoration of churches became a recurring theme in much of his fiction. Mr. Ouzel, the church warden for twenty-five years at St. Antholin's, has satisfied his congregation by spending little on building repairs, despite the archdeacon's warnings. After Ouzel's death a storm destroys the decaying structure, and the new rector does not appropriate sufficient funds for a properly constructed new building. Mr. Campo, the architect, designs a cheap modern church that quickly burns when the new stove fails. Fortunately, a benefactress provides sufficient funds to rebuild after the second disaster — with the condition that there be no pews.

The early Tractarians' distaste for pews is the central focus of *Milford Malvoisin; or, Pews and Pewholders* (1842). Paget warns in the novel's preface that "Pews are a never-ending, still beginning subject of animosity and ill-will" in that they are the cause of "making worldly distinctions between rich and poor." The desire for elaborate, high-walled pews, to which Paget refers contemptuously as "Pew Fever," had become frequent in wealthy Anglican churches. These pews resembled separate rooms and were frequently furnished with sofas, chairs, tables, and occasionally a fireplace, while the poor were relegated to wooden benches. Paget contrasts the institution of a pew system under Rector Kirkscrew with the healthy restoration of the church under the new curate, Mr. Till. The novel favors doing away with "the great unsightly packing-boxes which at present deform our Churches" and reflect

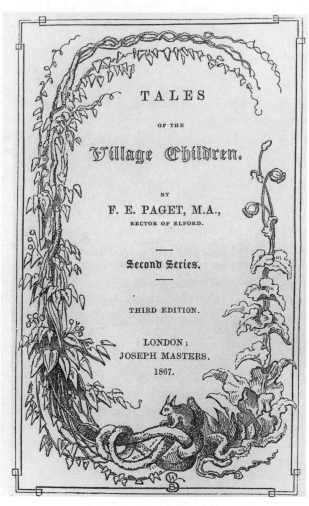

Title page for an early edition of Paget's popular moral tales (courtesy of the Lilly Library, Indiana University)

lains, he would later use this ploy in *Lucretia; or The Heroine of the Nineteenth Century* (1868), his satire on the sensational novel. In the preface to *The Warden of Berkingholt* Paget warns his High Church readers that they need to reconsider their responsibilities to the poor and working classes, noting that "If the country is to be saved at all . . . It will, under God, be saved by the Church's influence." The novel contrasts the hard-hearted utilitarian theories of Mr. Livingstone with the charity of the church under the direction of Warden Clinton and parishioners such as Aunt Amie. Paget insists that it is the Anglo-Catholic faith rather than Protestantism, socialism, or acts of Parliament that can reform England.

Despite the moral tone of his novels, Paget is a vivid writer and is capable of writing clever satire. He satirizes the excesses of Evangelical preachers in the figure of Rev. Lothario Swainham, who is so popular with his female parishioners that he has received forty-nine proposals and 753 pairs of embroidered slippers in a single year. Paget even ridicules the Tractarians and their habit of making themselves appear different and superior, as with the fashion of "wearing not crosses only, but crucifixes, as conspicuous as possible."

Paget returns to the theme of contrast between rich and poor in *The Pageant; or, Pleasure and Its Price, A Tale for the Upper Ranks of Society* (1843). Gertrude and Augusta, two sisters of the wealthy Blonderville family, prepare for an elaborate costume ball, but in the course of the novel they discover the appalling working conditions of their dressmakers. Paget makes explicit that upper-class indifference to the suffering of the working class is sinful, and his novel, similar to John Ruskin's *Unto This Last* (1862), is intended to alert readers to the exploitation of the urban working class.

In 1844 Paget began editing *The Juvenile Englishman's Library* for the publishing firm of Joseph Masters. The series comprises twenty-one volumes, which in the words of F. J. Harvey Darton were "designed to amuse and instruct, and at the same time adhere to sound Church of England doctrine." Besides providing religious instruction for youth, usually in the form of moral tales, *The Juvenile Englishman's Library* made traditional fairy tales available to children. Like the Henry Cole's Home Treasury series initiated in 1843, *The Juvenile Englishman's Library* was intended to provide children with imaginative literature and thus counteract what Paget felt was the exclusive focus on "useful" information found in a series of novels by Samuel Griswold Goodrich, writing under the pseudonym

"perverted taste, perverted feeling, and perverted principles." The novel's only illustrations reinforce the contrast, showing "Churches as they are" and "Churches as they were, and as they will be" — the latter being free of the detested pews and balconies. Paget argues that the pews of the wealthy minority have driven the poor from churches, a situation that will have the ultimate consequence of rendering cities "lawless and unmanageable."

In *The Warden of Berkingholt; or, Rich and Poor* (1843) Paget again addresses the social condition of England, offering the construction of more Anglican churches as the solution to class conflict. Joseph Ellis Baker has suggested that with Paget's combination of a crime story and a minor love story *The Warden of Berkingholt* marks "the crude beginnings of the true novel of the Oxford Movement." Although Paget uses his text to warn against writers of popular fiction who make heroes out of thieves and vil-

Peter Parley (beginning with *The Tales of Peter Parley,* 1827), and those publications it inspired.

The first title in *The Juvenile Englishman's Library* was Paget's *Tales of the Village Children, First Series* (1844), a popular three-volume collection of moral tales set in the village of Yateshull. In a series of interconnecting short stories, Paget examines the moral growth of a group of young boys. Under the guidance of Vicar Warlingham and the schoolmaster, Mr. Dilwyn, five boys discover valuable social and religious lessons through a series of adventures. Typical of the tales is "Singers," in which the boys sneak into the church belfry to hunt jackdaw eggs but are inadvertently locked in the tower and discover that they have been treating the church with less than proper reverence. In "The Wake" some boys decide to skip school to attend a local festival. Subsequently, they are involved in a serious cart accident with one boy fracturing his skull and never speaking again and the other becoming a "helpless cripple" destined to spend the rest of his life in a workhouse.

A second series of *Tales of the Village Children* (1845) also appeared in *The Juvenile Englishman's Library* and continued the characters' adventures and lessons, although the second series was intended for readers "a year or two older than those for whom the first series was written." Morality determines the action in these stories, as in "The April Fool," in which Frederick Sutton learns the folly of April Fool's pranks. Frederick is encouraged in his actions by his mother, who does not hesitate to tell white lies. In Paget's fiction, character flaws in children are usually the result of poor parenting, an issue he would later address in both *The Hope of the Katzekopfs* and *Luke Sharp.* Paget notes that the harm in carrying out an April Fool's prank is that "some deceit is employed," and Frederick learns that "there is no difference between a lie told to hide a fault, or to gain an end, and one which is spoke in jest, with no worse purpose than that of raising a laugh." Frederick's prank backfires, and he learns his moral lesson.

The second title in *The Juvenile Englishman's Library* was Paget's *The Hope of the Katzekopfs,* which appeared under the pseudonym William Churne of Staffordshire; the name was that of the registrar-general to the fairies in Richard Corbert's poem "The Fairies' Farewell" (1648). Paget's literary fairy tale, illustrated by William Bell Scott, was a success, and in 1845 a second edition was published as by Paget and with the obviously moral subtitle, *The Sorrows of Selfishness.* In the preface to the second edition Paget makes explicit his didactic intent behind writing the fairy tale: "It was an attempt under the guise of a Fairy-tale to lead young minds to a more wholesome train of thought than is commonly found at the present day in popular juvenile literature."

The story deals with the moral education of the spoiled Prince Eigenwillig, the only son of King Katzekopf and Queen Ninnilinda. Despite the Teutonic-sounding names of the characters, Paget patterned his fairy tale in the manner of French examples of the genre. Paget was the first English author to follow in this style, later used in Thackeray's *The Rose and the Ring,* Charles Dickens's *The Magic Fishbone* (1868), Tom Hood's *Petsetilla's Posy* (1870), Dinah Craik's *The Little Lame Prince* (1875), and Lang's *Prince Prigio* and *Prince Ricardo* (1893). While Paget borrowed from the French fairy court tradition, he developed an original tone by using humor to make the aristocracy look foolish. His antiaristocratic attitude, evident in his adult fiction, reappears in the superficial values of the upper classes that have corrupting influence on children, even in Fairyland.

The powerful fairy, Lady Abracadabra, is excluded from the royal christening but appears and insists on naming the child Eigenwillig. The king and queen reluctantly agree, as Abracadabra warns them of the dangers of spoiling their child. The first half of the tale centers on the parents and their failure to discipline their child, which results in Eigenwillig's removal to Fairyland for seven years under the supervision of Lady Abracadabra. The second half deals with Eigenwillig's attempts to acquire self-discipline. To counteract the indulgent environment of the court, Lady Abracadabra brings the poor but disciplined Witikind to court to become the prince's companion. *The Hope of the Katzekopfs* is a reworking of Thomas Day's *Sandford and Merton* (1783) in the form of a fairy tale, with Lady Abracadabra playing the role of Day's mentor, Reverend Barlow, but with a sense of humor that helps to deflate some of Paget's didacticism.

Transported to Fairyland, Eigenwillig learns that hard work, merit, and talent dictate rewards, not rank or birth. His greatest test is represented in an allegorical manner – he selects a tiny sprite named Selbst ("self") as a companion rather than a grave old gentleman. Eigenwillig is required to carry Selbst on his back, and the sprite becomes larger, heavier, and more unmanageable and ultimately threatens to destroy the boy if he does not conform to his will. It is only in a life-and-death struggle with Selbst that Eigenwillig ("self-willed") is forced to seek the help of the old gentleman, who later reveals himself to be Discipline. Paget's seriousness of purpose overshadows the entertainment value of the latter part of the fairy tale, and the humor and lively characters of the first two-thirds of the text are noticeably absent. The text argues that children are easily corrupted by poor parenting and stresses that happiness is to be found through work and self-reliance and the values of family and home.

The tale was popular enough to go through five editions. In *Aunt Judy's Magazine* Margaret Gatty praised it as "a charming story [that] ought to be much more widely known than it is. We cannot recommend it too highly to those who have not already made friends with it." In *What Books to Lend and What to Give* (1887) Charlotte Yonge proclaimed that it "Deserves to be classical for its fun and its moral." In his autobiography, *Something of Myself* (1937), Kipling recalls eagerly reading the book as a boy. Green has noted that the importance of *The Hope of the Katzekopfs* is "its influence, direct or oblique, on such greater writers" of literary fairy tales as Thackeray, Kipling, and Lang. Paget's fairy tale became the basis for *Eigenwillig, the Self-Willed,* a dramatic extravaganza that appeared in 1870, and a simplified version of the story titled *The Self-Willed Prince* (1916).

Luke Sharp, another title in *The Juvenile Englishman's Library,* was intended "for lads who are just leaving, or have lately left school, and who, on going out to service, or learn a trade, are sure to be exposed to the manifold trials and temptations which the Devil, the world, and the flesh put in the way of youth." Jeremiah Sharp wishes to have his clever son educated in the new method of education and sends him to the manufacturing town of Birsley, rather than having him educated by Mr. Dilwyn in the village of Yateshull, the setting of *Tales of the Village Children.* Luke is taught by Mr. Hampden under the new system of "educating children without religion," which leads to Luke's downfall. When Mr. Sharp's fortune disappears because of speculation, Luke must seek employment with his uncle, Mr. Atkins, a grocer. Although he is a clever boy, Luke lacks conduct and character and is easily led astray by Barney Ford, a dishonest shop man. Tempted into dishonesty, Luke is removed from his uncle's establishment. He descends the economic ladder, becomes involved with the Chartists, and finishes his life deported and dying in Convicts' Hospital. It is only on his deathbed that he realizes that "*knowledge without religion* is POISON and DEATH."

As an established writer and editor of children's books, Paget used the prefaces of his books to disseminate his surprisingly progressive views on writing for children. His introduction to the first edition of *The Hope of the Katzekopfs* is an early and important call for the reintroduction of the fairy tale as children's reading. In the preface to the *Tales of the Village Children, First Series,* Paget lists two faults that "run through the whole mass of children's books: they are written in a style above the capacity, or in language above the rank of those to whom they are addressed; or else represent children with virtues and vices beyond their years." These criticisms, however, could be leveled against the priggish and articulate characters of *Tales of the Village Children,* despite Paget's insistence that they are "neither wholly good, nor wholly bad – often very wild and thoughtless."

In the preface to *Tales of the Village Children, Second Series,* Paget objects to the notion of "writing down to the intellects of children," which he considers a "very absurd and mischievous process" that is "wholly unnecessary." He stresses that children's writers should adopt the language of childhood in their books and suggests that if a writer's language is clear and simple and the vocabulary is within a child's grasp, then it is not difficult to lead children to understand things frequently considered above them. Paget is thus an early voice against condescension in children's literature, observing, "Children are as capable of understanding deep things as adults; in some respects, more so," reminding his reader that a child is to be distinguished from an adult "less by an *inferiority* than by a *difference* in capacity."

Despite his progressive theories concerning children's literature, Paget's children's books are overburdened by his constant use of fiction as a medium to promote the religious beliefs of the Anglo-Catholic church. An anonymously published essay in *Fraser's Magazine* titled "Religious Stories" (1848) characterizes this chief flaw of Paget's fiction as "Writing hastily, writing for a party, and being sure of a certain measure of applause and circulation, secured for him by his opinions independently of any literary merit, he was tempted to disregard those qualities which would have given his stories a value as works of art."

While his overt use of didacticism and the uneven literary quality of his fiction would place him in the second rank of nineteenth-century children's writers, Paget remains historically significant to the field. His importance to children's literature is twofold: as the editor of *The Juvenile Englishman's Library,* the influential children's series that helped reintroduce more imaginative literature in general and fairy tales in particular to children's writing in the first half of the nineteenth century; and as a children's author of Tractarian fiction. His most significant children's texts, *The Hope of the Katzekopfs, Tales of the Village Children,* and *Luke Sharp,* were all published as volumes in his children's series. *The Hope of the Katzekopfs* especially, with its combination of didacticism from the moral tale and an imaginative use of characters, setting, and humor from the fairy tale, proved to be a powerful model for many writers of later Victorian literary fairy tales for children.

References:

Gillian Avery and Angel Bull, *Nineteenth-Century Children* (London: Hodder & Stoughton, 1965);

Joseph Ellis Baker, *The Novel and the Oxford Movement* (Princeton: Princeton University Press, 1932), pp. 9–22;

F. J. Harvey Darton, *Children's Books in England,* third edition (Cambridge: Cambridge University Press, 1982), pp. 262–263;

Roger Lancelyn Green, "Hope of the Katzekopfs," *Notes and Queries,* new series 11 (25 March 1944): 152–153;

Green, *Tellers of Tales* (London: Edmund Ward, 1946), pp. 24–26;

Margaret M. Maison, *The Victorian Vision: Studies in the Religious Novel* (New York: Sheed & Ward, 1961), pp. 11–30;

Patrick Scott, "Victorian Didacticism and Family Structure: Francis Paget's *The Pageant,* an Early Young Adult Novel," in *The Child and the Family: Selected Papers From the 1988 International Conference of the Children's Literature Association,* edited by Susan R. Gannon and Ruth Anne Thompson (New York: Pace University, 1989), pp. 34–38;

Judith St. John, Preface to *The Hope of the Katzekopfs,* by Paget (New York: Johnson Reprint Corporation, 1968);

Robert Lee Wolff, *Gains and Losses: Novels of Faith and Doubt in Victorian England* (New York: Garland, 1977), pp. 114–116.

Mayne Reid

(4 April 1818 – 22 October 1883)

Peter D. Sieruta
Wayne State University

See also the Reid entry in *DLB 21: Victorian Novelists Before 1885.*

BOOKS: *Love's Martyr: A Tragedy* (Philadelphia: Printed for the author, 1849);

War Life; or, The Adventures of a Light Infantry Officer (New York: Townsend, 1849); republished as *The Rifle Rangers; or, Adventures of an Officer in Southern Mexico*, 2 volumes (London: Shoberl, 1850; New York: DeWitt, 1855);

The Scalp Hunters; or, Romantic Adventures in Northern Mexico, 3 volumes (London: Skeet, 1851; Philadelphia: Lippincott, Grambo, 1851);

The Desert Home; or, The Adventures of a Lost Family in the Wilderness (London: Bogue, 1852; Boston: Ticknor & Fields, 1864);

The Boy Hunters; or, Adventures in Search of a White Buffalo (London: Bogue, 1853; Boston: Ticknor, 1854);

The Young Voyageurs; or, The Boy Hunters in the North (London: Bogue, 1854; Boston: Ticknor & Fields, 1857);

The Forest Exiles; or, The Perils of a Peruvian Family (London: Bogue, 1854; Boston: Ticknor & Fields, 1855);

The Bush Boys; or, The History and Adventures of a Cape Farmer and His Family in the Wild Karoos of Southern Africa (London: Bogue, 1855; Boston: Ticknor & Fields, 1856);

The Young Yagers; or, A Narrative of Hunting Adventures in Southern Africa (London: Bogue, 1856; Boston: Ticknor & Fields, 1857);

The Hunters' Feast; or, Conversations around the Camp-Fire (New York: DeWitt & Davenport, 1856);

The Quadroon; or, A Lover's Adventures in Louisiana, 3 volumes (London: Hyde, 1856; New York: DeWitt, 1856); republished as *Love's Vengeance* (New York: Carleton, 1880);

The Plant Hunters; or, Adventures among the Himalaya Mountains (London: Ward & Lock, 1857; Boston: Ticknor & Fields, 1858);

Mayne Reid

The War Trail; or, The Hunt of the Wild Horse (New York: DeWitt, 1858; London: Routledge, 1860);

Ran Away to Sea: An Autobiography for Boys (London: Brown, 1858; Boston: Ticknor & Fields, 1858);

The Boy Tar; or, A Voyage in the Dark (London: W. Kent, 1859; Boston: Ticknor & Fields, 1859);

Wild Life; or, Adventures on the Frontier, as Charles Beach (New York: DeWitt, 1859; London: Bentley, 1873);

Oceola, 3 volumes (London: Hurst & Blackett, 1859); republished as *Osceola, the Seminole; or The Red Fawn of the Flower Land* (New York: Carleton, 1875); republished as *The Half-Blood* (London: Chapman & Hall, 1861);

Odd People: Being a Popular Description of Singular Races of Man (London: Routledge, 1860); republished as *The Man-Eaters and Other Odd People* (New York: Miller, 1860);

The Wood Rangers; or, The Trappers of Sonora, 3 volumes (London: Hurst & Blackett; 1860; New York: DeWitt, 1860);

Bruin; or, The Great Bear Hunt (London: Routledge, 1861; Boston: Ticknor & Fields, 1861);

Despard the Sportsman (London: Lea, 1861);

A Hero in Spite of Himself, 3 volumes (London: Hurst & Blackett, 1861); republished as *The Tiger-Hunter* (London: Clarke, 1862; New York: De-Witt, 1865);

The Wild Huntress; or, Love in the Wilderness, 3 volumes (London: R. Bentley, 1861; New York: DeWitt, 1862); republished as *Wild Huntress; or, The Big Squatter's Vengeance* (New York: Beadle & Adams, 1882);

The Maroon; or, Planter Life in Jamaica, 3 volumes (London: Hurst & Blackett, 1862; New York: DeWitt, 1864);

Andrew Deverel: The History of an Adventurer in New Guinea, 2 volumes, as Charles Beach (London: Bentley, 1863);

Croquet (London: Skeet, 1864);

Lost Lenore; or, The Adventures of a Rolling Stone, 3 volumes, as Charles Beach (London: Skeet, 1864; New York: Carleton, 1872);

The Cliff Climbers; or, The Lone Home in the Himalayas (London: Ward & Lock, 1864; Boston: Ticknor & Fields, 1864);

The Ocean Waifs: A Story of Adventure on Land and Sea (London: D. Bryce, 1864; Boston: Ticknor & Fields, 1864);

The White Gauntlet: A Romance, 3 volumes (London: Skeet, 1864; New York: Carleton, 1868);

Left to the World, 3 volumes, as Charles Beach (London: Maxwell, 1865);

The Boy Slaves (London: C. H. Clarke, 1865; Boston: Ticknor & Fields, 1865);

The Headless Horseman: A Strange Tale of Texas, 2 volumes (volume 1, London: Chapman & Hall, 1865; volume 2, London: Bentley, 1865; New York: DeWitt, 1867);

Afloat in the Forest; or, A Voyage among the Tree-Tops (Boston: Ticknor & Fields, 1866);

The Giraffe Hunters, 3 volumes (Boston: Ticknor & Fields, 1866; London: Hurst & Blackett, 1867);

The Bandolero; or, A Marriage among the Mountains (London: Bentley, 1866); republished as *The Mountain Marriage* (Glasgow: Grand Colosseum Warehouse, n.d.);

The Guerilla Chief and Other Tales (London: Darton, 1867);

Quadrupeds: What They Are and Where Found (London: T. Nelson, 1867);

Now or Never: The Trials and Perilous Adventures of Frederick Lonsdale, as Charles Beach (London: Virtue, 1868);

The Child Wife: A Tale of the Two Worlds (London: Ward & Lock, 1868; New York: Sheldon, 1869);

The Rival Captains (New York: Munro, 1868);

White Squaw (New York: Beadle & Adams, 1868); republished, with *Yellow Chief,* as *The White Squaw and the Yellow Chief* (London: Clarke, 1871); republished as *Blue Dick; or The Yellow Chief's Vengeance* (New York: Beadle & Adams, 1879);

The Helpless Hand; or, Backwoods Retribution (New York: Beadle & Adams, 1868); republished as *The Fatal Cord: A Tale of Backwoods Retribution* (London: C. Brown, 1869);

The Planter Pirate: A Souvenir of the Mississippi (New York: Beadle & Adams, 1868); republished as *The Land Pirates; or, The League of Devil's Island* (New York: Beadle & Adams, 1879);

The Creole Forger: A Tale of the Cresent City (New York: Munro, 1868);

Yellow Chief (New York: Beadle & Adams, 1869); republished, with *White Squaw,* as *The White Squaw and the Yellow Chief* (London: Clarke, 1871); republished as *Blue Dick; or The Yellow Chief's Vengeance* (New York: Beadle & Adams, 1879);

The Way to Win: A Story of Adventure Afloat and Ashore, as Charles Beach (London: Lockwood, 1869);

The Castaways: A Story of Adventure in the Wilds of Borneo (London: T. Nelson, 1870; New York: Sheldon, 1870);

Popular Adventure Stories (London: Simpkin, Marshall, Hamilton, Kent, 1870);

The Rangers and Regulators of the Tanaha; or, Life among the Lawless: A Tale of the Republic of Texas (New York: Carleton, 1870; London: S. Low, 1870);

The Lone Ranche: A Tale of the 'Staked Plain', 2 volumes (London: Chapman & Hall, 1871; New York: Carleton, 1884);

The Finger of Fate: A Romance, 2 volumes (London: Chapman & Hall, 1872; New York: Munro, 1885); revised as *The Star of Empire: A Romance* (London: Maxwell, 1888);

The Cuban Patriot; or, The Beautiful Creole (New York: Beadle & Adams, 1873);

The Death Shot: A Romance of Forest and Prairie, 3 volumes (London: Chapman & Hall, 1873); republished as *The Death Shot: A Story Retold* (London: Ward, Lock & Tyler, 1874);

Pitzmaroon; or, The Magic Hammer, as Charles Beach (Springfield, Mass.: Whitney & Adams, 1874);

The Island Pirate: A Tale of the Mississippi (New York: Beadle & Adams, 1874);

The Flag of Distress: A Tale of the South Sea, 3 volumes (London: Tinsley, 1876); abridged and republished as *The Specter Barque: A Tale of the Pacific* (New York: Beadle & Adams, 1879);

Gwen Wynn: A Romance of the Wye, 3 volumes (London: Tinsley, 1877);

The Wild-Horse Hunters, by Reid and Frederick Whittaker (New York: Beadle & Adams, 1877);

Waifs of the World; or, Adventures Afloat and Ashore, as Charles Beach (London: Warne, 1878); republished as *Too Good for Anything* (London: Warne, n.d.);

Gaspar the Gaucho: A Tale of the Gran Chaco (London: Routledge, 1879);

The Captain of the Rifles; or, The Queen of the Lakes (New York: Beadle & Adams, 1879); republished as *The Queen of the Lakes: A Romance of the Mexican Valley* (London: Mullan, 1880);

The Free Lances: A Romance of the Mexican Valley, 3 volumes (London: Remington, 1881); revised and expanded as *Cris Rock; or, A Lover in Chains* (New York: Bonner, 1889);

The Ocean Hunters; or, The Chase of Leviathan (New York: Beadle & Adams, 1881); republished as *The Chase of Leviathan; or, Adventures in the Ocean* (London: Routledge, 1885);

The Gold Seeker's Guide; or, The Lost Mountain (New York: Beadle & Adams, 1882); republished as *The Lost Mountain: A Tale of Sonora* (London: Routledge, 1885);

The Land of Fire: A Tale of Adventure (London: Warne, 1884);

The Vee-Boers: A Tale of Adventure in Southern Africa (London: Routledge, 1885);

The Pierced Heart and Other Stories (London: Maxwell, 1885);

The Black Mustanger, by Reid and Whittaker (New York: Beadle & Adams, 1885);

No Quarter!, 3 volumes (London: Sonnenschein, 1888; New York: Hurst, 1888);

The Naturalist in Siluria (London: Sonnenschein, 1889; Philadelphia: Gebbie, 1890);

Popular Adventure Tales (London: Simpkin, 1890);

Stories of Strange Adventures, by Reid and others (New York: J. Miller, n.d.);

Trapped in a Tree and Other Stories (London: Miles, n.d.).

PLAY PRODUCTIONS: *Love's Martyr,* Philadelphia, Walnut Street Theater, 23 October 1848;

The Maroon, London, Royal Victoria Theater, 1 April 1865.

OTHER: "Toast to the Army and Navy," in *American Thanksgiving Dinner* (London: Ridgeway, 1863), pp. 69–84;

"A Flying Visit to Florida," in *Illustrated Travels: A Record of Discovery, Geography, and Adventure,* volume 4, edited by Henry Walter Bates (London: Cassell, 1872), pp. 72–78;

"A Zigzag Journey through Mexico," in *Wonderful Adventures: A Series of Narratives of Personal Experiences Among Native Tribes of America* (London: Cassell, 1872), pp. 215–313;

Frederick Whittaker, *The Cadet Button: A Romance of American Army Life,* edited by Reid (New York: Sheldon, 1878).

Thomas Mayne Reid, who published most of his works as "Captain Mayne Reid," was one of the most prolific and well-known authors of the Victorian Era. Although he wrote both adult and juvenile books, Reid would eventually regret the years he spent writing for children, claiming that his efforts in the field prevented him from achieving major critical acclaim. It is pointless to differentiate between Reid's adult and juvenile works, because many of the romances and adventures he originally wrote for adults were later abridged, sanitized, or rewritten as children's books. Even the volumes that were not revised for children were sought out and read by young fans of the author. Conversely, many adults enjoyed reading his juvenile works. Though Reid came to be known primarily as a "children's author," most nineteenth-century readers made little distinction between the adult and juvenile books in the author's canon.

Born 4 April 1818 in Ballyroney, County Down, Northern Ireland, to Rev. Thomas Mayne Reid and his wife (maiden name Rutherford), the author grew up in a family that had been called to the Presbyterian ministry for several generations. Reid was expected to enter the profession, but after attending the Royal Academical Institution in Belfast for four years he realized that he was not suited for the ministry. Yearning for adventure and travel, he left the institution and returned to Ballyroney, where he opened a local day school and sought his parents' permission to journey to America.

In December 1839 Reid sailed to the United States. Although his literary output during the next

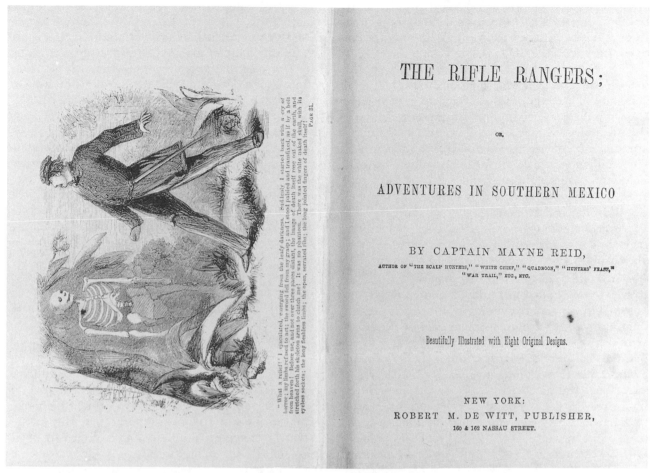

Frontispiece and title page for the retitled second American edition of Reid's first novel, based on his experiences in the Mexican-American War

decade was minimal, his experiences in the new world directly influenced most of his later work and helped create his public persona as a daring adventurer. Reid's early jobs included working in a New Orleans corn factory (he was dismissed for refusing to ship slaves); serving as a home tutor in Nashville, Tennessee; running his own school; and clerking in stores. So many legends have sprung up around the author's life – many of which he created or fostered himself – that it is difficult to ascertain the truth about Reid's American experiences. It is said that he embarked on trading expeditions with Native Americans in the western states and that John Audubon once accompanied him on a lengthy game-hunting excursion. After briefly working as an actor in Ohio, Reid relocated in 1843 to Philadelphia, where he struck up a friendship with Edgar Allan Poe and, during the next three years, began to publish poetry and stories in *Godey's* and *Graham's* magazines. He also

wrote a five-act play, *Love's Martyr,* which was staged in 1848 and later self-published.

Reid's most significant experiences of the era occurred in the military. He joined the First New York Volunteer Regiment as a second lieutenant in December 1846 and was by most claims – particularly his own – a brave and accomplished soldier. While serving in the army, he was a war correspondent for a newspaper, *Spirit of the Times,* which published several of his pieces under the pseudonym "Ecolier." He was praised as a hero at the Battle of Chapultepec, where he was severely wounded in the thigh. During his recuperation Reid immersed himself in the Mexican culture that he later explored in many of his novels.

He left the army as a captain in 1848 and spent several months on the East Coast writing for periodicals. He also wrote *War Life* (1849), a little-known volume that served as an early draft for his first major work, *The Rifle Rangers* (1850).

But adventure continued to beckon, and Reid set sail for Europe on 27 June 1849 in hopes of joining an ongoing Bavarian revolution. By the time he arrived, the revolution had ended.

In England Reid found a publisher for *The Rifle Rangers* and experienced great success with this fictionalized account of his experiences in the American military. The book's protagonist, Henry Haller, shares the basic circumstances of Reid's wartime adventures as a volunteer soldier in the Mexican-American War, but his exploits – which include fighting an alligator and enduring grisly tortures – are so outrageous that they are clearly fictional. In the course of two volumes, Haller scouts for mules, falls in love with a Mexican woman, engages in countless battles, and repeatedly escapes from capture.

The Rifle Rangers is the prototypical Reid novel, establishing a formula for many of his later works. The plot is busy with adventure, yet a great amount of time is spent describing minute details of natural history, geography, and social culture. The characterizations are pithy, but usually remain types, rather than unique individuals. The novel is sensational and not particularly challenging in literary terms, but it is nonetheless atmospheric and readable. It is easy to understand why English readers would be captivated by the view of the new world presented in Reid's novels, while American readers would feel a sense of proprietorship and pride.

After writing a second adult novel featuring Henry Haller, *The Scalp Hunters* (1851), the author published his first book intended for a young audience. Many editions of *The Desert Home* (1852) carried the caption title "The English Family Robinson," marking the novel as a "robinsonnade." After a lengthy opening, in which an unnamed narrator describes the topography of the American desert, he introduces a family he has encountered living alone in an oasis. The story is then given over to a first-person account by Robert Rolfe, an Englishman who immigrated to the United States and settled in the wilderness with his family. Vivid descriptions of building a log cabin, hunting, interacting with nature, and surviving the elements are given juvenile appeal because Rolfe's children play prominent roles in the story. After ten years alone in the oasis, the family relocates to Saint Louis, where the children are educated and find marriage partners, before returning to their wilderness home. The concept that wilderness life is preferable to civilization is a continuing theme in the author's body of work.

In 1853 Reid married fifteen-year-old Elizabeth Hyde, whom he had known for two years. Reid's romantic fascination with young girls is apparent in many of his novels, and, by all accounts, his marriage seems to have been a happy one. After the author's death, his wife published two fond biographical volumes. Married life did not alter Reid's love of adventure. At one point he made serious plans to smuggle a Hungarian revolutionary out of England. Although that scheme never came to fruition, there was no shortage of fictional adventure in the books he continued to write at a sustained fast pace. He also wrote serials for magazines such as *Youth's Companion* and *Boy's Journal* that were later expanded into full-length children's novels. Among his notable books of the era were *The Boy Hunters* (1853), which takes three brothers on a hunting expedition that is part travelogue and part natural history study. A sequel, *The Young Voyageurs* (1854), sends the brothers to Canada. Although the stories contain much adventure, they are meant to be instructive in geography, wildlife, and botany. This device frequently slows the plots.

In addition to his juvenile works, adult romances, and adventures, Reid published several works, including *Lost Lenore* (1864), under the name Charles Beach. Reid contended that the manuscripts were given to him by a mysterious stranger he called "Cannibal Charlie," although many readers suspected the works were actually penned by Reid. In *Captain Mayne Reid* (1978) Joan Steele proposes that the stylistic differences between Reid's work and the Charles Beach novels indicate "they may be plagiarisms or translations from a foreign author." Whatever the case, many of the Beach volumes later listed Reid's name on the title page.

Despite the success of his books, Reid declared bankruptcy in November 1866. The author was noted for living beyond his means, as evidenced by "The Ranche," an expensive Mexican hacienda he designed and built in Gerrard's Cross, Buckinghamshire. He was equally extravagant in his personal wardrobe, which included such affectations as sombreros and expensive shirt studs. Charles Ollivant, a fan of Reid's who became a close friend, devised a plan to save the author from destitution. He formed a committee that placed an advertisement in the London *Times* beseeching all of Reid's readers to purchase his latest book, *The Headless Horseman: A Strange Tale of Texas* (1865). The author's career was revived by this variant of the Washington Irving tale, which turned out to be Reid's best-selling volume and one of his most critically acclaimed works.

After being cleared of debt, Reid attempted publishing a journal, the *Little Times,* but it lasted for only twenty-two issues. Seeking to regain his fortune, he made his second journey to America, where he sought work writing dime novels for the publisher Beadle and Adams. Reid and his wife settled in Rhode Island, but although the author was thrilled to be back in his adopted homeland, Elizabeth Reid was extremely discontent. Her husband began publishing dime novels such as *White Squaw* (1868) and *The Helpless Hand* (1868), wrote for periodicals, and founded and edited *Onward: A Magazine for the Young Manhood of America.* The failure of this publication after two years was followed by a serious inflammation of his war wound and psychological difficulties.

On 22 October 1870 Reid and his wife returned to England, but the homecoming was not happy. The author was hospitalized for several months with "melancholia"; his physical state worsened because of his war injury; and he wrote little new fiction. There were scattered successes — such as a series of articles on "The Rural Life of England" — but his most productive days were behind him and his finances remained precarious. After a few years spent as a "gentleman farmer" in Herefordshire, Reid moved to London, where he died 22 October 1883.

More than one hundred years after the author's death, his work has fallen into obscurity. There have been attempted revivals, such as the publication of several Reid volumes in the 1967 "American Fiction Series," published by Gregg Press, and recent decades have also seen translations of his work published in Russia, eastern Europe, and Israel. Yet, in general, even his most exciting books seem too slow for contemporary readers, because of the ponderous relating of geographical and natural history facts. In addition, while his writing is competent and sometimes quite good, it never reaches the pinnacle of great literary works. During Reid's lifetime, authors such as Alexandre Dumas *père* and Robert Louis Stevenson were said to be fans of his work, yet Stevenson's adventure novels — which were influenced by Reid's books — are of a sufficiently higher caliber that they remain known and read, while Reid's work has been forgotten.

Nevertheless, Reid must still be considered a notable figure in nineteenth-century letters. As an English writer, he examined and enlightened many aspects of the United States and displayed a social conscience in his writing; many of his works condemn the American slavery system — although his Native American characters seldom stray from the unfortunate stereotypes of the era. Perhaps one of his most unusual achievements is publishing books that bridged generations. Except for a handful of modern classics, few twentieth-century books are enjoyed equally by readers of all ages. Yet in the nineteenth century, Reid's books blurred the distinction between adult and children's books and were read and enjoyed by all.

Bibliography:

Joan Steele, "Mayne Reid: A Revised Bibliography," *Bulletin of Bibliography,* 29 (July–September 1972): 95–100.

Biographies:

Elizabeth Reid, *Mayne Reid: A Memoir of His Life* (London: Ward & Downey, 1890);

Elizabeth Reid and Charles H. Coe, *Captain Mayne Reid: His Life and Adventures* (London: Greening, 1900).

References:

Maltus Questell Holyake, "Captain Mayne Reid: Soldier and Novelist," *Strand,* 2 (July 1891): 93–102;

Vincent Starrett, "Moustache and Saber," in his *Bookman's Holiday* (New York: Random House, 1942), pp. 167–182;

Joan Steele, *Captain Mayne Reid* (Boston: Twayne, 1978).

William Roscoe

(8 March 1753 – 30 June 1831)

Michael Scott Joseph
Rutgers University Libraries

BOOKS: *Ode, on the Institution of a Society in Liverpool, for the Encouragement of Designing, Drawing, Painting, &c. Read Before the Society, December 13th, 1773* (Liverpool, 1774);

Mount Pleasant, A Descriptive Poem (Warrington: J. Johnson, 1777);

The Wrongs of Africa (London: R. Faulder, 1787–1788); republished as *The Wrongs of Africa. A Poem. Part the First* (Philadelphia: J. James, 1788);

The Wrongs of Almoona, or The African's Revenge; a Narrative Poem, Founded on Historical Facts, as "A Friend to All Mankind" (Liverpool: H. Hodgson, 1788?);

A General View of the African Slave Trade (N.p., 1788);

Scriptural Refutation of a Pamphlet Lately Published by the Rev. Raymund Harris, intitled, "Scriptural Researches on the Licitness of the Slave Trade" (London, 1788);

The Life, Death, and Wonderful Atchievements of Edmund Burke. A New Ballad (N.p., 1792);

Thoughts on the Causes of the Present Failures (London: J. Johnson, 1793);

The Life of Lorenzo de' Medici Called the Magnificent (Liverpool: J. M'Creery, 1795 [i.e., 1796]; Philadelphia: Bronson & Chauncey, 1803); revised by Thomas Roscoe (London: Bohn, 1846);

Strictures on Mr. Burke's Two Letters Addressed to a Member of the Present Parliament (Philadelphia, 1797);

The Conspiracy of Gowrie, a Tragedy (London: J. Bell, 1800);

An Address Delivered before the Proprietors of the Botanic Garden in Liverpool (Liverpool, 1802);

The Life and Pontificate of Leo the Tenth (Liverpool, 1805; Philadelphia: E. Bronson, 1805–1806);

A New Arrangement of Plants of the Monandrian Class usually called "Scitamineae" (N.p., 1806);

The Butterfly's Ball and the Grasshopper's Feast (London: J. Harris, 1807; Philadelphia: B. C. Buzby, 1809);

Consideration of the Causes, Objects and Consequences of the Present War, and on the Expediency, or the Danger of Peace with France (London: T. Cadell & W. Davies, 1808; Philadelphia: Birch & Small, 1808);

Remarks on the Proposals Made to Great Britain, for Opening Negotiations for Peace, in the Year 1807 (London: T. Cadell & W. Davies, 1808);

Occasional Tracts Relative to the War Between Great Britain and France (London: T. Cadell, 1810);

Brief Observations on the Address to His Majesty Proposed by Earl Grey (Liverpool: M. Galway, 1810);

A Letter to Henry Brougham . . . on the Subject of Reform in the Representation of the People in Parliament (Liverpool: Printed for the author by M. Galway, 1811);

An Answer to a Letter From Mr. John Merritt, on the Subject of Parliamentary Reform (Liverpool: M. Galway, 1812);

A Review of the Speeches of the Right Hon. George Canning, on the Late Election for Liverpool, As Far As They Relate to the Questions of Peace and of Reform (Liverpool: T. Cadell & W. Davies, 1812);

On the Origins and Vicissitudes of Literature, Science, and Art, and Their Influence on the Present State of Society (London: I. M. Creery [i.e. M'Creery], 1818);

Observations on Penal Jurisprudence, and the Reformation of Criminals (London: T. Cadell & W. Davies, 1819);

Poems for Youth, by Roscoe and other members of his family (Liverpool: Robinson, 1820);

Memoir of Richard Roberts Jones, of Aberdaron, in the County of Carnarvon (London: Cadell, 1822);

Illustrations, Historical and Critical, of the Life of Lorenzo de' Medici, Called the Magnificent (London: T. Cadell, 1822);

Additional Observations on Penal Jurisprudence (London: T. Cadell & John and Arthur Arch, 1823–1825);

*A Letter to the Reverend William Lisle Bowles, A.M. . . .
in reply to His "Final Appeal to the Literary Public,
Relative to Pope"* (London: T. Cadell, 1825);

*Remarks on the Report of the Commissioners . . . to Visit the
State Prisons* (Liverpool: Harris, 1825);

*A Brief Statement of the Causes Which Have Led to the
Abandonment of the Celebrated System of Peniten-
tiary Discipline* (Liverpool: Harris, 1827).

Collection: *The Poetical Books of William Roscoe* (Liv-
erpool: Henry Young, 1853); republished as
The Poetical Works of William Roscoe (London:
Ward & Lock, 1857).

OTHER: Luigi Tansillo, *The Nurse a Poem,* translated by Roscoe (London: Cadell & Davies,
1798); revised as *The Pleasures of Hope by
Thomas Campbell, to Which Is Added The Nurse*
(New York: Evert Duyckinck, 1800);

Alexander Pope, *The Works of Alexander Pope,* edited
by Roscoe (London, 1824);

*Monandrian Plants of the Order "Scitamineae" Chiefly
Drawn from Living Specimens in the Botanic Garden
at Liverpool,* text by Roscoe (Liverpool: G.
Smith, 1828).

William Roscoe's poem *The Butterfly's Ball and
the Grasshopper's Feast* (1807) helped free English
children's literature from the pedagogical constraints that had ruled it since the middle of the
eighteenth century. The new awareness animating
Roscoe's poem — that fantasy and invention were
sufficiently worthwhile children's literary qualities
and that innocent pleasure could serve as the sole
purpose of reading — would become a hallmark of
English children's literature during the nineteenth
century, finding memorable and varied expression
within the airy visions of Clement Clarke Moore,
George MacDonald, and Lewis Carroll.

William Roscoe was born on 8 March 1753 at
the Old Bowling Green House, Mount Pleasant,
Liverpool. He was the only son of William and Elizabeth Roscoe. The elder William Roscoe owned an
extensive market garden and kept the popular
Bowling Green tavern. When six years old, Roscoe
was sent to schools in Liverpool, where he learned
reading and arithmetic. After leaving school before
his twelfth birthday, he learned something of car-
pentry and painting on china, as well.

Elizabeth Roscoe encouraged her son's reading. He learned a good deal of the works of William
Shakespeare by heart and bought copies of the *Spectator* and volumes of poetry by William Shenstone
and by "The Matchless Orinda" (Katherine Philips). In 1769 Roscoe was articled to John Eyes Jr.

and afterward to Peter Ellames, both attorneys of
Liverpool. His chief friend at the time was Francis
Holden, a young schoolmaster who instructed him
in French and persuaded him to study Italian. William Clarke and Richard Lowndes, two early
friends and lifelong associates, used to meet Roscoe
early in the morning to study the Latin classics before business hours.

In 1773 Roscoe cofounded a Liverpool society
for the encouragement of painting and design. In
1774 he was admitted as an attorney of the Court of
King's Bench and went into partnership in Liverpool, first with a Mr. Bannister, then with Samuel
Aspinall, and finally with Joshua Lace. In 1777 his
Mount Pleasant, A Descriptive Poem, modeled on John
Dyer's *Grongar Hill* (1726), was published. He also
wrote *Ode, on the Institution of a Society in Liverpool, for
the Encouragement of Designing, Drawing, Painting, &c.
Read Before the Society, December 13th, 1773* (1774), the
first of several denunciations of the slave trade.
These works were conventional, revealing no special quality or distinction; Roscoe would diligently
continue to write such verse throughout his life.

On 22 February 1781 Roscoe married Jane
Griffies, by whom he would have a family of seven
sons and three daughters. At about this time, he
began to collect rare books, notably Italian literature, early printed books, and prints. In 1784 he
was a promoter and vice president of a new society
for the advancement of painting and design, which
held exhibitions in Liverpool, and in 1785 he delivered lectures on the history of art. In several odes
and songs he endorsed the French Revolution, as in
*Strictures on Mr. Burke's Two Letters Addressed to a
Member of the Present Parliament* (1797). His song
"O'er the Vine-cover'd Hills and Gay Regions of
France" became popular.

The idea of writing a biography of Lorenzo
de'Medici had occurred to Roscoe at an early age,
and in 1790 he began to publish his principal work
at his own expense, at the press of John MacCreery
in Liverpool. The first edition of *The Life of Lorenzo
de'Medici Called the Magnificent* (1795), noted for its
typographical excellence, was published in February
1796 (dated 1795). The work established Roscoe's literary reputation, achieving a contemporary
status on a par with Ellis Farneworth's translation
of Gregorio Leti's *Life of Pope Sixtus the Fifth* (1754)
and Samuel Johnson's *Memoirs of Charles Frederick,
King of Prussia* (1786). Horace Walpole wrote enthusiastically to Roscoe, praising the book's "Grecian
simplicity" of style. The work was commended by
Thomas James Mathias and by Henry Fuseli — an
intimate of Roscoe's — in the *Analytical Review,* and

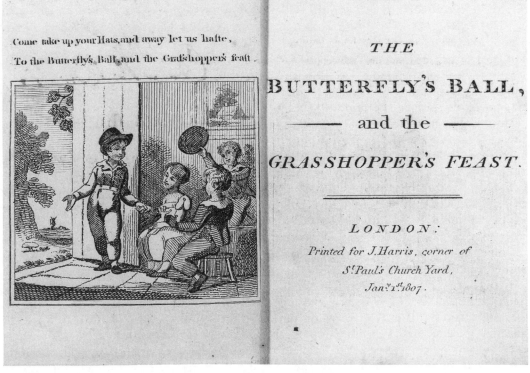

Cover, frontispiece, and title page for William Roscoe's most influential work for children, a poem stressing entertainment over didactic aims (courtesy of the Lilly Library, Indiana University)

in translation it found a European audience in Italy and Germany. Roscoe sold the copyright of the first edition for £1,200 to the publishers, Cadell and Davies, who brought out a second edition in 1796 and a third in 1799; many subsequent editions would follow.

In 1796 Roscoe retired from practicing law and in 1799 purchased Allerton Hall, a country home about six miles from Liverpool, which he restored in 1812, adding a library. He resumed the study of Greek, taken up in his middle age, and worked upon his biography of Leo X, begun about 1798. For this work Lord Holland and others procured material for him from Rome and Florence.

At the end of 1799, finding the Liverpool bank of Messrs. J. & W. Clarke in difficulties, Roscoe agreed to arrange their affairs and was induced to enter the bank as a partner and manager. He was thus again involved in business but found time for the study of botany. He struck up a friendship with the botanist Sir James Edward Smith, opened the Botanic Garden at Liverpool in 1802, and contributed to the *Transactions* of the Linnean Society, to which he was elected a fellow in 1805. Roscoe's botanical interest would continue to occupy him. In 1824 he proposed a new arrangement of the plants of the monandrian class, usually called *Scitamineae*, and Sir James Edward Smith would bestow the honor of naming an order of plant life, *Roscoea*, after him.

In 1805 Roscoe published his second great book, *The Life and Pontificate of Leo the Tenth*. The first impression of one thousand copies sold quickly, and Roscoe sold half of the copyright to Cadell and Davies for £2,000. A second edition appeared in 1806. *The Life and Pontificate of Leo the Tenth* was severely criticized in the *Edinburgh Review*, which accused Roscoe of harboring prejudice against Martin Luther, although with no apparent destructive effect upon its sales. In 1816–1817 Count Bossi produced an Italian translation with much additional matter. While this edition found a place on the *Index Expurgatorius*, the Catholic Church's notorious list of censored books, it nevertheless sold twenty-eight hundred copies in Italy.

In October 1806 Roscoe was elected a member of Parliament for Liverpool from the Whig Party. There, he voiced his opposition to slavery by supporting a bill to abolish the slave trade. He also contributed to the support of the African Institution, an antislavery organization. His antislavery stance, coupled with his support of the Catholic claims, made him many enemies in Parliament, and although Roscoe was nominated again, he failed to win reelection.

During this period Roscoe published the children's verse that was to outlive his other writings, *The Butterfly's Ball and the Grasshopper's Feast*, originally written to amuse his youngest son, Robert. In November 1806 it appeared in both the *Gentleman's Magazine,* which credited Roscoe with authorship, and the *Ladies Monthly Museum.* The poem soon attracted the attention of King George III, and the queen, who bid Sir George Smart, the composer, to set it to music for the young princesses Elizabeth, Augusta, and Mary.

Early in January 1807 John Harris, one of the most prolific of John Newbery's successors, published the poem as one of the first of his popular children's books. He had to choose between the text published in the *Gentleman's Magazine* and that of the *Ladies' Monthly Museum,* since there were slight discrepancies. Harris chose the former, as he happened to hold stock in the publication, and published the work in the small 5" by 4" format he favored at the time. Every page featured a copperplate engraving after fanciful drawings by William Mulready, depicting the various creatures either in human form or with humans riding on their backs, with Roscoe's verse inscribed at the top.

The sixteen couplets tell how various insects and other creatures make the journey to the ball, eat, dance, and are provided with light by "their watch-man, the Glow-worm" to return home. The poem has a roughly circular structure, beginning and ending with an address to the young reader. Following the initial invitation to attend the festivities is a sketch of the forest setting and a whimsical treatment of the assorted guests. Roscoe succinctly describes the feast, laid out on a mushroom table: "The viands were various to each of their taste / And the Bee brought the honey to sweeten the feast." He follows this with a similarly brief account of the ball; the lone dancer is not a butterfly — there is not a single butterfly or grasshopper in the poem — but the comically ponderous snail. With a nice lyrical conceit of evening giving "way to the shadows of night" and a final address to the reader urging him to hasten homeward, the poem concludes.

The gossamer-like insubstantiality of the poem's narrative is fortified by its quaint and homely inventiveness, a mood of midsummer languor, and a relaxed and intimate tone. Besides separating itself from the didactic school of children's literature popular at the time, *The Butterfly's Ball and the Grasshopper's Feast* is a poetical anachronism, having more in common with the classically inspired, idyllic poetry of Robert Herrick and Andrew

Marvell – Roscoe's predecessors by almost two centuries – than with the work of William Blake and William Wordsworth, his contemporaries. This poetic nostalgia chimes perfectly with the poem's air of gauzy fantasy and may perhaps account for part of its great appeal for children.

The book's popularity compelled Harris to reprint it many times in the months that followed, and in 1808 he brought out a new edition, revising and expanding the text and replacing Mulready's ingenious creatures with more-realistic ones – now universally judged to possess less charm. *The Butterfly's Ball and the Grasshopper's Feast* continued in popularity for many years: Harris describes an edition he published in 1841 as the twenty-first. Other publishers also produced editions, and the poem circulated in cheap copies as a chapbook.

American publishers produced pirated copies of *The Butterfly's Ball and the Grasshopper's Feast* as early as 1808 and as late as the mid 1860s; such successful American picture books as *The Cats' Party* (1865) and *The Dog's Grand Dinner Party* (1868) clearly reflect the original's wit and cheer – wearing a bit thin, however. In 1973 *The Butterfly's Ball and the Grasshopper's Feast* was revived, with spectacular illustrations by Alan Aldridge and a new verse text by William Plomer.

At the beginning of 1816 there was a run on Roscoe's bank, and on 25 January it suspended payments. Considerable sums were locked up in mining and landed property, and as the assets seemed ample, Roscoe accepted the creditors' request to resume management. To satisfy part of the claims, he sold his considerable library, consisting of books, prints, drawings, and paintings. His friends purchased a selection of Italian and other books at the sale, to the amount of £600, and offered them to him as a gift, which he refused. They were then presented in 1817 to the Liverpool Athenaeum to form a "Roscoe Collection."

In 1817 Roscoe was chosen to be the first president of the Liverpool Royal Institution. Meanwhile, although he had made large reimbursements to the creditors of his bank, his estate was determined to have been overvalued, and in 1819, when the remaining creditors pressed for payment, Roscoe and his partners were declared bankrupt. The allowance of Roscoe's "certificate of conformity" was petitioned against by two of the creditors, and to avoid arrest Roscoe confined himself indoors at his farm at Chat Moss. After some months the certificate was allowed, and he returned to Liverpool, dissolving his connection with the bank. At this time a hefty sum of £2,500 was raised by Dr.

Thomas Stewart Traill and other friends for the benefit of Roscoe and his family.

Roscoe was once more released from business cares, and in 1820 he began to prepare for his friend Mr. Coke a catalogue of the manuscripts at Holkham, Norfolk. In 1822 he published *Illustrations, Historical and Critical, of the Life of Lorenzo de'Medici, Called the Magnificent,* in which he defended Lorenzo, his hero, from the attacks of Sismondi. In 1824 the Royal Society of Literature elected Roscoe an honorary associate, and he was afterward awarded its gold medal. In the same year, he published a new edition of Alexander Pope's works with fairly infelicitous consequences. A controversy ensued between Roscoe and W. L. Bowles, who closed his case by publishing the biting *Lessons in Criticism to a 'Quarterly Reviewer.'* Later editors of Pope have been severely critical of Roscoe's efforts, as well, regarding him as an undiscriminating panegyrist of the poet's career and his annotations as misleading.

In December 1827 Roscoe suffered an attack of paralysis; he recovered, but was confined to his study. In June 1831 he was prostrated by influenza, and he died on 30 June at his house in Lodge Lane, Toxteth Park, Liverpool. He was buried in the ground attached to the chapel in Renshaw Street, Liverpool, whose services he had regularly attended.

Roscoe's writings stimulated a European interest in Italian literature and history, and his zeal for culture and art in his native place received a tribute in Liverpool on 8 March 1853, the Roscoe Centenary Festival. Thomas De Quincey, who rather disparages the Liverpool literary coterie to which Roscoe belonged, described him in about 1801 as "simple and manly in his demeanor," adding that, in spite of his boldness as a politician, there was "the feebleness of the mere belles-lettrist" in his views on many subjects. A Mrs. Hemans, who saw Roscoe in his latest years, speaks of him as "a delightful old man, with a fine Roman style of head" sitting in the study of his small house surrounded by busts, books, and flowers. It is perhaps this vision of Roscoe that serves him best, the neo-classical poet whose affectionate effort to amuse his young child rang in the dawn of levity in English children's literature.

Biographies:

Henry Roscoe, *Life of William Roscoe* (London: T. Cadell, 1833);

George Chandler, *William Roscoe of Liverpool* (London: Batsford, 1953).

Christina Georgina Rossetti

(5 December 1830 – 29 December 1894)

Jan Susina
Illinois State University

See also the Rossetti entry in *DLB 35: Victorian Poets After 1850.*

BOOKS: *Verses* (London: Privately printed at G. Polidori's, 1847);

Goblin Market and Other Poems (Cambridge & London: Macmillan, 1862);

The Prince's Progress and Other Poems (London: Macmillan, 1866);

Poems (Boston: Roberts, 1866);

Commonplace and Other Stories (London: Ellis, 1870; Boston: Roberts, 1870);

Sing-Song: A Nursery Rhyme Book (London: Routledge, 1872; Boston: Roberts, 1872; revised and enlarged edition, London: Macmillan, 1893);

Annus Domini: A Prayer for Each Day of the Year, Founded on a Text of Holy Scripture (Oxford & London: Parker, 1874);

Speaking Likenesses (London: Macmillan, 1874; Boston: Roberts, 1875);

Goblin Market, The Prince's Progress, and Other Poems (London & New York: Macmillan, 1875); republished as *Poems* (Boston: Roberts, 1876);

Seek and Find: A Double Series of Short Studies on the Benedicite (London & Brighton: Society for Promoting Christian Knowledge / New York: Young, 1879);

A Pageant and Other Poems (London: Macmillan, 1881; Boston: Roberts, 1881);

Called to be Saints: The Minor Festivals Devotionally Studied (London & Brighton: Society for Promoting Christian Knowledge / New York: Young, 1881);

Poems (Boston: Roberts, 1882);

Letter and Spirit: Notes on the Commandments (London & Brighton: Society for Promoting Christian Knowledge / New York: Young, 1883);

Time Flies: A Reading Diary (London & Brighton: Society for Promoting Christian Knowledge, 1885);

Poems (London & New York: Macmillan, 1890);

Christina Georgina Rossetti

The Face of the Deep: A Devotional Commentary on the Apocalypse (London & Brighton: Society for Promoting Christian Knowledge / New York: Young, 1893);

New Poems, Hitherto Unpublished or Uncollected, edited by William Michael Rossetti (London & New York: Macmillan, 1896);

Maude: Prose and Verse, edited by William Michael Rossetti (London: Bowden, 1897; enlarged edition, Chicago: Stone, 1897);

Poetical Works, edited by William Michael Rossetti (London & New York: Macmillan, 1904);

The Complete Poems of Christian Rossetti, 3 volumes, edited by R. W. Crump (Baton Rouge & London: Louisiana State University Press, 1979–1990).

Christina Georgina Rossetti is best known for her poetry on religious or inspirational themes. Her literary reputation has gradually increased since her death, and she has emerged as one of the finest British female poets of the nineteenth century. She is also considered, along with Gerard Manley Hopkins, as one of the two major religious poets of the nineteenth century. Because of her reticent nature, she is seen by many contemporary critics as the British equivalent of Emily Dickinson, although, unlike Dickinson, she was recognized as an important poetic voice during her lifetime. The 11 January 1865 *London Times* judged Rossetti and Jean Ingelow as the two foremost living women poets of the Victorian age. Critical recognition and reevaluation of Rossetti as a major Victorian poet is focused primarily on her adult work, while her two major children's texts, *Sing-Song: A Nursery Rhyme Book* (1872), a collection of poems, and *Speaking Likenesses* (1874), a collection of three literary fairy tales, are frequently overlooked. Although not specifically written for children, *Goblin Market and Other Poems* (1862) has also frequently been considered as children's literature.

Christina Rossetti was the youngest of four children of Gabriele Rossetti, an Italian exile living in London who earned his living as a professor of Italian and a Dante scholar at King's College, London. She was educated at home by her half-English, half-Italian mother, Frances Polidori Rossetti, to whom she was particularly close. Her elder brother, Dante Gabriel Rossetti, was the noted Pre-Raphaelite painter and poet. Her sister, Maria Francesca Rossetti, followed her father's literary interests and published *The Shadow of Dante* (1871), an introduction to the poet's work, and became a member of the Angelican Sisterhood in 1873. The younger brother, William Michael Rossetti, worked as a civil servant in the Excise Office and later functioned as the editor of the family manuscripts.

According to William Rossetti's memoir of his sister, Christina was "by far the least bookish of the family," but she showed an early facility for language. At age six Christina startled one of her mother's friends with her use of "a dictionary-word." Christina's first poem, "Cecilia never went to school / Without her gladiator," was composed orally at about the same time. Her first written work was a fairy tale entitled "The Dervise," which was inspired by her reading of the *Arabian Nights,*

one of her favorite books as a child. Even as a child Rossetti showed a marked preference for fairy tales and the fantastic over the moral tales that her mother encouraged her to read, such as Thomas Day's *Sandford and Merton* (1783) and Mary Martha Sherwood's *The Fairchild Family* (1818). Her oldest surviving work, dated 27 April 1842, is the poem "To My Mother," which was privately printed in 1847 by her maternal grandfather, Gaetano Polidori.

In 1848 Rossetti was engaged to James Collinson, a minor painter and member of the Pre-Raphaelite Brotherhood. However, her strong religious convictions prevented the marriage: Collins was Roman Catholic, while Rossetti was of the Tractarian Party of the Church of England. She began to submit poems for publication in 1848; seven were published in the *Germ,* the Pre-Raphaelite journal, under the pseudonym Ellen Alleyn, a name suggested by her brother Dante. Rossetti served as the model for several of her brother's paintings, the best known being *The Girlhood of Mary Virgin* (1849) and *Ecce Ancilla Domini (The Annunciation)* (1850).

The publication of her collection *Goblin Market and Other Poems,* with illustrations by Dante Rossetti, has been hailed as the first literary success of the Pre-Raphaelites. The title poem is a haunting and disturbing fairy tale of two sisters, Laura and Lizzie, who are tempted by the luscious fruits of the goblin men. While Rossetti denied that the poem was an allegory, the richly sensual language and overt sexual symbolism that permeate the poem have made it one of the most analyzed of Rossetti's works. Although neither "Goblin Market" nor any of the other poems in this volume were intended for children, "Goblin Market" has frequently appeared in children's anthologies of poetry because it utilizes fairy-tale conventions and characters. It also has been frequently read as a Christian allegory of temptation, fall, and redemption. Yet, as Jeanie Watson has noted, the overt text of the moral tale, which teaches spiritual and proper social conduct, is at odds with the fairy-tale subtext, which celebrates sensuality in a context of repressed eroticism. Lizzie sacrifices herself to the goblin men to redeem her fallen sister, Laura, who has tasted their forbidden fruit. While the poem ends with the moral "For there is no friend like a sister," the poem's frankly sexual subtext makes it atypical of the body of Rossetti's writing for children.

The success of *Goblin Market and Other Poems* led the way for the publication of Rossetti's second professionally published collection, *The Prince's Progress and Other Poems* (1866), which was also illustrated by her brother. It was during this period that Charles Bagot Cayley, a man of letters and translator of Dante, proposed to Rossetti. Once again she refused a marriage offer when she discovered that Cayley's religious faith was, in the words of William Rossetti, "either strictly wrong or woefully defective."

In 1870 Rossetti published *Commonplace and Other Stories,* a collection of tales written from 1852 to 1870. Two of the stories, "Nick" and "Hero: A Metamorphosis," are in the form of literary fairy tales. In "Nick" an envious man is given the opportunity to become anything he desires, and he uses his gift in a series of transformations to carry out his resentment against his neighbors; Nick's final wish is to become himself, and he is subsequently purged of his envy. "Hero" also involves transformations: the protagonist is granted her wish to be "the supreme object of admiration." When Hero finds herself changed into a diamond, she discovers that such admiration is also the root of greed, war, and death. Like Nick, she desires to return to her original state, having learned that admiration is not the most valuable quality. Although these tales are not intended for children, they show Rossetti using the literary fairy tale for didactic purposes. Rossetti's prose of this period is markedly inferior to her poetry, as her brother Dante noted when he remarked, "I think your proper business is to write poetry not *Commonplaces.*"

Since her adolescence Rossetti had been troubled with poor health; at one time she had convinced herself that she was dying of consumption. In 1864 she was misdiagnosed with tuberculosis. In 1871 she developed Graves' disease, which resulted in the darkening and discoloration of her skin and the protrusion of her eyes.

Rossetti's collection of nursery rhymes, *Sing-Song,* was published in 1872, with 120 illustrations by the Pre-Raphaelite artist Arthur Hughes. Rossetti had submitted the manuscript with her own illustrations, but she modestly added, "they are merely my own scratches and I cannot draw." The book was warmly praised in the press and reviewed by Sidney Colvin in the *Academy* along with Lewis Carroll's *Through the Looking-Glass* (1872) and Edward Lear's *More Nonsense* (1872). A second edition, with five additional poems, was published in 1893. Hughes's stunning black-and-white drawings richly complement Rossetti's text. Dante Rossetti remarked, "There is no man living who would have done my sister's book so divinely well."

The best-known poem from the collection is "Who Has Seen the Wind?," with its haunting lyric

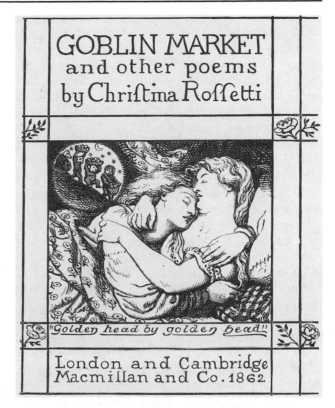

Title page for Rossetti's best-known work, illustrated by her brother Dante Gabriel Rossetti

that has become a standard in children's anthologies:

Who has seen the Wind?
Neither you nor I;
But when the trees bow down their heads
The wind is passing by.

Poems such as "If a Pig Wore a Wig" and "When Fishes Set Umbrellas Up" reflect Rossetti's interest in nonsense literature. Other poems, such as "A City Plum is Not a Plum" and "The Peacock Has a Score of Eyes," play with the incongruity of language. Dante Rossetti praised the poems as "admirable things, alternating between merest babyism and a sort of Blakish wisdom and tenderness."

The collection includes many rhymes intended to help young children learn useful bits of information such as the colors, seasons, time measurements, coins, and numbers (she would also produce "An Alphabet," published in the American children's magazine *For Very Little Folks* in 1875). Ralph Bellas observed that the reader of *Sing-Song* is made aware of the prevailing adult point of view and that the poems are primarily directed toward older children and adults, who, in turn, explain and teach them to younger children. Barbara Garlitz has noted that at least half the poems in the collection repeat the moral and sentimental themes that were the stock-in-trade of nineteenth-century children's poetry. She points out that although some of the poems reflect the trend toward the imagination and simple entertainment, in the manner of writers such as Carroll and Lear, much of the collection is firmly rooted in the didactic and sentimental tradition typified by Isaac Watts's *Divine Songs for Children* (1715) and Anne and Jane Taylor's *Original Poems for Infant Minds* (1804).

What is striking to contemporary readers is the large number of poems dealing with death. Dead babies or dead mothers are the frequent subjects of both Rossetti's lyrics and Hughes's illustrations, as in "My Baby Has a Father and a Mother," "A Baby's Cradle with No Baby in It," "Why Did Baby Die," "Three Little Children," and "Motherless Baby and Babyless Mother." R. Loring Taylor has observed that the poems in *Sing-Song* are "filled with images of death — grave mounds, empty cradles, farewell handshakes" and that Rossetti has the disconcerting tendency to equate sleep with death: there is an alarming ambiguity about whether children are merely sleeping or dead. It is frequently unclear if the hovering angels of such poems as "Angels at the Foot," "Baby Lies So Fast Asleep," or "Our Little Baby Fell Asleep" and the accompanying illustrations are intended to protect children as they sleep or have been summoned to snatch them away.

These melancholy poems reflect the high infant mortality rate of the Victorian period. Lila Hanft has noted that the resemblance between the angelic mothers and maternal angels in many of the poems may also suggest a hidden maternal ambivalence or wish for infanticide. Hanft notes that the publication of *Sing-Song* coincides with the passage of the Infant Life Protection Act of 1872, which was the result of the growing concern for the rising infanticide rate during the second half of the Victorian period.

Hughes also drew the illustrations for Rossetti's second children's book, *Speaking Likenesses,* one of many literary fairy tales published after the success of Carroll's *Alice's Adventures in Wonderland* (1865). The didactic emphasis in these three tales is clearly on punishment for improper conduct; it is even more pronounced than in *Sing-Song* and directed at a slightly older audience. A significant link between Rossetti's two children's texts is her overwhelming moral and didactic concerns. This connection has frequently been overlooked because many scholars examine only those poems in *Sing-Song* that resemble the nonsense poetry of Lear and Carroll.

In a letter to her brother Dante, Rossetti remarked that *Speaking Likenesses* was intended to be "merely a Christmas trifle, would-be in the *Alice* style with an eye to the market." The Rossetti family were friends of Carroll; he frequently visited their home and photographed various members of the family, including Christina. The Dormouse of *Alice's Adventures in Wonderland* was said by Michael to be based on Dante's pet wombat, which had the habit of falling asleep at the table. Carroll sent Rossetti a presentation copy of the book, which she seems to have admired and considered a "funny pretty book." She had originally intended to call her collection of three fairy tales "Nowhere" but was convinced by Dante Rossetti that there might be some confusion between her book and the recently published "free-thinking book" *Erewhon* (1872), by Samuel Butler. Rossetti changed the title and wrote to her publisher, Alexander Macmillan, explaining the meaning behind the new title:

> I really must adopt "Speaking Likenesses" as my title, this having met with some approval in my circle. Very likely you did not so deeply ponder upon my text as to remark that my small heroines perpetually encounter "speaking (literally *speaking*) likenesses" or embodiments or caricatures of themselves or their faults. This premised, I think the title boasts of point & neatness.

The fairy tales are narrated by a stern aunt who believes that stories for children ought to be educational as well as entertaining, as her five young nieces help with her knitting. There is a curious tension within the story frame between the aunt's obvious dislike of the fantastic and the young girls' desire for marvelous tales. The first and most grotesque of the fairy tales involves Flora, a self-centered eight-year-old girl celebrating her disastrous birthday party with a group of ill-mannered friends. Although Flora is given a large number of presents, she and her guests are unable to share and quickly become cross with one another. After a troublesome afternoon, Flora abandons her own party and discovers a yew tree with a lamp in its top branches and a door in its trunk. Entering, Flora discovers a large mirror-lined apartment, where a mad tea party of oddly shaped, antisocial children is taking place. The gathering is dominated by a spoiled young girl known as "the birthday Queen." The group plays a series of sadistic games, including "Hunt the Pincushion," in which Flora serves as the cushion, and "Self Help," in which the boys pursue the girls in an attempt to inflict pain. Awakened

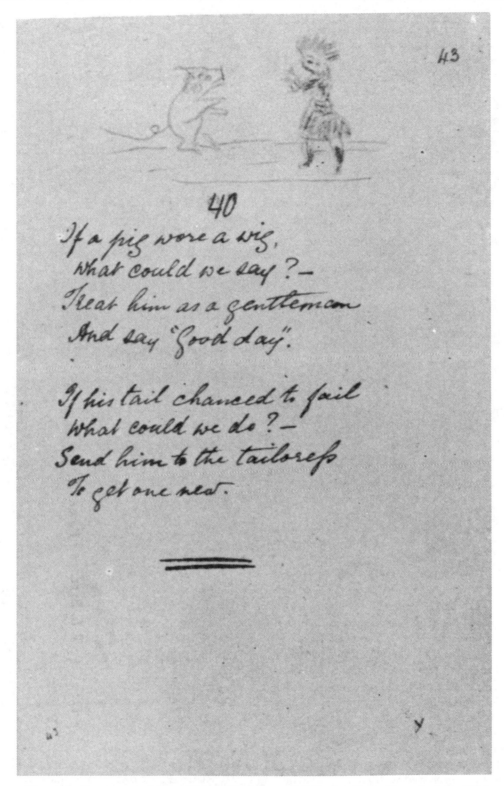

Manuscript for a nursery rhyme published in Sing-Song *(1872), from Rossetti's notebook for 1870
(British Library)*

Maggie the orphan and the hungry boy; illustration by Arthur Hughes for Rossetti's Speaking Likenesses *(1874)*

and chastised by this disturbing dream, Flora returns home and apologizes to her guests for her previous behavior.

The second tale is less overt in its use of punishment, but it is no less moralizing. Edith is an impetuous little girl who thinks of herself as quite mature. She rushes out of the house without permission to set up the kettle for a gypsy tea but loses most of her matches and is unable to light the fire. She is helped by animals of the forest, who correct her failure to fill the kettle before it is placed over the fire. Edith is ungrateful to her animal helpers, and they eventually desert her. The fire dies, but Edith is found by her nurse, who has come prepared with a box of matches, two fire wheels, and half a dozen newspapers. Edith finally realizes that she has much to learn from her elders and that if she volunteers for a task, it ought to be one for which she has the necessary equipment and knowledge.

Rossetti's final tale recounts the adventures of Maggie, an orphan who returns a package left at her grandmother's shop by the daughters of a wealthy doctor on Christmas Eve. Maggie is a Victorian version of Little Red Riding Hood who must fight off the temptation to sample some of the treats in the basket that do not belong to her. On her journey, Maggie confronts the figure of a hungry boy with an enormous mouth who demands some of the chocolate. After resisting her own desires, which appear in the form of "speaking likenesses," Maggie is given curt thanks at the door and turned away. The tale is an extreme version of the lesson that virtue is — or ought to be — its own reward. On her way home, Maggie befriends a pigeon, a puppy, and a kitten and learns that it is better to give comfort than to expect it from others.

Rossetti's fairy tales rank with those of Edward Knatchbull-Hugessen's *Stories for My Children*

(1869) and Lucy Clifford's *Anyhow Stories, Moral and Otherwise* (1882) as some of the most terrifying nineteenth-century fairy tales for children. While Rossetti felt that *Speaking Likenesses* was in the manner of *Alice's Adventures in Wonderland,* its tone is more obviously didactic, and the stories stress the value of punishment. U. C. Knoepflmacher has argued that Rossetti's excessive didacticism is actually an attempt to subvert and critique Carroll's book and that one should read *Speaking Likenesses* as an antagonistic and subversive text, a sort of antifantasy that takes Carroll's text to task. Whether meant as an imitation of *Alice's Adventures in Wonderland* or as a critique, *Speaking Likenesses* was not well received by the Victorian public and went through only one edition. Writing to a friend in 1875, John Ruskin commented that of the recently published children's books, "The *worst,* I consider Christina Rossetti's. I've kept that for the mere wonder of it: how could she or Arthur Hughes sink so low after their pretty nursery rhymes?" Rossetti exhibits what Gillian Avery has called the two most unattractive features of fairy tales of the period: "the tendency to gloat over the physically grotesque, and a determined insistence on punishment."

More juvenilia than finished adolescent novel, *Maude: Prose and Verse* (1897) is a fascinating autobiographical text that reveals much of the moody adolescence of the poet. Although written in 1850, *Maude* was not published until after Rossetti's death; William Rossetti, who edited the volume, termed it a "Tale for Girls." The author includes interpolated poems to break up the spiritual quest of the frail fifteen-year-old Maude, who, like Rossetti, excels in writing sonnets. William Rossetti considered the novella his sister's attempt to address the defects of her own character and to articulate her religious obligations. Maude's chief fault seems to be excessive pride in her literary accomplishments, which leads the sickly girl to intense bouts of guilt and self-recrimination. Her deep religious faith causes her to wonder if she lacks charity and question her pleasure in musical services. Maude assumes that her poor health is a result of her spiritual shortcomings. Her early death is hastened by a combination of religious doubts, ill health, and weakened condition caused by a carriage fall. *Maude* is a gloomy and perhaps morbid glimpse into the highly introspective and intensely spiritual adolescence of Rossetti.

In her fairy tales, and to a lesser extent in her poetry, Rossetti tended to write at children rather than to them, placing the need for improvement over that of entertainment. Rossetti is solidly Victorian in her attitudes and representations of children, although some critics point to a startling subversiveness embedded in the subtext of her fairy tales. There is a frequent impulse to improve children by providing them with information or social skills. Rossetti was part of the second wave of literary fairy tales that developed in the 1870s; they were written not for specific children, but for the children's market. In producing such texts, these authors created stories that met the approval of parents who purchased the books, but not necessarily of children who read them.

With the growing recognition of Christina Rossetti as a major poet of the nineteenth century, more attention is being directed toward her writing for children, with *Sing-Song* being considered her most significant work. It and Robert Louis Stevenson's *A Child's Garden of Verses* (1885) are usually deemed the two most significant collections of children's poetry published in England in the second half of the nineteenth century. The strength of Rossetti's poetry lies in her rich use of the imaginative possibilities of language. As Roderick McGillis has observed, the subtitle of the collection reminds readers that Rossetti's poems are linked with nursery rhymes because they reflect the verbal world of children, and it encourages them to participate in the play of language. At the same time, frequent references to infant mortality place the collection in the historical context of the Victorian acceptance, and even celebration, of death as an essential aspect of nineteenth-century children's literature.

Letters:

Rossetti Papers 1862 to 1870, edited by William Michael Rossetti (London: Sands, 1903);

The Family Letters of Christina Georgina Rossetti, edited by William Michael Rossetti (London: Brown, Langham, 1908);

Three Rossettis: Unpublished Letters to and from Dante Gabriel, Christina, William, edited by Janet Camp Troxell (Cambridge, Mass.: Harvard University Press, 1937);

The Rossetti-Macmillan Letters, edited by Lona Mosk Packer (Berkeley: University of California Press, 1963).

Bibliography:

Rebecca W. Crump, *Christina Rossetti: A Reference Guide* (Boston: G. K. Hall, 1976).

References:

Nina Auerbach and U. C. Knoepflmacher, *Forbidden Journeys: Fairy Tales and Fantasies by Victorian*

Women Writers (Chicago: University of Chicago Press, 1992), pp. 317–323;

Gillian Avery and Angela Bull, *Nineteenth-Century Children* (London: Hodder & Stoughton, 1965), pp. 47–48;

Georgina Battiscombe, *Christina Rossetti: A Divided Life* (London: Constable, 1981);

Ralph A. Bellas, *Christina Rossetti* (Boston: Twayne, 1977);

Steven Connor, " 'Speaking Likenesses': Language and Repetition in Christina Rossetti's *Goblin Market*," *Victorian Poetry,* 22 (Winter 1984): 439–448;

Diane D'Amico, "Christina Rossetti's *Maude:* A Reconsideration," *University of Dayton Review,* 15 (Spring 1981): 129–142;

Barbara Garlitz, "Christina Rossetti's *Sing-Song* and Nineteenth-Century Children's Poetry," *PMLA,* 70 (June 1955): 539–543;

Lila Hanft, "The Politics of Maternal Ambivalence in Christina Rossetti's *Sing-Song*," *Victorian Literature and Culture,* 19 (1991): 213–232;

Wendy R. Katz, "Muse from Nowhere: Christina Rossetti's Fantasy World in *Speaking Likenesses,*" *Journal of Pre-Raphaelite and Aesthetic Studies,* 5 (November 1984): 14–35;

Knoepflmacher, "Avenging Alice: Christina Rossetti and Lewis Carroll," *Nineteenth-Century Literature,* 41 (December 1986): 299–328;

Roderick McGillis, "Simple Surfaces: Christina Rossetti's Work for Children," in *The Achievement of Christina Rossetti,* edited by David A. Kent (Ithaca, N.Y.: Cornell University Press, 1987), pp. 208–230;

Lona Mosk Packer, *Christina Rossetti* (Berkeley: University of California Press, 1963);

William Michael Rossetti, "Memoir," in his *The Poetical Works of Christina Georgina Rossetti* (London: Macmillan, 1911), pp. xlv–lxxi;

Rossetti, *Some Reminiscences,* 2 volumes (London: Brown, Langham, 1906);

Sharon Smulders, "Sound, Sense, and Structure in Christina Rossetti's *Sing-Song,*" *Children's Literature,* 22 (1994): 3–26;

Thomas Burnett Swann, *Wonder and Whimsey: The Fantastic World of Christina Rossetti* (Francestown, N.H.: Marshall Jones, 1960);

R. Loring Taylor, "Preface," in *Sing-Song, Speaking Likenesses, Goblin Market,* by Rossetti (New York: Garland, 1974), pp. v–xviii;

Jeanie Watson, " 'Men Sell Not Such in Any Town': Christina Rossetti's Goblin Fruit of Fairy Tale," *Children's Literature,* 12 (1984): 61–77;

Marya Zaturenska, *Christina Rossetti: A Portrait Background* (New York: Macmillan, 1949).

Papers:

Several of Christina Georgina Rossetti's notebooks are located at the British Library, London, as is the manuscript for *Sing-Song*. Other notebooks are located at the Bodleian Library, Oxford. Other significant holdings of Rossetti manuscripts include those at the Harry Ransom Humanities Research Center, University of Texas at Austin; Princeton University; and the University of British Columbia.

John Ruskin

(8 February 1819 – 20 January 1900)

Marilynn Strasser Olson
Southwest Texas State University

See also the Ruskin entry in *DLB 55: Victorian Prose Writers Before 1867.*

SELECTED BOOKS*: *Salsette and Elephanta: A Prize Poem* (Oxford: Vincent, 1839);

Modern Painters, 5 volumes (London: Smith, Elder, 1843–1860; volumes 1–2, New York: Wiley & Putnam, 1847–1848; volumes 3–5, New York: Wiley, 1856–1860);

The Seven Lamps of Architecture (London: Smith, Elder, 1849; New York: Wiley, 1849);

Poems. J. R. Collected 1850 (London: Privately printed, 1850);

The King of the Golden River; or, The Black Brothers: A Legend of Stiria (London: Smith, Elder, 1851; New York: Wiley, 1860);

Notes on the Construction of Sheepfolds (London: Smith, Elder, 1851; New York: Wiley, 1851);

Examples of the Architecture of Venice, Selected, and Drawn to Measurement from the Edifices (London: Smith, Elder, 1851);

The Stones of Venice, 3 volumes (London: Smith, Elder, 1851–1853);

Pre-Raphaelitism (London: Smith, Elder, 1851–1853; New York: Wiley, 1851–1860);

Giotto and His Works in Padua (3 parts, London: Printed for the Arundel Society, 1853–1860; 1 volume, New York: Scribners, 1899);

Lectures on Architecture and Painting Delivered at Edinburgh in November 1853 (London: Smith, Elder, 1854; New York: Wiley, 1854);

The Opening of the Crystal Palace, Considered in Some of Its Relations to the Prospects of Art (London: Smith, Elder, 1854; New York: Alden, 1885);

Notes on Some of the Principal Pictures Exhibited in the Rooms of the Royal Academy: 1855 (London: Smith, Elder, 1855);

The Harbours of England (London: Gambart, 1856);

Notes on the Turner Gallery at Marlborough House, 1856 (London: Smith, Elder, 1857);

*This list excludes revised and enlarged editions.

John Ruskin (courtesy of the Lilly Library, Indiana University)

The Political Economy of Art, Being the Substance (with additions) of Two Lectures Delivered at Manchester, July 10th and 13th, 1857 (London: Smith, Elder, 1857; New York: Wiley & Halsted, 1858);

Notes on Some of the Principal Pictures Exhibited in the Rooms of the Royal Academy and the Society of Painters in Water Colours, No. III – 1857 (London: Smith, Elder, 1857);

Catalogue of the Turner Sketches in the National Gallery (London: Privately printed, 1857);

The Elements of Drawing in Three Letters to Beginners (London: Smith, Elder, 1857; New York: Wiley & Halsted, 1857);

Catalogue of the Sketches and Drawings by J. M. W. Turner, R.A., Exhibited in Marlborough House in the Year 1857–8 (London: Privately printed, 1857);

Notes on Some of the Principal Pictures Exhibited in the Rooms of the Royal Academy, the Old and New Societies of Painters in Water Colours, the Society of British Artists, and the French Exhibition, No. IV – 1858 (London: Smith, Elder, 1858);

Cambridge School of Art. Mr. Ruskin's Inaugural Address Delivered at Cambridge, Oct. 29, 1858 (Cambridge: Deighton, Bell / London: Bell & Daldy, 1858);

The Oxford Museum, by Ruskin and Henry W. Acland (London: Smith, Elder / Oxford: Parker, 1859);

The Unity of Art. By John Ruskin, Esq., M.A. Delivered at the Annual Meeting of the Manchester School of Art, February 22nd, 1859 (Manchester: Thos. Sowler, 1859);

The Two Paths: Being Lectures on Art, and Its Application to Decoration and Manufacture, Delivered in 1858–9 (London: Smith, Elder, 1859; New York: Wiley, 1859);

The Elements of Perspective Arranged for the Use of the Schools and Intended to be Read in Connexion with the First Three Books of Euclid (London: Smith, Elder, 1859; New York: Wiley, 1860);

Notes on Some of the Principal Pictures Exhibited in the Royal Academy, the Old and New Societies of Painters in Water Colours, the Society of British Artists, and the French Exhibition. No. V – 1859 (London: Smith, Elder, 1859);

"Unto This Last": Four Essays on the First Principles of Political Economy (London: Smith, Elder, 1862; New York: Wiley, 1866);

Sesame and Lilies: Two Lectures Delivered at Manchester in 1864 (London: Smith, Elder, 1865; New York: Wiley, 1865);

The Ethics of the Dust: Ten Lectures on Work, Traffic, and War (London: Smith, Elder, 1866; New York: Wiley, 1866);

The Crown of Wild Olive: Three Lectures on Work, Traffic, and War (London: Smith, Elder, 1866; New York: Wiley, 1866);

Time and Tide, By Weare and Tyne. Twenty-five Letters to a Working Man of Sunderland on the Laws of Work (London: Smith, Elder, 1867; New York: Wiley, 1868);

An Inquiry into Some of the Conditions at Present Affecting "the Study of Architecture" in our schools read at the Ordinary General Meeting of the Royal Institute of British Architects, May 15th, 1865 (New York: Wiley, 1867);

First Notes on the General Principles of Employment for the Destitute and Criminal Classes (London: Privately printed, 1868);

The Mystery of Life and Its Arts (New York: Wiley, 1869);

The Queen of the Air: Being a Study of the Greek Myths of Cloud and Storm (London: Smith, Elder, 1869; New York: Wiley, 1869);

Lectures on Art Delivered Before the University of Oxford in Hilary Term, 1870 (Oxford: Clarendon Press, 1870; New York: Wiley, 1870);

Fors Clavigera: Letters to the Workmen and Labourers of Great Britain, 96 letters (London: Printed for the author by Smith, Elder, 1871–1884; New York: Wiley, 1880, 1884–1886);

Munera Pulveris: Six Essays on the Elements of Political Economy (London: Printed for the author by Smith, Elder, 1872; New York: Wiley, 1872);

Instructions in Practice of Elementary Drawing, Arranged with Reference to the First Series of Examples in the Drawing Schools of the University of Oxford (Oxford: Privately printed, 1872);

Aratra Pentelici: Six Lectures on the Elements of Sculpture, Given Before the University of Oxford in Michaelmas Term, 1870 (London: Printed for the author by Smith, Elder, 1872; New York: Wiley, 1873);

The Relation between Michael Angelo and Tintoret: Seventh of the Course of Lectures on Sculpture Delivered at Oxford, 1870–71 (London: Printed for the author by Smith, Elder, 1872; New York: Alden, 1885);

The Eagle's Nest: Ten Lectures on the Relation of Natural Science to Art, Given Before the University of Oxford in Lent Term, 1872 (London: Printed for the author by Smith, Elder, 1872; New York: Wiley, 1873);

The Sepulchral Monuments of Italy: Monuments of the Cavalli Family in the Church of Santa Anastasia, Verona (London: Arundel Society, 1872);

Love's Meinie: Lectures on Greek and English Birds, 3 parts (lectures 1 & 2, Keston: George Allen, 1873; New York: Wiley, 1873; lecture 3, Orpington: George Allen, 1881); republished in 1 volume (Orpington: George Allen, 1881);

Ariadne Florentina: Six Lectures on Wood and Metal Engraving, with Appendix, 7 parts (lecture 1, Keston: George Allen, 1873; lectures 2–6 and appendix, Orpington: George Allen, 1874–

1876); republished in 1 volume (Orpington: George Allen, 1876; 2 volumes, New York: Wiley, 1874–1875);

The Poetry of Architecture: Cottage, Villa, etc. To Which is Added Suggestions on Works of Art, as Kata Phusin (New York: Wiley, 1873); republished as *The Poetry of Architecture: Or, The Architecture of the Nations of Europe Considered in its Association with Natural Scenery and National Character* (Orpington: George Allen, 1893);

Val d'Arno: Ten Lectures on the Tuscan Art Directly Antecedent to the Florentine Year of Victories, Given Before the University of Oxford in Michaelmas Term, 1873 (Orpington: George Allen, 1874; New York: Alden, 1885);

Notes on Some of the Principal Pictures Exhibited in the Rooms of the Royal Academy: 1875 (Orpington: George Allen / London: Ellis & Bond, 1875);

Mornings in Florence: Being Simple Studies of Christian Art, for English Travellers (6 parts, Orpington: George Allen, 1875–1877; 1 volume, New York: Wiley, 1877; Orpington: George Allen, 1885);

Deucalion: Collected Studies of the Lapse of Waves, and Life of Stones (8 parts, Orpington: George Allen, 1875–1883; parts 1–3 republished in 2 volumes, New York: Wiley, 1875–1877; parts 1–6 republished in 1 volume, Orpington: George Allen, 1879);

Proserpina: Studies of Wayside Flowers, While the Air Was Yet Pure Among the Alps, and in the Scotland and England which My Father Knew (10 parts, Orpington: George Allen, 1875–1886; parts 1–6 republished in 1 volume, 1879; New York: Alden, 1885);

Letter to Young Girls, A Reprint with Slight Additions, From Fors Clavigera (Orpington: George Allen, 1876);

Guide to the Principal Pictures in the Academy of Fine Arts at Venice, Arranged for English Travellers, 2 parts (Venice, 1877; Orpington: George Allen, 1882–1883);

The Laws of Fésole: A Familiar Treatise on the Elementary Principles and Practice of Drawing and Painting, as Determined by the Tuscan Master: Arranged for the Use of Schools (4 parts, Orpington: George Allen, 1877–1878; New York: Wiley, 1877–1878; 1 volume, Orpington: George Allen, 1879; New York: Wiley, 1879);

St. Mark's Rest. The History of Venice, Written for the Help of the Few Travellers Who Still Care About Her Monuments (6 parts, Orpington: George

Allen, 1877–1884; 1 volume, 1884; New York: Wiley, 1884);

Notes by Mr. Ruskin on His Drawings by the Late J. M. W. Turner, R.A. (London: Elzevir, 1878);

Notes by Mr. Ruskin on Samuel Prout and William Hunt, Illustrated by a Loan Collection of Drawings Exhibited at the Fine Art Society's Galleries (London: Fine Art Society, 1879);

Letters Addressed by Professor Ruskin, D.C.L., to the Clergy on the Lord's Prayer and the Church, edited by F. A. Malleson (N.p.: Privately printed, 1879);

Elements of English Prosody for Use in St. George's Schools. Explanatory of the Various Terms Used in "Rock Honeycomb" (Orpington: George Allen, 1880);

Arrows of the Chace, Being a Collection of Scattered Letters Published Chiefly in the Daily Newspapers, 1840–1880, 2 volumes (Orpington: George Allen, 1880; New York: Wiley, 1881);

"Our Fathers Have Told Us." Sketches of the History of Christendom for Boys and Girls Who Have Been Held at Its Fonts, Part I: The Bible of Amiens (5 parts, Orpington: George Allen, 1880–1885; 1 volume, New York: Alden, 1885);

Catalogue of the Collection of Siliceous Minerals Given to and Arranged for St. David's School, Reigate (Brantwood: Privately printed, 1883);

The Art of England: Lectures Given in Oxford, 6 lectures (Orpington: George Allen, 1883–1884; New York: Alden, 1885);

The Storm-Cloud of the Nineteenth Century: Two Lectures Delivered at the London Institution, February 4th and 11th, 1884 (2 parts, Orpington: George Allen, 1884; 1 volume, New York: Wiley, 1884);

The Pleasures of England: Lectures Given in Oxford (4 parts, Orpington: George Allen, 1884–1885; 1 volume, New York: Wiley, 1885);

On the Old Road: A Collection of Miscellaneous Essays, Pamphlets, Etc., Etc., Published 1834–1885, 2 volumes, edited by Alexander Wedderburn (Orpington: George Allen, 1885);

Praeterita: Outlines of Scenes and Thoughts Perhaps Worthy of Memory in My Past Life (28 parts, Orpington: George Allen, 1885–1889; 3 volumes, Orpington: George Allen, 1886–1889; New York: Wiley, 1886–1889);

Dilecta: Correspondence, Diary Notes, and Extracts from Books, Illustrating Praeterita, 3 parts (Orpington: George Allen, 1886–1889);

Verona and Other Lectures, edited by W. G. Collingwood (Orpington: George Allen, 1894; New York & London: Macmillan, 1894);

*Lectures on Landscape, Delivered at Oxford in Lent Term,
1871* (Orpington: George Allen, 1897);

The Diaries of John Ruskin, 3 volumes, edited by Joan
Evans and J. H. Whitehouse (Oxford: Oxford
University Press, 1956–1959);

The Brantwood Diary of John Ruskin, edited by Helen
Gill Viljoen (New Haven: Yale University
Press, 1970).

Collection: *The Works of John Ruskin,* Library Edition, 39 volumes, edited by E. T. Cook and
Alexander Wedderburn (London: George
Allen / New York: Longman, Green, 1903–
1912).

OTHER: Edgar Taylor, ed., *German Popular Stories,*
introduction by Ruskin (London: John Camden, 1869), pp. v–xiv;

Dame Wiggins of Lee and Her Seven Wonderful Cats,
with preface and additional verses by Ruskin
(Orpington: George Allen, 1885).

During his prolific career John Ruskin wrote
many more works for adults than those especially
for young people. He is, however, well known in
the field of children's literature because of his literary fairy tale *The King of the Golden River; or, The
Black Brothers: A Legend of Stiria* (1851). Ruskin
was interested in the education of children, particularly young girls, and he wrote works for their
instruction and essays and letters on the proper
method and aim of education. His essay about
fairy tales and review of other children's stories
promoted their importance, as did his friendship
with and employment of the children's illustrator
Kate Greenaway. Ruskin's universally acclaimed
position as an art critic and moralist meant that
his works were frequently given to children for
their instruction, and his influence on the editors
and authors who shaped their lives is incalcula-
ble.

John Ruskin was born in London on 8 February 1819, the only child of John James Ruskin, a
prosperous wine merchant with literary tastes, and
his evangelical, pious wife, Margaret. Ruskin's
childhood, as he describes it in *Praeterita: Outlines of
Scenes and Thoughts Perhaps Worthy of Memory in My
Past Life* (1885–1889), was indulgently guarded but
emotionally repressed, a pattern that enhanced the
precision of his perception but contributed to the
painful quality of his relationships in later life. Although modern critics may be correct in ascribing
the details Ruskin chose for inclusion in *Praeterita* to
the literary conventions of evangelical literature or
of spiritual autobiography, Ruskin's reader always

remembers the vision of the child trained never to
complain and deprived of most amusements, looking out the window at a drainpipe, tracing patterns
in the rugs, observing the family's holiday world
from a special seat in the family traveling carriage,
and studying chapters of the Bible every day with
his mother – a practice continued into his teenage
years and forming an essential portion of his education.

Ruskin briefly describes his childhood books,
especially the rhymes *Dame Wiggins of Lee* (1823)
and *Peacock at Home* (1807), Maria Edgeworth's
Frank and *Harry and Lucy* (both published in 1801),
Jeremiah Joyce's *Scientific Dialogues* (1800), *Seven Champions of Christendom* (1616; of interest in terms of his
later adopting the name "St. George's Guild" for his
social projects), and *German Popular Stories* (1823),
from which Ruskin copied George Cruikshank's
illustrations. *Harry and Lucy, Seven Champions,* and
Scientific Dialogues were models for his earliest writing. In *The Ethics of the Dust: Ten Lectures on Work,
Traffic, and War* (1866), *Fors Clavigera: Letters to the
Workmen and Labourers of Great Britain* (1871–1884),
his letters to his father, and his last series of Slade
lectures he further discusses stories that influenced
his early youth. David C. Hanson, in "Ruskin's
Praeterita and Landscape in Evangelical Children's
Education" (1989), traces the influence of Mary
Martha Sherwood's children's book *The History of
Henry Milner* (1822–1837) on Ruskin's view of his
own development.

Ruskin produced verses as early as his seventh year, one of which he quotes in *The Queen of the
Air: Being a Study of the Greek Myths of Cloud and Storm*
(1869). As a teenager he had verses published in a
gift annual titled *Friendship's Offering,* and he had articles on architecture and geology published in periodicals before he was twenty; he also won the New-
digate Prize for a poem he wrote at Oxford. An
often-mentioned book of Ruskin's youth was the
copy of Samuel Rogers's *Italy* he received for his
thirteenth birthday in 1832. The etchings accompanying the text were after works of J. M. W. Turner,
whose excellence as a painter is the subject of the
first volume of *Modern Painters* (1843–1860) and
many other Ruskin works.

Ruskin's family took extensive annual trips,
which inspired his early work on alpine scenery and
his lifelong interest in geology. Another formative
influence on his early life was his unrequited love
for Adèle Domecq, the daughter of one of his
father's business partners, which unhappily affected
ten years of his life beginning in 1836. In that year
Ruskin also matriculated at Christ Church, Oxford,

where he was accompanied by his mother. The Oxford experience, during which time Ruskin was mostly interested in drawing and geology and not particularly interested in the classical curriculum, gave him a great distaste for competitive examination. In his maturity he articulated his disapproval of such examinations in his plans for the schools of the St. George's Guild, as well as in his distaste for competitive rather than cooperative social and economic structures. His schooling was interrupted in 1840 by a lengthy family tour of temperate European countries because of fears that he might have contracted consumption, but he returned in 1842 to take his A.B.; more important, he published the first volume of *Modern Painters* (by "a graduate of Oxford") the following year, when he also received his M.A.

The King of the Golden River, Ruskin's best-known contribution to children's literature, belongs to the first period of the author's literary life, when he was more aware of the beauty of nature and art than of human misery. It was written in 1841 but published ten years later, possibly through the intervention of his father (the preface says "with the author's passive approval"). Although *The King of the Golden River* is one of his best-known works, he dismissed it as of no importance and protested that he was incapable of creative rather than critical work. This unusual dismissal of a good piece of writing and a pleasing story is the first of many reasons why critics have been interested in it. The story was solicited, apparently as a kind of teasing, by Euphemia Gray, the nine-year-old daughter of some Scottish friends of the family; she had married Ruskin by the time of its publication.

The tale's sources include German fairy tales, the works of Charles Dickens, and "Golden Water" in the *Arabian Nights*. It is the story of the youngest of three brothers, Gluck, who because of his obedience, kindness, and charity is rescued from an intolerable life with his brutal siblings. The brothers are first ruined and then turned into black stones for their cruelty and bad behavior by two diminutive but dynamic figures, South West Wind, Esquire, and the King of the Golden River. The Wind ruins the family farmland in the Treasure Valley as punishment for their inhospitality; the King restores it by changing the course of the Golden River to renew the land. There has been considerable speculation about the relation of *The King of the Golden River* to Ruskin's own psychological development — because Gluck does not marry at the end of the story but goes back to his patrimonial land; because he is a passive hero while his brothers are brutishly

Illustration by Richard Doyle for Ruskin's best-known contribution to children's literature, The King of the Golden River *(1851)*

masculine; and because Ruskin's parents were particularly pleased by the story but Ruskin allowed it to be published with extreme reluctance, not acknowledging that his present wife was the child who had asked for it.

It has been adequately demonstrated that Ruskin had ambivalent feelings about attaining manhood, and he certainly had unusually painful relationships with the women he loved, seeming more comfortable with them when they were young girls than when they had grown. He also remained in his family home until the death of his parents in advanced age. Thus, *The King of the Golden River,* written when he was in his early twenties, appears to have autobiographical importance. Ruskin's appreciation for alpine scenery in this story as well as the theme of the need for charity and kindness over the desire for gold also are entirely characteristic of the body of his later work. The story has long been deservedly popular.

Ruskin's fame as a young man rested upon his championship of the British painter J. M. W.

Turner, of mountain scenery, of Renaissance painting, and of medieval architecture. Like his art criticism, Ruskin's architectural criticism ultimately related the success of a work to its moral inspiration. It emphasized that an architectural style was the culmination of the spiritual beliefs and social practices of a culture. Between volumes of *Modern Painters* Ruskin published *The Seven Lamps of Architecture* (1849) and *The Stones of Venice* (1851–1853), after extensive sketching in Italy. Although the years from 1849, when he married Euphemia Gray, to 1854, when she had the marriage annulled on the grounds of nonconsummation, were thus years of critical celebrity and productivity for Ruskin, they closed in considerable pain as it became clear that his wife was unhappy in her marriage and in her relationship with the older Ruskins, information she made public. The year following her divorce from Ruskin, Effie married John Everett Millais, the Pre-Raphaelite painter. They had been brought together by Ruskin's enthusiasm for Pre-Raphaelite painting, which continued long after Millais's intervention in Ruskin's personal life. It was contemporaneously noted that Effie was the model for Millais's enormously popular Royal Academy entry of 1853, *The Order of Release.*

In the remainder of the 1850s Ruskin finished *Modern Painters* (volumes three and four in 1856, volume five in 1860), a task he perceived as a duty to his father, and he became increasingly active in lecturing upon and demonstrating the ideas he had published on art and architecture and their relation to right living. In 1854, for example, he began to give weekly drawing lessons at the Working Men's College, a Christian Socialist organization, a project he also convinced Dante Gabriel Rossetti to undertake. These lessons can be seen as Ruskin's first chance at classroom teaching; however, Ruskin was always a teacher, combining a disarming humility about his personal failures with great confidence in his ability to improve public perceptions. His teaching of children or the uneducated differs little from his stance toward adults or the especially well educated.

From 1854 to 1856 Ruskin returned to Oxford to oversee the design and take some part in the physical building of the new Oxford Science Museum, a work that was meant to demonstrate the superiority of the Gothic mode of architecture and the relation of the laborers (who were being given great creative freedom) to that work. He was not ultimately pleased with the museum, however, because inadequate funds were provided for its decoration

and current social conditions made it difficult to prepare laborers to undertake it.

He was often applied to for judgments about drawing, and he took on some pupils by correspondence. He also wrote a book, *The Elements of Drawing* (1857), which suggests the use of the Cruikshank illustrations to Grimm as models. The widespread practice of sketching scenery, particularly before the advent of easy photographic methods, meant that this book, as well as Ruskin's credo of naturalism and accuracy in drawing, had a large audience. Lewis Carroll, for example, gave a copy to his sister Mary Dodgson.

Henry Liddell, the father of Alice Liddell and her sisters, was made the dean of Christ Church in 1855 when Alice (for whom *Alice's Adventures in Wonderland* was written by Lewis Carroll) was three. Liddell and Ruskin had known each other since Ruskin's undergraduate days, and the girls were Ruskin's friends from their early years. Alice was Ruskin's drawing student, and she later studied at Ruskin's drawing school, founded in conjunction with his Slade Professorship, although Ruskin eventually quarreled with her father over her art training. Ruskin's first drawing pupil, however, was an Irish child named Rose La Touche. First as his friend and later as the object of his courtship, Rose provided the most important relationship in Ruskin's life from 1858 (four years after his divorce from Effie) until her death in 1875.

In 1860, his forty-first year, Ruskin entered the second part of his literary life with the publication of *"Unto This Last": Four Essays on the First Principles of Political Economy* (1862) in William Makepeace Thackeray's *Cornhill Magazine*. The work so inflamed the public that Thackeray was persuaded not to finish the series. Ruskin's social beliefs are credited with inspiring the Labour Party, and *"Unto This Last"* had a great influence on such people as Bernard Shaw and Mahatma Gandhi. At the time, however, the public that had been content to admire Ruskin's ethical approach to architecture and painting was deeply upset when he turned his attention to the evils of laissez-faire capitalism and the responsibility of masters for the well-being of their employees. Ruskin asserted that it was impossible to improve the way in which people saw and appreciated art and nature unless their way of life and their education were changed first.

From this point in his career, he paid more attention to educational theory, influences on childhood, and materials appropriate for the formation of the youngest minds. Ruskin's attacks on mercantilism, like his earlier realization that his narrow childhood faith was not in the truest sense what he believed, caused painful strains in his relationship with his parents. In his consideration of formative influences, he also came to see many weaknesses in his own rearing that had undermined his ability to function as an adult, which he discussed in his letters to his father as well as much later in *Fors Clavigera.* Ruskin's father died in 1864.

Ruskin published *Sesame and Lilies* in 1865 and *The Ethics of the Dust* in 1866, two works for and about children's education. "Of Kings' Treasuries," the first part of *Sesame and Lilies,* argues that the proper aim of education is becoming sensitive, merciful, and just by association with the best books, rather than being trained for a worldly position. "Of Queens' Gardens," a title which refers partly to Ruskin's theory that women grow organically ("you cannot hammer a girl into anything. She grows as a flower does") and partly to the idea that women are responsible for the ordering and nurturing of the world, is about female education.

Ruskin perceives the sexes as entirely different and complementary in their abilities, and he desires to educate them in ways that will enable them to build the home life that he saw essential for right development. This perception of the differences between the sexes, as well as his belief that women's essential intolerance of evil is a quality that will be hardened into worthless acquiescence if exposed to the same trials that men must undergo in the world, limits his present-day influence. His strength for modern readers lies in his championship of women's education ("let a girl's education be as serious as a boy's. You bring up your girls as if they were meant for sideboard ornaments, and then complain of their frivolity") and his insistence upon the equal importance of each sex at a time when there were few decent schools for women in England.

Ruskin saw a woman's particular abilities as right ordering and rightly judging the activities of mankind. For this reason, for example, he can later blame her for insufficiently disapproving of warfare because he believes in her power to end it. Ruskin insists that every woman and every man should be useful, and he makes it clear that no domestic "loaf-giver" should be capable of living happily in her own home while people have no food or cleanliness or clothing on the other side of that safe wall.

Ruskin's digression on the need for young women to leave theological study alone and to have spiritual humility is one of the most discussed portions of *Sesame and Lilies.* It appears to make reference to Rose La Touche, to whom Ruskin proposed on her eighteenth birthday in 1866, when he was in his middle forties. Her anxiety that Ruskin's beliefs and practice differed from the evangelical beliefs of her father was a source of great unhappiness in their relationship, and it contributed to her physical and mental ill health until her death in 1875. George MacDonald, the author of children's fantasies, attempted to ameliorate the situation.

Ruskin's interest in the education and beliefs of young women, however, was not always of so troubled or so personal a nature. *The Ethics of the Dust* is a discussion in dialogue form of crystals — their atomic structure and their creation. The book was modeled on the lectures Ruskin gave informally at the Winnington Hall girls' school near Manchester. Ruskin had met its founder, Margaret Bell, who was using *The Elements of Drawing* in the school's curriculum, in 1857. He first visited the school in 1859 and returned and lectured there regularly for the next ten years. The girls, in turn, prepared the index for the fifth volume of *Modern Painters V.* In their letters at the time of the publication of *The Ethics of the Dust,* the students and Bell comment upon and sometimes mildly protest over various aspects of the book, especially the degree to which the young girls in the book resemble the Winnington students.

Biographers disagree on the extent to which Ruskin's involvement with the Winnington girls was influenced by his love for Rose La Touche. As Joan Abse suggests in *John Ruskin: The Passionate Moralist* (1981), his letters suggest that there was much to be happy about in his relation with the school, a feeling that Edward Burne-Jones and other invited lecturers also shared. Ruskin was always alive to the pleasure of observing pretty unaffected young girls, but he also wanted students whose lives and ways of thinking might still be influenced. The Winnington letters reveal that Ruskin was quick to differentiate between the educational needs and talents of the students and to supply materials that would be of most help to their individual development. In *The Ethics of the Dust* and in his letters to the school he explicates Bible passages, recommends sections of *Modern Painters,* lends his Turners for their observation, corrects their sketches, and links natural science with human ethics. He wrote songs for the Winnington girls and arranged physical demonstrations (the girls arranged themselves into crystalline structures) and other laboratory-style learning methods.

The Ethics of the Dust, with chapters on crystal virtues and crystal sorrows, is partly geological de-

Drawing by Ruskin of Rose La Touche, to whom he proposed on her eighteenth birthday in 1866 (Education Trust, Ruskin Galleries, Bembridge)

scription and partly a discussion of how crystals demonstrate laws of nature that have ethical implication. Created from materials seen in ugly heaps outside manufacturing areas, crystals appear to Ruskin an indication that nature works to raise itself into a higher state. What was soot can become diamond; by analogy, what is human refuse *must* be raised by human mercy and justice to similar reclamation.

In the chapter "Home Virtues" Ruskin praises the children's stories of Maria Edgeworth that he evidently had often mentioned to the girls on former occasions. However, as in the Edgeworth passage in *Praeterita,* in which he notes that the reward of his obedience to his father's wishes in the negotiation for a painting was loss of the painting and erosion of family feeling, Ruskin measures Edgeworth's conclusions against real life and finds them unlike. He wants to be sure that the girls understand that right must be done for itself, not for reward, and that suffering for doing right is the real test that Edgeworth never asks of her characters.

In 1868 Ruskin wrote a preface to a new edition of the Grimms' *German Popular Stories* (1869). This volume included restored etchings of the Cruikshank illustrations and was in a format Rus-

kin had recommended to the publisher as convenient for young readers. The preface recommends fairy stories over contemporary stories because they have fewer negative qualities than the satiric, overtly moral, or sensational books being given to contemporary children, a judgment that could include *Alice's Adventures in Wonderland.* Ruskin says that a traditional story will be a valuable teacher to properly reared children:

> animating for them the material world with inextinguishable life, fortifying them against the glacial cold of selfish science, and preparing them submissively, and with no bitterness of astonishment, to behold, in later years, the mystery – divinely appointed to remain such to all human thought – of the fates that happen alike to the evil and the good.

Ruskin also thinks of such stories as close to the natural world he sees as the rightful environment for innocent childhood. Although Ruskin sees childhood as a state clearly different from adulthood, the personal appreciation and thoughtfulness that Ruskin brings to children's literature in his literary criticism is in itself a contribution to the validation of childhood and children's literature.

In 1869, when he was fifty, Ruskin was named the first Slade Professor of Art at Oxford, a role in which he produced and published public lectures until 1885, when he resigned the professorship after Oxford voted to approve vivisection in physiology courses. His professorship was interrupted, however, when he suffered a mental breakdown in 1878 after the publicity and anxiety surrounding a lawsuit by the American painter James Whistler protesting Ruskin's criticism of his work in *Fors Clavigera;* Ruskin resigned but was later reinstated.

Preferring to have control over publishing and marketing, Ruskin had published the first letter of *Fors Clavigera* in pamphlet form in 1871. He published ninety-six letters, which appeared regularly until 1878 – when they were interrupted because of the initial serious episode of delirium – and then continued from 1880 to 1884. Letters 91 and 93–96 include engravings of Kate Greenaway drawings. *Fors Clavigera* is of great interest because it extends Ruskin's educational and social theories and his dialogue with his audience. Using an intimate conversational style, Ruskin wrote about issues currently of interest to him and responded to letters from his readers. *Fors Clavigera* is the original source of some of the material in *Praeterita* and also Ruskin's original forum for discussing the education of children in the schools he envisioned for the St. George's Guild.

The guild was a utopian social project, like Ruskin's other practical social projects – including road building by Oxford undergraduates (including Oscar Wilde), street sweeping and tea selling in London, and clearing a polluted spring at Carshalton. Ruskin proposed to end urban unemployment by a renewal of an agrarian lifestyle without the trains and machines that reduced the dignity and need for human labor, made the countryside ugly, and brutalized the lives of the many for the benefit of a few. As in his work on female education, Ruskin's way of differentiating between social classes does not accord with modern aims, although the ecological and economic goals of the guild still appear desirable, and the problems it was to address have not been solved by other means.

In response to a reader request, the St. George's Guild oath was explained to children in "Letter to Young Girls" (16 March 1876), a pamphlet excerpt from *Fors Clavigera*. The young girls in question were to endeavor to please Christ in a world that falsely professed or had rendered obsolete this practice. (Ruskin had had a renewal of religious feelings at Assisi in 1874.) They were advised to keep calm under provocation, never to seek amusement but always to be ready to be amused, and to take care of things entrusted to them. They were also told to dress as plainly as their parents allowed, to employ the seamstresses in their country neighborhoods rather than fashionable city modistes, and to make attractive, good-quality clothing for the poor.

The St. George's Guild schools were meant to combat the problem of unemployed persons living under miserable conditions in cities. Because Ruskin felt that a preindustrial agricultural life was better than the degrading, idle city life and that the contemporary system of education encouraged people to look down on manual labor, the children in his country schools were not to be taught to read, although those who chose to learn on their own were to be provided with excellent literary and natural science books. Ruskin was not interested in pursuing reading and writing for their own sake. Letter 94 in *Fors Clavigera* reviews the need for music, geometry, astronomy, botany, zoology, and history (presented orally to the students or engaged in by practical learning methods) and decries the vulgar tendencies excited by undue stress on arithmetic. His 1873 Slade lectures, *Love's Meinie, Deucalion* (1875–1883), and *Proserpina* (1875–1886) were intended as textbooks for zoology, geology, and botany for the schools.

Letter 67 stresses the need to inculcate habits of obedience, reverence, and humility in students, but to do this without ranking the students against each other or otherwise engaging in competition. Ruskin experimented with his methods at a school in Coniston near Brantwood – the home he built shortly before the death of his mother in 1871 – until late in his life, but the St. George's Guild model never developed into the extensive social movement that he had desired. The failure of his social projects to attract the financial support of his admirers was a source of great sorrow to Ruskin, who saw his mission to change society and human perception as a failure, though he was in much demand as a lecturer and critic.

Two lectures that Ruskin gave in his sixties, during the resumption of *Fors Clavigera,* also have particular application to youth. The first, given at Eton on 6 November 1880, was published as *"Our Fathers Have Told Us." Sketches of the History of Christendom for Boys and Girls Who Have Been Held at Its Fonts, Part I: The Bible of Amiens* (1880–1885), later translated into French by Marcel Proust. It interprets the relation of the cathedral of Amiens to the citizens who built it and the significance of its structure to religious faith, and it contains passages on kindness to animals as well as to people.

His 1883 Slade lecture "Fairy Land" primarily discussed the strengths and weaknesses of Kate Greenaway's illustrations. It is part of the series that ended Ruskin's platform career; his last lectures evidenced increasing instability and presaged his serious mental breakdowns. It could be argued that the Slade Professor of Art should have been investigating French painters rather than a popular children's illustrator. The Greenaway lecture, however, like the one that followed it on journal illustrators (including Tenniel), can also be seen simply as a continuation of Ruskin's interest in educative influences. It was an attempt to look at the formative function of illustrations recently made available to every humble English home through improvements in the printing process. In this case, the public was both the still-malleable children and their already corrupted parents.

Although Ruskin saw many of Greenaway's shortcomings (in their subsequent lengthy correspondence he constantly told her that she spent too much time on clothes, ought to differentiate between the characters of the children she drew, ought to improve her ability to draw feet and natural backgrounds, and ought to improve in "descriptive real-

Self-caricature by Ruskin (Pierpont Morgan Library)

ity" rather than prettiness), the lecture praises her work. Ruskin preferred Greenaway pictures to those of many other illustrators, as they were devoid of the vulgarity of mercantilism and modern machinery while celebrating pastoral beauty and pastimes, and as they were exemplary in illustrating to a society abusing and exploiting its children what the right life of children ought to be. Greenaway's "fairy land" pictures were valuable because they were a reminder of the protected innocence, clean air, and agrarian beauty that ought to be every child's birthright.

In 1885 Ruskin wrote the preface to a facsimile edition of the anonymous picture book *Dame Wiggins of Lee and Her Seven Wonderful Cats* (1823), to which he had added four verses about the cats' education, illustrated by Greenaway sketches. Ruskin had commended the verse form of *Dame Wiggins* in letter 50 of *Fors Clavigera* and had approved it as relating "nothing that is sad, and . . . nothing that is ugly." In 1886, responding iconoclastically to Sir John Lubbock's lecture to workingmen on the one hundred best books, Ruskin stated that his own list would be headed by Edward Lear's "*Book of Nonsense* with its corollary carols." Ruskin's last great work, *Praeterita,* belongs to the period in his late sixties when he was often in the midst of breakdown (1885–1889) but had not yet become uncommunicative. While he was intermittently remembering and relating the story of his own sheltered childhood

and youth, Ruskin also corresponded (1887–1888) with an earnest and religious young art student, Kathleen Olander, to whom he gave art lessons and whom he hoped to marry, a relationship broken off by her parents and Ruskin's cousin Joanna Severn.

Although he did not write in the last decade before his death, Ruskin continued to have many visitors, friends, and correspondents, including Greenaway and some of the former Winnington students. In the late 1880s Ruskin continued to teach and plan curriculum for the Coniston School. In spite of his sadness that people had been entertained by but failed to be changed by his attempts to reform English life and perception, his celebrity was unfailing in his final years. His eightieth birthday on 8 February 1899 and his death on 20 January 1900 were occasions of elaborate national observances. Refusing interment at Westminster, Joanna buried her cousin near Brantwood, after his own wish.

Ruskin's view of the great separation between childhood and adulthood did not seem to hold true in his own case, nor is it any longer a dominant view. However, increased interest in children's literature has coincided with renewed interest in the Victorians, producing a body of work on Ruskin's childhood reading, his fairy tale, and his view of his own childhood in *Praeterita*. Similarly, interest in ecology, education, and animals has made Ruskin's concern with pollution of the environment, childhood learning, and the importance of nonhuman species seem particularly current.

In his own time Ruskin's ideas about the education of women, the goals and methods of education, the need for young people to engage in active social reform, the value of nature study, and the need to pursue truth to nature in drawing were widely disseminated by his admirers. If they were not recommended to young people in his own ubiquitous volumes or school adaptations, they were recommended at second- or third-hand by fiction writers and editors of children's works. By his own literary fairy tale and the fairy tales that he recommended for children's reading, Ruskin also encouraged the public to feel that imaginative literature for children was wholesome, and that writers of social realism for children had the power to engage one of the most brilliant minds of the age. A revival of interest in Ruskin's art and social criticism at the end of the twentieth century has encouraged a great many articles and books admiring his genius and breadth of vision, while attempting to explain his return to or failure to leave his childhood garden.

Both Ruskin's life and writing, in fact, may be said to have encouraged others to take children and their education seriously.

Letters:

Hortus Inclusus: Messages from the Wood to the Garden, Sent in Happy Days to the Sister Ladies of the Thwaite, Coniston, edited by Albert Fleming (Orpington: George Allen, 1887; New York: Wiley, 1887);

Letters of John Ruskin to Charles Eliot Norton, 2 volumes, edited by Charles Eliot Norton (Boston & New York: Houghton, Mifflin, 1904);

John Ruskin's Letters to Francesca and Memoirs of the Alexanders, edited by Lucia Gray Swett (Boston: Lothrop, Lee & Shepard, 1931);

The Gulf of Years: Letters from John Ruskin to Kathleen Olander, edited by Rayner Unwin (London: Allen & Unwin, 1953);

Ruskin's Letters from Venice, 1851–1852, edited by John L. Bradley (New Haven: Yale University Press, 1955);

Letters of John Ruskin to Lord and Lady Mount-Temple, edited by Bradley (Columbus: Ohio State University Press, 1964);

Dearest Mama Talbot, edited by Margaret Spence (London: Allen & Unwin, 1966);

The Winnington Letters: John Ruskin's Correspondence with Margaret Alexis Bell and the Children at Winnington Hall, edited by Van Akin Burd (Cambridge, Mass.: Harvard University Press, 1969);

Ruskin in Italy: Letters to His Parents, 1845, edited by Harold I. Shapiro (Oxford: Clarendon Press, 1972);

Sublime and Instructive, edited by Virginia Surtees (London: M. Joseph, 1972);

The Ruskin Family Letters: The Correspondence of John James Ruskin, His Wife, and Their Son, John, 1801–1843, 2 volumes, edited by Burd (Ithaca: Cornell University Press, 1973);

John Ruskin and Alfred Hunt, edited by Robert Secor (Victoria, B.C.: University of Victoria Press, 1982);

The Correspondence of Thomas Carlyle and John Ruskin, edited by George Allan Cate (Stanford, Cal.: Stanford University Press, 1982);

My Dearest Dora: Letters to Dora Livesey, Her Family and Friends 1860–1900 (Kendal, U.K.: Privately printed, 1984).

Bibliographies:

Thomas J. Wise and James P. Smart, *A Complete Bibliography of the Writings in Prose and Verse of John Ruskin, LL.D.,* 2 volumes (London: Privately printed, 1893);

Kirk H. Beetz, *John Ruskin: A Bibliography, 1900–1974* (Metuchen, N.J.: Scarecrow Press, 1976).

Biographies:

W. G. Collingwood, *The Life and Work of John Ruskin,* 2 volumes (London: Methuen, 1900);

E. T. Cook, *The Life of John Ruskin,* 2 volumes (London: George Allen, 1911);

Derrick Leon, *Ruskin: The Great Victorian* (London: Routledge & Kegan Paul, 1949);

Peter Quennell, *John Ruskin: The Portrait of a Prophet* (London: Collins, 1949);

Joan Evans, *John Ruskin* (New York: Oxford University Press, 1954);

John D. Rosenberg, *The Darkening Glass: A Portrait of Ruskin's Genius* (New York: Columbia University Press, 1961);

Patrick Conner, *Savage Ruskin* (Detroit: Wayne State University Press, 1979);

Joan Abse, *John Ruskin: The Passionate Moralist* (New York: Knopf, 1981);

John Dixon Hunt, *The Wider Sea: A Life of John Ruskin* (New York: Viking, 1982);

Tim Hilton, *John Ruskin: The Early Years* (New Haven: Yale University Press, 1985).

References:

Van Akin Burd, "Ruskin's Testament of His Boyhood Faith: *Sermons on the Pentateuch,*" in *New Approaches to Ruskin: Thirteen Essays,* edited by Robert Hewison (London: Routledge & Kegan Paul, 1981), pp. 1–16;

Francelia Butler, "From Fantasy to Reality: Ruskin's *King of the Golden River,* St. George's Guild, and Ruskin, Tennessee," *Children's Literature,* 1 (1972): 62–73;

Susan P. Casteras, "The Germ of a Museum: Arranged First for 'Workers in Iron': Ruskin's Museological Theories and the Curating of the Saint George's Museum," in *John Ruskin and the Victorian Eye,* edited by Harriet Welchel (New York: Abrams, 1992), pp. 184–210;

James S. Dearden, "*The King of the Golden River:* A Bio-Bibliographical Study," in *Studies in Ruskin,* edited by Robert Rhodes and Del Ivan Janick (Athens: Ohio University Press, 1982), pp. 32–59;

Jane Merrill Filstrup, "Thirst for Enchanted Views in Ruskin's *The King of the Golden River,*" *Children's Literature,* 8 (1980): 68–79;

Avrom Fleishman, *Figures of Autobiography: The Language of Self-Writing in Victorian and Modern England* (Berkeley: University of California Press, 1983), pp. 174–188;

Colin Gordon, *Beyond the Looking Glass: Reflections of Alice and Her Family* (San Diego: Harcourt Brace Jovanovich, 1982);

David C. Hanson, "Ruskin's *Praeterita* and Landscape in Evangelical Children's Education," *Nineteenth-Century Literature,* 44 (June 1989): 45–66;

Elizabeth K. Helsinger, "The Structure of Ruskin's *Praeterita,*" in *Approaches to Victorian Autobiography,* edited by George P. Landow (Athens: Ohio University Press, 1979), pp. 87–108;

William Jolly, *Ruskin on Education: Some Needed But Neglected Elements* (London: George Allen, 1894);

U. C. Knoepflmacher, "Resisting Growth through Fairy Tale in Ruskin's *The King of the Golden River,*" *Children's Literature,* 13 (1985): 3–30;

Patricia Miller, "The Importance of Being Earnest: The Fairy Tale in 19th Century England," *Children's Literature Association Quarterly,* 7 (Summer 1982): 11–14;

Linda H. Peterson, *Victorian Autobiography: The Tradition of Self-Interpretation* (New Haven: Yale University Press, 1986), pp. 60–90;

Suzanne Rahn, "The Sources of Ruskin's *Golden River,*" *Victorian Newsletter,* 68 (Fall 1985): 1–8;

Bruce B. Redford, "Ruskin Unparadized: Emblems of Eden in *Praeterita,*" *Studies in English Literature,* 22 (Autumn 1982): 675–687;

Jeffrey L. Spear, *The Dreams of an English Eden: Ruskin and His Tradition in Social Criticism* (New York: Columbia University Press, 1984).

Papers:
Notable holdings of John Ruskin's papers are at the Pierpont Morgan Library, New York; the Beinecke Library, Yale University; the Ruskin Gallery at Bembridge School, Isle of Wight; and the John Rylands Library, Manchester.

Anna Sewell

(30 March 1820 – 25 April 1878)

Lopa Prusty
Boston College

BOOK: *Black Beauty: The Autobiography of a Horse* (London: Jarrold, 1877); republished as *Black Beauty: His Grooms and Companions* (Boston: American Humane Society, 1890; Boston: D. Lothrop, 1890).

Anna Sewell's only book, *Black Beauty: The Autobiography of a Horse* (1877), has been considered as a work of humane literature, a moral tale, and an animal fable, which were all popular genres in the later nineteenth century. Unlike many of the works with which it has been compared, however, *Black Beauty* has come to be lauded as the best-loved animal story and a classic of children's literature. Its missionary aim to "induce kindness, sympathy and an understanding treatment of horses" was as timely as it was far-reaching: as the animal most relied upon for all modes of carriage and transport on both sides of the Atlantic, the horse was most apt to be abused.

The book was appropriated for its propagandistic capabilities first by George Angell, founder of the Massachusetts Society for the Prevention of Cruelty to Animals, and later by the Royal Society for the Prevention of Cruelty to Animals. Through its combination of technical details with the affective power of fiction, it influenced the abolition of the bearing rein and successfully pleaded for the kind treatment of horses. Anna Sewell's corollary desire to present the difficulties of cabmen in "a correct and telling manner" was realized when the book inspired London missionaries to establish cabmen's shelters providing systematic religious and temperance instruction. Although *Black Beauty* was not intended strictly for a juvenile audience, it was used as a reading book in boys' schools, no doubt for its moral and instructional value. The book outlived its purported missionary intent, however, as its author had created a work of the imagination whose aspects gave it lasting appeal.

Anna Sewell was born into the Quaker home of Isaac and Mary Sewell on 30 March 1820 in

Yarmouth, England. Isaac Sewell was an enterprising, if restless, businessman and banker whose financial misfortunes made for an itinerant family life for his wife and two children, Anna and Philip. Anna Sewell never married and, as was not uncommon for Victorian spinsters, never lived apart from her parents. As Isaac Sewell's salary did not afford formal education for both the Sewell children, Anna's early intellectual and moral training, until she reached the age of about twelve, took place under the tutelage of her resourceful and seemingly indefatigable mother. She received more-formal ed-

259

ucation for approximately three years, between the ages of twelve and fourteen. It was a time when her intellectual and artistic capabilities only began to be displayed; the promise she exhibited was left unrealized because of an unfortunate fall that would leave her a semi-invalid for the remainder of her life.

Sewell's training under the guidance of her mother gives insight not only into the origins of her characteristic courage and independence, but also possible sources of her imaginative and spiritual distresses. Mary Sewell was a follower of the Rousseauian educationists Richard Lovell Edgeworth and his daughter Maria. Undaunted by financial privation and zealous about her duty as a mother, she wrote a book called *Walks with Mama* in order to buy the Edgeworths' *Practical Education* (1798), the book she valued "above all others as a help" in her pedagogic endeavors. Anna and Philip Sewell were taught the Edgeworthian virtues of honesty, industry, thrift, self-reliance, independence, and courage. They were encouraged to keep themselves occupied without toys and storybooks, to learn the moral burden of wrongdoing and misconduct by suffering their "natural consequences," and to learn management of money. They were also inculcated with ideas of sacrifice and self-denial that their mother espoused; although the Sewells never knew real material comfort, the children were made conscious of their relative good fortune and once were even asked to give up their summer holiday at the seaside so that their vacation money could be donated to aid the Irish during the potato famine. Mary Sewell, confident of herself as a "heaven-taught mother," supported her dicta with examples from the Bible. Later in life Anna Sewell would suffer from extreme diffidence about the relinquishment of self to the putative will of God.

Anna Sewell's natural affinity with animals was surely reinforced through lessons in the subject her mother favored most: natural history. Mary Sewell saw divinity manifested in nature and believed that natural history "may always be made to lead happily and gracefully and tenderly to God, the Creator and Father, not through sermons, but through the things that He has made." She took her children on nature walks, during which plant, animal, and insect specimens were collected for the playroom. The Sewell children were taught early in life to be kind to animals, and Anna learned never to tolerate cruelty toward animals and the helpless, the sight of which, her niece Margaret Sewell relates, "roused her indignation almost to fury, and

wherever she was, or whoever she had to face, she would stop and scathe the culprit with burning words."

The three years of Anna Sewell's formal education constituted the happiest times of her life. In 1832, when she was twelve, the Sewells moved to Palatine Cottage at Stoke Newington. Acres of meadowland were turned into a farm, where Anna was able to indulge her interest in entomology by keeping bees. She went to school for the first time, where she found the company of girls her own age and was exposed to subjects such as French (she showed a gift for languages), mathematics, and drawing and painting, which had not been encompassed by her mother's tutorship. Her talent in drawing began to flower as she learned to paint landscapes in oil.

At about the age of fourteen, however, Sewell suffered a misfortune that altered the course of her life. On her return home from school she fell, severely hurting her ankle; the injury would lead to a life of semi-invalidism for the remainder of her years. She would never leave her parents' home or separate from her mother. Having learned to drive and ride horses on her maternal grandparents' farm at Buxton in Norfolk, she would come to rely on her pony and cart, which she drove unattended when carrying out her humanitarian work as an adult. Mary Sewell insists in her autobiography (included in Mrs. Bayly's *Life and Letters of Mary Sewell,* 1889) that her daughter's life had not been "discoloured" by her accident, and she affirms her faith in the divine purpose behind Anna's suffering: "the Blessed Lord saw that He could make a more exquisite character out of that noble, independent, courageous, capable creature by imprisoning it within the strictest limitations than by giving it the play of full development."

Apart from periods of recurrent lameness, Anna Sewell seems to have been generally hypochondriacal. She began to complain as a young woman of chest pains and weakness in her back and head. Interspersed with times of what Mrs. Bayly calls "enforced idleness" were periods of good health and activity. Contrary to the Quaker precept of plain living, Sewell seems to have enjoyed her sojourns for treatment in the rather worldly atmosphere of hydropathic centers in Germany and England. It seems noteworthy that, according to her mother, Sewell never looked ill. In her biography of Sewell, Susan Chitty surmises that hypochondria afforded refuge from activities that did not interest the girl. Sewell seems to have been troubled with guilt about pleasure, but, more profoundly, her ar-

"The moon had just risen above the hedge, and by its light I could see Smith lying a few yards beyond me."—*Page* 121.

BLACK BEAUTY:

HIS GROOMS AND COMPANIONS.

THE AUTOBIOGRAPHY OF A HORSE.

Translated from the Original Equine,

BY

ANNA SEWELL.

LONDON: JARROLD AND SONS,
3, PATERNOSTER BUILDINGS.

Cover, frontispiece, and title page for Sewell's popular novel (courtesy of the Lilly Library, Indiana University) tistic sensibility seems to have suffered from conflicts with the demand for austerity and self-abnegation, the edifying nature of which her mother had early inculcated.

Sewell's spiritual reconciliation to her misfortune as being part of a divine plan is not apparent from entries in the diary she kept from 1840 to 1845. Instead, her words suggest spiritual anguish, betraying guilt at her attraction to "the irresistible charm of worldly things," which might have extended to her desire for artistic expression and her fear of loss of selfhood in surrendering to the will of God. Her doubts may have been related to some degree to shifts in her mother's faith; Mary Sewell, in fact, left the Quakers for the Anglican Church in 1835, and Anna Sewell accompanied her mother to chapels of various denominations in the quest for spiritual restoration.

Sewell's few extant letters suggest the frustration of her predominantly artistic sensibility by her mother's disapproval and the requirements of faith. Mary Sewell had grown up in the atmosphere of strict Quaker censure of the expressive arts – painting, music, and literature. In a telling letter to her mother dated 23 September 1835, Anna alludes to Mary Sewell's disapproval of painting and passionately articulates the conflict of artistic desire with the denial of the means to create: "pray do not congratulate me on my wise resolution about not going on with my oil paints for I have heartedly repented of it since I have been here and seen all the fine oakes and elms with the bright colours of Autumn. . . . I am now always looking for something to make a picture of; what tints will harmonise together, what colours will do for this oak and ash and what for the distances. In fact I never enjoyed looking at the country so much before. It seems like another sense." Such effusiveness about the desire to create does not seem to have been uttered many more times. Guilt about the sense of self necessary for creative expression may have dwelled too closely with this desire.

Bayly's daughter, Elizabeth (Barrett) Bayly, noted Sewell's "artist instinct for form strongly developed," a gift that was evident in her remarkable drawings from nature and "made her an admirable critic of manner and arrangement in word-painting." As an adult, Sewell's literary energies were largely involved in being her mother's chief "critic and counsellor" – Mary Sewell was the popular author of what she called "homely ballads," written for the instruction and edification of the poor. Anna Sewell wrote only one serious poem and some unpublished stories in verse that combine humor and whimsicality with a darker sense of nature. None of these works were published in her lifetime, but they are recorded in Bayly's and Chitty's books. She had great love for the poetry of established poets – especially William Wordsworth, Samuel Taylor Coleridge, John Keats, and Alfred Tennyson – a fondness that Mary Sewell ultimately shared. Margaret Sewell recalls in her memoir of her aunt that both mother and daughter enjoyed reading and reciting poetry that they often learned by heart.

Anna Sewell lived at a time when humanitarian work often fell to the charge of Victorian gentlewomen. In her early twenties, when she lived at Brighton, she taught Sunday school, giving lessons in reading and writing as well as religious instruction to children of the poor, many of whom worked long hours in factories. In 1860, when she lived at a place called Blue Lodge near the village of Wick, she established a Working Man's Club, an evening institute providing instruction in reading, writing, and elementary biology to local miners and laborers. Sewell rode unattended in her pony cart three nights a week to give classes at Wick. She also became active with her mother in temperance work. After her retreat from the world, Sewell undertook a form of charity that her mother called the "Sixpenny Charity," the purpose behind which was to give regular help to the poor – if only sixpence – which the receiver could rely on and learn to manage.

By the time of the inception of the Sixpenny Charity, Sewell was confined to her house. Mary Sewell believed that her daughter had contracted a mortal disease at the age of fifty-one and that she succumbed to it seven years later. The exact nature of the illness remains mysterious. At the time Anna was impelled to write, although her artistic and literary productions were few. An entry in her diary for 6 November 1871 reveals that she had begun *Black Beauty:* "I am writing the life of a horse and getting dolls and boxes ready for Christmas." The book was in fact sometimes dictated and sometimes written in pencil on slips of paper to be transcribed into fair copy by Mary Sewell.

Black Beauty seems to have emerged from a strange confluence of events. Sewell gave up her horse and carriage and became a complete invalid; she also became fully dependent on her mother. In 1874 she experienced a spiritual revivification through which she seemed to become reconciled to her sufferings. She told Bayly, "He has shown me that I have a place in the household, I belong to the family of God, and my very frailty has given me a place among the weak ones in whom His strength is perfected. I know now the meaning of that word, 'No longer a servant, but a Son.' " This spiritual restitution seems to have ballasted her desire to write, and on 6 December 1876 she entered in her diary, "I am getting on with my little book, Black Beauty."

One of the work's acknowledged influences was an "Essay on Animals" by Horace Bushnell, an Anglican theologian. Bayly, impressed by the perfect accord between Sewell and her horse, had given a précis of Bushnell's work — a plea for kind treatment of animals as part of doing God's will — during a visit to the Sewells in 1863. Later Sewell wrote to Mrs. Bayly, "The thoughts you gave me from Horace Bushnell years ago have followed me entirely through the writing of my book, and have, more than anything else, helped me to feel it was worth a great effort to *try* at least, to bring the thoughts of men more in harmony with the purposes of God on this subject."

Sewell, apparently obeying the beckoning of her own imagination, chose to write not just an animal story but an animal autobiography. It is interesting that the work that emerged from her spiritual regeneration was not the straightforward didacticism of a homily or treatise, which would have accommodated sufficiently her mission. The novel form seems to have allowed Sewell to explore intricacies of her subject that a treatise or tract would not have permitted; it also allowed her, in curious juxtaposition to her deceivingly simple pious intention, to exercise her delight in words and written form. It is doubtful whether *Black Beauty* would have known its long-lasting success if it had been only a homiletic statement.

The story's title character and first-person narrator is a horse. After a life in which he has known relentless vicissitude, Black Beauty has been restored to a happier existence by the time he begins to relate his story. The book, however, ends with a poignant reminder of what he has lost through his movement away from a state of pastoral simplicity and innocence into the world of human beings. He knows the loss of his mother and "good, kind" Farmer Grey, under whose care he is reared up to the age of four. He endures first the unpleasant experiences of being broken in — having to wear a saddle, bridle, bit, and iron shoes — and later the distress of the bearing rein. One of his worst losses is that of his liberty, which he experiences at his first place of work, Squire Gordon's Birtwick Park: "week after week, month after month, and no doubt year after year, I must stand up in a stable night and

Anna and Mary Sewell

day except when I am wanted, and then I must be just as steady and quiet as any old horse who has worked twenty years." The mitigating factor is that at this early stage he knows only the kindness and consideration of men. His character, good breeding, and sanguine disposition are recognized, and his beauty, as well as his "sweet, good-tempered face" and "fine, intelligent eye," move Mrs. Gordon to name him "Black Beauty." He enjoys a felicitous relationship with human beings and the pleasure of companionship with other horses, Ginger, Merrylegs, Sir Oliver, and Justice.

His mother's warning, however, that "a horse never knows who may buy him, or who may drive him" proves to be prophetic, for Black Beauty not only loses the friendship and affection of human and equine companions, but his beauty is marred as well. At Earlshall, his next place of work, his life reaches a point of crisis. When he is ridden by an intemperate undercoachman, Reuben Smith, he falls and breaks his knees. Blemished by his scarred knees, he is considered unfit for a gentleman's stable, where appearance is a matter of consequence.

Deirdre Dwen Pitts, "Discerning the Animal of a Thousand Faces," *Children's Literature: An Annual of the Modern Language Association Seminar on Children's Literature and the Children's Literature Association,* 3 (1974): 169–172;

Frances Clark Sayers, "Books That Enchant: What Makes a Classic?," in *Summoned by Books: Essays and Speeches,* edited by Marjeanne Jensen Blinn (New York: Viking, 1965), pp. 151–161;

Margaret Sewell, "Recollections of Anna Sewell," in Anna Sewell's *Black Beauty: An Autobiography of a Horse* (London: Harrap, 1935), pp. 1–6;

Vincent Starrett, "*Black Beauty* and its Author," in his *Buried Caesars: Essays in Literary Appreciation* (New York: Books for Libraries, 1968), pp. 205–223;

Andrew Stibbs, "*Black Beauty:* Tales My Mother Told Me," *Children's Literature in Education,* 22 (Autumn 1976): 128–134;

John Rowe Townsend, "Articulate Animals," in his *Written for Children: An Outline of English-Language Children's Literature,* second revised edition (New York: Lippincott, 1983), pp. 103–113;

Nicholas Tucker, "Literature for Older Children (Ages 11–14)," in his *The Child and the Book: A Psychological and Literary Exploration* (Cambridge: Cambridge University Press, 1981), pp. 144–189.

Mary Martha Sherwood

(6 May 1775 – 20 September 1851)

Janis Dawson
Simon Fraser University

BOOKS: *The Traditions* (London: William Lane, 1795);

Margarita (London: William Lane, 1799);

The History of Susan Gray (Bath: Samuel Hazard, 1802); revised and corrected (Wellington, Salop: Houlston, 1815?; Portland: Shirley & Edwards, 1825);

The History of Little Henry and His Bearer (Wellington, Salop: Houlston, 1814; Andover, Mass.: Flagg & Gould, 1817);

The History of Lucy Clare (Wellington, Salop: Houlston, 1815);

The Memoirs of Sergeant Dale, His Daughter and the Orphan Mary (Wellington, Salop: Houlston, 1815; Boston: Samuel T. Armstrong, 1821);

The Ayah and Lady (Wellington, Salop: Houlston, 1816; Boston: Samuel T. Armstrong, 1822);

The History of Emily and Her Brothers (Wellington, Salop: Houlston, 1816; Philadelphia: Clark & Raser, 1819);

The History of Little George and His Penny (Wellington, Salop: Houlston, 1816; Portland: Wm. Hyde, 1820);

An Introduction to Astronomy (Wellington, Salop: Houlston, 1817);

Stories Explanatory of the Church Catechism (Wellington, Salop: Houlston, 1817; Burlington, N.J.: David Allinson, 1823);

The Infirmary (Wellington, Salop: Houlston, 1817?);

The History of Theophilis and Sophia (Wellington, Salop: Houlston, 1818; Andover, Mass.: Mark Newman, 1820);

The Indian Pilgrim (Wellington, Salop: Houlston, 1818); republished as *The Pilgrim of India* (Boston: James Loring, 1828);

An Introduction to Geography (Wellington, Salop: Houlston, 1818);

The Little Woodman and His Dog Caesar (Wellington, Salop: Houlston, 1818; Philadelphia: American Sunday School Union, 1826);

The Busy Bee (Wellington, Salop: Houlston, 1818);

Mary Martha Sherwood (courtesy of the Lilly Library, Indiana University)

A Drive in the Coach through the Streets of London (Wellington, Salop: Houlston, 1818);

The Rose (Wellington, Salop: Houlston, 1818; New York: Mahlon Day, 1833);

The History of the Fairchild Family: or The Child's Manual: Being a Collection of Stories Calculated to Shew the Importance and Effects of a Religious Education, 3 parts (London: John Hatchard, 1818, 1842, 1847; New York: W. Burgess, 1828);

A General Outline of Profane History (Wellington, Salop: Houlston, 1819);

The Two Sisters (Wellington, Salop: Houlston, 1819?);

The Hedge of Thorns (London: John Hatchard, 1819; New York: Samuel Wood, 1820);

The Errand Boy (Wellington, Salop: Houlston, 1819; Boston: Lincoln & Edmands, 1821);

The Little Sunday School Child's Reward (Wellington, Salop: Houlston, 1819);

The Orphan Boy (Wellington, Salop: Houlston, 1819; Boston: Samuel T. Armstrong, Crocker & Brewster, 1821);

The Wishing Cap (Wellington, Salop: Houlston, 1819; Newburyport, Mass.: W. & J. Gilman, 1820); revised as *The Wish, or Little Charles* (Philadelphia: American Sunday School Union, 1827);

Little Arthur (Wellington, Salop: Houlston, 1820);

The May-Bee (Wellington, Salop: Houlston, 1820);

The Nurserymaid's Diary (London: William Whittemore, 1820?);

Procrastination, or The Evil of Putting Off (London: William Whittemore, 1820?); republished as *Procrastination, or The Evil of Delay* (New York: General Protestant Episcopal Sunday School Union, 1829);

The Iron Cage (London: William Whittemore, 1820?; New York: General Protestant Episcopal Sunday School Union, 1842);

The Golden Clew (London: William Whittemore, 1820?; Boston: James Loring, 1831);

The Governess, or The Little Female Academy (Wellington, Salop: Houlston, 1820); republished as *The Governess, or The Young Female Academy* (New York: Printed for O. D. Cooke, Hartford, 1827);

The History of George Desmond (Wellington, Salop: Houlston, 1821; Philadelphia: American Sunday School Union, 1828?);

The Infant's Progress from the Valley of Destruction to Everlasting Glory (Wellington, Salop: Houlston, 1821; Boston: Samuel T. Armstrong, 1821);

Mrs. Sherwood's Primer, or First Book for Children (Wellington, Salop: Houlston, 1821; Hartford: H. & F. J. Huntington, 1828);

The Recaptured Negro (Wellington, Salop: Houlston, 1821; Boston: Samuel T. Armstrong, 1821);

Little Robert and the Owl (Wellington, Salop: Houlston, 1821; Boston: Samuel T. Armstrong, 1824);

Charles Lorraine, or The Young Soldier (London: William Whittemore, 1821; Boston: Samuel T. Armstrong, Crocker & Brewster, 1823);

The Orphans of Normandy, or Florentine and Lucie (London: John Hatchard, 1822; Hartford, Conn.: D. F. Robinson, 1827);

The History of Henry Milner, a Little Boy Who Was Not Brought Up According to the Fashions of This World (London: John Hatchard, 1822–1837);

Blind Richard (Wellington, Salop: Houlston, 1822?);

The Village Schoolmistress (Wellington, Salop: Houlston, 1822?);

Easy Questions for a Little Child (Wellington, Salop: Houlston, 1822);

The Penny Tract (London: William Whittemore, 1822?–1823; Boston: Samuel T. Armstrong, Crocker & Brewster, 1823);

The History of Mary Saunders (London: William Whittemore, 1822?–1823; Boston: Samuel T. Armstrong, 1823);

The Blind Man and Little George (London: William Whittemore, 1822?–1823; Boston: Samuel T. Armstrong, 1823);

The Potter's Common, or The Happy Choice (London: William Whittemore, 1822–1823; Philadelphia: American Sunday School Union, 1828?);

The Poor Man of Colour, or The Sufferings (London: William Whittemore, 1822–1830);

The History of Little Lucy and Her Dhaye (Wellington, Salop: Houlston, 1823; Boston: Samuel T. Armstrong, 1824);

The Infant's Grave, a Story of the Northern Part of France (Wellington, Salop: Houlston, 1823);

The Lady of the Manor (Wellington, Salop: Houlston, 1823–1829; Philadelphia: Towar & Hogan, 1829);

Pere La Chaise (Wellington, Salop: Houlston, 1823);

The Blessed Family (London: William Whittemore, 1823; Boston: Samuel T. Armstrong, 1823);

The Child's Magazine (London: Knight & Lacey, 1823–1824);

Bible History, or Scripture Its Own Interpreter (London: Knight & Lacey, 1823);

The History of Mrs. Catherine Crawley (Wellington, Salop: Houlston, 1824);

Content and Discontent (London: William Whittemore, 1824);

The Lambourne Bell (London: William Whittemore, 1824?);

The Little Beggars (London: William Whittemore, 1824; Philadelphia: American Sunday School Union, c. 1830);

Waste Not Want Not (London: William Whittemore, 1824);

My Uncle Timothy (London: Knight & Lacey, 1825);

Juliana Oakley (London: Knight & Lacey, 1825; Hartford: O. D. Cooke, 1825);

Clara Stephens, or the White Rose (Sabbath School Union for Scotland, 1825; Philadelphia: American Sunday School Union, 1827);

The Captive in Ceylon (Wellington, Salop: Houlston, 1826; New York: O. D. Cook, 1827);

The Gipsy Babes (Wellington, Salop: Houlston, 1826; Philadelphia: American Sunday School Union, 1827);

The Soldier's Orphan, or the History of Maria West (London: Dean & Munday, 1826; Portland: Shirley & Hyde, 1828);

A Chronology of Ancient History (London: Longman, Rees, Orme, Brown & Green, 1826–1827);

Julian Percival (Wellington, Salop: Houlston, 1826; Salem: Whipple & Lawrence, 1827);

The Two Dolls (Wellington, Salop: Houlston, 1826);

Ermina, or The Second Part of 'Juliana Oakley' (Philadelphia: American Sunday School Union, 1827); republished as *Ermina* (London & Wellington, Salop: Houlston, 1831);

The Pulpit and the Desk (Wellington, Salop: Houlston, 1827);

The Dry Ground (Wellington, Salop: Houlston, 1827; New Haven: S. Babcock, 1833);

Edward Mansfield (Wellington, Salop: Houlston, 1827; Salem: Whipple & Lawrence, 1827);

The Lady in the Arbour (Wellington, Salop: Houlston, 1827; New Haven: S. Babcock, 1833);

A Series of Questions and Answers Illustrative of the Church Catechism (Wellington, Salop: Houlston, 1827); republished as *Questions for Children with Answers from Scripture* (New Haven: S. Babcock, 1831);

Susannah, or, the Three Guardians (London: Longman, Rees, Orme, Brown & Green, 1827; Philadelphia: American Sunday School Union, 1829);

The Two Sisters, or Ellen and Sophia (London: Religious Tract Society, 1827; Philadelphia: American Sunday School Union, 1828);

Le Fevre (London: T. Hamilton, 1827);

The Fawns (Wellington, Salop: Houlston, 1828); republished as *The Two Fawns* (New Haven: Sidney's, 1833);

The Hills (Wellington, Salop: Houlston, 1828);

Home (Wellington, Salop: Houlston, 1828);

Poor Burruff (Wellington, Salop: Houlston, 1828);

The Rainbow (Wellington, Salop: Houlston, 1828);

Soffrona and Her Cat Muff (Wellington, Salop: Houlston, 1828);

The Rosebuds (Wellington, Salop: Houlston, 1828);

The Idiot Boy (Wellington, Salop: Houlston, 1828);

The Thunder Storm (Wellington, Salop: Houlston, 1828);

Arzoomund (Wellington, Salop: Houlston, 1828);

My Aunt Kate (Wellington, Salop: Houlston, 1828);

Southstone's Rock (Wellington, Salop: Houlston, 1828);

Theophilus (London: R. B. Seeley & W. Burnside, 1828);

Emancipation (Wellington, Salop: Houlston, 1829);

The Mourning Queen (Wellington, Salop: Houlston, 1829; New York: Harper, 1834);

The Orange Grove (Wellington, Salop: Houlston, 1829; New York: Protestant Episcopal Sunday School Union, 1842);

The Little Orphan (London: William Whittemore, 1829);

Little Sally (London: William Whittemore, 1829);

The Millennium, or Twelve Stories (London: T. Hamilton, 1829; New York: J. Leavit, 1829);

The Butterfly (Berwick-upon-Tweed: Thomas Melrose, 1829);

The Golden Chain (Berwick-upon-Tweed: Thomas Melrose, 1829);

Intimate Friends (London & Wellington, Salop: Houlston, 1830);

Roxobel, or English Manners and Customs Seventy Years Ago (London & Wellington, Salop: Houlston, 1830–1831; New York: Harper, 1831);

The Babes in the Woods of the New World (London & Wellington, Salop: Houlston, 1830?; New York: Mahlon Day, 1831);

The Stranger at Home (London & Wellington, Salop: Houlston, 1830?);

Katherine Seward (London & Wellington, Salop: Houlston, 1830; New York: N. B. Holmes, 1832);

The Hidden Treasure (London & Wellington, Salop: Houlston, 1830?);

A Mother's Duty (London & Wellington, Salop: Houlston, 1830?);

The Stolen Fruit (London & Wellington, Salop: Houlston, 1830?);

The Red Book (London: Religious Tract Society, 1830; New York: Pendleton & Hill, 1831);

The Flowers of the Forest (London: Religious Tract Society, 1830; Philadelphia: George Lattimer, 1833);

The Father's Eye (Berwick-upon-Tweed: Thomas Melrose, 1830);

The Mountain Ash (Berwick-upon-Tweed: Thomas Melrose, 1830);

Obedience (Berwick-upon-Tweed: Thomas Melrose, 1830);

The Two Paths, or The Lofty and The Lowly Way (Berwick-upon-Tweed: Thomas Melrose, 1830); republished as *The Lofty and The Lowly Way* (New York: John S. Taylor, 1839);

The Useful Little Girl and The Little Girl Who Was of No Use At All (Berwick-upon-Tweed: Thomas Melrose, 1830; New York: John S. Taylor, 1839);

Everything Out of Its Place (London & Wellington, Salop: Houlston, 1831);

Dudley Castle (London: Darton, 1832);

Emmeline (Berwick-upon-Tweed: Thomas Melrose, 1832);

The Convent of St. Clair (Berwick-upon-Tweed: Thomas Melrose, 1833);

Aleine, or le Bachen Holzli (Berwick-upon-Tweed: Thomas Melrose, 1833);

My Godmother (Berwick-upon-Tweed: Thomas Melrose, 1833);

The Little Momiere (London: John Hatchard, 1833);

Victoria (London: John Hatchard, 1833);

The Nun (London: Seeley & Burnside, 1833; Princeton: Moore Baker, 1834);

The Latter Days (London: Seeley & Burnside, 1833);

The Basket-Maker (Berwick-upon-Tweed: Thomas Melrose, 1834–1835);

The Monk of Cimies (London: Darton, 1834; New York: Harper, 1837);

The Red Morocco Shoes (Berwick-upon-Tweed: Thomas Melrose, 1835; New York: J. S. Taylor, 1839);

The Roman Baths, or the Two Orphans (Berwick-upon-Tweed: Thomas Melrose, 1835);

Saint Hospice (Berwick-upon-Tweed: Thomas Melrose, 1835);

The Violet Leaf (Berwick-upon-Tweed: Thomas Melrose, 1835);

Caroline Mordaunt, or The Governess (London: Darton, 1835);

Shanty the Blacksmith. A Tale of Other Times (London: Darton, 1835; New York: S. Taylor, 1839);

Social Tales for the Young (London: Darton, 1835; Philadelphia: J. Whetman, 1835);

Sabbaths on the Continent (London: Thomas Ward, 1835);

The Last Request of Emily (Berwick-upon-Tweed: Thomas Melrose, 1836);

The Well-Directed Sixpence (Berwick-upon-Tweed: Thomas Melrose, 1836);

The School Girl (Berwick-upon-Tweed: Thomas Melrose, 1836);

The Parson's Case of Jewels (Berwick-upon-Tweed: Thomas Melrose, 1837);

The Bible (London & Wellington, Salop: Houlston, 1838);

The Happy Family (London & Wellington, Salop: Houlston, 1838);

The Little Negroes (London & Wellington, Salop: Houlston, 1838);

The Indian Orphans (Berwick-upon-Tweed: Thomas Melrose, 1839);

Former and Latter Rain (London: Longman, Rees, Orme, Brown & Green, 1840);

Julietta di Lavenza (London: John Hatchard, 1841);

The Last Days of Boosy, the Bearer of Little Henry (London: Houlston, 1842); published as *The Last Days of Boosy: or The Sequel to Henry and his Bearer* (Philadelphia: American Sunday School Union, 1842);

Robert and Frederick (London: Seeley & Burnside, 1842);

The History of John Marten (London: John Hatchard, 1844);

The Fairy Knoll (London: H. K. Lewis, 1848);

The Story Book of Wonders (London: Thomas Nelson, 1849);

Jamie Gordon, or the Orphan (London: Seeley & Burnside, 1851);

The History of Master Henry, a Pleasing Narrative for the Young (Boston: Dayton & Wentworth, 1855);

The Life of Mrs. Sherwood, edited by Sophia Kelly (London: Darton, 1857);

The Life and Times of Mrs. Sherwood, edited by F. J. Harvey Darton (London: Wells, Gardner, Darton, 1910).

OTHER: *The Holiday Keepsake,* includes stories by Sherwood (London: Darton, 1841);

The Juvenile Forget-Me-Not, includes stories by Sherwood (London: Darton, 1842).

It is unfortunate that Mary Martha Sherwood is chiefly remembered today for *The History of the Fairchild Family* (1818), a book that has become infamous in the late twentieth century for extended deathbed scenes, rotting corpses, and other grisly and disturbing details. She is less often remembered as the author of more than four hundred titles, ranging from lengthy multivolume books to tales, tracts, texts, chapbooks, reward books, and periodical articles. While some of her efforts have been considered mediocre and even unreadable by twentieth-century critics, she has been acknowledged as a writer of considerable ability. *Caroline Mordaunt, or The Governess* (1835) has been compared to the novels of Jane Austen, and *Shanty the Blacksmith* (1835) is highly regarded as an exciting Gothic tale. It would be a mistake to regard the *History of the Fairchild Family* as representative of Sherwood's literary style, religious philosophy, or attitudes toward childhood and child rearing. Her literary career was hardly static, and many of her books and stories reflect her life experiences as well as developments in her personal philosophy.

Sherwood's literary output was no less than prodigious, considering that she spent many years in India with her husband's regiment, mothered a large family that included orphans as well as her own children, and taught tirelessly both in India and England. But her significance resides in more than the sheer volume of her work. Because Sherwood's works occupied such a dominant place in the nursery during her fifty-year writing career, it would not be unreasonable to argue that she helped shape the Victorian worldview. Many of her child readers became prominent statesmen, businessmen, clergymen, teachers, soldiers, missionaries, and writers.

Sherwood's early books were also popular in American nurseries until the 1840s. After that time, although they continued to be published by American firms, many Americans began to find her tales old-fashioned and distasteful, reflecting a social context and belief in the rightness of a fixed social order that seemed inappropriate. Moreover, authors offering moral instruction and entertainment from an American perspective began to compete successfully with Sherwood and other British and European authors. Louisa May Alcott's March family proved to be more interesting to American readers than the Fairchild family, and little Eva and Uncle Tom tugged at more hearts than little Henry and his bearer, Boosy.

Sherwood was born Mary Martha Butt on 6 May 1775, the eldest daughter and second child of the Reverend George Butt, rector of Stanford, near Worcester. Her ancestry was relatively distinguished and of considerable antiquity, as she relates in her autobiography. Her father was scholarly, cultured, and fond of society. He was a member of the Lichfield circle, which included prominent writers, thinkers, and educators of the day such as Erasmus Darwin, Richard Edgeworth, Anna Seward, and Thomas Day. Reverend Butt's close friends included members of the most important families in England, and at one point he became chaplain to King George III. His intellectual, literary, and social interests were maintained throughout his life, ultimately offering rich educational opportunities for his children. Martha Butt was the daughter of a wealthy merchant. Apparently she was sensitive about her lack of physical beauty and preferred to retire rather than join company. She had a good mind, however, which she cultivated by reading the important books of her day. Despite their obvious differences in temperament, the couple managed to create a secure and comfortable environment for their children.

Because of her parents' intellectual interests and her father's enlightened view of female education, Mary Butt was not discouraged from reading widely in her father's extensive library and joining in her brother's Latin and Greek lessons. She had a lively imagination, which was encouraged by her parents. She began to compose her own stories, many of them fairy tales, before she could write — her mother wrote them out for her — and as she grew older, she entertained young visitors with her own tales. As a grown woman she would tell stories to children on the veranda of her bungalow in India and wherever else her travels took her. Many of these stories were later published.

Butt's upbringing, though enlightened, was not permissive. She ate "the plainest possible food, such as dry bread and cold milk. I never sat on a chair in my mother's presence." Her mother carefully preserved her from knowledge of vice and ensured that she acquired the manners and social graces appropriate to her station. In order to correct her posture, Butt was required to wear an iron collar and a backboard strapped over the shoulders. She wore these "stocks," as she called the contraption, during the daytime from her sixth to thirteenth year. Yet she insisted that she was a cheerful child, and "when relieved from my collar, I not unseldom manifested my delight by starting from our hall-door, and taking a run for at least half a mile through the woods which adjoined our pleasure-grounds."

The natural beauty of Butt's first home afforded her real pleasure, and her parents allowed her considerable freedom to explore the countryside. A quick and observant child, she developed an appreciation for nature that she would employ as a writer. Her ability to describe the natural world around her, apparent even in simple tales such as *The Rose* (1818), as well as in her more complex stories, was one of her real strengths as a writer of didactic fiction.

By all accounts Butt's early life was thoroughly happy. She recorded in her autobiography many pleasant memories of tender moments with her parents, storytelling and games with her brother and sister, family excursions, and social engagements. Many of these experiences were later woven into her books and stories. The happy family, always at the heart of her work, reflected personal experience as much as nineteenth-century convention.

Frontispiece by Joseph Martin Kronheim for an 1866 edition of
The History of Little Henry and His Bearer; *the
popularity of the book in the United States rivaled
that of Harriet Beecher Stowe's* Uncle Tom's
Cabin *(1852).*

When she was sixteen, Butt and her sister, Lucy, were sent to the Abbey School at Reading, a respected school designed for the daughters of the clergy and minor gentry. Austen had been a pupil there only a few years previously. Mary acquired social graces and a good knowledge of conversational French. During the time that she and her sister were at the school, Reading was the destination of many of the French nobility fleeing the Revolution.

Following her return from school, Butt began to write seriously. Encouraged by her father, she completed *The Traditions* (1795), a two-volume book. Intended for adult readers, the work was published by subscription for the benefit of the master of Reading Abbey School, Mr. St. Quentin, who was facing financial ruin. The subscription was successful enough that he was able to set up a new school. Encouraged by the generally favorable re-

views, Butt began a second book, titled *Margarita* (1799). Both novels reflected what the author knew of society, and although they were romantic, they were considered appropriately moral.

The sudden death of Reverend Butt in 1795 brought an end to Mary's happy childhood. She had dearly loved her father, and he had supported her literary aspirations from early childhood. The family's lifestyle changed dramatically, as Mrs. Butt preferred a life of almost complete retirement. To offset some of the depression that enveloped the family after her father's death, Mary and her sister became involved in the Sunday school movement, which was still in its early stages. They were greatly affected at this time by the efforts of Hannah More to improve the lives of the poor through education. Butt developed a more serious attitude toward religion, as is reflected in her next two novels, *The History of Susan Gray* (1802) and *The History of Lucy Clare,* begun in 1802 as a companion work to *Susan Gray* but not completed until 1810.

Susan Gray, a tractlike novel, was originally written for the older girls in Butt's Sunday school class. It was designed, like More's tracts, to inculcate religious principles in the poor. The book was so popular that it was pirated several times before the author revised and "improved" it in 1816. Sarah Trimmer, the respected author of improving stories for children, expressed her approval of the book in the first volume of *The Guardian of Education* (1802). The publication of *Susan Gray* was a significant event in Mary's literary career, and at this point she began to write for children and young adults. By this time Lucy Butt was also writing religious and moral stories for children. Lucy was to develop her own literary career, writing extensively under her married name, Mrs. Cameron.

Not long after her father's death, Butt became reacquainted with her younger cousin Henry Sherwood, who had spent several years in France. On his return to England in 1798, Henry applied for and obtained a commission in the army. He soon left for the West Indies, where his regiment, the 53rd, was stationed, but is likely that he and Mary came to an understanding before his departure. Within six months of his return to England in 1803 the couple was married.

The marriage seems to have been a happy one. The Sherwoods were a devoted couple, and Henry encouraged and supported his wife's ambitions. For the first two years of their marriage, Mary Sherwood followed the regiment around England. Although she did not write much at this time, she did note many details and incidents of army life that she later incorporated into her books. She became even more serious in her religious devotions and began to study the Bible regularly. Her first child, named Mary Henrietta, was born in 1804. In April 1805 Sherwood was forced to leave her baby with her mother and sister when the regiment was ordered to India. This journey was to have a profound influence on Sherwood's personal life and literary career: she wrote some of her most popular stories while in India, and she collected anecdotes that were used in children's books and stories long after she returned to England.

Sherwood found the four-month voyage to India difficult and unpleasant. Her living quarters were cramped and confining, and she was ill for most of the voyage. Pregnancy contributed to her discomfort. Characteristically, she persevered with her study of the Scriptures, endeavored to teach a sailor's boy to read, and cared for her servant's baby. When the ship finally came to rest at Madras, Sherwood was taken ashore, and was dazzled by the exotic surroundings: "As an infant opening its eyes in a new world is unable to distinguish one thing from another or to comprehend any object it sees, so in a similar degree my first views of India seem strangely confused in my recollections."

From Madras the regiment traveled to Calcutta, where the Sherwoods remained for a month before traveling by boat to Dinapore. Sherwood actively recorded her impressions of everything she saw. Because she described India before the country experienced the full impact of the European presence, her journals, and even the children's stories written during this period of her life, have historical significance. It would be a mistake, however, to suggest that she had more than a superficial understanding of India, even though she lived there for a decade, or that her descriptions and interpretations were free of cultural bias. Her experience in India did not challenge her sense of British superiority; if anything, it reinforced it. Her perceptions of India were also colored by the loss of two of her infants, poor health, and her severe religious views. Within a short time of their arrival in Dinapore, she gave birth to her first son, Henry. Sherwood claimed that she never properly recovered her health after Henry's birth, and the baby suffered bouts of illness.

She found the climate difficult, at one point commenting that it had completely bleached her complexion. She wrote that the dampness gave off a sweet and sickening odor that depressed the spirits and caused headaches. She had an ample number of servants, but managing her household proved almost impossible until she understood something of the customs and learned how to communicate. Although she did not actually admit it as later generations of women in her position would, India probably frightened her. She reacted with horror to the poverty, disease, high infant and child mortality, and the non-Christian religious and social customs. She made no attempt to understand what she witnessed. Her contact with Indians was limited, and she tended to judge all Hindus and Muslims by her worst experiences. A strong-minded woman, she tried to control what she feared and could not understand. This meant engaging ever more intensely in those activities that were most familiar to her: teaching, writing, and studying her Bible.

She was greatly distressed by the fact that there was no provision made for the instruction or care of the children of British soldiers. The British government was not yet officially involved in governing India; much was still in the hands of the East India Company. Missionary work had not been encouraged by the company, and as army officers were not known for their religious enthusiasm, there was little interest in schools, teachers, or religious services. The situation was to change not long after Sherwood's arrival, but initially individuals were responsible for the education of British children in India.

With the support of her husband and the assistance of his clerk, Sherwood began to receive children in her home for three or four hours daily, and part of her veranda was converted into a schoolroom. She found the task a burden at times because of her health and the fact that she always seemed to have a baby to care for. Her school began with thirteen children and gradually increased to forty or fifty. The pupils included not only the children of soldiers and officers but also children of native origin. They ranged in age from the very young to adolescents, and on occasion illiterate soldiers attended. The school became an important part of Sherwood's life in India, and she established one wherever her husband's regiment was stationed.

The health of her children was a constant concern. Henry, never strong, succumbed to the effects of whooping cough before he was two. Another baby, Lucy, born in 1807, died of dysentery the following year. Sherwood grieved deeply for her two babies, and in many ways she never fully recovered from their lengthy sicknesses and ultimate deaths. It is probable that she relived their deaths every time she described the death of a beautiful, fair-haired child in a book or story. In addition, her severity of outlook was deeply influenced by the Calvinistic perspective of some of the regimental chaplains, in particular the pious Henry Martyn, who offered her considerable emotional and spiritual support during her time of trouble. Martyn died of dysentery in India in 1812, but he was remembered in some of Sherwood's stories and in the name of her son Henry Martyn Sherwood, born in 1813.

Sherwood wrote tirelessly during her years in India. Two early efforts included lengthy religious allegories based on John Bunyan's *The Pilgrim's Progress* (1678). The first, *The Infant's Progress,* was begun in 1806 when the author was at Berhampore and published in England in 1821. Like Bunyan's work, *The Infant's Progress* is told "in the similitude of a dream," and follows pilgrims through their trials to reach the City of God. But the book was intended for children, "to make them acquainted in an agreeable manner, with many of those awful mysteries of our holy Religion, the knowledge of which is necessary to your salvation." The pilgrims are three young children: Humble Mind, "not quite ten years old," and his two younger sisters, Playful and Peace. They are dogged every step of the way by In-bred Sin, who tempts them unmercifully with toys, novelties, and food. He causes the pilgrims to do all the things naughty children do: quarrel, disobey, overeat, covet, and ask too many questions.

The book might have been dreary, with its lengthy biblical quotations and its constant emphasis on sin and depravity, but an interesting tension is created in the character of In-bred Sin. Sometimes walking with the children, sometimes lurking behind, he is always plotting new temptations. Since neither the reader nor the pilgrims can be sure what he will do next, some young readers may have found his activities more interesting than the spiritual struggles of the little heroes, reading the book as an adventure story rather than as a guide to salvation. The book was popular because of its novelty and sentiment, and it remained Sunday reading for the rest of the century.

The second religious allegory was *The Indian Pilgrim,* begun in 1810 or 1811 and published in England in 1818. The idea for the book originated with a plan suggested by Henry Martyn and another chaplain, Daniel Corrie, to translate *The Pilgrim's Progress* into Hindustani, but it was eventually decided that a book reflecting an Indian context would be more successful in winning converts. The book was never published in India, but like Sherwood's earlier allegory, it became popular Sun-

day reading material and went through several British and American editions.

The Indian Pilgrim tells the story of the pilgrimage of Goonah Purist, or the Slave of Sin, from the City of the Wrath of God to the City of Mount Zion. Building on the tension of Bunyan's original theme, Sherwood added descriptions of Indian architecture, clothing, food, plant and animal life, and religious practices. Her descriptions were gruesome and sensational and must have provided exciting reading in middle-class Victorian parlors. Her treatment of the various religious faiths Goonah encounters reveals strong religious prejudices: Muslims and Jews receive better treatment than Hindus because of their belief in one God, but Roman Catholics fare little better than the Hindu idolaters. Chief among the faults of a Roman Catholic priest who tries to convert Goonah are his denial of the authority of the Scriptures, his refusal to give Goonah a Bible so that the pilgrim can read the word of God for himself, and his toleration of images of saints. *The Indian Pilgrim* was the last of Sherwood's long allegorical works, but she continued to write books and stories for home and school use. Her diaries indicate that she was able to work on more than one story at a time, many of which were first told to her children and only later written down.

Stories Explanatory of the Church Catechism, published in England in 1817, was originally written for use in Sherwood's school. Begun sometime between 1810 and 1812 and printed in Calcutta by 1814, the book is an excellent example of the author's ability to make the moral and religious tale – or in this case an explanation of the catechism – interesting and even entertaining, although that was not her first objective. She recounts in her autobiography how she had been "thoroughly perplexed by finding that the children could not understand any common English narrative without asking many questions," since they knew only the Indian context. Therefore, she used the pattern of writing approved by evangelical catechists, interspersing doctrine with stories from everyday life for ease of understanding, but she placed everything in a familiar Indian setting. The result was a lively and vivid collection of stories, liberally sprinkled with Indian terms, that became popular in England.

Stories Explanatory of the Church Catechism centers on six-year-old Mary Mills, her parents, and her godmother, Mrs. Browne. Like a responsible Christian godmother, Mrs. Browne concerns herself with the child's spiritual welfare as well as her physical needs. Mary learns the Ten Commandments through question-and-answer situations and examples drawn from the experiences of barracks life. One lesson demonstrates both the consequences of the failure of children to honor their fathers and mothers and the need for parents to gain control of their children at an early age: a boy, rendered uncontrollable and disobedient by his parents' failure to correct him when he was young, consumes a large quantity of spirits in the bazaar and succumbs to "the uncommon heat of the sun." *Stories Explanatory of the Church Catechism* gave Sherwood an opportunity to express her concern about the quality of family life and her views on the responsibilities and duties of each member to one another. Like other evangelicals, she believed that harmonious family relationships reflected man's relationship with God.

Despite the contrived nature of the stories, the scenes are vivid and colorful, and the character of little Mary is believable. Grisly details are not spared. Sherwood did not hesitate to describe corpses and how quickly they deteriorated in the heat of the Indian sun. She also describes the darker side of life in the barracks – idleness, drunkenness, neglect of children, the practice of dosing infants with alcohol or opium to keep them quiet (her own infant Henry narrowly escaped death by the latter means) – but all these things were well known to the children for whom the book was written. As Margaret Nancy Cutt notes in *Mrs. Sherwood and Her Books for Children* (1974), "Not until Kipling brought them to life again in the 1880s were the daily happenings in the married quarters depicted with such lively detail."

The Ayah and Lady, translated into Hindustani in 1813 and published in England in 1816, bears many similarities to *Stories Explanatory.* Here, too, the narrative is structured around an explanation of the Ten Commandments and aspects of the catechism. It also provides vivid descriptions of Indian scenes – particularly Indian domestic activities, customs, and manners – but it lacks the appeal contributed by a child character. Written for the use of servants in well-to-do English families living in India, the narrative focuses on an English lady and her maid, or ayah. The ayah is portrayed as sly, selfish, lazy, and untrustworthy. Her employers are well aware of her faults, yet they tolerate her. She is by far the most interesting character in the book, and her mistakes provide some of the entertainment value offered by child characters in other books. But the ayah is a grown woman, and modern readers are likely to find Sherwood's portrayal of an Indian maid condescending and even offensive.

One of Sherwood's best-known and most popular books, *The History of Little Henry and His Bearer,* was also written at this time and published in England in 1814 and the United States in 1817. The book went through many editions in a short time in both countries. At one point, its popularity in the United States even rivaled that of Harriet Beecher Stowe's *Uncle Tom's Cabin* (1852). Little Henry, the child hero, resembles her son Henry who had died in 1807. The story is sentimental, based on a theme Sherwood employed many times – that of the orphan or neglected child who tries to convert his or her elders. In this case, the orphaned and neglected Henry tries to convert his devoted native servant, Boosy. By his beautiful death he also influences his worldly foster mother to read the Bible and become more serious. *The History of Little Henry and His Bearer* is an interesting example of how the evangelical and romantic perspectives of childhood could exist together. Although Henry's heart is filled with sin (according to strict evangelical belief), he is a figure not unlike William Wordsworth's romantic child: sweet, innocent, wise, and physically beautiful.

The full story of Boosy's conversion was not told until 1842 in a sequel, *The Last Days of Boosy, the Bearer of Little Henry,* and with a sensitivity of which Sherwood was probably not capable at the height of her missionary zeal. Although Boosy had to become a Christian – there could be no compromise there – *The Last Days of Boosy* reflects an awareness of the difficulties faced by a prospective convert in India – loss of caste and rejection by family and community. The author's sympathetic portrayal of Boosy's loneliness and isolation is the strongest feature of an otherwise pedestrian work.

Another Indian tale that gained popularity for the novelty of the setting and its interesting child characters was *The Memoirs of Sergeant Dale, His Daughter and the Orphan Mary* (1815). The book was favorably reviewed in *The Salopian Magazine* (30 November 1815) as a work belonging to "a new era" in which "those who write for the capacities of children, have at last discovered, that common incidents well arranged, and common occurrences well related, are the most useful methods of instructing and improving the mind of infancy and youth." The story begins in India with infant Mary, a beautiful child with light curling hair and blue eyes, who is orphaned at a year and a half, shortly after her parents arrive at Cawnpore. She is neglected, dirty, and given spirits to keep her quiet.

The child's desperate state is relieved by Sarah, the motherless daughter of pious Sergeant Dale. Sarah, carefully raised by her father, is dutiful, devoted, and serious, unlike many of the girls

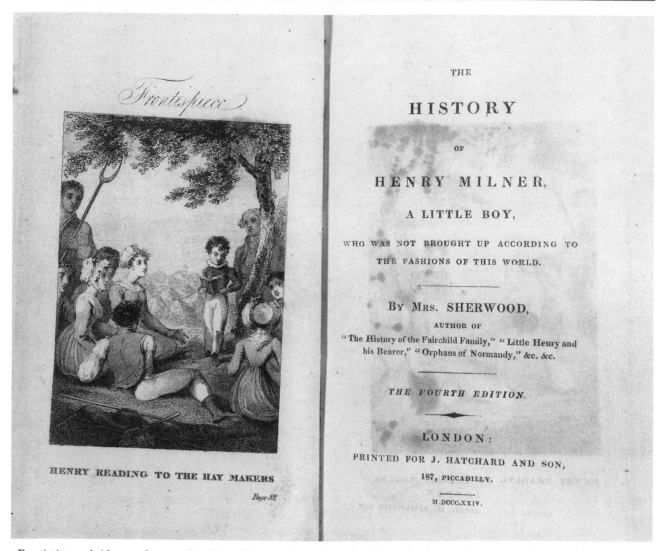

Frontispiece

HENRY READING TO THE HAY MAKERS

Page 52

THE

HISTORY

OF

HENRY MILNER,

A LITTLE BOY,

WHO WAS NOT BROUGHT UP ACCORDING TO
THE FASHIONS OF THIS WORLD.

BY MRS. SHERWOOD,

AUTHOR OF

"The History of the Fairchild Family," "Little Henry and
his Bearer," "Orphans of Normandy," &c. &c.

THE FOURTH EDITION.

LONDON:

PRINTED FOR J. HATCHARD AND SON,
187, PICCADILLY.

M.DCCC.XXIV.

Frontispiece and title page for an early edition of the book Sherwood began as a response to Thomas Day's The History of Sandford
and Merton *(1783–1789) (courtesy of the Lilly Library, Indiana University)*

and women of the barracks. She cares for Mary as tenderly as if the infant were her own and forgoes worldly pleasures for Mary's sake. Here, as in *Stories Explanatory,* barracks life is brought vividly to life. The book concludes in England, where Sergeant Dale must return for the sake of his health. There is a happy ending for all except two women of the barracks who had cruelly mocked Sergeant Dale and Sarah for their piety. They fail to return with the regiment, and Sergeant Dale is informed that they had become the victims of too much liquor and the heat of the Indian sun. Once again, as in so many of Sherwood's Indian stories, moral depravity is punished by death through the effects of the Indian climate.

The History of the Fairchild Family, the book so well remembered by nineteenth-century readers,

was begun as "The Child's Manual" in 1812. The work is a collection of stories centering on the serious-minded and pious Fairchilds and their three children, Lucy, Emily, and Henry. The first version of the book, completed in 1813 and published in England in 1818, quickly went through several editions and abridgments in Britain and the United States. It was translated into French and German in the 1830s. In 1822 the publisher requested a sequel, but it would be another twenty years before Sherwood completed parts II and III.

Unlike many of the stories Sherwood wrote while in India, *The Fairchild Family* was set in England. The book might have been subtitled "the Parent's Manual" rather than "the Child's Manual," for it must have served as a reference guide for many serious-minded parents. For twentieth-century readers it offers important information about evangelical values and attitudes toward all aspects of child rearing and education. The children are shown at their daily tasks, which are described in detail and assigned according to gender: Lucy and Emily polish the furniture and learn to sew with their mother, while Henry helps in the garden and learns Latin with his father. Through *The Fairchild Family* and other books, Sherwood supported and promoted the sex role stereotyping of her times.

The recital of these daily tasks could have made dull reading in less skillful hands, but Sherwood could imbue the mundane with dramatic quality. Her skill at vivid description raised her above the ordinary writer of moral tales, and her extensive experience with children enabled her to create realistic characters in Lucy, Emily, and Henry. Despite their precocious ability to quote lengthy passages from the Scriptures, their dutiful observance of the Sabbath, and their charity to the poor, the three children do rebel. They are sometimes greedy, disobedient, quarrelsome, covetous, envious, spiteful, and lazy.

Lucy, Emily, and Henry are naughty children, but they always receive their punishment – the aspect of the book that has prompted the most censure. Some of the discipline meted out in the book would be considered excessive, extreme, and psychologically damaging today. For example, Mr. Fairchild takes his children, who have been quarreling over a doll, to Blackwood to see what happened to a man who hated his brother. There, in a very thick and dark wood "stood a gibbet, on which the body of a man hung in chains: it had not yet fallen to pieces, although it had hung there some years." The clothing is intact, and even described in some detail, "but the face of the corpse was so shocking, that the children could not look at it." The children cry out, and Mr. Fairchild explains that "the man who hangs upon [the gibbet] is a murderer – one who first hated, and afterwards killed his brother!" Although the Blackwood scene is shocking to modern readers, it probably would not have been so to many children in the early part of the nineteenth century. As Cutt observes, "In the setting of its own time, *The History of the Fairchild Family* was realistic rather than terrifying." Nineteenth-century readers and critics commented, instead, on the book's humor, and the "very brightly written accounts of funerals." Charlotte Yonge noted Sherwood's "felicitous descriptions," "the gusto with which she dwells on new dolls," and "the absolutely sensational naughtiness of Henry, Lucy, and Emily."

It must be emphasized that for all its reputation and its importance as a nineteenth-century evangelical children's classic, *The History of the Fairchild Family* does not accurately represent Sherwood's perspective on child rearing and religious education. A gentler world inhabited by more-indulgent parents is portrayed in later books, including the sequels to *The Fairchild Family,* published in 1842 and 1847, in which the Fairchild family becomes more prosperous, and their activities consequently reflect their new status. The children are still naughty, but their misbehavior is less interesting and the consequences less severe. Sherwood's own fortunes had also improved by the time she came to write the sequels. Acknowledged as a successful writer of children's books by the time she left India, she eventually became the main financial support of the family.

The main interest of these later works lies in how much Sherwood's worldview had changed since her India days. While the 1818 edition reflects the evangelical perspective and the outlook of a woman still deeply affected by the deaths of her infants in India, the second and third parts, the latter a collaboration between Sherwood and her daughter Sophia Kelly, demonstrate that the author's religious views had changed considerably: she had turned to millenarianism and held a brighter view of the possibilities of salvation. Modern critics are often criticized for ignoring the latter parts of *The History of the Fairchild Family,* but many nineteenth- and early-twentieth-century editions of the work also chose to omit them, adding instead more illustrations to the first part.

In 1815 the Sherwoods began preparations to leave India. The long journey home does not seem to have been as arduous as the voyage out, in spite of the fact that their party was considerably larger, with their four children and three orphans in tow. In her autobiography Sherwood recalls her relief at the prospect of returning to what she considered a healthier climate for her children and her anticipation of her reception in England, where her books had produced, as she called it, "a sensation." There was also regret; she relates that "The children cried bitterly when they saw the shores receding, and truly we were all very sad."

The Sherwoods faced uncertainty about their future when they arrived in England. Sherwood's husband was not immediately assured of any income, so in order to ease their financial concerns she resolved to take in pupils. Much of her time for the next few years was taken up with teaching, writing, charity work, and domestic affairs. The deaths of Sherwood's mother and sister-in-law brought both sorrow and increased responsibilities as she took charge of her four motherless nephews. Her last child was born in 1819 but died early in 1820.

In spite of her difficulties, Sherwood found the time to write novels, Sunday school tracts, and short stories. She also wrote textbooks designed to impart knowledge and inculcate religious and moral principles. *An Introduction to Astronomy* (1817) and *An Introduction to Geography* (1818) include discussion of the Scriptures. Sherwood's determination in the textbooks to relate all knowledge to the Scriptures was characteristic of evangelical writing for children. It stemmed from a rejection of the idea that knowledge has its own value, or is an end in itself, and a suspicion of the classical or heathenish authors. Even though she had read the classics as a young girl, she came to disapprove of the emphasis given to them in education.

Mrs. Sherwood's Primer, or First Book for Children (1821) offers color illustrations, lists of letters, words, phrases, and sentences, progressing from the simple to the complex, as well as short stories with moral lessons incorporating words from the lists. It includes three short stories about a little girl named Margery, first written in India in 1806 and stressing obedience, kindness to animals, charity and respect for the elderly, and Sabbath observance. Their importance to children's literature rests in Sherwood's graded use of diction, sentence pattern, and complexity of ideas.

One of her most popular books, *The History of Henry Milner* (1822–1837), was begun as a response to *The History of Sandford and Merton* (1783–1789) by Thomas Day, a friend of her father's from the Lichfield days. Day's book was still influential, and a source of concern because it supported the educational ideas of Jean-Jacques Rousseau, whose writings Sherwood considered "the well-spring of infidelity." While Day emphasized the child's inherent goodness, Sherwood's concern was to expose original sin.

Her book's protagonist is orphaned and raised by a serious-minded evangelical clergyman, Mr. Dalben. Like the young Fairchilds, Henry is stubborn, naughty, and disobedient, and must be brought under control. Henry is a believable character and is consequently more interesting and entertaining than his eighteenth-century rivals, Harry Sandford and Tommy Merton. Henry fast loses his childish charm, however, as he grows up, proceeds through boarding school, and goes to Oxford. His trials with temper and stubbornness give way to serious spiritual trials, but Sherwood is really at her best when describing small children. Although the later parts of *Henry Milner* may be less interesting to the modern reader, the novel may be considered an early version of the schoolboy stories popularized in the 1850s by Thomas Hughes's *Tom Brown's School-Days* (1857).

Although Sherwood was determined to counteract Rousseau's influence, it is interesting to note that many of her character's early experiences resemble those of the hero of Rousseau's *Emile* (1762). Henry, like Emile, grows up in comfortable isolation and learns through carefully constructed dialogues, contrived situations, and the observation of natural phenomena. However, unlike Emile, who is represented as naturally good at birth, Henry Milner, as a descendant of Adam, is born utterly corrupt.

The History of Henry Milner sold well in America, but many American children became acquainted with the character through a series of short extracts published in the 1850s, each about twenty-four pages long and illustrated with woodcuts. Several of these titles were bound together in a single volume as *The History of Master Henry, a Pleasing Narrative for the Young* (1855).

The pernicious influence of Rousseau and his followers was only one of the issues Sherwood addressed in the years following her return from India. She had long detested Roman Catholicism, and had attacked it vigorously in *The Indian Pilgrim* and *The History of the Fairchild Family*. She launched a more sustained attack in the 1820s as a movement to allow Roman Catholics more civil liberties gained strength. The Catholic Emancipation Act of 1829, which permitted Catholics to vote, stand for Parliament, participate in municipal affairs, and sit in the House of Lords, alarmed a considerable segment of the population, including Sherwood. Three books she wrote in the early 1830s were particularly anti-Catholic: *Victoria* (1833), *The Nun* (1833), and *The Monk of Cimies* (1834). They were not entirely well received even by evangelicals. A reviewer in *The Christian Observer* (May 1837) found *The Monk of Cimies* "unfair and unconvincing."

Sherwood's understanding of Catholicism was as superficial as was her understanding of Hinduism. Although she traveled fairly extensively in Catholic countries after she returned from India, she retained a tourist's understanding of the faith. She demonstrated a lack of appreciation of the history, art, and architecture represented in Catholic churches, just as she had not shown any interest in Hindu temples except as haunts of Satan. Her writ-

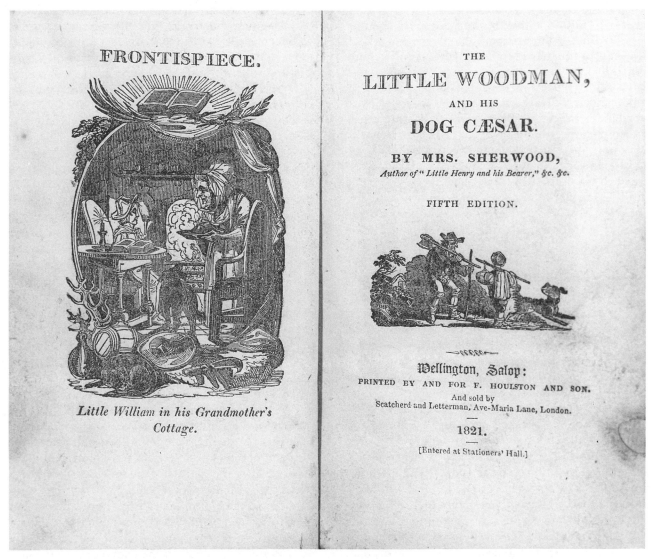

FRONTISPIECE.

Little William in his Grandmother's Cottage.

THE
LITTLE WOODMAN,
AND HIS
DOG CÆSAR.

BY MRS. SHERWOOD,
Author of " Little Henry and his Bearer," &c. &c.

FIFTH EDITION.

Wellington, Salop:
PRINTED BY AND FOR F. HOULSTON AND SON.
And sold by
Scatcherd and Letterman, Ave-Maria Lane, London.

1821.

[Entered at Stationers' Hall.]

Frontispiece and title page for an early edition of Sherwood's 1818 story about an orphan boy who is abandoned in a forest (courtesy of the Lilly Library, Indiana University)

ings suggest that she might even have confused the two religions.

It has been argued that some of Sherwood's dislike of the Catholic Church could have been inspired by vanity; because Roman Catholicism did not encourage interpretation of the Scriptures by lay persons, her position was challenged. By the 1820s she was confident of the correctness of her interpretations, and her study of scriptural emblems or symbols and her firm belief in biblical prophecy were reflected in several books written at this time. *The Millennium* (1829) was, in fact, a collection of twelve stories "designed to make easy to the youthful reader of the Holy Scriptures, some of the most beautiful and interesting portions of sacred proph-

ecy" and to explain the concept of the millennium, or thousand-year reign of Christ on earth.

Not all of Sherwood's shorter works had stern messages, and in the years following her return from India, her tales increasingly reflect a modification of her religious views and a less austere attitude toward life. Some of her penny books, as well as her more developed stories, offer gentler themes that had figured in her early works, such as kindness to orphans, to the afflicted, and to animals. *The Fawns* (1828) and *Soffrona and Her Cat Muff* (1828) stress man's responsibility to animals, while *The Idiot Boy* (1828) emphasizes humane treatment of a mentally defective child.

Some of her later books and stories also reflect her childhood love of fairy tales and a persistent strain of romanticism that strict evangelicalism had not managed to erase. *The Rose,* first published in 1818 as a penny tract, is an unusual moral fairy tale set deep in a wild wood on a moonlit night. Fairies, dressed in "white velvet robes, with borders of precious stones," gather to watch their queen bestow "the never-fading Rose on her who has spent the last twelve months in the most profitable manner." Although many fairies come forward to claim the Rose, the queen bestows it on a modest fairy who has spent her time training her children in wisdom, knowledge, and the acquisition of virtuous habits. In spite of its ultimate compliance with evangelical convention, *The Rose* is a remarkable little book demonstrating the author's descriptive powers and ability to create atmosphere.

The Lady in the Arbour (1827), another moral tale, also creates a fairy-tale or folktale atmosphere, with a neglected orphan, a cruel foster mother, a beautiful arbor in the middle of a deep, dark wood, and a kind but mysterious old woman. A similar setting and folk conventions are used in *The Little Woodman and His Dog Caesar* (1818), in which a pious little orphan boy is taken deep into the forest and abandoned by his six cruel brothers. He is saved from wolves by his courageous dog, Caesar, and together they find refuge in the cottage of an old woman who is discovered to be the little orphan's grandmother. The two live happily together, studying the Bible and caring for one another, until the old woman's death. The cruel brothers reappear many years later, but in a sorry state. The orphan, now a grown man with a family, offers them forgiveness in the spirit of a true Christian.

Mystery, intrigue, and dramatic tension are created in two stories involving stolen babies and gypsies. Both *The Gipsy Babes* (1826) and *Shanty the Blacksmith* employ the fear and suspicion traditionally inspired by the gypsy, but Sherwood presents them in a more generous light than many contemporary works. Evangelical doctrine is minimal in both tales. *The Gipsy Babes,* a romantic fireside tale with a happy ending, features an old gypsy woman who is kind and loving toward little children. *Shanty the Blacksmith,* in contrast, is a more complex Gothic romance that includes sinister and mysterious characters, ruins, a lonely blacksmith's forge in an isolated part of northern England, and a stolen baby abandoned by a gypsy. Despite the atmosphere of gloom and mystery created at the beginning of the book, there are touches of humor. One critic has remarked that more stories like *Shanty the Blacksmith,* one of the best examples of Sherwood's skillful use of description, would have assured the author a permanent place in children's literature.

Sherwood continued her literary activities to the end of her long life, but several of her books published in the 1840s also bear her daughter Sophia's name, in the forms of "Mrs. Streeton" or "Mrs. Kelly." She continued to devote a great deal of her time to the study of the Scriptures. Her husband, always supportive and encouraging, assisted her in interpreting the Bible through the preparation of a Hebrew-English concordance. His death in 1849 might have been unbearable without her unshakable religious faith. In her later years Sherwood came to believe in unconditional salvation for those who accepted Christ as their Savior. Her beliefs, always strongly stated, alienated her from her neighbors and evangelical societies, but she remained convinced of the rightness of her views. No clergyman was summoned to her deathbed on 20 September 1851.

Sherwood's influence on nineteenth-century children's literature and her contribution to what is often referred to as "the Victorian frame of mind" were considerable. She was one of the most popular and prolific writers of her time and a dominant force in the nursery for at least half a century. Many of her books and stories were read with interest even after the middle of the nineteenth century, when the original evangelical fervor that had contributed to their popularity had waned. Christian moralizing aside, Sherwood could tell a good story, rich in color, description, and atmosphere. Her Indian stories were read for the exotic detail they provided as well as for Christian instruction.

Books such as *Stories Explanatory of the Church Catechism, The Ayah and Lady*, and *The Indian Pilgrim* are still enjoyable, and they remain significant because they offer a unique perspective on Anglo-Indian relations in the early years of the nineteenth century. Sherwood's missionary stories influenced later children's writers, including Charlotte Maria Tucker ("A.L.O.E."), an evangelical missionary who also wrote stories about India, and possibly Rudyard Kipling. Indeed, few nineteenth-century children's writers could have been unfamiliar with Sherwood's work, given her prodigious literary output and the wide range of subjects she chose to address. Her influence extended not only to evangelical tracts, but also to school stories, domestic stories, historical fiction, and even the didactic fantasy or fairy story popularized by George MacDonald. Though her books are no longer widely read, she is regarded as one of the most significant authors of children's literature of the nineteenth century.

Biographies:

Naomi Royde Smith, *The State of Mind of Mrs. Sherwood* (London: Macmillan, 1946);

Margaret Nancy Cutt, *Mrs. Sherwood and Her Books for Children* (London: Oxford University Press, 1974).

References:

J. S. Bratton, *The Impact of Victorian Children's Fiction* (London: Croom Helm, 1981);

Margaret Nancy Cutt, *Ministering Angels. A Study of Nineteenth-Century Evangelical Writing for Children* (Wormley Broxbourne, Herts.: Five Owls Press, 1979);

F. J. Harvey Darton, *Children's Books in England. Five Centuries of Social Life,* third edition, revised by Brian Alderson (Cambridge: Cambridge University Press, 1982);

Patricia Demers, "Mrs. Sherwood and Hesba Stretton: The Letter and the Spirit of Evangelical Writing of and for Children," in *Romanticism and Children's Literature in Nineteenth-Century England,* edited by James Holt McGavran Jr. (Athens: University of Georgia Press, 1991), pp. 129–149;

David C. Hanson, "Ruskin's *Praeterita* and Landscape in Evangelical Children's Fiction," *Nineteenth-Century Literature,* 44 (June 1989): 45–66;

Lynne Vallone, " 'A Humble Spirit under Correction': Tracts, Hymns, and the Ideology of Evangelical Fiction for Children, 1780–1820," *Lion and the Unicorn,* 15 (December 1991): 72–95.

Papers:

Mary Martha Sherwood's multivolume manuscript journal is in the Children's Literature Collection at the University of California, Los Angeles.

Catherine Sinclair

(17 April 1800 – 6 August 1864)

Judith Gero John
Southwest Missouri State University

BOOKS: *Charlie Seymour; or, The Good Aunt and the Bad Aunt* (Edinburgh: Waugh & Innes, 1832; New York: Carter, 1842); republished as *Charlie Seymour; or, The Good and Bad Choice* (London: Ipswich, 1856);

Modern Accomplishments, or the March of Intellect (Edinburgh: Waugh & Innes, 1836; New York: Carter, 1836);

Modern Society: or, The March of Intellect (Edinburgh: Waugh & Innes, 1837; New York: Carter, 1837);

Hill and Valley, or Hours in England and Wales (Edinburgh: Whyte, 1838; New York: Carter, 1838);

Holiday House; a Series of Tales (Edinburgh: Whyte, 1839; New York: Carter, 1839); republished as *Holiday House: A Book for the Young* (London: Ipswich, 1856);

Scotland and the Scotch; or, the Western Circuit (Edinburgh: Whyte, 1840; New York: Appleton, 1840);

Shetland and the Shetlanders; or, The Northern Circuit (Edinburgh: Whyte, 1840; New York: Appleton, 1840);

Modern Flirtations; or, A Month at Harrowgate (Edinburgh: Whyte, 1841; New York: Stringer & Townsend, 1841); republished as *Flirtations in Fashionable Life* (Philadelphia: Peterson, 1863);

Scotch Courtiers and the Court (Edinburgh: Whyte, 1842);

Jane Bouverie; or, Prosperity and Adversity (Edinburgh: Whyte, 1846; New York: Harper, 1851); republished as *Jane Bouverie, and How She Became an Old Maid* (London: Ipswich, 1855);

The Lives of the Caesars; or, the Juvenile Plutarch (London, 1847); abbreviated as *Anecdotes of the Caesars* (London: Ipswich, 1858);

The Journey of Life (London: Marshall, 1847);

The Business of Life (London: Longman, Brown, Green & Longmans, 1848);

Sir Edward Graham; or, Railway Speculators (London: Longman, Brown, Green & Longmans, 1849;

New York: Harper, 1850); republished as *The Mysterious Marriage; or, Sir Edward Graham* (London: Ipswich, 1854; New York: Beeton, 1854);

Lord and Lady Harcourt; or, Country Hospitalities (London: Bentley, 1850; New York: Hart, 1851); republished as *Country Hospitalities; or, Lord and Lady Harcourt* (London: Ipswich, [1856]);

The Kaleidoscope of Anecdotes and Aphorisms (London: Bentley, 1851);

Beatrice; or, The Unknown Relatives (London: Bentley, 1852; New York: DeWitt);

Popish Legends or Bible Truths (London: Longman, 1852);

The Priest and the Curate; or, The Two Diaries, Common Sense Tracts 1 (London, 1853);

Lady Mary Pierrepoint, Common Sense Tracts 2 (London, 1853);

Frank Vansittart; or, The Model Schoolboys, Common Sense Tracts 3 (London, 1853);

London Homes: Including The Murder Hole; The Drowning Dragon; The Priest and the Curate; Lady Mary Pierrepoint; and Frank Vansittart (London: Bentley, 1853);

Memoir of the Right Hon. Sir John Sinclair, Bart; with an Account of His Writings and Personal Exertions for Social and Agricultural Improvement in Scotland (Edinburgh: Chambers, 1853);

The Cabman's Holiday: A Tale (London: Ipswich, 1855);

Cross Purposes, a Novel (London: Bentley, 1855); republished as *Torchester Abbey; or Cross Purposes, A Tale* (London: Ipswich, 1857);

Modern Superstition (London: Ipswich, 1857); republished as *Memoirs of the English Bible* (London: Ipswich, 1858);

Sketches and Stories of Scotland and the Scotch, and Shetland and the Shetlanders (London: Ipswich, 1859);

Sketches and Stories of Wales and the Welsh (London: Ipswich, 1860);

Letters (Edinburgh: James Wood, 1861–1864);

The First of April Picture Letter (Edinburgh, 1864).

Catherine Sinclair was a prolific and popular writer during her lifetime. Her early children's book *Holiday House: a Series of Tales* (1839), which includes the "Nonsensical Story of Giants and Fairies," marked a turning point in the history of children's literature. Those who objected to whimsy and imaginative literature for children had a difficult time finding fault with a story that was highly moral and instructive, and yet allowed children the right to be young and boisterous and make mistakes at the same time.

Catherine Sinclair was born on 17 April 1800 in Edinburgh, Scotland, the fourth daughter of Diana Macdonald Sinclair and Sir John Sinclair, a politician and the president of the Board of Agriculture. At the age of fourteen Catherine became her father's secretary; she held that position until his death in 1835. She never married, but devoted her life to her father, her writing, and acts of charity. Sinclair was both an enthusiastic Protestant and a writer with a vivid and lively imagination. These nearly conflicting elements of her personality helped her create novels that remain enjoyable, in spite of the moral tone she assumes throughout most of them.

Although *Holiday House* is the novel for which she is remembered, nearly all of her works were written for young people, with a special emphasis on attracting them to the right path rather then forcing them to it. If she were writing today, Sinclair would probably be considered a young adult author, since a majority of her books stress the pitfalls of growing up and treat the dangers faced by young people, especially young ladies, as they prepare to enter the adult world. Sinclair's novels are filled with details of setting and place that enliven the characters and plot and involve the reader in the final denouement. Her attention to detail is highlighted in her several guidebooks, which describe her travels around England, Scotland, and Wales. These books are steeped in the history and folklore of the regions.

Many of Sinclair's tendencies as a writer are found in her first book, *Charlie Seymour; or, The Good Aunt and the Bad Aunt* (1832), which was written, as were many of her early books, for her nephew, George Frederick Boyle, and her niece, Diana Boyle. She did not publish another book before her father's death in 1835; soon thereafter, however, she produced two lengthy but well-received novels: *Modern Accomplishments, or the March of Intellect* (1836) and its conclusion, *Modern Society: or, The March of Intellect* (1837).

Title page for Sinclair's best-known work, a series of tales she had told to her niece and nephew

Modern Accomplishments is the story of three worldly sisters and their Christian sister-in-law, Olivia Neville, but its focus is on the next generation, in the characters of Matilda Howard and Eleanor Fitz-Patrick. The two girls are raised as "modern society" dictates, with emphasis on ornamentation, pseudointellectual pursuits, and whimsical religious values. They also are influenced by their purely Christian and long-suffering Aunt Olivia, whose felicity has been destroyed by tribulations, but whose peace has been restored through contemplation of the next world. As with many books of this type, the girls have two options: the ways of the world or the ways of Protestantism. Sinclair does not even attempt to show any connection between being a good Christian and receiving earthly rewards. Eleanor, who takes on the shallow attributes of her worldly mother and aunts, marries well and inherits land and wealth beyond imagination, but never knows happiness. Matilda, in contrast, follows in the footsteps of Olivia and finds peace and contentment in the simple life.

As novels aimed at young women standing on the brink of maturity, *Modern Accomplishments* and *Modern Society* do not reject social life. Aunt Olivia encourages her nieces to enjoy themselves and to enjoy life; her concern is that without some guidance society and life might overwhelm the girls. Rather than adopting a purely didactic tone, Sinclair allows events to unfold and lets the reader see the results of making shallow choices. Aunt Olivia is the spokesperson for the right way to live. She does not condemn others, but is straightforward and honest in speaking out against what she sees happening to her nieces. The book presents the Christian way of life in its most romantic light – a Christian loves more fully, a Christian marriage is happier, and a Christian husband loves his wife more devotedly. This attitude must have been attractive to young girls daydreaming about marriage.

Sinclair's *Hill and Valley, or Hours in England and Wales* (1838) was initially written to a Scottish cousin during the summer of 1833. Along with her other travel books – *Scotland and the Scotch; or, the Western Circuit* (1840); *Shetland and the Shetlanders; or, The Northern Circuit* (1840); the combined, revised edition, *Sketches and Stories of Scotland and the Scotch, and Shetland and the Shetlanders* (1859); and *Sketches and Stories of Wales and the Welsh* (1860) – *Hill and Valley* details not just the popular and the less frequented travel spots in the various countries, but also includes history, legends, and discussions of local customs and people. Sinclair often interjects her thoughts and reactions to particular sights and enlivens her account through dialogue and commentary.

Holiday House (1839) is the written version of a series of tales Sinclair had told her niece and nephew – quite likely about some of their own adventures – with recurring characters, especially the young protagonists Harry and Laura Graham. Ultimately, it is a book about growing up. It is the story of three nearly orphaned children (Harry and Laura have an older brother, Frank) and their lives under the care of their happy Uncle David; their loving grandmother, Lady Harriet; and their vicious nurse, Mrs. Crabtree. Even though their mother is dead and their father is absent, Harry and Laura manage to turn out well; their rambunctious natures and the beatings by Mrs. Crabtree cannot destroy their natural goodness, which is nurtured and enhanced by the love of their grandmother and uncle.

Harry and Laura have a variety of adventures, including visits to Holiday House in the country, and more-universal experiences, such as Harry setting fire

to the nursery and Laura cutting her own hair. The highlight of the book for those tracing the origins of imaginative literature for children is Uncle David's "Nonsensical Story of Giants and Fairies," in which Master No-book is tempted from home by the fairy Do-nothing and saved by the fairy Teach-all from the giant Snap-em-up who devours lazy, fat, selfish children. *Holiday House* ends with the death of Frank, the return of the absent father, and the maturing of the children, especially Laura.

One of Sinclair's main focuses in the book is the treatment and education of children. As she had already shown in *Modern Accomplishments* and *Modern Society,* she did not think highly of the prevalent methods of education or child rearing. Mrs. Crabtree, with her suppression of natural childish spirits and daily whippings, quickly becomes the villain of the piece, although she proves to be devoted to the children, especially Frank, and shows that she is a good-hearted, if misguided, nursemaid. The children learn through experience and the shame of hurting their beloved grandmother that they must be good in order to feel good.

Although heavily moral, the collection is hailed as one of the first books for children intended chiefly for pleasure, and it is groundbreaking in not condemning children for their natural inclinations for play or to get into mischief. Harry and Laura are seen as basically good children with high spirits and a great desire to have fun. While most books of the times polarized children as good or bad, obedient or disobedient, Sinclair created stories in which children are allowed to laugh and play and experience life. This is not to say that she refrained from the didactic – in fact, even her "nonsensical" story is allegorical in nature, as the names suggest, and the lesson to be learned is obvious – but she believed that setting a good example and giving loving attention would help shape children just as well, if not better, than frequent spankings. As a result, her child characters, unlike naughty children in other stories of the times, grow up as caring Christian people.

Holiday House surprises many historians and critics because it seems so far removed from what was generally written for children in the mid 1800s, but the motivation for this unusual book becomes clear in an examination of some of Sinclair's other works. A devout Christian, Sinclair was strongly anti-Catholic and used her writing to examine and expose "papists" as dishonest and deceitful. One of the weapons the Roman Catholic Church had available was its storehouse of legends of saints and martyrs. Sinclair recognized in these stories a strong ap-

Page from one of Sinclair's picture letters for children (1861–1864), her final and most popular project

peal to the imagination, particularly to that of a child, and this recognition led her to break from the conventional literature of her times. Although *Holiday House* may show the effects of the Romantic movement on children's books, it was primarily Sinclair's interest in turning the imagination to salvation that prompted her to write this predecessor of the imaginative children's literature published in England during the rest of the century.

Popish Legends or Bible Truths (1852), *Modern Superstition* (1857), and the scathing *Beatrice* (1852) make it very clear that Sinclair was horrified at the Catholic Church's ability to turn the natural imagination of children into a tool for mind control. She saw in the bland and boring stories given to children by strict Protestants — where all bad children are condemned and the imagination is banished — the annihilation of the "right," Protestant way of life; hence, her interest in writing literature that appealed to childish fancy and retained its ability to improve the child.

The introduction to *Beatrice* claims the work is a "fictitious narrative" based on fact. Following the favorable reception of *Popish Legends or Bible Truths*, Sinclair reiterates what she knows to be "true of the irreconcilable hostility with which the Italian school of superstition looks upon the moral principles and domestic peace of a happy English fireside." She believes she must expose the horrors of the Catholic Church — especially Jesuits — and its plans to "waylay young ladies."

This three-part novel of more than a thousand pages weaves an interesting but predictable plot of misplaced heirs and heiresses and loves lost and found. But the root of the book is the horrifying war waged by the Catholics to control the world by any means possible. It is difficult to believe the author's claim that she has evidence of Jesuit plans for kidnapping, murder, and mind control, but there is no doubt about her sincerity or fear of the Catholic Church. It is this book that explains, better than any other, why Sinclair is eager to find and to write imaginative literature that upholds her Protestant ideals. She greatly fears the Catholic Church's ability to lure children away by the romantic and imaginative nature of its "superstitions."

Most of Sinclair's other works are difficult to find in the United States, and although some dedicated scholars may search for them, few others will. All of these works reveal the author's interest in teaching children, especially young girls, and on setting them on the right path to heaven. *Jane Bouverie* (1846), *Modern Flirtations* (1841), *Lord and Lady Harcourt; or, Country Hospitalities* (1850), and, in some respects, *Beatrice* all perform this function. *Jane Bouverie,* and explanation for why a young woman never marries, is probably partly autobiographical. Jane spends her life caring for her father and the young man she loves, whose father forbids their marriage and who dies an untimely death far from home. Jane spends the rest of her life, as Sinclair did, performing charitable acts and caring for others.

While the salvation of young women was frequently on Sinclair's mind and in her books, she wrote for young men as well, as in her first book, *Charlie Seymour.* The noble but wasteful death of Frank at the end of *Holiday House* was undoubtedly reminiscent of the death of Sinclair's brother, James, to whom she dedicated the second edition of the book. She also wrote *Frank Vansittart; or, The Model Schoolboys* (1853) and several variations on a book titled *The Lives of the Caesars* (1847) for young men.

Other books by Sinclair are unabashedly religious tracts. *The Journey of Life* (1847) and *The Business of Life* (1848) are not stories so much as conversations and advice for living. *The Kaleidoscope of Anecdotes and Aphorisms* (1851) is exactly what its title implies — page upon page of quotations and parables about living. Sinclair's final and most popular projects were her *Letters* (1861–1864) for children. These books, in which certain words were left out and replaced with pictures, were extremely popular, selling one hundred thousand each. Although most modern critics find them unexciting, they assured the author a place in the nursery for many years.

Today, however, Catherine Sinclair is primarily remembered for *Holiday House,* which introduced the elements of pleasure and imagination in children's books. Few of Sinclair's books are still available or read in the United States. Interest in her works is mostly limited to tracing her place in the history and development of children's literature.

References:

Louise Frances Field, *The Child and His Book: Some Account of The History and Progress of Children's Literature in England* (Detroit: Singing Tree Press, 1968);

Roger Lancelyn Green, *Tellers of Tales: British Authors of Children's Books from 1800 to 1964,* revised edition (New York: Franklin Watts, 1965), pp. 16–21;

Mary F. Thwaite, *From Primer to Pleasure in Reading: An Introduction to the History of Children's Books in England from the Invention of Printing to 1914 with an Outline of Some Developments in Other Countries* (Boston: Horn Book, 1972).

Hesba Stretton
(Sarah Smith)

(27 July 1832 – 8 October 1911)

Leslie Howsam
University of Windsor

BOOKS: *Fern's Hollow* (London: Religious Tract Society, 1864);

Enoch Roden's Training (London: Religious Tract Society, 1865);

The Children of Cloverley (London: Religious Tract Society, 1865); abridged and republished as *The Children of Lake Huron; or, The Cousins at Cloverley* (New York: Phillips & Hunt, n.d.; Cincinnati: Cranston & Stowe, n.d.);

The Clives of Burcot: A Novel, 3 volumes (London: Tinsley, 1867);

Jessica's First Prayer (London: Religious Tract Society, 1867);

Pilgrim Street, a Story of Manchester Life (London: Religious Tract Society, 1867);

Little Meg's Children (London: Religious Tract Society, 1868);

Alone in London (London: Religious Tract Society, 1869);

David Lloyd's Last Will (London: Sampson Low & Marston, 1869);

Max Krömer: A Story of the Siege of Strasburg (London: Religious Tract Society, 1871);

Michel Lorio's Cross (London: H. S. King, 1873);

The King's Servants (London: H. S. King, 1873);

The Wonderful Life (London: Religious Tract Society, 1875);

The Crew of the Dolphin (London: H. S. King, 1876; New York: Dodd, Mead, 1876);

Cobwebs and Cables (London: Religious Tract Society, 1881; New York: Dodd, Mead, 1881);

Under the Old Roof (London: Religious Tract Society, 1882);

The Highway of Sorrow. At the Close of the Nineteenth Century: A Story of Modern Russia (London: Cassell, 1894);

In the Hollow of His Hand: A Story of the Stundists (London: Religious Tract Society, 1897);

Jessica's Mother (London: Religious Tract Society, 1904).

Hesba Stretton in the 1890s

Hesba Stretton's children's story *Jessica's First Prayer* (1867) was popular with Victorian readers of all ages, and it influenced a generation of Victorian writers. Stretton (the pseudonym used by Sarah Smith) was the author of many periodical publications and more than fifty books. Her reputation may be summed up in Lord Shaftesbury's comment in *Seed Time and Harvest* (1911) that *Jessica's First Prayer* "will hardly find a rival for nature, simplicity, pathos and depth of Christian feeling." But Stretton was more than a sentimentalist: she was a skilled stylist who used vivid characterization, complex plotting, and engaging humor to construct her powerful narratives, and she was a vehement polemicist who used her stories to call for the redress of social injustice.

The name "Hesba" was created by Sarah Smith out of the initial letters of her name and those of her brother and three sisters; the surname was derived from Church Stretton, the name of a neighboring village in her home county of Shropshire. Smith was born on 27 July 1832 in Wellington. Her father, Benjamin Smith, was a printer with a local firm that specialized in evangelical literature. Later he became a bookseller and publisher, whose business included operating the local post office. These activities found their way into the realistic detail of many of his daughter's novels and stories. Her mother, Anne Bakewell Smith, was a strict Methodist and an evangelical of the old school, and her influence on her daughter's religious belief was the more profound because she died when Sarah was nine years of age.

The Smith home was a gathering place for intellectuals and literary people. Sarah Smith was educated in a nearby girls' school, but its resources were supplemented by the books always to be found in her family's home. She remained unmarried and began in her twenties to earn her living by writing. The need to do this was greater after 1862, when Benjamin Smith retired and the family experienced a decline in its standard of living. Elizabeth Smith left Wellington for Manchester in 1863 to become a governess, and her sister Sarah, then aged thirty-one, followed and continued to publish stories and tales. The two women spent three years there and then settled in London.

Hesba Stretton's first published story, "The Lucky Leg," appeared in Charles Dickens's journal *Household Words* in March 1859. Recent research has disposed of the well-worn anecdote that Elizabeth Smith sent "The Lucky Leg" to Dickens unsolicited and without her sister's knowledge, collecting an unlooked-for five pounds. Surviving documents demonstrate that Sarah began submitting stories to editors during the 1850s, applying the family's knowledge as retailers to the market for periodicals. Early stories were published by Dickens in *All the Year Round,* as well as in evangelical periodicals such as *The Sunday Magazine* and *The Leisure Hour.* There is, however, no evidence that Hesba Stretton knew Dickens personally. Later, when her work became more sensational and unsuitable for religious publications, she submitted it to the *Temple Bar.* Stretton's business records also demonstrate that she was prepared to engage in litigation with editors who failed to pay for her work.

Some of her early stories were obviously autobiographical, such as "The Postmaster's Daughter" and "A Provincial Post Office." They demonstrated what J. S. Bratton calls "vivid domesticity" and Stretton's "capacity for recalling intense childish feelings." *Fern's Hollow* (1864), her first children's book, written just before the move to Manchester in October 1863, is located in a hill community on the Welsh border, where most working-class people had long since lost their land. The hero, Stephen Fern, is the exception. He is the grandson of a returned convict, whose wife held onto their land in her husband's absence. Stephen is threatened with the loss of his inherited holding to the local landlord, James Wyley, who also manages his mining pits with insufficient attention to safety. Stephen proves his honor and Christian morality and finishes up in command of his own property and holding a position of trust as Wyley's bailiff.

In *Enoch Roden's Training* (1865) Hesba Stretton drew upon her knowledge of printing. The title character is apprenticed to Mr. Drury, a printer and bookseller in a town based on Shrewsbury and the publisher of the *Shadbury News.* Enoch enjoys his educational opportunities, working "in the midst of books and printing all the day long," until his employer becomes bankrupt.

The third novel, *The Children of Cloverley* (1865), is set initially in the United States during the Civil War, in a small farmhouse on the shores of Lake Huron. The family of Captain Bakewell is broken up by his wife's death, and his son, Ben, and daughter, Annie, travel to England to live with their uncle James Wyley at Church Cloverley. Ben represents the supposed values of the United States (hard work and sturdy independence) and Annie, those of England (where drink and unemployment combine to degrade the rural laboring class, and snobbery and selfishness distinguish the rural gentry) as they become established at Cloverley. There are temptations for adults as well as children, but they are overcome by exhortations about the will of Christ. The story ends with the reunion of the children with their father.

Jessica's First Prayer was first published in 1866 in the journal *Sunday at Home* and reprinted in book form by the Religious Tract Society in 1867. Jessica is a child of the London streets who is neglected by her mother, a drunken actress who named her daughter after Shylock's daughter in William Shakespeare's *Merchant of Venice* (circa 1596–1597). Jessica is befriended by Daniel, a man whose besetting sin is the love of money. One source of his income is a coffee stall, where he offers Jessica a meal, impressed by her honesty. She later accidentally discovers his second occupation – as caretaker of a large Methodist chapel – and begins to ask questions about what happens there. The answer, that ladies and gentlemen go there to pray, evokes a further question: what is a prayer? Jessica's ignorance about even the most basic of religious teaching was disturbing for Victorian readers; certainly it upsets the other child characters in the story, the minister's daughters. They befriend Jessica and then realize she is too ragged to be allowed to sit in their pew; she is relegated to the steps of the pulpit. When assured that she is entitled to offer a prayer, Jessica asks, "Oh God! I want to know more about you. And please pay Mr. Daniel for all the warm coffee he's given me." In this story it is the adult characters – especially Daniel, whose religion has only been on the surface – who are saved by Jessica's simple and trusting piety. The institutionalized chapels and churches are revealed to be at fault, as their strict notions of worldly respectability and class consciousness interfere with their commitment to the Christian gospel. Jessica, the uncorrupted innocent, teaches lessons both to Daniel and to the minister.

The book was tremendously popular, selling around two million copies by the end of the century. Because the Religious Tract Society had purchased the copyright, they collected most of the profits, although many pirated editions also appeared. Stretton once remarked that "Truly all men are cheats, especially publishers." She arranged to be paid by the thousand for her later books. *Jessica's First Prayer* was translated into most of the languages of Europe and into braille, as well as into several Asian and African languages for missionary use. Czar Alexander II required Russian educational authorities to place a copy in every school. In *Jessica's Mother* (1904), a sequel, the title character turns up at Daniel and Jessica's happy home, insisting on reclaiming her daughter. The drunken and dissolute woman's exposure to her child's purity leads her to commit suicide, providing an opportunity for the other characters to reexamine their Christian devotion in the light of Jessica's virtue.

In 1867 Stretton also published two adult novels and another powerful book for children, *Pilgrim Street, a Story of Manchester Life,* which is longer and more substantial than *Jessica's First Prayer.* Its hero is a boy of the streets, Tom Haslam, who is "no better than a heathen we send missionaries to." Tom is befriended by the kindly Philip Hope and entrusted to

Daniel and Jessica; illustration by A. W. Bayes for Stretton's Jessica's First Prayer *(1867)*

the supervision of the police officer Banner. Banner, like Mr. Daniel in London, is religious but lacks the warmth of the child characters, whose closeness to God is evidenced by their direct experience and forthright attitudes. Initially improved by exposure to Christian teaching, Tom falters when he develops a love of money and is tempted to swindle a customer. He is also distressed about the impending return of his convict father. Tom runs off to Liverpool, nearly dies of neglect, and eventually returns to Manchester to be nursed by Banner, whose own judgmental soul is saved by the simple piety of his charge. Tom dies in a fire set by his vengeful, unrepentant father, and the remaining characters settle down to tending his grave.

Most of Stretton's children's books were published by the Religious Tract Society, and many of her stories appeared in its periodicals. Founded in 1799, the Religious Tract Society was by the mid nineteenth century committed to circulating not only improving tracts but also religious works more broadly defined. Stretton's writing, which was always "improving," as well as being intensely poignant and engagingly entertaining, was among the best of what the society published, as well as the most popular. The society did not print publication dates on its title pages, which makes scholarly differentiation among the various editions difficult.

After the success of *Jessica's First Prayer*, Hesba Stretton also wrote fiction for adults. In fact, she was more interested in her adult novels than in tract fiction, which she regarded as a money-spinner. Her adult books had a circle of devoted admirers. Charles Kegan Paul, in the essay "On English Prose Style" (1891), places Stretton with Cardinal Newman, Walter Pater, and Thomas Hardy as one of the best contemporary stylists. Her first three-volume novel, *Paul's Courtship* (1867), again reflects the author's knowledge of printing and bookselling. *David Lloyd's Last Will* (1869) is set in Manchester during the period of unemployment in the 1860s known as the cotton famine and is concerned with the disposition of a miserly uncle's wealth. The complex plot involves a love story, a family's passage from comfortable respectability to poverty and back again, and the trial and imprisonment of a young man, Mark Fletcher, whose struggle over questions of duty and justice is presented in sympathetic detail. *Michel Lorio's Cross* (1873), a tale of heroism set at St. Michael's Mount in Normandy, was the author's personal favorite of her works.

Two other important children's books were *Little Meg's Children* (1868) and *Alone in London* (1869), which incorporate reformist political messages. In the former, Meg, whose mother dies in the opening chapter, has charge of her brothers and sisters and must endure terrible poverty while patiently awaiting their father's return. Their neighbor, Kitty, is a prostitute, who remains unrepentant in her occupation and her drunkenness, and is even indirectly responsible for the death of Meg's baby sister. She is finally saved when Meg persuades her to pray for forgiveness. *Alone in London* presents a pair of neglected children: a little girl, Dolly, whose piety serves to regenerate her grandfather as he struggles to look after her; and an older boy, Tony. Dolly dies because there is no bed for her in the Children's Hospital. These two stories generated combined sales of around 750,000 copies.

Some of Stretton's other books also express her political interests. She dedicated *Max Krömer: A Story of the Siege of Strasburg* (1871) to her "noble countrymen and countrywomen who are spending themselves – not their property merely – in aiding the distressed peasantry of France." The occasion was the Franco-Prussian War, and the first-person narrator is the fifteen-year-old son of an Englishwoman and a German explorer. *Under the Old Roof* (1882), the tragic story of a good Christian woman driven from her own home by the cruelty of her stepson, is a commentary on the injustice of the law before the passage in 1882 of the Married Women's Property Act. Through the story of a woman who buys back a house originally owned by her father and then earns a living outside the home while her husband, a shoemaker, takes care of their child, Stretton reveals her sympathy with contemporary feminist movements. In 1892 she also collected funds for the relief of a famine in Russia. Stretton raised £1,000 for this cause and later published a book about village life in Russia, *The Highway of Sorrow. At the Close of the Nineteenth-Century: A Story of Modern Russia* (1894).

The political cause with which Hesba Stretton was most closely associated was that of child abuse and poverty. She was one of the founders in 1884 of the London branch of the National Society for the Prevention of Cruelty to Children. Stretton wrote to the London *Times* in January and again in May of that year about the cruelty and neglect of children and described the foundation in Liverpool of a society for its prevention. It was time, she said, for a national society that would "deliver us as a nation from the curse and crime, the shame and sin, of neglected and oppressed childhood." She attended the July 1884 meeting when the National Society began and remained on the executive board until 1894.

Hesba and Elizabeth Stretton (the latter changed her name from Smith) enjoyed traveling, particularly to Italy and Switzerland. They remained close to their siblings, nieces, and nephews. They moved to Richmond, outside London, in 1892. Hesba Stretton died there on 8 October 1911, and her sister died the same year.

Stretton wrote with passion about the injustices children suffered in the urban slums of industrial England. She appealed to young readers by putting the Christian message into the mouths and personalities of her child characters, charging children with the responsibility of saving the adults around them and, by implication, the society in which they lived. Her reputation, however, is only gradually being reclaimed from what Margaret Nancy Cutt calls the legend of tedious modesty and worthy benevolence. A second generation of readers, force-fed *Jessica's First Prayer* in Sunday school editions, was primarily struck by the work's pathetic imagery and ostentatious piety; but Stretton's child contemporaries who read the work experienced the author's reformist zeal as well as her engaging writing. Serious bibliographical and textual work on Stretton's books remains to be undertaken; such research will no doubt demonstrate the great interest of this popular author to the history of publishing, and particularly to that of children's literature.

References:

J. S. Bratton, "Hesba Stretton's Journalism," *Victorian Periodicals Review,* 21 (Summer 1979): 60–70;

Bratton, *The Impact of Victorian Children's Fiction* (London: Croom Helm, 1981);

Margaret Nancy Cutt, *Ministering Angels: A Study of Nineteenth-Century Evangelical Writing for Children* (Wormley: Five Owls Press, 1979);

Robert Lee Wolff, *Gains and Losses: Novels of Faith and Doubt in Victorian England* (New York: Garland, 1977), pp. 240–244.

Papers:

The "Log Books," in which Hesba Stretton's business and personal records were kept from 1859 to 1871, are located at the Shropshire County Library (Mss. 5556/1–9). A few manuscript letters survive in the Osborne Collection of Children's Books, Toronto Public Libraries; and in the British Library.

Ann Taylor

(30 January 1782 – 20 December 1866)

and

Jane Taylor

(23 September 1783 – 12 April 1824)

Judith A. Overmier
University of Oklahoma

BOOKS – by Ann and Jane Taylor: *Original Poems for Infant Minds,* 2 volumes (London: Darton & Harvey, 1804–1805; Philadelphia: Kimber, Conrad, 1806);

Rural Scenes; or, A Peep Into the Country (London: Darton & Harvey, 1805; New York: S. Wood, 1823);

Rhymes for the Nursery (London: Darton & Harvey, 1806; Hartford: P. B. Gleason, 1813);

Limed Twigs to Catch Young Birds (London: Darton & Harvey, 1808; Philadelphia: Johnson & Warner, 1811);

City Scenes; or, A Peep Into London (London: Darton & Harvey, 1809; Philadelphia: J. P. Parke, 1809);

Hymns for Infant Minds (London: T. Conder, 1810; Boston: Monroe, Francis & Parker [1810]); republished as *Meddlesome Matty and Other Poems for Infant Minds* (London: John Lane, 1925; New York: Viking, 1926);

The Associate Minstrals, by Ann and Jane Taylor, Josiah Conder, and others (London: T. Conder, 1810);

Signor Topsy Turvy's Wonderful Magic Lantern (London: Tabart, 1810; Philadelphia: W. Charles, 1811);

Original Hymns for Sunday Schools (London: J. Conder, 1812); republished as *Original Hymns for Sabbath Schools* (Boston: S. T. Armstrong, 1820).

BOOKS – by Ann Taylor: *Wedding Among the Flowers* (London: Darton & Harvey, 1808);

Hymns for Infant Schools (London: B. J. Holdsworth, 1827);

Original Anniversary Hymns (London: B. J. Holdsworth, 1827);

Ann Taylor (courtesy of the Lilly Library, Indiana University)

The Convalescent; Twelve Letters on Recovery from Sickness (London: Jackson & Walford, 1839);

Seven Blessings for Little Children (London: Jackson & Walford, 1844);

Memoir of the Rev. Joseph Gilbert (London: Jackson & Walford, 1853).

BOOKS – by Jane Taylor: *Display: A Tale for Young People* (London: Taylor & Hessey, 1815; Boston: J. Eliot, 1815);

Essays in Rhyme, on Morals and Manners (London: Taylor & Hessey, 1816; Boston: Wells & Lilly, 1816);

The Contributions of Q. Q. to a Periodical Work (London: B. J. Holdsworth, 1824; New York: E. Bliss & E. White, 1826).

Goodness, humor, and a knowledge of children's foibles (and children's pleasure in reading about appropriate punishments) characterize the writing of Ann and Jane Taylor, the first well-known and widely read children's poets. In addition to their poetry, they published essays, short stories, reviews, an autobiography, and a "novel," but best remembered of all their works are Jane's classic poem "The Star" (1804) and Ann's affecting poetic tribute, "My Mother" (1806).

Ann was born in Islington on 30 January 1782 and Jane, in Holborn on 23 September 1783 to Ann Martin Taylor and Isaac Taylor, an engraver, painter, and minister; his 1791 portrait of his daughters hangs in the National Portrait Gallery, London. Edith Sitwell wrote that they appear in the portrait as "very serious-minded, good little girls."

Although Isaac and Ann Taylor disapproved of their daughters' desire to become authors, they were allowed to write as long as the demands of housework, religion, family activities, schooling, and the practice of engraving (which their father thought would be an appropriate profession for them) had been satisfied. The girls would literally squeeze their writing into the margins of their schoolwork, and Ann noted, "I must confess to having had a pencil and paper generally so near at hand that a flying thought could be caught by a feather." In fact, not long after Ann and Jane's first writing success, the entire family – six children and both parents – found themselves successfully "squeezing in" writing.

Ann and Jane's siblings were their oldest brother, Isaac, who became a prolific writer and was author of the popular *Natural History of Enthusiasm* (1829); their younger brother, Martin; the youngest brother, Jefferys, who also wrote children's books, the best known of which is *Aesop in Rhyme* (1820); and the youngest child, Jemima. The family lived in various towns and regions of England, including London, the village of Lavenham in Suffolk, Colchester and Ongar in Essex, and Ilfracome in Devon. They were all avid readers and writers; their mother instituted the practice of reading aloud at the table. The Taylors were also committed to education, and their father not only educated his own children but he also eventually gave home lectures to twenty or thirty children at a time on such topics as history, geometry, astronomy, and fortifications. Ann and Jane both wrote as children for their own pleasure and for family members and special occasions. The two girls helped form a literary group, the Umbelliferous Society (an umbellifer is a member of the carrot family) in 1798. Monthly meetings were held by the Taylor children and friends during which they read and discussed literature, including their own writings.

In 1799 one of Ann Taylor's poems was published in the *Minor's Pocket Book,* an annual publication for young people, as a solution to a riddle that had appeared in the 1798 edition. Ann had other material published there, and her brother Isaac, although he considered the *Minor's Pocket Book* a "humble" part of literature, also sent in a poem that appeared in 1803 and was much praised. Finally Jane submitted "The Beggar Boy" in response to the poetry contest in the 1803 edition. It won second prize, her sister Ann winning first place with "The Cripple Child's Complaint"; both poems were published in the 1804 edition.

In 1804 the publisher of the *Minor's Pocket Book,* William Darton, wrote to Isaac Taylor and invited the children to submit enough poems for a book. The result was *Original Poems for Infant Minds* (1804), with a second volume the following year. The book was enormously successful, going rapidly through multiple printings and editions. Most of the poems were by Ann and Jane, but unbeknownst to the Taylors, Darton added a few poems by Adelaide O'Keeffe, daughter of John O'Keeffe, an Irish dramatist, and by Bernard Barton, a Quaker poet. Evidence is ample that *Original Poems for Infant Minds* was widely read in circles that mattered. Sara Coleridge, daughter of Samuel Taylor Coleridge, wrote that she was "fond of reading the *Original Poems* of the Miss Taylors" and that she memorized and recited them for her mother's friends. The volumes sustained their success throughout the century and into the next, with a centenary issue of *Original Poems for Infant Minds,* including an introduction by the essayist and literary critic Edward Verrall Lucas, published in 1904.

A long-term relationship was established between the firm of Darton and Harvey and the Taylor family. Several Taylors were commissioned to do engravings for the publishers, and they contributed to the *Minor's Pocket Book,* for which Ann served as editor for several years before her marriage. Darton and Harvey published Ann and Jane's first five jointly written books, including *Original Poems for Infant Minds, Rural Scenes; or, A Peep Into the Country* (1805), *Rhymes for the Nursery* (1806), *Limed Twigs to Catch Young Birds* (1808), and *City Scenes; or, A Peep Into London* (1809), as well as Ann's independently written book *Wedding Among the Flowers* (1808).

The poetry and prose of *Rural Scenes* convey realistic descriptions of the inhabitants and the daily activities of a typical rural community, such as "The Butcher," "The Barber," "The Cows," "Churning," and "Thrashing." In *City Scenes* visitors from the

Jane Taylor; engraving after a portrait by her father (courtesy of Special Collections, Thomas Cooper Library, University of South Carolina)

countryside are regaled with the big city sights (as in "Westminster Abbey" and "St. Paul's Cathedral"), shops ("The Book-Stall"), and trades ("The Coach-Maker"), but they are also warned about urban dangers, such as pickpockets. Both of these works convey a palpable sense of time and place, as well as of an individual's place in the community; they were illustrated by Ann, Jane, and their brother Isaac.

Rhymes for the Nursery seems at first entirely a volume of cautionary verse; the poems have such titles as "Sulking," "The Undutiful Boy," "Playing With Fire," and "To a Little Girl That Liked to Look in the Glass." However, it also contains many charming, cheerful poems, such as Jane's "The Star." *Limed Twigs,* another of Ann and Jane's volumes for very young children, is written in simple three- and four-letter words as dialogues between parents and children on topics such as "The Careful Ant," "Old Dobbin," and "Learning to Read." *Wedding Among the Flowers* was written by Ann in response to, according to her, a wave of mediocre imitations of the *Butterfly's Ball and the Grasshopper's Feast* (1807), a popular imaginative book by William Roscoe.

It was during this period of their lives that the young poets were allowed to spend more time writ-

ing and to have their own quiet areas for working. When Jane fitted out her writing space in an unoccupied attic, she wrote that she placed "one chair for myself, and another for my muse." Ann continued a dual interest in art and literature, but in 1807 she visited London and was introduced to several authors, after which she wrote, "I was wedded to literature, so far as literature would condescend to the alliance."

The first poem in the sisters' next joint work, *Hymns for Infant Minds* (1810), is Ann's "A Child's Hymn of Praise," the first verse of which reads: "I thank the goodness and the grace, / Which on my birth have smiled, / And made me, in these Christian days, / A happy English child." It is followed by seventy "hymns" on the subjects of sickness, temptation, sorrow for a fault, selfishness, anger, and impatience, including the maudlin "A Child's Lamentation for the Death of a Dear Mother" and that popular poem of dire consequence, Ann's "Meddlesome Matty." This book, too, was immediately successful and went through many editions, including republication in 1925 with an introduction by Edith Sitwell.

Other publications on which Ann and Jane worked include the book *The Associate Minstrals* (1810), to which they contributed nineteen of the fifty-two poems. This volume was a joint effort with their friend Josiah Conder and several other friends in their literary and social circle. The book was highly praised, and Sir Walter Scott and Robert Southey both wrote to Conder with praise for the poems. Ann and Jane were commissioned to revise an eighteenth-century book of verse, and the result was *Signor Topsy Turvy's Wonderful Magic Lantern* (1810), a book of entertaining poetry. They added amusing poems of their own, as well as revising the existing material so thoroughly that it became their own, and bibliographers now assign the work to them.

Their volume *Original Hymns for Sunday Schools* (1812) was written in simplified language to reach younger children. The poems include such typical Taylor subjects as "Thanks to Teachers" and "God Punishes Liars." Jane wrote that her method of writing was to shut her eyes and imagine a child and its words. She reports that sometimes it worked, but when it failed, she would give up and say, "Now you may go, my dear, I shall finish the hymn myself!"

On 24 December 1813 Ann Taylor married the Reverend Joseph Gilbert, a Congregational minister, and the sisters' writing habits changed substantially. That winter Jane accompanied her brother Isaac to Ilfracombe, in Devon, where the weather was gentler for his ill health. While there Jane spent several hours a day writing *Display: A Tale For Young People* (1815), her first independently written vol-

SIGNOR TOPSY-TURVY'S

WONDERFUL

MAGIC LANTERN;

OR,

The World turned upside down.

BY THE AUTHOR OF " MY MOTHER," AND OTHER POEMS.

ILLUSTRATED WITH TWENTY-FOUR ENGRAVINGS.

LONDON:

PRINTED FOR TABART & Co. AT THE JUVENILE AND SCHOOL
LIBRARY, NO. 157, NEW BOND-STREET; AND TO BE HAD
OF ALL BOOKSELLERS;
By B. McMillan, Bow Street, Covent Garden.

1810.

[Price 3s. 6d. Bound.]

FRONTISPIECE

Frontispiece and title page for the book of verse that the Taylors began as a revision of an eighteenth-century collection (courtesy of the Lilly Library, Indiana University)

ume. The novel — called a tale since novels were not then approved of — tells how Elizabeth, a vain, self-centered young girl, learns important lessons about life. *Display* was enormously popular and well received critically. In 1982 Walford wrote, "the writing is exceptionally piquant, terse, and vigorous and the studies of character inimitable."

Essays in Rhyme, on Morals and Manners (1816) was Jane Taylor's next undertaking. Her brother Isaac recounts that "Jane never wrote anything with so much zest and excitement as these pieces. While employed on them she was almost lost to other interests." Jane's verse essays cover egotism, experience, accomplishment, and prejudice. In the latter poem Jane's recurring advocacy of education and reading led her to assert that one's prejudice "depends on what we read," and that "If people would but read" prejudice would be less of a problem. The volume was as well received as her other writings. The year after its publication John Keats wrote to ask his sister "How do you like Miss Taylor's *'Essays in Rhyme?'* I just looked into the book and it appeared to me most suitable to you — especially since I remembered your liking for those pleasant little things, the

'Original Poems.' The essays are the more mature productions of the same hand."

Jane's brother Isaac wrote that after Jane and her style had matured, "She continued to address herself to childhood and youth . . . within this humbler sphere, she thought herself safe." Jane began writing "improving essays" for the *Youth's Magazine* in 1816. They were so successful that she was invited to become a regular contributor; her brother Isaac reports that "She dreaded the bondage" and was afraid of the effect on her writing of the loss of spontaneity. Nevertheless, she accepted the invitation and regularly contributed essays until 1822. Her topics are varied; a few of the essays are on specific Bible verses, but most have titles such as "Government of the Thoughts" or "Pleasure and Happiness." In Jane's essay "Letter Addressed to a Young Lady, Who Had Requested Advice on the Choice of Her Pursuits," reading is once again advocated — "judicious reading." She cautions her young readers against reading novels. She recognizes that one's reading is "regulated by the libraries to which they happen to have access," and in the essays "A Letter to a Friend" and "Conversation in a Library," she comments on the importance of being within easy reach of a good library: "This is an advantage which I have never fully possessed; but I have availed myself of what came in my way."

These essays, like Taylor's other writings, were widely read and proved influential. Robert Browning said his poem "Rephan" was "suggested by very early recollection of a prose story (How It Strikes a Stranger) by the noble woman and imaginative writer Jane Taylor." Browning also said her poems were "the most perfect things of their kind in the English language." Modern literary critic Stuart Curran writes that Jane "Taylor's capacity to reveal the inner life as a thing is, it could be asserted, unrivaled in English literature before Dickens."

Ann Taylor Gilbert published no poetry for some time after her marriage, but she was invited to write an article for the *Eclectic Review,* and she contributed several reviews. Thus, Ann wrote literary criticism until her first child was born in October 1814, when she gave up all writing for a time, commenting, "Never mind, the dear little child is worth volumes of fame." Gilbert kept busy with family, religion, and civic works, the latter including the establishment of the Free Library in Nottingham. She was cognizant of artistic, literary, religious, and political movements of the period, and her position on the issues is often evident in her personal and public writings. She was, for instance, a supporter of the Corn Laws; she was not a supporter of women's right to vote. As a supporter of animal welfare, she had often used her wicked sense of humor to good effect in poems such as "The Last Dying Speech and Confession of Poor Puss" (1805). In this poem, a cat swears, with his paw over his heart, that he had been unaware of the enormity of his crime, having thought all along that "birds and mice were on purpose for eating." In "The Mare Turned Farrier" (1810), the horse avenges her discomfort during shoeing by sitting on the farrier and shoeing him. Revenge takes a more ominous turn in "The Cook Cooked" (1810), a poem in which a hare leads a turkey, some oysters and eels, and a turtle in revolt; they dredge and brown the cook.

Eventually Gilbert was able to return to writing; she produced poems, essays, and reviews and in 1827 published two volumes of poetry, *Hymns for Infant Schools* and *Original Anniversary Hymns.* In 1839 she wrote *The Convalescent; Twelve Letters on Recovery from Sickness,* which contains reflections based on her personal experience with illness and death. Her brother Isaac wrote to her of his pleasure that "you have returned to your vocation and left (as I heartily hope for ever) the mending of stockings to hands that cannot so well handle the pen."

Ann Taylor Gilbert's and Jane Taylor's books were reviewed in a variety of journals, including the *Literary Panorama,* the *Christian Observer,* the *Critical Review,* the *British Critic,* the *Monthly Mirror,* the *Augustan Review,* and the *Eclectic Review.* Several of their books were translated into Dutch, Russian, French, and German, and a few were republished until well into the twentieth century. Although their complete works are not currently in print, individual poems, most frequently "The Star," still appear in collections.

Letters:
Correspondence Between a Mother and Her Daughter (London: Taylor & Hessey, 1817; New York: W. B. Gilley, 1818);
Memoirs and Poetical Remains of the Late Jane Taylor, With Extracts From Her Correspondence, 2 volumes, edited by Isaac Taylor, (London: B. J. Holdsworth, 1825).

Biographies:
Anne Katherine Curteis Elwood, *Memoirs of the Literary Ladies of England,* volume 2 (London: H. Colburn, 1843), pp. 262–275;
Rev. Isaac Taylor, ed., *The Family Pen; Memorials, Biographical and Literary, of the Taylor Family, of Onger,* 2 volumes (London: Jackson, Walford & Hodder, 1867);
Josiah Gilbert, ed., *Autobiography and Other Memorials of Mrs. Gilbert (formerly Ann Taylor),* 2 volumes (London: H. S. King, 1874);
L. B. Walford, *Four Biographies from 'Blackwood'* (Edinburgh: W. Blackwood, 1888), pp. 3–71;
Doris Mary Armitage, *The Taylors of Ongar* (Cambridge: W. Heffer, 1939);
Christina Duff Stewart, *Ann Taylor Gilbert's Album* (New York: Garland, 1978).

References:
Stuart Curran, "The I Altered," in *Romanticism and Feminism,* edited by Anne K. Mellor (Bloomington: Indiana University Press, 1988), pp. 192–194;
Edmund Gosse, *Leaves and Fruit* (London: Heinemann, 1927), pp. 185–191;
Bradford Keyes Mudge, *Sara Coleridge, A Victorian Daughter* (New Haven: Yale University Press, 1989), p. 255;
Christina Duff Stewart, *The Taylors of Ongar; An Analytical Bio-Bibliography,* 2 volumes (New York: Garland, 1975);
L. B. Walford, *Twelve English Authoresses* (London: Longmans, Green, 1892), pp. 185–191.

William Makepeace Thackeray

(18 July 1811 – 24 December 1863)

Craig Howes
University of Hawaii at Manoa

See also the Thackeray entries in *DLB 21: Victorian Novelists Before 1885; DLB 55: Victorian Prose Writers Before 1867;* and *DLB 159: British Short Fiction Writers, 1800–1880.*

BOOKS: *Flore et Zéphyr: Ballet Mythologique par Théophile Wagstaffe* (London: Mitchell, 1836);

The Yellowplush Correspondence, as Charles J. Yellowplush (Philadelphia: Carey & Hart, 1838);

Reminiscences of Major Gahagan, as Goliah O'Grady Gahagan (Philadelphia: Carey & Hart, 1839);

An Essay on the Genius of George Cruikshank (London: Hooper, 1840);

The Paris Sketch Book, by Mr. Titmarsh, 2 volumes (London: Macrone, 1840; New York: Appleton, 1852);

Comic Tales and Sketches, Edited and Illustrated by Mr. Michael Angelo Titmarsh, 2 volumes (London: Cunningham, 1841);

The Second Funeral of Napoleon, in Three Letters to Miss Smith of London; and The Chronicle of the Drum, by Mr. M. A. Titmarsh (London: Cunningham, 1841); republished as *The Second Funeral of Napoleon, by M. A. Titmarsh and Critical Reviews* (New York: Lovell, 1883);

The Irish Sketch Book, by Mr. M. A. Titmarsh (2 volumes, London: Chapman & Hall, 1843; 1 volume, New York: Winchester, 1843);

Jeames's Diary (New York: Taylor, 1846);

Notes of a Journey from Cornhill to Grand Cairo, by Way of Lisbon, Athens, Constantinople, and Jerusalem, Performed in the Steamers of the Peninsular and Oriental Company, by Mr. M. A. Titmarsh (London: Chapman & Hall, 1846; New York: Wiley & Putnam, 1846);

Mrs. Perkins's Ball, by Mr. M. A. Titmarsh (London: Chapman & Hall, 1847);

Vanity Fair: A Novel without a Hero (19 monthly parts, London: Bradbury & Evans, 1847–1848; 2 volumes, New York: Harper, 1848);

The Book of Snobs (London: Punch Office, 1848; New York: Appleton, 1852);

William Makepeace Thackeray

Our Street, by Mr. M. A. Titmarsh (London: Chapman & Hall, 1848);

The Great Hoggarty Diamond (New York: Harper, 1848); republished as *The History of Samuel Titmarsh and the Great Hoggarty Diamond* (London: Bradbury & Evans, 1849);

The History of Pendennis: His Fortunes and Misfortunes, His Friends and His Greatest Enemy (23 monthly parts, London: Bradbury & Evans, 1848–1850; 2 volumes, New York: Harper, 1850);

Doctor Birch and His Young Friends, by Mr. M. A. Titmarsh (London: Chapman & Hall, 1849; New York: Appleton, 1853);

Miscellanies: Prose and Verse, 8 volumes (Leipzig: Tauchnitz, 1849–1857);

The Kickleburys on the Rhine, by Mr. M. A. Titmarsh (London: Smith, Elder, 1850; New York: Stringer & Townsend, 1851);

Stubbs's Calendar; or, The Fatal Boots (New York: Stringer & Townsend, 1850);

Rebecca and Rowena: A Romance upon Romance, by Mr. M. A. Titmarsh (London: Chapman & Hall, 1850; New York: Appleton, 1853);

The History of Henry Esmond, Esq., a Colonel in the Service of Her Majesty Q. Anne, Written by Himself (3 volumes, London: Smith, Elder, 1852; 1 volume, New York: Harper, 1852);

The Confessions of Fitz-Boodle; and Some Passages in the Life of Major Gahagan (New York: Appleton, 1852);

A Shabby Genteel Story and Other Tales (New York: Appleton, 1852);

Men's Wives (New York: Appleton, 1852);

The Luck of Barry Lyndon: A Romance of the Last Century, 2 volumes (New York: Appleton, 1852–1853);

Jeames's Diary, A Legend of the Rhine, and Rebecca and Rowena (New York: Appleton, 1853);

Mr. Brown's Letters to a Young Man about Town; with the Proser and Other Papers (New York: Appleton, 1853);

Punch's Prize Novelists, The Fat Contributor, and Travels in London (New York: Appleton, 1853);

The English Humourists of the Eighteenth Century: A Series of Lectures Delivered in England, Scotland, and the United States of America (London: Smith, Elder, 1853; New York: Harper, 1853);

The Newcomes: Memoirs of a Most Respectable Family, Edited by Arthur Pendennis Esqre (23 monthly parts, London: Bradbury & Evans, 1853–1855; 2 volumes, New York: Harper, 1855);

The Rose and the Ring; or, The History of Prince Giglio and Prince Bulbo: A Fireside Pantomime for Great and Small Children (London: Smith, Elder, 1855; New York: Harper, 1855);

Miscellanies: Prose and Verse, 4 volumes (London: Bradbury & Evans, 1855–1857);

Ballads (Boston: Ticknor & Fields, 1856);

Christmas Books (London: Chapman & Hall, 1857; Philadelphia: Lippincott, 1872);

The Virginians: A Tale of the Last Century (24 monthly parts, London: Bradbury & Evans, 1857–1859; 1 volume, New York: Harper, 1859);

The Four Georges; Sketches of Manners, Morals, Court and Town Life (New York: Harper, 1860; London: Smith, Elder, 1861);

Lovel the Widower (New York: Harper, 1860; London: Smith, Elder, 1861);

The Adventures of Philip on His Way through the World; Shewing Who Robbed Him, Who Helped Him, and Who Passed Him By (3 volumes, London: Smith, Elder, 1862; 1 volume, New York: Harper, 1862);

Roundabout Papers (London: Smith, Elder, 1863; New York: Harper, 1863);

Denis Duval (New York: Harper, 1864; London: Smith, Elder, 1867);

Early and Late Papers Hitherto Uncollected, edited by James T. Fields (Boston: Ticknor & Fields, 1867);

Miscellanies, Volume IV (Boston: Osgood, 1870);

The Orphan of Pimlico; and Other Sketches, Fragments, and Drawings, with notes by A. I. Thackeray (London: Smith, Elder, 1876);

Sultan Stork and Other Stories and Sketches (1829–1844), Now First Collected, edited by R. H. Sheppard (London: Redway, 1887);

Loose Sketches, An Eastern Adventure, Etc. (London: Sabin, 1894);

The Hitherto Unidentified Contributions of W. M. Thackeray to Punch, with a Complete Authoritative Bibliography from 1845 to 1848, edited by M. H. Spielmann (London & New York: Harper, 1899);

Mr. Thackeray's Writings in the "National Standard" and the "Constitutional," edited by W. T. Spencer (London: Spencer, 1899);

Stray Papers: Being Stories, Reviews, Verses, and Sketches 1821–47, edited by Lewis S. Benjamin as Lewis Melville (London: Hutchinson, 1901; Philadelphia: Jacobs, 1901);

The New Sketch Book: Being Essays Now First Collected from the "Foreign Quarterly Review," edited by R. S. Garnett (London: Rivers, 1906);

The Rose and the Ring: Reproduced in Facsimile from the Author's Original Illustrated Manuscript in the Pierpont Morgan Library (New York: Pierpont Morgan Library, 1947);

Thackeray's Contributions to the "Morning Chronicle," edited by Gordon N. Ray (Urbana: University of Illinois Press, 1955).

SELECTED PERIODICAL PUBLICATIONS –
UNCOLLECTED: "A Word on the Annuals," *Fraser's Magazine,* 16 (December 1837): 757–763;

"Our Annual Execution," *Fraser's Magazine,* 19 (January 1839): 57–67;

"On Some Illustrated Children's Books," *Fraser's Magazine,* 33 (April 1846): 495–502;

"A Grumble about the Christmas-Books," *Fraser's Magazine,* 35 (January 1847): 111–126.

William Makepeace Thackeray's status as a writer, illustrator, and critic of children's literature is problematic. Throughout his career he adopted and parodied the genres most associated in his day with juvenile audiences. Fairy tales, *Arabian Nights* imitations, sequels to famous fables and romances, and Christmas books poured from his pen. So too did personal essays and reviews that took childhood and its literature for their subjects. Though his "Fireside Pantomime" in *The Rose and the Ring* (1855) proved to be his only enduring work written for the young, Thackeray's frequent and often ironic excursions into fable and tale made him one of Victorian England's most astute commentators on children's literature.

His upbringing suggests why Thackeray's attitude toward children's literature often oscillates between sarcasm and nostalgia. He was born on 18 July 1811 in Calcutta, the only child of Richmond Makepeace Thackeray, one of the many young Englishmen seeking to make their fortunes with the British East India Company, and Anne Becher Thackeray, one of the many Englishwomen who ventured to India to marry one of these young men. Richmond died when Thackeray was four; fifteen months later the boy was sent to England for schooling. He was reunited with his mother before his ninth birthday, when she returned to England with her second husband, Capt. Henry Carmichael-Smyth. Removed from the school he was attending, in early 1822 Thackeray entered Charterhouse, the renowned English institution that served as the model for the many fictional schools Thackeray would later create to expose the brutality and student bullying he experienced.

A dead father, an absent mother, and a prestigious English school all tempered Thackeray's opinions about the joys of childhood. Throughout his life he maintained that books and pictures had been his refuge and salvation. In an 1840 essay on George Cruikshank, the twenty-nine-year-old Thackeray adopted a heavily elegiac tone about his childhood reading. He found Cruikshank's art the source of "misty moralities, reflections, and sad and pleasant remembrances." Each illustration recalls childhood holidays, sports, and pantomimes. Cruikshank's comic drawings for Pierce Egan's *Life in London* (1821) remained some of Thackeray's favorites for the rest of his life.

Though children's publishing already had a distinguished history before Thackeray was born, he in fact believed that he had grown up just before the age of children's books. In an 1854 tribute to artist John Leech, Thackeray recalled the amusements available during his Regency childhood. Illustrated editions of the works of William Shakespeare, caricatures and political cartoons by Thomas Rowlandson or Cruikshank, and old prints by James Gillray, Henry William Bunbury, and George Woodward entertained the eyes. Books written for the young were tomes such as Maria Edgeworth's *The Parent's Assistant* (1795), Mrs. Barbauld's and John Aikin's *Evenings at Home* (1792), or Arnaud Berquin's *L'Ami des Enfans* (1782–1783). Small wonder, then, that novels and stories not necessarily written for children were Thackeray's favorites. The first book he remembered reading was Jane Porter's *The Scottish Chiefs* (1810), which was soon followed by works written by Miguel de Cervantes, Henry Fielding, Tobias Smollett, and Fanny Burney, as well as by contemporary page-turners such as Ann Radcliffe's *The Mysteries of Udolpho* (1794) and Porter's *Thaddeus of Warsaw* (1803). But Sir Walter Scott took firmest hold of Thackeray's imagination. *Waverley* (1814), *Quentin Durward* (1823), and *The Heart of Midlothian* (1818) were favorites, and later, in his own *Rebecca and Rowena* (1850), Thackeray would write a sequel to *Ivanhoe*. James Fenimore Cooper's Leatherstocking Tales, Alexandre Dumas's romances, and Eugene Sue's *Mysteries of Paris* (1842–1843) also absorbed him, and like so many others, he fell under the spell of the *Arabian Nights*.

Uncertainty and misfortunes severely tested Thackeray's love for romance as he entered adulthood. He lasted less than two years at Trinity College, Cambridge, leaving with massive gambling debts. After time on the Continent he entered the Middle Temple in 1831, but the law proved unappealing, and he drifted toward his love of art and literature. In 1832 he was back in France, reading, painting, and gambling; in 1833 he became editor of the *National Standard and Journal of Literature, Science, Music, Theatricals, and the Fine Arts,* which survived for nine months. That same year the failure of the Indian financial houses erased the patrimony that his gambling had already eaten into. In 1835 Thackeray fell in love with young Isabella Shawe, who was living in Paris with her widowed mother. Since marriage depended on his ability to support a family, he began testing the waters as an illustrator and as a journalist for the *Constitutional and Public Ledger,* a London radical newspaper in which his stepfather had invested. The marriage took place in August 1836, and a daughter, Anne Isabella, was born in June 1837. A second daughter, Jane, was born in July 1838 but died in infancy; Harriet Marian (Minny) was born in May 1840.

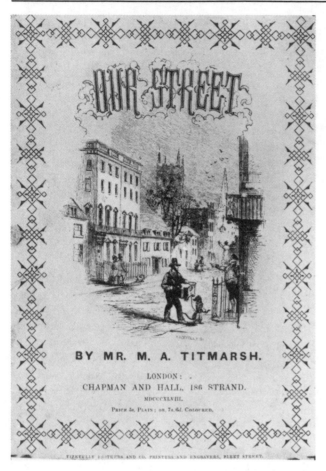

Title page for Thackeray's second Christmas book

When he began writing in earnest, Thackeray was a twenty-six-year-old husband and father with memories of a melancholy childhood and a restless and financially irresponsible youth, as well as a firm conviction that he was prematurely aged. When his attention turned to children's literature, he displayed both a yearning for a time of play and wonder and a grim sarcasm that lampooned sentiment and stressed the cruelty and ordinariness of childhood. His annual *Fraser's Magazine* reviews of the various holiday collections and books of beauty tended toward ridicule. In 1837 he denounced the "miserable mediocrity" and "feeble verse" in these publications and condemned the artwork for encouraging "bad taste in the public, bad engraving, and worse painting." The intended audience only fueled his anger: "Is every year to bring more nonsense like this, for foolish parents to give their foolish children; for dull people to dawdle over till the dinner-bell rings; to add something to the trash on my lady's drawing-room table, or in Miss's bookcase?" The title of his review of 1838's publica-

tions, "Our Annual Execution," suggests that a year had not changed his opinions. Shortly afterward, though, Thackeray was himself writing for publications with a sizable juvenile readership. Two slight stories — "Stubbs's Calendar; or, the Fatal Boots" and "Barber Cox and the Cutting of his Comb" — in the 1839 and 1840 volumes of George Cruikshank's *Comic Annual* were little more than excuses for the master's illustrations.

In three more ambitious pieces Thackeray exploited with varying success literary forms associated with childhood. "Sultan Stork, Being the One Thousand and Second Night" appeared in *Ainsworth's Magazine* in February 1842. In this light parody of the *Arabian Nights,* a king and a vizier gain the power to transform themselves, but they become trapped in the form of storks until they encounter a princess who has been turned into an owl. Magic words and promises of love restore everyone to human form, and the king marries the princess. Some of Thackeray's favorite parodic techniques, however, give "Sultan Stork" a certain bite: incongruity, anachronism, exaggeration, and deflation.

Thackeray's second parody, "Miss Tickletoby's Lectures on English History," in which the mistress of a girl's school makes faintly humorous remarks on British history, was not as successful. Though the supposed audience is juvenile, the assumed reader is adult, since knowledge of the events is necessary for understanding the humor. This tedious series, which represented Thackeray's first sustained contribution to *Punch,* was discontinued after four months in October 1842. "Bluebeard's Ghost," published in the October 1843 issue of *Fraser's Magazine,* has a plot barely worth noting: two rival suitors plot to marry the wealthy widow of the infamous Bluebeard, and one of them does. Far more amusing is Mrs. Bluebeard's performance as a mourning widow. She encases herself and her household in the deepest and most expensive mourning, erects a splendid monument for her husband, and denounces her vulgar brothers, who in the process of saving her life had cruelly cut down "the best of husbands."

The seldom-discussed "A Legend of the Rhine," from *George Cruikshank's Table-Book* for 1845, is Thackeray's first lengthy excursion into what he calls "the grey limbo of romance." As the narrator admits, the plot comes from Alexandre Dumas's *Othon l'Archer* (1840), but the debt is small. The melancholy undercutting of romance begins in the first paragraph, which sets the story in "the good old days of chivalry" but then describes time's impact on the characters before they have even been introduced:

> Their golden hair first changed to silver, and then the silver dropped off and disappeared for ever; their elegant legs, so slim and active in the dance, became swollen and gouty, and then, from being swollen and gouty, dwindled down to bare bone-shanks; the roses left their cheeks, and then their cheeks disappeared, and left their skulls, and then their skulls powdered into dust, and all sign of them was gone. And as it was with them, so shall it be with us.

Similar jolts keep the reader alert but unsteady as the tale unfolds. Though romance heroes always perform remarkable feats, Thackeray's heroic descriptions are exaggerated to the point of absurdity. He also savages romance conventions simply by calling attention to them. When for lack of space the description of a great competition gets cut short, he refers the reader "to the account of the tournament in the ingenious novel of 'Ivanhoe,' where the above phenomena are described at length." Similarly, after the hero's father sinks "lifeless to the floor" at the news of his son's drowning, the next chapter undercuts the melodrama. "It must be clear to the dullest intellect" that the father's fears were groundless: "No, young Otto was *not* drowned. Was ever hero of romantic story done to death so early in the tale?" One final technique, a lengthy allusion to the Christmas pantomimes, would appear prominently in many of Thackeray's later works. Like Signor Clown, conventional romance heroes have impeccable timing: "they rescue virgins just as ogres are on the point of devouring them; they manage to be present at Court and interesting ceremonies, and to see the most interesting people at the most interesting moment; directly an adventure is necessary for them, that adventure occurs."

That Thackeray would link romance with the pantomime is not surprising, for by 1845 the Christmas stage extravaganza had been triumphantly joined by literary entertainments for the holiday season aimed at the same youthful audience. The reason was Charles Dickens, whose *A Christmas Carol* (1843) redefined Christmas by stressing its transcendent importance for children. In February 1844 Thackeray wrote that Scrooge's story had "so spread over England by this time, that no sceptic, no *Fraser's Magazine* . . . could review it down." The book's creation of a huge domestic audience for short seasonal tales featuring comedy, sentiment, and fantasy, however, soon produced a host of imitators. Thackeray was of two minds about Christmas books. In a three-part review for the *Morning Chronicle* in December 1845, he compared the appearance of "a hundred new Christmas volumes, in beautiful bindings, with beautiful pictures" to the spectacular holiday profusion of food, candy, and sweets.

A concern with cheap facade arises, however, when Thackeray praises John Edward Taylor's *The Fairy Ring* (1846) for remaining true to "the old form of the fairy tale, and the child-like simplicity and wonder of narration which constitute its main charm, and which has been ruined by that knowing modern slang and *goguenard* air with which later authors have polluted that sacred fairy ground." In a review of Mrs. Gore's *The Snow Storm, a Tale of Christmas* (1845), Thackeray forges the link between theatrical sentimentality and holiday cheer to ridicule the book's close. He marvels at the villagers' jubilation when a mysterious person, who "has disappeared for fifty years (and with rather a bad character)," returns at the last moment to bail out the plot.

When looking at contemporary juvenile literature Thackeray could be affectionate, caustic, and sometimes both. An 1846 *Fraser's Magazine* review celebrates the "collection of treasures" available to juvenile readers thanks to publishers such as Joseph Cundall; writers and editors such as Felix Summerly (Sir Henry Cole), Mrs. Harriet Myrtle, and Ambrose Merton (William John Thomas); and artists such as Thomas Webster, Henry James Townshend, John Absolon, Charles West Cope, John Callcot Horsley, Richard Redgrave, Henry Corbould, John Franklin, and Frederick Tayler.

On the other hand, his "A Grumble about the Christmas-Books" (1847) begins with a rant: "Curses on all fairies! . . . I will never swallow another one as long as I live! Perdition seize all benevolence! Be hanged to the Good and the True! Fling me every drop of the milk of human kindness out of window! – horrible, curdling slops, away with them! Kick old Father Christmas out of doors, the abominable old impostor!" Yet even this scrooge in the making insists on a benevolent recipe for how such books should close:

> Kill your people off as much as you like; but always bring 'em to life again. Belabour your villains as you please. . . . But they must always amend, and you must be reconciled to them in the last scene, when the spangled fairy comes out of the revolving star, and, uttering the magic octosyllabic incantations of reconcilement, vanishes into an elysium of blue fire.

Testing out just how far this pantomime vision could be extended would become one of Thacker-

*Betsinda; Princess Angelica; the queen, Lady Gruffanuff; King Valoroso; and Prince
Giglio; illustration by Thackeray for* The Rose and the Ring *(1854)*

ay's greatest challenges – both in his own Christmas books and in his major novels.

Thackeray's first five Christmas books were *Mrs. Perkins's Ball* (1847), *Our Street* (1848), *Doctor Birch and His Young Friends* (1849), *Rebecca and Rowena,* and *The Kickleburys on the Rhine* (1850). The sixth and most significant was *The Rose and the Ring.* As Gordon N. Ray recommends, these books "should be read in their pretty original format: the type large and heavily leaded, Thackeray's quaint illustrations coloured by hand, and the whole bound in glazed white boards." The drawings, which Thackeray always found easier to produce than text, dominate the first three volumes. In *Mrs. Perkins's Ball* the plot is only the thinnest of threads holding together short character descriptions accompanied by full-page portraits of the guests. If anything, *Our Street* has even less plot, merely introducing the reader to the residents of a thinly disguised version of Thackeray's own Kensington neighborhood. One of his favorite narrative frames

is used in *Doctor Birch and His Young Friends,* with its portraits of generic schoolboys and teachers. The shy narrator, an instructor, secretly loves the ingenue, in this case Doctor Birch's ill-treated niece, but watches sadly when a younger and infinitely more suitable lover eventually whisks her away. The narrator of *The Kickleburys on the Rhine,* a series of drawings and longer prose vignettes recording a farcical European tour, suffers the same fate.

What sets these four volumes apart from most Christmas books is Thackeray's apparent lack of interest in appealing to the genre's assumed juvenile audience. One possible reason for this puzzling fact appears in *Doctor Birch and His Young Friends,* the book whose subject actually is children. In "The End of the Play," the book's poetic epilogue, Thackeray prepares his "young friends" for the roles that "Fate ere long shall bid you play" by insisting that "the griefs, the joys" of boys are "not less keen," nor are their "hopes more vain, than those of men." Childhood, in short, teaches human beings that life is fundamentally unfair. Though such sentiments are hardly the stuff of Christmas cheer, they certainly agree with Thackeray's strong sense of how mingled childhood's emotions are – a sense caught perfectly when he wishes young readers of *Doctor Birch* "health, and love, and mirth, / As fits the solemn Christmas tide."

Rebecca and Rowena: A Romance upon Romance is even less festive. When a severe illness in September 1849 interrupted the monthly installments of *The History of Pendennis* (1848–1850) and threatened to break the string of Christmas books, Thackeray turned to his "Proposals for a Continuation of Ivanhoe," a two-part fantasia that he had published in *Fraser's Magazine* in 1846. He then asked Richard "Dicky" Doyle to do the illustrations, while he revised the "Proposals." Despite all this cobbling, *Rebecca and Rowena* is a dark but remarkably sustained example of Thackeray at midcareer. The story's original spur was unfulfilled desire. After condemning Dickens and George P. R. James for ending their novels by marrying off their young heroes and heroines, Thackeray turns happily to Alexandre Dumas, "who carries his heroes from early youth down to the most venerable old age; and does not let them rest until they are so old, that it is full time the poor fellows should get a little peace and quiet." Following Dumas's example, he proposes to continue *Ivanhoe,* largely because he never accepted that the beautiful and heroic Rebecca could disappear before Rowena, whom he considers unworthy of Ivanhoe and her place as heroine.

In keeping with the sentiments expressed in *Doctor Birch and His Young Friends,* Thackeray both gratifies and frustrates his desire to do Rebecca justice. To begin with, the whole story is set within a Christmas pantomime frame, which for Thackeray always has a mixed significance. Doyle's frontispiece, showing the characters transformed into Clown, Harlequin, Columbine, and Pantaloon, seems cheery enough. The story's first chapter is called "The Overture – Commencement of the Business," and in the final chapter, "The End of the Performance," Thackeray promises to satisfy "that generous public which likes to see virtue righted, true love rewarded, and the brilliant Fairy descend out of the blazing chariot at the end of the pantomime, and make Harlequin and Columbine happy."

But Thackeray also sharply distinquishes between what romance readers or pantomime audiences want and what they know to be the case. For such people, "It is only hope which is real, and reality is a bitterness and a deceit," because they realize that "through life's shifting scenes, no fairy comes

down to make *us* comfortable at the close of the performance." Bitterness is certainly dominant in *Rebecca and Rowena,* as Thackeray swiftly tarnishes Scott's heroic characters. Richard the Lionhearted appears as a violent reprobate; Robin Hood has become a "conscientious magistrate" and "the strictest game-proprietor in all the Riding," who happily and anachronistically sends poachers off to Botany Bay; and self-righteous, humorless Rowena delights in tormenting her husband, Wilfred of Ivanhoe, about Rebecca's love for him. Worn down by this assault, Wilfred decides to join Richard on the Continent, where he is laying siege to the town of Chalus. This long scene not only ridicules the exploits of romance heroes, who in this case wallow in the blood of hundreds, but also mocks the bravery of the victims.

Wilfred falls into a six-year coma. When he awakes, he disguises himself as a friar and returns to Rotherwood, where Rowena is happier with her "stupid and boozy" second husband, Athelstane. Wilfred leaves, but shortly afterward King John attacks the estate, leaving Athelstane dead and Rowena imprisoned. When Wilfred eventually finds her she is dying, but she extorts from him one last vow: " 'Promise me, then,' gasped Rowena, staring wildly at him, 'that you never will marry a Jewess!' "

By now the story is three-quarters told, and Rebecca has not appeared. The narrator attacks this problem with a lightning charge to Europe, where Wilfred fights nobly, even if some warriors felt "that he did not persecute the Jews as so religious a knight should." In Spain he continues his habit of killing hundreds of people a day, then searching the Jewish quarter for Rebecca. Eventually her father, Isaac, appears as the negotiator for a Moorish nobleman trying to ransom his daughter from Wilfred's host. During this gruesome scene, as the host murders the daughter for insulting him, while Ivanhoe catches hold of Isaac, who declares that Rebecca is dead.

She is not, however; in fact, Rebecca has been refusing for years to marry wealthy Moors or Jews. When forced to explain why, she reveals that she has converted to Christianity – so much for Rowena's deathbed demand – and can only marry someone of the faith she now shares with dear Wilfred. In a distinctly Thackerayan manner, the story ends in a happy but thoroughly unsatisfying manner. Invoking the pantomime again, Thackeray announces that "the fairy in the pretty pink tights and spangled muslin is getting into the brilliant revolving chariot of the realms of bliss," as the audience scuffles to leave the pit. Events onstage are equally mixed.

THE RIVALS.

Princess Angelica, Prince Giglio, and Prince Bulbo; illustration by Thackeray for The Rose and the Ring

When Wilfred finally fights his way to Rebecca, she lays her head on his heart in a manner that moves the narrator, who for "five-and-twenty years" has loved Rebecca "and longed to see her righted." Yet, with one more turn of the screw, Thackeray provides a conclusion that would be almost inconceivable in a Christmas book written by anyone else: although Rebecca and Wilfred marry, the narrator adds, "I don't think they had any other children, or were subsequently very boisterously happy. Of some sort of happiness melancholy is a characteristic, and I think these were a solemn pair, and died rather early." For this reason, above all, *Rebecca and Rowena* represents a limit to Thackeray's parodic treatments of romance narratives. The desire for happiness and the fact of dashed hopes could hardly be twisted more tightly together.

The Rose and the Ring; or, The History of Prince Giglio and Prince Bulbo: A Fireside Pantomime for Great and Small Children is more overtly a children's book than anything else Thackeray wrote. One reason is biographical: while Thackeray was in Rome during the Christmas season of 1853, his daughters organized a Twelfth Night party. Since the baker could not supply the traditional comic figures that accompany the cakes, Thackeray was enlisted to draw "the King, the Queen, the Lover, the Lady, the Dandy, the Captain, and so on." After the party he picked up the "little painted figures" and "began placing them in order and making a story to fit them." Soon he was writing his narrative, then sharing it chapter by chapter with Edith Story, a little girl who, like Thackeray, was recovering from malarial fever. He continued to work on what he called his "Fairy Tale" after leaving Rome in February, reading the installments to his daughters. That fall he revised the manuscript and selected and prepared the illustrations for his last and most successful Christmas book.

The book's announced intentions are strikingly modest. Since most children would soon be returning to school, it proclaims, "for a brief holiday, let us laugh and be as pleasant as we can." This prevailing tone makes *The Rose and the Ring* the most genial of Thackeray's fantasy fictions, though irony and the grotesque make their appearance. The story is a storehouse of fairy-tale motifs. At the time of their births, Prince Giglio, heir to the throne of Paflagonia, and Princess Rosalba, heir to the throne of Crim Tartary, receive the precious gift of "a little misfortune" from the Fairy Blackstick. Giglio's misfortune is having to play Hamlet to his usurping uncle, King Valoroso; Rosalba's misfortune is exile and obscurity after the Duke of Padella overthrows her father. To complicate matters, Blackstick had many years before given a magical ring to Giglio's mother and a magical rose to the mother of Prince Bulbo, the son of the Duke of Padella. These objects make whoever owns them irresistibly attractive.

In both the text and the illustrations the Twelfth Night figures have developed into Christmas pantomime figures. Names are descriptive and outrageous. In addition to Valoroso and Giglio, the Paflagonian court boasts Lady Gruffanuff, Prime Minister Glumboso, Chancellor Squaretoso, and Kutasoff Hedzoff, the Captain of the Guard. Rosalba's Crim Tartary boasts such noble families as the Spinachi, the Articiocchi, the Family of Sauerkraut, and the House of Broccoli. These characters act out typical pantomime situations. Unaware of her true identity, poor Rosalba becomes "Betsinda," a serving maid in Valoroso's palace. When she accidentally acquires the ring, she has to fight off the suddenly enamored Giglio and Prince Bulbo, and she actually smashes Valoroso to the floor with a warming pan. In response, the fiercely jealous queen, Princess Angelica, and Lady Gruffanuff drive her out into the wilderness.

This same ring almost traps Giglio into marrying Lady Gruffanuff, the ugly villain of the piece. A pantomime transformation, however, saves him when Blackstick, who years before had turned Gruffanuff's rude footman husband into a door knocker, turns him back into a human being, and Lady Gruffanuff is a married woman once more. Characters are constantly and miraculously escaping capture or death. The drawings are often highly theatrical tableaux, which mix fairly realistic figures, Giglio and Rosalba, and with a cast of caricatures – Gruffanuff, Hedzoff, Valoroso, Padella, and, most notably Bulbo, who resembles one of the pantomime's popular Big Heads.

These influences blend with Thackeray's favorite routines. Anachronisms run rampant throughout this story set "ten or twenty thousand years ago": characters read about important events in the newspapers, and the court painter is Tomaso Lorenzo, an allusion to Sir Thomas Lawrence, Sir Joshua Reynolds's successor as royal portraitist. Exaggeration and deflation repeatedly occur. From the moment he demands his throne, Giglio, "as more becoming his majestic station," speaks blank verse and starts off with a speech that keeps an entire army spellbound "for three days and three nights." An even more absurd example occurs when Princess Angelica faints and is revived with boiling water.

Some deflations are in the spirit of Thackeray's earlier lampoons. When facing an imposing Giglio on the battlefield, King Padella quite reasonably points out that "If . . . you ride a fairy horse, and wear fairy armour, what on earth is the use of my hitting you? I may as well give myself up a prisoner at once." Other deflations, however, have a more homely feel. For instance, the description and illustrations of poor Prince Bulbo's last night before his supposed execution reveal an angry, self-pitying, but touchingly pathetic figure who climbs upon a pile of tables, bed, chairs, and hats for a last look out between the bars of his cell.

By mixing the ingredients of the fairy tale, Christmas book, and pantomime together with his own ironic perspective on human motivation, Thackeray helped to create a fantasy literature that played an important role, according to Stephen Prickett, "in bridging the divided halves of the Victorian psyche." Like his other writings, *The Rose and the Ring* explicitly calls into question its own formal and ethical artifice, and Prickett notes: "The elements of self-parody, the use of fantasy both to present a 'serious' moral, and, simultaneously to satirize the magical means by which the virtuous (and hard-working!) are rewarded, and the wicked and idle punished" became central in fantasy literature over the next fifty years. C. N. Manlove goes

further, claiming that *The Rose and the Ring* marks the transition from the traditional to the modern fairy tale.

In the years that followed, Thackeray's literary reputation grew as the quality of his writing declined. Though rewarding financially, his lecture tours of Great Britain and the United States exhausted him, and stress forced him to resign the lucrative editorship of *Cornhill Magazine*. His novels from this period were all sequels of a sort and drew heavily on earlier themes. His roundabout essays in the *Cornhill Magazine* were best suited to his abilities at this time. Many of his remarks on children's literature and his own memories of reading appear in these late pieces. Though his health had been uncertain for more than a decade, Thackeray died suddenly, apparently of a cerebral hemorrhage, on 24 December 1863.

The most important point to make about Thackeray's children's writing is that it always threatens to melt into his other works – or vice versa. Juliet McMaster has referred to *The Rose and the Ring* as "Quintessential Thackeray" because of the authorial tone, the undercutting of the heroic by the domestic, the attack on snobbery and false pretensions, the similarities between the fairy tale figures and characters from the major novels, and the handling of narrative. It is just as true, though, that Thackeray's best-known works are profoundly influenced by his meditations on the literature of childhood. The close of *Vanity Fair* is an excellent example: "Come, children, let us shut up the box and the puppets, for our play is played out." Just as evocative, however, is *The Newcomes* (1853–1855), the novel written at the same time as *The Rose and the Ring*. "The Overture" that begins this massive social novel is "a farrago of old fables," in which Aesop's characters tumble over each other until some critics rise up and denounce the mess. The narrator responds by remarking that even children know that the fable should precede the moral, and so "our wolves and lambs, our foxes and lions, our roaring donkeys, our billing ringdoves, our motherly partlets, and crowing chanticleers" should take the stage without further critical positioning. The novel's close provides a fitting conclusion for a discussion of Thackeray's relationship to children's literature:

The Poet of Fable-land rewards and punishes absolutely. He splendidly deals out bags of sovereigns, which won't buy anything; belabours wicked backs with awful blows, which do not hurt; endows heroines with preternatural beauty, and creates heroes, who, if ugly sometimes, yet possess a thousand good qualities, and usually end by being immensely rich; makes the hero and heroine happy at last, and happy ever after. Ah, happy, harmless Fable-land, where these things are!

Letters:

The Letters and Private Papers of William Makepeace Thackeray, 4 volumes, edited by Gordon N. Ray (London: Oxford University Press, 1945-1946).

Bibliographies:

Henry S. Van Duzer, *A Thackeray Library* (Port Washington, N.Y.: Kennikat Press, 1965);

Edward M. White, "Thackeray's Contributions to *Fraser's Magazine,*" *Studies in Bibliography,* 19 (1966): 67-84;

Dudley Flamm, *Thackeray's Critics: An Annotated Bibliography of British and American Criticism 1836-1901* (Chapel Hill: University of North Carolina Press, 1967);

John C. Olmsted, *Thackeray and His Twentieth-Century Critics: An Annotated Bibliography, 1900-1975* (New York & London: Garland, 1977);

Sheldon Goldfarb, *William Makepeace Thackeray: An Annotated Bibliography 1976-1987* (New York: Garland, 1989).

Biographies:

Lionel Stevenson, *The Showman of Vanity Fair* (New York: Scribners, 1947);

Gordon N. Ray, *William Makepeace Thackeray: The Uses of Adversity* (New York: McGraw-Hill, 1955);

Ray, *William Makepeace Thackeray: The Age of Wisdom* (New York: McGraw-Hill, 1958);

Ann Monsarrat, *An Uneasy Victorian: Thackeray the Man* (New York: Dodd, Mead, 1980).

References:

Edwin M. Eigner, *The Dickens Pantomime* (Berkeley: University of California Press, 1989);

Gerald Frow, *"Oh, Yes It Is!": A History of Pantomime* (London: British Broadcasting Corporation, 1985);

Edgar F. Harden, ed., *Annotations for the Selected Works of William Makepeace Thackeray: The Complete Novels, the Major Non-Fictional Prose, and Se-* lected Shorter Pieces, 2 volumes (New York: Garland, 1990);

Donald Hawes, "Thackeray and the Annuals," *Ariel,* 1 (January 1976): 3-31;

John Loofbourow, *Thackeray and the Form of Fiction* (Princeton: Princeton University Press, 1964);

C. N. Manlove, *The Impulse of Fantasy Literature* (Kent, Ohio: Kent State University Press, 1983), pp. 9-14;

David Mayer, *Harlequin in His Element: The English Pantomime, 1806-1836* (Cambridge, Mass.: Harvard University Press, 1969);

Juliet McMaster, "*The Rose and the Ring:* Quintessential Thackeray," *Mosaic,* 9 (Summer 1976): 157-165;

S. A. Muresianu, *The History of the Victorian Christmas Book* (New York: Garland, 1987), pp. 88-144;

Stephen Prickett, *Victorian Fantasy* (Bloomington: Indiana University Press, 1979), pp. 66-72;

Gail D. Sorensen, "Thackeray's *The Rose and the Ring:* A Novelist's Fairy Tale," *Mythlore,* 57 (Spring 1989): 37-38, 43;

Ellen Tremper, "Commitment and Escape: The Fairy Tales of Thackeray, Dickens, and Wilde," *Lion and the Unicorn,* 2 (Spring 1978): 38-47.

Papers:

The manuscript for William Makepeace Thackeray's *The Rose and the Ring,* complete with the original illustrations, is held at the Pierpont Morgan library. Another substantial resource for Thackeray manuscripts is the Harry Ransom Humanities Research Center of the University of Texas at Austin, which holds manuscript materials and proof plates for several of the Christmas books. Several institutions have extensive collections of manuscripts, publication materials, and correspondence in Great Britain, including the British Library, the Charterhouse School Library, the National Library of Scotland, the *Punch* archive, and Trinity College, Cambridge. Important collections in the United States include those at Harvard University, the Huntington Library, the New York Public Library, New York University, Princeton University, and Yale University.

Charlotte Elizabeth Tonna
("Charlotte Elizabeth")

(1 October 1790 – 12 July 1846)

Lois Rauch Gibson
Coker College

and

Madelyn Holmes
George Washington University

BOOKS: *The Shepherd Boy; and The Deluge* (London: Westley, 1823);

Zadoc, The Outcast of Israel: A Tale (London: James Duncan & J. Nisbet, 1825);

Osric: A Missionary Tale; with The Garden, and Other Poems (Dublin: W. Curry, 1825?; London: J. Nisbet, 1826; New York: Baker & Scribner, J. S. Taylor, 1845);

Anne Bell: or, the Faults (Dublin: Bentham & Hardy, 1826); revised by D. P. Kidder (New York: Lane & Tippett, 1847);

Consistency (London: J. Hatchard, 1826; Boston: Crocker & Brewster, 1831);

The Grandfather's Tales (London: F. Westley & A. H. Davis, 1826);

Izram, A Mexican Tale; and Other Poems (London: J. Nisbet, 1826; New York: J. S. Taylor, 1845);

The Net of Lemons (London: J. Nisbet, 1826);

Perseverance; or Walter and His Little School (London: J. Nisbet, 1826);

Rachel. A Tale (London: J. Nisbet, 1826); republished as *Rachel; a Tale* (Boston: Crocker & Brewster, 1828); republished as *The Flower of Innocence; or, Rachel. A True Narrative: With Other Tales* (New York: J. S. Taylor, 1841);

Allen M'Leod, The Highland Soldier (Boston: Crocker & Brewster, 1827);

The Bird's Nest (Dublin: J. & M. Porteous, 1827);

Edward, The Orphan Boy; A Tale, Founded on Facts (Clapham: W. Hands, 1827);

The Hen and Her Chickens (Dublin: T. I. White, 1827; New York: American Tract Society, 1850);

Little Frank, The Irish Boy (London: F. Westley, 1827);

The System: A Tale of the West Indies (London: F. Westley, 1827);

Eng.ᵈ By T. Bowar.

Charlotte Eliz.ᵗᵉ Tonna

A Visit to St. George's Chapel, Windsor, on the Evening Succeeding the Funeral of His Late Royal Highness the Duke of York (London: J. Dennett, 1827);

A Friendly Address to Converts from the Roman Catholic Church (Dublin: T. I. White, 1828);

The Willow Tree (Dublin: J. & M. Porteous, 1828);

The Fortune Teller (Dublin: J. & M. Porteous, 1829);

The Rockite, An Irish Story (London: J. Nisbet, 1829; New York: J. S. Taylor, 1844; enlarged edition, London: J. Nisbet, 1846);

The Swan (Dublin: J. & M. Porteous, 1829; New York: American Tract Society, 1850s);

The Burying Ground (Dublin: T. I. White, 1830; New York: American Tract Society, 1840s);

Little Oaths (Dublin: J. & M. Porteous, 1830; New York: American Tract Society, 1840s);

Maternal Martyrdom: A Fact, Ilustrative of the Improved Spirit of Popery, In the Nineteenth Century, as C. E. (N.p., 1830?);

A Respectful Appeal to the Primates and Prelates of the Church, on the Present Crisis (London: J. Dennett, 1830?);

Tales and Illustrations, 2 volumes (London: J. Nisbet, 1830; New York: J. S. Taylor, 1843);

Works, 2 volumes (New York, 1830); enlarged as *The Works of Charlotte Elizabeth* (New York: M. W. Dodd, 1844);

An Address to the Christian Friends and Supporters of the British and Foreign Bible Society, on the Connexion between Socinians and Arians and that Institution (London: J. Nisbet, 1831);

The Baby (Dublin: J. Porteous, 1831);

The Fragments (Dublin: T. I. White, 1831);

The Glow-worm (Dublin: T. I. White, 1831); revised by Kidder (New York: Lane & Tippett, 1848);

A Letter to a Friend, Containing a Few Heads for Consideration, on Subjects that Trouble the Church (London: William Crofts, 1831);

"Try Again" (Dublin: J. Porteous, 1831);

The Wasp (Dublin: T. I. White, 1831);

The Bible the Best Book (Dublin: J. Porteous, 1832; New York: American Tract Society, 1850s);

The Bow and the Cloud (Dublin: J. Porteous, 1832);

Combination: A Tale, Founded on Facts (Dublin: Religious Tract and Book Society for Ireland, 1832; New York: M. W. Dodd, 1844);

The Dying Sheep (Dublin: Religious Tract and Book Society for Ireland, 1832);

The Girl's Best Ornament: With Other Sketches (Boston: J. Loring, 1832);

Ireland's Crisis (London, 1832);

The Museum (Dublin: Religious Tract and Book Society for Ireland, 1832); republished as *Pleasure and Profit, or Time Well Spent* (New York: Taylor & Gould, 1835); republished as *Glimpses of the Past* (London: Seeley, 1839; New York: J. S. Taylor, 1841);

Short Stories for Children, 2 volumes (Dublin, 1832; London: Houlston, 1852; New York: American Tract Society, n.d.);

Derry, a Tale of the Revolution (London: J. Nisbet, 1833); republished as *The Siege of Derry; or, Sufferings of the Protestants: A Tale of the Revolution* (New York: J. S. Taylor, 1841);

The Happy Mute; or, the Dumb Child's Appeal (London: L. B. Seeley, 1833); republished as *Happy Mute* (Boston, 1842);

The Oak-grove (Dublin: Religious Tract and Book Society for Ireland, 1833);

White Lies (Dublin: Religious Tract and Book Society for Ireland, 1833); republished as *White Lies; Little Oaths and The Bee* (Philadelphia: Presbyterian Board of Publication, n.d.);

Good and Bad Luck (Dublin: Religious Tract and Book Society for Ireland, 1834);

Grumbling (Dublin: Religious Tract and Book Society for Ireland, 1834);

A Few Words on the Eightieth Psalm (London: R. B. Seeley & W. Burnside, 1835);

The Mole (Dublin: Religious Tract and Book Society for Ireland, 1835);

The Newfoundland Fisherman. A True Story (London: Religious Tract Society, 1835); revised by Kidder as *The Newfoundland Fisherman* (New York: Lane & Tippett, 1846);

Chapters on Flowers (London: R. B. Seeley & W. Burnside, 1836); republished as *Floral Biography; or Chapters on Flowers* (New York: M. W. Dodd, 1840); enlarged as *The Flower Garden; or Chapters on Flowers* (New York: M. W. Dodd, 1840);

The Deserter (Dublin: Religious Tract and Book Society for Ireland, 1836; New York: M. W. Dodd, 1845);

The Industrious Artist (Dublin: Religious Tract and Book Society for Ireland, 1836);

Letter Writing (Dublin: Religious Tract and Book Society for Ireland, 1836; New York: Scribners, n.d.);

Alice Benden, or, The Bowed Shilling (London: R. B. Seeley & W. Burnside, 1838; New York: J. S. Taylor, 1841);

Letters from Ireland, MDCCCXXXVII (London: R. B. Seeley & W. Burnside, 1838; New York: J. S. Taylor, 1843);

Passing Thoughts (London: James Burns/W. Edwards, 1838; New York: M. W. Dodd, 1841);

The Lady Flora Hastings. A Brief Sketch (London: L. & G. Seeley, 1839);

The Simple Flower (New York: American Tract Society, 1840; New York: J. S. Taylor, 1842);

Conformity: A Tale (London: W. H. Dalton, 1841; New York: M. W. Dodd, 1842);

Dangers and Duties. A Tale (London: L. & G. Seeley, 1841; New York: M. W. Dodd, 1842);

Falsehood and Truth (Liverpool: Henry Perris, 1841; New York: M. W. Dodd, 1841);

Helen Fleetwood (London: R. B. Seeley & W. Burnside, 1841; New York: M. W. Dodd, 1844);

A Peep Into Number Ninety (Philadelphia: Hooker & Agnew, 1841);

Personal Recollections (London: R. B. Seeley & W. Burnside, 1841; New York: J. S. Taylor, 1842; enlarged, London: R. B. Seeley & W. Burnside, 1847); republished as *Life of Charlotte Elizabeth, as Contained in her Personal Recollections* and as *Personal Recollections, with Explanatory Notes* (New York: M. W. Dodd, 1848);

Philip and His Garden: and Other Tales Suitable for Sabbath Schools (New York: J. S. Taylor, 1841; London: J. Hogg, 1861);

Backbiting (New York: J. S. Taylor, 1842); republished in *Backbiting Reproved, The Visit, and Other Sketches* (Philadelphia: Presbyterian Board of Publication, 1860s);

The Bee (New York: General Protestant Episcopal Sunday School Union, 1842);

"Principalities and Powers in Heavenly Places" (London: R. B. Seeley & W. Burnside, 1842; New York: J. S. Taylor, 1842);

The Glory of Israel; or, Letters to Jewish Children on the Early History of Their Nation (Philadelphia: American Sunday School Union, 1843);

Israel's Ordinances. A Few Thoughts on Their Perpetuity Respectfully Suggested in a Letter to the Right Rev., the Bishop of Jerusalem (London: Seeley, Burnside, & Seeley, 1843; New York: Labagh, 1844);

Judah's Lion (London: R. B. Seeley & W. Burnside, 1843; New York: M. W. Dodd, 1843);

The Perils of the Nation; an Appeal to the Legislature, the Clergy, and the Higher and Middle Classes, anonymous (London: Seeley, Burnside & Seeley, 1843);

Promising and Performing. A True Narrative (New York: J. S. Taylor, 1843);

Second Causes; or, Up and Be Doing (Dublin: John Robertson, 1843; New York: M. W. Dodd, 1843);

The Wrongs of Woman, 2 volumes (London: W. H. Dalton, 1843; New York: M. W. Dodd, 1843–1844); republished as *The Wrongs of Women* (New York: M. W. Dodd, 1852);

The Church Visible in All Ages (London: Seeley, Burnside & Seeley, 1844; New York: M. W. Dodd, 1845);

The Female Martyrs of the English Reformation (New York: J. S. Taylor, 1844);

Kindness to Animals (London: Religious Tract Society, 1844); republished as *Kindness to Animals; or, The Sin of Cruelty Exposed and Rebuked* (Philadelphia: American Sunday School Union,

1845); revised, with illustrations (London: S. W. Partridge, 1876);

Mesmerism. A Letter to Miss Martineau (London: Seeley, Burnside & Seeley, 1844; Philadelphia: Martien, 1847);

Ridley, Latimer, Cranmer, and Other English Martyrs (New York: J. S. Taylor, 1844);

The Yew-tree, and Other Stories (New York: M. W. Dodd, 1844);

The Convent Bell: and Other Poems (New York: J. S. Taylor, 1845);

Judaea Capta. An Historical Sketch of the Siege and Destruction of Jerusalem by the Romans (London: W. H. Dalton, 1845; New York: J. S. Taylor);

Posthumous and Other Poems (London: Seeley, Burnside & Seeley, 1846; New York: M. W. Dodd, 1847);

Richard and Rover, revised by Kidder (New York: Lane & Tippett, 1846);

The Snow-Ball, revised by Kidder (New York: Lane & Tippett, 1846);

Days of Old (Philadelphia: Jewish Publication Society, 1847);

The Minor Poems of Charlotte Elizabeth, Written Especially for Juvenile Readers (Dublin: P. D. Hardy, 1848);

War With the Saints (London: Seeleys, 1848; New York: Dodd, Mead, 1848);

Humility Before Honor, and Other Tales and Illustrations. With a Brief Memoir of the Author by William B. Sprague (Albany, N.Y.: Erastus H. Pease, 1849);

James Orwell, the Mountain Cottager (New York: J. S. Taylor, 1840s?);

Stories from the Bible; to Which Is Added, Paul, the Martyr of Palestine (London: F. Warne, 1840s); republished, with illustrations by William Harvey (London: J. Hogg, 1861);

Memoir of John Britt: The Happy Mute Compiled from the Writings, Letters, and Conversation of Charlotte Elizabeth (London: Seeleys, 1850; Philadelphia: American Sunday School Union, 1850);

Bible Characteristics (London: Partridge & Oakey, 1851);

The Peep of Day (Gabon, W. Africa: Press of the A.B.C.F.M., 1852);

Wants and Wishes, revised by Kidder (New York: Carlton & Phillips, 1854);

Juvenile Stories for Juvenile Readers (Dublin: P. D. Hardy, 1858);

The Red Berries (New York: American Tract Society, 1850s?);

Juvenile Tales for Juvenile Readers (London: J. Hogg, 1861);

Little Tales for Little Readers (Edinburgh: Gall & Inglis, 1861);

The Boat (New York: American Tract Society, n.d.);

The Star (New York: J. S. Taylor, n.d.);

The Two Carpenters (New York: General Protestant Episcopal Sunday School Union, n.d.);

The Two Servants (New York: General Protestant Episcopal Sunday School Union, n.d.).

OTHER: John Foxe, *The English Martyrology*, 2 volumes, abridged by Tonna (London: R. B. Seeley & W. Burnside, 1837; Philadelphia: Presbyterian Board of Publication, 1843).

When she died on 12 July 1846, Charlotte Elizabeth Browne Phelan Tonna had long been recognized as a prolific and significant evangelical writer for children and adults. A year before her death, an article published in the July 1845 *Christian Examiner* proclaimed that her writings had secured "an unhesitating reception among most of those called Evangelical Christians" and that they were to be found in "the libraries and schools of the largest denominations in England and America." Individual works by "Charlotte Elizabeth" (her baptismal name, under which she published) were translated into such diverse languages as French, Italian, Marathi (in Bombay), and the Mpongwe language of Gabon in West Africa. Even her admirers commented on the sometimes offensively dogmatic and tactless way she approached any belief different from her own, but the tract societies and other publishers for whom she wrote clearly recognized a market for her work. Charlotte Elizabeth is also remembered for her part in bringing much-needed attention to the plight of English factory workers in the 1840s and for her popular editorship of *The Christian Lady's Magazine* from 1834 until her death.

Born on 1 October 1790 in Norwich, England, Charlotte Elizabeth Browne was the daughter of the Reverend Michael Browne, an Anglican priest and a minor canon at Norwich Cathedral. Her mother was the daughter of a Dr. Murray, an eminent physician. The influences of her comfortable childhood in a Tory, royalist, Church-of-England family are reflected throughout Charlotte Elizabeth's writings. She vividly describes her religious, political, and family relations in *Personal Recollections* (1841), which Harriet Beecher Stowe, in an introduction to the 1844 edition of the collected works, places "at the head of her writings."

Because Charlotte Elizabeth wrote these memoirs after her religious conversion, her experiences are interpreted in a fervently evangelical manner with zealous Bible study and Low Church practices at the center of her life and work. She comments early in her *Personal Recollections* on how appropriate it was that "probably one of the first objects traced on the retina of my infant eye" was "the stern-looking gateway of that strong building where the glorious martyrs of Mary's day were imprisoned." She remembers a childhood walk past Lollard's Pit with her father and younger brother, John. Her father noted that "there Mary burnt good people alive for refusing to worship wooden images," and she asked, "Papa, may I be a martyr?"

Her fascination with martyrs continued throughout her career as a writer. Not only did she publish an 1837 abridgment of John Foxe's *The English Martyrology* (1516–1587) and a separate selection called *The Female Martyrs of the English Reformation* (1844), but several of her characters die after much suffering, at least partly as a result of their faith – most notably the title character of *Helen Fleetwood* (1841). Other characters, usually female, are clearly spokespersons for the author. Their ruling passions match Charlotte Elizabeth's, which biographer William B. Sprague describes as "to do good and to glorify God." These are spiritual people who are familiar enough with the Bible to quote it spontaneously and often, in an effort to convert and save more-worldly characters. Examples in children's books include Mary Sedley in *The Simple Flower* (1840) and Sarah Roberts and her parents in *Falsehood and Truth* (1841).

In addition to religion, Charlotte Elizabeth's childhood passions included gardens and flowers, nature in general, books, and her brother, John Murray Browne. Her descriptions of her brother's physical beauty and charm and of their intense fraternal bonds appear in several places in *Personal Recollections*. Her deep despair at his early death by drowning led at least one friend to accuse her of worshiping him as an idol, an accusation she vehemently and bitterly denies in her memoir. But her comments about her brother are intense enough to suggest an unusually strong attachment, and her comments about sibling relationships, both in her memoir and in her stories, suggest that her relationship with her brother was by far the most important one in her life.

Examples of her feelings for gardening appear most obviously in such children's stories as *The Simple Flower* and *Philip and His Garden* (1841), but also in many other tales, through her precise and loving descriptions of landscape. Certain favorite flowers, such as heartsease, appear frequently, sometimes for their symbolic value and sometimes as samples of the beauty of God's creation. In *Chapters on Flowers* (1836), Charlotte Elizabeth associates people she knows with specific flowers, discussing the qualities of each that led to her choices. An avid gardener, she considered her garden far more than a hobby: "Next after the blessed Bible, a flower-garden is to me the most eloquent of books – a volume teeming with instruction, consolation, and reproof."

Nature appears often in Charlotte Elizabeth's work, particularly when she is teaching small readers how to live. In such stories as *The Bee* (1842), *The Swan* (1829), *The Wasp* (1831), *The Bow and the Cloud* (1832), *The Willow Tree* (1828), and *The Hen and Her Chickens* (1827), Charlotte Elizabeth uses nature in religious analogies just as earlier writers for children such as John Bunyan and Isaac Watts had done. Such analogies appear in both her prose and her poems, and often a poem appears as a kind of coda to a story or lecture.

Charlotte Elizabeth's child characters spend most of their time outdoors in the countryside, which the author associates with healthy robustness. Yet despite her own rural upbringing, Charlotte Elizabeth was not a healthy child. She was completely blind for several months during her sixth year, and at the age of ten she permanently lost her hearing – the result, she believed, of medical treatments for her other ailments. Her deafness led to her interest in educating deaf children and had a profound effect on her as a writer, freeing her from distractions but making the creation of realistic dialogue difficult.

Charlotte Elizabeth's years at Norwich ended abruptly in 1812 with what she describes as her "first sorrow," her father's death. She and her mother moved to London, where Charlotte met Capt. George Phelan, whom she married six months later. She followed her husband to colonial Nova Scotia, Canada, where he was stationed in the British army for two years. Captain Phelan, an Irishman by birth, then moved from Canada to Ireland, where he was involved in a lawsuit concerning his estate near Kilkenny. Though the marriage was not happy, it did introduce Charlotte Elizabeth to the land and people of Ireland. The five years she spent there, from 1819 to 1824, were crucial in her development: her conversion to Evangelical Protestantism, her rabid anti-Catholicism, her love of the Irish people, and the commencement of her writing career all occurred during this period.

Although she had serious reservations about moving to Ireland, she credits her dramatic change of attitude to the events and people she encountered: "I found the Irish to be frank, warm and affectionate beyond any [race] I had ever met with." Her religious conversion, however, impacted more fundamentally on her writing career. Left alone on her husband's estate while he was in Dublin, she developed an acute case of melancholy. Within six months she "experienced the mighty power of God in a way truly marvellous." From then on she had a mission: to convert everyone, especially Irish Catholics, to Evangelical Protestantism.

She began writing for the Dublin Tract Society in the early 1820s, composing her first "complete little story" from seven o'clock to three in the morning one long winter night. The secretary of the society was "commendatory of my tract" but "recommended frequent intercourse with the peasantry, of whose habits and modes of expression I was evidently ignorant . . . I then mentioned my loss of hearing as a bar to this branch of usefulness." Nonetheless, Charlotte Elizabeth continued to write tracts and poetry, her multiple editions clear evidence of her success.

A few months later, Charlotte Elizabeth formally separated from her husband when he was sent abroad with the army and she "declined to cross the Atlantic a second time." Her mother came to live with her in Ireland. She reminisces that "from this period I became chiefly dependent on my own exertions." She assumed the pen name of Charlotte Elizabeth to keep Captain Phelan from claiming a share of her earnings.

In 1823 she met an Irish deaf and dumb boy, John Britt, who was eleven years old and whom she converted from Roman Catholicism. When she and her mother returned permanently to live in England, Charlotte Elizabeth took Britt, in effect adopting him as a son. Her many references to him in memoirs, letters, conversations, and stories were collected and published in narrative form as *Memoir of John Britt: The Happy Mute* (1850), after Charlotte Elizabeth's death. He also appears in *Kindness to Animals* (1844), where his behavior is presented as a model.

Their first residence in England was in Clifton near Bristol, where, in the mid 1820s, Charlotte Elizabeth met Hannah More, who also wrote religious tracts and moral tales and with whom Charlotte Elizabeth is sometimes compared. By this time, the more worldly More had left behind a successful career as a dramatist and educator to become equally successful as an evangelical founder of Sunday schools, writer of religious tracts, and opponent of slavery. Unlike More, however, whose lively, fluently written tales contain well-developed, interesting plots and colorful characters, Charlotte Elizabeth's

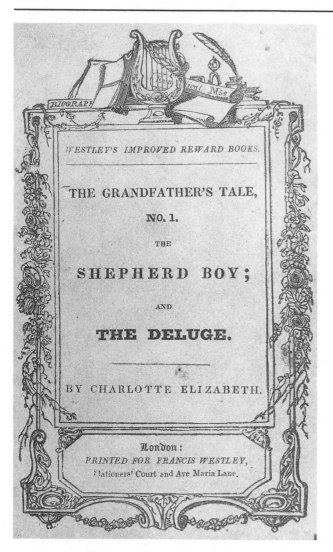

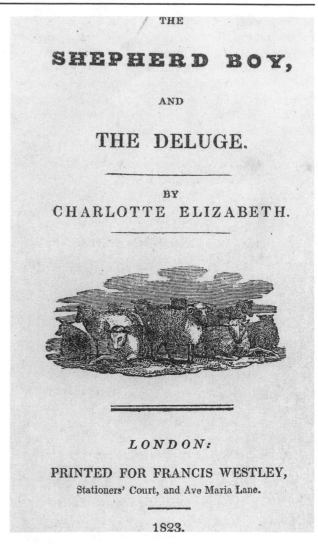

Cover and title page for Charlotte Elizabeth's first book (courtesy of the Lilly Library, Indiana University)

evangelical message dominates all she wrote. In tales for children or novels for adults, the religious message overshadows the plot, and the characters are rarely individualized, remaining instead vehicles for the message.

Charlotte Elizabeth's stories for children fit into one of several categories: Bible stories, such as "The Star," "The Golden Image," and "The Faithful Steward" (all included in *Tales and Illustrations,* 1830); moral tales (a designation Charlotte Elizabeth disliked), such as *Backbiting* (1842), *Kindness to Animals, The Simple Flower,* and *Anne Bell: or, the Faults* (1826), written to help socialize the young, according to biblical precepts; cautionary tales, such as "The Boat" and "The Red Berries" (both included as stories in *Tales and Illustrations*); and sermonlike lectures, such as "Where Are You Going?" (in *Tales and Illustrations*) and *The Bird's Nest*

(1827), written in the sometimes gentle, sometimes threatening tradition of James Janeway.

Each story makes a moral point and all are generously peppered with biblical quotes and allusions. Only the cautionary tales and a few longer stories more suitable for older readers (*Falsehood and Truth,* 1841; *Combination,* 1832) involve much plot. Characters are generic types rather than fleshed-out individuals, but children often act realistically: they argue with siblings and are jealous, claim "it's not my fault," and sometimes disobey parental warnings. They also ask naive questions, allowing Charlotte Elizabeth to use a kind of modified Socratic dialogue, in which adults help children learn proper behavior and beliefs. Such dialogue is used extensively in *The Museum* (1832).

Charlotte Elizabeth pleased her Protestant audiences, and several of her books were even translated and taken to Italy, where *The Simple Flower* and other "humble penny books" were placed on the Papal Index Expurgatorious, to the author's joy and amazement. As she points out in her memoir, *The Simple Flower* is not even in the anti-Catholic mold of many of her books, focusing instead on the long, painful process by which young Emma Merton learns to accept financial reverses and adapt, like her favorite flower, to less comfortable and commodious surroundings; she must, her mother explains, "rise above the vain things of this world" and be less self-indulgent. In the course of her adaptation, Emma learns to stop venting her frustrations on the one remaining servant, an orphan girl, and to become a nicer person. As Charlotte Elizabeth says, it is a "very simple narrative" and one of her least zealous.

Writing seemed to come even more easily to Charlotte Elizabeth during the years after her beloved brother returned to England from seven years' army service in Portugal. He was assigned to Sandhurst Military College, and Charlotte Elizabeth, her mother, and John Britt followed him there, moving into a cottage at Bagshot Heath. In her *Personal Recollections,* she says of this fruitful period in her writing career: "In the course of the two years and two months of my residence under my brother's roof, I wrote the *Rockite, The System, Izram, Consistency, Perseverance, Allan M'Leod, Zadoc,* and upwards of thirty little books and tracts, besides contributions to various periodicals." Her brother also wrote a book during this time, *An Historical View of the Revolutions of Portugal Since the Close of the Peninsular War* (1827) published as "By an Eyewitness."

This joyous period of Charlotte Elizabeth's life ended with her brother's departure for army service in Ireland. Six months later, in June 1827, she received a letter announcing his death by drowning. Charlotte Elizabeth adopted his young children, but she never fully recovered from her loss. Her descriptions of her despair at his death and the poignancy of her attempts to convince herself that her beloved brother was "saved" at the time he died are among the most emotionally moving of her writings, particularly when she comments about these feelings in her introduction to a book for his young son.

She also wrote an autobiographical story, "The Boat," based on a childhood incident recounted in her memoirs, when she had actually saved her brother from drowning. It is among her most powerful tales, using suspense and a climactic plot to keep readers involved, despite the sermonizing interruptions. When John falls into a river be-

cause he has foolishly disobeyed his parents' directive to stay out of boats, his sister, Bess, tries desperately to pull him out, but she is in grave danger of being pulled in herself. Just as they seem about to drown, Charlotte Elizabeth stops the narrative and says, "Now see, my little readers, what an easy thing it is to join hand in hand in sin, but how impossible for sinners to deliver themselves, or each other. . . . If God had not taken pity on these faulty children, they would have been deep in the cold waters, dead and stiff before night; and if the Lord Jesus did not show compassion to you, and offer you salvation through his precious blood, you would have no way to escape from the far more deep and horrible pit that burns with eternal fire." Finally, two men rescue the children.

Her evangelical writings and works continued. Following the passage of the Catholic Emancipation Act in 1829, Charlotte Elizabeth channeled her energy into evangelical service and educational activities. She started a Sunday school in her cottage and did charity work in the Irish ghetto in London, culminating in the establishment of a Protestant Church in St. Giles in the early 1830s.

When John Britt died at nineteen in February 1831, Charlotte Elizabeth moved to London. In 1832 her antitrade-union novel *Combination* was published, and by 1834, because of her reputation as a "fighting Protestant," she was offered the position of founding editor of *The Christian Lady's Magazine.* From that time on, most of her writings appeared first in the magazine. She wrote serialized adult fiction, travel articles, *Chapters on Flowers,* and political editorials with a Tory perspective.

In the 1840s Charlotte Elizabeth's writings started to be published in the United States. The American Tract Society published several collections of her children's stories, illustrating them with attractive woodcuts. One of her stories was abridged and included in the 1843 edition of McGuffey's *Eclectic Third Reader.* The story, originally published as "Try Again," is here titled "Perseverance." It is narrated by an aunt who takes her nephew John and niece Lucy out to fly a kite. All of the usual kite-flying problems occur: the tail gets entangled in a tree; the wind shifts; John slackens his hold on the string; and repeatedly the kite falls flat onto the ground. But the aunt keeps encouraging the frustrated John and Lucy to "Try again!" The obedient children finally enjoy a few moments of excellent kite flying. The story concludes with its undisguised moral: "Yes, my dear children, I wish to teach you the value of PERSEVERANCE, even when nothing more depends upon it than the flying of a kite. Whenever you fail in your attempts to do any good thing, let your motto be TRY AGAIN." Following this story in McGuffey's *Eclectic Third Reader* is a T. H. Palmer poem that includes the popular line, "If at first you don't succeed, try, try again."

While Charlotte Elizabeth's children's stories were establishing her reputation in the United States, the 1840s in England were marked by social upheaval with a growing consciousness of the untenable division between rich and poor. Charlotte Elizabeth contributed her own Tory, evangelical slant to the debates about social change. In her 1841 social realist novel, *Helen Fleetwood,* originally serialized in *The Christian Lady's Magazine,* she incorporates many of her interests, including the superiority of rural over urban life, the domestic role of women, the dangers of Popery, the hatred of unions, and, of course, the urgency of being born again through Christ. Although the novel is flawed by many of the stylistic faults of her children's books, including thin characterization and long sermons disrupting the plot, the author's detailed descriptions of the miseries of living and working in a factory mill town in 1830s England are of interest. Her book testifies to the weaknesses of the Factory Act of 1833, particularly emphasizing the problems of women, and helped guarantee enactment of the Ten Hour Bill of 1847. Today the novel remains a valuable document of social history, useful because of its graphic portrayal of children's and women's factory conditions, based upon government documents.

In April 1843 Charlotte Elizabeth published anonymously a treatise entitled *The Perils of the Nation* and subsequently in *The Wrongs of Woman,* she described the abominable living and working conditions of female laborers in London. The four parts of the book – Milliners and Dressmakers, The Forsaken Home, The Little Pin-headers, and the Lacerunners – draw attention to working conditions outside of factories. These works and Charlotte Elizabeth's editorial comments in *The Christian Lady's Magazine* helped gather support for passage of the Factory Acts of 1844, 1847, and 1848.

In 1841, when she was immersed in writing these reformist works, Charlotte Elizabeth became the editor of the *Protestant Magazine.* In the same year, she married Lewis Hippolytus Joseph Tonna, a religious writer twenty-two years her junior. Her first husband had died in 1837, and this second marriage was apparently a happy one. Tonna shared her evangelical and millenarian views. They also shared a respect and sympathy for the Jews, a

belief that Jews might retain their traditional rituals and still reach salvation through acceptance of Jesus Christ as Messiah, and an antipathy toward anti-Semitism. This led some people to believe, erroneously, that Lewis Tonna was Jewish. The Tonnas' views about Jews are developed in *Judah's Lion* (1843), which was Charlotte Elizabeth's final and perhaps most sophisticated book-length work of fiction. Sprague believes that it is upon this book "which her highest reputation as a writer must depend." He proclaims, "It is full of bold, striking, and beautiful thought, and withal discovers a familiarity with that noblest of all sciences, Theology." A smaller literary achievement of this period is her proselytizing book for children called *The Glory of Israel; or, Letters to Jewish Children on the Early History of Their Nation* (1843).

In his memoir, Lewis Tonna anticipates Sprague's impression of the intensity of Charlotte Elizabeth's concern for improving conditions of Jews worldwide and for "bringing them into the fold," in Sprague's words. He remarks particularly on a letter she wrote in 1844 to the Emperor Nicholas on behalf of improved treatment for Jews in Russia. Tonna also notes his wife's close friendship with Sir Moses Montefiore and his wife, who were among her last visitors before her death.

In 1841 Charlotte Elizabeth published two books for older children, *Conformity* and *Falsehood and Truth.* Both portray with some complexity adolescents' internal conflicts about their faith and the satisfactory resolution of those conflicts. For the remainder of her life Charlotte Elizabeth devoted herself to her garden, the evangelical movement, and her editorship of *The Christian Lady's Magazine.* She was diagnosed with cancer, and in June 1846 she wrote a farewell letter to her readers, in which she joyously faced her impending death. At her request she was carried to Ramsgate for a last visit to the sea. She died there on 12 July.

An October 1846 obituary in *Gentleman's Magazine* described Charlotte Elizabeth as "a very successful religious writer," several of whose books had "gone through many editions." In fact, new editions of her work continued to appear long after her death, including the seventh edition of her collected works in 1849, an edition of *Helen Fleetwood* in 1874, an edition of *Chapters on Flowers* in 1886, and an 1890 printing of *Judah's Lion* that the publisher advertised as the "thirtieth thousand." At least one collection of children's stories was republished in New York as late as 1908 by the Protestant Episcopal Sunday School Union, and a reprint of *Falsehood and Truth* and *Conformity* in one volume appeared in 1975.

Charlotte Elizabeth selected the inscription for her tombstone, which Sprague quotes: "Here lie the mortal remains of Charlotte Elizabeth, the beloved wife of Lewis Hypolytus Joseph Tonna, who died on the 12th of July, 1846, LOOKING UNTO JESUS." It is a fitting epitaph for a woman who devoted her life to evangelical works and deeds, and who is remembered far more for her religious than her literary achievements.

Biographies:

Lewis Hippolytus Joseph Tonna, *A Memoir of Charlotte Elizabeth, Embracing the Period from the Close of Her Personal Recollections to Her Death* (New York: M. W. Dodd, 1847);

William B. Sprague, D.D., "Biographical Sketch of Charlotte Elizabeth," in Tonna's *Humility Before Honor and Other Tales and Illustrations* (Albany: Erastus H. Pease, 1849), pp. 144–195.

References:

Monica Correa Fryckstedt, "Charlotte Elizabeth Tonna & *The Christian Lady's Magazine,*" *Victorian Periodicals Review,* 14 (Summer 1981): 43–51;

E. B. H., "Charlotte Elizabeth and Her Writings," *Christian Examiner,* 39 (July 1845): 28–46;

Deborah Kaplan, "The Woman Worker in Charlotte Elizabeth's Fiction," *Mosaic: A Journal for the Interdisciplinary Study of Literature,* 18 (Spring 1985): 51–63;

Joseph Kestner, *Protest and Reform: The British Social Narrative by Women, 1827–1867* (Madison: University of Wisconsin Press, 1985);

Ellen Moers, *Literary Women* (Garden City, N.Y.: Doubleday, 1977);

Harriet Beecher Stowe, introduction to *The Works of Charlotte Elizabeth,* volume 1 (New York: M. W. Dodd, 1844);

Mona Wilson, *Jane Austen and Some Contemporaries* (Norwood, Pa.: Norwood Editions, 1974), pp. 182–204.

Charlotte Maria Tucker
("A. L. O. E.")
(8 May 1821 – 2 December 1893)

Judith Overmier
University of Oklahoma

BOOKS: *The Claremont Tales: Or, Illustrations of the Beatitudes* (Edinburgh: Gall & Inglis, 1852);

Angus Tarlton; or, Illustrations of the Fruits of the Spirit (Edinburgh: Gall & Inglis, 1853; New York: R. Carter, 1862);

Wings and Stings; A Tale for the Young (London: T. Nelson, 1855; New York: R. Carter, 1856);

Walter Binning, the Adopted Son; or, Illustrations of the Lord's Prayer (Edinburgh: Gall & Inglis, 1856; New York: R. Carter, 1856);

True Heroism (Edinburgh: Gall & Inglis, 1856; New York: R. Carter, 1856);

The Giant-Killer; or, The Battle Which All Must Fight (London: T. Nelson, 1856; New York: R. Carter, 1867);

Daybreak in Britain (London: Religious Tract Society, 1857); republished as *The Chief's Daughter; or, Daybreak in Britain* (New York: R. Carter, 1866); republished as *Imogen; or, Daybreak in Britain* (New York: General Protestant Episcopal Sunday School Union and Church Book Society, 1862?);

The Story of a Needle (London: T. Nelson, 1857; New York: R. Carter, 1862);

The Rambles of a Rat (London: T. Nelson, 1857; New York: R. Carter, 1858);

Futtypore; or, The City of Victory (London: Society for Promoting Christian Knowledge, 1858);

The Mine; or, Darkness and Light (London: T. Nelson, 1858; New York: General Protestant Episcopal Sunday School Union and Church Book Society, 1859);

Eddie Ellerslie; or, Old Friends With New Faces (London: T. Nelson, 1858; New York: General Protestant Episcopal Sunday School Union and Church Book Society, 1859);

Precepts in Practice; or, Stories Illustrating the Proverbs (London: T. Nelson, 1858; New York: T. Nelson, 1859);

Idols in the Heart (London: T. Nelson, 1859; New York: R. Carter, 1863);

Whispering Unseen; or, Be Ye Doers of the Word, and Not Hearers Only (London: T. Nelson, 1859);

Parliament in the Playroom (London: T. Nelson, 1860; New York: R. Carter, 1864);

316

My Neighbour's Shoes; or, Feeling for Others. A Tale (London: Nelson, 1861; New York: T. Nelson, 1862);

The Crown of Success; or, Four Heads to Furnish (London: Nelson, 1863; New York: R. Carter, 1863);

Exiles in Babylon; or, Children of Light (London: T. Nelson, 1864; New York: T. Nelson, 1873);

Fairy Know-a-Bit (London: T. Nelson, 1865; New York: T. Nelson, 1866);

Rescued from Egypt (London: T. Nelson, 1865; New York: T. Nelson, 1866);

Triumph Over Midian (London: T. Nelson, 1866; New York: T. Nelson, 1867);

David Aspinall, the Wanderer in Africa. A Tale Illustrating the Thirty-Second Psalm (Edinburgh: Gall & Inglis, 1866; New York: R. Carter, 1869);

Hymns and Poems (Edinburgh: Gall & Inglis, 1867; London: T. Nelson, 1868);

House Beautiful; or, The Bible Museum (London: T. Nelson, 1867; New York: R. Carter, 1868);

The Lake of the Woods: A Tale Illustrative of the Twelfth Chapter of Romans (Edinburgh: Gall & Inglis, 1867); republished as *The Lake of the Woods; A Story of the Backwoods* (Chicago: Fleming H. Revell, 1870s);

Places Passed by Pilgrims; Twelve Tales Illustrating the Pilgrim's Progress (London: T. Nelson, 1868);

Hebrew Heroes: A Tale Founded on Jewish History (London: T. Nelson, 1868; New York: R. Carter, 1869);

The Golden Fleece; or, Who Wins the Prize (London: T. Nelson, 1869; New York: Dutton, 1869);

Claudia (London: T. Nelson, 1869; New York: R. Carter, 1870);

Cyril Ashley (London: T. Nelson, 1870; New York: T. Nelson, 1896);

Freedom: A Tale of the Early Christians (London: Gall & Inglis, 1871);

The Lady of Provence; or Humbled and Healed. A Tale of the First French Revolution (London: T. Nelson, 1871; New York: T. Nelson, 1894);

Edith and Her Ayah, and Other Stories (London: T. Nelson, 1872);

The City of Nocross and Its Famous Physician (London: T. Nelson, 1872; New York: R. Carter, 1873);

The Spanish Cavalier; A Story of Seville (London: T. Nelson, 1874; New York: T. Nelson, 1875);

Fairy Frisket; or, Peeps at Insect Life (London: T. Nelson, 1874; New York: R. Carter, 1875);

Haunted Rooms. A Tale (London: T. Nelson, 1875; New York: R. Carter, 1876);

A Wreath of Indian Stories (London: T. Nelson, 1876);

Jai Singh, the Brave Sikh; and Other Stories (Madras: Christian Vernacular Education Society, 1877);

Pomegranates from the Punjab; Indian Stories (Chicago: F. H. Revell, 1878; Edinburgh: Gall & Inglis, n.d.);

The Zenana Reader (Madras: Christian Vernacular Education Society, 1880);

Little Bullets from Batala and Seven Perils Passed (London: T. Nelson, 1880; New York: R. Carter, 1883);

Life in the Eagle's Nest; A Tale of Afghanistan (London: Gall & Inglis, 1883; New York: R. Carter, 1884);

Life in the White Bear's Den; A Tale of Labrador (London: Gall & Inglis, 1884);

Harold Hartley (London: Gall & Inglis, 1885);

Pictures of St. Peter in an English Home (London: T. Nelson, 1886);

The Hartley Brothers; or, The Knights of Saint John (Edinburgh: Gall & Inglis, 1888);

Driven into Exile: A Story of the Huguenots (London: T. Nelson, 1888);

Harold's Bride. A Tale (London: T. Nelson, 1889);

Beyond the Black Waters; A Tale (London: T. Nelson, 1890; New York: T. Nelson, 1890);

The Blacksmith of Boniface Lane (London: T. Nelson, 1891);

The Iron Chain and the Golden; A Tale (London: T. Nelson, 1892);

The Two Pilgrims to Kashi, and Other Stories (London & Madras: Christian Literature Society for India, 1901).

Charlotte Maria Tucker, whose books were published under the acronym A.L.O.E. (A Lady of England), forged a successful and personally rewarding life and career both in England and India. She was the author of more than a hundred popular works of children's fiction (as well as nearly fifty fiction and nonfiction titles for adults) and was a respected missionary to India, even though she did not publish her first book until she was thirty and did not immigrate to India until age fifty-four.

Charlotte Maria Tucker was born on 8 May 1821 at Friern Hatch, Barnet, Hertfordshire. The daughter of Jane Boswell Tucker and Henry St. George Tucker, Charlotte Tucker was one of ten children. She corresponded extensively with her siblings and with other family members and friends, who saved her letters; she destroyed the letters she received from them, however. The available information about her life derives largely from letters

Tucker wrote to her sister Dorothea Laura Tucker Hamilton. Tucker's biographer, Agnes Giberne, also solicited recollections and copies of letters from relatives and friends.

Tucker's father was born in Bermuda and sent to England for schooling at age ten. Plans for his education and subsequent career were destroyed by an interfering aunt, who sent him to India at age fourteen. He did not return to England until 1810, when he was thirty-nine years old. He had by then achieved success in India and was an expert in Indian affairs and finance; that expertise eventually led to his directorship in the East India Company. The recurrence of characters who overcome great obstacles to achieve success in Charlotte Tucker's fiction and her choice of India for her missionary work probably had their roots in her father's life.

Henry St. George Tucker married Jane Boswell, a Scottish woman, in 1811; he was forty and she about twenty-one. They went to India the following year, but in 1815 they returned to Edinburgh and lived there until 1819 or 1820. The family lived for a short transition period in Friern Hatch, where Charlotte Tucker was born, and in 1822 moved to London to 3 Upper Portand Place. J. S. Bratton describes it as a "lavish establishment," but this must refer to the period after 1837, because Giberne states that the family found it difficult to make ends meet until that year, when they unexpectedly inherited funds from a friend.

The Tucker children formed a self-contained group, without many young friends outside their family. Giberne reports that their father discouraged outside friends and encouraged the children to entertain each other, which they did, although the family circle began to diminish as early as 1831, when the eldest son, Henry Carre, went to India, followed in 1842 by Robert Tudor and St. George. Among the family's entertainments were the production of a family magazine and the writing and acting of plays, some of which their father had written and published. Charlotte Tucker, a leader among the children, wrote verses and stories for the family from childhood. In her late teens and early twenties she followed her father's lead and wrote plays for the family to stage, including "The Pretender" (1842), published in full in her biography.

Henry St. George Tucker is reported to have had an aversion to girls going to school, so Charlotte and her sisters were educated at home. Sometimes they had a governess or a master, but much of their study was done independently. Although Charlotte does not often speak of her education or reading habits in her correspondence, the knowledge of history, geography, and science displayed in her written works suggests that she was well educated. There is some evidence also that she read extensively. She is reported to have been extremely fond of the works of William Shakespeare, and her admiration of John Bunyan's *Pilgrim's Progress* (1678) is apparent in the style and content of much of her own writing. In one of her letters Tucker writes about reading a romance by a Miss Martineau set in Haiti – undoubtedly Harriet Martineau's *The Hour and the Man* (1841), based on the life of Toussaint L'Ouverture. Additional evidence of the variety of Tucker's reading is found in the authors or titles she recommended in letters to a niece, which included Sir Walter Scott and Elizabeth Sewell, as well as Harriet Beecher Stowe's *Uncle Tom's Cabin* (1852), "If you are allowed to read it."

Although the Tucker children may have had few friends their age while young, as young adults they moved in a broad social circle. The family led an active upper-middle-class social life, which included the mandatory calls and calling cards, teas, lunches, open houses, dinner parties, and balls. However, in 1847 Charlotte began to care for the three children of her widowed brother, Robert – Louis, Charley, and two-year-old Letitia – whom the Tucker family called "The Robins." Charlotte also began to feel uneasy about the continual round of social entertainments and received permission from her parents to be excused from some of the occasions. The following year she formally converted and became an evangelical. She and her older sister Fanny began "visiting" the Marylebone workhouse, probably in the following year, after Charlotte had overcome her parents' initial objections.

Charlotte's youngest brother, William, married in 1850. The wedding took place in Brussels, and Charlotte took her first trip abroad to attend, accompanied by her brother St. George, who was home from India. Charlotte went to Paris in August 1855 for the French Exhibition, to Canada in 1875 to visit one of the "Robins," and then to India. That she delighted in travel and faraway places is evident from her descriptions in letters home and by her choice of foreign settings such as Afghanistan, France, Canada, Labrador, Africa, Spain, and India for her fiction.

On 14 June 1851 Charlotte Tucker's father died. Within six months she had, with her mother's approval and encouragement, submitted the manuscript of *The Claremont Tales: Or, Illustrations of the Beatitudes* (1852) to the young Scottish publishing firm of William and Robert Chambers. The stories in the collection concern a fictional family consisting

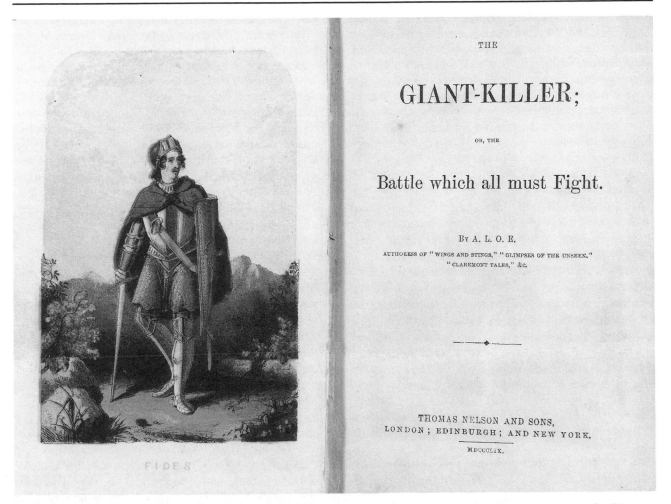

THE

GIANT-KILLER;

OR, THE

Battle which all must Fight.

By A. L. O. E.

AUTHORESS OF "WINGS AND STINGS," "GLIMPSES OF THE UNSEEN,"
"CLAREMONT TALES," &c.

THOMAS NELSON AND SONS,
LONDON; EDINBURGH; AND NEW YORK.
MDCCCLIX.

Frontispiece and title page for Tucker's 1856 story in which the battles of a hero are paralleled by the moral struggles of children (courtesy of the Lilly Library, Indiana University)

of Mrs. Claremont, her three children, their visiting aunt, Mrs. Mason, and her four children. The Mason children have been less stringently brought up and prove to be more problematic, with the lessons of cause and effect made quite clear. In her preface Tucker writes of the need to reach young minds "through the medium of a simple story."

In her cover letter she says that she wrote the stories for the young children she was in charge of. The book did not fit with the Chambers publishing line, so they forwarded it to Gall and Inglis, who published it. When Tucker finally saw a copy on 24 May 1853, she immediately wrote the publishers and offered them another manuscript. She also inquired about the possibility of "very cheap" copies of *The Claremont Tales* being made available for the poor or for Ragged Schools. The idea of providing inexpensive reading material for the underprivileged was one she pursued throughout her writing and missionary careers. A later letter comments on

her pleasure that the book was "favorably received in America." In fact, an American reviewer wrote in the *Independent,* "The writings of A.L.O.E. are so well known and approved that it is unnecessary to speak of their general excellence."

Tucker mentions in a letter dated 1 September 1854 that her brother Henry had the book translated into Hindustani for Indian readers and later, in 1857, that Henry had written from Benares to her publishers requesting multiple copies of her works for distribution in India. Thus, from the beginning of her writing career she was reaching audiences in England, America, and India, in English and in translations including Indian languages, French, and Swedish (published in Chicago for a Swedish-American audience). This pattern of success would continue for four decades.

Tucker's first efforts at using the allegorical style appear in *The Claremont Tales*. Later, in the preface to *Eddie Ellerslie; or, Old Friends With New*

Faces (1858), a retelling of old stories, she writes, "Allegory keeps the mind as it were on tiptoe" and that it is one of the best methods of "strengthening the minds of children." By 1858 she had achieved success with such allegorical works as *Wings and Stings; A Tale for the Young* (1855), in which the character development of a little girl is paralleled by the story of similar growth in a bee, and *The Giant Killer; or, The Battle Which All Must Fight* (1856), in which a pitched battle is fought not only by the giant killer, but by children who are beset by such problems as impatience, greed, and pride.

She continued writing allegories throughout her career. Surely the most charming and amusing of these is *The Crown of Success; or, Four Heads to Furnish* (1863), in which four children spend several months in the care of Mr. Learning, who drinks ink and eats paper for breakfast. He provides each of them with a little cottage to furnish the Villa of the Head and supplies them with magic purses of time that they can spend in the Town of Education. The character lessons and humor arise from the ordinariness of all that goes awry with choosing wallpaper and materials and then hanging it properly. *Places Passed by Pilgrims; Twelve Tales Illustrating the Pilgrim's Progress* (1868) and *The City of Nocross and Its Famous Physician* (1872) are undoubtedly Tucker's most direct literary descendants of John Bunyan. The latter features a young man who has just purchased his fifth edition of *The Pilgrim's Progress* and is daydreaming an exciting as well as instructive pilgrimage that includes a love story.

In addition to allegory, Tucker utilizes the family setting, religion, foreign lands, history, and science in her stories, always with the intent to teach through entertaining. The children of the family in *Parliament in the Playroom* (1860) are vastly entertaining and enterprising. While their parents are away, they establish a government, elect themselves its officials, and pass taxes that include one on sins, which for them (and Tucker) means such moral lapses as laziness, pride, selfishness, greed, and haste. The book has a weak ending involving an escaped leopard in the garden, but the typical children's squabbles and resolutions that precede it are realistic. History and religion were also combined in several books, such as *Daybreak in Britain* (1857), set in England in pre-Christian times, and *Driven Into Exile: A Story of the Huguenots* (1888), set in France and England during the expulsion of the Protestants from France.

Giberne asserts that Tucker developed an interest in science sometime before she was twenty-one (and as a result tried to learn chemistry), and that throughout her life she tried to maintain this interest, even though she was not encouraged by her family. Her correspondence includes frequent references to natural-history topics, such as a trip to the botanical gardens, a meteor she saw, or information about wasps. She wrote to her sister Dorothea Laura Hamilton, "Tell dear Otho [Hamilton's son] that I shall be charmed if he makes the discovery of a magenta-coloured caterpillar, or a mauve earwig; and that as it will be ten times as curious as the *Spongmenta Padella,* it ought to have a Latin name ten times as long."

Tucker wrote several children's books on natural-history topics, including *Wings and Stings; A Tale for the Young, Fairy Know-a-Bit* (1865), and *Fairy Frisket; or, Peeps at Insect Life* (1874). In the preface to *Fairy Know-a-Bit* she cites the sources used for the scientific information and professes that her intent in writing the book is to "lure" her young readers to seek more scientific knowledge when they are older. The fanciful fairy character entertains children, but the inclusion of an index, with entries such as *anthers, chloroform, Copernicus, fermentation,* and *Saturn,* confirms the educational intent of the author. *Fairy Frisket; or, Peeps at Insect Life,* which covers butterflies, moths, ants, and termites, also includes fairy characters, although the author notes that her readers will not expect actually to see the latter. She cites the publisher Charles Knight's series Library of Entertaining Knowledge and J. G. Wood's *Homes Without Hands* (1866) as her main sources. That Tucker includes her sources and worries about their currency indicates that she understands the requirements of the scientific culture.

Tucker incorporates natural history into her novels, as well. *Harold's Bride. A Tale* (1889) includes incidents based on the natural history of India, such as problems with white ants, and the first story in *Pomegranates From the Punjab; Indian Stories* (1878) features the demonstration of a microscope, under which the characters view a hair, a piece of cloth, a moth's wing, and a drop of water. The latter view causes a Hindu character great distress when he discovers there are millions of microscopic living things in the drop of water.

After her mother's death on 24 July 1869 and the sale of the family home, Tucker lived for six years with her brother St. George, who had retired from India in 1869, and his family, much of that time at Binfield in Berkshire, near Bracknell. She visited the poor and an Infant School in Bracknell and continued her writing. Her niece reminisces about her role in their home: "As we grew older she would help us with our charades and games, planning wonderful card games herself, and ornamenting them with brush and stencil. It was she who introduced us to Shakespeare. . . . It was during this time that she wrote *The Haunted House* [presumably *Haunted Rooms,* 1875], which thrilled me with so much horror, that it was not until years after that I learnt there was a spiritual meaning underlying the tale."

Although moral lessons pervade all her works, Tucker's treatment of religion varies. When meant to assume a major role, it is sometimes incorporated into the story and sometimes constitutes a text alternating with the story. Her entirely religious works — such as *House Beautiful; or, The Bible Museum* (1867), a retelling of well-known Bible stories — are not usually aimed at children. In *The Mine; or, Darkness and Light* (1858), which is basically an exciting adventure story, such religious themes as conversion and moral lessons are incorporated into the plot. Conversions, whether of religion or of character, occur with some frequency in Tucker's works. *The Mine,* like many of her stories, was considered appropriate for a Sunday school prize. Although Tucker is usually tolerant and nonjudgmental in her treatment of other religions and cultures, she evidences a strong anti-Catholic bias in many of her books and an anti-Spanish bias in one: *The Spanish Cavalier; A Story of Seville* (1874) includes aspersions on lazy Spaniards as well as against Catholicism.

Emma Marshall suggests that the long, heavy-handed moralizing or religious portions of Tucker's books may have been skipped by children. It seems entirely possible that those novels with alternating plots and biblical stories were not always read in their entirety. For instance, in *Exiles in Babylon; or, Children of Light* (1864), set in the town of Wildwaste, the biblical story of Daniel alternates with the adventures of the Holdich family. Similarly, in *Rescued From Egypt* (1865), once again set in the town of Wildwaste, the story of the Madden family alternates with the life of Moses. Tucker acknowledges in her preface that she is aware of the "young readers who prefer a story to a sermon" and asks them not to pass over the sermon. The reviewer in the *Independent* says of *Rescued From Egypt,* "The fact that the initials A.L.O.E. appear upon the title-page is presumptive and strong evidence that the story is well told, and that the lessons taught are true and useful."

After more than twenty years as a successful author, at age fifty-four Tucker decided to go to India as an unpaid missionary for the Church of England. She had sufficient funds to do so; in fact, she reportedly contributed all the proceeds from her writing to charities. She began her study of Hindustani (and eventually extended her knowledge of Indian languages to Punjabi), destroyed all her personal papers, visited one of the Robins in Canada, and then set out for Bombay. She arrived in October 1875 and proceeded overland to Amritsar, where she arrived on 1 November 1875, having written a small treatise, "The Church Built Out of One Brick," on the way. Whether this particular manuscript was ever shared beyond her missionary circle in published form is unknown. Amritsar was a large city, near which she lived for two years. The missionaries there were expecting Tucker and welcomed her; they had recognized her name and that she was the author A.L.O.E. before she arrived, for they had read her books as children.

Two years later, on 6 December 1876, she moved to Batala; it was an outstation, a walled city of about twenty-five thousand people, located twenty-four miles east of Amritsar and fifty miles from the Himalayas. The missionaries were the only Europeans there. Tucker helped with the Baring High School for native Christian boys, established in 1878, and then helped found and endowed (at fifty pounds a year) the mission's "plough" school for boys not yet converted. Her main missionary work was to visit Zenana, a portion of the house where high-caste Indian women were kept in seclusion. She also wrote allegories and parables especially for the Indian people. These were translated into various Indian languages, and the Christian Literary Society and the Punjab Religious Book Society published them; the *Dictionary of National Biography* reports that they sold well.

Tucker submitted some of these stories for publication in England, in an attempt to educate the British about Indian life. *A Wreath of Indian Stories* (1876) is a collection of such stories, with unfamiliar terms defined in footnotes. *Pomegranates From the Punjab* was also written for the people of India. *Harold's Bride,* on the other hand, is clearly aimed at a British audience. The story is about the young missionary Harold Hartley, one of Tucker's few recurring characters, and his new bride, Alicia, whom he takes to India. The headstrong Alicia learns lessons about India and about herself and eventually makes her contribution to society by visiting Zenana. Once again, footnotes provide information about India and the author's personal experiences with Indians who converted and were later harassed or killed. The preface confirms that the story is based on Tucker's eyewitness accounts. Among other reasons for writing this book she cites the need to alert prospective missionary wives to the extreme hardships waiting for them in India.

In 1893 Tucker became ill with a respiratory sickness and died on 2 December. She was buried in Batala, as she had requested. Her books were extremely popular during her lifetime and after: she was placed in the same category as the Brontë sisters, George Eliot, Elizabeth Cleghorn Gaskell, and Juliana Horatia Ewing by contemporary women authors and critics, such as Margaret Oliphant. Both Marshall, writing in 1897, and J. S. Bratton, writing in 1981, consider that Tucker's readers appreciated her allegorical style and her books. Although Tucker's works are not widely read today, Bratton's assessment suggests that her successful introduction of imaginative richness into didactic literature influenced other authors and established her as

the forerunner of Charles Kingsley and George MacDonald.

Biography:

Agnes Giberne, *A Lady of England: The Life and Letters of Charlotte Maria Tucker* (London: Hodder & Stoughton, 1895).

References:

J. S. Bratton, *The Impact of Victorian Children's Fiction* (London: Croom Helm, 1981), pp. 70–79;

Margaret Nancy Cutt, *Ministering Angels: A Study of Nineteenth-Century Evangelical Writing for Children* (Wormely: Five Owls Press, 1979), pp. 75–98;

Emma Marshall, " 'A.L.O.E.' (Miss Tucker)," in *Women Novelists of Queen Victoria's Reign,* edited by Margaret Oliphant (London: Hurst & Blackett, 1897), pp. 293–297.

Charlotte Mary Yonge

(11 August 1823 – 20 March 1901)

Claudia Nelson
Southwest Texas State University

See also the Yonge entry in *DLB 18: Victorian Novelists After 1885*.

BOOKS: *Le Château de Melville, ou, Recréations du Cabinet d'Etude* (London: Simpkin, 1839);

Abbeychurch, or, Self-Control and Self-Conceit (London: Burns, 1844);

Scenes and Characters, or, Eighteen Months at Beechcroft (London: Mozley, 1847); republished as *Beechcroft* (New York: Appleton, 1856);

The Kings of England: A History for Young Children (London: Mozley, 1848);

Henrietta's Wish, or, Domineering: A Tale (London: Masters, 1850; New York: Munro, 1885);

Kenneth, or, The Rear Guard of the Grand Army (London: Parker, 1850; New York: Appleton, 1855);

Langley School (London: Mozley, 1850);

Landmarks of History, I: Ancient History from the Earliest Times to the Mahometan Conquest (London: Mozley, 1852; Philadelphia: Leypoldt, 1863);

The Two Guardians, or, Home in This World (London: Masters, 1852; New York: Appleton, 1855);

Landmarks of History, II: Middle Ages, from the Reign of Charlemagne to That of Charles V (London: Mozley, 1853; New York: Leypoldt & Holt, 1867);

The Heir of Redclyffe (London: Parker, 1853; New York: Appleton, 1853);

The Herb of the Field (London: Mozley, 1853; New York: Macmillan, 1887);

The Little Duke, or, Richard the Fearless (London: Parker, 1854); republished as *Richard the Fearless, or, The Little Duke* (New York: Appleton, 1856);

The Castle Builders, or, The Deferred Confirmation (London: Mozley, 1854; New York: Appleton, 1855);

Heartsease, or, The Brother's Wife (London: Parker, 1854; New York: Appleton, 1854);

The Lances of Lynwood (London: Parker, 1855; New York: Appleton, 1856);

Charlotte Mary Yonge

The History of the Life and Death of the Good Knight Sir Thomas Thumb (Edinburgh: Constable, 1855; New York, 1856);

The Railroad Children (London, 1855);

Ben Sylvester's Word (London: Mozley, 1856; New York: Appleton, 1859);

The Daisy Chain, or, Aspirations: A Family Chronicle (London: Parker, 1856; New York: Appleton, 1856);

Harriet and Her Sister (London: Mozley, circa 1856);

Leonard the Lion-Heart, or, Bravery Put to the Test (London: Mozley, 1856; Philadelphia: American Sunday-School Union, circa 1860);

Dynevor Terrace, or, The Clue of Life (London: Parker, 1857; New York: Appleton, 1857);

Landmarks of History, III: Modern History, from the Beginning of the Reformation to the Accession of Napoleon III (London: Mozley, 1857; New York: Leypoldt & Holt, 1868);

The Instructive Picture Book, or, Lessons from the Vegetable World (Edinburgh: Edmonston & Douglas, 1857);

The Christmas Mummers (London: Mozley, 1858; New York: Pott, 1876);

Conversations on the Catechism, 2 volumes (London: Mozley, 1859);

Friarswood Post Office (London: Mozley, 1860; New York: Appleton, 1860);

Hopes and Fears, or, Scenes from the Life of a Spinster (London: Parker, 1860; New York: Appleton, 1861);

The Pigeon Pie (London: Mozley, 1860; Boston: Roberts, 1864);

The Young Stepmother, or, A Chronicle of Mistakes (London: Longmans, Green, 1861; New York: Appleton, 1862);

The Stokesley Secret, or, How the Pig Paid the Rent (London: Mozley, 1861; New York: Appleton, 1862);

Countess Kate (London: Mozley, 1862; Boston: Loring, 1865);

The Chosen People: A Compendium of Sacred and Church History for School Children (London: Mozley, 1862; New York: Pott & Amery, circa 1868);

Conversations on the Catechism: III, Means of Grace (London: Mozley, 1862);

The Wars of Wapsburgh (London: Groombridge, 1862);

A History of Christian Names (London: Macmillan, 1862; revised edition, London: Macmillan, 1884; New York: Macmillan, 1885);

Sea Spleenwort and Other Stories (London: Groombridge, 1862);

One Story by Two Authors, or, A Tale without a Moral, by Yonge and Jean Ingelow (London: Masters, 1862);

The Trial: More Links of the Daisy Chain (London: Macmillan, 1864; New York: Appleton, 1864);

A Book of Golden Deeds of All Times and All Lands (London & New York: Macmillan, 1864);

The Apple of Discord: A Play (London: Groombridge, 1864);

Historical Dramas (London: Groombridge, 1864; New York: Pott & Amery, n.d.) – comprises "The Mice at Play," "The Apple of Discord," and "The Strayed Falcon";

The Clever Woman of the Family (London: Macmillan, 1865; New York: Appleton, 1865);

The Prince and the Page: A Story of the Last Crusade (London: Macmillan, 1865; New York: Macmillan, 1875);

The Dove in the Eagle's Nest (London: Macmillan, 1866; New York: Appleton, 1866);

The Danvers Papers: An Invention (London: Macmillan, 1867);

A Shilling Book of Golden Deeds (London: Macmillan, 1867);

The Six Cushions (London: Mozley, 1867; Boston: Lee & Shepherd, n.d.);

Cameos from English History, First Series: From Rollo to Edward (London: Macmillan, 1868; Philadelphia: Lippincott, 1868);

The Chaplet of Pearls, or, The White and Black Ribaumont (London: Macmillan, 1868; New York: Appleton, 1869);

New Ground: Kaffirland (London: Mozley, 1868; New York: Pott & Amery, 1869);

The Pupils of St. John the Divine (London: Macmillan, 1868; Philadelphia: Lippincott, 1868);

A Book of Worthies, Gathered from the Old Histories and Now Written Out Anew (London & New York: Macmillan, 1869);

Keynotes of the First Lessons for Every Day in the Year (London: Society for Promoting Christian Knowledge, 1869);

The Seal, or, The Inward Spiritual Grace of Confirmation (London, 1869);

Questions on the Catechism (London: Mozley, 1869);

The Caged Lion (London: Macmillan, 1870; New York: Appleton, 1870);

Cameos from English History, Second Series: The Wars in France (London & New York: Macmillan, 1871);

Pioneers and Founders, or, Recent Workers in the Mission Field (London & New York: Macmillan, 1871);

A Parallel History of France and England, Consisting of Outlines and Dates (London & New York: Macmillan, 1871);

Little Lucy's Wonderful Globe (London & New York: Macmillan, 1871);

Musings over "The Christian Year" and "Lyra Innocentium" Together with a Few Gleanings of Recollections of the Rev. J. Keble, Gathered by Several Friends (Oxford: Parker, 1871; New York: Appleton, 1871);

Scripture Readings for Schools and Families, with Comments, First Series: Genesis to Deuteronomy (London & New York: Macmillan, 1871);

Scripture Readings for Schools and Families, with Comments, Second Series: From Joshua to Solomon (London & New York: Macmillan, 1872);

A History of France, volume 8 of *Historical Course for Schools,* edited by Edward A. Freeman (London, 1872; New York: Holt, 1879);

P's and Q's, or, The Question of Putting Upon (London & New York: Macmillan, 1872);

Questions on the Prayer-Book (London: Mozley, 1872);

In Memoriam Bishop Patteson: Being with Additions the Substance of a Memoir Published in the "Literary Churchman" (London: Skeffington, 1872);

The Mystery of the Cavern (London, 1872);

The Pillars of the House, or, Under Wode, Under Rode (London: Macmillan, 1873; New York: Macmillan, 1874);

Aunt Charlotte's Stories of English History for the Little Ones (London: Ward, 1873); republished as *Young Folks' History of England* (New York: Estes & Lauriat, 1879); republished as *Popular History of England* (Boston: Estes & Lauriat, 1894);

Life of John Coleridge Patteson, Missionary Bishop of the Melanesian Islands (London & New York: Macmillan, 1873); revised as *Sketches of the Life of Bishop Patteson in Melanesia* (London: Society for Promoting Christian Knowledge, 1875);

Questions on the Collects (London: Mozley, 1874);

Questions on the Epistles (London: Mozley, 1874);

Scripture Readings for Schools, with Comments, Third Series: The Kings and the Prophets (London & New York: Macmillan, 1874);

Lady Hester, or, Ursula's Narrative (London & New York: Macmillan, 1874);

Aunt Charlotte's Stories of French History for the Little Ones (London: Ward, 1874); republished as *Young Folks' History of France* (Boston: Estes & Lauriat, circa 1876–1881); republished as *Child's History of France* (New York: Lovell, 1881); republished as *Popular History of France* (Boston: Estes & Lauriat, 1894);

Questions on the Gospels (London: Mozley, 1875);

My Young Alcides: A Faded Photograph (London: Macmillan, 1875; New York: Macmillan, 1876);

Aunt Charlotte's Stories of Bible History for the Little Ones (London: Ward, 1875); republished as *Young Folks' Bible History* (Boston: Lothrop, 1880);

Aunt Charlotte's Stories of Greek History for the Little Ones (London: Ward, 1875; New York: Ward, 1879); republished as *Young Folks' History of Greece* (New York: Nelson & Phillips, 1878); republished as *Popular History of Greece* (Boston: Estes & Lauriat, 1894);

The Three Brides (London: Macmillan, 1876; New York: Appleton, 1876);

Eighteen Centuries of Beginnings of Church History (London: Mozley & Smith, 1876; New York: Pott, 1876);

Aunt Charlotte's Scripture Readings (N.p., 1876);

Scripture Readings for Schools and Families, with Comments, Fourth Series: The Gospel Times (London: Macmillan, 1876);

Worthies of English History (N.p., 1876);

Worthies of Ancient History (N.p., 1876);

Aunt Charlotte's Stories of Roman History for the Little Ones (London: Ward, 1877); republished as *Stories of Roman History for the Little Ones* (New York: Estes & Lauriat, 1877); republished as *Young Folks' History of Rome* (Boston: Lothrop, 1879); republished as *Popular History of Rome* (Boston: Estes & Lauriat, 1894);

Aunt Charlotte's Stories of German History for the Little Ones (London: Ward, 1877); republished as *Young Folks' History of Germany* (Boston: Lothrop, 1878); republished as *Child's History of Germany* (New York: Hurst, circa 1882); republished as *Popular History of Germany* (Boston: Estes & Lauriat, 1894);

Cameos from English History, Third Series: The Wars of the Roses (London & New York: Macmillan, 1877);

Womankind (London: Mozley & Smith, 1877; New York: Macmillan, 1877);

The Story of the Christians and Moors of Spain (London & New York: Macmillan, 1878);

The Disturbing Element, or, Chronicles of the Blue-bell Society (London: Ward, 1878; New York: Appleton, 1879);

A History of France, edited by J. R. Green (London: Macmillan, 1878; New York: Appleton, 1882);

Burnt Out: A Story for Mothers' Meetings (London: Smith, 1879);

Magnum Bonum, or, Mother Carey's Brood (London: Macmillan, 1879; New York: Macmillan, 1880);

Short English Grammar for Use in Schools (London: Longmans, 1879);

Scripture Readings for Schools and Families, with Comments, Fifth Series: Apostolic Times (London & New York: Macmillan, 1879);

Cameos from English History, Fourth Series: Reformation Times (London & New York: Macmillan, 1879);

Love and Life: An Old Story in Eighteenth-Century Costume (London & New York: Macmillan, 1880);

Buy a Broom/Kaspar's Summer Dream/The Boy Bishop (Rochester, N.Y.: Fitch, 1880);

Bye-Words: A Collection of Tales New and Old (London: Macmillan, 1880);

Verses on the Gospel for Sundays and Holy Days (London: Smith, 1880);

Mary and Norah, or, Queen Katharine's School (N.p., circa 1880);

Cheap Jack (London: Smith, 1881);

Lads and Lasses of Langley (London: Smith, 1881; New York: Young, 1882);

Aunt Charlotte's Evenings at Home with the Poets: A Collection of Poems for the Young, with Conversations Arranged in Twenty-Five Evenings (London: Ward, 1881);

How to Teach the New Testament (London: National Society, 1881; New York: Pott, 1889);

Practical Work in Sunday Schools (London: National Society, 1881); republished as *Practical Work in Schools* (New York: Kellogg, 1888);

Frank's Debt (London: Smith, 1881);

Wolf (London: Smith, 1881);

English History Reading-Books, Adapted to the Requirements of the New Code: Standards II–VI, and Supplemental Reading Book, 2 volumes (London: National Society, 1881, 1883);

Questions on the Psalms (London: Smith, 1881);

Given to Hospitality (London: Smith, 1882);

Sowing and Sewing: A Sexagesima Story (London: Smith, 1882);

Talks about the Laws We Live Under, or, At Langley Night-School (London: Smith, 1882);

Unknown to History: A Story of the Captivity of Mary of Scotland (London & New York: Macmillan, 1882);

Langley Little Ones: Six Stories (London: Smith, 1882);

Pickle and His Page Boy, or, Unlooked For: A Story (London: Smith, 1882; New York: Dutton, 1883);

A Pictorial History of the World's Great Nations from the Earliest Dates to the Present Time (N.p., 1882; New York: Hess, 1894);

Landmarks of Recent History, 1770–1883 (London: Smith, 1883);

Aunt Charlotte's Stories of American History, by Yonge and J. H. Hastings Weld (London: Ward, 1883; New York: Appleton, 1883);

Langley Adventures (London: Smith, 1883; New York: Dutton, 1884);

The Miz-Maze, or, The Winkworth Puzzle: A Story in Letters by Nine Authors, by Yonge and others (London & New York: Macmillan, 1883);

Stray Pearls: Memoirs of Margaret de Ribaumont, Viscountess of Bellaise (London & New York: Macmillan, 1883);

English Church History, Adapted for Use in Day and Sunday Schools, first series (London: National Society, 1883);

Cameos from English History, Fifth Series: England and Spain (London & New York: Macmillan, 1883);

The Armourer's 'Prentices (London & New York: Macmillan, 1884);

The Daisy Chain Birthday Book (London: Smith, 1885);

English History Reading-Books, Adapted to the Requirements of the New Code: Standards II–VI, and Supplemental Reading Book, volume 3 (London: National Society, 1885); republished as *Westminster Historical Reading-Books*, 2 volumes (London: National Society, 1891–1892);

Nuttie's Father (London & New York: Macmillan, 1885);

The Two Sides of the Shield (London & New York: Macmillan, 1885);

A Key to the Waverley Novels (Boston: Ginn, Heath, 1885);

Astray: A Tale of a Country Town, by Yonge, Mary Bramston, Christabel Coleridge, and Esmé Stuart [Amélie Leroy] (London: Hatchards, 1886; New York: Dutton, 1887);

Chantry House (London & New York: Macmillan, 1886);

The Little Rick-Burners (London: Skeffington, 1886);

A Modern Telemachus (London & New York: Macmillan, 1886);

Teachings on the Catechism: For the Little Ones (London: Smith, 1886);

The Victorian Half-Century: A Jubilee Book (London & New York: Macmillan, 1886);

Cameos from English History, Sixth Series: Forty Years of Stewart Rule (London & New York: Macmillan, 1887);

What Books to Lend and What to Give (London: National Society, 1887);

Under the Storm, or, Steadfast's Charge (London: National Society, 1887; New York: Whittaker, 1887);

Deacon's Book of Dates: A Manual of the World's Chief Historical Landmarks, and an Outline of Universal History (London: Deacon, 1888);

Beechcroft at Rockstone (London: Macmillan, 1888; New York: Macmillan, 1889);

Conversations on the Prayer Book (N.p., 1888);

Hannah More (London: Allen, 1888; Boston: Roberts, 1888);

Nurse's Memories (London: Eyre & Spottiswoode, 1888; New York: Young, 1888);

Our New Mistress, or, Changes at Brookfield Earl (London: National Society, 1888; New York: Whittaker, 1888);

Preparation of Prayer-Book Lessons (London: Smith & Innes, 1888);

A Reputed Changeling, or, Three Seventh Years Two Centuries Ago (London & New York: Macmillan, 1889);

The Parent's Power: Address to the Conference of the Mothers' Union (Winchester: Warren, 1889);

Neighbour's Fare (London: Skeffington, 1889);

The Cunning Woman's Grandson: A Tale of Cheddar a Hundred Years Ago (London: National Society, 1889; New York: Whittaker, 1889);

Cameos from English History, Seventh Series: The Rebellion and Restoration (London & New York: Macmillan, 1890);

Life of H.R.H. the Prince Consort (London: Allen, 1890);

More Bywords (London: Macmillan, 1890; New York: Macmillan, 1891);

The Slaves of Sabinus: Jew and Gentile (London: National Society, 1890; New York: Whittaker, 1890);

The Constable's Tower, or, The Times of Magna Charta (London: National Society, 1891; New York: Whittaker, 1891);

Old Times at Otterbourne (Winchester: Warren, 1891);

Simple Stories Relating to English History (London: Longmans, 1891);

Twelve Stories from Early English History (London: National Society, 1891);

Twenty Stories and Biographies from 1066 to 1485 (N.p., 1891);

Two Penniless Princesses (London & New York: Macmillan, 1891);

The Cross Roads, or, A Choice in Life (London: National Society, 1892; New York: Whittaker, 1892);

An Old Woman's Outlook in a Hampshire Village (London & New York: Macmillan, 1892);

That Stick (London & New York: Macmillan, 1892);

The Hanoverian Period, with Biographies of Leading Persons (London: National Society, 1892);

The Stuart Period, with Biographies of Leading Persons (London: National Society, 1892);

The Tudor Period, with Biographies of Leading Persons (London: National Society, 1892);

Chimes for the Mothers: A Reading for Every Day in the Year (London: Gardner, 1893);

The Girl's Little Book (London: Skeffington, 1893; New York: Pott, n.d.);

Grisly Grisell, or, The Laidly Lady of Whitburn: A Tale of the Wars of the Roses (London & New York: Macmillan, 1893);

The Strolling Players: A Harmony of Contrasts, by Yonge and Christabel Coleridge (London & New York: Macmillan, 1893);

The Treasures in the Marshes (London: National Society, 1893; New York: Whittaker, 1893);

The Rubies of St. Lô (London & New York: Macmillan, 1894);

The Story of Easter (London: Ward, 1894);

The Cook and the Captive, or, Attalus the Hostage (London: National Society, 1894; New York: Whittaker, 1894);

The Long Vacation (London & New York: Macmillan, 1895);

The Carbonels (London: National Society, 1895; New York: Whittaker, 1895);

Cameos from English History, Eighth Series: The End of the Stewarts (London & New York: Macmillan, 1896);

The Wardship of Steepcombe (London: National Society, 1896; New York: Whittaker, 1896);

The Release, or, Caroline's French Kindred (London & New York: Macmillan, 1896);

The Pilgrimage of the Ben Beriah (London & New York: Macmillan, 1897);

Founded on Paper, or, Uphill and Downhill between the Two Jubilees (London: National Society, 1897; New York: Whittaker, 1897);

John Keble's Parishes: A History of Hursley and Otterbourne (London & New York: Macmillan, 1898);

The Patriots of Palestine: A Story of the Maccabees (London: National Society, 1898; New York: Whittaker, 1898);

Cameos from English History, Ninth Series: The Eighteenth Century (London & New York: Macmillan, 1899);

Scenes from "Kenneth" (London: Arnold, 1899);

The Herd Boy and His Hermit (London: National Society, 1899; New York: Whittaker, 1899);

The Making of a Missionary, or, Day Dreams in Earnest: A Story of Mission Work in China (London: National Society, 1900; New York: Whittaker, 1900);

Modern Broods, or, Developments Unlooked For (London & New York: Macmillan, 1900);

Last Heartsease Leaves (Bournemouth: Sydenham's Royal Marine Library, 1900);

Reasons Why I Am a Catholic and Not a Roman Catholic (London: Wells, Gardner, Darton, 1901);

Midsummer Day (N.p., n.d.);

Hints on the Religious Education of Children of the Wealthier Classes (N.p., n.d.);

A Langley Story (N.p., n.d.).

Leonard's dream; illustration by "J. B." for Yonge's The
Lances of Lynwood *(1855)*

was primarily conducted through her publications. These began in 1838, when in order to raise money to benefit Otterbourne School (which the senior Yonges had founded), Frances Yonge suggested that stories Charlotte had written as a French exercise might be privately printed and sold to friends and to those attending a charitable bazaar. The result was *Le Château de Melville* (1839), of which the young author wrote to a cousin, "I hope the story is not very foolish, but I am in hopes that it has a little better *moralité* than the French stories by the French themselves usually have." Yonge's writing career thus started in the path it was to follow for the next sixty-odd years: her theme was "*moralité*"; her object was charitable; and her story was marked by vivid characterization and lively dialogue – a talent that she would employ even in such unlikely contexts as the *Conversations on the Catechism* (1859, 1862).

Yonge's literary aspirations, however, caused some anxiety to her family, as her grandmother (a clergyman's widow) thought earning money by writing was "unladylike," while her father required her to explain that her motive for writing was nei-

ther vanity nor avarice, but rather "the wish to do good." As Elaine Showalter has noted in *A Literature of Their Own: British Women Novelists from Brontë to Lessing* (1977), the decision that Yonge would publish anonymously and contribute the bulk of her profits to good causes (missionary ships, religious colleges) helped to fix her forever in a "female and subordinate role" of dependency and modesty. Afraid of vanity, her parents had encouraged the child to believe herself ugly and stupid; as an adult, Yonge remained reluctant to show pride in herself or her productions.

Yonge's works stress women's need to embrace an ostensibly inferior role – while suggesting at the same time that for women and men alike, sacrifice, subordination, and suffering bring the soul closer to God. This "feminine, familial value system," as Catherine Sandbach-Dahlström calls it, unites religion with the values associated primarily with Victorian womanhood to console and inspire those readers for whom duty may sometimes seem too heavy. Women (and men whose lives somehow approximate the feminine), Yonge's writings continually suggest, have the advantage where salvation is concerned because they are more likely to understand self-abnegation and self-discipline.

In the fifteen years following her first book Yonge produced a variety of fiction and nonfiction: stories published in the *Magazine for the Young* (founded in 1842 by Anne Mozley, whose brother Richard's publishing firm accepted several of Yonge's books), volumes of history, and full-length novels. While these early works were moderately successful in financial terms, they by no means established their author as the household word she later became. They are chiefly interesting today, perhaps, for their connection with what came after them. Thus *Abbeychurch* (1844), the major incident of which is the unwise attendance of some of the girl characters at a Mechanics' Institute lecture, explores themes of vital importance in Yonge's oeuvre, such as filial obedience and the problem of bad parenting; *Scenes and Characters* (1847) introduces the Mohun family, whose history Yonge was to chronicle further in *The Two Sides of the Shield* (1885), *Beechcroft at Rockstone* (1888), *The Long Vacation* (1895), and *Modern Broods* (1900); *Langley School* (1850) is the first in a series of village stories, running through *Sewing and Sowing* (1882) and *Pickle and His Page Boy* (1882), designed to interest middle-class girls in parish work.

With the publication of *The Heir of Redclyffe* (1853), however, Yonge advanced from the ranks of writers of pleasing and instructive works for youthful readers to the status of national celebrity. Characteristically, her reaction to her own success was to consult Keble on the possibility that the world's praise might induce "vainglory"; he prescribed prayer and introspection, two activities always congenial to her. Like so many of Yonge's novels, *The Heir of Redclyffe* combines lively domestic portraiture with Christian allegory; it also draws upon chivalric romance, as in its recurring invocations of Friedrich de la Motte Fouqué's *Sintram* (1815), a work for which Yonge was to write an introduction in 1896.

The Heir of Redclyffe tells the story of Guy Morville, heir at once to a landed estate and to an unfortunate family tendency to hot temper, who upon his grandfather's death goes to live with his guardians, the Edmonstones. There Guy forms ties that will shape his later life: he becomes another son to Mrs. Edmonstone, befriends and cheers the invalid Charles, falls in love with Amy, and – most significant – runs afoul of his cousin and heir, Philip Morville. Philip's inability to appreciate Guy arises from vanity, pride, and the gravest sin in the Yongean calendar, "self-sufficiency" (or irreligion).

Guy, it turns out, is a modern-day saint; his humility has enabled him to conquer his faults and desires and to think of others' good before his own. While talented and personable, Philip is by no means the hero he thinks himself, and only after Guy lays down his own life to nurse Philip through a fever does the latter awaken to his errors, which range from jealous stupidity (in the manifold obstacles he has unjustifiably placed in Guy's way) to unfilial conduct (in having engaged himself to Amy's sister without her parents' knowledge) to criminal recklessness (in exposing himself to the fever) and to the ultimate cause of all these flaws, spiritual arrogance.

The story of Guy's widespread effect for good had an enormous impact on the Victorian reading public. Countless young men took him for their model (among them William Morris, then a student at Oxford, and Dante Gabriel Rossetti); according to Yonge's disciple and biographer Christabel Coleridge, the novel accompanied many youthful officers to the encampments of the Crimean War. Jo March is discovered weeping over the novel in British editions of Louisa May Alcott's *Little Women* (1868–1869), and thirty years after the publication of *The Heir of Redclyffe,* Yonge was still receiving fan letters in its praise from German princesses. This response says much for Yonge's ability to make didacticism not merely palatable but irresistible; as Coleridge points out, she had the rare ability to infuse goodness with interest. Barbara Dennis refines this

comment by remarking that in Yonge's world, "the romantic *is* domestic," or vice versa – an ideal trait for a novelist whose era turned home life into a religious cult.

As this glance at the reception of *The Heir of Redclyffe* suggests, Yonge's contemporaries never considered her a writer for women or children alone. Charles Kingsley, for instance – of whom Yonge herself disapproved – called *Heartsease* (1854) "the most delightful and wholesome novel I ever read"; statesmen and prelates admired her work; and most present-day critics recognize her, in Elliot Engel's words, as "an important heir of the Oxford Movement," whose readership was defined at least as much by belief as by age or gender. Nevertheless, her connection with the Anglican magazine *The Monthly Packet,* which she edited from its founding in 1851 until 1890, linked her especially to that periodical's readership: middle-class girls between fifteen and twenty-five years old.

The Monthly Packet, Yonge wrote in its first issue, was meant as an aid in character formation, "a companion in times of recreation, which may help you to perceive how to bring your religious principles to bear upon your daily life, may show you the examples, both good and evil, of historical persons." From its inception, then, it was a crucial part of Yonge's "ministry," and reached an unusually clearly defined demographic segment of her readership. The "home daughters" who followed Yonge's serialized novels and histories in its pages often came from backgrounds resembling her own. Indeed, as Julia Courtney has noted, one group of young women (known as the Goslings) who especially identified with Yonge's positions and aims, and who moved beyond *The Monthly Packet* to produce their own manuscript magazine under her guidance, consisted mostly of girls related to her or to each other and of their network of friends.

The first volume of *The Monthly Packet* began the serial publication of one of Yonge's own favorites among her works, *The Little Duke* (1854). This historical tale, set in tenth-century France and depicting the early life of Duke Richard of Normandy (great-grandfather of William the Conqueror), might at first seem improbable fare for the girls who subscribed to the magazine: there are no major female characters, and the central issue is the construction of the ideal knight. But it soon becomes evident that the achievements demanded of Richard by the turbulent and treacherous society in which he finds himself are not so much the martial ones of swordplay and cunning as they are the same person-

Yonge with one of her Sunday school classes in the early 1870s

ality traits Victorian society asked of middle-class women: patience, gentleness, consideration.

That Yonge's historical tales link the domestic profile of her peers with the blood and thunder of past adventure has laid her open to accusations of ahistoricism. But her fondness for costume drama suggests less a flawed historical imagination than a conviction that religious principle is timeless – and perhaps a further desire to comfort girls who may believe themselves condemned to boredom. Victorian girls might legitimately have felt that history was peculiarly "theirs," as their lessons typically stressed this subject, while at mid century boys' public schools omitted it from their curricula. For girls, then, historical novels provided a legitimate form of escapism because they combined adventure with edification. In addition, since Yonge's excursions into history are so thoroughly imbued with Tractarian and Victorian ideals, readers could transfer the sense of excitement induced by the exotic settings and martial incidents to their own lives, as the same principles clearly underlay both.

Moreover, insofar as the novels often enforce identification with male protagonists, girls could conclude that the ethical standards governing their own lives must also govern the lives of their virtuous brothers. It is striking that Yonge bestowed these "home values" equally upon her female and male creations, in a manner suggesting that she considered gender differences a matter more of lifestyle than of biology. Her heroes are often gentle and domestically inclined; her heroines hoydenish, clumsy, and spirited. This acknowledgment that not all girls find it easy to manifest the docility that Victorian society demanded of them is frequently a shaping force in Yonge's fiction, whether set in the ninth century or in the nineteenth.

Hence many of the Victorian chronicles provide a detailed description of family life instead of a dramatic plot; for Yonge, excitement is interior rather than exterior. For example, *The Castle Builders* (1854), a novel serialized in *The Monthly Packet* at the same time as *The Little Duke*, hinges on the delayed confirmation of two sisters who have not yet learned the difficult art of self-examination. Although the climax of the tale is the drowning of the girls' stepbrother, Frank, the importance of this event is not its physical drama but its moral effect: it teaches Kate a better sense of duty and purpose, while it throws Emmeline into a despondency from which only her saintly brother-in-law can rouse her. When the confirmation finally takes place, Yonge makes it clear that only spiritual experience is meaningful — and such experience is open to all, adolescents as well as adults, women as well as men.

Yonge's next pair of novels, *Heartsease* and *The Lances of Lynwood* (1855), recapitulate these issues of androgyny and again conclude that, in men and women alike, a feminine gentleness is the mark of moral superiority. Thus, in the domestic tale *Heartsease,* Theodora Martindale conforms more to male than to female stereotypes — she is rebellious, "princely," unconventional, and proud; she bullies her teachers, leads her brother into bad company, treats love lightly, and finds it hard to express affection — until at last she is set on the true path by her meek, despised sister-in-law, Violet. Conversely, *The Lances of Lynwood,* set in fourteenth-century England and France, follows the career of a delicate young knight primarily notable for his "woman's" heart, "girl's" physique, and pious self-forgetfulness. Both narratives ratify feminine values while teaching that they have little to do with gender.

At about the time that *The Heir of Redclyffe* was published, *The Monthly Packet* began serializing the other work that cemented Yonge's reputation, *The Daisy Chain,* which appeared in book form in 1856. *The Daisy Chain* introduced the Mays, a large family that would appear again in *The Trial* (1864) and that would also infiltrate other families' stories, such as the Underwood saga in *The Pillars of the House* (1873). Such populous clans recall Yonge's pleasure in visiting her ten second cousins in Devon, who were her closest playmates as a child; in addition, they advance the theme of the androgyny of virtue explored in her earlier works.

Thus the best-loved figure of *The Daisy Chain,* Etheldred (third daughter and fifth child of Dr. Thomas May), at first combines brilliant academic prowess and a strong likeness to her father with utter domestic incompetence, while her eldest brother, Richard, reverses these traits. The novel describes the moral development of the senior members of the family, from Dr. May down to the eighth child, Tom, after Mrs. May's death in a carriage accident. The more-active personalities find that they must renounce part of the self in order to fulfill God's plan for them. Thus Margaret becomes an in-

valid and finally succeeds in relinquishing her desire to be first within the family; Ethel gives up her cherished study of Greek to have more time for philanthropy and housekeeping; Norman eschews worldly success to go as a missionary to New Zealand; Dr. May learns the patience and gentleness necessary to bringing up his large brood alone; and Flora, secretly the most self-absorbed of the lot, is only brought to a true sense of her duty by the tragic death of her neglected little daughter.

Conversely, the family's more-passive spirits, Richard and Tom, come to recognize the dangers of moral timidity. As in so many of Yonge's works, error is no respecter of gender: male and female characters alike must strive for self-sacrifice. Indeed, one reason the Mays took such a hold on the public imagination — and their admirers ranged from Agatha Christie and E. Nesbit to Henry James — is surely Yonge's awareness that gender stereotypes only make life more difficult for the individual. The awkward and eager Ethel and the gentle and unintellectual Richard do not fit naturally into the social patterns ordained for them. But their acceptance of these burdens and constraints makes them all the more worthy, and like-minded readers may console themselves with the thought that they are engaged in conforming to the divine will.

The Mays' spiritual progress is mirrored by the ultimate achievement of Ethel's pet project: the building of a church to serve the working-class population of Cocksmoor. Yonge inherited this interest from her father, who had designed and largely funded St. Matthew's Church in Otterbourne (consecrated in 1838). The combined focus of *The Daisy Chain* on church-building and warm father/child relationships takes on some poignancy in that William Yonge died suddenly in February 1854, while his daughter was engaged in writing the novel.

The loss inaugurated a series of changes in Yonge's life. Her brother Julian (whose departure for the Crimean War may have hastened their father's fatal stroke) was invalided out of the army and subsequently married in 1858, bringing his wife back to live in his childhood home; Yonge and her mother accordingly moved down the street to set up housekeeping for themselves. In 1866 the Kebles died, and two years later Frances Yonge followed them after an illness that had left her progressively less capable mentally.

Some critics have found that Yonge's powers substantially diminished after she lost her father and her confessor, both of whom had exercised editorial and moral control over her writing. But this judgment seems questionable. It was after her

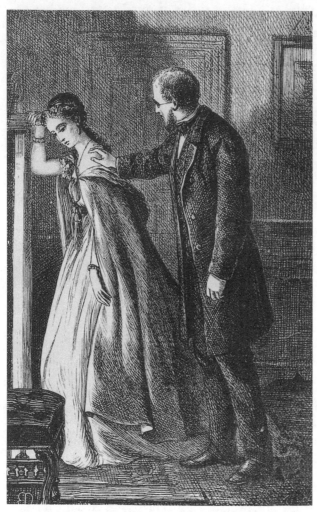

Dr. May and Flora; illustration for Yonge's best-known work,
The Daisy Chain *(1856)*

father's death that she produced two of her liveliest novels for younger children: *The Stokesley Secret, or, How the Pig Paid the Rent* (1861) and *Countess Kate* (1862), both serialized in the *Magazine for the Young* between 1860 and 1862. The former, which begins with the memorable line, "How can a pig pay the rent?," describes the charitable efforts of a group of children who are saving to buy a pig for a poor woman; the latter, whose eponymous protagonist has much in common with Yonge as a child, deals with the misadventures of a gawky bookworm who inherits a title before she has achieved the self-control and understanding that accompany true gentility. As with all Yonge's best writing, the two stories perform their didactic function with considerable humor and vivid reportage.

Other notable books of this period include *A History of Christian Names* (1862), which remained a standard work on this subject for a considerable

time; *The Trial,* which partakes of the mid-Victorian interest in mystery and the law; *The Clever Woman of the Family* (1865), a study of the dangers lying in wait for women who misdirect their energies in a society that appears to offer little of interest for talented women to do; and *The Dove in the Eagle's Nest* (1866), about the taming of a fifteenth-century family of German robber barons by a timid burgher girl. The last-named work again suggests the appeal of history for adventure-loving young women; if Rachel Curtis of *The Clever Woman of the Family* discovers that reading aloud to her husband's uncle is among the most important contributions she can make, Christina Sorel of *The Dove in the Eagle's Nest* manages single-handedly to bring the von Adlerstein family out of the Middle Ages and into the Renaissance. All of these works demonstrate that William Yonge's death had little effect on the range of his daughter's interests or the fecundity of her pen.

Similarly, Keble's death by no means immediately impeded Yonge's creative flow. In the early 1870s, for instance, she was at work not only on writings about the teaching of Scripture and on nonfiction historical texts, but also on less formulaic projects, including a biography of her distant cousin John Coleridge Patteson (a missionary bishop killed by Maori tribesmen in 1871, and the model for Norman May) and the longest and one of the best of her family chronicles, *The Pillars of the House*. Such was Yonge's fluency in writing that she typically had three works in hand at once – she would write a page of one, put it aside to dry, write a page of the second, then the third, and begin the cycle anew. Her admirer Ethel Romanes recounts the story "of Miss Yonge coming in to a meal after a morning's writing, and saying: 'I have had a dreadful day; I have killed the Bishop and Felix [the hero of *The Pillars of the House*].'"

Indeed, Felix's death clearly stood for Yonge as an example of Christian devotion and martyrdom. With his sister Wilmet, Felix is one of "the pillars of the house" of Underwood, as they are the two oldest of an orphaned family of thirteen. Felix's willingness to live for others is immediately manifest when he undertakes to support his siblings by going to work for a printer. Meanwhile, Wilmet manages their scanty housekeeping and brings up the younger children, many of whom show considerable talent for art, music, and religion – which Yonge, of course, sees as the ultimate inspiration for all worthy creative endeavor. While Felix eventually succeeds to the family estate, he continues to devote himself to the others' interests until he finally dies of a lung complaint.

Felix, a bachelor who relinquishes romance because one of his brothers is attracted to his love interest, may be said to be wedded to his family. But the same could be said of some of his siblings: Wilmet and Robina marry John and William Harewood, who are half-brothers, while Lance marries Gertrude May; Bernard marries Phyllis Merrifield; and Stella marries Charles Audley – all of these spouses belonging to families whose stories Yonge had traced elsewhere, and who may thus be considered "family" within her fictional oeuvre. Four of the children remain single. This consuming interest in clan unity and corresponding distrust of exogamy not only recall Yonge's membership in a devoted extended family but also help to explain her appeal for mid-Victorian girls (to whom the family was often the world) and for her adult contemporaries, as the era saw the family bond as the root of government, civilization, language, and even biology. At the same time, the emotional circumscription of Yonge's fiction takes its toll: her forays outside the middle class or outside England – Peru in *Dynevor Terrace* (1857), New York and Indiana in *The Trial*, or China in *The Making of a Missionary* (1900) – often lack the inside knowledge that contributes so much to her domestic works.

The same year that *The Pillars of the House* appeared in book form, Yonge's sister-in-law's sister, Gertrude Walter, moved from the Julian Yonge home to Charlotte's house, Elderfield. Yonge scholars Margaret Mare and Alicia Percival consider this event a striking example of "Yonge's instinct for self-immolation," since Walter's invalidism meant that Yonge not only found herself distracted by nursing duties but also lost the use of her guest room. The change in lifestyle thus had a potentially stultifying effect by curtailing Yonge's association with erstwhile house guests such as pioneer educator Elizabeth Wordsworth. Coleridge, on the other hand, notes that Yonge greatly prized Walter's companionship, and Walter, who described herself as "Char's wife," filled the combined roles of secretary and literary critic as well as close friend.

Walter's presence seems to have been no hindrance to Yonge's productivity; she continued to pour out volumes of fiction, histories, textbooks, religious guides, biographies, and translations from French. In addition, she remained the guiding spirit behind *The Monthly Packet* (which between 1880 and 1885 counted Lewis Carroll among its contributors) until she reluctantly gave over its editorship to Coleridge; she promptly filled the gap in her time with the editorship of *Mothers in Council*. Notable among her later works are *Womankind* (1877), a

Yonge's grave in the Otterbourne churchyard

meditation on women's spiritual lives from youth to old age; *Magnum Bonum* (1879), which suffers from a disjointed plot but nonetheless presents one of Yonge's most interesting families; and *What Books to Lend and What to Give* (1887), a guide for librarians and prize-book donors that provides insight into her understanding of what constitutes literature's worth.

While her popularity continued high, especially among girls – she ranked high in a list of favorite authors in a *Girl's Realm* poll of 1898 – Yonge's most important novels were behind her. Gillian Avery argues that Yonge was perennially "hostile to new experience," and certainly her circle of friends and family narrowed rather than widened as time went on. Julian Yonge died in 1892 (after years of financial difficulty that diminished his sister's exchequer), Gertrude Walter, in 1897. Appropriately enough, Yonge proved unable to outlast the Victorian era, whose religious and domestic ideals she had so faithfully chronicled; she died two months after the queen, on 20 March 1901, and was buried in Otterbourne churchyard on the thirty-fifth anniversary of Keble's death.

Charlotte Yonge's work is not to everyone's taste. While her contemporaries regarded her as an important novelist and moral guide, as well as a talented historian and liturgical expert, mid-twentieth-century critics often scorned her. Q. D. Leavis, writing in 1944, dismissed Yonge as "a day-dreamer with a writing itch that compensated her for a peculiarly starved life." Over the last several decades, however, Yonge has received increasingly respectful attention from scholars of literature and social history. Feminists in particular have found valuable her complex and sympathetic portrayals of Victorian family life. While her readership is now considerably smaller than it was in her own time (particularly among children and adult men), Yonge continues to win devotees – a circumstance at which no one who shares her belief in the significance of the home should wonder.

Biographies:

Christabel Coleridge, *Charlotte Mary Yonge: Her Life and Letters* (London & New York: Macmillan, 1903);

Ethel Romanes, *Charlotte Mary Yonge: An Appreciation* (London: Mowbray, 1908);

Georgina Battiscombe, *Charlotte Mary Yonge: The Story of an Uneventful Life* (London: Constable, 1943);

Margaret Mare and Alicia C. Percival, *Victorian Best-Seller: The World of Charlotte M. Yonge* (London: Harrap, 1947).

References:

Gillian Avery, "Charlotte Mary Yonge 1823–1901," in *Writers for Children: Critical Studies of Major Authors Since the Seventeenth Century*, edited by Jane M. Bingham (New York: Scribners, 1988), pp. 625–631;

Georgina Battiscombe and Marghanita Laski, eds., *A Chaplet for Charlotte Yonge* (London: Cresset, 1965);

David Brownell, "The Two Worlds of Charlotte Yonge," in *The Worlds of Victorian Fiction,* edited by Jerome H. Buckley (Cambridge: Harvard University Press, 1975), pp. 165–178;

Raymond Chapman, "A Tractarian Parish," in his *Faith and Revolt: Studies in the Literary Influence of the Oxford Movement* (London: Weidenfeld & Nicolson, 1970), pp. 58–87;

Julia Courtney, "The *Barnacle:* A Manuscript Magazine of the 1860s," in *The Girl's Own: Cultural Histories of the Anglo-American Girl, 1830–1915,* edited by Claudia Nelson and Lynne Vallone (Athens: University of Georgia Press, 1994), pp. 71–97;

Barbara Dennis, *Charlotte Yonge (1823–1901), Novelist of the Oxford Movement: A Literature of Victorian Culture and Society* (Lewiston: Mellen, 1992);

Dennis, "The Two Voices of Charlotte Yonge," *Durham University Journal,* new series 34 (March 1973): 181–188;

Elliot Engel, "Heir of the Oxford Movement: Charlotte Mary Yonge's *The Heir of Redclyffe,*" *Etudes Anglaises,* 33 (April–June 1980): 132–141;

Q. D. Leavis, "Charlotte Yonge and 'Christian Discrimination,'" *Scrutiny,* 12 (Spring 1944): 152–160;

Catherine Sandbach-Dahlström, *Be Good Sweet Maid: Charlotte Yonge's Domestic Fiction, a Study in Dogmatic Purpose and Fictional Form* (Stockholm: Almqvist & Wiksell, 1984);

June Sturrock, "A Personal View of Women's Education, 1838–1900: Charlotte Yonge's Novels," *Victorians' Institute Journal,* 7 (1979): 7–18.

APPENDIX

Children's Illustrators, 1800–1880

Children's Illustrators, 1800–1880

Gwyneth Evans
Malaspina University College

The rapid expansion of the market for printed books in nineteenth-century England and widespread public eagerness to have both fiction and nonfiction accompanied by prints or engravings led to a great increase both in the number of book illustrators and in the technical resources available to them. While adult literature rejoiced in the enhancement of the printed text by such artists as George Cruikshank, Hablot Knight Browne ("Phiz"), Dante Gabriel Rossetti, and William Makepeace Thackeray (who illustrated many of his own novels), a variety of books for children were also largely and often lavishly illustrated, sometimes by the same artists. Both picture books, which were much affected by the development of a successful color-printing process by Edmund Evans late in the century, and children's novels and informational works were enriched by fine-detailed, humorous, or romantic drawings that had been transferred onto the woodblock or engraving plate and reproduced for children's pleasure.

Public demand and commercial pressures often resulted in unequal quality of work or in crude reproduction of an original. Nonetheless, in addition to the well-known names of the period such as Randolph Caldecott, Walter Crane, and Kate Greenaway, there were many lesser illustrators who produced memorable children's books. Sometimes illustrating their own texts, they more often responded with highly trained artistic sympathy to the ideas, mood, and characters created by someone else. The best-known collaboration on a nineteenth-century children's book is that between Lewis Carroll and Sir John Tenniel, but Arthur Hughes's illustrations for George MacDonald's books, or those of Samuel Williams for Elizabeth Turner's poetry had an equally significant effect on how these books were perceived.

Tenniel, like many other such illustrators, was a cartoonist for *Punch;* Williams and others among the older artists worked in the Bewick tradition of woodcuts depicting nature and rural life; and Hughes was a Pre-Raphaelite painter with a visionary sense of association between the world of childhood and the supernatural. These different strains of satiric humor, naturalistic detail, and visionary exaltation are to be found in English illustration throughout the nineteenth century, contributing to the making of fine and even extraordinary children's books. Williams and the Dalziel brothers, Edward, George, and Thomas, were better known in their time as engravers than as illustrators in their own right; they were accomplished draftsmen, however, and they advanced the art of children's book illustration in various ways.

Preeminently a wood engraver and designer, Samuel Williams (1788–1853) produced some fine work for children in his busy career, which spanned the Regency and early Victorian periods. Although recently John Harvey and Jane R. Cohen have discussed his influential contribution to Charles Dickens's *The Old Curiosity Shop* (1841). His children's books have thus far received little attention. He was born in Colchester, an Essex market town, on 23 February 1788. His working-class family apprenticed him to a local printer named Marsden, but the boy spent his free time on his real interest — drawing and engraving on wood. Eventually, he decided to risk making art his life's work rather than a hobby and established himself in Colchester as a designer and engraver of woodcuts.

He proved successful enough to move to London in 1819, where he became, according to the *Dictionary of National Biography,* "one of the ablest and best employed of English wood engravers, specially excelling in landscape work." Like other wood engravers of the period, Williams was assisted in his work by other family members, including his four sons, his sister Ann Mary Williams, and his younger brother, Thomas.

Williams's facility as an engraver carried over into an ease and ingenuity in executing his own drawings. In the early 1820s he was responsible for the illustrations of two volumes that appealed to both adults and children: Whittingham's edition of *Robinson Crusoe* (1822) and Sarah Trimmer's *Natural History* (1823–1824). The subjects of these volumes reappear in Williams's later work: he illustrated a

Naughty Sam; illustration by Williams for Elizabeth Turner's The Daisy; or Cautionary Stories
in Verse *(1830); courtesy of Special Collections, Thomas Cooper
Library, University of South Carolina*

lively robinsonnade for children, Jeffrey Taylor's *The Young Islanders* (1842), and throughout his career he was noted for his drawings of nature – particularly trees and landscapes – which he often included as backgrounds in his vignettes of child and family life.

The golden age of English fantasy was yet to come, and Williams is essentially a realistic artist, excelling in the depiction of natural scenes and vignettes of children's behavior. While Williams's draftsmanship occasionally falters, particularly in the figure drawing, this is a common problem with wood engravings of the period, often attributable to the pressures of production and the difficulties of transferring drawings to the woodblock. For the most part, Williams's work is characterized by fine detail and careful execution. He was never a caricaturist, as were such successors as Browne, Charles Henry Bennett, and Tenniel, nor are his figures of children as lively as some created by the later artists. Nonetheless, Williams's illustrations show a real understanding of the pleasures and woes of childhood. The emotions conveyed through his children's facial expressions, though not always apparent in their rather stylized gestures, are convincing.

Two of Williams's most appealing sets of drawings for and about children accompany the 1830 republication of the mild didactic verses of

Elizabeth Turner in two small, elegantly produced books called *The Daisy; or, Cautionary Stories, in Verse* (1830) and *The Cowslip, or More Cautionary Stories, in Verse* (1830). Williams's sympathy for children is well conveyed in the vignettes; the drawings are effectively composed to focus on the child's emotion. Though set in the context of a household or outdoor scene, they convey much visual information without seeming cluttered. Williams's skill is especially evident in his handling of light and shadow, a technique that, according to William James Linton, generally distinguished his woodcuts: light, from a clearly defined source, usually shines upon the well-behaved children, while the naughty are in a shaded area. In "The Purloiner," however, a shaft of sunlight reveals a culprit in the cupboard, helping himself to raspberry jam.

Williams also illustrated several books in the Peter Parley series, by Samuel Griswold Goodrich and others. His art in these volumes ranges outside the English domestic and rural scene to depict life in the tropics and other exotic subjects. In Ann Fraser Tyler's *Leila; or, The Island* (1841), Williams makes an appealing subject out of the familiar act of a girl feeding chickens in an unfamiliar tropical setting. Mary Elizabeth Southwell Leathley's *Little Mary Grown Older* (1832) includes a realistic and not unsympathetic portrayal of an African American, which was relatively unusual in a period when dark-skinned races tended to be caricatured. Williams's characteristic strengths, however, are his lovingly detailed studies of the natural world, as in the dramatic landscape on the title page of Goodrich's *Wit Bought; or, The Life and Adventures of Robert Merry* (circa 1845). After a long and productive work life, Williams died in London on 19 September 1853, but he lived long enough to see several strong new illustrators devoting a significant part of their careers to supplying the rapidly expanding market for children's books.

Undoubtedly, the most renowned workshop of British wood engravers in the nineteenth century was that of the Dalziel family, whose principal members – George (1815–1902), Edward (1817–1905), and Thomas (1823–1906) – engraved thousands of drawings by other artists, as well as working from their own designs. The Dalziel brothers were born in Wooler, Northumberland, to a father who had in midlife taken up art as a profession, and they were raised in Newcastle upon Tyne. Newcastle had also been the home of Thomas Bewick, who at the turn of the century had revived and greatly extended the possibilities of wood engraving, and the Dalziels were influenced by his work. Seven of the eight Dalziel sons became professional artists and/or engravers.

In 1835, at the age of nineteen, George Dalziel went to London as a pupil of the wood engraver Charles Gray, who had been Bewick's pupil; four years later George set up his own business and was soon joined by his brother Edward, with whom he formed a partnership that lasted more than fifty-five years and produced many finely illustrated books. Virtually all of Tenniel's illustrations, for example, apart from those in *Punch,* were engraved by the Dalziels, as were those of Richard Doyle, and a chapter of Percy Muir's *Victorian Illustrated Books* (1971) titled "The Dalziel Era" suggests the brothers' scope and influence. In 1852 the two oldest brothers were joined in business by John, who died in 1869, and in 1860 by Thomas, who had been trained as a copperplate engraver but became the one brother known primarily as an illustrator, or designer, rather than strictly an engraver of woodblocks.

In *A History of Children's Book Illustration* (1988), Joyce Irene Whalley and Tessa Rose Chester stress that in considering the illustrations of this time "the importance of the engraver should never be overlooked, since in the end it is his interpretation of the artist's original sketch that we see and it was his hand that could make or mar the finished picture." A common practice of the time was to include the

"The Genie Brings the Hatchet and Cord"; illustration by Thomas Dalziel for The Arabian Nights Entertainments: Dalziels' Illustrated Edition *(1864)*

engraver's name on many of the illustrations, even when the artist's name is absent. Artists were at times displeased by the treatment their drawings received at the hands of the engravers. Forrest Reid has compiled some of the irritated remarks of Dante Gabriel Rossetti on what he saw as the Dalziels' mistreatment of his drawings:

> These engravers! What ministers of wrath! Your drawing comes to them, like Agag, delicately, and is hewn in pieces before the Lord Harry. I took more pains with one block lately than I had done with anything for a long while. It came back to me on paper, the other day, with Dalziel performing his cannibal jig in the corner, and I have really felt like an invalid ever since. As yet, I fare best with W. J. Linton. He keeps stomack aches for you, but Dalziel deals in fevers and agues.

Rossetti's view was not, however, shared by most illustrators, whose appreciative letters to the Dalziels are quoted extensively in the biographical memoir *The Brothers Dalziel: A Record of Work 1840–1890* (1901).

The Dalziels' influence extended beyond the engraving of illustrations to commissioning them

Illustration by Alfred Crowquill for his fairy tale "Heinrich; or The Love of Gold" (courtesy of the Lilly Library, Indiana University)

from artists. They produced lavish editions such as *The Arabian Nights Entertainments: Dalziels' Illustrated Edition* (1864) and *Dalziel's Bible Gallery* (1880), whose illustrators included such major figures of the period as Tenniel, A. B. Houghton, G. J. Pinwell, John Everett Millais, and William Holman Hunt. These two volumes were part of a series called Dalziel's Fine Art Books. Designed to appeal to the whole family, these volumes are landmarks in the history of children's books as well as of illustration in general. Unlike Edmund Evans, who had an engraving workshop and his own press, the Dalziels had to make arrangements with publishers to print their books, until they established their own small printing office, the Camden Press, in 1857. Through their commissions to artists and their promotion of fine-art books, the Dalziels, according to Gordon N. Ray, "became the leading patrons of book illustrators in general, as well as a sort of special providence to a few of them."

While the Dalziels are now known principally for their work as engravers and promoters of fine illustrated editions, all four of the brothers active in the firm – Edward, George, John, and Thomas – also designed illustrations, as did Edward's son, E. G.

Dalziel. Thomas, however, was the only one to make his living primarily by painting and drawing. He contributed heavily to many of the firm's volumes, including *The Bible Gallery,* and helped to illustrate *National Nursery Rhymes and Nursery Songs* (1870) and *Christmas Carols* (1871). Reid refers dismissively to "some forty others, unimportant children's tales for the most part," as "high-class journeyman work." Thomas Dalziel's chief success was in his creation of evocative landscapes and natural scenes. Edward was less prolific and skilled as an illustrator than Thomas, but he contributed to many of the same collections, such as *The Arabian Nights* and *National Nursery Rhymes,* and drew children with particular delicacy and charm.

In his fifty-year-long working career Alfred Henry Forrester (1804-1872), better known as "Alfred Crowquill," wrote and illustrated many books for children, as well as working as a newspaper artist, a writer and illustrator of books for adults, a painter, a sculptor, and a designer for the theater. Despite his considerable output, his reputation has not survived as well as those of his contemporaries. References to him by Graham Everitt and Ray, and in the *Dictionary of National Biography,* for example, tend to disparage him in relation to other comic artists such as Browne, John Leech, and Tenniel.

The nom de plume "Alfred Crowquill" was first used jointly by Forrester and his older brother, Charles Robert Forrester (1803-1850). The brothers were born in London, sons of a public notary working on the Royal Exchange, and they were educated at a private school in Islington. Both followed their father into his profession, but Alfred, unlike Charles, never became a sworn notary. He broke his connection with the city in 1839, although he retained a close relationship with his brother. The financial success of the family business enabled him to practice his chosen professions of literature and art as a privileged amateur.

Alfred's abilities in these latter fields became evident early; at eighteen he began writing for periodicals such as *The Hive* and *The Mirror,* and he studied drawing, modeling, and wood and steel engraving, contributing caricatures to periodicals and illustrating *Der Freishutz Travestied* in 1824. When Alfred illustrated his brother's contributions to *Bentley's Miscellany* in 1840 (the woodcuts were later published in two volumes as *The Phantasmagoria of Fun,* 1843), they began to use "Alfred Crowquill" as a joint name; after Charles retired from literary life in 1843, however, the name came to be understood as referring to Alfred Forrester only. One of the brothers' collaborative works was aimed at children: *The Pictorial Grammar* (1842) has a fairly staid text by Charles, enlivened by Alfred's comical illustrations.

Crowquill was an early contributor to the comic and satiric weekly *Punch,* founded in 1841, and indeed many of the important children's book illustrators to follow – including Doyle, Bennett, Leech, and Tenniel – were "*Punch* men." Crowquill left *Punch* in 1844 to join the literary and pictorial staff of the *Illustrated London News.* His books for children began to appear in 1842 and quickly became his best-known works. He published many series in the 1850s, such as the cheaply produced Alfred Crowquill's Fairy Tales, Comic Nursery Tales, and Little Plays for Little Actors, as well as more carefully executed and expensively produced volumes such as Miss Corner's *Familiar Fables: In Easy Language, Suited to the Juvenile Mind* (1854) and his own *Fairy Footsteps: or Lessons from Legends* (1861). The quality of Crowquill's work varies considerably. He seems to have enjoyed drawing groups of people in action, although he never had John Leech's ability to portray gesture and movement. Like all the *Punch* caricaturists, he excelled at depicting comical human physiognomies, expressing a range of character and emotion. His animal characters are competently drawn (as in *Picture Fables,* 1854) but lack the expressiveness achieved by Bennett or Tenniel.

Crowquill was particularly successful in some of his illustrations for fairy tales and tall tales, such as an edition of *The Travels and Surprising Adventures of Baron Munchausen* (1859) and a similar volume of mock travel narratives, Constantino Giuseppe Beschi's *Strange Surprising Adventures of the Venerable Gooroo Simple, and His Five Disciples, Noodle, Doodle, Wiseacre, Zany, and Foozle* (1861). Absurd adventures clearly appealed to Crowquill; they are depicted literally, in a matter-of-fact style. The Gooroo Simple pictures are particularly detailed and lively, with some woodcuts set directly into the text and others on separate plates. This volume differs from some of Crowquill's earlier work in depicting black characters fairly realistically; his Friday in an 1844 child's version of *Robinson Crusoe* by F. W. N. Bayley is grotesque, as are the black figures in his unpleasantly racist volume *Drolleries for Young England* (1854). Crowquill was also attracted to the moralistic fairy tale, such as his book *Gruffel Swillendrinken: Or the Reproof of the Beasts* (1856), in which a lion teaches a drunken wife-beater that even the lowest of the animals would scorn such behavior.

Another aspect of Crowquill's life that influenced his book illustration was his involvement with the theatre. Graham Everitt notes that "most of the Christmas pantomimes of his time were indebted to him for clever designs, devices, and effects." Crowquill illustrated at least two series of fairy tales in dramatic form, intended to be acted by children. Not surprisingly, the figures in these little books tend to exhibit theatrical poses.

Forrester was apparently a delightful individual: according to Everitt, he "was talented and clever, – a universal favourite. He could draw, he could write; he was an admirable vocalist, setting the table in a roar with his medley of songs." Two of his early children's books, *The Pictorial Grammar* (1842), done with John Leech, and *Alfred Crowquill's Pictorial Arithmetic* (1843), undoubtedly entertained many a child, as did *Alfred Crowquill's Comic History of the Kings and Queens of England,* a folding "panorama" with verses (circa 1850). While he never achieved the rank of a great illustrator, Crowquill's humor and the spirit of carefree willingness conveyed in his designs delighted many children of his day and helped to set the tone of playfulness and fantasy that came into English children's literature in the mid nineteenth century. Forrester died in London on 26 May 1872.

Although best known as the illustrator of most of Charles Dickens's novels, Hablot Knight Browne (1815–1882), or "Phiz," was a prolific artist who did a considerable amount of work for children, much of it of high quality. The pseudonym Phiz was taken to fit with Dickens's pen name "Boz"; either Browne's real name or Phiz appears, apparently indiscriminately, on title pages of his children's books. Energy, humor, and a delight in human oddity characterize Browne's illustrations for both adults and children; his pictures are typically filled with characters and details, but in his best work all of the elements of the picture work together to convey an impression of the abundance and variety of life. Because his work for Dickens is so well known, Browne's drawings have come to characterize Victorian illustration for many people.

Born on 15 June 1815 at Kennington, Surrey, Browne was the ninth son and the thirteenth of fourteen children. He received his unusual first name, Hablot (sometimes erroneously spelled Hablôt), in memory of a French officer to whom his sister was engaged, but who was killed at Waterloo in the year of the artist's birth. The Browne family was of Huguenot descent and comfortably middle class; in the economic depression following the Napoleonic wars, however, the artist's father, William Loder Browne, suffered financially. Hablot Browne attended a private school in Botesdale, Suffolk, run

Illustration by Hablot Knight Browne for James Greenwood's
The Little Ragamuffin *(1866)*

a memorable collaboration that lasted through twenty years and ten novels. Dickens's was the controlling hand in their relationship, directing Browne closely as to the subjects and appearance of his drawings, but Browne's suggestions could alter the novelist's mind. For years the two were close friends, traveling together and looking for new material for their books, as in the trip they took to Yorkshire to gather impressions for the brutal school in *The Life and Adventures of Nicholas Nickleby* (1839).

Browne was also the principal illustrator for the novels of Charles Lever, one of which – *St. Patrick's Eve* (1845) – makes a dramatic representation for younger readers of the problems of absentee land ownership in Ireland. Browne worked for other novelists, including Thackeray, Anthony Trollope, and Robert Smith Surtees. He was noted for his engraved plates, dense with characters and activity but also exhibiting fine and expressive detail, particularly of facial features. Like many illustrators of his generation, Browne drew from memory rather than using models, and he developed a remarkably acute eye for the revealing gesture or movement; Leech, the great sporting illustrator, once said, "I wish I could draw horses like Browne."

In 1840 Browne married a Miss Reynolds, and in 1846 he moved from London to Thornton Heath, Surrey, to provide healthier and less hectic surroundings for his rapidly expanding family. His children's books began to appear in the early 1850s, when he was at the height of his powers. His twenty-four hand-colored engravings for Jane Euphemia Saxby's *Aunt Effie's Rhymes for Little Children* (1852) reveal his skill in a delightful variety of genres – anthropomorphized animals, animated carpenter's tools and alphabet letters, and the realistic depiction of domestic scenes, with natural-looking children in many activities and moods.

Browne's illustrations for J. C. Maitland's *The Doll and Her Friends; or Memories of the Lady Seraphina* (1852), Harriet Myrtle's *Home and Its Pleasures: Simple Stories for Young People* (1852), Mary and Elizabeth Kirby's *The Talking Bird; or, The Little Girl Who Knew What Was Going to Happen* (1856), and Matilda Barbara Betham-Edwards's *Snow-Flakes and the Stories They Told the Children* (1862) reveal his gentle humor and intimate sympathy with the pleasures and concerns of a young child's home life, as well as his capacity for fantasizing the child's familiar surroundings in animated dolls and snowflakes. Excursions into more overtly fantastic subjects, as in Anna Eliza Kempe Stothard's *A Peep at the Pixies; or,*

by the Reverend William Haddock, who recognized and encouraged the boy's artistic gifts and remained a lifelong friend. Browne was apprenticed to an engraver named Finden, under whom he learned the technical craft of engraving and developed his skill in drawing. In 1833, at the age of eighteen, he was awarded the Isis Medal of the Society of Arts for his engraving "John Gilpin's Ride."

Leaving his apprenticeship early, Browne set up business in partnership with another Finden pupil, Robert Young, who was to engrave much of Browne's work and handle business affairs throughout Browne's career. The suicide of Robert Seymour left a vacancy for an illustrator to work with Dickens on the monthly parts of *The Posthumous Papers of the Pickwick Club* (1836–1837); Browne, only twenty-one, was chosen over applicants including Thackeray and the young John Leech. Thus began

Legends of the West (1854) or "Tom Thumb" in Henry W. Dulcken's *Our Favourite Fairy Tales and Famous Histories* (1858), show Browne's inventiveness as a fairy illustrator; it is unfortunate that his pictures for *Grimm's Goblins* (1861) in Vickers's Fairy Books for Boys and Girls series were cheaply and unattractively reproduced and spoiled by the crude color overprinting (despite the publishers' assertion that "some of [Phiz'] designs in this work will be acknowledged in after years as his masterpieces").

Overwork — a common problem for the professional illustrator in the mid-Victorian period — and a reluctance to adapt his style to the prevailing fashions of the 1860s led to a falling-off in Browne's popularity. He was dropped by Dickens in 1864, and his work on the novels of Trollope and Lever was also terminated for various reasons. Browne frequently had to resort to hackwork and the treatment of uncongenial subjects. His name, once so potent, is sometimes not acknowledged on title pages, although immediately after his death Routledge capitalized on the nostalgia it aroused by reissuing some of his children's work done in the 1850s. Even in his later years, however, Browne was capable of outstanding illustrations, such as those done for James Greenwood's children's novel *The Little Ragamuffin* (1866).

The following year Browne was stricken with paralysis, apparently a form of polio; although he recovered only partial use of his fingers, he bravely continued to work, until a small annuity granted him by fellow artists from the Royal Academy enabled him to retire to Brighton a few years before his death. A modest, shy, and unworldly man, Browne came increasingly to shrink from social contact, finding happiness in his work and family life, although he was of a good-natured disposition and kept good friends throughout life. In addition to illustrating more than two hundred books, he contributed many illustrations for periodicals and did some work in watercolor and oils.

As is evident from many sketches published in *Punch* and elsewhere, John Leech (1817–1864) had a great interest in children; he enjoyed depicting the sturdy London street urchin quite as much as poking fun at the cossetted middle-class Miss, and his quick eye and kindly humor captured on paper a great variety of Victorian children. A prolific and immensely popular illustrator, Leech unfortunately did few books specifically for children; many of the works he did illustrate, however, such as Dickens's Christmas books, continue to appeal to readers of all ages.

Woodcut illustration by John Leech for Percival Leigh's Jack the Giant Killer *(1843)*

Of Irish descent, John Leech's family had been settled in London for several generations, and his grandfather built the London Coffee House on Ludgate Hill into a prosperous restaurant and hotel. John's father, however, was not such a successful businessman, although during the years immediately after the artist's birth on 29 August 1817, the family — which eventually included a younger brother and five sisters — was still well-off. Life in the stimulating environment of the Coffee House encouraged young John Leech's interest in human character and social behavior. His gifts manifested themselves and were recognized early. Before he was ten, his drawings were shown to John Flaxman, the eminent artist, who, according to Simon Houfe's biography, declared, "Do not let him be cramped by drawing-lessons; let his genius follow its own bent. He will astonish the world."

In January 1825 Leech was sent to Charterhouse School, where Thackeray was an older pupil. Despite his physical delicacy, Leech was more interested in sports than in drawing or academic subjects. On leaving Charterhouse in 1832 Leech became a medical student, attending lectures at St. Bartholomew's Hospital, where he joined a group of lively fellow students including Percival Leigh, Albert Smith, and Gilbert à Beckett, whose writings he would eventually illustrate. The careful drawings he made for anatomy classes were virtually Leech's only training as an artist; his natural ability, however, was so great that when his father's bankruptcy obliged him to leave his medical studies at the age of eighteen to earn a living, he was soon able to support himself through selling caricatures and sketches.

The founding of *Punch* in 1841 provided Leech with an ideal outlet for developing his humorous, gently satiric vision of English social and family life, and he soon became the artistic mainstay of the magazine. His marriage to the pretty and graceful Annie Eaton in May 1842 contributed to the perceptiveness evident in Leech's humorous depiction of the small quirks and follies of the Victorian middle-class family. The Leeches were devasted by the death in 1849 of their first child, Rose, before her second birthday; their second daughter, Ada, was not born until 1854, followed by a son, John, in 1855. The lengthy period of childlessness during his early marriage may have encouraged Leech's interest in drawing children, who are so numerous in his *Punch* drawings, and in the production of some children's books in the 1840s.

Leech's twelve woodcuts illustrating Leigh's *Jack the Giant Killer* (1843) show not only his skill as a draftsman but also a strong vein of fantasy. Young Jack has the jauntiness of the street urchins Leech portrayed in his *Punch* cartoons, but the diverse and comical giants Jack encounters are the chief delight of this little book. One giant has two heads – on top of each other, rather than side-by-side – while another red-nosed giant peers through spectacles. Leech's treatment of fantasy in the steel engravings for *Punch's Snapdragons* is again charming and inventive.

Whimsy rather than fantasy is, however, the general characteristic of Leech's illustrations. Older children could enjoy the humorous treatment of academic subjects in Leigh's Comic Grammars, and in Gilbert Abbott à Beckett's *Comic History of England* (1847) and *Comic History of Rome* (1852). Beckett's punning, facetious, and lengthy text wears a little thin, but Leech's sense of absurdity enlivens the pages through dozens of woodcuts, generally showing a fallible human side of the famous characters of history. King Harold, for instance, is seasick, while William the Conqueror trips and falls flat at Hastings. Leech's humor is never cruel, and his pictures imply a degree of sympathy with his characters' predicaments. While enough background detail is given to set the social and historical milieu, Leech's

apt and economical line vividly conveys the character and the emotion of the central figures.

Leech's most memorable collaboration was with a popular novelist and fellow hunting enthusiast, Robert Smith Surtees. In such novels as *Mr. Sponge's Sporting Tour* (1853), *Handley Cross* (1854), and *'Ask Mama': or, The Richest Commoner in England* (1858), the two men worked out a fertile partnership, in which Surtees incorporated references in his text to Leech's illustrations. Leech also contributed illustrations to all of Dickens's Christmas books and to lesser novels and literary sketches by his *Punch* colleagues. Although successful in his work and popular throughout England for his weekly *Punch* sketches, Leech was burdened by having to support his improvident father and sisters, as well as his own family. Overwork contributed to angina attacks, which led to his death at the age of forty-seven on 29 October 1864.

Another important children's illustrator who worked on *Punch* was the fantasist Richard Doyle (1824–1883). Known throughout his life as Dick or Dicky, he came from a remarkable family of artists: his father, John, was a painter who, as "H.B.," was for some years England's best-known creator of political sketches. Several of Richard's siblings had careers in the arts, and his nephew was Arthur Conan Doyle, the creator of Sherlock Holmes. John Doyle took great pains to develop the abilities of his seven children, educating them at home with tutors and governesses but also taking an active personal interest in their progress. Each of them wrote him a weekly illustrated letter, and each read, exhibited a painting, or performed music in a Sunday family talent show.

Dick Doyle's Journal (1885), a revision of the letters Doyle wrote to his father in 1840, reveals not only a wonderful comic fantasy in the decoration of its pages and its whimsical elaboration of the author's doubts and fears but also the strong moral pressure he was under to fulfill his father's high expectations. The family was Roman Catholic; John Doyle had moved from Ireland to London in 1822 to further his career but instilled in all his children a strong sense of loyalty to their church – a loyalty that was to have a major effect on his oldest son's career.

Doyle showed such remarkable ability that he was able while still only sixteen to arrange for the publication of his first book, *The Tournament; or the Days of Chivalry Revived* (1840), consisting of seven humorous lithographs on the subject of the ill-fated Eglington Tournament. As in much of Dick's work, the main pictures are framed by whimsical borders depicting elfish creatures. This seemingly inexhaustible fund of delicately fantastic figures and activities is one side of his early development; on the other side, he was actively interested in the social scene, and he often walked through the London streets, gathering impressions to record in his sketchbooks. His interest in animals took him to the London zoo, and he read the newly published work of Grandville. Other favorite books of Doyle's youth were Keightley's *Fairy Mythology* (1828) and Croker's *Fairy Legends and Traditions of the South of Ireland* (1825-1828); the works of Sir Walter Scott, full of romance, chivalry, and interest in the legendary and supernatural, also fascinated the young artist.

At the age of eighteen Doyle chose a pseudonym, Dick Kitcat, for his artistic work. That year he collaborated with Leech on copperplate etchings for W. H. Maxwell's comic novel *The Fortunes of Hector O'Halloran and His Man Mark Antony O'Toole* (1843), and he was hired to do drawings for *Punch*. As he had no experience of drawing on woodblocks for engraving, Doyle took lessons from the engraver Joseph Swain. Doyle was an excessively shy and excitable pupil who had great difficulty concentrating on the work at hand, and these qualities were to hamper him throughout his life, resulting in incomplete assignments and aborted projects. Nonetheless, during his seven years with *Punch* Doyle gained confidence and a broader range of social relationships and produced much highly admired work; the design he submitted at the age of twenty was used as the cover of *Punch* for more than one hundred years.

Dickens was sufficiently taken with Doyle's *Punch* drawings to commission him as an illustrator for three of his Christmas books; Doyle, naturally, took the more fantastic subjects, such as the chapter title from *The Chimes: A Goblin Story of Some Bells That Rang an Old Year Out and a New Year In* (1845), which shows a crowd of "dwarf phantoms, spirits, elfin creatures . . . leaping, flying, dropping, pouring from the Bells." Also naturally appealing to Doyle was the opportunity to illustrate J. E. Taylor's 1845 translation of some of the Grimm brothers' fairy tales and the Montalba *Fairy Tales from All Nations* (1849), republished after Doyle's death as *The Doyle Fairy Book*. Thackeray, reviewing the former for *The Morning Chronicle* on 26 December 1845, helped to establish Doyle's subsequent reputation as a fairy artist: "We read every now and then in these legends of certain princes and princesses who are carried off by the little people for awhile, and kept in fairy land. This must have been surely Mr. Doyle's

The murder of the giant; illustration by Doyle for his Story of Jack and the Giants *(1850)*

case, and he must have had the advantage of pencils and paper during his banishment. If any man knows the people and country, he does."

In the late 1840s and early 1850s Doyle was at his most prolific, and he produced four other notable children's books: the illustrations for Mark Lemon's fairy tale, *The Enchanted Doll* (1849); for Thackeray's humorous Ivanhoe sequel, *Rebecca and Rowena: A Romance Upon Romance* (1849); for his own lively version of *The Story of Jack and the Giants* (1850); and for John Ruskin's ecological fairy tale, *The King of the Golden River; or the Black Brothers; a Legend of Stiria* (1851). Doyle's work is characterized by elaborate borders and title pages, with fantastic figures entwined by vegetation. The detail is meticulous, and fine lines and carefully balanced composition show Doyle's lifelong delight in embodying lively, sometimes sentimental – and at other times grotesque – images.

The fertility of Doyle's imagination made it difficult for him to complete individual projects,

Illustration by Charles Henry Bennett for Darcy W. Thompson's Fun and Earnest; or
Rhymes with Reason *(1865)*

however, as he always had so many other ideas he wanted to work on. His exquisite pictures for the story of Sleeping Beauty, eventually published by Routledge as *An Old Fairy Tale Told Anew in Pictures and Verse* (1865), had been promised to the Dalziels for publication in 1850, but Doyle procrastinated so long that the project was finally abandoned.

When Doyle resigned from *Punch* in 1850 – in protest over the magazine's satiric treatment of the pope – he turned exclusively to book illustration and watercolor painting. His comical sketches of the three young Englishmen and their mishaps, which had begun to appear in *Punch,* were published with great success as *The Foreign Tour of Brown, Jones, and Robinson* (1854). The small, naive artist named Brown is a humorous self-portrait. Doyle was selected to depict the everyday adventures of other young men in Thomas Hughes's *The Scouring of the White Horse, or the Long Vacation of a London Clerk* (1859), and Thackeray commissioned him to illustrate his novel *The Newcomes: Memoirs of a Most Respectable Family* (1854–1855).

Doyle rather mechanically illustrated one other children's book, E. H. K. Knatchbull-Hugessen's

Higgledy-Piggledy (1876), but the most imaginative work of his later period was not intended specifically for children. This was *In Fairyland: A Series of Pictures from the Elf World with a Poem by William Allingham* (1869), a collection of drawings exquisitely printed in color by Edmund Evans, who used up to twelve color blocks to achieve the depth and delicacy of color in each picture. The publishers had arranged for the Irish poet William Allingham to write a text for the book, but as neither Doyle nor Allingham had the opportunity to see the other's work first, neither was particularly pleased with the result; the pictures were republished in 1884 – with a story Andrew Lang wrote to fit them – as *The Princess Nobody.*

In his later years Doyle gave up book illustration to concentrate on his watercolor paintings. He never married but was very fond of and popular with the children of his friends and relatives, and he gave considerable help to the medical career of his promising nephew, Arthur Conan Doyle, although distressed by Arthur's rejection of Roman Catholicism. He died from an apoplectic seizure on 11 December 1883.

Another "*Punch* man," Charles Henry Bennett (1829–1867), worked prolifically as an illustrator and writer from the late 1850s until his premature death in 1867. Much of Bennett's best children's work rose out of his situation in those years as father of a rapidly increasing young family, and many of his prefaces and dedications make affectionate reference to the children for whom the stories were originally produced. Many of his picture books have a simplicity and childlike directness in the designs, which differ from the more elaborate decorative styles and sophisticated whimsy characteristic of the period. His technique shows a rapid development during the relatively short time in which he produced children's books, and in several respects he anticipates the work of major children's illustrators to follow.

Bennett apparently had no formal training as an artist; under the great illustrator George Cruikshank, however, Bennett learned to engrave plates for etching and to cut his own woodblocks and thus was relatively unusual among Victorian illustrators in being able to engrave his own pictures. In his chapter on Bennett in *Sing a Song of Sixpence: The English Picture-Book Tradition and Randolph Caldecott* (1986), Brian Alderson speculates, however, that the inadequate engraving and color reproduction of some of Bennett's early children's books by the Edmund Evans firm may have impeded Bennett's development as a picture-book artist, and he notes that after 1858 Bennett seems to have shunned the color-printing process and left the color to be added by hand.

By his early twenties Bennett was contributing humorous pictures to *Diogenes, The Comic Times, Comic News,* and *The Illustrated Times.* A set of drawings from the last, published in book form in 1857 as *Shadows,* launched Bennett's career as a popular creator of picture books. The book's text comprises only a brief caption for each drawing; the nature of the pictures, however, represents Bennett's interest in emblems, or pictures used to represent a spiritual or moral concept. *Shadows* presents drawings of individual human figures, each of which casts a shadow that looks like something else: a sharp-nosed woman in a bonnet casts a shadow of "The Goose," while a self-satisfied dandy casts that of "A Bantum." Beyond the immediate humor of the incongruity between the subject and the unflattering shadow each casts is a satiric commentary by the artist on the foibles of human nature. The distorted appearance of most of the characters in *Shadows* is caused by extremes of dress, or by facial features revealing personality traits such as prudishness,

greed, or gin-tippling; these traits lead Bennett's subjects to cast shadows that disclose their real selves. The beer drinker's crooked arm makes his shadow appear as that of a jug of his favorite brew, and the greedy child is shown by his shadow to be a pig. In its combination of visual games with a moral concern, and an appeal to readers of widely differing ages, *Shadows* looks forward to the late-twentieth-century work of Anthony Browne.

The emblematic approach to art is also evident in Bennett's illustrations for *The Fables of Aesop and Others, Translated into Human Nature* (1857) – the frontispiece to which depicts a man seeing in a mirror the reflection of a fox – and in the 1861 edition of Francis Quarles's book of emblems, which reminds the reader that "an Emblem is but a silent parable"; it also governs his portraits of the characters in an 1860 edition of John Bunyan's *Pilgrim's Progress.* As an illustrator of children's books, however, Bennett developed another side of his talent – his gift for nonsense and whimsical animal drawings, as in *The Frog Who Would a Wooing Go* (circa 1858). Bennett's ability to capture personality and mood is engagingly revealed in the child figures appearing in the corners of the pages of *Old Nurse's Book of Rhymes, Jingles and Ditties* (1858), which its dedication describes as representing "all the different sorts of boys and girls that I could easily call to mind." Bennett seems to have more readily called to mind boys than girls, since the girls in this charming set of child portraits are less interesting and less frequent than the boys; this emphasis on the masculine is generally characteristic of Bennett's work.

The influence of Heinrich Hoffmann's *Struwwelpeter* (1845) is evident in *The Sad History of Greedy Jem and All His Little Brothers* (1858), in which Bennett's comic verses and cartoonlike picture sequences reveal the awful fates of seven naughty boys who are transformed into various animals or objects symbolizing their behavior: Talkative Toby becomes a parrot and Crooked Christopher who slouches is folded into a parcel. Some of Bennett's most appealing books are the works of nonsense and fantasy produced in collaboration with his family. *The Stories That Little Breeches Told and the Pictures Which Charles Bennett Drew for Them* (1863) is a collection of tales in a frame narrative that reveals Bennett's warm relationship with children. Morals to the animal fables are supplied by various family members. The drawings of animals are more skillful and expressive than those in earlier books, and the volume is attractively produced, with fine detail in the engraving. The popularity of *Little Breeches* led to several further collections: *The Book of Blockheads*

*Alice meets the caterpillar; illustration by John Tenniel for
Lewis Carroll's* Alice's Adventures
in Wonderland *(1866)*

(1863) is an alphabet book, with stories about sillies like Alfred the Archer and Isaac the Idler, while *The Sorrowful Ending of Noodledoo* (1865) gives facetious explanations of birdcalls and animal sounds. Bennett's text in this book frequently refers his audience to elements in the accompanying illustration:

> "M-MORE milk to-morrow MOR-NING."
> "Stupid old Cow!" cried the Fish, "you Cows are the most useless things on the face of the earth."
> But just look all round the picture, not forgetting the cheese that is crumbling away at the bottom, and see how that silly little Fish was made to alter his mind.

A similar device of riddling through pictures was used in one of Bennett's early picture books, *The Nine Lives of a Cat: A Tale of Wonder* (1860). One of Bennett's last books, *Lightsome and the Little Golden Lady* (1867), includes twenty-four of his most delicate woodcuts, some set into the text and others on full colored pages. The whimsical subject of this three-chapter story and its pictures shows the

author's continuing delight in absurd characters and fantastic explanations, but fantasy predominates over nonsense – suggesting the direction Bennett's art might have taken had he lived longer.

Bennett's unexpected and early death on 2 April 1867, leaving a family of eight children in financial distress, caused his friends to rally round and revealed how highly he and his work were admired by his fellow artists. A petition for a Civil List pension for Bennett's widow was signed by Charles Kingsley and John Everett Millais, among others, while Bennett's former colleagues at *Punch* staged benefit nights superintended by Sir Arthur Sullivan. While for a century after his death Bennett's reputation was overshadowed by the popularity of contemporaries such as Randolph Caldecott, a revival of interest in this versatile humorist seems to be taking place.

John Tenniel (1820–1914) is remembered as the illustrator of only two children's books, but they are books that ensure his place in any history of children's literature. His acceptance of the commission to illustrate *Alice's Adventures in Wonderland* (1865), a children's story by an obscure Oxford don named Charles Dodgson, writing as "Lewis Carroll," did not seem at the time to be his life's most significant undertaking, and he at first declined to do the sequel, *Through the Looking-Glass, and What Alice Found There* (1872), but it is because of his pictures for these books that Tenniel's name is still well known more than a century later.

Like the rest of this group of Victorian illustrators, Tenniel had little formal training in art but was largely self-taught. He was born on 28 February 1820 in Kensington, the third and youngest son of a well-regarded dancing master and instructor in arms, and he retained a lifelong interest in costume and armor. After attending a private school in Kensington, Tenniel was enrolled at the Schools of the Royal Academy of Art, but he did not remain long as he felt there was no real teaching. Instead, he joined the Clipstone Street Life Academy, where he studied life drawing alongside Charles Keene, who became an important illustrator of the 1860s and a lifelong friend. Tenniel attended anatomy lectures, examined the Elgin marbles and other classical sculpture at the British Museum, and traveled to Munich to study for a short time. At the age of sixteen he exhibited and sold an oil painting at the Society of British Artists, and in the following year he had a narrative painting, a scene from Sir Walter Scott's *The Fortunes of Nigel*, accepted for exhibition at the Royal Academy. This promising beginning to an artistic career was confirmed in 1845 when Tenniel received a commission for paintings in the Houses of Parliament.

Despite these successes in the field of "high art," Tenniel seems to have been strongly drawn to the work of illustration. As a boy he had done an impressive set of drawings for Bunyan's *Pilgrim's Progress* (since lost), and in the 1840s he began to receive some significant commissions – for example, to work on S. C. Hall's *Book of British Ballads* (1842), to illustrate the story of "The Children in the Wood" for James Burns's *Book of Nursery Tales* (1845), and to illustrate an 1854 edition of La Motte-Fouqué's *Undine*.

Most significant, Tenniel produced more than one hundred fine wood engravings for the Reverend Thomas James's version of *Aesop's Fables* (1852), a contribution graciously acknowledged in the author's introduction, which describes the collaboration as "a pleasure which has arisen no less from the kindly spirit of Mr. Tenniel's co-operation, than from the happy results of his skill." The Aesop illustrations attracted the attention of Mark Lemon, the editor of *Punch*, who offered Tenniel a position. After the resignation of Richard Doyle in 1850, Tenniel became, with John Leech, one of the two editorial cartoonists for *Punch*; in what was perhaps a foretaste of his later fame as a children's illustrator, his earliest cartoon represented Lord John Russell as Jack the Giant-Killer. Tenniel remained with the magazine for more than fifty years, retiring in 1901.

While fencing with his father in 1840, Tenniel was injured and lost the sight of his right eye, but he always minimized this disability. Fortunately, Tenniel's artistic career was well begun before the accident occurred. Like Browne and Leech, Tenniel drew from memory rather than from models; his drawing is marked by clarity and simplicity of line and a strong sense of composition. Despite the popularity of the Alice books, Tenniel's contemporaries generally considered his major achievement as an illustrator to be his engravings for Thomas Moore's oriental romance, *Lalla Rookh* (1861).

Although Tenniel was noted for being a genial and even-tempered man, his collaboration with Carroll on *Alice's Adventures in Wonderland* sometimes strained that temper. While in 1865 Carroll was unknown outside Oxford, Tenniel was a national figure thanks to his weekly cartoon in *Punch*, and the early reviews of Carroll's book had much more to say about the illustrations than the text. The two men collaborated closely: Carroll selected the subjects for illustration and corresponded frequently with Tenniel about his drawings, suggesting for ex-

ample that Alice have "less crinoline" in one picture and that the "White Knight must not have whiskers; he must not be made to look old." Tenniel sometimes rejected Carroll's instructions, however, and the Knight retained his whiskers; the artist also made suggestions affecting the text, such as deleting a section of *Through the Looking-Glass* about a wasp in a wig. It was at Tenniel's urging that Carroll rejected the first printing of *Alice's Adventures in Wonderland* on the grounds that the pictures were not clearly reproduced.

Tenniel's representation of Wonderland seems to have been influenced by Carroll's drawings for his original manuscript, "Alice's Adventures Under Ground," but many other influences have been proposed, such as resemblances between the Duchess and the painting of "A Grotesque Old Woman" by (or after) Quentin Massys and between the White Knight and one of Tenniel's *Punch* colleagues, Ponny Mayhew. Alice seems to have been drawn from a composite of several models, and a similar little girl appears in an 1864 *Punch* illustration. The careful design of the illustrations and their somewhat flat, factual quality counterbalance the absurdist fantasy of the text. Although many other fine illustrators such as Arthur Rackham have illustrated the Alice books, Tenniel's illustrations have never been surpassed either in popular or in critical opinion.

Despite the success of *Alice's Adventures in Wonderland*, Tenniel was reluctant to undertake the illustration of its sequel, and Carroll approached Richard Doyle, Joseph Noel Paton, and others before returning to Tenniel, offering to pay his publishers for the artist's time for five months. Eventually Tenniel did undertake the commission, but *Through the Looking-Glass* was to be nearly his last work as an illustrator. When Carroll approached him about yet another book, Stuart Dodgson Collingwood quotes Tenniel as replying, "It is a curious fact that with 'Through the Looking-Glass' the faculty of making drawings for book illustration departed from me, and, notwithstanding all sorts of tempting inducements, I have done nothing in that direction since." Tenniel was knighted in 1893, the only Victorian illustrator, or "black and white" artist, to be so honored. He died on 25 February 1914.

Unlike any of the other illustrators considered here, Arthur Hughes (1832–1915) is equally remembered in the late twentieth century for his work as a painter, one of the later Pre-Raphaelites whose vividly colored and emotionally charged works are widely reproduced. But just as Tenniel's illustra-

Flora shaking hands with a door knocker; illustration by Arthur Hughes for Christina Rossetti's Speaking Likenesses *(1874)*

only fourteen he was permitted to study under Alfred Stevens at the school of design at Somerset House. The following year he was accepted into the Royal Academy schools. Although his technical skill in drawing never matched that of such self-trained illustrators as Leech and Tenniel, Hughes's formal instruction in painting undoubtedly helped him to the career of a "serious" painter that some of the other illustrators had sought but not achieved. Hughes began exhibiting at the Royal Academy in 1849 and continued to have one or more paintings accepted for the annual exhibition there almost every year for the following half-century. These paintings, like those of other Pre-Raphaelite artists, have been rediscovered and newly appreciated in the late twentieth century, after a period of neglect.

The publication in 1850 of the first issue of *The Germ,* the periodical that served briefly as the mouthpiece for the newly formed Pre-Raphaelite Brotherhood, had a great effect on Hughes, and he readily and faithfully adopted the brotherhood's principles of fidelity to nature and attention to detail, as well as its enthusiasm for medieval and literary subject matter. He participated in the painting of the Oxford Union frescoes and joined Sir John Everett Millais and Dante Gabriel Rossetti in contributing illustrations to *The Music Master: A Love Story and Two Series of Day and Night Songs* (1855), a volume of poetry by Rossetti's friend William Allingham. Hughes's most effective illustration in the volume, a group of fairies dancing beside a pond in the moonlight, accompanies "The Fairies," a well-known poem that begins:

Up the airy mountain,
And down the rushy glen,
We dare not go a-hunting
For fear of little men.

As the poem has become a children's classic, the woodcut thus might well be considered Hughes's first illustration for children. In its eerie atmosphere, in the shadowy, supernatural forms of the fairies, and in the delicately detailed bluebells framing the scene, the woodcut anticipates Hughes's later achievement in MacDonald's fantasies.

Hughes married Tryphena Foord in 1855, and they eventually had two sons and three daughters. The artist's fondness for children is evident in his painting quite as much as in his children's book illustration: the child figures in oil paintings such as "Home from the Sea" and "The Rescue" demonstrate the artist's empathy with his young subjects. Living quietly with his family on the outskirts of London, Hughes worked at his painting and re-

tions remain the standard in modern editions of the Alice books, so Hughes's illustrations for George MacDonald's *Dealings with the Fairies* (1867), *The Princess and the Goblin* (1871), and *At the Back of the North Wind* (1871) have retained their popularity through many generations. Despite a long, productive life as a painter, Hughes's career as a book illustrator was practically confined to the years 1867 to 1874; during this short time, however, he did some remarkable work, especially in books for children. His approach to fantasy has a spiritual quality, quite distinct from the whimsy, prettiness, or grotesquerie of most nineteenth-century fantasy illustrations.

Although his father's family was of Welsh descent, from the border town of Oswestry, Arthur, the third and youngest son, was born in London and educated at Archbishop Tenison's grammar school in Long Acre. From an early age he showed great enthusiasm for art, such that when he was ceived considerable praise and patronage: his paintings were often sold directly from the studio. William Morris purchased "April Love" (now in the Tate Gallery), and Ruskin was enthusiastic about his work. For ten years Hughes also held a position as examiner for the South Kensington art schools. He also took students, among whom was Sydney Prior Hall, who helped his teacher illustrate an 1869 edition of Thomas Hughes's *Tom Brown's School Days*. The most striking of Arthur Hughes's contributions to this edition is, surprisingly, not any of the figures – whose sensitive and ethereal quality hardly embodies the author's vision of Rugby boys – but rather a landscape scene, showing the great sweep of horizon and sky above White Horse Hill.

After *The Music Master* Hughes received more commissions to illustrate poetry, including Alfred Tennyson's *Enoch Arden* (1864) and – at the suggestion of William Michael Rossetti – Christina Rossetti's book of children's verse, *Sing-Song. A Nursery Rhyme Book* (1872). The 120 tiny illustrations to the latter delighted Ruskin, but he was distressed by Rossetti and Hughes's next collaboration, the three nightmarish stories of *Speaking Likenesses* (1874). Always at his best in evoking an atmosphere of the supernatural, Hughes did vigorous drawings, full of swirling shapes, to present the frightening fairy children at the party and in the wood, and a curiously disturbing woodcut of Flora shaking hands with an animate door knocker.

Among Hughes's most remarkable fantasy illustrations are those he did for MacDonald's *At the Back of the North Wind* (1870). Again, there is a contrast between a realistically drawn child and a supernatural being who is identified with the forms of Nature. The North Wind always has masses of swirling, Pre-Raphaelite hair and is a powerful female presence, both maternal and subtly erotic. Although Hughes was often criticized for the stiffness of his figure drawing and was said to be happier drawing horses than people, Forrest Reid points out that the remarkable quality of his vision and his empathy with the imaginative side of childhood more than compensates for deficiencies in technique.

At the Back of the North Wind and another MacDonald/Hughes fantasy, *The Princess and the Goblin*, were originally published in the magazine *Good Words for the Young*, which MacDonald edited for several years; Hughes contributed 231 drawings to the first five volumes, as well as a cover design. He also contributed a frontispiece to each of the volumes of the Uniform Edition of Anne Thackeray Richie's novels. After 1874, however, Hughes practically gave up illustration, until approached after the turn of the century by Greville MacDonald to illustrate a 1905 republication of his father's *Phantastes: A Faerie Romance for Men and Women*. "I know of no other living artist who is capable of portraying the spirit of *Phantastes*," Greville wrote in the preface, "and every reader of this edition will, I believe, feel that the illustrations are part of the romance, and will gain through them some perception of the brotherhood between George MacDonald and Arthur Hughes." Hughes also contributed several delicate, humorous, and richly detailed decorations and vignettes to Lilia Scott MacDonald's *Babies' Classics* (1904) and went on to illustrate three of Greville's fairy tales, which are the concluding works of a lifetime devoted to the imaginative apprehension of the beauty and mystery of the world. Hughes died on 22 December 1915.

The literature of nineteenth-century England was uniquely enriched by the collaboration of visual and literary artists. Neither before nor since has adult literature been so abundantly illustrated, and most artists moved freely between adult and juvenile books, finding these categories more fluid and overlapping than they became in the century following. Significant technical advances, including the development of steel plate engraving and color printing, combined with the great demand for their work and offered major illustrators the opportunity to experiment and develop in many directions. The disadvantage of this wealth of opportunity was that some illustrators suffered badly from overwork, and most of those discussed here responded at times to economic pressures and publication deadlines by churning out inferior drawings. Nonetheless, their children's illustrations considered as a whole represent a remarkable achievement in the history of children's literature. Their work has a vitality, directness, and attention to detail that not only has been immensely influential, but also still retains its power to touch and delight the viewer.

Biographies:

E. G. Kitton, *Hablot Knight Browne ('Phiz'), a Memoir* (London: Redway, 1882);

Frederick George Kitton, *John Leech, Artist Humorist: A Biographical Sketch* (London: Redway, 1883);

David Croal Thomson, *The Life and Labours of Hablot Knight Browne* (London: Chapman & Hall, 1884);

W. P. Frith, *John Leech, His Life and Works*, 2 volumes (London: Bentley, 1891);

George Dalziel and Edward Dalziel, *The Brothers Dalziel: A Record of Work 1840–1890* (London: Methuen, 1901);

Cosmo Monkhouse, *The Life and Work of Sir John Tenniel* (London: Art Journal, 1901);

Edgar Browne, *Phiz and Dickens as They Appeared to Edgar Browne* (London: Nisbet, 1913);

Daria Hambourg, *Richard Doyle: His Life and Work* (London: Arts & Technics, 1948);

Francis Sarzano, *Sir John Tenniel* (London: Art & Technics, 1948);

Rodney Engen, *Sir John Tenniel* (Aldershot: Scolar / Brookfield, Vt.: Gower, 1991).

References:

Brian Alderson, *Sing a Song for Sixpence: The English Picture-Book Tradition and Randolph Caldecott* (Cambridge: Cambridge University Press, 1986);

John Barr, *Illustrated Children's Books* (London: British Library, 1986);

John Buchanan-Brown, *Phiz! Illustrator of Dickens' World* (New York: Scribners, 1978);

Jane R. Cohen, "Samuel Williams," in her *Charles Dickens and His Original Illustrators* (Columbus: Ohio State University Press, 1980);

Morton N. Cohen, ed., *The Letters of Lewis Carroll,* 2 volumes (New York: Oxford University Press, 1979);

Stuart Dodgson Collingwood, *The Life and Letters of Lewis Carroll* (London: Unwin, 1898);

Morna Daniels, *Victorian Book Illustration* (London: British Library, 1988);

Eric de Mare, *The Victorian Woodblock Illustrators* (London: Fraser, 1980);

The Diaries of Lewis Carroll, 2 volumes, edited by Roger Lancelyn Green (Westport, Conn.: Greenwood Press, 1971);

Rodney Engen, *Richard Doyle* (Stroud: Catalpa Press, 1983);

Graham Everitt, *English Caricaturists and Graphic Humourists of the Nineteenth Century* (London: Sonnenschein, Le Bas & Lowrey, 1886);

Kate Flint, "Arthur Hughes as Illustrator for Children," in *Children and Their Books: A Celebration of the Work of Iona and Peter Opie,* edited by Gillian Avery and Julia Briggs (Oxford: Clarendon Press, 1989), pp. 201–220;

John Harvey, *Victorian Novelists and Their Illustrators* (London: Sidgwick & Jackson, 1970);

Michael Patrick Hearn, "Alice's Other Parent: John Tenniel as Lewis Carroll's Illustrator," *American Book Collector,* 4 (May–June 1983): 11–20;

Edward Hodnett, *Image and Text: Studies in the Illustration of English Literature* (London: Scolar, 1982);

Simon Houfe, *The Dictionary of British Book Illustrators and Caricaturists 1800–1914,* revised edition (Woodbridge, Suffolk: Antique Collectors Club, 1981);

Houfe, *John Leech and the Victorian Scene* (Woodbridge, Suffolk: Antique Collectors Club, 1984);

Kenneth Lindley, *The Woodblock Engravers* (Newton Abbot: David & Charles, 1970);

William James Linton, *The Masters of Wood-Engraving* (London: B. F. Stevens, 1889);

Bertha E. Mahony and others, *Illustrators of Children's Books 1744–1945* (Boston: Horn Book, 1947);

Roderick F. McGillis, "Tenniel's Turned Rabbit: A Reading of *Alice* with Tenniel's Help," *English Studies in Canada,* 3 (1977): 326–335;

Percy Muir, *English Children's Books 1600 to 1900* (London: Batsford / New York: Frederick A. Praeger, 1954);

Muir, *Victorian Illustrated Books* (London: Batsford, 1971);

Gordon N. Ray, *The Illustrator and the Book in England From 1790 to 1914* (London: Constable, 1976);

Forrest Reid, *Illustrators of the Eighteen Sixties: An Illustrated Survey of the Work of 58 British Artists* (London: Faber & Gwyer, 1928);

June Rose, *The Drawings of John Leech* (London: Art & Technics, 1950);

Janet Adam Smith, *Children's Illustrated Books* (London: Collins, 1948);

Joyce Irene Whalley and Tessa Rose Chester, *A History of Children's Book Illustration* (London: John Murray, 1988).

Books for Further Reading

Alderson, Brian. *Sing a Song for Sixpence: The English Picture-Book Tradition and Randolph Caldecott*. Cambridge: Cambridge University Press, 1986.

Auerbach, Nina. *Woman and the Demon: The Life of a Victorian Myth*. Cambridge, Mass. & London: Harvard University Press, 1982.

Auerbach and U. C. Knoepflmacher. *Forbidden Journeys: Fairy Tales and Fantasies by Victorian Women Writers*. Chicago: University of Chicago Press, 1992.

Avery, Gillian. *Childhood's Pattern: A Study of the Heroes and Heroines of Children's Fiction, 1770–1950*. London: Hodder & Stoughton, 1975.

Avery. *The Echoing Green: Memories of Victorian Youth*. New York: Viking, 1974.

Avery and Angela Bull. *Nineteenth Century Children: Heroes and Heroines in English Children's Stories 1780–1900*. London: Hodder & Stoughton, 1965.

Barr, John. *Illustrated Children's Books*. London: British Library, 1986.

Bingham, Jane. *Writers for Children: Critical Studies of Major Authors Since the Seventeenth Century*. New York: Scribners, 1988.

Bradley, Ian. *The Call to Seriousness: The Evangelical Impact on the Victorians*. New York: Macmillan, 1976.

Brantlinger, Patrick. *Rule of Darkness: British Literature and Imperialism, 1830–1914*. Ithaca & London: Cornell University Press, 1988.

Bratton, J. S. *The Impact of Victorian Children's Fiction*. London: Croom Helm, 1981.

Brownell, David. *The Worlds of Victorian Fiction*. Cambridge, Mass.: Harvard University Press, 1975.

Buckley, Jerome Hamilton. *The Victorian Temper: A Study in Literary Culture*. Cambridge, Mass.: Harvard University Press, 1969.

Carpenter, Humphrey. *Secret Gardens: A Study of the Golden Age of Children's Literature*. London: Allen & Unwin / Boston: Houghton Mifflin, 1985.

Carpenter and Mari Prichard. *The Oxford Companion to Children's Literature*. Oxford: Oxford University Press, 1984.

Chapman, Raymond. *Faith and Revolt: Studies in the Literary Influence of the Oxford Movement*. London: Weidenfeld & Nicolson, 1970.

Colby, Vineta. *Yesterday's Woman: Domestic Realism in the English Novel*. Princeton, N.J.: Princeton University Press, 1974.

Cox, Jack. *Take a Cold Tub, Sir! The Story of the Boy's Own Paper*. Guildford: Lutterworth Press, 1983.

Crow, Duncan. *The Victorian Woman*. London: Allen & Unwin, 1971.

Cutt, Margaret Nancy. *Ministering Angels: A Study of Nineteenth-Century Evangelical Writing for Children*. Wormley Broxbourne: Five Owls Press, 1979.

Daniels, Morna. *Victorian Book Illustration*. London: British Library, 1988.

Darton, F. J. Harvey. *Children's Books in England: Five Centuries of Social Life,* third edition. Revised by Alderson. Cambridge: Cambridge University Press, 1982.

Drotner, Kirsten. *English Children and Their Magazines, 1751–1945*. New Haven & London: Yale University Press, 1982.

Duffy, Maureen. *The Erotic World of Faerie*. London: Hodder & Stoughton, 1962.

Dusinberre, Juliet. *Alice to the Lighthouse: Children's Books and Radical Experiments in Art*. New York: St. Martin's Press, 1987.

Dyhouse, Carol. *Girls Growing Up in Late Victorian and Edwardian England*. London: Routledge & Kegan Paul, 1981.

Frey, Charles H., and John Griffith. *The Literary Heritage of Childhood: An Appraisal of Children's Classics in the Western Tradition*. New York: Greenwood Press, 1987.

Gathorne-Hardy, Jonathan. *The Public School Phenomenon 597–1977*. London: Hodder & Stoughton, 1977.

Green, Roger Lancelyn. *Tellers of Tales: Children's Books and Their Authors from 1800–1964*. London: Edmund Ward, 1965.

Grylls, David. *Guardians and Angels: Parents and Children in Nineteenth-Century Literature*. London & Boston: Faber & Faber, 1978.

Honig, Edith Lazaros. *Breaking the Angelic Image: Woman Power in Victorian Children's Fantasy*. New York: Greenwood Press, 1988.

Houghton, Walter E. *The Victorian Frame of Mind 1830–1870*. New Haven: Yale University Press, 1957.

Jay, Elizabeth. *The Religion of the Heart: Anglican Evangelicalism and the Nineteenth-Century Novel*. Oxford: Clarendon Press, 1979.

Kestner, Joseph. *Protest and Reform: The British Social Narrative by Women, 1827–1867*. Madison: University of Wisconsin Press, 1985.

Laqueur, T. W. *Religion and Respectability: Sunday Schools and Working Class Culture*. New Haven: Yale University Press, 1976.

Mahony, Bertha E., and others, comps. *Illustrators of Children's Books 1744–1945*. Boston: Horn Book, 1947.

Maison, Margaret M. *The Victorian Vision: Studies in the Religious Novel*. New York: Sheed & Ward, 1961.

McCann, P., ed. *Popular Education and Socialization in the Nineteenth Century*. Cambridge: Cambridge University Press, 1977.

McGavran, James Holt, ed. *Romanticism and Children's Literature in Nineteenth-Century England*. Athens: University of Georgia Press, 1991.

Miall, Antony, and Peter Miall. *The Victorian Nursery Book*. New York: Pantheon, 1980.

Moers, Ellen. *Literary Women*. Garden City, N.Y.: Doubleday, 1976.

Muir, Percy. *English Children's Books, 1600–1900*. London: Batsford / New York: Praeger, 1954.

Muresianu, S. A. *The History of the Victorian Christmas Book*. New York: Garland, 1987.

Musgrave, P. W. *From Brown to Bunter: The Life and Death of the School Story*. London & Boston: Routledge & Kegan Paul, 1985.

Nelson, Claudia. *Boys Will Be Girls: The Feminine Ethic and British Children's Fiction, 1857–1917*. New Brunswick, N.J.: Rutgers University Press, 1991.

Pattison, Robert. *The Child Figure in English Literature*. Athens: University of Georgia Press, 1978.

Pickering, Samuel F. Jr. *Moral Instruction and Fiction for Children, 1749–1820*. Athens: University of Georgia Press, 1993.

Pickering. *The Moral Tradition in English Fiction, 1785–1850*. Hanover, N.H.: University Press of New England, 1976.

Pinchbeck, Ivy, and Margaret Hewitt. *Children in English Society,* volume 2. London: Routledge & Kegan Paul / Toronto: University of Toronto Press, 1973.

Prickett, Stephen. *Victorian Fantasy*. Bloomington: Indiana University Press, 1979.

Quigly, Isabel. *The Heirs of Tom Brown: The English School Story*. London: Chatto & Windus, 1982.

Reader, William Joseph. *Victorian England*. London: Batsford/Putnam, 1974.

Reed, John R. *Old School Ties: The Public School in British Literature*. Syracuse: Syracuse University Press, 1964.

Renier, Anne. *Friendship's Offering: An Essay on the Annuals and Gift Books of the Century*. London: Private Libraries Association, 1964.

Richards, Jeffrey. *Happiest Days: The Public Schools in English Fiction*. Manchester: Manchester University Press, 1988.

Rowbotham, Judith. *Good Girls Make Good Wives: Guidance for Girls in Victorian Fiction*. Oxford: Blackwell, 1989.

Salway, Lance. *A Peculiar Gift: Nineteenth-Century Writings on Books for Children*. Harmondsworth: Kestrel/Penguin, 1976.

Showalter, Elaine. *A Literature of Their Own: British Women Novelists from Brontë to Lessing*. Princeton, N.J.: Princeton University Press, 1977.

Smith, Janet Adams. *Children's Illustrated Books*. London: Collins, 1948.

Street, Brian. *The Savage in Literature*. London: Routledge & Kegan Paul, 1975.

Summerfield, Geoffrey. *Fantasy and Reason: Children's Literature in the Eighteenth Century.* Athens: University of Georgia Press, 1985.

Townsend, John Rowe. *Written for Children: An Outline of English Children's Literature,* fourth edition. New York: HarperCollins, 1992.

Vance, Norman. *The Sinews of the Spirit: The Ideal of Christian Manliness in Victorian Literature and Religious Thought.* Cambridge: Cambridge University Press, 1985.

Walvin, James. *A Child's World: A Social History of English Childhood, 1800–1914.* Harmondsworth, Middlesex: Penguin, 1982.

Whalley, Joyce Irene, and Tessa Rose Chester. *A History of Children's Book Illustration.* London: John Murray, 1988.

Wolff, Robert Lee. *Gains and Losses: Novels of Faith and Doubt in Victorian England.* New York: Garland, 1977.

Zipes, Jack. *Fairy Tales and the Art of Subversion.* New York: Wildman, 1983.

Contributors

Celia Catlett Anderson...*Eastern Connecticut State University*
George R. Bodmer ....*Indiana University Northwest*
Joel D. Chaston..*Southwest Missouri State University*
Diana A. Chlebek...*University of Akron*
Janis Dawson...*Simon Fraser University*
Patricia Demers...*University of Alberta*
Gwyneth Evans..*Malaspina University College*
Adele M. Fasick ....*University of Toronto*
Lois Rauch Gibson...*Coker College*
A. Waller Hastings...*Northern State University*
Madelyn Holmes ....*George Washington University*
Craig Howes...*University of Hawaii at Manoa*
Leslie Howsam...*University of Windsor*
Douglas Ivison ....*Université de Montréal*
Judith Gero John ....*Southwest Missouri State University*
Michael Scott Joseph..*Rutgers University Libraries*
Frederick Rankin MacFadden Jr. ....*Coppin State College*
Roderick McGillis ....*University of Calgary*
Ann R. Montanaro...*Rutgers University*
Claudia Nelson ....*Southwest Texas State University*
Marilynn Strasser Olson ....*Southwest Texas State University*
Judith A. Overmier ....*University of Oklahoma*
Lopa Prusty ....*Boston College*
Brendan A. Rapple...*Boston College*
Alan Richardson ....*Boston College*
Peter D. Sieruta...*Wayne State University*
Carolyn Sigler ....*Kansas State University*
Karen Patricia Smith....................................*Queens College, City University of New York*
Nigel Spence ....*University of New England*
Jan Susina..*Illinois State University*
Nicola D. Thompson ....*State University of New York, College at Cortland*
Linda J. Turzynski ....*Rutgers University*
Kay E. Vandergrift...*Rutgers University*
Judy Anne White..*Morgan State University*
Naomi J. Wood...*Kansas State University*

Cumulative Index

Dictionary of Literary Biography, Volumes 1-163
Dictionary of Literary Biography Yearbook, 1980-1994
Dictionary of Literary Biography Documentary Series, Volumes 1-13

Cumulative Index

DLB before number: *Dictionary of Literary Biography*, Volumes 1-163
Y before number: *Dictionary of Literary Biography Yearbook*, 1980-1994
DS before number: *Dictionary of Literary Biography Documentary Series*, Volumes 1-13

A

Abbey Press DLB-49

The Abbey Theatre and Irish Drama,
    1900-1945 ....DLB-10

Abbot, Willis J. 1863-1934 ....DLB-29

Abbott, Jacob 1803-1879 ....DLB-1

Abbott, Lee K. 1947- DLB-130

Abbott, Lyman 1835-1922 ....DLB-79

Abbott, Robert S. 1868-1940 ....DLB-29, 91

Abelard, Peter circa 1079-1142 .....DLB-115

Abelard-Schuman DLB-46

Abell, Arunah S. 1806-1888 ....DLB-43

Abercrombie, Lascelles 1881-1938 ...DLB-19

Aberdeen University Press
    Limited DLB-106

Abish, Walter 1931- DLB-130

Ablesimov, Aleksandr Onisimovich
    1742-1783 ....DLB-150

Abrahams, Peter 1919- DLB-117

Abrams, M. H. 1912- DLB-67

Abrogans circa 790-800 ....DLB-148

Abse, Dannie 1923- DLB-27

Academy Chicago Publishers DLB-46

Accrocca, Elio Filippo 1923- DLB-128

Ace Books DLB-46

Achebe, Chinua 1930- DLB-117

Achtenberg, Herbert 1938- DLB-124

Ackerman, Diane 1948- DLB-120

Ackroyd, Peter 1949- DLB-155

Acorn, Milton 1923-1986 ....DLB-53

Acosta, Oscar Zeta 1935?- DLB-82

Actors Theatre of Louisville DLB-7

Adair, James 1709?-1783? DLB-30

Adam, Graeme Mercer 1839-1912 ...DLB-99

Adame, Leonard 1947- DLB-82

Adamic, Louis 1898-1951 ....DLB-9

Adams, Alice 1926- Y-86

Adams, Brooks 1848-1927 ....DLB-47

Adams, Charles Francis, Jr.
    1835-1915 ....DLB-47

Adams, Douglas 1952- Y-83

Adams, Franklin P. 1881-1960 ......DLB-29

Adams, Henry 1838-1918 ....DLB-12, 47

Adams, Herbert Baxter 1850-1901 ...DLB-47

Adams, J. S. and C.
    [publishing house] DLB-49

Adams, James Truslow 1878-1949 ...DLB-17

Adams, John 1735-1826 ....DLB-31

Adams, John Quincy 1767-1848 .....DLB-37

Adams, Léonie 1899-1988 ....DLB-48

Adams, Levi 1802-1832 ....DLB-99

Adams, Samuel 1722-1803 ......DLB-31, 43

Adams, Thomas
    1582 or 1583-1652 ....DLB-151

Adams, William Taylor 1822-1897 ..DLB-42

Adamson, Sir John 1867-1950 ......DLB-98

Adcock, Arthur St. John
    1864-1930 ....DLB-135

Adcock, Betty 1938- DLB-105

Adcock, Betty, Certain Gifts DLB-105

Adcock, Fleur 1934- DLB-40

Addison, Joseph 1672-1719 ....DLB-101

Ade, George 1866-1944 ....DLB-11, 25

Adeler, Max (see Clark, Charles Heber)

Adonias Filho 1915-1990 ....DLB-145

Advance Publishing Company DLB-49

AE 1867-1935 ....DLB-19

Ælfric circa 955-circa 1010 ....DLB-146

Aesthetic Poetry (1873), by
    Walter Pater DLB-35

After Dinner Opera Company Y-92

Afro-American Literary Critics:
    An Introduction DLB-33

Agassiz, Jean Louis Rodolphe
    1807-1873 ....DLB-1

Agee, James 1909-1955 ......DLB-2, 26, 152

The Agee Legacy: A Conference at
    the University of Tennessee
    at Knoxville Y-89

Aguilera Malta, Demetrio
    1909-1981 ....DLB-145

Ai 1947- DLB-120

Aichinger, Ilse 1921- DLB-85

Aidoo, Ama Ata 1942 ....DLB-117

Aiken, Conrad 1889-1973 ....DLB-9, 45, 102

Aiken, Joan 1924- DLB-161

Aikin, Lucy 1781-1864 ....DLB-144, 163

Ainsworth, William Harrison
    1805-1882 ....DLB-21

Aitken, George A. 1860-1917 ......DLB-149

Aitken, Robert [publishing house] ...DLB-49

Akenside, Mark 1721-1770 ....DLB-109

Akins, Zoë 1886-1958 ....DLB-26

Alabaster, William 1568-1640 ......DLB-132

Alain-Fournier 1886-1914 ....DLB-65

Alarcón, Francisco X. 1954- DLB-122

Alba, Nanina 1915-1968 ....DLB-41

Albee, Edward 1928- DLB-7

Albert the Great circa 1200-1280 ...DLB-115

Alberti, Rafael 1902- DLB-108

Alcott, Amos Bronson 1799-1888 .....DLB-1

Alcott, Louisa May
    1832-1888 ....DLB-1, 42, 79

Alcott, William Andrus 1798-1859 ....DLB-1

Alcuin circa 732-804 ....DLB-148

Alden, Henry Mills 1836-1919 ......DLB-79

Alden, Isabella 1841-1930 ....DLB-42

Alden, John B. [publishing house] DLB-49

Alden, Beardsley and Company DLB-49

Aldington, Richard
    1892-1962 ....DLB-20, 36, 100, 149

Aldis, Dorothy 1896-1966 .... DLB-22

Aldiss, Brian W. 1925- DLB-14

Aldrich, Thomas Bailey
    1836-1907 .... DLB-42, 71, 74, 79

Alegría, Ciro 1909-1967 .... DLB-113

Alegría, Claribel 1924- DLB-145

Aleixandre, Vicente 1898-1984 .... DLB-108

Aleramo, Sibilla 1876-1960 .... DLB-114

Alexander, Charles 1868-1923 ...... DLB-91

Alexander, Charles Wesley
    [publishing house] DLB-49

Alexander, James 1691-1756 .... DLB-24

Alexander, Lloyd 1924- DLB-52

Alexander, Sir William, Earl of Stirling
    1577?-1640 .... DLB-121

Alexis, Willibald 1798-1871 .... DLB-133

Alfred, King 849-899 .... DLB-146

Alger, Horatio, Jr. 1832-1899 .... DLB-42

Algonquin Books of Chapel Hill DLB-46

Algren, Nelson
    1909-1981 .... DLB-9; Y-81, 82

Allan, Andrew 1907-1974 .... DLB-88

Allan, Ted 1916- DLB-68

Allbeury, Ted 1917- DLB-87

Alldritt, Keith 1935- DLB-14

Allen, Ethan 1738-1789 .... DLB-31

Allen, Frederick Lewis 1890-1954 .. DLB-137

Allen, Gay Wilson 1903- DLB-103

Allen, George 1808-1876 .... DLB-59

Allen, George [publishing house] ... DLB-106

Allen, George, and Unwin
    Limited DLB-112

Allen, Grant 1848-1899 .... DLB-70, 92

Allen, Henry W. 1912- Y-85

Allen, Hervey 1889-1949 .... DLB-9, 45

Allen, James 1739-1808 .... DLB-31

Allen, James Lane 1849-1925 .... DLB-71

Allen, Jay Presson 1922- DLB-26

Allen, John, and Company DLB-49

Allen, Samuel W. 1917- DLB-41

Allen, Woody 1935- DLB-44

Allende, Isabel 1942- DLB-145

Alline, Henry 1748-1784 .... DLB-99

Allingham, Margery 1904-1966 ..... DLB-77

Allingham, William 1824-1889 ...... DLB-35

Allison, W. L. [publishing house] ... DLB-49

The *Alliterative Morte Arthure* and
    the *Stanzaic Morte Arthur*
    circa 1350-1400 .... DLB-146

Allott, Kenneth 1912-1973 .... DLB-20

Allston, Washington 1779-1843 ...... DLB-1

Almon, John [publishing house] DLB-154

Alonzo, Dámaso 1898-1990 .... DLB-108

Alsop, George 1636-post 1673 .... DLB-24

Alsop, Richard 1761-1815 .... DLB-37

Altemus, Henry, and Company DLB-49

Altenberg, Peter 1885-1919 .... DLB-81

Altolaguirre, Manuel 1905-1959 .... DLB-108

Aluko, T. M. 1918- DLB-117

Alurista 1947- DLB-82

Alvarez, A. 1929- DLB-14, 40

Amadi, Elechi 1934- DLB-117

Amado, Jorge 1912- DLB-113

Ambler, Eric 1909- DLB-77

*America: or, a Poem on the Settlement of the
    British Colonies* (1780?), by Timothy
    Dwight DLB-37

American Conservatory Theatre DLB-7

American Fiction and the 1930s DLB-9

American Humor: A Historical Survey
    East and Northeast
    South and Southwest
    Midwest
    West DLB-11

The American Library in Paris Y-93

American News Company DLB-49

The American Poets' Corner: The First
    Three Years (1983-1986) Y-86

American Proletarian Culture:
    The 1930s DS-11

American Publishing Company DLB-49

American Stationers' Company DLB-49

American Sunday-School Union DLB-49

American Temperance Union DLB-49

American Tract Society DLB-49

The American Writers Congress
    (9-12 October 1981) Y-81

The American Writers Congress: A Report
    on Continuing Business Y-81

Ames, Fisher 1758-1808 .... DLB-37

Ames, Mary Clemmer 1831-1884 .... DLB-23

Amini, Johari M. 1935- DLB-41

Amis, Kingsley 1922-
    .... DLB-15, 27, 100, 139

Amis, Martin 1949- DLB-14

Ammons, A. R. 1926- DLB-5

Amory, Thomas 1691?-1788 .... DLB-39

Anaya, Rudolfo A. 1937- DLB-82

Ancrene Riwle circa 1200-1225 ...... DLB-146

Andersch, Alfred 1914-1980 .... DLB-69

Anderson, Margaret 1886-1973 ... DLB-4, 91

Anderson, Maxwell 1888-1959 .... DLB-7

Anderson, Patrick 1915-1979 .... DLB-68

Anderson, Paul Y. 1893-1938 .... DLB-29

Anderson, Poul 1926- DLB-8

Anderson, Robert 1750-1830 ...... DLB-142

Anderson, Robert 1917- DLB-7

Anderson, Sherwood
    1876-1941 .... DLB-4, 9, 86; DS-1

Andreas-Salomé, Lou 1861-1937 .... DLB-66

Andres, Stefan 1906-1970 .... DLB-69

Andreu, Blanca 1959- DLB-134

Andrewes, Lancelot 1555-1626 ..... DLB-151

Andrews, Charles M. 1863-1943 ..... DLB-17

Andrews, Miles Peter ?-1814 .... DLB-89

Andrian, Leopold von 1875-1951 .... DLB-81

Andrić, Ivo 1892-1975 .... DLB-147

Andrieux, Louis (see Aragon, Louis)

Andrus, Silas, and Son DLB-49

Angell, James Burrill 1829-1916 ...... DLB-64

Angelou, Maya 1928- DLB-38

Anger, Jane flourished 1589 .... DLB-136

Angers, Félicité (see Conan, Laure)

Anglo-Norman Literature in the Development
    of Middle English Literature DLB-146

The Anglo-Saxon Chronicle
    circa 890-1154 .... DLB-146

The "Angry Young Men" DLB-15

Angus and Robertson (UK)
    Limited DLB-112

Anhalt, Edward 1914- DLB-26

Anners, Henry F. [publishing house] ...DLB-49

Annolied between 1077 and 1081 .... DLB-148

Anselm of Canterbury 1033-1109 ...DLB-115

Anstey, F. 1856-1934 .... DLB-141

Anthony, Michael 1932- DLB-125

Anthony, Piers 1934- DLB-8

Anthony Burgess's *99 Novels*:
    An Opinion Poll Y-84

Antin, Mary 1881-1949 .... Y-84

Antschel, Paul (see Celan, Paul)

Anyidoho, Kofi 1947- DLB-157

Anzaldúa, Gloria 1942- DLB-122

Anzengruber, Ludwig 1839-1889 ...DLB-129

Apodaca, Rudy S. 1939- DLB-82

Apple, Max 1941- DLB-130

Appleton, D., and Company DLB-49

Appleton-Century-Crofts DLB-46

Applewhite, James 1935- DLB-105

Apple-wood Books DLB-46

Aquin, Hubert 1929-1977 .... DLB-53

Aquinas, Thomas 1224 or
    1225-1274 .... DLB-115

Aragon, Louis 1897-1982 .... DLB-72

Arbor House Publishing
    Company DLB-46

Arbuthnot, John 1667-1735 .... DLB-101

Arcadia House DLB-46

Arce, Julio G. (see Ulica, Jorge)

Archer, William 1856-1924 .... DLB-10

The Archpoet circa 1130?-? DLB-148

Archpriest Avvakum (Petrovich)
    1620?-1682 .... DLB-150

Arden, John 1930- DLB-13

Arden of Faversham DLB-62

Ardis Publishers Y-89

Ardizzone, Edward 1900-1979 ..... DLB-160

Arellano, Juan Estevan 1947- DLB-122

The Arena Publishing Company DLB-49

Arena Stage DLB-7

Arenas, Reinaldo 1943-1990 ...... DLB-145

Arensberg, Ann 1937- Y-82

Arguedas, José María 1911-1969 ... DLB-113

Argueta, Manilio 1936- DLB-145

Arias, Ron 1941- DLB-82

Arland, Marcel 1899-1986 .... DLB-72

Arlen, Michael 1895-1956 .. DLB-36, 77, 162

Armah, Ayi Kwei 1939- DLB-117

Der arme Hartmann
    ?-after 1150 .... DLB-148

Armed Services Editions DLB-46

Armstrong, Richard 1903- DLB-160

Arndt, Ernst Moritz 1769-1860 ..... DLB-90

Arnim, Achim von 1781-1831 .... DLB-90

Arnim, Bettina von 1785-1859 ...... DLB-90

Arno Press DLB-46

Arnold, Edwin 1832-1904 .... DLB-35

Arnold, Matthew 1822-1888 ..... DLB-32, 57

Arnold, Thomas 1795-1842 .... DLB-55

Arnold, Edward
    [publishing house] DLB-112

Arnow, Harriette Simpson
    1908-1986 .... DLB-6

Arp, Bill (see Smith, Charles Henry)

Arreola, Juan José 1918- DLB-113

Arrowsmith, J. W.
    [publishing house] DLB-106

Arthur, Timothy Shay
    1809-1885 ....DLB-3, 42, 79; DS-13

The Arthurian Tradition and Its European
    Context DLB-138

Artmann, H. C. 1921- DLB-85

Arvin, Newton 1900-1963 .... DLB-103

As I See It, by Carolyn Cassady DLB-16

Asch, Nathan 1902-1964 .... DLB-4, 28

Ash, John 1948- DLB-40

Ashbery, John 1927- DLB-5; Y-81

Ashendene Press DLB-112

Asher, Sandy 1942- Y-83

Ashton, Winifred (see Dane, Clemence)

Asimov, Isaac 1920-1992 .... DLB-8; Y-92

Askew, Anne circa 1521-1546 ..... DLB-136

Asselin, Olivar 1874-1937 .... DLB-92

Asturias, Miguel Angel
    1899-1974 .... DLB-113

Atheneum Publishers DLB-46

Atherton, Gertrude 1857-1948 .... DLB-9, 78

Athlone Press DLB-112

Atkins, Josiah circa 1755-1781 ...... DLB-31

Atkins, Russell 1926- DLB-41

The Atlantic Monthly Press DLB-46

Attaway, William 1911-1986 .... DLB-76

Atwood, Margaret 1939- DLB-53

Aubert, Alvin 1930- DLB-41

Aubert de Gaspé, Phillipe-Ignace-François
    1814-1841 .... DLB-99

Aubert de Gaspé, Phillipe-Joseph
    1786-1871 .... DLB-99

Aubin, Napoléon 1812-1890 .... DLB-99

Aubin, Penelope 1685-circa 1731 .... DLB-39

Aubrey-Fletcher, Henry Lancelot
    (see Wade, Henry)

Auchincloss, Louis 1917- DLB-2; Y-80

Auden, W. H. 1907-1973 ....DLB-10, 20

Audio Art in America: A Personal
    Memoir Y-85

Auerbach, Berthold 1812-1882 ..... DLB-133

Auernheimer, Raoul 1876-1948 ...... DLB-81

Augustine 354-430 .... DLB-115

Austen, Jane 1775-1817 .... DLB-116

Austin, Alfred 1835-1913 .... DLB-35

Austin, Mary 1868-1934 ....DLB-9, 78

Austin, William 1778-1841 .... DLB-74

The Author's Apology for His Book
    (1684), by John Bunyan DLB-39

An Author's Response, by
    Ronald Sukenick Y-82

Authors and Newspapers
    Association DLB-46

Authors' Publishing Company DLB-49

Avalon Books DLB-46

Avendaño, Fausto 1941- DLB-82

Averroës 1126-1198 .... DLB-115

Avery, Gillian 1926- DLB-161

Avicenna 980-1037 .... DLB-115

Avison, Margaret 1918- DLB-53

Avon Books DLB-46

Awdry, Wilbert Vere 1911- DLB-160

Awoonor, Kofi 1935- DLB-117

Ayckbourn, Alan 1939- DLB-13

Aymé, Marcel 1902-1967 .... DLB-72

Aytoun, Sir Robert 1570-1638 ...... DLB-121

Aytoun, William Edmondstoune
    1813-1865 ....DLB-32, 159

B

B. V. (see Thomson, James)

Babbitt, Irving 1865-1933 .... DLB-63

Babbitt, Natalie 1932- DLB-52

Babcock, John [publishing house] DLB-49

Baca, Jimmy Santiago 1952- DLB-122

Bache, Benjamin Franklin
    1769-1798 .... DLB-43

Bachmann, Ingeborg 1926-1973 ..... DLB-85

Bacon, Delia 1811-1859 .... DLB-1

Bacon, Francis 1561-1626 .... DLB-151

Bacon, Roger circa
    1214/1220-1292 .... DLB-115

Bacon, Sir Nicholas
circa 1510-1579 .... DLB-132

Bacon, Thomas circa 1700-1768 .... DLB-31

Badger, Richard G.,
and Company DLB-49

Bage, Robert 1728-1801 .... DLB-39

Bagehot, Walter 1826-1877 .... DLB-55

Bagley, Desmond 1923-1983 .... DLB-87

Bagnold, Enid 1889-1981 ...... DLB-13, 160

Bagryana, Elisaveta 1893-1991 ..... DLB-147

Bahr, Hermann 1863-1934 ..... DLB-81, 118

Bailey, Alfred Goldsworthy
1905- DLB-68

Bailey, Francis [publishing house] ... DLB-49

Bailey, H. C. 1878-1961 .... DLB-77

Bailey, Jacob 1731-1808 .... DLB-99

Bailey, Paul 1937- DLB-14

Bailey, Philip James 1816-1902 ..... DLB-32

Baillargeon, Pierre 1916-1967 .... DLB-88

Baillie, Hugh 1890-1966 .... DLB-29

Baillie, Joanna 1762-1851 .... DLB-93

Bailyn, Bernard 1922- DLB-17

Bainbridge, Beryl 1933- DLB-14

Baird, Irene 1901-1981 .... DLB-68

Baker, Augustine 1575-1641 .... DLB-151

Baker, Carlos 1909-1987 .... DLB-103

Baker, David 1954- DLB-120

Baker, Herschel C. 1914-1990 ..... DLB-111

Baker, Houston A., Jr. 1943- DLB-67

Baker, Walter H., Company
("Baker's Plays") DLB-49

The Baker and Taylor Company DLB-49

Balaban, John 1943- DLB-120

Bald, Wambly 1902- DLB-4

Balderston, John 1889-1954 .... DLB-26

Baldwin, James
1924-1987 .... DLB-2, 7, 33; Y-87

Baldwin, Joseph Glover
1815-1864 .... DLB-3, 11

Baldwin, William
circa 1515-1563 .... DLB-132

Bale, John 1495-1563 .... DLB-132

Balestrini, Nanni 1935- DLB-128

Ballantine Books DLB-46

Ballantyne, R. M. 1825-1894 ...... DLB-163

Ballard, J. G. 1930- DLB-14

Ballerini, Luigi 1940- DLB-128

Ballou, Maturin Murray
1820-1895 .... DLB-79

Ballou, Robert O.
[publishing house] DLB-46

Balzac, Honoré de 1799-1855 ...... DLB-119

Bambara, Toni Cade 1939- DLB-38

Bancroft, A. L., and
Company DLB-49

Bancroft, George
1800-1891 ....DLB-1, 30, 59

Bancroft, Hubert Howe
1832-1918 ....DLB-47, 140

Bangs, John Kendrick
1862-1922 ....DLB-11, 79

Banim, John 1798-1842 ...DLB-116, 158, 159

Banim, Michael 1796-1874 ....DLB-158, 159

Banks, John circa 1653-1706 .... DLB-80

Banks, Russell 1940- DLB-130

Bannerman, Helen 1862-1946 ..... DLB-141

Bantam Books DLB-46

Banville, John 1945- DLB-14

Baraka, Amiri
1934- DLB-5, 7, 16, 38; DS-8

Barbauld, Anna Laetitia
1743-1825 ...... DLB-107, 109, 142, 158

Barbeau, Marius 1883-1969 .... DLB-92

Barber, John Warner 1798-1885 ..... DLB-30

Bàrberi Squarotti, Giorgio
1929- DLB-128

Barbey d'Aurevilly, Jules-Amédée
1808-1889 .... DLB-119

Barbour, John circa 1316-1395 .... DLB-146

Barbour, Ralph Henry
1870-1944 .... DLB-22

Barbusse, Henri 1873-1935 .... DLB-65

Barclay, Alexander
circa 1475-1552 .... DLB-132

Barclay, E. E., and Company DLB-49

Bardeen, C. W.
[publishing house] DLB-49

Barham, Richard Harris
1788-1845 .... DLB-159

Baring, Maurice 1874-1945 .... DLB-34

Baring-Gould, Sabine 1834-1924 .... DLB-156

Barker, A. L. 1918- DLB-14, 139

Barker, George 1913-1991 .... DLB-20

Barker, Harley Granville
1877-1946 .... DLB-10

Barker, Howard 1946- DLB-13

Barker, James Nelson 1784-1858 ..... DLB-37

Barker, Jane 1652-1727 .... DLB-39, 131

Barker, William
circa 1520-after 1576 .... DLB-132

Barker, Arthur, Limited DLB-112

Barkov, Ivan Semenovich
1732-1768 ....DLB-150

Barks, Coleman 1937- DLB-5

Barlach, Ernst 1870-1938 ...... DLB-56, 118

Barlow, Joel 1754-1812 ....DLB-37

Barnard, John 1681-1770 ....DLB-24

Barne, Kitty (Mary Catherine Barne)
1883-1957 ....DLB-160

Barnes, Barnabe 1571-1609 ....DLB-132

Barnes, Djuna 1892-1982 ...... DLB-4, 9, 45

Barnes, Julian 1946- Y-93

Barnes, Margaret Ayer 1886-1967 .....DLB-9

Barnes, Peter 1931- DLB-13

Barnes, William 1801-1886 ....DLB-32

Barnes, A. S., and Company DLB-49

Barnes and Noble Books DLB-46

Barnet, Miguel 1940- DLB-145

Barney, Natalie 1876-1972 ....DLB-4

Baron, Richard W.,
Publishing Company DLB-46

Barr, Robert 1850-1912 .... DLB-70, 92

Barral, Carlos 1928-1989 ....DLB-134

Barrax, Gerald William
1933- DLB-41, 120

Barrès, Maurice 1862-1923 ....DLB-123

Barrett, Eaton Stannard
1786-1820 ....DLB-116

Barrie, J. M. 1860-1937 .... DLB-10, 141, 156

Barrie and Jenkins DLB-112

Barrio, Raymond 1921- DLB-82

Barrios, Gregg 1945- DLB-122

Barry, Philip 1896-1949 ....DLB-7

Barry, Robertine (see Françoise)

Barse and Hopkins DLB-46

Barstow, Stan 1928- DLB-14, 139

Barth, John 1930- DLB-2

Barthelme, Donald
1931-1989 .... DLB-2; Y-80, 89

Barthelme, Frederick 1943- Y-85

Bartholomew, Frank 1898-1985 .....DLB-127

Bartlett, John 1820-1905 ....DLB-1

Bartol, Cyrus Augustus 1813-1900 ....DLB-1

Barton, Bernard 1784-1849 ....DLB-96

Barton, Thomas Pennant
1803-1869 ....DLB-140

Bartram, John 1699-1777 ....DLB-31

Bartram, William 1739-1823 ....DLB-37

Basic Books DLB-46

Basille, Theodore (see Becon, Thomas)

Bass, T. J. 1932- Y-81

Bassani, Giorgio 1916- DLB-128

Basse, William circa 1583-1653 .....DLB-121

Bassett, John Spencer 1867-1928 .....DLB-17

Bassler, Thomas Joseph (see Bass, T. J.)

Bate, Walter Jackson 1918- DLB-67, 103

Bateman, Stephen
circa 1510-1584 ....DLB-136

Bates, H. E. 1905-1974 ....DLB-162

Bates, Katharine Lee 1859-1929 .....DLB-71

Batsford, B. T.
[publishing house] DLB-106

Battiscombe, Georgina 1905- DLB-155

The Battle of Maldon circa 1000 .....DLB-146

Bauer, Bruno 1809-1882 ....DLB-133

Bauer, Wolfgang 1941- DLB-124

Baum, L. Frank 1856-1919 ....DLB-22

Baum, Vicki 1888-1960 ....DLB-85

Baumbach, Jonathan 1933- Y-80

Bausch, Richard 1945- DLB-130

Bawden, Nina 1925- DLB-14, 161

Bax, Clifford 1886-1962 ....DLB-10, 100

Baxter, Charles 1947- DLB-130

Bayer, Eleanor (see Perry, Eleanor)

Bayer, Konrad 1932-1964 ....DLB-85

Baynes, Pauline 1922- DLB-160

Bazin, Hervé 1911- DLB-83

Beach, Sylvia 1887-1962 ....DLB-4

Beacon Press DLB-49

Beadle and Adams DLB-49

Beagle, Peter S. 1939- Y-80

Beal, M. F. 1937- Y-81

Beale, Howard K. 1899-1959 ....DLB-17

Beard, Charles A. 1874-1948 ....DLB-17

A Beat Chronology: The First Twenty-five
Years, 1944-1969 ....DLB-16

Beattie, Ann 1947- Y-82

Beattie, James 1735-1803 ....DLB-109

Beauchemin, Nérée 1850-1931 ....DLB-92

Beauchemin, Yves 1941- DLB-60

Beaugrand, Honoré 1848-1906 ......DLB-99

Beaulieu, Victor-Lévy 1945- DLB-53

Beaumont, Francis circa 1584-1616
and Fletcher, John 1579-1625 ...DLB-58

Beaumont, Sir John 1583?-1627 ....DLB-121

Beaumont, Joseph 1616–1699 ......DLB-126

Beauvoir, Simone de
1908-1986 ....DLB-72; Y-86

Becher, Ulrich 1910- DLB-69

Becker, Carl 1873-1945 ....DLB-17

Becker, Jurek 1937- DLB-75

Becker, Jurgen 1932- DLB-75

Beckett, Samuel
1906-1989 ....DLB-13, 15; Y-90

Beckford, William 1760-1844 ....DLB-39

Beckham, Barry 1944- DLB-33

Becon, Thomas circa 1512-1567 ....DLB-136

Beddoes, Thomas 1760-1808 ......DLB-158

Beddoes, Thomas Lovell
1803-1849 ....DLB-96

Bede circa 673-735 ....DLB-146

Beecher, Catharine Esther
1800-1878 ....DLB-1

Beecher, Henry Ward
1813-1887 ....DLB-3, 43

Beer, George L. 1872-1920 ....DLB-47

Beer, Patricia 1919- DLB-40

Beerbohm, Max 1872-1956 .....DLB-34, 100

Beer-Hofmann, Richard
1866-1945 ....DLB-81

Beers, Henry A. 1847-1926 ....DLB-71

Beeton, S. O. [publishing house] ...DLB-106

Bégon, Elisabeth 1696-1755 ....DLB-99

Behan, Brendan 1923-1964 ....DLB-13

Behn, Aphra 1640?-1689 ....DLB-39, 80, 131

Behn, Harry 1898-1973 ....DLB-61

Behrman, S. N. 1893-1973 ....DLB-7, 44

Belaney, Archibald Stansfeld (see Grey Owl)

Belasco, David 1853-1931 ....DLB-7

Belford, Clarke and Company DLB-49

Belitt, Ben 1911- DLB-5

Belknap, Jeremy 1744-1798 ......DLB-30, 37

Bell, Clive 1881-1964 ....DS-10

Bell, James Madison 1826-1902 .....DLB-50

Bell, Marvin 1937- DLB-5

Bell, Millicent 1919- DLB-111

Bell, Quentin 1910- DLB-155

Bell, Vanessa 1879-1961 ....DS-10

Bell, George, and Sons DLB-106

Bell, Robert [publishing house] DLB-49

Bellamy, Edward 1850-1898 ....DLB-12

Bellamy, Joseph 1719-1790 ....DLB-31

Bellezza, Dario 1944- DLB-128

La Belle Assemblée 1806-1837 ....DLB-110

Belloc, Hilaire
1870-1953 ....DLB-19, 100, 141

Bellow, Saul
1915- DLB-2, 28; Y-82; DS-3

Belmont Productions DLB-46

Bemelmans, Ludwig 1898-1962 ......DLB-22

Bemis, Samuel Flagg 1891-1973 ....DLB-17

Bemrose, William
[publishing house] DLB-106

Benchley, Robert 1889-1945 ....DLB-11

Benedetti, Mario 1920- DLB-113

Benedictus, David 1938- DLB-14

Benedikt, Michael 1935- DLB-5

Benét, Stephen Vincent
1898-1943 ....DLB-4, 48, 102

Benét, William Rose 1886-1950 .....DLB-45

Benford, Gregory 1941- Y-82

Benjamin, Park 1809-1864 .....DLB-3, 59, 73

Benlowes, Edward 1602-1676 ......DLB-126

Benn, Gottfried 1886-1956 ....DLB-56

Benn Brothers Limited DLB-106

Bennett, Arnold
1867-1931 ....DLB-10, 34, 98, 135

Bennett, Charles 1899- DLB-44

Bennett, Gwendolyn 1902- DLB-51

Bennett, Hal 1930- DLB-33

Bennett, James Gordon 1795-1872 ...DLB-43

Bennett, James Gordon, Jr.
1841-1918 ....DLB-23

Bennett, John 1865-1956 ....DLB-42

Bennett, Louise 1919- DLB-117

Benoit, Jacques 1941- DLB-60

Benson, A. C. 1862-1925 ....DLB-98

Benson, E. F. 1867-1940 ....DLB-135, 153

Benson, Jackson J. 1930- DLB-111

Benson, Robert Hugh 1871-1914 ...DLB-153

Benson, Stella 1892-1933 ....DLB-36, 162

Bentham, Jeremy 1748-1832 ...DLB-107, 158

Bentley, E. C. 1875-1956 .... DLB-70

Bentley, Richard
[publishing house] DLB-106

Benton, Robert 1932- and Newman,
David 1937- DLB-44

Benziger Brothers DLB-49

Beowulf circa 900-1000
or 790-825 .... DLB-146

Beresford, Anne 1929- DLB-40

Beresford, John Davys
1873-1947 .... DLB-162

Beresford-Howe, Constance
1922- DLB-88

Berford, R. G., Company DLB-49

Berg, Stephen 1934- DLB-5

Bergengruen, Werner 1892-1964 .... DLB-56

Berger, John 1926- DLB-14

Berger, Meyer 1898-1959 .... DLB-29

Berger, Thomas 1924- DLB-2; Y-80

Berkeley, Anthony 1893-1971 ...... DLB-77

Berkeley, George 1685-1753 .... DLB-31, 101

The Berkley Publishing
Corporation DLB-46

Berlin, Lucia 1936- DLB-130

Bernal, Vicente J. 1888-1915 .... DLB-82

Bernanos, Georges 1888-1948 ...... DLB-72

Bernard, Harry 1898-1979 .... DLB-92

Bernard, John 1756-1828 .... DLB-37

Bernard of Chartres
circa 1060-1124? DLB-115

Bernhard, Thomas
1931-1989 .... DLB-85, 124

Berriault, Gina 1926- DLB-130

Berrigan, Daniel 1921- DLB-5

Berrigan, Ted 1934-1983 ....DLB-5

Berry, Wendell 1934- DLB-5, 6

Berryman, John 1914-1972 .... DLB-48

Bersianik, Louky 1930- DLB-60

Bertolucci, Attilio 1911- DLB-128

Berton, Pierre 1920- DLB-68

Besant, Sir Walter 1836-1901 ...... DLB-135

Bessette, Gerard 1920- DLB-53

Bessie, Alvah 1904-1985 .... DLB-26

Bester, Alfred 1913-1987 ....DLB-8

The Bestseller Lists: An Assessment Y-84

Betjeman, John 1906-1984 .... DLB-20; Y-84

Betocchi, Carlo 1899-1986 .... DLB-128

Bettarini, Mariella 1942- DLB-128

Betts, Doris 1932- Y-82

Beveridge, Albert J. 1862-1927 ...... DLB-17

Beverley, Robert
circa 1673-1722 .... DLB-24, 30

Beyle, Marie-Henri (see Stendhal)

Bianco, Margery Williams
1881-1944 .... DLB-160

Bibaud, Adèle 1854-1941 .... DLB-92

Bibaud, Michel 1782-1857 .... DLB-99

Bibliographical and Textual Scholarship
Since World War II Y-89

The Bicentennial of James Fenimore
Cooper: An International
Celebration Y-89

Bichsel, Peter 1935- DLB-75

Bickerstaff, Isaac John
1733-circa 1808 .... DLB-89

Biddle, Drexel [publishing house] DLB-49

Bidwell, Walter Hilliard
1798-1881 .... DLB-79

Bienek, Horst 1930- DLB-75

Bierbaum, Otto Julius 1865-1910 .... DLB-66

Bierce, Ambrose
1842-1914? DLB-11, 12, 23, 71, 74

Bigelow, William F. 1879-1966 ...... DLB-91

Biggle, Lloyd, Jr. 1923- DLB-8

Biglow, Hosea (see Lowell, James Russell)

Bigongiari, Piero 1914- DLB-128

Billinger, Richard 1890-1965 .... DLB-124

Billings, John Shaw 1898-1975 ..... DLB-137

Billings, Josh (see Shaw, Henry Wheeler)

Binding, Rudolf G. 1867-1938 ...... DLB-66

Bingham, Caleb 1757-1817 .... DLB-42

Bingham, George Barry
1906-1988 .... DLB-127

Bingley, William
[publishing house] DLB-154

Binyon, Laurence 1869-1943 .... DLB-19

Biographia Brittanica DLB-142

Biographical Documents I Y-84

Biographical Documents II Y-85

Bioren, John [publishing house] DLB-49

Bioy Casares, Adolfo 1914- DLB-113

Bird, William 1888-1963 .... DLB-4

Birney, Earle 1904- DLB-88

Birrell, Augustine 1850-1933 .... DLB-98

Bishop, Elizabeth 1911-1979 .... DLB-5

Bishop, John Peale 1892-1944 .. DLB-4, 9, 45

Bismarck, Otto von 1815-1898 .....DLB-129

Bisset, Robert 1759-1805 ....DLB-142

Bissett, Bill 1939- DLB-53

Bitzius, Albert (see Gotthelf, Jeremias)

Black, David (D. M.) 1941- DLB-40

Black, Winifred 1863-1936 ....DLB-25

Black, Walter J.
[publishing house] DLB-46

The Black Aesthetic: Background DS-8

The Black Arts Movement, by
Larry Neal DLB-38

Black Theaters and Theater Organizations in
America, 1961-1982:
A Research List DLB-38

Black Theatre: A Forum
[excerpts] DLB-38

Blackamore, Arthur 1679-? DLB-24, 39

Blackburn, Alexander L. 1929- Y-85

Blackburn, Paul 1926-1971 .... DLB-16; Y-81

Blackburn, Thomas 1916-1977 ......DLB-27

Blackmore, R. D. 1825-1900 ....DLB-18

Blackmore, Sir Richard
1654-1729 ....DLB-131

Blackmur, R. P. 1904-1965 ....DLB-63

Blackwell, Basil, Publisher DLB-106

Blackwood, Algernon Henry
1869-1951 .... DLB-153, 156

Blackwood, Caroline 1931- DLB-14

Blackwood, William, and
Sons, Ltd. DLB-154

Blackwood's Edinburgh Magazine
1817-1980 ....DLB-110

Blair, Eric Arthur (see Orwell, George)

Blair, Francis Preston 1791-1876 .....DLB-43

Blair, James circa 1655-1743 ....DLB-24

Blair, John Durburrow 1759-1823 ....DLB-37

Blais, Marie-Claire 1939- DLB-53

Blaise, Clark 1940- DLB-53

Blake, Nicholas 1904-1972 ....DLB-77
(see Day Lewis, C.)

Blake, William
1757-1827 .... DLB-93, 154, 163

The Blakiston Company DLB-49

Blanchot, Maurice 1907- DLB-72

Blanckenburg, Christian Friedrich von
1744-1796 ....DLB-94

Bledsoe, Albert Taylor
1809-1877 .... DLB-3, 79

Blelock and Company DLB-49

Blennerhassett, Margaret Agnew
   1773-1842 ....DLB-99

Bles, Geoffrey
   [publishing house] DLB-112

The Blickling Homilies
   circa 971 ....DLB-146

Blish, James 1921-1975 ....DLB-8

Bliss, E., and E. White
   [publishing house] DLB-49

Bliven, Bruce 1889-1977 ....DLB-137

Bloch, Robert 1917-1994 ....DLB-44

Block, Rudolph (see Lessing, Bruno)

Blondal, Patricia 1926-1959 ....DLB-88

Bloom, Harold 1930- DLB-67

Bloomer, Amelia 1818-1894 ....DLB-79

Bloomfield, Robert 1766-1823 ....DLB-93

Bloomsbury Group DS-10

Blotner, Joseph 1923- DLB-111

Bloy, Léon 1846-1917 ....DLB-123

Blume, Judy 1938- DLB-52

Blunck, Hans Friedrich 1888-1961 ...DLB-66

Blunden, Edmund
   1896-1974 .... DLB-20, 100, 155

Blunt, Wilfrid Scawen 1840-1922 ....DLB-19

Bly, Nellie (see Cochrane, Elizabeth)

Bly, Robert 1926- DLB-5

Blyton, Enid 1897-1968 ....DLB-160

Boaden, James 1762-1839 ....DLB-89

Boas, Frederick S. 1862-1957 ....DLB-149

The Bobbs-Merrill Archive at the
   Lilly Library, Indiana University Y-90

The Bobbs-Merrill Company DLB-46

Bobrov, Semen Sergeevich
   1763?-1810 ....DLB-150

Bobrowski, Johannes 1917-1965 .....DLB-75

Bodenheim, Maxwell 1892-1954 ...DLB-9, 45

Bodenstedt, Friedrich von
   1819-1892 ....DLB-129

Bodini, Vittorio 1914-1970 ....DLB-128

Bodkin, M. McDonnell
   1850-1933 ....DLB-70

Bodley Head DLB-112

Bodmer, Johann Jakob 1698-1783 ....DLB-97

Bodmershof, Imma von 1895-1982 ...DLB-85

Bodsworth, Fred 1918- DLB-68

Boehm, Sydney 1908- DLB-44

Boer, Charles 1939- DLB-5

Boethius circa 480-circa 524 .... DLB-115

Boethius of Dacia circa 1240-? DLB-115

Bogan, Louise 1897-1970 .... DLB-45

Bogarde, Dirk 1921- DLB-14

Bogdanovich, Ippolit Fedorovich
   circa 1743-1803 .... DLB-150

Bogue, David [publishing house] ... DLB-106

Bohn, H. G. [publishing house] DLB-106

Boie, Heinrich Christian
   1744-1806 .... DLB-94

Bok, Edward W. 1863-1930 .... DLB-91

Boland, Eavan 1944- DLB-40

Bolingbroke, Henry St. John, Viscount
   1678-1751 .... DLB-101

Böll, Heinrich 1917-1985 ..... Y-85, DLB-69

Bolling, Robert 1738-1775 .... DLB-31

Bolotov, Andrei Timofeevich
   1738-1833 .... DLB-150

Bolt, Carol 1941- DLB-60

Bolt, Robert 1924- DLB-13

Bolton, Herbert E. 1870-1953 .... DLB-17

Bonaventura DLB-90

Bonaventure circa 1217-1274 ...... DLB-115

Bond, Edward 1934- DLB-13

Bond, Michael 1926- DLB-161

Boni, Albert and Charles
   [publishing house] DLB-46

Boni and Liveright DLB-46

Robert Bonner's Sons DLB-49

Bontemps, Arna 1902-1973 ...... DLB-48, 51

The Book League of America DLB-46

Book Reviewing in America: I Y-87

Book Reviewing in America: II Y-88

Book Reviewing in America: III Y-89

Book Reviewing in America: IV Y-90

Book Reviewing in America: V Y-91

Book Reviewing in America: VI Y-92

Book Reviewing in America: VII Y-93

Book Reviewing in America: VIII Y-94

Book Supply Company DLB-49

The Book Trade History Group Y-93

The Booker Prize
   Address by Anthony Thwaite,
   Chairman of the Booker Prize Judges
   Comments from Former Booker
   Prize Winners Y-86

Boorde, Andrew circa 1490-1549 ...DLB-136

Boorstin, Daniel J. 1914- DLB-17

Booth, Mary L. 1831-1889 ....DLB-79

Booth, Philip 1925- Y-82

Booth, Wayne C. 1921- DLB-67

Borchardt, Rudolf 1877-1945 ....DLB-66

Borchert, Wolfgang
   1921-1947 ....DLB-69, 124

Borel, Pétrus 1809-1859 ....DLB-119

Borges, Jorge Luis
   1899-1986 ....DLB-113; Y-86

Börne, Ludwig 1786-1837 ....DLB-90

Borrow, George 1803-1881 ......DLB-21, 55

Bosch, Juan 1909- DLB-145

Bosco, Henri 1888-1976 ....DLB-72

Bosco, Monique 1927- DLB-53

Boston, Lucy M. 1892-1990 ....DLB-161

Boswell, James 1740-1795 .....DLB-104, 142

Botev, Khristo 1847-1876 ....DLB-147

Botta, Anne C. Lynch 1815-1891 .....DLB-3

Bottomley, Gordon 1874-1948 ......DLB-10

Bottoms, David 1949- DLB-120; Y-83

Bottrall, Ronald 1906- DLB-20

Boucher, Anthony 1911-1968 ....DLB-8

Boucher, Jonathan 1738-1804 ....DLB-31

Boucher de Boucherville, George
   1814-1894 ....DLB-99

Boudreau, Daniel (see Coste, Donat)

Bourassa, Napoléon 1827-1916 ......DLB-99

Bourget, Paul 1852-1935 ....DLB-123

Bourinot, John George 1837-1902 ....DLB-99

Bourjaily, Vance 1922- DLB-2, 143

Bourne, Edward Gaylord
   1860-1908 ....DLB-47

Bourne, Randolph 1886-1918 ....DLB-63

Bousoño, Carlos 1923- DLB-108

Bousquet, Joë 1897-1950 ....DLB-72

Bova, Ben 1932- Y-81

Bovard, Oliver K. 1872-1945 ....DLB-25

Bove, Emmanuel 1898-1945 ....DLB-72

Bowen, Elizabeth 1899-1973 ....DLB-15, 162

Bowen, Francis 1811-1890 ....DLB-1, 59

Bowen, John 1924- DLB-13

Bowen, Marjorie 1886-1952 ....DLB-153

Bowen-Merrill Company DLB-49

Bowering, George 1935- DLB-53

Bowers, Claude G. 1878-1958 . . . . . . DLB-17

Bowers, Edgar 1924- DLB-5

Bowers, Fredson Thayer
1905-1991 . . . . DLB-140; Y-91

Bowles, Paul 1910- DLB-5, 6

Bowles, Samuel III 1826-1878 . . . . . . DLB-43

Bowles, William Lisles 1762-1850 . . . DLB-93

Bowman, Louise Morey
1882-1944 . . . . DLB-68

Boyd, James 1888-1944 . . . . .DLB-9

Boyd, John 1919- DLB-8

Boyd, Thomas 1898-1935 . . . . .DLB-9

Boyesen, Hjalmar Hjorth
1848-1895 . . . . .DLB-12, 71; DS-13

Boyle, Kay
1902-1992 . . . . . . .DLB-4, 9, 48, 86; Y-93

Boyle, Roger, Earl of Orrery
1621-1679 . . . . DLB-80

Boyle, T. Coraghessan 1948- Y-86

Brackenbury, Alison 1953- DLB-40

Brackenridge, Hugh Henry
1748-1816 . . . . DLB-11, 37

Brackett, Charles 1892-1969 . . . . DLB-26

Brackett, Leigh 1915-1978 . . . . DLB-8, 26

Bradburn, John
[publishing house] DLB-49

Bradbury, Malcolm 1932- DLB-14

Bradbury, Ray 1920- DLB-2, 8

Bradbury and Evans DLB-106

Braddon, Mary Elizabeth
1835-1915 . . . . DLB-18, 70, 156

Bradford, Andrew 1686-1742 . . . . DLB-43, 73

Bradford, Gamaliel 1863-1932 . . . . . . DLB-17

Bradford, John 1749-1830 . . . . DLB-43

Bradford, Roark 1896-1948 . . . . DLB-86

Bradford, William 1590-1657 . . . . DLB-24, 30

Bradford, William III
1719-1791 . . . . DLB-43, 73

Bradlaugh, Charles 1833-1891 . . . . . . DLB-57

Bradley, David 1950- DLB-33

Bradley, Marion Zimmer 1930- DLB-8

Bradley, William Aspenwall
1878-1939 . . . . .DLB-4

Bradley, Ira, and Company DLB-49

Bradley, J. W., and Company DLB-49

Bradstreet, Anne
1612 or 1613-1672 . . . . DLB-24

Bradwardine, Thomas circa
1295-1349 . . . . .DLB-115

Brady, Frank 1924-1986 . . . . .DLB-111

Brady, Frederic A.
[publishing house] DLB-49

Bragg, Melvyn 1939- DLB-14

Brainard, Charles H.
[publishing house] DLB-49

Braine, John 1922-1986 . . . . . . .DLB-15; Y-86

Braithwait, Richard 1588-1673 . . . . .DLB-151

Braithwaite, William Stanley
1878-1962 . . . . .DLB-50, 54

Braker, Ulrich 1735-1798 . . . . DLB-94

Bramah, Ernest 1868-1942 . . . . DLB-70

Branagan, Thomas 1774-1843 . . . . . . DLB-37

Branch, William Blackwell
1927- DLB-76

Branden Press DLB-46

Brathwaite, Edward Kamau
1930- DLB-125

Brault, Jacques 1933- DLB-53

Braun, Volker 1939- DLB-75

Brautigan, Richard
1935-1984 . . . . DLB-2, 5; Y-80, 84

Braxton, Joanne M. 1950- DLB-41

Bray, Anne Eliza 1790-1883 . . . . . . .DLB-116

Bray, Thomas 1656-1730 . . . . DLB-24

Braziller, George
[publishing house] DLB-46

The Bread Loaf Writers'
Conference 1983 . . . . .Y-84

The Break-Up of the Novel (1922),
by John Middleton Murry DLB-36

Breasted, James Henry 1865-1935 . . . DLB-47

Brecht, Bertolt 1898-1956 . . . . . .DLB-56, 124

Bredel, Willi 1901-1964 . . . . DLB-56

Breitinger, Johann Jakob
1701-1776 . . . . DLB-97

Bremser, Bonnie 1939- DLB-16

Bremser, Ray 1934- DLB-16

Brentano, Bernard von
1901-1964 . . . . DLB-56

Brentano, Clemens 1778-1842 . . . . . . DLB-90

Brentano's DLB-49

Brenton, Howard 1942- DLB-13

Breton, André 1896-1966 . . . . DLB-65

Breton, Nicholas
circa 1555-circa 1626 . . . . .DLB-136

The Breton Lays
1300-early fifteenth century DLB-146

Brewer, Warren and Putnam DLB-46

Brewster, Elizabeth 1922- DLB-60

Bridgers, Sue Ellen 1942- DLB-52

Bridges, Robert 1844-1930 . . . . . . DLB-19, 98

Bridie, James 1888-1951 . . . . .DLB-10

Briggs, Charles Frederick
1804-1877 . . . . .DLB-3

Brighouse, Harold 1882-1958 . . . . .DLB-10

Bright, Mary Chavelita Dunne
(see Egerton, George)

Brimmer, B. J., Company DLB-46

Brines, Francisco 1932- DLB-134

Brinley, George, Jr. 1817-1875 . . . . . .DLB-140

Brinnin, John Malcolm 1916- DLB-48

Brisbane, Albert 1809-1890 . . . . .DLB-3

Brisbane, Arthur 1864-1936 . . . . .DLB-25

British Academy DLB-112

The British Library and the Regular
Readers' Group Y-91

The British Critic 1793-1843 . . . . .DLB-110

*The British Review and London
Critical Journal* 1811-1825 . . . . . . .DLB-110

Brito, Aristeo 1942- DLB-122

Broadway Publishing Company DLB-46

Broch, Hermann 1886-1951 . . . . DLB-85, 124

Brochu, André 1942- DLB-53

Brock, Edwin 1927- DLB-40

Brod, Max 1884-1968 . . . . .DLB-81

Brodber, Erna 1940- DLB-157

Brodhead, John R. 1814-1873 . . . . . . .DLB-30

Brodkey, Harold 1930- DLB-130

Brome, Richard circa 1590-1652 . . . . .DLB-58

Brome, Vincent 1910- DLB-155

Bromfield, Louis 1896-1956 . . . . DLB-4, 9, 86

Broner, E. M. 1930- DLB-28

Bronnen, Arnolt 1895-1959 . . . . .DLB-124

Brontë, Anne 1820-1849 . . . . .DLB-21

Brontë, Charlotte 1816-1855 . . . DLB-21, 159

Brontë, Emily 1818-1848 . . . . DLB-21, 32

Brooke, Frances 1724-1789 . . . . . . DLB-39, 99

Brooke, Henry 1703?-1783 . . . . .DLB-39

Brooke, L. Leslie 1862-1940 . . . . . . .DLB-141

Brooke, Rupert 1887-1915 . . . . .DLB-19

Brooker, Bertram 1888-1955 . . . . . . .DLB-88

Brooke-Rose, Christine 1926- DLB-14

Brookner, Anita 1928- Y-87

Brooks, Charles Timothy
1813-1883 ....DLB-1

Brooks, Cleanth 1906-1994 ....DLB-63; Y-94

Brooks, Gwendolyn 1917- DLB-5, 76

Brooks, Jeremy 1926- DLB-14

Brooks, Mel 1926- DLB-26

Brooks, Noah 1830-1903 .... DLB-42; DS-13

Brooks, Richard 1912-1992 ....DLB-44

Brooks, Van Wyck
1886-1963 .... DLB-45, 63, 103

Brophy, Brigid 1929- DLB-14

Brossard, Chandler 1922-1993 ......DLB-16

Brossard, Nicole 1943- DLB-53

Broster, Dorothy Kathleen
1877-1950 ....DLB-160

Brother Antoninus (see Everson, William)

Brougham and Vaux, Henry Peter
Brougham, Baron
1778-1868 ....DLB-110, 158

Brougham, John 1810-1880 ....DLB-11

Broughton, James 1913- DLB-5

Broughton, Rhoda 1840-1920 ....DLB-18

Broun, Heywood 1888-1939 ....DLB-29

Brown, Alice 1856-1948 ....DLB-78

Brown, Bob 1886-1959 ....DLB-4, 45

Brown, Cecil 1943- DLB-33

Brown, Charles Brockden
1771-1810 .... DLB-37, 59, 73

Brown, Christy 1932-1981 ....DLB-14

Brown, Dee 1908- Y-80

Brown, Frank London 1927-1962 ....DLB-76

Brown, Fredric 1906-1972 ....DLB-8

Brown, George Mackay
1921- DLB-14, 27, 139

Brown, Harry 1917-1986 ....DLB-26

Brown, Marcia 1918- DLB-61

Brown, Margaret Wise
1910-1952 ....DLB-22

Brown, Morna Doris (see Ferrars, Elizabeth)

Brown, Oliver Madox
1855-1874 ....DLB-21

Brown, Sterling
1901-1989 .... DLB-48, 51, 63

Brown, T. E. 1830-1897 ....DLB-35

Brown, William Hill 1765-1793 .....DLB-37

Brown, William Wells
1814-1884 .... DLB-3, 50

Browne, Charles Farrar
1834-1867 .... DLB-11

Browne, Francis Fisher
1843-1913 .... DLB-79

Browne, Michael Dennis
1940- DLB-40

Browne, Sir Thomas 1605-1682 .... DLB-151

Browne, William, of Tavistock
1590-1645 .... DLB-121

Browne, Wynyard 1911-1964 .... DLB-13

Browne and Nolan DLB-106

Brownell, W. C. 1851-1928 .... DLB-71

Browning, Elizabeth Barrett
1806-1861 .... DLB-32

Browning, Robert
1812-1889 .... DLB-32, 163

Brownjohn, Allan 1931- DLB-40

Brownson, Orestes Augustus
1803-1876 .... DLB-1, 59, 73

Bruccoli, Matthew J. 1931- DLB-103

Bruce, Charles 1906-1971 .... DLB-68

Bruce, Leo 1903-1979 .... DLB-77

Bruce, Philip Alexander
1856-1933 .... DLB-47

Bruce Humphries
[publishing house] DLB-46

Bruce-Novoa, Juan 1944- DLB-82

Bruckman, Clyde 1894-1955 .... DLB-26

Bruckner, Ferdinand 1891-1958 .... DLB-118

Brundage, John Herbert (see Herbert, John)

Brutus, Dennis 1924- DLB-117

Bryant, Arthur 1899-1985 .... DLB-149

Bryant, William Cullen
1794-1878 .... DLB-3, 43, 59

Bryce Echenique, Alfredo
1939- DLB-145

Brydges, Sir Samuel Egerton
1762-1837 .... DLB-107

Buchan, John 1875-1940 ....DLB-34, 70, 156

Buchanan, George 1506-1582 ...... DLB-132

Buchanan, Robert 1841-1901 .... DLB-18, 35

Buchman, Sidney 1902-1975 .... DLB-26

Buck, Pearl S. 1892-1973 .... DLB-9, 102

Büchner, Georg 1813-1837 .... DLB-133

Bucke, Charles 1781-1846 .... DLB-110

Bucke, Richard Maurice
1837-1902 .... DLB-99

Buckingham, Joseph Tinker 1779-1861 and
Buckingham, Edwin
1810-1833 ....DLB-73

Buckler, Ernest 1908-1984 ....DLB-68

Buckley, William F., Jr.
1925- DLB-137; Y-80

Buckminster, Joseph Stevens
1784-1812 ....DLB-37

Buckner, Robert 1906- DLB-26

Budd, Thomas ?-1698 ....DLB-24

Budrys, A. J. 1931- DLB-8

Buechner, Frederick 1926- Y-80

Buell, John 1927- DLB-53

Buffum, Job [publishing house] DLB-49

Bugnet, Georges 1879-1981 ....DLB-92

Buies, Arthur 1840-1901 ....DLB-99

Building the New British Library
at St Pancras Y-94

Bukowski, Charles 1920-1994 ....DLB-5, 130

Bullins, Ed 1935- DLB-7, 38

Bulwer-Lytton, Edward (also Edward Bulwer)
1803-1873 ....DLB-21

Bumpus, Jerry 1937- Y-81

Bunce and Brother DLB-49

Bunner, H. C. 1855-1896 ....DLB-78, 79

Bunting, Basil 1900-1985 ....DLB-20

Bunyan, John 1628-1688 ....DLB-39

Burch, Robert 1925- DLB-52

Burciaga, José Antonio 1940- DLB-82

Bürger, Gottfried August
1747-1794 ....DLB-94

Burgess, Anthony 1917-1993 ....DLB-14

Burgess, Gelett 1866-1951 ....DLB-11

Burgess, John W. 1844-1931 ....DLB-47

Burgess, Thornton W.
1874-1965 ....DLB-22

Burgess, Stringer and Company DLB-49

Burk, John Daly circa 1772-1808 ....DLB-37

Burke, Edmund 1729?-1797 ....DLB-104

Burke, Kenneth 1897-1993 ......DLB-45, 63

Burlingame, Edward Livermore
1848-1922 ....DLB-79

Burnet, Gilbert 1643-1715 ....DLB-101

Burnett, Frances Hodgson
1849-1924 .... DLB-42, 141; DS-13

Burnett, W. R. 1899-1982 ....DLB-9

Burnett, Whit 1899-1973 and
Martha Foley 1897-1977 ....DLB-137

Burney, Fanny 1752-1840 .... DLB-39

Burns, Alan 1929- DLB-14

Burns, John Horne 1916-1953 .... Y-85

Burns, Robert 1759-1796 .... DLB-109

Burns and Oates DLB-106

Burnshaw, Stanley 1906- DLB-48

Burr, C. Chauncey 1815?-1883 ..... DLB-79

Burroughs, Edgar Rice 1875-1950 .....DLB-8

Burroughs, John 1837-1921 .... DLB-64

Burroughs, Margaret T. G.
1917- DLB-41

Burroughs, William S., Jr.
1947-1981 .... DLB-16

Burroughs, William Seward
1914- DLB-2, 8, 16, 152; Y-81

Burroway, Janet 1936- DLB-6

Burt, Maxwell S. 1882-1954 .... DLB-86

Burt, A. L., and Company DLB-49

Burton, Hester 1913- DLB-161

Burton, Miles (see Rhode, John)

Burton, Richard F. 1821-1890 ...... DLB-55

Burton, Robert 1577-1640 .... DLB-151

Burton, Virginia Lee 1909-1968 ..... DLB-22

Burton, William Evans
1804-1860 .... DLB-73

Burwell, Adam Hood 1790-1849 .... DLB-99

Bury, Lady Charlotte
1775-1861 .... DLB-116

Busch, Frederick 1941- DLB-6

Busch, Niven 1903-1991 .... DLB-44

Bushnell, Horace 1802-1876 .... DS-13

Bussieres, Arthur de 1877-1913 ..... DLB-92

Butler, Juan 1942-1981 .... DLB-53

Butler, Octavia E. 1947- DLB-33

Butler, Samuel 1613-1680 ..... DLB-101, 126

Butler, Samuel 1835-1902 .... DLB-18, 57

Butler, E. H., and Company DLB-49

Butor, Michel 1926- DLB-83

Butterworth, Hezekiah 1839-1905 ... DLB-42

Buttitta, Ignazio 1899- DLB-114

Byars, Betsy 1928- DLB-52

Byatt, A. S. 1936- DLB-14

Byles, Mather 1707-1788 .... DLB-24

Bynner, Witter 1881-1968 .... DLB-54

Byrd, William II 1674-1744 .... DLB-24, 140

Byrne, John Keyes (see Leonard, Hugh)

Byron, George Gordon, Lord
1788-1824 ....DLB-96, 110

C

Caballero Bonald, José Manuel
1926- DLB-108

Cabañero, Eladio 1930- DLB-134

Cabell, James Branch
1879-1958 ....DLB-9, 78

Cabeza de Baca, Manuel
1853-1915 ....DLB-122

Cabeza de Baca Gilbert, Fabiola
1898- DLB-122

Cable, George Washington
1844-1925 .... DLB-12, 74; DS-13

Cabrera, Lydia 1900-1991 ....DLB-145

Cabrera Infante, Guillermo
1929- DLB-113

Cadell [publishing house] DLB-154

Cady, Edwin H. 1917- DLB-103

Caedmon flourished 658-680 ......DLB-146

Caedmon School circa 660-899 .....DLB-146

Cahan, Abraham
1860-1951 ....DLB-9, 25, 28

Cain, George 1943- DLB-33

Caldecott, Randolph 1846-1886 ....DLB-163

Calder, John
(Publishers), Limited DLB-112

Caldwell, Ben 1937- DLB-38

Caldwell, Erskine 1903-1987 ......DLB-9, 86

Caldwell, H. M., Company DLB-49

Calhoun, John C. 1782-1850 ....DLB-3

Calisher, Hortense 1911- DLB-2

A Call to Letters and an Invitation
to the Electric Chair,
by Siegfried Mandel DLB-75

Callaghan, Morley 1903-1990 ....DLB-68

Callaloo Y-87

Calmer, Edgar 1907- DLB-4

Calverley, C. S. 1831-1884 ....DLB-35

Calvert, George Henry
1803-1889 ....DLB-1, 64

Cambridge Press DLB-49

Cambridge Songs (Carmina Cantabrigensia)
circa 1050 ....DLB-148

Camden House: An Interview with
James Hardin Y-92

Cameron, Eleanor 1912- DLB-52

Cameron, George Frederick
1854-1885 ....DLB-99

Cameron, Lucy Lyttelton
1781-1858 ....DLB-163

Cameron, William Bleasdell
1862-1951 ....DLB-99

Camm, John 1718-1778 ....DLB-31

Campana, Dino 1885-1932 ....DLB-114

Campbell, Gabrielle Margaret Vere
(see Shearing, Joseph, and Bowen, Marjorie)

Campbell, James Dykes
1838-1895 ....DLB-144

Campbell, James Edwin
1867-1896 ....DLB-50

Campbell, John 1653-1728 ....DLB-43

Campbell, John W., Jr.
1910-1971 ....DLB-8

Campbell, Roy 1901-1957 ....DLB-20

Campbell, Thomas
1777-1844 .... DLB-93, 144

Campbell, William Wilfred
1858-1918 ....DLB-92

Campion, Thomas 1567-1620 ....DLB-58

Camus, Albert 1913-1960 ....DLB-72

Canby, Henry Seidel 1878-1961 .....DLB-91

Candelaria, Cordelia 1943- DLB-82

Candelaria, Nash 1928- DLB-82

Candour in English Fiction (1890),
by Thomas Hardy DLB-18

Canetti, Elias 1905-1994 .... DLB-85, 124

Canham, Erwin Dain
1904-1982 ....DLB-127

Cankar, Ivan 1876-1918 ....DLB-147

Cannan, Gilbert 1884-1955 ....DLB-10

Cannell, Kathleen 1891-1974 ....DLB-4

Cannell, Skipwith 1887-1957 ....DLB-45

Canning, George 1770-1827 ....DLB-158

Cantwell, Robert 1908-1978 ....DLB-9

Cape, Jonathan, and Harrison Smith
[publishing house] DLB-46

Cape, Jonathan, Limited DLB-112

Capen, Joseph 1658-1725 ....DLB-24

Capes, Bernard 1854-1918 ....DLB-156

Capote, Truman
1924-1984 .... DLB-2; Y-80, 84

Caproni, Giorgio 1912-1990 ....DLB-128

Cardarelli, Vincenzo 1887-1959 ....DLB-114

Cárdenas, Reyes 1948- DLB-122

Cardinal, Marie 1929- DLB-83

Carew, Jan 1920- DLB-157

Carew, Thomas
1594 or 1595-1640 ....DLB-126

Carey, Henry
circa 1687-1689-1743 ....DLB-84

Carey, Mathew 1760-1839 ....DLB-37, 73

Carey and Hart DLB-49

Carey, M., and Company DLB-49

Carlell, Lodowick 1602-1675 ....DLB-58

Carleton, William 1794-1869 ......DLB-159

Carleton, G. W.
[publishing house] DLB-49

Carlile, Richard 1790-1843 ....DLB-110, 158

Carlyle, Jane Welsh 1801-1866 ......DLB-55

Carlyle, Thomas 1795-1881 .....DLB-55, 144

Carman, Bliss 1861-1929 ....DLB-92

Carmina Burana circa 1230 ....DLB-138

Carnero, Guillermo 1947- DLB-108

Carossa, Hans 1878-1956 ....DLB-66

Carpenter, Humphrey 1946- DLB-155

Carpenter, Stephen Cullen
?-1820? DLB-73

Carpentier, Alejo 1904-1980 ....DLB-113

Carrier, Roch 1937- DLB-53

Carrillo, Adolfo 1855-1926 ....DLB-122

Carroll, Gladys Hasty 1904- DLB-9

Carroll, John 1735-1815 ....DLB-37

Carroll, John 1809-1884 ....DLB-99

Carroll, Lewis 1832-1898 ....DLB-18, 163

Carroll, Paul 1927- DLB-16

Carroll, Paul Vincent 1900-1968 .....DLB-10

Carroll and Graf Publishers DLB-46

Carruth, Hayden 1921- DLB-5

Carryl, Charles E. 1841-1920 ....DLB-42

Carswell, Catherine 1879-1946 ......DLB-36

Carter, Angela 1940-1992 ....DLB-14

Carter, Elizabeth 1717-1806 ....DLB-109

Carter, Henry (see Leslie, Frank)

Carter, Hodding, Jr. 1907-1972 .....DLB-127

Carter, Landon 1710-1778 ....DLB-31

Carter, Lin 1930- Y-81

Carter, Martin 1927- DLB-117

Carter and Hendee DLB-49

Carter, Robert, and Brothers DLB-49

Cartwright, John 1740-1824 ....DLB-158

Cartwright, William circa
1611-1643 ....DLB-126

Caruthers, William Alexander
1802-1846 .... DLB-3

Carver, Jonathan 1710-1780 .... DLB-31

Carver, Raymond
1938-1988 ....DLB-130; Y-84, 88

Cary, Joyce 1888-1957 .... DLB-15, 100

Cary, Patrick 1623?-1657 .... DLB-131

Casey, Juanita 1925- DLB-14

Casey, Michael 1947- DLB-5

Cassady, Carolyn 1923- DLB-16

Cassady, Neal 1926-1968 .... DLB-16

Cassell and Company DLB-106

Cassell Publishing Company DLB-49

Cassill, R. V. 1919- DLB-6

Cassity, Turner 1929- DLB-105

The Castle of Perserverance
circa 1400-1425 .... DLB-146

Castellano, Olivia 1944- DLB-122

Castellanos, Rosario 1925-1974 .... DLB-113

Castillo, Ana 1953- DLB-122

Castlemon, Harry (see Fosdick, Charles Austin)

Caswall, Edward 1814-1878 .... DLB-32

Catacalos, Rosemary 1944- DLB-122

Cather, Willa
1873-1947 ....DLB-9, 54, 78; DS-1

Catherine II (Ekaterina Alekseevna), "The
Great," Empress of Russia
1729-1796 .... DLB-150

Catherwood, Mary Hartwell
1847-1902 .... DLB-78

Catledge, Turner 1901-1983 .... DLB-127

Cattafi, Bartolo 1922-1979 .... DLB-128

Catton, Bruce 1899-1978 .... DLB-17

Causley, Charles 1917- DLB-27

Caute, David 1936- DLB-14

Cavendish, Duchess of Newcastle,
Margaret Lucas 1623-1673 .... DLB-131

Cawein, Madison 1865-1914 .... DLB-54

The Caxton Printers, Limited DLB-46

Cayrol, Jean 1911- DLB-83

Cecil, Lord David 1902-1986 ...... DLB-155

Celan, Paul 1920-1970 .... DLB-69

Celaya, Gabriel 1911-1991 .... DLB-108

Céline, Louis-Ferdinand
1894-1961 .... DLB-72

The Celtic Background to Medieval English
Literature DLB-146

Center for Bibliographical Studies and
Research at the University of
California, Riverside Y-91

The Center for the Book in the Library
of Congress Y-93

Center for the Book Research Y-84

Centlivre, Susanna 1669?-1723 ......DLB-84

The Century Company DLB-49

Cernuda, Luis 1902-1963 ....DLB-134

Cervantes, Lorna Dee 1954- DLB-82

Chacel, Rosa 1898- DLB-134

Chacón, Eusebio 1869-1948 ....DLB-82

Chacón, Felipe Maximiliano
1873-? DLB-82

Challans, Eileen Mary (see Renault, Mary)

Chalmers, George 1742-1825 ....DLB-30

Chamberlain, Samuel S.
1851-1916 ....DLB-25

Chamberland, Paul 1939- DLB-60

Chamberlin, William Henry
1897-1969 ....DLB-29

Chambers, Charles Haddon
1860-1921 ....DLB-10

Chambers, W. and R.
[publishing house] DLB-106

Chamisso, Albert von
1781-1838 ....DLB-90

Champfleury 1821-1889 ....DLB-119

Chandler, Harry 1864-1944 ....DLB-29

Chandler, Norman 1899-1973 ......DLB-127

Chandler, Otis 1927- DLB-127

Chandler, Raymond 1888-1959 .... DS-6

Channing, Edward 1856-1931 ......DLB-17

Channing, Edward Tyrrell
1790-1856 ....DLB-1, 59

Channing, William Ellery
1780-1842 ....DLB-1, 59

Channing, William Ellery, II
1817-1901 .... DLB-1

Channing, William Henry
1810-1884 ....DLB-1, 59

Chaplin, Charlie 1889-1977 ....DLB-44

Chapman, George
1559 or 1560 - 1634 ....DLB-62, 121

Chapman, John DLB-106

Chapman, William 1850-1917 ....DLB-99

Chapman and Hall DLB-106

Chappell, Fred 1936- DLB-6, 105

Chappell, Fred, A Detail
in a Poem DLB-105

Charbonneau, Jean 1875-1960 ...... DLB-92

Charbonneau, Robert 1911-1967 .... DLB-68

Charles, Gerda 1914- DLB-14

Charles, William
[publishing house] DLB-49

The Charles Wood Affair:
A Playwright Revived Y-83

Charlotte Forten: Pages from
her Diary DLB-50

Charteris, Leslie 1907-1993 .... DLB-77

Charyn, Jerome 1937- Y-83

Chase, Borden 1900-1971 .... DLB-26

Chase, Edna Woolman
1877-1957 .... DLB-91

Chase-Riboud, Barbara 1936- DLB-33

Chateaubriand, François-René de
1768-1848 .... DLB-119

Chatterton, Thomas 1752-1770 .... DLB-109

Chatto and Windus DLB-106

Chaucer, Geoffrey 1340?-1400 ..... DLB-146

Chauncy, Charles 1705-1787 .... DLB-24

Chauveau, Pierre-Joseph-Olivier
1820-1890 .... DLB-99

Chávez, Denise 1948- DLB-122

Chávez, Fray Angélico 1910- DLB-82

Chayefsky, Paddy
1923-1981 .... DLB-7, 44; Y-81

Cheever, Ezekiel 1615-1708 .... DLB-24

Cheever, George Barrell
1807-1890 .... DLB-59

Cheever, John
1912-1982 .... DLB-2, 102; Y-80, 82

Cheever, Susan 1943- Y-82

Cheke, Sir John 1514-1557 .... DLB-132

Chelsea House DLB-46

Cheney, Ednah Dow (Littlehale)
1824-1904 ....DLB-1

Cheney, Harriet Vaughn
1796-1889 .... DLB-99

Cherry, Kelly 1940 .... Y-83

Cherryh, C. J. 1942- Y-80

Chesnutt, Charles Waddell
1858-1932 .... DLB-12, 50, 78

Chester, Alfred 1928-1971 .... DLB-130

Chester, George Randolph
1869-1924 .... DLB-78

The Chester Plays circa 1505-1532;
revisions until 1575 .... DLB-146

Chesterfield, Philip Dormer Stanhope,
Fourth Earl of 1694-1773 ...... DLB-104

Chesterton, G. K.
1874-1936 ... DLB-10, 19, 34, 70, 98, 149

Chettle, Henry
circa 1560-circa 1607 .... DLB-136

Chew, Ada Nield 1870-1945 .... DLB-135

Cheyney, Edward P. 1861-1947 ..... DLB-47

Chicano History DLB-82

Chicano Language DLB-82

Child, Francis James
1825-1896 .... DLB-1, 64

Child, Lydia Maria
1802-1880 .... DLB-1, 74

Child, Philip 1898-1978 .... DLB-68

Childers, Erskine 1870-1922 .... DLB-70

Children's Book Awards
and Prizes DLB-61

Children's Illustrators,
1800-1880 .... DLB-163

Childress, Alice 1920-1994 ...... DLB-7, 38

Childs, George W. 1829-1894 ...... DLB-23

Chilton Book Company DLB-46

Chinweizu 1943- DLB-157

Chitham, Edward 1932- DLB-155

Chittenden, Hiram Martin
1858-1917 .... DLB-47

Chivers, Thomas Holley
1809-1858 .... DLB-3

Chopin, Kate 1850-1904 .... DLB-12, 78

Chopin, Rene 1885-1953 .... DLB-92

Choquette, Adrienne 1915-1973 ..... DLB-68

Choquette, Robert 1905- DLB-68

The Christian Publishing
Company DLB-49

Christie, Agatha 1890-1976 ...... DLB-13, 77

Christus und die Samariterin
circa 950 .... DLB-148

Chulkov, Mikhail Dmitrievich
1743?-1792 .... DLB-150

Church, Benjamin 1734-1778 .... DLB-31

Church, Francis Pharcellus
1839-1906 .... DLB-79

Church, William Conant
1836-1917 .... DLB-79

Churchill, Caryl 1938- DLB-13

Churchill, Charles 1731-1764 ..... DLB-109

Churchill, Sir Winston
1874-1965 .... DLB-100

Churchyard, Thomas
1520?-1604 .... DLB-132

Churton, E., and Company DLB-106

Chute, Marchette 1909-1994 ...... DLB-103

Ciardi, John 1916-1986 .... DLB-5; Y-86

Cibber, Colley 1671-1757 .... DLB-84

Cima, Annalisa 1941- DLB-128

Cirese, Eugenio 1884-1955 .... DLB-114

Cisneros, Sandra 1954- DLB-122, 152

City Lights Books DLB-46

Cixous, Hélène 1937- DLB-83

Clampitt, Amy 1920-1994 .... DLB-105

Clapper, Raymond 1892-1944 ...... DLB-29

Clare, John 1793-1864 .... DLB-55, 96

Clarendon, Edward Hyde, Earl of
1609-1674 .... DLB-101

Clark, Alfred Alexander Gordon
(see Hare, Cyril)

Clark, Ann Nolan 1896- DLB-52

Clark, Catherine Anthony
1892-1977 .... DLB-68

Clark, Charles Heber
1841-1915 .... DLB-11

Clark, Davis Wasgatt 1812-1871 ..... DLB-79

Clark, Eleanor 1913- DLB-6

Clark, J. P. 1935- DLB-117

Clark, Lewis Gaylord
1808-1873 .... DLB-3, 64, 73

Clark, Walter Van Tilburg
1909-1971 .... DLB-9

Clark, C. M., Publishing
Company DLB-46

Clarke, Austin 1896-1974 .... DLB-10, 20

Clarke, Austin C. 1934- DLB-53, 125

Clarke, Gillian 1937- DLB-40

Clarke, James Freeman
1810-1888 .... DLB-1, 59

Clarke, Pauline 1921- DLB-161

Clarke, Rebecca Sophia
1833-1906 .... DLB-42

Clarke, Robert, and Company DLB-49

Clarkson, Thomas 1760-1846 ..... DLB-158

Claudius, Matthias 1740-1815 ...... DLB-97

Clausen, Andy 1943- DLB-16

Claxton, Remsen and
Haffelfinger DLB-49

Clay, Cassius Marcellus
1810-1903 .... DLB-43

Cleary, Beverly 1916- DLB-52

Cleaver, Vera 1919- and
Cleaver, Bill 1920-1981 .... DLB-52

Cleland, John 1710-1789 .... DLB-39

Clemens, Samuel Langhorne
1835-1910 .... DLB-11, 12, 23, 64, 74

Clement, Hal 1922- DLB-8

Clemo, Jack 1916- DLB-27

Cleveland, John 1613-1658 ....DLB-126

Cliff, Michelle 1946- DLB-157

Clifford, Lady Anne 1590-1676 .....DLB-151

Clifford, James L. 1901-1978 ....DLB-103

Clifford, Lucy 1853?-1929 .....DLB-135, 141

Clifton, Lucille 1936- DLB-5, 41

Clode, Edward J.
[publishing house] DLB-46

Clough, Arthur Hugh 1819-1861 ....DLB-32

Cloutier, Cécile 1930- DLB-60

Clutton-Brock, Arthur
1868-1924 ....DLB-98

Coates, Robert M.
1897-1973 .... DLB-4, 9, 102

Coatsworth, Elizabeth 1893- DLB-22

Cobb, Charles E., Jr. 1943- DLB-41

Cobb, Frank I. 1869-1923 ....DLB-25

Cobb, Irvin S.
1876-1944 .... DLB-11, 25, 86

Cobbett, William 1763-1835 ....DLB-43, 107

Cochran, Thomas C. 1902- DLB-17

Cochrane, Elizabeth 1867-1922 ......DLB-25

Cockerill, John A. 1845-1896 ....DLB-23

Cocteau, Jean 1889-1963 ....DLB-65

Coderre, Emile (see Jean Narrache)

Coffee, Lenore J. 1900?-1984 ....DLB-44

Coffin, Robert P. Tristram
1892-1955 ....DLB-45

Cogswell, Fred 1917- DLB-60

Cogswell, Mason Fitch
1761-1830 ....DLB-37

Cohen, Arthur A. 1928-1986 ....DLB-28

Cohen, Leonard 1934- DLB-53

Cohen, Matt 1942- DLB-53

Colden, Cadwallader
1688-1776 ....DLB-24, 30

Cole, Barry 1936- DLB-14

Cole, George Watson
1850-1939 ....DLB-140

Colegate, Isabel 1931- DLB-14

Coleman, Emily Holmes
1899-1974 ....DLB-4

Coleman, Wanda 1946- DLB-130

Coleridge, Hartley 1796-1849 ....DLB-96

Coleridge, Mary 1861-1907 ..... DLB-19, 98

Coleridge, Samuel Taylor
1772-1834 .... DLB-93, 107

Colet, John 1467-1519 .... DLB-132

Colette 1873-1954 .... DLB-65

Colette, Sidonie Gabrielle (see Colette)

Colinas, Antonio 1946- DLB-134

Collier, John 1901-1980 .... DLB-77

Collier, Mary 1690-1762 .... DLB-95

Collier, Robert J. 1876-1918 .... DLB-91

Collier, P. F. [publishing house] DLB-49

Collin and Small DLB-49

Collingwood, W. G. 1854-1932 .... DLB-149

Collins, An floruit circa 1653 ...... DLB-131

Collins, Merle 1950- DLB-157

Collins, Mortimer 1827-1876 .... DLB-21, 35

Collins, Wilkie 1824-1889 ... DLB-18, 70, 159

Collins, William 1721-1759 .... DLB-109

Collins, William, Sons and
Company DLB-154

Collins, Isaac [publishing house] DLB-49

Collyer, Mary 1716?-1763? DLB-39

Colman, Benjamin 1673-1747 .... DLB-24

Colman, George, the Elder
1732-1794 .... DLB-89

Colman, George, the Younger
1762-1836 .... DLB-89

Colman, S. [publishing house] DLB-49

Colombo, John Robert 1936- DLB-53

Colquhoun, Patrick 1745-1820 ..... DLB-158

Colter, Cyrus 1910- DLB-33

Colum, Padraic 1881-1972 .... DLB-19

Colvin, Sir Sidney 1845-1927 ...... DLB-149

Colwin, Laurie 1944-1992 .... Y-80

Comden, Betty 1919- and Green,
Adolph 1918- DLB-44

Comi, Girolamo 1890-1968 .... DLB-114

The Comic Tradition Continued
[in the British Novel] DLB-15

Commager, Henry Steele
1902- DLB-17

The Commercialization of the Image of
Revolt, by Kenneth Rexroth DLB-16

Community and Commentators: Black
Theatre and Its Critics DLB-38

Compton-Burnett, Ivy
1884?-1969 .... DLB-36

Conan, Laure 1845-1924 .... DLB-99

Conde, Carmen 1901- DLB-108

Conference on Modern Biography Y-85

Congreve, William
1670-1729 ....DLB-39, 84

Conkey, W. B., Company DLB-49

Connell, Evan S., Jr. 1924- DLB-2; Y-81

Connelly, Marc 1890-1980 .....DLB-7; Y-80

Connolly, Cyril 1903-1974 ....DLB-98

Connolly, James B. 1868-1957 ......DLB-78

Connor, Ralph 1860-1937 ....DLB-92

Connor, Tony 1930- DLB-40

Conquest, Robert 1917- DLB-27

Conrad, Joseph
1857-1924 .... DLB-10, 34, 98, 156

Conrad, John, and Company DLB-49

Conroy, Jack 1899-1990 ....Y-81

Conroy, Pat 1945- DLB-6

The Consolidation of Opinion: Critical
Responses to the Modernists DLB-36

Constable, Henry 1562-1613 ....DLB-136

Constable and Company
Limited DLB-112

Constable, Archibald, and
Company DLB-154

Constant, Benjamin 1767-1830 .....DLB-119

Constant de Rebecque, Henri-Benjamin de
(see Constant, Benjamin)

Constantine, David 1944- DLB-40

Constantin-Weyer, Maurice
1881-1964 ....DLB-92

Contempo Caravan: Kites in
a Windstorm Y-85

A Contemporary Flourescence of Chicano
Literature Y-84

The Continental Publishing
Company DLB-49

A Conversation with Chaim Potok Y-84

Conversations with Publishers I: An Interview
with Patrick O'Connor Y-84

Conversations with Publishers II: An Interview
with Charles Scribner III Y-94

Conversations with Rare Book Dealers I: An
Interview with Glenn Horowitz Y-90

Conversations with Rare Book Dealers II: An
Interview with Ralph Sipper Y-94

The Conversion of an Unpolitical Man,
by W. H. Bruford DLB-66

Conway, Moncure Daniel
1832-1907 ....DLB-1

Cook, Ebenezer
circa 1667-circa 1732 ....DLB-24

Cook, Edward Tyas 1857-1919 .... DLB-149

Cook, Michael 1933- DLB-53

Cook, David C., Publishing
    Company DLB-49

Cooke, George Willis 1848-1923 .... DLB-71

Cooke, Increase, and Company DLB-49

Cooke, John Esten 1830-1886 ....DLB-3

Cooke, Philip Pendleton
    1816-1850 .... DLB-3, 59

Cooke, Rose Terry
    1827-1892 .... DLB-12, 74

Coolbrith, Ina 1841-1928 .... DLB-54

Cooley, Peter 1940- DLB-105

Cooley, Peter, Into the Mirror DLB-105

Coolidge, Susan (see Woolsey, Sarah Chauncy)

Coolidge, George
    [publishing house] DLB-49

Cooper, Giles 1918-1966 .... DLB-13

Cooper, James Fenimore 1789-1851 ...DLB-3

Cooper, Kent 1880-1965 .... DLB-29

Cooper, Susan 1935- DLB-161

Coote, J. [publishing house] DLB-154

Coover, Robert 1932- DLB-2; Y-81

Copeland and Day DLB-49

Copland, Robert 1470?-1548 ...... DLB-136

Coppard, A. E. 1878-1957 .... DLB-162

Coppel, Alfred 1921- Y-83

Coppola, Francis Ford 1939- DLB-44

Corazzini, Sergio 1886-1907 .... DLB-114

Corbett, Richard 1582-1635 .... DLB-121

Corcoran, Barbara 1911- DLB-52

Corelli, Marie 1855-1924 ...... DLB-34, 156

Corle, Edwin 1906-1956 .... Y-85

Corman, Cid 1924- DLB-5

Cormier, Robert 1925- DLB-52

Corn, Alfred 1943- DLB-120; Y-80

Cornish, Sam 1935- DLB-41

Cornish, William
    circa 1465-circa 1524 .... DLB-132

Cornwall, Barry (see Procter, Bryan Waller)

Cornwallis, Sir William, the Younger
    circa 1579-1614 .... DLB-151

Cornwell, David John Moore
    (see le Carré, John)

Corpi, Lucha 1945- DLB-82

Corrington, John William 1932- DLB-6

Corrothers, James D. 1869-1917 .... DLB-50

Corso, Gregory 1930- DLB-5, 16

Cortázar, Julio 1914-1984 .... DLB-113

Cortez, Jayne 1936- DLB-41

Corvo, Baron (see Rolfe, Frederick William)

Cory, Annie Sophie (see Cross, Victoria)

Cory, William Johnson
    1823-1892 .... DLB-35

Coryate, Thomas 1577?-1617 ...... DLB-151

Cosin, John 1595-1672 .... DLB-151

Cosmopolitan Book Corporation DLB-46

Costain, Thomas B. 1885-1965 .... DLB-9

Coste, Donat 1912-1957 .... DLB-88

Cota-Cárdenas, Margarita
    1941- DLB-122

Cotter, Joseph Seamon, Sr.
    1861-1949 .... DLB-50

Cotter, Joseph Seamon, Jr.
    1895-1919 .... DLB-50

Cottle, Joseph [publishing house] ... DLB-154

Cotton, Charles 1630-1687 .... DLB-131

Cotton, John 1584-1652 .... DLB-24

Coulter, John 1888-1980 .... DLB-68

Cournos, John 1881-1966 .... DLB-54

Cousins, Margaret 1905- DLB-137

Cousins, Norman 1915-1990 .... DLB-137

Coventry, Francis 1725-1754 .... DLB-39

Coverly, N. [publishing house] DLB-49

Covici-Friede DLB-46

Coward, Noel 1899-1973 .... DLB-10

Coward, McCann and
    Geoghegan DLB-46

Cowles, Gardner 1861-1946 .... DLB-29

Cowles, Gardner ("Mike"), Jr.
    1903-1985 ....DLB-127, 137

Cowley, Abraham
    1618-1667 ....DLB-131, 151

Cowley, Hannah 1743-1809 .... DLB-89

Cowley, Malcolm
    1898-1989 .... DLB-4, 48; Y-81, 89

Cowper, William 1731-1800 ...DLB-104, 109

Cox, A. B. (see Berkeley, Anthony)

Cox, James McMahon
    1903-1974 .... DLB-127

Cox, James Middleton
    1870-1957 .... DLB-127

Cox, Palmer 1840-1924 .... DLB-42

Coxe, Louis 1918-1993 .... DLB-5

Coxe, Tench 1755-1824 .... DLB-37

Cozzens, James Gould
    1903-1978 .... DLB-9; Y-84; DS-2

Crabbe, George 1754-1832 ....DLB-93

Crackanthorpe, Hubert
    1870-1896 ....DLB-135

Craddock, Charles Egbert
    (see Murfree, Mary N.)

Cradock, Thomas 1718-1770 ....DLB-31

Craig, Daniel H. 1811-1895 ....DLB-43

Craik, Dinah Maria
    1826-1887 .... DLB-35, 136

Cranch, Christopher Pearse
    1813-1892 .... DLB-1, 42

Crane, Hart 1899-1932 .... DLB-4, 48

Crane, R. S. 1886-1967 ....DLB-63

Crane, Stephen 1871-1900 ... DLB-12, 54, 78

Crane, Walter 1845-1915 ....DLB-163

Cranmer, Thomas 1489-1556 ......DLB-132

Crapsey, Adelaide 1878-1914 .... DLB-54

Crashaw, Richard
    1612 or 1613-1649 ....DLB-126

Craven, Avery 1885-1980 ....DLB-17

Crawford, Charles
    1752-circa 1815 ....DLB-31

Crawford, F. Marion 1854-1909 .....DLB-71

Crawford, Isabel Valancy
    1850-1887 ....DLB-92

Crawley, Alan 1887-1975 ....DLB-68

Crayon, Geoffrey (see Irving, Washington)

Creasey, John 1908-1973 ....DLB-77

Creative Age Press DLB-46

Creech, William
    [publishing house] DLB-154

Creel, George 1876-1953 ....DLB-25

Creeley, Robert 1926- DLB-5, 16

Creelman, James 1859-1915 ....DLB-23

Cregan, David 1931- DLB-13

Creighton, Donald Grant
    1902-1979 ....DLB-88

Cremazie, Octave 1827-1879 ....DLB-99

Crémer, Victoriano 1909?- DLB-108

Crescas, Hasdai
    circa 1340-1412? DLB-115

Crespo, Angel 1926- DLB-134

Cresset Press DLB-112

Cresswell, Helen 1934- DLB-161

Crèvecoeur, Michel Guillaume Jean de
    1735-1813 ....DLB-37

Crews, Harry 1935- DLB-6, 143

Crichton, Michael 1942- Y-81

A Crisis of Culture: The Changing Role
of Religion in the New Republic
.............................DLB-37

Crispin, Edmund 1921-1978 ....DLB-87

Cristofer, Michael 1946- DLB-7

"The Critic as Artist" (1891), by
Oscar Wilde DLB-57

"Criticism In Relation To Novels" (1863),
by G. H. Lewes DLB-21

Crnjanski, Miloš 1893-1977 ....DLB-147

Crockett, David (Davy)
1786-1836 ....DLB-3, 11

Croft-Cooke, Rupert (see Bruce, Leo)

Crofts, Freeman Wills
1879-1957 ....DLB-77

Croker, John Wilson 1780-1857 ....DLB-110

Croly, George 1780-1860 ....DLB-159

Croly, Herbert 1869-1930 ....DLB-91

Croly, Jane Cunningham
1829-1901 ....DLB-23

Crompton, Richmal 1890-1969 .....DLB-160

Crosby, Caresse 1892-1970 ....DLB-48

Crosby, Caresse 1892-1970 and Crosby,
Harry 1898-1929 ....DLB-4

Crosby, Harry 1898-1929 ....DLB-48

Cross, Gillian 1945- DLB-161

Cross, Victoria 1868-1952 ....DLB-135

Crossley-Holland, Kevin
1941- DLB-40, 161

Crothers, Rachel 1878-1958 ....DLB-7

Crowell, Thomas Y., Company DLB-49

Crowley, John 1942- Y-82

Crowley, Mart 1935- DLB-7

Crown Publishers DLB-46

Crowne, John 1641-1712 ....DLB-80

Crowninshield, Edward Augustus
1817-1859 ....DLB-140

Crowninshield, Frank 1872-1947 ....DLB-91

Croy, Homer 1883-1965 ....DLB-4

Crumley, James 1939- Y-84

Cruz, Victor Hernández 1949- DLB-41

Csokor, Franz Theodor
1885-1969 ....DLB-81

Cuala Press DLB-112

Cullen, Countee 1903-1946 ... DLB-4, 48, 51

Culler, Jonathan D. 1944- DLB-67

The Cult of Biography
Excerpts from the Second Folio Debate:
"Biographies are generally a disease of
English Literature" – Germaine Greer,
Victoria Glendinning, Auberon Waugh,
and Richard Holmes Y-86

Cumberland, Richard 1732-1811 .... DLB-89

Cummings, E. E. 1894-1962 ...... DLB-4, 48

Cummings, Ray 1887-1957 .... DLB-8

Cummings and Hilliard DLB-49

Cummins, Maria Susanna
1827-1866 ....DLB-42

Cundall, Joseph
[publishing house] DLB-106

Cuney, Waring 1906-1976 .... DLB-51

Cuney-Hare, Maude 1874-1936 ..... DLB-52

Cunningham, Allan
1784-1842 .... DLB-116, 144

Cunningham, J. V. 1911- DLB-5

Cunningham, Peter F.
[publishing house] DLB-49

Cunquiero, Alvaro 1911-1981 ..... DLB-134

Cuomo, George 1929- Y-80

Cupples and Leon DLB-46

Cupples, Upham and Company DLB-49

Cuppy, Will 1884-1949 .... DLB-11

Curll, Edmund
[publishing house] DLB-154

Currie, James 1756-1805 .... DLB-142

Currie, Mary Montgomerie Lamb Singleton,
Lady Currie (see Fane, Violet)

Cursor Mundi circa 1300 .... DLB-146

Curti, Merle E. 1897- DLB-17

Curtis, Anthony 1926- DLB-155

Curtis, Cyrus H. K. 1850-1933 ..... DLB-91

Curtis, George William
1824-1892 .... DLB-1, 43

Curzon, Sarah Anne 1833-1898 ..... DLB-99

Cynewulf circa 770-840 .... DLB-146

D

D. M. Thomas: The Plagiarism
Controversy Y-82

Dabit, Eugène 1898-1936 .... DLB-65

Daborne, Robert circa 1580-1628 .... DLB-58

Dacey, Philip 1939- DLB-105

Dacey, Philip, Eyes Across Centuries:
Contemporary Poetry and "That
Vision Thing" DLB-105

Daggett, Rollin M. 1831-1901 .... DLB-79

D'Aguiar, Fred 1960- DLB-157

Dahl, Roald 1916-1990 ....DLB-139

Dahlberg, Edward 1900-1977 ....DLB-48

Dahn, Felix 1834-1912 ....DLB-129

Dale, Peter 1938- DLB-40

Dall, Caroline Wells (Healey)
1822-1912 ....DLB-1

Dallas, E. S. 1828-1879 ....DLB-55

The Dallas Theater Center DLB-7

D'Alton, Louis 1900-1951 ....DLB-10

Daly, T. A. 1871-1948 ....DLB-11

Damon, S. Foster 1893-1971 ....DLB-45

Damrell, William S.
[publishing house] DLB-49

Dana, Charles A. 1819-1897 ......DLB-3, 23

Dana, Richard Henry, Jr
1815-1882 ....DLB-1

Dandridge, Ray Garfield DLB-51

Dane, Clemence 1887-1965 ....DLB-10

Danforth, John 1660-1730 ....DLB-24

Danforth, Samuel, I 1626-1674 ......DLB-24

Danforth, Samuel, II 1666-1727 .....DLB-24

Dangerous Years: London Theater,
1939-1945 ....DLB-10

Daniel, John M. 1825-1865 ....DLB-43

Daniel, Samuel
1562 or 1563-1619 ....DLB-62

Daniel Press DLB-106

Daniells, Roy 1902-1979 ....DLB-68

Daniels, Jim 1956- DLB-120

Daniels, Jonathan 1902-1981 ....DLB-127

Daniels, Josephus 1862-1948 ....DLB-29

Dannay, Frederic 1905-1982 and
Manfred B. Lee 1905-1971 .....DLB-137

Danner, Margaret Esse 1915- DLB-41

Dantin, Louis 1865-1945 ....DLB-92

D'Arcy, Ella circa 1857-1937 ....DLB-135

Darley, George 1795-1846 ....DLB-96

Darwin, Charles 1809-1882 ....DLB-57

Darwin, Erasmus 1731-1802 ....DLB-93

Daryush, Elizabeth 1887-1977 ....DLB-20

Dashkova, Ekaterina Romanovna
(née Vorontsova) 1743-1810 ....DLB-150

Dashwood, Edmée Elizabeth Monica
de la Pasture (see Delafield, E. M.)

Daudet, Alphonse 1840-1897 ....DLB-123

d'Aulaire, Edgar Parin 1898- and
d'Aulaire, Ingri 1904- DLB-22

Davenant, Sir William
1606-1668 .... DLB-58, 126

Davenport, Guy 1927- DLB-130

Davenport, Robert ?-? DLB-58

Daves, Delmer 1904-1977 .... DLB-26

Davey, Frank 1940- DLB-53

Davidson, Avram 1923-1993 ....DLB-8

Davidson, Donald 1893-1968 .... DLB-45

Davidson, John 1857-1909 .... DLB-19

Davidson, Lionel 1922- DLB-14

Davie, Donald 1922- DLB-27

Davie, Elspeth 1919- DLB-139

Davies, John, of Hereford
1565?-1618 .... DLB-121

Davies, Rhys 1901-1978 .... DLB-139

Davies, Robertson 1913- DLB-68

Davies, Samuel 1723-1761 .... DLB-31

Davies, Thomas 1712?-1785 ... DLB-142, 154

Davies, W. H. 1871-1940 .... DLB-19

Davies, Peter, Limited DLB-112

Daviot, Gordon 1896?-1952 .... DLB-10
(see also Tey, Josephine)

Davis, Charles A. 1795-1867 .... DLB-11

Davis, Clyde Brion 1894-1962 ....DLB-9

Davis, Dick 1945- DLB-40

Davis, Frank Marshall 1905-? DLB-51

Davis, H. L. 1894-1960 ....DLB-9

Davis, John 1774-1854 .... DLB-37

Davis, Lydia 1947- DLB-130

Davis, Margaret Thomson 1926- .. DLB-14

Davis, Ossie 1917- DLB-7, 38

Davis, Paxton 1925-1994 .... Y-94

Davis, Rebecca Harding
1831-1910 .... DLB-74

Davis, Richard Harding
1864-1916 .... DLB-12, 23, 78, 79; DS-13

Davis, Samuel Cole 1764-1809 ...... DLB-37

Davison, Peter 1928- DLB-5

Davys, Mary 1674-1732 .... DLB-39

DAW Books DLB-46

Dawson, Ernest 1882-1947 .... DLB-140

Dawson, Fielding 1930- DLB-130

Dawson, William 1704-1752 .... DLB-31

Day, Benjamin Henry 1810-1889 .... DLB-43

Day, Clarence 1874-1935 .... DLB-11

Day, Dorothy 1897-1980 .... DLB-29

Day, Frank Parker 1881-1950 .... DLB-92

Day, John circa 1574-circa 1640 ..... DLB-62

Day Lewis, C. 1904-1972 ....DLB-15, 20
(see also Blake, Nicholas)

Day, Thomas 1748-1789 .... DLB-39

Day, The John, Company DLB-46

Day, Mahlon [publishing house] DLB-49

Deacon, William Arthur
1890-1977 .... DLB-68

Deal, Borden 1922-1985 .... DLB-6

de Angeli, Marguerite 1889-1987 .... DLB-22

De Angelis, Milo 1951- DLB-128

De Bow, James Dunwoody Brownson
1820-1867 ....DLB-3, 79

de Bruyn, Günter 1926- DLB-75

de Camp, L. Sprague 1907- DLB-8

The Decay of Lying (1889),
by Oscar Wilde [excerpt] DLB-18

Dedication, *Ferdinand Count Fathom* (1753),
by Tobias Smollett DLB-39

Dedication, *The History of Pompey the Little*
(1751), by Francis Coventry DLB-39

Dedication, *Lasselia* (1723), by Eliza
Haywood [excerpt] DLB-39

Dedication, *The Wanderer* (1814),
by Fanny Burney DLB-39

Dee, John 1527-1609 .... DLB-136

Deeping, George Warwick
1877-1950 .... DLB 153

Defense of *Amelia* (1752), by
Henry Fielding DLB-39

Defoe, Daniel 1660-1731 ....DLB-39, 95, 101

de Fontaine, Felix Gregory
1834-1896 .... DLB-43

De Forest, John William
1826-1906 .... DLB-12

DeFrees, Madeline 1919- DLB-105

DeFrees, Madeline, The Poet's Kaleidoscope:
The Element of Surprise in the Making
of the Poem DLB-105

de Graff, Robert 1895-1981 ....Y-81

de Graft, Joe 1924-1978 .... DLB-117

De Heinrico circa 980? DLB-148

Deighton, Len 1929- DLB-87

DeJong, Meindert 1906-1991 .... DLB-52

Dekker, Thomas circa 1572-1632 .... DLB-62

Delacorte, Jr., George T.
1894-1991 .... DLB-91

Delafield, E. M. 1890-1943 ....DLB-34

Delahaye, Guy 1888-1969 ....DLB-92

de la Mare, Walter
1873-1956 .... DLB-19, 153, 162

Deland, Margaret 1857-1945 ....DLB-78

Delaney, Shelagh 1939- DLB-13

Delany, Martin Robinson
1812-1885 ....DLB-50

Delany, Samuel R. 1942- DLB-8, 33

de la Roche, Mazo 1879-1961 ......DLB-68

Delbanco, Nicholas 1942- DLB-6

De León, Nephtal 1945- DLB-82

Delgado, Abelardo Barrientos
1931- DLB-82

De Libero, Libero 1906-1981 ....DLB-114

DeLillo, Don 1936- DLB-6

de Lisser H. G. 1878-1944 ....DLB-117

Dell, Floyd 1887-1969 ....DLB-9

Dell Publishing Company DLB-46

delle Grazie, Marie Eugene
1864-1931 ....DLB-81

del Rey, Lester 1915-1993 ....DLB-8

Del Vecchio, John M. 1947- DS-9

de Man, Paul 1919-1983 ....DLB-67

Demby, William 1922- DLB-33

Deming, Philander 1829-1915 ....DLB-74

Demorest, William Jennings
1822-1895 ....DLB-79

De Morgan, William 1839-1917 .....DLB-153

Denham, Sir John
1615-1669 .... DLB-58, 126

Denison, Merrill 1893-1975 ....DLB-92

Denison, T. S., and Company DLB-49

Dennie, Joseph
1768-1812 .... DLB-37, 43, 59, 73

Dennis, John 1658-1734 ....DLB-101

Dennis, Nigel 1912-1989 .... DLB-13, 15

Dent, Tom 1932- DLB-38

Dent, J. M., and Sons DLB-112

Denton, Daniel circa 1626-1703 ......DLB-24

DePaola, Tomie 1934- DLB-61

De Quincey, Thomas
1785-1859 .... DLB-110, 144

Derby, George Horatio
1823-1861 ....DLB-11

Derby, J. C., and Company DLB-49

Derby and Miller DLB-49

Derleth, August 1909-1971 . . . . DLB-9

The Derrydale Press DLB-46

Derzhavin, Gavriil Romanovich
    1743-1816 . . . . DLB-150

Desaulniers, Gonsalve
    1863-1934 . . . . DLB-92

Desbiens, Jean-Paul 1927- DLB-53

des Forêts, Louis-Rene 1918- DLB-83

DesRochers, Alfred 1901-1978 . . . . . . DLB-68

Desrosiers, Léo-Paul 1896-1967 . . . . . DLB-68

Destouches, Louis-Ferdinand
    (see Céline, Louis-Ferdinand)

De Tabley, Lord 1835-1895 . . . . DLB-35

Deutsch, Babette 1895-1982 . . . . DLB-45

Deutsch, André, Limited DLB-112

Deveaux, Alexis 1948- DLB-38

The Development of the Author's Copyright
    in Britain DLB-154

The Development of Lighting in the Staging
    of Drama, 1900-1945 . . . . DLB-10

de Vere, Aubrey 1814-1902 . . . . DLB-35

Devereux, second Earl of Essex, Robert
    1565-1601 . . . . DLB-136

The Devin-Adair Company DLB-46

De Voto, Bernard 1897-1955 . . . . DLB-9

De Vries, Peter 1910-1993 . . . . . DLB-6; Y-82

Dewdney, Christopher 1951- DLB-60

Dewdney, Selwyn 1909-1979 . . . . DLB-68

DeWitt, Robert M., Publisher DLB-49

DeWolfe, Fiske and Company DLB-49

Dexter, Colin 1930- DLB-87

de Young, M. H. 1849-1925 . . . . DLB-25

Dhlomo, H. I. E. 1903-1956 . . . . DLB-157

Dhuoda circa 803-after 843 . . . . DLB-148

The Dial Press DLB-46

Diamond, I. A. L. 1920-1988 . . . . . . DLB-26

Di Cicco, Pier Giorgio 1949- DLB-60

Dick, Philip K. 1928-1982 . . . . DLB-8

Dick and Fitzgerald DLB-49

Dickens, Charles
    1812-1870 . . . . DLB-21, 55, 70, 159

Dickinson, Peter 1927- DLB-161

Dickey, James
    1923- DLB-5; Y-82, 93; DS-7

Dickey, William 1928-1994 . . . . DLB-5

Dickinson, Emily 1830-1886 . . . . DLB-1

Dickinson, John 1732-1808 . . . . DLB-31

Dickinson, Jonathan 1688-1747 . . . . . DLB-24

Dickinson, Patric 1914- DLB-27

Dickinson, Peter 1927- DLB-87

Dicks, John [publishing house] DLB-106

Dickson, Gordon R. 1923- DLB-8

*Dictionary of Literary Biography
    Yearbook Awards* Y-92, 93

The Dictionary of National Biography
    . . . . DLB-144

Didion, Joan 1934- DLB-2; Y-81, 86

Di Donato, Pietro 1911- DLB-9

Diego, Gerardo 1896-1987 . . . . DLB-134

Digges, Thomas circa 1546-1595 . . . DLB-136

Dillard, Annie 1945- Y-80

Dillard, R. H. W. 1937- DLB-5

Dillingham, Charles T.,
    Company DLB-49

The Dillingham, G. W.,
    Company DLB-49

Dilly, Edward and Charles
    [publishing house] DLB-154

Dilthey, Wilhelm 1833-1911 . . . . . . DLB-129

Dingelstedt, Franz von
    1814-1881 . . . . DLB-133

Dintenfass, Mark 1941- Y-84

Diogenes, Jr. (see Brougham, John)

DiPrima, Diane 1934- DLB-5, 16

Disch, Thomas M. 1940- DLB-8

Disney, Walt 1901-1966 . . . . DLB-22

Disraeli, Benjamin 1804-1881 . . . . DLB-21, 55

D'Israeli, Isaac 1766-1848 . . . . DLB-107

Ditzen, Rudolf (see Fallada, Hans)

Dix, Dorothea Lynde 1802-1887 . . . . . DLB-1

Dix, Dorothy (see Gilmer,
    Elizabeth Meriwether)

Dix, Edwards and Company DLB-49

Dixon, Paige (see Corcoran, Barbara)

Dixon, Richard Watson
    1833-1900 . . . . DLB-19

Dixon, Stephen 1936- DLB-130

Dmitriev, Ivan Ivanovich
    1760-1837 . . . . DLB-150

Dobell, Sydney 1824-1874 . . . . DLB-32

Döblin, Alfred 1878-1957 . . . . DLB-66

Dobson, Austin
    1840-1921 . . . . DLB-35, 144

Doctorow, E. L. 1931- DLB-2, 28; Y-80

Dodd, William E. 1869-1940 . . . . DLB-17

Dodd, Anne [publishing house] DLB-154

Dodd, Mead and Company DLB-49

Doderer, Heimito von 1896-1968 . . . . DLB-85

Dodge, Mary Mapes
    1831?-1905 . . . . DLB-42, 79; DS-13

Dodge, B. W., and Company DLB-46

Dodge Publishing Company DLB-49

Dodgson, Charles Lutwidge
    (see Carroll, Lewis)

Dodsley, Robert 1703-1764 . . . . DLB-95

Dodsley, R. [publishing house] DLB-154

Dodson, Owen 1914-1983 . . . . DLB-76

Doesticks, Q. K. Philander, P. B.
    (see Thomson, Mortimer)

Doheny, Carrie Estelle
    1875-1958 . . . . DLB-140

Domínguez, Sylvia Maida
    1935- DLB-122

Donahoe, Patrick
    [publishing house] DLB-49

Donald, David H. 1920- DLB-17

Donaldson, Scott 1928- DLB-111

Donleavy, J. P. 1926- DLB-6

Donnadieu, Marguerite (see Duras,
    Marguerite)

Donne, John 1572-1631 . . . . DLB-121, 151

Donnelley, R. R., and Sons
    Company DLB-49

Donnelly, Ignatius 1831-1901 . . . . . . DLB-12

Donohue and Henneberry DLB-49

Donoso, José 1924- DLB-113

Doolady, M. [publishing house] DLB-49

Dooley, Ebon (see Ebon)

Doolittle, Hilda 1886-1961 . . . . DLB-4, 45

Doplicher, Fabio 1938- DLB-128

Dor, Milo 1923- DLB-85

Doran, George H., Company DLB-46

Dorgelès, Roland 1886-1973 . . . . DLB-65

Dorn, Edward 1929- DLB-5

Dorr, Rheta Childe 1866-1948 . . . . . . DLB-25

Dorset and Middlesex, Charles Sackville,
    Lord Buckhurst,
    Earl of 1643-1706 . . . . DLB-131

Dorst, Tankred 1925- DLB-75, 124

Dos Passos, John
    1896-1970 . . . . DLB-4, 9; DS-1

Doubleday and Company DLB-49

Dougall, Lily 1858-1923 . . . . DLB-92

Etherege, George 1636-circa 1692 . . . DLB-80

Ethridge, Mark, Sr. 1896-1981 . . . . . DLB-127

Ets, Marie Hall 1893- DLB-22

Etter, David 1928- DLB-105

Eudora Welty: Eye of the Storyteller . . . Y-87

Eugene O'Neill Memorial Theater
Center .DLB-7

Eugene O'Neill's Letters: A Review Y-88

Eupolemius
flourished circa 1095 . . . . DLB-148

Evans, Caradoc 1878-1945 . . . . DLB-162

Evans, Donald 1884-1921 . . . . DLB-54

Evans, George Henry 1805-1856 . . . . DLB-43

Evans, Hubert 1892-1986 . . . . DLB-92

Evans, Mari 1923- DLB-41

Evans, Mary Ann (see Eliot, George)

Evans, Nathaniel 1742-1767 . . . . DLB-31

Evans, Sebastian 1830-1909 . . . . DLB-35

Evans, M., and Company DLB-46

Everett, Alexander Hill
790-1847 . . . . DLB-59

Everett, Edward 1794-1865 . . . . . . DLB-1, 59

Everson, R. G. 1903- DLB-88

Everson, William 1912-1994 . . . . . DLB-5, 16

Every Man His Own Poet; or, The
Inspired Singer's Recipe Book (1877),
by W. H. Mallock DLB-35

Ewart, Gavin 1916- DLB-40

Ewing, Juliana Horatia
1841-1885 . . . . DLB-21, 163

The Examiner 1808-1881 . . . . DLB-110

Exley, Frederick
1929-1992 . . . . DLB-143; Y-81

Experiment in the Novel (1929),
by John D. Beresford DLB-36

Eyre and Spottiswoode DLB-106

Ezzo ?-after 1065 . . . . DLB-148

F

"F. Scott Fitzgerald: St. Paul's Native Son
and Distinguished American Writer":
University of Minnesota Conference,
29-31 October 1982 . . . . Y-82

Faber, Frederick William
1814-1863 . . . . DLB-32

Faber and Faber Limited DLB-112

Faccio, Rena (see Aleramo, Sibilla)

Fagundo, Ana María 1938- DLB-134

Fair, Ronald L. 1932- DLB-33

Fairfax, Beatrice (see Manning, Marie)

Fairlie, Gerard 1899-1983 . . . . DLB-77

Fallada, Hans 1893-1947 . . . . DLB-56

Fancher, Betsy 1928- Y-83

Fane, Violet 1843-1905 . . . . DLB-35

Fanfrolico Press DLB-112

Fanning, Katherine 1927 . . . . DLB-127

Fanshawe, Sir Richard
1608-1666 . . . . DLB-126

Fantasy Press Publishers DLB-46

Fante, John 1909-1983 . . . . DLB-130; Y-83

Al-Farabi circa 870-950 . . . . DLB-115

Farah, Nuruddin 1945- DLB-125

Farber, Norma 1909-1984 . . . . DLB-61

Farigoule, Louis (see Romains, Jules)

Farjeon, Eleanor 1881-1965 . . . . DLB-160

Farley, Walter 1920-1989 . . . . DLB-22

Farmer, Penelope 1939- DLB-161

Farmer, Philip José 1918- DLB-8

Farquhar, George circa 1677-1707 . . . DLB-84

Farquharson, Martha (see Finley, Martha)

Farrar, Frederic William
1831-1903 . . . . DLB-163

Farrar and Rinehart DLB-46

Farrar, Straus and Giroux DLB-46

Farrell, James T.
1904-1979 . . . . DLB-4, 9, 86; DS-2

Farrell, J. G. 1935-1979 . . . . DLB-14

Fast, Howard 1914- DLB-9

Faulkner, William 1897-1962
. . . . DLB-9, 11, 44, 102; DS-2; Y-86

Faulkner, George
[publishing house] DLB-154

Fauset, Jessie Redmon 1882-1961 . . . . DLB-51

Faust, Irvin 1924- DLB-2, 28; Y-80

Fawcett Books DLB-46

Fearing, Kenneth 1902-1961 . . . . DLB-9

Federal Writers' Project DLB-46

Federman, Raymond 1928- Y-80

Feiffer, Jules 1929- DLB-7, 44

Feinberg, Charles E. 1899-1988 . . . . . . .Y-88

Feinstein, Elaine 1930- DLB-14, 40

Felipe, Léon 1884-1968 . . . . DLB-108

Fell, Frederick, Publishers DLB-46

Felltham, Owen 1602?-1668 . . .DLB-126, 151

Fels, Ludwig 1946- DLB-75

Felton, Cornelius Conway
1807-1862 .DLB-1

Fennario, David 1947- DLB-60

Fenno, John 1751-1798 . . . . .DLB-43

Fenno, R. F., and Company DLB-49

Fenton, Geoffrey 1539?-1608 . . . . . .DLB-136

Fenton, James 1949- DLB-40

Ferber, Edna 1885-1968 . . . . . . DLB-9, 28, 86

Ferdinand, Vallery III (see Salaam, Kalamu ya)

Ferguson, Sir Samuel 1810-1886 . . . . .DLB-32

Ferguson, William Scott
1875-1954 .DLB-47

Fergusson, Robert 1750-1774 . . . . . . .DLB-109

Ferland, Albert 1872-1943 . . . . .DLB-92

Ferlinghetti, Lawrence 1919- DLB-5, 16

Fern, Fanny (see Parton, Sara Payson Willis)

Ferrars, Elizabeth 1907- DLB-87

Ferré, Rosario 1942- DLB-145

Ferret, E., and Company DLB-49

Ferrier, Susan 1782-1854 . . . . .DLB-116

Ferrini, Vincent 1913- DLB-48

Ferron, Jacques 1921-1985 . . . . .DLB-60

Ferron, Madeleine 1922- DLB-53

Fetridge and Company DLB-49

Feuchtersleben, Ernst Freiherr von
1806-1849 . . . . .DLB-133

Feuchtwanger, Lion 1884-1958 . . . . . .DLB-66

Feuerbach, Ludwig 1804-1872 . . . . . .DLB-133

Fichte, Johann Gottlieb
1762-1814 . . . . .DLB-90

Ficke, Arthur Davison 1883-1945 . . . .DLB-54

Fiction Best-Sellers, 1910-1945 . . . . . . .DLB-9

Fiction into Film, 1928-1975: A List of Movies
Based on the Works of Authors in
British Novelists, 1930-1959 . . . . . . .DLB-15

Fiedler, Leslie A. 1917- DLB-28, 67

Field, Edward 1924- DLB-105

Field, Edward, The Poetry File DLB-105

Field, Eugene
1850-1895 . . . . . . .DLB-23, 42, 140; DS-13

Field, Marshall, III 1893-1956 . . . . . .DLB-127

Field, Marshall, IV 1916-1965 . . . . . .DLB-127

Field, Marshall, V 1941- DLB-127

Field, Nathan 1587-1619 or 1620 . . . . .DLB-58

Field, Rachel 1894-1942 . . . . DLB-9, 22

A Field Guide to Recent Schools of American
Poetry Y-86

Fielding, Henry
 1707-1754 .... DLB-39, 84, 101

Fielding, Sarah 1710-1768 .... DLB-39

Fields, James Thomas 1817-1881 ..... DLB-1

Fields, Julia 1938- DLB-41

Fields, W. C. 1880-1946 .... DLB-44

Fields, Osgood and Company DLB-49

Fifty Penguin Years Y-85

Figes, Eva 1932- DLB-14

Figuera, Angela 1902-1984 .... DLB-108

Filmer, Sir Robert 1586-1653 ...... DLB-151

Filson, John circa 1753-1788 .... DLB-37

Finch, Anne, Countess of Winchilsea
 1661-1720 .... DLB-95

Finch, Robert 1900- DLB-88

Findley, Timothy 1930- DLB-53

Finlay, Ian Hamilton 1925- DLB-40

Finley, Martha 1828-1909 .... DLB-42

Finney, Jack 1911- DLB-8

Finney, Walter Braden (see Finney, Jack)

Firbank, Ronald 1886-1926 .... DLB-36

Firmin, Giles 1615-1697 .... DLB-24

First Edition Library/Collectors'
 Reprints, Inc. Y-91

First International F. Scott Fitzgerald
 Conference Y-92

First Strauss "Livings" Awarded to Cynthia
 Ozick and Raymond Carver
 An Interview with Cynthia Ozick
 An Interview with Raymond
 Carver Y-83

Fischer, Karoline Auguste Fernandine
 1764-1842 .... DLB-94

Fish, Stanley 1938- DLB-67

Fishacre, Richard 1205-1248 .... DLB-115

Fisher, Clay (see Allen, Henry W.)

Fisher, Dorothy Canfield
 1879-1958 .... DLB-9, 102

Fisher, Leonard Everett 1924- DLB-61

Fisher, Roy 1930- DLB-40

Fisher, Rudolph 1897-1934 ..... DLB-51, 102

Fisher, Sydney George 1856-1927 ... DLB-47

Fisher, Vardis 1895-1968 .... DLB-9

Fiske, John 1608-1677 .... DLB-24

Fiske, John 1842-1901 .... DLB-47, 64

Fitch, Thomas circa 1700-1774 ..... DLB-31

Fitch, William Clyde 1865-1909 ...... DLB-7

FitzGerald, Edward 1809-1883 ...... DLB-32

Fitzgerald, F. Scott
 1896-1940 ..... DLB-4, 9, 86; Y-81; DS-1

Fitzgerald, Penelope 1916- DLB-14

Fitzgerald, Robert 1910-1985 .... Y-80

Fitzgerald, Thomas 1819-1891 ..... DLB-23

Fitzgerald, Zelda Sayre 1900-1948 ...... Y-84

Fitzhugh, Louise 1928-1974 .... DLB-52

Fitzhugh, William
 circa 1651-1701 .... DLB-24

Flanagan, Thomas 1923- Y-80

Flanner, Hildegarde 1899-1987 ..... DLB-48

Flanner, Janet 1892-1978 .... DLB-4

Flaubert, Gustave 1821-1880 ..... DLB-119

Flavin, Martin 1883-1967 .... DLB-9

Fleck, Konrad (flourished circa 1220)
 .... DLB-138

Flecker, James Elroy 1884-1915 .. DLB-10, 19

Fleeson, Doris 1901-1970 .... DLB-29

Fleißer, Marieluise 1901-1974 ... DLB-56, 124

Fleming, Ian 1908-1964 .... DLB-87

The Fleshly School of Poetry and Other
 Phenomena of the Day (1872), by Robert
 Buchanan DLB-35

The Fleshly School of Poetry: Mr. D. G.
 Rossetti (1871), by Thomas Maitland
 (Robert Buchanan) DLB-35

Fletcher, Giles, the Elder
 1546-1611 .... DLB-136

Fletcher, Giles, the Younger
 1585 or 1586 - 1623 .... DLB-121

Fletcher, J. S. 1863-1935 .... DLB-70

Fletcher, John (see Beaumont, Francis)

Fletcher, John Gould 1886-1950 ... DLB-4, 45

Fletcher, Phineas 1582-1650 .... DLB-121

Flieg, Helmut (see Heym, Stefan)

Flint, F. S. 1885-1960 .... DLB-19

Flint, Timothy 1780-1840 .... DLB-734

Foix, J. V. 1893-1987 .... DLB-134

Foley, Martha (see Burnett, Whit, and
 Martha Foley)

Folger, Henry Clay 1857-1930 ..... DLB-140

Folio Society DLB-112

Follen, Eliza Lee (Cabot) 1787-1860 .. DLB-1

Follett, Ken 1949- Y-81, DLB-87

Follett Publishing Company DLB-46

Folsom, John West
 [publishing house] DLB-49

Fontane, Theodor 1819-1898 ...... DLB-129

Fonvisin, Denis Ivanovich
 1744 or 1745-1792 .... DLB-150

Foote, Horton 1916- DLB-26

Foote, Samuel 1721-1777 .... DLB-89

Foote, Shelby 1916- DLB-2, 17

Forbes, Calvin 1945- DLB-41

Forbes, Ester 1891-1967 .... DLB-22

Forbes and Company DLB-49

Force, Peter 1790-1868 .... DLB-30

Forché, Carolyn 1950- DLB-5

Ford, Charles Henri 1913- DLB-4, 48

Ford, Corey 1902-1969 .... DLB-11

Ford, Ford Madox
 1873-1939 .... DLB-34, 98, 162

Ford, Jesse Hill 1928- DLB-6

Ford, John 1586-? DLB-58

Ford, R. A. D. 1915- DLB-88

Ford, Worthington C. 1858-1941 .... DLB-47

Ford, J. B., and Company DLB-49

Fords, Howard, and Hulbert DLB-49

Foreman, Carl 1914-1984 .... DLB-26

Forester, Frank (see Herbert, Henry William)

Fornés, María Irene 1930- DLB-7

Forrest, Leon 1937- DLB-33

Forster, E. M.
 1879-1970 ...... DLB-34, 98, 162; DS-10

Forster, Georg 1754-1794 .... DLB-94

Forster, John 1812-1876 .... DLB-144

Forster, Margaret 1938- DLB-155

Forsyth, Frederick 1938- DLB-87

Forten, Charlotte L. 1837-1914 ...... DLB-50

Fortini, Franco 1917- DLB-128

Fortune, T. Thomas 1856-1928 ..... DLB-23

Fosdick, Charles Austin
 1842-1915 .... DLB-42

Foster, Genevieve 1893-1979 .... DLB-61

Foster, Hannah Webster
 1758-1840 .... DLB-37

Foster, John 1648-1681 .... DLB-24

Foster, Michael 1904-1956 .... DLB-9

Foulis, Robert and Andrew / R. and A.
 [publishing house] DLB-154

Fouqué, Caroline de la Motte
 1774-1831 .... DLB-90

Fouqué, Friedrich de la Motte
 1777-1843 .... DLB-90

Four Essays on the Beat Generation,
by John Clellon Holmes DLB-16

Four Seas Company DLB-46

Four Winds Press DLB-46

Fournier, Henri Alban (see Alain-Fournier)

Fowler and Wells Company DLB-49

Fowles, John 1926- DLB-14, 139

Fox, John, Jr. 1862 or
1863-1919 .... DLB-9; DS-13

Fox, Paula 1923- DLB-52

Fox, Richard Kyle 1846-1922 .... DLB-79

Fox, William Price 1926- DLB-2; Y-81

Fox, Richard K.
[publishing house] DLB-49

Foxe, John 1517-1587 .... DLB-132

Fraenkel, Michael 1896-1957 ....DLB-4

France, Anatole 1844-1924 .... DLB-123

France, Richard 1938- DLB-7

Francis, Convers 1795-1863 ....DLB-1

Francis, Dick 1920- DLB-87

Francis, Jeffrey, Lord 1773-1850 ... DLB-107

Francis, C. S. [publishing house] DLB-49

François 1863-1910 .... DLB-92

François, Louise von 1817-1893 .... DLB-129

Francke, Kuno 1855-1930 .... DLB-71

Frank, Bruno 1887-1945 .... DLB-118

Frank, Leonhard 1882-1961 .... DLB-56, 118

Frank, Melvin (see Panama, Norman)

Frank, Waldo 1889-1967 .... DLB-9, 63

Franken, Rose 1895?-1988 .... Y-84

Franklin, Benjamin
1706-1790 .... DLB-24, 43, 73

Franklin, James 1697-1735 .... DLB-43

Franklin Library DLB-46

Frantz, Ralph Jules 1902-1979 ....DLB-4

Franzos, Karl Emil 1848-1904 ..... DLB-129

Fraser, G. S. 1915-1980 .... DLB-27

Frattini, Alberto 1922- DLB-128

Frau Ava ?-1127 .... DLB-148

Frayn, Michael 1933- DLB-13, 14

Frederic, Harold
1856-1898 ....DLB-12, 23; DS-13

Freeling, Nicolas 1927- DLB-87

Freeman, Douglas Southall
1886-1953 .... DLB-17

Freeman, Legh Richmond
1842-1915 .... DLB-23

Freeman, Mary E. Wilkins
1852-1930 ....DLB-12, 78

Freeman, R. Austin 1862-1943 ...... DLB-70

Freidank circa 1170-circa 1233 ..... DLB-138

Freiligrath, Ferdinand 1810-1876 ... DLB-133

French, Alice 1850-1934 ......DLB-74; DS-13

French, David 1939- DLB-53

French, James [publishing house] DLB-49

French, Samuel [publishing house] ... DLB-49

Samuel French, Limited DLB-106

Freneau, Philip 1752-1832 ....DLB-37, 43

Freni, Melo 1934- DLB-128

Freytag, Gustav 1816-1895 .... DLB-129

Fried, Erich 1921-1988 .... DLB-85

Friedman, Bruce Jay 1930- DLB-2, 28

Friedrich von Hausen
circa 1171-1190 .... DLB-138

Friel, Brian 1929- DLB-13

Friend, Krebs 1895?-1967? DLB-4

Fries, Fritz Rudolf 1935- DLB-75

Fringe and Alternative Theater
in Great Britain DLB-13

Frisch, Max 1911-1991 ....DLB-69, 124

Frischmuth, Barbara 1941- DLB-85

Fritz, Jean 1915- DLB-52

Fromentin, Eugene 1820-1876 ...... DLB-123

From The Gay Science, by
E. S. Dallas DLB-21

Frost, A. B. 1851-1928 ....DS-13

Frost, Robert 1874-1963 ....DLB-54; DS-7

Frothingham, Octavius Brooks
1822-1895 .... DLB-1

Froude, James Anthony
1818-1894 ....DLB-18, 57, 144

Fry, Christopher 1907- DLB-13

Fry, Roger 1866-1934 ....DS-10

Frye, Northrop 1912-1991 ....DLB-67, 68

Fuchs, Daniel
1909-1993 .... DLB-9, 26, 28; Y-93

Fuentes, Carlos 1928- DLB-113

Fuertes, Gloria 1918- DLB-108

The Fugitives and the Agrarians:
The First Exhibition Y-85

Fuller, Charles H., Jr. 1939- DLB-38

Fuller, Henry Blake 1857-1929 ...... DLB-12

Fuller, John 1937- DLB-40

Fuller, Roy 1912-1991 ....DLB-15, 20

Fuller, Samuel 1912- DLB-26

Fuller, Sarah Margaret, Marchesa
D'Ossoli 1810-1850 ...... DLB-1, 59, 73

Fuller, Thomas 1608-1661 ....DLB-151

Fulton, Len 1934- Y-86

Fulton, Robin 1937- DLB-40

Furbank, P. N. 1920- DLB-155

Furman, Laura 1945- Y-86

Furness, Horace Howard
1833-1912 ....DLB-64

Furness, William Henry 1802-1896 ....DLB-1

Furthman, Jules 1888-1966 ....DLB-26

The Future of the Novel (1899), by
Henry James DLB-18

Fyleman, Rose 1877-1957 ....DLB-160

G

The G. Ross Roy Scottish Poetry
Collection at the University of
South Carolina Y-89

Gaddis, William 1922- DLB-2

Gág, Wanda 1893-1946.............DLB-22

Gagnon, Madeleine 1938- DLB-60

Gaine, Hugh 1726-1807 ....DLB-43

Gaine, Hugh [publishing house] DLB-49

Gaines, Ernest J.
1933- DLB-2, 33, 152; Y-80

Gaiser, Gerd 1908-1976 ....DLB-69

Galarza, Ernesto 1905-1984 ....DLB-122

Galaxy Science Fiction Novels DLB-46

Gale, Zona 1874-1938 .... DLB-9, 78

Gall, Louise von 1815-1855 ....DLB-133

Gallagher, Tess 1943- DLB-120

Gallagher, Wes 1911- DLB-127

Gallagher, William Davis
1808-1894 ....DLB-73

Gallant, Mavis 1922- DLB-53

Gallico, Paul 1897-1976 ....DLB-9

Galsworthy, John
1867-1933 ....DLB-10, 34, 98, 162

Galt, John 1779-1839 .... DLB-99, 116

Galvin, Brendan 1938- DLB-5

Gambit DLB-46

Gamboa, Reymundo 1948- DLB-122

Gammer Gurton's Needle DLB-62

Gannett, Frank E. 1876-1957 ....DLB-29

Gaos, Vicente 1919-1980 ....DLB-134

García, Lionel G. 1935- DLB-82

García Lorca, Federico
    1898-1936 ....DLB-108

García Márquez, Gabriel
    1928- DLB-113

Gardam, Jane 1928- DLB-14, 161

Garden, Alexander
    circa 1685-1756 ....DLB-31

Gardner, John 1933-1982 ....DLB-2; Y-82

Garfield, Leon 1921- DLB-161

Garis, Howard R. 1873-1962 ....DLB-22

Garland, Hamlin
    1860-1940 .... DLB-12, 71, 78

Garneau, Francis-Xavier
    1809-1866 ....DLB-99

Garneau, Hector de Saint-Denys
    1912-1943 ....DLB-88

Garneau, Michel 1939- DLB-53

Garner, Alan 1934- DLB-161

Garner, Hugh 1913-1979 ....DLB-68

Garnett, David 1892-1981 ....DLB-34

Garnett, Eve 1900-1991 ....DLB-160

Garraty, John A. 1920- DLB-17

Garrett, George
    1929- DLB-2, 5, 130, 152; Y-83

Garrick, David 1717-1779 ....DLB-84

Garrison, William Lloyd
    1805-1879 ....DLB-1, 43

Garro, Elena 1920- DLB-145

Garth, Samuel 1661-1719 ....DLB-95

Garve, Andrew 1908- DLB-87

Gary, Romain 1914-1980 ....DLB-83

Gascoigne, George 1539?-1577 .....DLB-136

Gascoyne, David 1916- DLB-20

Gaskell, Elizabeth Cleghorn
    1810-1865 .... DLB-21, 144, 159

Gaspey, Thomas 1788-1871 ....DLB-116

Gass, William Howard 1924- DLB-2

Gates, Doris 1901- DLB-22

Gates, Henry Louis, Jr. 1950- DLB-67

Gates, Lewis E. 1860-1924 ....DLB-71

Gatto, Alfonso 1909-1976 ....DLB-114

Gautier, Théophile 1811-1872 ......DLB-119

Gauvreau, Claude 1925-1971 ....DLB-88

The *Gawain*-Poet
    flourished circa 1350-1400 ......DLB-146

Gay, Ebenezer 1696-1787 ....DLB-24

Gay, John 1685-1732 .... DLB-84, 95

The Gay Science (1866), by E. S. Dallas
    [excerpt] DLB-21

Gayarré, Charles E. A. 1805-1895 ... DLB-30

Gaylord, Edward King
    1873-1974 ....DLB-127

Gaylord, Edward Lewis 1919- ... DLB-127

Gaylord, Charles
    [publishing house] DLB-49

Geddes, Gary 1940- DLB-60

Geddes, Virgil 1897- DLB-4

Gedeon (Georgii Andreevich Krinovsky)
    circa 1730-1763 ....DLB-150

Geibel, Emanuel 1815-1884 ....DLB-129

Geis, Bernard, Associates DLB-46

Geisel, Theodor Seuss
    1904-1991 ....DLB-61; Y-91

Gelb, Arthur 1924- DLB-103

Gelb, Barbara 1926- DLB-103

Gelber, Jack 1932- DLB-7

Gelinas, Gratien 1909- DLB-88

Gellert, Christian Füerchtegott
    1715-1769 ....DLB-97

Gellhorn, Martha 1908- Y-82

Gems, Pam 1925- DLB-13

A General Idea of the College of Mirania (1753),
    by William Smith [excerpts] DLB-31

Genet, Jean 1910-1986 .... DLB-72; Y-86

Genevoix, Maurice 1890-1980 ..... DLB-65

Genovese, Eugene D. 1930- DLB-17

Gent, Peter 1942- Y-82

Geoffrey of Monmouth
    circa 1100-1155 ....DLB-146

George, Henry 1839-1897 ....DLB-23

George, Jean Craighead 1919- DLB-52

Georgslied 896? DLB-148

Gerhardie, William 1895-1977 ...... DLB-36

Gérin, Winifred 1901-1981 .... DLB-155

Gérin-Lajoie, Antoine 1824-1882 .... DLB-99

German Drama 800-1280 ....DLB-138

German Drama from Naturalism
    to Fascism: 1889-1933 ....DLB-118

German Literature and Culture from
    Charlemagne to the Early Courtly
    Period DLB-148

German Radio Play, The DLB-124

German Transformation from the Baroque
    to the Enlightenment, The DLB-97

The Germanic Epic and Old English Heroic
    Poetry: *Widseth, Waldere*, and *The
    Fight at Finnsburg* DLB-146

Germanophilism, by Hans Kohn DLB-66

Gernsback, Hugo 1884-1967 .....DLB-8, 137

Gerould, Katharine Fullerton
    1879-1944 ....DLB-78

Gerrish, Samuel [publishing house] ..DLB-49

Gerrold, David 1944- DLB-8

Gersonides 1288-1344 ....DLB-115

Gerstäcker, Friedrich 1816-1872 ....DLB-129

Gerstenberg, Heinrich Wilhelm von
    1737-1823 ....DLB-97

Gervinus, Georg Gottfried
    1805-1871 ....DLB-133

Geßner, Salomon 1730-1788 ....DLB-97

Geston, Mark S. 1946- DLB-8

Al-Ghazali 1058-1111 ....DLB-115

Gibbon, Edward 1737-1794 ....DLB-104

Gibbon, John Murray 1875-1952 ....DLB-92

Gibbon, Lewis Grassic (see Mitchell,
    James Leslie)

Gibbons, Floyd 1887-1939 ....DLB-25

Gibbons, Reginald 1947- DLB-120

Gibbons, William ?-? DLB-73

Gibson, Charles Dana 1867-1944 ..... DS-13

Gibson, Charles Dana 1867-1944 ..... DS-13

Gibson, Graeme 1934- DLB-53

Gibson, Margaret 1944- DLB-120

Gibson, Wilfrid 1878-1962 ....DLB-19

Gibson, William 1914- DLB-7

Gide, André 1869-1951 ....DLB-65

Giguère, Diane 1937- DLB-53

Giguère, Roland 1929- DLB-60

Gil de Biedma, Jaime 1929-1990 ....DLB-108

Gil-Albert, Juan 1906- DLB-134

Gilbert, Anthony 1899-1973 ....DLB-77

Gilbert, Michael 1912- DLB-87

Gilbert, Sandra M. 1936- DLB-120

Gilbert, Sir Humphrey
    1537-1583 ....DLB-136

Gilchrist, Alexander
    1828-1861 ....DLB-144

Gilchrist, Ellen 1935- DLB-130

Gilder, Jeannette L. 1849-1916 ......DLB-79

Gilder, Richard Watson
    1844-1909 ....DLB-64, 79

Gildersleeve, Basil 1831-1924 . . . . DLB-71

Giles, Henry 1809-1882 . . . . DLB-64

Giles of Rome circa 1243-1316 . . . . . DLB-115

Gilfillan, George 1813-1878 . . . . DLB-144

Gill, Eric 1882-1940 . . . . DLB-98

Gill, William F., Company DLB-49

Gillespie, A. Lincoln, Jr.
    1895-1950 . . . . .DLB-4

Gilliam, Florence ?-? DLB-4

Gilliatt, Penelope 1932-1993 . . . . DLB-14

Gillott, Jacky 1939-1980 . . . . DLB-14

Gilman, Caroline H. 1794-1888 . . . DLB-3, 73

Gilman, W. and J.
    [publishing house] DLB-49

Gilmer, Elizabeth Meriwether
    1861-1951 . . . . DLB-29

Gilmer, Francis Walker
    1790-1826 . . . . DLB-37

Gilroy, Frank D. 1925- DLB-7

Gimferrer, Pere (Pedro) 1945- . . . DLB-134

Gingrich, Arnold 1903-1976 . . . . DLB-137

Ginsberg, Allen 1926- DLB-5, 16

Ginzkey, Franz Karl 1871-1963 . . . . . DLB-81

Gioia, Dana 1950- DLB-120

Giono, Jean 1895-1970 . . . . DLB-72

Giotti, Virgilio 1885-1957 . . . . DLB-114

Giovanni, Nikki 1943- DLB-5, 41

Gipson, Lawrence Henry
    1880-1971 . . . . DLB-17

Girard, Rodolphe 1879-1956 . . . . DLB-92

Giraudoux, Jean 1882-1944 . . . . DLB-65

Gissing, George 1857-1903 . . . . . DLB-18, 135

Giudici, Giovanni 1924- DLB-128

Giuliani, Alfredo 1924- DLB-128

Gladstone, William Ewart
    1809-1898 . . . . DLB-57

Glaeser, Ernst 1902-1963 . . . . DLB-69

Glanville, Brian 1931- DLB-15, 139

Glapthorne, Henry 1610-1643? DLB-58

Glasgow, Ellen 1873-1945 . . . . DLB-9, 12

Glaspell, Susan 1876-1948 . . . . . DLB-7, 9, 78

Glass, Montague 1877-1934 . . . . DLB-11

Glassco, John 1909-1981 . . . . DLB-68

Glauser, Friedrich 1896-1938 . . . . DLB-56

F. Gleason's Publishing Hall DLB-49

Gleim, Johann Wilhelm Ludwig
    1719-1803 . . . . DLB-97

Glendinning, Victoria 1937- DLB-155

Glover, Richard 1712-1785 . . . . DLB-95

Glück, Louise 1943- DLB-5

Glyn, Elinor 1864-1943 . . . . DLB-153

Gobineau, Joseph-Arthur de
    1816-1882 . . . . DLB-123

Godbout, Jacques 1933- DLB-53

Goddard, Morrill 1865-1937 . . . . DLB-25

Goddard, William 1740-1817 . . . . DLB-43

Godden, Rumer 1907- DLB-161

Godey, Louis A. 1804-1878 . . . . DLB-73

Godey and McMichael DLB-49

Godfrey, Dave 1938- DLB-60

Godfrey, Thomas 1736-1763 . . . . DLB-31

Godine, David R., Publisher DLB-46

Godkin, E. L. 1831-1902 . . . . DLB-79

Godolphin, Sidney 1610-1643 . . . . . . DLB-126

Godwin, Gail 1937- DLB-6

Godwin, Mary Jane Clairmont
    1766-1841 . . . . DLB-163

Godwin, Parke 1816-1904 . . . . DLB-3, 64

Godwin, William
    1756-1836 . . . DLB-39, 104, 142, 158, 163

Godwin, M. J., and Company DLB-154

Goering, Reinhard 1887-1936 . . . . . . DLB-118

Goes, Albrecht 1908- DLB-69

Goethe, Johann Wolfgang von
    1749-1832 . . . . DLB-94

Goetz, Curt 1888-1960 . . . . DLB-124

Goffe, Thomas circa 1592-1629 . . . . . DLB-58

Goffstein, M. B. 1940- DLB-61

Gogarty, Oliver St. John
    1878-1957 . . . . DLB-15, 19

Goines, Donald 1937-1974 . . . . DLB-33

Gold, Herbert 1924- DLB-2; Y-81

Gold, Michael 1893-1967 . . . . DLB-9, 28

Goldbarth, Albert 1948- DLB-120

Goldberg, Dick 1947- DLB-7

Golden Cockerel Press DLB-112

Golding, Arthur 1536-1606 . . . . DLB-136

Golding, William 1911-1993 . . . .DLB-15, 100

Goldman, William 1931- DLB-44

Goldsmith, Oliver
    1730?-1774 . . . DLB-39, 89, 104, 109, 142

Goldsmith, Oliver 1794-1861 . . . . . . DLB-99

Goldsmith Publishing Company DLB-46

Gollancz, Victor, Limited DLB-112

Gómez-Quiñones, Juan 1942- DLB-122

Gomme, Laurence James
    [publishing house] DLB-46

Goncourt, Edmond de 1822-1896 . . .DLB-123

Goncourt, Jules de 1830-1870 . . . . .DLB-123

Gonzales, Rodolfo "Corky"
    1928- DLB-122

González, Angel 1925- DLB-108

Gonzalez, Genaro 1949- DLB-122

Gonzalez, Ray 1952- DLB-122

González de Mireles, Jovita
    1899-1983 . . . . .DLB-122

González-T., César A. 1931- DLB-82

Goodison, Lorna 1947- DLB-157

Goodman, Paul 1911-1972 . . . . .DLB-130

The Goodman Theatre DLB-7

Goodrich, Frances 1891-1984 and
    Hackett, Albert 1900- DLB-26

Goodrich, Samuel Griswold
    1793-1860 . . . . DLB-1, 42, 73

Goodrich, S. G. [publishing house] . . .DLB-49

Goodspeed, C. E., and Company DLB-49

Goodwin, Stephen 1943- Y-82

Googe, Barnabe 1540-1594 . . . . .DLB-132

Gookin, Daniel 1612-1687 . . . . .DLB-24

Gordon, Caroline
    1895-1981 . . . . DLB-4, 9, 102; Y-81

Gordon, Giles 1940- DLB-14, 139

Gordon, Lyndall 1941- DLB-155

Gordon, Mary 1949- DLB-6; Y-81

Gordone, Charles 1925- DLB-7

Gore, Catherine 1800-1861 . . . . .DLB-116

Gorey, Edward 1925- DLB-61

Görres, Joseph 1776-1848 . . . . .DLB-90

Gosse, Edmund 1849-1928 . . . . . DLB-57, 144

Gotlieb, Phyllis 1926- DLB-88

Gottfried von Straßburg
    died before 1230 . . . . .DLB-138

Gotthelf, Jeremias 1797-1854 . . . . . . .DLB-133

Gottschalk circa 804/808-869 . . . . . . .DLB-148

Gottsched, Johann Christoph
    1700-1766 .DLB-97

Götz, Johann Nikolaus
    1721-1781 .DLB-97

Gould, Wallace 1882-1940 . . . . .DLB-54

Govoni, Corrado 1884-1965 . . . . . . .DLB-114

Gower, John circa 1330-1408 . . . . . . .DLB-146

Goyen, William 1915-1983 . . . . .DLB-2; Y-83

Goytisolo, José Augustín 1928- . . .DLB-134

Gozzano, Guido 1883-1916 . . . . . . .DLB-114

Grabbe, Christian Dietrich
1801-1836 . . . . .DLB-133

Gracq, Julien 1910- DLB-83

Grady, Henry W. 1850-1889 . . . . . . .DLB-23

Graf, Oskar Maria 1894-1967 . . . . . . .DLB-56

Graf Rudolf between circa 1170
and circa 1185 . . . . .DLB-148

Graham, George Rex 1813-1894 . . . . .DLB-73

Graham, Gwethalyn 1913-1965 . . . . . .DLB-88

Graham, Jorie 1951- DLB-120

Graham, Katharine 1917- DLB-127

Graham, Lorenz 1902-1989 . . . . .DLB-76

Graham, Philip 1915-1963 . . . . .DLB-127

Graham, R. B. Cunninghame
1852-1936 . . . . .DLB-98, 135

Graham, Shirley 1896-1977 . . . . .DLB-76

Graham, W. S. 1918- DLB-20

Graham, William H.
[publishing house] DLB-49

Graham, Winston 1910- DLB-77

Grahame, Kenneth
1859-1932 . . . . .DLB-34, 141

Grainger, Martin Allerdale
1874-1941 . . . . .DLB-92

Gramatky, Hardie 1907-1979 . . . . . . .DLB-22

Grand, Sarah 1854-1943 . . . . .DLB-135

Grandbois, Alain 1900-1975 . . . . . . .DLB-92

Grange, John circa 1556-? DLB-136

Granich, Irwin (see Gold, Michael)

Grant, Duncan 1885-1978 . . . . DS-10

Grant, George 1918-1988 . . . . .DLB-88

Grant, George Monro 1835-1902 . . . .DLB-99

Grant, Harry J. 1881-1963 . . . . .DLB-29

Grant, James Edward 1905-1966 . . . . .DLB-26

Grass, Günter 1927- DLB-75, 124

Grasty, Charles H. 1863-1924 . . . . . . .DLB-25

Grau, Shirley Ann 1929- DLB-2

Graves, John 1920- Y-83

Graves, Richard 1715-1804 . . . . .DLB-39

Graves, Robert
1895-1985 . . . . DLB-20, 100; Y-85

Gray, Asa 1810-1888 . . . . .DLB-1

Gray, David 1838-1861 . . . . .DLB-32

Gray, Simon 1936- DLB-13

Gray, Thomas 1716-1771 . . . . DLB-109

Grayson, William J. 1788-1863 . . . DLB-3, 64

The Great Bibliographers Series Y-93

The Great War and the Theater, 1914-1918
[Great Britain] DLB-10

Greeley, Horace 1811-1872 . . . . DLB-3, 43

Green, Adolph (see Comden, Betty)

Green, Duff 1791-1875 . . . . DLB-43

Green, Gerald 1922- DLB-28

Green, Henry 1905-1973 . . . . DLB-15

Green, Jonas 1712-1767 . . . . DLB-31

Green, Joseph 1706-1780 . . . . DLB-31

Green, Julien 1900- DLB-4, 72

Green, Paul 1894-1981 . . . . . DLB-7, 9; Y-81

Green, T. and S.
[publishing house] DLB-49

Green, Timothy
[publishing house] DLB-49

Greenaway, Kate 1846-1901 . . . . DLB-141

Greenberg: Publisher DLB-46

Green Tiger Press DLB-46

Greene, Asa 1789-1838 . . . . DLB-11

Greene, Benjamin H.
[publishing house] DLB-49

Greene, Graham 1904-1991
. . . . DLB-13, 15, 77, 100, 162; Y-85, Y-91

Greene, Robert 1558-1592 . . . . DLB-62

Greenhow, Robert 1800-1854 . . . . DLB-30

Greenough, Horatio 1805-1852 . . . . . . DLB-1

Greenwell, Dora 1821-1882 . . . . DLB-35

Greenwillow Books DLB-46

Greenwood, Grace (see Lippincott, Sara Jane
Clarke)

Greenwood, Walter 1903-1974 . . . . . . DLB-10

Greer, Ben 1948- DLB-6

Greg, W. R. 1809-1881 . . . . DLB-55

Gregg Press DLB-46

Gregory, Isabella Augusta
Persse, Lady 1852-1932 . . . . DLB-10

Gregory, Horace 1898-1982 . . . . DLB-48

Gregory of Rimini
circa 1300-1358 . . . . DLB-115

Gregynog Press DLB-112

Grenfell, Wilfred Thomason
1865-1940 . . . . DLB-92

Greve, Felix Paul (see Grove, Frederick Philip)

Greville, Fulke, First Lord Brooke
1554-1628 . . . . .DLB-62

Grey, Lady Jane 1537-1554 . . . . .DLB-132

Grey Owl 1888-1938 . . . . .DLB-92

Grey, Zane 1872-1939 . . . . .DLB-9

Grey Walls Press DLB-112

Grier, Eldon 1917- DLB-88

Grieve, C. M. (see MacDiarmid, Hugh)

Griffin, Gerald 1803-1840 . . . . .DLB-159

Griffith, Elizabeth 1727?-1793 . . . .DLB-39, 89

Griffiths, Trevor 1935- DLB-13

Griffiths, Ralph
[publishing house] DLB-154

Griggs, S. C., and Company DLB-49

Griggs, Sutton Elbert 1872-1930 . . . . .DLB-50

Grignon, Claude-Henri 1894-1976 . . .DLB-68

Grigson, Geoffrey 1905- DLB-27

Grillparzer, Franz 1791-1872 . . . . . . .DLB-133

Grimald, Nicholas
circa 1519-circa 1562 . . . . .DLB-136

Grimké, Angelina Weld
1880-1958 . . . . .DLB-50, 54

Grimm, Hans 1875-1959 . . . . .DLB-66

Grimm, Jacob 1785-1863 . . . . .DLB-90

Grimm, Wilhelm 1786-1859 . . . . .DLB-90

Grindal, Edmund
1519 or 1520-1583 . . . . .DLB-132

Griswold, Rufus Wilmot
1815-1857 . . . . .DLB-3, 59

Gross, Milt 1895-1953 . . . . .DLB-11

Grosset and Dunlap DLB-49

Grossman Publishers DLB-46

Grosseteste, Robert
circa 1160-1253 . . . . .DLB-115

Grosvenor, Gilbert H. 1875-1966 . . . .DLB-91

Groth, Klaus 1819-1899 . . . . .DLB-129

Groulx, Lionel 1878-1967 . . . . .DLB-68

Grove, Frederick Philip 1879-1949 . . .DLB-92

Grove Press DLB-46

Grubb, Davis 1919-1980 . . . . .DLB-6

Gruelle, Johnny 1880-1938 . . . . .DLB-22

Grymeston, Elizabeth
before 1563-before 1604 . . . . . . .DLB-136

Guare, John 1938- DLB-7

Guerra, Tonino 1920- DLB-128

Guest, Barbara 1920- DLB-5

Guèvremont, Germaine
1893-1968 . . . . DLB-68

Guidacci, Margherita 1921-1992 . . . DLB-128

Guide to the Archives of Publishers, Journals,
and Literary Agents in North American
Libraries Y-93

Guillén, Jorge 1893-1984 . . . . DLB-108

Guilloux, Louis 1899-1980 . . . . DLB-72

Guilpin, Everard
circa 1572-after 1608? DLB-136

Guiney, Louise Imogen 1861-1920 . . DLB-54

Guiterman, Arthur 1871-1943 . . . . . . DLB-11

Günderrode, Caroline von
1780-1806 . . . . DLB-90

Gundulić, Ivan 1589-1638 . . . . DLB-147

Gunn, Bill 1934-1989 . . . . DLB-38

Gunn, James E. 1923- DLB-8

Gunn, Neil M. 1891-1973 . . . . DLB-15

Gunn, Thom 1929- DLB-27

Gunnars, Kristjana 1948- DLB-60

Gurik, Robert 1932- DLB-60

Gustafson, Ralph 1909- DLB-88

Gütersloh, Albert Paris 1887-1973 . . . DLB-81

Guthrie, A. B., Jr. 1901- DLB-6

Guthrie, Ramon 1896-1973 . . . . .DLB-4

The Guthrie Theater DLB-7

Gutzkow, Karl 1811-1878 . . . . DLB-133

Guy, Ray 1939- DLB-60

Guy, Rosa 1925- DLB-33

Guyot, Arnold 1807-1884 . . . . .DS-13

Gwynne, Erskine 1898-1948 . . . . .DLB-4

Gyles, John 1680-1755 . . . . DLB-99

Gysin, Brion 1916- DLB-16

H

H. D. (see Doolittle, Hilda)

Habington, William 1605-1654 . . . . DLB-126

Hacker, Marilyn 1942- DLB-120

Hackett, Albert (see Goodrich, Frances)

Hacks, Peter 1928- DLB-124

Hadas, Rachel 1948- DLB-120

Hadden, Briton 1898-1929 . . . . DLB-91

Hagelstange, Rudolf 1912-1984 . . . . . DLB-69

Haggard, H. Rider 1856-1925 . . . .DLB-70, 156

Haggard, William 1907-1993 . . . . Y-93

Hahn-Hahn, Ida Gräfin von
1805-1880 . . . . DLB-133

Haig-Brown, Roderick 1908-1976 . . . . DLB-88

Haight, Gordon S. 1901-1985 . . . . . DLB-103

Hailey, Arthur 1920- DLB-88; Y-82

Haines, John 1924- DLB-5

Hake, Edward
flourished 1566-1604 . . . . DLB-136

Hake, Thomas Gordon 1809-1895 . . . DLB-32

Hakluyt, Richard 1552?-1616 . . . . . . DLB-136

Halbe, Max 1865-1944 . . . . DLB-118

Haldane, J. B. S. 1892-1964 . . . . DLB-160

Haldeman, Joe 1943- DLB-8

Haldeman-Julius Company DLB-46

Hale, E. J., and Son DLB-49

Hale, Edward Everett
1822-1909 . . . . .DLB-1, 42, 74

Hale, Kathleen 1898- DLB-160

Hale, Leo Thomas (see Ebon)

Hale, Lucretia Peabody
1820-1900 . . . . DLB-42

Hale, Nancy 1908-1988 . . . .DLB-86; Y-80, 88

Hale, Sarah Josepha (Buell)
1788-1879 . . . . .DLB-1, 42, 73

Hales, John 1584-1656 . . . . DLB-151

Haley, Alex 1921-1992 . . . . DLB-38

Haliburton, Thomas Chandler
1796-1865 . . . . .DLB-11, 99

Hall, Anna Maria 1800-1881 . . . . DLB-159

Hall, Donald 1928- DLB-5

Hall, Edward 1497-1547 . . . . DLB-132

Hall, James 1793-1868 . . . . .DLB-73, 74

Hall, Joseph 1574-1656 . . . . . . .DLB-121, 151

Hall, Samuel [publishing house] DLB-49

Hallam, Arthur Henry 1811-1833 . . . . DLB-32

Halleck, Fitz-Greene 1790-1867 . . . . . .DLB-3

Hallmark Editions DLB-46

Halper, Albert 1904-1984 . . . . .DLB-9

Halperin, John William 1941- DLB-111

Halstead, Murat 1829-1908 . . . . DLB-23

Hamann, Johann Georg 1730-1788 . . DLB-97

Hamburger, Michael 1924- DLB-27

Hamilton, Alexander 1712-1756 . . . . . DLB-31

Hamilton, Alexander 1755?-1804 . . . . DLB-37

Hamilton, Cicely 1872-1952 . . . . DLB-10

Hamilton, Edmond 1904-1977 . . . . . . .DLB-8

Hamilton, Elizabeth
1758-1816 . . . . DLB-116, 158

Hamilton, Gail (see Corcoran, Barbara)

Hamilton, Ian 1938- DLB-40, 155

Hamilton, Patrick 1904-1962 . . . . . . .DLB-10

Hamilton, Virginia 1936- DLB-33, 52

Hamilton, Hamish, Limited DLB-112

Hammett, Dashiell 1894-1961 . . . . .DS-6

Dashiell Hammett:
An Appeal in TAC Y-91

Hammon, Jupiter 1711-died between
1790 and 1806 . . . . DLB-31, 50

Hammond, John ?-1663 . . . . .DLB-24

Hamner, Earl 1923- DLB-6

Hampton, Christopher 1946- DLB-13

Handel-Mazzetti, Enrica von
1871-1955 . . . . .DLB-81

Handke, Peter 1942- DLB-85, 124

Handlin, Oscar 1915- DLB-17

Hankin, St. John 1869-1909 . . . . .DLB-10

Hanley, Clifford 1922- DLB-14

Hannah, Barry 1942- DLB-6

Hannay, James 1827-1873 . . . . .DLB-21

Hansberry, Lorraine 1930-1965 . . . DLB-7, 38

Hapgood, Norman 1868-1937 . . . . . . .DLB-91

Harcourt Brace Jovanovich DLB-46

Hardenberg, Friedrich von (see Novalis)

Harding, Walter 1917- DLB-111

Hardwick, Elizabeth 1916- DLB-6

Hardy, Thomas 1840-1928 . . .DLB-18, 19, 135

Hare, Cyril 1900-1958 . . . . .DLB-77

Hare, David 1947- DLB-13

Hargrove, Marion 1919- DLB-11

Häring, Georg Wilhelm Heinrich (see Alexis,
Willibald)

Harington, Donald 1935- DLB-152

Harington, Sir John 1560-1612 . . . . .DLB-136

Harjo, Joy 1951- DLB-120

Harlow, Robert 1923- DLB-60

Harman, Thomas
flourished 1566-1573 . . . . .DLB-136

Harness, Charles L. 1915- DLB-8

Harnett, Cynthia 1893-1981 . . . . . . .DLB-161

Harper, Fletcher 1806-1877 . . . . .DLB-79

Harper, Frances Ellen Watkins
1825-1911 . . . . .DLB-50

Harper, Michael S. 1938- DLB-41

Harper and Brothers DLB-49

Harraden, Beatrice 1864-1943 . . . . . .DLB-153

Harrap, George G., and Company
Limited DLB-112

Harriot, Thomas 1560-1621 . . . . . . .DLB-136

Harris, Benjamin ?-circa 1720 . . . .DLB-42, 43

Harris, Christie 1907- DLB-88

Harris, Frank 1856-1931 . . . . .DLB-156

Harris, George Washington
1814-1869 . . . . .DLB-3, 11

Harris, Joel Chandler
1848-1908 . . . . DLB-11, 23, 42, 78, 91

Harris, Mark 1922- DLB-2; Y-80

Harris, Wilson 1921- DLB-117

Harrison, Charles Yale
1898-1954 . . . . .DLB-68

Harrison, Frederic 1831-1923 . . . . . . .DLB-57

Harrison, Harry 1925- DLB-8

Harrison, Jim 1937- Y-82

Harrison, Mary St. Leger Kingsley (see Malet,
Lucas)

Harrison, Paul Carter 1936- DLB-38

Harrison, Susan Frances
1859-1935 . . . . .DLB-99

Harrison, Tony 1937- DLB-40

Harrison, William 1535-1593 . . . . . .DLB-136

Harrison, James P., Company DLB-49

Harrisse, Henry 1829-1910 . . . . .DLB-47

Harsent, David 1942- DLB-40

Hart, Albert Bushnell 1854-1943 . . . . .DLB-17

Hart, Julia Catherine 1796-1867 . . . . .DLB-99

Hart, Moss 1904-1961 . . . . .DLB-7

Hart, Oliver 1723-1795 . . . . .DLB-31

Hart-Davis, Rupert, Limited DLB-112

Harte, Bret 1836-1902 . . . DLB-12, 64, 74, 79

Harte, Edward Holmead 1922- . . .DLB-127

Harte, Houston Harriman
1927- DLB-127

Hartlaub, Felix 1913-1945 . . . . .DLB-56

Hartlebon, Otto Erich
1864-1905 . . . . .DLB-118

Hartley, L. P. 1895-1972 . . . . . .DLB-15, 139

Hartley, Marsden 1877-1943 . . . . .DLB-54

Hartling, Peter 1933- DLB-75

Hartman, Geoffrey H. 1929- DLB-67

Hartmann, Sadakichi 1867-1944 . . . . .DLB-54

Hartmann von Aue
circa 1160-circa 1205 . . . . DLB-138

Harvey, Jean-Charles 1891-1967 . . . . DLB-88

Harvill Press Limited DLB-112

Harwood, Lee 1939- DLB-40

Harwood, Ronald 1934- DLB-13

Haskins, Charles Homer
1870-1937 . . . . DLB-47

Hass, Robert 1941- DLB-105

The Hatch-Billops Collection DLB-76

Hathaway, William 1944- DLB-120

Hauff, Wilhelm 1802-1827 . . . . DLB-90

A Haughty and Proud Generation (1922),
by Ford Madox Hueffer DLB-36

Hauptmann, Carl
1858-1921 . . . . DLB-66, 118

Hauptmann, Gerhart
1862-1946 . . . . DLB-66, 118

Hauser, Marianne 1910- Y-83

Hawes, Stephen
1475?-before 1529 . . . . DLB-132

Hawker, Robert Stephen
1803-1875 . . . . DLB-32

Hawkes, John 1925- DLB-2, 7; Y-80

Hawkesworth, John 1720-1773 . . . . . DLB-142

Hawkins, Sir Anthony Hope (see Hope,
Anthony)

Hawkins, Sir John
1719-1789 . . . . DLB-104, 142

Hawkins, Walter Everette 1883-? . . . DLB-50

Hawthorne, Nathaniel
1804-1864 . . . . DLB-1, 74

Hay, John 1838-1905 . . . . DLB-12, 47

Hayden, Robert 1913-1980 . . . . DLB-5, 76

Haydon, Benjamin Robert
1786-1846 . . . . DLB-110

Hayes, John Michael 1919- DLB-26

Hayley, William 1745-1820 . . . . DLB-93, 142

Haym, Rudolf 1821-1901 . . . . DLB-129

Hayman, Robert 1575-1629 . . . . DLB-99

Hayman, Ronald 1932- DLB-155

Hayne, Paul Hamilton
1830-1886 . . . . DLB-3, 64, 79

Hays, Mary 1760-1843 . . . . . . DLB-142, 158

Haywood, Eliza 1693?-1756 . . . . DLB-39

Hazard, Willis P. [publishing house] . . .DLB-49

Hazlitt, William 1778-1830 . . . . DLB-110, 158

Hazzard, Shirley 1931- Y-82

Head, Bessie 1937-1986 . . . . DLB-117

Headley, Joel T. 1813-1897 . . DLB-30; DS-13

Heaney, Seamus 1939- DLB-40

Heard, Nathan C. 1936- DLB-33

Hearn, Lafcadio 1850-1904 . . . . . .DLB-12, 78

Hearne, John 1926- DLB-117

Hearne, Samuel 1745-1792 . . . . .DLB-99

Hearst, William Randolph
1863-1951 . . . . .DLB-25

Hearst, William Randolph, Jr
1908-1993 . . . . .DLB-127

Heath, Catherine 1924- DLB-14

Heath, Roy A. K. 1926- DLB-117

Heath-Stubbs, John 1918- DLB-27

Heavysege, Charles 1816-1876 . . . . . .DLB-99

Hebbel, Friedrich 1813-1863 . . . . . . .DLB-129

Hebel, Johann Peter 1760-1826 . . . . . .DLB-90

Hébert, Anne 1916- DLB-68

Hébert, Jacques 1923- DLB-53

Hecht, Anthony 1923- DLB-5

Hecht, Ben 1894-1964
. . . . .DLB-7, 9, 25, 26, 28, 86

Hecker, Isaac Thomas 1819-1888 . . . . .DLB-1

Hedge, Frederic Henry
1805-1890 . . . . .DLB-1, 59

Hefner, Hugh M. 1926- DLB-137

Hegel, Georg Wilhelm Friedrich
1770-1831 . . . . .DLB-90

Heidish, Marcy 1947- Y-82

Heißenbüttel 1921- DLB-75

Hein, Christoph 1944- DLB-124

Heine, Heinrich 1797-1856 . . . . .DLB-90

Heinemann, Larry 1944- DS-9

Heinemann, William, Limited DLB-112

Heinlein, Robert A. 1907-1988 . . . . . .DLB-8

Heinrich von dem Türlîn
flourished circa 1230 . . . . .DLB-138

Heinrich von Melk
flourished after 1160 . . . . .DLB-148

Heinrich von Veldeke
circa 1145-circa 1190 . . . . .DLB-138

Heinrich, Willi 1920- DLB-75

Heiskell, John 1872-1972 . . . . .DLB-127

Heinse, Wilhelm 1746-1803 . . . . .DLB-94

Heliand circa 850 . . . . .DLB-148

Heller, Joseph 1923- DLB-2, 28; Y-80

Hellman, Lillian 1906-1984 . . . . .DLB-7; Y-84

Helprin, Mark 1947- Y-85

Helwig, David 1938- DLB-60

Hemans, Felicia 1793-1835 . . . . DLB-96

Hemingway, Ernest 1899-1961
. . . . DLB-4, 9, 102; Y-81, 87; DS-1

Hemingway: Twenty-Five Years
Later Y-85

Hémon, Louis 1880-1913 . . . . DLB-92

Hemphill, Paul 1936- Y-87

Hénault, Gilles 1920- DLB-88

Henchman, Daniel 1689-1761 . . . . . . DLB-24

Henderson, Alice Corbin
1881-1949 . . . . DLB-54

Henderson, Archibald
1877-1963 . . . . DLB-103

Henderson, David 1942- DLB-41

Henderson, George Wylie
1904- DLB-51

Henderson, Zenna 1917-1983 . . . . . . .DLB-8

Henisch, Peter 1943- DLB-85

Henley, Beth 1952- Y-86

Henley, William Ernest
1849-1903 . . . . DLB-19

Henniker, Florence 1855-1923 . . . . . DLB-135

Henry, Alexander 1739-1824 . . . . DLB-99

Henry, Buck 1930- DLB-26

Henry VIII of England
1491-1547 . . . . DLB-132

Henry, Marguerite 1902- DLB-22

Henry, O. (see Porter, William Sydney)

Henry of Ghent
circa 1217-1229 - 1293 . . . . DLB-115

Henry, Robert Selph 1889-1970 . . . . . DLB-17

Henry, Will (see Allen, Henry W.)

Henryson, Robert
1420s or 1430s-circa 1505 . . . . . DLB-146

Henschke, Alfred (see Klabund)

Hensley, Sophie Almon 1866-1946 . . DLB-99

Henty, G. A. 1832?-1902 . . . . . . DLB-18, 141

Hentz, Caroline Lee 1800-1856 . . . . . .DLB-3

Herbert, Alan Patrick 1890-1971 . . . . DLB-10

Herbert, Edward, Lord, of Cherbury
1582-1648 . . . . DLB-121, 151

Herbert, Frank 1920-1986 . . . . .DLB-8

Herbert, George 1593-1633 . . . . DLB-126

Herbert, Henry William
1807-1858 . . . . DLB-3, 73

Herbert, John 1926- DLB-53

Herbst, Josephine 1892-1969 . . . . .DLB-9

Herburger, Gunter 1932- DLB-75, 124

Hercules, Frank E. M. 1917- DLB-33

Herder, Johann Gottfried
1744-1803 . . . . DLB-97

Herder, B., Book Company DLB-49

Herford, Charles Harold
1853-1931 . . . . DLB-149

Hergesheimer, Joseph
1880-1954 . . . . .DLB-9, 102

Heritage Press DLB-46

Hermann the Lame 1013-1054 . . . . . DLB-148

Hermes, Johann Timotheus
1738-1821 . . . . DLB-97

Hermlin, Stephan 1915- DLB-69

Hernández, Alfonso C. 1938- DLB-122

Hernández, Inés 1947- DLB-122

Hernández, Miguel 1910-1942 . . . . . DLB-134

Hernton, Calvin C. 1932- DLB-38

"The Hero as Man of Letters: Johnson,
Rousseau, Burns" (1841), by Thomas
Carlyle [excerpt] DLB-57

The Hero as Poet. Dante; Shakspeare (1841),
by Thomas Carlyle DLB-32

Heron, Robert 1764-1807 . . . . .DLB-142

Herrera, Juan Felipe 1948- DLB-122

Herrick, Robert 1591-1674 . . . . DLB-126

Herrick, Robert 1868-1938 . . . .DLB-9, 12, 78

Herrick, William 1915- Y-83

Herrick, E. R., and Company DLB-49

Herrmann, John 1900-1959 . . . . DLB-4

Hersey, John 1914-1993 . . . . DLB-6

Hertel, François 1905-1985 . . . . DLB-68

Hervé-Bazin, Jean Pierre Marie (see Bazin,
Hervé)

Hervey, John, Lord 1696-1743 . . . . . DLB-101

Herwig, Georg 1817-1875 . . . . DLB-133

Herzog, Emile Salomon Wilhelm (see Maurois,
André)

Hesse, Hermann 1877-1962 . . . . DLB-66

Hewat, Alexander
circa 1743-circa 1824 . . . . DLB-30

Hewitt, John 1907- DLB-27

Hewlett, Maurice 1861-1923 . . . .DLB-34, 156

Heyen, William 1940- DLB-5

Heyer, Georgette 1902-1974 . . . . DLB-77

Heym, Stefan 1913- DLB-69

Heyse, Paul 1830-1914 . . . . DLB-129

Heytesbury, William
circa 1310-1372 or 1373 . . . . . . .DLB-115

Heyward, Dorothy 1890-1961 . . . . . . .DLB-7

Heyward, DuBose
1885-1940 . . . . DLB-7, 9, 45

Heywood, John 1497?-1580? DLB-136

Heywood, Thomas
1573 or 1574-1641 . . . . .DLB-62

Hibbs, Ben 1901-1975 . . . . .DLB-137

Hichens, Robert S. 1864-1950 . . . . . .DLB-153

Hickman, William Albert
1877-1957 . . . . .DLB-92

Hidalgo, José Luis 1919-1947 . . . . . . .DLB-108

Hiebert, Paul 1892-1987 . . . . .DLB-68

Hierro, José 1922- DLB-108

Higgins, Aidan 1927- DLB-14

Higgins, Colin 1941-1988 . . . . .DLB-26

Higgins, George V. 1939- DLB-2; Y-81

Higginson, Thomas Wentworth
1823-1911 . . . . DLB-1, 64

Highwater, Jamake 1942?- . . . DLB-52; Y-85

Hijuelos, Oscar 1951- DLB-145

Hildegard von Bingen
1098-1179 . . . . .DLB-148

Das Hildesbrandslied circa 820 . . . . . . .DLB-148

Hildesheimer, Wolfgang
1916-1991 . . . . DLB-69, 124

Hildreth, Richard
1807-1865 . . . . DLB-1, 30, 59

Hill, Aaron 1685-1750 . . . . .DLB-84

Hill, Geoffrey 1932- DLB-40

Hill, "Sir" John 1714?-1775 . . . . .DLB-39

Hill, Leslie 1880-1960 . . . . .DLB-51

Hill, Susan 1942- DLB-14, 139

Hill, Walter 1942- DLB-44

Hill and Wang DLB-46

Hill, George M., Company DLB-49

Hill, Lawrence, and Company,
Publishers DLB-46

Hillberry, Conrad 1928- DLB-120

Hilliard, Gray and Company DLB-49

Hills, Lee 1906- DLB-127

Hillyer, Robert 1895-1961 . . . . .DLB-54

Hilton, James 1900-1954 . . . . DLB-34, 77

Hilton, Walter died 1396 . . . . .DLB-146

Hilton and Company DLB-49

Himes, Chester
1909-1984 . . . . DLB-2, 76, 143

Hine, Daryl 1936- DLB-60

Hingley, Ronald 1920- DLB-155

Hinojosa-Smith, Rolando
1929- DLB-82

Hippel, Theodor Gottlieb von
1741-1796 ....DLB-97

Hirsch, E. D., Jr. 1928- DLB-67

Hirsch, Edward 1950- DLB-120

The History of the Adventures of Joseph Andrews
(1742), by Henry Fielding
[excerpt] DLB-39

Hoagland, Edward 1932- DLB-6

Hoagland, Everett H., III 1942- DLB-41

Hoban, Russell 1925- DLB-52

Hobbes, Thomas 1588-1679 ....DLB-151

Hobby, Oveta 1905- DLB-127

Hobby, William 1878-1964 ....DLB-127

Hobsbaum, Philip 1932- DLB-40

Hobson, Laura Z. 1900- DLB-28

Hoby, Thomas 1530-1566 ....DLB-132

Hoccleve, Thomas
circa 1368-circa 1437 ....DLB-146

Hochhuth, Rolf 1931- DLB-124

Hochman, Sandra 1936- DLB-5

Hodder and Stoughton, Limited DLB-106

Hodgins, Jack 1938- DLB-60

Hodgman, Helen 1945- DLB-14

Hodgskin, Thomas 1787-1869 .....DLB-158

Hodgson, Ralph 1871-1962 ....DLB-19

Hodgson, William Hope
1877-1918 .... DLB-70, 153, 156

Hoffenstein, Samuel 1890-1947 .....DLB-11

Hoffman, Charles Fenno
1806-1884 ....DLB-3

Hoffman, Daniel 1923- DLB-5

Hoffmann, E. T. A. 1776-1822 ......DLB-90

Hofmann, Michael 1957- DLB-40

Hofmannsthal, Hugo von
1874-1929 ....DLB-81, 118

Hofstadter, Richard 1916-1970 ......DLB-17

Hogan, Desmond 1950- DLB-14

Hogan and Thompson DLB-49

Hogarth Press DLB-112

Hogg, James 1770-1835 ... DLB-93, 116, 159

Hohl, Ludwig 1904-1980 ....DLB-56

Holbrook, David 1923- DLB-14, 40

Holcroft, Thomas
1745-1809 ....DLB-39, 89, 158

Holden, Jonathan 1941- DLB-105

Holden, Jonathan, Contemporary
Verse Story-telling DLB-105

Holden, Molly 1927-1981 ....DLB-40

Hölderlin, Friedrich 1770-1843 .....DLB-90

Holiday House DLB-46

Holland, J. G. 1819-1881 ....DS-13

Holland, Norman N. 1927- DLB-67

Hollander, John 1929- DLB-5

Holley, Marietta 1836-1926 ....DLB-11

Hollingsworth, Margaret 1940- DLB-60

Hollo, Anselm 1934- DLB-40

Holloway, Emory 1885-1977 ......DLB-103

Holloway, John 1920- DLB-27

Holloway House Publishing
Company DLB-46

Holme, Constance 1880-1955 ....DLB-34

Holmes, Abraham S. 1821?-1908 ....DLB-99

Holmes, John Clellon 1926-1988 ....DLB-16

Holmes, Oliver Wendell
1809-1894 ....DLB-1

Holmes, Richard 1945- DLB-155

Holroyd, Michael 1935- DLB-155

Holst, Hermann E. von
1841-1904 ....DLB-47

Holt, John 1721-1784 ....DLB-43

Holt, Henry, and Company DLB-49

Holt, Rinehart and Winston DLB-46

Holthusen, Hans Egon 1913- DLB-69

Hölty, Ludwig Christoph Heinrich
1748-1776 ....DLB-94

Holz, Arno 1863-1929 ....DLB-118

Home, Henry, Lord Kames (see Kames, Henry
Home, Lord)

Home, John 1722-1808 ....DLB-84

Home, William Douglas 1912- DLB-13

Home Publishing Company DLB-49

Homes, Geoffrey (see Mainwaring, Daniel)

Honan, Park 1928- DLB-111

Hone, William 1780-1842 .....DLB-110, 158

Hongo, Garrett Kaoru 1951- DLB-120

Honig, Edwin 1919- DLB-5

Hood, Hugh 1928- DLB-53

Hood, Thomas 1799-1845 ....DLB-96

Hook, Theodore 1788-1841 ....DLB-116

Hooker, Jeremy 1941- DLB-40

Hooker, Richard 1554-1600 ....DLB-132

Hooker, Thomas 1586-1647 ....DLB-24

Hooper, Johnson Jones
1815-1862 ....DLB-3, 11

Hope, Anthony 1863-1933 .....DLB-153, 156

Hopkins, Gerard Manley
1844-1889 ....DLB-35, 57

Hopkins, John (see Sternhold, Thomas)

Hopkins, Lemuel 1750-1801 ....DLB-37

Hopkins, Pauline Elizabeth
1859-1930 ....DLB-50

Hopkins, Samuel 1721-1803 ....DLB-31

Hopkins, John H., and Son DLB-46

Hopkinson, Francis 1737-1791 ......DLB-31

Horgan, Paul 1903- DLB-102; Y-85

Horizon Press DLB-46

Horne, Frank 1899-1974 ....DLB-51

Horne, Richard Henry (Hengist)
1802 or 1803-1884 ....DLB-32

Hornung, E. W. 1866-1921 ....DLB-70

Horovitz, Israel 1939- DLB-7

Horton, George Moses
1797?-1883? DLB-50

Horváth, Ödön von
1901-1938 ....DLB-85, 124

Horwood, Harold 1923- DLB-60

Hosford, E. and E.
[publishing house] DLB-49

Hoskyns, John 1566-1638 ....DLB-121

Hotchkiss and Company DLB-49

Hough, Emerson 1857-1923 ....DLB-9

Houghton Mifflin Company DLB-49

Houghton, Stanley 1881-1913 ....DLB-10

Household, Geoffrey 1900-1988 .....DLB-87

Housman, A. E. 1859-1936 ....DLB-19

Housman, Laurence 1865-1959 ......DLB-10

Houwald, Ernst von 1778-1845 ......DLB-90

Hovey, Richard 1864-1900 ....DLB-54

Howard, Donald R. 1927-1987 .....DLB-111

Howard, Maureen 1930- Y-83

Howard, Richard 1929- DLB-5

Howard, Roy W. 1883-1964 ....DLB-29

Howard, Sidney 1891-1939 ....DLB-7, 26

Howe, E. W. 1853-1937 ....DLB-12, 25

Howe, Henry 1816-1893 ....DLB-30

Howe, Irving 1920-1993 ....DLB-67

Howe, Joseph 1804-1873 .... DLB-99

Howe, Julia Ward 1819-1910 ....DLB-1

Howe, Percival Presland
    1886-1944 .... DLB-149

Howe, Susan 1937- DLB-120

Howell, Clark, Sr. 1863-1936 .... DLB-25

Howell, Evan P. 1839-1905 .... DLB-23

Howell, James 1594?-1666 .... DLB-151

Howell, Warren Richardson
    1912-1984 .... DLB-140

Howell, Soskin and Company DLB-46

Howells, William Dean
    1837-1920 .... DLB-12, 64, 74, 79

Howitt, William 1792-1879 and
    Howitt, Mary 1799-1888 ...... DLB-110

Hoyem, Andrew 1935- DLB-5

Hoyos, Angela de 1940- DLB-82

Hoyt, Palmer 1897-1979 .... DLB-127

Hoyt, Henry [publishing house] DLB-49

Hrabanus Maurus 776?-856 .... DLB-148

Hrotsvit of Gandersheim
    circa 935-circa 1000 .... DLB-148

Hubbard, Elbert 1856-1915 .... DLB-91

Hubbard, Kin 1868-1930 .... DLB-11

Hubbard, William circa 1621-1704 .. DLB-24

Huber, Therese 1764-1829 .... DLB-90

Huch, Friedrich 1873-1913 .... DLB-66

Huch, Ricarda 1864-1947 .... DLB-66

Huck at 100: How Old Is
    Huckleberry Finn? Y-85

Huddle, David 1942- DLB-130

Hudgins, Andrew 1951- DLB-120

Hudson, Henry Norman
    1814-1886 .... DLB-64

Hudson, W. H. 1841-1922 ..... DLB-98, 153

Hudson and Goodwin DLB-49

Huebsch, B. W.
    [publishing house] DLB-46

Hughes, David 1930- DLB-14

Hughes, John 1677-1720 .... DLB-84

Hughes, Langston
    1902-1967 ....DLB-4, 7, 48, 51, 86

Hughes, Richard 1900-1976 .... DLB-15, 161

Hughes, Ted 1930- DLB-40, 161

Hughes, Thomas 1822-1896 .... DLB-18, 163

Hugo, Richard 1923-1982 ....DLB-5

Hugo, Victor 1802-1885 .... DLB-119

Hugo Awards and Nebula Awards DLB-8

Hull, Richard 1896-1973 .... DLB-77

Hulme, T. E. 1883-1917 .... DLB-19

Humboldt, Alexander von
    1769-1859 .... DLB-90

Humboldt, Wilhelm von
    1767-1835 .... DLB-90

Hume, David 1711-1776 .... DLB-104

Hume, Fergus 1859-1932 .... DLB-70

Hummer, T. R. 1950- DLB-120

Humorous Book Illustration DLB-11

Humphrey, William 1924- DLB-6

Humphreys, David 1752-1818 ..... DLB-37

Humphreys, Emyr 1919- DLB-15

Huncke, Herbert 1915- DLB-16

Huneker, James Gibbons
    1857-1921 .... DLB-71

Hunt, Irene 1907- DLB-52

Hunt, Leigh 1784-1859 ....DLB-96, 110, 144

Hunt, Violet 1862-1942 .... DLB-162

Hunt, William Gibbes 1791-1833 .... DLB-73

Hunter, Evan 1926- Y-82

Hunter, Jim 1939- DLB-14

Hunter, Kristin 1931- DLB-33

Hunter, Mollie 1922- DLB-161

Hunter, N. C. 1908-1971 .... DLB-10

Hunter-Duvar, John 1821-1899 ..... DLB-99

Huntington, Henry E.
    1850-1927 .... DLB-140

Hurd and Houghton DLB-49

Hurst, Fannie 1889-1968 .... DLB-86

Hurst and Blackett DLB-106

Hurst and Company DLB-49

Hurston, Zora Neale
    1901?-1960 ....DLB-51, 86

Husson, Jules-François-Félix (see Champfleury)

Huston, John 1906-1987 .... DLB-26

Hutcheson, Francis 1694-1746 ...... DLB-31

Hutchinson, Thomas
    1711-1780 ....DLB-30, 31

Hutchinson and Company
    (Publishers) Limited DLB-112

Hutton, Richard Holt 1826-1897 .... DLB-57

Huxley, Aldous
    1894-1963 ....DLB-36, 100, 162

Huxley, Elspeth Josceline 1907- DLB-77

Huxley, T. H. 1825-1895 .... DLB-57

Huyghue, Douglas Smith
    1816-1891 ....DLB-99

Huysmans, Joris-Karl 1848-1907 ....DLB-123

Hyman, Trina Schart 1939- DLB-61

I

Iavorsky, Stefan 1658-1722 ....DLB-150

Ibn Bajja circa 1077-1138 ....DLB-115

Ibn Gabirol, Solomon
    circa 1021-circa 1058 ....DLB-115

The Iconography of Science-Fiction
    Art DLB-8

Iffland, August Wilhelm
    1759-1814 ....DLB-94

Ignatow, David 1914- DLB-5

Ike, Chukwuemeka 1931- DLB-157

Iles, Francis (see Berkeley, Anthony)

The Illustration of Early German
    Literary Manuscripts,
    circa 1150-circa 1300 ....DLB-148

Imbs, Bravig 1904-1946 ....DLB-4

Imbuga, Francis D. 1947- DLB-157

Immermann, Karl 1796-1840 ......DLB-133

Inchbald, Elizabeth 1753-1821 ... DLB-39, 89

Inge, William 1913-1973 ....DLB-7

Ingelow, Jean 1820-1897 .... DLB-35, 163

Ingersoll, Ralph 1900-1985 ....DLB-127

The Ingersoll Prizes Y-84

Ingoldsby, Thomas (see Barham, Richard
    Harris)

Ingraham, Joseph Holt 1809-1860 .....DLB-3

Inman, John 1805-1850 ....DLB-73

Innerhofer, Franz 1944- DLB-85

Innis, Harold Adams 1894-1952 .....DLB-88

Innis, Mary Quayle 1899-1972 ......DLB-88

International Publishers Company ...DLB-46

An Interview with David Rabe Y-91

An Interview with George Greenfield,
    Literary Agent Y-91

An Interview with James Ellroy Y-91

An Interview with Peter S. Prescott Y-86

An Interview with Russell Hoban Y-90

An Interview with Tom Jenks Y-86

Introduction to Paul Laurence Dunbar,
    Lyrics of Lowly Life (1896),
    by William Dean Howells DLB-50

Introductory Essay: *Letters of Percy Bysshe Shelley* (1852), by Robert Browning DLB-32

Introductory Letters from the Second Edition of *Pamela* (1741), by Samuel Richardson DLB-39

Irving, John 1942- DLB-6; Y-82

Irving, Washington 1783-1859 . . . . .DLB-3, 11, 30, 59, 73, 74

Irwin, Grace 1907- DLB-68

Irwin, Will 1873-1948 . . . . .DLB-25

Isherwood, Christopher 1904-1986 . . . . .DLB-15; Y-86

The Island Trees Case: A Symposium on School Library Censorship
An Interview with Judith Krug
An Interview with Phyllis Schlafly
An Interview with Edward B. Jenkinson
An Interview with Lamarr Mooneyham
An Interview with Harriet Bernstein Y-82

Islas, Arturo 1938-1991 . . . . .DLB-122

Ivers, M. J., and Company DLB-49

Iyayi, Festus 1947- DLB-157

J

Jackmon, Marvin E. (see Marvin X)

Jacks, L. P. 1860-1955 . . . . .DLB-135

Jackson, Angela 1951- DLB-41

Jackson, Helen Hunt 1830-1885 . . . . .DLB-42, 47

Jackson, Holbrook 1874-1948 . . . . . . .DLB-98

Jackson, Laura Riding 1901-1991 . . . .DLB-48

Jackson, Shirley 1919-1965 . . . . .DLB-6

Jacob, Piers Anthony Dillingham (see Anthony, Piers)

Jacobi, Friedrich Heinrich 1743-1819 . . . . .DLB-94

Jacobi, Johann Georg 1740-1841 . . . . .DLB-97

Jacobs, Joseph 1854-1916 . . . . .DLB-141

Jacobs, W. W. 1863-1943 . . . . .DLB-135

Jacobs, George W., and Company . . .DLB-49

Jacobson, Dan 1929- DLB-14

Jahier, Piero 1884-1966 . . . . .DLB-114

Jahnn, Hans Henny 1894-1959 . . . . .DLB-56, 124

Jakes, John 1932- Y-83

James, C. L. R. 1901-1989 . . . . .DLB-125

James, George P. R. 1801-1860 . . . . .DLB-116

James, Henry 1843-1916 . . . . . . .DLB-12, 71, 74; DS-13

James, John circa 1633-1729 . . . . .DLB-24

The James Jones Society Y-92

James, M. R. 1862-1936 . . . . .DLB-156

James, P. D. 1920- DLB-87

James Joyce Centenary: Dublin, 1982 . . . Y-82

James Joyce Conference Y-85

James VI of Scotland, I of England 1566-1625 . . . . DLB-151

James, U. P. [publishing house] DLB-49

Jameson, Anna 1794-1860 . . . . .DLB-99

Jameson, Fredric 1934- DLB-67

Jameson, J. Franklin 1859-1937 . . . . .DLB-17

Jameson, Storm 1891-1986 . . . . .DLB-36

Janés, Clara 1940- DLB-134

Jaramillo, Cleofas M. 1878-1956 . . .DLB-122

Jarman, Mark 1952- DLB-120

Jarrell, Randall 1914-1965 . . . . . . .DLB-48, 52

Jarrold and Sons DLB-106

Jasmin, Claude 1930- DLB-60

Jay, John 1745-1829 . . . . .DLB-31

Jefferies, Richard 1848-1887 . . . .DLB-98, 141

Jeffers, Lance 1919-1985 . . . . .DLB-41

Jeffers, Robinson 1887-1962 . . . . . . .DLB-45

Jefferson, Thomas 1743-1826 . . . . . . .DLB-31

Jelinek, Elfriede 1946- DLB-85

Jellicoe, Ann 1927- DLB-13

Jenkins, Elizabeth 1905- DLB-155

Jenkins, Robin 1912- DLB-14

Jenkins, William Fitzgerald (see Leinster, Murray)

Jenkins, Herbert, Limited DLB-112

Jennings, Elizabeth 1926- DLB-27

Jens, Walter 1923- DLB-69

Jensen, Merrill 1905-1980 . . . . .DLB-17

Jephson, Robert 1736-1803 . . . . .DLB-89

Jerome, Jerome K. 1859-1927 . . . . .DLB-10, 34, 135

Jerome, Judson 1927-1991 . . . . .DLB-105

Jerome, Judson, Reflections: After a Tornado DLB-105

Jerrold, Douglas 1803-1857 . . . .DLB-158, 159

Jesse, F. Tennyson 1888-1958 . . . . . .DLB-77

Jewett, Sarah Orne 1849-1909 . . .DLB-12, 74

Jewett, John P., and Company DLB-49

The Jewish Publication Society DLB-49

Jewitt, John Rodgers 1783-1821 . . . . .DLB-99

Jewsbury, Geraldine 1812-1880 . . . . . .DLB-21

Jhabvala, Ruth Prawer 1927- DLB-139

Jiménez, Juan Ramón 1881-1958 . . . .DLB-134

Joans, Ted 1928- DLB-16, 41

John, Eugenie (see Marlitt, E.)

John of Dumbleton circa 1310-circa 1349 . . . . .DLB-115

John Edward Bruce: Three Documents DLB-50

John O'Hara's Pottsville Journalism Y-88

John Steinbeck Research Center Y-85

John Webster: The Melbourne Manuscript Y-86

Johns, Captain W. E. 1893-1968 . . . .DLB-160

Johnson, B. S. 1933-1973 . . . . . . .DLB-14, 40

Johnson, Charles 1679-1748 . . . . . . .DLB-84

Johnson, Charles R. 1948- DLB-33

Johnson, Charles S. 1893-1956 . . .DLB-51, 91

Johnson, Denis 1949- DLB-120

Johnson, Diane 1934- Y-80

Johnson, Edgar 1901- DLB-103

Johnson, Edward 1598-1672 . . . . .DLB-24

Johnson, Fenton 1888-1958 . . . . . .DLB-45, 50

Johnson, Georgia Douglas 1886-1966 . . . . .DLB-51

Johnson, Gerald W. 1890-1980 . . . . . .DLB-29

Johnson, Helene 1907- DLB-51

Johnson, James Weldon 1871-1938 . . . . .DLB-51

Johnson, John H. 1918- DLB-137

Johnson, Linton Kwesi 1952- DLB-157

Johnson, Lionel 1867-1902 . . . . .DLB-19

Johnson, Nunnally 1897-1977 . . . . . . .DLB-26

Johnson, Owen 1878-1952 . . . . .Y-87

Johnson, Pamela Hansford 1912- DLB-15

Johnson, Pauline 1861-1913 . . . . .DLB-92

Johnson, Samuel 1696-1772 . . . . .DLB-24

Johnson, Samuel 1709-1784 . . . . .DLB-39, 95, 104, 142

Johnson, Samuel 1822-1882 . . . . .DLB-1

Johnson, Uwe 1934-1984 . . . . .DLB-75

Johnson, Benjamin [publishing house] DLB-49

Johnson, Benjamin, Jacob, and Robert [publishing house] DLB-49

Johnson, Jacob, and Company DLB-49

Johnson, Joseph [publishing house] ...DLB-154

Johnston, Annie Fellows 1863-1931 .. DLB-42

Johnston, Basil H. 1929- DLB-60

Johnston, Denis 1901-1984 .... DLB-10

Johnston, George 1913- DLB-88

Johnston, Jennifer 1930- DLB-14

Johnston, Mary 1870-1936 ....DLB-9

Johnston, Richard Malcolm
1822-1898 .... DLB-74

Johnstone, Charles 1719?-1800? DLB-39

Johst, Hanns 1890-1978 .... DLB-124

Jolas, Eugene 1894-1952 .... DLB-4, 45

Jones, Alice C. 1853-1933 .... DLB-92

Jones, Charles C., Jr. 1831-1893 .... DLB-30

Jones, D. G. 1929- DLB-53

Jones, David 1895-1974 .... DLB-20, 100

Jones, Diana Wynne 1934- DLB-161

Jones, Ebenezer 1820-1860 .... DLB-32

Jones, Ernest 1819-1868 .... DLB-32

Jones, Gayl 1949- DLB-33

Jones, Glyn 1905- DLB-15

Jones, Gwyn 1907- DLB-15, 139

Jones, Henry Arthur 1851-1929 ..... DLB-10

Jones, Hugh circa 1692-1760 .... DLB-24

Jones, James 1921-1977 .... DLB-2, 143

Jones, Jenkin Lloyd 1911- DLB-127

Jones, LeRoi (see Baraka, Amiri)

Jones, Lewis 1897-1939 .... DLB-15

Jones, Madison 1925- DLB-152

Jones, Major Joseph (see Thompson, William
Tappan)

Jones, Preston 1936-1979 ....DLB-7

Jones, Rodney 1950- DLB-120

Jones, Sir William 1746-1794 ...... DLB-109

Jones, William Alfred 1817-1900 .... DLB-59

Jones's Publishing House DLB-49

Jong, Erica 1942- DLB-2, 5, 28, 152

Jonke, Gert F. 1946- DLB-85

Jonson, Ben 1572?-1637 .... DLB-62, 121

Jordan, June 1936- DLB-38

Joseph, Jenny 1932- DLB-40

Joseph, Michael, Limited DLB-112

Josephson, Matthew 1899-1978 ......DLB-4

Josiah Allen's Wife (see Holley, Marietta)

Josipovici, Gabriel 1940- DLB-14

Josselyn, John ?-1675 .... DLB-24

Joudry, Patricia 1921- DLB-88

Jovine, Giuseppe 1922- DLB-128

Joyaux, Philippe (see Sollers, Philippe)

Joyce, Adrien (see Eastman, Carol)

Joyce, James
1882-1941 .... DLB-10, 19, 36, 162

Judd, Sylvester 1813-1853 .... DLB-1

Judd, Orange, Publishing
Company DLB-49

Judith circa 930 .... DLB-146

Julian of Norwich
1342-circa 1420 .... DLB-1146

Julian Symons at Eighty Y-92

June, Jennie (see Croly, Jane Cunningham)

Jung, Franz 1888-1963 .... DLB-118

Jünger, Ernst 1895- DLB-56

Der jüngere Titurel circa 1275 .... DLB-138

Jung-Stilling, Johann Heinrich
1740-1817 .... DLB-94

Justice, Donald 1925- Y-83

The Juvenile Library (see Godwin, M. J., and
Company)

K

Kacew, Romain (see Gary, Romain)

Kafka, Franz 1883-1924 .... DLB-81

Kaiser, Georg 1878-1945 .... DLB-124

Kaiserchronik circca 1147 .... DLB-148

Kalechofsky, Roberta 1931- DLB-28

Kaler, James Otis 1848-1912 .... DLB-12

Kames, Henry Home, Lord
1696-1782 ....DLB-31, 104

Kandel, Lenore 1932- DLB-16

Kanin, Garson 1912- DLB-7

Kant, Hermann 1926- DLB-75

Kant, Immanuel 1724-1804 .... DLB-94

Kantemir, Antiokh Dmitrievich
1708-1744 .... DLB-150

Kantor, Mackinlay 1904-1977 ....DLB-9, 102

Kaplan, Fred 1937- DLB-111

Kaplan, Johanna 1942- DLB-28

Kaplan, Justin 1925- DLB-111

Kapnist, Vasilii Vasilevich
1758?-1823 .... DLB-150

Karadžić, Vuk Stefanović
1787-1864 ....DLB-147

Karamzin, Nikolai Mikhailovich
1766-1826 ....DLB-150

Karsch, Anna Louisa 1722-1791 .....DLB-97

Kasack, Hermann 1896-1966 ....DLB-69

Kaschnitz, Marie Luise 1901-1974 ....DLB-69

Kaštelan, Jure 1919-1990 ....DLB-147

Kästner, Erich 1899-1974 ....DLB-56

Kattan, Naim 1928- DLB-53

Katz, Steve 1935- Y-83

Kauffman, Janet 1945- Y-86

Kauffmann, Samuel 1898-1971 .....DLB-127

Kaufman, Bob 1925- DLB-16, 41

Kaufman, George S. 1889-1961 ....DLB-7

Kavanagh, P. J. 1931- DLB-40

Kavanagh, Patrick 1904-1967 .... DLB-15, 20

Kaye-Smith, Sheila 1887-1956 ....DLB-36

Kazin, Alfred 1915- DLB-67

Keane, John B. 1928- DLB-13

Keary, Annie 1825-1879 ....DLB-163

Keating, H. R. F. 1926- DLB-87

Keats, Ezra Jack 1916-1983 ....DLB-61

Keats, John 1795-1821 .... DLB-96, 110

Keble, John 1792-1866 .... DLB-32, 55

Keeble, John 1944- Y-83

Keeffe, Barrie 1945- DLB-13

Keeley, James 1867-1934 ....DLB-25

W. B. Keen, Cooke
and Company DLB-49

Keillor, Garrison 1942- Y-87

Keith, Marian 1874?-1961 ....DLB-92

Keller, Gary D. 1943- DLB-82

Keller, Gottfried 1819-1890 ....DLB-129

Kelley, Edith Summers 1884-1956 .....DLB-9

Kelley, William Melvin 1937- DLB-33

Kellogg, Ansel Nash 1832-1886 ......DLB-23

Kellogg, Steven 1941- DLB-61

Kelly, George 1887-1974 ....DLB-7

Kelly, Hugh 1739-1777 ....DLB-89

Kelly, Robert 1935- DLB-5, 130

Kelly, Piet and Company DLB-49

Kelmscott Press DLB-112

Kemble, Fanny 1809-1893 ....DLB-32

Kemelman, Harry 1908- DLB-28

Kempe, Margery circa 1373-1438 .... DLB-146

Kempner, Friederike 1836-1904 .... DLB-129

Kempowski, Walter 1929- DLB-75

Kendall, Claude [publishing company] DLB-46

Kendell, George 1809-1867 .... DLB-43

Kenedy, P. J., and Sons DLB-49

Kennedy, Adrienne 1931- DLB-38

Kennedy, John Pendleton 1795-1870 ... DLB-3

Kennedy, Leo 1907- DLB-88

Kennedy, Margaret 1896-1967 ...... DLB-36

Kennedy, Patrick 1801-1873 .... DLB-159

Kennedy, Richard S. 1920- DLB-111

Kennedy, William 1928- DLB-143; Y-85

Kennedy, X. J. 1929- DLB-5

Kennelly, Brendan 1936- DLB-40

Kenner, Hugh 1923- DLB-67

Kennerley, Mitchell [publishing house] DLB-46

Kent, Frank R. 1877-1958 .... DLB-29

Kenyon, Jane 1947- DLB-120

Keppler and Schwartzmann DLB-49

Kerner, Justinus 1776-1862 .... DLB-90

Kerouac, Jack 1922-1969 ... DLB-2, 16; DS-3

Kerouac, Jan 1952- DLB-16

Kerr, Orpheus C. (see Newell, Robert Henry)

Kerr, Charles H., and Company DLB-49

Kesey, Ken 1935- DLB-2, 16

Kessel, Joseph 1898-1979 .... DLB-72

Kessel, Martin 1901- DLB-56

Kesten, Hermann 1900- DLB-56

Keun, Irmgard 1905-1982 .... DLB-69

Key and Biddle DLB-49

Keynes, John Maynard 1883-1946 .... DS-10

Keyserling, Eduard von 1855-1918 ... DLB-66

Khan, Ismith 1925- DLB-125

Khemnitser, Ivan Ivanovich 1745-1784 .... DLB-150

Kheraskov, Mikhail Matveevich 1733-1807 .... DLB-150

Khvostov, Dmitrii Ivanovich 1757-1835 .... DLB-150

Kidd, Adam 1802?-1831 .... DLB-99

Kidd, William [publishing house] DLB-106

Kiely, Benedict 1919- DLB-15

Kiggins and Kellogg DLB-49

Kiley, Jed 1889-1962 .... DLB-4

Kilgore, Bernard 1908-1967 .... DLB-127

Killens, John Oliver 1916- DLB-33

Killigrew, Anne 1660-1685 .... DLB-131

Killigrew, Thomas 1612-1683 .... DLB-58

Kilmer, Joyce 1886-1918 .... DLB-45

Kilwardby, Robert circa 1215-1279 .... DLB-115

Kincaid, Jamaica 1949- DLB-157

King, Clarence 1842-1901 .... DLB-12

King, Florence 1936 .... Y-85

King, Francis 1923- DLB-15, 139

King, Grace 1852-1932 .... DLB-12, 78

King, Henry 1592-1669 .... DLB-126

King, Stephen 1947- DLB-143; Y-80

King, Woodie, Jr. 1937- DLB-38

King, Solomon [publishing house] ... DLB-49

Kinglake, Alexander William 1809-1891 .... DLB-55

Kingsley, Charles 1819-1875 .... DLB-21, 32, 163

Kingsley, Henry 1830-1876 .... DLB-21

Kingsley, Sidney 1906- DLB-7

Kingsmill, Hugh 1889-1949 .... DLB-149

Kingston, Maxine Hong 1940- Y-80

Kingston, William Henry Giles 1814-1880 .... DLB-163

Kinnell, Galway 1927- DLB-5; Y-87

Kinsella, Thomas 1928- DLB-27

Kipling, Rudyard 1865-1936 .... DLB-19, 34, 141, 156

Kipphardt, Heinar 1922-1982 ...... DLB-124

Kirby, William 1817-1906 .... DLB-99

Kirk, John Foster 1824-1904 .... DLB-79

Kirkconnell, Watson 1895-1977 ..... DLB-68

Kirkland, Caroline M. 1801-1864 .... DLB-3, 73, 74; DS-13

Kirkland, Joseph 1830-1893 .... DLB-12

Kirkpatrick, Clayton 1915- DLB-127

Kirkup, James 1918- DLB-27

Kirouac, Conrad (see Marie-Victorin, Frère)

Kirsch, Sarah 1935- DLB-75

Kirst, Hans Hellmut 1914-1989 ..... DLB-69

Kitcat, Mabel Greenhow 1859-1922 .... DLB-135

Kitchin, C. H. B. 1895-1967 .... DLB-77

Kizer, Carolyn 1925- DLB-5

Klabund 1890-1928 .... DLB-66

Klappert, Peter 1942- DLB-5

Klass, Philip (see Tenn, William)

Klein, A. M. 1909-1972 .... DLB-68

Kleist, Ewald von 1715-1759 .... DLB-97

Kleist, Heinrich von 1777-1811 ...... DLB-90

Klinger, Friedrich Maximilian 1752-1831 .... DLB-94

Klopstock, Friedrich Gottlieb 1724-1803 .... DLB-97

Klopstock, Meta 1728-1758 .... DLB-97

Kluge, Alexander 1932- DLB-75

Knapp, Joseph Palmer 1864-1951 .... DLB-91

Knapp, Samuel Lorenzo 1783-1838 .... DLB-59

Knapton, J. J. and P. [publishing house] DLB-154

Kniazhnin, Iakov Borisovich 1740-1791 .... DLB-150

Knickerbocker, Diedrich (see Irving, Washington)

Knigge, Adolph Franz Friedrich Ludwig, Freiherr von 1752-1796 .... DLB-94

Knight, Damon 1922- DLB-8

Knight, Etheridge 1931-1992 .... DLB-41

Knight, John S. 1894-1981 .... DLB-29

Knight, Sarah Kemble 1666-1727 .... DLB-24

Knight, Charles, and Company DLB-106

Knister, Raymond 1899-1932 ...... DLB-68

Knoblock, Edward 1874-1945 .... DLB-10

Knopf, Alfred A. 1892-1984 .... Y-84

Knopf, Alfred A. [publishing house] DLB-46

Knowles, John 1926- DLB-6

Knox, Frank 1874-1944 .... DLB-29

Knox, John circa 1514-1572 .... DLB-132

Knox, John Armoy 1850-1906 .... DLB-23

Knox, Ronald Arbuthnott 1888-1957 .... DLB-77

Kober, Arthur 1900-1975 .... DLB-11

Kocbek, Edvard 1904-1981 .... DLB-147

Koch, Howard 1902- DLB-26

Koch, Kenneth 1925- DLB-5

Koenigsberg, Moses 1879-1945 ...... DLB-25

Koeppen, Wolfgang 1906- DLB-69

Koertge, Ronald 1940- DLB-105

Koestler, Arthur 1905-1983 .... Y-83

Kokoschka, Oskar 1886-1980 ...... DLB-124

Kolb, Annette 1870-1967 .... DLB-66

Kolbenheyer, Erwin Guido
1878-1962 .... DLB-66, 124

Kolleritsch, Alfred 1931- DLB-85

Kolodny, Annette 1941- DLB-67

Komarov, Matvei
circa 1730-1812 .... DLB-150

Komroff, Manuel 1890-1974 ....DLB-4

Komunyakaa, Yusef 1947- DLB-120

Konigsburg, E. L. 1930- DLB-52

Konrad von Würzburg
circa 1230-1287 .... DLB-138

Konstantinov, Aleko 1863-1897 .... DLB-147

Kooser, Ted 1939- DLB-105

Kopit, Arthur 1937- DLB-7

Kops, Bernard 1926?- DLB-13

Kornbluth, C. M. 1923-1958 ....DLB-8

Körner, Theodor 1791-1813 .... DLB-90

Kornfeld, Paul 1889-1942 .... DLB-118

Kosinski, Jerzy 1933-1991 ...... DLB-2; Y-82

Kosovel, Srečko 1904-1926 .... DLB-147

Kostrov, Ermil Ivanovich
1755-1796 .... DLB-150

Kotzebue, August von 1761-1819 ... DLB-94

Kovačić, Ante 1854-1889 .... DLB-147

Kraf, Elaine 1946- Y-81

Kranjčević, Silvije Strahimir
1865-1908 .... DLB-147

Krasna, Norman 1909-1984 .... DLB-26

Kraus, Karl 1874-1936 .... DLB-118

Krauss, Ruth 1911-1993 .... DLB-52

Kreisel, Henry 1922- DLB-88

Kreuder, Ernst 1903-1972 .... DLB-69

Kreymborg, Alfred 1883-1966 .... DLB-4, 54

Krieger, Murray 1923- DLB-67

Krim, Seymour 1922-1989 .... DLB-16

Krleža, Miroslav 1893-1981 .... DLB-147

Krock, Arthur 1886-1974 .... DLB-29

Kroetsch, Robert 1927- DLB-53

Krutch, Joseph Wood 1893-1970 .... DLB-63

Krylov, Ivan Andreevich
1769-1844 .... DLB-150

Kubin, Alfred 1877-1959 .... DLB-81

Kubrick, Stanley 1928- DLB-26

Kudrun circa 1230-1240 .... DLB-138

Kumin, Maxine 1925- DLB-5

Kunene, Mazisi 1930- DLB-117

Kunitz, Stanley 1905- DLB-48

Kunjufu, Johari M. (see Amini, Johari M.)

Kunnert, Gunter 1929- DLB-75

Kunze, Reiner 1933- DLB-75

Kupferberg, Tuli 1923- DLB-16

Kürnberger, Ferdinand
1821-1879 .... DLB-129

Kurz, Isolde 1853-1944 .... DLB-66

Kusenberg, Kurt 1904-1983 .... DLB-69

Kuttner, Henry 1915-1958 .... DLB-8

Kyd, Thomas 1558-1594 .... DLB-62

Kyftin, Maurice
circa 1560?-1598 .... DLB-136

Kyger, Joanne 1934- DLB-16

Kyne, Peter B. 1880-1957 .... DLB-78

L

L. E. L. (see Landon, Letitia Elizabeth)

Laberge, Albert 1871-1960 .... DLB-68

Laberge, Marie 1950- DLB-60

Lacombe, Patrice (see Trullier-Lacombe,
Joseph Patrice)

Lacretelle, Jacques de 1888-1985 ..... DLB-65

Ladd, Joseph Brown 1764-1786 ..... DLB-37

La Farge, Oliver 1901-1963 .... DLB-9

Lafferty, R. A. 1914- DLB-8

La Guma, Alex 1925-1985 .... DLB-117

Lahaise, Guillaume (see Delahaye, Guy)

Lahontan, Louis-Armand de Lom d'Arce,
Baron de 1666-1715? DLB-99

Laing, Kojo 1946- DLB-157

Laird, Carobeth 1895- Y-82

Laird and Lee DLB-49

Lalonde, Michèle 1937- DLB-60

Lamantia, Philip 1927- DLB-16

Lamb, Charles
1775-1834 ....DLB-93, 107, 163

Lamb, Lady Caroline 1785-1828 ... DLB-116

Lamb, Mary 1764-1874 .... DLB-163

Lambert, Betty 1933-1983 .... DLB-60

Lamming, George 1927- DLB-125

L'Amour, Louis 1908?- Y-80

Lampman, Archibald 1861-1899 ..... DLB-92

Lamson, Wolffe and Company DLB-49

Lancer Books DLB-46

Landesman, Jay 1919- and
Landesman, Fran 1927- DLB-16

Landon, Letitia Elizabeth 1802-1838 ..DLB-96

Landor, Walter Savage
1775-1864 .... DLB-93, 107

Landry, Napoléon-P. 1884-1956 .....DLB-92

Lane, Charles 1800-1870 ....DLB-1

Lane, Laurence W. 1890-1967 ......DLB-91

Lane, M. Travis 1934- DLB-60

Lane, Patrick 1939- DLB-53

Lane, Pinkie Gordon 1923- DLB-41

Lane, John, Company DLB-49

Laney, Al 1896- DLB-4

Lang, Andrew 1844-1912 ...... DLB-98, 141

Langevin, André 1927- DLB-60

Langgässer, Elisabeth 1899-1950 .....DLB-69

Langhorne, John 1735-1779 ....DLB-109

Langland, William
circa 1330-circa 1400 ....DLB-146

Langton, Anna 1804-1893 ....DLB-99

Lanham, Edwin 1904-1979 ....DLB-4

Lanier, Sidney 1842-1881 .... DLB-64; DS-13

Lanyer, Aemilia 1569-1645 ....DLB-121

Lapointe, Gatien 1931-1983 ....DLB-88

Lapointe, Paul-Marie 1929- DLB-88

Lardner, Ring 1885-1933 .... DLB-11, 25, 86

Lardner, Ring, Jr. 1915- DLB-26

Lardner 100: Ring Lardner
Centennial Symposium Y-85

Larkin, Philip 1922-1985 ....DLB-27

La Roche, Sophie von 1730-1807 ....DLB-94

La Rocque, Gilbert 1943-1984 ......DLB-60

Laroque de Roquebrune, Robert (see Roquebrune, Robert de)

Larrick, Nancy 1910- DLB-61

Larsen, Nella 1893-1964 ....DLB-51

Lasker-Schüler, Else
1869-1945 .... DLB-66, 124

Lasnier, Rina 1915- DLB-88

Lassalle, Ferdinand 1825-1864 ......DLB-129

Lathrop, Dorothy P. 1891-1980 ......DLB-22

Lathrop, George Parsons
1851-1898 ....DLB-71

Lathrop, John, Jr. 1772-1820 ....DLB-37

Latimer, Hugh 1492?-1555 ....DLB-136

Latimore, Jewel Christine McLawler
(see Amini, Johari M.)

Latymer, William 1498-1583 . . . . . . .DLB-132

Laube, Heinrich 1806-1884 . . . . .DLB-133

Laughlin, James 1914- DLB-48

Laumer, Keith 1925- DLB-8

Laurence, Margaret 1926-1987 . . . . . .DLB-53

Laurents, Arthur 1918- DLB-26

Laurie, Annie (see Black, Winifred)

Laut, Agnes Christiana 1871-1936 . . .DLB-92

Lavater, Johann Kaspar 1741-1801 . . .DLB-97

Lavin, Mary 1912- DLB-15

Lawes, Henry 1596-1662 . . . . .DLB-126

Lawless, Anthony (see MacDonald, Philip)

Lawrence, D. H.
1885-1930 . . . . . .DLB-10, 19, 36, 98, 162

Lawrence, David 1888-1973 . . . . .DLB-29

Lawrence, Seymour 1926-1994 . . . . .Y-94

Lawson, John ?-1711 . . . . .DLB-24

Lawson, Robert 1892-1957 . . . . .DLB-22

Lawson, Victor F. 1850-1925 . . . . .DLB-25

Layton, Irving 1912- DLB-88

LaZamon flourished circa 1200 . . . . .DLB-146

Lazarević, Laza K. 1851-1890 . . . . . .DLB-147

Lea, Henry Charles 1825-1909 . . . . . .DLB-47

Lea, Sydney 1942- DLB-120

Lea, Tom 1907- DLB-6

Leacock, John 1729-1802 . . . . .DLB-31

Leacock, Stephen 1869-1944 . . . . .DLB-92

Lead, Jane Ward 1623-1704 . . . . .DLB-131

Leadenhall Press DLB-106

Leapor, Mary 1722-1746 . . . . .DLB-109

Lear, Edward 1812-1888 . . . . . .DLB-32, 163

Leary, Timothy 1920- DLB-16

Leary, W. A., and Company DLB-49

Léautaud, Paul 1872-1956 . . . . .DLB-65

Leavitt, David 1961- DLB-130

Leavitt and Allen DLB-49

le Carré, John 1931- DLB-87

Lécavelé, Roland (see Dorgeles, Roland)

Lechlitner, Ruth 1901- DLB-48

Leclerc, Félix 1914- DLB-60

Le Clézio, J. M. G. 1940- DLB-83

Lectures on Rhetoric and Belles Lettres (1783),
by Hugh Blair [excerpts] DLB-31

Leder, Rudolf (see Hermlin, Stephan)

Lederer, Charles 1910-1976 . . . . DLB-26

Ledwidge, Francis 1887-1917 . . . . DLB-20

Lee, Dennis 1939- DLB-53

Lee, Don L. (see Madhubuti, Haki R.)

Lee, George W. 1894-1976 . . . . DLB-51

Lee, Harper 1926- DLB-6

Lee, Harriet (1757-1851) and
Lee, Sophia (1750-1824) DLB-39

Lee, Laurie 1914- DLB-27

Lee, Manfred B. (see Dannay, Frederic, and
Manfred B. Lee)

Lee, Nathaniel circa 1645 - 1692 . . . . DLB-80

Lee, Sir Sidney 1859-1926 . . . . DLB-149

Lee, Sir Sidney, "Principles of Biography," in
Elizabethan and Other Essays DLB-149

Lee, Vernon 1856-1935 . . . .DLB-57, 153, 156

Lee and Shepard DLB-49

Le Fanu, Joseph Sheridan
1814-1873 . . . . .DLB-21, 70, 159

Leffland, Ella 1931- Y-84

le Fort, Gertrud von 1876-1971 . . . . . DLB-66

Le Gallienne, Richard 1866-1947 . . . . . DLB-4

Legaré, Hugh Swinton
1797-1843 . . . . .DLB-3, 59, 73

Legaré, James M. 1823-1859 . . . . DLB-3

The Legends of the Saints and a Medieval
Christian Worldview DLB-148

Léger, Antoine-J. 1880-1950 . . . . DLB-88

Le Guin, Ursula K. 1929- DLB-8, 52

Lehman, Ernest 1920- DLB-44

Lehmann, John 1907- DLB-27, 100

Lehmann, Rosamond 1901-1990 . . . . DLB-15

Lehmann, Wilhelm 1882-1968 . . . . . . DLB-56

Lehmann, John, Limited DLB-112

Leiber, Fritz 1910-1992 . . . . DLB-8

Leicester University Press DLB-112

Leinster, Murray 1896-1975 . . . . DLB-8

Leisewitz, Johann Anton
1752-1806 . . . . DLB-94

Leitch, Maurice 1933- DLB-14

Leithauser, Brad 1943- DLB-120

Leland, Charles G. 1824-1903 . . . . . . DLB-11

Leland, John 1503?-1552 . . . . DLB-136

Lemay, Pamphile 1837-1918 . . . . DLB-99

Lemelin, Roger 1919- DLB-88

Lemon, Mark 1809-1870 . . . . DLB-163

Le Moine, James MacPherson
1825-1912 . . . . .DLB-99

Le Moyne, Jean 1913- DLB-88

L'Engle, Madeleine 1918- DLB-52

Lennart, Isobel 1915-1971 . . . . .DLB-44

Lennox, Charlotte
1729 or 1730-1804 . . . . .DLB-39

Lenox, James 1800-1880 . . . . .DLB-140

Lenski, Lois 1893-1974 . . . . .DLB-22

Lenz, Hermann 1913- DLB-69

Lenz, J. M. R. 1751-1792 . . . . .DLB-94

Lenz, Siegfried 1926- DLB-75

Leonard, Hugh 1926- DLB-13

Leonard, William Ellery
1876-1944 . . . . .DLB-54

Leonowens, Anna 1834-1914 . . . . .DLB-99

LePan, Douglas 1914- DLB-88

Leprohon, Rosanna Eleanor
1829-1879 . . . . .DLB-99

Le Queux, William 1864-1927 . . . . . .DLB-70

Lerner, Max 1902-1992 . . . . .DLB-29

Lernet-Holenia, Alexander
1897-1976 . . . . .DLB-85

Le Rossignol, James 1866-1969 . . . . . .DLB-92

Lescarbot, Marc circa 1570-1642 . . . .DLB-99

LeSeur, William Dawson
1840-1917 . . . . .DLB-92

LeSieg, Theo. (see Geisel, Theodor Seuss)

Leslie, Frank 1821-1880 . . . . .DLB-43, 79

Leslie, Frank, Publishing House DLB-49

Lesperance, John 1835?-1891 . . . . . . .DLB-99

Lessing, Bruno 1870-1940 . . . . .DLB-28

Lessing, Doris 1919- . . . DLB-15, 139; Y-85

Lessing, Gotthold Ephraim
1729-1781 . . . . .DLB-97

Lettau, Reinhard 1929- DLB-75

Letter from Japan Y-94

Letter to [Samuel] Richardson on *Clarissa*
(1748), by Henry Fielding DLB-39

Lever, Charles 1806-1872 . . . . .DLB-21

Leverson, Ada 1862-1933 . . . . .DLB-153

Levertov, Denise 1923- DLB-5

Levi, Peter 1931- DLB-40

Levien, Sonya 1888-1960 . . . . .DLB-44

Levin, Meyer 1905-1981 . . . .DLB-9, 28; Y-81

Levine, Norman 1923- DLB-88

Levine, Philip 1928- DLB-5

Levis, Larry 1946- DLB-120

Levy, Amy 1861-1889 .... DLB-156

Levy, Benn Wolfe
1900-1973 .... DLB-13; Y-81

Lewald, Fanny 1811-1889 .... DLB-129

Lewes, George Henry
1817-1878 .... DLB-55, 144

Lewis, Alfred H. 1857-1914 .... DLB-25

Lewis, Alun 1915-1944 .... DLB-20, 162

Lewis, C. Day (see Day Lewis, C.)

Lewis, C. S. 1898-1963 .... DLB-15, 100, 160

Lewis, Charles B. 1842-1924 .... DLB-11

Lewis, Henry Clay 1825-1850 .... DLB-3

Lewis, Janet 1899- Y-87

Lewis, Matthew Gregory
1775-1818 .... DLB-39, 158

Lewis, R. W. B. 1917- DLB-111

Lewis, Richard circa 1700-1734 ..... DLB-24

Lewis, Sinclair
1885-1951 .... DLB-9, 102; DS-1

Lewis, Wilmarth Sheldon
1895-1979 .... DLB-140

Lewis, Wyndham 1882-1957 .... DLB-15

Lewisohn, Ludwig
1882-1955 .... DLB-4, 9, 28, 102

Lezama Lima, José 1910-1976 ..... DLB-113

The Library of America DLB-46

The Licensing Act of 1737 .... DLB-84

Lichtenberg, Georg Christoph
1742-1799 .... DLB-94

Liebling, A. J. 1904-1963 .... DLB-4

Lieutenant Murray (see Ballou, Maturin
Murray)

Lighthall, William Douw
1857-1954 .... DLB-92

Lilar, Françoise (see Mallet-Joris, Françoise)

Lillo, George 1691-1739 .... DLB-84

Lilly, J. K., Jr. 1893-1966 .... DLB-140

Lilly, Wait and Company DLB-49

Lily, William circa 1468-1522 ..... DLB-132

Limited Editions Club DLB-46

Lincoln and Edmands DLB-49

Lindsay, Jack 1900- Y-84

Lindsay, Sir David
circa 1485-1555 .... DLB-132

Lindsay, Vachel 1879-1931 .... DLB-54

Linebarger, Paul Myron Anthony (see Smith,
Cordwainer)

Link, Arthur S. 1920- DLB-17

Linn, John Blair 1777-1804 .... DLB-37

Lins, Osman 1924-1978 .... DLB-145

Linton, Eliza Lynn 1822-1898 .... DLB-18

Linton, William James 1812-1897 .... DLB-32

Lion Books DLB-46

Lionni, Leo 1910- DLB-61

Lippincott, Sara Jane Clarke
1823-1904 .... DLB-43

Lippincott, J. B., Company DLB-49

Lippmann, Walter 1889-1974 .... DLB-29

Lipton, Lawrence 1898-1975 .... DLB-16

Liscow, Christian Ludwig
1701-1760 .... DLB-97

Lish, Gordon 1934- DLB-130

Lispector, Clarice 1925-1977 ...... DLB-113

The Literary Chronicle and Weekly Review
1819-1828 .... DLB-110

Literary Documents: William Faulkner
and the People-to-People
Program Y-86

Literary Documents II: *Library Journal*
Statements and Questionnaires from
First Novelists Y-87

Literary Effects of World War II
[British novel] DLB-15

Literary Prizes [British] DLB-15

Literary Research Archives: The Humanities
Research Center, University of
Texas Y-82

Literary Research Archives II: Berg
Collection of English and American
Literature of the New York Public
Library Y-83

Literary Research Archives III:
The Lilly Library Y-84

Literary Research Archives IV:
The John Carter Brown Library Y-85

Literary Research Archives V:
Kent State Special Collections Y-86

Literary Research Archives VI: The Modern
Literary Manuscripts Collection in the
Special Collections of the Washington
University Libraries Y-87

Literary Research Archives VII:
The University of Virginia
Libraries Y-91

Literary Research Archives VIII:
The Henry E. Huntington
Library Y-92

"Literary Style" (1857), by William
Forsyth [excerpt] DLB-57

Literatura Chicanesca: The View From
Without DLB-82

Literature at Nurse, or Circulating Morals (1885),
by George Moore DLB-18

Littell, Eliakim 1797-1870 .... DLB-79

Littell, Robert S. 1831-1896 .... DLB-79

Little, Brown and Company DLB-49

Littlewood, Joan 1914- DLB-13

Lively, Penelope 1933- DLB-14, 161

Liverpool University Press DLB-112

The Lives of the Poets DLB-142

Livesay, Dorothy 1909- DLB-68

Livesay, Florence Randal
1874-1953 .... DLB-92

Livings, Henry 1929- DLB-13

Livingston, Anne Howe
1763-1841 .... DLB-37

Livingston, Myra Cohn 1926- DLB-61

Livingston, William 1723-1790 ..... DLB-31

Liyong, Taban lo (see Taban lo Liyong)

Lizárraga, Sylvia S. 1925- DLB-82

Llewellyn, Richard 1906-1983 ...... DLB-15

Lloyd, Edward
[publishing house] DLB-106

Lobel, Arnold 1933- DLB-61

Lochridge, Betsy Hopkins (see Fancher, Betsy)

Locke, David Ross 1833-1888 ... DLB-11, 23

Locke, John 1632-1704 .... DLB-31, 101

Locke, Richard Adams 1800-1871 ....DLB-43

Locker-Lampson, Frederick
1821-1895 .... DLB-35

Lockhart, John Gibson
1794-1854 .... DLB-110, 116 144

Lockridge, Ross, Jr.
1914-1948 .... DLB-143; Y-80

Locrine and *Selimus* DLB-62

Lodge, David 1935- DLB-14

Lodge, George Cabot 1873-1909 ..... DLB-54

Lodge, Henry Cabot 1850-1924 ..... DLB-47

Loeb, Harold 1891-1974 .... DLB-4

Loeb, William 1905-1981 .... DLB-127

Lofting, Hugh 1886-1947 .... DLB-160

Logan, James 1674-1751 .... DLB-24, 140

Logan, John 1923- DLB-5

Logan, William 1950- DLB-120

Logue, Christopher 1926- DLB-27

Lomonosov, Mikhail Vasil'evich
1711-1765 .... DLB-150

London, Jack 1876-1916 ...... DLB-8, 12, 78

The London Magazine 1820-1829 . . . . . DLB-110

Long, Haniel 1888-1956 . . . . DLB-45

Long, Ray 1878-1935 . . . . DLB-137

Long, H., and Brother DLB-49

Longfellow, Henry Wadsworth
1807-1882 . . . . DLB-1, 59

Longfellow, Samuel 1819-1892 . . . . DLB-1

Longford, Elizabeth 1906- DLB-155

Longley, Michael 1939- DLB-40

Longman, T. [publishing house] DLB-154

Longmans, Green and Company DLB-49

Longmore, George 1793?-1867 . . . . . . DLB-99

Longstreet, Augustus Baldwin
1790-1870 . . . . DLB-3, 11, 74

Longworth, D. [publishing house] DLB-49

Lonsdale, Frederick 1881-1954 . . . . . . DLB-10

A Look at the Contemporary Black Theatre
Movement DLB-38

Loos, Anita 1893-1981 . . . . DLB-11, 26; Y-81

Lopate, Phillip 1943- Y-80

López, Diana (see Isabella, Ríos)

Loranger, Jean-Aubert 1896-1942 . . . . DLB-92

Lorca, Federico García 1898-1936 . . . DLB-108

Lord, John Keast 1818-1872 . . . . DLB-99

The Lord Chamberlain's Office and Stage
Censorship in England DLB-10

Lorde, Audre 1934-1992 . . . . DLB-41

Lorimer, George Horace
1867-1939 . . . . DLB-91

Loring, A. K. [publishing house] DLB-49

Loring and Mussey DLB-46

Lossing, Benson J. 1813-1891 . . . . DLB-30

Lothar, Ernst 1890-1974 . . . . DLB-81

Lothrop, Harriet M. 1844-1924 . . . . . . DLB-42

Lothrop, D., and Company DLB-49

Loti, Pierre 1850-1923 . . . . DLB-123

The Lounger, no. 20 (1785), by Henry
Mackenzie DLB-39

Lounsbury, Thomas R. 1838-1915 . . . DLB-71

Louÿs, Pierre 1870-1925 . . . . DLB-123

Lovelace, Earl 1935- DLB-125

Lovelace, Richard 1618-1657 . . . . DLB-131

Lovell, Coryell and Company DLB-49

Lovell, John W., Company DLB-49

Lover, Samuel 1797-1868 . . . . DLB-159

Lovesey, Peter 1936- DLB-87

Lovingood, Sut (see Harris,
George Washington)

Low, Samuel 1765-? DLB-37

Lowell, Amy 1874-1925 . . . . DLB-54, 140

Lowell, James Russell
1819-1891 . . . . DLB-1, 11, 64, 79

Lowell, Robert 1917-1977 . . . . DLB-5

Lowenfels, Walter 1897-1976 . . . . DLB-4

Lowndes, Marie Belloc 1868-1947 . . . DLB-70

Lowry, Lois 1937- DLB-52

Lowry, Malcolm 1909-1957 . . . . DLB-15

Lowther, Pat 1935-1975 . . . . DLB-53

Loy, Mina 1882-1966 . . . . DLB-4, 54

Lozeau, Albert 1878-1924 . . . . DLB-92

Lubbock, Percy 1879-1965 . . . . DLB-149

Lucas, E. V. 1868-1938 . . . . DLB-98, 149, 153

Lucas, Fielding, Jr.
[publishing house] DLB-49

Luce, Henry R. 1898-1967 . . . . DLB-91

Luce, John W., and Company DLB-46

Lucie-Smith, Edward 1933- DLB-40

Lucini, Gian Pietro 1867-1914 . . . . . DLB-114

Ludlum, Robert 1927- Y-82

Ludus de Antichristo circa 1160 . . . . . DLB-148

Ludvigson, Susan 1942- DLB-120

Ludwig, Jack 1922- DLB-60

Ludwig, Otto 1813-1865 . . . . DLB-129

Ludwigslied 881 or 882 . . . . DLB-148

Luera, Yolanda 1953- DLB-122

Luft, Lya 1938- DLB-145

Luke, Peter 1919- DLB-13

Lupton, F. M., Company DLB-49

Lupus of Ferrières
circa 805-circa 862 . . . . DLB-148

Lurie, Alison 1926- DLB-2

Luzi, Mario 1914- DLB-128

L'vov, Nikolai Aleksandrovich
1751-1803 . . . . DLB-150

Lyall, Gavin 1932- DLB-87

Lydgate, John circa 1370-1450 . . . . . DLB-146

Lyly, John circa 1554-1606 . . . . DLB-62

Lynch, Patricia 1898-1972 . . . . DLB-160

Lynd, Robert 1879-1949 . . . . DLB-98

Lyon, Matthew 1749-1822 . . . . DLB-43

Lytle, Andrew 1902- DLB-6

Lytton, Edward (see Bulwer-Lytton, Edward)

Lytton, Edward Robert Bulwer
1831-1891 . . . . DLB-32

M

Maass, Joachim 1901-1972 . . . . DLB-69

Mabie, Hamilton Wright
1845-1916 . . . . DLB-71

Mac A'Ghobhainn, Iain (see Smith, Iain
Crichton)

MacArthur, Charles
1895-1956 . . . . DLB-7, 25, 44

Macaulay, Catherine 1731-1791 . . . . DLB-104

Macaulay, David 1945- DLB-61

Macaulay, Rose 1881-1958 . . . . DLB-36

Macaulay, Thomas Babington
1800-1859 . . . . DLB-32, 55

Macaulay Company DLB-46

MacBeth, George 1932- DLB-40

Macbeth, Madge 1880-1965 . . . . DLB-92

MacCaig, Norman 1910- DLB-27

MacDiarmid, Hugh 1892-1978 . . . . . DLB-20

MacDonald, Cynthia 1928- DLB-105

MacDonald, George
1824-1905 . . . . DLB-18, 163

MacDonald, John D.
1916-1986 . . . . DLB-8; Y-86

MacDonald, Philip 1899?-1980 . . . . . DLB-77

Macdonald, Ross (see Millar, Kenneth)

MacDonald, Wilson 1880-1967 . . . . . DLB-92

Macdonald and Company
(Publishers) DLB-112

MacEwen, Gwendolyn 1941- DLB-53

Macfadden, Bernarr
1868-1955 . . . . DLB-25, 91

MacGregor, Mary Esther (see Keith, Marian)

Machado, Antonio 1875-1939 . . . . . DLB-108

Machado, Manuel 1874-1947 . . . . . DLB-108

Machar, Agnes Maule 1837-1927 . . . DLB-92

Machen, Arthur Llewelyn Jones
1863-1947 . . . . DLB-36, 156

MacInnes, Colin 1914-1976 . . . . DLB-14

MacInnes, Helen 1907-1985 . . . . DLB-87

Mack, Maynard 1909- DLB-111

Mackall, Leonard L. 1879-1937 . . . . DLB-140

MacKaye, Percy 1875-1956 . . . . DLB-54

Macken, Walter 1915-1967 . . . . DLB-13

Mackenzie, Alexander 1763-1820 . . . DLB-99

Mackenzie, Compton
 1883-1972 .... DLB-34, 100

Mackenzie, Henry 1745-1831 .... DLB-39

Mackey, William Wellington
 1937- DLB-38

Mackintosh, Elizabeth (see Tey, Josephine)

Mackintosh, Sir James
 1765-1832 .... DLB-158

Maclaren, Ian (see Watson, John)

Macklin, Charles 1699-1797 .... DLB-89

MacLean, Katherine Anne 1925- DLB-8

MacLeish, Archibald
 1892-1982 .... DLB-4, 7, 45; Y-82

MacLennan, Hugh 1907-1990 ...... DLB-68

Macleod, Fiona (see Sharp, William)

MacLeod, Alistair 1936- DLB-60

Macleod, Norman 1906-1985 ....DLB-4

Macmillan and Company DLB-106

The Macmillan Company DLB-49

Macmillan's English Men of Letters,
 First Series (1878-1892) DLB-144

MacNamara, Brinsley 1890-1963 .... DLB-10

MacNeice, Louis 1907-1963 ..... DLB-10, 20

MacPhail, Andrew 1864-1938 ...... DLB-92

Macpherson, James 1736-1796 ..... DLB-109

Macpherson, Jay 1931- DLB-53

Macpherson, Jeanie 1884-1946 ...... DLB-44

Macrae Smith Company DLB-46

Macrone, John
 [publishing house] DLB-106

MacShane, Frank 1927- DLB-111

Macy-Masius DLB-46

Madden, David 1933- DLB-6

Maddow, Ben 1909-1992 .... DLB-44

Maddux, Rachel 1912-1983 .... Y-93

Madgett, Naomi Long 1923- DLB-76

Madhubuti, Haki R.
 1942- DLB-5, 41; DS-8

Madison, James 1751-1836 .... DLB-37

Maginn, William 1794-1842 ... DLB-110, 159

Mahan, Alfred Thayer 1840-1914 ... DLB-47

Maheux-Forcier, Louise 1929- DLB-60

Mahin, John Lee 1902-1984 .... DLB-44

Mahon, Derek 1941- DLB-40

Maikov, Vasilii Ivanovich
 1728-1778 .... DLB-150

Mailer, Norman
 1923- DLB-2, 16, 28; Y-80, 83; DS-3

Maillet, Adrienne 1885-1963 .... DLB-68

Maimonides, Moses 1138-1204 ..... DLB-115

Maillet, Antonine 1929- DLB-60

Maillu, David G. 1939- DLB-157

Main Selections of the Book-of-the-Month
 Club, 1926-1945 .... DLB-9

Main Trends in Twentieth-Century Book
 Clubs DLB-46

Mainwaring, Daniel 1902-1977 ...... DLB-44

Mair, Charles 1838-1927 .... DLB-99

Mais, Roger 1905-1955 .... DLB-125

Major, Andre 1942- DLB-60

Major, Clarence 1936- DLB-33

Major, Kevin 1949- DLB-60

Major Books DLB-46

Makemie, Francis circa 1658-1708 ... DLB-24

The Making of a People, by
 J. M. Ritchie DLB-66

Maksimović, Desanka 1898-1993 ... DLB-147

Malamud, Bernard
 1914-1986 ..... DLB-2, 28, 152; Y-80, 86

Malet, Lucas 1852-1931 .... DLB-153

Malleson, Lucy Beatrice (see Gilbert, Anthony)

Mallet-Joris, Françoise 1930- DLB-83

Mallock, W. H. 1849-1923 ......DLB-18, 57

Malone, Dumas 1892-1986 .... DLB-17

Malone, Edmond 1741-1812 .... DLB-142

Malory, Sir Thomas
 circa 1400-1410 - 1471 .... DLB-146

Malraux, André 1901-1976 .... DLB-72

Malthus, Thomas Robert
 1766-1834 ....DLB-107, 158

Maltz, Albert 1908-1985 .... DLB-102

Malzberg, Barry N. 1939- DLB-8

Mamet, David 1947- DLB-7

Manaka, Matsemela 1956- DLB-157

Manchester University Press DLB-112

Mandel, Eli 1922- DLB-53

Mandeville, Bernard 1670-1733 .... DLB-101

Mandeville, Sir John
 mid fourteenth century DLB-146

Mandiargues, André Pieyre de
 1909- DLB-83

Manfred, Frederick 1912-1994 .... DLB-6

Mangan, Sherry 1904-1961 .... DLB-4

Mankiewicz, Herman 1897-1953 .....DLB-26

Mankiewicz, Joseph L. 1909-1993 ....DLB-44

Mankowitz, Wolf 1924- DLB-15

Manley, Delarivière
 1672?-1724 .... DLB-39, 80

Mann, Abby 1927- DLB-44

Mann, Heinrich 1871-1950 ..... DLB-66, 118

Mann, Horace 1796-1859 ....DLB-1

Mann, Klaus 1906-1949 ....DLB-56

Mann, Thomas 1875-1955 ....DLB-66

Mann, William D'Alton
 1839-1920 ....DLB-137

Manning, Marie 1873?-1945 ....DLB-29

Manning and Loring DLB-49

Mannyng, Robert
 flourished 1303-1338 ....DLB-146

Mano, D. Keith 1942- DLB-6

Manor Books DLB-46

Mansfield, Katherine 1888-1923 ....DLB-162

Mapanje, Jack 1944- DLB-157

March, William 1893-1954 .... DLB-9, 86

Marchand, Leslie A. 1900- DLB-103

Marchant, Bessie 1862-1941 ....DLB-160

Marchessault, Jovette 1938- DLB-60

Marcus, Frank 1928- DLB-13

Marden, Orison Swett
 1850-1924 ....DLB-137

Marechera, Dambudzo
 1952-1987 ....DLB-157

Marek, Richard, Books DLB-46

Mares, E. A. 1938- DLB-122

Mariani, Paul 1940- DLB-111

Marie-Victorin, Frère 1885-1944 .....DLB-92

Marin, Biagio 1891-1985 ....DLB-128

Marincović, Ranko 1913- DLB-147

Marinetti, Filippo Tommaso
 1876-1944 ....DLB-114

Marion, Frances 1886-1973 ....DLB-44

Marius, Richard C. 1933- Y-85

The Mark Taper Forum DLB-7

Mark Twain on Perpetual Copyright ... Y-92

Markfield, Wallace 1926- DLB-2, 28

Markham, Edwin 1852-1940 ....DLB-54

Markle, Fletcher 1921-1991 ... DLB-68; Y-91

Marlatt, Daphne 1942- DLB-60

Marlitt, E. 1825-1887 ....DLB-129

Marlowe, Christopher 1564-1593 . . . . DLB-62

Marlyn, John 1912- DLB-88

Marmion, Shakerley 1603-1639 . . . . . . DLB-58

Der Marner
before 1230-circa 1287 . . . . DLB-138

The *Marprelate Tracts* 1588-1589 . . . . DLB-132

Marquand, John P. 1893-1960 . . . . DLB-9, 102

Marqués, René 1919-1979 . . . . DLB-113

Marquis, Don 1878-1937 . . . . DLB-11, 25

Marriott, Anne 1913- DLB-68

Marryat, Frederick 1792-1848 . . . DLB-21, 163

Marsh, George Perkins
1801-1882 . . . . DLB-1, 64

Marsh, James 1794-1842 . . . . DLB-1, 59

Marsh, Capen, Lyon and Webb DLB-49

Marsh, Ngaio 1899-1982 . . . . DLB-77

Marshall, Edison 1894-1967 . . . . DLB-102

Marshall, Edward 1932- DLB-16

Marshall, Emma 1828-1899 . . . . DLB-163

Marshall, James 1942-1992 . . . . DLB-61

Marshall, Joyce 1913- DLB-88

Marshall, Paule 1929- DLB-33, 157

Marshall, Tom 1938- DLB-60

Marsilius of Padua
circa 1275-circa 1342 . . . . DLB-115

Marson, Una 1905-1965 . . . . DLB-157

Marston, John 1576-1634 . . . . DLB-58

Marston, Philip Bourke 1850-1887 . . . DLB-35

Martens, Kurt 1870-1945 . . . . DLB-66

Martien, William S.
[publishing house] DLB-49

Martin, Abe (see Hubbard, Kin)

Martin, Charles 1942- DLB-120

Martin, Claire 1914- DLB-60

Martin, Jay 1935- DLB-111

Martin, Violet Florence (see Ross, Martin)

Martin du Gard, Roger 1881-1958 . . . DLB-65

Martineau, Harriet
1802-1876 . . . . DLB-21, 55, 159, 163

Martínez, Eliud 1935- DLB-122

Martínez, Max 1943- DLB-82

Martyn, Edward 1859-1923 . . . . DLB-10

Marvell, Andrew 1621-1678 . . . . . . DLB-131

Marvin X 1944- DLB-38

Marx, Karl 1818-1883 . . . . DLB-129

Marzials, Theo 1850-1920 . . . . DLB-35

Masefield, John
1878-1967 . . . . DLB-10, 19, 153, 160

Mason, A. E. W. 1865-1948 . . . . DLB-70

Mason, Bobbie Ann 1940- Y-87

Mason, William 1725-1797 . . . . DLB-142

Mason Brothers DLB-49

Massey, Gerald 1828-1907 . . . . DLB-32

Massinger, Philip 1583-1640 . . . . DLB-58

Masson, David 1822-1907 . . . . DLB-144

Masters, Edgar Lee 1868-1950 . . . . . . DLB-54

Mather, Cotton
1663-1728 . . . . DLB-24, 30, 140

Mather, Increase 1639-1723 . . . . DLB-24

Mather, Richard 1596-1669 . . . . DLB-24

Matheson, Richard 1926- DLB-8, 44

Matheus, John F. 1887- DLB-51

Mathews, Cornelius
1817?-1889 . . . . DLB-3, 64

Mathews, Elkin
[publishing house] DLB-112

Mathias, Roland 1915- DLB-27

Mathis, June 1892-1927 . . . . DLB-44

Mathis, Sharon Bell 1937- DLB-33

Matoš, Antun Gustav 1873-1914 . . . DLB-147

The Matter of England
1240-1400 . . . . DLB-146

The Matter of Rome
early twelfth to late fifteenth
century DLB-146

Matthews, Brander
1852-1929 . . . . DLB-71, 78; DS-13

Matthews, Jack 1925- DLB-6

Matthews, William 1942- DLB-5

Matthiessen, F. O. 1902-1950 . . . . . . DLB-63

Matthiessen, Peter 1927- DLB-6

Maugham, W. Somerset
1874-1965 . . . . . DLB-10, 36, 77, 100, 162

Maupassant, Guy de 1850-1893 . . . . DLB-123

Mauriac, Claude 1914- DLB-83

Mauriac, François 1885-1970 . . . . . . DLB-65

Maurice, Frederick Denison
1805-1872 . . . . DLB-55

Maurois, André 1885-1967 . . . . DLB-65

Maury, James 1718-1769 . . . . DLB-31

Mavor, Elizabeth 1927- DLB-14

Mavor, Osborne Henry (see Bridie, James)

Maxwell, H. [publishing house] DLB-49

Maxwell, John [publishing house] . . DLB-106

Maxwell, William 1908- Y-80

May, Elaine 1932- DLB-44

May, Karl 1842-1912 . . . . DLB-129

May, Thomas 1595 or 1596-1650 . . . . DLB-58

Mayer, Mercer 1943- DLB-61

Mayer, O. B. 1818-1891 . . . . DLB-3

Mayes, Herbert R. 1900-1987 . . . . . . DLB-137

Mayes, Wendell 1919-1992 . . . . DLB-26

Mayfield, Julian 1928-1984 . . . . DLB-33; Y-84

Mayhew, Henry 1812-1887 . . . . . . DLB-18, 55

Mayhew, Jonathan 1720-1766 . . . . . . DLB-31

Mayne, Jasper 1604-1672 . . . . DLB-126

Mayne, Seymour 1944- DLB-60

Mayor, Flora Macdonald
1872-1932 . . . . DLB-36

Mayrocker, Friederike 1924- DLB-85

Mazrui, Ali A. 1933- DLB-125

Mažuranić, Ivan 1814-1890 . . . . DLB-147

Mazursky, Paul 1930- DLB-44

McAlmon, Robert 1896-1956 . . . . . DLB-4, 45

McArthur, Peter 1866-1924 . . . . DLB-92

McBride, Robert M., and
Company DLB-46

McCaffrey, Anne 1926- DLB-8

McCarthy, Cormac 1933- DLB-6, 143

McCarthy, Mary 1912-1989 . . . . DLB-2; Y-81

McCay, Winsor 1871-1934 . . . . DLB-22

McClatchy, C. K. 1858-1936 . . . . DLB-25

McClellan, George Marion
1860-1934 . . . . DLB-50

McCloskey, Robert 1914- DLB-22

McClung, Nellie Letitia 1873-1951 . . . DLB-92

McClure, Joanna 1930- DLB-16

McClure, Michael 1932- DLB-16

McClure, Phillips and Company DLB-46

McClure, S. S. 1857-1949 . . . . DLB-91

McClurg, A. C., and Company DLB-49

McCluskey, John A., Jr. 1944- DLB-33

McCollum, Michael A. 1946 . . . . Y-87

McConnell, William C. 1917- DLB-88

McCord, David 1897- DLB-61

McCorkle, Jill 1958- Y-87

McCorkle, Samuel Eusebius
1746-1811 . . . . DLB-37

McCormick, Anne O'Hare
1880-1954 . . . . DLB-29

McCormick, Robert R. 1880-1955 . . . DLB-29

McCourt, Edward 1907-1972 . . . . DLB-88

McCoy, Horace 1897-1955 . . . . .DLB-9

McCrae, John 1872-1918 . . . . DLB-92

McCullagh, Joseph B. 1842-1896 . . . . DLB-23

McCullers, Carson 1917-1967 . . . . . DLB-2, 7

McCulloch, Thomas 1776-1843 . . . . . DLB-99

McDonald, Forrest 1927- DLB-17

McDonald, Walter
1934- DLB-105, DS-9

McDonald, Walter, Getting Started:
Accepting the Regions You Own—
or Which Own You DLB-105

McDougall, Colin 1917-1984 . . . . DLB-68

McDowell, Obolensky DLB-46

McEwan, Ian 1948- DLB-14

McFadden, David 1940- DLB-60

McFall, Frances Elizabeth Clarke
(see Grand, Sarah)

McFarlane, Leslie 1902-1977 . . . . DLB-88

McFee, William 1881-1966 . . . . DLB-153

McGahern, John 1934- DLB-14

McGee, Thomas D'Arcy
1825-1868 . . . . DLB-99

McGeehan, W. O. 1879-1933 . . . . DLB-25

McGill, Ralph 1898-1969 . . . . DLB-29

McGinley, Phyllis 1905-1978 . . . . DLB-11, 48

McGirt, James E. 1874-1930 . . . . DLB-50

McGlashan and Gill DLB-106

McGough, Roger 1937- DLB-40

McGraw-Hill DLB-46

McGuane, Thomas 1939- DLB-2; Y-80

McGuckian, Medbh 1950- DLB-40

McGuffey, William Holmes
1800-1873 . . . . DLB-42

McIlvanney, William 1936- DLB-14

McIlwraith, Jean Newton
1859-1938 . . . . DLB-92

McIntyre, James 1827-1906 . . . . DLB-99

McIntyre, O. O. 1884-1938 . . . . DLB-25

McKay, Claude
1889-1948 . . . . DLB-4, 45, 51, 117

The David McKay Company DLB-49

McKean, William V. 1820-1903 . . . . . DLB-23

McKinley, Robin 1952- DLB-52

McLachlan, Alexander 1818-1896 . . . DLB-99

McLaren, Floris Clark 1904-1978 . . . DLB-68

McLaverty, Michael 1907- DLB-15

McLean, John R. 1848-1916 . . . . DLB-23

McLean, William L. 1852-1931 . . . . . DLB-25

McLennan, William 1856-1904 . . . . . DLB-92

McLoughlin Brothers DLB-49

McLuhan, Marshall 1911-1980 . . . . . DLB-88

McMaster, John Bach 1852-1932 . . . . DLB-47

McMurtry, Larry
1936- DLB-2, 143; Y-80, 87

McNally, Terrence 1939- DLB-7

McNeil, Florence 1937- DLB-60

McNeile, Herman Cyril
1888-1937 . . . . DLB-77

McPherson, James Alan 1943- DLB-38

McPherson, Sandra 1943- Y-86

McWhirter, George 1939- DLB-60

McWilliams, Carey 1905-1980 . . . . . DLB-137

Mead, L. T. 1844-1914 . . . . DLB-141

Mead, Matthew 1924- DLB-40

Mead, Taylor ?- DLB-16

Mechthild von Magdeburg
circa 1207-circa 1282 . . . . DLB-138

Medill, Joseph 1823-1899 . . . . DLB-43

Medoff, Mark 1940- DLB-7

Meek, Alexander Beaufort
1814-1865 . . . . DLB-3

Meeke, Mary ?-1816? DLB-116

Meinke, Peter 1932- DLB-5

Mejia Vallejo, Manuel 1923- DLB-113

Melançon, Robert 1947- DLB-60

Mell, Max 1882-1971 . . . . .DLB-81, 124

Mellow, James R. 1926- DLB-111

Meltzer, David 1937- DLB-16

Meltzer, Milton 1915- DLB-61

Melville, Herman 1819-1891 . . . . . .DLB-3, 74

Memoirs of Life and Literature (1920),
by W. H. Mallock [excerpt] DLB-57

Mencken, H. L.
1880-1956 . . . . DLB-11, 29, 63, 137

Mencken and Nietzsche: An Unpublished
Excerpt from H. L. Mencken's *My Life
as Author and Editor* Y-93

Mendelssohn, Moses 1729-1786 . . . . . DLB-97

Méndez M., Miguel 1930- DLB-82

Mercer, Cecil William (see Yates, Dornford)

Mercer, David 1928-1980 . . . . DLB-13

Mercer, John 1704-1768 . . . . DLB-31

Meredith, George
1828-1909 . . . . .DLB-18, 35, 57, 159

Meredith, Owen (see Lytton, Edward Robert
Bulwer)

Meredith, William 1919- DLB-5

Mérimée, Prosper 1803-1870 . . . . . . .DLB-119

Merivale, John Herman
1779-1844 . . . . .DLB-96

Meriwether, Louise 1923- DLB-33

Merlin Press DLB-112

Merriam, Eve 1916-1992 . . . . .DLB-61

The Merriam Company DLB-49

Merrill, James 1926- DLB-5; Y-85

Merrill and Baker DLB-49

The Mershon Company DLB-49

Merton, Thomas 1915-1968 . . . DLB-48; Y-81

Merwin, W. S. 1927- DLB-5

Messner, Julian [publishing house] . . .DLB-46

Metcalf, J. [publishing house] DLB-49

Metcalf, John 1938- DLB-60

The Methodist Book Concern DLB-49

Methuen and Company DLB-112

Mew, Charlotte 1869-1928 . . . . . DLB-19, 135

Mewshaw, Michael 1943- Y-80

Meyer, Conrad Ferdinand
1825-1898 . . . . .DLB-129

Meyer, E. Y. 1946- DLB-75

Meyer, Eugene 1875-1959 . . . . .DLB-29

Meyer, Michael 1921- DLB-155

Meyers, Jeffrey 1939- DLB-111

Meynell, Alice
1847-1922 . . . . DLB-19, 98

Meynell, Viola 1885-1956 . . . . .DLB-153

Meyrink, Gustav 1868-1932 . . . . .DLB-81

Michaels, Leonard 1933- DLB-130

Micheaux, Oscar 1884-1951 . . . . .DLB-50

Michel of Northgate, Dan
circa 1265-circa 1340 . . . . .DLB-146

Micheline, Jack 1929- DLB-16

Michener, James A. 1907?- DLB-6

Micklejohn, George
circa 1717-1818 . . . . .DLB-31

Middle English Literature:
An Introduction DLB-146

The Middle English Lyric DLB-146

Middle Hill Press DLB-106

Middleton, Christopher 1926- DLB-40

Middleton, Richard 1882-1911 . . . . . DLB-156

Middleton, Stanley 1919- DLB-14

Middleton, Thomas 1580-1627 . . . . . . DLB-58

Miegel, Agnes 1879-1964 . . . . DLB-56

Miles, Josephine 1911-1985 . . . . DLB-48

Milius, John 1944- DLB-44

Mill, James 1773-1836 . . . . DLB-107, 158

Mill, John Stuart 1806-1873 . . . . DLB-55

Millar, Kenneth
 1915-1983 . . . . DLB-2; Y-83; DS-6

Millar, Andrew
 [publishing house] DLB-154

Millay, Edna St. Vincent
 1892-1950 . . . . DLB-45

Miller, Arthur 1915- DLB-7

Miller, Caroline 1903-1992 . . . . DLB-9

Miller, Eugene Ethelbert 1950- DLB-41

Miller, Heather Ross 1939- DLB-120

Miller, Henry 1891-1980 . . . . DLB-4, 9; Y-80

Miller, J. Hillis 1928- DLB-67

Miller, James [publishing house] DLB-49

Miller, Jason 1939- DLB-7

Miller, May 1899- DLB-41

Miller, Paul 1906-1991 . . . . DLB-127

Miller, Perry 1905-1963 . . . . DLB-17, 63

Miller, Sue 1943- DLB-143

Miller, Walter M., Jr. 1923- DLB-8

Miller, Webb 1892-1940 . . . . DLB-29

Millhauser, Steven 1943- DLB-2

Millican, Arthenia J. Bates
 1920- DLB-38

Mills and Boon DLB-112

Milman, Henry Hart 1796-1868 . . . . . DLB-96

Milne, A. A.
 1882-1956 . . . . DLB-10, 77, 100, 160

Milner, Ron 1938- DLB-38

Milner, William
 [publishing house] DLB-106

Milnes, Richard Monckton (Lord Houghton)
 1809-1885 . . . . DLB-32

Milton, John 1608-1674 . . . . DLB-131, 151

The Minerva Press DLB-154

Minnesang circa 1150-1280 . . . . DLB-138

Minns, Susan 1839-1938 . . . . DLB-140

Minor Illustrators, 1880-1914 . . . . . . DLB-141

Minor Poets of the Earlier Seventeenth
 Century DLB-121

Minton, Balch and Company DLB-46

Mirbeau, Octave 1848-1917 . . . . DLB-123

Mirk, John died after 1414? DLB-146

Miron, Gaston 1928- DLB-60

Mitchel, Jonathan 1624-1668 . . . . DLB-24

Mitchell, Adrian 1932- DLB-40

Mitchell, Donald Grant
 1822-1908 . . . . DLB-1; DS-13

Mitchell, Gladys 1901-1983 . . . . DLB-77

Mitchell, James Leslie 1901-1935 . . . . DLB-15

Mitchell, John (see Slater, Patrick)

Mitchell, John Ames 1845-1918 . . . . . DLB-79

Mitchell, Julian 1935- DLB-14

Mitchell, Ken 1940- DLB-60

Mitchell, Langdon 1862-1935 . . . . DLB-7

Mitchell, Loften 1919- DLB-38

Mitchell, Margaret 1900-1949 . . . . DLB-9

Mitchell, W. O. 1914- DLB-88

Mitchison, Naomi Margaret (Haldane)
 1897- DLB-160

Mitford, Mary Russell
 1787-1855 . . . . DLB-110, 116

Mittelholzer, Edgar 1909-1965 . . . . . DLB-117

Mitterer, Erika 1906- DLB-85

Mitterer, Felix 1948- DLB-124

Mizener, Arthur 1907-1988 . . . . DLB-103

Modern Age Books DLB-46

"Modern English Prose" (1876),
 by George Saintsbury DLB-57

The Modern Language Association of America
 Celebrates Its Centennial Y-84

The Modern Library DLB-46

"Modern Novelists – Great and Small" (1855),
 by Margaret Oliphant DLB-21

"Modern Style" (1857), by Cockburn
 Thomson [excerpt] DLB-57

The Modernists (1932), by Joseph Warren
 Beach DLB-36

Modiano, Patrick 1945- DLB-83

Moffat, Yard and Company DLB-46

Moffet, Thomas 1553-1604 . . . . DLB-136

Mohr, Nicholasa 1938- DLB-145

Moix, Ana María 1947- DLB-134

Molesworth, Louisa 1839-1921 . . . . DLB-135

Möllhausen, Balduin 1825-1905 . . . . DLB-129

Momaday, N. Scott 1934- DLB-143

Monkhouse, Allan 1858-1936 . . . . . . DLB-10

Monro, Harold 1879-1932 . . . . DLB-19

Monroe, Harriet 1860-1936 . . . . . DLB-54, 91

Monsarrat, Nicholas 1910-1979 . . . . DLB-15

Montagu, Lady Mary Wortley
 1689-1762 . . . . DLB-95, 101

Montague, John 1929- DLB-40

Montale, Eugenio 1896-1981 . . . . . . DLB-114

Monterroso, Augusto 1921- DLB-145

Montgomery, James
 1771-1854 . . . . DLB-93, 158

Montgomery, John 1919- DLB-16

Montgomery, Lucy Maud
 1874-1942 . . . . DLB-92

Montgomery, Marion 1925- DLB-6

Montgomery, Robert Bruce (see Crispin,
 Edmund)

Montherlant, Henry de 1896-1972 . . . DLB-72

The Monthly Review 1749-1844 . . . . . DLB-110

Montigny, Louvigny de 1876-1955 . . . DLB-92

Montoya, José 1932- DLB-122

Moodie, John Wedderburn Dunbar
 1797-1869 . . . . DLB-99

Moodie, Susanna 1803-1885 . . . . DLB-99

Moody, Joshua circa 1633-1697 . . . . DLB-24

Moody, William Vaughn
 1869-1910 . . . . DLB-7, 54

Moorcock, Michael 1939- DLB-14

Moore, Catherine L. 1911- DLB-8

Moore, Clement Clarke 1779-1863 . . . DLB-42

Moore, Dora Mavor 1888-1979 . . . . DLB-92

Moore, George
 1852-1933 . . . . DLB-10, 18, 57, 135

Moore, Marianne
 1887-1972 . . . . DLB-45; DS-7

Moore, Mavor 1919- DLB-88

Moore, Richard 1927- DLB-105

Moore, Richard, The No Self, the Little Self,
 and the Poets DLB-105

Moore, T. Sturge 1870-1944 . . . . DLB-19

Moore, Thomas 1779-1852 . . . . . DLB-96, 144

Moore, Ward 1903-1978 . . . . DLB-8

Moore, Wilstach, Keys and
 Company DLB-49

The Moorland-Spingarn Research
 Center DLB-76

Moorman, Mary C. 1905-1994 . . . . . DLB-155

Moraga, Cherríe 1952- DLB-82

Morales, Alejandro 1944- DLB-82

Morales, Mario Roberto 1947- ... DLB-145

Morales, Rafael 1919- DLB-108

Morality Plays: *Mankind* circa 1450-1500 and *Everyman* circa 1500 .... DLB-146

More, Hannah 1745-1833 .... DLB-107, 109, 116, 158

More, Henry 1614-1687 .... DLB-126

More, Sir Thomas 1477 or 1478-1535 .... DLB-136

Moreno, Dorinda 1939- DLB-122

Morency, Pierre 1942- DLB-60

Moretti, Marino 1885-1979 .... DLB-114

Morgan, Berry 1919- DLB-6

Morgan, Charles 1894-1958 .... DLB-34, 100

Morgan, Edmund S. 1916- DLB-17

Morgan, Edwin 1920- DLB-27

Morgan, John Pierpont 1837-1913 .... DLB-140

Morgan, John Pierpont, Jr. 1867-1943 .... DLB-140

Morgan, Robert 1944- DLB-120

Morgan, Sydney Owenson, Lady 1776?-1859 .... DLB-116, 158

Morgner, Irmtraud 1933- DLB-75

Morier, James Justinian 1782 or 1783?-1849 .... DLB-116

Mörike, Eduard 1804-1875 .... DLB-133

Morin, Paul 1889-1963 .... DLB-92

Morison, Richard 1514?-1556 ..... DLB-136

Morison, Samuel Eliot 1887-1976 ... DLB-17

Moritz, Karl Philipp 1756-1793 ..... DLB-94

Moriz von Craûn circa 1220-1230 .... DLB-138

Morley, Christopher 1890-1957 ...... .DLB-9

Morley, John 1838-1923 .... DLB-57, 144

Morris, George Pope 1802-1864 .... DLB-73

Morris, Lewis 1833-1907 .... DLB-35

Morris, Richard B. 1904-1989 ...... DLB-17

Morris, William 1834-1896 .... DLB-18, 35, 57, 156

Morris, Willie 1934- Y-80

Morris, Wright 1910- DLB-2; Y-81

Morrison, Arthur 1863-1945 ... DLB-70, 135

Morrison, Charles Clayton 1874-1966 .... DLB-91

Morrison, Toni 1931- DLB-6, 33, 143; Y-81

Morrow, William, and Company ... DLB-46

Morse, James Herbert 1841-1923 .... DLB-71

Morse, Jedidiah 1761-1826 .... DLB-37

Morse, John T., Jr. 1840-1937 ...... DLB-47

Mortimer, Favell Lee 1802-1878 .... DLB-163

Mortimer, John 1923- DLB-13

Morton, Carlos 1942- DLB-122

Morton, John P., and Company DLB-49

Morton, Nathaniel 1613-1685 .... DLB-24

Morton, Sarah Wentworth 1759-1846 .... DLB-37

Morton, Thomas circa 1579-circa 1647 .... DLB-24

Möser, Justus 1720-1794 .... DLB-97

Mosley, Nicholas 1923- DLB-14

Moss, Arthur 1889-1969 .... DLB-4

Moss, Howard 1922-1987 .... DLB-5

Moss, Thylias 1954- DLB-120

The Most Powerful Book Review in America [*New York Times Book Review*] Y-82

Motion, Andrew 1952- DLB-40

Motley, John Lothrop 1814-1877 .... DLB-1, 30, 59

Motley, Willard 1909-1965 .... DLB-76, 143

Motte, Benjamin Jr. [publishing house] DLB-154

Motteux, Peter Anthony 1663-1718 .... DLB-80

Mottram, R. H. 1883-1971 .... DLB-36

Mouré, Erin 1955- DLB-60

Movies from Books, 1920-1974 .... DLB-9

Mowat, Farley 1921- DLB-68

Mowbray, A. R., and Company, Limited DLB-106

Mowrer, Edgar Ansel 1892-1977 .... DLB-29

Mowrer, Paul Scott 1887-1971 ...... DLB-29

Moxon, Edward [publishing house] DLB-106

Mphahlele, Es'kia (Ezekiel) 1919- DLB-125

Mtshali, Oswald Mbuyiseni 1940- DLB-125

Mucedorus DLB-62

Mudford, William 1782-1848 ...... DLB-159

Mueller, Lisel 1924- DLB-105

Muhajir, El (see Marvin X)

Muhajir, Nazzam Al Fitnah (see Marvin X)

Mühlbach, Luise 1814-1873 ...... DLB-133

Muir, Edwin 1887-1959 .... DLB-20, 100

Muir, Helen 1937- DLB-14

Mukherjee, Bharati 1940- DLB-60

Muldoon, Paul 1951- DLB-40

Müller, Friedrich (see Müller, Maler)

Müller, Heiner 1929- DLB-124

Müller, Maler 1749-1825 .... DLB-94

Müller, Wilhelm 1794-1827 .... DLB-90

Mumford, Lewis 1895-1990 .... DLB-63

Munby, Arthur Joseph 1828-1910 .... DLB-35

Munday, Anthony 1560-1633 .... DLB-62

Mundt, Clara (see Mühlbach, Luise)

Mundt, Theodore 1808-1861 .... DLB-133

Munford, Robert circa 1737-1783 .... DLB-31

Mungoshi, Charles 1947- DLB-157

Munonye, John 1929- DLB-117

Munro, Alice 1931- DLB-53

Munro, H. H. 1870-1916 ...... DLB-34, 162

Munro, Neil 1864-1930 .... DLB-156

Munro, George [publishing house] DLB-49

Munro, Norman L. [publishing house] DLB-49

Munroe, James, and Company DLB-49

Munroe, Kirk 1850-1930 .... DLB-42

Munroe and Francis DLB-49

Munsell, Joel [publishing house] DLB-49

Munsey, Frank A. 1854-1925 .... DLB-25, 91

Munsey, Frank A., and Company DLB-49

Murav'ev, Mikhail Nikitich 1757-1807 .... DLB-150

Murdoch, Iris 1919- DLB-14

Murdoch, Rupert 1931- DLB-127

Murfree, Mary N. 1850-1922 .... DLB-12, 74

Murger, Henry 1822-1861 .... DLB-119

Murger, Louis-Henri (see Murger, Henry)

Muro, Amado 1915-1971 .... DLB-82

Murphy, Arthur 1727-1805 .... DLB-89, 142

Murphy, Beatrice M. 1908- DLB-76

Murphy, Emily 1868-1933 .... DLB-99

Murphy, John H., III 1916- DLB-127

Murphy, John, and Company DLB-49

Murphy, Richard 1927-1993 .... DLB-40

Murray, Albert L. 1916- DLB-38

Murray, Gilbert 1866-1957 .... DLB-10

Murray, Judith Sargent 1751-1820 . . . DLB-37

Murray, Pauli 1910-1985 . . . . DLB-41

Murray, John [publishing house] DLB-154

Murry, John Middleton
 1889-1957 . . . . DLB-149

Musäus, Johann Karl August
 1735-1787 . . . . DLB-97

Muschg, Adolf 1934- DLB-75

The Music of *Minnesang* DLB-138

Musil, Robert 1880-1942 . . . . DLB-81, 124

Muspilli circa 790-circa 850 . . . . DLB-148

Mussey, Benjamin B., and
 Company DLB-49

Mwangi, Meja 1948- DLB-125

Myers, Gustavus 1872-1942 . . . . DLB-47

Myers, L. H. 1881-1944 . . . . DLB-15

Myers, Walter Dean 1937- DLB-33

N

Nabbes, Thomas circa 1605-1641 . . . . DLB-58

Nabl, Franz 1883-1974 . . . . DLB-81

Nabokov, Vladimir
 1899-1977 . . . . . DLB-2; Y-80, Y-91; DS-3

Nabokov Festival at Cornell Y-83

The Vladimir Nabokov Archive
 in the Berg Collection Y-91

Nafis and Cornish DLB-49

Naipaul, Shiva 1945-1985 . . . . . DLB-157; Y-85

Naipaul, V. S. 1932- DLB-125; Y-85

Nancrede, Joseph
 [publishing house] DLB-49

Naranjo, Carmen 1930- DLB-145

Narrache, Jean 1893-1970 . . . . DLB-92

Nasby, Petroleum Vesuvius (see Locke, David
 Ross)

Nash, Ogden 1902-1971 . . . . DLB-11

Nash, Eveleigh
 [publishing house] DLB-112

Nast, Conde 1873-1942 . . . . DLB-91

Nastasijević, Momčilo 1894-1938 . . . DLB-147

Nathan, George Jean 1882-1958 . . . . DLB-137

Nathan, Robert 1894-1985 . . . . DLB-9

The National Jewish Book Awards Y-85

The National Theatre and the Royal
 Shakespeare Company: The
 National Companies DLB-13

Naughton, Bill 1910- DLB-13

Nazor, Vladimir 1876-1949 . . . . DLB-147

Ndebele, Njabulo 1948- DLB-157

Neagoe, Peter 1881-1960 . . . . DLB-4

Neal, John 1793-1876 . . . . DLB-1, 59

Neal, Joseph C. 1807-1847 . . . . DLB-11

Neal, Larry 1937-1981 . . . . DLB-38

The Neale Publishing Company DLB-49

Neely, F. Tennyson
 [publishing house] DLB-49

Negri, Ada 1870-1945 . . . . DLB-114

"The Negro as a Writer," by
 G. M. McClellan DLB-50

"Negro Poets and Their Poetry," by
 Wallace Thurman DLB-50

Neidhart von Reuental
 circa 1185-circa 1240 . . . . DLB-138

Neihardt, John G. 1881-1973 . . . . . DLB-9, 54

Neledinsky-Meletsky, Iurii Aleksandrovich
 1752-1828 . . . . DLB-150

Nelligan, Emile 1879-1941 . . . . DLB-92

Nelson, Alice Moore Dunbar
 1875-1935 . . . . DLB-50

Nelson, Thomas, and Sons [U.S.] . . . DLB-49

Nelson, Thomas, and Sons [U.K.] . . DLB-106

Nelson, William 1908-1978 . . . . DLB-103

Nelson, William Rockhill
 1841-1915 . . . . DLB-23

Nemerov, Howard 1920-1991 . . . DLB-5, 6; Y-83

Nesbit, E. 1858-1924 . . . . DLB-141, 153

Ness, Evaline 1911-1986 . . . . DLB-61

Nestroy, Johann 1801-1862 . . . . DLB-133

Neugeboren, Jay 1938- DLB-28

Neumann, Alfred 1895-1952 . . . . DLB-56

Nevins, Allan 1890-1971 . . . . DLB-17

Nevinson, Henry Woodd
 1856-1941 . . . . DLB-135

The New American Library DLB-46

New Approaches to Biography: Challenges
 from Critical Theory, USC Conference
 on Literary Studies, 1990 . . . . Y-90

New Directions Publishing
 Corporation DLB-46

A New Edition of *Huck Finn* Y-85

New Forces at Work in the American Theatre:
 1915-1925 . . . . DLB-7

New Literary Periodicals:
 A Report for 1987 . . . . Y-87

New Literary Periodicals:
 A Report for 1988 . . . . Y-88

New Literary Periodicals:
 A Report for 1989 . . . . Y-89

New Literary Periodicals:
 A Report for 1990 . . . . Y-90

New Literary Periodicals:
 A Report for 1991 . . . . Y-91

New Literary Periodicals:
 A Report for 1992 . . . . Y-92

New Literary Periodicals:
 A Report for 1993 . . . . Y-93

The New Monthly Magazine
 1814-1884 . . . . DLB-110

The New *Ulysses* Y-84

The New Variorum Shakespeare Y-85

A New Voice: The Center for the Book's First
 Five Years Y-83

The New Wave [Science Fiction] DLB-8

New York City Bookshops in the 1930s and
 1940s: The Recollections of Walter
 Goldwater Y-93

Newbery, John
 [publishing house] DLB-154

Newbolt, Henry 1862-1938 . . . . DLB-19

Newbound, Bernard Slade (see Slade, Bernard)

Newby, P. H. 1918- DLB-15

Newby, Thomas Cautley
 [publishing house] DLB-106

Newcomb, Charles King 1820-1894 . . . DLB-1

Newell, Peter 1862-1924 . . . . DLB-42

Newell, Robert Henry 1836-1901 . . . . DLB-11

Newhouse, Samuel I. 1895-1979 . . . . DLB-127

Newman, Cecil Earl 1903-1976 . . . . . DLB-127

Newman, David (see Benton, Robert)

Newman, Frances 1883-1928 . . . . Y-80

Newman, John Henry
 1801-1890 . . . . DLB-18, 32, 55

Newman, Mark [publishing house] . . . DLB-49

Newnes, George, Limited DLB-112

Newsome, Effie Lee 1885-1979 . . . . . . DLB-76

Newspaper Syndication of American
 Humor DLB-11

Newton, A. Edward 1864-1940 . . . . . DLB-140

Ngugi wa Thiong'o 1938- DLB-125

The *Nibelungenlied* and the *Klage*
 circa 1200 . . . . DLB-138

Nichol, B. P. 1944- DLB-53

Nicholas of Cusa 1401-1464 . . . . DLB-115

Nichols, Dudley 1895-1960 . . . . DLB-26

Nichols, Grace 1950- DLB-157

Nichols, John 1940- Y-82

Nichols, Mary Sargeant (Neal) Gove 1810-
1884 .... DLB-1

Nichols, Peter 1927- DLB-13

Nichols, Roy F. 1896-1973 .... DLB-17

Nichols, Ruth 1948- DLB-60

Nicholson, Norman 1914- DLB-27

Nicholson, William 1872-1949 ..... DLB-141

Ní Chuilleanáin, Eiléan 1942- DLB-40

Nicol, Eric 1919- DLB-68

Nicolai, Friedrich 1733-1811 .... DLB-97

Nicolay, John G. 1832-1901 and
Hay, John 1838-1905 .... DLB-47

Nicolson, Harold 1886-1968 ... DLB-100, 149

Nicolson, Nigel 1917- DLB-155

Niebuhr, Reinhold 1892-1971 ...... DLB-17

Niedecker, Lorine 1903-1970 .... DLB-48

Nieman, Lucius W. 1857-1935 ...... DLB-25

Nietzsche, Friedrich 1844-1900 .... DLB-129

Niggli, Josefina 1910- Y-80

Nikolev, Nikolai Petrovich
1758-1815 .... DLB-150

Niles, Hezekiah 1777-1839 .... DLB-43

Nims, John Frederick 1913- DLB-5

Nin, Anaïs 1903-1977 .... DLB-2, 4, 152

1985: The Year of the Mystery:
A Symposium Y-85

Nissenson, Hugh 1933- DLB-28

Niven, Frederick John 1878-1944 ... DLB-92

Niven, Larry 1938- DLB-8

Nizan, Paul 1905-1940 .... DLB-72

Njegoš, Petar II Petrović
1813-1851 .... DLB-147

Nkosi, Lewis 1936- DLB-157

Nobel Peace Prize
The 1986 Nobel Peace Prize
Nobel Lecture 1986: Hope, Despair   and
Memory
Tributes from Abraham Bernstein,
Norman Lamm, and
John R. Silber Y-86

The Nobel Prize and Literary Politics ... Y-86

Nobel Prize in Literature
The 1982 Nobel Prize in Literature
Announcement by the Swedish Academy
of the Nobel Prize Nobel Lecture 1982:
The Solitude of Latin America Excerpt
from *One Hundred Years of Solitude* The
Magical World of Macondo A Tribute
to Gabriel García Márquez Y-82

The 1983 Nobel Prize in Literature
Announcement by the Swedish Academy
Nobel Lecture 1983 The Stature of
William Golding Y-83

The 1984 Nobel Prize in Literature
Announcement by the Swedish Academy
Jaroslav Seifert Through the Eyes of the
English-Speaking Reader
Three Poems by Jaroslav Seifert Y-84

The 1985 Nobel Prize in Literature
Announcement by the Swedish Academy
Nobel Lecture 1985 .... Y-85

The 1986 Nobel Prize in Literature
Nobel Lecture 1986: This Past Must
Address Its Present Y-86

The 1987 Nobel Prize in Literature
Nobel Lecture 1987 .... Y-87

The 1988 Nobel Prize in Literature
Nobel Lecture 1988 .... Y-88

The 1989 Nobel Prize in Literature
Nobel Lecture 1989 .... Y-89

The 1990 Nobel Prize in Literature
Nobel Lecture 1990 .... Y-90

The 1991 Nobel Prize in Literature
Nobel Lecture 1991 .... Y-91

The 1992 Nobel Prize in Literature
Nobel Lecture 1992 .... Y-92

The 1993 Nobel Prize in Literature
Nobel Lecture 1993 .... Y-93

The 1994 Nobel Prize in Literature
Nobel Lecture 1994 .... Y-94

Nodier, Charles 1780-1844 .... DLB-119

Noel, Roden 1834-1894 .... DLB-35

Nolan, William F. 1928- DLB-8

Noland, C. F. M. 1810?-1858 .... DLB-11

Nonesuch Press DLB-112

Noonday Press DLB-46

Noone, John 1936- DLB-14

Nora, Eugenio de 1923- DLB-134

Nordhoff, Charles 1887-1947 ...... DLB-9

Norman, Charles 1904- DLB-111

Norman, Marsha 1947- Y-84

Norris, Charles G. 1881-1945 .... DLB-9

Norris, Frank 1870-1902 .... DLB-12

Norris, Leslie 1921- DLB-27

Norse, Harold 1916- DLB-16

North Point Press DLB-46

Nortje, Arthur 1942-1970 .... DLB-125

Norton, Alice Mary (see Norton, Andre)

Norton, Andre 1912- DLB-8, 52

Norton, Andrews 1786-1853 .... DLB-1

Norton, Caroline 1808-1877 .... DLB-21, 159

Norton, Charles Eliot 1827-1908 .. DLB-1, 64

Norton, John 1606-1663 .... DLB-24

Norton, Mary 1903-1992 .... DLB-160

Norton, Thomas (see Sackville, Thomas)

Norton, W. W., and Company DLB-46

Norwood, Robert 1874-1932 .... DLB-92

Nossack, Hans Erich 1901-1977 ...... DLB-69

Notker Balbulus circa 840-912 ..... DLB-148

Notker III of Saint Gall
circa 950-1022 .... DLB-148

Notker von Zweifalten ?-1095 ...... DLB-148

A Note on Technique (1926), by
Elizabeth A. Drew [excerpts] DLB-36

Nourse, Alan E. 1928- DLB-8

Novak, Vjenceslav 1859-1905 ...... DLB-147

Novalis 1772-1801 .... DLB-90

Novaro, Mario 1868-1944 .... DLB-114

Novás Calvo, Lino 1903-1983 ...... DLB-145

"The Novel in [Robert Browning's] 'The Ring
and the Book' " (1912), by
Henry James DLB-32

The Novel of Impressionism,
by Jethro Bithell DLB-66

Novel-Reading: *The Works of Charles Dickens,
The Works of W. Makepeace Thackeray* (1879),
by Anthony Trollope DLB-21

The Novels of Dorothy Richardson (1918), by
May Sinclair DLB-36

Novels with a Purpose (1864), by Justin
M'Carthy DLB-21

Noventa, Giacomo 1898-1960 ...... DLB-114

Novikov, Nikolai Ivanovich
1744-1818 .... DLB-150

Nowlan, Alden 1933-1983 .... DLB-53

Noyes, Alfred 1880-1958 .... DLB-20

Noyes, Crosby S. 1825-1908 .... DLB-23

Noyes, Nicholas 1647-1717 .... DLB-24

Noyes, Theodore W. 1858-1946 ..... DLB-29

N-Town Plays
circa 1468 to early sixteenth
century DLB-146

Nugent, Frank 1908-1965 .... DLB-44

Nusic, Branislav 1864-1938 .... DLB-147

Nutt, David [publishing house] DLB-106

Nwapa, Flora 1931- DLB-125

Nye, Edgar Wilson (Bill)
1850-1896 .... DLB-11, 23

Nye, Naomi Shihab 1952- DLB-120

Nye, Robert 1939- DLB-14

O

Oakes, Urian circa 1631-1681 ....DLB-24

Oates, Joyce Carol
1938- DLB-2, 5, 130; Y-81

Ober, William 1920-1993 ....Y-93

Oberholtzer, Ellis Paxson
1868-1936 ....DLB-47

Obradović, Dositej 1740?-1811 .....DLB-147

O'Brien, Edna 1932- DLB-14

O'Brien, Fitz-James 1828-1862 ....DLB-74

O'Brien, Kate 1897-1974 ....DLB-15

O'Brien, Tim
1946- DLB-152; Y-80; DS-9

O'Casey, Sean 1880-1964 ....DLB-10

Ochs, Adolph S. 1858-1935 ....DLB-25

Ochs-Oakes, George Washington
1861-1931 ....DLB-137

O'Connor, Flannery
1925-1964 ..... DLB-2, 152; Y-80; DS-12

O'Connor, Frank 1903-1966 ....DLB-162

Octopus Publishing Group DLB-112

Odell, Jonathan 1737-1818 ....DLB-31, 99

O'Dell, Scott 1903-1989 ....DLB-52

Odets, Clifford 1906-1963 ....DLB-7, 26

Odhams Press Limited DLB-112

O'Donnell, Peter 1920- DLB-87

O'Donovan, Michael (see O'Connor, Frank)

O'Faolain, Julia 1932- DLB-14

O'Faolain, Sean 1900- DLB-15, 162

Off Broadway and Off-Off Broadway .DLB-7

Off-Loop Theatres DLB-7

Offord, Carl Ruthven 1910- DLB-76

O'Flaherty, Liam
1896-1984 .... DLB-36, 162; Y-84

Ogilvie, J. S., and Company DLB-49

Ogot, Grace 1930- DLB-125

O'Grady, Desmond 1935- DLB-40

Ogunyemi, Wale 1939- DLB-157

O'Hagan, Howard 1902-1982 ....DLB-68

O'Hara, Frank 1926-1966 ....DLB-5, 16

O'Hara, John 1905-1970 .... DLB-9, 86; DS-2

Okara, Gabriel 1921- DLB-125

O'Keeffe, John 1747-1833 ....DLB-89

Okigbo, Christopher 1930-1967 .... DLB-125

Okot p'Bitek 1931-1982 .... DLB-125

Okpewho, Isidore 1941- DLB-157

Okri, Ben 1959- DLB-157

Olaudah Equiano and Unfinished Journeys:
The Slave-Narrative Tradition and
Twentieth-Century Continuities, by
Paul Edwards and Pauline T.
Wangman DLB-117

Old English Literature:
An Introduction DLB-146

Old English Riddles
eighth to tenth centuries DLB-146

Old Franklin Publishing House DLB-49

Old German Genesis and Old German Exodus
circa 1050-circa 1130 .... DLB-148

Old High German Charms and
Blessings DLB-148

The Old High German Isidor
circa 790-800 .... DLB-148

Older, Fremont 1856-1935 .... DLB-25

Oldham, John 1653-1683 .... DLB-131

Olds, Sharon 1942- DLB-120

Oliphant, Laurence 1829?-1888 ..... DLB-18

Oliphant, Margaret 1828-1897 ...... DLB-18

Oliver, Chad 1928- DLB-8

Oliver, Mary 1935- DLB-5

Ollier, Claude 1922- DLB-83

Olsen, Tillie 1913?- DLB-28; Y-80

Olson, Charles 1910-1970 .... DLB-5, 16

Olson, Elder 1909- DLB-48, 63

Omotoso, Kole 1943- DLB-125

"On Art in Fiction "(1838),
by Edward Bulwer DLB-21

On Learning to Write Y-88

On Some of the Characteristics of Modern
Poetry and On the Lyrical Poems of
Alfred Tennyson (1831), by Arthur
Henry Hallam DLB-32

"On Style in English Prose" (1898), by
Frederic Harrison DLB-57

"On Style in Literature: Its Technical
Elements" (1885), by Robert Louis
Stevenson DLB-57

"On the Writing of Essays" (1862),
by Alexander Smith DLB-57

Ondaatje, Michael 1943- DLB-60

O'Neill, Eugene 1888-1953 .... DLB-7

Onetti, Juan Carlos 1909-1994 ..... DLB-113

Onions, George Oliver
1872-1961 .... DLB-153

Onofri, Arturo 1885-1928 ....DLB-114

Opie, Amelia 1769-1853 ......DLB-116, 159

Oppen, George 1908-1984 ....DLB-5

Oppenheim, E. Phillips 1866-1946 ...DLB-70

Oppenheim, James 1882-1932 ....DLB-28

Oppenheimer, Joel 1930- DLB-5

Optic, Oliver (see Adams, William Taylor)

Orczy, Emma, Baroness
1865-1947 ....DLB-70

Origo, Iris 1902-1988 ....DLB-155

Orlovitz, Gil 1918-1973 ....DLB-2, 5

Orlovsky, Peter 1933- DLB-16

Ormond, John 1923- DLB-27

Ornitz, Samuel 1890-1957 ....DLB-28, 44

Ortiz, Simon 1941- DLB-120

Ortnit and Wolfdietrich
circa 1225-1250 ....DLB-138

Orton, Joe 1933-1967 ....DLB-13

Orwell, George 1903-1950 ....DLB-15, 98

The Orwell Year Y-84

Ory, Carlos Edmundo de 1923- ...DLB-134

Osbey, Brenda Marie 1957- DLB-120

Osbon, B. S. 1827-1912 ....DLB-43

Osborne, John 1929-1994 ....DLB-13

Osgood, Herbert L. 1855-1918 ......DLB-47

Osgood, James R., and
Company DLB-49

Osgood, McIlvaine and
Company DLB-112

O'Shaughnessy, Arthur
1844-1881 ....DLB-35

O'Shea, Patrick
[publishing house] DLB-49

Osipov, Nikolai Petrovich
1751-1799 ....DLB-150

Osofisan, Femi 1946- DLB-125

Ostenso, Martha 1900-1963 ....DLB-92

Ostriker, Alicia 1937- DLB-120

Osundare, Niyi 1947- DLB-157

Oswald, Eleazer 1755-1795 ....DLB-43

Otero, Blas de 1916-1979 ....DLB-134

Otero, Miguel Antonio
1859-1944 ....DLB-82

Otero Silva, Miguel 1908-1985 .....DLB-145

Otfried von Weißenburg
circa 800-circa 875? DLB-148

Otis, James (see Kaler, James Otis)

Otis, James, Jr. 1725-1783 . . . . DLB-31

Otis, Broaders and Company DLB-49

Ottaway, James 1911- DLB-127

Ottendorfer, Oswald 1826-1900 . . . . . DLB-23

Otto-Peters, Louise 1819-1895 . . . . . DLB-129

Otway, Thomas 1652-1685 . . . . DLB-80

Ouellette, Fernand 1930- DLB-60

Ouida 1839-1908 . . . . DLB-18, 156

Outing Publishing Company DLB-46

Outlaw Days, by Joyce Johnson DLB-16

Overbury, Sir Thomas
circa 1581-1613 . . . . DLB-151

The Overlook Press DLB-46

Overview of U.S. Book Publishing,
1910-1945 . . . . DLB-9

Owen, Guy 1925- DLB-5

Owen, John 1564-1622 . . . . DLB-121

Owen, John [publishing house] DLB-49

Owen, Robert 1771-1858 . . . . . DLB-107, 158

Owen, Wilfred 1893-1918 . . . . DLB-20

Owen, Peter, Limited DLB-112

The Owl and the Nightingale
circa 1189-1199 . . . . DLB-146

Owsley, Frank L. 1890-1956 . . . . DLB-17

Ozerov, Vladislav Aleksandrovich
1769-1816 . . . . DLB-150

Ozick, Cynthia 1928- DLB-28, 152; Y-82

P

Pacey, Desmond 1917-1975 . . . . DLB-88

Pack, Robert 1929- DLB-5

Packaging Papa: *The Garden of Eden* Y-86

Padell Publishing Company DLB-46

Padgett, Ron 1942- DLB-5

Padilla, Ernesto Chávez 1944- . . . DLB-122

Page, L. C., and Company DLB-49

Page, P. K. 1916- DLB-68

Page, Thomas Nelson
1853-1922 . . . . .DLB-12, 78; DS-13

Page, Walter Hines 1855-1918 . . . DLB-71, 91

Paget, Francis Edward
1806-1882 . . . . DLB-163

Paget, Violet (see Lee, Vernon)

Pagliarani, Elio 1927- DLB-128

Pain, Barry 1864-1928 . . . . DLB-135

Pain, Philip ?-circa 1666 . . . . DLB-24

Paine, Robert Treat, Jr. 1773-1811 . . . DLB-37

Paine, Thomas
1737-1809 . . . . DLB-31, 43, 73, 158

Painter, George D. 1914- DLB-155

Painter, William 1540?-1594 . . . . DLB-136

Palazzeschi, Aldo 1885-1974 . . . . DLB-114

Paley, Grace 1922- DLB-28

Palfrey, John Gorham
1796-1881 . . . . .DLB-1, 30

Palgrave, Francis Turner
1824-1897 . . . . DLB-35

Paltock, Robert 1697-1767 . . . . DLB-39

Pan Books Limited DLB-112

Panamaa, Norman 1914- and
Frank, Melvin 1913-1988 . . . . DLB-26

Pancake, Breece D'J 1952-1979 . . . . . DLB-130

Panero, Leopoldo 1909-1962 . . . . DLB-108

Pangborn, Edgar 1909-1976 . . . . DLB-8

"Panic Among the Philistines": A Postscript,
An Interview with Bryan Griffin Y-81

Panneton, Philippe (see Ringuet)

Panshin, Alexei 1940- DLB-8

Pansy (see Alden, Isabella)

Pantheon Books DLB-46

Paperback Library DLB-46

Paperback Science Fiction DLB-8

Paquet, Alfons 1881-1944 . . . . DLB-66

Paradis, Suzanne 1936- DLB-53

Pareja Diezcanseco, Alfredo
1908-1993 . . . . DLB-145

Parents' Magazine Press DLB-46

Parisian Theater, Fall 1984: Toward
A New Baroque Y-85

Parizeau, Alice 1930- DLB-60

Parke, John 1754-1789 . . . . DLB-31

Parker, Dorothy
1893-1967 . . . . .DLB-11, 45, 86

Parker, Gilbert 1860-1932 . . . . DLB-99

Parker, James 1714-1770 . . . . DLB-43

Parker, Theodore 1810-1860 . . . . DLB-1

Parker, William Riley 1906-1968 . . . DLB-103

Parker, J. H. [publishing house] DLB-106

Parker, John [publishing house] DLB-106

Parkman, Francis, Jr.
1823-1893 . . . . .DLB-1, 30

Parks, Gordon 1912- DLB-33

Parks, William 1698-1750 . . . . .DLB-43

Parks, William [publishing house] DLB-49

Parley, Peter (see Goodrich, Samuel Griswold)

Parnell, Thomas 1679-1718 . . . . .DLB-95

Parr, Catherine 1513?-1548 . . . . . . .DLB-136

Parrington, Vernon L.
1871-1929 . . . . DLB-17, 63

Parronchi, Alessandro 1914- DLB-128

Partridge, S. W., and Company DLB-106

Parton, James 1822-1891 . . . . .DLB-30

Parton, Sara Payson Willis
1811-1872 . . . . DLB-43, 74

Pasolini, Pier Paolo 1922- DLB-128

Pastan, Linda 1932- DLB-5

Paston, George 1860-1936 . . . . .DLB-149

The *Paston Letters* 1422-1509 . . . . . . .DLB-146

Pastorius, Francis Daniel
1651-circa 1720 . . . . .DLB-24

Patchen, Kenneth 1911-1972 . . . . DLB-16, 48

Pater, Walter 1839-1894 . . . . DLB-57, 156

Paterson, Katherine 1932- DLB-52

Patmore, Coventry 1823-1896 . . . DLB-35, 98

Paton, Joseph Noel 1821-1901 . . . . . .DLB-35

Paton Walsh, Jill 1937- DLB-161

Patrick, Edwin Hill ("Ted")
1901-1964 . . . . .DLB-137

Patrick, John 1906- DLB-7

Pattee, Fred Lewis 1863-1950 . . . . . . .DLB-71

Pattern and Paradigm: History as
Design, by Judith Ryan DLB-75

Patterson, Alicia 1906-1963 . . . . . . .DLB-127

Patterson, Eleanor Medill
1881-1948 . . . . .DLB-29

Patterson, Eugene 1923- DLB-127

Patterson, Joseph Medill
1879-1946 . . . . .DLB-29

Pattillo, Henry 1726-1801 . . . . .DLB-37

Paul, Elliot 1891-1958 . . . . .DLB-4

Paul, Jean (see Richter, Johann Paul Friedrich)

Paul, Kegan, Trench, Trubner and Company
Limited .DLB-106

Paul, Peter, Book Company DLB-49

Paul, Stanley, and Company
Limited .DLB-112

Paulding, James Kirke
1778-1860 . . . . DLB-3, 59, 74

Paulin, Tom 1949- DLB-40

Pauper, Peter, Press DLB-46

Pavese, Cesare 1908-1950 ....DLB-128

Paxton, John 1911-1985 ....DLB-44

Payn, James 1830-1898 ....DLB-18

Payne, John 1842-1916 ....DLB-35

Payne, John Howard 1791-1852 .....DLB-37

Payson and Clarke DLB-46

Peabody, Elizabeth Palmer
    1804-1894 ....DLB-1

Peabody, Elizabeth Palmer
    [publishing house] DLB-49

Peabody, Oliver William Bourn
    1799-1848 ....DLB-59

Peace, Roger 1899-1968 ....DLB-127

Peacham, Henry 1578-1644? DLB-151

Peachtree Publishers, Limited DLB-46

Peacock, Molly 1947- DLB-120

Peacock, Thomas Love
    1785-1866 ....DLB-96, 116

Pead, Deuel ?-1727 ....DLB-24

Peake, Mervyn 1911-1968 ......DLB-15, 160

Pear Tree Press DLB-112

Pearce, Philippa 1920- DLB-161

Pearson, H. B. [publishing house] DLB-49

Pearson, Hesketh 1887-1964 ......DLB-149

Peck, George W. 1840-1916 ......DLB-23, 42

Peck, H. C., and Theo. Bliss
    [publishing house] DLB-49

Peck, Harry Thurston
    1856-1914 ....DLB-71, 91

Peele, George 1556-1596 ....DLB-62

Pellegrini and Cudahy DLB-46

Pelletier, Aimé (see Vac, Bertrand)

Pemberton, Sir Max 1863-1950 ......DLB-70

Penguin Books [U.S.] DLB-46

Penguin Books [U.K.] DLB-112

Penn Publishing Company DLB-49

Penn, William 1644-1718 ....DLB-24

Penna, Sandro 1906-1977 ....DLB-114

Penner, Jonathan 1940- Y-83

Pennington, Lee 1939- Y-82

Pepys, Samuel 1633-1703 ....DLB-101

Percy, Thomas 1729-1811 ....DLB-104

Percy, Walker 1916-1990 ... DLB-2; Y-80, 90

Perec, Georges 1936-1982 ....DLB-83

Perelman, S. J. 1904-1979 ....DLB-11, 44

Perez, Raymundo "Tigre"
    1946- DLB-122

Peri Rossi, Cristina 1941- DLB-145

Periodicals of the Beat Generation ... DLB-16

Perkins, Eugene 1932- DLB-41

Perkoff, Stuart Z. 1930-1974 ....DLB-16

Perley, Moses Henry 1804-1862 .....DLB-99

Permabooks DLB-46

Perrin, Alice 1867-1934 ....DLB-156

Perry, Bliss 1860-1954 ....DLB-71

Perry, Eleanor 1915-1981 ....DLB-44

Perry, Sampson 1747-1823 ....DLB-158

"Personal Style" (1890), by John Addington
    Symonds DLB-57

Perutz, Leo 1882-1957 ....DLB-81

Pesetsky, Bette 1932- DLB-130

Pestalozzi, Johann Heinrich
    1746-1827 ....DLB-94

Peter, Laurence J. 1919-1990 ....DLB-53

Peter of Spain circa 1205-1277 ..... DLB-115

Peterkin, Julia 1880-1961 ....DLB-9

Peters, Lenrie 1932- DLB-117

Peters, Robert 1924- DLB-105

Peters, Robert, Foreword to
    Ludwig of Bavaria DLB-105

Petersham, Maud 1889-1971 and
    Petersham, Miska 1888-1960 .... DLB-22

Peterson, Charles Jacobs
    1819-1887 ....DLB-79

Peterson, Len 1917- DLB-88

Peterson, Louis 1922- DLB-76

Peterson, T. B., and Brothers DLB-49

Petitclair, Pierre 1813-1860 ....DLB-99

Petrov, Gavriil 1730-1801 ....DLB-150

Petrov, Vasilii Petrovich
    1736-1799 ....DLB-150

Petrović, Rastko 1898-1949 ....DLB-147

Petruslied circa 854? DLB-148

Petry, Ann 1908- DLB-76

Pettie, George circa 1548-1589 ..... DLB-136

Peyton, K. M. 1929- DLB-161

Pfaffe Konrad
    flourished circa 1172 ....DLB-148

Pfaffe Lamprecht
    flourished circa 1150 ....DLB-148

Pforzheimer, Carl H. 1879-1957 ... DLB-140

Phaidon Press Limited DLB-112

Pharr, Robert Deane 1916-1992 ..... DLB-33

Phelps, Elizabeth Stuart
    1844-1911 ....DLB-74

Philip, Marlene Nourbese
    1947- DLB-157

Philippe, Charles-Louis
    1874-1909 ....DLB-65

Philips, John 1676-1708 ....DLB-95

Philips, Katherine 1632-1664 ....DLB-131

Phillips, Caryl 1958- DLB-157

Phillips, David Graham
    1867-1911 ....DLB-9, 12

Phillips, Jayne Anne 1952- Y-80

Phillips, Robert 1938- DLB-105

Phillips, Robert, Finding, Losing,
    Reclaiming: A Note on My
    Poems DLB-105

Phillips, Stephen 1864-1915 ....DLB-10

Phillips, Ulrich B. 1877-1934 ....DLB-17

Phillips, Willard 1784-1873 ....DLB-59

Phillips, William 1907- DLB-137

Phillips, Sampson and Company DLB-49

Phillpotts, Eden
    1862-1960 .... DLB-10, 70, 135, 153

Philosophical Library DLB-46

"The Philosophy of Style" (1852), by
    Herbert Spencer DLB-57

Phinney, Elihu [publishing house] ...DLB-49

Phoenix, John (see Derby, George Horatio)

PHYLON (Fourth Quarter, 1950),
    The Negro in Literature:
    The Current Scene DLB-76

Physiologus
    circa 1070-circa 1150 ....DLB-148

Piccolo, Lucio 1903-1969 ....DLB-114

Pickard, Tom 1946- DLB-40

Pickering, William
    [publishing house] DLB-106

Pickthall, Marjorie 1883-1922 ....DLB-92

Pictorial Printing Company DLB-49

Piel, Gerard 1915- DLB-137

Piercy, Marge 1936- DLB-120

Pierro, Albino 1916- DLB-128

Pignotti, Lamberto 1926- DLB-128

Pike, Albert 1809-1891 ....DLB-74

Pilon, Jean-Guy 1930- DLB-60

Pinckney, Josephine 1895-1957 ....DLB-6

Pindar, Peter (see Wolcot, John)

Pinero, Arthur Wing 1855-1934 .....DLB-10

Pinget, Robert 1919- DLB-83

Pinnacle Books DLB-46

Piñon, Nélida 1935- DLB-145

Pinsky, Robert 1940- Y-82

Pinter, Harold 1930- DLB-13

Piontek, Heinz 1925- DLB-75

Piozzi, Hester Lynch [Thrale]
　　1741-1821 .... DLB-104, 142

Piper, H. Beam 1904-1964 ....DLB-8

Piper, Watty DLB-22

Pisar, Samuel 1929- Y-83

Pitkin, Timothy 1766-1847 .... DLB-30

The Pitt Poetry Series: Poetry Publishing
　　Today Y-85

Pitter, Ruth 1897- DLB-20

Pix, Mary 1666-1709 .... DLB-80

Plaatje, Sol T. 1876-1932 .... DLB-125

The Place of Realism in Fiction (1895), by
　　George Gissing DLB-18

Plante, David 1940- Y-83

Platen, August von 1796-1835 ...... DLB-90

Plath, Sylvia 1932-1963 .... DLB-5, 6, 152

Platon 1737-1812 .... DLB-150

Platt and Munk Company DLB-46

Playboy Press DLB-46

Plays, Playwrights, and Playgoers ... DLB-84

Playwrights and Professors, by
　　Tom Stoppard DLB-13

Playwrights on the Theater DLB-80

Der Pleier flourished circa 1250 .... DLB-138

Plenzdorf, Ulrich 1934- DLB-75

Plessen, Elizabeth 1944- DLB-75

Pliévier, Theodor 1892-1955 .... DLB-69

Plomer, William 1903-1973 .... DLB-20, 162

Plumly, Stanley 1939- DLB-5

Plumpp, Sterling D. 1940- DLB-41

Plunkett, James 1920- DLB-14

Plymell, Charles 1935- DLB-16

Pocket Books DLB-46

Poe, Edgar Allan
　　1809-1849 .... DLB-3, 59, 73, 74

Poe, James 1921-1980 .... DLB-44

The Poet Laureate of the United States
　　Statements from Former Consultants
　　in Poetry Y-86

Pohl, Frederik 1919- DLB-8

Poirier, Louis (see Gracq, Julien)

Polanyi, Michael 1891-1976 .... DLB-100

Pole, Reginald 1500-1558 .... DLB-132

Poliakoff, Stephen 1952- DLB-13

Polidori, John William
　　1795-1821 .... DLB-116

Polite, Carlene Hatcher 1932- DLB-33

Pollard, Edward A. 1832-1872 ..... DLB-30

Pollard, Percival 1869-1911 .... DLB-71

Pollard and Moss DLB-49

Pollock, Sharon 1936- DLB-60

Polonsky, Abraham 1910- DLB-26

Polotsky, Simeon 1629-1680 .... DLB-150

Ponce, Mary Helen 1938- DLB-122

Ponce-Montoya, Juanita 1949- DLB-122

Ponet, John 1516?-1556 .... DLB-132

Poniatowski, Elena 1933- DLB-113

Pony Stories DLB-160

Poole, Ernest 1880-1950 .... DLB-9

Poore, Benjamin Perley
　　1820-1887 .... DLB-23

Pope, Abbie Hanscom
　　1858-1894 .... DLB-140

Pope, Alexander 1688-1744 .....DLB-95, 101

Popov, Mikhail Ivanovich
　　1742-circa 1790 .... DLB-150

Popular Library DLB-46

Porlock, Martin (see MacDonald, Philip)

Porpoise Press DLB-112

Porta, Antonio 1935-1989 .... DLB-128

Porter, Anna Maria
　　1780-1832 .... DLB-116, 159

Porter, Eleanor H. 1868-1920 .... DLB-9

Porter, Henry ?-? DLB-62

Porter, Jane 1776-1850 .... DLB-116, 159

Porter, Katherine Anne
　　1890-1980 ... DLB-4, 9, 102; Y-80; DS-12

Porter, Peter 1929- DLB-40

Porter, William Sydney
　　1862-1910 .... DLB-12, 78, 79

Porter, William T. 1809-1858 ..... DLB-3, 43

Porter and Coates DLB-49

Portis, Charles 1933- DLB-6

Postl, Carl (see Sealsfield, Carl)

Poston, Ted 1906-1974 .... DLB-51

Postscript to [the Third Edition of] Clarissa
　　(1751), by Samuel Richardson ... DLB-39

Potok, Chaim 1929- DLB-28, 152; Y-84

Potter, Beatrix 1866-1943 .... DLB-141

Potter, David M. 1910-1971 ....DLB-17

Potter, John E., and Company DLB-49

Pottle, Frederick A.
　　1897-1987 .... DLB-103; Y-87

Poulin, Jacques 1937- DLB-60

Pound, Ezra 1885-1972 .... DLB-4, 45, 63

Powell, Anthony 1905- DLB-15

Powers, J. F. 1917- DLB-130

Pownall, David 1938- DLB-14

Powys, John Cowper 1872-1963 .....DLB-15

Powys, Llewelyn 1884-1939 ....DLB-98

Powys, T. F. 1875-1953 .... DLB-36, 162

Poynter, Nelson 1903-1978 ....DLB-127

The Practice of Biography: An Interview
　　with Stanley Weintraub Y-82

The Practice of Biography II: An Interview
　　with B. L. Reid Y-83

The Practice of Biography III: An Interview
　　with Humphrey Carpenter Y-84

The Practice of Biography IV: An Interview
　　with William Manchester Y-85

The Practice of Biography V: An Interview
　　with Justin Kaplan Y-86

The Practice of Biography VI: An Interview
　　with David Herbert Donald Y-87

The Practice of Biography VII: An Interview
　　with John Caldwell Guilds Y-92

The Practice of Biography VIII: An Interview
　　with Joan Mellen Y-94

Prados, Emilio 1899-1962 ....DLB-134

Praed, Winthrop Mackworth
　　1802-1839 ....DLB-96

Praeger Publishers DLB-46

Pratt, E. J. 1882-1964 ....DLB-92

Pratt, Samuel Jackson 1749-1814 .....DLB-39

Preface to Alwyn (1780), by
　　Thomas Holcroft DLB-39

Preface to Colonel Jack (1722), by
　　Daniel Defoe DLB-39

Preface to Evelina (1778), by
　　Fanny Burney DLB-39

Preface to Ferdinand Count Fathom (1753), by
　　Tobias Smollett DLB-39

Preface to Incognita (1692), by
　　William Congreve DLB-39

Preface to Joseph Andrews (1742), by
　　Henry Fielding DLB-39

Preface to Moll Flanders (1722), by
　　Daniel Defoe DLB-39

Preface to Poems (1853), by
　　Matthew Arnold DLB-32

Preface to *Robinson Crusoe* (1719), by
Daniel Defoe DLB-39

Preface to *Roderick Random* (1748), by
Tobias Smollett DLB-39

Preface to *Roxana* (1724), by
Daniel Defoe DLB-39

Preface to *St. Leon* (1799), by
William Godwin DLB-39

Preface to Sarah Fielding's *Familiar Letters*
(1747), by Henry Fielding
[excerpt] DLB-39

Preface to Sarah Fielding's *The Adventures of
David Simple* (1744), by
Henry Fielding DLB-39

Preface to *The Cry* (1754), by
Sarah Fielding DLB-39

Preface to *The Delicate Distress* (1769), by
Elizabeth Griffin DLB-39

Preface to *The Disguis'd Prince* (1733), by
Eliza Haywood [excerpt] DLB-39

Preface to *The Farther Adventures of Robinson
Crusoe* (1719), by Daniel Defoe . . . DLB-39

Preface to the First Edition of *Pamela* (1740), by
Samuel Richardson DLB-39

Preface to the First Edition of *The Castle of
Otranto* (1764), by
Horace Walpole DLB-39

Preface to *The History of Romances* (1715), by
Pierre Daniel Huet [excerpts] DLB-39

Preface to *The Life of Charlotta du Pont* (1723),
by Penelope Aubin DLB-39

Preface to *The Old English Baron* (1778), by
Clara Reeve DLB-39

Preface to the Second Edition of *The Castle of
Otranto* (1765), by Horace
Walpole DLB-39

Preface to *The Secret History, of Queen Zarah,
and the Zarazians* (1705), by Delariviere
Manley DLB-39

Preface to the Third Edition of *Clarissa* (1751),
by Samuel Richardson
[excerpt] DLB-39

Preface to *The Works of Mrs. Davys* (1725), by
Mary Davys DLB-39

Preface to Volume 1 of *Clarissa* (1747), by
Samuel Richardson DLB-39

Preface to Volume 3 of *Clarissa* (1748), by
Samuel Richardson DLB-39

Préfontaine, Yves 1937- DLB-53

Prelutsky, Jack 1940- DLB-61

Premisses, by Michael Hamburger . . . DLB-66

Prentice, George D. 1802-1870 . . . . . DLB-43

Prentice-Hall DLB-46

Prescott, William Hickling
1796-1859 . . . . DLB-1, 30, 59

The Present State of the English Novel (1892),
by George Saintsbury DLB-18

Prešeren, Francè 1800-1849 . . . . DLB-147

Preston, Thomas 1537-1598 . . . . DLB-62

Price, Reynolds 1933- DLB-2

Price, Richard 1723-1791 . . . . DLB-158

Price, Richard 1949- Y-81

Priest, Christopher 1943- DLB-14

Priestley, J. B. 1894-1984
. . . . DLB-10, 34, 77, 100, 139; Y-84

Prime, Benjamin Young 1733-1791 . . DLB-31

Primrose, Diana
floruit circa 1630 . . . . DLB-126

Prince, F. T. 1912- DLB-20

Prince, Thomas 1687-1758 . . . . . DLB-24, 140

The Principles of Success in Literature (1865), by
George Henry Lewes [excerpt] . . DLB-57

Prior, Matthew 1664-1721 . . . . DLB-95

Pritchard, William H. 1932- DLB-111

Pritchett, V. S. 1900- DLB-15, 139

Procter, Adelaide Anne 1825-1864 . . . DLB-32

Procter, Bryan Waller
1787-1874 . . . . DLB-96, 144

The Profession of Authorship:
Scribblers for Bread Y-89

The Progress of Romance (1785), by Clara Reeve
[excerpt] DLB-39

Prokopovich, Feofan 1681?-1736 . . . DLB-150

Prokosch, Frederic 1906-1989 . . . . . DLB-48

The Proletarian Novel DLB-9

Propper, Dan 1937- DLB-16

The Prospect of Peace (1778), by
Joel Barlow DLB-37

Proud, Robert 1728-1813 . . . . DLB-30

Proust, Marcel 1871-1922 . . . . DLB 65

Prynne, J. H. 1936- DLB-40

Przybyszewski, Stanisław
1868-1927 . . . . DLB-66

Pseudo-Dionysius the Areopagite floruit
circa 500 . . . . DLB-115

The Public Lending Right in America
Statement by Sen. Charles McC.
Mathias, Jr. PLR and the Meaning
of Literary Property Statements on
PLR by American Writers Y-83

The Public Lending Right in the United Kingdom Public Lending Right: The First Year
in the United Kingdom Y-83

The Publication of English
Renaissance Plays DLB-62

Publications and Social Movements
[Transcendentalism] DLB-1

Publishers and Agents: The Columbia
Connection Y-87

A Publisher's Archives: G. P. Putnam . . Y-92

Publishing Fiction at LSU Press Y-87

Pückler-Muskau, Hermann von
1785-1871 . . . . DLB-133

Pugh, Edwin William 1874-1930 . . . DLB-135

Pugin, A. Welby 1812-1852 . . . . DLB-55

Puig, Manuel 1932-1990 . . . . DLB-113

Pulitzer, Joseph 1847-1911 . . . . DLB-23

Pulitzer, Joseph, Jr. 1885-1955 . . . . . DLB-29

Pulitzer Prizes for the Novel,
1917-1945 . . . . DLB-9

Pulliam, Eugene 1889-1975 . . . . DLB-127

Purchas, Samuel 1577?-1626 . . . . . . DLB-151

Purdy, Al 1918- DLB-88

Purdy, James 1923- DLB-2

Purdy, Ken W. 1913-1972 . . . . DLB-137

Pusey, Edward Bouverie
1800-1882 . . . . DLB-55

Putnam, George Palmer
1814-1872 . . . . DLB-3, 79

Putnam, Samuel 1892-1950 . . . . DLB-4

G. P. Putnam's Sons [U.S.] DLB-49

G. P. Putnam's Sons [U.K.] DLB-106

Puzo, Mario 1920- DLB-6

Pyle, Ernie 1900-1945 . . . . DLB-29

Pyle, Howard 1853-1911 . . . . DLB-42; DS-13

Pym, Barbara 1913-1980 . . . . . . DLB-14; Y-87

Pynchon, Thomas 1937- DLB-2

Pyramid Books DLB-46

Pyrnelle, Louise-Clarke 1850-1907 . . DLB-42

Q

Quad, M. (see Lewis, Charles B.)

Quarles, Francis 1592-1644 . . . . DLB-126

The Quarterly Review
1809-1967 . . . . DLB-110

Quasimodo, Salvatore 1901-1968 . . . DLB-114

Queen, Ellery (see Dannay, Frederic, and
Manfred B. Lee)

The Queen City Publishing House . . . DLB-49

Queneau, Raymond 1903-1976 . . . . . DLB-72

Quennell, Sir Peter 1905-1993 . . . . . DLB-155

Quesnel, Joseph 1746-1809 .... DLB-99

The Question of American Copyright
   in the Nineteenth Century
    Headnote
    Preface, by George Haven Putnam
    The Evolution of Copyright, by Brander
      Matthews
    Summary of Copyright Legislation in
      the United States, by R. R. Bowker
    Analysis of the Provisions of the
      Copyright Law of 1891, by
      George Haven Putnam
    The Contest for International Copyright,
      by George Haven Putnam
    Cheap Books and Good Books,
      by Brander Matthews DLB-49

Quiller-Couch, Sir Arthur Thomas
   1863-1944 .... DLB-135, 153

Quin, Ann 1936-1973 .... DLB-14

Quincy, Samuel, of Georgia ?-? DLB-31

Quincy, Samuel, of Massachusetts
   1734-1789 .... DLB-31

Quinn, Anthony 1915- DLB-122

Quintana, Leroy V. 1944- DLB-82

Quintana, Miguel de 1671-1748
   A Forerunner of Chicano
   Literature DLB-122

Quist, Harlin, Books DLB-46

Quoirez, Françoise (see Sagan, Françcise)

R

Raabe, Wilhelm 1831-1910 .... DLB-129

Rabe, David 1940- DLB-7

Raboni, Giovanni 1932- DLB-128

Rachilde 1860-1953 .... DLB-123

Racin, Kočo 1908-1943 .... DLB-147

Rackham, Arthur 1867-1939 ...... DLB-141

Radcliffe, Ann 1764-1823 .... DLB-39

Raddall, Thomas 1903- DLB-68

Radiguet, Raymond 1903-1923 ..... DLB-65

Radishchev, Aleksandr Nikolaevich
   1749-1802 .... DLB-150

Radványi, Netty Reiling (see Seghers, Anna)

Rahv, Philip 1908-1973 .... DLB-137

Raimund, Ferdinand Jakob
   1790-1836 .... DLB-90

Raine, Craig 1944- DLB-40

Raine, Kathleen 1908- DLB-20

Rainolde, Richard
   circa 1530-1606 .... DLB-136

Rakić, Milan 1876-1938 .... DLB-147

Ralph, Julian 1853-1903 .... DLB-23

Ralph Waldo Emerson in 1982 ....Y-82

Ramat, Silvio 1939- DLB-128

Rambler, no. 4 (1750), by Samuel Johnson
   [excerpt] DLB-39

Ramée, Marie Louise de la (see Ouida)

Ramírez, Sergío 1942- DLB-145

Ramke, Bin 1947- DLB-120

Ramler, Karl Wilhelm 1725-1798 .... DLB-97

Ramon Ribeyro, Julio 1929- DLB-145

Ramous, Mario 1924- DLB-128

Rampersad, Arnold 1941- DLB-111

Ramsay, Allan 1684 or 1685-1758 ... DLB-95

Ramsay, David 1749-1815 .... DLB-30

Ranck, Katherine Quintana
   1942- DLB-122

Rand, Avery and Company DLB-49

Rand McNally and Company DLB-49

Randall, David Anton
   1905-1975 .... DLB-140

Randall, Dudley 1914- DLB-41

Randall, Henry S. 1811-1876 ...... DLB-30

Randall, James G. 1881-1953 ...... DLB-17

The Randall Jarrell Symposium: A Small
   Collection of Randall Jarrells
   Excerpts From Papers Delivered at
   the Randall Jarrell
   Symposium Y-86

Randolph, A. Philip 1889-1979 ...... DLB-91

Randolph, Anson D. F.
   [publishing house] DLB-49

Randolph, Thomas 1605-1635 ..DLB-58, 126

Random House DLB-46

Ranlet, Henry [publishing house] DLB-49

Ransom, John Crowe
   1888-1974 ....DLB-45, 63

Ransome, Arthur 1884-1967 .... DLB-160

Raphael, Frederic 1931- DLB-14

Raphaelson, Samson 1896-1983 ..... DLB-44

Raskin, Ellen 1928-1984 .... DLB-52

Rastell, John 1475?-1536 .... DLB-136

Rattigan, Terence 1911-1977 .... DLB-13

Rawlings, Marjorie Kinnan
   1896-1953 ....DLB-9, 22, 102

Raworth, Tom 1938- DLB-40

Ray, David 1932- DLB-5

Ray, Gordon Norton
   1915-1986 ....DLB-103, 140

Ray, Henrietta Cordelia
   1849-1916 ....DLB-50

Raymond, Henry J. 1820-1869 ... DLB-43, 79

Raymond Chandler Centenary Tributes
   from Michael Avallone, James Elroy, Joe
   Gores,
   and William F. Nolan Y-88

Reach, Angus 1821-1856 ....DLB-70

Read, Herbert 1893-1968 ...... DLB-20, 149

Read, Herbert, "The Practice of Biography," in
   *The English Sense of Humour and Other
   Essays* DLB-149

Read, Opie 1852-1939 ....DLB-23

Read, Piers Paul 1941- DLB-14

Reade, Charles 1814-1884 ....DLB-21

Reader's Digest Condensed
   Books DLB-46

Reading, Peter 1946- DLB-40

Reaney, James 1926- DLB-68

Rèbora, Clemente 1885-1957 ....DLB-114

Rechy, John 1934- DLB-122; Y-82

The Recovery of Literature: Criticism in the
   1990s: A Symposium Y-91

Redding, J. Saunders
   1906-1988 .... DLB-63, 76

Redfield, J. S. [publishing house] DLB-49

Redgrove, Peter 1932- DLB-40

Redmon, Anne 1943- Y-86

Redmond, Eugene B. 1937- DLB-41

Redpath, James [publishing house] ...DLB-49

Reed, Henry 1808-1854 ....DLB-59

Reed, Henry 1914- DLB-27

Reed, Ishmael 1938- DLB-2, 5, 33; DS-8

Reed, Sampson 1800-1880 ....DLB-1

Reed, Talbot Baines 1852-1893 .....DLB-141

Reedy, William Marion 1862-1920 ...DLB-91

Reese, Lizette Woodworth
   1856-1935 ....DLB-54

Reese, Thomas 1742-1796 ....DLB-37

Reeve, Clara 1729-1807 ....DLB-39

Reeves, James 1909-1978 ....DLB-161

Reeves, John 1926- DLB-88

Regnery, Henry, Company DLB-46

Rehberg, Hans 1901-1963 ....DLB-124

Rehfisch, Hans José 1891-1960 .....DLB-124

Reid, Alastair 1926- DLB-27

Reid, B. L. 1918-1990 ....DLB-111

Reid, Christopher 1949- DLB-40

Reid, Forrest 1875-1947 . . . . .DLB-153

Reid, Helen Rogers 1882-1970 . . . . . .DLB-29

Reid, James ?-? DLB-31

Reid, Mayne 1818-1883 . . . . .DLB-21, 163

Reid, Thomas 1710-1796 . . . . .DLB-31

Reid, V. S. (Vic) 1913-1987 . . . . . . .DLB-125

Reid, Whitelaw 1837-1912 . . . . .DLB-23

Reilly and Lee Publishing
    Company .DLB-46

Reimann, Brigitte 1933-1973 . . . . . . .DLB-75

Reinmar der Alte
    circa 1165-circa 1205 . . . . .DLB-138

Reinmar von Zweter
    circa 1200-circa 1250 . . . . .DLB-138

Reisch, Walter 1903-1983 . . . . .DLB-44

Remarque, Erich Maria 1898-1970 . . .DLB-56

"Re-meeting of Old Friends": The Jack
    Kerouac Conference Y-82

Remington, Frederic 1861-1909 . . . . .DLB-12

Renaud, Jacques 1943- DLB-60

Renault, Mary 1905-1983 . . . . .Y-83

Rendell, Ruth 1930- DLB-87

Representative Men and Women: A Historical
    Perspective on the British Novel,
    1930-1960 . . . . .DLB-15

(Re-)Publishing Orwell Y-86

Reuter, Fritz 1810-1874 . . . . .DLB-129

Reuter, Gabriele 1859-1941 . . . . .DLB-66

Revell, Fleming H., Company DLB-49

Reventlow, Franziska Gräfin zu
    1871-1918 . . . . .DLB-66

Review of Reviews Office DLB-112

Review of [Samuel Richardson's] *Clarissa*
    (1748), by Henry Fielding DLB-39

The Revolt (1937), by Mary Colum
    [excerpts] .DLB-36

Rexroth, Kenneth
    1905-1982 . . . . .DLB-16, 48; Y-82

Rey, H. A. 1898-1977 . . . . .DLB-22

Reynal and Hitchcock DLB-46

Reynolds, G. W. M. 1814-1879 . . . . . .DLB-21

Reynolds, John Hamilton
    1794-1852 . . . . .DLB-96

Reynolds, Mack 1917- DLB-8

Reynolds, Sir Joshua 1723-1792 . . . .DLB-104

Reznikoff, Charles 1894-1976 . . . .DLB-28, 45

"Rhetoric" (1828; revised, 1859), by
    Thomas de Quincey [excerpt] . . .DLB-57

Rhett, Robert Barnwell 1800-1876 . . .DLB-43

Rhode, John 1884-1964 . . . . .DLB-77

Rhodes, James Ford 1848-1927 . . . . .DLB-47

Rhys, Jean 1890-1979 . . . . .DLB-36, 117, 162

Ricardo, David 1772-1823 . . . .DLB-107, 158

Ricardou, Jean 1932- DLB-83

Rice, Elmer 1892-1967 . . . . .DLB-4, 7

Rice, Grantland 1880-1954 . . . . .DLB-29

Rich, Adrienne 1929- DLB-5, 67

Richards, David Adams 1950- DLB-53

Richards, George circa 1760-1814 . . .DLB-37

Richards, I. A. 1893-1979 . . . . .DLB-27

Richards, Laura E. 1850-1943 . . . . . .DLB-42

Richards, William Carey
    1818-1892 . . . . .DLB-73

Richards, Grant
    [publishing house] DLB-112

Richardson, Charles F. 1851-1913 . . .DLB-71

Richardson, Dorothy M.
    1873-1957 . . . . .DLB-36

Richardson, Jack 1935- DLB-7

Richardson, John 1796-1852 . . . . . . .DLB-99

Richardson, Samuel
    1689-1761 . . . . .DLB-39, 154

Richardson, Willis 1889-1977 . . . . . . .DLB-51

Riche, Barnabe 1542-1617 . . . . .DLB-136

Richler, Mordecai 1931- DLB-53

Richter, Conrad 1890-1968 . . . . .DLB-9

Richter, Hans Werner 1908- DLB-69

Richter, Johann Paul Friedrich
    1763-1825 . . . . .DLB-94

Rickerby, Joseph
    [publishing house] DLB-106

Rickword, Edgell 1898-1982 . . . . .DLB-20

Riddell, Charlotte 1832-1906 . . . . . .DLB-156

Riddell, John (see Ford, Corey)

Ridge, Lola 1873-1941 . . . . .DLB-54

Ridge, William Pett 1859-1930 . . . . .DLB-135

Riding, Laura (see Jackson, Laura Riding)

Ridler, Anne 1912- DLB-27

Ridruego, Dionisio 1912-1975 . . . . .DLB-108

Riel, Louis 1844-1885 . . . . .DLB-99

Riffaterre, Michael 1924- DLB-67

Riis, Jacob 1849-1914 . . . . .DLB-23

Riker, John C. [publishing house] . . .DLB-49

Riley, John 1938-1978 . . . . .DLB-40

Rilke, Rainer Maria 1875-1926 . . . . .DLB-81

Rinehart and Company DLB-46

Ringuet 1895-1960 . . . . .DLB-68

Ringwood, Gwen Pharis
    1910-1984 . . . . .DLB-88

Rinser, Luise 1911- DLB-69

Ríos, Alberto 1952- DLB-122

Ríos, Isabella 1948- DLB-82

Ripley, Arthur 1895-1961 . . . . .DLB-44

Ripley, George 1802-1880 . . . . .DLB-1, 64, 73

The Rising Glory of America:
    Three Poems DLB-37

The Rising Glory of America: Written in 1771
    (1786), by Hugh Henry Brackenridge and
    Philip Freneau DLB-37

Riskin, Robert 1897-1955 . . . . .DLB-26

Risse, Heinz 1898- DLB-69

Ritchie, Anna Mowatt 1819-1870 . . . . .DLB-3

Ritchie, Anne Thackeray
    1837-1919 . . . . .DLB-18

Ritchie, Thomas 1778-1854 . . . . .DLB-43

Rites of Passage
    [on William Saroyan] Y-83

The Ritz Paris Hemingway Award Y-85

Rivard, Adjutor 1868-1945 . . . . .DLB-92

Rive, Richard 1931-1989 . . . . .DLB-125

Rivera, Marina 1942- DLB-122

Rivera, Tomás 1935-1984 . . . . .DLB-82

Rivers, Conrad Kent 1933-1968 . . . . .DLB-41

Riverside Press DLB-49

Rivington, James circa 1724-1802 . . . .DLB-43

Rivington, Charles
    [publishing house] DLB-154

Rivkin, Allen 1903-1990 . . . . .DLB-26

Roa Bastos, Augusto 1917- DLB-113

Robbe-Grillet, Alain 1922- DLB-83

Robbins, Tom 1936- Y-80

Roberts, Charles G. D. 1860-1943 . . .DLB-92

Roberts, Dorothy 1906-1993 . . . . . . .DLB-88

Roberts, Elizabeth Madox
    1881-1941 . . . . .DLB-9, 54, 102

Roberts, Kenneth 1885-1957 . . . . .DLB-9

Roberts, William 1767-1849 . . . . . . .DLB-142

Roberts Brothers DLB-49

Roberts, James [publishing house] . .DLB-154

Robertson, A. M., and Company DLB-49

Robertson, William 1721-1793 . . . . .DLB-104

Robinson, Casey 1903-1979 . . . . .DLB-44

Robinson, Edwin Arlington
1869-1935 .... DLB-54

Robinson, Henry Crabb
1775-1867 .... DLB-107

Robinson, James Harvey
1863-1936 .... DLB-47

Robinson, Lennox 1886-1958 .... DLB-10

Robinson, Mabel Louise
1874-1962 .... DLB-22

Robinson, Mary 1758-1800 .... DLB-158

Robinson, Therese
1797-1870 .... DLB-59, 133

Robison, Mary 1949- DLB-130

Roblès, Emmanuel 1914- DLB-83

Roccatagliata Ceccardi, Ceccardo
1871-1919 .... DLB-114

Rochester, John Wilmot, Earl of
1647-1680 .... DLB-131

Rock, Howard 1911-1976 .... DLB-127

Rodgers, Carolyn M. 1945- DLB-41

Rodgers, W. R. 1909-1969 .... DLB-20

Rodríguez, Claudio 1934- DLB-134

Rodriguez, Richard 1944- DLB-82

Rodríguez Julia, Edgardo
1946- DLB-145

Roethke, Theodore 1908-1963 ....DLB-5

Rogers, Pattiann 1940- DLB-105

Rogers, Samuel 1763-1855 .... DLB-93

Rogers, Will 1879-1935 .... DLB-11

Rohmer, Sax 1883-1959 .... DLB-70

Roiphe, Anne 1935- Y-80

Rojas, Arnold R. 1896-1988 .... DLB-82

Rolfe, Frederick William
1860-1913 .... DLB-34, 156

Rolland, Romain 1866-1944 .... DLB-65

Rolle, Richard
circa 1290-1300 - 1340 .... DLB-146

Rolvaag, O. E. 1876-1931 ....DLB-9

Romains, Jules 1885-1972 .... DLB-65

Roman, A., and Company DLB-49

Romano, Octavio 1923- DLB-122

Romero, Leo 1950- DLB-122

Romero, Lin 1947- DLB-122

Romero, Orlando 1945- DLB-82

Rook, Clarence 1863-1915 .... DLB-135

Roosevelt, Theodore 1858-1919 .... DLB-47

Root, Waverley 1903-1982 ....DLB-4

Root, William Pitt 1941- DLB-120

Roquebrune, Robert de 1889-1978 ... DLB-68

Rosa, João Guimarães
1908-1967 .... DLB-113

Rosales, Luis 1910-1992 .... DLB-134

Roscoe, William 1753-1831 .... DLB-163

Rose, Reginald 1920- DLB-26

Rosegger, Peter 1843-1918 .... DLB-129

Rosei, Peter 1946- DLB-85

Rosen, Norma 1925- DLB-28

Rosenbach, A. S. W. 1876-1952 .... DLB-140

Rosenberg, Isaac 1890-1918 .... DLB-20

Rosenfeld, Isaac 1918-1956 .... DLB-28

Rosenthal, M. L. 1917- DLB-5

Ross, Alexander 1591-1654 .... DLB-151

Ross, Harold 1892-1951 .... DLB-137

Ross, Leonard Q. (see Rosten, Leo)

Ross, Martin 1862-1915 .... DLB-135

Ross, Sinclair 1908- DLB-88

Ross, W. W. E. 1894-1966 .... DLB-88

Rosselli, Amelia 1930- DLB-128

Rossen, Robert 1908-1966 .... DLB-26

Rossetti, Christina Georgina
1830-1894 ....DLB-35, 163

Rossetti, Dante Gabriel 1828-1882 ... DLB-35

Rossner, Judith 1935- DLB-6

Rosten, Leo 1908- DLB-11

Rostenberg, Leona 1908- DLB-140

Rostovsky, Dimitrii 1651-1709 ..... DLB-150

Bertram Rota and His Bookshop Y-91

Roth, Gerhard 1942- DLB-85, 124

Roth, Henry 1906?- DLB-28

Roth, Joseph 1894-1939 .... DLB-85

Roth, Philip 1933- DLB-2, 28; Y-82

Rothenberg, Jerome 1931- DLB-5

Rotimi, Ola 1938- DLB-125

Routhier, Adolphe-Basile
1839-1920 .... DLB-99

Routier, Simone 1901-1987 .... DLB-88

Routledge, George, and Sons DLB-106

Roversi, Roberto 1923- DLB-128

Rowe, Elizabeth Singer
1674-1737 ....DLB-39, 95

Rowe, Nicholas 1674-1718 .... DLB-84

Rowlands, Samuel
circa 1570-1630 .... DLB-121

Rowlandson, Mary
circa 1635-circa 1678 ....DLB-24

Rowley, William circa 1585-1626 ....DLB-58

Rowse, A. L. 1903- DLB-155

Rowson, Susanna Haswell
circa 1762-1824 ....DLB-37

Roy, Camille 1870-1943 ....DLB-92

Roy, Gabrielle 1909-1983 ....DLB-68

Roy, Jules 1907- DLB-83

The Royal Court Theatre and the English
Stage Company DLB-13

The Royal Court Theatre and the New
Drama DLB-10

The Royal Shakespeare Company
at the Swan Y-88

Royall, Anne 1769-1854 ....DLB-43

The Roycroft Printing Shop DLB-49

Royster, Vermont 1914- DLB-127

Ruark, Gibbons 1941- DLB-120

Ruban, Vasilii Grigorevich
1742-1795 ....DLB-150

Rubens, Bernice 1928- DLB-14

Rudd and Carleton DLB-49

Rudkin, David 1936- DLB-13

Rudolf von Ems
circa 1200-circa 1254 ....DLB-138

Ruffin, Josephine St. Pierre
1842-1924 ....DLB-79

Ruganda, John 1941- DLB-157

Ruggles, Henry Joseph 1813-1906 ....DLB-64

Rukeyser, Muriel 1913-1980 ....DLB-48

Rule, Jane 1931- DLB-60

Rulfo, Juan 1918-1986 ....DLB-113

Rumaker, Michael 1932- DLB-16

Rumens, Carol 1944- DLB-40

Runyon, Damon 1880-1946 ..... DLB-11, 86

Ruodlieb circa 1050-1075 ....DLB-148

Rush, Benjamin 1746-1813 ....DLB-37

Rusk, Ralph L. 1888-1962 ....DLB-103

Ruskin, John 1819-1900 .... DLB-55, 163

Russ, Joanna 1937- DLB-8

Russell, B. B., and Company DLB-49

Russell, Benjamin 1761-1845 ....DLB-43

Russell, Bertrand 1872-1970 ....DLB-100

Russell, Charles Edward
1860-1941 ....DLB-25

Russell, George William (see AE)

Russell, R. H., and Son DLB-49

Rutherford, Mark 1831-1913 ....DLB-18

Ryan, Michael 1946- Y-82

Ryan, Oscar 1904- DLB-68

Ryga, George 1932- DLB-60

Rymer, Thomas 1643?-1713 ....DLB-101

Ryskind, Morrie 1895-1985 ....DLB-26

Rzhevsky, Aleksei Andreevich
    1737-1804 ....DLB-150

S

The Saalfield Publishing
    Company DLB-46

Saba, Umberto 1883-1957 ....DLB-114

Sábato, Ernesto 1911- DLB-145

Saberhagen, Fred 1930- DLB-8

Sackler, Howard 1929-1982 ....DLB-7

Sackville, Thomas 1536-1608 ......DLB-132

Sackville, Thomas 1536-1608
    and Norton, Thomas
    1532-1584 ....DLB-62

Sackville-West, V. 1892-1962 ....DLB-34

Sadlier, D. and J., and Company DLB-49

Sadlier, Mary Anne 1820-1903 ......DLB-99

Sadoff, Ira 1945- DLB-120

Saenz, Jaime 1921-1986 ....DLB-145

Saffin, John circa 1626-1710 ....DLB-24

Sagan, Françoise 1935- DLB-83

Sage, Robert 1899-1962 ....DLB-4

Sagel, Jim 1947- DLB-82

Sagendorph, Robb Hansell
    1900-1970 ....DLB-137

Sahagún, Carlos 1938- DLB-108

Sahkomaapii, Piitai (see Highwater, Jamake)

Sahl, Hans 1902- DLB-69

Said, Edward W. 1935- DLB-67

Saiko, George 1892-1962 ....DLB-85

St. Dominic's Press DLB-112

Saint-Exupéry, Antoine de
    1900-1944 ....DLB-72

St. Johns, Adela Rogers 1894-1988 ...DLB-29

St. Martin's Press DLB-46

St. Omer, Garth 1931- DLB-117

Saint Pierre, Michel de 1916-1987 ....DLB-83

Saintsbury, George
    1845-1933 ....DLB-57, 149

Saki (see Munro, H. H.)

Salaam, Kalamu ya 1947- DLB-38

Salas, Floyd 1931- DLB-82

Sálaz-Marquez, Rubén 1935- DLB-122

Salemson, Harold J. 1910-1988 ......DLB-4

Salinas, Luis Omar 1937- DLB-82

Salinas, Pedro 1891-1951 ....DLB-134

Salinger, J. D. 1919- DLB-2, 102

Salkey, Andrew 1928- DLB-125

Salt, Waldo 1914- DLB-44

Salter, James 1925- DLB-130

Salter, Mary Jo 1954- DLB-120

Salustri, Carlo Alberto (see Trilussa)

Salverson, Laura Goodman
    1890-1970 ....DLB-92

Sampson, Richard Henry (see Hull, Richard)

Samuels, Ernest 1903- DLB-111

Sanborn, Franklin Benjamin
    1831-1917 ....DLB-1

Sánchez, Luis Rafael 1936- DLB-145

Sánchez, Philomeno "Phil"
    1917- DLB-122

Sánchez, Ricardo 1941- DLB-82

Sanchez, Sonia 1934- DLB-41; DS-8

Sand, George 1804-1876 ....DLB-119

Sandburg, Carl 1878-1967 ......DLB-17, 54

Sanders, Ed 1939- DLB-16

Sandoz, Mari 1896-1966 ....DLB-9

Sandwell, B. K. 1876-1954 ....DLB-92

Sandys, George 1578-1644 .....DLB-24, 121

Sangster, Charles 1822-1893 ....DLB-99

Sanguineti, Edoardo 1930- DLB-128

Sansom, William 1912-1976 ....DLB-139

Santayana, George
    1863-1952 ....DLB-54, 71; DS-13

Santiago, Danny 1911-1988 ....DLB-122

Santmyer, Helen Hooven 1895-1986 ....Y-84

Sapir, Edward 1884-1939 ....DLB-92

Sapper (see McNeile, Herman Cyril)

Sarduy, Severo 1937- DLB-113

Sargent, Pamela 1948- DLB-8

Saro-Wiwa, Ken 1941- DLB-157

Saroyan, William
    1908-1981 ....DLB-7, 9, 86; Y-81

Sarraute, Nathalie 1900- DLB-83

Sarrazin, Albertine 1937-1967 ......DLB-83

Sarton, May 1912- DLB-48; Y-81

Sartre, Jean-Paul 1905-1980 ....DLB-72

Sassoon, Siegfried 1886-1967 .....DLB-20

Saturday Review Press DLB-46

Saunders, James 1925- DLB-13

Saunders, John Monk 1897-1940 ....DLB-26

Saunders, Margaret Marshall
    1861-1947 ....DLB-92

Saunders and Otley DLB-106

Savage, James 1784-1873 ....DLB-30

Savage, Marmion W. 1803?-1872 ....DLB-21

Savage, Richard 1697?-1743 ....DLB-95

Savard, Félix-Antoine 1896-1982 ....DLB-68

Saville, (Leonard) Malcolm
    1901-1982 ....DLB-160

Sawyer, Ruth 1880-1970 ....DLB-22

Sayers, Dorothy L.
    1893-1957 ....DLB-10, 36, 77, 100

Sayles, John Thomas 1950- DLB-44

Sbarbaro, Camillo 1888-1967 ......DLB-114

Scannell, Vernon 1922- DLB-27

Scarry, Richard 1919-1994 ....DLB-61

Schaeffer, Albrecht 1885-1950 ....DLB-66

Schaeffer, Susan Fromberg 1941- ...DLB-28

Schaff, Philip 1819-1893 ....DS-13

Schaper, Edzard 1908-1984 ....DLB-69

Scharf, J. Thomas 1843-1898 ....DLB-47

Scheffel, Joseph Viktor von
    1826-1886 ....DLB-129

Schelling, Friedrich Wilhelm Joseph von
    1775-1854 ....DLB-90

Scherer, Wilhelm 1841-1886 ....DLB-129

Schickele, René 1883-1940 ....DLB-66

Schiff, Dorothy 1903-1989 ....DLB-127

Schiller, Friedrich 1759-1805 ....DLB-94

Schlaf, Johannes 1862-1941 ....DLB-118

Schlegel, August Wilhelm
    1767-1845 ....DLB-94

Schlegel, Dorothea 1763-1839 ....DLB-90

Schlegel, Friedrich 1772-1829 ....DLB-90

Schleiermacher, Friedrich
    1768-1834 ....DLB-90

Schlesinger, Arthur M., Jr. 1917- ...DLB-17

Schlumberger, Jean 1877-1968 ......DLB-65

Schmid, Eduard Hermann Wilhelm (see
    Edschmid, Kasimir)

Schmidt, Arno 1914-1979 ....DLB-69

Schmidt, Johann Kaspar (see Stirner, Max)

Schmidt, Michael 1947- DLB-40

Schmidtbonn, Wilhelm August
1876-1952 .... DLB-118

Schmitz, James H. 1911- DLB-8

Schnackenberg, Gjertrud 1953- ... DLB-120

Schnitzler, Arthur 1862-1931 ... DLB-81, 118

Schnurre, Wolfdietrich 1920- DLB-69

Schocken Books DLB-46

Schönbeck, Virgilio (see Giotti, Virgilio)

School Stories, 1914-1960 .... DLB-160

Schönherr, Karl 1867-1943 .... DLB-118

Scholartis Press DLB-112

The Schomburg Center for Research
in Black Culture DLB-76

Schopenhauer, Arthur 1788-1860 ... DLB-90

Schopenhauer, Johanna 1766-1838 .. DLB-90

Schorer, Mark 1908-1977 .... DLB-103

Schouler, James 1839-1920 .... DLB-47

Schrader, Paul 1946- DLB-44

Schreiner, Olive 1855-1920 ..... DLB-18, 156

Schroeder, Andreas 1946- DLB-53

Schubart, Christian Friedrich Daniel
1739-1791 .... DLB-97

Schubert, Gotthilf Heinrich
1780-1860 .... DLB-90

Schücking, Levin 1814-1883 .... DLB-133

Schulberg, Budd
1914- DLB-6, 26, 28; Y-81

Schulte, F. J., and Company DLB-49

Schurz, Carl 1829-1906 .... DLB-23

Schuyler, George S. 1895-1977 ... DLB-29, 51

Schuyler, James 1923-1991 .... DLB-5

Schwartz, Delmore 1913-1966 ... DLB-28, 48

Schwartz, Jonathan 1938- Y-82

Schwob, Marcel 1867-1905 .... DLB-123

Science Fantasy DLB-8

Science-Fiction Fandom and
Conventions DLB-8

Science-Fiction Fanzines: The Time
Binders DLB-8

Science-Fiction Films DLB-8

Science Fiction Writers of America and the
Nebula Awards DLB-8

Scot, Reginald circa 1538-1599 ..... DLB-136

Scotellaro, Rocco 1923-1953 .... DLB-128

Scott, Dennis 1939-1991 .... DLB-125

Scott, Dixon 1881-1915 .... DLB-98

Scott, Duncan Campbell
1862-1947 .... DLB-92

Scott, Evelyn 1893-1963 .... DLB-9, 48

Scott, F. R. 1899-1985 .... DLB-88

Scott, Frederick George
1861-1944 .... DLB-92

Scott, Geoffrey 1884-1929 .... DLB-149

Scott, Harvey W. 1838-1910 .... DLB-23

Scott, Paul 1920-1978 .... DLB-14

Scott, Sarah 1723-1795 .... DLB-39

Scott, Tom 1918- DLB-27

Scott, Sir Walter
1771-1832 ... DLB-93, 107, 116, 144, 159

Scott, William Bell 1811-1890 .... DLB-32

Scott, Walter, Publishing
Company Limited DLB-112

Scott, William R.
[publishing house] DLB-46

Scott-Heron, Gil 1949- DLB-41

Charles Scribner's Sons DLB-49

Scripps, E. W. 1854-1926 .... DLB-25

Scudder, Horace Elisha
1838-1902 .... DLB-42, 71

Scudder, Vida Dutton 1861-1954 .... DLB-71

Scupham, Peter 1933- DLB-40

Seabrook, William 1886-1945 .... DLB-4

Seabury, Samuel 1729-1796 .... DLB-31

The Seafarer circa 970 .... DLB-146

Sealsfield, Charles 1793-1864 ...... DLB-133

Sears, Edward I. 1819?-1876 .... DLB-79

Sears Publishing Company DLB-46

Seaton, George 1911-1979 .... DLB-44

Seaton, William Winston
1785-1866 .... DLB-43

Secker, Martin, and Warburg
Limited DLB-112

Secker, Martin [publishing house] .. DLB-112

Second-Generation Minor Poets of the
Seventeenth Century DLB-126

Sedgwick, Arthur George
1844-1915 .... DLB-64

Sedgwick, Catharine Maria
1789-1867 .... DLB-1, 74

Sedgwick, Ellery 1872-1930 .... DLB-91

Sedley, Sir Charles 1639-1701 ...... DLB-131

Seeger, Alan 1888-1916 .... DLB-45

Seers, Eugene (see Dantin, Louis)

Segal, Erich 1937- Y-86

Seghers, Anna 1900-1983 .... DLB-69

Seid, Ruth (see Sinclair, Jo)

Seidel, Frederick Lewis 1936- Y-84

Seidel, Ina 1885-1974 .... DLB-56

Seigenthaler, John 1927- DLB-127

Seizin Press DLB-112

Séjour, Victor 1817-1874 .... DLB-50

Séjour Marcou et Ferrand, Juan Victor (see
Séjour, Victor)

Selby, Hubert, Jr. 1928- DLB-2

Selden, George 1929-1989 .... DLB-52

Selected English-Language Little Magazines
and Newspapers [France,
1920-1939] DLB-4

Selected Humorous Magazines
(1820-1950) DLB-11

Selected Science-Fiction Magazines and
Anthologies DLB-8

Self, Edwin F. 1920- DLB-137

Seligman, Edwin R. A. 1861-1939 .... DLB-47

Seltzer, Chester E. (see Muro, Amado)

Seltzer, Thomas
[publishing house] DLB-46

Selvon, Sam 1923-1994 .... DLB-125

Senancour, Etienne de 1770-1846 ... DLB-119

Sendak, Maurice 1928- DLB-61

Senécal, Eva 1905- DLB-92

Sengstacke, John 1912- DLB-127

Senior, Olive 1941- DLB-157

Šenoa, August 1838-1881 .... DLB-147

"Sensation Novels" (1863), by
H. L. Manse DLB-21

Sepamla, Sipho 1932- DLB-157

Seredy, Kate 1899-1975 .... DLB-22

Sereni, Vittorio 1913-1983 .... DLB-128

Serling, Rod 1924-1975 .... DLB-26

Serote, Mongane Wally 1944- DLB-125

Serraillier, Ian 1912-1994 .... DLB-161

Serrano, Nina 1934- DLB-122

Service, Robert 1874-1958 .... DLB-92

Seth, Vikram 1952- DLB-120

Seton, Ernest Thompson
1860-1942 .... DLB-92; DS-13

Settle, Mary Lee 1918- DLB-6

Seume, Johann Gottfried
1763-1810 .... DLB-94

Seuss, Dr. (see Geisel, Theodor Seuss)

The Seventy-fifth Anniversary of the Armistice:
The Wilfred Owen Centenary and the
Great War Exhibit at the University of
Virginia Y-93

Sewall, Joseph 1688-1769 ....DLB-24

Sewall, Richard B. 1908- DLB-111

Sewell, Anna 1820-1878 ....DLB-163

Sewell, Samuel 1652-1730 ....DLB-24

Sex, Class, Politics, and Religion [in the
British Novel, 1930-1959] DLB-15

Sexton, Anne 1928-1974 ....DLB-5

Seymour-Smith, Martin 1928- DLB-155

Shaara, Michael 1929-1988 ....Y-83

Shadwell, Thomas 1641?-1692 ......DLB-80

Shaffer, Anthony 1926- DLB-13

Shaffer, Peter 1926- DLB-13

Shaftesbury, Anthony Ashley Cooper,
Third Earl of 1671-1713 ....DLB-101

Shairp, Mordaunt 1887-1939 ....DLB-10

Shakespeare, William 1564-1616 .....DLB-62

The Shakespeare Globe Trust Y-93

Shakespeare Head Press DLB-112

Shakhovskoi, Aleksandr Aleksandrovich
1777-1846 ....DLB-150

Shange, Ntozake 1948- DLB-38

Shapiro, Karl 1913- DLB-48

Sharon Publications DLB-46

Sharp, Margery 1905-1991 ....DLB-161

Sharp, William 1855-1905 ....DLB-156

Sharpe, Tom 1928- DLB-14

Shaw, Albert 1857-1947 ....DLB-91

Shaw, Bernard 1856-1950 ....DLB-10, 57

Shaw, Henry Wheeler 1818-1885 ....DLB-11

Shaw, Joseph T. 1874-1952 ....DLB-137

Shaw, Irwin 1913-1984 .... DLB-6, 102; Y-84

Shaw, Robert 1927-1978 ....DLB-13, 14

Shaw, Robert B. 1947- DLB-120

Shawn, William 1907-1992 ....DLB-137

Shay, Frank [publishing house] DLB-46

Shea, John Gilmary 1824-1892 ......DLB-30

Sheaffer, Louis 1912-1993 ....DLB-103

Shearing, Joseph 1886-1952 ....DLB-70

Shebbeare, John 1709-1788 ....DLB-39

Sheckley, Robert 1928- DLB-8

Shedd, William G. T. 1820-1894 ....DLB-64

Sheed, Wilfred 1930- DLB-6

Sheed and Ward [U.S.] DLB-46

Sheed and Ward Limited [U.K.] ... DLB-112

Sheldon, Alice B. (see Tiptree, James, Jr.)

Sheldon, Edward 1886-1946 ....DLB-7

Sheldon and Company DLB-49

Shelley, Mary Wollstonecraft
1797-1851 ....DLB-110, 116, 159

Shelley, Percy Bysshe
1792-1822 ....DLB-96, 110, 158

Shelnutt, Eve 1941- DLB-130

Shenstone, William 1714-1763 ......DLB-95

Shepard, Ernest Howard
1879-1976 ....DLB-160

Shepard, Sam 1943- DLB-7

Shepard, Thomas I,
1604 or 1605-1649 ....DLB-24

Shepard, Thomas II, 1635-1677 .....DLB-24

Shepard, Clark and Brown DLB-49

Shepherd, Luke
flourished 1547-1554 ....DLB-136

Sherburne, Edward 1616-1702 .....DLB-131

Sheridan, Frances 1724-1766 .... DLB-39, 84

Sheridan, Richard Brinsley
1751-1816 ....DLB-89

Sherman, Francis 1871-1926 ....DLB-92

Sherriff, R. C. 1896-1975 ....DLB-10

Sherry, Norman 1935- DLB-155

Sherwood, Mary Martha
1775-1851 ....DLB-163

Sherwood, Robert 1896-1955 .....DLB-7, 26

Shiel, M. P. 1865-1947 ....DLB-153

Shiels, George 1886-1949 ....DLB-10

Shillaber, B.[enjamin] P.[enhallow]
1814-1890 ....DLB-1, 11

Shine, Ted 1931- DLB-38

Ship, Reuben 1915-1975 ....DLB-88

Shirer, William L. 1904-1993 ....DLB-4

Shirinsky-Shikhmatov, Sergii Aleksandrovich
1783-1837 ....DLB-150

Shirley, James 1596-1666 ....DLB-58

Shishkov, Aleksandr Semenovich
1753-1841 ....DLB-150

Shockley, Ann Allen 1927- DLB-33

Shorthouse, Joseph Henry
1834-1903 ....DLB-18

Showalter, Elaine 1941- DLB-67

Shulevitz, Uri 1935- DLB-61

Shulman, Max 1919-1988 ....DLB-11

Shute, Henry A. 1856-1943 ....DLB-9

Shuttle, Penelope 1947- DLB-14, 40

Sibbes, Richard 1577-1635 ....DLB-151

Sidgwick and Jackson Limited DLB-112

Sidney, Margaret (see Lothrop, Harriet M.)

Sidney's Press DLB-49

Siegfried Loraine Sassoon: A Centenary Essay
Tributes from Vivien F. Clarke and
Michael Thorpe Y-86

Sierra, Rubén 1946- DLB-122

Sierra Club Books DLB-49

Siger of Brabant
circa 1240-circa 1284 ....DLB-115

Sigourney, Lydia Howard (Huntley)
1791-1865 ....DLB-1, 42, 73

Silkin, Jon 1930- DLB-27

Silko, Leslie Marmon 1948- DLB-143

Silliphant, Stirling 1918- DLB-26

Sillitoe, Alan 1928- DLB-14, 139

Silman, Roberta 1934- DLB-28

Silva, Beverly 1930- DLB-122

Silverberg, Robert 1935- DLB-8

Silverman, Kenneth 1936- DLB-111

Simak, Clifford D. 1904-1988 ....DLB-8

Simcoe, Elizabeth 1762-1850 ....DLB-99

Simcox, George Augustus
1841-1905 ....DLB-35

Sime, Jessie Georgina 1868-1958 .....DLB-92

Simenon, Georges
1903-1989 ....DLB-72; Y-89

Simic, Charles 1938- DLB-105

Simic, Charles,
Images and "Images" DLB-105

Simmel, Johannes Mario 1924- DLB-69

Simmons, Ernest J. 1903-1972 ......DLB-103

Simmons, Herbert Alfred 1930- DLB-33

Simmons, James 1933- DLB-40

Simms, William Gilmore
1806-1870 ....DLB-3, 30, 59, 73

Simms and M'Intyre DLB-106

Simon, Claude 1913- DLB-83

Simon, Neil 1927- DLB-7

Simon and Schuster DLB-46

Simons, Katherine Drayton Mayrant
1890-1969 ....Y-83

Simpkin and Marshall
[publishing house] DLB-154

Simpson, Helen 1897-1940 .... DLB-77

Simpson, Louis 1923- DLB-5

Simpson, N. F. 1919- DLB-13

Sims, George 1923- DLB-87

Sims, George Robert
1847-1922 .... DLB-35, 70, 135

Sinán, Rogelio 1904- DLB-145

Sinclair, Andrew 1935- DLB-14

Sinclair, Bertrand William
1881-1972 .... DLB-92

Sinclair, Catherine
1800-1864 .... DLB-163

Sinclair, Jo 1913- DLB-28

Sinclair Lewis Centennial
Conference Y-85

Sinclair, Lister 1921- DLB-88

Sinclair, May 1863-1946 .... DLB-36, 135

Sinclair, Upton 1878-1968 .... DLB-9

Sinclair, Upton [publishing house] ... DLB-46

Singer, Isaac Bashevis
1904-1991 .... DLB-6, 28, 52; Y-91

Singmaster, Elsie 1879-1958 .... DLB-9

Sinisgalli, Leonardo 1908-1981 .... DLB-114

Siodmak, Curt 1902- DLB-44

Sissman, L. E. 1928-1976 .... DLB-5

Sisson, C. H. 1914- DLB-27

Sitwell, Edith 1887-1964 .... DLB-20

Sitwell, Osbert 1892-1969 .... DLB-100

Skármeta, Antonio 1940- DLB-145

Skeffington, William
[publishing house] DLB-106

Skelton, John 1463-1529 .... DLB-136

Skelton, Robin 1925- DLB-27, 53

Skinner, Constance Lindsay
1877-1939 .... DLB-92

Skinner, John Stuart 1788-1851 ..... DLB-73

Skipsey, Joseph 1832-1903 .... DLB-35

Slade, Bernard 1930- DLB-53

Slater, Patrick 1880-1951 .... DLB-68

Slaveykov, Pencho 1866-1912 ..... DLB-147

Slavitt, David 1935- DLB-5, 6

Sleigh, Burrows Willcocks Arthur
1821-1869 .... DLB-99

A Slender Thread of Hope: The Kennedy
Center Black Theatre Project ... DLB-38

Slesinger, Tess 1905-1945 .... DLB-102

Slick, Sam (see Haliburton, Thomas Chandler)

Sloane, William, Associates DLB-46

Small, Maynard and Company DLB-49

Small Presses in Great Britain and Ireland,
1960-1985 .... DLB-40

Small Presses I: Jargon Society Y-84

Small Presses II: The Spirit That Moves Us
Press Y-85

Small Presses III: Pushcart Press Y-87

Smart, Christopher 1722-1771 ..... DLB-109

Smart, David A. 1892-1957 .... DLB-137

Smart, Elizabeth 1913-1986 .... DLB-88

Smellie, William
[publishing house] DLB-154

Smiles, Samuel 1812-1904 .... DLB-55

Smith, A. J. M. 1902-1980 .... DLB-88

Smith, Adam 1723-1790 .... DLB-104

Smith, Alexander 1829-1867 ..... DLB-32, 55

Smith, Betty 1896-1972 .... Y-82

Smith, Carol Sturm 1938- Y-81

Smith, Charles Henry 1826-1903 .... DLB-11

Smith, Charlotte 1749-1806 ..... DLB-39, 109

Smith, Cordwainer 1913-1966 .... DLB-8

Smith, Dave 1942- DLB-5

Smith, Dodie 1896- DLB-10

Smith, Doris Buchanan 1934- DLB-52

Smith, E. E. 1890-1965 .... DLB-8

Smith, Elihu Hubbard 1771-1798 .... DLB-37

Smith, Elizabeth Oakes (Prince)
1806-1893 .... DLB-1

Smith, F. Hopkinson 1838-1915 .... DS-13

Smith, George D. 1870-1920 .... DLB-140

Smith, George O. 1911-1981 .... DLB-8

Smith, Goldwin 1823-1910 .... DLB-99

Smith, H. Allen 1907-1976 ..... DLB-11, 29

Smith, Hazel Brannon 1914- DLB-127

Smith, Horatio (Horace)
1779-1849 .... DLB-116

Smith, Horatio (Horace) 1779-1849 and
James Smith 1775-1839 .... DLB-96

Smith, Iain Crichton
1928- DLB-40, 139

Smith, J. Allen 1860-1924 .... DLB-47

Smith, John 1580-1631 .... DLB-24, 30

Smith, Josiah 1704-1781 .... DLB-24

Smith, Ken 1938- DLB-40

Smith, Lee 1944- DLB-143; Y-83

Smith, Logan Pearsall 1865-1946 .... DLB-98

Smith, Mark 1935- Y-82

Smith, Michael 1698-circa 1771 ..... DLB-31

Smith, Red 1905-1982 .... DLB-29

Smith, Roswell 1829-1892 .... DLB-79

Smith, Samuel Harrison
1772-1845 .... DLB-43

Smith, Samuel Stanhope
1751-1819 .... DLB-37

Smith, Sarah (see Stretton, Hesba)

Smith, Seba 1792-1868 .... DLB-1, 11

Smith, Sir Thomas 1513-1577 ..... DLB-132

Smith, Stevie 1902-1971 .... DLB-20

Smith, Sydney 1771-1845 .... DLB-107

Smith, Sydney Goodsir 1915-1975 ...DLB-27

Smith, William
flourished 1595-1597 .... DLB-136

Smith, William 1727-1803 .... DLB-31

Smith, William 1728-1793 .... DLB-30

Smith, William Gardner
1927-1974 .... DLB-76

Smith, William Henry
1808-1872 .... DLB-159

Smith, William Jay 1918- DLB-5

Smith, Elder and Company DLB-154

Smith, Harrison, and Robert Haas
[publishing house] DLB-46

Smith, J. Stilman, and Company DLB-49

Smith, W. B., and Company DLB-49

Smith, W. H., and Son DLB-106

Smithers, Leonard
[publishing house] DLB-112

Smollett, Tobias 1721-1771 .... DLB-39, 104

Snellings, Rolland (see Touré, Askia
Muhammad)

Snodgrass, W. D. 1926- DLB-5

Snow, C. P. 1905-1980 .... DLB-15, 77

Snyder, Gary 1930- DLB-5, 16

Sobiloff, Hy 1912-1970 .... DLB-48

The Society for Textual Scholarship and
TEXT Y-87

The Society for the History of Authorship,
Reading and Publishing Y-92

Soffici, Ardengo 1879-1964 .... DLB-114

Sofola, 'Zulu 1938- DLB-157

Solano, Solita 1888-1975 .... DLB-4

Sollers, Philippe 1936- DLB-83

Solmi, Sergio 1899-1981 .... DLB-114

Solomon, Carl 1928- DLB-16

Solway, David 1941- DLB-53

Solzhenitsyn and America Y-85

Somerville, Edith Œnone
1858-1949 ....DLB-135

Sontag, Susan 1933- DLB-2, 67

Sorrentino, Gilbert 1929- DLB-5; Y-80

Sorge, Reinhard Johannes
1892-1916 ....DLB-118

Sotheby, William 1757-1833 ....DLB-93

Soto, Gary 1952- DLB-82

Sources for the Study of Tudor and Stuart
Drama DLB-62

Souster, Raymond 1921- DLB-88

The *South English Legendary*
circa thirteenth-fifteenth
centuries DLB-146

Southerland, Ellease 1943- DLB-33

Southern, Terry 1924- DLB-2

Southern Writers Between the
Wars DLB-9

Southerne, Thomas 1659-1746 ......DLB-80

Southey, Caroline Anne Bowles
1786-1854 ....DLB-116

Southey, Robert
1774-1843 ....DLB-93, 107, 142

Sowande, Bode 1948- DLB-157

Soyfer, Jura 1912-1939 ....DLB-124

Soyinka, Wole 1934- ... DLB-125; Y-86, 87

Spacks, Barry 1931- DLB-105

Spalding, Frances 1950- DLB-155

Spark, Muriel 1918- DLB-15, 139

Sparks, Jared 1789-1866 ....DLB-1, 30

Sparshott, Francis 1926- DLB-60

Späth, Gerold 1939- DLB-75

Spatola, Adriano 1941-1988 ....DLB-128

Spaziani, Maria Luisa 1924- DLB-128

The Spectator 1828- DLB-110

Spedding, James 1808-1881 ....DLB-144

Speght, Rachel 1597-after 1630 .....DLB-126

Spellman, A. B. 1935- DLB-41

Spence, Thomas 1750-1814 ....DLB-158

Spencer, Anne 1882-1975 ....DLB-51, 54

Spencer, Elizabeth 1921- DLB-6

Spencer, Herbert 1820-1903 ....DLB-57

Spencer, Scott 1945- Y-86

Spender, J. A. 1862-1942 ....DLB-98

Spender, Stephen 1909- DLB-20

Sperr, Martin 1944- DLB-124

Spicer, Jack 1925-1965 ....DLB-5, 16

Spielberg, Peter 1929- Y-81

Spielhagen, Friedrich 1829-1911 ... DLB-129

"*Spielmannsepen*"
(circa 1152-circa 1500) DLB-148

Spier, Peter 1927- DLB-61

Spinrad, Norman 1940- DLB-8

Spires, Elizabeth 1952- DLB-120

Spitteler, Carl 1845-1924 ....DLB-129

Spivak, Lawrence E. 1900- DLB-137

Spofford, Harriet Prescott
1835-1921 ....DLB-74

Squibob (see Derby, George Horatio)

Stacpoole, H. de Vere
1863-1951 ....DLB-153

Staël, Germaine de 1766-1817 .....DLB-119

Staël-Holstein, Anne-Louise Germaine de
(see Staël, Germaine de)

Stafford, Jean 1915-1979 ....DLB-2

Stafford, William 1914- DLB-5

Stage Censorship: "The Rejected Statement"
(1911), by Bernard Shaw
[excerpts] DLB-10

Stallings, Laurence 1894-1968 .... DLB-7, 44

Stallworthy, Jon 1935- DLB-40

Stampp, Kenneth M. 1912- DLB-17

Stanford, Ann 1916- DLB-5

Stanković, Borisav ("Bora")
1876-1927 ....DLB-147

Stanley, Henry M. 1841-1904 ....DS-13

Stanley, Thomas 1625-1678 ....DLB-131

Stannard, Martin 1947- DLB-155

Stanton, Elizabeth Cady
1815-1902 ....DLB-79

Stanton, Frank L. 1857-1927 .... DLB-25

Stanton, Maura 1946- DLB-120

Stapledon, Olaf 1886-1950 ....DLB-15

Star Spangled Banner Office DLB-49

Starkey, Thomas
circa 1499-1538 .... DLB-132

Starkweather, David 1935- DLB-7

Statements on the Art of Poetry DLB-54

Stead, Robert J. C. 1880-1959 ......DLB-92

Steadman, Mark 1930- DLB-6

The Stealthy School of Criticism (1871), by
Dante Gabriel Rossetti DLB-35

Stearns, Harold E. 1891-1943 ....DLB-4

Stedman, Edmund Clarence
1833-1908 ....DLB-64

Steegmuller, Francis 1906-1994 .....DLB-111

Steel, Flora Annie
1847-1929 ....DLB-153, 156

Steele, Max 1922- Y-80

Steele, Richard 1672-1729 ......DLB-84, 101

Steele, Timothy 1948- DLB-120

Steele, Wilbur Daniel 1886-1970 .....DLB-86

Steere, Richard circa 1643-1721 .....DLB-24

Stegner, Wallace 1909-1993 .....DLB-9; Y-93

Stehr, Hermann 1864-1940 ....DLB-66

Steig, William 1907- DLB-61

Stein, Gertrude 1874-1946 .....DLB-4, 54, 86

Stein, Leo 1872-1947 ....DLB-4

Stein and Day Publishers DLB-46

Steinbeck, John 1902-1968 ... DLB-7, 9; DS-2

Steiner, George 1929- DLB-67

Stendhal 1783-1842 ....DLB-119

Stephen Crane: A Revaluation Virginia
Tech Conference, 1989 ....Y-89

Stephen, Leslie 1832-1904 ......DLB-57, 144

Stephens, Alexander H. 1812-1883 ...DLB-47

Stephens, Ann 1810-1886 ....DLB-3, 73

Stephens, Charles Asbury
1844?-1931 ....DLB-42

Stephens, James
1882?-1950 .... DLB-19, 153, 162

Sterling, George 1869-1926 ....DLB-54

Sterling, James 1701-1763 ....DLB-24

Sterling, John 1806-1844 ....DLB-116

Stern, Gerald 1925- DLB-105

Stern, Madeleine B. 1912- DLB-111, 140

Stern, Gerald, Living in Ruin DLB-105

Stern, Richard 1928- Y-87

Stern, Stewart 1922- DLB-26

Sterne, Laurence 1713-1768 ....DLB-39

Sternheim, Carl 1878-1942 .....DLB-56, 118

Sternhold, Thomas ?-1549 and
John Hopkins ?-1570 ....DLB-132

Stevens, Henry 1819-1886 ....DLB-140

Stevens, Wallace 1879-1955 ....DLB-54

Stevenson, Anne 1933- DLB-40

Stevenson, Lionel 1902-1973 ....DLB-155

Stevenson, Robert Louis
1850-1894 ....DLB-18, 57, 141, 156; DS-13

Stewart, Donald Ogden
1894-1980 . . . . DLB-4, 11, 26

Stewart, Dugald 1753-1828 . . . . DLB-31

Stewart, George, Jr. 1848-1906 . . . . . . DLB-99

Stewart, George R. 1895-1980 . . . . .DLB-8

Stewart and Kidd Company DLB-46

Stewart, Randall 1896-1964 . . . . DLB-103

Stickney, Trumbull 1874-1904 . . . . . DLB-54

Stifter, Adalbert 1805-1868 . . . . DLB-133

Stiles, Ezra 1727-1795 . . . . DLB-31

Still, James 1906- DLB-9

Stirner, Max 1806-1856 . . . . DLB-129

Stith, William 1707-1755 . . . . DLB-31

Stock, Elliot [publishing house] DLB-106

Stockton, Frank R.
1834-1902 . . . . .DLB-42, 74; DS-13

Stoddard, Ashbel
[publishing house] DLB-49

Stoddard, Richard Henry
1825-1903 . . . . DLB-3, 64; DS-13

Stoddard, Solomon 1643-1729 . . . . . . DLB-24

Stoker, Bram 1847-1912 . . . . DLB-36, 70

Stokes, Frederick A., Company DLB-49

Stokes, Thomas L. 1898-1958 . . . . . . DLB-29

Stokesbury, Leon 1945- DLB-120

Stolberg, Christian Graf zu
1748-1821 . . . . DLB-94

Stolberg, Friedrich Leopold Graf zu
1750-1819 . . . . DLB-94

Stone, Herbert S., and Company DLB-49

Stone, Lucy 1818-1893 . . . . DLB-79

Stone, Melville 1848-1929 . . . . DLB-25

Stone, Robert 1937- DLB-152

Stone, Ruth 1915- DLB-105

Stone, Samuel 1602-1663 . . . . DLB-24

Stone and Kimball DLB-49

Stoppard, Tom 1937- DLB-13; Y-85

Storey, Anthony 1928- DLB-14

Storey, David 1933- DLB-13, 14

Storm, Theodor 1817-1888 . . . . DLB-129

Story, Thomas circa 1670-1742 . . . . . DLB-31

Story, William Wetmore 1819-1895 . . .DLB-1

Storytelling: A Contemporary
Renaissance Y-84

Stoughton, William 1631-1701 . . . . . . DLB-24

Stow, John 1525-1605 . . . . DLB-132

Stowe, Harriet Beecher
1811-1896 . . . . DLB-1, 12, 42, 74

Stowe, Leland 1899- DLB-29

Stoyanov, Dimitŭr Ivanov (see Elin Pelin)

Strachey, Lytton
1880-1932 . . . . .DLB-149; DS-10

Strachey, Lytton, Preface to Eminent
Victorians DLB-149

Strahan and Company DLB-106

Strahan, William
[publishing house] DLB-154

Strand, Mark 1934- DLB-5

The Strasbourg Oaths 842 . . . . DLB-148

Stratemeyer, Edward 1862-1930 . . . . DLB-42

Stratton and Barnard DLB-49

Straub, Peter 1943- Y-84

Strauß, Botho 1944- DLB-124

Strauß, David Friedrich
1808-1874 . . . . DLB-133

The Strawberry Hill Press DLB-154

Streatfeild, Noel 1895-1986 . . . . DLB-160

Street, Cecil John Charles (see Rhode, John)

Street, G. S. 1867-1936 . . . . DLB-135

Street and Smith DLB-49

Streeter, Edward 1891-1976 . . . . DLB-11

Streeter, Thomas Winthrop
1883-1965 . . . . DLB-140

Stretton, Hesba 1832-1911 . . . . DLB-163

Stribling, T. S. 1881-1965 . . . . .DLB-9

Der Stricker circa 1190-circa 1250 . . DLB-138

Strickland, Samuel 1804-1867 . . . . . . DLB-99

Stringer and Townsend DLB-49

Stringer, Arthur 1874-1950 . . . . DLB-92

Strittmatter, Erwin 1912- DLB-69

Strode, William 1630-1645 . . . . DLB-126

Strother, David Hunter 1816-1888 . . . . DLB-3

Strouse, Jean 1945- DLB-111

Stuart, Dabney 1937- DLB-105

Stuart, Dabney, Knots into Webs: Some Autobiographical Sources DLB-105

Stuart, Jesse
1906-1984 . . . . DLB-9, 48, 102; Y-84

Stuart, Lyle [publishing house] DLB-46

Stubbs, Harry Clement (see Clement, Hal)

Studio DLB-112

The Study of Poetry (1880), by
Matthew Arnold DLB-35

Sturgeon, Theodore
1918-1985 . . . . DLB-8; Y-85

Sturges, Preston 1898-1959 . . . . .DLB-26

"Style" (1840; revised, 1859), by
Thomas de Quincey [excerpt] DLB-57

"Style" (1888), by Walter Pater DLB-57

Style (1897), by Walter Raleigh
[excerpt] DLB-57

"Style" (1877), by T. H. Wright
[excerpt] DLB-57

"Le Style c'est l'homme" (1892), by
W. H. Mallock DLB-57

Styron, William 1925- . . . DLB-2, 143; Y-80

Suárez, Mario 1925- DLB-82

Such, Peter 1939- DLB-60

Suckling, Sir John 1609-1641? . . DLB-58, 126

Suckow, Ruth 1892-1960 . . . . DLB-9, 102

Sudermann, Hermann 1857-1928 . . .DLB-118

Sue, Eugène 1804-1857 . . . . .DLB-119

Sue, Marie-Joseph (see Sue, Eugène)

Suggs, Simon (see Hooper, Johnson Jones)

Sukenick, Ronald 1932- Y-81

Suknaski, Andrew 1942- DLB-53

Sullivan, Alan 1868-1947 . . . . .DLB-92

Sullivan, C. Gardner 1886-1965 . . . . .DLB-26

Sullivan, Frank 1892-1976 . . . . .DLB-11

Sulte, Benjamin 1841-1923 . . . . .DLB-99

Sulzberger, Arthur Hays
1891-1968 . . . . .DLB-127

Sulzberger, Arthur Ochs 1926- DLB-127

Sulzer, Johann Georg 1720-1779 . . . . .DLB-97

Sumarokov, Aleksandr Petrovich
1717-1777 . . . . .DLB-150

Summers, Hollis 1916- DLB-6

Sumner, Henry A.
[publishing house] DLB-49

Surtees, Robert Smith 1803-1864 . . . . .DLB-21

A Survey of Poetry Anthologies,
1879-1960 . . . . .DLB-54

Surveys of the Year's Biographies

A Transit of Poets and Others: American
Biography in 1982 . . . . Y-82

The Year in Literary Biography . . . Y-83–Y-94

Survey of the Year's Book Publishing

The Year in Book Publishing Y-86

Survey of the Year's Children's Books

The Year in Children's Books Y-92–Y-94

Surveys of the Year's Drama

The Year in Drama
.... Y-82–Y-85, Y-87–Y-94

The Year in London Theatre Y-92

Surveys of the Year's Fiction

The Year's Work in Fiction:
A Survey Y-82

The Year in Fiction: A Biased View Y-83

The Year in Fiction ... Y-84–Y-86, Y-89, Y-94

The Year in the
Novel Y-87, Y-88, Y-90–Y-93

The Year in Short Stories Y-87

The Year in the
Short Story Y-88, Y-90–Y-93

Survey of the Year's Literary Theory

The Year in Literary Theory Y-92–Y-93

Surveys of the Year's Poetry

The Year's Work in American
Poetry.........................Y-82

The Year in Poetry Y-83–Y-92, Y-94

Sutherland, Efua Theodora
1924- DLB-117

Sutherland, John 1919-1956 ....DLB-68

Sutro, Alfred 1863-1933 ....DLB-10

Swados, Harvey 1920-1972 ....DLB-2

Swain, Charles 1801-1874 ....DLB-32

Swallow Press DLB-46

Swan Sonnenschein Limited DLB-106

Swanberg, W. A. 1907- DLB-103

Swenson, May 1919-1989 ....DLB-5

Swerling, Jo 1897- DLB-44

Swift, Jonathan
1667-1745 .... DLB-39, 95, 101

Swinburne, A. C. 1837-1909 .....DLB-35, 57

Swineshead, Richard floruit
circa 1350 ....DLB-115

Swinnerton, Frank 1884-1982 ....DLB-34

Swisshelm, Jane Grey 1815-1884 .....DLB-43

Swope, Herbert Bayard 1882-1958 ...DLB-25

Swords, T. and J., and Company DLB-49

Swords, Thomas 1763-1843 and
Swords, James ?-1844 ....DLB-73

Sylvester, Josuah
1562 or 1563 - 1618 ....DLB-121

Symonds, Emily Morse (see Paston, George)

Symonds, John Addington
1840-1893 ....DLB-57, 144

Symons, A. J. A. 1900-1941 ....DLB-149

Symons, Arthur
1865-1945 .... DLB-19, 57, 149

Symons, Julian
1912-1994 ....DLB-87, 155; Y-92

Symons, Scott 1933- DLB-53

A Symposium on *The Columbia History of
the Novel* Y-92

Synge, John Millington
1871-1909 ....DLB-10, 19

Synge Summer School: J. M. Synge and the
Irish Theater, Rathdrum, County Wiclow,
Ireland Y-93

Syrett, Netta 1865-1943 ....DLB-135

T

Taban lo Liyong 1939?- DLB-125

Taché, Joseph-Charles 1820-1894 ...DLB-99

Tafolla, Carmen 1951- DLB-82

Taggard, Genevieve 1894-1948 .....DLB-45

Tagger, Theodor (see Bruckner, Ferdinand)

Tait, J. Selwin, and Sons DLB-49

Tait's Edinburgh Magazine
1832-1861 ....DLB-110

The Takarazaka Revue Company Y-91

Tallent, Elizabeth 1954- DLB-130

Talvj 1797-1870 ....DLB-59, 133

Taradash, Daniel 1913- DLB-44

Tarbell, Ida M. 1857-1944 ....DLB-47

Tardivel, Jules-Paul 1851-1905 ......DLB-99

Targan, Barry 1932- DLB-130

Tarkington, Booth 1869-1946 ....DLB-9, 102

Tashlin, Frank 1913-1972 ....DLB-44

Tate, Allen 1899-1979 ....DLB-4, 45, 63

Tate, James 1943- DLB-5

Tate, Nahum circa 1652-1715 ......DLB-80

Tatian circa 830 ....DLB-148

Tavčar, Ivan 1851-1923 ....DLB-147

Taylor, Ann 1782-1866 ....DLB-163

Taylor, Bayard 1825-1878 ....DLB-3

Taylor, Bert Leston 1866-1921 ......DLB-25

Taylor, Charles H. 1846-1921 ......DLB-25

Taylor, Edward circa 1642-1729 ....DLB-24

Taylor, Elizabeth 1912-1975 ....DLB-139

Taylor, Henry 1942- DLB-5

Taylor, Sir Henry 1800-1886 ....DLB-32

Taylor, Jane 1783-1824 ....DLB-163

Taylor, Jeremy circa 1613-1667 ....DLB-151

Taylor, John
1577 or 1578 - 1653 ....DLB-121

Taylor, Mildred D. ?- DLB-52

Taylor, Peter 1917-1994 ....Y-81, Y-94

Taylor, William, and Company DLB-49

Taylor-Made Shakespeare? Or Is
"Shall I Die?" the Long-Lost Text
of Bottom's Dream? Y-85

Teasdale, Sara 1884-1933 ....DLB-45

The Tea-Table (1725), by Eliza Haywood
[excerpt] DLB-39

Telles, Lygia Fagundes 1924- DLB-113

Temple, Sir William 1628-1699 ....DLB-101

Tenn, William 1919- DLB-8

Tennant, Emma 1937- DLB-14

Tenney, Tabitha Gilman
1762-1837 ....DLB-37

Tennyson, Alfred 1809-1892 ....DLB-32

Tennyson, Frederick 1807-1898 .....DLB-32

Terhune, Albert Payson 1872-1942 ...DLB-9

Terhune, Mary Virginia 1830-1922 ... DS-13

Terry, Megan 1932- DLB-7

Terson, Peter 1932- DLB-13

Tesich, Steve 1943- Y-83

Tessa, Delio 1886-1939 ....DLB-114

Testori, Giovanni 1923-1993 ......DLB-128

Tey, Josephine 1896?-1952 ....DLB-77

Thacher, James 1754-1844 ....DLB-37

Thackeray, William Makepeace
1811-1863 .... DLB-21, 55, 159, 163

Thames and Hudson Limited DLB-112

Thanet, Octave (see French, Alice)

The Theater in Shakespeare's
Time........................DLB-62

The Theatre Guild DLB-7

Thegan and the Astronomer
flourished circa 850 ....DLB-148

Thelwall, John 1764-1834 ......DLB-93, 158

Theodulf circa 760-circa 821 ....DLB-148

Theriault, Yves 1915-1983 ....DLB-88

Thério, Adrien 1925- DLB-53

Theroux, Paul 1941- DLB-2

Thibaudeau, Colleen 1925- DLB-88

Thielen, Benedict 1903-1965 ....DLB-102

Thiong'o Ngugi wa (see Ngugi wa Thiong'o)

Third-Generation Minor Poets of the
Seventeenth Century DLB-131

Thoma, Ludwig 1867-1921 ....DLB-66

Thoma, Richard 1902- DLB-4

Thomas, Audrey 1935- DLB-60

Thomas, D. M. 1935- DLB-40

Thomas, Dylan
1914-1953 .... DLB-13, 20, 139

Thomas, Edward
1878-1917 .... DLB-19, 98, 156

Thomas, Gwyn 1913-1981 .... DLB-15

Thomas, Isaiah 1750-1831 ...... DLB-43, 73

Thomas, Isaiah [publishing house] .. DLB-49

Thomas, John 1900-1932 .... DLB-4

Thomas, Joyce Carol 1938- DLB-33

Thomas, Lorenzo 1944- DLB-41

Thomas, R. S. 1915- DLB-27

Thomasîn von Zerclære
circa 1186-circa 1259 .... DLB-138

Thompson, David 1770-1857 .... DLB-99

Thompson, Dorothy 1893-1961 ..... DLB-29

Thompson, Francis 1859-1907 ...... DLB-19

Thompson, George Selden (see Selden, George)

Thompson, John 1938-1976 .... DLB-60

Thompson, John R. 1823-1873 ... DLB-3, 73

Thompson, Lawrance 1906-1973 ... DLB-103

Thompson, Maurice
1844-1901 .... DLB-71, 74

Thompson, Ruth Plumly
1891-1976 .... DLB-22

Thompson, Thomas Phillips
1843-1933 .... DLB-99

Thompson, William 1775-1833 .... DLB-158

Thompson, William Tappan
1812-1882 .... DLB-3, 11

Thomson, Edward William
1849-1924 .... DLB-92

Thomson, James 1700-1748 .... DLB-95

Thomson, James 1834-1882 .... DLB-35

Thomson, Mortimer 1831-1875 ..... DLB-11

Thoreau, Henry David 1817-1862 ....DLB-1

Thorpe, Thomas Bangs
1815-1878 .... DLB-3, 11

Thoughts on Poetry and Its Varieties (1833),
by John Stuart Mill DLB-32

Thrale, Hester Lynch (see Piozzi, Hester
Lynch [Thrale])

Thümmel, Moritz August von
1738-1817 .... DLB-97

Thurber, James
1894-1961 ....DLB-4, 11, 22, 102

Thurman, Wallace 1902-1934 ...... DLB-51

Thwaite, Anthony 1930- DLB-40

Thwaites, Reuben Gold
1853-1913 .... DLB-47

Ticknor, George
1791-1871 ....DLB-1, 59, 140

Ticknor and Fields DLB-49

Ticknor and Fields (revived) DLB-46

Tieck, Ludwig 1773-1853 .... DLB-90

Tietjens, Eunice 1884-1944 .... DLB-54

Tilney, Edmund circa 1536-1610 ... DLB-136

Tilt, Charles [publishing house] DLB-106

Tilton, J. E., and Company DLB-49

Time and Western Man (1927), by Wyndham
Lewis [excerpts] DLB-36

Time-Life Books DLB-46

Times Books DLB-46

Timothy, Peter circa 1725-1782 ..... DLB-43

Timrod, Henry 1828-1867 .... DLB-3

Tinker, Chauncey Brewster
1876-1963 .... DLB-140

Tinsley Brothers DLB-106

Tiptree, James, Jr. 1915-1987 .... DLB-8

Titus, Edward William 1870-1952 .... DLB-4

Tlali, Miriam 1933- DLB-157

Todd, Barbara Euphan
1890-1976 .... DLB-160

Toklas, Alice B. 1877-1967 .... DLB-4

Tolkien, J. R. R. 1892-1973 .....DLB-15, 160

Toller, Ernst 1893-1939 .... DLB-124

Tollet, Elizabeth 1694-1754 .... DLB-95

Tolson, Melvin B. 1898-1966 ....DLB-48, 76

Tom Jones (1749), by Henry Fielding
[excerpt] DLB-39

Tomalin, Claire 1933- DLB-155

Tomlinson, Charles 1927- DLB-40

Tomlinson, H. M. 1873-1958 ...DLB-36, 100

Tompkins, Abel [publishing house] .. DLB-49

Tompson, Benjamin 1642-1714 ...... DLB-24

Tonks, Rosemary 1932- DLB-14

Tonna, Charlotte Elizabeth
1790-1846 .... DLB-163

Toole, John Kennedy 1937-1969 ....Y-81

Toomer, Jean 1894-1967 ....DLB-45, 51

Tor Books DLB-46

Torberg, Friedrich 1908-1979 ...... DLB-85

Torrence, Ridgely 1874-1950 .... DLB-54

Torres-Metzger, Joseph V.
1933- DLB-122

Toth, Susan Allen 1940- Y-86

Tough-Guy Literature DLB-9

Touré, Askia Muhammad 1938- DLB-41

Tourgée, Albion W. 1838-1905 ......DLB-79

Tourneur, Cyril circa 1580-1626 .....DLB-58

Tournier, Michel 1924- DLB-83

Tousey, Frank [publishing house] DLB-49

Tower Publications DLB-46

Towne, Benjamin circa 1740-1793 ....DLB-43

Towne, Robert 1936- DLB-44

The Townely Plays
fifteenth and sixteenth
centuries DLB-146

Townshend, Aurelian
by 1583 - circa 1651 ....DLB-121

Tracy, Honor 1913- DLB-15

Traherne, Thomas 1637?-1674 .....DLB-131

Traill, Catharine Parr 1802-1899 .....DLB-99

Train, Arthur 1875-1945 ....DLB-86

The Transatlantic Publishing
Company DLB-49

Transcendentalists, American DS-5

Translators of the Twelfth Century:
Literary Issues Raised and Impact
Created DLB-115

Traven, B.
1882? or 1890?-1969? DLB-9, 56

Travers, Ben 1886-1980 ....DLB-10

Travers, P. L. (Pamela Lyndon)
1899- DLB-160

Trediakovsky, Vasilii Kirillovich
1703-1769 ....DLB-150

Treece, Henry 1911-1966 ....DLB-160

Trejo, Ernesto 1950- DLB-122

Trelawny, Edward John
1792-1881 ....DLB-110, 116, 144

Tremain, Rose 1943- DLB-14

Tremblay, Michel 1942- DLB-60

Trends in Twentieth-Century
Mass Market Publishing DLB-46

Trent, William P. 1862-1939 ....DLB-47

Trescot, William Henry
1822-1898 ....DLB-30

Trevelyan, Sir George Otto
1838-1928 ....DLB-144

Trevisa, John
circa 1342-circa 1402 ....DLB-146

Trevor, William 1928- DLB-14, 139

Trierer Floyris circa 1170-1180 ....DLB-138

Trilling, Lionel 1905-1975 . . . . . . .DLB-28, 63

Trilussa 1871-1950 . . . . .DLB-114

Trimmer, Sarah 1741-1810 . . . . . . .DLB-158

Triolet, Elsa 1896-1970 . . . . .DLB-72

Tripp, John 1927- DLB-40

Trocchi, Alexander 1925- DLB-15

Trollope, Anthony
1815-1882 . . . . DLB-21, 57, 159

Trollope, Frances 1779-1863 . . . . . . .DLB-21

Troop, Elizabeth 1931- DLB-14

Trotter, Catharine 1679-1749 . . . . . . .DLB-84

Trotti, Lamar 1898-1952 . . . . .DLB-44

Trottier, Pierre 1925- DLB-60

Troupe, Quincy Thomas, Jr.
1943- DLB-41

Trow, John F., and Company DLB-49

Truillier-Lacombe, Joseph-Patrice
1807-1863 . . . . .DLB-99

Trumbo, Dalton 1905-1976 . . . . .DLB-26

Trumbull, Benjamin 1735-1820 . . . . . .DLB-30

Trumbull, John 1750-1831 . . . . .DLB-31

T. S. Eliot Centennial Y-88

Tucholsky, Kurt 1890-1935 . . . . .DLB-56

Tucker, Charlotte Maria
1821-1893 . . . . .DLB-163

Tucker, George 1775-1861 . . . . . . .DLB-3, 30

Tucker, Nathaniel Beverley
1784-1851 . . . . .DLB-3

Tucker, St. George 1752-1827 . . . . . . .DLB-37

Tuckerman, Henry Theodore
1813-1871 . . . . .DLB-64

Tunis, John R. 1889-1975 . . . . .DLB-22

Tunstall, Cuthbert 1474-1559 . . . . . .DLB-132

Tuohy, Frank 1925- DLB-14, 139

Tupper, Martin F. 1810-1889 . . . . . . .DLB-32

Turbyfill, Mark 1896- DLB-45

Turco, Lewis 1934- Y-84

Turnbull, Andrew 1921-1970 . . . . . .DLB-103

Turnbull, Gael 1928- DLB-40

Turner, Arlin 1909-1980 . . . . .DLB-103

Turner, Charles (Tennyson)
1808-1879 . . . . .DLB-32

Turner, Frederick 1943- DLB-40

Turner, Frederick Jackson
1861-1932 . . . . .DLB-17

Turner, Joseph Addison
1826-1868 . . . . .DLB-79

Turpin, Waters Edward
1910-1968 . . . . .DLB-51

Turrini, Peter 1944- DLB-124

Tutuola, Amos 1920- DLB-125

Twain, Mark (see Clemens,
Samuel Langhorne)

The 'Twenties and Berlin, by
Alex Natan DLB-66

Tyler, Anne 1941- DLB-6, 143; Y-82

Tyler, Moses Coit 1835-1900 . . . . DLB-47, 64

Tyler, Royall 1757-1826 . . . . .DLB-37

Tylor, Edward Burnett 1832-1917 . . . DLB-57

Tynan, Katharine 1861-1931 . . . . . . DLB-153

Tyndale, William
circa 1494-1536 . . . . .DLB-132

U

Udall, Nicholas 1504-1556 . . . . DLB-62

Uhland, Ludwig 1787-1862 . . . . DLB-90

Uhse, Bodo 1904-1963 . . . . DLB-69

Ujević, Augustin ("Tin")
1891-1955 . . . . DLB-147

Ulibarrí, Sabine R. 1919- DLB-82

Ulica, Jorge 1870-1926 . . . . DLB-82

Ulizio, B. George 1889-1969 . . . . DLB-140

Ulrich von Liechtenstein
circa 1200-circa 1275 . . . . DLB-138

Ulrich von Zatzikhoven
before 1194-after 1214 . . . . DLB-138

Unamuno, Miguel de 1864-1936 . . . DLB-108

Under the Microscope (1872), by
A. C. Swinburne DLB-35

Unger, Friederike Helene
1741-1813 . . . . DLB-94

Ungaretti, Giuseppe 1888-1970 . . . . DLB-114

United States Book Company DLB-49

Universal Publishing and Distributing
Corporation DLB-46

The University of Iowa Writers' Workshop
Golden Jubilee Y-86

The University of South Carolina
Press Y-94

University of Wales Press DLB-112

"The Unknown Public" (1858), by
Wilkie Collins [excerpt] DLB-57

Unruh, Fritz von 1885-1970 . . . . DLB-56, 118

Unspeakable Practices II: The Festival of
Vanguard Narrative at Brown
University Y-93

Unwin, T. Fisher
[publishing house] DLB-106

Upchurch, Boyd B. (see Boyd, John)

Updike, John
1932- DLB-2, 5, 143; Y-80, 82; DS-3

Upton, Bertha 1849-1912 . . . . DLB-141

Upton, Charles 1948- DLB-16

Upton, Florence K. 1873-1922 . . . . .DLB-141

Upward, Allen 1863-1926 . . . . .DLB-36

Urista, Alberto Baltazar (see Alurista)

Urzidil, Johannes 1896-1976 . . . . . . .DLB-85

Urquhart, Fred 1912- DLB-139

The Uses of Facsimile Y-90

Usk, Thomas died 1388 . . . . .DLB-146

Uslar Pietri, Arturo 1906- DLB-113

Ustinov, Peter 1921- DLB-13

Uttley, Alison 1884-1976 . . . . .DLB-160

Uz, Johann Peter 1720-1796 . . . . .DLB-97

V

Vac, Bertrand 1914- DLB-88

Vail, Laurence 1891-1968 . . . . .DLB-4

Vailland, Roger 1907-1965 . . . . .DLB-83

Vajda, Ernest 1887-1954 . . . . .DLB-44

Valdés, Gina 1943- DLB-122

Valdez, Luis Miguel 1940- DLB-122

Valduga, Patrizia 1953- DLB-128

Valente, José Angel 1929- DLB-108

Valenzuela, Luisa 1938- DLB-113

Valeri, Diego 1887-1976 . . . . .DLB-128

Valgardson, W. D. 1939- DLB-60

Valle, Víctor Manuel 1950- DLB-122

Valle-Inclán, Ramón del
1866-1936 . . . . .DLB-134

Vallejo, Armando 1949- DLB-122

Vallès, Jules 1832-1885 . . . . .DLB-123

Vallette, Marguerite Eymery (see Rachilde)

Valverde, José María 1926- DLB-108

Van Allsburg, Chris 1949- DLB-61

Van Anda, Carr 1864-1945 . . . . .DLB-25

Van Doren, Mark 1894-1972 . . . . . . .DLB-45

van Druten, John 1901-1957 . . . . . . .DLB-10

Van Duyn, Mona 1921- DLB-5

Van Dyke, Henry
1852-1933 . . . . DLB-71; DS-13

Van Dyke, Henry 1928- DLB-33

van Itallie, Jean-Claude 1936- DLB-7

Van Rensselaer, Mariana Griswold
1851-1934 .... DLB-47

Van Rensselaer, Mrs. Schuyler (see Van
Rensselaer, Mariana Griswold)

Van Vechten, Carl 1880-1964 ..... DLB-4, 9

van Vogt, A. E. 1912- DLB-8

Vanbrugh, Sir John 1664-1726 ...... DLB-80

Vance, Jack 1916?- DLB-8

Vane, Sutton 1888-1963 .... DLB-10

Vanguard Press DLB-46

Vann, Robert L. 1879-1940 .... DLB-29

Vargas, Llosa, Mario 1936- DLB-145

Varley, John 1947- Y-81

Varnhagen von Ense, Karl August
1785-1858 .... DLB-90

Varnhagen von Ense, Rahel
1771-1833 .... DLB-90

Vásquez Montalbán, Manuel
1939- DLB-134

Vassa, Gustavus (see Equiano, Olaudah)

Vassalli, Sebastiano 1941- DLB-128

Vaughan, Henry 1621-1695 .... DLB-131

Vaughan, Thomas 1621-1666 ..... DLB-131

Vaux, Thomas, Lord 1509-1556 ... DLB-132

Vazov, Ivan 1850-1921 .... DLB-147

Vega, Janine Pommy 1942- DLB-16

Veiller, Anthony 1903-1965 .... DLB-44

Velásquez-Trevino, Gloria
1949- DLB-122

Veloz Maggiolo, Marcio 1936- ... DLB-145

Venegas, Daniel ?-? DLB-82

Vergil, Polydore circa 1470-1555 ... DLB-132

Veríssimo, Erico 1905-1975 .... DLB-145

Verne, Jules 1828-1905 .... DLB-123

Verplanck, Gulian C. 1786-1870 .... DLB-59

Very, Jones 1813-1880 .... DLB-1

Vian, Boris 1920-1959 .... DLB-72

Vickers, Roy 1888?-1965 .... DLB-77

Victoria 1819-1901 .... DLB-55

Victoria Press DLB-106

Vidal, Gore 1925- DLB-6, 152

Viebig, Clara 1860-1952 .... DLB-66

Viereck, George Sylvester
1884-1962 .... DLB-54

Viereck, Peter 1916- DLB-5

Viets, Roger 1738-1811 .... DLB-99

Viewpoint: Politics and Performance, by
David Edgar DLB-13

Vigil-Piñon, Evangelina 1949- DLB-122

Vigneault, Gilles 1928- DLB-60

Vigny, Alfred de 1797-1863 .... DLB-119

Vigolo, Giorgio 1894-1983 .... DLB-114

The Viking Press DLB-46

Villanueva, Alma Luz 1944- DLB-122

Villanueva, Tino 1941- DLB-82

Villard, Henry 1835-1900 .... DLB-23

Villard, Oswald Garrison
1872-1949 .... DLB-25, 91

Villarreal, José Antonio 1924- DLB-82

Villegas de Magnón, Leonor
1876-1955 .... DLB-122

Villemaire, Yolande 1949- DLB-60

Villena, Luis Antonio de 1951- ... DLB-134

Villiers de l'Isle-Adam, Jean-Marie
Mathias Philippe-Auguste, Comte de
1838-1889 .... DLB-123

Villiers, George, Second Duke
of Buckingham 1628-1687 .... DLB-80

Vine Press DLB-112

Viorst, Judith ?- DLB-52

Vipont, Elfrida (Elfrida Vipont Foulds,
Charles Vipont) 1902-1992 ..... DLB-160

Viramontes, Helena María
1954- DLB-122

Vischer, Friedrich Theodor
1807-1887 .... DLB-133

Vivanco, Luis Felipe 1907-1975 .... DLB-108

Viviani, Cesare 1947- DLB-128

Vizetelly and Company DLB-106

Voaden, Herman 1903- DLB-88

Voigt, Ellen Bryant 1943- DLB-120

Vojnović, Ivo 1857-1929 .... DLB-147

Volkoff, Vladimir 1932- DLB-83

Volland, P. F., Company DLB-46

von der Grün, Max 1926- DLB-75

Vonnegut, Kurt
1922- DLB-2, 8, 152; Y-80; DS-3

Voranc, Prežihov 1893-1950 .... DLB-147

Voß, Johann Heinrich 1751-1826 .... DLB-90

Vroman, Mary Elizabeth
circa 1924-1967 .... DLB-33

W

Wace, Robert ("Maistre")
circa 1100-circa 1175 .... DLB-146

Wackenroder, Wilhelm Heinrich
1773-1798 .... DLB-90

Wackernagel, Wilhelm
1806-1869 .... DLB-133

Waddington, Miriam 1917- DLB-68

Wade, Henry 1887-1969 .... DLB-77

Wagenknecht, Edward 1900- DLB-103

Wagner, Heinrich Leopold
1747-1779 .... DLB-94

Wagner, Henry R. 1862-1957 ..... DLB-140

Wagner, Richard 1813-1883 .... DLB-129

Wagoner, David 1926- DLB-5

Wah, Fred 1939- DLB-60

Waiblinger, Wilhelm 1804-1830 .... DLB-90

Wain, John
1925-1994 .... DLB-15, 27, 139, 155

Wainwright, Jeffrey 1944- DLB-40

Waite, Peirce and Company DLB-49

Wakoski, Diane 1937- DLB-5

Walahfrid Strabo circa 808-849 .... DLB-148

Walck, Henry Z. DLB-46

Walcott, Derek
1930- DLB-117; Y-81, 92

Waldman, Anne 1945- DLB-16

Walker, Alice 1944- DLB-6, 33, 143

Walker, George F. 1947- DLB-60

Walker, Joseph A. 1935- DLB-38

Walker, Margaret 1915- DLB-76, 152

Walker, Ted 1934- DLB-40

Walker and Company DLB-49

Walker, Evans and Cogswell
Company DLB-49

Walker, John Brisben 1847-1931 ..... DLB-79

Wallace, Dewitt 1889-1981 and
Lila Acheson Wallace
1889-1984 .... DLB-137

Wallace, Edgar 1875-1932 .... DLB-70

Wallace, Lila Acheson (see Wallace, Dewitt,
and Lila Acheson Wallace)

Wallant, Edward Lewis
1926-1962 .... DLB-2, 28, 143

Waller, Edmund 1606-1687 .... DLB-126

Walpole, Horace 1717-1797 .... DLB-39, 104

Walpole, Hugh 1884-1941 .... DLB-34

Walrond, Eric 1898-1966 .... DLB-51

Walser, Martin 1927- DLB-75, 124

Walser, Robert 1878-1956 ....DLB-66

Walsh, Ernest 1895-1926 ....DLB-4, 45

Walsh, Robert 1784-1859 ....DLB-59

Waltharius circa 825 ....DLB-148

Walters, Henry 1848-1931 ....DLB-140

Walther von der Vogelweide
  circa 1170-circa 1230 ....DLB-138

Walton, Izaak 1593-1683 ....DLB-151

Wambaugh, Joseph 1937- DLB-6; Y-83

Waniek, Marilyn Nelson 1946- ...DLB-120

Warburton, William 1698-1779 ....DLB-104

Ward, Aileen 1919- DLB-111

Ward, Artemus (see Browne, Charles Farrar)

Ward, Arthur Henry Sarsfield
  (see Rohmer, Sax)

Ward, Douglas Turner 1930- DLB-7, 38

Ward, Lynd 1905-1985 ....DLB-22

Ward, Lock and Company DLB-106

Ward, Mrs. Humphry 1851-1920 ....DLB-18

Ward, Nathaniel circa 1578-1652 ....DLB-24

Ward, Theodore 1902-1983 ....DLB-76

Wardle, Ralph 1909-1988 ....DLB-103

Ware, William 1797-1852 ....DLB-1

Warne, Frederick, and
  Company [U.S.] DLB-49

Warne, Frederick, and
  Company [U.K.] DLB-106

Warner, Charles Dudley
  1829-1900 ....DLB-64

Warner, Rex 1905- DLB-15

Warner, Susan Bogert
  1819-1885 ....DLB-3, 42

Warner, Sylvia Townsend
  1893-1978 ....DLB-34, 139

Warner Books DLB-46

Warr, Bertram 1917-1943 ....DLB-88

Warren, John Byrne Leicester (see De Tabley,
  Lord)

Warren, Lella 1899-1982 ....Y-83

Warren, Mercy Otis 1728-1814 .....DLB-31

Warren, Robert Penn
  1905-1989 .....DLB-2, 48, 152; Y-80, 89

Die Wartburgkrieg
  circa 1230-circa 1280 ....DLB-138

Warton, Joseph 1722-1800 .....DLB-104, 109

Warton, Thomas 1728-1790 ...DLB-104, 109

Washington, George 1732-1799 .....DLB-31

Wassermann, Jakob 1873-1934 ..... DLB-66

Wasson, David Atwood 1823-1887 ... DLB-1

Waterhouse, Keith 1929- DLB-13, 15

Waterman, Andrew 1940- DLB-40

Waters, Frank 1902- Y-86

Waters, Michael 1949- DLB-120

Watkins, Tobias 1780-1855 .... DLB-73

Watkins, Vernon 1906-1967 .... DLB-20

Watmough, David 1926- DLB-53

Watson, James Wreford (see Wreford, James)

Watson, John 1850-1907 .... DLB-156

Watson, Sheila 1909- DLB-60

Watson, Thomas 1545?-1592 ...... DLB-132

Watson, Wilfred 1911- DLB-60

Watt, W. J., and Company DLB-46

Watterson, Henry 1840-1921 ...... DLB-25

Watts, Alan 1915-1973 .... DLB-16

Watts, Franklin [publishing house] .. DLB-46

Watts, Isaac 1674-1748 .... DLB-95

Waugh, Auberon 1939- DLB-14

Waugh, Evelyn 1903-1966 ..... DLB-15, 162

Way and Williams DLB-49

Wayman, Tom 1945- DLB-53

Weatherly, Tom 1942- DLB-41

Weaver, Gordon 1937- DLB-130

Weaver, Robert 1921- DLB-88

Webb, Frank J. ?-? DLB-50

Webb, James Watson 1802-1884 .... DLB-43

Webb, Mary 1881-1927 .... DLB-34

Webb, Phyllis 1927- DLB-53

Webb, Walter Prescott 1888-1963 ... DLB-17

Webbe, William ?-1591 .... DLB-132

Webster, Augusta 1837-1894 .... DLB-35

Webster, Charles L.,
  and Company DLB-49

Webster, John
  1579 or 1580-1634? DLB-58

Webster, Noah
  1758-1843 ....DLB-1, 37, 42, 43, 73

Wedekind, Frank 1864-1918 ...... DLB-118

Weeks, Edward Augustus, Jr.
  1898-1989 .... DLB-137

Weems, Mason Locke
  1759-1825 ....DLB-30, 37, 42

Weerth, Georg 1822-1856 .... DLB-129

Weidenfeld and Nicolson DLB-112

Weidman, Jerome 1913- DLB-28

Weigl, Bruce 1949- DLB-120

Weinbaum, Stanley Grauman
  1902-1935 ....DLB-8

Weintraub, Stanley 1929- DLB-111

Weisenborn, Gunther
  1902-1969 ....DLB-69, 124

Weiß, Ernst 1882-1940 ....DLB-81

Weiss, John 1818-1879 ....DLB-1

Weiss, Peter 1916-1982 ....DLB-69, 124

Weiss, Theodore 1916- DLB-5

Weisse, Christian Felix 1726-1804 ...DLB-97

Weitling, Wilhelm 1808-1871 ......DLB-129

Welch, Lew 1926-1971? DLB-16

Weldon, Fay 1931- DLB-14

Wellek, René 1903- DLB-63

Wells, Carolyn 1862-1942 ....DLB-11

Wells, Charles Jeremiah
  circa 1800-1879 ....DLB-32

Wells, Gabriel 1862-1946 ....DLB-140

Wells, H. G. 1866-1946 .... DLB-34, 70, 156

Wells, Robert 1947- DLB-40

Wells-Barnett, Ida B. 1862-1931 .....DLB-23

Welty, Eudora
  1909- DLB-2, 102, 143; Y-87; DS-12

Wendell, Barrett 1855-1921 ....DLB-71

Wentworth, Patricia 1878-1961 ......DLB-77

Werfel, Franz 1890-1945 ....DLB-81, 124

The Werner Company DLB-49

Werner, Zacharias 1768-1823 ....DLB-94

Wersba, Barbara 1932- DLB-52

Wescott, Glenway 1901- DLB-4, 9, 102

Wesker, Arnold 1932- DLB-13

Wesley, Charles 1707-1788 ....DLB-95

Wesley, John 1703-1791 ....DLB-104

Wesley, Richard 1945- DLB-38

Wessels, A., and Company DLB-46

Wessobrunner Gebet
  circa 787-815 ....DLB-148

West, Anthony 1914-1988 ....DLB-15

West, Dorothy 1907- DLB-76

West, Jessamyn 1902-1984 ......DLB-6; Y-84

West, Mae 1892-1980 ....DLB-44

West, Nathanael 1903-1940 .....DLB-4, 9, 28

West, Paul 1930- DLB-14

West, Rebecca 1892-1983 .....DLB-36; Y-83

West and Johnson DLB-49

Western Publishing Company DLB-46

The Westminster Review 1824-1914 ... DLB-110

Wetherald, Agnes Ethelwyn
1857-1940 .... DLB-99

Wetherell, Elizabeth
(see Warner, Susan Bogert)

Wetzel, Friedrich Gottlob
1779-1819 .... DLB-90

Weyman, Stanley J.
1855-1928 .... DLB-141, 156

Wezel, Johann Karl 1747-1819 ...... DLB-94

Whalen, Philip 1923- DLB-16

Whalley, George 1915-1983 .... DLB-88

Wharton, Edith
1862-1937 .... DLB-4, 9, 12, 78; DS-13

Wharton, William 1920s?- Y-80

What's Really Wrong With Bestseller
Lists Y-84

Wheatley, Dennis Yates
1897-1977 .... DLB-77

Wheatley, Phillis
circa 1754-1784 .... DLB-31, 50

Wheeler, Anna Doyle
1785-1848? DLB-158

Wheeler, Charles Stearns
1816-1843 ....DLB-1

Wheeler, Monroe 1900-1988 ....DLB-4

Wheelock, John Hall 1886-1978 .... DLB-45

Wheelwright, John
circa 1592-1679 .... DLB-24

Wheelwright, J. B. 1897-1940 .... DLB-45

Whetstone, Colonel Pete
(see Noland, C. F. M.)

Whetstone, George 1550-1587 ..... DLB-136

Whicher, Stephen E. 1915-1961 .... DLB-111

Whipple, Edwin Percy
1819-1886 .... DLB-1, 64

Whitaker, Alexander 1585-1617 .... DLB-24

Whitaker, Daniel K. 1801-1881 ..... DLB-73

Whitcher, Frances Miriam
1814-1852 .... DLB-11

White, Andrew 1579-1656 .... DLB-24

White, Andrew Dickson
1832-1918 .... DLB-47

White, E. B. 1899-1985 .... DLB-11, 22

White, Edgar B. 1947- DLB-38

White, Ethel Lina 1887-1944 ...... DLB-77

White, Henry Kirke 1785-1806 ..... DLB-96

White, Horace 1834-1916 .... DLB-23

White, Phyllis Dorothy James
(see James, P. D.)

White, Richard Grant 1821-1885 .... DLB-64

White, T. H. 1906-1964 .... DLB-160

White, Walter 1893-1955 .... DLB-51

White, William, and Company DLB-49

White, William Allen
1868-1944 .... DLB-9, 25

White, William Anthony Parker (see Boucher,
Anthony)

White, William Hale (see Rutherford, Mark)

Whitechurch, Victor L.
1868-1933 .... DLB-70

Whitehead, Alfred North
1861-1947 .... DLB-100

Whitehead, James 1936- Y-81

Whitehead, William
1715-1785 .... DLB-84, 109

Whitfield, James Monroe
1822-1871 .... DLB-50

Whitgift, John circa 1533-1604 ..... DLB-132

Whiting, John 1917-1963 .... DLB-13

Whiting, Samuel 1597-1679 .... DLB-24

Whitlock, Brand 1869-1934 .... DLB-12

Whitman, Albert, and Company DLB-46

Whitman, Albery Allson
1851-1901 .... DLB-50

Whitman, Alden 1913-1990 ....Y-91

Whitman, Sarah Helen (Power)
1803-1878 .... DLB-1

Whitman, Walt 1819-1892 .... DLB-3, 64

Whitman Publishing Company DLB-46

Whitney, Geoffrey
1548 or 1552?-1601 .... DLB-136

Whitney, Isabella
flourished 1566-1573 .... DLB-136

Whitney, John Hay 1904-1982 ..... DLB-127

Whittemore, Reed 1919- DLB-5

Whittier, John Greenleaf 1807-1892 ... DLB-1

Whittlesey House DLB-46

Who Runs American Literature? Y-94

Wideman, John Edgar
1941- DLB-33, 143

Widener, Harry Elkins 1885-1912 ... DLB-140

Wiebe, Rudy 1934- DLB-60

Wiechert, Ernst 1887-1950 .... DLB-56

Wied, Martina 1882-1957 .... DLB-85

Wieland, Christoph Martin
1733-1813 .... DLB-97

Wienbarg, Ludolf 1802-1872 ....DLB-133

Wieners, John 1934- DLB-16

Wier, Ester 1910- DLB-52

Wiesel, Elie 1928- DLB-83; Y-87

Wiggin, Kate Douglas 1856-1923 ....DLB-42

Wigglesworth, Michael 1631-1705 ...DLB-24

Wilberforce, William 1759-1833 ...DLB-158

Wilbrandt, Adolf 1837-1911 ....DLB-129

Wilbur, Richard 1921- DLB-5

Wild, Peter 1940- DLB-5

Wilde, Oscar
1854-1900 ... DLB-10, 19, 34, 57, 141, 156

Wilde, Richard Henry
1789-1847 .... DLB-3, 59

Wilde, W. A., Company DLB-49

Wilder, Billy 1906- DLB-26

Wilder, Laura Ingalls 1867-1957 .....DLB-22

Wilder, Thornton 1897-1975 .... DLB-4, 7, 9

Wildgans, Anton 1881-1932 ....DLB-118

Wiley, Bell Irvin 1906-1980 ....DLB-17

Wiley, John, and Sons DLB-49

Wilhelm, Kate 1928- DLB-8

Wilkes, George 1817-1885 ....DLB-79

Wilkinson, Anne 1910-1961 ....DLB-88

Wilkinson, Sylvia 1940- Y-86

Wilkinson, William Cleaver
1833-1920 ....DLB-71

Willard, Barbara 1909-1994 ....DLB-161

Willard, L. [publishing house] DLB-49

Willard, Nancy 1936- DLB-5, 52

Willard, Samuel 1640-1707 ....DLB-24

William of Auvergne 1190-1249 ....DLB-115

William of Conches
circa 1090-circa 1154 ....DLB-115

William of Ockham
circa 1285-1347 ....DLB-115

William of Sherwood
1200/1205 - 1266/1271 ....DLB-115

The William Chavrat American Fiction
Collection at the Ohio State University
Libraries Y-92

Williams, A., and Company DLB-49

Williams, Ben Ames 1889-1953 .....DLB-102

Williams, C. K. 1936- DLB-5

Williams, Chancellor 1905- DLB-76

Williams, Charles
1886-1945 .... DLB-100, 153

132 *Sixteenth-Century British Nondramatic Writers, First Series,* edited by David A. Richardson (1993)

133 *Nineteenth-Century German Writers to 1840,* edited by James Hardin and Siegfried Mews (1993)

134 *Twentieth-Century Spanish Poets, Second Series,* edited by Jerry Phillips Winfield (1994)

135 *British Short-Fiction Writers, 1880–1914: The Realist Tradition,* edited by William B. Thesing (1994)

136 *Sixteenth-Century British Nondramatic Writers, Second Series,* edited by David A. Richardson (1994)

137 *American Magazine Journalists, 1900–1960, Second Series,* edited by Sam G. Riley (1994)

138 *German Writers and Works of the High Middle Ages: 1170–1280,* edited by James Hardin and Will Hasty (1994)

139 *British Short-Fiction Writers, 1945–1980,* edited by Dean Baldwin (1994)

140 *American Book-Collectors and Bibliographers, First Series,* edited by Joseph Rosenblum (1994)

141 *British Children's Writers, 1880–1914,* edited by Laura M. Zaidman (1994)

142 *Eighteenth-Century British Literary Biographers,* edited by Steven Serafin (1994)

143 *...paper Publishers, 1950-... Perry J. Ashley (1993)*

144 *...tury Italian Poets, Second ... by Giovanna Wedel ...auco Cambon, and An- ...(1993)*

145 *...entury German Writers, ...edited by James Hardin ...d Mews (1993)*

146 *...Short-Story Writers Since ...r II,* edited by Patrick ...1993)

147 *...h-Century British Nondramatic ...ird Series,* edited by M. ...Hester (1993)

148 *German Writers and Works of the Early Middle Ages: 800–1170,* edited by Will Hasty and James Hardin (1994)

149 *Late Nineteenth- and Early Twentieth-Century British Literary Biographers,* edited by Steven Serafin (1995)

150 *Early Modern Russian Writers, Late Seventeenth and Eighteenth Centuries,* edited by Marcus C. Levitt (1995)

151 *British Prose Writers of the Early Seventeenth Century,* edited by Clayton D. Lein (1995)

152 *American Novelists Since World War II, Fourth Series,* edited by James and Wanda Giles (1995)

153 *Late-Victorian and Edwardian British Novelists, First Series,* edited by George M. Johnson (1995)

154 *The British Literary Book Trade, 1700–1820,* edited by James K. Bracken and Joel Silver (1995)

155 *Twentieth-Century British Literary Biographers,* edited by Steven Serafin (1995)

156 *British Short-Fiction Writers, 1880–1914: The Romantic Tradition,* edited by William F. Naufftus (1995)

157 *Twentieth-Century Caribbean and Black African Writers, Third Series,* edited by Bernth Lindfors and Reinhard Sander (1995)

158 *British Reform Writers, 1789–1832,* edited by Gary Kelly and Edd Applegate (1995)

159 *British Short Fiction Writers, 1800–1880,* edited by John R. Greenfield (1996)

160 *British Children's Writers, 1914–1960,* edited by Donald R. Hettinga and Gary D. Schmidt (1996)

161 *British Children's Writers Since 1960, First Series,* edited by Caroline Hunt (1996)

162 *British Short-Fiction Writers, 1915–1945,* edited by John H. Rogers (1996)

163 *British Children's Writers, 1800–1880,* edited by Meena Khorana (1996)

Documentary Series

...ood Anderson, Willa Cather, John ...Passos, Theodore Dreiser, F. Scott ...rald, Ernest Hemingway, Sinclair ..., edited by Margaret A. Van ...erp (1982)

2 *James Gould Cozzens, James T. Farrell, William Faulkner, John O'Hara, John Steinbeck, Thomas Wolfe, Richard Wright,* edited by Margaret A. Van Antwerp (1982)

Williams, Denis 1923- DLB-117

Williams, Emlyn 1905- DLB-10, 77

Williams, Garth 1912- DLB-22

Williams, George Washington 1849-1891 ....DLB-47

Williams, Heathcote 1941- DLB-13

Williams, Helen Maria 1761-1827 ....DLB-158

Williams, Hugo 1942- DLB-40

Williams, Isaac 1802-1865 ....DLB-32

Williams, Joan 1928- DLB-6

Williams, John A. 1925- DLB-2, 33

Williams, John E. 1922-1994 ....DLB-6

Williams, Jonathan 1929- DLB-5

Williams, Miller 1930- DLB-105

Williams, Raymond 1921- DLB-14

Williams, Roger circa 1603-1683 .....DLB-24

Williams, Samm-Art 1946- DLB-38

Williams, Sherley Anne 1944- DLB-41

Williams, T. Harry 1909-1979 .....DLB-17

Williams, Tennessee 1911-1983 ....DLB-7; Y-83; DS-4

Williams, Ursula Moray 1911- DLB-160

Williams, Valentine 1883-1946 ......DLB-77

Williams, William Appleman 1921- DLB-17

Williams, William Carlos 1883-1963 ....DLB-4, 16, 54, 86

Williams, Wirt 1921- DLB-6

Williams Brothers DLB-49

Williamson, Jack 1908- DLB-8

Willingham, Calder Baynard, Jr. 1922- DLB-2, 44

William of Ebersberg circa 1020-1085 ....DLB-148

Willis, Nathaniel Parker 1806-1867 .....DLB-3, 59, 73, 74; DS-13

Willkomm, Ernst 1810-1886 ....DLB-133

Wilmer, Clive 1945- DLB-40

Wilson, A. N. 1950- DLB-14, 155

Wilson, Angus 1913-1991 ....DLB-15, 139, 155

Wilson, Arthur 1595-1652 ....DLB-58

Wilson, Augusta Jane Evans 1835-1909 ....DLB-42

Wilson, Colin 1931- DLB-14

Wilson, Edmund 1895-1972 ....DLB-63

Wilson, Ethel 1888-1980 ....DLB-68

Wilson, Harriet E. Adams 1828?-1863? DLB-50

Wilson, Harry Leon 1867-1939 ......DLB-9

Wilson, John 1588-1667 ....DLB-24

Wilson, John 1785-1854 ....DLB-110

Wilson, Lanford 1937- DLB-7

Wilson, Margaret 1882-1973 ....DLB-9

Wilson, Michael 1914-1978 ....DLB-44

Wilson, Mona 1872-1954 ....DLB-149

Wilson, Thomas 1523 or 1524-1581 ....DLB-132

Wilson, Woodrow 1856-1924 ....DLB-47

Wilson, Effingham [publishing house] DLB-154

Wimsatt, William K., Jr. 1907-1975 ....DLB-63

Winchell, Walter 1897-1972 ....DLB-29

Winchester, J. [publishing house] DLB-49

Winckelmann, Johann Joachim 1717-1768 ....DLB-97

Windham, Donald 1920- DLB-6

Wingate, Allan [publishing house] ..DLB-112

Winnifrith, Tom 1938- DLB-155

Winsloe, Christa 1888-1944 ....DLB-124

Winsor, Justin 1831-1897 ....DLB-47

John C. Winston Company DLB-49

Winters, Yvor 1900-1968 ....DLB-48

Winthrop, John 1588-1649 ......DLB-24, 30

Winthrop, John, Jr. 1606-1676 ......DLB-24

Wirt, William 1772-1834 ....DLB-37

Wise, John 1652-1725 ....DLB-24

Wiseman, Adele 1928- DLB-88

Wishart and Company DLB-112

Wisner, George 1812-1849 ....DLB-43

Wister, Owen 1860-1938 ....DLB-9, 78

Wither, George 1588-1667 ....DLB-121

Witherspoon, John 1723-1794 ......DLB-31

Withrow, William Henry 1839-1908 ...DLB-99

Wittig, Monique 1935- DLB-83

Wodehouse, P. G. 1881-1975 ....DLB-34, 162

Wohmann, Gabriele 1932- DLB-75

Woiwode, Larry 1941- DLB-6

Wolcot, John 1738-1819 ......DLB-109

Wolcott, Roger 1679-1767 ....DLB-24

Wolf, Christa 1929- DLB-75

Wolf, Friedrich 1888-1953 ....DLB-124

Wolfe, Gene 1931- DLB-8

Wolfe, Thomas 1900-1938 ......DLB-9, 102; Y-85; DS-2

Wolfe, Tom 1931- DLB-152

Wolff, Helen 1906-1994 ....Y-94

Wolff, Tobias 1945- DLB-130

Wolfram von Eschenbach circa 1170-after 1220 ....DLB-138

Wolfram von Eschenbach's *Parzival:* Prologue and Book 3 ....DLB-138

Wollstonecraft, Mary 1759-1797 ....DLB-39, 104, 158

Wondratschek, Wolf 1943- DLB-75

Wood, Benjamin 1820-1900 ....DLB-23

Wood, Charles 1932- DLB-13

Wood, Mrs. Henry 1814-1887 ......DLB-18

Wood, Joanna E. 1867-1927 ....DLB-92

Wood, Samuel [publishing house] DLB-49

Wood, William ?-? DLB-24

Woodberry, George Edward 1855-1930 ....DLB-71, 103

Woodbridge, Benjamin 1622-1684 ...DLB-24

Woodcock, George 1912- DLB-88

Woodhull, Victoria C. 1838-1927 ....DLB-79

Woodmason, Charles circa 1720-? ...DLB-31

Woodress, Jr., James Leslie 1916- DLB-111

Woodson, Carter G. 1875-1950 .....DLB-17

Woodward, C. Vann 1908- DLB-17

Wooler, Thomas 1785 or 1786-1853 ....DLB-158

Woolf, David (see Maddow, Ben)

Woolf, Leonard 1880-1969 ....DLB-100; DS-10

Woolf, Virginia 1882-1941 .....DLB-36, 100, 162; DS-10

Woolf, Virginia, "The New Biography," *New York Herald Tribune,* 30 October 1927 ....DLB-149

Woollcott, Alexander 1887-1943 .....DLB-29

Woolman, John 1720-1772 ....DLB-31

Woolner, Thomas 1825-1892 ....DLB-35

Woolsey, Sarah Chauncy 1835-1905 ....DLB-42

Woolson, Constance Fenimore 1840-1894 ....DLB-12, 74

Worcester, Joseph Emerson 1784-1865 ....DLB-1

Cumulative Index

Wordsworth, Dorothy
    1771-1855 . . . . DLB-107

Wordsworth, Elizabeth
    1840-1932 . . . . DLB-98

Wordsworth, William
    1770-1850 . . . . DLB-93, 107

The Works of the Rev. John Witherspoon
    (1800-1801) [excerpts] DLB-31

A World Chronology of Important Science
    Fiction Works (1818-1979) DLB-8

World Publishing Company DLB-46

Worthington, R., and Company DLB-49

Wotton, Sir Henry 1568-1639 . . . . . DLB-121

Wouk, Herman 1915- Y-82

Wreford, James 1915- DLB-88

Wren, Percival Christopher
    1885-1941 . . . . DLB-153

Wrenn, John Henry 1841-1911 . . . . DLB-140

Wright, C. D. 1949- DLB-120

Wright, Charles 1935- Y-82

Wright, Charles Stevenson 1932- DLB-33

Wright, Frances 1795-1852 . . . . DLB-73

Wright, Harold Bell 1872-1944 . . . . . . .DLB-9

Wright, James 1927-1980 . . . . .DLB-5

Wright, Jay 1935- DLB-41

Wright, Louis B. 1899-1984 . . . . DLB-17

Wright, Richard
    1908-1960 . . . . .DLB-76, 102; DS-2

Wright, Richard B. 1937- DLB-53

Wright, Sarah Elizabeth 1928- DLB-33

Writers and Politics: 1871-1918,
    by Ronald Gray DLB-66

Writers and their Copyright Holders:
    the WATCH Project Y-94

Writers' Forum Y-85

Writing for the Theatre, by
    Harold Pinter DLB-13

Wroth, Lady Mary 1587-1653 . . . . . DLB-121

Wyatt, Sir Thomas
    circa 1503-1542 . . . . DLB-132

Wycherley, William 1641-1715 . . . . . . DLB-80

Wyclif, John
    circa 1335-31 December 1384 . . . DLB-146

Wylie, Elinor 1885-1928 . . . . .DLB-9, 45

Wylie, Philip 1902-1971 . . . . .DLB-9

Wyllie, John Cook 1908-1968 . . . . . . DLB-140

Y

Yates, Dornford 1885-1960 . . . . .DLB-77, 153

Yates, J. Michael 1938- DLB-60

Yates, Richard 1926-1992 . . .DLB-2; Y-81, 92

Yavorov, Peyo 1878-1914 . . . . .DLB-147

Yearsley, Ann 1753-1806 . . . . .DLB-109

Yeats, William Butler
    1865-1939 . . . . DLB-10, 19, 98, 156

Yep, Laurence 1948- DLB-52

Yerby, Frank 1916-1991 . . . . DLB-76

Yezierska, Anzia 1885-1970 . . . . DLB-28

Yolen, Jane 1939- DLB-52

Yonge, Charlotte Mary
    1823-1901 . . . . .DLB-18, 163

The York Cycle
    circa 1376-circa 1569 . . . . .DLB-146

A Yorkshire Tragedy DLB-58

Yoseloff, Thomas
    [publishing house] DLB-46

Young, Al 1939- DLB-33

Young, Arthur 1741-1820 . . . . .DLB-158

Young, Edward 1683-1765 . . . . DLB-95

Young, Stark 1881-1963 . . . . .DLB-9, 102

Young, Waldeman 1880-1938 . . . . DLB-26

Young, William [publishing house] . . DLB-49

Yourcenar, Marguerite
    1903-1987 . . . . .DLB-72; Y-88

"You've Never Had It So Good," Gusted by
    "Winds of Change": British Fiction in the
    1950s, 1960s, and After DLB-14

Yovkov, Yordan 1880-1937 . . . . .DLB-147

Z

Zachariä, Friedrich Wilhelm
    1726-1777 .DLB-97

Zamora, Bernice 1938- DLB-82

Zand, Herbert 1923-1970 . . . . .DLB-85

Zangwill, Israel 1864-1926 . . . . . DLB-10, 135

Zanzotto, Andrea 1921- DLB-128

Zapata Olivella, Manuel 1920- DLB-113

Zebra Books DLB-46

Zebrowski, George 1945- DLB-8

Zech, Paul 1881-1946 . . . . .DLB-56

Zeidner, Lisa 1955- DLB-120

Zelazny, Roger 1937-1995 . . . . .DLB-8

Zenger, John Peter 1697-1746 . . . DLB-24, 43

Zieber, G. B., and Company DLB-49

Zieroth, Dale 1946- DLB-60

Zimmer, Paul 1934- DLB-5

Zindel, Paul 1936- DLB-7, 52

Zola, Emile 1840-1902 . . . . .DLB-123

Zolotow, Charlotte 1915- DLB-52

Zschokke, Heinrich 1771-1848 . . . . . .DLB-94

Zubly, John Joachim 1724-1781 . . . . .DLB-31

Zu-Bolton II, Ahmos 1936- DLB-41

Zuckmayer, Carl 1896-1977 . . . . DLB-56, 124

Zukofsky, Louis 1904-1978 . . . . .DLB-5

Župančič, Oton 1878-1949 . . . . .DLB-147

zur Mühlen, Hermynia 1883-1951 . . . .DLB-56

Zweig, Arnold 1887-1968 . . . . .DLB-66

Zweig, Stefan 1881-1942 . . . . DLB-81, 118

ISBN 0-8103-9358-1

90000

9 780810 393585

(Continued from front endshe

117 *Twentieth-Century Caribbean a
     African Writers, First Series, e
     Bernth Lindfors and R
     Sander (1992)

118 *Twentieth-Century German
     1889-1918, edited by Wo
     Elfe and James Hardin (19

119 *Nineteenth-Century French
     ers: Romanticism and Rea
     1860, edited by Cathar
     Brosman (1992)

120 *American Poets Since W
     Third Series, edited by
     (1992)

121 *Seventeenth-Century Briti
     Poets, First Series, e
     Thomas Hester (1992

122 *Chicano Writers, Second
     Francisco A. Lome
     Shirley (1992)

123 *Nineteenth-Century Fr
     ers: Naturalism and
     1900, edited by C
     Brosman (1992)

124 *Twentieth-Century
     1919-1992, edited
     Elfe and James H

125 *Twentieth-Century,
     African Writers,
     by Bernth Lind
     Sander (1993)

126 *Seventeenth-Cent
     Poets, Second S
     Thomas Heste

127 *American News
     1990, edited by

128 *Twentieth-Cen
     Series, edited
     De Stasio, G
     tonio Illiano

129 *Nineteenth-C
     1841-1900,
     and Siegfri

130 *American
     World W
     Meanor

131 *Seventeen
     Poets, T
     Thomas

1   *She
     Do
     Fi
     L*